Health, United States, 2016

With Chartbook on Long-term Trends in Health

U.S. DEPARTMENT OF HEALTH AND HUMAN SERVICES
Centers for Disease Control and Prevention
National Center for Health Statistics

June 2017
DHHS Publication No. 2017–1232

U.S. Department of Health and Human Services

Thomas E. Price, M.D.
Secretary

Centers for Disease Control and Prevention

Anne Schuchat, M.D. (RADM, U.S. Public Health Service)
Acting Director

National Center for Health Statistics

Charles J. Rothwell, M.S., M.B.A.
Director

For sale by the Superintendent of Documents, U.S. Government Publishing Office
Internet: bookstore.gpo.gov Phone: toll free (866) 512-1800; DC area (202) 512-1800
Fax: (202) 512-2104 Mail: Stop IDCC, Washington, DC 20402-0001

ISBN 978-0-16-093977-8

Preface

Health, United States, 2016 is the 40th report on the health status of the nation and is submitted by the Secretary of the Department of Health and Human Services to the President and the Congress of the United States in compliance with Section 308 of the Public Health Service Act. This report was compiled by the Centers for Disease Control and Prevention's (CDC) National Center for Health Statistics (NCHS).

The *Health, United States* series presents an annual overview of national trends in health statistics. The report contains a Chartbook that assesses the nation's health by presenting trends and current information on selected measures of morbidity, mortality, health care utilization and access, health risk factors, prevention, health insurance, and personal health care expenditures. This year's Chartbook focuses on long-term trends in health. The report also contains 114 Trend Tables organized around four major subject areas: health status and determinants, health care utilization, health care resources, and health care expenditures. A companion report—*Health, United States*: In Brief—features information extracted from the full report. The complete report and related data products are available on the *Health, United States* website at: http://www.cdc.gov/nchs/hus.htm.

The 2016 Edition

Health, United States, 2016 contains a summary At a Glance table that displays recent data on selected indicators of health and their determinants, cross-referenced to tables in the report. This is followed by a Highlights section, which focuses on both long-term trends and current data on topics of public health interest and illustrates the breadth of material included in *Health, United States*. The other major sections are a Chartbook, detailed Trend Tables, two Appendixes, and an Index. The major sections of the 2016 report are described below.

Chartbook

The 2016 Chartbook contains 27 figures on long-term trends in health. As *Health, United States* enters its 40th year of reporting on the health of the nation, this year's Chartbook focuses on trends in health and health care since 1975. Examining long-term trends in health informs the development and implementation of effective health policies and programs. The Chartbook has been grouped into five sections. The first section (Figures 1–5) presents an overview of the demographic and socioeconomic factors that have influenced the health of the nation over the last 40 years. The second section (Figures 6–14) focuses on health status and determinants: life expectancy, infant mortality, leading causes of death, birth rates, cigarette smoking, obesity, untreated dental caries, diabetes prevalence, and uncontrolled hypertension. The third section (Figures 15–19) presents trends in health care utilization: use of prescription drugs, health care and emergency department visits, overnight hospital stays, and cancer screening tests. The fourth section (Figures 20–22) focuses on changes in health care resources: hospitals, primary and specialist physicians, and nursing homes. The fifth section (Figures 23–27) describes trends in health care expenditures: personal health care expenditures, mental health and substance use expenditures, Medicare managed care enrollment by state, and health insurance coverage.

Trend Tables

The Chartbook is followed by 114 detailed Trend Tables that highlight major trends in health statistics. Comparability across editions of *Health, United States* is fostered by including similar Trend Tables in each volume, and timeliness is maintained by improving the content of tables to reflect key topics in public health. An important criterion used in selecting these tables is the availability of comparable national data over a period of several years.

Appendixes

Appendix I. Data Sources describes each data source used in *Health, United States, 2016* and provides references for further information about the sources. Data sources are listed alphabetically within two broad categories: Government Sources, and Private and Global Sources.

Appendix II. Definitions and Methods is an alphabetical listing of selected terms used in *Health, United States, 2016*. It also contains information on the statistical methodologies used in the report.

Index

The Index to the Trend Tables and Chartbook figures is a useful tool for locating data by topic. Tables and figures are cross-referenced by such topics as child and adolescent health; older population aged 65 and over; women's health; men's health; state data; American Indian or Alaska Native, Asian, black or African American, Hispanic-origin, and white populations; education; injury; disability; and metropolitan and nonmetropolitan data. Many of the Index topics are also available as conveniently grouped data packages on the *Health, United States* website at: http://www.cdc.gov/nchs/hus.htm.

Data Considerations

Racial and Ethnic Data

Many tables in *Health, United States* present data according to race and Hispanic origin, consistent with a department-wide emphasis on ensuring that health data on racial and ethnic minority populations are presented whenever possible. Trend data on race and ethnicity are presented in the greatest detail possible after taking into account the quality of the data, the amount of missing data, and the number of observations. These issues significantly affect the availability of reportable data for certain populations, such as the Native Hawaiian or Other Pacific Islander populations and the American Indian or Alaska Native populations. Standards for the classification of federal data on race and ethnicity are described in an appendix. (See Appendix II, Race.)

Education and Income Data

Many Trend Tables in *Health, United States* present data according to socioeconomic status, using education and family income as proxy measures. Education and income data are generally obtained directly from survey respondents and are not usually available from records-based data collection systems. (See Appendix II, Education; Family income; Poverty.)

Disability Data

Disability can include the presence of physical or mental impairments that limit a person's ability to perform an important activity and affect the use of or need for support, accommodation, or intervention to improve functioning. Information on disability in the U.S. population is critical to health planning and policy. Disability may be measured based on a specific disability or a composite measure designed to identify persons with any of a variety of disabilities. *Health, United States* includes data from the National Health Interview Survey to examine specific types of disability and to create composite disability measures consistent with two of the conceptual components that have been identified in disability models and legislation: basic actions difficulty and complex activity limitation.

Basic actions difficulty captures limitations or difficulties in movement and sensory, emotional, or mental functioning that are associated with a health problem. Complex activity limitation describes limitations or restrictions in a person's ability to participate fully in social role activities such as working or maintaining a household. *Health, United States, 2016* includes the following disability-related information: basic actions difficulty and complex activity limitation (Table 42), vision and hearing limitations for adults (Tables 43 and 44), and disability-related information for Medicare enrollees (Table 108), Medicaid recipients (Table 109), and veterans with service-connected disabilities (Table 111). For more information on disability statistics, see Altman and Bernstein (1) and Brault (2).

Statistical Significance

All statements in the text describing differences, or lack thereof, in estimates indicate that statistical testing was performed. Differences between two point estimates were determined to be statistically significant at the 0.05 level using two-sided significance tests (z-tests) without correction for multiple comparisons. Data tables include point estimates and standard errors for users who would like to perform additional statistical tests. In the text, the standard terminology used when a difference between two point estimates was tested is, "Between (estimate 1) and (estimate 2)." For example, the statement "Between 2014 and 2015" indicates that the difference between the point estimate for 2014 and that for 2015 was tested for statistical significance.

The statistical significance of a time trend was assessed using weighted least squares regression applied to data for all years in the time period. (For a description of the trend testing technique, see the Technical Notes that follow the Chartbook.) The terminology used in the text to indicate testing of a trend is "During (time period 1)–(time period 2)." For example, the statement "During 2005–2015" indicates that a statistical test of trend was conducted that included estimates for all 11 years in the time period. Because statistically significant differences or trends are partly a function of sample size (i.e., the larger the sample, the smaller the change that can be detected), statistically significant differences or trends do not necessarily have public health significance (3).

Terms such as "similar," "stable," and "no difference" indicate that the statistics being compared were not significantly different. Lack of comment regarding the difference between statistics does not necessarily suggest that the difference was tested and found to not be significant.

Overall estimates generally have relatively small standard errors, but estimates for certain population subgroups may be based on small numbers and have relatively large standard errors. Although numbers of births and deaths from the Vital Statistics System represent complete counts (except for births in those states where data are based on a 50% sample for selected years) and are not subject to sampling error, the counts are subject to random variation, which means that the number of events that actually occur in a given year may be considered as one of a large series of possible results that could have arisen under the same circumstances. When the number of events is small and the probability of such an event is small, considerable caution must be observed in interpreting the conditions described by the estimates. Estimates that are unreliable because of large standard errors or small numbers of events are noted with an asterisk. The criteria used to designate or suppress unreliable estimates are indicated in the table footnotes.

For NCHS surveys, point estimates and their corresponding variances were calculated using the SUDAAN software package (4), which takes into consideration the complex survey design. Standard errors for other surveys or data sets were computed using the methodology recommended by the programs providing the data, or were provided directly by those programs. Standard errors are available for selected tables in the spreadsheet version on the *Health, United States* website at: http://www.cdc.gov/nchs/hus.htm.

Accessing *Health, United States*

Health, United States can be accessed in its entirety at: http://www.cdc.gov/nchs/hus.htm. The website is a user-friendly resource for *Health, United States* and related products. In addition to the full report, the website contains data conveniently organized and grouped by topic. The Chartbook figures are provided as PowerPoint slides, and the Trend Tables and Chartbook data tables are provided as spreadsheet and PDF files. Many spreadsheet files include additional years of data not shown in the printed report, along with standard errors where available. Visitors to the website can join the *Health, United States* e-mail list (https://www.cdc.gov/nchs/hus/hus_electronic_mailing.htm) to receive announcements about release dates and notices of updates. Previous editions of *Health, United States,* and their Chartbooks, can also be accessed from the website.

Printed copies of *Health, United States* can be purchased from the U.S. Government Printing Office at: http://bookstore.gpo.gov.

Questions?

If you have questions about *Health, United States* or related data products, please contact:

Office of Information Services
Information Dissemination Staff
National Center for Health Statistics
Centers for Disease Control and Prevention
3311 Toledo Road
Hyattsville, MD 20782–2064
Phone: 1–800–CDC–INFO (1–800–232–4636)
TTY: 1–888–232–6348
Internet: http://www.cdc.gov/nchs
Online request form:
https://wwwn.cdc.gov/dcs/ContactUs/Form
For e-mail updates on NCHS publication releases, subscribe online at:
http://www.cdc.gov/nchs/govdelivery.htm.

References

1. Altman B, Bernstein A. Disability and health in the United States, 2001–2005. Hyattsville, MD: NCHS; 2008.
2. Brault MW. Americans with disabilities: 2010. Current population reports, P70–131. Washington, DC: U.S. Census Bureau; 2012.
3. CDC. Youth Risk Behavior Surveillance System (YRBSS). Interpretation of YRBS trend data. Atlanta, GA; 2014.
4. RTI International. SUDAAN (Release 11.0.0) [computer software]; 2012.

Acknowledgments

Overall responsibility for planning and coordinating the content of this volume rested with the National Center for Health Statistics' (NCHS) Office of Analysis and Epidemiology, under the direction of Julia S. Holmes and Irma E. Arispe.

Production of **Health, United States, 2016** was managed by Sheila J. Franco, Virginia M. Freid, Julia S. Holmes, and Hashini S. Khajuria. Preparation of the volume, including highlights, trend tables, appendixes, and index, was completed by Shilpa Bengeri, Mary Ann Bush, La-Tonya D. Curl, Anne K. Driscoll, Catherine R. Duran, Sheila J. Franco, Virginia M. Freid, Nancy Han, Hashini S. Khajuria, Ji-Eun Kim, Florence Lee, Xianfen Li, Anita L. Powell, Ilene B. Rosen, and Ashley M. Woodall. Administrative and word processing assistance was provided by Lillie C. Featherstone.

Production of the **Chartbook** was managed by Sheila J. Franco and Virginia M. Freid. Data, analysis, and text for specific charts were provided by Shilpa Bengeri, Mary Ann Bush, La-Tonya D. Curl, Anne K. Driscoll, Catherine R. Duran, Sheila J. Franco, Virginia M. Freid, Nancy Han, Hashini S. Khajuria, Ji-Eun Kim, Florence Lee, Xianfen Li, Diane M. Makuc, and Ashley M. Woodall.

Publication assistance was provided by CDC/OPHSS/ NCHS/OD/Office of Information Services (OIS) and Office of Information Technology (OIT). Cover design was provided by Sarah Hinkle. Printing was managed by Nathanael Brown (CDC/OD/OADC). Publication production was performed under contract with Karna, LLC. Electronic access through the NCHS website was provided by Shilpa Bengeri, Christine J. Brown (CDC/OPHSS/NCHS/OD/OMO), La-Tonya D. Curl, Virginia M. Freid, Elom L. Lawson, Florence Lee, Anthony Lipphardt, Anita L. Powell, Ilene B. Rosen, Brian Tsai (CDC/ OPHSS/NCHS/OD), and Ashley M. Woodall.

Data and technical assistance were provided by staff of the following NCHS organizations: *Division of Health Care Statistics*: Jill Ashman, Lauren Harris-Kojetin, Pinyao Rui, Susan M. Schappert, Manisha Sengupta, and Victor V. Shigaev; *Division of Health and Nutrition Examination Surveys*: Namanjeet Ahluwalia, Margaret D. Carroll, Mark S. Eberhardt, Eleanor B. Fleming, Qiuping Gu, Brian K. Kit, Cynthia L. Ogden, and Ryne Paulose-Ram; *Division of Health Interview Statistics*: Veronica Benson, Debra Blackwell, Barbara Bloom, Robin A. Cohen, Jacqueline Lucas, Tina Norris, Jeannine Schiller, Charlotte Schoenborn, Maria Villarroel, Brian Ward, and Emily Zammitti; *Division of Vital Statistics*: Robert N. Anderson, Joyce A. Arbertha, Elizabeth Arias, Amy M. Branum, Anjani Chandra, Sally C. Curtin, Kimberly Daniels, Anne K. Driscoll, Elizabeth Gregory, Annie Liu, Joyce A. Martin, T.J. Mathews, Arialdi M. Miniño, Steven J. Steimel, and Margaret Warner; *Office of Analysis and Epidemiology*: Holly Hedegaard, Deborah D. Ingram, Ellen A. Kramarow, Laura A. Pratt, and Cheryl V. Rose; *Office of the Center Director*: Juan Albertorio and Francis C. Notzon; and *Office of Research and Methodology*: Meena Khare.

Additional data and technical assistance were provided by the following organizations of the Centers for Disease Control and Prevention (CDC): *National Center for Chronic Disease Prevention and Health Promotion*: Tara Jatlaoui; *National Center for HIV/AIDS, Viral Hepatitis, STD, and TB Prevention*: Jim Braxton, Lori Elmore, Anna Satcher Johnson, Sarah Kidd, Jennifer Ludovic, Rodney Presley, Elizabeth Torrone, Hillard Weinstock, and the Surveillance and Data Management Branch; *National Center for Immunization and Respiratory Diseases*: Laurie D. Elam-Evans, Holly A. Hill, James Singleton, and David Yankey; *Office of Public Health Scientific Services, Center for Surveillance, Epidemiology, and Laboratory Services*: Ruth Ann Jajosky; by the following organizations within the Department of Health and Human Services: *Agency for Healthcare Research and Quality*: Kellyn V. Carper and Anne Elixhauser; *Centers for Medicare & Medicaid Services*: Aaron C. Catlin, Tony Dean, Maria Diacogiannis, Micah B. Hartman, Deborah Kidd, Barbara S. Klees, Jennifer W. Lazio, Anne B. Martin, Debra Reed-Gillette, Joseph F. Regan, Jeffrey S. Silverman, Christopher J. Truffer, and Lekha S. Whittle; *National Institutes of Health*: Nadia Howlander and Marsha Lopez; *Substance Abuse and Mental Health Services Administration*: Mitchell Berger, Christopher D. Carroll, Beth Han, and Neil Russell; and by the following governmental and nongovernmental organizations: *U.S. Census Bureau*: Bernadette Proctor; *Bureau of Labor Statistics*: Elizabeth A. Ashack, Ryan Farrell, Matt Gunter, Jesus Ranon, and Audrey Watson; *Department of Veterans Affairs*: Tom Garin and Susan Sullivan; *American Association of Colleges of Pharmacy*: Nancy T. Nguyen, Danielle A. Taylor, and Jamie N. Taylor; *American Association of Colleges of Osteopathic Medicine*: Lindsey Jurd; *American Association of Colleges of Podiatric Medicine*: Moraith G. North; *American Dental Association*: Adriana R. Menezes and Bradley Munson; *Association of American Medical Colleges*: Brianna Gunter; *Association of Schools and Colleges of Optometry*: Joanne C. Zuckerman; *Association of Schools & Programs of Public Health*: Christine M. Plepys; *University of Michigan, Monitoring the Future*: Lloyd Johnston and Ginger Maggio; and *Cowles Research Group*: C. McKeen Cowles.

Special Acknowledgment

The *Health, United States* team would like to recognize **Virginia (Ginny) M. Freid** and **Ilene B. Rosen**, who recently retired from the National Center for Health Statistics. Ginny contributed to *Health, United States* for more than 30 years, providing direction and guidance for the report. Her analytical and statistical skills were key to maintaining *Health, United States* as the gold standard for reporting on health in the United States. Ilene provided meticulous administrative and production support for *Health, United States* for nearly 10 years, including the critical task of report distribution to key partners and stakeholders. We wish them the very best in their retirement!

Contents

Contents

At a Glance Table and Highlights

Chartbook on Long-term Trends in Health

Trend Tables

List of Chartbook Figures

Population Characteristics

Mortality

Natality

Health Risk Factors

Morbidity

Utilization

Prevention

Health Care Resources

Personal Health Care Expenditures

Health Insurance

List of Trend Tables

Health Status and Determinants

Determinants and Measures of Health

Utilization of Health Resources

Ambulatory Care

Inpatient Care

Health Care Resources

Personnel

Health Care Expenditures and Payers

	Value (year)		*Health, United States, 2016* Table No.
Life Expectancy and Mortality			
Life expectancy, in years			Table 15
At birth	76.8 (2000)	78.9 (2014)	78.8 (2015)
Infant deaths per 1,000 live births			Table 11
All infants	6.91 (2000)	5.82 (2014)	5.90 (2015)
Deaths per 100,000 population,[1] age-adjusted			Table 17
All causes	869.0 (2000)	724.6 (2014)	733.1 (2015)
Heart disease	257.6 (2000)	167.0 (2014)	168.5 (2015)
Cancer	199.6 (2000)	161.2 (2014)	158.5 (2015)
Chronic lower respiratory diseases	44.2 (2000)	40.5 (2014)	41.6 (2015)
Unintentional injuries	34.9 (2000)	40.5 (2014)	43.2 (2015)
Stroke	60.9 (2000)	36.5 (2014)	37.6 (2015)
Alzheimer's disease	18.1 (2000)	25.4 (2014)	29.4 (2015)
Diabetes	25.0 (2000)	20.9 (2014)	21.3 (2015)
Influenza and pneumonia	23.7 (2000)	15.1 (2014)	15.2 (2015)
Nephritis, nephrotic syndrome, and nephrosis	13.5 (2000)	13.2 (2014)	13.4 (2015)
Suicide	10.4 (2000)	13.0 (2014)	13.3 (2015)
Morbidity and Risk Factors			
Fair or poor health, percent			Table 45
All ages	8.9 (2000)	9.8 (2014)	10.1 (2015)
65 years and over	26.9 (2000)	21.7 (2014)	21.8 (2015)
Heart disease (ever told), percent			Table 38
18 years and over	11.3 (2000–2001)	11.4 (2012–2013)	11.6 (2014–2015)
65 years and over	30.9 (2000–2001)	29.8 (2012–2013)	29.2 (2014–2015)
Cancer (ever told), percent			Table 38
18 years and over	5.0 (2000–2001)	6.4 (2012–2013)	6.5 (2014–2015)
65 years and over	15.2 (2000–2001)	18.4 (2012–2013)	18.4 (2014–2015)
Hypertension,[2] percent			Table 54
20 years and over	30.2 (1999–2002)	32.2 (2007–2010)	33.0 (2011–2014)
Diabetes,[3] percent			Table 40
20 years and over	9.8 (1999–2002)	12.0 (2007–2010)	12.6 (2011–2014)
Hypercholesterolemia,[4] percent			Table 55
20 years and over	25.0 (1999–2002)	28.7 (2007–2010)	29.8 (2011–2014)
Obese, percent			Tables 58 and 59
Obese,[5] 20 years and over	30.5 (1999–2002)	34.9 (2007–2010)	36.5 (2011–2014)
Obese (BMI at or above sex- and age-specific 95th percentile):			
2–5 years	10.3 (1999–2002)	11.1 (2007–2010)	8.9 (2011–2014)
6–11 years	15.9 (1999–2002)	18.8 (2007–2010)	17.5 (2011–2014)
12–19 years	16.0 (1999–2002)	18.2 (2007–2010)	20.5 (2011–2014)
Cigarette smoking, percent			Table 47
18 years and over	23.2 (2000)	16.8 (2014)	15.1 (2015)
Aerobic activity and muscle strengthening,[6] met both guidelines, percent			Table 57
18 years and over	15.1 (2000)	20.9 (2014)	20.9 (2015)

[1] Causes are ordered by the number of deaths in 2015.
[2] Having measured high blood pressure (systolic pressure of at least 140 mm Hg or diastolic pressure of at least 90 mm Hg) and/or respondent report of taking antihypertensive medication.
[3] Includes physician-diagnosed and undiagnosed diabetes (fasting plasma glucose of at least 126 mg/dL or a hemoglobin A1c of at least 6.5%).
[4] Having high serum total cholesterol of 240 mg/dL or greater and/or respondent report of taking cholesterol-lowering medication.
[5] Obesity is a body mass index (BMI) greater than or equal to 30 for adults. Height and weight are measured rather than self-reported.
[6] Federal guidelines recommend at least 150 minutes of moderate-intensity or 75 minutes of vigorous-intensity aerobic physical activity a week and muscle-strengthening activities at least twice a week.

	Value (year)			*Health, United States, 2016* Table No.
Health Care Utilization				
No health care visit in past 12 months, percent				Table 65
Under 18 years	12.3 (2000)	7.9 (2014)	7.9 (2015)	
18–44 years	23.4 (2000)	23.2 (2014)	23.3 (2015)	
45–64 years	14.9 (2000)	15.0 (2014)	13.7 (2015)	
65 years and over	7.4 (2000)	5.6 (2014)	5.5 (2015)	
Emergency room visit in past 12 months, percent				Tables 73 and 74
Under 18 years	20.3 (2000)	16.7 (2014)	16.9 (2015)	
18–44 years	20.5 (2000)	18.4 (2014)	18.6 (2015)	
45–64 years	17.6 (2000)	17.5 (2014)	17.4 (2015)	
65 years and over	23.7 (2000)	21.2 (2014)	21.8 (2015)	
Dental visit in past year, percent				Table 78
2–17 years	74.1 (2000)	83.0 (2014)	84.7 (2015)	
18–64 years	65.1 (2000)	62.0 (2014)	64.0 (2015)	
65 years and over	56.6 (2000)	62.4 (2014)	62.7 (2015)	
Prescription drug in past 30 days, percent				Table 79
Under 18 years	23.8 (1999–2002)	24.0 (2007–2010)	21.5 (2011–2014)	
18–44 years	35.9 (1999–2002)	38.7 (2007–2010)	37.1 (2011–2014)	
45–64 years	64.1 (1999–2002)	66.2 (2007–2010)	69.0 (2011–2014)	
65 years and over	84.7 (1999–2002)	89.7 (2007–2010)	90.6 (2011–2014)	
Hospitalization in past year, percent				Table 81
18–44 years	7.0 (2000)	5.8 (2014)	5.8 (2015)	
45–64 years	8.4 (2000)	7.4 (2014)	7.7 (2015)	
65 years and over	18.2 (2000)	15.3 (2014)	15.2 (2015)	
Health Insurance and Access to Care				
Uninsured, percent				Table 105
Under 65 years	17.0 (2000)	13.3 (2014)	10.6 (2015)	
Under 18 years	12.6 (2000)	5.4 (2014)	4.5 (2015)	
18–44 years	22.4 (2000)	19.7 (2014)	15.9 (2015)	
45–64 years	12.6 (2000)	11.8 (2014)	9.0 (2015)	
Delay or nonreceipt of needed medical care in past 12 months due to cost, percent				Table 63
Under 18 years	4.6 (2000)	2.8 (2014)	2.7 (2015)	
18–44 years	9.5 (2000)	10.7 (2014)	9.5 (2015)	
45–64 years	8.8 (2000)	11.7 (2014)	10.3 (2015)	
65 years and over	4.5 (2000)	4.3 (2014)	4.1 (2015)	
Health Care Resources				
Community hospital beds per 1,000 population[7]				Table 90
United States	2.9 (2000)	2.5 (2013)	2.5 (2014)	
Highest state	6.0 (ND) (2000)	5.6 (DC) (2013)	5.4 (DC) (2014)	
Lowest state	1.9 (NM,NV,OR,UT,WA) (2000)	1.7 (OR,WA) (2013)	1.7 (OR,WA) (2014)	
Health Care Expenditures				
Personal health care expenditures, in dollars				Table 95
Total, in trillions	$1.2 (2000)	$2.6 (2014)	$2.7 (2015)	
Per capita	$4,121 (2000)	$8,050 (2014)	$8,468 (2015)	

[7] Copyright 2016. Used with permission of Health Forum LLC, an affiliate of the American Hospital Association.

NOTES: Estimates in this table are taken from the PDF, printed, or spreadsheet version of the cited tables. For more information and the spreadsheet version of the tables, see the *Health, United States* website: http://www.cdc.gov/nchs/hus/index.htm.

Highlights

This Highlights section includes data from the four major areas included in the report: health status and determinants, utilization of health resources, health care resources, and health care expenditures and payers. As *Health, United States* enters its 40th year of reporting on the health of the nation, this year's Highlights section presents trends in health from 1975 or the earliest year possible, given data availability and comparability issues. The Highlights focus on both trends and current data on topics of public health interest and illustrate the breadth of material included in *Health, United States*. Each highlight includes a reference to the detailed trend table or figure where definitions of terms and additional data can be obtained.

Health Status and Determinants

Life Expectancy and Mortality

Between 1975 and 2015, life expectancy at birth increased from 72.6 to 78.8 years for the total U.S. population. For males, life expectancy increased from 68.8 years in 1975 to 76.3 years in 2015, and for females, life expectancy increased from 76.6 years in 1975 to 81.2 years in 2015 (Table 15).

Life expectancy at birth decreased 0.1 years overall between 2014 and 2015. For males, life expectancy declined 0.2 years from 76.5 years in 2014 to 76.3 years in 2015, and for females, life expectancy decreased 0.1 years, from 81.3 years in 2014 to 81.2 years in 2015 (Table 15).

Between 1975 and 2015, life expectancy at birth increased more for the black than for the white population, thereby narrowing the gap in life expectancy between these two racial groups. In 1975, life expectancy at birth for the white population was 6.6 years longer than for the black population; by 2015, the difference had narrowed to 3.5 years (Figure 6).

Between 2014 and 2015, life expectancy at birth was stable at 82.0 years for Hispanic persons, decreased 0.2 years to 78.7 years for non-Hispanic white persons, and decreased 0.2 years to 75.1 years for non-Hispanic black persons (Table 15).

Between 1975 and 2015, the infant mortality rate decreased 63%, from 16.07 to 5.90 deaths per 1,000 live births and the neonatal mortality rate (among infants under age 28 days) decreased 66%, from 11.58 to 3.93. Between 1975 and 2015, the postneonatal mortality rate (among infants aged 28 days through 11 months) decreased 56%, from 4.49 to 1.96 (Figure 7).

Despite declines in infant mortality for all racial and ethnic groups, infants of non-Hispanic black mothers (10.93 infant deaths per 1,000 live births) had the highest infant mortality rates compared with the other racial and ethnic groups in 2014 (Figure 7 and Table 10).

Between 1975 and 2015, the age-adjusted heart disease death rate decreased 61% from 431.2 to 168.5 deaths per 100,000 population; and the age-adjusted cancer death rate decreased 21% from 200.1 to 158.5 deaths per 100,000 population. Throughout 1975–2015, heart disease and cancer were the first and second leading causes of death. In 2015, these two causes accounted for 45% of all deaths (Figure 8 and Table 19).

The age-adjusted drug poisoning death rate involving opioid analgesics increased from 1.4 to 5.4 deaths per 100,000 population between 1999 and 2010, decreased to 5.1 in 2012 and 2013, then increased to 5.9 in 2014, and to 7.0 in 2015. The age-adjusted drug poisoning death rate involving heroin doubled from 0.7 to 1.4 deaths per 100,000 resident population between 1999 and 2011 and then continued to increase to 4.1 in 2015 (Table 27).

In 2015, the 10 leading causes of death were heart disease, cancer, chronic lower respiratory diseases, unintentional injuries, stroke, Alzheimer's disease, diabetes, influenza and pneumonia, kidney disease, and suicide. These 10 causes of death accounted for 74% of the 2.7 million deaths in 2015 (Figure 8 and Table 19).

Between 2014 and 2015, age-adjusted death rates increased for eight of the ten leading causes. The only decrease in age-adjusted death rates among the 10 leading causes of death between 2014 and 2015 was for cancer; the rate for influenza and pneumonia did not change significantly (Table 17).

Between 2014 and 2015, the age-adjusted suicide death rate increased 2%, from 13.0 to 13.3 deaths per 100,000 resident population. Among adolescents and adults aged 15–24, suicide death rates increased 8% between 2014 and 2015 (Table 30).

Fertility and Natality

Between 1975 and 2015, the birth rate among teenagers aged 15–19 fell 60%, from 55.6 to 22.3 live births per 1,000 females—a record low for the United States (Figure 9).

In 1975, 7.38% of infants were low-birthweight (weighing less than 2,500 grams [5.5 pounds] at birth) compared with 8.07% in 2015. Low-birthweight was more common among infants of non-Hispanic black mothers (13.35%) and Puerto Rican mothers (9.42%) than among infants of mothers in other racial and ethnic groups in 2015 (Table 5).

Health Risk Factors for the Noninstitutionalized Population

Children

From 1988–1994 to 2003–2004, the percentage of children and adolescents aged 2–19 with obesity increased from 10.0% to 17.1%, and then was stable from 2003–2004 to 2013–2014. The percentage of children and adolescents with obesity was 17.2% in 2013–2014 (Figure 11).

In 2015, 4.2% of adolescents aged 12–17 reported smoking cigarettes in the past month. Smoking prevalence has declined since 2002, when 13.0% of adolescents reported smoking cigarettes in the past month (Table 50).

In 2015, e-cigarette use in the past month was reported by 16.2% of 12th graders, 14.0% of 10th graders, and 9.5% of 8th graders (Table 51).

Adults

Between 1988–1994 and 2013–2014, the percentage of adults aged 20 and over with Grade 1 obesity (a body mass index [BMI] of 30.0–34.9) increased from 14.8% to 20.7%. Those with Grade 2 obesity (BMI of 35.0–39.9) rose from 5.2% to 9.5%, and those with Grade 3 obesity (BMI of 40 or higher) increased from 2.9% to 7.6% (percentages are age-adjusted) (Figure 11).

Between 1974 and 2015, the age-adjusted prevalence of current cigarette smoking declined from 36.9% to 15.6% among persons aged 25 and over. Current cigarette smoking declined as educational attainment increased, from 25.6% of adults aged 25 and over without a high school diploma or GED to 5.9% of those with a Bachelor's degree or higher in 2015 (Figure 10 and Table 48).

Measures of Health and Disease Prevalence for the Noninstitutionalized Population

Between 1997–1999 and 2013–2015, the percentage of children and adolescents under age 18 with a food allergy increased from 3.4% to 5.6%. During the same period, the percentage of children and adolescents under age 18 with a skin allergy increased from 7.4% to 11.8% (Table 35).

For children and adolescents aged 5–19 living below the federal poverty level, the percentage with untreated dental caries declined steadily from 39.0% in 1988–1994 to 24.7% in 2011–2014 (Figure 12).

Between 1997–1999 and 2013–2015, the percentage of children and adolescents aged 5–17 diagnosed with attention deficit/hyperactivity disorder increased from 6.5% to 10.4% (Table 35).

From 1988–1994 to 2011–2014, the age-adjusted percentage of adults aged 20 and over with hypertension who had uncontrolled high blood pressure decreased for both men (83.2% to 58.1%) and women (68.5% to 45.5%). Throughout the period, among those with hypertension, men had a higher percentage with uncontrolled blood pressure than women (Figure 14 and Table 54).

Between 1988–1994 and 2011–2014, the age-adjusted prevalence of total diabetes among adults aged 20 and over increased from 8.8% to 11.9%. In both time periods, the age-adjusted prevalence of total diabetes was higher among non-Hispanic black and Mexican origin adults compared with non-Hispanic white adults (Figure 13 and Table 40).

Utilization of Health Resources for the Noninstitutionalized Population

Use of Health Care Services

Between 1997 and 2015, the percentage of persons who had no health care visits in the past 12 months decreased from 16.5% to 14.6%. In 2015, 7.9% of children and adolescents under age 18, 23.3% of adults aged 18–44, 13.7% of those aged 45–64, and 5.5% of adults aged 65 and over had no health care visits in the past 12 months (Table 65).

Between 1975 and 2015, the percentage of males and females under age 75 with an overnight hospital stay in the prior 12 months declined, while remaining stable among those aged 75 and over. Hospitalization use generally increased with age, from 2.1% of boys and girls aged under 18 to 20.3% of men and 17.7% of women aged 75 and over in 2015 (Figure 18).

Between 1988–1994 and 2013–2014, the percent of adults who had taken at least one prescription drug in the past 30 days increased for adults aged 18–44, adults aged 45–64, and adults aged 65 and over. In 2013–2014, 36.5% of adults aged 18–44 years, 69.6% of adults aged 45–64 years, and 90.8% of adults aged 65 years and over had taken at least one prescription drug (Figure 15).

Between 1997 and 2015, the percentage of persons aged 2 and over who had a dental visit in the past year increased from 65.1% to 68.2%. In 2015, 84.7% of children aged 2–17 years, 64.0% of adults aged 18–64, and 62.7% of adults aged 65 and over had visited a dentist in the past year (Table 78).

Use of Preventive Medical Care Services for the Noninstitutionalized Population

Between 2008 and 2015, receipt of the full series of human papillomavirus (HPV) vaccine for adolescents aged 13–17 increased among females from 17.9% to 41.9% (Table 67). The HPV vaccine was first recommended for adolescent males in October 2011; receipt of the full series for males aged 13–17 increased from 1.3% in 2011 to 28.1% in 2015.

Between 2010 and 2015, the percentage of adults aged 18 and over who had received an influenza vaccination in the past 12 months increased from 35.8% to 43.2%. In 2015, influenza vaccination increased with age, with 30.9% of those aged 18–44, 45.1% of those aged 45–64, and 69.1% of those aged 65 and over reporting an influenza vaccination in the past 12 months (Table 68).

Between 2000 and 2015, the percent of adults aged 50–75 with a colorectal cancer test or procedure approximately doubled for each of the four racial and ethnic groups. In 2015, 52.1% of non-Hispanic Asian and 47.4% of Hispanic adults aged 50–75 had a colorectal cancer test, compared with 60.3% of non-Hispanic black and 65.6% of non-Hispanic white adults aged 50–75 (Figure 19).

Difficulty Accessing Needed Medical Care Due to Cost for the Noninstitutionalized Population

The percentage of adults aged 18–64 who reported delaying or not receiving needed medical care due to cost increased from 10.7% in 1997 to 14.7% in 2010 and then declined to 9.8% in 2015 (Table 63).

Health Care Resources

Between 2001 and 2015, the number of professionally active dentists in the United States increased from 57.32 to 60.89 dentists per 100,000 civilian population. In 2015, the number of dentists per 100,000 population ranged from 40.93 in Arkansas to 89.85 in the District of Columbia (Table 86).

The average length of community hospital stays fell from 7.7 days in 1975 to 5.5 days in 2014. The occupancy rate for community hospitals declined from 75.0% in 1975 to 64.8% in 1985 and then to 62.8% in 2014 (Figure 20).

Between 1995 and 2015, the U.S. nursing home occupancy rate decreased from 84.5% to 80.3%. In 2015, nursing home occupancy rates were highest in North Dakota (92.7%), the District of Columbia (91.8%), Rhode Island (91.4%), and South Dakota (91.4%). The lowest occupancy rates in 2015 were in Oregon (60.1%), Utah (63.9%), Indiana (64.3%), and Idaho (64.9%) (Table 92).

Health Care Expenditures and Payers

Health Care Expenditures

Between 1975 and 2015, national health expenditures as a percent of gross domestic product (GDP) increased from 7.9% to 17.8% (Table 93).

Between 1975 and 2015, the percentage of personal health care expenditures for hospital care decreased from 45.3% to 38.1%; the percentage of expenditures for prescription drugs increased from 7.1% to 11.9%; the percentage of expenditures for nursing care facilities and continuing care retirement communities decreased from 7.1% to 5.8%; and the percentage of expenditures for physician and clinical services remained stable (22.4%–23.4%) (Table 94).

Between 2000 and 2014, the average inflation-adjusted cost for the entire hospitalization involving a heart valve procedure increased from $44,609 to $51,896; a coronary artery bypass graft procedure increased from $32,520 to $41,932; cardiac pacemaker or defibrillator insertion, revision, replacement, or removal increased from $28,757 to $34,974; and spinal fusion increased from $18,119 to $28,949 (Table 96).

Health Care Payers

Between 1975 and 2015, the share of all personal health care expenditures paid by private insurance increased from 24.5% to 34.8%; by Medicare increased from 13.8% to 22.3%; and by Medicaid increased from 11.3% to 17.9%. The share paid by consumers out-of-pocket decreased from 32.9% to 12.4% during the same period (Figure 23 and Table 95).

Between 1986 and 2014, the share of mental health expenditures paid for inpatient care decreased from 41% to 16%; residential treatment decreased from 22% to 12%; outpatient treatment increased from 24% to 35%; and the share paid for retail prescription drugs increased from 8% to 27% (Figure 24).

Between 1986 and 2014, the share of substance use disorder expenditures paid for inpatient care decreased from 50% to 19%; outpatient treatment increased from 27% to 40%; residential treatment increased from 17% to 27%; and the share paid for retail prescription drugs increased from less than 1% to 5% (Figure 24).

Health Insurance Coverage for the Noninstitutionalized Population

Between 1978 and September 2016 (preliminary estimates), the percentage of children under age 18 with Medicaid coverage increased from 11.3% to 39.2% and the percentage of children who were uninsured decreased from 12.0% to

5.0% (Martinez ME, Zammitti EP, Cohen RA. Health insurance coverage: Early release of estimates from the National Health Interview Survey, January–September 2016. NCHS; 2017. Available from: https://www.cdc.gov/nchs/data/nhis/earlyrelease/insur201702.pdf; Figure 26; and unpublished data).

The percentage of adults aged 18–64 who were uninsured increased from 11.9% in 1978 to over 18% by the mid-1990s before climbing to more than 20% in the early years of the 2010 decade. The percentage then decreased to 12.3% in September 2016 (preliminary data) (Martinez ME, Zammitti EP, Cohen RA. Health insurance coverage: Early release of estimates from the National Health Interview Survey, January–September 2016. NCHS; 2017. Available from: https://www.cdc.gov/nchs/data/nhis/earlyrelease/insur201702.pdf; Figure 27).

A provision of the ACA requires insurers to extend dependent coverage on a family plan until age 26, effective in 2010. The percentage of adults aged 19–25 who were uninsured decreased from 33.8% in 2010 to 16.0% in 2015 (Table 105).

During January–September 2016 (preliminary data), 14.6% of adults aged 19–25 were uninsured (Martinez ME, Zammitti EP, Cohen RA. Health insurance coverage: Early release of estimates from the National Health Interview Survey, January–September 2016. NCHS; 2017. Available from: https://www.cdc.gov/nchs/data/nhis/earlyrelease/insur201702.pdf).

In 2015, Massachusetts (3.2%), the District of Columbia (4.0%), Hawaii (4.5%), and Vermont (5.0%) had the lowest percentages of persons uninsured (i.e., without public or private coverage) among those under age 65, while Florida (16.2%), Oklahoma (16.5%), and Texas (19.0%) had the highest percentages of persons uninsured (Table 114).

Chartbook on Long-term Trends in Health

Chartbook on Long-term Trends in Health

Introduction

As *Health, United States* enters its 40th year of reporting on the health of the nation, this year's Chartbook focuses on trends in health and health care since 1975. Examining long-term trends in health informs the development and implementation of effective health policies and programs. During the period since 1975, the nation has witnessed important changes in the characteristics of the national population which affect health and health care delivery in the United States. The fraction of the population aged 65 and over has increased and more older Americans are living longer with chronic health conditions. The nation has also become increasingly racially and ethnically diverse with a growing immigrant population (1,2). Socioeconomic and cultural differences among racial and ethnic groups in the United States influence patterns of disease, disability, and health care use (3). Changes in the distribution of persons living in poverty and near-poverty have implications for access to health care, health behaviors, and health outcomes. Finally, where Americans live has shifted over the past 40 years, with variations in health outcomes by metropolitan versus nonmetropolitan areas of the country (4,5).

The health of the Nation has improved in many respects over the past century, in part because of the significant resources devoted to public health programs, research, health education, and health care. Life expectancy in the United States has had a long-term upward trend, although the greatest increases were in the early part of the 20th century and gains have recently stalled for certain demographic subgroups (6). Many diseases have been controlled or their morbidity and mortality substantially reduced since 1975. Notable achievements in public health have included the control of vaccine-preventable diseases, lead poisoning prevention, and improvements in motor vehicle safety (7,8). The AIDS epidemic in the 1980s has since been controlled by prevention, testing, and treatment services including the use of highly active antiretroviral therapy (HAART) starting in 1996, which substantially reduced AIDS-related hospital admissions (9) and death rates (Table 17). Advances in medical technology, including diagnostic imaging technologies, procedures, and new prescription drugs have extended and improved the quality of countless lives. The decline in death rates from cardiovascular disease, stroke, and cancer (10) is a major public health achievement that resulted in large part from prevention efforts and improvements in early detection, treatment, and care, including changes in risk factors and lifestyle modifications (11). Yet, even as progress is made in improving life expectancy and quality of life, increased longevity is accompanied by increased prevalence of chronic conditions and their associated pain and disability.

Additionally, new threats have emerged—communicable diseases such as severe acute respiratory syndrome (SARS) in 2003, pandemic influenza A(H1N1)pdm09 (12) in 2009, and more recently the Ebola outbreak in 2014 and Zika virus in 2016, continue to pose ongoing health concerns. Other public health threats include the misuse of antibiotics and the rise of antibiotic resistance (13) and the increasing overuse of prescription opioid painkillers, contributing to a national drug overdose epidemic and rising drug poisoning deaths (14,15). Moreover, in recent years progress in some arenas—declines in infant and some cause-specific mortality, morbidity from certain chronic diseases, reduction in prevalence of risk factors including smoking and lack of exercise—has not been as rapid as in earlier years, or trends have been moving in the wrong direction. In addition, improvements have not been equally distributed by income, race, ethnicity, education, and geography (16,17).

Over the past 40 years *Health, United States* has provided an annual picture of the health of the United States, presenting trends in health status and health care utilization, resources, and expenditures and health insurance. The report has also identified variations in health status, modifiable risk factors, and health care utilization among people by age, race and ethnicity, gender, income level, and geographic location. Monitoring the health of the American people is an essential step in making sound health policy and setting research and program priorities.

Figures in the *Health, United States, 2016* Chartbook are from multiple data systems, and 40-year trends are not always possible given data availability and comparability issues. Charts have been grouped into five sections. The first section (Figures 1–5) presents an overview of the demographic and socioeconomic factors that have influenced the health of the nation over the last 40 years. The second section (Figures 6–14) focuses on health status and determinants: life expectancy, birth rates, leading causes of death, infant mortality, cigarette smoking, obesity, untreated dental caries, diabetes prevalence, and uncontrolled hypertension. The third section (Figures 15–19) presents trends in health care utilization: use of prescription drugs, health care and emergency department visits, overnight hospital stays, and cancer screening tests. The fourth section (Figures 20–22) focuses on changes in health care resources: hospitals, primary and specialist physicians, and nursing homes. The fifth section (Figures 23–27) describes trends in health care expenditures: personal health care expenditures, mental health and substance use expenditures, Medicare managed care enrollment by state, and health insurance coverage. This collection of charts provides a long-term look at changes in the health of the nation and the condition of the U.S. health system. Ensuring healthier and safer lives in the future will require continuing efforts to monitor health outcomes and the many factors affecting health and health care.

Population Characteristics
Population by Sex and Age

Between 1975 and 2015, the U.S. population grew from 216.0 million to 321.4 million and the percentage aged 65 and over increased for both males and females.

The aging of the population has important consequences for the health of the nation (18). The increase in the fraction of the population aged 65 and over, particularly those aged 85 and older (the oldest old), suggests a growing number of older Americans living longer with chronic health conditions, placing pressure on both the acute and long-term care delivery systems, and public and private payers. The rectangularization of the population pyramid occurring between 1975 and 2015 reflects longer life spans and lower birth rates, although the U.S. decline in fertility has not been as extensive as other developed countries (19).

From 1975 to 2015, the number of Americans aged 65 and over more than doubled from 22.6 million to 47.8 million (See data table for Figure 1). By 2030, it is projected that one in five Americans will be 65 or older (20). Within the population aged 65 and over, those 85 and over have experienced the most rapid growth, particularly among women. While the proportion of both men and women 85 and older increased between 1975 and 2015, in both time periods there are more women than men aged 85 and older. By 2015, 2.5% of the female population was 85 and older (4.1 million) compared to 1.4% of the male population aged 85 and over (2.2 million).

Figure 1. Population, by sex and five-year age groups: United States, 1975 and 2015

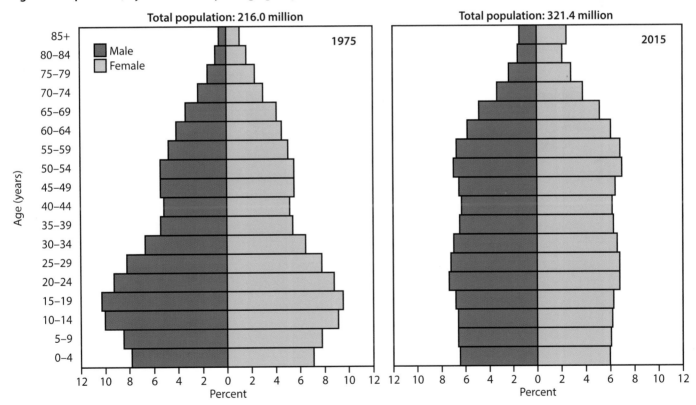

NOTES: Resident Population. See data table for Figure 1.

SOURCE: U.S. Census Bureau 1975 intercensal estimates of the July 1, 1975 resident population; 2015 postcensal estimates of the July 1, 2015 resident population.

Excel and PowerPoint: http://www.cdc.gov/nchs/hus/contents2016.htm#fig01

Population Characteristics
Population by Race and Ethnic Group

Between 1980 and 2015, the U.S. population became more diverse as the percentage of the population in racial and ethnic minority groups (including non-Hispanic black, Hispanic, non-Hispanic Asian, and all other non-Hispanic persons) grew among all age groups.

The racial and ethnic composition of the population has implications for the health care system because many risk factors, including health behaviors, disease prevalence, mortality rates, health insurance coverage, and access to and utilization of health services, differ substantially by race and ethnicity (*Health, United States, 2016* Trend Tables). The U.S. population is becoming more ethnically and racially diverse (3). In 1980, 20.1% of the population identified as racial or ethnic minorities; in 2015, 38.4% of the population identified as racial or ethnic minorities (Figure 2). This growing diversity also has implications for the health care workforce given the importance of providing culturally competent care to all race and ethnic groups (21).

Non-Hispanic whites remain the largest racial and ethnic group, although the population of people who identified as non-Hispanic white declined among all age groups from 1980 to 2015. Diversity is highest among children and adolescents aged 0–17: between 1980 and 2015, the non-Hispanic white share of the population aged 0–17 decreased by 31% and the Hispanic share nearly tripled. By 2015, just over one-half of the child and adolescent population was non-Hispanic white and one-quarter was Hispanic. Over the same time frame, among adults aged 18–64, the non-Hispanic white share of the population decreased by 24% and the Hispanic share of the population nearly tripled. By 2015, 61.5% of the 18–64 population was non-Hispanic white and 17.3% was Hispanic. Among adults aged 65 and over, the non-Hispanic white share of the population decreased by 12% between 1980 and 2015 and the Hispanic share of the population nearly tripled. By 2015, just over three-quarters of the older adult population was non-Hispanic white, 8.8% was non-Hispanic black, and 7.9% was Hispanic.

Figure 2. Population, by race and Hispanic origin and age: United States, 1980, 1990, 2000, and 2015

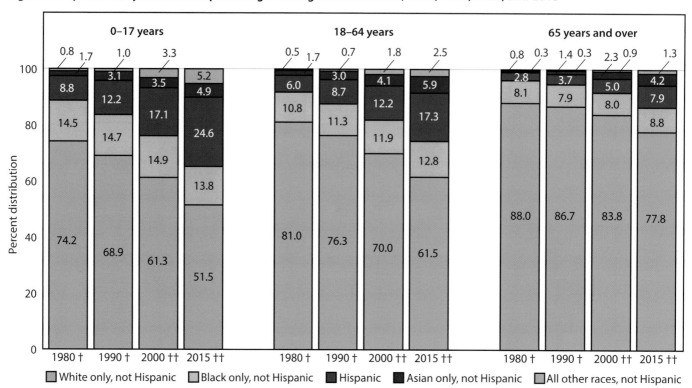

NOTES: Resident population. Persons of Hispanic origin may be of any race. Race data for 2000 and 2015 are not directly comparable with data from 1980 and 1990 because of the use of different Standards for classifying race.

†1980 and 1990: Data were tabulated based on the 1977 Standards with four single race categories; the category non-Hispanic Asian only includes non-Hispanic Pacific Islander only persons. Non-Hispanic All other races includes non-Hispanic American Indian or Alaska Native only.

††2000 and 2015: Data were tabulated based on the 1997 Standards with five single race groups and the option to report more than one race. Non-Hispanic All other races includes non-Hispanic Native Hawaiian or Other Pacific Islander only, non-Hispanic American Indian or Alaska Native only, and non-Hispanic multiple race (shown combined in the chart due to small numbers and displayed separately in the data table). See data table for Figure 2.

SOURCE: U.S. Census Bureau decennial estimates 1980, 1990, and 2000; postcensal estimates 2015.

Excel and PowerPoint: http://www.cdc.gov/nchs/hus/contents2016.htm#fig02

Population Characteristics
Foreign-Born Population

Since 1970, the foreign-born share of the population residing in the United States has nearly tripled, increasing from 4.7% of the population to 13.5% of the population in 2015.

The increasing racial and ethnic diversity in the U.S. population is due in part to the immigrant population who are more likely to be from racial and ethnic minority groups. Foreign-born immigrants are often younger and healthier than native-born Americans, explained in part by the healthy immigrant effect—that those who immigrate are healthier than those who do not (22,23). However, addressing the health and health care needs of an increasingly diverse immigrant population can be challenging given different socioeconomic circumstances, immigration statuses, and federal and state policies related to access to health care (24).

Since 1970, the foreign-born share of the population residing in the United States has nearly tripled, from 4.7% to 13.5% in 2015. The distribution of country of origin of immigrants has changed between 1970 and 2015. In 1970, 61.7% of immigrants living in the U.S. were from Europe, 19.4% were from Latin America, and 8.9% were from Asia. By 2015, European immigrants made up a smaller share of the foreign-born population (11.1%), while Latin Americans accounted for more than one-half (51.1%) and Asians accounted for nearly one-third (30.6%) of all immigrants.

Figure 3. Foreign-born population: United States, selected years 1970–2015

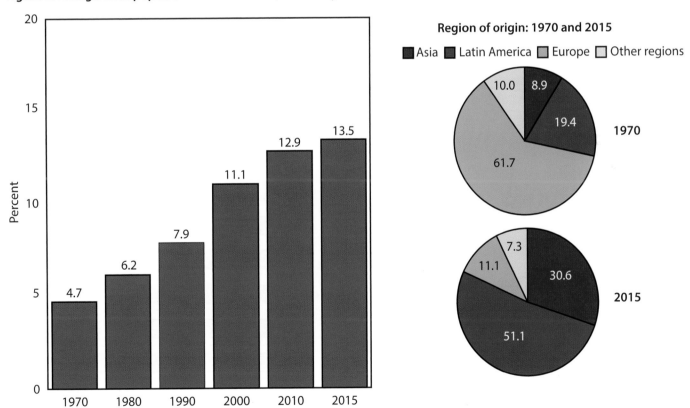

NOTES: Resident population for 1970–2000 and civilian noninstitutionalized population for 2010 and 2015. The foreign-born population includes anyone who is not a U.S. citizen at birth (including naturalized citizens, lawful permanent residents, temporary migrants, humanitarian migrants, and undocumented migrants) among those with region of birth reported. Region of origin "Other" includes Africa, Oceania, and Northern America. See data table for Figure 3.

SOURCE: U.S. Census Bureau, Decennial Census 1970–2000; American Community Survey (ACS) 2010 and 2015.

Excel and PowerPoint: http://www.cdc.gov/nchs/hus/contents2016.htm#fig03

Population Characteristics

Population by Poverty

During 1975–2015, children under age 18 were more likely to live in poverty than adults aged 18–64, and 65 and over.

The relationship between socioeconomic status and health is well established (25,26). Although in some cases illness can lead to poverty, more often poverty is associated with poor health (25–28). Poverty and low income are related to many aspects of health, including access to care, preventive health care, insurance coverage, and health status (26). Children and adults with income below or near 100% of poverty experience worse health outcomes compared with those with higher income levels (Tables 35, 38–46, 102–105).

During 1975–2015, the percent of children under age 18 living in poverty reached a high of 22.7% in 1993, declined to 16.2% in 2000, rose to 22.0% in 2010, and then declined to

19.7% in 2015. Between 1975 and 2015, the percent of adults aged 18–64 living in poverty increased by 35%, from 9.2% in 1975 to 12.4% in 2015. In contrast, adults aged 65 and over experienced a 42% decline in poverty, from 15.3% in 1975 to 8.8% in 2015—due in part to Social Security's cost-of-living adjustments (COLAs), which went into effect in 1975 (29).

In 2015, the percent of persons living below 200% of the poverty level differed significantly by age and gender. Approximately 42% of children, 28% of adults aged 18–64, and 31% of adults aged 65 and over were living below 200% of poverty. Among adults aged 18–64 and 65 and over, a higher percent of women were living below 200% of poverty compared to men in 2015. In contrast, the percent of those living below 200% of poverty were similar for both boys and girls under age 18.

Figure 4. Population, by percent of poverty level and age: United States, 1975–2015

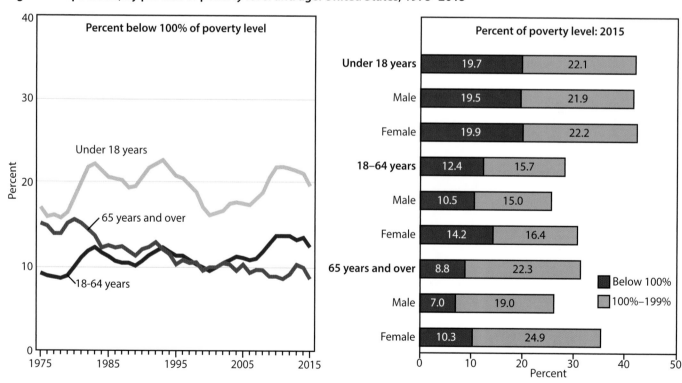

NOTES: Percent of poverty level is based on family income and family size and composition using U.S. Census Bureau poverty thresholds. See data table for Figure 4 and Appendix II, Poverty.

Excel and PowerPoint: http://www.cdc.gov/nchs/hus/contents2016.htm#fig04

SOURCE: U.S. Census Bureau, Current Population Survey, Annual Social and Economic Supplements.

Population Characteristics
Population by Urban-Rural Residence

Between 1970 and 2015, the rural (nonmetropolitan) share of the population declined almost by one-half, from 26.8% to 14.4%, while the suburban share of the population doubled from 12.3% to 24.8%.

Health differences between urban and rural communities have persisted over time (4). The rural population is generally older and poorer than the urban population (28,30). Rural residents have higher injury and smoking rates, and are more likely to lack health insurance, among other health differences (4; Table 105). In addition, the supply of physicians and other health care services differs in urban and rural areas (30). Physicians in rural areas are less likely to be specialists, and mental health providers are less available in rural areas (30). Within metropolitan areas, most of the population growth has occurred in the suburbs of large (population of 1 million or more) metropolitan areas. The population in suburbs are generally wealthier and healthier than inner city areas in large metropolitan areas (4).

Between 1970 and 2015, the percentage of the population living in metropolitan (urban) counties increased by 17% to 85.6% in 2015 and the percentage living in nonmetropolitan (rural) counties declined by 46% to 14.4% in 2015. During this same time period, the percentage of Americans living in suburbs (large fringe metropolitan counties) doubled from 12.3% to 24.8%. In 2015, more than one-half (55.6%) of the U.S. population resided in the inner cities or suburbs of large metropolitan statistical areas of 1 million or more population. Thirty percent of the population lived in medium or small metropolitan areas. An additional 8.5% of the population lived in nonmetropolitan areas with a small city or town and 5.9% lived in the most rural areas.

Figure 5. Population, by urbanization level: United States, 1970, 1980, 1990, 2000, and 2015

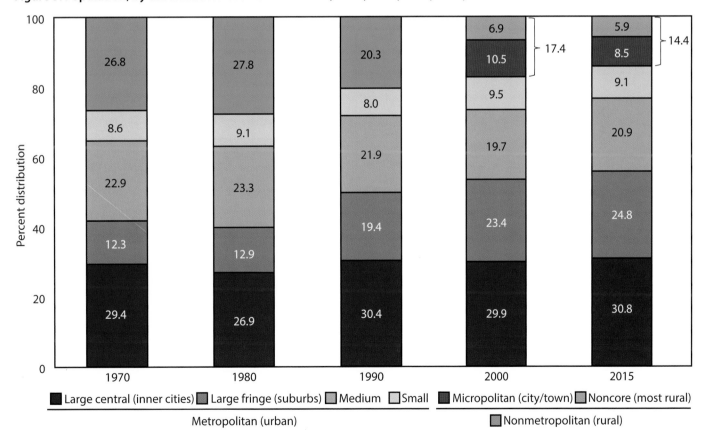

NOTES: The categories micropolitan and noncore were not used in 1970, 1980, and 1990; therefore, total nonmetropolitan population is shown. See data table for Figure 5.

SOURCE: U.S. Census Bureau; 1970 and 1980 data from Department of Agriculture Economic Research Service reports.

Excel and PowerPoint: http://www.cdc.gov/nchs/hus/contents2016.htm#fig05

Mortality
Life Expectancy at Birth

The gap in life expectancy at birth between white persons and black persons persists, but has narrowed since 1975; in 2015, life expectancy was longer for Hispanic persons than for non-Hispanic white and non-Hispanic black persons.

Life expectancy is a measure often used to gauge the overall health of a population. Life expectancy at birth represents the average number of years that a group of infants would live if the group were to experience the age-specific death rates present in the year of birth (31). Differences in life expectancy among various demographic subpopulations, including racial and ethnic groups, may reflect differences in a range of factors such as socioeconomic status, access to medical care, and the prevalence of specific risk factors in a particular subpopulation (32).

During 1975–2015, life expectancy at birth in the United States increased from 68.8 to 76.3 years for males and from 76.6 to 81.2 years for females (Table 15 and data table for Figure 6). During this period, life expectancy at birth for males and females was longer for white persons than for black persons. Racial disparities in life expectancy at birth persisted for both males and females in 2015, but continued to narrow.

Life expectancy at birth was 7.1 years longer for white males than for black males in 1975, and 4.4 years longer for white males than for black males in 2015. In 1975, life expectancy at birth was 6.0 years longer for white females than for black females, and 2.8 years longer for white females than for black females in 2015.

In 2015, Hispanic males and females had the longest life expectancy at birth (79.3 and 84.3, respectively) and non-Hispanic black males (71.8) and females (78.1) had the shortest. In 2015, life expectancy at birth was 7.5 years longer for Hispanic males than for non-Hispanic black males and 6.2 years longer for Hispanic females than non-Hispanic black females.

Figure 6. Life expectancy at birth, by sex, race and Hispanic origin: United States, 1975–2015

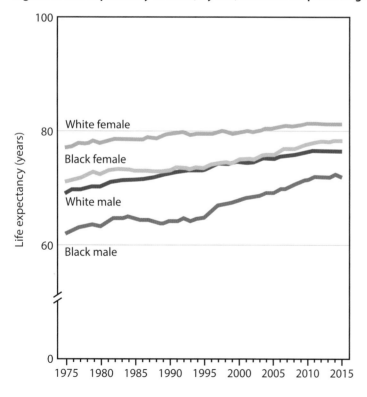

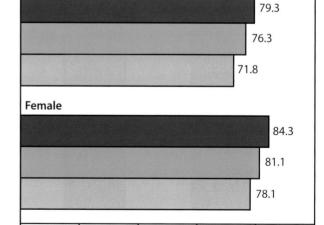

NOTES: Life expectancy data by Hispanic origin were available starting in 2006 and were corrected to address racial and ethnic misclassification. Life expectancy estimates for white and black persons in 2014 and 2015 are based on preliminary Medicare data. See data table for Figure 6.

SOURCE: NCHS, National Vital Statistics System (NVSS).

Excel and PowerPoint: http://www.cdc.gov/nchs/hus/contents2016.htm#fig06

Mortality

Infant Mortality

Between 1975 and 2015, the infant mortality rate declined 63% to reach an historic low, but the rate of decline has slowed since the mid-1990s.

Infant mortality, the death of a baby before his or her first birthday, is an important indicator of the health and well-being of a country. It is used as an indicator of maternal health, community health status, and the availability of quality health services and medical technology (33,34).

Between 1975 and 2015, the infant mortality rate decreased 63% to 5.90 infant deaths per 1,000 live births in 2015. The infant mortality rate has declined more slowly since the mid-1990s, with average annual declines of 0.8% per year during 1996–2007 and 1.8% per year during 2007–2015, compared with 4.7% per year during 1975–1982.

During 1975–2015, the neonatal mortality rate (death rate among infants under 28 days, a subset of infant mortality) declined 66% to 3.93 infant deaths per 1,000 live births

in 2015, and the postneonatal mortality rate (death rate among infants 28 days through 11 months, a subset of infant mortality) declined 56% to 1.96 infant deaths per 1,000 live births in 2015. The neonatal mortality rate has declined more slowly since the mid-1990s, similar to the overall infant mortality rate, while the postneonatal mortality rate declined during 1975–1998, followed by periods of stability and decline during 1998–2015.

Although the infant mortality rate has declined for all racial and ethnic groups (Table 10), rates for infants of non-Hispanic black (10.93 in 2014) and non-Hispanic American Indian or Alaska Native (7.66 in 2014) mothers remain higher than the rates for infants of non-Hispanic white (4.89 in 2014), Hispanic (5.01 in 2014), and non-Hispanic Asian or Pacific Islander (3.68 in 2014) mothers.

Figure 7. Infant mortality rates, by infant age at death and race and Hispanic origin of mother: United States, 1975–2015

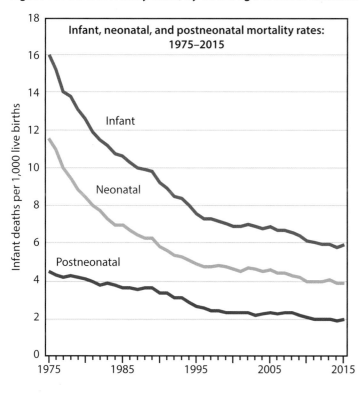

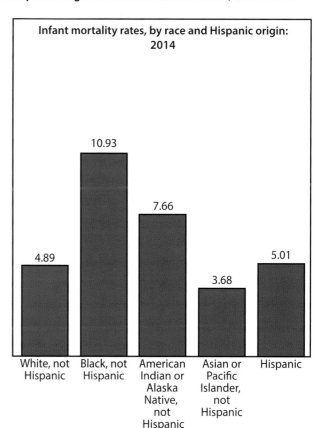

NOTES: Infant (under 1 year of age), neonatal (under 28 days), and postneonatal (28 days–11 months) rates are based on the number of deaths from the mortality file and the number of births from the natality file. Infant mortality rates by race and Hispanic origin are from the Linked Birth/Infant Death data set, in which the most recent data available is 2014. See data table for Figure 7.

SOURCE: NCHS, National Vital Statistics System (NVSS).

Excel and PowerPoint: http://www.cdc.gov/nchs/hus/contents2016.htm#fig07

Mortality
Leading Causes of Death

Heart disease and cancer have remained the top two leading causes of death for the past 40 years.

Cause of death rankings present the most frequently occurring causes of death and illustrate the relative burden of a specific cause of death compared to other causes (35). Because rankings measure the mortality burden relative to other causes, a rank for a specific cause of death may decline over time, even if its death rate has not changed, or its rank may remain the same over time even if its death rate is declining. Rankings may vary by age, sex, and racial and ethnic group (Tables 19 and 20).

In 1975, the five leading causes of death were heart disease, cancer, stroke, unintentional injuries, and influenza and pneumonia. In 2015, the five leading causes of death were heart disease, cancer, chronic lower respiratory diseases, unintentional injuries, and stroke. Throughout 1975–2015, heart disease and cancer remained the top two leading causes of death. The age-adjusted death rate for heart disease declined during 1975–2011, and then stabilized during 2011–2015 (23.4% of deaths in 2015). The age-adjusted death rate for cancer increased during 1975–1990, followed by periods of stability and decline during 1990–2000, and finally

a steady decline during 2000–2015 (22.0% of deaths in 2015). Greater declines in heart disease than cancer mortality during 1975–2015 have narrowed the gap between heart disease and cancer deaths.

Between 1975 and 2015, stroke shifted from being the third to the fifth leading cause of death (5.2% of deaths in 2015). The age-adjusted death rate for stroke declined by 70% during 1975–2015. Unintentional injuries was the fourth leading cause of death in both 1975 and 2015 (5.4% of deaths in 2015). The age-adjusted death rate for unintentional injuries declined between 1975 and the mid-1990s, followed by increasing death rates through 2015. Between 1975 and 2015, influenza and pneumonia shifted from being the fifth to the eighth leading cause of death (2.1% of deaths in 2015). Chronic lower respiratory diseases was the third leading cause of death in 2015 (5.7% of deaths). The age-adjusted death rate for chronic lower respiratory disease decreased steadily during 2000–2015. The remaining top ten leading causes of death in 2015 include Alzheimer's disease (4.1%); diabetes mellitus (2.9%); nephritis, nephrotic syndrome, and nephrosis (1.8%); and suicide (1.6%).

Figure 8. Leading causes of death in 1975 and 2015: United States, 1975–2015

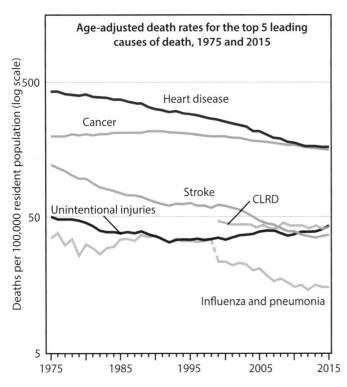

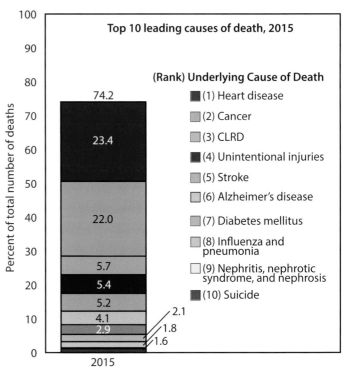

NOTES: Underlying causes of death are based on the *International Classification of Diseases, 8th Revision* (ICD–8) for 1975–1978, ICD–9 for 1979–1998, and ICD–10 for 1999–2015. Due to coding changes for chronic lower respiratory diseases (CLRD) between ICD–9 and ICD–10, which prevent the direct comparison of trends prior to 1998 and after 1999, rates for CLRD are only shown for 1999 onwards. Influenza and Pneumonia coding rules changed starting in 1999 resulting in a decreased number of deaths coded to the cause. See data table for Figure 8.

SOURCE: NCHS, National Vital Statistics System (NVSS).

Excel and PowerPoint: http://www.cdc.gov/nchs/hus/contents2016.htm#fig08

Natality

Birth Rates

Between 1975 and 2015, the birth rates among women aged 15–19, 20–24, and 25–29 declined, with the smallest percent decline among women aged 25–29, while birth rates among women aged 30–34, 35–39, and 40–44 increased.

Changing patterns in social and cultural norms, such as increases in educational attainment and contraceptive use, have contributed to the decline in birth rates among younger women and the increase in birth rates among older women (36).

The birth rate among teens aged 15–19 declined by 64% between 1991 and 2015, after a period of increasing birth rates during 1987–1991. By 2015, the teen birth rate was 22.3 live births per 1,000 females, a record low for the country. While the birth rate among women aged 20–24 has also declined during much of the period 1975–2015 to 76.8 births in 2015, the birth rate among women aged 25–29 had stable, declining, and increasing periods during 1975–2006, followed by a decline during 2006–2015 (104.3 births in 2015).

Between 1975 and 2015, the birth rate declined by 60% for teens aged 15–19, 32% for women aged 20–24, and 4% for women aged 25–29. Between 1975–2015, the birth rate among women aged 30–34 doubled (101.5 births in 2015) and the birth rate among women aged 35–39 and 40–44 more than doubled (51.8 births and 11.0 births, respectively, in 2015).

In 2015, nearly 30% of the first live-births to non-Hispanic American Indian or Alaska Native mothers (27.3%) and one-fifth of the first live-births to non-Hispanic black (19.5%) and Hispanic (21.2%) mothers occurred under age 20. More than one-half of the first live-births to Asian or Pacific Islander mothers (52.5%) and more than one-third of first live-births to non-Hispanic white mothers (34.8%) occurred at the age of 30 years and over. Non-Hispanic Asian or Pacific Islander mothers were the least likely to have their first live-birth under age 20 (2.4%) and the most likely to have their first live-birth at the age of 40 and over (3.2%).

Figure 9. Birth rates, by age of mother and age at first live-birth: United States, 1975–2015

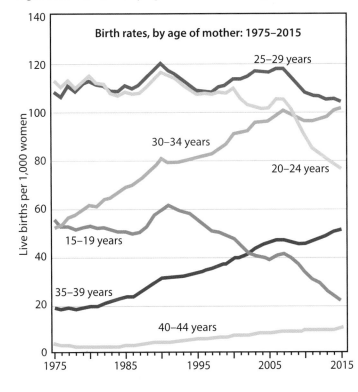

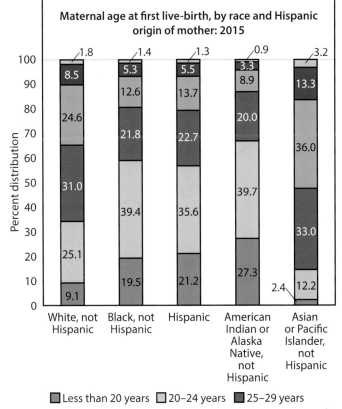

NOTE: See data table for Figure 9.

SOURCE: NCHS, National Vital Statistics System (NVSS).

Excel and PowerPoint: http://www.cdc.gov/nchs/hus/contents2016.htm#fig09

Health Risk Factors
Current Cigarette Smoking

The prevalence of smoking declined among men and women aged 25 and over at each education level between 1974 and 2015; however, men and women with no high school diploma were more than four times as likely to smoke as those with a bachelor's degree or higher in 2015.

Smoking is the leading cause of preventable disease, disability, and death in the United States (37). It is associated with an increased risk of heart disease, stroke, lung and other types of cancers, and chronic lung diseases (38). Between 1974 and 2015, the age-adjusted prevalence of smoking among persons aged 25 and over decreased from 36.9% to 15.6% (Table 48 and data table for Figure 10). Smoking declined among men and women at each education level during 1974–2015; however, the magnitude of annual decline in the prevalence of smoking has been smaller since the early 1990s among men with a high school education or higher and among women with some college or higher education.

In 2015, the age-adjusted percent of men aged 25 and over who were current smokers ranged from 6.6% of those with a bachelor's degree or higher (21.7 percentage points lower than 1974) to 28.6% of those with no high school diploma (23.7 percentage points lower than 1974). Among women aged 25 and over, the age-adjusted percent of current smokers in 2015 ranged from 5.3% of those with a bachelor's degree or higher (20.6 percentage points lower than 1974) to 22.6% of those with no high school diploma (14.0 percentage points lower than 1974).

In 2015, both men and women aged 25 and over with no high school diploma were more than four times as likely to smoke as those with a bachelor's degree or higher. Although the difference in smoking prevalence between men and women has narrowed since 1974, men were more likely than women to smoke at each education level, except for those with some college where the prevalence of smoking was similar.

Figure 10. Cigarette smoking among adults aged 25 years and over, by sex and education level: United States, 1974–2015

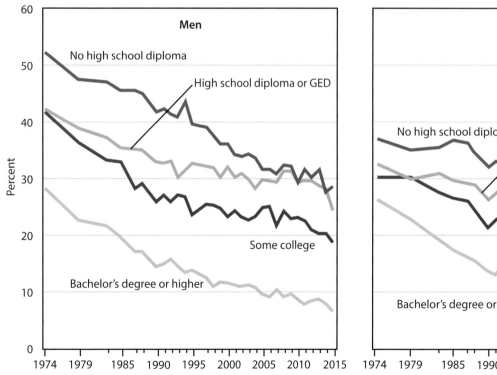
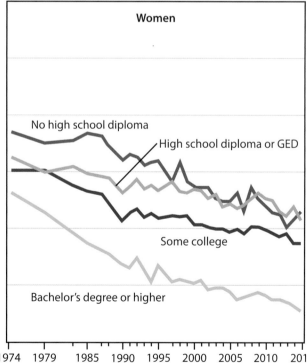

NOTES: Current cigarette smokers are defined as ever smoking 100 cigarettes in their lifetime and now smoke every day or some days. Educational categories shown are for 1997 and subsequent years. GED is General Educational Development high school equivalency diploma. Prior to 1997, the educational categories were less than 12 years completed, 12 years completed, 13–15 years, 16 years or more. Estimates are age-adjusted. See data table for Figure 10.

Excel and PowerPoint: http://www.cdc.gov/nchs/hus/contents2016.htm#fig10

SOURCE: NCHS, *Health, United States, 2016*, Table 48. Data from the National Health Interview Survey (NHIS).

Health Risk Factors
Children, Adolescents, and Adults with Obesity

The percentage of children and adolescents aged 2–19 with obesity increased from 1988–1994 to 2003–2004 and then remained stable through 2013–2014; for adults aged 20 and over, the age-adjusted percentage with obesity increased from 22.9% in 1988–1994 to 37.8% in 2013–2014.

Excess body weight in children is associated with excess morbidity during childhood and excess body weight in adulthood (39–42). Among adults, obesity is a significant risk factor for numerous chronic diseases and conditions including cardiovascular disease, diabetes, and cancer (43–46). Obesity is a major public health challenge for the United States and many other countries (47–49). During 1988–1994 through 2003–2004, the percentage of children and adolescents aged 2–19 with obesity increased

from 10.0% to 17.1%, and then was stable from 2003–2004 to 2013–2014. The percentage of children and adolescents with obesity was 17.2% in 2013–2014.

For adults aged 20 and over, the age-adjusted percentage with obesity increased steadily from 22.9% in 1988–1994 to 37.8% in 2013–2014. For adults aged 20 and over, the age-adjusted percentage with grade 1 obesity increased from 14.8% in 1988–1994 to 20.0% in 2003–2004, and then stabilized. In 2013–2014, the age-adjusted percentage of adults with grade 1 obesity was 20.7%. The age-adjusted percentage of adults with grade 2 obesity increased steadily from 5.2% in 1988–1994 to 9.5% in 2013–2014. The age-adjusted percentage of adults with grade 3 obesity more than doubled from 2.9% in 1988–1994 to 7.6% in 2013–2014.

Figure 11. Obesity among children and adolescents aged 2–19 and adults aged 20 years and over: United States, 1988–1994 through 2013–2014

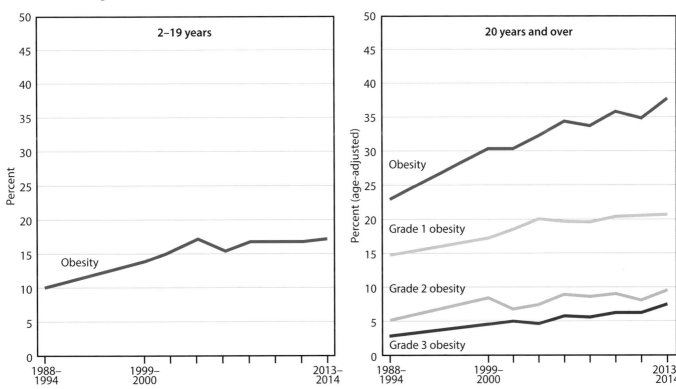

NOTES: For children and adolescents aged 2–19, obesity is defined as a body mass index (BMI) at or above the sex- and age-specific 95th percentile of the CDC growth charts. For adults, obesity is defined as a BMI at or above 30; grade 1 obesity is a BMI from 30.0 to 34.9; grade 2 obesity is a BMI from 35.0 to 39.9; and grade 3 obesity is a BMI greater than or equal to 40.0. Estimates for adults are age-adjusted. See data table for Figure 11.

SOURCE: NCHS, National Health and Nutrition Examination Survey (NHANES).

Excel and PowerPoint: http://www.cdc.gov/nchs/hus/contents2016.htm#fig11

Health Risk Factors
Untreated Dental Caries

Untreated dental caries increases with decreasing family income for children and adolescents aged 5–19 and for adults aged 20 and over.

Oral health is integral to an individual's overall health and well-being (50). The presence of dental caries, or tooth decay, is one of the most common chronic conditions in the United States (50). Possible causes of dental caries include high levels of bacteria in the mouth and frequent consumption of high-sugar foods and drink (51). Preventive measures include community water fluoridation, limiting consumption of high-sugar foods and drink, use of dental sealants, and regular oral care (50,52,53). Utilization of dental visits varies with family income, those with lower family income being less likely to have had a recent dental visit (Table 78) and more likely to delay needed dental care due to cost (Table 63) than those with higher family income.

The percentage of children and adolescents aged 5–19 with untreated dental caries declined steadily from 1988–1994 to 2011–2014 for those living below 100% of the poverty threshold, while remaining stable from 1988–1994 to 1999–2004, and then declining for those at 100%–199% of poverty. The percentage of children and adolescents aged 5–19 with untreated dental caries remained stable over the entire time

period in the two highest income groups. In 2011–2014, among children and adolescents aged 5–19, the percentage with untreated dental caries ranged from 9.1% for those at 400% or more of poverty to 24.7% for those living below poverty. Between 1988–1994 and 2011–2014, the difference between the highest and lowest percentage of untreated dental caries narrowed from 28.6 percentage points to 15.6 percentage points (16).

The age-adjusted percentage of adults with untreated dental caries was similar in 1988–1994 and 2011–2014 for all income levels. Similar to the pattern for children and adolescents, untreated dental caries among adults is inversely related to family income. During 1988–1994 through 2011–2014, among adults aged 20 and over, the age-adjusted percentage of untreated dental caries was highest among those living below 100% of the poverty threshold (49.7% in 2011–2014) and lowest among those at 400% or more of poverty (13.3% in 2011–2014). The disparity in untreated dental caries between the highest and lowest poverty groups remained stable between 1988–1994 and 2011–2014 (36.4 percentage points in 2011–2014).

Figure 12. Untreated dental caries among children and adolescents aged 5–19 years and adults aged 20 and over, by percent of poverty level: United States, 1988–1994, 1999–2004, and 2011–2014

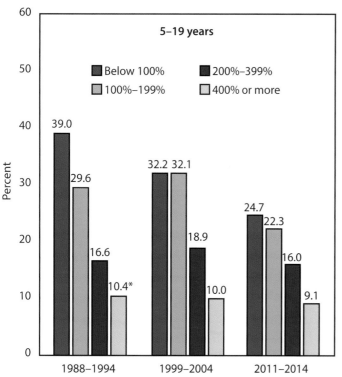

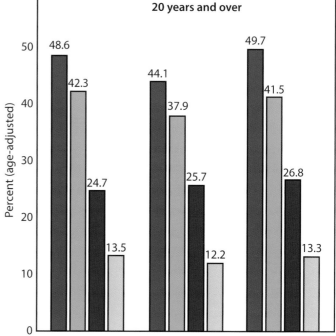

* Relative standard error (RSE) of 20%–30%.

NOTES: Estimates for adults are age-adjusted. Untreated dental caries refers to decay on the crown or enamel surface of a tooth (i.e., coronal caries) that has not been treated or filled. Decay in the root (i.e., root caries) was not included. The presence of caries was evaluated in primary and permanent teeth for persons aged 5 and over. Persons who were classified as edentulous were excluded. See data table for Figure 12.

SOURCE: NCHS, National Health and Nutrition Examination Survey (NHANES).

Excel and PowerPoint: http://www.cdc.gov/nchs/hus/contents2016.htm#fig12

Morbidity
Diabetes

In both 1988–1994 and 2011–2014, the prevalence of diabetes was higher among non-Hispanic black and Mexican origin adults compared to non-Hispanic white adults.

Diabetes is a group of conditions in which insulin is not adequately secreted or utilized by the body (54). Long-term complications of high glucose levels and diabetes include cardiovascular disease, renal failure, nerve damage, and retinal damage (54,55). Diabetes was the 7th leading cause of death in 2015 (Figure 8). Treatment guidelines for diabetes include recommendations for dietary modifications, physical activity, weight loss (if overweight), and the use of medication (54,55). In order to manage the disease and avoid or delay long-term complications, ongoing medical care is recommended (56).

Between 1988–1994 and 2011–2014, the overall prevalence of total diabetes increased 35% to 11.9%, but among racial and ethnic groups the increase was significant only for non-Hispanic white adults. The prevalence of physician-diagnosed diabetes increased among non-Hispanic white and black

adults from 1988–1994 to 2011–2014 and did not increase significantly among Mexican origin adults. The prevalence of undiagnosed diabetes decreased among non-Hispanic white and black adults over this time frame while remaining stable among Mexican origin adults.

In 2011–2014, approximately 1 in 9 adults in the United States had diabetes. The prevalence of total diabetes was higher among non-Hispanic black, non-Hispanic Asian, and Mexican origin adults than non-Hispanic white adults. The prevalence of both diagnosed and undiagnosed diabetes also was higher among non-Hispanic black, non-Hispanic Asian, and Mexican origin adults than non-Hispanic white adults.

Figure 13. Diabetes prevalence among adults aged 20 years and over, by diagnosis status and race and Hispanic origin: United States, 1988–1994 and 2011–2014

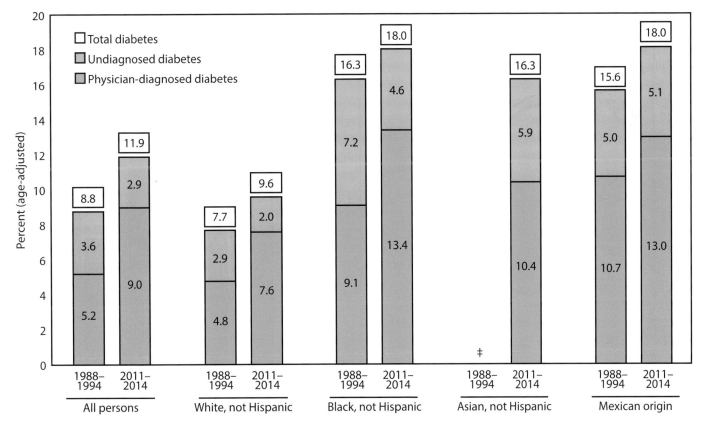

‡Estimates are not available for non-Hispanic Asian persons in 1988–1994.

SOURCE: NCHS, National Health and Nutrition Examination Survey (NHANES).

NOTES: Estimates are age-adjusted. See Appendix II, Diabetes. See data table for Figure 13 and Table 40.

Excel and PowerPoint: http://www.cdc.gov/nchs/hus/contents2016.htm#fig13

Morbidity
Uncontrolled Hypertension

During 1988–1994 through 2011–2014, the age-adjusted percentage of uncontrolled high blood pressure among adults aged 20 and over with hypertension decreased for all adults and for men and women separately; in 2011–2014, the prevalence of uncontrolled high blood pressure among men and women with hypertension varied by age.

Hypertension is an important risk factor for cardiovascular disease, stroke, kidney failure, and other health conditions (57,58) and can lead to premature death (59,60). In 2011–2014, 84.1% of adults with hypertension were aware of their status, and 76.1% were taking medication to lower their blood pressure (61).

During 1988–1994 through 2011–2014, the age-adjusted percentage of adults aged 20 and over with hypertension who had uncontrolled high blood pressure decreased steadily from 77.2% to 52.8%. Among men with hypertension, the age-adjusted percentage with uncontrolled high blood pressure decreased steadily from 83.2% in 1988–1994 to

58.1% in 2011–2014. Among women with hypertension, the age-adjusted percentage with uncontrolled high blood pressure declined from 68.5% in 1988–1994 to 45.5% in 2011–2014. However, for women, the magnitude of the decline changed over this period. During 1988–1994 through 2011–2014, among those with hypertension, the age-adjusted percentage of uncontrolled hypertension was higher for men than for women.

In 2011–2014, the pattern by age for uncontrolled high blood pressure among those with hypertension differed among men and women. Among men with hypertension, the prevalence of uncontrolled high blood pressure was higher for those in the two youngest age groups than for those of other ages. Among women with hypertension, the prevalence of uncontrolled hypertension was higher for women aged 75 and over than for women aged 35–44, 45–64, and 65–74 years; the prevalence of uncontrolled hypertension was not significantly different for women in the youngest and oldest age groups.

Figure 14. Uncontrolled high blood pressure among adults aged 20 and over with hypertension, by sex and age: United States, 1988–1994 through 2011–2014

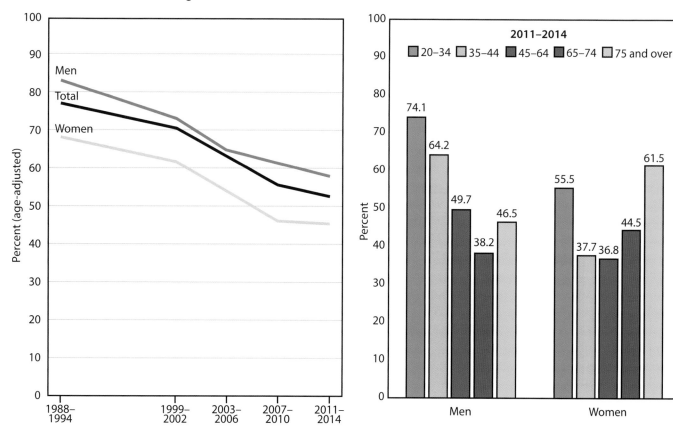

NOTES: Uncontrolled high blood pressure among persons with hypertension is defined as measured systolic pressure of at least 140 mm Hg or diastolic pressure of at least 90 mm Hg, among those with measured high blood pressure or reporting taking antihypertensive medication. Estimates for the left figure are age-adjusted. See data table for Figure 14.

Excel and PowerPoint: http://www.cdc.gov/nchs/hus/contents2016.htm#fig14

SOURCE: NCHS, National Health and Nutrition Examination Survey (NHANES).

Utilization
Prescription Drugs

In 2013–2014, 36.5% of adults aged 18–44, 69.6% of adults aged 45–64, and 90.8% of those aged 65 and over took a prescription drug in the past month—up from levels in 1988–1994.

Prescription drug use over the past 40 years has been affected by many factors, including medical need, prescription drug development, increased direct-to-consumer advertising, and expansions in health insurance and prescription drug coverage (62–64). Even though Americans are now living longer lives, a greater fraction of older Americans are living with several chronic conditions that may require multiple medications. As prescription drug use increases, however, so do concerns about polypharmacy. Polypharmacy—which is commonly defined as taking five or more drugs—increases the risk of drug interactions, adverse drug events, nonadherence, and reduced functional capacity (65).

Between 1988–1994 and 2013–2014, the use of at least one prescription drug in the past 30 days increased 5.2 percentage points for adults aged 18–44, 14.8 percentage points for adults aged 45–64, and 17.2 percentage points for adults aged 65 and over. For adults aged 45–64, use of at least one prescription drug during the past 30 days

increased throughout the period, while for adults aged 18–44 and 65 and over, use initially increased before remaining stable in recent years. For adults aged 18–44, use of at least one prescription drug remained stable from 2007–2008 to 2013–2014, while for adults aged 65 and over, use of at least one prescription drug remained stable from 2003–2004 to 2013–2014.

Between 1988–1994 and 2013–2014, the percent of adults reporting the use of five or more prescription drugs in the past 30 days rose—by 2.7 percentage points for adults aged 18–44, 12.8 percentage points for adults aged 45–64, and 28.4 percentage points for adults aged 65 and over. In contrast, the percentage of adults reporting the use of one to four prescription drugs between these two periods remained stable for adults aged 18–44 and 45–64, while decreasing for adults aged 65 and over.

Figure 15. Prescription drug use in the past 30 days among adults aged 18 and over, by age and number of drugs taken: United States, 1988–1994 through 2013–2014

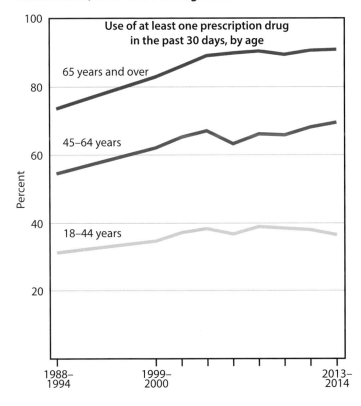

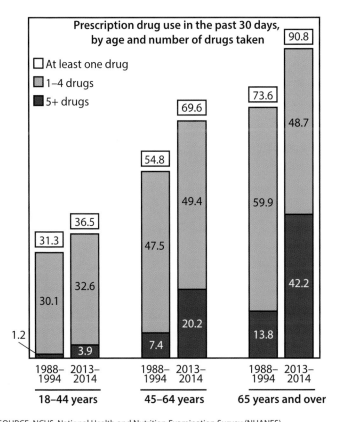

NOTES: Respondent-reported use of prescription drugs in the past 30 days. See Appendix II, Drug. See data table for Figure 15.

SOURCE: NCHS, National Health and Nutrition Examination Survey (NHANES).

Excel and PowerPoint: http://www.cdc.gov/nchs/hus/contents2016.htm#fig15

Utilization
Health Provider Visits

Between 1997 and 2015, the percent of persons with a health care visit in the past 12 months increased for each of five provider types among children and adults aged 65 and over. Among adults aged 18–64, the percent with a visit to a dentist remained stable and the percent with a visit to the other four provider types increased.

Visits to health providers are influenced by a variety of factors including patient characteristics, supply and distribution of providers, and health care affordability. Since the 1990s, shifts in disease prevalence have increased the need for chronic care management, while expansions to health insurance coverage have rendered health services more affordable for those previously uninsured (66,67). Increases in the supply of selected provider types have also increased the potential for utilization, although geographic differences in the distribution of providers may create disparities in utilization by urban/rural status (68,69).

In 1997, 2006, and 2015, the percent of persons with one or more visits to generalist physicians in the past year was higher than the percent with visits to specialist physicians, eye doctors, or mental health providers among children aged 2–17, adults aged 18–64, and adults 65 and over. The percent

of persons with a mental health provider visit was lower than that for any other type of provider; in 2015, 8.7% of children, 8.8% of adults aged 18–64, and 4.8% of those 65 and over reported a visit to a mental health provider in the past year.

Among all three age groups, the percent with a health care visit in the past year increased overall between 1997 and 2015 for each of the provider types shown with the exception of dental visits among adults aged 18–64, which remained stable. After a decrease in the percent of adults aged 18–64 with a dental visit between 1997 and 2006 (from 64.1% to 62.4%), the percent increased to 64.0% between 2006 and 2015.

Figure 16. Health care visits in the past 12 months among children aged 2–17 and adults aged 18 and over, by age and provider type: United States, 1997, 2006, and 2015

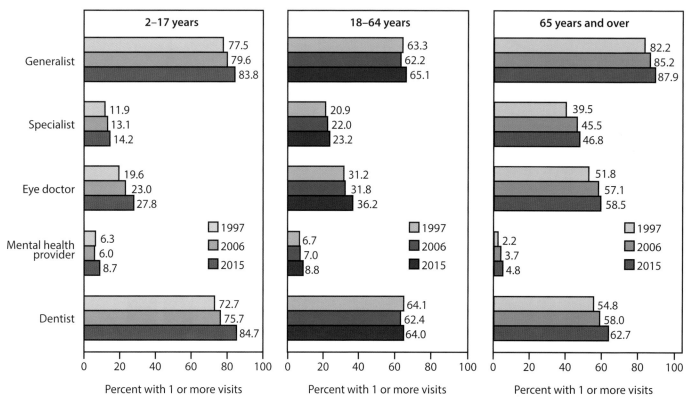

NOTE: See data table for Figure 16.

SOURCE: NCHS, National Health Interview Survey (NHIS).

Excel and PowerPoint: http://www.cdc.gov/nchs/hus/contents2016.htm#fig16

Utilization
Emergency Departments

The percent of children and adults aged 18–64 with an ED visit in the past year decreased during all or recent parts of the period 1997–2015, regardless of insurance coverage, with the exception of ED use among adults without health insurance, which remained stable.

Emergency departments (EDs) provide services to individuals with emergency health needs or who are seeking after-hours care. Additionally, EDs provide a safety net for those who have difficulty accessing alternative sources of care (70,71). Over the past 40 years, many health policies have impacted ED use. For instance, the 1986 Emergency Medical Treatment and Labor Act required providers to administer emergency care regardless of the patient's ability to pay, while the 1997 Balanced Budget Act instructed some managed care plans to pay for emergency services as long as a "prudent layperson" standard was met (72,73).

Among children, the percent with an ED visit in the past year has decreased in recent years, although the year in which the decrease began varied by type of insurance. For children with Medicaid, ED use decreased an average of 1.0 percentage point per year from 2009–2015; for children with private insurance, ED use decreased an average of 0.5 percentage points per year from 2002–2015; and for children

without health insurance, ED use decreased an average of 0.2 percentage points per year from 1997–2015.

Among adults aged 18–64, the percent with an ED visit decreased for those with Medicaid coverage as well as those with private insurance. Among adults with Medicaid, ED use remained stable from 1997–2010 before decreasing an average of 1.0 percentage point per year from 2010–2015, and among adults with private insurance, ED use decreased an average of 0.1 percentage points per year from 1997–2015. In contrast, ED use among adults without health insurance remained stable throughout 1997–2015.

From 1997–2015, children and adults with Medicaid coverage were more likely than those with private or no health insurance to have an ED visit in the past year. In 2015, 22.8% of children with Medicaid had a recent ED visit compared with 14.3% of children without health insurance and 12.5% of children with private insurance. For adults aged 18–64 in 2015, 34.8% of those with Medicaid had a recent ED visit, compared with 14.0% of those with private insurance and 18.2% of those without health insurance.

Figure 17. Emergency department visits in the past 12 months for persons under age 65, by age and type of coverage: United States, 1997–2015

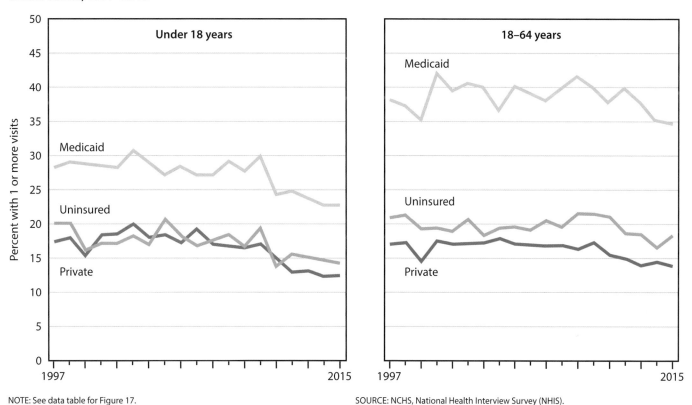

NOTE: See data table for Figure 17.

SOURCE: NCHS, National Health Interview Survey (NHIS).

Excel and PowerPoint: http://www.cdc.gov/nchs/hus/contents2016.htm#fig17

Utilization
Hospital Stays

The percentage of persons with an overnight hospital stay was lower in 2015 than in 1975 for males and females under age 75, and was not significantly different in 2015 than in 1975 for males and females aged 75 and over.

The U.S. population is aging, and there is a concurrent increase in the prevalence of chronic conditions, both of which suggest an increasing demand for hospital care (74) (Figure 1; Table 39). However, payment changes by private insurers and government programs have tended to reduce the number and length of hospitals stays. These efforts include Medicare's prospective payment system which reduced payments, and managed care policies, such as physician financial incentives and utilization review, designed to reduce the use of hospital care (75) (Figure 25). In addition, technological innovations and changes in practice patterns and patient preferences have shifted some formerly hospital inpatient procedures to outpatient settings, further reducing inpatient hospital stays (66,76).

Among males in all age groups and females aged 18–44 and 65–74 the percentage of persons with a hospital stay had periods of stability and decline during 1975–2015. Among females aged 1–17 the percentage with a hospital

stay declined throughout 1975–2015, while among females aged 45–64 and 75 and over the percentage with a hospital stay increased for specific time periods during 1975–2010; however, focusing on more recent trends, the percentage with a hospital stay has declined since 2010 for women aged 45–64 and since 2003 for women aged 75 and over. For men and women under age 75 the percentage with a hospital stay was lower in 2015 than in 1975; for men and women aged 75 and over, the difference between the percentage with one or more hospital stays in 1975 and 2015 was not statistically significant.

In 2015, the percentage of the population with at least one hospital stay in the past 12 months was similar for boys and girls under 18 and for men and women aged 45–64. Hospital use was higher among men than women, aged 65–74 and aged 75 and over. Women of childbearing age (18–44) were almost three times as likely to have had a hospital stay in the past year as men in this age group.

Figure 18. Overnight hospital stays in the past 12 months, by sex and age: United States, 1975–2015

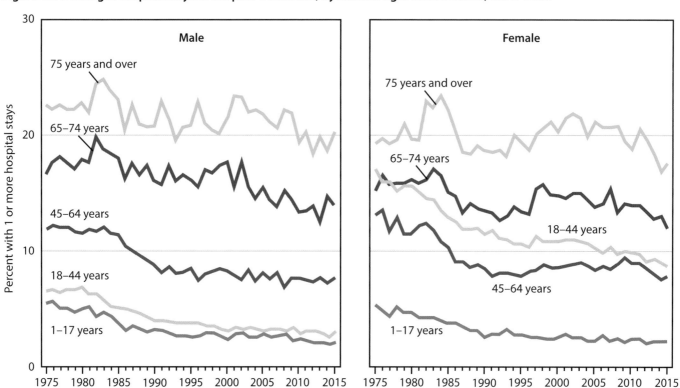

NOTES: Hospitalizations include those relating to deliveries. Because persons who had a hospitalization and subsequently died or were institutionalized are not included in the National Health Interview Survey, the estimates shown will vary from those based on a survey of hospital discharges. The difference will be larger for older persons. See data table for Figure 18.

SOURCE: NCHS, National Health Interview Survey (NHIS).

Excel and PowerPoint: http://www.cdc.gov/nchs/hus/contents2016.htm#fig18

Prevention
Use of Mammography and Colorectal Tests and Procedures

While use of mammograms and use of colorectal cancer tests and procedures have increased for all racial and ethnic groups, disparities in utilization persist in 2015.

Although breast cancer and colorectal cancer remain among the leading causes of cancer deaths in the U.S., advancements in and increased utilization of cancer screening tests have, in part, contributed to decreasing cancer death rates since the 1980s (77,78). During the 1990s, initiatives such as the National Breast and Cervical Cancer Early Detection Program increased educational outreach and financial subsidies for breast and cervical cancer screening among the population's most vulnerable women (79). Periodic screening increases the likelihood of detecting cancers at earlier stages and enables less invasive treatment, though the recommendations— which include the age of initiation and interval between screenings—have changed over time (80–82).

During 1987–2015, the percent of women aged 40–74 with a mammogram in the past two years increased through the mid-1990s for all four racial and ethnic groups before either continuing to increase (non-Hispanic Asian women),

decreasing (non-Hispanic white women), or stabilizing (Hispanic and non-Hispanic black women) in recent years. In 2015, the percent of women aged 40–74 with a mammogram in the past two years ranged from approximately 63% for non-Hispanic Asian women and Hispanic women to 72.3% for non-Hispanic black women. (See data table for Figure 19.)

The percent of adults aged 50–75 with a colorectal cancer test or procedure—either a fecal occult blood test in the past year, a sigmoidoscopy in the past 5 years with fecal occult blood test (FOBT) in the past 3 years, or a colonoscopy in the past 10 years—approximately doubled between 2000 and 2015 for all four racial and ethnic groups. However, racial and ethnic disparities in utilization remain; in 2015, 52.1% of non-Hispanic Asian and 47.4% of Hispanic adults aged 50–75 had a colorectal cancer test, compared with 60.3% of non-Hispanic black and 65.6% of non-Hispanic white adults aged 50–75.

Figure 19. Mammography use and colorectal cancer testing use, by race and Hispanic origin: United States, selected years 1987–2015

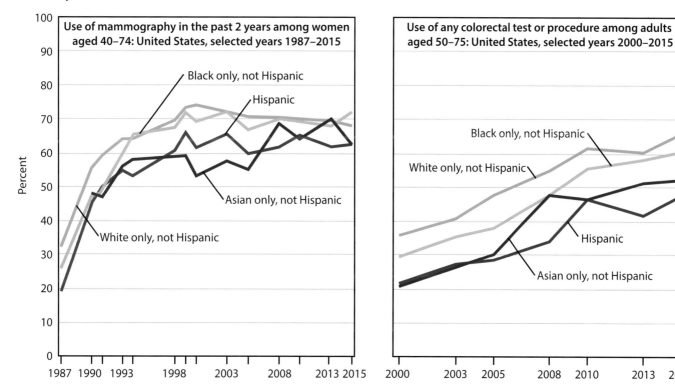

NOTES: Prior to 1999, data were tabulated according to the 1977 Standards with four racial groups, and the Asian category included Native Hawaiian or Other Pacific Islander. Mammography data for Asian only, not Hispanic in 1987 are not shown because they are unreliable. Data for colorectal testing are presented starting in 2000 due to changes in available examinations prior to 2000. Mammograms and colorectal cancer testing and procedures may be used for diagnostic or screening purposes. It is not possible to determine the purpose of the test in NHIS. See data table for Figure 19.

SOURCE: NCHS, National Health Interview Survey (NHIS).

Excel and PowerPoint: http://www.cdc.gov/nchs/hus/contents2016.htm#fig19

Health Care Resources
Hospitals

The number of community hospital beds per 1,000 resident population fell by almost one-half and average length of stay fell by almost one-third between 1975 and 2014 to 2.5 beds per population and 5.5 days per hospital stay in 2014.

Hospital care has undergone substantial changes in the past 40 years (76). This transformation has been driven by a variety of forces, including payment system reforms, technological advancements in medical care, modifications to practice patterns, and changes in consumer preferences (66). In 1983, Medicare implemented a prospective payment system for hospital care which paid a flat rate per case based on diagnosis instead of reimbursing costs (75). Increased managed care penetration, especially in private plans, put further pressure on hospitals to manage costs. Hospitals responded to managed care penetration by consolidating (83). In the past four decades, technological innovations have reduced recovery times and allowed some formerly hospital inpatient procedures, such as laparoscopic surgery and cataract removal, to take place in outpatient settings (66).

Changes in practice patterns and consumer preferences have also shifted some care from hospitals to alternative sites, such as post-acute care settings, nursing homes, and home health care (66). These forces have combined to encourage efficiency in hospital care and reduced incentives for longer hospital stays.

Between 1975 and 2014, community hospital beds per resident population, average length of stay, and occupancy rate declined. As a result of closures and consolidation, the number of community hospitals has also declined by 16%, from 5,875 in 1975 to 4,926 in 2014 (Table 89). During the same time frame, the number of community hospital beds per 1,000 resident population was almost cut in half from 4.6 to 2.5 (Figure 20). The average length of stay declined from 7.7 days in 1975 to 5.5 days in 2014. Occupancy rates for community hospitals averaged 62.8% in 2014—a 16% decline from 1975, although much of the decline took place during the mid-1980s.

Figure 20. Community hospital beds, average length of stay, and occupancy rate: United States, selected years 1975–2014

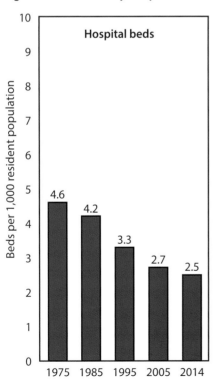
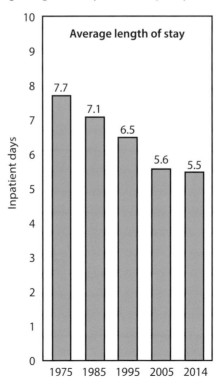
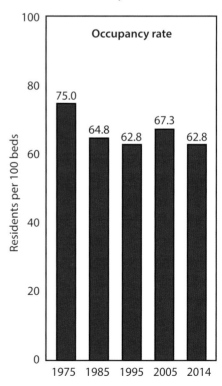

NOTE: See data table for Figure 20.

SOURCE: American Hospital Association (AHA) [Reprinted from AHA Hospital Statistics by permission, Copyright 1976, 1986, 1998, 2007, and 2016 by Health Forum, LLC, an American Hospital Association Company].

Excel and PowerPoint: http://www.cdc.gov/nchs/hus/contents2016.htm#fig20

Health Care Resources
Active Primary Care Generalist and Specialist Physicians

Between 1975 and 2013, the number of primary care generalist physicians per 10,000 population increased by 53% and the number of specialists per 10,000 population increased by 90%.

An adequate supply of physicians is necessary to provide quality health care. In addition to the number of physicians, the geographic distribution and specialty mix affect the adequacy of the supply. The need for physician services is growing, due to population growth, higher utilization due to higher rates of insurance coverage, and the aging population (84). Research suggests that the supply of primary care physicians is not keeping up with this demand (85–87).

Since 1975, the overall supply of active physicians in the United States nearly doubled, from 15.5 to 27.0 physicians per 10,000 population in 2013. Between 1975 and 2013, the number of primary care generalist physicians per 10,000 population increased by 53% and the number of specialists per 10,000 population increased by 90%. Because of the faster growth in specialist physicians compared with primary care generalist physicians during this period, the percentage of physicians who were specialists increased from 57.4% in 1975 to 62.6% in 2013.

Figure 21. Active primary care generalist and specialist physicians, by self-designated specialty: United States, selected years 1975–2013

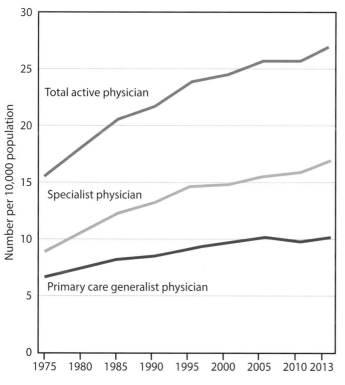
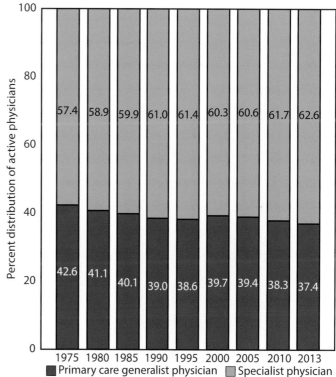

NOTES: Primary care generalist physicians include family medicine, internal medicine, obstetrics and gynecology, and pediatrics. Specialists include all other specialties and primary care subspecialists. Excludes physicians who are inactive, and physicians who did not provide generalist/specialist information. See data table for Figure 21.

SOURCE: American Medical Association (AMA) [Copyright 1976, 1982, 1986, 1992, 1997, 2003, 2007, 2012, and 2015: Used with permission of the AMA].

Excel and PowerPoint: http://www.cdc.gov/nchs/hus/contents2016.htm#fig21

Health Care Resources
Nursing Homes

From 1977 to 2014, the number of nursing home residents aged 65 and over per 1,000 population aged 65 and over fell by about one-half.

Long-term care (LTC) services fill a crucial role by delivering needed health care, personal care, housing, and supportive services to those with chronic conditions, disabilities, and, especially, frail older persons with age-related conditions (66). Long-term care services are available in several different settings, including the home and other residential care settings, the community, and institutions. Long-term care services are provided by adult day care centers and home health agencies; residential care settings, such as assisted living or continuing care communities; in-home or in-facility hospice care organizations; and by nursing homes (88). Until recently, nursing home care has been a key component of LTC, especially for older adults. However, although the U.S. population aged 65 and over increased from 10.6% to 14.9% in 2015 (18,89–91; Figure 1), use of nursing home care began to decline as early as 2000 (Figure 22)(66,92). A variety of factors likely contributed to this ongoing decline, including changes in consumer care preferences and the availability of additional long-term care options with the growth of residential care communities, such as assisted living (88,92,93).

As a result of closures and consolidation, the number of nursing homes declined by 15% between 1977 and 2014 (94,95). From 1977 to 2014, the number of nursing home beds per 1,000 population aged 65 and over, and the number of nursing home residents aged 65 and over per 1,000 population aged 65 and over declined, as did the nursing home occupancy rate (that is, number of nursing home residents per 100 nursing home beds). The number of nursing home beds per 1,000 population aged 65 and over decreased by 40%, from 59.7 in 1977 to 36.0 beds per 1,000 population aged 65 and over in 2014. The number of nursing home residents aged 65 and over per 1,000 population aged 65 and over declined by 47% from 47.1 in 1977 to 25.2 residents per 1,000 population aged 65 and over in 2014. The nursing home occupancy rate fell by 11% to 82.3%.

Figure 22. Nursing home beds, residents, and occupancy rate: United States, selected years 1977–2014

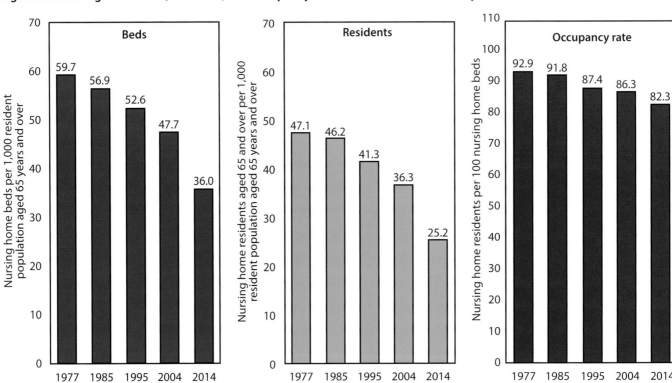

NOTE: See data table for Figure 22.

SOURCE: NCHS, National Nursing Home Survey (NNHS) for 1977, 1985, 1995, and 2004 data; National Study of Long-Term Care Providers (NSLTCP) for 2014.

Excel and PowerPoint: http://www.cdc.gov/nchs/hus/contents2016.htm#fig22

Personal Health Care Expenditures
Source of Funds and Type of Expenditure

Between 1975 and 2015, U.S. health care spending changed in terms of who paid for care and the type of care that was paid for.

The United States spent $2.7 trillion on personal health care for an average of $8,468 per person in 2015; in contrast in 1975, the United States spent $113 billion, on average $514 per person (96). In 2015, 17.8% of the U.S. Gross Domestic Product (GDP) was spent on national health care—more than twice the percentage in 1975 (7.9% of GDP) (96). More is spent on health care in the United States, in terms of a percentage of GDP, than any other developed country for which data are collected by the Organisation of Economic Co-operation and Development (OECD) (97).

Between 1975 and 2015, the share of personal health care expenditures paid by private health insurance increased from 24.5% to 34.8% and the share paid by Medicare increased from 13.8% to 22.3%. In addition, the share the federal government paid for Medicaid increased from 6.2% to 11.6% and the share that states paid for Medicaid increased from 5.1% to 6.7%. During the same period, the share paid out of

pocket by consumers decreased from 32.9% to 12.4%, and the remaining share paid by other sources decreased from 17.5% to 12.2%.

Between 1975 and 2015, the share of personal health care expenditures paid for hospital care decreased from 45.3% to 38.1%, the share for nursing care facilities and continuing care retirement communities decreased from 7.1% to 5.8%, and the share for dental services decreased from 7.1% to 4.3%. During the same period the share of personal health care expenditures paid for prescription drugs increased from 7.1% to 11.9%, for home health care increased from 0.5% to 3.3%, and for other types of care increased from 10.6% to 13.2%. During this period, about one-quarter (22.4%–23.4%) of personal health care expenditures were paid for physician and clinical services.

Figure 23. Personal health care expenditures, by source of funds and type of expenditure: United States, 1975, 1995, and 2015

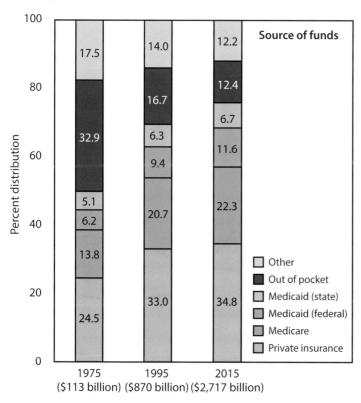

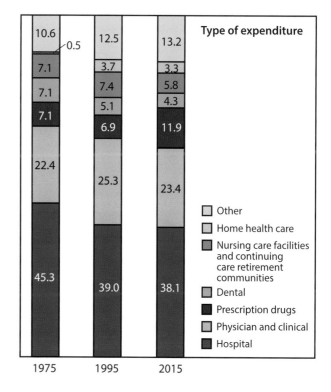

NOTES: Personal health care expenditures are outlays for goods and services relating directly to patient care. Other sources include Department of Defense, Department of Veterans Affairs, and other third party payers and programs. Medicaid includes expenditures for the Children's Health Insurance Program (CHIP). Other types of expenditures include other professional services; other health, residential, and personal care; and durable and nondurable medical equipment and products. Personal health care expenditures are in current dollars and are not adjusted for inflation. See data table for Figure 23.

SOURCE: Centers for Medicare & Medicaid Services, National Health Expenditures Accounts (NHEA).

Excel and PowerPoint: http://www.cdc.gov/nchs/hus/contents2016.htm#fig23

Personal Health Care Expenditures
Mental Health and Substance Use Disorder Expenditures

Between 1986 and 2014, the share of mental health and substance use disorder spending for inpatient services decreased, while the share for outpatient services and retail prescription drugs increased.

Mental health and substance use disorders are serious, potentially disabling or fatal, and costly on a personal and societal level (98–101; Tables 27 and 30). Mental illness and substance use disorders affect a significant segment of the U.S. population (102,103). Mental health and substance use disorders are amenable to treatment (104–107), however, treatment can be costly and not always readily available (108–113). The Paul Wellstone and Pete Domenici Mental Health Parity and Addiction Equity Act of 2008 (114) and the ACA (115) included provisions to expand access to mental health and substance abuse coverage and treatment. In 2013, 14.6% of noninstitutionalized adults received any type of mental health treatment and 1.3% received any type of substance use treatment (102).

In 2014, $186 billion was spent on mental health treatment, representing 6.4% of all health spending* (116). Between 1986 and 2014, the share of mental health expenditures paid

for inpatient care decreased from 41% to 16%; residential treatment decreased from 22% to 12%; outpatient treatment increased from 24% to 35%; and retail prescription drug spending increased from 8% to 27%.

In 2014, $34 billion was spent on substance use disorder treatment, representing 1.2% of all health spending*. Between 1986 and 2014, the share of substance use disorder expenditures paid for inpatient care decreased from 50% to 19%; outpatient treatment increased from 27% to 40%; residential treatment increased from 17% to 27%; and retail prescription drug spending increased from less than 1% to 5%.

*All health spending is defined here as health consumption expenditures (national health expenditures minus investments for structures and research). See Table 94.

Figure 24. Mental health and substance use disorder expenditures, by type of expenditure: United States, selected years, 1986–2014

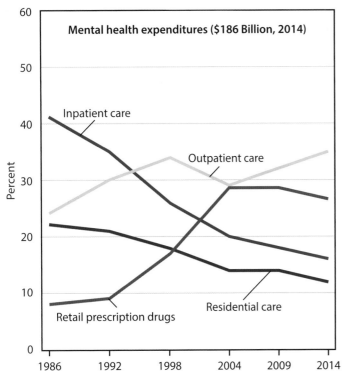

NOTE: See data table for Figure 24.

Excel and PowerPoint: http://www.cdc.gov/nchs/hus/contents2016.htm#fig24

SOURCE: Substance Abuse and Mental Health Services Administration (SAMHSA), Behavioral Health Spending and Use Accounts (BHSUA).

Health Insurance
Medicare Managed Care Enrollment

In 2015, more than three in ten (31.3%) Medicare beneficiaries were enrolled in Medicare managed care plans, with participation varying substantially across states.

Medicare provides health insurance coverage to most persons aged 65 and over, in addition to those under age 65 with long-standing disabilities and certain serious medical conditions. In 2015, the Medicare program (117) covered 55.3 million persons (118), with the majority enrolled in the traditional Medicare program (Part A and Part B) (119–121). Annually, nearly all Medicare beneficiaries have the choice to enroll (or disenroll) in Medicare managed care programs offered in their area (originally referred to as Medicare Part C or Medicare + Choice, and now called Medicare Advantage [MA]). MA plans provide the same coverage as the traditional Medicare program, generally through a restricted care network, and may offer extra coverage including vision, dental, and prescription drug coverage.

Enrollment in MA plans is affected by the availability of a plan in the enrollee's county (which was limited in the early years of the program, especially in rural areas) and by having premiums and cost sharing low enough, or benefits generous enough, to attract beneficiaries from traditional Medicare (122–124). Increased participation in MA programs in the mid-to-late 1990s mimicked the general growth in managed care

participation and then in the late 1990s MA participation fell with wide-spread managed care "backlash" against managed care cost containment practices, such as prior authorization (123,125). In 2003, MA payments were increased and enrollment grew (120). In recent years, MA plan choices have become increasingly varied and include health maintenance organizations (HMOs), preferred provider organizations (PPOs), private fee-for-service plans (PFFS), special needs, HMO point-of-service plans, and Medical Savings Account plans (126).

Nationwide between 1994 and 1999, the percentage of Medicare enrollees participating in managed care plans more than doubled from 7.9% to 18.2%, and then decreased steadily to 13.0% by 2004. Between 2004 and 2015, the percentage of enrollees in managed care plans more than doubled, increasing from 13.0% to 31.3%.

In 2015, the percentage of Medicare enrollees participating in managed care plans varied across states, ranging from 1.0% in Alaska to 53.8% in Minnesota. The 13 states in the top quartile with the highest percentage of Medicare managed care enrollees in 2015 were: Tennessee, Rhode Island, Colorado, New York, Wisconsin, Arizona, Florida, Pennsylvania, California, Ohio, Oregon, Hawaii, and Minnesota.

Figure 25. Medicare enrollees in managed care: United States, 1994–2015

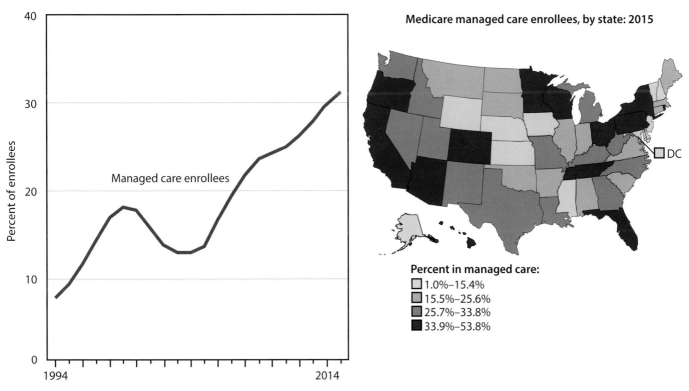

Medicare managed care enrollees, by state: 2015

Percent in managed care:
- 1.0%–15.4%
- 15.5%–25.6%
- 25.7%–33.8%
- 33.9%–53.8%

NOTE: See data table for Figure 25.

Excel and PowerPoint: http://www.cdc.gov/nchs/hus/contents2016.htm#fig25

SOURCE: Centers for Medicare & Medicaid Services, Medicare Administrative Data.

Health Insurance

Coverage Among Children Under Age 18

Between 1978 and September 2016 (preliminary data), the percentage of children under age 18 who were uninsured decreased; the percentage with Medicaid coverage increased, while the percentage with private coverage decreased.

Children and adolescents need regular and ongoing healthcare to provide routine preventive care, such as age-appropriate vaccinations; to offer health and developmental guidance; to screen for health conditions; to control and to treat acute and chronic conditions; and to provide injury care (127). Historically, children have been more likely than adults (Figure 27) to have coverage primarily because they have been more likely to qualify for Medicaid, enacted in 1966 (128). Starting in 1997, the Children's Health Insurance Program has provided coverage to eligible low-income, uninsured children who do not qualify for Medicaid (129).

Between 1978 and September 2016 (130,131) the percentage of uninsured children decreased 7.0 percentage points from 12.0% to 5.0%; Medicaid coverage increased 27.9 percentage points from 11.3% to 39.2% while private coverage decreased 21.6 percentage points from 75.1% to 53.5%; private workplace coverage, which is the largest component of private coverage, decreased 18.4 percentage points from 67.6% to 49.2%. For children, the percentage uninsured increased 0.4 percentage points per year on average during 1978–1990, and then decreased 0.4 percentage points per year on average during 1990–September 2016. The decrease in the percentage uninsured starting in 1990 was primarily due to increases in Medicaid coverage during most of the period 1990–2012. Increases in Medicaid coverage were larger than decreases in private coverage during that period.

Figure 26. Health insurance coverage among children under age 18, by type of coverage: United States, selected years 1978–September 2016 (preliminary data)

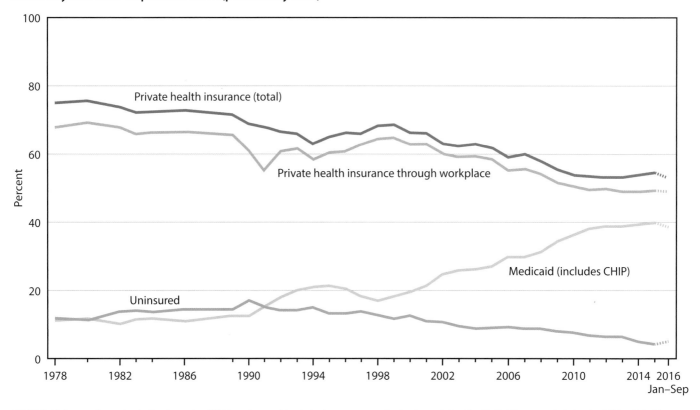

NOTES: Preliminary estimates for the first 9 months of 2016 are shown with a dashed line (130,131). Health insurance coverage, definitions, and questionnaires have changed over time. Insurance status is at the time of interview except for 1990–1996, when it is for the month prior to interview. Private workplace coverage includes private coverage originally obtained through a present or former employer or union, self-employment, or a professional association. The Medicaid category includes the Children's Health Insurance Program (CHIP), which was enacted in 1997. Persons classified with Private or Medicaid coverage may also have other types of coverage. See data table for Figure 26.

SOURCE: NCHS, National Health Interview Survey (NHIS).

Excel and PowerPoint: http://www.cdc.gov/nchs/hus/contents2016.htm#fig26

Health Insurance
Coverage Among Adults Aged 18–64

Between 2010 and September 2016 (preliminary data), the percentage of adults aged 18–64 who were uninsured decreased, while both private and Medicaid coverage increased.

Adults aged 18–64 were historically more likely to be uninsured than children and adolescents because they were less likely to qualify for public coverage, primarily Medicaid (Figure 27) (128,132,133). Passage of the Affordable Care Act (ACA) in 2010 (115) authorized states to expand Medicaid eligibility to low income adults to 138% of the federal poverty level (134) and established the health insurance marketplace in 2014. The health insurance marketplace offered deductible and copayment subsidies for people at 139%–250% of the federal poverty level and tax credits for people at 139%–400% of the federal poverty level without offers of affordable coverage through an employer. However, in states that did not expand Medicaid, subsidies and premiums are offered to those at 100%–250% and 100%–400% of the federal poverty level, respectively.

For adults aged 18–64, the percentage uninsured increased from 11.9% in 1978 to 18.8% in 1993 and 22.3% in 2010, followed by a decline of 10 percentage points to 12.3% in September 2016. Both private and Medicaid coverage increased during 2010–September 2016. Overall, between 1978 and September 2016, private coverage decreased 12.4 percentage points from 81.4% to 69.0%; private workplace coverage, the largest component of private coverage, decreased 10.5 percentage points from 71.4% to 60.9%; and Medicaid coverage increased 9.7 percentage points from 4.4% to 14.1%. Despite changes in the percent uninsured during 1978–September 2016, the percent uninsured was similar in 1978 and September 2016 (11.9% and 12.3%, respectively).

Figure 27. Health insurance coverage among adults aged 18–64, by type of coverage: United States, selected years 1978–September 2016 (preliminary data)

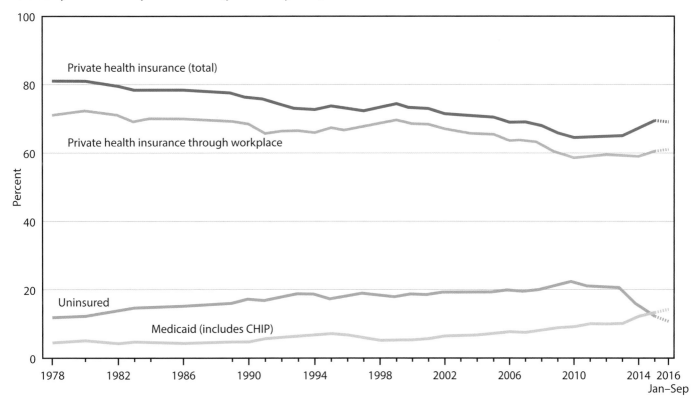

NOTES: Preliminary estimates for the first 9 months of 2016 are shown with a dashed line (130,131). Health insurance coverage, definitions, and questionnaires have changed over time. Insurance status is at the time of interview except for 1990–1996, when it is for the month prior to interview. Private workplace coverage includes private coverage originally obtained through a present or former employer or union, self-employment, or a professional association. Medicaid includes the Children's Health Insurance Program (CHIP), which was enacted in 1997. Persons classified with Private or Medicaid coverage may also have other types of coverage. See data table for Figure 27.

SOURCE: NCHS, National Health Interview Survey (NHIS).

Excel and PowerPoint: http://www.cdc.gov/nchs/hus/contents2016.htm#fig27

Chartbook Data Tables

Data table for Figure 1 (page 1 of 2). Population, by sex and five-year age groups: United States, 1975 and 2015

Excel and PowerPoint: http://www.cdc.gov/nchs/hus/contents2016.htm#fig01

Year and age group	Both sexes	Male	Female
1975		Percent	
0–4 years	7.5	7.8	7.1
5–9 years	8.1	8.5	7.8
10–14 years	9.6	10.0	9.1
15–19 years	9.9	10.3	9.5
20–24 years	9.0	9.3	8.8
25–29 years	8.0	8.2	7.8
30–34 years	6.6	6.7	6.5
35–39 years	5.4	5.4	5.4
40–44 years	5.2	5.2	5.2
45–49 years	5.5	5.4	5.5
50–54 years	5.5	5.4	5.6
55–59 years	4.9	4.8	5.1
60–64 years	4.4	4.1	4.5
65–69 years	3.8	3.4	4.1
70–74 years	2.7	2.3	3.0
75–79 years	2.0	1.6	2.3
80–84 years	1.3	0.9	1.6
85 years and over	0.8	0.6	1.1
2015			
0–4 years	6.2	6.4	6.0
5–9 years	6.4	6.6	6.1
10–14 years	6.4	6.6	6.2
15–19 years	6.6	6.8	6.3
20–24 years	7.1	7.4	6.8
25–29 years	7.0	7.2	6.8
30–34 years	6.7	6.9	6.6
35–39 years	6.3	6.4	6.3
40–44 years	6.3	6.3	6.2
45–49 years	6.5	6.5	6.4
50–54 years	6.9	6.9	7.0
55–59 years	6.8	6.7	6.9
60–64 years	5.9	5.8	6.1
65–69 years	5.0	4.8	5.2
70–74 years	3.6	3.3	3.8
75–79 years	2.5	2.3	2.8
80–84 years	1.8	1.5	2.1
85 years and over	2.0	1.4	2.5

See footnotes at end of table.

Excel and PowerPoint: *http://www.cdc.gov/nchs/hus/contents2016.htm#fig01*

Year and age group	Both sexes	Male	Female
1975	Population, in millions		
0–4 years	16.1	8.2	7.9
5–9 years	17.6	9.0	8.6
10–14 years	20.6	10.5	10.1
15–19 years	21.3	10.8	10.5
20–24 years	19.5	9.8	9.7
25–29 years	17.3	8.6	8.7
30–34 years	14.2	7.0	7.2
35–39 years	11.6	5.7	5.9
40–44 years	11.2	5.5	5.7
45–49 years	11.8	5.7	6.1
50–54 years	12.0	5.7	6.2
55–59 years	10.6	5.0	5.6
60–64 years	9.4	4.4	5.0
65–69 years	8.1	3.6	4.5
70–74 years	5.8	2.4	3.3
75–79 years	4.2	1.7	2.6
80–84 years	2.7	1.0	1.7
85 years and over	1.8	0.6	1.2
2015			
0–4 years	19.9	10.2	9.7
5–9 years	20.5	10.5	10.0
10–14 years	20.6	10.5	10.1
15–19 years	21.1	10.8	10.3
20–24 years	22.7	11.7	11.1
25–29 years	22.5	11.4	11.1
30–34 years	21.7	10.9	10.8
35–39 years	20.4	10.2	10.2
40–44 years	20.2	10.0	10.2
45–49 years	20.9	10.3	10.5
50–54 years	22.3	11.0	11.4
55–59 years	21.8	10.6	11.2
60–64 years	19.1	9.1	10.0
65–69 years	16.1	7.6	8.5
70–74 years	11.5	5.3	6.2
75–79 years	8.1	3.6	4.5
80–84 years	5.8	2.4	3.4
85 years and over	6.3	2.2	4.1

NOTE: Resident population.

SOURCE: U.S. Census Bureau 1975 intercensal estimates of the July 1, 1975 resident population; 2015 postcensal estimates of the July 1, 2015 resident population. See Appendix I. Population Census and Population Estimates.

Data table for Figure 2. Population, by race and Hispanic origin and age: United States, 1980, 1990, 2000, and 2015

Excel and PowerPoint: http://www.cdc.gov/nchs/hus/contents2016.htm#fig02

		Race and Hispanic origin						
			Not Hispanic or Latino					
							All other races, by detailed race	
Age and year	Hispanic	White only	Black only	Asian only	All other races (total)	Native Hawaiian or Other Pacific Islander only	American Indian or Alaska Native only	Multiple Race
All ages					Percent			
1980 †	6.4	79.9	11.5	1.6	0.6	- - -	0.6	- - -
1990 †	9.0	75.7	11.8	2.8	0.7	- - -	0.7	- - -
2000 ††	12.5	69.5	12.2	3.7	2.0	0.1	0.7	1.2
2015 ††	17.6	61.6	12.4	5.4	3.0	0.2	0.7	2.0
0–17 years								
1980 †	8.8	74.2	14.5	1.7	0.8	- - -	0.8	- - -
1990 †	12.2	68.9	14.7	3.1	1.0	- - -	1.0	- - -
2000 ††	17.1	61.3	14.9	3.5	3.3	0.2	1.0	2.2
2015 ††	24.6	51.5	13.8	4.9	5.2	0.2	0.9	4.1
18–64 years								
1980 †	6.0	81.0	10.8	1.7	0.5	- - -	0.5	- - -
1990 †	8.7	76.3	11.3	3.0	0.7	- - -	0.7	- - -
2000 ††	12.2	70.0	11.9	4.1	1.8	0.1	0.7	1.0
2015 ††	17.3	61.5	12.8	5.9	2.5	0.2	0.7	1.6
65 years and over								
1980 †	2.8	88.0	8.1	0.8	0.3	- - -	0.3	- - -
1990 †	3.7	86.7	7.9	1.4	0.3	- - -	0.3	- - -
2000 ††	5.0	83.8	8.0	2.3	0.9	0.1	0.4	0.5
2015 ††	7.9	77.8	8.8	4.2	1.3	0.1	0.5	0.7

- - - Data not available.

† In 1980 and 1990, data were tabulated based on the 1977 Standards with four single race categories; the category non-Hispanic Asian only includes non-Hispanic Pacific Islander only persons. Non-Hispanic All other races includes non-Hispanic American Indian or Alaska Native only.

†† In 2000 and 2015, data were tabulated based on the 1997 Standards with five single race groups and the option to report more than one race. Non-Hispanic All other races includes non-Hispanic Native Hawaiian or Other Pacific Islander only, non-Hispanic American Indian or Alaska Native only, and non-Hispanic multiple race (shown combined in the chart due to small numbers and displayed separately in the data table). See Appendix I, Population Census and Population Estimates, Appendix II, Hispanic origin; Race.

NOTES: Resident population. Persons of Hispanic origin may be of any race. Race data for 2000 and 2015 are not directly comparable with data from 1980 and 1990 because of the use of different Standards for classifying race.

SOURCE: U.S. Census Bureau decennial estimates 1980, 1990, and 2000; postcensal estimates 2015. See Appendix I. Population Census and Population Estimates.

Data table for Figure 3. Foreign-born population: United States, selected years 1970–2015

Excel and PowerPoint: http://www.cdc.gov/nchs/hus/contents2016.htm#fig03

Year	Percent
1970	4.7
1980	6.2
1990	7.9
2000	11.1
2010	12.9
2015	13.5
Year and region of origin	
1970	
Asia	8.9
Latin America	19.4
Europe	61.7
Other	10.0
2015	
Asia	30.6
Latin America	51.1
Europe	11.1
Other	7.3

NOTES: Resident population for 1970–2000 and civilian noninstitutionalized population for 2010 and 2015. The foreign-born population includes anyone who is not a U.S. citizen at birth (including naturalized citizens, lawful permanent residents, temporary migrants, humanitarian migrants, and undocumented migrants) among those with region of birth reported. Region of origin 'Other' includes Africa, Oceania, and Northern America. For a list of countries and dependencies included under 'Latin America', see https://www.census.gov/content/dam/Census/library/publications/2011/acs/acsbr10-15.pdf.

SOURCE: U.S. Census Bureau, Decennial Census 1970–2000; American Community Survey (ACS) 2010 and 2015. See Appendix I, American Community Survey (ACS); Population Census and Population Estimates.

Data table for Figure 4. Population, by percent of poverty level and age: United States, 1975–2015

Excel and PowerPoint: http://www.cdc.gov/nchs/hus/contents2016.htm#fig04

| Year | Percent below 100% of the poverty level | | |
| | Age | | |
	Under 18 years	18–64 years	65 years and over
	Percent		
1975	17.1	9.2	15.3
1976	16.0	9.0	15.0
1977	16.2	8.8	14.1
1978	15.9	8.7	14.0
1979	16.4	8.9	15.2
1980	18.3	10.1	15.7
1981	20.0	11.1	15.3
1982	21.9	12.0	14.6
1983	22.3	12.4	13.8
1984	21.5	11.7	12.4
1985	20.7	11.3	12.6
1986	20.5	10.8	12.4
1987	20.3	10.6	12.5
1988	19.5	10.5	12.0
1989	19.6	10.2	11.4
1990	20.6	10.7	12.2
1991	21.8	11.4	12.4
1992	22.3	11.9	12.9
1993	22.7	12.4	12.2
1994	21.8	11.9	11.7
1995	20.8	11.4	10.5
1996	20.6	11.4	10.8
1997	19.9	10.9	10.5
1998	18.9	10.5	10.5
1999	17.1	10.1	9.7
2000	16.2	9.6	9.9
2001	16.3	10.1	10.1
2002	16.7	10.6	10.4
2003	17.6	10.8	10.2
2004	17.8	11.3	9.8
2005	17.6	11.1	10.1
2006	17.4	10.8	9.4
2007	18.0	10.9	9.7
2008	19.0	11.7	9.7
2009	20.7	12.9	8.9
2010	22.0	13.8	8.9
2011	21.9	13.7	8.7
2012	21.8	13.7	9.1
2013	21.5	13.3	10.2
2014	21.1	13.5	10.0
2015	19.7	12.4	8.8

| Age and sex | Percent of poverty level: 2015 | |
	Below 100%	100%–199%
	Percent	
Under 18 years	19.7	22.1
Male.	19.5	21.9
Female	19.9	22.2
18–64 years	12.4	15.7
Male.	10.5	15.0
Female	14.2	16.4
65 years and over	8.8	22.3
Male.	7.0	19.0
Female	10.3	24.9

NOTES: Civilian noninstitutionalized population. Percent of poverty level is based on family income and family size and composition using U.S. Census Bureau poverty thresholds. See Appendix II, Poverty.

SOURCE: U.S. Census Bureau, Current Population Survey, Annual Social and Economic Supplements. Available from: http://www.census.gov/data/tables/time-series/demo/income-poverty/historical-poverty-people.html. See Appendix I, Current Population Survey (CPS).

Data table for Figure 5. Population, by urbanization level: United States, 1970, 1980, 1990, 2000, and 2015

Excel and PowerPoint: http://www.cdc.gov/nchs/hus/contents2016.htm#fig05

Urban-rural category	1970	1980	1990	2000	2015
	Percent of population				
Metropolitan (urban)	73.2	72.2	79.7	82.6	85.6
Large central (inner cities)	29.4	26.9	30.4	29.9	30.8
Large fringe (suburbs)	12.3	12.9	19.4	23.4	24.8
Medium	22.9	23.3	21.9	19.7	20.9
Small	8.6	9.1	8.0	9.5	9.1
Nonmetropolitan (rural)	26.8	27.8	20.3	17.4	14.4
Micropolitan (city/town)	- - -	- - -	- - -	10.5	8.5
Noncore (most rural)	- - -	- - -	- - -	6.9	5.9

- - - Data not available.

NOTES: Resident population data are presented. The categories micropolitan and noncore were not used in 1970, 1980, and 1990; therefore, total nonmetropolitan population is shown. The 2000 Office of Management and Budget metropolitan classification system included major changes, including the introduction of the micropolitan category. Therefore, the nonmetropolitan categories for 1990 and earlier are not strictly analogous to subsequent data. The 1990 NCHS urban-rural classification scheme for counties was applied to 1990 population data. The 2006 NCHS urban-rural classification scheme for counties was applied to 2000 population data. The 2013 NCHS urban-rural classification scheme for counties was applied to 2015 population data. Available from: http://www.cdc.gov/nchs/data_access/urban_rural.htm.

SOURCE: U.S. Census Bureau; 1970 and 1980 from Department of Agriculture Economic Research Service reports, available from: http://naldc.nal.usda.gov/naldc/download.xhtml?id=CAT10847914&.

Data table for Figure 6 (page 1 of 2). Life Expectancy at birth, by sex, race and Hispanic origin: United States, 1975–2015

Excel and PowerPoint: http://www.cdc.gov/nchs/hus/contents2016.htm#fig06

Year	All races Both sexes	All races Male	All races Female	White Both sexes	White Male	White Female	Black or African American Both sexes	Black or African American Male	Black or African American Female
	Life expectancy (years)								
1975	72.6	68.8	76.6	73.4	69.5	77.3	66.8	62.4	71.3
1976	72.9	69.1	76.8	73.6	69.9	77.5	67.2	62.9	71.6
1977	73.3	69.5	77.2	74.0	70.2	77.9	67.7	63.4	72.0
1978	73.5	69.6	77.3	74.1	70.4	78.0	68.1	63.7	72.4
1979	73.9	70.0	77.8	74.6	70.8	78.4	68.5	64.0	72.9
1980	73.7	70.0	77.4	74.4	70.7	78.1	68.1	63.8	72.5
1981	74.1	70.4	77.8	74.8	71.1	78.4	68.9	64.5	73.2
1982	74.5	70.8	78.1	75.1	71.5	78.7	69.4	65.1	73.6
1983	74.6	71.0	78.1	75.2	71.6	78.7	69.4	65.2	73.5
1984	74.7	71.1	78.2	75.3	71.8	78.7	69.5	65.3	73.6
1985	74.7	71.1	78.2	75.3	71.8	78.7	69.3	65.0	73.4
1986	74.7	71.2	78.2	75.4	71.9	78.8	69.1	64.8	73.4
1987	74.9	71.4	78.3	75.6	72.1	78.9	69.1	64.7	73.4
1988	74.9	71.4	78.3	75.6	72.2	78.9	68.9	64.4	73.2
1989	75.1	71.7	78.5	75.9	72.5	79.2	68.8	64.3	73.3
1990	75.4	71.8	78.8	76.1	72.7	79.4	69.1	64.5	73.6
1991	75.5	72.0	78.9	76.3	72.9	79.6	69.3	64.6	73.8
1992	75.8	72.3	79.1	76.5	73.2	79.8	69.6	65.0	73.9
1993	75.5	72.2	78.8	76.3	73.1	79.5	69.2	64.6	73.7
1994	75.7	72.4	79.0	76.5	73.3	79.6	69.5	64.9	73.9
1995	75.8	72.5	78.9	76.5	73.4	79.6	69.6	65.2	73.9
1996	76.1	73.1	79.1	76.8	73.9	79.7	70.2	66.1	74.2
1997	76.5	73.6	79.4	77.1	74.3	79.9	71.1	67.2	74.7
1998	76.7	73.8	79.5	77.3	74.5	80.0	71.3	67.6	74.8
1999	76.7	73.9	79.4	77.3	74.6	79.9	71.4	67.8	74.7
2000	76.8	74.1	79.3	77.3	74.7	79.9	71.8	68.2	75.1
2001	77.0	74.3	79.5	77.5	74.9	80.0	72.0	68.5	75.3
2002	77.0	74.4	79.6	77.5	74.9	80.1	72.2	68.7	75.4
2003	77.2	74.5	79.7	77.7	75.1	80.2	72.4	68.9	75.7
2004	77.6	75.0	80.1	78.1	75.5	80.5	72.9	69.4	76.1
2005	77.6	75.0	80.1	78.0	75.5	80.5	73.0	69.5	76.2
2006	77.8	75.2	80.3	78.3	75.8	80.7	73.4	69.9	76.7
2007	78.1	75.5	80.6	78.5	76.0	80.9	73.8	70.3	77.0
2008	78.2	75.6	80.6	78.5	76.1	80.9	74.3	70.9	77.3
2009	78.5	76.0	80.9	78.8	76.4	81.2	74.7	71.4	77.7
2010	78.7	76.2	81.0	78.9	76.5	81.3	75.1	71.8	78.0
2011	78.7	76.3	81.1	79.0	76.6	81.3	75.3	72.2	78.2
2012	78.8	76.4	81.2	79.1	76.7	81.4	75.5	72.3	78.4
2013[1]	78.8	76.4	81.2	79.0	76.7	81.4	75.5	72.3	78.4
2014[1]	78.9	76.5	81.3	79.1	76.7	81.4	75.6	72.5	78.5
2015[1]	78.8	76.3	81.2	79.0	76.6	81.3	75.5	72.2	78.5

See footnotes at end of table.

Data table for Figure 6 (page 2 of 2). Life Expectancy at birth, by sex, race and Hispanic origin: United States, 1975–2015

Excel and PowerPoint: http://www.cdc.gov/nchs/hus/contents2016.htm#fig06

| | Hispanic or Latino[2] | | | Not Hispanic or Latino | | | | | |
| | | | | White | | | Black or African American | | |
	Both sexes	Male	Female	Both sexes	Male	Female	Both sexes	Male	Female
2015[1]	82.0	79.3	84.3	78.7	76.3	81.1	75.1	71.8	78.1

[1] Life expectancy estimates for 2013 are based on final Medicare data. Life expectancy estimates for 2014 and 2015 are based on preliminary Medicare data.
[2] Persons of Hispanic origin may be of any race. See Appendix II, Hispanic origin. Life expectancies for the Hispanic population are adjusted for underreporting of Hispanic ethnicity on the death certificate, but are not adjusted to account for the potential effects of return migration. To address the effects of age misstatement at the oldest ages, the probability of death for Hispanic persons age 80 and over is estimated as a function of non-Hispanic white mortality with the use of the Brass relational logit model. See Appendix II, Race, for a discussion of sources of bias in death rates by race and Hispanic origin.

NOTES: Populations for computing life expectancy for 1991–1999 are 1990-based postcensal estimates of the U.S. resident population. Populations for computing life expectancy for 2001–2009 were based on intercensal population estimates of the U.S. resident population. Populations for computing life expectancy for 2010 were based on 2010 census counts. Life expectancy for 2011 and beyond was computed using 2010-based postcensal estimates. See Appendix I, Population Census and Population Estimates. In 1997, life table methodology was revised to construct complete life tables by single years of age that extend to age 100. (Anderson RN. Method for constructing complete annual U.S. life tables. NCHS. Vital Health Stat 2(129). 1999.) Previously, abridged life tables were constructed for 5-year age groups ending with 85 years and over. In 2000, the life table methodology was revised. The revised methodology is similar to that developed for the 1999–2001 decennial life tables. In 2008, the life table methodology was further refined. See Appendix II, Life expectancy. Starting with 2003 data, some states allowed the reporting of more than one race on the death certificate. The multiple-race data for these states were bridged to the single-race categories of the 1977 Office of Management and Budget standards, for comparability with other states. The race groups, white and black include persons of Hispanic and non-Hispanic origin. See Appendix II, Race. Life expectancy is not currently available for persons of other racial and ethnic groups. Also see Table 15. Estimates for 2001 and onwards were revised based on the methodology used in the 2008 life table report. Life expectancy for 2001–2012 was calculated using data from Medicare to supplement vital statistics and census data. Starting with *Health, United States, 2016*, life expectancy estimates for 2010–2012, except as noted in Table 15, were revised to take into account updated race and Hispanic origin classification ratios. See Arias E, Heron M, Hakes JK. The validity of race and Hispanic-origin reporting on death certificates in the United States: An update. NCHS. Vital Health Stat 2(172). 2016. Available from: http://www.cdc.gov/nchs/data/series/sr_02/sr02_172.pdf.

SOURCE: NCHS, National Vital Statistics System, public-use Mortality Files; Grove RD, Hetzel AM. Vital statistics rates in the United States, 1940–1960. Washington, DC: U.S. Government Printing Office, 1968; Arias E. United States life tables by Hispanic origin. Vital health statistics; vol 2 no 152. Hyattsville, MD: NCHS. 2010; United States Life Tables, 2001–2009 (using revised intercensal population estimates and a new methodology implemented with the final 2008 life tables); United States Life Tables, 2010–2012 (using a new methodology implemented with the final 2008 life tables and updated race and Hispanic origin classification ratios); United States Life Tables, 2013, forthcoming (using a new methodology implemented with the final 2008 life tables and updated race and Hispanic origin classification ratios). Life table reports available from: http://www.cdc.gov/nchs/products/life_tables.htm; (for 2014 life expectancy) Xu J, Murphy SL, Kochanek KD, Arias E. Mortality in the United States, 2015. NCHS data brief, no 267. Hyattsville, MD: NCHS; 2016. Murphy SL, Kochanek KD, Xu JQ, Curtin SC. Deaths: Final data for 2015. National vital statistics reports. Hyattsville, MD: NCHS; 2017. Available from: http://www.cdc.gov/nchs/products/nvsr.htm; unpublished 2015 life expectancy estimates for white and black persons at birth. See Appendix I, National Vital Statistics System (NVSS).

Data table for Figure 7. Infant mortality rates, by infant age at death and race and Hispanic origin of mother: United States, 1975–2015

Excel and PowerPoint: http://www.cdc.gov/nchs/hus/contents2016.htm#fig07

Year	Infant [1]	Neonatal [1]	Postneonatal [1]
	Infant deaths per 1,000 live births		
1975	16.07	11.58	4.49
1976	15.24	10.92	4.32
1977	14.12	9.88	4.24
1978	13.78	9.49	4.30
1979	13.07	8.87	4.20
1980	12.60	8.48	4.13
1981	11.93	8.02	3.91
1982	11.52	7.70	3.82
1983	11.16	7.28	3.88
1984	10.79	7.00	3.79
1985	10.64	6.96	3.68
1986	10.35	6.71	3.64
1987	10.08	6.46	3.62
1988	9.95	6.32	3.64
1989	9.81	6.23	3.59
1990	9.22	5.85	3.38
1991	8.94	5.59	3.35
1992	8.52	5.37	3.14
1993	8.37	5.29	3.07
1994	8.02	5.12	2.90
1995	7.59	4.91	2.67
1996	7.32	4.77	2.55
1997	7.23	4.77	2.45
1998	7.20	4.80	2.40
1999	7.06	4.73	2.33
2000	6.91	4.63	2.28
2001	6.85	4.54	2.31
2002	6.97	4.66	2.31
2003	6.85	4.62	2.23
2004	6.79	4.52	2.27
2005	6.87	4.54	2.34
2006	6.69	4.45	2.24
2007	6.75	4.42	2.34
2008	6.61	4.29	2.32
2009	6.39	4.18	2.22
2010	6.15	4.05	2.10
2011	6.07	4.06	2.01
2012	5.98	4.01	1.97
2013	5.96	4.04	1.93
2014	5.82	3.94	1.88
2015	5.90	3.93	1.96

Year	Race and Hispanic origin of mother [2]				
		Not Hispanic or Latina			
	Hispanic or Latina	White	Black or African American	Asian or Pacific Islander	American Indian or Alaska Native
	Infant deaths per 1,000 live births [1]				
2014	5.01	4.89	10.93	3.68	7.66

[1] Infant (under 1 year of age), neonatal (under 28 days), and postneonatal (28 days–11 months).

[2] Persons of Hispanic origin may be of any race. Starting with 2003 data, some states reported multiple-race data. The multiple-race data for these states were bridged to the single-race categories of the 1977 Office of Management and Budget standards, for comparability with other states. See Appendix II, Hispanic origin; Race.

NOTES: Infant, neonatal, and postneonatal rates are based on the number of deaths from the mortality file and the number of births from the natality file. Infant mortality rates by race and Hispanic origin are from the Linked Birth/Infant Death data set, in which the most recent data available is 2014.

SOURCE: NCHS, National Vital Statistics System (NVSS). See Appendix I, National Vital Statistics System (NVSS).

Data table for Figure 8 (page 1 of 3). Leading causes of death in 1975 and 2015: United States, 1975–2015

Excel and PowerPoint: http://www.cdc.gov/nchs/hus/contents2016.htm#fig08

Age-adjusted death rates for the top 5 leading causes of death, 1975 and 2015

| Year | Cause of death [1] | | | | | |
	Heart disease	Cancer	Cerebrovascular diseases (Stroke)	Unintentional injuries	Influenza and pneumonia [2]	Chronic lower respiratory diseases [3]
	Age-adjusted deaths per 100,000 resident population [4]					
1975	431.2	200.1	123.5	50.8	35.0	- - -
1976	426.9	202.5	117.4	48.7	38.8	- - -
1977	413.7	203.5	110.4	48.8	31.0	- - -
1978	409.9	204.9	103.7	48.9	34.5	- - -
1979	401.6	204.0	97.3	47.9	26.1	- - -
1980	412.1	207.9	96.2	46.4	31.4	- - -
1981	397.0	206.4	89.5	43.4	30.0	- - -
1982	389.1	208.3	84.2	40.1	26.5	- - -
1983	388.9	209.1	81.2	39.1	29.8	- - -
1984	378.8	210.8	78.7	38.8	30.6	- - -
1985	374.9	211.3	76.4	38.5	34.5	- - -
1986	365.1	211.5	73.1	38.6	34.8	- - -
1987	355.9	211.7	71.6	38.2	33.8	- - -
1988	352.5	212.5	70.6	38.9	37.3	- - -
1989	332.0	214.2	66.9	37.7	35.9	- - -
1990	321.8	216.0	65.3	36.3	36.8	- - -
1991	312.5	215.2	62.9	34.7	34.7	- - -
1992	304.0	213.5	61.5	33.2	32.8	- - -
1993	308.1	213.5	62.7	34.2	35.0	- - -
1994	297.5	211.7	62.6	34.2	33.6	- - -
1995	293.4	209.9	63.1	34.4	33.4	- - -
1996	285.7	206.7	62.5	34.5	32.9	- - -
1997	277.7	203.4	61.1	34.2	33.3	- - -
1998	271.3	200.7	59.3	34.5	34.6	- - -
1999	266.5	200.8	61.6	35.3	23.5	45.4
2000	257.6	199.6	60.9	34.9	23.7	44.2
2001	249.5	196.5	58.4	35.7	22.2	43.9
2002	244.6	194.3	57.2	37.1	23.2	43.9
2003	236.3	190.9	54.6	37.6	22.6	43.7
2004	221.6	186.8	51.2	38.1	20.4	41.6
2005	216.8	185.1	48.0	39.5	21.0	43.9
2006	205.5	181.8	44.8	40.2	18.4	41.0
2007	196.1	179.3	43.5	40.4	16.8	41.4
2008	192.1	176.4	42.1	39.2	17.6	44.7
2009	182.8	173.5	39.6	37.5	16.5	42.7
2010	179.1	172.8	39.1	38.0	15.1	42.2
2011	173.7	169.0	37.9	39.1	15.7	42.5
2012	170.5	166.5	36.9	39.1	14.4	41.5
2013	169.8	163.2	36.2	39.4	15.9	42.1
2014	167.0	161.2	36.5	40.5	15.1	40.5
2015	168.5	158.5	37.6	43.2	15.2	41.6

See footnotes at end of table.

Excel and PowerPoint: *http://www.cdc.gov/nchs/hus/contents2016.htm#fig08*

Age-adjusted death rates for the top 5 leading causes of death, 1975 and 2015

Year	Cause of death[1]					
	Heart disease	Cancer	Cerebrovascular diseases (Stroke)	Unintentional injuries	Influenza and pneumonia[2]	Chronic lower respiratory diseases[3]
	Standard error					
1975	0.5	0.3	0.3	0.2	0.2	- - -
1976	0.5	0.3	0.3	0.2	0.2	- - -
1977	0.5	0.3	0.3	0.2	0.1	- - -
1978	0.5	0.3	0.3	0.2	0.1	- - -
1979	0.5	0.3	0.2	0.2	0.1	- - -
1980	0.5	0.3	0.2	0.2	0.1	- - -
1981	0.5	0.3	0.2	0.1	0.1	- - -
1982	0.5	0.3	0.2	0.1	0.1	- - -
1983	0.5	0.3	0.2	0.1	0.1	- - -
1984	0.4	0.3	0.2	0.1	0.1	- - -
1985	0.4	0.3	0.2	0.1	0.1	- - -
1986	0.4	0.3	0.2	0.1	0.1	- - -
1987	0.4	0.3	0.2	0.1	0.1	- - -
1988	0.4	0.3	0.2	0.1	0.1	- - -
1989	0.4	0.3	0.2	0.1	0.1	- - -
1990	0.4	0.3	0.2	0.1	0.1	- - -
1991	0.4	0.3	0.2	0.1	0.1	- - -
1992	0.4	0.3	0.2	0.1	0.1	- - -
1993	0.4	0.3	0.2	0.1	0.1	- - -
1994	0.3	0.3	0.2	0.1	0.1	- - -
1995	0.3	0.3	0.2	0.1	0.1	- - -
1996	0.3	0.3	0.2	0.1	0.1	- - -
1997	0.3	0.3	0.2	0.1	0.1	- - -
1998	0.3	0.3	0.1	0.1	0.1	- - -
1999	0.3	0.3	0.2	0.1	0.1	0.1
2000	0.3	0.3	0.1	0.1	0.1	0.1
2001	0.3	0.3	0.1	0.1	0.1	0.1
2002	0.3	0.3	0.1	0.1	0.1	0.1
2003	0.3	0.3	0.1	0.1	0.1	0.1
2004	0.3	0.3	0.1	0.1	0.1	0.1
2005	0.3	0.2	0.1	0.1	0.1	0.1
2006	0.3	0.2	0.1	0.1	0.1	0.1
2007	0.3	0.2	0.1	0.1	0.1	0.1
2008	0.2	0.2	0.1	0.1	0.1	0.1
2009	0.2	0.2	0.1	0.1	0.1	0.1
2010	0.2	0.2	0.1	0.1	0.1	0.1
2011	0.2	0.2	0.1	0.1	0.1	0.1
2012	0.2	0.2	0.1	0.1	0.1	0.1
2013	0.2	0.2	0.1	0.1	0.1	0.1
2014	0.2	0.2	0.1	0.1	0.1	0.1
2015	0.2	0.2	0.1	0.1	0.1	0.1

See footnotes at end of table.

Data table for Figure 8 (page 3 of 3). Leading causes of death in 1975 and 2015: United States, 1975–2015

Excel and PowerPoint: http://www.cdc.gov/nchs/hus/contents2016.htm#fig08

Top 10 leading causes of death, 2015

Rank order	Cause of death [1]	Deaths	Percent
Rank	All causes	2,712,630	100.0
1	Heart disease	633,842	23.4
2	Cancer	595,930	22.0
3	Chronic lower respiratory diseases	155,041	5.7
4	Unintentional injuries.	146,571	5.4
5	Stroke.	140,323	5.2
6	Alzheimer's disease	110,561	4.1
7	Diabetes mellitus	79,535	2.9
8	Influenza and pneumonia	57,062	2.1
9	Nephritis, nephrotic syndrome, and nephrosis.	49,959	1.8
10	Suicide	44,193	1.6

- - - Data not available.

[1] Underlying causes of death are based on the *International Classification of Diseases, 8th Revision* (ICD–8) for 1975–1978 estimates, ICD–9 for 1979–1998 estimates, and ICD–10 for 1999–2015 estimates.

[2] Starting with 1999 data, the rules for selecting influenza and pneumonia as the underlying cause of death changed, resulting in a decrease in the number of deaths for pneumonia. Therefore, trend data for this cause of death should be interpreted with caution. For more information, see Comparability of cause of death between ICD–9 and ICD–10: preliminary estimates, available from: http://www.cdc.gov/nchs/data/nvsr/nvsr49/nvsr49_02.pdf.

[3] Starting with 1999 data, the rules for selecting CLRD and Pneumonia as the underlying cause of death changed, resulting in an increase in the number of deaths for CLRD and a decrease in the number of deaths for pneumonia. Therefore, trend data for these two causes of death should be interpreted with caution. For more information, see Comparability of cause of death between ICD–9 and ICD–10 in Appendix II, Table V.

[4] Estimates are age-adjusted to the year 2000 standard population using four age groups: 25–34 years, 35–44 years, 45–64 years, and 65 years and over. See Appendix II, Age adjustment.

NOTES: For cause of death codes based on the ICD–8 in 1975 and ICD–10 in 2015, see Appendix II, Cause of death; Cause-of-death ranking; Table III; Table IV. Starting with 2003 data, some states allowed the reporting of more than one race on the death certificate. The multiple-race data for these states were bridged to the single-race categories of the 1977 Office of Management and Budget standards, for comparability with other states. The race groups, white, black, Asian or Pacific Islander, and American Indian or Alaska Native, include persons of Hispanic and non-Hispanic origin. Persons of Hispanic origin may be of any race. See Appendix II, Race; Hispanic origin.

SOURCE: NCHS, National Vital Statistics System: Final Mortality Statistics, 1975. Monthly Vital Statistics Report, 25(Suppl. 11). 1977. Public-use 2015 Mortality File. Murphy SL, Kochanek KD, Xu JQ, Curtin SC. Deaths: Final data for 2015. National vital statistics reports. Hyattsville, MD: NCHS; 2017. Available from: http://www.cdc.gov/nchs/products/nvsr.htm. See Appendix I, National Vital Statistics System (NVSS).

Data table for Figure 9 (page 1 of 3). Birth rates, by age of mother and age at first live-birth: United States, 1975–2015

Excel and PowerPoint: *http://www.cdc.gov/nchs/hus/contents2016.htm#fig09*

Birth rates, by age of mother: 1975–2015

	Age of mother					
	15–19	20–24	25–29	30–34	35–39	40–44
Year	Live births per 1,000 women					
1975	55.6	113.0	108.2	52.3	19.5	4.6
1976	52.8	110.3	106.2	53.6	19.0	4.3
1977	52.8	112.9	111.0	56.4	19.2	4.2
1978	51.5	109.9	108.5	57.8	19.0	3.9
1979	52.3	112.8	111.4	60.3	19.5	3.9
1980	53.0	115.1	112.9	61.9	19.8	3.9
1981	52.2	112.2	111.5	61.4	20.0	3.8
1982	52.4	111.6	111.0	64.1	21.2	3.9
1983	51.4	107.8	108.5	64.9	22.0	3.9
1984	50.6	106.8	108.7	67.0	22.9	3.9
1985	51.0	108.3	111.0	69.1	24.0	4.0
1986	50.2	107.4	109.8	70.1	24.4	4.1
1987	50.6	107.9	111.6	72.1	26.3	4.4
1988	53.0	110.2	114.4	74.8	28.1	4.8
1989	57.3	113.8	117.6	77.4	29.9	5.2
1990	59.9	116.5	120.2	80.8	31.7	5.5
1991	61.8	115.3	117.2	79.2	31.9	5.5
1992	60.3	113.7	115.7	79.6	32.3	5.9
1993	59.0	111.3	113.2	79.9	32.7	6.1
1994	58.2	109.2	111.0	80.4	33.4	6.4
1995	56.0	107.5	108.8	81.1	34.0	6.6
1996	53.5	107.8	108.6	82.1	34.9	6.8
1997	51.3	107.3	108.3	83.0	35.7	7.1
1998	50.3	108.4	110.2	85.2	36.9	7.4
1999	48.8	107.9	111.2	87.1	37.8	7.4
2000	47.7	109.7	113.5	91.2	39.7	8.0
2001	45.0	105.6	113.8	91.8	40.5	8.1
2002	42.6	103.1	114.7	92.6	41.6	8.3
2003	41.1	102.3	116.7	95.7	43.9	8.7
2004	40.5	101.5	116.5	96.2	45.5	9.0
2005	39.7	101.8	116.5	96.7	46.4	9.1
2006	41.1	105.5	118.0	98.9	47.5	9.4
2007	41.5	105.4	118.1	100.6	47.6	9.6
2008	40.2	101.8	115.0	99.4	46.8	9.9
2009	37.9	96.2	111.5	97.5	46.1	10.0
2010	34.2	90.0	108.3	96.5	45.9	10.2
2011	31.3	85.3	107.2	96.5	47.2	10.3
2012	29.4	83.1	106.5	97.3	48.3	10.4
2013	26.5	80.7	105.5	98.0	49.3	10.4
2014	24.2	79.0	105.8	100.8	51.0	10.6
2015	22.3	76.8	104.3	101.5	51.8	11.0

See footnotes at end of table.

Excel and PowerPoint: http://www.cdc.gov/nchs/hus/contents2016.htm#fig09

Birth rates, by age of mother: 1975–2015

	Age of mother					
	15–19	20–24	25–29	30–34	35–39	40–44
Year	Standard error					
1975	0.07	0.11	0.11	0.09	0.06	0.03
1976	0.07	0.11	0.11	0.09	0.06	0.03
1977	0.07	0.11	0.11	0.08	0.06	0.03
1978	0.07	0.10	0.11	0.08	0.05	0.03
1979	0.07	0.10	0.11	0.08	0.05	0.03
1980	0.07	0.10	0.11	0.08	0.05	0.03
1981	0.07	0.10	0.10	0.08	0.05	0.02
1982	0.07	0.10	0.10	0.08	0.05	0.02
1983	0.07	0.10	0.10	0.08	0.05	0.02
1984	0.07	0.10	0.10	0.08	0.05	0.02
1985	0.07	0.10	0.10	0.08	0.05	0.02
1986	0.07	0.10	0.10	0.08	0.05	0.02
1987	0.07	0.10	0.10	0.08	0.05	0.02
1988	0.08	0.11	0.10	0.08	0.05	0.02
1989	0.08	0.11	0.10	0.08	0.06	0.02
1990	0.08	0.11	0.11	0.09	0.06	0.02
1991	0.09	0.11	0.11	0.08	0.06	0.02
1992	0.08	0.11	0.11	0.08	0.06	0.02
1993	0.08	0.11	0.11	0.08	0.05	0.03
1994	0.08	0.11	0.11	0.08	0.05	0.03
1995	0.08	0.11	0.11	0.09	0.05	0.03
1996	0.08	0.11	0.10	0.09	0.06	0.03
1997	0.07	0.11	0.10	0.09	0.06	0.03
1998	0.07	0.11	0.11	0.09	0.06	0.03
1999	0.07	0.11	0.11	0.09	0.06	0.03
2000	0.07	0.11	0.11	0.09	0.06	0.03
2001	0.07	0.10	0.11	0.09	0.06	0.03
2002	0.07	0.10	0.11	0.09	0.06	0.03
2003	0.06	0.10	0.11	0.10	0.06	0.03
2004	0.06	0.10	0.11	0.10	0.07	0.03
2005	0.06	0.10	0.11	0.10	0.07	0.03
2006	0.06	0.10	0.11	0.10	0.07	0.03
2007	0.06	0.10	0.11	0.10	0.07	0.03
2008	0.06	0.10	0.11	0.10	0.07	0.03
2009	0.06	0.10	0.10	0.10	0.07	0.03
2010	0.06	0.09	0.10	0.10	0.07	0.03
2011	0.05	0.09	0.10	0.10	0.07	0.03
2012	0.05	0.09	0.10	0.10	0.07	0.03
2013	0.05	0.09	0.10	0.10	0.07	0.03
2014	0.05	0.08	0.10	0.10	0.07	0.03
2015	0.05	0.08	0.10	0.10	0.07	0.03

See footnotes at end of table.

Data table for Figure 9 (page 3 of 3). Birth rates, by age of mother and age at first live-birth: United States, 1975–2015

Excel and PowerPoint: http://www.cdc.gov/nchs/hus/contents2016.htm#fig09

Maternal age at first live-birth, by race and Hispanic origin of mother: 2015

| | | Race and Hispanic origin of mother[2] | | | | |
| | | | Not Hispanic or Latina | | | |
Year	Hispanic or Latina	White	Black or African American	American Indian or Alaska Native	Asian or Pacific Islander
All ages	100.0	100.0	100.0	100.0	100.0
		Percent distribution			
Less than 20 years	21.2	9.1	19.5	27.3	2.4
20–24 years	35.6	25.1	39.4	39.7	12.2
25–29 years	22.7	31.0	21.8	20.0	33.0
30–34 years	13.7	24.6	12.6	8.9	36.0
35–39 years	5.5	8.5	5.3	3.3	13.3
40 years and over	1.3	1.8	1.4	0.9	3.2
		Standard error			
Less than 20 years	0.07	0.03	0.09	0.41	0.04
20–24 years	0.09	0.05	0.11	0.45	0.10
25–29 years	0.08	0.05	0.09	0.37	0.14
30–34 years	0.06	0.05	0.07	0.26	0.14
35–39 years	0.04	0.03	0.05	0.16	0.10
40 years and over	0.02	0.01	0.03	0.09	0.05

[1] Persons of Hispanic origin may be of any race. Starting with 2003 data, some states reported multiple-race data. The multiple-race data for these states were bridged to the single-race categories of the 1977 Office of Management and Budget standards, for comparability with other states. See Appendix II, Hispanic origin; Race.

NOTES: Starting with 1970 data, births to persons who were not residents of the 50 states and the District of Columbia are excluded. Starting with *Health, United States, 2003*, rates for 1991–1999 were revised using intercensal population estimates based on the 1990 and 2000 censuses. Rates for 2000 were based on bridged-race April 1, 2000 census counts. Starting with *Health, United States, 2012*, rates for 2001–2009 were revised using intercensal population estimates based on the 2000 and 2010 censuses. Rates for 2010 were based on bridged-race April 1, 2010 census counts. Rates for 2011 and beyond were computed using 2010-based postcensal estimates. See Appendix I, Population Census and Population Estimates. Data for additional years are available. See the Excel spreadsheet on the *Health, United States* website at: http://www.cdc.gov/nchs/hus.htm. Race and Hispanic origin are reported separately on birth certificates. Race categories are consistent with 1977 Office of Management and Budget standards. Forty-nine states and the District of Columbia reported multiple-race data for 2014 that were bridged to single race categories for comparability with other states. Persons of Hispanic origin may be of any race. In this table, Hispanic women are classified only by place of origin; non-Hispanic women are classified by race. See Technical Notes in Births: Final Data for 2015, available from: http://www.cdc.gov/nchs/data/nvsr/nvsr66/nvsr66_01.pdf.

SOURCE: NCHS, National Vital Statistics System, public-use Birth File. Martin JA, Hamilton BE, Osterman MJK, Driscoll AK. Births: Final data for 2015. National vital statistics report; vol 66, no 1. Hyattsville, MD: NCHS. 2017; Available from: http://www.cdc.gov/nchs/data/nvsr/nvsr66/nvsr66_01.pdf. See Appendix I, National Vital Statistics System (NVSS).

Data table for Figure 10. Cigarette smoking among adults aged 25 years and over, by sex and education level: United States, selected years 1974–2015

Excel and PowerPoint: http://www.cdc.gov/nchs/hus/contents2016.htm#fig10

Sex and education level	1974[1]	1979[1]	1985[1]	1990[1]	1995[1]	2000	2005	2010	2015
25 years and over, age-adjusted[2]	Percent of adults who were current cigarette smokers[3]								
Both sexes[4]	36.9	33.1	30.0	25.4	24.5	22.6	20.3	19.2	15.6
No high school diploma or GED.	43.7	40.7	40.8	36.7	35.6	31.6	28.2	26.9	25.6
High school diploma or GED	36.2	33.6	32.0	29.1	29.1	29.2	27.0	27.0	22.9
Some college, no bachelor's degree	35.9	33.2	29.5	23.4	22.6	21.7	21.8	21.3	17.9
Bachelor's degree or higher.	27.2	22.6	18.5	13.9	13.6	10.9	9.1	8.3	5.9
Men[4].	42.9	37.3	32.8	28.2	26.4	24.7	22.7	21.0	17.1
No high school diploma or GED.	52.3	47.6	45.7	42.0	39.7	36.0	31.7	29.7	28.6
High school diploma or GED	42.4	38.9	35.5	33.1	32.7	32.1	29.9	29.3	24.3
Some college, no bachelor's degree	41.8	36.5	32.9	25.9	23.7	23.3	24.9	23.2	18.7
Bachelor's degree or higher.	28.3	22.7	19.6	14.5	13.8	11.6	9.7	8.7	6.6
Women[4].	32.0	29.5	27.5	22.9	22.9	20.5	18.0	17.5	14.3
No high school diploma or GED.	36.6	34.8	36.5	31.8	31.7	27.1	24.6	23.7	22.6
High school diploma or GED	32.2	29.8	29.5	26.1	26.4	26.6	24.1	24.9	21.2
Some college, no bachelor's degree	30.1	30.0	26.3	21.0	21.6	20.4	19.1	19.6	17.2
Bachelor's degree or higher.	25.9	22.5	17.1	13.3	13.3	10.1	8.5	7.9	5.3
	Standard error								
Both sexes[4]	0.3	0.4	0.3	0.3	0.4	0.3	0.3	0.3	0.3
No high school diploma or GED.	0.6	0.8	0.8	0.7	1.1	0.8	0.8	0.9	1.0
High school diploma or GED	0.6	0.6	0.6	0.4	0.7	0.6	0.6	0.7	0.7
Some college, no bachelor's degree	1.0	0.9	0.8	0.6	0.8	0.5	0.5	0.6	0.5
Bachelor's degree or higher.	0.8	0.8	0.7	0.5	0.7	0.4	0.4	0.4	0.3
Men[4].	0.5	0.5	0.5	0.4	0.6	0.5	0.5	0.5	0.5
No high school diploma or GED.	0.9	1.1	1.2	1.1	1.7	1.2	1.2	1.3	1.5
High school diploma or GED	1.0	0.9	0.9	0.7	1.1	0.9	0.9	1.1	1.0
Some college, no bachelor's degree	1.7	1.5	1.2	0.9	1.3	0.8	0.9	0.9	0.8
Bachelor's degree or higher.	1.2	1.0	0.9	0.7	0.9	0.6	0.5	0.5	0.5
Women[4].	0.4	0.5	0.4	0.3	0.6	0.4	0.4	0.4	0.4
No high school diploma or GED.	0.8	0.9	1.0	0.9	1.4	1.0	1.1	1.3	1.2
High school diploma or GED	0.8	0.7	0.7	0.5	0.9	0.8	0.8	0.9	1.0
Some college, no bachelor's degree	1.4	1.1	0.9	0.7	1.1	0.7	0.7	0.8	0.7
Bachelor's degree or higher.	1.4	1.1	1.0	0.7	0.9	0.5	0.5	0.5	0.4

[1] Data prior to 1997 are not strictly comparable with data for later years due to the 1997 questionnaire redesign. See Appendix I, National Health Interview Survey (NHIS).

[2] Estimates are age-adjusted to the year 2000 standard population using four age groups: 25–34 years, 35–44 years, 45–64 years, and 65 years and over. See Appendix II, Age adjustment. For age groups where smoking was 0% or 100%, the age-adjustment procedure was modified to substitute the percentage smoking from the next lower education group.

[3] Starting with 1993 data (shown in spreadsheet version of Table 48), current cigarette smokers were defined as ever smoking 100 cigarettes in their lifetime and smoking now every day or some days. For previous definition, see Appendix II, Cigarette smoking.

[4] Includes unknown education level. Education categories shown are for 1997 (shown in spreadsheet version of Table 48) and subsequent years. GED is General Educational Development high school equivalency diploma. In 1974–1995, the following categories based on number of years of school completed were used: less than 12 years, 12 years, 13–15 years, 16 years or more. See Appendix II, Education.

NOTES: Estimates are age-adjusted. The data table only presents selected years of data for Figure 10. For additional data years, see the Excel spreadsheet version of Table 48 on the *Health, United States* website at: http://www.cdc.gov/nchs/hus.htm.

SOURCE: NCHS, National Health Interview Survey. Data are from the following questionnaire supplements: hypertension (1974), smoking (1979), alcohol and health practices (1983), health promotion and disease prevention (1985, 1990–1991), cancer control and cancer epidemiology (1992), and year 2000 objectives (1993–1995). Starting with 1997, data are from the family core and sample adult questionnaires. See Appendix I, National Health Interview Survey (NHIS).

Data table for Figure 11. Obesity among children and adolescents aged 2–19 and adults aged 20 and over: United States, 1988–1994 through 2013–2014

Excel and PowerPoint: http://www.cdc.gov/nchs/hus/contents2016.htm#fig11

Age and obesity	1988–1994 Percent	SE	1999–2000 Percent	SE	2001–2002 Percent	SE	2003–2004 Percent	SE	2005–2006 Percent	SE	2007–2008 Percent	SE	2009–2010 Percent	SE	2011–2012 Percent	SE	2013–2014 Percent	SE
2–19 years with obesity[1]	10.0	0.5	13.9	0.9	15.4	0.9	17.1	1.3	15.5	1.3	16.8	1.3	16.9	0.7	16.9	1.0	17.2	1.1
20 years and over, age-adjusted[2,3]:																		
Obesity (all grades)	22.9	0.7	30.5	1.5	30.5	1.2	32.3	1.2	34.4	1.4	33.7	1.1	35.7	0.9	34.9	1.3	37.8	0.9
Grade 1 obesity	14.8	0.4	17.3	0.8	18.4	0.8	20.0	0.7	19.6	0.7	19.5	0.6	20.3	0.7	20.5	0.9	20.7	0.7
Grade 2 obesity	5.2	0.4	8.5	0.6	6.9	0.6	7.4	0.5	8.9	0.7	8.6	0.5	9.1	0.5	8.1	0.5	9.5	0.4
Grade 3 obesity	2.9	0.2	4.7	0.6	5.1	0.5	4.8	0.6	5.9	0.5	5.6	0.4	6.3	0.3	6.3	0.5	7.6	0.7
20 years and over, crude[2]:																		
Obesity (all grades)	22.3	0.7	30.3	1.5	30.6	1.1	32.3	1.2	34.7	1.4	33.9	1.1	35.9	0.9	35.1	1.4	37.9	0.8
Grade 1 obesity	14.4	0.4	17.2	0.8	18.5	0.8	20.0	0.8	19.7	0.7	19.6	0.6	20.5	0.7	20.6	0.9	20.8	0.7
Grade 2 obesity	5.1	0.4	8.4	0.5	7.0	0.6	7.4	0.5	9.0	0.7	8.6	0.5	9.1	0.5	8.2	0.5	9.5	0.4
Grade 3 obesity	2.8	0.2	4.7	0.6	5.2	0.5	4.9	0.6	6.0	0.5	5.7	0.4	6.3	0.2	6.4	0.6	7.7	0.7

SE is standard error.

[1] Obesity among children aged 2–19 is defined as body mass index (BMI) at or above the sex- and age-specific 95th percentile from the 2000 CDC Growth Charts: United States. Kuczmarski RJ, Ogden CL, Guo SS, Grummer–Strawn LM, Flegal KM, Mei Z, Wei R, Curtin LR, Roche AF, Johnson CL. 2000 CDC Growth Charts for the United States: methods and development. Vital Health Stat 11. 2002 May;(246):1–190. Available at: http://www.cdc.gov/nchs/data/series/sr_11/sr11_246.pdf. In *Health, United States*, the NHANES variable, Body Mass Index, is used to assign persons to BMI categories.

[2] Obesity among adults is defined as body mass index (BMI) greater than or equal to 30.0. Grade 1 obesity is defined as BMI from 30.0 to 34.9; Grade 2 obesity is defined as BMI from 35.0 to 39.9; and Grade 3 obesity is defined as BMI greater than or equal to 40.0. In *Health, United States*, the NHANES variable, Body Mass Index, is used to assign persons to BMI categories. See Appendix II, Body mass index (BMI).

[3] Estimates are age-adjusted to the year 2000 standard population using five age groups: 20–34 years, 35–44 years, 45–54 years, 55–64 years, and 65 years and over.

NOTE: Also see Tables 58 and 59.

SOURCE: NCHS, National Health and Nutrition Examination Survey. See Appendix I, National Health and Nutrition Examination Survey (NHANES).

Data table for Figure 12. Untreated dental caries among children and adolescents aged 5–19 and adults aged 20 and over, by percent of poverty level: United States, 1988–1994, 1999–2004, and 2011–2014

Excel and PowerPoint: http://www.cdc.gov/nchs/hus/contents2016.htm#fig12

Age and percent of poverty level [1]	1988–1994		1999–2004		2011–2014	
	Percent	SE	Percent	SE	Percent	SE
5–19 years.	24.3	1.0	23.6	0.9	18.6	1.1
Percent of poverty level:						
Below 100%	39.0	1.7	32.2	1.3	24.7	1.2
100%–199%	29.6	2.0	32.1	1.8	22.3	1.7
200%–399%	16.6	1.1	18.9	1.4	16.0	1.5
400% or more	*10.4	2.2	10.0	1.1	9.1	1.4
20 years and over, age-adjusted [2].	27.9	1.0	25.2	0.9	28.5	1.2
Percent of poverty level:						
Below 100%	48.6	2.0	44.1	1.8	49.7	1.8
100%–199%	42.3	1.7	37.9	1.3	41.5	1.7
200%–399%	24.7	1.2	25.7	1.1	26.8	1.5
400% or more	13.5	0.9	12.2	0.9	13.3	1.1
20 years and over, crude	28.2	1.1	25.5	1.0	28.4	1.2
Percent of poverty level:						
Below 100%	48.0	2.1	44.4	1.9	48.7	2.0
100%–199%	42.6	1.7	37.3	1.2	41.3	1.8
200%–399%	24.6	1.2	25.7	1.1	26.7	1.5
400% or more	13.1	1.0	12.0	1.0	13.0	1.1

SE is standard error.

* Estimates are considered unreliable. Data preceded by an asterisk have a relative standard error of 20%–30%.

[1] Percent of poverty level was calculated by dividing family income by the U.S. Department of Health and Human Services' poverty guideline specific to family size, as well as the appropriate year, and state. See Appendix II, Family income; Poverty.

[2] Estimates are age-adjusted to the year 2000 standard population using five age groups: 20–34 years, 35–49 years, 50–64 years, 65–74 years, and 75 years and over.

NOTES: Also see Table 60. Untreated dental caries refers to decay on the crown or enamel surface of a tooth (i.e., coronal caries) that has not been treated or filled. Decay in the root (i.e., root caries) was not included. The presence of caries was evaluated in primary and permanent teeth for persons aged 5 and older. The third molars were not included. Persons without at least one natural tooth (primary or permanent) were classified as edentulous (without any teeth) and were excluded. The majority of edentulous persons are aged 65 and over. Age-adjusted estimates of edentulism among persons aged 65 and over are 34% in 1988–1994, 27% in 1999–2004, and 18% in 2011–2014.

SOURCE: NCHS, National Health and Nutrition Examination Survey. See Appendix I, National Health and Nutrition Examination Survey (NHANES).

Data table for Figure 13. Diabetes prevalence among adults aged 20 years and over, by diagnosis status and race and Hispanic origin: United States, 1988–1994 and 2011–2014

Excel and PowerPoint: http://www.cdc.gov/nchs/hus/contents2016.htm#fig13

Race and Hispanic origin [4]	Total diabetes [1]				Physician-diagnosed diabetes [2]				Undiagnosed diabetes [3]			
	1988–1994		2011–2014		1988–1994		2011–2014		1988–1994		2011–2014	
	Percent	SE	Percent	SE	Percent	SE	Percent	SE	Percent	SE	Percent	SE
	Percent of population											
All persons.	8.8	0.5	11.9	0.6	5.2	0.4	9.0	0.6	3.6	0.3	2.9	0.3
Not Hispanic or Latino:												
White only.	7.7	0.6	9.6	0.7	4.8	0.5	7.6	0.7	2.9	0.3	2.0	0.3
Black or African American only. . .	16.3	0.9	18.0	1.3	9.1	0.7	13.4	0.8	7.2	0.5	4.6	0.8
Asian only.	- - -	- - -	16.3	1.4	- - -	- - -	10.4	1.0	- - -	- - -	5.9	1.1
Hispanic or Latino:												
Mexican origin	15.6	0.9	18.0	1.7	10.7	0.9	13.0	1.0	5.0	0.7	5.1	1.0

SE is standard error.

- - - Data not available.

[1] Total diabetes includes those with either physician-diagnosed or undiagnosed diabetes.

[2] Physician-diagnosed diabetes was obtained by self-report and excludes women who were only told they had diabetes while pregnant.

[3] Undiagnosed diabetes is defined as a fasting plasma glucose (FPG) of at least 126 mg/dL or a hemoglobin A1c of at least 6.5% and no reported physician diagnosis. Respondents had fasted for at least 8 hours and less than 24 hours at the time of blood draw.

[4] From 1976 to 2006, the NHANES sample was designed to provide estimates specifically for persons of Mexican origin. Beginning in 2007, NHANES allows for reporting of both total Hispanics and Mexican Americans. Beginning 2011–2012, the NHANES sample was designed to provide estimates for Asian Americans.

NOTES: All persons includes persons of all other races and Hispanic origins not shown separately. For more information, see Appendix II, Diabetes. Estimates are age-adjusted to the year 2000 standard population using three age groups: 20–44 years, 45–64 years, and 65 years and over. See Table 40.

SOURCE: NCHS, National Health and Nutrition Examination Survey. See Appendix I, National Health and Nutrition Examination Survey (NHANES).

Data table for Figure 14. Uncontrolled high blood pressure among adults aged 20 and over with hypertension, by sex and age: United States, 1988–1994 through 2011–2014

Excel and PowerPoint: http://www.cdc.gov/nchs/hus/contents2016.htm#fig14

	Uncontrolled high blood pressure among adults aged 20 and over with hypertension [1]									
	1988–1994		1999–2002		2003–2006		2007–2010		2011–2014	
Sex and age	Percent	SE	Percent	SE	Percent	SE	Percent	SE	Percent	SE
	Percent of population									
20 years and over, age-adjusted [2]										
Both sexes.	77.2	1.4	70.6	1.7	63.3	1.9	55.8	1.8	52.8	1.9
Men.	83.2	1.6	73.3	1.8	65.0	2.3	61.4	2.1	58.1	1.9
Women	68.5	2.2	61.8	3.4	53.6	4.1	46.3	2.7	45.5	3.1
20 years and over, crude										
Both sexes.	73.9	1.0	67.3	1.5	58.6	1.4	49.3	1.2	47.0	1.8
Men.	79.3	1.3	67.1	1.9	58.4	2.1	52.3	1.6	49.9	2.1
Women	68.8	1.6	67.4	1.7	58.8	1.3	46.4	1.3	44.3	1.9

	2011–2014	
Sex and age	Percent	SE
Men:		
20–34 years.	74.1	4.6
35–44 years.	64.2	5.1
45–64 years.	49.7	3.1
65–74 years.	38.2	3.1
75 years and over.	46.5	4.4
Women:		
20–34 years.	55.5	8.0
35–44 years.	37.7	3.7
45–64 years.	36.8	2.7
65–74 years.	44.5	2.8
75 years and over.	61.5	3.0

SE is standard error.

[1] Uncontrolled high blood pressure among adults with hypertension is defined as measured systolic pressure of at least 140 mm Hg or diastolic pressure of at least 90 mm Hg, among those with measured high blood pressure or reporting taking antihypertensive medication.

[2] Estimates are age-adjusted to the year 2000 standard population using five age groups: 20–34 years, 35–44 years, 45–54 years, 55–64 years, and 65 years and over. Age-adjusted estimates in this table may differ from other age-adjusted estimates based on the same data and presented elsewhere if different age groups are used in the adjustment procedure. See Appendix II, Age adjustment; Blood pressure, high. Also see Table 54.

SOURCE: NCHS, National Health and Nutrition Examination Survey. See Appendix I, National Health and Nutrition Examination Survey (NHANES).

Data table for Figure 15. Prescription drug use in the past 30 days among adults aged 18 and over, by age and number of drugs taken: United States, 1988–1994 through 2013–2014

Excel and PowerPoint: http://www.cdc.gov/nchs/hus/contents2016.htm#fig15

Use of at least one prescription drug in the past 30 days, by age

Age	1988–1994	1999–2000	2001–2002	2003–2004	2005–2006	2007–2008	2009–2010	2011–2012	2013–2014
					Percent				
18–44 years	31.3	34.7	37.0	38.3	36.6	39.0	38.4	37.7	36.5
45–64 years	54.8	62.1	65.3	67.1	63.3	66.3	66.0	68.4	69.6
65 years and over	73.6	83.9	85.7	88.8	90.0	90.3	89.1	90.4	90.8
					Standard error				
18–44 years	0.8	1.4	2.3	1.3	1.1	1.2	2.0	1.6	1.3
45–64 years	1.0	2.1	2.3	1.4	1.0	2.0	1.5	1.2	1.4
65 years and over	0.9	1.2	1.3	1.2	0.9	0.9	0.8	1.3	1.1

Prescription drug use in the past 30 days, by age and number of drugs taken

Age and number of drugs taken	1988–1994		2013–2014	
18–44 years	*Percent*	*SE*	*Percent*	*SE*
At least one prescription drug.	31.3	0.8	36.5	1.3
One to four prescription drugs	30.1	0.7	32.6	1.2
Five or more prescription drugs	1.2	0.2	3.9	0.6
45–64 years				
At least one prescription drug.	54.8	1.0	69.6	1.4
One to four prescription drugs	47.5	1.1	49.4	1.3
Five or more prescription drugs	7.4	0.5	20.2	1.4
65 years and over				
At least one prescription drug.	73.6	0.9	90.8	1.1
One to four prescription drugs	59.9	0.9	48.7	1.8
Five or more prescription drugs	13.8	0.7	42.2	1.9

SE is standard error.

NOTE: See Appendix II, Drug.

SOURCE: NCHS, National Health and Nutrition Examination Survey. See Appendix I, National Health and Nutrition Examination Survey (NHANES).

Data table for Figure 16. Health care visits in the past 12 months among children aged 2–17 and adults aged 18 and over, by age and provider type: United States, 1997, 2006, and 2015

Excel and PowerPoint: *http://www.cdc.gov/nchs/hus/contents2016.htm#fig16*

Age and provider type [1]	1997 Percent	1997 SE	2006 Percent	2006 SE	2015 Percent	2015 SE
2–17 years	Percent with 1 or more visits					
Generalist	77.5	0.5	79.6	0.6	83.8	0.5
Specialist	11.9	0.4	13.1	0.5	14.2	0.5
Eye doctor.	19.6	0.5	23.0	0.6	27.8	0.6
Mental health provider.	6.3	0.3	6.0	0.3	8.7	0.4
Dentist.	72.7	0.5	75.7	0.6	84.7	0.5
18–64 years						
Generalist	63.3	0.4	62.2	0.5	65.1	0.4
Specialist	20.9	0.3	22.0	0.4	23.2	0.4
Eye doctor.	31.2	0.3	31.8	0.5	36.2	0.4
Mental health provider.	6.7	0.2	7.0	0.2	8.8	0.3
Dentist.	64.1	0.4	62.4	0.5	64.0	0.4
65 years and over						
Generalist	82.2	0.5	85.2	0.7	87.9	0.5
Specialist	39.5	0.7	45.5	1.0	46.8	0.8
Eye doctor.	51.8	0.7	57.1	1.0	58.5	0.7
Mental health provider.	2.2	0.2	3.7	0.3	4.8	0.3
Dentist.	54.8	0.7	58.0	0.9	62.7	0.8

SE is standard error.

[1] Generalist includes providers practicing general practice, family medicine, and internal medicine. Specialist includes providers specializing in a particular disease or problem. Eye doctor includes optometrists and ophthalmologists. Mental health providers include psychiatrists, psychologists, psychiatric nurses, clinical social workers, and other mental health professionals. Dentist includes orthodontists, oral surgeons, dental hygienists, and other dental specialists.

NOTES: Respondents were asked a series of questions about the different types of health care contacts they have had in the past 12 months: "During the past 12 months, have you seen or talked to any of the following health care providers about your own/your child's health?".

SOURCE: NCHS, National Health Interview Survey. See Appendix I, National Health Interview Survey (NHIS).

Data table for Figure 17 (page 1 of 2). Emergency department visits in the past 12 months for persons under age 65, by age and type of coverage: United States, 1997–2015

Excel and PowerPoint: http://www.cdc.gov/nchs/hus/contents2016.htm#fig17

Age and year	Insurance status at time of interview [1]		
	Medicaid [2]	Uninsured [3]	Private
Under 18	Percent with 1 or more emergency department visits		
1997	28.2	20.2	17.5
1998	29.0	20.1	17.9
1999	28.8	16.4	15.4
2000	28.6	17.2	18.4
2001	28.3	17.3	18.6
2002	30.7	18.2	20.0
2003	28.9	17.1	18.1
2004	27.2	20.7	18.5
2005	28.5	18.4	17.4
2006	27.2	16.8	19.2
2007	27.3	17.7	17.1
2008	29.1	18.4	16.8
2009	27.8	16.8	16.6
2010	30.0	19.4	17.1
2011	24.4	13.8	14.9
2012	24.8	15.6	13.0
2013	24.0	15.1	13.2
2014	22.9	14.7	12.4
2015	22.8	14.3	12.5
18–64 years			
1997	38.0	21.0	16.9
1998	37.2	21.3	17.2
1999	35.2	19.2	14.5
2000	41.9	19.5	17.5
2001	39.5	19.0	17.1
2002	40.5	20.8	17.3
2003	39.8	18.3	17.3
2004	36.5	19.5	17.8
2005	40.0	19.6	17.1
2006	38.9	19.2	17.0
2007	38.0	20.5	16.8
2008	39.8	19.5	16.8
2009	41.5	21.6	16.4
2010	39.8	21.5	17.2
2011	37.7	21.1	15.5
2012	39.7	18.7	14.9
2013	37.7	18.5	14.0
2014	35.2	16.6	14.4
2015	34.8	18.2	14.0

See footnotes at end of table.

Data table for Figure 17 (page 2 of 2). Emergency department visits in the past 12 months for persons under age 65, by age and type of coverage: United States, 1997–2015

Excel and PowerPoint: http://www.cdc.gov/nchs/hus/contents2016.htm#fig17

Age and year	Insurance status at time of interview [1]		
	Medicaid [2]	Uninsured [3]	Private
Under 18	Standard error		
1997	1.1	1.0	0.5
1998	1.2	1.1	0.5
1999	1.2	1.1	0.5
2000	1.1	1.1	0.5
2001	1.1	1.2	0.5
2002	1.0	1.3	0.5
2003	1.0	1.2	0.5
2004	1.0	1.6	0.5
2005	1.0	1.4	0.5
2006	1.1	1.4	0.8
2007	1.1	1.6	0.6
2008	1.1	1.8	0.6
2009	1.0	1.6	0.6
2010	1.0	1.6	0.6
2011	0.8	1.3	0.5
2012	0.8	1.5	0.6
2013	0.8	1.6	0.5
2014	0.8	1.7	0.6
2015	0.8	1.8	0.6
18–64 years			
1997	1.3	0.6	0.3
1998	1.4	0.7	0.3
1999	1.4	0.7	0.3
2000	1.5	0.7	0.3
2001	1.3	0.7	0.3
2002	1.3	0.7	0.3
2003	1.3	0.7	0.4
2004	1.3	0.7	0.4
2005	1.3	0.7	0.3
2006	1.4	0.8	0.4
2007	1.4	0.8	0.4
2008	1.6	0.8	0.4
2009	1.4	0.8	0.4
2010	1.2	0.7	0.4
2011	1.2	0.7	0.3
2012	1.2	0.7	0.4
2013	1.1	0.7	0.4
2014	1.1	0.7	0.4
2015	1.1	0.9	0.4

[1] Health insurance categories are mutually exclusive. Persons who reported both Medicaid and private coverage are classified as having private coverage.

[2] Children's Health Insurance Plan (CHIP) and state-sponsored health plan coverage are included as Medicaid coverage.

[3] Persons not covered by private insurance, Medicaid, CHIP, state-sponsored or other government-sponsored health plans, Medicare, or military plans are considered to have no health insurance coverage. Persons with only Indian Health Service coverage are considered to have no health insurance coverage.

NOTE: See Appendix II, Health insurance coverage.

SOURCE: NCHS, National Health Interview Survey. See Appendix I, National Health Interview Survey (NHIS).

Data table for Figure 18 (page 1 of 4). Overnight hospital stays in the past 12 months, by sex and age: United States, 1975–2015

Excel and PowerPoint: http://www.cdc.gov/nchs/hus/contents2016.htm#fig18

Gender and year	Age				
	1–17 years	18–44 years	45–64 years	65–74 years	75 years and over
Male	Percent with 1 or more overnight hospital stays				
1975	5.5	6.5	11.8	16.6	22.6
1976	5.6	6.6	12.2	17.7	22.3
1977	5.1	6.5	12.1	18.2	22.6
1978	5.1	6.6	12.1	17.7	22.4
1979	4.7	6.6	11.7	17.2	22.3
1980	5.0	6.8	11.6	17.9	22.8
1981	5.1	6.3	11.8	17.7	22.0
1982	4.4	6.3	11.7	19.9	24.5
1983	4.7	5.7	12.1	18.9	24.9
1984	4.4	5.2	11.5	18.5	23.9
1985	3.8	5.1	11.4	18.1	23.2
1986	3.2	5.0	10.5	16.3	20.5
1987	3.5	4.8	10.0	17.6	22.6
1988	3.3	4.6	9.6	16.6	21.0
1989	3.0	4.3	9.1	17.4	20.8
1990	3.2	4.0	8.8	16.1	20.8
1991	3.1	4.0	8.2	15.8	23.2
1992	2.9	3.9	8.6	17.4	21.5
1993	2.7	3.8	8.1	16.1	19.4
1994	2.7	3.8	8.2	16.6	20.7
1995	2.6	3.8	8.5	16.2	20.9
1996	2.7	3.8	7.5	15.6	23.1
1997	2.9	3.6	8.0	17.1	21.1
1998	2.9	3.6	8.2	16.8	20.5
1999	2.7	3.3	8.5	17.4	20.2
2000	2.4	3.1	8.3	17.7	21.6
2001	2.8	3.4	7.9	15.5	23.5
2002	2.9	3.3	7.6	17.7	23.4
2003	2.5	3.4	8.4	15.6	22.0
2004	2.5	3.3	7.4	14.6	22.3
2005	2.8	3.2	8.1	15.5	21.9
2006	2.6	3.3	7.7	14.4	21.2
2007	2.7	3.3	8.1	13.9	20.7
2008	2.8	3.2	6.9	15.2	22.3
2009	2.3	3.4	7.7	14.5	22.0
2010	2.4	2.9	7.7	13.4	19.4
2011	2.3	3.1	7.6	13.5	20.3
2012	2.1	3.1	7.4	13.9	18.3
2013	2.1	2.9	7.7	12.5	20.0
2014	2.0	2.6	7.3	14.8	18.6
2015	2.1	3.1	7.7	13.9	20.3

See footnotes at end of table.

Data table for Figure 18 (page 2 of 4). Overnight hospital stays in the past 12 months, by sex and age: United States, 1975–2015

Excel and PowerPoint: http://www.cdc.gov/nchs/hus/contents2016.htm#fig18

Gender and year	Age				
	1–17 years	*18–44 years*	*45–64 years*	*65–74 years*	*75 years and over*
Female	Percent with 1 or more overnight hospital stays				
1975	5.3	17.1	12.9	14.9	19.2
1976	4.7	16.0	13.4	16.4	19.6
1977	4.3	15.8	11.6	15.7	19.2
1978	5.0	15.1	12.7	15.8	19.5
1979	4.6	15.5	11.4	15.8	20.9
1980	4.6	15.5	11.5	16.1	19.6
1981	4.2	15.0	12.0	15.8	19.5
1982	4.3	14.4	12.3	16.1	22.9
1983	4.2	14.3	11.7	17.0	22.3
1984	3.9	13.5	10.8	16.5	23.3
1985	3.7	12.8	10.2	15.0	22.1
1986	3.7	12.4	9.0	14.6	20.1
1987	3.4	11.8	9.0	13.2	18.4
1988	3.1	11.8	8.5	14.0	18.3
1989	3.0	11.9	8.7	13.6	19.0
1990	2.6	11.4	8.4	13.4	18.6
1991	2.7	11.7	7.8	13.2	18.5
1992	2.7	11.0	8.0	12.6	18.6
1993	3.1	10.9	8.0	12.9	18.0
1994	2.7	10.6	7.9	13.7	19.9
1995	2.7	10.6	7.7	13.3	19.3
1996	2.6	10.3	8.1	13.1	18.6
1997	2.6	11.2	8.3	15.3	20.0
1998	2.5	10.8	8.7	15.7	20.6
1999	2.4	10.8	8.5	14.8	21.1
2000	2.5	10.8	8.5	14.7	20.2
2001	2.7	10.9	8.7	14.5	21.4
2002	2.4	10.9	8.8	14.9	21.8
2003	2.4	10.8	8.9	14.9	21.4
2004	2.2	10.6	8.7	14.3	19.7
2005	2.2	10.2	8.3	13.7	21.1
2006	2.6	9.8	8.5	14.0	20.6
2007	2.2	10.2	8.4	15.3	20.6
2008	2.3	9.7	8.8	13.2	20.7
2009	2.1	9.9	9.3	14.0	19.4
2010	2.3	9.8	8.9	13.9	18.7
2011	2.3	9.7	8.9	13.9	20.4
2012	2.0	9.0	8.4	13.3	19.5
2013	2.1	9.2	8.0	12.7	18.3
2014	2.1	8.9	7.5	12.9	16.8
2015	2.1	8.5	7.8	11.7	17.7

See footnotes at end of table.

Data table for Figure 18 (page 3 of 4). Overnight hospital stays in the past 12 months, by sex and age: United States, 1975–2015

Excel and PowerPoint: http://www.cdc.gov/nchs/hus/contents2016.htm#fig18

Gender and year	Age				
	1–17 years	18–44 years	45–64 years	65–74 years	75 years and over
Male	Standard error				
1975	0.2	0.2	0.3	0.7	1.1
1976	0.2	0.3	0.4	0.7	1.0
1977	0.2	0.3	0.4	0.8	1.0
1978	0.3	0.3	0.5	0.7	1.1
1979	0.3	0.3	0.4	0.7	1.1
1980	0.2	0.2	0.4	0.7	1.1
1981	0.3	0.3	0.4	0.7	1.1
1982	0.2	0.2	0.3	0.7	1.0
1983	0.2	0.2	0.4	0.7	1.0
1984	0.2	0.2	0.3	0.8	1.0
1985	0.2	0.2	0.4	0.7	1.2
1986	0.2	0.2	0.4	0.9	1.3
1987	0.2	0.2	0.3	0.6	0.9
1988	0.2	0.1	0.3	0.6	0.9
1989	0.1	0.1	0.3	0.7	1.0
1990	0.1	0.1	0.3	0.7	0.9
1991	0.1	0.1	0.3	0.6	1.0
1992	0.1	0.1	0.3	0.6	0.9
1993	0.2	0.1	0.3	0.6	1.0
1994	0.1	0.1	0.3	0.6	0.9
1995	0.1	0.1	0.3	0.7	1.0
1996	0.2	0.2	0.4	0.9	1.3
1997	0.2	0.2	0.3	0.7	0.9
1998	0.2	0.1	0.3	0.7	1.0
1999	0.2	0.1	0.3	0.8	1.0
2000	0.1	0.1	0.3	0.8	1.0
2001	0.2	0.1	0.3	0.7	1.0
2002	0.2	0.2	0.3	0.8	1.0
2003	0.2	0.2	0.3	0.8	1.0
2004	0.2	0.1	0.3	0.7	1.0
2005	0.2	0.1	0.3	0.8	1.0
2006	0.2	0.2	0.3	0.9	1.2
2007	0.2	0.2	0.3	0.8	1.2
2008	0.2	0.2	0.3	0.8	1.1
2009	0.2	0.2	0.3	0.8	1.1
2010	0.2	0.1	0.3	0.7	1.0
2011	0.1	0.1	0.3	0.7	0.9
2012	0.1	0.2	0.3	0.7	0.9
2013	0.1	0.2	0.3	0.6	1.0
2014	0.1	0.1	0.3	0.7	0.9
2015	0.2	0.2	0.3	0.7	0.9

See footnotes at end of table.

Data table for Figure 18 (page 4 of 4). Overnight hospital stays in the past 12 months, by sex and age: United States, 1975–2015

Excel and PowerPoint: http://www.cdc.gov/nchs/hus/contents2016.htm#fig18

Gender and year	Age				
	1–17 years	18–44 years	45–64 years	65–74 years	75 years and over
Female	Standard error				
1975	0.2	0.3	0.3	0.5	0.8
1976	0.2	0.4	0.5	0.6	0.8
1977	0.2	0.4	0.4	0.6	0.7
1978	0.3	0.4	0.5	0.5	0.8
1979	0.3	0.4	0.4	0.6	0.8
1980	0.2	0.3	0.3	0.6	0.8
1981	0.3	0.4	0.4	0.6	0.8
1982	0.2	0.3	0.4	0.6	0.9
1983	0.2	0.3	0.4	0.7	0.8
1984	0.2	0.3	0.3	0.5	0.8
1985	0.2	0.3	0.3	0.6	1.0
1986	0.2	0.3	0.4	0.8	1.0
1987	0.1	0.2	0.3	0.5	0.7
1988	0.1	0.2	0.3	0.5	0.6
1989	0.2	0.2	0.3	0.5	0.7
1990	0.1	0.2	0.3	0.5	0.7
1991	0.1	0.2	0.3	0.5	0.7
1992	0.1	0.2	0.3	0.5	0.7
1993	0.2	0.2	0.3	0.5	0.7
1994	0.1	0.2	0.3	0.5	0.7
1995	0.1	0.2	0.3	0.6	0.8
1996	0.2	0.3	0.4	0.7	0.9
1997	0.2	0.2	0.3	0.6	0.7
1998	0.1	0.2	0.3	0.6	0.8
1999	0.2	0.2	0.3	0.7	0.8
2000	0.2	0.2	0.3	0.7	0.9
2001	0.2	0.2	0.3	0.6	0.8
2002	0.2	0.3	0.3	0.7	0.8
2003	0.2	0.3	0.3	0.7	0.8
2004	0.2	0.3	0.3	0.7	0.8
2005	0.2	0.3	0.3	0.6	0.8
2006	0.2	0.3	0.3	0.7	1.0
2007	0.2	0.3	0.3	0.8	0.9
2008	0.2	0.3	0.3	0.7	0.9
2009	0.2	0.3	0.3	0.7	0.9
2010	0.2	0.3	0.3	0.7	0.8
2011	0.2	0.2	0.3	0.6	0.8
2012	0.1	0.2	0.3	0.6	0.8
2013	0.2	0.3	0.3	0.6	0.8
2014	0.2	0.2	0.3	0.6	0.7
2015	0.2	0.2	0.3	0.6	0.7

NOTES: Estimates for hospital stays include those relating to deliveries but exclude stays for institutionalized persons as well as stays that ended in death. Consequently, the estimates shown will vary from those based on a survey of hospital discharges. The difference will be larger for older persons, since they have greater likelihood of being institutionalized and higher death rates than younger persons. See Appendix II, Hospital utilization; Table 81.

SOURCE: NCHS, National Health Interview Survey. See Appendix I, National Health Interview Survey (NHIS).

Data table for Figure 19. Mammography use and colorectal cancer testing use, by race and Hispanic origin: United States, selected years 1987–2015

Excel and PowerPoint: http://www.cdc.gov/nchs/hus/contents2016.htm#fig19

Use of mammography in the past 2 years among women aged 40–74: United States, selected years 1987–2015

Year	Hispanic or Latino	Race and Hispanic origin [1]		
		Not Hispanic or Latino		
		White only	Black only	Asian only
	Percent of women having a mammogram within the past 2 years [2]			
1987	19.3	32.5	25.6	*
1990	45.3	55.7	47.1	47.7
1991	49.9	59.4	48.8	47.0
1993	55.0	64.2	59.6	56.3
1994	53.6	64.4	65.4	58.1
1998	60.9	69.9	67.7	59.0
1999	66.1	73.4	72.0	59.3
2000	61.5	74.1	69.3	53.4
2003	65.5	72.2	72.3	57.8
2005	59.6	70.6	66.9	55.4
2008	61.7	70.5	70.1	69.0
2010	65.2	69.9	69.5	64.1
2013	62.1	69.6	68.1	70.4
2015	62.8	68.2	72.3	62.7
	Standard error			
1987	2.4	0.8	2.2	*
1990	2.5	0.7	1.6	4.8
1991	2.5	0.7	1.6	4.2
1993	3.4	0.8	2.3	5.7
1994	3.7	0.8	2.1	5.5
1998	1.7	0.7	1.6	4.2
1999	1.9	0.7	1.6	4.5
2000	1.8	0.7	1.6	4.5
2003	1.7	0.7	1.6	3.9
2005	1.8	0.7	1.6	3.8
2008	2.2	0.9	1.8	3.3
2010	1.7	0.9	1.5	2.7
2013	1.5	0.8	1.7	2.4
2015	1.7	0.8	1.6	3.0

Use of any colorectal test or procedure among adults aged 50–75: United States, selected years 2000–2015

Year	Hispanic or Latino	White only	Black only	Asian only
	Percent of adults with any colorectal test or procedure [3]			
2000 [4]	21.7	35.7	29.7	20.6
2003	27.2	41.0	35.3	26.3
2005	28.5	47.4	38.0	30.0
2008	34.0	54.8	47.4	47.3
2010	46.5	61.3	55.3	46.6
2013	41.5	60.4	58.2	51.2
2015	47.4	65.6	60.3	52.1
	Standard error			
2000 [4]	1.7	0.7	1.8	3.4
2003	1.7	0.7	1.7	3.7
2005	1.8	0.7	1.7	3.4
2008	2.0	0.8	2.0	3.4
2010	1.9	0.8	1.6	2.9
2013	1.7	0.7	1.5	2.7
2015	1.8	0.8	1.5	2.8

* Estimates are considered unreliable. Data not shown have an RSE greater than 30%.

[1] Starting with 1999 data, race-specific estimates are tabulated according to the 1997 *Revisions to the Standards for the Classification of Federal Data on Race and Ethnicity* and are not strictly comparable with estimates for earlier years. Prior to 1999, data were tabulated according to the 1977 Standards with four racial groups, and the Asian only category included Native Hawaiian or Other Pacific Islander. Estimates for single-race categories prior to 1999 included persons who reported one race or, if they reported more than one race, identified one race as best representing their race. See Appendix II, Hispanic origin; Race.

[2] Questions concerning use of mammography differed slightly on the National Health Interview Survey across the survey years. See Appendix II, Mammography. Data prior to 1997 are not strictly comparable with data for later years due to the 1997 questionnaire redesign.

[3] Adults with a colorectal test or procedure are those who reported a home fecal occult blood test (FOBT) in the past year, a sigmoidoscopy procedure in the past five years with FOBT in the past three years, or a colonoscopy in the past 10 years. Questions concerning colorectal testing differed slightly on the National Health Interview Survey across survey years. See Appendix II, Colorectal tests or procedures.

[4] Colorectal cancer testing data begin in 2000 due to changes in available procedures prior to 2000.

SOURCE: NCHS, National Health Interview Survey. See Appendix I, National Health Interview Survey (NHIS).

Data table for Figure 20. Community hospital beds, average length of stay, and occupancy rate: United States, selected years 1975–2014

Excel and PowerPoint: http://www.cdc.gov/nchs/hus/contents2016.htm#fig20

Characteristic	1975	1985	1995	2005	2014
Beds per 1,000 population	4.6	4.2	3.3	2.7	2.5
Average length of stay (days)	7.7	7.1	6.5	5.6	5.5
Occupancy rate	75.0	64.8	62.8	67.3	62.8
Beds (thousands)	942	1,001	873	802	787

NOTES: Average length of stay is the number of inpatient days divided by the number of admissions. Occupancy rate is the average daily census divided by the number of hospital beds, cribs, and pediatric bassinets set up and staffed on the last day of the reporting period, expressed as a percentage. For 1975, 1985, and 1995 data, civilian population is used for beds per 1,000 population and resident population is used for 2005 and 2014 data. See Appendix II, Average length of stay; Occupancy rate. See Table 89.

SOURCE: American Hospital Association (AHA). Annual Survey of Hospitals. Hospital Statistics, 1976, 1986, 1998, 2007, and 2016 editions. Chicago, IL. [Reprinted from AHA Hospital Statistics by permission, Copyright 1976, 1986, 1998, 2007, and 2016 by Health Forum, LLC, an American Hospital Association Company.] See Appendix I, American Hospital Association (AHA) Annual Survey of Hospitals.

Data table for Figure 21. Active primary care generalist and specialist physicians, by self-designated specialty: United States, selected years 1975–2013

Excel and PowerPoint: http://www.cdc.gov/nchs/hus/contents2016.htm#fig21

Characteristic	1975	1980	1985	1990	1995	2000	2005	2010	2013
	Number per 10,000 population								
Total active physicians	15.5	17.9	20.5	21.7	23.8	24.5	25.7	25.7	27.0
Primary care generalist physician	6.6	7.4	8.2	8.5	9.2	9.7	10.1	9.9	10.1
Specialist physician.	8.9	10.6	12.3	13.2	14.6	14.8	15.6	15.9	16.9
	Percent distribution								
Total active physicians	100.0	100.0	100.0	100.0	100.0	100.0	100.0	100.0	100.0
Primary care generalist physician	42.6	41.1	40.1	39.0	38.6	39.7	39.4	38.3	37.4
Specialist physician.	57.4	58.9	59.9	61.0	61.4	60.3	60.6	61.7	62.6

NOTES: Rates per 10,000 civilian population for 1975 to 2010. For 2013, rates per 10,000 resident population. Primary care generalist physicians include family medicine, internal medicine, obstetrics and gynecology, and pediatrics. Specialists include all other specialties and primary care subspecialists. Excludes physicians who are inactive or who did not provide generalist/specialist information. See Appendix II, Physician specialty.

SOURCE: American Medical Association (AMA): Physician distribution and medical licensure in the U.S., 1975; Physician characteristics and distribution in the U.S., 1981, 1986, 1992, 1997, 2002–2003, 2007, 2012, 2015 editions; Department of Physician Practice and Communications Information, Division of Survey and Data Resources, AMA. [Copyright 1976, 1982, 1986, 1992, 1997, 2003, 2007, 2012, and 2015: Used with permission of the AMA.] See Appendix I, American Medical Association (AMA) Physician Masterfile.

Data table for Figure 22. Nursing home beds, residents, and occupancy rate: United States, selected years 1977–2014

Excel and PowerPoint: http://www.cdc.gov/nchs/hus/contents2016.htm#fig22

Characteristic	1977	1985	1995	2004	2014
Beds per 1,000 population aged 65 years and over	59.7	56.9	52.6	47.7	36.0
Nursing home residents aged 65 years and over per 1,000 population aged 65 years and over	47.1	46.2	41.3	36.3	25.2
Occupancy rate	92.9	91.8	87.4	86.3	82.3
Beds (thousands)	1,402.4	1,624.2	1,770.9	1,730.0	1,663.3
Nursing home residents all ages (thousands)	1,303.1	1,491.4	1,548.6	1,492.2	1,369.7
Nursing home residents aged 65 years and over (thousands)	1,126.0	1,318.3	1,385.4	1,317.2	1,162.9
Population aged 65 years and over (in millions).	23.5	28.5	33.6	36.3	46.2

NOTES: Rates are for resident population. Occupancy rate is the percentage of beds occupied (number of nursing home residents per 100 nursing home beds). See Appendix II, Occupancy rate.

SOURCE: NCHS, the National Nursing Home Survey (NNHS) for 1977, 1985, 1995, and 2004 data, available from: http://www.cdc.gov/nchs/data/nnhsd/nursinghomes1973-2004.pdf; https://www.cdc.gov/nchs/data/series/sr_13/sr13_102.pdf; http://www.cdc.gov/nchs/data/ad/ad280.pdf; https://www.cdc.gov/nchs/data/ad/ad289.pdf; http://www.cdc.gov/nchs/data/series/sr_13/sr13_167.pdf; the National Study of Long-Term Care Providers for 2014, available from: http://www.cdc.gov/nchs/data/series/sr_03/sr03_038.pdf. See Appendix I, National Study of Long-Term Care Providers (NSLTCP) and National Nursing Home Survey (NNHS).

Data table for Figure 23. Personal health care expenditures, by source of funds and type of expenditure: United States, 1975, 1995, and 2015

Excel and PowerPoint: http://www.cdc.gov/nchs/hus/contents2016.htm#fig23

Source of funds and type of expenditure	1975	1995	2015
		Amount, in billions	
Personal health care expenditures[1]	$113	$870	$2,717
Source of funds:		Percent distribution	
All sources of funds	100.0	100.0	100.0
Private health insurance	24.5	33.0	34.8
Medicare	13.8	20.7	22.3
Medicaid, total[2]	11.3	15.7	18.3
Medicaid (federal)	6.2	9.4	11.6
Medicaid (state)	5.1	6.3	6.7
Out of pocket	32.9	16.7	12.4
All other sources of funds[3]	17.5	14.0	12.2
Type of expenditure:			
All types of expenditures	100.0	100.0	100.0
Hospital	45.3	39.0	38.1
Physician and clinical	22.4	25.3	23.4
Prescription drugs	7.1	6.9	11.9
Dental	7.1	5.1	4.3
Nursing care facilities and continuing care retirement communities	7.1	7.4	5.8
Home health care	0.5	3.7	3.3
All other types of expenditures[4]	10.6	12.5	13.2

[1] Personal health care expenditures are in current dollars and are not adjusted for inflation.
[2] Medicaid includes expenditures for the Children's Health Insurance Program (CHIP).
[3] Other sources include Department of Defense, Department of Veterans Affairs, and other third party payers and programs.
[4] Other types of expenditures include other professional services; other health, residential, and personal care; and durable and nondurable medical equipment and products.

NOTES: Personal health care expenditures are outlays for goods and services relating directly to patient care. See Appendix II, Health expenditures, national; Table 95.

SOURCE: Centers for Medicare & Medicaid Services, National Health Expenditure Accounts. See Appendix I, National Health Expenditure Accounts (NHEA).

Data table for Figure 24. Mental health and substance use disorder expenditures, by type of expenditure: United States, selected years 1986–2014

Excel and PowerPoint: http://www.cdc.gov/nchs/hus/contents2016.htm#fig24

Type of expenditures	1986	1992	1998	2004	2009	2014	1986	1992	1998	2004	2009	2014
Mental health expenditures	Amount, in millions						Percent distribution					
All mental health expenditures .	$32,444	$51,936	$68,956	$111,412	$145,126	$186,089	100	100	100	100	100	100
Inpatient care[1]	13,260	18,370	18,054	21,863	25,837	30,274	41	35	26	20	18	16
Outpatient care[2]	7,884	15,716	23,226	32,865	47,322	65,525	24	30	34	29	32	35
Residential care[3]	7,216	10,868	12,272	15,625	19,707	23,246	22	21	18	14	14	12
Retail prescription drugs[4] . .	2,564	4,538	11,670	31,965	42,027	51,102	8	9	17	29	29	27
Insurance administration[5] . .	1,520	2,444	3,733	9,094	10,233	15,942	5	5	5	8	7	9
Substance use disorder expenditures	Amount, in millions						Percent distribution					
All substance use disorder expenditures	$9,082	$13,392	$14,713	$18,764	$25,132	$33,891	100	100	100	100	100	100
Inpatient care[1]	4,553	4,500	3,076	3,766	5,174	6,419	50	34	21	20	21	19
Outpatient care[2]	2,431	4,966	6,932	7,587	9,652	13,633	27	37	47	40	38	40
Residential care[3]	1,578	3,390	4,006	5,946	7,893	9,264	17	25	27	32	31	27
Retail prescription drugs[4] . .	3	4	5	11	889	1,818	<1	<1	<1	<1	4	5
Insurance administration[5] . .	517	532	695	1,455	1,525	2,757	6	4	5	8	6	8

[1] Inpatient expenditures are spending for care provided in an acute medical care unit or setting of a general hospital or in specialty mental health or substance use disorder hospitals.

[2] Outpatient expenditures are spending for care provided in settings such as hospital outpatient departments, emergency departments, or offices and clinics of physicians and other medical professionals. This category includes partial hospitalization and intensive outpatient services offered by hospital outpatient departments as well as case management and intensive outpatient services offered by health clinics and specialty mental health and substance use disorder centers. Care provided by home health providers was counted as outpatient service.

[3] Residential expenditures are spending for therapeutic care provided by licensed health professionals in a 24-hour care setting, including residential care in specialty mental health and substance use disorder centers and all nursing home care. Starting in 2009, this category was broadened to encompass residential treatment facilities that included residential substance use disorder and mental health facilities. Trends for residential treatment expenditures should be interpreted with caution.

[4] Retail prescription drug expenditures are spending for psychotherapeutic and substance use disorder medications sold in retail establishments such as community pharmacies, mass merchandise retailers, grocery stores, or through mail order pharmacies. Excluded were sales through hospital pharmacies (which were counted with hospital expenditures), exclusive-to-patient HMOs, and nursing home pharmacies (which were counted where the pharmacy was located). Methadone is not included in retail prescription drug expenditures for substance abuse treatment. Instead, it is captured in the estimates of specialty substance use disorder treatment centers.

[5] Insurance administration covers the cost of running various government health care programs, the net cost of private health insurance, and the administrative costs associated with operating philanthropic organizations that provide donations for health care.

NOTES: Mental health and substance use disorder expenditures focus on spending for treatment as opposed to disease burden. These expenditures exclude comorbid health costs and other costs of patient care such as job training, subsidized housing, lost wages, and lost productivity. Mental health and substance use disorder spending was based on the following principal or primary diagnosis codes from the *International Classification of Diseases, 9th Revision, Clinical Modification* (ICD–9–CM): 291–292, 295–304, 305.2–305.9, 306–314, 648.3, 648.4.

SOURCE: Substance Abuse and Mental Health Services Administration (SAMHSA), Behavioral Health and Spending Use Accounts. Substance Abuse and Mental Health Services Administration. Behavioral health spending and use accounts, 1986–2014. HHS Publication no. SMA-16-4975. Rockville, MD: SAMHSA; 2016. Available from: http://store.samhsa.gov/shin/content/SMA16-4975/SMA16-4975.pdf. See Appendix I, Behavioral Health Spending and Use Accounts (BHSUA).

Data table for Figure 25 (page 1 of 2). Medicare enrollees in managed care: United States, 1994–2015

Excel and PowerPoint: http://wwwcdcgov/nchs/hus/contents2016htm#fig25

Medicare enrollees in managed care

Year	Percent of enrollees
1994	7.9
1995	9.5
1996	11.8
1997	14.5
1998	17.1
1999	18.2
2000	17.8
2001	15.8
2002	13.9
2003	13.1
2004	13.0
2005	13.7
2006	16.9
2007	19.5
2008	21.9
2009	23.7
2010	24.3
2011	25.0
2012	26.4
2013	28.0
2014	29.9
2015	31.3

See footnotes at end of table.

Data table for Figure 25 (page 2 of 2). Medicare enrollees in managed care: United States, 1994–2015

Excel and PowerPoint: *http://wwwcdcgov/nchs/hus/contents2016htm#fig25*

Medicare enrollees in managed care, by state: 2015

State	Percent of enrollees
Alabama	25.3
Alaska	1.0
Arizona	38.1
Arkansas	20.1
California	40.5
Colorado	36.9
Connecticut	25.6
Delaware	8.3
District of Columbia	13.1
Florida	39.8
Georgia	31.5
Hawaii	45.8
Idaho	32.6
Illinois	21.0
Indiana	23.8
Iowa	14.9
Kansas	13.7
Kentucky	26.2
Louisiana	30.1
Maine	22.9
Maryland	8.7
Massachusetts	20.9
Michigan	33.3
Minnesota	53.8
Mississippi	14.7
Missouri	28.3
Montana	18.3
Nebraska	12.3
Nevada	33.1
New Hampshire	7.5
New Jersey	15.4
New Mexico	31.7
New York	37.0
North Carolina	29.8
North Dakota	16.9
Ohio	41.0
Oklahoma	16.9
Oregon	43.8
Pennsylvania	39.9
Rhode Island	35.1
South Carolina	23.2
South Dakota	19.0
Tennessee	34.3
Texas	31.8
Utah	33.8
Vermont	7.5
Virginia	18.1
Washington	30.0
West Virginia	26.8
Wisconsin	37.9
Wyoming	3.9

NOTES: Prior to 2004, enrollment and percentage of enrollees in managed care were based on a 5% annual Denominator File derived from the Centers for Medicare & Medicaid Services' (CMS) Enrollment Database. Starting with 2004 data, the enrollee counts were pulled from the 100% Denominator File. See Appendix II, Managed care; Table 112. State is based on residence of the beneficiary.

SOURCE: Centers for Medicare & Medicaid Services; Office of Research, Development, and Information. Health Care Financing Review: Medicare and Medicaid Statistical Supplements for publication years 1996 to 2010; Center for Strategic Planning. Medicare & Medicaid Research Review: Medicare and Medicaid Statistical Supplement for publication year 2011; Office of Information Products and Data Analytics. Medicare and Medicaid Statistical Supplements for publication year 2012. Data for 2013–2015 are unpublished. See Appendix I, Medicare Administrative Data.

Data table for Figure 26 (page 1 of 2). Health insurance coverage among children under age 18, by type of coverage: United States, selected years 1978–September 2016 (preliminary data)

Excel and PowerPoint: *http://www.cdc.gov/nchs/hus/contents2016.htm#fig26*

Year	Type of coverage			
	Private (total)[1]	Private (workplace)[1]	Medicaid[2]	Uninsured[3]
	Percent			
1978	75.1	67.6	11.3	12.0
1980	75.7	69.1	11.8	11.6
1982	74.0	67.8	10.4	14.0
1983	72.5	66.0	11.6	14.2
1984	72.6	66.5	11.9	13.9
1986	72.7	66.6	11.2	14.5
1989	71.8	65.8	12.6	14.7
1990	68.9	60.9	12.7	17.1
1991	68.1	55.2	15.3	15.4
1992	66.7	60.9	18.1	14.2
1993	66.1	61.7	20.2	14.2
1994	63.2	58.5	21.2	15.0
1995	65.2	60.4	21.5	13.4
1996	66.4	61.1	20.7	13.3
1997	66.1	62.8	18.4	14.0
1998	68.4	64.3	17.1	12.7
1999	68.8	65.0	18.1	11.9
2000[4]	66.6	63.0	19.6	12.6
2001[4]	66.3	63.0	21.5	11.2
2002[4]	63.5	60.4	24.8	10.9
2003	63.0	59.4	26.0	9.8
2004	63.2	59.6	26.4	9.2
2005	62.1	58.6	27.2	9.3
2006	59.4	55.5	29.9	9.5
2007	59.8	55.8	29.8	9.0
2008	58.4	54.4	31.3	9.0
2009	55.8	51.8	34.5	8.2
2010	54.1	50.7	36.4	7.8
2011	53.7	49.7	38.2	7.0
2012	53.4	49.9	38.9	6.6
2013	53.2	49.3	38.9	6.6
2014	53.7	49.3	39.4	5.4
2015	54.6	49.6	39.9	4.5
2016, Jan–Sep[5]	53.5	49.2	39.2	5.0

See footnotes at end of table.

Data table for Figure 26 (page 2 of 2). Health insurance coverage among children under age 18, by type of coverage: United States, selected years 1978–September 2016 (preliminary data)

Excel and PowerPoint: http://www.cdc.gov/nchs/hus/contents2016.htm#fig26

Year	Type of coverage			
	Private (total)[1]	Private (workplace)[1]	Medicaid[2]	Uninsured[3]
	Standard error			
1978	1.0	1.0	0.7	0.6
1980	0.9	0.9	0.7	0.6
1982	0.9	0.9	0.7	0.6
1983	1.0	1.1	0.7	0.7
1984	0.9	0.9	0.6	0.5
1986	0.9	0.9	0.5	0.6
1989	0.6	0.6	0.4	0.5
1990	0.6	0.6	0.4	0.4
1991	0.6	0.7	0.4	0.4
1992	0.6	0.6	0.5	0.3
1993	0.7	0.7	0.7	0.4
1994	0.6	0.6	0.5	0.4
1995	0.6	0.6	0.5	0.3
1996	0.7	0.8	0.6	0.4
1997	0.6	0.6	0.5	0.3
1998	0.6	0.6	0.5	0.3
1999	0.5	0.5	0.4	0.3
2000[4]	0.5	0.5	0.5	0.3
2001[4]	0.6	0.5	0.5	0.4
2002[4]	0.6	0.6	0.5	0.3
2003	0.6	0.6	0.5	0.3
2004	0.6	0.6	0.5	0.3
2005	0.6	0.6	0.5	0.3
2006	0.7	0.7	0.7	0.3
2007	0.7	0.7	0.6	0.4
2008	0.7	0.7	0.7	0.4
2009	0.8	0.8	0.7	0.4
2010	0.7	0.7	0.6	0.3
2011	0.7	0.7	0.7	0.3
2012	0.6	0.6	0.6	0.3
2013	0.7	0.7	0.6	0.3
2014	0.6	0.6	0.6	0.2
2015	0.7	0.7	0.7	0.2
2016, Jan–Sep[5]	0.9	0.9	0.8	0.4

[1] Respondents were considered to be covered by private coverage if they indicated private coverage or, prior to 1997, if they were covered by a single-service hospital plan. This category excludes plans that paid for only one type of specialized service, such as accidents or dental care. Private health insurance includes managed care such as health maintenance organizations (HMOs). Private workplace coverage includes private coverage originally obtained through a present or former employer or union or starting in 1997, through the workplace, self-employment, or a professional association. Starting in 2014, an additional question on the health insurance marketplace was added to the questionnaire for those respondents who did not indicate that their health plan was obtained through a present or former employer, union, self-employment, or professional association. Starting in 2015, an additional answer category was added to the question on how a health plan was originally obtained to allow a respondent to indicate that their plan was obtained through the Health Insurance Marketplace or state-based exchange.

[2] Until 1996, persons were defined as having Medicaid or other public assistance coverage if they indicated that they had either Medicaid or other public assistance or if they reported receiving Aid to Families with Dependent Children (AFDC) or Supplemental Security Income (SSI). After welfare reform in late 1996, Medicaid was delinked from AFDC and SSI. Starting in 1997, persons were considered to be covered by Medicaid if they reported Medicaid or a state-sponsored health program. Starting in 1999, persons were considered covered by Medicaid if they reported coverage by the Children's Health Insurance Program (CHIP), which was originally enacted in 1997. CHIP funding is currently extended through 2017. See Appendix II, Children's Health Insurance Program (CHIP). Beginning in quarter 3 of the 2004 NHIS, persons under age 65 with no reported coverage were asked explicitly about Medicaid coverage. Estimates for 2004 and subsequent years were calculated with the additional information from this question. Estimates are presented for 1978 and onwards because that was the first year direct questions were included on Medicaid and Medicare coverage (for persons under age 65 years).

[3] Persons not covered by private insurance, Medicaid, Children's Health Insurance Program (CHIP), public assistance (through 1996), state-sponsored or other government-sponsored health plans (starting in 1997), Medicare, or military plans are considered to have no health insurance coverage. Persons with only Indian Health Service coverage are considered to have no health insurance coverage.

[4] Estimates for 2000-2002 were calculated using 2000-based sample weights and may differ from estimates in other reports that used 1990-based sample weights for 2000-2002 estimates.

[5] Preliminary data based on the National Health Interview Survey's Early Release program. Estimates based on the preliminary 9-month file may differ from estimates based on the final annual file and have larger standard errors associated with them than standard errors based on a final annual file. Available from: Martinez ME, Zammitti EP, Cohen RA. Health insurance coverage: Early release of estimates from the National Health Interview Survey, January–September 2016. NCHS. February 2017. Available from: https://www.cdc.gov/nchs/data/nhis/earlyrelease/insur201702.pdf; and National Health Interview Survey, 2016 preliminary file. For more information, visit: http://www.cdc.gov/nchs/nhis/htm.

NOTES: Health insurance coverage, definitions, and questionnaires have changed over time. Health insurance status is at the time of interview except for 1990–1996, when it is for the month prior to interview. Persons classified with Private or Medicaid coverage may also have other types of coverage. Respondents who did not report coverage under a type of plan and had unknown coverage under private or Medicaid were considered to have unknown coverage. Persons had to be known on health insurance coverage to be classified as having private coverage, Medicaid, or being uninsured. See Appendix II, Health insurance coverage; Tables 102–105. For more information on historic health insurance trends, see: Cohen RA, Makuc DM, Bernstein AB, Bilheimer LT, Powell-Griner E. Health insurance coverage trends, 1959–2007: Estimates from the National Health Interview Survey. National health statistics reports; no 17. Hyattsville, MD: NCHS. 2009. Available from: http://www.cdc.gov/nchs/data/nhsr/nhsr017.pdf.

SOURCE: NCHS, National Health Interview Survey. See Appendix I, National Health Interview Survey (NHIS).

Data table for Figure 27 (page 1 of 2). Health insurance coverage among adults aged 18–64, by type of coverage: United States, selected years 1978–September 2016 (preliminary data)

Excel and PowerPoint: http://www.cdc.gov/nchs/hus/contents2016.htm#fig27

Year	Private (total)[1]	Private (workplace)[1]	Medicaid[2]	Uninsured[3]
		Percent		
1978	81.4	71.4	4.4	11.9
1980	81.2	72.4	4.9	12.2
1982	79.9	71.4	4.1	13.8
1983	78.8	69.5	4.7	14.7
1984	78.6	70.3	4.5	14.8
1986	78.6	70.4	4.3	15.2
1989	77.6	69.4	4.9	16.0
1990	76.5	68.8	4.7	17.2
1991	76.0	66.0	5.6	16.8
1992	74.3	66.6	6.2	17.7
1993	73.2	66.8	6.5	18.8
1994	72.9	66.2	6.8	18.6
1995	73.9	67.6	7.1	17.3
1996	73.3	66.9	6.8	18.3
1997	72.7	68.0	5.9	19.0
1998	73.8	68.9	5.3	18.3
1999	74.6	69.8	5.3	17.9
2000[4]	73.5	68.8	5.2	18.9
2001[4]	73.3	68.6	5.7	18.5
2002[4]	71.9	67.4	6.5	19.3
2003	71.4	66.5	6.6	19.3
2004	71.1	65.8	6.8	19.3
2005	70.7	65.7	7.2	19.3
2006	69.1	63.9	7.7	20.0
2007	69.5	63.9	7.5	19.6
2008	68.5	62.9	8.1	19.9
2009	66.2	60.4	8.9	21.2
2010	64.7	58.9	9.2	22.3
2011	65.0	59.1	9.9	21.2
2012	65.1	59.6	10.0	20.9
2013	65.1	59.5	10.2	20.5
2014	67.4	59.2	12.1	16.3
2015	69.7	60.4	13.2	13.0
2016, Jan–Sep[5]	69.0	60.9	14.1	12.3

See footnotes at end of table.

Data table for Figure 27 (page 2 of 2). Health insurance coverage among adults aged 18–64, by type of coverage: United States, selected years 1978–September 2016 (preliminary data)

Excel and PowerPoint: http://www.cdc.gov/nchs/hus/contents2016.htm#fig27

Year	Type of coverage			
	Private (total)[1]	Private (workplace)[1]	Medicaid[2]	Uninsured[3]
	Standard error			
1978	0.6	0.7	0.3	0.4
1980	0.6	0.7	0.3	0.4
1982	0.6	0.6	0.3	0.4
1983	0.7	0.7	0.3	0.5
1984	0.5	0.5	0.2	0.4
1986	0.5	0.6	0.2	0.4
1989	0.3	0.3	0.1	0.2
1990	0.3	0.3	0.1	0.2
1991	0.3	0.3	0.2	0.2
1992	0.3	0.3	0.2	0.3
1993	0.4	0.4	0.2	0.3
1994	0.4	0.4	0.2	0.3
1995	0.3	0.4	0.2	0.2
1996	0.4	0.5	0.2	0.3
1997	0.3	0.3	0.2	0.2
1998	0.3	0.3	0.1	0.3
1999	0.3	0.3	0.1	0.3
2000[4]	0.3	0.3	0.1	0.3
2001[4]	0.3	0.3	0.1	0.3
2002[4]	0.3	0.3	0.2	0.3
2003	0.3	0.4	0.2	0.3
2004	0.3	0.4	0.2	0.3
2005	0.3	0.3	0.2	0.3
2006	0.4	0.4	0.2	0.3
2007	0.4	0.4	0.2	0.3
2008	0.4	0.4	0.2	0.3
2009	0.4	0.4	0.2	0.3
2010	0.4	0.4	0.2	0.3
2011	0.4	0.4	0.2	0.3
2012	0.4	0.4	0.2	0.3
2013	0.4	0.4	0.2	0.3
2014	0.4	0.4	0.2	0.3
2015	0.4	0.4	0.3	0.2
2016, Jan–Sep[5]	0.5	0.5	0.4	0.4

[1] Respondents were considered to be covered by private coverage if they indicated private coverage or, prior to 1997, if they were covered by a single-service hospital plan. This category excludes plans that paid for only one type of specialized service, such as accidents or dental care. Private health insurance includes managed care such as health maintenance organizations (HMOs). Private workplace coverage includes private coverage originally obtained through a present or former employer or union or starting in 1997, through the workplace, self-employment, or a professional association. Starting in 2014, an additional question on the health insurance marketplace was added to the questionnaire for those respondents who did not indicate that their health plan was obtained through a present or former employer, union, self-employment, or professional association. Starting in 2015, an additional answer category was added to the question on how a health plan was originally obtained to allow a respondent to indicate that their plan was obtained through the Health Insurance Marketplace or state-based exchange.

[2] Until 1996, persons were defined as having Medicaid or other public assistance coverage if they indicated that they had either Medicaid or other public assistance or if they reported receiving Aid to Families with Dependent Children (AFDC) or Supplemental Security Income (SSI). After welfare reform in late 1996, Medicaid was delinked from AFDC and SSI. Starting in 1997, persons were considered to be covered by Medicaid if they reported Medicaid or a state-sponsored health program. Starting in 1999, persons were considered covered by Medicaid if they reported coverage by the Children's Health Insurance Program (CHIP), which was originally enacted in 1997. CHIP funding is currently extended through 2017. See Appendix II, Children's Health Insurance Program (CHIP). Beginning in quarter 3 of the 2004 NHIS, persons under age 65 with no reported coverage were asked explicitly about Medicaid coverage. Estimates for 2004 and subsequent years were calculated with the additional information from this question. Estimates are presented for 1978 and onwards because that was the first year direct questions were included on Medicaid and Medicare coverage (for persons under age 65 years).

[3] Persons not covered by private insurance, Medicaid, Children's Health Insurance Program (CHIP), public assistance (through 1996), state-sponsored or other government-sponsored health plans (starting in 1997), Medicare, or military plans are considered to have no health insurance coverage. Persons with only Indian Health Service coverage are considered to have no health insurance coverage.

[4] Estimates for 2000-2002 were calculated using 2000-based sample weights and may differ from estimates in other reports that used 1990-based sample weights for 2000-2002 estimates.

[5] Preliminary data based on the National Health Interview Survey's Early Release program. Estimates based on the preliminary 9-month file may differ from estimates based on the final annual file and have larger standard errors associated with them than standard errors based on a final annual file. Available from: Martinez ME, Zammitti EP, Cohen RA. Health insurance coverage: Early release of estimates from the National Health Interview Survey, January–September 2016. NCHS. February 2017. Available from: https://www.cdc.gov/nchs/data/nhis/earlyrelease/insur201702.pdf; and National Health Interview Survey, 2016 preliminary file. For more information, visit: http://www.cdc.gov/nchs/nhis.htm.

NOTES: Health insurance coverage, definitions, and questionnaires have changed over time. Health insurance status is at the time of interview except for 1990–1996, when it is for the month prior to interview. Persons classified with Private or Medicaid coverage may also have other types of coverage. Respondents who did not report coverage under a type of plan and had unknown coverage under private or Medicaid were considered to have unknown coverage. Persons had to be known on health insurance coverage to be classified as having private coverage, Medicaid, or being uninsured. See Appendix II, Health insurance coverage; Tables 102–105. For more information on historic health insurance trends, see: Cohen RA, Makuc DM, Bernstein AB, Bilheimer LT, Powell-Griner E. Health insurance coverage trends, 1959–2007: Estimates from the National Health Interview Survey. National health statistics reports; no 17. Hyattsville, MD: NCHS. 2009. Available from: http://www.cdc.gov/nchs/data/nhsr/nhsr017.pdf.

SOURCE: NCHS, National Health Interview Survey. See Appendix I, National Health Interview Survey (NHIS).

Technical Notes

Data Sources

Data for the *Health, United States, 2016*, Chartbook come from many surveys and data systems and cover a broad range of years. Detailed descriptions of the data sources included in the Chartbook are provided in Appendix I. Data Sources. Additional information clarifying and qualifying the data is included in the table notes and in Appendix II. Definitions and Methods.

Data Presentation

Many measures in the Chartbook are shown for people in specific age groups because of the strong effect of age on most health outcomes. In some cases, age-adjusted rates and age-adjusted percentages are computed to eliminate differences in observed rates that result from age differences in population composition (see Appendix II, Age adjustment). Age-adjusted rates and age-adjusted percentages are noted as such in the text; rates and percentages without this notation are crude rates and crude percentages. For some charts, data years are combined to increase sample size and the reliability of the estimates. Some charts present time trends, and others focus on differences in estimates among population subgroups for the most recent time period available. Trends are generally shown on a linear scale to emphasize absolute differences over time.

Point estimates and standard errors for Chartbook figures are available either in the Trend Table and Excel spreadsheet specified in the note below the chart, or in the Chartbook data tables section. Chartbook data tables may include additional data that were not graphed because of space considerations.

Reliability of Estimates

Overall estimates generally have relatively small sampling errors, but estimates for certain population subgroups may be based on small numbers and have relatively large sampling errors. Numbers of deaths obtained from the National Vital Statistics System represent complete counts and therefore are not subject to sampling error. They are, however, subject to random variation, which means that the number of events that actually occur in a given year may be considered as one of a large series of possible results that could have arisen under the same circumstances. When the number of events is small and the probability of such an event is small, considerable caution must be observed in interpreting the conditions described by the charts. Estimates that are unreliable because of large sampling

errors or small numbers of events have been noted with an asterisk. The criteria used to designate or suppress unreliable estimates are indicated in the notes to the applicable tables or charts.

For NCHS surveys, point estimates and their corresponding variances were calculated using the SUDAAN software package, which takes into consideration the complex survey design (135). Standard errors for other surveys or data sets were computed using the methodology recommended by the programs providing the data, or were provided directly by those programs.

Statistical Testing

Data trends can be analyzed in many ways. The approaches used in the Chartbook to analyze trends in health measures depend on the data source and the number of data points. Trend analyses of data from the National Vital Statistics System and the National Health Interview Survey are based on aggregated point estimates and their standard errors. Trend analyses of data from the National Health and Nutrition Examination Survey are based on record-level data. If data from at least seven time points were available, then one objective of the trend analysis was to identify time points when changes in trend occurred.

For trend analyses of data on birth, infant mortality, and death rates from the National Vital Statistics System (Figures 7–9) and data from the National Health Interview Survey (Figures 10, 17–19, 26, 27), increases or decreases in the estimates during the entire time period shown are assessed by the weighted least squares regression method in the National Cancer Institute's Joinpoint software (with Grid search and either permutation model selection for 10 or more time points or BIC criterion model selection for fewer than 10 time points). Joinpoint software identifies the number and location of joinpoints when changes in trend have occurred. The maximum number of joinpoints searched for was limited to four or fewer, based on the number of available time points. For more information on Joinpoint, see: http://surveillance.cancer.gov/joinpoint. Trend analyses using weighted least squares regression were carried out on the log scale for birth, infant mortality, and death rates so that results provide estimates of annual percent change. For the charts based on the National Health Interview Survey, trend analyses were carried out on the linear scale and results provide estimates of annual percentage point change. A limitation of using aggregated data and Joinpoint software alone for trend analysis of the National Health Interview Survey is that this approach does not account for year-to-year correlation or use the proper degrees of freedom for statistical testing.

For trend analyses from the National Health and Nutrition Examination Survey (NHANES) (Figures 11 and 15), with nine time points, increases or decreases in the estimates during the entire period shown were assessed using polynomial regression (SUDAAN PROC REGRESS). Linear trends were tested separately and quadratic trends were tested with both linear and quadratic terms in the models. If a quadratic trend was significant, Joinpoint software was used to find an inflection point, and the difference in slopes between the two segments on either side of the inflection point was assessed using piecewise linear regression (SUDAAN PROC REGRESS). For trend analyses based on three to five time points from the NHANES, linear and quadratic trends were assessed using polynomial regression. If a quadratic trend was significant, pairwise differences between percents were tested using z-tests to obtain additional information regarding changes in the trend.

For other charts either the difference between two points was assessed for statistical significance using z-tests or the statistical testing methods recommended by the data systems were used. For analyses that show two time points, differences between the two points were assessed for statistical significance at the 0.05 level using two-sided significance tests (z-tests) without correction for multiple comparisons. For data sources with no standard errors, generally relative differences greater than 10% are discussed in the text. Chartbook data tables include point estimates and standard errors, when available, for users who would like to perform additional statistical tests.

Terms such as "similar," "stable," and "no difference" used in the text indicate that the statistics being compared were not significantly different. Lack of comment regarding the difference between statistics does not necessarily suggest that the difference was tested and found to be not significant. Because statistically significant differences or trends are partly a function of sample size (the larger the sample, the smaller the change that can be detected), they do not necessarily have public health significance (136).

References

1. Trevelyan E, Gambino C, Gryn T, Larsen L, Acosta Y, Grieco E, Harris D, Walters N. Characteristics of the U.S. population by generational status: 2013, Current Population Survey Reports, P23–214, US Census Bureau, Washington DC; 2016.

2. Cohn D, Caumont A. 10 demographic trends that are shaping the U.S. and the world. Washington, DC: Pew Research Center; 2016.

3. Crimmins EM, Hayward MD, Seeman TE. Race/ethnicity, socioeconomic status, and health. In Critical Perspectives on Racial and Ethnic Differences in Late Life. National Academies Press; 2004.

4. Ingram DD, Franco SJ. NCHS urban-rural classification scheme for counties. Hyattsville, MD: NCHS; 2014.

5. Dixon J, Welch N. Researching the rural-metropolitan health differential using the 'social determinants of health'. Aust J Rural Health 2000;8(5):254–60.

6. Arias E. Changes in life expectancy by race and Hispanic origin in the United States, 2013–2014. NCHS data brief, no 244. Hyattsville, MD: NCHS; 2016.

7. Koppaka R. Ten great public health achievements—United States, 2001–2010. MMWR 2011; 60(19);619–23.

8. CDC. Achievements in public health, 1900–1999 Motor-vehicle safety: A 20th century public health achievement. MMWR 1999;48(18);369–74.

9. Berry SA, Fleishman JA, Moore RD, Gebo KA. Trends in reasons for hospitalization in multisite United States cohort of persons living with HIV 2001–2008. J Acquir Immune Defic Syndr 2012;59(4):368–75.

10. National Cancer Institute. Cancer statistics. [website] Last updated March 14, 2016, https://www.cancer.gov/about-cancer/understanding/statistics.

11. CDC. Achievements in public health, 1900–1999: Decline in deaths from heart disease and stroke—United States, 1900-1999. MMWR 1999;48(30);649–56.

12. CDC. Public health then and now: Celebrating 50 years of MMWR at CDC. MMWR 2011;60(Suppl):1–120.

13. Ventola CL. The antibiotic crisis. Pharm Therapeut 2015;40(4):277–83.

14. Rossen LM, Bastian B, Warner M, Khan D, Chong Y. Drug poisoning mortality: United States, 1999–2014. NCHS. 2016. [website] Last updated March 30, 2016, https://blogs.cdc.gov/nchs-data-visualization/drug-poisoning-mortality/.

15. American Society of Addiction Medicine. Opioid addiction 2016 facts and figures. [website] Accessed December 15, 2016, http://www.asam.org/docs/default-source/advocacy/opioid-addiction-disease-facts-figures.pdf.

16. NCHS. Health, United States, 2015: With special feature on racial and ethnic health disparities. Hyattsville, MD; 2016.

17. Moy E, Garcia MC, Bastian B, Rossen LM, Ingram DD, Faul M, et al. Leading causes of death in nonmetropolitan and metropolitan areas — United States, 1999–2014. MMWR Surveill Summ 2017;66(No. SS-1):1–8.

18. Ortman JM, Velkoff VA, Hogan H. An aging nation: The older population in the United States. Current Population Reports, P25–1140. Washington, DC: Census Bureau; 2014.

19. Mather M. The decline in U.S. fertility. Washington, DC: Population Research Board; 2014.

20. Colby SL, Ortman JM. Projections of the size and composition of the U.S. population: 2014 to 2060, Current Population Reports, P25–1143, US Census Bureau, Washington DC; 2014.

21. Betancourt JR, Green AR, Carrillo JE, Ananeh-Firempong O. Defining cultural competence: a practical framework for addressing racial/ethnic disparities in health and health care. Public Health Rep 2003;118(4):293–302.

22. Markides KS, Eschbach K. Aging, migration, and mortality: Current status of research on the Hispanic paradox. J Gerontol Series B: Psychological Sciences and Social Sciences 2005;60(Spec No 2):S68–S75.

23. Singh GK, Rodriguez-Lainz A, Kogan MD. Immigrant health inequalities in the United States: Use of eight major national data systems. Sci World J 2013;2013:1–21.

24. Derose GP, Escarce JJ, Lurie N. Immigrants and health care: Sources of vulnerability. Health Aff 2007;26(5):1258–68.

25. Ross CE, Wu C. The links between education and health. Am Sociol Rev 1995;60(5):719–45.

26. Wood D. Effect of child and family poverty on child health in the United States. Pediatrics 2003;112(3 Part 2):707–11.

27. Smith JP. Unraveling the SES–health connection. Popul Dev Rev 2004;30(Suppl):108–32.

28. CDC. CDC health disparities and inequalities report — United States, 2013. MMWR 2013;62(Suppl 3):1–187.

29. Boccia R, Greszler R. Social security benefits and the impact of the chained CPI. Backgrounder, no 2799. Washington, DC: The Heritage Foundation; 2013.

30. Reschovsky JD, Staiti AB. Access and quality: Does rural America lag behind? Health Aff 2005; 24(4):1128–39.

31. Arias E, Heron M, Xu JQ. United States life tables, 2012. National vital statistics reports; vol 65 no 83. Hyattsville, MD: NCHS; 2016.

32. Mehta NK, House JS, Elliott MR. Dynamics of health behaviours and socioeconomic differences in mortality in the USA. J Epidemiol Community Health 2015;69(5):416–22.

33. Singh GK, van Dyck PC. Infant mortality in the United States, 1935–2007: Over seven decades of progress and disparities. Rockville, MD: HHS, Health Resources and Services Administration, Maternal and Child Health Bureau; 2010.

34. Association of Maternal & Child Health Programs. Celebrating the legacy, shaping the future: 75 years of state and federal partnership to improve maternal and child health. Washington, DC; 2010.

35. Kockanek KD, Murphy SL, Xu JQ, Tejada-Vera B. Deaths: Final Data for 2014. National vital statistics reports; vol 65 no 5. Hyattsville, MD: NCHS; 2016.

36. Sweeney MM, Raley RK. Race, ethnicity, and the changing context of childbearing in the United States. Annu Rev Sociol 2014;40:539–58.

37. HHS. The health consequences of smoking: 50 years of progress. A Report of the Surgeon General. Atlanta, GA: CDC, National Center for Chronic Disease Prevention and Health Promotion, Office on Smoking and Health; 2014.

38. HHS. How tobacco smoke causes disease: The biology and behavioral basis for smoking-attributable disease: A report of the Surgeon General. Atlanta, GA: CDC, National Center for Chronic Disease Prevention and Health Promotion, Office on Smoking and Health; 2010.

39. Freedman DS, Mei Z, Srinivasan SR, Berenson GS, Dietz WH. Cardiovascular risk factors and excess adiposity among overweight children and adolescents: The Bogalusa Heart Study. J Pediatr 2007;150(1):12–7.

40. Engeland A, Bjørge T, Tverdal A, Søgaard AJ. Obesity in adolescence and adulthood and the risk of adult mortality. Epidemiology 2004;15(1):79–85.

41. Kuczmarski RJ, Ogden CL, Guo SS, et al. 2000 CDC growth charts for the United States: Methods and development. Hyattsville, MD: NCHS. Vital Health Stat 11(246); 2002.

42. Barlow SE; Expert Committee. Expert Committee recommendations regarding the prevention, assessment, and treatment of child and adolescent overweight and obesity: Summary report. Pediatrics 2007;120(suppl 4):S164–92.

43. National Heart, Lung, and Blood Institute; National Institute of Diabetes and Digestive and Kidney Diseases. Clinical guidelines on the identification, evaluation, and treatment of overweight and obesity in adults: The evidence report. NIH pub no 98–4083. Bethesda, MD: National Institutes of Health; 1998.

44. Jensen MD, Ryan DH, Apovian CM, Ard JD, Comuzzie AG, Donato KA, et al. 2013 AHA/ACC/TOS guideline for the management of overweight and obesity in adults: A report of the American College of Cardiology/American Heart Association Task Force on Practice Guidelines and the Obesity Society. Circulation 2014;129(25 suppl 2):S102–40.

45. HHS. The Surgeon General's vision for a healthy and fit nation. Rockville, MD: HHS, Office of the Surgeon General; 2010.

46. Flegal KM, Graubard BI, Williamson DF, Gail MH. Excess deaths associated with underweight, overweight, and obesity. JAMA 2005;293(15):1861–7.

47. Carroll MD, Navaneelan T, Bryan S, Ogden CL. Prevalence of obesity among children and adolescents in Canada and the United States. NCHS data brief, no 211. Hyattsville, MD: NCHS; 2015.

48. World Health Organization. Health topics: Obesity. [website] Accessed December 15, 2016, http://www.who.int/topics/obesity/en/.

49. Ogden CL, Carroll MD, Lawman HG, Fryar CD, Kruszon-Moran D, Kit BK, Flegal KM. Trends in obesity prevalence among children and adolescents in the United States, 1988–1994 through 2013–2014. JAMA 2016;315(21):2292–9.

50. HHS. Oral health in America: A report of the Surgeon General. Executive Summary. Rockville, MD: National Institute of Dental and Craniofacial Research, National Institutes of Health; 2000.

51. Rugg-Gunn A. Dental caries: Strategies to control this preventable disease. Acta Med Acad 2013;42(2):117–30.

52. CDC. Achievements in public health, 1900–1999: Fluoridation of drinking water to prevent dental caries. MMWR 1999;48(41); 933–40.

53. Dye BA, Thornton-Evans G, Li X, Iafolla TJ. Dental caries and sealant prevalence in children and adolescents in the United States, 2011–2012. NCHS data brief, no 191. Hyattsville, MD: NCHS; 2015.

54. American Diabetes Association. Standards of medical care in diabetes—2014. Diabetes Care 2014;37(suppl 1):S14–80.

55. Chamberlain JJ, Rhinehart AS, Shaefer CF Jr, Neuman A. Diagnosis and management of diabetes: synopsis of the 2016 American Diabetes Association standards of medical care in diabetes. Ann Intern Med 2016;164(8):542–52.

56. Villarroel MA, Vahratian A, Ward BW. Health care utilization among U.S. adults with diagnosed diabetes, 2013. NCHS data brief, no 183. Hyattsville, MD: NCHS; 2015.

57. National High Blood Pressure Education Program. Seventh report of the Joint National Committee on Prevention, Detection, Evaluation, and Treatment of High Blood Pressure: Complete report. NIH pub no 04–5230. Bethesda, MD: National Institutes of Health, National Heart, Lung, and Blood Institute; 2004.

58. Nwankwo T, Yoon SS, Burt V, Gu Q. Hypertension among adults in the United States: National Health and Nutrition Examination Survey, 2011–2012. NCHS data brief, no 133. Hyattsville, MD: NCHS; 2013.

59. Ingram DD, Montresor-Lopez JA. Differences in stroke mortality among adults aged 45 and over: United States, 2010–2013. NCHS data brief, no 207. Hyattsville, MD: NCHS; 2015.

60. Kung HC, Xu JQ. Hypertension-related mortality in the United States, 2000–2013. NCHS data brief, no 193. Hyattsville, MD: NCHS; 2015.

61. NCHS. National Health and Nutrition Examination Survey. Hyattsville, MD. [unpublished analysis].

62. Wilkes M, Bell R, Kravitz R. Direct-to-consumer prescription drug advertising: trends, impact, and implications. Health Aff 2000;19(2):1–19.

63. Mulcahy NW, Eibner C, Finegold K. Gaining coverage through Medicaid or private insurance increased prescription use and lowered out-of-pocket spending. Health Aff 2016;35(8):1–16.

64. Lichtenberg FR, Sun SX. The impact of Medicare Part D on prescription drug use by the elderly. Health Aff 2016;26(6):1735–44.

65. Maher RL, Hanlon J, Hajjar E. Clinical consequences of polypharmacy in elderly. Expert Opin Drug Saf 2014;13(1):1–11.

66. Bernstein AB, Hing E, Moss AJ, Allen KF, Siller AB, Tiggle RB. Health care in America: Trends in utilization. Hyattsville, MD: NCHS; 2003.

67. Hofer AN, Abraham JM, Moscovice I. Expansion of coverage under the Patient Protection and Affordable Care Act and Primary Care Utilization. Milbank Q 2011;89(1):69–89.

68. Continelli T, McGinnis S, Holmes T. The effect of local primary care physician supply on the utilization of preventive health services in the United States. Health Place 2010;16(5):942–51.

69. Eberhardt MS, Ingram DD, Makuc DM, et al. Urban and rural health chartbook. Health, United States, 2001. Hyattsville, MD: NCHS; 2001.

70. Tang N, Stein J, Hsia RY, Maselli, JH, Gonzales R. Trends and characteristics of US emergency department visits, 1997-2007. JAMA 2010;304(6):664–70.

71. Institute of Medicine. Hospital-based emergency care: At the breaking point. Washington, DC: National Academies Press; 2007.

72. Centers for Medicare & Medicaid Services. Emergency medical treatment & labor act (EMTALA). [website] Last updated March 26, 2012, https://www.cms.gov/Regulations-and-Guidance/ Legislation/EMTALA/.

73. Balanced Budget Act of 1997. Pub L No 105–33, 111 Stat 251, 105; 1997.

74. Weiss AJ, Elixhauser A. Overview of hospital stays in the United States, 2012. Healthcare Cost and Utilization Project Statistical Brief, no. 180. Rockville, MD: Agency for Healthcare Research and Quality; 2014.

75. Gilman BH. Hospital response to DRG refinements: The impact of multiple reimbursement incentives on inpatient length of stay. Health Econ 2000;9(4):277–94.

76. Leonard K. Hospital of yesterday: The biggest changes in health care. U.S. News & World Report. July 15, 2014.

77. National Cancer Institute. Surveillance, Epidemiology, and End Results Program stat fact sheets: Cancer of any site. [website] Accessed December 15, 2016, http://seer.cancer.gov/statfacts/ html/all.html.

78. American Cancer Society. Cancer facts & figures 2016. Atlanta, GA: ACS; 2016.

79. CDC. Division of Cancer Prevention and Control, Centers for Disease Control and Prevention. National Breast and Cervical Cancer Early Detection Program (NBCCEDP): About the program. [website] Last updated September 9, 2016, https:// www.cdc.gov/cancer/nbccedp/about.htm.

80. National Cancer Institute. Cancer screening. [website] Last updated April 29, 2015, https://www.cancer.gov/about-cancer/screening.

81. Siu AL. Screening for Breast Cancer: U.S. Preventive Services Task Force. Recommendation statement. Ann Intern Med 2016;64(4):279-96.

82. Bibbins-Domingo K, Grossman DC, Curry SJ, Davidson KW, Epling JW Jr., Garcia FA, et al. Screening for Colorectal Cancer: U.S. Preventive Services Task Force. Recommendation statement. JAMA 2016;315(23):2564-75.

83. Ginsburg PB. Competition in health care: Its evolution over the past decade. Health Aff 2005;24(6):1512–22.

84. Government Accountability Office. Health care workforce: Comprehensive planning by HHS needed to meet national needs. GAO-16-17. Washington, DC; 2015.

85. HHS. Health Resources and Services Administration, National Center for Health Workforce Analysis. Projecting the supply and demand for primary care practitioners through 2020. Rockville, MD; 2013.

86. Medicare Payment Advisory Commission. Report to the Congress: Medicare and the health care delivery system. March 2016. Washington, DC: MedPAC; 2016.

87. Colwill JM, Cultice JM, Kruse RL. Will generalist physician supply meet demands of an increasing and aging population? Health Aff 2008;27(3):232–41.

88. Harris-Kojetin L, Sengupta M, Park-Lee E, Valverde R. Long-term care services in the United States: 2013 overview. NCHS. Vital Health Stat 3(37); 2013.

89. Census Bureau. Statistical abstract of the United States: 1977. 98th edition. Washington, DC: Census Bureau; 1977.

90. Werner CA. The older population 2010. 2010 Census Briefs. Washington, DC: Census Bureau; 2011.

91. He W, Goodkind D, Kowal P. An aging world: 2015. International Population Reports, P95/16-1. Washington, DC: Census Bureau; 2016.

92. McCormick JC, Chulis GS. MCBS highlights: Growth in residential alternatives to nursing homes: 2001. Health Care Financ R 2003;24(4):143–50.

93. Bishop CE. Where are the missing elders? The decline in nursing home use, 1985 and 1995. Health Aff 1999;18(4):146–55.

94. NCHS. National Nursing Home Survey. Table 1. Number of nursing homes, beds, current residents, and discharges: United States, selected years 1973–2004.

95. Harris-Kojetin L, Sengupta M, Park-Lee E, et al. Long-term care providers and services users in the United States: Data from the National Study of Long-Term Care Providers, 2013–2014. Hyattsville, MD: NCHS. Vital Health Stat 3(38); 2016.

96. Centers for Medicare & Medicaid Services, Office of the Actuary, National Health Statistics Group. [website] Last updated December 6, 2016, https://www.cms.gov/Research-Statistics-Data-and-Systems/Statistics-Trends-and-Reports/ NationalHealthExpendData/NationalHealthAccountsHistorical. html.

97. Organisation for Economic Co-Operation and Development. OECD.STAT. [website] Accessed May 23, 2016, http://stats. oecd.org/Index.aspx?DataSetCode=SHA.

98. National Institute of Mental Health. The numbers count: Mental disorders in America. Bethesda, MD: National Institutes of Health; 2013.

99. Kessler RC, Heeringa S, Lakoma MD, Petukhova M, Rupp AE, Schoenbaum M, et al. Individual and societal effects of mental disorders on earnings in the United States: Results from the National Comorbidity Survey Replication. Am J Psychiatry 2008;165(6):703–11.

100. Druss BG, Walker ER. Mental disorders and medical comorbidity. Research synthesis report no 21. Princeton, NJ: Robert Wood Johnson Foundation; 2011.

101. HHS. Mental health: Culture, race, and ethnicity: A supplement to Mental Health: A Report of the Surgeon General. Rockville, MD: HHS, Substance Abuse and Mental Health Services Administration, Center for Mental Health Services; 2001.

102. Center for Behavioral Health Statistics and Quality. Behavioral health trends in the United States: Results from the 2014 National Survey on Drug Use and Health. Rockville, MD: HHS Publication No. SMA 15-4927, NSDUH Series H-50; 2015.

103. HHS. Office of the Surgeon General, Facing addiction in America: The Surgeon General's report on alcohol, drugs, and health. Washington, DC: HHS; November 2016.

104. Substance Abuse and Mental Health Services Administration, Health Resources and Services Administration. Center for Integrated Health Solutions. Innovations in addictions treatment: Addictions treatment providers working with integrated primary care services. Rockville, MD: HHS; 2013.

105. Substance Abuse and Mental Health Services Administration. Behavioral health treatment and services. [website] Last updated October 19, 2015, http://www.samhsa.gov/treatment.

106. National Institute on Drug Abuse. Principles of drug addiction treatment: A research-based guide (third edition). NIH Publication No. 12–4180. Bethesda, MD: NIH; 2012.

107. HHS. 2012 National strategy for suicide prevention: Goals and objectives for action. Washington, D.C.: HHS, Office of the Surgeon General and National Action Alliance for Suicide Prevention; 2012.

108. Padwa H, Urada D, Gauthier P, Rieckmann T, Hurley B, Crèvecouer-MacPhail D, Rawson RA. Organizing publicly funded substance use disorder treatment in the United States: Moving toward a service system approach. J Subst Abuse Treat 2016;69:9–18.

109. Government Accountability Office. Veterans affairs: Better understanding needed to enhance services to veterans readjusting to civilian life. GAO-14-676. Washington, DC; 2014.

110. Huskamp HA, Iglehart JK. Mental health and substance-use reforms — Milestones reached, challenges ahead. N Engl J Med 2016;375(7):688–95.

111. Iza M. Probability and predictors of first treatment contact for anxiety disorders in the United States: Analysis of data from the National Epidemiologic Survey on Alcohol and Related Conditions (NESARC). J Clin Psychiatry 2013;74(11);1093–100.

112. Wang PS, Berglund P, Olfson M, Pincus HA, Wells KB, Kessler RC. Failure and delay in initial treatment contact after first onset of mental disorders in the National Comorbidity Survey Replication. Arch Gen Psychiatry 2005;62(6):606–13.

113. Burrows E, Suh R, Hamann D. Health care workforce distribution and shortage issues in rural America. National Rural Health Association Policy Brief; 2012.

114. Paul Wellstone and Pete Domenici Mental Health Parity and Addiction Equity Act of 2008. Sections 511 & 512 of the Tax Extenders and Alternative Minimum Tax Relief Act of 2008 (Division C of Pub. L. 110-343).

115. Patient Protection and Affordable Care Act. Pub L No 111–148, 124 Stat 119, 132; 2010.

116. Substance Abuse and Mental Health Services Administration. Behavioral health spending and use accounts, 1986-2014. HHS Publication no SMA-16-4975. Rockville, MD: Substance Abuse and Mental Health Services Administration; 2016.

117. Centers for Medicare & Medicaid Services. Medicare & you 2016. [website] Accessed December 10, 2016, http://www.medicare.org/medicare-program/medicare-2016-handbook.html.

118. The Boards of Trustees, Federal Hospital Insurance and Federal Supplementary Medical Insurance Trust Funds. The 2016 annual report of the boards of trustees of the federal hospital insurance and federal supplementary medical insurance trust funds. Baltimore, MD: CMS; 2016.

119. Centers for Medicare & Medicaid Services. Medicare & Medicaid milestones. Baltimore, MD: CMS; 2015.

120. Blumental D, Davis K, Guterman S. Medicare at 50—Origins and evolution. N Engl J Med 2015;372(5):479–86.

121. Ginsburg PB, Rivlin AM. Challenges for Medicare at 50. N Engl J Med 2015;373(21):1993–5.

122. Kaiser Family Foundation. Medicare Advantage: Fact sheet. Menlo Park, CA: KFF; 2016.

123. Zarabozo C. Milestones in Medicare managed care. Health Care Financ R 2000;22(1):61–7.

124. McGuire TG, Newhouse JP, Sinaiko AD. An economic history of Medicare Part C. Milbank Q 2011;89(2):289–32.

125. Blendon RJ, Brodie M, Benson JM, Altman DE, Levitt L, Hoff T, Hugick L. Understanding the managed care backlash. Health Aff 1998:17(4):80–94.

126. Jacobson G, Swoope C, Perry M, Slosar MC. How are seniors choosing and changing health insurance plans? Menlo Park, CA: Kaiser Family Foundation; 2014.

127. American Academy of Pediatrics. 2016 recommendations for preventive pediatric healthcare. Pediatrics 2016;137(1):25–7.

128. Title XIX of the Social Security Act, 42 U.S.C. 1396 et seq.

129. Title XXI of the Social Security Act, 42 U.S.C. 1397aa-1397mm.

130. Martinez ME, Zammitti EP, Cohen RA. Health insurance coverage: Early release of estimates from the National Health Interview Survey, January–September 2016. Hyattsville, MD: NCHS; 2017.

131. NCHS. National Health Interview Survey. Hyattsville, MD. [unpublished analysis].

132. Kaiser Commission on Medicaid and the Uninsured. The uninsured and the difference health insurance makes. Menlo Park, CA: Kaiser Family Foundation; 2012.

133. Centers for Medicare & Medicaid Services. Children's Health Insurance Program (CHIP). Baltimore, MD. [website] Accessed January 13, 2017, https://www.medicaid.gov/chip/chip-program-information.html.

134. Kaiser Family Foundation. A guide to the Supreme Court's decision on the ACA's Medicaid expansion. Menlo Park, CA; 2012.

135. RTI International. SUDAAN (Release 11.0.0) [computer software]; 2012.

136. CDC. Youth Risk Behavior Surveillance System (YRBSS). Interpretation of YRBS trend data. Atlanta, GA; 2014.

Table 1 (page 1 of 3). Resident population, by age, sex, race, and Hispanic origin: United States, selected years 1950–2015

Excel and PDF versions (with more data years and standard errors when available): http://www.cdc.gov/nchs/hus/contents2016.htm#001.

[Data are based on the decennial census updated with data from multiple sources]

Sex, race, Hispanic origin, and year	Total resident population	Under 1 year	1–4 years	5–14 years	15–24 years	25–34 years	35–44 years	45–54 years	55–64 years	65–74 years	75–84 years	85 years and over
All persons						Number, in thousands						
1950	150,697	3,147	13,017	24,319	22,098	23,759	21,450	17,343	13,370	8,340	3,278	577
1960	179,323	4,112	16,209	35,465	24,020	22,818	24,081	20,485	15,572	10,997	4,633	929
1970	203,212	3,485	13,669	40,746	35,441	24,907	23,088	23,220	18,590	12,435	6,119	1,511
1980	226,546	3,534	12,815	34,942	42,487	37,082	25,635	22,800	21,703	15,581	7,729	2,240
1990	248,710	3,946	14,812	35,095	37,013	43,161	37,435	25,057	21,113	18,045	10,012	3,021
2000	281,422	3,806	15,370	41,078	39,184	39,892	45,149	37,678	24,275	18,391	12,361	4,240
2010	308,746	3,944	16,257	41,026	43,626	41,064	41,071	45,007	36,483	21,713	13,061	5,493
2013	316,129	3,942	15,926	41,221	43,954	42,845	40,453	43,768	39,316	25,217	13,447	6,041
2014	318,857	3,948	15,929	41,191	43,980	43,517	40,513	43,459	40,078	26,398	13,683	6,162
2015	321,419	3,978	15,929	41,110	43,848	44,137	40,590	43,188	40,878	27,551	13,923	6,287
Male												
1950	74,833	1,602	6,634	12,375	10,918	11,597	10,588	8,655	6,697	4,024	1,507	237
1960	88,331	2,090	8,240	18,029	11,906	11,179	11,755	10,093	7,537	5,116	2,025	362
1970	98,912	1,778	6,968	20,759	17,551	12,217	11,231	11,199	8,793	5,437	2,436	542
1980	110,053	1,806	6,556	17,855	21,419	18,382	12,570	11,009	10,152	6,757	2,867	682
1990	121,239	2,018	7,581	17,971	18,915	21,564	18,510	12,232	9,955	7,907	3,745	841
2000	138,054	1,949	7,862	21,043	20,079	20,121	22,448	18,497	11,645	8,303	4,879	1,227
2010	151,781	2,014	8,305	20,970	22,318	20,632	20,436	22,142	17,601	10,097	5,477	1,790
2013	155,652	2,017	8,136	21,061	22,525	21,641	20,145	21,569	18,957	11,798	5,761	2,042
2014	156,936	2,018	8,138	21,030	22,523	21,970	20,159	21,425	19,322	12,349	5,893	2,109
2015	158,229	2,035	8,142	20,980	22,466	22,299	20,204	21,299	19,715	12,892	6,024	2,174
Female												
1950	75,864	1,545	6,383	11,944	11,181	12,162	10,863	8,688	6,672	4,316	1,771	340
1960	90,992	2,022	7,969	17,437	12,114	11,639	12,326	10,393	8,036	5,881	2,609	567
1970	104,300	1,707	6,701	19,986	17,890	12,690	11,857	12,021	9,797	6,998	3,683	969
1980	116,493	1,727	6,259	17,087	21,068	18,700	13,065	11,791	11,551	8,824	4,862	1,559
1990	127,471	1,928	7,231	17,124	18,098	21,596	18,925	12,824	11,158	10,139	6,267	2,180
2000	143,368	1,857	7,508	20,034	19,105	19,771	22,701	19,181	12,629	10,088	7,482	3,013
2010	156,964	1,930	7,952	20,056	21,309	20,432	20,635	22,864	18,882	11,617	7,584	3,704
2013	160,477	1,925	7,791	20,160	21,429	21,203	20,307	22,198	20,360	13,419	7,686	3,999
2014	161,921	1,930	7,791	20,161	21,456	21,546	20,354	22,034	20,756	14,049	7,789	4,053
2015	163,190	1,943	7,787	20,130	21,382	21,838	20,386	21,889	21,163	14,658	7,900	4,113
White male												
1950	67,129	1,400	5,845	10,860	9,689	10,430	9,529	7,836	6,180	3,736	1,406	218
1960	78,367	1,784	7,065	15,659	10,483	9,940	10,564	9,114	6,850	4,702	1,875	331
1970	86,721	1,501	5,873	17,667	15,232	10,775	9,979	10,090	7,958	4,916	2,243	487
1980	94,976	1,487	5,402	14,773	18,123	15,940	11,010	9,774	9,151	6,096	2,600	621
1990	102,143	1,604	6,071	14,467	15,389	18,071	15,819	10,624	8,813	7,127	3,397	760
2000	113,445	1,524	6,143	16,428	15,942	16,232	18,568	15,670	10,067	7,343	4,419	1,109
2010	121,403	1,518	6,281	16,043	17,069	16,139	16,208	18,096	14,840	8,726	4,866	1,617
2013	123,559	1,509	6,101	16,000	17,093	16,764	15,813	17,447	15,787	10,160	5,056	1,830
2014	124,143	1,505	6,089	15,925	17,034	16,907	15,747	17,265	16,034	10,603	5,152	1,883
2015	124,790	1,520	6,085	15,846	16,952	17,052	15,716	17,101	16,309	11,033	5,244	1,934
White female												
1950	67,813	1,341	5,599	10,431	9,821	10,851	9,719	7,868	6,168	4,031	1,669	314
1960	80,465	1,714	6,795	15,068	10,596	10,204	11,000	9,364	7,327	5,428	2,441	527
1970	91,028	1,434	5,615	16,912	15,420	11,004	10,349	10,756	8,853	6,366	3,429	890
1980	99,835	1,412	5,127	14,057	17,653	15,896	11,232	10,285	10,325	7,951	4,457	1,440
1990	106,561	1,524	5,762	13,706	14,599	17,757	15,834	10,946	9,698	9,048	5,687	2,001
2000	116,641	1,447	5,839	15,576	14,966	15,574	18,386	15,921	10,731	8,757	6,715	2,729
2010	124,020	1,451	5,993	15,270	16,153	15,552	15,941	18,311	15,586	9,846	6,601	3,314
2013	125,785	1,440	5,826	15,247	16,146	16,021	15,489	17,569	16,588	11,319	6,603	3,537
2014	126,488	1,439	5,816	15,203	16,129	16,204	15,444	17,362	16,849	11,805	6,667	3,569
2015	127,085	1,450	5,807	15,141	16,043	16,344	15,395	17,173	17,126	12,267	6,734	3,604

See footnotes at end of table.

Excel and PDF versions (with more data years and standard errors when available): http://www.cdc.gov/nchs/hus/contents2016.htm#001.

[Data are based on the decennial census updated with data from multiple sources]

Sex, race, Hispanic origin, and year	Total resident population	Age										
		Under 1 year	1–4 years	5–14 years	15–24 years	25–34 years	35–44 years	45–54 years	55–64 years	65–74 years	75–84 years	85 years and over
Black or African American male						Number, in thousands						
1950	7,300	- - -	[1]944	1,442	1,162	1,105	1,003	772	459	299	[2]113	- - -
1960	9,114	281	1,082	2,185	1,305	1,120	1,086	891	617	382	137	29
1970	10,748	245	975	2,784	2,041	1,226	1,084	979	739	461	169	46
1980	12,585	269	967	2,614	2,807	1,967	1,235	1,024	854	567	228	53
1990	14,420	322	1,164	2,700	2,669	2,592	1,962	1,175	878	614	277	66
2000	17,407	313	1,271	3,454	2,932	2,586	2,705	1,957	1,090	683	330	87
2010	20,101	341	1,388	3,408	3,591	2,801	2,639	2,708	1,832	886	396	110
2013	20,935	346	1,381	3,447	3,720	3,019	2,629	2,693	2,092	1,038	439	129
2014	21,241	347	1,383	3,458	3,735	3,122	2,661	2,681	2,162	1,099	456	136
2015	21,518	351	1,384	3,457	3,727	3,225	2,691	2,674	2,231	1,164	473	142
Black or African American female												
1950	7,745	- - -	[1]941	1,446	1,300	1,260	1,112	796	443	322	[2]125	- - -
1960	9,758	283	1,085	2,191	1,404	1,300	1,229	974	663	430	160	38
1970	11,832	243	970	2,773	2,196	1,456	1,309	1,134	868	582	230	71
1980	14,046	266	951	2,578	2,937	2,267	1,488	1,258	1,059	776	360	106
1990	16,063	316	1,137	2,641	2,700	2,905	2,279	1,416	1,135	884	495	156
2000	19,187	302	1,228	3,348	2,971	2,866	3,055	2,274	1,353	971	587	233
2010	21,965	330	1,343	3,292	3,568	3,066	2,962	3,056	2,197	1,192	675	282
2013	22,762	331	1,333	3,333	3,630	3,224	2,950	3,043	2,499	1,378	723	318
2014	23,069	332	1,333	3,349	3,630	3,305	2,984	3,029	2,578	1,460	741	328
2015	23,345	336	1,336	3,350	3,607	3,383	3,013	3,022	2,654	1,544	763	339
American Indian or Alaska Native male												
1980	702	17	59	153	161	114	75	53	37	22	9	2
1990	1,024	24	88	206	192	183	140	86	55	32	13	3
2000	1,488	28	109	301	271	229	229	165	88	45	18	5
2010	2,143	39	160	381	392	336	290	264	167	76	29	7
2013	2,240	40	157	388	396	356	299	272	194	95	35	9
2014	2,269	40	156	389	395	362	302	274	201	102	37	10
2015	2,299	40	156	389	393	367	307	276	210	108	40	11
American Indian or Alaska Native female												
1980	718	16	57	149	158	118	79	57	41	27	12	4
1990	1,041	24	85	200	178	186	148	92	61	41	21	6
2000	1,496	26	106	293	254	219	236	174	95	54	28	10
2010	2,121	38	156	370	364	316	282	273	179	87	41	14
2013	2,217	39	153	378	374	329	288	277	209	107	48	18
2014	2,250	38	152	379	376	335	291	277	218	114	50	19
2015	2,279	39	151	380	376	340	295	278	227	122	53	20
Asian or Pacific Islander male												
1980	1,814	35	130	321	334	366	252	159	110	72	30	6
1990	3,652	68	258	598	665	718	588	347	208	133	57	12
2000	5,713	84	339	861	934	1,073	947	705	399	231	112	27
2010	8,134	116	476	1,138	1,266	1,356	1,299	1,075	761	409	186	55
2013	8,917	121	497	1,226	1,316	1,503	1,405	1,158	884	504	230	73
2014	9,284	127	510	1,257	1,359	1,580	1,449	1,205	925	545	248	80
2015	9,622	124	517	1,288	1,394	1,655	1,490	1,248	965	586	267	87

See footnotes at end of table.

Table 1 (page 3 of 3). Resident population, by age, sex, race, and Hispanic origin: United States, selected years 1950–2015

Excel and PDF versions (with more data years and standard errors when available): http://www.cdc.gov/nchs/hus/contents2016.htm#001.

[Data are based on the decennial census updated with data from multiple sources]

Sex, race, Hispanic origin, and year	Total resident population	Age										
		Under 1 year	1–4 years	5–14 years	15–24 years	25–34 years	35–44 years	45–54 years	55–64 years	65–74 years	75–84 years	85 years and over
Asian or Pacific Islander female					Number, in thousands							
1980	1,915	34	127	307	325	423	269	192	126	71	33	9
1990	3,805	65	247	578	621	749	664	371	264	166	65	17
2000	6,044	81	336	817	914	1,112	1,024	812	451	305	152	41
2010	8,859	110	460	1,124	1,223	1,498	1,450	1,223	920	491	267	93
2013	9,713	116	479	1,202	1,279	1,628	1,580	1,309	1,064	615	313	127
2014	10,114	121	489	1,230	1,322	1,702	1,634	1,366	1,111	670	331	138
2015	10,480	118	493	1,259	1,357	1,771	1,684	1,417	1,155	726	350	150
Hispanic or Latino male												
1980	7,280	187	661	1,530	1,646	1,256	761	570	364	200	86	19
1990	11,388	279	980	2,128	2,376	2,310	1,471	818	551	312	131	32
2000	18,162	395	1,506	3,469	3,564	3,494	2,653	1,551	804	474	203	50
2010	25,619	515	2,094	4,755	4,648	4,419	3,734	2,736	1,535	735	352	95
2013	27,461	518	2,091	5,049	4,826	4,638	3,996	3,070	1,840	898	407	127
2014	28,018	517	2,097	5,107	4,868	4,666	4,083	3,194	1,955	964	428	140
2015	28,603	523	2,099	5,171	4,912	4,710	4,179	3,301	2,076	1,030	448	152
Hispanic or Latina female												
1980	7,329	181	634	1,482	1,546	1,249	805	615	411	257	117	30
1990	10,966	268	939	2,039	2,028	2,073	1,448	868	632	403	209	59
2000	17,144	376	1,441	3,318	3,017	3,016	2,476	1,585	907	603	303	101
2010	24,859	497	2,008	4,561	4,206	4,016	3,564	2,728	1,679	914	510	176
2013	26,610	496	2,013	4,844	4,449	4,124	3,794	3,011	1,979	1,089	580	230
2014	27,370	496	2,021	4,920	4,551	4,215	3,910	3,136	2,099	1,166	607	248
2015	27,989	501	2,020	4,987	4,617	4,273	3,997	3,239	2,214	1,242	633	267
White, not Hispanic or Latino male												
1980	88,035	1,308	4,772	13,317	16,554	14,739	10,284	9,229	8,803	5,906	2,519	603
1990	91,743	1,351	5,181	12,525	13,219	15,967	14,481	9,875	8,303	6,837	3,275	729
2000	96,551	1,163	4,761	13,238	12,628	12,958	16,088	14,223	9,312	6,894	4,225	1,062
2010	98,386	1,067	4,438	11,817	12,930	12,171	12,813	15,606	13,434	8,045	4,536	1,528
2013	98,937	1,058	4,270	11,529	12,794	12,612	12,193	14,654	14,108	9,332	4,677	1,711
2014	99,042	1,055	4,254	11,409	12,700	12,739	12,055	14,359	14,252	9,715	4,753	1,752
2015	99,182	1,064	4,249	11,279	12,578	12,849	11,943	14,100	14,417	10,085	4,827	1,791
White, not Hispanic or Latina female												
1980	92,872	1,240	4,522	12,647	16,185	14,711	10,468	9,700	9,935	7,707	4,345	1,411
1990	96,557	1,280	4,909	11,846	12,749	15,872	14,520	10,153	9,116	8,674	5,491	1,945
2000	100,774	1,102	4,517	12,529	12,183	12,778	16,089	14,446	9,879	8,188	6,429	2,633
2010	101,741	1,016	4,225	11,219	12,426	11,972	12,718	15,839	14,049	9,000	6,125	3,150
2013	101,982	1,007	4,063	10,958	12,194	12,358	12,073	14,844	14,785	10,314	6,064	3,321
2014	102,007	1,007	4,047	10,852	12,083	12,460	11,927	14,522	14,938	10,730	6,102	3,338
2015	102,060	1,014	4,039	10,735	11,936	12,551	11,806	14,242	15,113	11,124	6,146	3,354

- - - Data not available.
[1] Population for age group under 5 years.
[2] Population for age group 75 years and over.

NOTES: The race groups, white, black, American Indian or Alaska Native, and Asian or Pacific Islander, include persons of Hispanic and non-Hispanic origin. Persons of Hispanic origin may be of any race. Starting with *Health, United States, 2003*, population estimates for 1991–1999 are intercensal estimates based on the 1990 and 2000 censuses. Starting with *Health, United States, 2012*, population estimates for 2001–2009 are intercensal estimates based on the 2000 and 2010 censuses. Population estimates for 2011 and beyond are 2010-based postcensal estimates. Population figures are census counts as of April 1 for 1950, 1960, 1970, 1980, and 1990. For 2000 and 2010, population estimates are bridged-race April 1 census counts. Estimates for other years are as of July 1. See Appendix I, Population Census and Population Estimates. Populations for age groups may not sum to the total due to rounding. Unrounded population figures are available in the spreadsheet version of this table. Available from: http://www.cdc.gov/nchs/hus.htm. Data for additional years are available. See the Excel spreadsheet on the *Health, United States* website at: http://www.cdc.gov/nchs/hus.htm.

SOURCE: U.S. Census Bureau: 1950 Nonwhite Population by Race. Special Report P-E, No. 3B. Washington, DC: U.S. Government Printing Office, 1951; U.S. Census of Population: 1960, Number of Inhabitants, PC(1)-A1, United States Summary, 1964; 1970, Number of Inhabitants, Final Report PC(1)-A1, United States Summary, 1971; U.S. population estimates, by age, sex, race, and Hispanic origin: 1980 to 1991. Current population reports, series P-25, no 1095. Washington, DC: U.S. Government Printing Office, Feb. 1993; NCHS. Estimates of the July 1, 1991–July 1, 1999; April 1, 2000; July 1, 2001–July 1, 2009; April 1, 2010; July 1, 2011–July 1, 2015 United States resident population by age, sex, race, and Hispanic origin, prepared under a collaborative arrangement with the U.S. Census Bureau, Population Estimates Program. Available from: http://www.cdc.gov/nchs/nvss/bridged_race.htm. See Appendix I, Population Census and Population Estimates.

Table 2 (page 1 of 2). Persons below poverty level, by selected characteristics, race, and Hispanic origin: United States, selected years 1973–2015

Excel and PDF versions (with more data years and standard errors when available): http://www.cdc.gov/nchs/hus/contents2016.htm#002.

[Data are based on household interviews of a sample of the civilian noninstitutionalized population]

Selected characteristic, race, and Hispanic origin [1]	1973	1980	1990	2000 [2]	2010 [4]	2013(1) [4]	2013(2) [4,5]	2014 [5]	2015 [5]
All persons	\multicolumn{9}{c}{Percent below poverty}
All races	11.1	13.0	13.5	11.3	15.1	14.5	14.8	14.8	13.5
White only	8.4	10.2	10.7	9.5	13.0	12.3	12.9	12.7	11.6
Black or African American only	31.4	32.5	31.9	22.5	27.4	27.2	25.2	26.2	24.1
Asian only	- - -	- - -	12.2	9.9	12.2	10.5	13.1	12.0	11.4
Hispanic or Latino	21.9	25.7	28.1	21.5	26.5	23.5	24.7	23.6	21.4
Mexican	- - -	- - -	28.1	22.9	- - -	- - -	- - -	- - -	- - -
Puerto Rican	- - -	- - -	40.6	25.6	- - -	- - -	- - -	- - -	- - -
White only, not Hispanic or Latino	7.5	9.1	8.8	7.4	9.9	9.6	10.0	10.1	9.1
Related children under age 18 in families									
All races	14.2	17.9	19.9	15.6	21.5	19.5	20.9	20.7	19.2
White only	9.7	13.4	15.1	12.4	17.9	15.9	18.4	17.4	16.7
Black or African American only	40.6	42.1	44.2	30.9	39.0	38.0	33.8	37.1	32.7
Asian only	- - -	- - -	17.0	12.5	14.0	9.8	14.4	13.4	11.4
Hispanic or Latino	27.8	33.0	37.7	27.6	34.3	30.0	32.2	31.3	28.6
Mexican	- - -	- - -	35.5	29.5	- - -	- - -	- - -	- - -	- - -
Puerto Rican	- - -	- - -	56.7	32.1	- - -	- - -	- - -	- - -	- - -
White only, not Hispanic or Latino	- - -	11.3	11.6	8.5	11.7	10.1	12.7	11.9	11.5
Related children under age 18 in families with female householder and no husband present									
All races	- - -	50.8	53.4	40.1	46.6	45.8	47.4	46.5	42.6
White only	- - -	41.6	45.9	33.9	43.3	41.6	46.5	42.9	40.9
Black or African American only	- - -	64.8	64.7	49.3	53.2	54.0	49.6	52.8	46.1
Asian only	- - -	- - -	32.2	38.0	36.9	22.7	47.4	32.4	25.7
Hispanic or Latino	- - -	65.0	68.4	49.8	56.3	52.3	53.4	53.3	48.7
Mexican	- - -	- - -	62.4	51.4	- - -	- - -	- - -	- - -	- - -
Puerto Rican	- - -	- - -	82.7	55.3	- - -	- - -	- - -	- - -	- - -
White only, not Hispanic or Latino	- - -	- - -	39.6	28.0	34.7	33.6	39.5	35.8	34.8
All persons	\multicolumn{9}{c}{Number below poverty, in thousands}
All races	22,973	29,272	33,585	31,581	46,343	45,318	46,269	46,657	43,123
White only	15,142	19,699	22,326	21,645	31,083	29,936	31,287	31,089	28,566
Black or African American only	7,388	8,579	9,837	7,982	10,746	11,041	10,186	10,755	10,020
Asian only	- - -	- - -	858	1,258	1,899	1,785	2,255	2,137	2,078
Hispanic or Latino	2,366	3,491	6,006	7,747	13,522	12,744	13,356	13,104	12,133
Mexican	- - -	- - -	3,764	5,460	- - -	- - -	- - -	- - -	- - -
Puerto Rican	- - -	- - -	966	814	- - -	- - -	- - -	- - -	- - -
White only, not Hispanic or Latino	12,864	16,365	16,622	14,366	19,251	18,796	19,552	19,652	17,786
Related children under age 18 in families									
All races	9,453	11,114	12,715	11,005	15,598	14,142	15,116	14,987	13,962
White only	5,462	6,817	7,696	6,834	9,590	8,428	9,702	9,172	8,838
Black or African American only	3,822	3,906	4,412	3,495	4,271	4,153	3,678	4,036	3,571
Asian only	- - -	- - -	356	407	477	354	538	492	420
Hispanic or Latino	1,364	1,718	2,750	3,342	5,815	5,273	5,638	5,522	5,139
Mexican	- - -	- - -	1,733	2,537	- - -	- - -	- - -	- - -	- - -
Puerto Rican	- - -	- - -	490	329	- - -	- - -	- - -	- - -	- - -
White only, not Hispanic or Latino	- - -	5,174	5,106	3,715	4,544	3,833	4,784	4,440	4,301

See footnotes at end of table.

Table 2 (page 2 of 2). Persons below poverty level, by selected characteristics, race, and Hispanic origin: United States, selected years 1973–2015

Excel and PDF versions (with more data years and standard errors when available): *http://www.cdc.gov/nchs/hus/contents2016.htm#002.*

[Data are based on household interviews of a sample of the civilian noninstitutionalized population]

Selected characteristic, race, and Hispanic origin[1]	1973	1980	1990	2000[2]	2010[4]	2013(1)[4]	2013(2)[4,5]	2014[5]	2015[5]
Related children under age 18 in families with female householder and no husband present	Number below poverty, in thousands								
All races	- - -	5,866	7,363	6,300	8,603	8,305	9,025	8,491	7,854
White only	- - -	2,813	3,597	3,090	4,495	4,316	5,155	4,426	4,278
Black or African American only	- - -	2,944	3,543	2,908	3,252	3,180	2,964	3,121	2,777
Asian only	- - -	- - -	80	162	141	89	159	136	74
Hispanic or Latino	- - -	809	1,314	1,407	2,707	2,763	3,069	2,739	2,463
Mexican	- - -	- - -	615	938	- - -	- - -	- - -	- - -	- - -
Puerto Rican	- - -	- - -	382	242	- - -	- - -	- - -	- - -	- - -
White only, not Hispanic or Latino	- - -	- - -	2,411	1,832	2,209	2,001	2,477	2,174	2,198

- - - Data not available.

[1] The race groups white, black, and Asian include persons of Hispanic and non-Hispanic origin. Persons of Hispanic origin may be of any race. For 2002 and later years, race-specific estimates are tabulated according to the 1997 *Revisions to the Standards for the Classification of Federal Data on Race and Ethnicity* and are not strictly compatible with estimates for earlier years. Starting with 2002 data, the CPS allowed respondents to report more than one race; however, race-specific estimates shown in the table were for respondents who reported one race. Prior to 2002, race-specific estimates were tabulated according to the 1977 Standards, and the Asian only category included Native Hawaiian or Other Pacific Islander. Race-specific estimates prior to 2002 were based on the Current Population Survey question, which allowed respondents to report only one race group. See Appendix II, Hispanic origin; Race.

[2] Implementation of 28,000-household sample expansion.

[3] Data for 2004 (shown in spreadsheet version) reflect a correction to the weights in the 2005 Annual Social and Economic (ASEC) Supplement of the Current Population Survey. See Appendix I, Current Population Survey (CPS).

[4] For 2013 data, the CPS ASEC used a split panel to test a new set of income questions. Estimates for 2013 shown in the column labeled (1) are based on the approximately 68,000 addresses that received questions consistent with those used to create estimates for 2012 and earlier. Estimates for 2013 shown in the column labeled (2) are based on the approximately 30,000 addresses that received the new set of income questions. The vertical line in the table indicates the introduction of the new set of income questions into the ASEC estimates. For more information, see the CPS website at: http://www.census.gov/cps.

[5] Data for 2013(2) and beyond are based on a redesigned questionnaire that includes the new set of income questions; therefore data trends need to be interpreted with caution. For more information on the redesigned questionnaire and the impact of the new income questions on poverty estimates, see: http://www.census.gov/content/dam/Census/library/publications/2015/demo/p60-252.pdf.

NOTES: Estimates of poverty for 1992–1998 were prepared using the 1990 census population controls. Estimates for 1999–2009 were prepared using the Census 2000-based population controls. Estimates for 2010 and beyond were prepared using the Census 2010-based population controls. Poverty level is based on family income and family size using U.S. Census Bureau poverty thresholds. See Appendix II, Poverty. Poverty estimates based on a supplemental poverty measure are available from the U.S. Census Bureau. In 2011–2013, an estimated 30.1% of American Indian or Alaska Native only persons (1,005,000 persons) were living below the poverty level, and an estimated 15.9% of Native Hawaiian or Other Pacific Islander only persons (176,000 persons) were living below the poverty level. Due to the redesign of the CPS ASEC income questions, 2013 is the last year that data were available to compute three-year estimates for the American Indian or Alaska Native only populations and the Native Hawaiian or Other Pacific Islander populations. Estimates for these groups will not be updated until 2016 estimates are available. Data for additional years are available. See the Excel spreadsheet on the *Health, United States* website at: http://www.cdc.gov/nchs/hus.htm.

SOURCE: U.S. Census Bureau, Current Population Survey, Annual Social and Economic Supplement; Proctor BD, Semega JL, Kollar MA. Income and poverty in the United States: 2015. Current Population Reports, P60–256. Washington, DC: U.S. Government Printing Office. 2016. Available from: http://www.census.gov/content/dam/Census/library/publications/2016/demo/p60-256.pdf. See Appendix I, Current Population Survey (CPS).

Table 3 (page 1 of 3). Crude birth rates, fertility rates, and birth rates, by age, race, and Hispanic origin of mother: United States, selected years 1950–2015

Excel and PDF versions (with more data years and standard errors when available): http://www.cdc.gov/nchs/hus/contents2016.htm#003.

[Data are based on birth certificates]

Race, Hispanic origin, and year	Crude birth rate [1]	Fertility rate [2]	10–14 years	15–19 years			20–24 years	25–29 years	30–34 years	35–39 years	40–44 years	45–54 years [3]
				Total	15–17 years	18–19 years						
All races				Live births per 1,000 women								
1950	24.1	106.2	1.0	81.6	40.7	132.7	196.6	166.1	103.7	52.9	15.1	1.2
1960	23.7	118.0	0.8	89.1	43.9	166.7	258.1	197.4	112.7	56.2	15.5	0.9
1970	18.4	87.9	1.2	68.3	38.8	114.7	167.8	145.1	73.3	31.7	8.1	0.5
1980	15.9	68.4	1.1	53.0	32.5	82.1	115.1	112.9	61.9	19.8	3.9	0.2
1990	16.7	70.9	1.4	59.9	37.5	88.6	116.5	120.2	80.8	31.7	5.5	0.2
1995	14.6	64.6	1.3	56.0	35.5	87.7	107.5	108.8	81.1	34.0	6.6	0.3
2000	14.4	65.9	0.9	47.7	26.9	78.1	109.7	113.5	91.2	39.7	8.0	0.5
2005	14.0	66.7	0.6	39.7	21.1	68.4	101.8	116.5	96.7	46.4	9.1	0.6
2010	13.0	64.1	0.4	34.2	17.3	58.2	90.0	108.3	96.5	45.9	10.2	0.7
2012	12.6	63.0	0.4	29.4	14.1	51.4	83.1	106.5	97.3	48.3	10.4	0.7
2013	12.4	62.5	0.3	26.5	12.3	47.1	80.7	105.5	98.0	49.3	10.4	0.8
2014	12.5	62.9	0.3	24.2	10.9	43.8	79.0	105.8	100.8	51.0	10.6	0.8
2015	12.4	62.5	0.2	22.3	9.9	40.7	76.8	104.3	101.5	51.8	11.0	0.8
Race of child: [4] White												
1950	23.0	102.3	0.4	70.0	31.3	120.5	190.4	165.1	102.6	51.4	14.5	1.0
1960	22.7	113.2	0.4	79.4	35.5	154.6	252.8	194.9	109.6	54.0	14.7	0.8
1970	17.4	84.1	0.5	57.4	29.2	101.5	163.4	145.9	71.9	30.0	7.5	0.4
1980	14.9	64.7	0.6	44.7	25.2	72.1	109.5	112.4	60.4	18.5	3.4	0.2
Race of mother: [5] White												
1980	15.1	65.6	0.6	45.4	25.5	73.2	111.1	113.8	61.2	18.8	3.5	0.2
1990	15.8	68.3	0.7	50.8	29.5	78.0	109.8	120.7	81.7	31.5	5.2	0.2
1995	14.1	63.6	0.8	49.5	29.6	80.2	104.7	111.7	83.3	34.2	6.4	0.3
2000	13.9	65.3	0.6	43.2	23.3	72.3	106.6	116.7	94.6	40.2	7.9	0.4
2005	13.6	66.8	0.5	36.7	18.8	64.0	99.9	120.7	100.7	47.6	9.0	0.6
2010	12.5	64.4	0.3	31.9	15.8	54.8	87.9	111.9	100.5	46.4	10.0	0.6
2012	12.1	63.0	0.3	27.4	13.0	48.3	80.8	109.2	100.2	48.5	10.0	0.7
2013	12.0	62.7	0.2	24.9	11.3	44.7	78.5	108.3	101.3	49.6	10.1	0.7
2014	12.0	63.2	0.2	23.0	10.2	42.0	77.3	108.6	103.9	51.2	10.2	0.7
2015	12.0	63.1	0.2	21.3	9.2	39.3	75.3	107.6	104.8	52.2	10.6	0.8
Race of child: [4] Black or African American												
1960	31.9	153.5	4.3	156.1	- - -	- - -	295.4	218.6	137.1	73.9	21.9	1.1
1970	25.3	115.4	5.2	140.7	101.4	204.9	202.7	136.3	79.6	41.9	12.5	1.0
1980	22.1	88.1	4.3	100.0	73.6	138.8	146.3	109.1	62.9	24.5	5.8	0.3
Race of mother: [5] Black or African American												
1980	21.3	84.7	4.3	97.8	72.5	135.1	140.0	103.9	59.9	23.5	5.6	0.3
1990	22.4	86.8	4.9	112.8	82.3	152.9	160.2	115.5	68.7	28.1	5.5	0.3
1995	17.8	71.0	4.1	94.4	68.5	135.0	133.7	95.6	63.0	28.4	6.0	0.3
2000	17.0	70.0	2.3	77.4	49.0	118.8	141.3	100.3	65.4	31.5	7.2	0.4
2005	16.1	68.5	1.6	60.1	34.5	101.2	129.5	107.0	70.2	35.1	8.4	0.5
2010	15.1	66.3	1.0	51.1	27.3	84.8	118.1	101.8	73.0	36.4	9.3	0.7
2012	14.7	65.1	0.8	44.0	22.0	74.4	108.7	101.7	75.1	39.2	9.7	0.7
2013	14.5	64.7	0.7	39.1	19.0	67.3	105.5	102.6	77.3	40.5	10.0	0.8
2014	14.5	64.6	0.6	35.1	16.7	61.9	102.6	103.1	79.4	42.6	10.2	0.8
2015	14.3	64.0	0.5	32.0	15.3	57.1	100.2	101.8	81.0	43.4	10.7	0.9
American Indian or Alaska Native mother [5]												
1980	20.7	82.7	1.9	82.2	51.5	129.5	143.7	106.6	61.8	28.1	8.2	*
1990	18.9	76.2	1.6	81.1	48.5	129.3	148.7	110.3	61.5	27.5	5.9	*
1995	15.3	63.0	1.6	72.9	44.6	122.2	123.1	91.6	56.5	24.3	5.5	*
2000	14.0	58.7	1.1	58.3	34.1	97.1	117.2	91.8	55.5	24.6	5.7	0.3
2005	12.6	53.6	0.8	46.0	26.3	78.0	102.9	86.3	51.8	23.3	5.4	0.3
2010	11.0	48.6	0.5	38.7	20.1	66.1	91.0	74.4	48.4	22.3	5.2	0.3
2012	10.5	47.0	0.5	34.9	17.0	60.5	81.7	73.9	49.7	23.3	5.5	0.5
2013	10.3	46.4	0.4	31.1	15.9	53.3	78.9	75.6	50.4	24.7	5.5	0.3
2014	9.9	44.8	0.3	27.3	13.2	48.6	73.2	74.7	52.3	24.1	5.5	0.3
2015	9.7	43.9	0.3	25.7	12.7	45.8	70.2	73.2	51.7	25.2	5.8	0.4

See footnotes at end of table.

Table 3 (page 2 of 3). Crude birth rates, fertility rates, and birth rates, by age, race, and Hispanic origin of mother: United States, selected years 1950–2015

Excel and PDF versions (with more data years and standard errors when available): http://www.cdc.gov/nchs/hus/contents2016.htm#003.

[Data are based on birth certificates]

Race, Hispanic origin, and year	Crude birth rate[1]	Fertility rate[2]	10–14 years	Total	15–17 years	18–19 years	20–24 years	25–29 years	30–34 years	35–39 years	40–44 years	45–54 years[3]
					15–19 years							
								Age of mother				

Asian or Pacific Islander mother[5]

Live births per 1,000 women

Year												
1980	19.9	73.2	0.3	26.2	12.0	46.2	93.3	127.4	96.0	38.3	8.5	0.7
1990	19.0	69.6	0.7	26.4	16.0	40.2	79.2	126.3	106.5	49.6	10.7	1.1
1995	16.7	62.6	0.7	25.5	15.6	40.1	64.2	103.7	102.3	50.1	11.8	0.8
2000	17.1	65.8	0.3	20.5	11.6	32.6	60.3	108.4	116.5	59.0	12.6	0.8
2005	15.9	63.0	0.2	15.4	7.7	26.4	52.9	96.6	115.3	61.8	13.7	1.0
2010	14.5	59.2	0.1	10.9	5.1	18.7	42.6	91.5	113.6	62.8	15.1	1.2
2012	15.1	62.2	0.1	9.7	4.1	17.7	41.4	95.8	121.3	68.1	16.1	1.4
2013	14.3	59.2	0.1	8.7	3.7	16.1	39.1	89.5	114.6	66.6	16.1	1.5
2014	14.6	60.7	0.1	7.7	3.3	13.9	37.5	90.0	121.3	68.9	16.1	1.5
2015	14.0	58.5	0.1	6.9	2.7	12.8	35.6	84.1	117.4	67.6	15.9	1.6

Hispanic or Latina mother[5,6]

Year												
1980	23.5	95.4	1.7	82.2	52.1	126.9	156.4	132.1	83.2	39.9	10.6	0.7
1990	26.7	107.7	2.4	100.3	65.9	147.7	181.0	153.0	98.3	45.3	10.9	0.7
1995	24.1	98.8	2.6	99.3	68.3	145.4	171.9	140.4	90.5	43.7	10.7	0.6
2000	23.1	95.9	1.7	87.3	55.5	132.6	161.3	139.9	97.1	46.6	11.5	0.6
2005	22.9	96.4	1.3	76.5	45.8	124.4	161.1	147.0	105.6	53.3	12.8	0.8
2010	18.7	80.2	0.8	55.7	32.3	90.7	126.1	125.3	96.6	51.7	13.0	0.8
2012	17.1	74.4	0.6	46.3	25.5	77.2	111.5	119.6	94.3	51.6	13.2	0.8
2013	16.7	72.9	0.5	41.7	22.0	70.8	107.2	119.1	94.8	52.4	13.3	0.8
2014	16.5	72.1	0.4	38.0	19.3	66.1	104.5	118.7	96.5	53.6	13.5	0.9
2015	16.3	71.7	0.4	34.9	17.4	61.9	102.1	119.3	98.6	54.5	14.0	0.9

White, not Hispanic or Latina mother[5,6]

Year												
1980	14.2	62.4	0.4	41.2	22.4	67.7	105.5	110.6	59.9	17.7	3.0	0.1
1990	14.4	62.8	0.5	42.5	23.2	66.6	97.5	115.3	79.4	30.0	4.7	0.2
1995	12.5	57.5	0.4	39.3	22.0	66.2	90.2	105.1	81.5	32.8	5.9	0.3
2000	12.2	58.5	0.3	32.6	15.8	57.5	91.2	109.4	93.2	38.8	7.3	0.4
2005	11.6	59.0	0.2	26.0	11.5	48.0	82.7	111.7	98.4	46.0	8.3	0.5
2010	10.9	58.7	0.2	23.5	10.0	42.5	74.9	105.8	99.9	44.1	9.2	0.6
2012	10.7	58.6	0.2	20.5	8.4	37.9	70.2	104.4	100.5	46.8	9.1	0.6
2013	10.7	58.7	0.1	18.6	7.4	35.0	68.3	103.5	101.9	48.0	9.1	0.7
2014	10.8	59.5	0.1	17.3	6.7	32.9	67.1	103.9	104.7	49.6	9.1	0.7
2015	10.7	59.3	0.1	16.0	6.0	30.6	65.0	102.3	105.1	50.6	9.4	0.7

Black or African American, not Hispanic or Latina mother[5,6]

Year												
1980	22.9	90.7	4.6	105.1	77.2	146.5	152.2	111.7	65.2	25.8	5.8	0.3
1990	23.0	89.0	5.0	116.2	84.9	157.5	165.1	118.4	70.2	28.7	5.6	0.3
1995	18.2	72.8	4.2	97.2	70.4	139.2	137.8	98.5	64.4	28.8	6.1	0.3
2000	17.3	71.4	2.4	79.2	50.1	121.9	145.4	102.8	66.5	31.8	7.2	0.4
2005	15.8	67.2	1.6	59.4	34.1	100.2	127.9	105.5	68.8	34.2	8.2	0.5
2010	15.1	66.6	1.0	51.5	27.4	85.6	119.4	102.5	73.6	36.4	9.2	0.7
2012	14.6	65.0	0.8	43.9	21.9	74.1	109.0	101.7	75.1	38.9	9.6	0.7
2013	14.4	64.6	0.7	39.0	18.9	67.0	105.6	102.7	77.3	40.3	9.9	0.8
2014	14.4	64.5	0.6	34.9	16.6	61.5	102.8	103.3	79.6	42.5	10.1	0.9
2015	14.2	64.1	0.6	31.8	15.3	56.7	100.2	102.0	81.6	43.6	10.7	0.9

See footnotes at end of table.

Table 3 (page 3 of 3). Crude birth rates, fertility rates, and birth rates, by age, race, and Hispanic origin of mother: United States, selected years 1950–2015

Excel and PDF versions (with more data years and standard errors when available): http://www.cdc.gov/nchs/hus/contents2016.htm#003.

[Data are based on birth certificates]

- - - Data not available.

* Rates based on fewer than 20 births are considered unreliable and are not shown.

[1] Live births per 1,000 population.

[2] Total number of live births regardless of age of mother per 1,000 women aged 15–44.

[3] Prior to 1997, data are for live births to mothers aged 45–49 per 1,000 women aged 45–49. In subsequent years, rates were computed by dividing the number of births to women aged 45 and over by the population of women aged 45–49. See Appendix II, Age.

[4] Live births are tabulated by race of child. See Appendix II, Race.

[5] Live births are tabulated by race and/or Hispanic origin of mother. See Appendix II, Race.

[6] Prior to 1993, data from states that did not report Hispanic origin on the birth certificate were excluded. See Appendix II, Hispanic origin. Rates in 1985 were not calculated because estimates for the Hispanic and non-Hispanic populations were not available.

NOTES: Data are based on births adjusted for underregistration for 1950 and on registered births for all other years. Starting with 1970 data, births to persons who were not residents of the 50 states and the District of Columbia are excluded. Starting with *Health, United States, 2003*, rates for 1991–1999 were revised using intercensal population estimates based on the 1990 and 2000 censuses. Rates for 2000 were based on bridged-race April 1, 2000 census counts. Starting with *Health, United States, 2012*, rates for 2001–2009 were revised using intercensal population estimates based on the 2000 and 2010 censuses. Rates for 2010 were based on bridged-race April 1, 2010 census counts. Rates for 2011 and beyond were computed using 2010-based postcensal estimates. See Appendix I, Population Census and Population Estimates. The race groups, white, black, American Indian or Alaska Native, and Asian or Pacific Islander, include persons of Hispanic and non-Hispanic origin. Persons of Hispanic origin may be of any race. Starting with 2003 data, some states reported multiple-race data. The multiple-race data for these states were bridged to the single-race categories of the 1977 Office of Management and Budget standards, for comparability with other states. See Appendix II, Race. Interpretation of trend data for Hispanic women should take into consideration expansion of reporting areas. Data for additional years are available. See the Excel spreadsheet on the *Health, United States* website at: http://www.cdc.gov/nchs/hus.htm.

SOURCE: NCHS, National Vital Statistics System, public-use Birth File. Martin JA, Hamilton BE, Osterman MJK, Driscoll AK, Mathews TJ. Births: Final data for 2015. National vital statistics report, vol 66, no 1. Hyattsville, MD: NCHS. 2017. Available from: http://www.cdc.gov/nchs/data/nvsr/nvsr66/nvsr66_01.pdf. Ventura SJ. Births of Hispanic parentage, 1980 and 1985. Monthly vital statistics report; vol 32 no 6 and vol 36 no 11, suppl. Public Health Service. Hyattsville, MD. 1983 and 1988; Available from: http://www.cdc.gov/nchs/data/mvsr/supp/mv32_06sacc.pdf and http://www.cdc.gov/nchs/data/mvsr/supp/mv36_11s.pdf. Internet release of: Vital statistics of the United States, 2003, vol 1, Natality, Tables 1–1 and 1–7; available from: http://www.cdc.gov/nchs/products/vsus.htm#electronic. See Appendix I, National Vital Statistics System (NVSS).

Table 4. Nonmarital childbearing, by detailed race and Hispanic origin of mother, and maternal age: United States, selected years 1970–2015

Excel and PDF versions (with more data years and standard errors when available): http://www.cdc.gov/nchs/hus/contents2016.htm#004.

[Data are based on birth certificates]

Maternal race, Hispanic origin, and age	1970	1980	1990	1995	2000	2005	2010	2013	2014	2015
	Live births per 1,000 unmarried women aged 15–44 [1]									
All races and origins	26.4	29.4	43.8	44.3	44.1	47.2	47.5	44.3	43.9	43.4
White [2]	13.9	18.1	32.9	37.0	38.2	43.2	44.5	40.8	40.6	40.4
Black or African American [2]	95.5	81.1	90.5	74.5	70.5	67.2	65.3	61.7	61.5	59.6
Asian or Pacific Islander	- - -	- - -	- - -	- - -	20.9	22.8	22.3	21.8	21.7	20.4
Hispanic or Latina [3]	- - -	- - -	89.6	88.8	87.2	96.2	80.6	69.9	68.5	67.4
White, not Hispanic or Latina [3]	- - -	- - -	24.4	28.1	28.0	30.4	32.9	31.7	31.8	31.6
	Percent of live births to unmarried mothers									
All races and origins	10.7	18.4	28.0	32.2	33.2	36.9	40.8	40.6	40.2	40.3
White	5.5	11.2	20.4	25.3	27.1	31.7	35.9	35.8	35.7	35.8
Black or African American	37.5	56.1	66.5	69.9	68.5	69.3	72.1	71.0	70.4	70.1
American Indian or Alaska Native	22.4	39.2	53.6	57.2	58.4	63.5	65.6	66.4	65.7	65.8
Asian or Pacific Islander [4]	- - -	7.3	13.2	16.3	14.8	16.2	17.0	17.0	16.4	16.4
Hispanic or Latina [3]	- - -	23.6	36.7	40.8	42.7	48.0	53.4	53.2	52.9	53.0
Mexican	- - -	20.3	33.3	38.1	40.7	46.7	52.0	51.9	51.6	51.5
Puerto Rican	- - -	46.3	55.9	60.0	59.6	61.7	65.2	64.6	63.9	64.2
Cuban	- - -	10.0	18.2	23.8	27.3	36.4	47.0	50.1	49.8	50.7
Central and South American	- - -	27.1	41.2	44.1	44.7	49.2	51.8	50.1	50.4	51.0
Other and unknown Hispanic or Latina . .	- - -	22.4	37.2	44.0	46.2	48.6	56.3	56.1	55.5	55.1
Not Hispanic or Latina: [3]										
White	- - -	9.5	16.9	21.2	22.1	25.3	29.0	29.3	29.2	29.2
Black or African American	- - -	57.2	66.7	70.0	68.7	69.9	72.5	71.5	70.9	70.5
	Number of live births, in thousands									
Live births to unmarried mothers	399	666	1,165	1,254	1,347	1,527	1,633	1,596	1,605	1,602
Maternal age	Percent distribution of live births to unmarried mothers									
Under 20 years	50.1	40.8	30.9	30.9	28.0	23.1	20.1	15.4	13.9	12.9
20–24 years	31.8	35.6	34.7	34.5	37.4	38.3	36.8	36.8	36.1	35.0
25 years and over	18.1	23.5	34.4	34.7	34.6	38.7	43.1	47.9	50.0	52.1

- - - Data not available.

[1] Rates computed by dividing births to unmarried mothers, regardless of age of mother, by the population of unmarried women aged 15–44. Population data for unmarried American Indian or Alaska Native women are not available for rate calculations. Prior to 2000, population data for unmarried Asian or Pacific Islander women were not available for rate calculations.

[2] For 1970 and 1975 (shown in spreadsheet version), birth rates are by race of child.

[3] Prior to 1993, data from states that did not report Hispanic origin on the birth certificate were excluded. See Appendix II, Hispanic origin. Data for non-Hispanic white and non-Hispanic black women for years prior to 1989 are not nationally representative and are provided solely for comparison with Hispanic data.

[4] Estimates are not available for Asian or Pacific Islander subgroups because not all states have adopted the 2003 revision of the U.S. Standard Certificate of Live Birth. See Appendix II, Race.

NOTES: National estimates for 1970 and 1975 (shown in spreadsheet version) for unmarried mothers are based on births occurring in states reporting marital status of mother. Changes in reporting procedures for marital status occurred in some states during the 1990s. Data for states in which marital status was not reported have been inferred and included with data from the remaining states. See Appendix II, Marital status. Interpretation of trend data for Hispanic births should take into consideration expansion of reporting areas. The race groups, white, black, American Indian or Alaska Native, and Asian or Pacific Islander, include persons of Hispanic and non-Hispanic origin. Persons of Hispanic origin may be of any race. Starting with 2003 data, some states reported multiple-race data. The multiple-race data for these states were bridged to the single-race categories of the 1977 Office of Management and Budget standards, for comparability with other states. See Appendix II, Race. Starting with *Health, United States, 2003*, rates for 1991–1999 were revised using intercensal population estimates based on the 1990 and 2000 censuses. Rates for 2000 were based on bridged-race April 1, 2000 census counts. Starting with *Health, United States, 2012*, rates for 2001–2009 were revised using intercensal population estimates based on the 2000 and 2010 censuses. Rates for 2010 were based on 2010 bridged-race April 2010 census counts. Rates for 2011 and beyond were computed using 2010-based postcensal estimates. Data for additional years are available. See the Excel spreadsheet on the *Health, United States* website at: http://www.cdc.gov/nchs/hus.htm.

SOURCE: NCHS, National Vital Statistics System, public-use Birth File. Martin JA, Hamilton BE, Osterman MJK, Driscoll AK, Mathews TJ. Births: Final data for 2015. National vital statistics report, vol 66, no 1. Hyattsville, MD: NCHS. 2017. Available from: http://www.cdc.gov/nchs/data/nvsr/nvsr66/nvsr66_01.pdf. Hamilton BE, Sutton PD, Ventura SJ. Revised birth and fertility rates for the 1990s and new rates for Hispanic populations, 2000 and 2001: United States. National vital statistics reports; vol 51 no 12. Hyattsville, MD: NCHS. 2003; Available from: http://www.cdc.gov/nchs/data/nvsr/nvsr51/nvsr51_12.pdf. Births: Final data for each data year 1997–2007. National vital statistics reports. Hyattsville, MD; Final natality statistics for each data year 1993–1996. Monthly vital statistics report. Hyattsville, MD; Ventura SJ. Births to unmarried mothers: United States, 1980–1992. Vital Health Stat 21(53). 1995. See Appendix I, National Vital Statistics System (NVSS).

Table 5. Low birthweight live births, by detailed race and Hispanic origin of mother: United States, selected years 1970–2015

Excel and PDF versions (with more data years and standard errors when available): http://www.cdc.gov/nchs/hus/contents2016.htm#005.

[Data are based on birth certificates]

Birthweight, maternal race, and Hispanic origin	1970	1975	1980	1990	2000	2005	2010	2013	2014	2015
Low birthweight (less than 2,500 grams)					Percent of live births [1]					
All races	7.93	7.38	6.84	6.97	7.57	8.19	8.15	8.02	8.00	8.07
White	6.85	6.27	5.72	5.70	6.55	7.16	7.08	7.00	6.98	7.00
Black or African American.	13.90	13.19	12.69	13.25	12.99	13.59	13.21	12.76	12.83	13.03
American Indian or Alaska Native	7.97	6.41	6.44	6.11	6.76	7.36	7.61	7.48	7.65	7.53
Asian or Pacific Islander [2]	- - -	- - -	6.68	6.45	7.31	7.98	8.49	8.34	8.05	8.40
Hispanic or Latina [3]	- - -	- - -	6.12	6.06	6.41	6.88	6.97	7.09	7.05	7.21
Mexican.	- - -	- - -	5.62	5.55	6.01	6.49	6.49	6.62	6.58	6.81
Puerto Rican	- - -	- - -	8.95	8.99	9.30	9.92	9.55	9.38	9.54	9.42
Cuban	- - -	- - -	5.62	5.67	6.49	7.64	7.30	7.35	7.48	7.16
Central and South American.	- - -	- - -	5.76	5.84	6.34	6.78	6.55	6.85	6.68	6.74
Other and unknown Hispanic or Latina . .	- - -	- - -	6.96	6.87	7.84	8.27	8.38	7.99	7.94	8.13
Not Hispanic or Latina: [3]										
White	- - -	- - -	5.69	5.61	6.60	7.29	7.14	6.98	6.96	6.93
Black or African American	- - -	- - -	12.71	13.32	13.13	14.02	13.53	13.08	13.17	13.35
Very low birthweight (less than 1,500 grams)										
All races	1.17	1.16	1.15	1.27	1.43	1.49	1.45	1.41	1.40	1.40
White	0.95	0.92	0.90	0.95	1.14	1.20	1.17	1.14	1.14	1.12
Black or African American.	2.40	2.40	2.48	2.92	3.07	3.15	2.90	2.82	2.79	2.81
American Indian or Alaska Native	0.98	0.95	0.92	1.01	1.16	1.17	1.28	1.32	1.27	1.27
Asian or Pacific Islander [2]	- - -	- - -	0.92	0.87	1.05	1.14	1.17	1.18	1.15	1.13
Hispanic or Latina [3]	- - -	- - -	0.98	1.03	1.14	1.20	1.20	1.21	1.23	1.23
Mexican.	- - -	- - -	0.92	0.92	1.03	1.12	1.09	1.13	1.13	1.13
Puerto Rican	- - -	- - -	1.29	1.62	1.93	1.87	1.82	1.65	1.86	1.73
Cuban	- - -	- - -	1.02	1.20	1.21	1.50	1.42	1.27	1.45	1.38
Central and South American.	- - -	- - -	0.99	1.05	1.20	1.19	1.09	1.15	1.12	1.13
Other and unknown Hispanic or Latina . .	- - -	- - -	1.01	1.09	1.42	1.36	1.46	1.37	1.38	1.44
Not Hispanic or Latina: [3]										
White	- - -	- - -	0.87	0.93	1.14	1.21	1.16	1.11	1.10	1.09
Black or African American	- - -	- - -	2.47	2.93	3.10	3.27	2.98	2.90	2.87	2.89

- - - Data not available.

[1] Excludes live births with unknown birthweight. Percentage based on live births with known birthweight. See Appendix II, Birthweight.

[2] Estimates are not available for Asian or Pacific Islander subgroups because not all states have adopted the 2003 revision of the U.S. Standard Certificate of Live Birth. See Appendix II, Race.

[3] Prior to 1993, data from states that did not report Hispanic origin on the birth certificate were excluded. See Appendix II, Hispanic origin. Data for non-Hispanic white and non-Hispanic black women for years prior to 1989 are not nationally representative and are provided solely for comparison with Hispanic data.

NOTES: The race groups, white, black, American Indian or Alaska Native, and Asian or Pacific Islander, include persons of Hispanic and non-Hispanic origin. Persons of Hispanic origin may be of any race. Starting with 2003 data, some states reported multiple-race data. The multiple-race data for these states were bridged to the single-race categories of the 1977 Office of Management and Budget standards, for comparability with other states. See Appendix II, Race. Interpretation of trend data for Hispanic births should take into consideration expansion of reporting areas. Data for additional years are available. See the Excel spreadsheet on the *Health, United States* website at: http://www.cdc.gov/nchs/hus.htm.

SOURCE: NCHS, National Vital Statistics System, public-use Birth File. Martin JA, Hamilton BE, Osterman MJK, Driscoll AK, Mathews TJ. Births: Final data for 2015. National vital statistics report, vol 66, no 1. Hyattsville, MD: NCHS. 2017. Available from: http://www.cdc.gov/nchs/data/nvsr/nvsr66/nvsr66_01.pdf. See Appendix I, National Vital Statistics System (NVSS).

Table 6 (page 1 of 3). Low birthweight live births, by race and Hispanic origin of mother, state, and territory: United States and U.S. dependent areas, 2000–2002, 2003–2005, and 2013–2015

Excel and PDF versions (with more data years and standard errors when available): http://www.cdc.gov/nchs/hus/contents2016.htm#006.

[Data are based on birth certificates]

| | All races | | | Not Hispanic or Latina | | | | | |
| | | | | White | | | Black or African American | | |
State and territory	2000–2002	2003–2005	2013–2015	2000–2002	2003–2005	2013–2015	2000–2002	2003–2005	2013–2015
	Percent of live births weighing less than 2,500 grams [1]								
United States [2]	7.69	8.07	8.03	6.75	7.18	6.96	13.19	13.77	13.20
Alabama	9.75	10.35	10.17	7.77	8.46	8.03	14.10	15.02	15.17
Alaska	5.71	6.02	5.81	4.84	5.34	5.37	10.70	11.74	8.15
Arizona	6.91	7.05	7.03	6.78	7.01	6.58	13.16	12.38	11.77
Arkansas	8.64	9.04	8.95	7.48	7.83	7.71	13.81	14.86	14.59
California	6.29	6.71	6.78	5.86	6.30	5.91	11.66	12.46	11.46
Colorado	8.60	9.04	8.86	8.24	8.81	8.35	14.59	15.20	13.48
Connecticut.	7.52	7.74	7.79	6.48	6.60	6.58	12.28	12.88	12.23
Delaware	9.29	9.31	8.63	7.80	7.62	7.05	14.08	14.32	12.72
District of Columbia . .	11.85	11.06	9.76	6.35	6.28	6.19	14.60	13.96	12.83
Florida	8.18	8.59	8.60	6.98	7.38	7.16	12.58	13.28	13.11
Georgia	8.79	9.27	9.47	6.92	7.44	7.14	12.98	13.81	13.69
Hawaii	7.98	8.23	8.15	6.17	6.42	5.88	11.01	11.44	11.90
Idaho.	6.41	6.65	6.64	6.29	6.60	6.49	*	*7.03	9.39
Illinois	8.04	8.40	8.22	6.74	7.22	6.85	14.04	14.70	13.76
Indiana.	7.54	8.10	7.97	6.95	7.54	7.33	12.89	13.46	12.87
Iowa	6.39	6.92	6.68	6.19	6.72	6.36	11.77	12.22	10.85
Kansas	6.96	7.28	6.96	6.66	6.97	6.56	12.37	13.42	12.39
Kentucky	8.38	8.86	8.71	7.84	8.50	8.33	13.84	13.52	13.40
Louisiana	10.40	11.02	10.67	7.56	8.12	8.02	14.44	15.33	15.20
Maine	6.12	6.58	7.20	6.13	6.57	7.04	*9.47	8.47	9.87
Maryland	8.88	9.17	8.54	6.79	7.19	6.61	13.00	13.13	11.95
Massachusetts.	7.26	7.77	7.54	6.56	7.15	6.76	11.54	11.82	10.45
Michigan	7.94	8.28	8.36	6.55	7.00	6.98	14.24	14.43	13.74
Minnesota.	6.23	6.43	6.46	5.80	5.93	5.86	10.54	10.71	9.32
Mississippi	10.82	11.62	11.42	7.97	8.67	8.07	14.48	15.60	16.05
Missouri	7.74	8.12	8.18	6.79	7.18	7.10	13.27	13.90	14.07
Montana.	6.65	7.02	7.28	6.60	6.81	6.90	*	*15.58	*13.58
Nebraska	6.88	6.97	6.73	6.52	6.76	6.19	13.07	12.16	12.05
Nevada	7.44	8.11	8.28	7.19	7.78	7.59	13.40	13.98	13.32
New Hampshire	6.40	6.65	6.87	6.24	6.59	6.77	10.58	10.85	10.14
New Jersey	7.89	8.19	8.14	6.59	7.11	6.88	13.20	13.48	12.42
New Mexico	7.99	8.38	8.79	7.89	8.33	8.50	13.88	15.01	14.47
New York	7.76	8.11	7.88	6.48	6.82	6.50	12.02	12.78	12.08
North Carolina	8.90	9.07	8.92	7.49	7.73	7.39	13.83	14.33	13.74
North Dakota	6.28	6.49	6.26	6.13	6.37	6.08	*9.02	*9.43	8.41
Ohio	8.07	8.51	8.49	7.08	7.53	7.33	13.45	13.83	13.61
Oklahoma.	7.75	7.92	7.96	7.35	7.63	7.53	13.57	13.62	13.34
Oregon	5.65	6.09	6.31	5.44	6.02	5.99	10.32	11.16	9.47
Pennsylvania	7.93	8.20	8.15	6.78	7.06	6.98	13.79	13.67	12.96
Rhode Island	7.47	8.12	7.19	6.75	7.39	6.30	12.32	11.22	10.63
South Carolina	9.74	10.15	9.55	7.40	7.82	7.38	14.29	15.19	14.39
South Dakota.	6.58	6.71	6.31	6.37	6.62	6.00	*11.51	*7.27	8.06
Tennessee	9.20	9.35	9.09	7.95	8.26	7.86	14.23	14.51	14.19
Texas	7.54	8.07	8.25	6.81	7.43	7.23	12.82	13.91	13.16
Utah	6.48	6.68	7.00	6.28	6.45	6.68	13.09	12.05	9.48
Vermont	6.15	6.57	6.80	6.12	6.55	6.63	*	*	*9.01
Virginia	7.90	8.23	7.91	6.54	7.01	6.57	12.56	12.83	12.29
Washington.	5.75	6.13	6.43	5.43	5.63	5.89	10.34	10.63	9.87
West Virginia	8.60	9.16	9.36	8.39	9.03	9.21	13.81	13.15	13.58
Wisconsin.	6.58	6.93	7.20	5.83	6.18	6.27	13.25	13.59	14.04
Wyoming	8.35	8.71	8.79	8.12	8.74	8.45	*13.29	*	*10.55
American Samoa [3] . .	3.51	3.75	3.68	- - -	- - -	- - -	- - -	- - -	- - -
Guam [3].	7.88	8.81	8.65	*4.13	*4.01	*	*	*	*
Northern Marianas [3] . .	8.05	7.55	7.73	- - -	- - -	–	- - -	- - -	–
Puerto Rico [3]	11.14	11.92	10.63	- - -	- - -	10.83	- - -	- - -	14.07
Virgin Islands [3]	10.21	11.14	- - -	*8.37	*5.90	- - -	9.89	12.51	- - -

See footnotes at end of table.

Table 6 (page 2 of 3). Low birthweight live births, by race and Hispanic origin of mother, state, and territory: United States and U.S. dependent areas, 2000–2002, 2003–2005, and 2013–2015

Excel and PDF versions (with more data years and standard errors when available): http://www.cdc.gov/nchs/hus/contents2016.htm#006.

[Data are based on birth certificates]

State and territory	Hispanic or Latina[4]			American Indian or Alaska Native[5]			Asian or Pacific Islander[5]		
	2000–2002	2003–2005	2013–2015	2000–2002	2003–2005	2013–2015	2000–2002	2003–2005	2013–2015
	Percent of live births weighing less than 2,500 grams[1]								
United States[2]	6.48	6.79	7.12	7.11	7.39	7.55	7.54	7.89	8.26
Alabama.	6.95	6.92	6.96	9.68	10.53	8.51	7.38	8.02	8.96
Alaska	6.07	5.31	5.80	5.81	5.86	6.25	7.33	6.57	6.51
Arizona	6.56	6.69	6.79	6.85	7.11	7.01	7.95	7.92	8.31
Arkansas	5.79	6.54	6.45	8.11	8.86	6.77	7.73	6.74	9.09
California	5.66	6.10	6.40	6.21	6.49	7.12	7.15	7.42	7.57
Colorado	8.33	8.53	8.72	9.05	9.45	9.40	10.17	10.26	10.96
Connecticut.	8.25	8.49	8.18	10.06	7.45	11.11	8.07	7.83	8.08
Delaware	6.81	7.03	7.08	*	*	*	9.89	9.33	7.96
District of Columbia . .	8.04	7.46	7.37	*	*	*	*7.00	8.97	6.99
Florida.	6.61	6.98	7.27	7.11	7.38	6.75	8.35	8.73	8.86
Georgia	5.77	5.96	6.85	9.29	9.00	9.66	8.18	8.35	8.39
Hawaii	8.00	8.34	8.35	*4.99	*	*	8.45	8.84	9.03
Idaho.	6.95	6.67	7.01	6.15	8.31	7.26	7.38	6.67	7.16
Illinois	6.31	6.60	6.92	8.60	9.46	7.81	8.49	8.28	9.20
Indiana.	6.09	6.33	6.70	*7.74	*10.00	*9.41	7.41	7.87	7.68
Iowa	6.01	6.12	6.20	7.23	9.15	6.29	7.13	7.71	8.24
Kansas	5.93	6.09	6.02	6.20	7.09	5.27	6.69	7.34	8.16
Kentucky	7.73	6.85	6.38	*7.17	*8.54	*9.35	7.75	7.56	8.01
Louisiana	6.56	7.62	6.98	9.06	10.11	7.46	7.89	8.46	8.97
Maine	*6.03	*4.74	*7.23	*	*	*9.31	*5.46	8.69	9.32
Maryland	6.73	7.18	7.06	9.74	10.87	6.68	7.42	7.93	8.21
Massachusetts.	8.37	8.41	8.20	*7.11	*7.62	*7.16	7.57	7.63	8.14
Michigan	6.26	6.46	7.11	7.26	6.98	7.58	7.46	8.33	8.73
Minnesota.	6.02	5.70	6.34	7.10	6.87	8.40	7.28	7.43	7.48
Mississippi	6.61	6.42	6.64	7.30	6.24	*6.07	6.83	8.06	7.65
Missouri	6.18	6.33	6.89	8.67	7.63	8.54	7.34	7.61	7.84
Montana.	7.44	8.63	7.58	7.14	7.80	9.05	*5.95	*8.70	*9.93
Nebraska	6.30	6.20	6.46	7.27	6.78	6.82	8.05	7.61	8.03
Nevada	6.34	6.74	7.15	6.80	7.58	7.02	7.56	10.35	9.28
New Hampshire	4.84	6.55	6.78	*	*	*	5.95	7.75	7.79
New Jersey	7.15	7.27	7.50	11.09	9.83	10.52	7.57	8.10	8.96
New Mexico	8.13	8.45	8.91	6.88	7.32	7.87	7.67	8.60	9.50
New York	7.38	7.59	7.72	7.81	7.31	7.45	7.33	7.89	8.26
North Carolina	6.13	6.27	6.75	10.30	11.01	10.90	8.20	7.77	8.09
North Dakota	*8.10	*5.84	5.75	6.62	6.78	6.75	*	*8.39	6.62
Ohio	7.20	7.13	7.85	8.86	10.22	9.64	7.86	8.27	8.59
Oklahoma.	6.41	6.46	6.92	6.48	6.69	7.01	7.87	6.82	7.94
Oregon	5.54	5.43	6.41	7.23	7.34	6.85	6.78	7.00	7.84
Pennsylvania	8.97	9.00	8.75	9.15	10.95	9.92	7.48	7.99	8.70
Rhode Island	7.20	8.61	7.79	*10.32	13.66	*8.86	9.31	10.11	7.98
South Carolina	6.87	6.66	6.68	10.22	10.75	*7.38	8.02	8.13	8.62
South Dakota.	6.89	5.94	7.07	6.84	7.04	6.95	*11.39	*9.50	8.38
Tennessee	6.28	6.04	6.61	*7.11	*6.63	8.11	8.60	7.76	8.06
Texas	6.88	7.23	7.62	6.67	7.33	6.63	7.78	8.33	9.45
Utah	7.20	7.26	7.72	6.37	7.46	7.67	7.23	8.20	8.68
Vermont.	*	*	*8.98	*	*	*	*	*8.08	*9.57
Virginia	6.07	6.28	6.58	*10.73	*9.20	7.92	7.50	7.71	8.15
Washington.	5.31	5.93	6.11	7.08	7.31	7.48	6.37	6.90	7.85
West Virginia	*	*6.06	8.67	*	*	*	9.16	*9.51	*7.22
Wisconsin.	6.13	6.34	6.69	6.12	6.04	6.56	6.97	7.50	7.72
Wyoming	8.81	8.43	9.72	9.55	8.39	10.30	*12.04	*	*9.84
American Samoa[3] . . .	- - -	- - -	- - -	- - -	- - -	–	3.46	3.75	3.66
Guam[3].	*	*	*	*	–	*	7.78	9.33	9.16
Northern Marianas[3] . .	- - -	- - -	–	- - -	- - -	–	8.12	7.65	7.83
Puerto Rico[3]	- - -	- - -	10.59	- - -	- - -	*	- - -	- - -	*
Virgin Islands[3]	10.84	8.29	- - -	*12.50	–	- - -	*	*	- - -

See footnotes at end of table.

Table 6 (page 3 of 3). Low birthweight live births, by race and Hispanic origin of mother, state, and territory: United States and U.S. dependent areas, 2000–2002, 2003–2005, and 2013–2015

Excel and PDF versions (with more data years and standard errors when available): http://www.cdc.gov/nchs/hus/contents2016.htm#006.

[Data are based on birth certificates]

---

* Percentages preceded by an asterisk are based on fewer than 50 births. Percentages not shown are based on fewer than 20 births.
- - - Data not available.
− Quantity zero.
[1] Excludes live births with unknown birthweight.
[2] Excludes data for American Samoa, Guam, Northern Marianas, Puerto Rico, and Virgin Islands.
[3] Comparable data were not available for all time periods and racial and ethnicity groups. Therefore, only selected low birthweight percentages are presented for the territories.
[4] Persons of Hispanic origin may be of any race. See Appendix II, Hispanic origin.
[5] Includes persons of Hispanic and non-Hispanic origin.

NOTES: For information on low birthweight live births by state, see Table I-9 in Martin JA, Hamilton BE, Osterman MJK, Driscoll AK, Mathews TJ. Births: Final data for 2015. National vital statistics report, vol 66, no 1. Hyattsville, MD: NCHS. 2017. Available from: http://www.cdc.gov/nchs/data/nvsr/nvsr66/nvsr66_01.pdf. Starting with 2003 data, some states and territories reported multiple-race data. The multiple-race data for these areas were bridged to the single-race categories of the 1977 Office of Management and Budget standards, for comparability with other areas. See Appendix II, Race. Data for the territories are shown by race and ethnicity only if race-specific data are available for all years in the 3-year period. Data for additional years are available. See the Excel spreadsheet on the *Health, United States* website at: http://www.cdc.gov/nchs/hus.htm.

SOURCE: NCHS, National Vital Statistics System, public-use Birth File. Martin JA, Hamilton BE, Osterman MJK, Driscoll AK, Mathews TJ. Births: Final data for 2015. National vital statistics report, vol 66, no 1. Hyattsville, MD: NCHS. 2017. Available from: http://www.cdc.gov/nchs/data/nvsr/nvsr66/nvsr66_01.pdf. See Appendix I, National Vital Statistics System (NVSS).

Table 7. Legal abortions, legal abortion rates, and legal abortion ratios: United States and 47 continuous reporting areas, 2004–2013

Excel and PDF versions (with more data years and standard errors when available): http://www.cdc.gov/nchs/hus/contents2016.htm#007.

[Data are based on reporting by state health departments and by hospitals and other medical facilities]

Data provider	2004	2005	2006	2007	2008	2009	2010	2011	2012	2013
	Number of legal abortions reported, in thousands									
Centers for Disease Control and Prevention (CDC)[1]	839	820	852	828	826	789	766	730	699	664
Guttmacher Institute[2]	1,222	1,206	1,242	1,210	1,212	1,152	1,103	1,059	- - -	- - -
	CDC 47 continuous reporting areas[3]									
Number of legal abortions reported, in thousands	818	808	835	819	817	779	755	720	688	653
Number of legal abortions per 1,000 women aged 15–44.	15.9	15.7	16.2	15.8	15.8	15.0	14.6	13.9	13.2	12.5
Number of legal abortions per 1,000 live births	241	236	237	229	232	227	227	219	210	200

- - - Data not available.

[1] Overall trends presented in this table should be interpreted with caution because of the different numbers of reporting areas that provided data to CDC in different years. The following states did not report abortion data to CDC in the specified year: California (2004–2013), Louisiana (2005), Maryland (2007–2013), New Hampshire (2004–2013), and West Virginia (2004). For 2006, the number of legal abortions is greater than reported in the 2006 report because of numbers subsequently provided by Louisiana. For 2009, the number of legal abortions is greater than reported in the 2009 report because of numbers subsequently provided by Delaware.

[2] No surveys were conducted in 2006 or 2009. Data for those years were estimated by interpolation. See Appendix I, Guttmacher Institute Abortion Provider Census.

[3] Because overall trends in abortion data are affected by the number of reporting areas that provide data to CDC on an annual basis, CDC also presents estimates for the 47 reporting areas that provided data for the entire period from 2004 to 2013. The 47 continuous reporting areas include all states except California, Louisiana, Maryland, New Hampshire, and West Virginia. The District of Columbia and New York City are included in the 47 continuous reporting areas.

NOTES: Each year, CDC requests abortion data from the central health agencies of 52 reporting areas (the 50 states, the District of Columbia, and New York City). This information is provided voluntarily to CDC. See the annual Abortion Surveillance reports for more information on the characteristic-specific list of reporting areas. Available from: http://www.cdc.gov/reproductivehealth/Data_Stats/Abortion.htm. For methodological differences between CDC and the Guttmacher Institute Abortion Provider Census, see Appendix I, Abortion Surveillance System; Guttmacher Institute Abortion Provider Census. Some data were revised and differ from previous editions of *Health, United States*.

SOURCE: CDC, National Center for Chronic Disease Prevention and Health Promotion. CDC. Abortion surveillance–United States, 2013. MMWR 2016;65(SS12);1–44. Available from: http://www.cdc.gov/mmwr/volumes/65/ss/ss6512a1.htm. Guttmacher Institute Abortion Provider Survey. Perspect Sex Reprod Health 2014;46(1):3–14. Available from: http://www.guttmacher.org/pubs/journals/psrh.46e0414.pdf. See Appendix I, Abortion Surveillance System; Guttmacher Institute Abortion Provider Census.

Table 8 (page 1 of 6). Contraceptive use in the past month among women aged 15–44, by age, race and Hispanic origin, and method of contraception: United States, selected years 1982 through 2011–2015

Excel and PDF versions (with more data years and standard errors when available): http://www.cdc.gov/nchs/hus/contents2016.htm#008.

[Data are based on household interviews of samples of women of childbearing age]

Race and Hispanic origin and year [1]	Age, in years				
	15–44	15–19	20–24	25–34	35–44
	Number of women, in thousands				
All women: [2]					
1982	54,099	9,521	10,629	19,644	14,305
1995	60,201	8,961	9,041	20,758	21,440
2002	61,561	9,834	9,840	19,522	22,365
2006–2010	61,755	10,478	10,365	19,722	21,190
2011–2015	61,263	9,482	10,454	21,091	20,236
Not Hispanic or Latina:					
White only:					
1982	41,279	7,010	8,081	14,945	11,243
1995	42,154	5,865	6,020	14,471	15,798
2002	39,498	6,069	5,938	12,073	15,418
2006–2010	37,384	6,034	6,173	11,953	13,224
2011–2015	34,087	4,925	5,594	11,809	11,759
Black or African American only:					
1982	6,825	1,383	1,456	2,392	1,593
1995	8,060	1,334	1,305	2,780	2,641
2002	8,250	1,409	1,396	2,587	2,857
2006–2010	8,451	1,566	1,493	2,621	2,771
2011–2015	8,407	1,370	1,572	2,863	2,603
Hispanic or Latina: [3]					
1982	4,393	886	811	1,677	1,018
1995	6,702	1,150	1,163	2,450	1,940
2002	9,107	1,521	1,632	3,249	2,705
2006–2010	10,474	1,904	1,734	3,611	3,225
2011–2015	12,303	2,169	2,176	4,137	3,822
	Percent of women using contraception				
All women: [2]					
1982	55.7	24.2	55.8	66.7	61.6
1995	64.2	29.8	63.5	71.1	72.3
2002	61.9	31.5	60.7	68.6	69.9
2006–2010	62.2	30.5	58.3	67.3	74.9
2011–2015	61.6	33.2	62.7	66.1	69.6
Not Hispanic or Latina:					
White only:					
1982	57.3	23.6	58.7	67.8	63.5
1995	66.2	30.5	65.4	72.9	73.6
2002	64.6	35.0	66.3	69.9	71.4
2006–2010	65.6	35.1	62.7	69.7	77.2
2011–2015	65.5	40.4	65.8	68.7	72.7
Black or African American only:					
1982	51.6	29.8	52.3	63.5	52.0
1995	62.3	36.1	67.6	66.8	68.3
2002	57.6	32.9	50.8	67.9	63.8
2006–2010	54.2	25.5	50.0	60.9	66.2
2011–2015	56.5	28.4	59.0	63.1	62.4
Hispanic or Latina: [3]					
1982	50.6	*	*36.8	67.2	59.0
1995	59.0	26.1	50.6	69.2	70.8
2002	59.0	20.4	57.4	66.2	72.9
2006–2010	59.7	22.3	54.0	66.0	77.7
2011–2015	57.6	22.1	58.5	64.5	69.8

See footnotes at end of table.

Table 8 (page 2 of 6). Contraceptive use in the past month among women aged 15–44, by age, race and Hispanic origin, and method of contraception: United States, selected years 1982 through 2011–2015

Excel and PDF versions (with more data years and standard errors when available): http://www.cdc.gov/nchs/hus/contents2016.htm#008.

[Data are based on household interviews of samples of women of childbearing age]

Race and Hispanic origin and year [1]	Age, in years				
	15–44	15–19	20–24	25–34	35–44
	Number of women using contraception or not using contraception and sexually active, in thousands [4]				
All women: [2]					
1982	- - -	- - -	- - -	- - -	- - -
1995	41,796	3,341	6,272	15,687	16,495
2002	42,683	3,775	6,798	14,857	17,252
2006–2010	43,145	3,896	6,944	14,785	17,520
2011–2015	42,063	3,709	7,351	15,503	15,500
Not Hispanic or Latina:					
White only:					
1982	- - -	- - -	- - -	- - -	- - -
1995	29,994	2,202	4,276	11,194	12,322
2002	28,079	2,519	4,329	9,224	12,006
2006–2010	27,105	2,471	4,341	9,105	11,188
2011–2015	24,479	2,224	4,092	8,893	9,271
Black or African American only:					
1982	- - -	- - -	- - -	- - -	- - -
1995	5,579	598	967	2,039	1,975
2002	5,611	564	949	1,978	2,121
2006–2010	5,526	517	939	1,946	2,124
2011–2015	5,487	496	1,086	2,030	1,874
Hispanic or Latina: [3]					
1982	- - -	- - -	- - -	- - -	- - -
1995	4,330	409	685	1,794	1,442
2002	6,075	405	1,070	2,462	2,138
2006–2010	6,978	563	1,076	2,656	2,683
2011–2015	8,136	665	1,455	3,064	2,952
	Percent of women using contraception among women using contraception or not using contraception and sexually active [4]				
All women: [2]					
1982	- - -	- - -	- - -	- - -	- - -
1995	92.5	80.2	91.7	94.0	93.9
2002	89.3	82.0	87.9	90.2	90.7
2006–2010	89.0	82.0	87.0	89.8	90.6
2011–2015	89.7	84.9	89.1	89.9	90.9
Not Hispanic or Latina:					
White only:					
1982	- - -	- - -	- - -	- - -	- - -
1995	93.0	81.7	93.0	93.9	94.2
2002	90.9	84.4	90.9	91.5	91.7
2006–2010	90.5	85.7	89.1	91.6	91.2
2011–2015	91.2	89.4	90.0	91.3	92.2
Black or African American only:					
1982	- - -	- - -	- - -	- - -	- - -
1995	90.0	80.0	91.3	91.6	90.9
2002	84.7	82.2	74.8	88.9	86.0
2006–2010	82.8	77.3	79.4	82.1	86.3
2011–2015	86.5	78.5	85.4	89.0	86.6
Hispanic or Latina: [3]					
1982	- - -	- - -	- - -	- - -	- - -
1995	91.4	75.5	82.5	95.4	95.2
2002	88.4	76.4	87.5	87.4	92.3
2006–2010	89.6	75.5	87.0	89.7	93.4
2011–2015	87.1	72.0	87.5	87.1	90.4

See footnotes at end of table.

Table 8 (page 3 of 6). Contraceptive use in the past month among women aged 15–44, by age, race and Hispanic origin, and method of contraception: United States, selected years 1982 through 2011–2015

Excel and PDF versions (with more data years and standard errors when available): http://www.cdc.gov/nchs/hus/contents2016.htm#008.

[Data are based on household interviews of samples of women of childbearing age]

Method of contraception and year	Age, in years				
	15–44	15–19	20–24	25–34	35–44
Female sterilization	Percent of women using contraception				
1982	23.2	–	*4.5	22.1	43.5
1995	27.8	*	4.0	23.8	45.0
2002	27.0	–	3.6	21.6	45.8
2006–2010.	26.6	*	*2.6	22.9	44.0
2011–2015.	23.2	–	*1.9	20.1	41.3
Male sterilization					
1982	10.9	*	*3.6	10.1	19.9
1995	10.9	–	*	7.8	19.5
2002	10.2	–	*	7.2	18.2
2006–2010.	10.8	*	*	7.1	19.8
2011–2015.	8.2	–	*	3.9	17.9
Implant and other hormonal contraceptives[5]					
1982	. . .	. . .	. . .	. . .	. . .
1995	1.3	*	3.7	*1.3	*
2002	1.0	*	*	*1.7	*
2006–2010.	3.4	*4.7	6.4	4.4	*1.1
2011–2015.	4.7	*6.1	9.3	5.0	*1.9
Injectable[6]					
1982	. . .	. . .	. . .	. . .	. . .
1995	3.0	9.7	6.1	2.9	*0.8
2002	5.5	14.2	10.6	5.5	*1.9
2006–2010.	3.9	11.4	5.9	4.2	*1.3
2011–2015.	4.2	13.3	6.4	3.9	*1.5
Birth control pill[7]					
1982	28.0	63.9	55.1	25.7	*3.7
1995	27.0	43.8	52.1	33.4	8.7
2002	31.0	53.8	52.5	34.8	15.0
2006–2010.	28.4	53.6	47.3	30.5	14.3
2011–2015.	26.6	53.3	43.2	25.3	14.2
Intrauterine device					
1982	7.1	*	*4.2	9.7	6.9
1995	0.8	–	*	*0.8	1.1
2002	2.1	*	1.8	3.7	*1.3
2006–2010.	5.6	*	5.6	7.2	4.9
2011–2015.	11.5	*	11.3	15.2	9.9

See footnotes at end of table.

Table 8 (page 4 of 6). Contraceptive use in the past month among women aged 15–44, by age, race and Hispanic origin, and method of contraception: United States, selected years 1982 through 2011–2015

Excel and PDF versions (with more data years and standard errors when available): http://www.cdc.gov/nchs/hus/contents2016.htm#008.

[Data are based on household interviews of samples of women of childbearing age]

Method of contraception and year	Age, in years				
	15–44	15–19	20–24	25–34	35–44
Diaphragm	Percent of women using contraception				
1982	8.1	*6.0	10.2	10.3	4.0
1995	1.9	*	*	1.7	2.8
2002	*	–	*	*	*
2006–2010.	*	–	–	*	*
2011–2015.	*	–	*	*	*
Condom					
1982	12.0	20.8	10.7	11.4	11.3
1995	23.4	45.8	33.7	23.7	15.3
2002	23.8	44.6	36.0	23.1	15.6
2006–2010.	23.1	34.7	39.6	25.2	12.8
2011–2015.	22.2	34.0	32.9	23.9	12.8
Periodic abstinence-calendar rhythm					
1982	3.3	2.0	3.1	3.3	3.7
1995	3.3	*	*1.5	3.7	3.9
2002	2.0	*	*2.3	*1.7	*2.4
2006–2010.	1.7	*	*	2.0	2.1
2011–2015.	3.0	*	*3.4	3.2	2.8
Periodic abstinence-natural family planning					
1982	0.6	–	*	0.9	*
1995	*0.5	–	*	*0.7	*
2002	*0.4	–	–	*	*
2006–2010.	*	–	*	*	*
2011–2015.	*0.3	*	*	*	*
Withdrawal					
1982	2.0	2.9	3.0	1.8	1.3
1995	6.1	13.2	7.1	6.0	4.5
2002	8.8	15.0	11.9	10.7	4.7
2006–2010.	10.1	14.5	15.1	10.2	7.3
2011–2015.	14.0	17.2	20.2	16.1	8.4
Other methods[8]					
1982	4.9	2.6	5.4	4.8	5.3
1995	3.2	*	3.2	3.1	3.4
2002	1.7	*	*0.9	*1.5	*1.8
2006–2010.	0.6	*	*	*0.8	*
2011–2015.	1.1	*	*	*1.3	*

See footnotes at end of table.

Table 8 (page 5 of 6). Contraceptive use in the past month among women aged 15–44, by age, race and Hispanic origin, and method of contraception: United States, selected years 1982 through 2011–2015

Excel and PDF versions (with more data years and standard errors when available): http://www.cdc.gov/nchs/hus/contents2016.htm#008.

[Data are based on household interviews of samples of women of childbearing age]

Method of contraception and year	Not Hispanic or Latina [1]		Hispanic or Latina [3]
	White only	Black or African American only	
Female sterilization	Percent of women using contraception		
1982	22.0	30.0	23.0
1995	24.5	39.9	36.6
2002	23.9	39.2	33.8
2006–2010	23.6	37.3	31.7
2011–2015	20.7	30.9	28.2
Male sterilization			
1982	13.0	*1.5	*
1995	13.7	*1.8	*4.0
2002	12.9	*	4.7
2006–2010	14.2	*	5.8
2011–2015	11.2	*2.2	4.4
Implant and other hormonal contraceptives [5]			
1982	. . .	. . .	. . .
1995	*1.0	*2.4	*2.0
2002	*0.6	*	*2.6
2006–2010	3.0	4.7	3.3
2011–2015	4.3	5.2	5.3
Injectable [6]			
1982	. . .	. . .	. . .
1995	2.4	5.4	4.7
2002	4.3	9.4	7.8
2006–2010	2.5	8.9	6.0
2011–2015	2.8	10.0	5.0
Birth control pill [7]			
1982	26.4	37.9	30.2
1995	28.7	23.7	23.0
2002	34.9	23.1	22.0
2006–2010	33.1	18.7	20.2
2011–2015	30.9	19.5	18.3
Intrauterine device			
1982	5.8	9.3	19.2
1995	0.7	*	*
2002	1.7	*	5.3
2006–2010	5.6	5.0	6.8
2011–2015	11.4	8.8	14.3
Diaphragm			
1982	9.2	*3.2	*
1995	2.3	*	*
2002	*	*	–
2006–2010	*	*	*
2011–2015	–	–	*
Condom			
1982	13.1	6.3	*6.9
1995	22.5	24.9	21.2
2002	21.7	29.6	24.1
2006–2010	20.8	29.9	22.2
2011–2015	20.9	25.6	21.3
Periodic abstinence-calendar rhythm			
1982	3.2	2.9	3.9
1995	3.3	*1.7	3.2
2002	2.3	*	*
2006–2010	1.3	*	*2.7
2011–2015	2.9	*2.2	*2.1

See footnotes at end of table.

Table 8 (page 6 of 6). **Contraceptive use in the past month among women aged 15–44, by age, race and Hispanic origin, and method of contraception: United States, selected years 1982 through 2011–2015**

Excel and PDF versions (with more data years and standard errors when available): *http://www.cdc.gov/nchs/hus/contents2016.htm#008.*

[Data are based on household interviews of samples of women of childbearing age]

	Not Hispanic or Latina [1]		Hispanic or Latina [3]
Method of contraception and year	White only	Black or African American only	
Periodic abstinence-natural family planning	Percent of women using contraception		
1982	0.7	0.3	–
1995	0.7	*	*
2002	*	*	*
2006–2010	*	*	*
2011–2015	*	*	*
Withdrawal			
1982	2.1	1.3	2.6
1995	6.4	3.3	5.7
2002	9.5	4.8	6.3
2006–2010	10.3	7.1	10.4
2011–2015	13.8	12.4	13.9
Other methods [8]			
1982	4.6	7.3	5.0
1995	3.3	3.8	*2.2
2002	*1.7	*1.9	*1.2
2006–2010	0.6	*	*
2011–2015	*1.2	*	*

* Estimates are considered unreliable. Data preceded by an asterisk have a relative standard error (RSE) of 20%–30%. Data not shown have an RSE greater than 30% or based on fewer than 100 sample cases.

- - - Data not available.

– Quantity zero.

. . . Data not applicable.

[1] Starting with 1995 data, race-specific estimates are tabulated according to 1997 *Revisions to the Standards for the Classification of Federal Data on Race and Ethnicity* and are not strictly comparable with estimates for earlier years. Starting with 1995 data, race-specific estimates are for persons who reported only one racial group. Prior to data year 1995, data were tabulated according to the 1977 Standards. Estimates for single-race categories prior to 1995 included persons who reported one race or, if they reported more than one race, identified one race as best representing their race. See Appendix II, Race.

[2] Includes women of other or multiple race not shown separately.

[3] Persons of Hispanic origin may be of any race. See Appendix II, Hispanic origin.

[4] Includes women using contraception in the month of interview, or not using contraception in the month of interview but had sexual intercourse in the three months prior to interview.

[5] Data collected starting with the 1995 survey. Includes data about the contraceptive patch, with data collection starting in the 2002 survey, and the contraceptive ring, with data collection starting in the 2006–2010 survey.

[6] Data collected starting with the 1995 survey.

[7] In 2011–2015, includes the oral contraceptive pill only. In previous tables, includes the oral contraceptive pill and emergency contraception/morning-after pill.

[8] In 2011–2015, includes emergency contraception, female condom/vaginal pouch, foam, cervical cap, Today sponge, suppository or insert, jelly or cream (without diaphragm), and other method. In 2006–2010, includes the contraceptive ring, female condom/vaginal pouch, foam, cervical cap, Today brand sponge, suppository or insert, jelly or cream (without diaphragm), and other method. In 2002, includes female condom, foam, cervical cap, Today sponge, suppository or insert, jelly or cream (without diaphragm), or other method. In 1995, includes the female condom or vaginal pouch, foam, cervical cap, Today sponge, suppository or insert, jelly or cream, or other method. In 1988 (in spreadsheet version), includes foam, douche, Today sponge, suppository or insert, jelly or cream, or other method. In 1982, includes foam, douche, suppository or insert, or other method.

NOTES: Survey collects up to four methods of contraception used in the month of interview. See Appendix II, Contraception. Percents may not add to the total because more than one method could have been used in the month of interview. Standard errors for selected years are available in the spreadsheet version of this table. Available from: http://www.cdc.gov/nchs/hus.htm. Data for additional years are available. See the Excel spreadsheet on the *Health, United States* website at: http://www.cdc.gov/nchs/hus.htm.

SOURCE: NCHS, National Survey of Family Growth. See Appendix I, National Survey of Family Growth (NSFG).

Table 9. Breastfeeding among mothers aged 15–44, by year of baby's birth and selected characteristics of mother: United States, 1986–1988 through 2011–2013

Excel and PDF versions (with more data years and standard errors when available): http://www.cdc.gov/nchs/hus/contents2016.htm#009.

[Data are based on household interviews of samples of women of childbearing age]

Maternal characteristic	1986–1988	1989–1991	1992–1994	1995–1998	1999–2001	2002–2004	2005–2007	2008–2010	2011–2013
	Percent of babies breastfed								
Total	54.1	53.3	57.6	64.4	66.5	69.5	68.8	73.1	78.6
Age at baby's birth									
Under 20 years	28.4	34.7	41.0	49.5	47.3	60.0	50.7	64.5	68.6
20–24 years	48.2	44.3	50.0	55.9	59.3	61.4	64.3	64.0	72.3
25–29 years	58.2	56.4	57.4	68.1	63.5	71.1	70.6	75.0	79.8
30–44 years	68.6	66.0	70.2	72.8	80.0	77.1	76.2	80.4	82.9
Race and Hispanic origin[1]									
Not Hispanic or Latina:									
White only.	59.1	58.4	61.7	66.5	68.7	73.8	72.3	73.1	78.3
Black or African American only	22.3	22.4	26.1	47.9	45.3	42.3	46.2	52.7	60.1
Hispanic or Latina	55.6	57.0	63.8	71.2	76.0	76.6	73.7	77.4	84.8
Education[2]									
No high school diploma or GED	31.8	36.5	44.6	50.6	46.6	56.3	58.7	63.7	72.6
High school diploma or GED	47.4	45.5	51.1	55.9	61.6	61.2	55.4	64.9	71.0
Some college, no bachelor's degree . . .	62.2	61.4	64.3	70.1	75.6	68.1	72.7	71.7	77.8
Bachelor's degree or higher.	78.4	80.6	82.5	82.0	81.3	89.6	88.3	87.1	88.3
Geographic region[3]									
Northeast.	51.3	53.5	56.5	61.6	66.9	73.0	72.4	70.3	76.8
Midwest	52.3	49.6	51.7	61.7	61.9	66.0	66.2	68.2	74.6
South	44.6	43.6	48.6	58.1	60.9	62.2	62.6	69.2	74.9
West	71.4	69.5	77.3	78.1	78.9	83.3	79.0	84.6	89.0
	Percent of babies breastfed 3 months or more								
Total	34.6	31.8	33.6	45.8	48.4	50.6	46.6	50.2	56.6
Age at baby's birth									
Under 20 years	18.5	*10.5	*11.7	30.0	30.0	37.6	26.6	35.5	38.4
20–24 years	26.1	24.1	25.1	36.6	41.8	38.0	38.6	37.6	43.8
25–29 years	36.9	32.3	35.6	46.3	43.7	50.2	49.0	54.8	58.3
30–44 years	50.1	46.8	46.7	57.5	62.4	63.9	56.3	59.6	65.6
Race and Hispanic origin[1]									
Not Hispanic or Latina:									
White only.	37.7	35.2	36.6	47.8	49.7	54.5	49.5	48.4	57.8
Black or African American only	11.6	11.5	13.3	29.6	33.7	29.2	26.3	35.7	37.0
Hispanic or Latina	38.2	33.9	35.0	49.7	54.3	55.9	49.4	55.6	58.8
Education[2]									
No high school diploma or GED	21.8	17.6	25.2	33.9	37.0	39.9	41.3	42.8	50.8
High school diploma or GED	28.2	28.0	27.4	36.9	43.1	41.9	36.8	44.4	45.1
Some college, no bachelor's degree . . .	38.7	33.1	38.7	49.6	52.8	43.2	48.7	46.7	52.3
Bachelor's degree or higher.	55.0	56.1	59.3	64.5	64.1	75.9	65.8	63.7	73.9
Geographic region[3]									
Northeast.	29.9	37.2	36.4	48.2	48.8	59.9	51.5	46.9	57.7
Midwest	30.3	31.5	30.1	42.0	42.8	46.8	41.6	42.1	50.8
South	27.7	20.1	26.2	38.9	44.4	42.7	40.5	45.6	51.8
West	52.4	42.9	45.3	58.2	59.2	62.6	57.8	66.0	68.5

* Estimates are considered unreliable. Data preceded by an asterisk have a relative standard error of 20%–30%.

[1] Starting with 1995 data, race-specific estimates are tabulated according to 1997 *Revisions to the Standards for the Classification of Federal Data on Race and Ethnicity* and are not strictly comparable with estimates for earlier years. Starting with 1995 data, race-specific estimates are for persons who reported only one racial group. Prior to data year 1995, data were tabulated according to the 1977 Standards. Estimates for single race categories prior to 1995 included persons who reported one race or, if they reported more than one race, identified one race as best representing their race. See Appendix II, Race.

[2] Educational attainment is presented only for women aged 22–44. Education is as of date of interview. GED is General Educational Development high school equivalency diploma. See Appendix II, Education.

[3] See Appendix II, Geographic region.

NOTES: Data are based on single births to mothers aged 15–44 at interview, including those births that occurred when the mothers were younger than age 15. Data on breastfeeding for babies born in 1986–1994 are based on women interviewed for the 1995 National Survey of Family Growth (NSFG), also known as Cycle 5. Data for babies born in 1995–2001 are based on women interviewed for the 2002 NSFG, also known as Cycle 6. Data for babies born in 2002–2004 and 2005–2007 are based on women interviewed for the 2006–2010 NSFG, conducted after NSFG's transition from periodic to continuous interviewing. Data for babies born in 2008–2010 and 2011–2013 are based on women interviewed for the 2011–2015 NSFG. Data for babies born in 2008–2010 have been revised and differ from previous editions of *Health, United States*. Standard errors are available in the spreadsheet version of this table. Available from: http://www.cdc.gov/nchs/hus.htm.

SOURCE: NCHS, National Survey of Family Growth. See Appendix I, National Survey of Family Growth (NSFG).

Table 10 (page 1 of 2). Infant, neonatal, postneonatal, fetal, and perinatal mortality rates, by detailed race and Hispanic origin of mother: United States, selected years 1983–2014

Excel and PDF versions (with more data years and standard errors when available): http://www.cdc.gov/nchs/hus/contents2016.htm#010.

[Data are based on linked birth and death certificates for infants and fetal death records]

Maternal race and Hispanic origin	1983[1]	1985[1]	1990[1]	1995[2]	2000[2]	2005[2]	2010[2]	2013[2]	2014[2]
	Infant[3] deaths per 1,000 live births								
All mothers	10.9	10.4	8.9	7.6	6.9	6.9	6.1	6.0	5.8
White	9.3	8.9	7.3	6.3	5.7	5.7	5.2	5.1	4.9
Black or African American.	19.2	18.6	16.9	14.6	13.5	13.3	11.2	10.8	10.7
American Indian or Alaska Native	15.2	13.1	13.1	9.0	8.3	8.1	8.3	7.6	7.6
Asian or Pacific Islander[4]	8.3	7.8	6.6	5.3	4.9	4.9	4.3	4.1	3.9
Hispanic or Latina[5,6]	9.5	8.8	7.5	6.3	5.6	5.6	5.3	5.0	5.0
Mexican.	9.1	8.5	7.2	6.0	5.4	5.5	5.1	4.9	4.8
Puerto Rican	12.9	11.2	9.9	8.9	8.2	8.3	7.1	5.9	7.2
Cuban.	7.5	8.5	7.2	5.3	4.6	4.4	3.8	3.0	3.9
Central and South American	8.5	8.0	6.8	5.5	4.6	4.7	4.4	4.3	4.3
Other and unknown Hispanic or Latina. . . .	10.6	9.5	8.0	7.4	6.9	6.4	6.1	5.9	5.4
Not Hispanic or Latina:[6]									
White	9.2	8.6	7.2	6.3	5.7	5.8	5.2	5.1	4.9
Black or African American	19.1	18.3	16.9	14.7	13.6	13.6	11.5	11.1	10.9
	Neonatal[3] deaths per 1,000 live births								
All mothers	7.1	6.8	5.7	4.9	4.6	4.5	4.0	4.0	3.9
White	6.1	5.8	4.6	4.1	3.8	3.8	3.5	3.4	3.3
Black or African American.	12.5	12.3	11.1	9.6	9.1	8.9	7.3	7.3	7.3
American Indian or Alaska Native	7.5	6.1	6.1	4.0	4.4	4.0	4.3	4.1	4.1
Asian or Pacific Islander[4]	5.2	4.8	3.9	3.4	3.4	3.4	3.0	3.0	2.8
Hispanic or Latina[5,6]	6.2	5.7	4.8	4.1	3.8	3.9	3.6	3.6	3.5
Mexican.	5.9	5.4	4.5	3.9	3.6	3.8	3.5	3.5	3.5
Puerto Rican	8.7	7.6	6.9	6.1	5.8	5.9	4.8	4.2	5.0
Cuban.	*5.0	6.2	5.3	*3.6	*3.2	*3.1	*2.9	*2.3	2.6
Central and South American	5.8	5.6	4.4	3.7	3.3	3.2	3.0	3.1	3.1
Other and unknown Hispanic or Latina. . . .	6.4	5.6	5.0	4.8	4.6	4.3	4.0	4.0	3.7
Not Hispanic or Latina:[6]									
White	5.9	5.6	4.5	4.0	3.8	3.7	3.4	3.3	3.2
Black or African American	12.0	11.9	11.0	9.6	9.2	9.1	7.5	7.5	7.4
	Postneonatal[3] deaths per 1,000 live births								
All mothers	3.8	3.6	3.2	2.6	2.3	2.3	2.1	1.9	1.9
White	3.2	3.1	2.7	2.2	1.9	2.0	1.8	1.6	1.6
Black or African American.	6.7	6.3	5.9	5.0	4.3	4.3	3.9	3.5	3.4
American Indian or Alaska Native	7.7	7.0	7.0	5.1	3.9	4.0	4.0	3.5	3.5
Asian or Pacific Islander[4]	3.1	2.9	2.7	1.9	1.4	1.5	1.3	1.1	1.0
Hispanic or Latina[5,6]	3.3	3.2	2.7	2.1	1.8	1.8	1.7	1.5	1.5
Mexican.	3.2	3.2	2.7	2.1	1.8	1.7	1.6	1.4	1.4
Puerto Rican	4.2	3.5	3.0	2.8	2.4	2.4	2.3	1.7	2.2
Cuban.	*2.5	*2.3	*1.9	*1.7	*	*1.4	*	*	*1.3
Central and South American	2.6	2.4	2.4	1.9	1.4	1.5	1.4	1.2	1.1
Other and unknown Hispanic or Latina. . . .	4.2	3.9	3.0	2.6	2.3	2.1	2.1	1.9	1.7
Not Hispanic or Latina:[6]									
White	3.2	3.0	2.7	2.2	1.9	2.1	1.8	1.7	1.7
Black or African American	7.0	6.4	5.9	5.0	4.4	4.5	4.0	3.7	3.5

See footnotes at end of table.

Table 10 (page 2 of 2). Infant, neonatal, postneonatal, fetal, and perinatal mortality rates, by detailed race and Hispanic origin of mother: United States, selected years 1983–2014

Excel and PDF versions (with more data years and standard errors when available): http://www.cdc.gov/nchs/hus/contents2016.htm#010.

[Data are based on linked birth and death certificates for infants and fetal death records]

Maternal race and Hispanic origin	1983	1985	1990	1995	2000[7]	2005	2010	2013	2014
Fetal[8,9] deaths per 1,000 live births plus fetal deaths									
All mothers	- - -	- - -	- - -	7.0	6.6	6.2	6.0	6.0	6.0
Hispanic or Latina[5]	- - -	- - -	- - -	- - -	5.8	5.4	5.2	5.2	5.1
Not Hispanic or Latina:									
White	- - -	- - -	- - -	- - -	5.3	4.8	4.8	4.9	4.9
Black or African American	- - -	- - -	- - -	- - -	12.0	11.1	10.8	10.5	10.7
Late fetal[8,10] deaths per 1,000 live births plus late fetal deaths									
All mothers	- - -	- - -	- - -	3.6	3.3	3.0	3.0	3.0	2.8
Hispanic or Latina[5]	- - -	- - -	- - -	- - -	3.1	2.8	2.6	2.7	2.5
Not Hispanic or Latina:									
White	- - -	- - -	- - -	- - -	2.8	2.4	2.5	2.6	2.4
Black or African American	- - -	- - -	- - -	- - -	5.2	4.8	4.7	4.7	4.6
Perinatal[8,11] deaths per 1,000 live births plus late fetal deaths									
All mothers	- - -	- - -	- - -	7.6	7.0	6.6	6.2	6.2	6.0
Hispanic or Latina[5]	- - -	- - -	- - -	- - -	6.1	5.9	5.5	5.6	5.4
Not Hispanic or Latina:									
White	- - -	- - -	- - -	- - -	5.7	5.4	5.1	5.3	5.0
Black or African American	- - -	- - -	- - -	- - -	12.6	12.2	10.6	10.7	10.6

* Estimates are considered unreliable. Rates preceded by an asterisk are based on fewer than 50 deaths in the numerator. Rates not shown are based on fewer than 20 deaths in the numerator.

- - - Data not available.

[1] Rates based on unweighted birth cohort data.

[2] Rates based on a period file using weighted data. See Appendix I, National Vital Statistics System (NVSS), Linked Birth/Infant Death Data Set.

[3] Infant (under 1 year of age), neonatal (under 28 days), and postneonatal (28 days–11 months).

[4] Estimates are not available for Asian or Pacific Islander subgroups because not all states have adopted the 2003 revision of the U.S. Standard Certificate of Live Birth. See Appendix II, Race.

[5] Persons of Hispanic origin may be of any race.

[6] Prior to 1995, data are shown only for states with an Hispanic-origin item on their birth certificates. See Appendix II, Hispanic origin.

[7] Rates for 1999–2004 (shown in spreadsheet version) exclude data from Oklahoma, which did not report Hispanic origin on the fetal death report in those years.

[8] Starting with 2014 data, the obstetric estimate of gestation at delivery replaced the gestational age measure based on the date of the last normal menses, which was used for prior years. For more information on the impact of this change, see Appendix I, National Vital Statistic System (NVSS).

[9] Number of fetal deaths of 20 weeks or more gestation per 1,000 live births plus fetal deaths.

[10] Number of fetal deaths of 28 weeks or more gestation (late fetal deaths) per 1,000 live births plus late fetal deaths.

[11] Number of late fetal deaths plus infant deaths within 7 days of birth per 1,000 live births plus late fetal deaths.

NOTES: The race groups, white, black, American Indian or Alaska Native, and Asian or Pacific Islander include persons of Hispanic and non-Hispanic origin. Starting with 2003 data, some states reported multiple-race data. The multiple-race data for these states were bridged to the single-race categories of the 1977 Office of Management and Budget standards, for comparability with other states. See Appendix II, Race. National linked files do not exist for 1992–1994. Data for additional years are available. See the Excel spreadsheet on the *Health, United States* website at: http://www.cdc.gov/nchs/hus.htm.

SOURCE: NCHS, National Vital Statistics System, public-use Linked Birth/Infant Death Data Set, public-use Fetal Death File, public-use Birth File. National Center for Health Statistics. Mathews TJ, Driscoll AK. Trends in infant mortality in the United States, 2005–2014. NCHS data brief, no 279. Hyattsville, MD: NCHS; 2017. Available from: https://www.cdc.gov/nchs/products/databriefs.htm and National Center for Health Statistics. 2014 fetal death data set and user's guide. Hyattsville, MD: 2016. Available from: https://www.cdc.gov/nchs/data_access/vitalstatsonline.htm. See Appendix I, National Vital Statistics System (NVSS).

Table 11. Infant mortality rates, by race: United States, selected years 1950–2015

Excel and PDF versions (with more data years and standard errors when available): http://www.cdc.gov/nchs/hus/contents2016.htm#011.

[Data are based on death certificates and birth certificates]

Race and year	Infant [1]	Neonatal [1] Under 28 days	Neonatal [1] Under 7 days	Postneonatal [1]
All races			Deaths per 1,000 live births	
1950 [2]	29.2	20.5	17.8	8.7
1960 [2]	26.0	18.7	16.7	7.3
1970	20.0	15.1	13.6	4.9
1980	12.6	8.5	7.1	4.1
1990	9.2	5.8	4.8	3.4
1995	7.6	4.9	4.0	2.7
2000	6.9	4.6	3.7	2.3
2004	6.8	4.5	3.6	2.3
2005	6.9	4.5	3.6	2.3
2010	6.1	4.0	3.2	2.1
2012	6.0	4.0	3.3	2.0
2013	6.0	4.0	3.3	1.9
2014	5.8	3.9	3.2	1.9
2015	5.9	3.9	3.2	2.0
Race of child: [3] White				
1950 [2]	26.8	19.4	17.1	7.4
1960 [2]	22.9	17.2	15.6	5.7
1970	17.8	13.8	12.5	4.0
1980	11.0	7.5	6.2	3.5
Race of mother: [4] White				
1980	10.9	7.4	6.1	3.5
1990	7.6	4.8	3.9	2.8
1995	6.3	4.1	3.3	2.2
2000	5.7	3.8	3.0	1.9
2004	5.7	3.8	3.0	1.9
2005	5.7	3.8	3.0	1.9
2010	5.2	3.5	2.7	1.7
2012	5.1	3.5	2.8	1.6
2013	5.1	3.5	2.8	1.6
2014	4.9	3.4	2.7	1.6
2015	4.9	3.3	2.7	1.6
Race of child: [3] Black or African American				
1950 [2]	43.9	27.8	23.0	16.1
1960 [2]	44.3	27.8	23.7	16.5
1970	32.6	22.8	20.3	9.9
1980	21.4	14.1	11.9	7.3
Race of mother: [4] Black or African American				
1980	22.2	14.6	12.3	7.6
1990	18.0	11.6	9.7	6.4
1995	15.1	9.8	8.2	5.3
2000	14.1	9.4	7.6	4.7
2004	13.8	9.1	7.3	4.7
2005	13.7	9.1	7.3	4.7
2010	11.6	7.5	6.0	4.1
2012	11.2	7.3	6.0	3.9
2013	11.2	7.4	6.1	3.8
2014	11.0	7.3	6.0	3.7
2015	11.4	7.4	6.0	4.0

[1] Infant (under 1 year of age), neonatal (under 28 days), early neonatal (under 7 days), and postneonatal (28 days–11 months).
[2] Includes births and deaths of persons who were not residents of the 50 states and the District of Columbia.
[3] Infant deaths and live births are tabulated by race of infant. See Appendix II, Race.
[4] Infant deaths are tabulated by race of infant; live births are tabulated by race of mother. See Appendix II, Race.

NOTES: Infant mortality rates in this table are based on infant deaths from the mortality file (numerator) and live births from the natality file (denominator). Inconsistencies in reporting race for the same infant between the birth and death certificate can result in underestimated infant mortality rates for races other than white or black. Infant mortality rates for additional population groups are available from the Linked Birth/Infant Death Data Set and are presented in Table 10. Data for additional years are available. See the Excel spreadsheet on the *Health, United States* website at: http://www.cdc.gov/nchs/hus.htm.

SOURCE: NCHS, National Vital Statistics System, public-use Mortality File, public-use Birth File; Murphy SL, Kochanek KD, Xu JQ, Curtin SC. Deaths: Final data for 2015. National vital statistics reports. Hyattsville, MD: NCHS; 2017. Available from: http://www.cdc.gov/nchs/products/nvsr.htm. See Appendix I, National Vital Statistics System (NVSS).

Table 12 (page 1 of 3). **Infant mortality rates, by race and Hispanic origin of mother, state, and territory: United States and U.S. dependent areas, average annual 1989–1991, 2003–2005, and 2012–2014**

Excel and PDF versions (with more data years and standard errors when available): http://www.cdc.gov/nchs/hus/contents2016.htm#012.

[Data are based on linked birth and death certificates for infants]

| | All races | | | Not Hispanic or Latina | | | | | |
| | | | | White | | | Black or African American | | |
State and territory	1989–1991[1]	2003–2005[2]	2012–2014[2]	1989–1991[1]	2003–2005[2]	2012–2014[2]	1989–1991[1]	2003–2005[2]	2012–2014[2]
				Infant[3] deaths per 1,000 live births					
United States[4].	9.0	6.8	5.9	7.3	5.7	5.0	17.2	13.6	11.1
Alabama.	11.4	9.0	8.7	8.6	6.8	6.9	16.8	13.6	13.3
Alaska	9.2	6.5	5.8	7.2	5.3	4.2	*	*	*
Arizona	8.8	6.7	5.7	8.2	6.0	4.8	17.3	11.2	11.4
Arkansas	9.8	8.3	7.5	8.1	7.2	6.9	15.2	13.6	10.3
California	7.6	5.2	4.5	6.9	4.6	3.7	15.4	11.4	9.5
Colorado	8.7	6.3	4.8	8.0	5.2	4.1	16.7	16.3	10.0
Connecticut.	7.9	5.5	5.0	5.9	3.9	3.6	17.0	12.7	9.7
Delaware	11.2	9.0	6.9	8.2	6.5	4.7	20.1	16.8	11.9
District of Columbia . .	20.3	12.2	7.3	*8.2	*3.4	*2.6	23.9	17.2	10.9
Florida	9.4	7.2	6.1	7.2	5.8	5.1	16.2	12.9	10.5
Georgia	11.9	8.4	6.9	8.4	6.1	5.0	17.9	13.3	10.4
Hawaii	7.0	6.7	5.2	5.5	3.9	4.3	*13.6	*15.5	*12.6
Idaho.	8.9	6.1	5.5	8.9	6.1	5.2	*	*	*
Illinois	10.7	7.5	6.4	7.6	5.9	4.9	20.5	15.3	12.6
Indiana.	9.4	7.9	7.0	8.4	7.1	6.2	17.3	15.1	13.3
Iowa	8.2	5.4	4.8	7.8	5.1	4.5	15.8	*11.0	9.6
Kansas	8.5	7.1	6.3	7.8	6.7	5.7	15.4	14.3	12.9
Kentucky	8.7	6.8	6.9	8.1	6.4	6.5	14.4	10.9	11.2
Louisiana[5]	10.2	9.8	8.1	7.5	7.1	6.0	14.3	13.9	11.7
Maine	6.6	5.9	6.9	6.2	5.8	6.7	*	*	*
Maryland	9.1	8.0	6.5	6.3	5.2	4.2	15.0	13.7	10.6
Massachusetts	7.0	4.9	4.2	5.9	4.0	3.5	14.2	10.0	7.6
Michigan	10.5	8.0	6.8	7.7	6.2	5.3	20.7	16.4	12.6
Minnesota.	7.3	4.8	5.0	6.4	4.3	4.2	18.5	8.9	9.3
Mississippi	11.5	10.7	8.9	7.9	7.0	6.6	15.2	15.6	11.8
Missouri	9.7	7.6	6.4	8.0	6.6	5.5	18.0	13.8	11.4
Montana.	9.0	6.3	5.8	8.0	5.7	5.0	*	*	*
Nebraska	8.1	5.9	5.0	7.2	5.1	4.4	18.3	14.0	*8.7
Nevada	8.6	5.9	5.3	7.8	5.6	4.9	16.9	12.2	9.6
New Hampshire[5]. . . .	7.1	5.0	4.7	7.2	4.8	4.4	*	*	*
New Jersey	8.4	5.4	4.4	6.1	3.7	3.1	17.8	11.9	9.6
New Mexico	8.4	6.1	5.8	8.1	6.9	5.5	*17.2	*	*
New York	9.5	6.0	4.9	6.3	4.6	3.9	18.4	11.8	8.7
North Carolina	10.7	8.6	7.2	8.0	6.3	5.4	16.9	15.8	12.6
North Dakota	8.0	6.4	5.8	7.3	6.0	5.1	*	*	*
Ohio	9.0	7.8	7.2	7.7	6.4	6.0	16.2	15.6	13.0
Oklahoma[5]	8.0	7.9	7.5	7.3	7.5	6.9	12.7	13.0	12.7
Oregon	8.0	5.7	5.1	7.4	5.5	4.9	21.3	*8.6	*7.6
Pennsylvania	9.2	7.3	6.5	7.2	5.8	5.1	19.1	13.6	12.3
Rhode Island	8.7	6.2	5.8	7.5	4.5	4.3	*13.6	*10.8	*10.2
South Carolina	11.8	9.0	6.9	8.4	6.4	5.2	17.2	14.2	10.9
South Dakota.	9.5	7.2	6.8	7.5	6.2	5.5	*	*	*
Tennessee	10.2	8.9	7.0	7.8	7.0	5.9	18.2	16.3	11.7
Texas	7.9	6.5	5.8	6.9	5.9	5.1	14.1	12.4	10.9
Utah	7.0	4.9	5.0	6.8	4.5	4.5	*	*	*13.5
Vermont	6.6	5.4	4.4	6.3	5.3	4.4	*	*	*
Virginia	9.9	7.5	6.1	7.4	6.0	4.7	18.0	13.7	11.2
Washington.	8.0	5.4	4.8	7.4	5.0	4.4	15.1	9.0	8.5
West Virginia	9.1	7.7	7.2	8.8	7.5	7.2	*15.7	*12.0	*10.1
Wisconsin.	8.4	6.3	5.9	7.4	5.1	4.9	17.0	16.4	13.8
Wyoming	8.4	6.9	5.6	8.0	6.8	5.4	*	*	*
American Samoa[6] . . .	- - -	- - -	- - -	- - -	- - -	- - -	- - -	- - -	- - -
Guam[6].	- - -	11.1	9.7	- - -	*	*	- - -	*	*
Northern Marianas[6] . .	- - -	- - -	- - -	- - -	- - -	- - -	- - -	- - -	- - -
Puerto Rico[6]	- - -	8.9	7.8	- - -	- - -	7.1	- - -	- - -	- - -
Virgin Islands[6]	- - -	7.5	- - -	- - -	*	- - -	- - -	*	- - -

See footnotes at end of table.

Table 12 (page 2 of 3). Infant mortality rates, by race and Hispanic origin of mother, state, and territory: United States and U.S. dependent areas, average annual 1989–1991, 2003–2005, and 2012–2014

Excel and PDF versions (with more data years and standard errors when available): http://www.cdc.gov/nchs/hus/contents2016.htm#012.

[Data are based on linked birth and death certificates for infants]

State and territory	Hispanic or Latina[7]			American Indian or Alaska Native[8]			Asian or Pacific Islander[8]		
	1989–1991[1]	2003–2005[2]	2012–2014[2]	1989–1991[1]	2003–2005[2]	2012–2014[2]	1989–1991[1]	2003–2005[2]	2012–2014[2]
	Infant[3] deaths per 1,000 live births								
United States[4]	7.5	5.6	5.0	12.6	8.4	7.9	6.6	4.8	4.0
Alabama	*	7.7	5.9	*	*	*	*	*	*
Alaska	*	*	*	15.7	9.2	10.7	*	*	*
Arizona	8.0	6.7	5.6	11.4	8.3	8.2	*8.5	6.7	5.1
Arkansas	*	6.0	6.1	*	*	*	*	*	*7.6
California	7.0	5.0	4.5	11.0	6.2	5.4	6.4	4.2	3.5
Colorado	8.5	7.0	5.3	*16.5	*	*	*7.8	*5.7	*4.6
Connecticut	7.9	7.4	6.4	*	*	*	*	*	*
Delaware	*	*6.1	*4.9	*	*	*	*	*	*
District of Columbia . .	*8.8	*7.2	*5.4	*	*	*	*	*	*
Florida	7.1	5.2	4.4	*	*	*	*6.2	5.9	3.3
Georgia	9.0	5.5	5.2	*	*	*	*8.2	5.8	3.8
Hawaii	10.7	7.9	*4.5	*	*	*	7.1	7.2	5.3
Idaho	*7.2	6.2	6.3	*	*	*	*	*	*
Illinois	9.2	6.2	5.2	*	*	*	6.0	4.5	4.7
Indiana	*7.2	6.8	5.7	*	*	*	*	*	*5.8
Iowa	*11.9	*5.2	*3.8	*	*	*	*	*	*6.2
Kansas	8.7	6.2	6.6	*	*	*	*	*5.6	*
Kentucky	*	7.6	6.6	*	*	*	*	*	*
Louisiana[9]	- - -	*5.7	4.5	*	*	*	*	*	*5.8
Maine	*	*	*	*	*	*	*	*	*
Maryland	7.2	5.8	5.3	*	*	*	7.5	4.3	4.3
Massachusetts	8.3	6.5	5.1	*	*	*	5.7	3.8	3.1
Michigan	7.9	7.6	6.8	*10.7	*	*	*6.1	5.1	4.9
Minnesota	*8.4	4.3	5.4	17.3	*8.6	*10.6	*5.1	3.8	5.1
Mississippi	*	*	*7.9	*	*	*	*	*	*
Missouri	*9.1	6.6	6.3	*	*	*	*9.1	*6.1	*3.5
Montana	*	*	*	16.7	*9.3	*10.7	*	*	*
Nebraska	*8.8	5.7	5.5	*18.2	*	*	*	*	*
Nevada	7.0	4.5	4.4	*	*	*	*	*5.8	*4.3
New Hampshire[9]	- - -			*	*	*	*	*	*
New Jersey	7.5	5.2	4.4	*	*	*	5.6	5.0	3.2
New Mexico	7.8	5.3	5.9	9.8	7.6	5.0	*	*	*
New York	9.4	5.5	4.9	*15.2	*	*	6.4	3.9	3.3
North Carolina	*7.5	6.6	5.5	12.2	10.2	10.5	*6.3	5.9	4.0
North Dakota	*	*	*	*13.8	*8.6	*12.0	*	*	*
Ohio	8.0	6.5	6.7	*	*	*	*4.8	*4.5	4.5
Oklahoma[9]	- - -	6.0	6.3	7.8	7.9	7.1	*	*	*7.8
Oregon	8.5	5.5	5.2	*15.7	*11.0	*10.1	*8.4	*5.8	*4.1
Pennsylvania	10.9	7.6	6.9	*	*	*	7.8	4.9	3.8
Rhode Island	*7.2	7.4	*6.4	*	*	*	*	*	*
South Carolina	*	7.3	4.6	*	*	*	*	*	*
South Dakota	*	*	*	19.9	12.7	11.7	*	*	*
Tennessee	*	6.5	4.7	*	*	*	*	*8.1	*5.3
Texas	7.0	5.6	5.3	*	*	*	6.8	4.3	4.0
Utah	*7.0	5.8	5.4	*10.0	*	*	*10.7	*7.7	*6.9
Vermont	*	*	*	*	*	*	*	*	*
Virginia	7.6	5.4	5.0	*	*	*	6.0	4.5	3.9
Washington	7.6	4.9	4.5	19.6	9.5	8.8	6.2	4.8	4.1
West Virginia	*	*	*	*	*	*	*	*	*
Wisconsin	*7.3	6.1	4.8	*11.9	*8.2	*6.7	*6.7	*6.6	5.9
Wyoming	*	*	*	*	*	*	*	*	*
American Samoa[6] . . .	- - -	- - -	- - -	- - -	- - -	- - -	- - -	- - -	- - -
Guam[6]	- - -	*	*	- - -	*	*	- - -	11.5	10.2
Northern Marianas[6] . .	- - -	- - -	- - -	- - -	- - -	- - -	- - -	- - -	- - -
Puerto Rico[6]	- - -	- - -	7.8	- - -	- - -	*	- - -	- - -	- - -
Virgin Islands[6]	- - -	*	- - -	- - -	*	- - -	- - -	*	*

See footnotes at end of table.

Table 12 (page 3 of 3). Infant mortality rates, by race and Hispanic origin of mother, state, and territory: United States and U.S. dependent areas, average annual 1989–1991, 2003–2005, and 2012–2014

Excel and PDF versions (with more data years and standard errors when available): *http://www.cdc.gov/nchs/hus/contents2016.htm#012.*

[Data are based on linked birth and death certificates for infants]

---

* Estimates are considered unreliable. Rates preceded by an asterisk are based on fewer than 50 deaths in the numerator. Rates not shown are based on fewer than 20 deaths in the numerator.

- - - Data not available.

[1] Rates based on unweighted birth cohort data.

[2] Rates based on period file using weighted data. See Appendix I, National Vital Statistics System (NVSS), Linked Birth/Infant Death Data Set.

[3] Under 1 year of age.

[4] Excludes data for American Samoa, Guam, Northern Marianas, Puerto Rico, and Virgin Islands.

[5] Rates for white and black are substituted for non-Hispanic white and non-Hispanic black for Louisiana for 1989, Oklahoma for 1989–1990, and New Hampshire for 1989–1991.

[6] Comparable data were not available for all time periods and for all racial and ethnicity groups. Therefore, only selected rates are presented for the territories. Linked birth/infant death data are not available for American Samoa and Northern Marianas.

[7] Persons of Hispanic origin may be of any race. See Appendix II, Hispanic origin.

[8] Includes persons of Hispanic origin.

[9] Rates for Hispanic origin exclude data from states not reporting Hispanic origin on the birth certificate for 1 or more years in a 3-year period.

NOTES: Starting with 2003 data, some states reported multiple-race data. The multiple-race data for these states were bridged to the single-race categories of the 1977 Office of Management and Budget standards, for comparability with other states. See Appendix II, Race. National linked files do not exist for 1992–1994.

SOURCE: NCHS, National Vital Statistics System, public-use and nonpublic-use Linked Birth/Infant Death Data Set. National Center for Health Statistics. Mathews TJ, Driscoll AK. Trends in infant mortality in the United States, 2005-2014. NCHS data brief, no 279. Hyattsville, MD: NCHS; 2017. Available from: https://www.cdc.gov/nchs/products/databriefs.htm. See Appendix I, National Vital Statistics System (NVSS).

Table 13. Infant mortality rates and international rankings: Organisation for Economic Co-operation and Development (OECD) countries, selected years 1960–2013

Excel and PDF versions (with more data years and standard errors when available): http://www.cdc.gov/nchs/hus/contents2016.htm#013.

[Data are based on reporting by OECD countries]

Country[2]	1960	1970	1980	1990	2000	2010	2012	2013	International rankings[1] 1960	International rankings[1] 2013
	Infant[3] deaths per 1,000 live births									
Australia	20.2	17.9	10.7	8.2	5.2	4.1	3.3	3.6	5	16
Austria	37.5	25.9	14.3	7.8	4.8	3.9	3.2	3.1	19	10
Belgium	31.4	21.1	12.1	8.0	4.8	3.6	3.8	3.5	17	13
Canada	27.3	18.8	10.4	6.8	5.3	5.0	4.8	- - -	12	- - -
Chile	120.3	79.3	33.0	16.0	8.9	7.4	7.4	7.0	27	25
Czech Republic[4]	20.0	20.2	16.9	10.8	4.1	2.7	2.6	2.5	4	4
Denmark	21.5	14.2	8.4	7.5	5.3	3.4	3.4	3.5	8	13
Finland	21.0	13.2	7.6	5.6	3.8	2.3	2.4	1.8	6	1
France	27.7	18.2	10.0	7.3	4.5	3.6	3.5	- - -	13	- - -
Germany[5]	35.0	22.5	12.4	7.0	4.4	3.4	3.3	3.3	18	12
Greece	40.1	29.6	17.9	9.7	5.9	3.8	2.9	3.7	20	17
Hungary	47.6	35.9	23.2	14.8	9.2	5.3	4.9	5.0	23	22
Ireland	29.3	19.5	11.1	8.2	6.2	3.6	3.5	3.5	15	13
Israel[6]	- - -	24.2	15.6	9.9	5.5	3.7	3.6	3.1	- - -	10
Italy	43.9	29.6	14.6	8.1	4.3	3.0	2.9	2.9	22	7
Japan	30.7	13.1	7.5	4.6	3.2	2.3	2.2	2.1	16	2
Korea	- - -	45.0	- - -	- - -	- - -	3.2	2.9	3.0	- - -	9
Mexico	92.3	- - -	52.6	32.5	20.8	14.1	13.3	13.0	26	27
Netherlands	16.5	12.7	8.6	7.1	5.1	3.8	3.7	3.8	2	18
New Zealand	22.6	16.7	13.0	8.4	6.3	5.5	4.7	- - -	10	- - -
Norway	16.0	11.3	8.1	6.9	3.8	2.8	2.5	2.4	1	3
Poland	56.1	36.4	25.4	19.4	8.1	5.0	4.6	4.6	24	21
Portugal	77.5	55.5	24.3	10.9	5.5	2.5	3.4	2.9	25	7
Slovak Republic[4]	28.6	25.7	20.9	12.0	8.6	5.7	5.8	5.5	14	23
Spain	43.7	28.1	†12.3	7.6	4.4	3.2	3.1	2.7	21	5
Sweden	16.6	11.0	6.9	6.0	3.4	2.5	2.6	2.7	3	5
Switzerland	21.1	15.1	9.1	6.8	4.9	3.8	3.6	3.9	7	19
Turkey	- - -	- - -	- - -	- - -	28.4	12.0	11.6	10.8	- - -	26
United Kingdom	22.5	18.5	12.1	7.9	5.6	4.2	4.0	3.9	9	19
United States	26.0	20.0	12.6	9.2	6.9	6.1	6.0	6.0	11	24

- - - Data not available.

† Break in series. See OECD website for additional information. Available from: http://www.oecd.org/.

[1] Rankings are from lowest to highest infant mortality rates (IMR). Countries with the same IMR receive the same rank. The country with the next highest IMR is assigned the rank it would have received had the lower-ranked countries not been tied, i.e., skip a rank. The latest year's international rankings are based on 2013 data because that is the most current data year for which most countries have reported their final data to OECD. Countries without an estimate in the OECD database are omitted from ranking. Relative rankings for individual countries may be affected if not all countries have reported data to OECD.

[2] Refers to countries, territories, cities, or geographic areas with at least 2.5 million population in 2000 (United Nations, Department of Economic and Social Affairs, Population Division. World Urbanization Prospects: The 2014 Revision, Volume I: Comprehensive Tables. ST/ESA/SER.A/379. 2015. Available from: https://esa.un.org/unpd/wpp/Publications/Files/WPP2015_Volume-I_Comprehensive-Tables.pdf) and with complete counts of live births and infant deaths according to the United Nations Demographic Yearbook.

[3] The infant mortality rate is defined as the number of deaths of children under one year of age, expressed per 1,000 live births. Some of the international variation in infant mortality rates is due to variations among countries in registering practices for premature infants. See OECD website for additional information. Available at: http://www.oecd.org/.

[4] In 1993, Czechoslovakia was divided into two nations, the Czech Republic and Slovakia. Data for years prior to 1993 are from the Czech and Slovak regions of Czechoslovakia.

[5] Until 1990, estimates refer to the Federal Republic of Germany; from 1995 onward data refer to Germany after reunification.

[6] Statistical data for Israel are supplied by, and under the responsibility of, the relevant Israeli authorities. The use of such data by the OECD is without prejudice to the status of the Golan Heights, East Jerusalem, and Israeli settlements in the West Bank under the terms of international law.

NOTE: Some rates for selected countries and selected years were revised and differ from previous editions of *Health, United States*.

SOURCE: Organisation for Economic Co-operation and Development (OECD) Health Data 2016, incorporating revisions to the annual update, accessed on February 2, 2017. Available from: http://www.oecd.org/. See Appendix I, Organisation for Economic Co-operation and Development (OECD) Health Data.

Table 14 (page 1 of 2). Life expectancy at birth and at age 65, by sex: Organisation for Economic Co-operation and Development (OECD) countries, selected years 1980–2014

Excel and PDF versions (with more data years and standard errors when available): http://www.cdc.gov/nchs/hus/contents2016.htm#014.

[Data are based on reporting by OECD countries]

Country	Male					Female				
	1980	1990	2000	2013	2014	1980	1990	2000	2013	2014
At birth	Life expectancy, in years									
Australia	71.0	73.9	76.6	80.1	80.3	78.1	80.1	82.0	84.3	84.4
Austria	69.0	72.3	75.2	78.6	79.2	76.1	79.0	81.2	83.8	84.0
Belgium.	69.9	72.7	74.6	78.1	78.8	76.7	79.5	81.0	83.2	83.9
Canada.	71.7	74.4	76.3	- - -	- - -	78.9	80.8	81.7	- - -	- - -
Chile	- - -	69.4	73.7	†76.3	†76.4	- - -	76.5	80.0	†81.4	†81.6
Czech Republic[1]	66.9	67.6	71.6	75.2	75.8	74.0	75.5	78.5	81.3	82.0
Denmark	71.2	72.0	74.5	78.3	78.7	77.3	77.8	79.2	82.4	82.8
Estonia	64.2	64.7	65.6	72.8	72.4	74.3	74.9	76.4	81.7	81.9
Finland	69.2	71.0	74.2	78.0	78.4	78.0	79.0	81.2	84.1	84.1
France	70.2	72.8	75.3	79.0	††79.5	78.4	80.9	83.0	85.6	††86.0
Germany[2]	69.6	72.0	75.1	78.6	††78.7	76.2	78.5	81.2	83.2	††83.6
Greece	73.0	74.7	75.9	78.7	78.9	77.5	79.5	81.3	84.0	84.1
Hungary	65.5	65.2	67.5	72.2	72.3	72.8	73.8	76.2	79.1	79.4
Iceland	73.5	75.5	77.8	80.5	81.3	80.4	80.7	81.6	83.7	84.5
Ireland	70.1	72.1	74.0	†79.0	†79.3	75.6	77.7	79.2	†83.1	†83.5
Israel[3].	72.1	74.9	76.7	80.3	80.3	75.7	78.4	80.9	83.9	84.1
Italy	70.6	73.8	76.9	80.3	80.7	77.4	80.3	82.8	85.2	85.6
Japan.	73.4	75.9	77.7	80.2	80.5	78.8	81.9	84.6	86.6	86.8
Korea.	61.8	67.3	72.3	78.5	79.0	70.0	75.5	79.6	85.1	85.5
Latvia.	- - -	- - -	- - -	69.3	69.1	- - -	- - -	- - -	78.9	79.4
Luxembourg.	70.0	72.4	74.6	79.8	79.4	75.6	78.7	81.3	83.9	85.2
Mexico	64.1	67.0	70.5	71.7	72.1	70.2	74.0	76.1	77.4	77.5
Netherlands	72.5	73.8	75.6	79.5	80.0	79.2	80.2	80.7	83.2	83.5
New Zealand	70.1	72.5	75.9	79.5	†79.8	76.2	78.4	80.8	83.2	†83.4
Norway.	72.4	73.4	76.0	79.8	80.1	79.3	79.9	81.5	83.8	84.2
Poland	66.0	66.3	††69.6	73.0	73.7	74.4	75.3	††78.0	81.2	81.7
Portugal	67.9	70.6	73.3	77.6	†78.0	74.9	77.5	80.4	84.0	†84.4
Slovak Republic[1]	66.7	66.7	69.2	72.9	73.3	74.4	75.7	77.5	80.1	80.5
Slovenia	- - -	69.8	72.2	77.2	78.2	- - -	77.8	79.9	83.6	84.1
Spain	72.3	73.4	75.8	80.2	80.4	78.4	80.6	82.9	86.1	86.2
Sweden.	72.8	74.8	77.4	80.2	80.4	79.0	80.5	82.0	83.8	84.2
Switzerland	72.3	74.0	77.0	80.7	81.1	79.0	80.9	82.8	85.0	85.4
Turkey	55.8	††65.4	69.0	††75.3	75.3	60.3	††69.5	73.1	††80.7	80.7
United Kingdom.	70.2	72.9	75.5	†79.2	†79.5	76.2	78.5	80.3	†82.9	†83.2
United States	70.0	71.8	74.1	76.4	76.5	77.4	78.8	79.3	81.2	81.3

See footnotes at end of table.

Table 14 (page 2 of 2). Life expectancy at birth and at age 65, by sex: Organisation for Economic Co-operation and Development (OECD) countries, selected years 1980–2014

Excel and PDF versions (with more data years and standard errors when available): http://www.cdc.gov/nchs/hus/contents2016.htm#014.

[Data are based on reporting by OECD countries]

Country	Male					Female				
	1980	1990	2000	2013	2014	1980	1990	2000	2013	2014
At 65 years					Life expectancy, in years					
Australia	13.7	15.2	16.9	19.2	19.4	17.9	19.0	20.4	22.1	22.2
Austria	12.9	14.4	16.0	18.2	18.5	16.3	18.1	19.6	21.5	21.8
Belgium.	12.9	14.3	15.6	17.8	18.4	16.8	18.8	19.7	21.4	21.9
Canada.	14.5	15.7	16.5	- - -	- - -	18.9	19.9	20.2	- - -	- - -
Chile	- - -	13.7	15.5	†16.8	†16.8	- - -	17.2	19.3	†19.9	†20.0
Czech Republic[1]	11.2	11.7	13.7	15.7	16.1	14.4	15.3	17.2	19.3	19.8
Denmark	13.6	14.0	15.2	17.7	18.1	17.7	17.9	18.3	20.4	20.8
Estonia	11.8	12.0	12.7	15.2	15.2	15.6	15.8	17.1	20.3	20.4
Finland	12.6	13.8	15.5	18.0	18.2	17.0	17.8	19.5	21.8	21.7
France	13.6	15.5	16.8	19.3	††19.7	18.2	19.8	21.4	23.6	††24.0
Germany[2]	12.8	14.0	15.8	18.2	††18.2	16.3	17.7	19.6	21.1	††21.4
Greece	15.2	15.7	16.7	18.7	18.8	17.0	18.1	19.2	21.6	21.6
Hungary	11.6	12.1	13.0	14.5	14.6	14.7	15.4	16.7	18.4	18.6
Iceland	15.7	16.4	17.8	18.8	19.5	19.3	19.8	19.8	21.2	22.2
Ireland	12.6	13.3	14.6	†18.1	†18.4	15.7	17.0	18.0	†20.8	†21.1
Israel[3].	- - -	15.7	17.0	19.2	19.2	- - -	17.8	19.0	21.3	21.5
Italy	13.3	15.2	16.7	18.9	19.2	17.1	18.9	20.7	22.6	22.8
Japan.	14.6	16.2	17.5	19.1	19.3	17.7	20.0	22.4	24.0	24.2
Korea.	10.5	12.4	14.3	18.0	18.3	15.1	16.3	18.2	22.4	22.8
Latvia.	- - -	- - -	- - -	13.9	13.8	- - -	- - -	- - -	18.6	19.0
Luxembourg.	12.6	14.3	15.5	19.1	18.4	16.5	18.5	20.1	21.9	22.7
Mexico	15.4	16.0	16.5	16.7	16.7	17.0	18.0	18.4	18.6	18.6
Netherlands	13.7	14.4	15.4	18.2	18.6	18.0	19.1	19.3	21.2	21.4
New Zealand	13.2	14.6	16.4	18.9	†19.1	17.0	18.3	19.8	21.3	†21.5
Norway.	14.3	14.6	16.1	18.5	18.8	18.2	18.7	19.9	21.4	21.6
Poland	12.0	12.4	††13.5	15.5	15.9	15.5	16.2	††17.5	19.9	20.4
Portugal	13.1	14.0	15.4	17.8	†18.1	16.1	17.1	19.1	21.6	†21.9
Slovak Republic[1]	12.0	12.3	12.9	14.7	15.1	15.2	16.0	16.7	18.8	19.1
Slovenia	- - -	13.3	14.2	17.2	17.7	- - -	17.1	18.7	21.4	21.6
Spain	14.6	15.5	16.7	19.2	19.3	17.8	19.3	20.8	23.4	23.5
Sweden.	14.3	15.4	16.7	18.8	18.9	18.1	19.2	20.2	21.3	21.6
Switzerland	14.3	15.3	17.0	19.4	19.6	18.2	19.7	20.9	22.4	22.7
Turkey	11.7	††12.8	13.4	††16.2	16.2	12.8	††14.3	15.1	††19.5	19.4
United Kingdom.	12.6	14.0	15.8	†18.6	†18.8	16.6	17.9	19.0	†20.9	†21.3
United States	14.1	15.1	16.0	17.9	18.0	18.3	18.9	19.0	20.5	20.6

- - - Data not available.

† Data are estimated. See OECD website for updated data and additional information. Available at: http://www.oecd.org/.

†† Break in series. See OECD website for updated data and additional information. Available at: http://www.oecd.org/.

[1] In 1993, Czechoslovakia was divided into two nations, the Czech Republic and Slovakia. Data for years prior to 1993 are from the Czech and Slovak regions of Czechoslovakia.

[2] Until 1990, estimates refer to the Federal Republic of Germany; from 1995 onward data refer to Germany after reunification.

[3] Statistical data for Israel are supplied by, and under the responsibility of, the relevant Israeli authorities. The use of such data by OECD is without prejudice to the status of the Golan Heights, East Jerusalem, and Israeli settlements in the West Bank under the terms of international law.

NOTES: Differences in life expectancy may reflect differences in reporting and calculation methods, which can vary by country, in addition to actual differences in mortality rates. Therefore, ranks are not presented and comparisons among countries should be made with caution. See Appendix II, Life expectancy. Some estimates for selected countries and selected years were revised and differ from previous editions of *Health, United States*.

SOURCE: Organisation for Economic Co-operation and Development (OECD) Health Data 2016, OECD. StatExtracts, accessed on February 2, 2017. Available from: http://www.oecd.org/; NCHS. Vital statistics of the United States (selected years). Public Health Service. Washington, DC. See Appendix I, Organisation for Economic Co-operation and Development (OECD) Health Data.

Table 15 (page 1 of 2). Life expectancy at birth, at age 65, and at age 75, by sex, race, and Hispanic origin: United States, selected years 1900–2015

Excel and PDF versions (with more data years and standard errors when available): http://www.cdc.gov/nchs/hus/contents2016.htm#015.

[Data are based on death certificates]

Specified age and year	All races			White			Black or African American[1]		
	Both sexes	Male	Female	Both sexes	Male	Female	Both sexes	Male	Female
At birth				Life expectancy, in years					
1900[2,3]	47.3	46.3	48.3	47.6	46.6	48.7	33.0	32.5	33.5
1950[3]	68.2	65.6	71.1	69.1	66.5	72.2	60.8	59.1	62.9
1960[3]	69.7	66.6	73.1	70.6	67.4	74.1	63.6	61.1	66.3
1970	70.8	67.1	74.7	71.7	68.0	75.6	64.1	60.0	68.3
1975	72.6	68.8	76.6	73.4	69.5	77.3	66.8	62.4	71.3
1980	73.7	70.0	77.4	74.4	70.7	78.1	68.1	63.8	72.5
1990	75.4	71.8	78.8	76.1	72.7	79.4	69.1	64.5	73.6
1995	75.8	72.5	78.9	76.5	73.4	79.6	69.6	65.2	73.9
2000	76.8	74.1	79.3	77.3	74.7	79.9	71.8	68.2	75.1
2001	77.0	74.3	79.5	77.5	74.9	80.0	72.0	68.5	75.3
2002	77.0	74.4	79.6	77.5	74.9	80.1	72.2	68.7	75.4
2003	77.2	74.5	79.7	77.7	75.1	80.2	72.4	68.9	75.7
2004	77.6	75.0	80.1	78.1	75.5	80.5	72.9	69.4	76.1
2005	77.6	75.0	80.1	78.0	75.5	80.5	73.0	69.5	76.2
2006	77.8	75.2	80.3	78.3	75.8	80.7	73.4	69.9	76.7
2007	78.1	75.5	80.6	78.5	76.0	80.9	73.8	70.3	77.0
2008	78.2	75.6	80.6	78.5	76.1	80.9	74.3	70.9	77.3
2009	78.5	76.0	80.9	78.8	76.4	81.2	74.7	71.4	77.7
2010	78.7	76.2	81.0	78.9	76.5	81.3	75.1	71.8	78.0
2011	78.7	76.3	81.1	79.0	76.6	81.3	75.3	72.2	78.2
2012	78.8	76.4	81.2	79.1	76.7	81.4	75.5	72.3	78.4
2013[4]	78.8	76.4	81.2	79.0	76.7	81.4	75.5	72.3	78.4
2014[4]	78.9	76.5	81.3	79.1	76.7	81.4	75.6	72.5	78.5
2015[4]	78.8	76.3	81.2	79.0	76.6	81.3	75.5	72.2	78.5
At 65 years									
1950[3]	13.9	12.8	15.0	14.1	12.8	15.1	13.9	12.9	14.9
1960[3]	14.3	12.8	15.8	14.4	12.9	15.9	13.9	12.7	15.1
1970	15.2	13.1	17.0	15.2	13.1	17.1	14.2	12.5	15.7
1975	16.1	13.8	18.1	16.1	13.8	18.2	15.0	13.1	16.7
1980	16.4	14.1	18.3	16.5	14.2	18.4	15.1	13.0	16.8
1990	17.2	15.1	18.9	17.3	15.2	19.1	15.4	13.2	17.2
1995	17.4	15.6	18.9	17.6	15.7	19.1	15.6	13.6	17.1
2000	17.6	16.0	19.0	17.7	16.1	19.1	16.1	14.1	17.5
2001	17.9	16.2	19.2	18.0	16.3	19.3	16.2	14.2	17.7
2002	17.9	16.3	19.2	18.0	16.4	19.3	16.3	14.4	17.8
2003	18.1	16.5	19.3	18.2	16.6	19.4	16.5	14.5	18.0
2004	18.4	16.9	19.6	18.5	17.0	19.7	16.8	14.9	18.3
2005	18.4	16.9	19.6	18.5	17.0	19.7	16.9	15.0	18.3
2006	18.7	17.2	19.9	18.7	17.3	19.9	17.2	15.2	18.6
2007	18.8	17.4	20.0	18.9	17.4	20.1	17.3	15.4	18.8
2008	18.8	17.4	20.0	18.9	17.5	20.0	17.5	15.5	18.9
2009	19.1	17.7	20.3	19.2	17.7	20.3	17.8	15.9	19.2
2010	19.1	17.7	20.3	19.2	17.8	20.3	17.8	15.9	19.3
2011	19.2	17.8	20.3	19.2	17.8	20.3	18.0	16.2	19.4
2012	19.3	17.9	20.5	19.3	18.0	20.4	18.1	16.2	19.5
2013[4]	19.3	17.9	20.5	19.3	18.0	20.5	18.1	16.2	19.5
2014[4]	19.4	18.0	20.6	19.4	18.0	20.6	18.2	16.4	19.7
2015[4]	19.4	18.0	20.6	19.4	18.0	20.5	18.2	16.4	19.7
At 75 years									
1980	10.4	8.8	11.5	10.4	8.8	11.5	9.7	8.3	10.7
1990	10.9	9.4	12.0	11.0	9.4	12.0	10.2	8.6	11.2
1995	11.0	9.7	11.9	11.1	9.7	12.0	10.2	8.8	11.1
2000	11.0	9.8	11.8	11.0	9.8	11.9	10.4	9.0	11.3
2001	11.2	9.9	12.0	11.2	10.0	12.1	10.5	9.0	11.5
2002	11.2	10.0	12.0	11.2	10.0	12.1	10.5	9.1	11.5
2003	11.3	10.1	12.1	11.3	10.2	12.1	10.7	9.2	11.6
2004	11.5	10.4	12.4	11.6	10.4	12.4	10.9	9.4	11.8
2005	11.5	10.4	12.3	11.5	10.4	12.3	10.9	9.4	11.7
2006	11.7	10.6	12.5	11.7	10.6	12.5	11.1	9.6	12.0
2007	11.9	10.7	12.6	11.9	10.8	12.6	11.2	9.8	12.1
2008	11.8	10.7	12.6	11.8	10.7	12.6	11.3	9.8	12.2
2009	12.1	11.0	12.9	12.1	11.0	12.9	11.6	10.2	12.5
2010	12.1	11.0	12.9	12.1	11.0	12.8	11.6	10.2	12.5
2011	12.1	11.1	12.9	12.1	11.0	12.8	11.7	10.4	12.5
2012	12.2	11.2	12.9	12.1	11.1	12.9	11.8	10.4	12.7
2013[4]	12.2	11.2	12.9	12.1	11.1	12.9	11.8	10.4	12.7
2014[4]	12.3	11.2	13.1	12.2	11.2	13.0	11.9	10.6	12.8
2015[4]	12.3	11.2	13.0	12.2	11.2	13.0	11.9	10.6	12.8

See footnotes at end of table.

Excel and PDF versions (with more data years and standard errors when available): http://www.cdc.gov/nchs/hus/contents2016.htm#015.

[Data are based on death certificates]

Specified age and year	White, not Hispanic			Black, not Hispanic			Hispanic [5]		
	Both sexes	*Male*	*Female*	*Both sexes*	*Male*	*Female*	*Both sexes*	*Male*	*Female*
At birth				Life expectancy, in years					
2006	78.2	75.7	80.6	73.1	69.5	76.4	80.3	77.5	82.9
2007	78.4	75.9	80.8	73.5	69.9	76.7	80.7	77.8	83.2
2008	78.4	76.0	80.7	73.9	70.5	77.0	80.8	78.0	83.3
2009	78.7	76.3	81.0	74.4	71.0	77.4	81.1	78.4	83.5
2010	78.8	76.4	81.1	74.7	71.5	77.7	81.7	78.8	84.3
2011	78.7	76.4	81.1	75.0	71.8	77.8	81.8	79.2	84.2
2012	78.9	76.5	81.2	75.1	71.9	78.1	81.9	79.3	84.3
2013 [4,6]	78.8	76.5	81.2	75.1	71.9	78.1	81.9	79.2	84.2
2014 [4,6]	78.9	76.5	81.2	75.3	72.1	78.2	82.0	79.4	84.4
2015 [4,6]	78.7	76.3	81.1	75.1	71.8	78.1	82.0	79.3	84.3
At 65 years									
2006	18.7	17.2	19.9	17.1	15.1	18.5	20.2	18.5	21.5
2007	18.8	17.4	20.0	17.2	15.3	18.7	20.5	18.7	21.7
2008	18.8	17.4	20.0	17.4	15.4	18.8	20.4	18.7	21.6
2009	19.1	17.7	20.3	17.7	15.8	19.1	20.7	19.0	21.9
2010	19.1	17.7	20.3	17.7	15.8	19.1	21.2	19.2	22.6
2011	19.1	17.8	20.3	17.9	16.1	19.2	21.2	19.5	22.5
2012	19.3	17.9	20.4	18.0	16.1	19.4	21.0	19.5	22.1
2013 [4,6]	19.3	17.9	20.4	18.0	16.1	19.4	21.3	19.5	22.5
2014 [4,6]	19.3	18.0	20.5	18.1	16.3	19.5	21.5	19.7	22.8
2015 [4,6]	19.3	18.0	20.5	18.1	16.2	19.6	21.4	19.7	22.7
At 75 years									
2006	11.7	10.6	12.5	11.1	9.6	12.0	13.0	11.7	13.7
2007	11.8	10.7	12.6	11.2	9.7	12.1	13.1	11.8	13.8
2008	11.8	10.7	12.6	11.3	9.8	12.2	13.0	11.7	13.8
2009	12.0	11.0	12.8	11.6	10.1	12.4	13.3	12.0	14.1
2010	12.0	11.0	12.8	11.6	10.1	12.5	13.7	12.2	14.7
2011	12.0	11.0	12.8	11.7	10.4	12.5	13.7	12.4	14.5
2012	12.1	11.1	12.9	11.7	10.4	12.6	13.5	12.3	14.2
2013 [4,6]	12.1	11.1	12.9	11.7	10.3	12.6	13.7	12.4	14.5
2014 [4,6]	12.2	11.2	13.0	11.9	10.5	12.7	13.9	12.6	14.8
2015 [4,6]	12.2	11.2	12.9	11.8	10.5	12.7	13.9	12.7	14.7

[1] Data shown for 1900–1960 are for the nonwhite population. Data for 1970 onwards are for the Black or African American population only.

[2] Death registration area only. The death registration area increased from 10 states and the District of Columbia (D.C.) in 1900 to the coterminous United States in 1933. See Appendix II, Registration area.

[3] Includes deaths of persons who were not residents of the 50 states and D.C.

[4] Life expectancy estimates for 2013 are based on final Medicare data. Life expectancy estimates for 2014 and 2015 are based on preliminary Medicare data.

[5] Hispanic origin was added to the U.S. standard death certificate in 1989 and was adopted by every state in 1997. Life expectancies for the Hispanic population are adjusted for underreporting on the death certificate of Hispanic ethnicity, but are not adjusted to account for the potential effects of return migration. To address the effects of age misstatement at the oldest ages, the probability of death for Hispanic persons older than 80 years is estimated as a function of non-Hispanic white mortality with the use of the Brass relational logit model. See Appendix II, Hispanic origin. See Appendix II, Race, for a discussion of sources of bias in death rates by race and Hispanic origin.

[6] Tables by Hispanic origin are adjusted for race and Hispanic origin misclassification with classification ratios. Life expectancy estimates for 2010–2015 use the 2016 classification ratios. See NOTES section of this table.

NOTES: Populations for computing life expectancy for 1991–1999 are 1990-based postcensal estimates of the U.S. resident population. Starting with *Health, United States, 2012*, populations for computing life expectancy for 2001–2009 were based on revised intercensal population estimates of the U.S. resident population. Populations for computing life expectancy for 2010 were based on 2010 census counts. Life expectancy for 2011 and beyond was computed using 2010-based postcensal estimates. See Appendix I, Population Census and Population Estimates. In 1997, life table methodology was revised to construct complete life tables by single years of age that extend to age 100. (Anderson RN. Method for constructing complete annual U.S. life tables. NCHS. Vital Health Stat 2(129). 1999.) Previously, abridged life tables were constructed for 5-year age groups ending with 85 years and over. In 2000, the life table methodology was revised. The revised methodology is similar to that developed for the 1999–2001 decennial life tables. In 2008, the life table methodology was further refined. Estimates for 2001 and onwards were revised based on the methodology used in the 2008 life table report. Life expectancy for 2001–2015, except as noted in footnote 4, was calculated using data from Medicare to supplement vital statistics and census data. Starting with *Health, United States, 2016*, life expectancy for 2010–2015 were revised to take into account updated race and Hispanic origin classification ratios. See Arias E, Heron M, Hakes JK. The validity of race and Hispanic origin reporting on death certificates in the United States: An update. NCHS. Vital Health Stat 2(172). 2016. Available from: http://www.cdc.gov/nchs/data/series/sr_02/sr02_172.pdf. See Appendix II, Life expectancy. Starting with 2003 data, some states allowed the reporting of more than one race on the death certificate. The multiple-race data for these states were bridged to the single-race categories of the 1977 Office of Management and Budget standards, for comparability with other states. The race groups, white and black include persons of Hispanic and non-Hispanic origin. Persons of Hispanic origin may be of any race. See Appendix II, Race. Data for additional years are available. See the Excel spreadsheet on the *Health, United States* website at: http://www.cdc.gov/nchs/hus.htm. Some data were revised and differ from previous editions of *Health, United States*.

SOURCE: NCHS, National Vital Statistics System, public-use Mortality Files; Grove RD, Hetzel AM. Vital statistics rates in the United States, 1940–1960. Washington, DC: U.S. Government Printing Office, 1968; Arias E. United States life tables by Hispanic origin. Vital health statistics; vol 2 no 152. Hyattsville, MD: NCHS. 2010; United States Life Tables, 2001–2009 (using revised intercensal population estimates and a new methodology implemented with the final 2008 life tables); United States Life Tables, 2010–2012 (using a new methodology implemented with the final 2008 life tables and updated race and Hispanic origin classification ratios); United States Life Tables, 2013, forthcoming (using a new methodology implemented with the final 2008 life tables and updated race and Hispanic origin classification ratios). Life table reports available from: http://www.cdc.gov/nchs/products/life_tables.htm; (for 2014 life expectancy) Xu J, Murphy SL, Kochanek KD, Arias E. Mortality in the United States, 2015. NCHS data brief, no 267. Hyattsville, MD: NCHS; 2016. Murphy SL, Kochanek KD, Xu JQ, Curtin SC. Deaths: Final data for 2015. National vital statistics reports. Hyattsville, MD: NCHS; 2017. Available from: http://www.cdc.gov/nchs/products/nvsr.htm; unpublished 2015 life expectancy estimates for white and black persons at birth, at age 65, and at age 75. See Appendix I, National Vital Statistics System (NVSS).

Table 16 (page 1 of 2). Age-adjusted death rates, by race, Hispanic origin, state, and territory: United States and U.S. dependent areas, average annual 1979–1981, 1989–1991, and 2013–2015

Excel and PDF versions (with more data years and standard errors when available): http://www.cdc.gov/nchs/hus/contents2016.htm#016.

[Data are based on death certificates]

State and territory	All persons 1979–1981	All persons 1989–1991	All persons 2013–2015	White 2013–2015	Black or African American 2013–2015	American Indian or Alaska Native[1] 2013–2015	Asian or Pacific Islander[1] 2013–2015	Hispanic or Latino[1] 2013–2015	White, not Hispanic or Latino[1] 2013–2015
			Age-adjusted death rate per 100,000 population[2]						
United States[3].	1,022.8	942.2	729.9	730.5	853.9	594.1	395.9	527.8	747.7
Alabama.	1,091.2	1,037.9	919.5	906.1	994.8	326.9	219.6	346.2	914.8
Alaska	1,087.4	944.6	736.2	680.9	657.1	1,169.7	479.3	356.7	690.3
Arizona	951.5	873.5	669.2	663.9	763.4	843.4	376.0	590.1	672.1
Arkansas	1,017.0	996.3	893.1	885.0	992.6	250.2	519.6	303.2	894.6
California	975.5	911.0	619.1	651.4	807.6	380.2	394.5	514.4	686.4
Colorado	941.1	856.1	661.7	667.6	741.6	462.4	389.0	652.5	663.1
Connecticut.	961.5	857.5	649.6	655.2	683.2	194.9	311.7	519.8	657.0
Delaware	1,069.7	1,001.9	734.2	733.2	790.5	*	329.3	403.9	739.9
District of Columbia	1,243.1	1,255.3	748.1	463.6	969.7	*	345.4	362.8	458.7
Florida	960.8	870.9	662.7	657.8	741.2	285.2	331.9	507.4	694.7
Georgia	1,094.3	1,037.4	805.4	795.0	869.3	205.7	394.4	316.2	816.0
Hawaii	801.2	752.2	589.2	652.8	532.6	*	568.5	828.2	638.3
Idaho.	936.7	856.6	727.4	731.7	413.7	716.4	411.6	486.7	741.0
Illinois	1,063.7	973.8	726.1	712.9	915.0	127.1	370.6	451.2	730.9
Indiana.	1,048.3	962.0	829.5	824.6	951.2	192.3	384.2	461.3	833.2
Iowa	919.9	848.2	723.8	722.7	877.9	540.7	447.3	382.9	727.3
Kansas	940.1	867.2	763.8	756.2	936.0	1,127.3	445.5	528.0	763.2
Kentucky	1,088.9	1,024.5	910.3	915.8	914.6	161.2	390.9	319.9	921.2
Louisiana	1,132.6	1,074.6	888.5	844.7	1,019.3	367.4	423.5	393.5	859.9
Maine	1,002.9	918.7	758.9	762.4	464.6	793.4	292.6	243.3	762.2
Maryland	1,063.3	985.2	705.1	692.6	799.8	253.5	338.3	312.2	708.3
Massachusetts.	982.6	884.8	670.5	689.5	583.9	289.7	353.1	446.0	684.3
Michigan	1,050.2	966.0	783.5	763.8	961.9	819.5	341.1	623.9	763.8
Minnesota.	892.9	825.2	650.6	643.3	736.0	1,066.6	480.1	402.4	645.5
Mississippi	1,108.7	1,071.4	953.6	919.5	1,029.8	740.6	494.2	243.4	929.7
Missouri.	1,033.7	952.4	810.6	799.6	956.7	376.2	399.9	417.0	804.9
Montana.	1,013.6	890.2	751.9	726.0	*	1,268.9	413.6	511.8	721.6
Nebraska	930.6	867.9	724.1	719.5	892.9	823.8	365.9	450.7	726.7
Nevada	1,077.4	1,017.4	758.5	788.5	815.1	525.1	429.9	462.1	845.3
New Hampshire	982.3	891.7	702.1	711.2	374.2	*	331.4	243.6	715.3
New Jersey.	1,047.5	956.0	669.3	677.4	791.2	148.2	317.1	460.0	697.3
New Mexico	967.1	891.9	740.8	736.5	707.7	826.1	339.0	709.4	729.0
New York	1,051.8	973.7	643.2	663.9	654.8	180.0	354.6	492.2	663.4
North Carolina	1,050.4	986.0	781.2	761.8	884.9	759.9	374.2	321.2	774.4
North Dakota	922.4	818.4	699.7	677.8	397.1	1,278.2	504.2	527.9	677.3
Ohio	1,070.6	967.4	816.6	808.3	932.6	249.8	368.1	468.6	811.4
Oklahoma.	1,025.6	961.4	904.2	890.9	1,014.5	1,015.8	478.2	522.3	903.6
Oregon	953.9	893.0	715.5	724.5	761.3	674.7	424.7	450.3	734.3
Pennsylvania	1,076.4	963.4	760.0	751.9	908.1	280.3	390.2	563.2	748.5
Rhode Island	990.8	889.6	710.8	726.9	474.7	560.3	402.8	404.2	733.9
South Carolina	1,104.6	1,030.0	835.6	808.2	942.6	351.4	365.6	368.2	818.9
South Dakota.	941.9	846.4	701.7	664.1	273.7	1,283.2	375.5	254.1	667.9
Tennessee	1,045.5	1,011.8	882.5	875.4	967.1	229.2	394.1	338.4	882.4
Texas	1,014.9	947.6	747.2	748.5	889.8	150.7	383.6	626.6	787.0
Utah	924.9	823.2	710.7	714.5	600.7	713.0	543.3	538.9	724.0
Vermont	990.2	908.6	706.7	711.1	497.0	*	375.3	329.3	713.2
Virginia	1,054.0	963.1	721.3	714.6	847.4	283.7	364.3	350.1	725.5
Washington.	947.7	869.4	679.9	694.1	734.4	856.5	418.6	454.0	702.5
West Virginia	1,100.3	1,031.5	932.0	935.3	981.0	*	276.2	226.6	940.2
Wisconsin.	956.4	879.1	716.0	702.9	948.6	958.6	499.8	449.4	706.6
Wyoming	1,016.1	897.4	740.8	742.9	333.2	1,042.5	*	533.9	752.0
American Samoa[4].	- - -	- - -	1,042.0	- - -	- - -	- - -	- - -	- - -	- - -
Guam[4].	- - -	- - -	793.4	- - -	- - -	- - -	- - -	- - -	- - -
Northern Marianas[4]	- - -	- - -	861.3	- - -	- - -	- - -	- - -	- - -	- - -
Puerto Rico[4]	- - -	- - -	656.4	- - -	- - -	- - -	- - -	- - -	- - -
Virgin Islands[4]	- - -	- - -	†644.0	- - -	- - -	- - -	- - -	- - -	- - -

See footnotes at end of table.

Table 16 (page 2 of 2). Age-adjusted death rates, by race, Hispanic origin, state, and territory: United States and U.S. dependent areas, average annual 1979–1981, 1989–1991, and 2013–2015

Excel and PDF versions (with more data years and standard errors when available): http://www.cdc.gov/nchs/hus/contents2016.htm#016.

[Data are based on death certificates]

- - - Data not available.

[†] Rate shown is for 2010–2012 because death data were not available for the Virgin Islands for 2013 and 2014.

[*] Prior to 2009–2011 (shown in spreadsheet file), data for states with populations under 10,000 in the middle year of a 3-year period, or fewer than 50 deaths for the 3-year period, are considered unreliable and are not shown. Starting with 2009–2011 estimates (shown in spreadsheet file), data for states with an average population for the 3-year period of under 10,000, or fewer than 50 deaths for the 3-year period, are considered unreliable and are not shown.

[1] Death rates for Hispanic, American Indian or Alaska Native, and Asian or Pacific Islander persons should be interpreted with caution because of inconsistencies in reporting Hispanic origin or race on the death certificate (death rate numerators) compared with population figures (death rate denominators). The net effect of misclassification is an underestimation of deaths and death rates for races other than white and black. See Appendix II, Race, for a detailed discussion of sources of bias in death rates by race and Hispanic origin.

[2] Age-adjusted average annual death rates are calculated using the year 2000 standard population. Prior to 2001, age-adjusted rates were calculated using standard million proportions based on rounded population numbers. Starting with 2001 data, unrounded population numbers are used to calculate age-adjusted rates. Age-adjusted rates for Puerto Rico, Virgin Islands, Guam, American Samoa, and Northern Marianas were computed by applying the age-specific death rates to the U.S. standard population combining the age groups for age 75 and over. For the territories, age groups were not available for those age 75 and over by age. See Appendix II, Age adjustment. Prior to 2009–2011 (shown in spreadsheet file), denominators for rates are resident population estimates for the middle year of each 3-year period, multiplied by 3. Starting with 2009–2011 estimates (shown in spreadsheet file), denominators for rates are the 3-year average population. See Appendix I, Population Census and Population Estimates.

[3] Excludes data for American Samoa, Guam, Northern Marianas, Puerto Rico, and Virgin Islands.

[4] Comparable population data were not available for all time periods and for all racial and ethnicity groups. Therefore, only selected rates are presented for the territories.

NOTES: The race groups, white, black, American Indian or Alaska Native, and Asian or Pacific Islander, include persons of Hispanic and non-Hispanic origin. Persons of Hispanic origin may be of any race. United States, state, and territory rates for 2011 and beyond were calculated using 2010-based postcensal population estimates. Starting with 2003 data, some states began to collect information on more than one race on the death certificate, according to 1997 Office of Management and Budget (OMB) standards. The multiple-race data for these states were bridged to the single-race categories of the 1977 OMB standards, for comparability with other states. See Appendix II, Race. Rates are rounded at the end of the calculation process. They may differ from rates based on the same data presented elsewhere if rounding is done earlier in the calculation process. Data for additional years are available. See the Excel spreadsheet on the *Health, United States* website at: http://www.cdc.gov/nchs/hus.htm.

SOURCE: NCHS, National Vital Statistics System; numerator data from annual public-use and nonpublic-use Mortality Files; denominator data from state population estimates prepared by the U.S. Census Bureau 1980 from April 1, 1980 MARS Census File; 1990 from April 1, 1990 MARS Census File; 2011 and beyond from 2010-based postcensal bridged-race files. Available from: http://www.cdc.gov/nchs/nvss/bridged_race.htm. For the territories (except for Puerto Rico) populations are from the U.S. Census Bureau. International data base. 2010. Available from: http://www.census.gov/population/international/. For Puerto Rico, populations are from U.S. Census Bureau. Puerto Rico Commonwealth characteristics. See Appendix I, National Vital Statistics System (NVSS).

Table 17 (page 1 of 4). Age-adjusted death rates for selected causes of death, by sex, race, and Hispanic origin: United States, selected years 1950–2015

Excel and PDF versions (with more data years and standard errors when available): http://www.cdc.gov/nchs/hus/contents2016.htm#017.

[Data are based on death certificates]

Sex, race, Hispanic origin, and cause of death [1]	1950 [2,3]	1960 [2,3]	1970 [3]	1980 [3]	1990 [3]	2000 [4]	2005 [4]	2010 [4]	2014 [4]	2015 [4]
All persons	Age-adjusted death rate per 100,000 population [5]									
All causes	1,446.0	1,339.2	1,222.6	1,039.1	938.7	869.0	815.0	747.0	724.6	733.1
Diseases of heart	588.8	559.0	492.7	412.1	321.8	257.6	216.8	179.1	167.0	168.5
Ischemic heart disease	- - -	- - -	- - -	345.2	249.6	186.8	148.2	113.6	98.8	97.2
Cerebrovascular diseases	180.7	177.9	147.7	96.2	65.3	60.9	48.0	39.1	36.5	37.6
Malignant neoplasms	193.9	193.9	198.6	207.9	216.0	199.6	185.1	172.8	161.2	158.5
Trachea, bronchus, and lung	15.0	24.1	37.1	49.9	59.3	56.1	52.7	47.6	42.1	40.5
Colon, rectum, and anus	- - -	30.3	28.9	27.4	24.5	20.8	17.7	15.8	14.3	14.2
Chronic lower respiratory diseases [6]	- - -	- - -	- - -	28.3	37.2	44.2	43.9	42.2	40.5	41.6
Influenza and pneumonia [7]	48.1	53.7	41.7	31.4	36.8	23.7	21.0	15.1	15.1	15.2
Chronic liver disease and cirrhosis	11.3	13.3	17.8	15.1	11.1	9.5	8.9	9.4	10.4	10.8
Diabetes mellitus [8]	23.1	22.5	24.3	18.1	20.7	25.0	24.9	20.8	20.9	21.3
Alzheimer's disease	- - -	- - -	- - -	†	†	18.1	24.0	25.1	25.4	29.4
Human immunodeficiency virus (HIV) disease	. . .	. . .	. . .	. . .	10.2	5.2	4.2	2.6	2.0	1.9
Unintentional injuries	78.0	62.3	60.1	46.4	36.3	34.9	39.5	38.0	40.5	43.2
Motor vehicle-related injuries	24.6	23.1	27.6	22.3	18.5	15.4	15.2	11.3	10.8	11.4
Poisoning	2.5	1.7	2.8	1.9	2.3	4.5	8.0	10.6	13.1	14.8
Nephritis, nephrotic syndrome, and nephrosis [8]	- - -	- - -	- - -	9.1	9.3	13.5	14.7	15.3	13.2	13.4
Suicide [9]	13.2	12.5	13.1	12.2	12.5	10.4	10.9	12.1	13.0	13.3
Homicide [9]	5.1	5.0	8.8	10.4	9.4	5.9	6.1	5.3	5.1	5.7
Male										
All causes	1,674.2	1,609.0	1,542.1	1,348.1	1,202.8	1,053.8	971.9	887.1	855.1	863.2
Diseases of heart	699.0	687.6	634.0	538.9	412.4	320.0	268.2	225.1	210.9	211.8
Ischemic heart disease	- - -	- - -	- - -	459.7	328.2	241.4	192.3	151.3	133.5	131.2
Cerebrovascular diseases	186.4	186.1	157.4	102.2	68.5	62.4	48.4	39.3	36.9	37.8
Malignant neoplasms	208.1	225.1	247.6	271.2	280.4	248.9	227.2	209.9	192.9	189.2
Trachea, bronchus, and lung	24.6	43.6	67.5	85.2	91.1	76.7	69.1	60.3	51.7	49.5
Colon, rectum, and anus	- - -	31.8	32.3	32.8	30.4	25.1	21.2	19.0	16.9	16.8
Prostate	28.6	28.7	28.8	32.8	38.4	30.4	25.3	21.9	19.0	18.8
Chronic lower respiratory diseases [6]	- - -	- - -	- - -	49.9	55.4	55.8	52.2	48.7	45.4	46.0
Influenza and pneumonia [7]	55.0	65.8	54.0	42.1	47.8	28.9	24.9	18.2	17.8	17.7
Chronic liver disease and cirrhosis	15.0	18.5	24.8	21.3	15.9	13.4	12.4	12.9	14.1	14.5
Diabetes mellitus [8]	18.8	19.9	23.0	18.1	21.7	27.8	28.8	24.9	25.6	26.2
Alzheimer's disease	- - -	- - -	- - -	†	†	15.2	19.5	21.0	20.6	23.7
Human immunodeficiency virus (HIV) disease	. . .	. . .	. . .	. . .	18.5	7.9	6.3	3.8	3.0	2.8
Unintentional injuries	101.8	85.5	87.4	69.0	52.9	49.3	55.0	51.5	54.6	58.7
Motor vehicle-related injuries	38.5	35.4	41.5	33.6	26.5	21.7	21.9	16.2	15.8	16.7
Poisoning	3.3	2.3	3.9	2.7	3.5	6.6	10.8	13.8	17.3	19.8
Nephritis, nephrotic syndrome, and nephrosis [8]	- - -	- - -	- - -	12.2	12.1	16.9	18.1	18.7	16.2	16.3
Suicide [9]	21.2	20.0	19.8	19.9	21.5	17.7	18.1	19.8	20.7	21.1
Homicide [9]	7.9	7.5	14.3	16.6	14.8	9.0	9.7	8.4	8.0	9.1
Female										
All causes	1,236.0	1,105.3	971.4	817.9	750.9	731.4	692.3	634.9	616.7	624.2
Diseases of heart	486.6	447.0	381.6	320.8	257.0	210.9	177.5	143.3	131.8	133.6
Ischemic heart disease	- - -	- - -	- - -	263.1	193.9	146.5	115.0	84.9	71.6	70.5
Cerebrovascular diseases	175.8	170.7	140.0	91.7	62.6	59.1	47.0	38.3	35.6	36.9
Malignant neoplasms	182.3	168.7	163.2	166.7	175.7	167.6	156.7	146.7	138.1	135.9
Trachea, bronchus, and lung	5.8	7.5	13.1	24.4	37.1	41.3	40.6	38.1	34.7	33.5
Colon, rectum, and anus	- - -	29.1	26.5	23.8	20.6	17.7	15.0	13.3	12.1	12.1
Breast	31.9	31.7	32.1	31.9	33.3	26.8	24.2	22.1	20.6	20.3
Chronic lower respiratory diseases [6]	- - -	- - -	- - -	14.9	26.6	37.4	38.7	38.0	37.1	38.6
Influenza and pneumonia [7]	41.9	43.8	32.7	25.1	30.5	20.7	18.6	13.1	13.2	13.5
Chronic liver disease and cirrhosis	7.8	8.7	11.9	9.9	7.1	6.2	5.8	6.2	7.1	7.6
Diabetes mellitus [8]	27.0	24.7	25.1	18.0	19.9	23.0	21.9	17.6	17.2	17.3
Alzheimer's disease	- - -	- - -	- - -	†	†	19.3	26.2	27.3	28.3	32.8
Human immunodeficiency virus (HIV) disease	. . .	. . .	. . .	. . .	2.2	2.5	2.3	1.4	1.1	1.0
Unintentional injuries	54.0	40.0	35.1	26.1	21.5	22.0	25.3	25.6	27.3	28.7
Motor vehicle-related injuries	11.5	11.7	14.9	11.8	11.0	9.5	8.9	6.5	6.1	6.4
Poisoning	1.7	1.1	1.8	1.3	1.2	2.5	5.1	7.5	9.1	9.8
Nephritis, nephrotic syndrome, and nephrosis [8]	- - -	- - -	- - -	7.3	7.7	11.5	12.6	13.0	11.1	11.3
Suicide [9]	5.6	5.6	7.4	5.7	4.8	4.0	4.4	5.0	5.8	6.0
Homicide [9]	2.4	2.6	3.7	4.4	4.0	2.8	2.5	2.3	2.1	2.2

See footnotes at end of table.

Table 17 (page 2 of 4). **Age-adjusted death rates for selected causes of death, by sex, race, and Hispanic origin: United States, selected years 1950–2015**

Excel and PDF versions (with more data years and standard errors when available): http://www.cdc.gov/nchs/hus/contents2016.htm#017.

[Data are based on death certificates]

Sex, race, Hispanic origin, and cause of death [1]	1950 [2,3]	1960 [2,3]	1970 [3]	1980 [3]	1990 [3]	2000 [4]	2005 [4]	2010 [4]	2014 [4]	2015 [4]
White [10]	Age-adjusted death rate per 100,000 population [5]									
All causes	1,410.8	1,311.3	1,193.3	1,012.7	909.8	849.8	801.1	741.8	725.4	735.0
Diseases of heart	586.0	559.0	492.2	409.4	317.0	253.4	213.2	176.9	165.9	167.9
Ischemic heart disease	- - -	- - -	- - -	347.6	249.7	185.6	147.3	113.5	99.3	98.0
Cerebrovascular diseases	175.5	172.7	143.5	93.2	62.8	58.8	46.0	37.7	35.2	36.4
Malignant neoplasms	194.6	193.1	196.7	204.2	211.6	197.2	183.9	172.4	161.9	159.4
Trachea, bronchus, and lung	15.2	24.0	36.7	49.2	58.6	56.2	53.2	48.3	42.9	41.4
Colon, rectum, and anus	- - -	30.9	29.2	27.4	24.1	20.3	17.1	15.3	14.0	13.9
Chronic lower respiratory diseases [6]	- - -	- - -	- - -	29.3	38.3	46.0	46.0	44.6	43.1	44.5
Influenza and pneumonia [7]	44.8	50.4	39.8	30.9	36.4	23.5	20.9	14.9	15.1	15.2
Chronic liver disease and cirrhosis	11.5	13.2	16.6	13.9	10.5	9.6	9.2	9.9	11.2	11.7
Diabetes mellitus [8]	22.9	21.7	22.9	16.7	18.8	22.8	22.8	19.0	19.3	19.6
Alzheimer's disease	- - -	- - -	- - -	†	†	18.8	24.7	26.0	26.4	30.5
Human immunodeficiency virus (HIV) disease	. . .	. . .	. . .	. . .	8.3	2.8	2.2	1.4	1.1	1.1
Unintentional injuries	77.0	60.4	57.8	45.3	35.5	35.1	40.7	40.3	43.1	46.0
Motor vehicle-related injuries	24.4	22.9	27.1	22.6	18.5	15.6	15.7	11.7	11.1	11.7
Poisoning	2.4	1.6	2.4	1.8	2.1	4.5	8.5	11.9	14.8	16.7
Nephritis, nephrotic syndrome, and nephrosis [8]	- - -	- - -	- - -	8.0	8.3	12.1	13.2	14.0	12.1	12.2
Suicide [9]	13.9	13.1	13.8	13.0	13.4	11.3	12.1	13.6	14.7	15.1
Homicide [9]	2.6	2.7	4.7	6.7	5.5	3.6	3.7	3.3	3.0	3.3
Black or African American [10]										
All causes	1,722.1	1,577.5	1,518.1	1,314.8	1,250.3	1,121.4	1,035.1	898.2	849.3	851.9
Diseases of heart	588.7	548.3	512.0	455.3	391.5	324.8	278.0	224.9	206.3	205.1
Ischemic heart disease	- - -	- - -	- - -	334.5	267.0	218.3	175.7	131.2	112.8	108.9
Cerebrovascular diseases	233.6	235.2	197.1	129.1	91.6	81.9	67.0	53.0	49.7	50.8
Malignant neoplasms	176.4	199.1	225.3	256.4	279.5	248.5	223.5	203.8	185.6	180.1
Trachea, bronchus, and lung	11.1	23.7	41.3	59.7	72.4	64.0	58.1	51.4	44.5	42.0
Colon, rectum, and anus	- - -	22.8	26.1	28.3	30.6	28.2	25.1	21.8	18.6	18.8
Chronic lower respiratory diseases [6]	- - -	- - -	- - -	19.2	28.1	31.6	31.1	29.0	28.4	28.9
Influenza and pneumonia [7]	76.7	81.1	57.2	34.4	39.4	25.6	22.6	16.8	16.1	15.9
Chronic liver disease and cirrhosis	9.0	13.6	28.1	25.0	16.5	9.4	7.6	6.7	7.2	7.4
Diabetes mellitus [8]	23.5	30.9	38.8	32.7	40.5	49.5	47.5	38.7	37.3	37.0
Alzheimer's disease	- - -	- - -	- - -	†	†	13.0	20.8	20.6	22.3	26.6
Human immunodeficiency virus (HIV) disease	. . .	. . .	. . .	. . .	26.7	23.3	19.2	11.6	8.3	7.9
Unintentional injuries	79.9	74.0	78.3	57.6	43.8	37.7	38.8	31.3	33.7	36.8
Motor vehicle-related injuries	26.0	24.2	31.1	20.2	18.8	15.7	14.4	10.9	11.1	12.2
Poisoning	2.8	2.9	5.8	3.1	4.1	6.0	8.1	7.3	9.6	11.1
Nephritis, nephrotic syndrome, and nephrosis [8]	- - -	- - -	- - -	20.9	19.8	28.7	30.3	29.3	24.6	25.4
Suicide [9]	4.5	5.0	6.2	6.5	7.1	5.5	5.2	5.2	5.5	5.6
Homicide [9]	28.3	26.0	44.0	39.0	36.3	20.5	21.1	17.7	17.2	19.8
American Indian or Alaska Native [10]										
All causes	- - -	- - -	- - -	867.0	716.3	709.3	701.1	628.3	594.1	596.9
Diseases of heart	- - -	- - -	- - -	240.6	200.6	178.2	156.6	128.6	119.1	118.5
Ischemic heart disease	- - -	- - -	- - -	173.6	139.1	129.1	106.1	84.9	76.4	73.4
Cerebrovascular diseases	- - -	- - -	- - -	57.8	40.7	45.0	38.8	28.1	25.4	24.7
Malignant neoplasms	- - -	- - -	- - -	113.7	121.8	127.8	128.8	122.4	106.7	107.9
Trachea, bronchus, and lung	- - -	- - -	- - -	20.7	30.9	32.3	35.3	33.1	27.8	26.7
Colon, rectum, and anus	- - -	- - -	- - -	9.5	12.0	13.4	12.6	11.7	10.9	11.1
Chronic lower respiratory diseases [6]	- - -	- - -	- - -	14.2	25.4	32.8	31.6	33.8	29.9	30.9
Influenza and pneumonia [7]	- - -	- - -	- - -	44.4	36.1	22.3	23.6	15.9	15.1	12.5
Chronic liver disease and cirrhosis	- - -	- - -	- - -	45.3	24.1	24.3	21.6	22.8	24.2	26.4
Diabetes mellitus [8]	- - -	- - -	- - -	29.6	34.1	41.5	44.1	36.4	31.3	34.2
Alzheimer's disease	- - -	- - -	- - -	†	†	9.1	15.0	17.2	15.2	15.4
Human immunodeficiency virus (HIV) disease	. . .	. . .	. . .	. . .	1.8	2.2	2.5	1.6	1.2	1.4
Unintentional injuries	- - -	- - -	- - -	99.0	62.6	51.3	51.3	46.9	49.5	50.7
Motor vehicle-related injuries	- - -	- - -	- - -	54.5	32.5	27.3	22.6	15.7	16.6	16.9
Poisoning	- - -	- - -	- - -	2.3	3.2	4.7	8.6	13.0	15.5	16.1
Nephritis, nephrotic syndrome, and nephrosis [8]	- - -	- - -	- - -	12.2	11.6	15.0	15.6	16.4	12.4	12.2
Suicide [9]	- - -	- - -	- - -	11.9	11.7	9.8	10.7	10.8	10.9	12.6
Homicide [9]	- - -	- - -	- - -	15.5	10.4	6.8	6.8	5.7	5.8	6.2

See footnotes at end of table.

Excel and PDF versions (with more data years and standard errors when available): http://www.cdc.gov/nchs/hus/contents2016.htm#017.

[Data are based on death certificates]

Sex, race, Hispanic origin, and cause of death [1]	1950 [2,3]	1960 [2,3]	1970 [3]	1980 [3]	1990 [3]	2000 [4]	2005 [4]	2010 [4]	2014 [4]	2015 [4]
Asian or Pacific Islander [10]				Age-adjusted death rate per 100,000 population [5]						
All causes	- - -	- - -	- - -	589.9	582.0	506.4	459.6	424.3	388.3	394.8
Diseases of heart	- - -	- - -	- - -	202.1	181.7	146.0	119.7	100.9	86.1	86.5
Ischemic heart disease	- - -	- - -	- - -	168.2	139.6	109.6	85.6	68.7	55.1	54.9
Cerebrovascular diseases	- - -	- - -	- - -	66.1	56.9	52.9	40.8	33.2	28.3	29.8
Malignant neoplasms	- - -	- - -	- - -	126.1	134.2	121.9	113.2	108.9	98.9	99.0
Trachea, bronchus, and lung	- - -	- - -	- - -	28.4	30.2	28.1	26.3	24.8	22.7	22.2
Colon, rectum, and anus	- - -	- - -	- - -	16.4	14.4	12.7	11.5	11.4	9.5	9.8
Chronic lower respiratory diseases [6]	- - -	- - -	- - -	12.9	19.4	18.6	15.9	13.9	12.5	12.2
Influenza and pneumonia [7]	- - -	- - -	- - -	24.0	31.4	19.7	16.8	14.4	12.9	14.0
Chronic liver disease and cirrhosis	- - -	- - -	- - -	6.1	5.2	3.5	3.6	3.2	3.5	3.3
Diabetes mellitus [8]	- - -	- - -	- - -	12.6	14.6	16.4	17.3	15.5	15.0	15.7
Alzheimer's disease	- - -	- - -	- - -	†	†	5.5	8.5	10.9	12.1	14.7
Human immunodeficiency virus (HIV) disease	. . .	. . .	. . .	. . .	2.2	0.6	0.6	0.4	0.3	0.4
Unintentional injuries	- - -	- - -	- - -	27.0	23.9	17.9	18.1	15.0	15.1	16.1
Motor vehicle-related injuries	- - -	- - -	- - -	13.9	14.0	8.6	7.5	5.1	4.6	4.9
Poisoning	- - -	- - -	- - -	0.5	0.7	0.7	1.3	1.4	2.0	2.4
Nephritis, nephrotic syndrome, and nephrosis [8]	- - -	- - -	- - -	7.2	7.1	8.4	8.7	9.6	8.2	8.3
Suicide [9]	- - -	- - -	- - -	7.8	6.7	5.5	5.1	6.2	6.0	6.4
Homicide [9]	- - -	- - -	- - -	5.9	5.0	3.0	2.8	1.8	1.5	1.6
Hispanic or Latino [10,11]										
All causes	- - -	- - -	- - -	- - -	692.0	665.7	627.6	558.6	523.3	525.3
Diseases of heart	- - -	- - -	- - -	- - -	217.1	196.0	170.4	132.8	116.0	116.9
Ischemic heart disease	- - -	- - -	- - -	- - -	173.3	153.2	127.9	92.3	75.3	74.5
Cerebrovascular diseases	- - -	- - -	- - -	- - -	45.2	46.4	38.6	32.1	30.2	32.3
Malignant neoplasms	- - -	- - -	- - -	- - -	136.8	134.9	127.9	119.7	112.4	110.3
Trachea, bronchus, and lung	- - -	- - -	- - -	- - -	26.5	24.8	23.3	20.4	18.3	17.8
Colon, rectum, and anus	- - -	- - -	- - -	- - -	14.7	14.1	13.1	12.3	11.1	10.9
Chronic lower respiratory diseases [6]	- - -	- - -	- - -	- - -	19.3	21.1	20.9	19.6	17.5	17.7
Influenza and pneumonia [7]	- - -	- - -	- - -	- - -	29.7	20.6	18.5	13.7	12.8	11.4
Chronic liver disease and cirrhosis	- - -	- - -	- - -	- - -	18.3	16.5	14.1	13.7	14.5	14.9
Diabetes mellitus [8]	- - -	- - -	- - -	- - -	28.2	36.9	35.4	27.1	25.1	25.2
Alzheimer's disease	- - -	- - -	- - -	- - -	†	10.4	15.6	18.5	19.8	24.2
Human immunodeficiency virus (HIV) disease	. . .	. . .	. . .	. . .	16.3	6.7	4.8	2.8	2.0	1.8
Unintentional injuries	- - -	- - -	- - -	- - -	34.6	30.1	31.8	25.8	26.8	28.6
Motor vehicle-related injuries	- - -	- - -	- - -	- - -	19.5	14.7	14.6	9.6	9.6	10.2
Poisoning	- - -	- - -	- - -	- - -	3.2	4.1	5.2	5.6	6.8	7.7
Nephritis, nephrotic syndrome, and nephrosis [8]	- - -	- - -	- - -	- - -	8.4	11.8	12.8	14.1	11.1	11.4
Suicide [9]	- - -	- - -	- - -	- - -	7.8	5.9	5.6	5.9	6.3	6.2
Homicide [9]	- - -	- - -	- - -	- - -	16.2	7.5	7.4	5.3	4.5	4.9
White, not Hispanic or Latino [11]										
All causes	- - -	- - -	- - -	- - -	914.5	855.5	810.1	755.0	742.8	753.2
Diseases of heart	- - -	- - -	- - -	- - -	319.7	255.5	215.5	179.9	169.9	171.9
Ischemic heart disease	- - -	- - -	- - -	- - -	251.9	186.6	148.3	115.0	101.2	99.7
Cerebrovascular diseases	- - -	- - -	- - -	- - -	63.5	59.0	46.2	37.8	35.4	36.4
Malignant neoplasms	- - -	- - -	- - -	- - -	215.4	200.6	187.8	176.5	166.2	163.7
Trachea, bronchus, and lung	- - -	- - -	- - -	- - -	60.3	58.2	55.5	50.8	45.4	43.8
Colon, rectum, and anus	- - -	- - -	- - -	- - -	24.6	20.5	17.4	15.5	14.3	14.1
Chronic lower respiratory diseases [6]	- - -	- - -	- - -	- - -	39.2	47.2	47.7	46.6	45.4	46.9
Influenza and pneumonia [7]	- - -	- - -	- - -	- - -	36.5	23.5	21.0	14.9	15.1	15.4
Chronic liver disease and cirrhosis	- - -	- - -	- - -	- - -	9.9	9.0	8.7	9.4	10.6	11.1
Diabetes mellitus [8]	- - -	- - -	- - -	- - -	18.3	21.8	21.8	18.2	18.6	18.9
Alzheimer's disease	- - -	- - -	- - -	- - -	†	19.1	25.1	26.4	26.8	30.8
Human immunodeficiency virus (HIV) disease	. . .	. . .	. . .	. . .	7.4	2.2	1.8	1.1	0.9	0.9
Unintentional injuries	- - -	- - -	- - -	- - -	35.0	35.3	41.5	42.4	45.8	49.0
Motor vehicle-related injuries	- - -	- - -	- - -	- - -	18.2	15.6	15.7	11.9	11.3	11.8
Poisoning	- - -	- - -	- - -	- - -	2.0	4.6	9.1	13.3	16.7	18.8
Nephritis, nephrotic syndrome, and nephrosis [8]	- - -	- - -	- - -	- - -	8.1	12.0	13.1	13.8	12.1	12.2
Suicide [9]	- - -	- - -	- - -	- - -	13.8	12.0	13.0	15.0	16.4	17.0
Homicide [9]	- - -	- - -	- - -	- - -	4.0	2.8	2.7	2.5	2.5	2.6

See footnotes at end of table.

Table 17 (page 4 of 4). Age-adjusted death rates for selected causes of death, by sex, race, and Hispanic origin: United States, selected years 1950–2015

Excel and PDF versions (with more data years and standard errors when available): *http://www.cdc.gov/nchs/hus/contents2016.htm#017.*

[Data are based on death certificates]

- - - Data not available.

[†] Data for Alzheimer's disease are only presented for data years 1999 and beyond due to large differences in death rates caused by changes in the *International Classification of Diseases* (ICD) coding of the causes of death between ICD–9 and ICD–10. See Appendix II, Cause of death; Comparability ratio; Table IV; Table V.

. . . Category not applicable.

[1] Underlying cause of death code numbers are based on the applicable revision of the ICD for data years shown. See Appendix II, Cause of death; Table III; Table IV.

[2] Includes deaths of persons who were not residents of the 50 states and the District of Columbia (D.C.).

[3] Underlying cause of death was coded according to the 6th Revision of the ICD in 1950, 7th Revision in 1960, 8th Revision in 1970, and 9th Revision in 1980–1998. See Appendix II, Cause of death; Table III; Table IV.

[4] Starting with 1999 data, cause of death is coded according to ICD–10. See Appendix II, Cause of death; Comparability ratio; Table IV; Table V.

[5] Age-adjusted rates are calculated using the year 2000 standard population. Prior to 2001, age-adjusted rates were calculated using standard million proportions based on rounded population numbers. Starting with 2001 data, unrounded population numbers are used to calculate age-adjusted rates. See Appendix II, Age adjustment.

[6] Between 1998 and 1999, the cause of death title for Chronic obstructive pulmonary diseases in the ICD–9 was renamed to Chronic lower respiratory diseases (CLRD) in ICD–10.

[7] Starting with 1999 data, the rules for selecting CLRD and Pneumonia as the underlying cause of death changed, resulting in an increase in the number of deaths for CLRD and a decrease in the number of deaths for pneumonia. Therefore, trend data for these two causes of death should be interpreted with caution. For more information, see Comparability of cause of death between the 9th and 10th revisions of the *International Classification of Diseases* in Appendix II, Table V.

[8] Starting with 2011 data, the rules for selecting Renal failure as the underlying cause of death were changed, affecting the number of deaths in the Nephritis, nephrotic syndrome, and nephrosis and Diabetes categories. These changes directly affect deaths with mention of Renal failure and other associated conditions, such as Diabetes mellitus with renal complications. The result is a decrease in the number of deaths for Nephritis, nephrotic syndrome, and nephrosis and an increase in the number of deaths for Diabetes mellitus. Therefore, trend data for these two causes of death should be interpreted with caution. For more information, see Technical Notes in Deaths: Final data for 2011, available from: http://www.cdc.gov/nchs/data/nvsr/nvsr63/nvsr63_03.pdf.

[9] Figures for 2001 (in Excel spreadsheet on the Web) include September 11-related deaths for which death certificates were filed as of October 24, 2002. See Appendix II, Cause of death; Table IV for terrorism-related ICD–10 codes.

[10] The race groups, white, black, Asian or Pacific Islander, and American Indian or Alaska Native, include persons of Hispanic and non-Hispanic origin. Persons of Hispanic origin may be of any race. Death rates for Hispanic, American Indian or Alaska Native, and Asian or Pacific Islander persons should be interpreted with caution because of inconsistencies in reporting Hispanic origin or race on the death certificate (death rate numerators) compared with population figures (death rate denominators). The net effect of misclassification is an underestimation of deaths and death rates for races other than white and black. See Appendix II, Race, for a detailed discussion of sources of bias in death rates by race and Hispanic origin.

[11] Prior to 1997, data from states that did not report Hispanic origin on the death certificate were excluded. See Appendix II, Hispanic origin.

NOTES: Starting with *Health, United States, 2003*, rates for 1991–1999 were revised using intercensal population estimates based on the 1990 and 2000 censuses. For 2000, population estimates are bridged-race April 1 census counts. Starting with *Health, United States, 2012*, rates for 2001–2009 were revised using intercensal population estimates based on the 2000 and 2010 censuses. For 2010, population estimates are bridged-race April 1 census counts. Rates for 2011 and beyond were computed using 2010-based postcensal estimates. See Appendix I, Population Census and Population Estimates. Starting with 2003 data, some states began to collect information on more than one race on the death certificate, according to 1997 Office of Management and Budget (OMB) standards. The multiple-race data for these states were bridged to the single-race categories of the 1977 OMB standards, for comparability with other states. See Appendix II, Race. Data for additional years are available. See the Excel spreadsheet on the *Health, United States* website at: http://www.cdc.gov/nchs/hus.htm. Some data have been revised and differ from previous editions of *Health, United States*.

SOURCE: NCHS, National Vital Statistics System; Grove RD, Hetzel AM. Vital statistics rates in the United States, 1940–1960. Washington, DC: U.S. Government Printing Office. 1968; numerator data from National Vital Statistics System, annual public-use Mortality Files; denominator data from national population estimates for race groups from Table 1 and unpublished Hispanic population estimates for 1985–1996 prepared by the Housing and Household Economic Statistics Division, U.S. Census Bureau; Murphy SL, Kochanek KD, Xu JQ, Curtin SC. Deaths: Final data for 2015. National vital statistics reports. Hyattsville, MD: NCHS; 2017. Available from: http://www.cdc.gov/nchs/products/nvsr.htm. See Appendix I, National Vital Statistics System (NVSS).

Table 18 (page 1 of 4). Years of potential life lost before age 75 for selected causes of death, by sex, race, and Hispanic origin: United States, selected years 1980–2015

Excel and PDF versions (with more data years and standard errors when available): *http://www.cdc.gov/nchs/hus/contents2016.htm#018.*

[Data are based on death certificates]

Sex, race, Hispanic origin, and cause of death [2]	Crude 2015 [3]	Age-adjusted [1] 1980 [2]	1990 [2]	2000 [3]	2010 [3]	2014 [3]	2015 [3]
All persons	Years lost before age 75 per 100,000 population under age 75						
All causes	7,214.0	10,448.4	9,085.5	7,578.1	6,642.9	6,622.1	6,757.7
Diseases of heart	1,090.7	2,238.7	1,617.7	1,253.0	972.4	952.0	956.6
Ischemic heart disease	622.5	1,729.3	1,153.6	841.8	577.3	537.1	530.3
Cerebrovascular diseases	183.0	357.5	259.6	223.3	169.3	160.1	161.0
Malignant neoplasms	1,501.2	2,108.8	2,003.8	1,674.1	1,395.8	1,310.4	1,283.3
Trachea, bronchus, and lung	342.1	548.5	561.4	443.1	331.3	287.7	273.4
Colorectal	140.6	190.0	164.7	141.9	125.0	122.2	123.3
Prostate [4]	59.1	84.9	96.8	63.6	52.2	47.6	46.7
Breast [5]	272.0	463.2	451.6	332.6	262.4	245.9	241.9
Chronic lower respiratory diseases	217.1	169.1	187.4	188.1	172.4	174.1	175.9
Influenza and pneumonia	81.7	160.2	141.5	87.1	71.4	93.3	74.2
Chronic liver disease and cirrhosis	205.9	300.3	196.9	164.1	163.9	180.7	190.3
Diabetes mellitus [6]	200.8	134.4	155.9	178.4	158.2	170.8	176.2
Alzheimer's disease	17.1	†	†	10.9	11.7	11.4	13.0
Human immunodeficiency virus (HIV) disease	50.2	. . .	383.8	174.6	76.6	55.0	50.4
Unintentional injuries	1,139.2	1,543.5	1,162.1	1,026.5	1,025.2	1,080.1	1,172.0
Motor vehicle-related injuries	394.4	912.9	716.4	574.3	400.6	383.0	404.9
Poisoning	510.4	68.0	81.2	163.6	379.7	465.8	531.2
Nephritis, nephrotic syndrome, and nephrosis [6]	79.6	- - -	50.4	70.7	73.1	66.7	69.3
Suicide [7]	418.7	392.0	393.1	334.5	385.2	413.6	428.6
Homicide [7]	241.8	425.5	417.4	266.5	239.0	224.5	251.9
Male							
All causes	8,960.1	13,777.2	11,973.5	9,572.2	8,329.5	8,276.4	8,474.7
Diseases of heart	1,482.8	3,352.1	2,356.0	1,766.0	1,370.8	1,326.9	1,327.6
Ischemic heart disease	895.4	2,715.1	1,766.3	1,255.4	864.8	797.6	784.1
Cerebrovascular diseases	204.3	396.7	286.6	244.6	190.7	184.9	183.1
Malignant neoplasms	1,583.8	2,360.8	2,214.6	1,810.8	1,500.8	1,396.9	1,365.3
Trachea, bronchus, and lung	385.2	821.1	764.8	554.9	390.5	331.8	315.8
Colorectal	161.7	214.9	194.3	167.3	148.0	144.3	144.2
Prostate	59.1	84.9	96.8	63.6	52.2	47.6	46.7
Chronic lower respiratory diseases	221.5	235.1	224.8	206.0	182.8	182.8	184.5
Influenza and pneumonia	92.9	202.5	180.0	102.8	82.6	103.7	85.6
Chronic liver disease and cirrhosis	270.8	415.0	283.9	236.9	226.9	242.6	252.5
Diabetes mellitus [6]	245.9	140.4	170.4	203.8	194.8	214.0	220.7
Alzheimer's disease	14.7	†	†	10.6	10.7	10.3	11.7
Human immunodeficiency virus (HIV) disease	72.8	. . .	686.2	258.9	109.5	79.0	72.7
Unintentional injuries	1,608.3	2,342.7	1,715.1	1,475.6	1,432.1	1,509.6	1,642.4
Motor vehicle-related injuries	571.5	1,359.7	1,018.4	796.4	569.2	550.4	579.7
Poisoning	697.2	96.4	123.6	242.1	503.8	623.8	722.2
Nephritis, nephrotic syndrome, and nephrosis [6]	90.7	- - -	58.9	81.1	82.3	78.6	80.3
Suicide [7]	643.4	605.6	634.8	539.1	607.0	635.1	654.2
Homicide [7]	397.5	675.0	658.0	410.5	380.3	357.3	407.0
Female							
All causes	5,481.1	7,350.3	6,333.1	5,644.6	4,994.0	4,999.8	5,070.7
Diseases of heart	701.5	1,246.0	948.5	774.6	593.6	595.2	603.4
Ischemic heart disease	351.6	852.1	600.3	457.6	305.2	290.2	289.7
Cerebrovascular diseases	161.8	324.0	235.9	203.9	149.1	136.5	140.1
Malignant neoplasms	1,419.2	1,896.8	1,826.6	1,555.3	1,301.0	1,232.6	1,209.8
Trachea, bronchus, and lung	299.3	310.4	382.2	342.1	276.9	247.1	234.4
Colorectal	119.6	168.7	138.7	118.7	103.4	101.4	103.6
Breast	272.0	463.2	451.6	332.6	262.4	245.9	241.9
Chronic lower respiratory diseases	212.8	114.0	155.9	172.3	162.8	166.1	167.9
Influenza and pneumonia	70.7	122.0	106.2	72.3	60.7	83.4	63.1
Chronic liver disease and cirrhosis	141.6	194.5	115.1	94.5	103.5	121.5	130.6
Diabetes mellitus [6]	156.0	128.5	142.3	154.4	123.5	129.6	133.8
Alzheimer's disease	19.5	†	†	11.1	12.6	12.5	14.1
Human immunodeficiency virus (HIV) disease	27.8	. . .	87.8	92.0	44.4	31.6	28.7
Unintentional injuries	673.6	755.3	607.4	573.2	616.4	647.5	698.3
Motor vehicle-related injuries	218.7	470.4	411.6	348.5	230.5	213.6	228.1
Poisoning	325.0	40.2	39.1	85.0	255.1	306.6	338.9
Nephritis, nephrotic syndrome, and nephrosis [6]	68.7	- - -	42.4	60.8	64.6	55.3	58.8
Suicide [7]	195.7	184.2	153.3	129.1	163.7	191.2	201.7
Homicide [7]	87.3	181.3	174.3	118.9	94.9	88.7	93.1

See footnotes at end of table.

Table 18 (page 2 of 4). **Years of potential life lost before age 75 for selected causes of death, by sex, race, and Hispanic origin: United States, selected years 1980–2015**

Excel and PDF versions (with more data years and standard errors when available): http://www.cdc.gov/nchs/hus/contents2016.htm#018.

[Data are based on death certificates]

Sex, race, Hispanic origin, and cause of death[2]	Crude	Age-adjusted[1]					
	2015[3]	1980[2]	1990[2]	2000[3]	2010[3]	2014[3]	2015[3]
White[8]	Years lost before age 75 per 100,000 population under age 75						
All causes	7,090.6	9,554.1	8,159.5	6,949.5	6,342.8	6,390.1	6,514.8
Diseases of heart	1,056.0	2,100.8	1,490.3	1,149.4	900.9	883.0	889.0
Ischemic heart disease	635.4	1,682.7	1,113.4	805.3	563.7	524.8	519.2
Cerebrovascular diseases	163.3	300.7	213.1	187.1	142.7	138.1	137.9
Malignant neoplasms	1,549.3	2,035.9	1,929.3	1,627.8	1,375.8	1,301.5	1,274.9
Trachea, bronchus, and lung	365.1	529.9	544.2	436.3	332.8	291.0	277.8
Colorectal	140.7	186.8	157.8	134.1	118.4	117.6	119.3
Prostate[4]	55.2	74.8	86.6	54.3	45.3	41.8	40.9
Breast[5]	263.7	460.2	441.7	315.6	245.0	230.3	226.7
Chronic lower respiratory diseases	236.7	165.4	182.3	185.3	176.1	178.7	180.1
Influenza and pneumonia	79.6	130.8	116.9	77.7	66.7	90.1	70.2
Chronic liver disease and cirrhosis	228.2	257.3	175.8	162.7	173.5	195.1	206.3
Diabetes mellitus[6]	186.5	115.7	133.7	155.6	139.0	152.6	157.5
Alzheimer's disease	19.2	†	†	11.4	12.4	12.0	13.6
Human immunodeficiency virus (HIV) disease	27.6	. . .	309.0	94.7	39.9	30.2	27.3
Unintentional injuries	1,208.7	1,520.4	1,139.7	1,031.8	1,098.6	1,156.4	1,258.9
Motor vehicle-related injuries	398.5	939.9	726.7	586.1	419.0	395.9	415.4
Poisoning	578.7	64.9	74.4	167.2	435.4	534.7	610.6
Nephritis, nephrotic syndrome, and nephrosis[6]	66.5	- - -	37.0	52.5	57.4	53.6	55.2
Suicide[7]	469.3	414.5	417.7	362.0	430.8	468.3	484.7
Homicide[7]	127.3	271.7	234.9	156.6	138.7	125.7	135.9
Black or African American[8]							
All causes	9,764.6	17,873.4	16,593.0	12,897.1	9,832.5	9,490.6	9,702.3
Diseases of heart	1,613.8	3,619.9	2,891.8	2,275.2	1,691.1	1,638.9	1,637.9
Ischemic heart disease	737.4	2,305.1	1,676.1	1,300.1	818.8	756.5	740.4
Cerebrovascular diseases	318.0	883.2	656.4	507.0	358.1	322.3	322.9
Malignant neoplasms	1,610.4	2,946.1	2,894.8	2,294.7	1,796.7	1,651.6	1,598.8
Trachea, bronchus, and lung	328.8	776.0	811.3	593.0	405.6	340.8	318.3
Colorectal	171.3	232.3	241.8	222.4	188.6	176.5	172.9
Prostate[4]	102.4	200.3	223.5	171.0	127.3	109.0	106.9
Breast[5]	378.6	524.2	592.9	500.0	420.8	386.7	379.2
Chronic lower respiratory diseases	201.7	203.7	240.6	232.7	187.7	193.6	198.3
Influenza and pneumonia	114.9	384.9	330.8	161.2	109.8	130.9	114.5
Chronic liver disease and cirrhosis	121.6	644.0	371.8	185.6	120.2	120.4	122.5
Diabetes mellitus[6]	325.5	305.3	361.5	383.4	316.4	321.4	329.6
Alzheimer's disease	12.6	†	†	8.3	10.0	11.2	13.0
Human immunodeficiency virus (HIV) disease	192.4	. . .	1,014.7	763.3	329.5	222.9	203.5
Unintentional injuries	1,081.0	1,751.5	1,392.7	1,152.8	896.7	986.8	1,082.6
Motor vehicle-related injuries	457.4	750.2	699.5	580.8	393.4	404.6	450.7
Poisoning	326.8	99.4	144.3	196.6	218.9	289.7	342.1
Nephritis, nephrotic syndrome, and nephrosis[6]	172.9	- - -	160.9	216.9	193.2	167.1	174.6
Suicide[7]	218.5	238.0	261.4	208.7	196.4	209.0	216.1
Homicide[7]	942.0	1,580.8	1,612.9	941.6	821.2	785.1	907.4
American Indian or Alaska Native[8]							
All causes	6,895.3	13,390.9	9,506.2	7,758.2	6,771.3	6,954.0	7,176.2
Diseases of heart	770.5	1,819.9	1,391.0	1,030.1	820.6	822.2	850.0
Ischemic heart disease	437.5	1,208.2	901.8	709.3	487.6	492.0	487.5
Cerebrovascular diseases	124.3	269.3	223.3	198.1	129.7	123.2	138.6
Malignant neoplasms	776.0	1,101.3	1,141.1	995.7	929.5	809.9	848.8
Trachea, bronchus, and lung	148.5	181.1	268.1	227.8	211.0	168.4	166.0
Colorectal	84.1	78.8	82.4	93.8	95.8	90.2	94.5
Prostate[4]	28.3	66.7	42.0	44.5	36.8	39.0	32.6
Breast[5]	119.1	205.5	213.4	174.1	145.0	110.9	129.7
Chronic lower respiratory diseases	147.0	89.3	129.0	151.8	154.5	140.5	158.2
Influenza and pneumonia	69.5	307.9	206.3	124.0	99.3	129.0	75.5
Chronic liver disease and cirrhosis	543.8	1,190.3	535.1	519.4	510.8	549.9	605.3
Diabetes mellitus[6]	269.5	305.5	292.3	305.6	267.6	279.4	300.7
Alzheimer's disease	4.3	†	†	*	8.8	6.7	5.3
Human immunodeficiency virus (HIV) disease	33.2	. . .	70.1	68.4	46.1	29.5	36.2
Unintentional injuries	1,512.5	3,541.0	2,183.9	1,700.1	1,377.7	1,509.3	1,523.6
Motor vehicle-related injuries	652.8	2,102.4	1,301.5	1,032.2	570.6	605.4	638.0
Poisoning	516.1	92.9	119.5	180.1	449.6	537.8	543.5
Nephritis, nephrotic syndrome, and nephrosis[6]	67.2	- - -	88.5	102.0	81.7	80.5	74.1
Suicide[7]	513.0	515.0	495.9	403.1	437.9	437.1	497.7
Homicide[7]	263.2	628.9	434.2	278.5	256.4	239.0	256.2

See footnotes at end of table.

Excel and PDF versions (with more data years and standard errors when available): http://www.cdc.gov/nchs/hus/contents2016.htm#018.

[Data are based on death certificates]

Sex, race, Hispanic origin, and cause of death[2]	Crude 2015[3]	Age-adjusted[1]					
		1980[2]	1990[2]	2000[3]	2010[3]	2014[3]	2015[3]
Asian or Pacific Islander[8]		Years lost before age 75 per 100,000 population under age 75					
All causes	3,073.6	5,378.4	4,705.2	3,811.1	3,061.2	2,954.4	3,049.7
Diseases of heart	414.8	952.8	702.2	567.9	400.1	402.1	400.6
Ischemic heart disease	249.9	697.7	486.6	381.1	250.6	239.8	240.1
Cerebrovascular diseases.	133.8	266.9	233.5	199.4	148.3	121.8	129.5
Malignant neoplasms	839.1	1,218.6	1,166.4	1,033.8	874.7	799.4	809.9
Trachea, bronchus, and lung	137.1	238.2	204.7	185.8	148.2	136.5	130.5
Colorectal.	84.0	115.9	105.1	91.6	87.6	79.1	80.8
Prostate[4]	18.6	17.0	32.4	18.8	17.0	16.8	18.6
Breast[5]	165.6	222.2	216.5	200.8	156.9	160.6	155.1
Chronic lower respiratory diseases	29.1	56.4	72.8	56.5	33.2	32.7	28.0
Influenza and pneumonia	36.5	79.3	74.0	48.6	38.4	42.8	36.1
Chronic liver disease and cirrhosis.	45.5	85.6	72.4	44.8	41.7	41.6	44.0
Diabetes mellitus[6]	78.9	83.1	74.0	77.0	69.5	73.8	75.4
Alzheimer's disease	4.4	†	†	3.5	3.2	2.6	4.3
Human immunodeficiency virus (HIV) disease	11.2	. . .	77.0	19.9	10.7	9.8	11.0
Unintentional injuries.	336.8	742.7	636.6	425.7	303.0	307.0	328.6
Motor vehicle-related injuries	144.3	472.6	445.5	263.4	147.9	141.2	140.4
Poisoning	89.6	*	17.6	25.9	46.5	67.6	84.3
Nephritis, nephrotic syndrome, and nephrosis[6] . . .	33.6	- - -	26.7	33.6	38.1	29.1	32.3
Suicide[7]	229.9	217.1	200.6	168.6	199.7	203.1	222.0
Homicide[7]	61.5	201.1	205.8	113.1	68.8	59.7	60.6
Hispanic or Latino[8,9]							
All causes	4,452.8	- - -	7,963.3	6,037.6	4,795.1	4,676.8	4,750.4
Diseases of heart	474.5	- - -	1,082.0	821.3	598.1	567.9	578.0
Ischemic heart disease	268.9	- - -	756.6	564.6	366.6	334.1	339.9
Cerebrovascular diseases.	116.9	- - -	238.0	207.8	150.4	140.2	141.1
Malignant neoplasms	752.0	- - -	1,232.2	1,098.2	951.2	909.3	900.6
Trachea, bronchus, and lung	74.6	- - -	193.7	152.1	115.0	96.8	96.9
Colorectal.	75.5	- - -	100.2	101.4	94.0	87.4	92.4
Prostate[4]	26.0	- - -	47.7	42.9	38.2	36.5	37.8
Breast[5]	143.0	- - -	299.3	230.7	180.0	183.4	169.0
Chronic lower respiratory diseases	44.3	- - -	78.8	68.5	59.6	52.7	54.3
Influenza and pneumonia	47.9	- - -	130.1	76.0	57.5	79.1	54.3
Chronic liver disease and cirrhosis.	182.7	- - -	329.1	252.1	201.6	216.4	219.2
Diabetes mellitus[6]	130.9	- - -	177.8	215.6	158.5	160.9	163.1
Alzheimer's disease	6.8	- - -	†	6.9	8.4	8.9	10.2
Human immunodeficiency virus (HIV) disease	41.6	. . .	600.1	209.4	74.9	49.5	47.0
Unintentional injuries.	827.8	- - -	1,190.6	920.1	708.7	740.1	808.7
Motor vehicle-related injuries	392.1	- - -	740.8	540.2	340.3	348.3	370.7
Poisoning	263.2	- - -	121.9	145.9	191.2	234.1	269.1
Nephritis, nephrotic syndrome, and nephrosis[6] . . .	49.0	- - -	54.4	62.0	67.7	56.3	60.1
Suicide[7]	221.6	- - -	256.2	188.5	193.6	214.3	215.4
Homicide[7]	229.1	- - -	720.8	335.1	238.0	197.6	213.5
White, not Hispanic or Latino[9]							
All causes	7,661.5	- - -	8,022.5	6,960.5	6,545.3	6,659.4	6,799.9
Diseases of heart	1,193.0	- - -	1,504.0	1,175.1	943.2	932.4	939.2
Ischemic heart disease	721.6	- - -	1,127.2	824.7	590.8	553.6	546.4
Cerebrovascular diseases.	172.0	- - -	210.1	183.0	139.1	134.9	134.1
Malignant neoplasms	1,737.4	- - -	1,974.1	1,668.4	1,421.5	1,349.1	1,320.0
Trachea, bronchus, and lung	439.1	- - -	566.8	460.3	359.1	318.6	304.0
Colorectal.	155.7	- - -	162.1	136.2	121.2	122.3	123.0
Prostate[4]	62.4	- - -	89.2	54.9	45.9	42.2	41.0
Breast[5]	291.1	- - -	451.5	322.3	252.6	235.4	234.1
Chronic lower respiratory diseases	285.4	- - -	188.1	193.8	189.1	195.9	197.1
Influenza and pneumonia	86.3	- - -	112.3	76.4	67.8	91.1	72.3
Chronic liver disease and cirrhosis.	234.4	- - -	162.4	150.9	166.9	188.6	200.7
Diabetes mellitus[6]	197.1	- - -	131.2	150.2	136.7	150.6	156.2
Alzheimer's disease	22.2	- - -	†	11.7	12.7	12.3	13.8
Human immunodeficiency virus (HIV) disease	22.4	. . .	271.2	76.0	31.3	24.7	21.1
Unintentional injuries.	1,285.9	- - -	1,114.7	1,041.4	1,183.0	1,253.8	1,365.1
Motor vehicle-related injuries	390.8	- - -	715.7	588.8	430.6	398.9	417.6
Poisoning	652.3	- - -	68.3	169.4	494.0	613.2	700.8
Nephritis, nephrotic syndrome, and nephrosis[6] . . .	69.8	- - -	34.5	51.1	55.3	52.7	53.7
Suicide[7]	529.2	- - -	433.0	389.2	483.8	531.3	554.1
Homicide[7]	96.1	- - -	162.0	113.2	103.4	98.4	106.2

See footnotes at end of table.

Excel and PDF versions (with more data years and standard errors when available): http://www.cdc.gov/nchs/hus/contents2016.htm#018.

[Data are based on death certificates]

. . . Category not applicable.

- - - Data not available.

[†] Data for Alzheimer's disease are only presented for data years 1999 and beyond due to large differences in death rates caused by changes in the coding of this cause of death between ICD–9 and ICD–10. See Appendix II, Cause of death; Comparability ratio; Table IV; Table V.

[*] Rates based on fewer than 20 deaths are considered unreliable and are not shown.

[1] Age-adjusted rates are calculated using the year 2000 standard population. Prior to 2001, age-adjusted rates were calculated using standard million proportions based on rounded population numbers. Starting with 2001 data, unrounded population numbers are used to calculate age-adjusted rates. See Appendix II, Age adjustment.

[2] Underlying cause of death was coded according to the 9th Revision of the *International Classification of Diseases* (ICD) in 1980–1998. See Appendix II, Cause of death; Table III; Table IV.

[3] Starting with 1999 data, cause of death is coded according to ICD–10. See Appendix II, Cause of death; Comparability ratio; Table IV; Table V.

[4] Rate for male population only.

[5] Rate for female population only.

[6] Starting with 2011 data, the rules for selecting Renal failure as the underlying cause of death were changed, affecting the number of deaths in the Nephritis, nephrotic syndrome, and nephrosis and Diabetes categories. These changes directly affect deaths with mention of Renal failure and other associated conditions, such as Diabetes mellitus with renal complications. The result is a decrease in the number of deaths for Nephritis, nephrotic syndrome, and nephrosis and an increase in the number of deaths for Diabetes mellitus. Therefore, trend data for these two causes of death should be interpreted with caution. For more information, see Technical Notes in Deaths: Preliminary data for 2011, available from: http://www.cdc.gov/nchs/data/nvsr/nvsr61/nvsr61_06.pdf.

[7] Figures for 2001 (in Excel spreadsheet on the Web) include September 11-related deaths for which death certificates were filed as of October 24, 2002. See Appendix II, Cause of death; Table IV for terrorism-related ICD–10 codes.

[8] The race groups, white, black, Asian or Pacific Islander, and American Indian or Alaska Native, include persons of Hispanic and non-Hispanic origin. Persons of Hispanic origin may be of any race. Death rates for Hispanic, American Indian or Alaska Native, and Asian or Pacific Islander persons should be interpreted with caution because of inconsistencies in reporting Hispanic origin or race on the death certificate (death rate numerators) compared with population figures (death rate denominators). The net effect of misclassification is an underestimation of deaths and death rates for races other than white and black. See Appendix II, Race, for a detailed discussion of sources of bias in death rates by race and Hispanic origin.

[9] Prior to 1997, data from states that did not report Hispanic origin on the death certificate were excluded. See Appendix II, Hispanic origin.

NOTES: Starting with *Health, United States, 2003*, rates for 1991–1999 were revised using intercensal population estimates based on the 1990 and 2000 censuses. For 2000, population estimates are bridged-race April 1 census counts. Starting with *Health, United States, 2012*, rates for 2001–2009 were revised using intercensal population estimates based on the 2000 and 2010 censuses. For 2010, population estimates are bridged-race April 1 census counts. Rates for 2011 and beyond were computed using 2010-based postcensal estimates. See Appendix I, Population Census and Population Estimates. See Appendix II, Years of potential life lost (YPLL) for definition and method of calculation. Starting with 2003 data, some states began to collect information on more than one race on the death certificate, according to 1997 Office of Management and Budget (OMB) standards. The multiple-race data for these states were bridged to the single-race categories of the 1977 OMB standards, for comparability with other states. See Appendix II, Race. Rates are rounded at the end of the calculation process. They may differ from rates based on the same data presented elsewhere if rounding is done earlier in the calculation process. Data for additional years are available. See the Excel spreadsheet on the *Health, United States* website at: http://www.cdc.gov/nchs/hus.htm. Some data have been revised and differ from previous editions of *Health, United States*.

SOURCE: NCHS, National Vital Statistics System; numerator data from annual public-use Mortality Files; denominator data from national population estimates for race groups from Table 1 and unpublished Hispanic population estimates for 1990–1996 prepared by the Housing and Household Economic Statistics Division, U.S. Census Bureau. See Appendix I, National Vital Statistics System (NVSS).

Table 19 (page 1 of 4). Leading causes of death and numbers of deaths, by sex, race, and Hispanic origin: United States, 1980 and 2015

Excel and PDF versions (with more data years and standard errors when available): http://www.cdc.gov/nchs/hus/contents2016.htm#019.

[Data are based on death certificates]

Sex, race, Hispanic origin, and rank order	1980 Cause of death	1980 Deaths	2015 Cause of death	2015 Deaths
All persons				
Rank	All causes	1,989,841	All causes	2,712,630
1	Diseases of heart	761,085	Diseases of heart	633,842
2	Malignant neoplasms	416,509	Malignant neoplasms	595,930
3	Cerebrovascular diseases	170,225	Chronic lower respiratory diseases [1,2]	155,041
4	Unintentional injuries	105,718	Unintentional injuries	146,571
5	Chronic obstructive pulmonary diseases [1]	56,050	Cerebrovascular diseases	140,323
6	Pneumonia and influenza [2]	54,619	Alzheimer's disease	110,561
7	Diabetes mellitus	34,851	Diabetes mellitus [3]	79,535
8	Chronic liver disease and cirrhosis	30,583	Influenza and pneumonia [2]	57,062
9	Atherosclerosis	29,449	Nephritis, nephrotic syndrome, and nephrosis [3]	49,959
10	Suicide	26,869	Suicide	44,193
Male				
Rank	All causes	1,075,078	All causes	1,373,404
1	Diseases of heart	405,661	Diseases of heart	335,002
2	Malignant neoplasms	225,948	Malignant neoplasms	313,818
3	Unintentional injuries	74,180	Unintentional injuries	92,919
4	Cerebrovascular diseases	69,973	Chronic lower respiratory diseases [1,2]	72,498
5	Chronic obstructive pulmonary diseases [1]	38,625	Cerebrovascular diseases	58,288
6	Pneumonia and influenza [2]	27,574	Diabetes mellitus [3]	43,123
7	Suicide	20,505	Suicide	33,994
8	Chronic liver disease and cirrhosis	19,768	Alzheimer's disease	33,690
9	Homicide	18,779	Influenza and pneumonia [2]	26,903
10	Diabetes mellitus	14,325	Chronic liver disease and cirrhosis	25,666
Female				
Rank	All causes	914,763	All causes	1,339,226
1	Diseases of heart	355,424	Diseases of heart	298,840
2	Malignant neoplasms	190,561	Malignant neoplasms	282,112
3	Cerebrovascular diseases	100,252	Chronic lower respiratory diseases [1,2]	82,543
4	Unintentional injuries	31,538	Cerebrovascular diseases	82,035
5	Pneumonia and influenza [2]	27,045	Alzheimer's disease	76,871
6	Diabetes mellitus	20,526	Unintentional injuries	53,652
7	Atherosclerosis	17,848	Diabetes mellitus [3]	36,412
8	Chronic obstructive pulmonary diseases [1]	17,425	Influenza and pneumonia [2]	30,159
9	Chronic liver disease and cirrhosis	10,815	Nephritis, nephrotic syndrome, and nephrosis [3]	24,518
10	Certain conditions originating in the perinatal period	9,815	Septicemia	21,388
White				
Rank	All causes	1,738,607	All causes	2,306,861
1	Diseases of heart	683,347	Diseases of heart	540,857
2	Malignant neoplasms	368,162	Malignant neoplasms	505,613
3	Cerebrovascular diseases	148,734	Chronic lower respiratory diseases [1,2]	141,766
4	Unintentional injuries	90,122	Unintentional injuries	125,773
5	Chronic obstructive pulmonary diseases [1]	52,375	Cerebrovascular diseases	116,788
6	Pneumonia and influenza [2]	48,369	Alzheimer's disease	99,866
7	Diabetes mellitus	28,868	Diabetes mellitus [3]	61,938
8	Atherosclerosis	27,069	Influenza and pneumonia [2]	48,877
9	Chronic liver disease and cirrhosis	25,240	Suicide	39,796
10	Suicide	24,829	Nephritis, nephrotic syndrome, and nephrosis [3]	39,078
Black or African American				
Rank	All causes	233,135	All causes	320,072
1	Diseases of heart	72,956	Diseases of heart	75,249
2	Malignant neoplasms	45,037	Malignant neoplasms	69,389
3	Cerebrovascular diseases	20,135	Cerebrovascular diseases	17,988
4	Unintentional injuries	13,480	Unintentional injuries	15,745
5	Homicide	10,172	Diabetes mellitus [3]	13,869
6	Certain conditions originating in the perinatal period	6,961	Chronic lower respiratory diseases [1,2]	10,475
7	Pneumonia and influenza [2]	5,648	Homicide	9,173
8	Diabetes mellitus	5,544	Nephritis, nephrotic syndrome, and nephrosis [3]	9,170
9	Chronic liver disease and cirrhosis	4,790	Alzheimer's disease	8,156
10	Nephritis, nephrotic syndrome, and nephrosis	3,416	Septicemia	6,647

See footnotes at end of table.

Table 19 (page 2 of 4). Leading causes of death and numbers of deaths, by sex, race, and Hispanic origin: United States, 1980 and 2015

Excel and PDF versions (with more data years and standard errors when available): http://www.cdc.gov/nchs/hus/contents2016.htm#019.

[Data are based on death certificates]

Sex, race, Hispanic origin, and rank order	1980		2015	
	Cause of death	Deaths	Cause of death	Deaths
American Indian or Alaska Native				
Rank	All causes	6,923	All causes	19,016
1	Diseases of heart	1,494	Diseases of heart	3,463
2	Unintentional injuries	1,290	Malignant neoplasms	3,358
3	Malignant neoplasms	770	Unintentional injuries	2,078
4	Chronic liver disease and cirrhosis.	410	Diabetes mellitus[3]	1,087
5	Cerebrovascular diseases.	322	Chronic liver disease and cirrhosis	1,061
6	Pneumonia and influenza[2]	257	Chronic lower respiratory diseases[1,2]	883
7	Homicide.	217	Cerebrovascular diseases	676
8	Diabetes mellitus	210	Suicide	577
9	Certain conditions originating in the perinatal period .	199	Nephritis, nephrotic syndrome, and nephrosis[3]	352
10	Suicide	181	Influenza and pneumonia[2]	342
Asian or Pacific Islander				
Rank	All causes	11,071	All causes	66,681
1	Diseases of heart	3,265	Malignant neoplasms	17,570
2	Malignant neoplasms	2,522	Diseases of heart	14,273
3	Cerebrovascular diseases.	1,028	Cerebrovascular diseases	4,871
4	Unintentional injuries	810	Unintentional injuries	2,975
5	Pneumonia and influenza[2]	342	Diabetes mellitus[3]	2,641
6	Suicide	249	Alzheimer's disease	2,212
7	Certain conditions originating in the perinatal period .	246	Influenza and pneumonia[2]	2,202
8	Diabetes mellitus	227	Chronic lower respiratory diseases[1,2]	1,917
9	Homicide.	211	Nephritis, nephrotic syndrome, and nephrosis[3]	1,359
10	Chronic obstructive pulmonary diseases[1]	207	Suicide	1,316
Hispanic or Latino				
Rank	- - -	- - -	All causes.	179,457
1	- - -	- - -	Malignant neoplasms	37,804
2	- - -	- - -	Diseases of heart	36,401
3	- - -	- - -	Unintentional injuries	13,806
4	- - -	- - -	Cerebrovascular diseases	9,795
5	- - -	- - -	Diabetes mellitus[3]	8,278
6	- - -	- - -	Alzheimer's disease	6,444
7	- - -	- - -	Chronic liver disease and cirrhosis	6,018
8	- - -	- - -	Chronic lower respiratory diseases[1,2]	5,159
9	- - -	- - -	Nephritis, nephrotic syndrome, and nephrosis[3]	3,581
10	- - -	- - -	Influenza and pneumonia[2]	3,497
White male				
Rank	All causes	933,878	All causes.	1,164,176
1	Diseases of heart	364,679	Diseases of heart	285,884
2	Malignant neoplasms	198,188	Malignant neoplasms	267,885
3	Unintentional injuries	62,963	Unintentional injuries	78,887
4	Cerebrovascular diseases.	60,095	Chronic lower respiratory diseases[1,2]	65,680
5	Chronic obstructive pulmonary diseases[1]	35,977	Cerebrovascular diseases	47,713
6	Pneumonia and influenza[2]	23,810	Diabetes mellitus[3]	34,299
7	Suicide	18,901	Alzheimer's disease	30,710
8	Chronic liver disease and cirrhosis.	16,407	Suicide	30,658
9	Diabetes mellitus	12,125	Influenza and pneumonia[2]	22,794
10	Atherosclerosis	10,543	Chronic liver disease and cirrhosis	22,681
Black or African American male				
Rank	All causes	130,138	All causes.	164,670
1	Diseases of heart	37,877	Diseases of heart	39,325
2	Malignant neoplasms	25,861	Malignant neoplasms	35,250
3	Unintentional injuries	9,701	Unintentional injuries	10,779
4	Cerebrovascular diseases.	9,194	Cerebrovascular diseases	8,073
5	Homicide.	8,274	Homicide	8,021
6	Certain conditions originating in the perinatal period .	3,869	Diabetes mellitus[3]	6,909
7	Pneumonia and influenza[2]	3,386	Chronic lower respiratory diseases[1,2]	5,328
8	Chronic liver disease and cirrhosis.	3,020	Nephritis, nephrotic syndrome, and nephrosis[3]	4,401
9	Chronic obstructive pulmonary diseases[1]	2,429	Septicemia	3,098
10	Diabetes mellitus	2,010	Influenza and pneumonia[2]	2,787

See footnotes at end of table.

Table 19 (page 3 of 4). Leading causes of death and numbers of deaths, by sex, race, and Hispanic origin: United States, 1980 and 2015

Excel and PDF versions (with more data years and standard errors when available): http://www.cdc.gov/nchs/hus/contents2016.htm#019.

[Data are based on death certificates]

Sex, race, Hispanic origin, and rank order	1980 Cause of death	1980 Deaths	2015 Cause of death	2015 Deaths
American Indian or Alaska Native male				
Rank	All causes	4,193	All causes	10,451
1	Unintentional injuries	946	Diseases of heart	2,009
2	Diseases of heart	917	Malignant neoplasms	1,781
3	Malignant neoplasms	408	Unintentional injuries	1,364
4	Chronic liver disease and cirrhosis	239	Chronic liver disease and cirrhosis	598
5	Cerebrovascular diseases	163	Diabetes mellitus [3]	573
6	Homicide	162	Suicide	426
7	Pneumonia and influenza [2]	148	Chronic lower respiratory diseases [1,2]	408
8	Suicide	147	Cerebrovascular diseases	308
9	Certain conditions originating in the perinatal period	107	Homicide	228
10	Diabetes mellitus	86	Influenza and pneumonia [2]	189
Asian or Pacific Islander male				
Rank	All causes	6,809	All causes	34,107
1	Diseases of heart	2,174	Malignant neoplasms	8,902
2	Malignant neoplasms	1,485	Diseases of heart	7,784
3	Unintentional injuries	556	Cerebrovascular diseases	2,194
4	Cerebrovascular diseases	521	Unintentional injuries	1,889
5	Pneumonia and influenza [2]	227	Diabetes mellitus [3]	1,342
6	Suicide	159	Influenza and pneumonia [2]	1,133
7	Chronic obstructive pulmonary diseases [1]	158	Chronic lower respiratory diseases [1,2]	1,082
8	Homicide	151	Suicide	887
9	Certain conditions originating in the perinatal period	128	Alzheimer's disease	688
10	Diabetes mellitus	103	Nephritis, nephrotic syndrome, and nephrosis [3]	672
Hispanic or Latino male				
Rank	---	---	All causes	98,170
1	---	---	Diseases of heart	20,225
2	---	---	Malignant neoplasms	19,847
3	---	---	Unintentional injuries	10,067
4	---	---	Cerebrovascular diseases	4,544
5	---	---	Diabetes mellitus [3]	4,426
6	---	---	Chronic liver disease and cirrhosis	4,109
7	---	---	Chronic lower respiratory diseases [1,2]	2,606
8	---	---	Suicide	2,587
9	---	---	Homicide	2,391
10	---	---	Alzheimer's disease	2,035
White female				
Rank	All causes	804,729	All causes	1,142,685
1	Diseases of heart	318,668	Diseases of heart	254,973
2	Malignant neoplasms	169,974	Malignant neoplasms	237,728
3	Cerebrovascular diseases	88,639	Chronic lower respiratory diseases [1,2]	76,086
4	Unintentional injuries	27,159	Alzheimer's disease	69,156
5	Pneumonia and influenza [2]	24,559	Cerebrovascular diseases	69,075
6	Diabetes mellitus	16,743	Unintentional injuries	46,886
7	Atherosclerosis	16,526	Diabetes mellitus [3]	27,639
8	Chronic obstructive pulmonary diseases [1]	16,398	Influenza and pneumonia [2]	26,083
9	Chronic liver disease and cirrhosis	8,833	Nephritis, nephrotic syndrome, and nephrosis [3]	18,876
10	Certain conditions originating in the perinatal period	6,512	Septicemia	17,282
Black or African American female				
Rank	All causes	102,997	All causes	155,402
1	Diseases of heart	35,079	Diseases of heart	35,924
2	Malignant neoplasms	19,176	Malignant neoplasms	34,139
3	Cerebrovascular diseases	10,941	Cerebrovascular diseases	9,915
4	Unintentional injuries	3,779	Diabetes mellitus [3]	6,960
5	Diabetes mellitus	3,534	Alzheimer's disease	5,973
6	Certain conditions originating in the perinatal period	3,092	Chronic lower respiratory diseases [1,2]	5,147
7	Pneumonia and influenza [2]	2,262	Unintentional injuries	4,966
8	Homicide	1,898	Nephritis, nephrotic syndrome, and nephrosis [3]	4,769
9	Chronic liver disease and cirrhosis	1,770	Septicemia	3,549
10	Nephritis, nephrotic syndrome, and nephrosis	1,722	Essential hypertension and hypertensive renal disease	3,175

See footnotes at end of table.

Table 19 (page 4 of 4). Leading causes of death and numbers of deaths, by sex, race, and Hispanic origin: United States, 1980 and 2015

Excel and PDF versions (with more data years and standard errors when available): http://www.cdc.gov/nchs/hus/contents2016.htm#019.

[Data are based on death certificates]

Sex, race, Hispanic origin, and rank order	1980		2015	
	Cause of death	Deaths	Cause of death	Deaths
American Indian or Alaska Native female				
Rank	All causes	2,730	All causes	8,565
1	Diseases of heart	577	Malignant neoplasms	1,577
2	Malignant neoplasms	362	Diseases of heart	1,454
3	Unintentional injuries	344	Unintentional injuries	714
4	Chronic liver disease and cirrhosis	171	Diabetes mellitus[3]	514
5	Cerebrovascular diseases	159	Chronic lower respiratory diseases[1,2]	475
6	Diabetes mellitus	124	Chronic liver disease and cirrhosis	463
7	Pneumonia and influenza[2]	109	Cerebrovascular diseases	368
8	Certain conditions originating in the perinatal period	92	Alzheimer's disease	218
9	Nephritis, nephrotic syndrome, and nephrosis	56	Nephritis, nephrotic syndrome, and nephrosis[3]	186
10	Homicide	55	Septicemia	167
Asian or Pacific Islander female				
Rank	All causes	4,262	All causes	32,574
1	Diseases of heart	1,091	Malignant neoplasms	8,668
2	Malignant neoplasms	1,037	Diseases of heart	6,489
3	Cerebrovascular diseases	507	Cerebrovascular diseases	2,677
4	Unintentional injuries	254	Alzheimer's disease	1,524
5	Diabetes mellitus	124	Diabetes mellitus[3]	1,299
6	Certain conditions originating in the perinatal period	118	Unintentional injuries	1,086
7	Pneumonia and influenza[2]	115	Influenza and pneumonia[2]	1,069
8	Congenital anomalies	104	Chronic lower respiratory diseases[1,2]	835
9	Suicide	90	Nephritis, nephrotic syndrome, and nephrosis[3]	687
10	Homicide	60	Essential hypertension and hypertensive renal disease	635
Hispanic or Latina female				
Rank	- - -	- - -	All causes	81,287
1	- - -	- - -	Malignant neoplasms	17,957
2	- - -	- - -	Diseases of heart	16,176
3	- - -	- - -	Cerebrovascular diseases	5,251
4	- - -	- - -	Alzheimer's disease	4,409
5	- - -	- - -	Diabetes mellitus[3]	3,852
6	- - -	- - -	Unintentional injuries	3,739
7	- - -	- - -	Chronic lower respiratory diseases[1,2]	2,553
8	- - -	- - -	Chronic liver disease and cirrhosis	1,909
9	- - -	- - -	Influenza and pneumonia[2]	1,762
10	- - -	- - -	Nephritis, nephrotic syndrome, and nephrosis[3]	1,744

- - - Data not available. Complete coverage of all states for the Hispanic origin variable began in 1997.

[1] Between 1998 and 1999, the cause of death title for Chronic obstructive pulmonary diseases in the *International Classification of Diseases, 9th Revision* (ICD–9) was renamed to Chronic lower respiratory diseases (CLRD) in ICD–10.

[2] Starting with 1999 data, the rules for selecting CLRD and Pneumonia as the underlying cause of death changed, resulting in an increase in the number of deaths for CLRD and a decrease in the number of deaths for pneumonia. Therefore, trend data for these two causes of death should be interpreted with caution. For more information, see Comparability of cause of death between ICD–9 and ICD–10 in Appendix II, Table V.

[3] Starting with 2011 data, the rules for selecting Renal failure as the underlying cause of death were changed, affecting the number of deaths in the Nephritis, nephrotic syndrome, and nephrosis and Diabetes categories. These changes directly affect deaths with mention of Renal failure and other associated conditions, such as Diabetes mellitus with renal complications. The result is a decrease in the number of deaths for Nephritis, nephrotic syndrome, and nephrosis and an increase in the number of deaths for Diabetes mellitus. Therefore, trend data for these two causes of death should be interpreted with caution. For more information, see Technical Notes in Deaths: Final data for 2011, available from: http://www.cdc.gov/nchs/data/nvsr/nvsr63/nvsr63_03.pdf.

NOTES: For cause of death codes based on the ICD–9 in 1980 and ICD–10 in 2015, see Appendix II, Cause of death; Cause-of-death ranking; Table III; Table IV. Starting with 2003 data, some states began to collect information on more than one race on the death certificate, according to 1997 Office of Management and Budget (OMB) standards. The multiple-race data for these states were bridged to the single-race categories of the 1977 OMB standards, for comparability with other states. The race groups, white, black, Asian or Pacific Islander, and American Indian or Alaska Native, include persons of Hispanic and non-Hispanic origin. Persons of Hispanic origin may be of any race. See Appendix II, Race; Hispanic origin.

SOURCE: NCHS, National Vital Statistics System: Vital statistics of the United States, vol II, mortality, part A, 1980. Washington, DC: Public Health Service. 1985. Public-use 2015 Mortality File. Murphy SL, Kochanek KD, Xu JQ, Curtin SC. Deaths: Final data for 2015. National vital statistics reports. Hyattsville, MD: NCHS; 2017. Available from: http://www.cdc.gov/nchs/products/nvsr.htm. See Appendix I, National Vital Statistics System (NVSS).

Table 20 (page 1 of 2). Leading causes of death and numbers of deaths, by age: United States, 1980 and 2015

Excel and PDF versions (with more data years and standard errors when available): http://www.cdc.gov/nchs/hus/contents2016.htm#020.

[Data are based on death certificates]

Age and rank order	1980 Cause of death	1980 Deaths	2015 Cause of death	2015 Deaths
Under 1 year				
Rank	All causes	45,526	All causes	23,455
1	Congenital anomalies	9,220	Congenital malformations/deformations/ chromosomal abnormalities	4,825
2	Sudden infant death syndrome	5,510	Disorders related to short gestation and low birth weight	4,084
3	Respiratory distress syndrome	4,989	Sudden infant death syndrome	1,568
4	Disorders relating to short gestation and unspecified low birthweight	3,648	Newborn affected by maternal complications of pregnancy	1,522
5	Newborn affected by maternal complications of pregnancy	1,572	Unintentional injuries	1,291
6	Intrauterine hypoxia and birth asphyxia	1,497	Newborn affected by complications of placenta, cord, and membranes	910
7	Unintentional injuries	1,166	Bacterial sepsis of newborn	599
8	Birth trauma	1,058	Respiratory distress of newborn	462
9	Pneumonia and influenza[1]	1,012	Diseases of circulatory system	428
10	Newborn affected by complications of placenta, cord, and membranes	985	Neonatal hemorrhage	406
1–4 years				
Rank	All causes	8,187	All causes	3,965
1	Unintentional injuries	3,313	Unintentional injuries	1,235
2	Congenital anomalies	1,026	Congenital malformations/deformations/ chromosomal abnormalities	435
3	Malignant neoplasms	573	Homicide	369
4	Diseases of heart	338	Malignant neoplasms	354
5	Homicide	319	Diseases of heart	147
6	Pneumonia and influenza[1]	267	Influenza and pneumonia[1]	88
7	Meningitis	223	Septicemia	54
8	Meningococcal infection	110	Conditions originating in perinatal period	50
9	Certain conditions originating in the perinatal period	84	Cerebrovascular diseases	42
10	Septicemia	71	Chronic lower respiratory diseases[1,2]	40
5–14 years				
Rank	All causes	10,689	All causes	5,411
1	Unintentional injuries	5,224	Unintentional injuries	1,518
2	Malignant neoplasms	1,497	Malignant neoplasms	865
3	Congenital anomalies	561	Suicide	413
4	Homicide	415	Congenital malformations/deformations/ chromosomal abnormalities	337
5	Diseases of heart	330	Homicide	298
6	Pneumonia and influenza[1]	194	Diseases of heart	210
7	Suicide	142	Chronic lower respiratory diseases[1,2]	173
8	Benign neoplasms	104	Cerebrovascular diseases	84
9	Cerebrovascular diseases	95	Influenza and pneumonia[1]	83
10	Chronic obstructive pulmonary diseases[2]	85	In situ neoplasms/benign neoplasms/neoplasms of uncertain/unknown behavior	72
15–24 years				
Rank	All causes	49,027	All causes	30,494
1	Unintentional injuries	26,206	Unintentional injuries	12,514
2	Homicide	6,537	Suicide	5,491
3	Suicide	5,239	Homicide	4,733
4	Malignant neoplasms	2,683	Malignant neoplasms	1,469
5	Diseases of heart	1,223	Diseases of heart	997
6	Congenital anomalies	600	Congenital malformations/deformations/ chromosomal abnormalities	386
7	Cerebrovascular diseases	418	Chronic lower respiratory diseases[1,2]	202
8	Pneumonia and influenza[1]	348	Diabetes mellitus[3]	196
9	Chronic obstructive pulmonary diseases[2]	141	Influenza and pneumonia[1]	184
10	Anemias	133	Cerebrovascular diseases	166

See footnotes at end of table.

Table 20 (page 2 of 2). Leading causes of death and numbers of deaths, by age: United States, 1980 and 2015

Excel and PDF versions (with more data years and standard errors when available): *http://www.cdc.gov/nchs/hus/contents2016.htm#020.*

[Data are based on death certificates]

Age and rank order	1980		2015	
	Cause of death	Deaths	Cause of death	Deaths
25–44 years				
Rank	All causes	108,658	All causes	124,605
1	Unintentional injuries	26,722	Unintentional injuries	37,613
2	Malignant neoplasms	17,551	Malignant neoplasms	14,613
3	Diseases of heart	14,513	Diseases of heart	13,909
4	Homicide	10,983	Suicide	13,883
5	Suicide	9,855	Homicide	7,758
6	Chronic liver disease and cirrhosis	4,782	Chronic liver disease and cirrhosis	3,705
7	Cerebrovascular diseases	3,154	Diabetes mellitus[3]	2,784
8	Diabetes mellitus	1,472	Cerebrovascular diseases	2,355
9	Pneumonia and influenza[1]	1,467	Human immunodeficiency virus (HIV) disease	1,584
10	Congenital anomalies	817	Septicemia	1,208
45–64 years				
Rank	All causes	425,338	All causes	532,279
1	Diseases of heart	148,322	Malignant neoplasms	159,176
2	Malignant neoplasms	135,675	Diseases of heart	111,120
3	Cerebrovascular diseases	19,909	Unintentional injuries	40,987
4	Unintentional injuries	18,140	Chronic liver disease and cirrhosis	22,152
5	Chronic liver disease and cirrhosis	16,089	Chronic lower respiratory diseases[1,2]	21,802
6	Chronic obstructive pulmonary diseases[2]	11,514	Diabetes mellitus[3]	20,378
7	Diabetes mellitus	7,977	Cerebrovascular diseases	17,423
8	Suicide	7,079	Suicide	16,490
9	Pneumonia and influenza[1]	5,804	Septicemia	8,316
10	Homicide	4,019	Nephritis, nephrotic syndrome, and nephrosis[3]	7,576
65 years and over				
Rank	All causes	1,341,848	All causes	1,992,283
1	Diseases of heart	595,406	Diseases of heart	507,138
2	Malignant neoplasms	258,389	Malignant neoplasms	419,389
3	Cerebrovascular diseases	146,417	Chronic lower respiratory diseases[1,2]	131,804
4	Pneumonia and influenza[1]	45,512	Cerebrovascular diseases	120,156
5	Chronic obstructive pulmonary diseases[2]	43,587	Alzheimer's disease	109,495
6	Atherosclerosis	28,081	Diabetes mellitus[3]	56,142
7	Diabetes mellitus	25,216	Unintentional injuries	51,395
8	Unintentional injuries	24,844	Influenza and pneumonia	48,774
9	Nephritis, nephrotic syndrome, and nephrosis	12,968	Nephritis, nephrotic syndrome, and nephrosis[3]	41,258
10	Chronic liver disease and cirrhosis	9,519	Septicemia	30,817

[1] Starting with 1999 data, the rules for selecting CLRD and Pneumonia as the underlying cause of death changed, resulting in an increase in the number of deaths for CLRD and a decrease in the number of deaths for pneumonia. Therefore, trend data for these two causes of death should be interpreted with caution. For more information, see Comparability of cause of death between the 9th and 10th revisions of the *International Classification of Diseases* in Appendix II, Table V.

[2] Between 1998 and 1999, the cause of death title for Chronic obstructive pulmonary diseases in the ICD–9 was renamed to Chronic lower respiratory diseases (CLRD) in ICD–10.

[3] Starting with 2011 data, the rules for selecting Renal failure as the underlying cause of death were changed, affecting the number of deaths in the Nephritis, nephrotic syndrome, and nephrosis and Diabetes categories. These changes directly affect deaths with mention of Renal failure and other associated conditions, such as Diabetes mellitus with renal complications. The result is a decrease in the number of deaths for Nephritis, nephrotic syndrome, and nephrosis and an increase in the number of deaths for Diabetes mellitus. Therefore, trend data for these two causes of death should be interpreted with caution. For more information, see Technical Notes in Deaths: Final data for 2011, available from: http://www.cdc.gov/nchs/data/nvsr/nvsr63/nvsr63_03.pdf.

NOTE: For cause of death codes based on the ICD–9 in 1980 and ICD–10 in 2015, see Appendix II, Cause of death; Cause-of-death ranking; Table III; Table IV.

SOURCE: NCHS, National Vital Statistics System: Vital statistics of the United States, vol II, mortality, part A, 1980. Washington, DC: Public Health Service. 1985. Public-use 2015 Mortality File. Murphy SL, Kochanek KD, Xu JQ, Curtin SC. Deaths: Final data for 2015. National vital statistics reports. Hyattsville, MD: NCHS; 2017. Available from: http://www.cdc.gov/nchs/products/nvsr.htm. See Appendix I, National Vital Statistics System (NVSS).

Table 21 (page 1 of 4). Death rates for all causes, by sex, race, Hispanic origin, and age: United States, selected years 1950–2015

Excel and PDF versions (with more data years and standard errors when available): http://www.cdc.gov/nchs/hus/contents2016.htm#021.

[Data are based on death certificates]

Sex, race, Hispanic origin, and age	1950 [1]	1960 [1]	1970	1980	1990	2000	2014	2015
All persons	_		Deaths per 100,000 resident population					
All ages, age-adjusted [2]	1,446.0	1,339.2	1,222.6	1,039.1	938.7	869.0	724.6	733.1
All ages, crude	963.8	954.7	945.3	878.3	863.8	854.0	823.7	844.0
Under 1 year.	3,299.2	2,696.4	2,142.4	1,288.3	971.9	736.7	588.0	589.6
1–4 years.	139.4	109.1	84.5	63.9	46.8	32.4	24.0	24.9
5–14 years	60.1	46.6	41.3	30.6	24.0	18.0	12.7	13.2
15–24 years	128.1	106.3	127.7	115.4	99.2	79.9	65.5	69.5
25–34 years	178.7	146.4	157.4	135.5	139.2	101.4	108.4	116.7
35–44 years	358.7	299.4	314.5	227.9	223.2	198.9	175.2	180.1
45–54 years	853.9	756.0	730.0	584.0	473.4	425.6	404.8	404.0
55–64 years	1,901.0	1,735.1	1,658.8	1,346.3	1,196.9	992.2	870.3	875.3
65–74 years	4,104.3	3,822.1	3,582.7	2,994.9	2,648.6	2,399.1	1,786.3	1,796.8
75–84 years	9,331.1	8,745.2	8,004.4	6,692.6	6,007.2	5,666.5	4,564.2	4,579.2
85 years and over.	20,196.9	19,857.5	16,344.9	15,980.3	15,327.4	15,524.4	13,407.9	13,673.9
Male								
All ages, age-adjusted [2]	1,674.2	1,609.0	1,542.1	1,348.1	1,202.8	1,053.8	855.1	863.2
All ages, crude	1,106.1	1,104.5	1,090.3	976.9	918.4	853.0	846.4	868.0
Under 1 year.	3,728.0	3,059.3	2,410.0	1,428.5	1,082.8	806.5	638.6	639.2
1–4 years.	151.7	119.5	93.2	72.6	52.4	35.9	26.7	28.0
5–14 years	70.9	55.7	50.5	36.7	28.5	20.9	14.9	15.0
15–24 years	167.9	152.1	188.5	172.3	147.4	114.9	93.8	99.5
25–34 years	216.5	187.9	215.3	196.1	204.3	138.6	148.8	160.5
35–44 years	428.8	372.8	402.6	299.2	310.4	255.2	216.7	226.0
45–54 years	1,067.1	992.2	958.5	767.3	610.3	542.8	496.5	495.6
55–64 years	2,395.3	2,309.5	2,282.7	1,815.1	1,553.4	1,230.7	1,098.2	1,103.9
65–74 years	4,931.4	4,914.4	4,873.8	4,105.2	3,491.5	2,979.6	2,175.5	2,190.0
75–84 years	10,426.0	10,178.4	10,010.2	8,816.7	7,888.6	6,972.6	5,369.2	5,376.3
85 years and over.	21,636.0	21,186.3	17,821.5	18,801.1	18,056.6	17,501.4	14,642.2	14,795.8
Female								
All ages, age-adjusted [2]	1,236.0	1,105.3	971.4	817.9	750.9	731.4	616.7	624.2
All ages, crude	823.5	809.2	807.8	785.3	812.0	855.0	801.7	820.7
Under 1 year.	2,854.6	2,321.3	1,863.7	1,141.7	855.7	663.4	535.0	537.7
1–4 years.	126.7	98.4	75.4	54.7	41.0	28.7	21.3	21.6
5–14 years	48.9	37.3	31.8	24.2	19.3	15.0	10.5	11.2
15–24 years	89.1	61.3	68.1	57.5	49.0	43.1	35.8	38.1
25–34 years	142.7	106.6	101.6	75.9	74.2	63.5	67.2	72.1
35–44 years	290.3	229.4	231.1	159.3	137.9	143.2	134.1	134.5
45–54 years	641.5	526.7	517.2	412.9	342.7	312.5	315.6	315.0
55–64 years	1,404.8	1,196.4	1,098.9	934.3	878.8	772.2	658.2	662.3
65–74 years	3,333.2	2,871.8	2,579.7	2,144.7	1,991.2	1,921.2	1,444.2	1,450.9
75–84 years	8,399.6	7,633.1	6,677.6	5,440.1	4,883.1	4,814.7	3,955.1	3,971.3
85 years and over.	19,194.7	19,008.4	15,518.0	14,746.9	14,274.3	14,719.2	12,765.7	13,080.8
White male [3]								
All ages, age-adjusted [2]	1,642.5	1,586.0	1,513.7	1,317.6	1,165.9	1,029.4	853.4	861.9
All ages, crude	1,089.5	1,098.5	1,086.7	983.3	930.9	887.8	909.4	932.9
Under 1 year.	3,400.5	2,694.1	2,113.2	1,230.3	896.1	667.6	551.3	541.8
1–4 years.	135.5	104.9	83.6	66.1	45.9	32.6	23.8	24.9
5–14 years	67.2	52.7	48.0	35.0	26.4	19.8	14.0	14.1
15–24 years	152.4	143.7	170.8	167.0	131.3	105.8	88.3	92.3
25–34 years	185.3	163.2	176.6	171.3	176.1	124.1	145.3	157.0
35–44 years	380.9	332.6	343.5	257.4	268.2	233.6	212.6	221.3
45–54 years	984.5	932.2	882.9	698.9	548.7	496.9	488.9	487.4
55–64 years	2,304.4	2,225.2	2,202.6	1,728.5	1,467.2	1,163.3	1,063.8	1,070.9
65–74 years	4,864.9	4,848.4	4,810.1	4,035.7	3,397.7	2,905.7	2,143.3	2,159.9
75–84 years	10,526.3	10,299.6	10,098.8	8,829.8	7,844.9	6,933.1	5,419.1	5,426.8
85 years and over.	22,116.3	21,750.0	18,551.7	19,097.3	18,268.3	17,716.4	15,000.3	15,202.8

See footnotes at end of table.

Table 21 (page 2 of 4). Death rates for all causes, by sex, race, Hispanic origin, and age: United States, selected years 1950–2015

Excel and PDF versions (with more data years and standard errors when available): http://www.cdc.gov/nchs/hus/contents2016.htm#021.

[Data are based on death certificates]

Sex, race, Hispanic origin, and age	1950[1]	1960[1]	1970	1980	1990	2000	2014	2015
Black or African American male[3]				Deaths per 100,000 resident population				
All ages, age-adjusted[2]	1,909.1	1,811.1	1,873.9	1,697.8	1,644.5	1,403.5	1,034.0	1,040.3
All ages, crude	1,257.7	1,181.7	1,186.6	1,034.1	1,008.0	834.1	742.6	765.3
Under 1 year.	- - -	5,306.8	4,298.9	2,586.7	2,112.4	1,567.6	1,125.4	1,150.2
1–4 years[4]	1,412.6	208.5	150.5	110.5	85.8	54.5	42.2	45.7
5–14 years	95.1	75.1	67.1	47.4	41.2	28.2	21.0	21.0
15–24 years	289.7	212.0	320.6	209.1	252.2	181.4	135.4	150.9
25–34 years	503.5	402.5	559.5	407.3	430.8	261.0	212.1	229.0
35–44 years	878.1	762.0	956.6	689.8	699.6	453.0	308.5	325.8
45–54 years	1,905.0	1,624.8	1,777.5	1,479.9	1,261.0	1,017.7	671.8	678.1
55–64 years	3,773.2	3,316.4	3,256.9	2,873.0	2,618.4	2,080.1	1,611.5	1,612.9
65–74 years	5,310.3	5,798.7	5,803.2	5,131.1	4,946.1	4,253.5	3,047.4	3,041.8
75–84 years[5]	10,101.9	8,605.1	9,454.9	9,231.6	9,129.5	8,486.0	6,172.6	6,204.5
85 years and over.	- - -	14,844.8	12,222.3	16,098.8	16,954.9	16,791.0	13,291.7	13,066.3
American Indian or Alaska Native male[3]								
All ages, age-adjusted[2]	- - -	- - -	- - -	1,111.5	916.2	841.5	685.4	693.6
All ages, crude	- - -	- - -	- - -	597.1	476.4	415.6	433.2	454.7
Under 1 year.	- - -	- - -	- - -	1,598.1	1,056.6	700.2	509.7	486.4
1–4 years.	- - -	- - -	- - -	82.7	77.4	44.9	41.0	35.2
5–14 years	- - -	- - -	- - -	43.7	33.4	20.2	12.3	15.2
15–24 years	- - -	- - -	- - -	311.1	219.8	136.2	103.8	101.1
25–34 years	- - -	- - -	- - -	360.6	256.1	179.1	179.1	191.4
35–44 years	- - -	- - -	- - -	556.8	365.4	295.2	264.4	281.4
45–54 years	- - -	- - -	- - -	871.3	619.9	520.0	508.5	543.5
55–64 years	- - -	- - -	- - -	1,547.5	1,211.3	1,090.4	984.7	994.2
65–74 years	- - -	- - -	- - -	2,968.4	2,461.7	2,478.3	1,830.2	1,840.6
75–84 years	- - -	- - -	- - -	5,607.0	5,389.2	5,351.2	4,097.9	4,171.0
85 years and over.	- - -	- - -	- - -	12,635.2	11,243.9	10,725.8	8,610.4	8,277.3
Asian or Pacific Islander male[3]								
All ages, age-adjusted[2]	- - -	- - -	- - -	786.5	716.4	624.2	462.0	467.6
All ages, crude	- - -	- - -	- - -	375.3	334.3	332.9	341.3	354.5
Under 1 year.	- - -	- - -	- - -	816.5	605.3	529.4	384.3	437.8
1–4 years.	- - -	- - -	- - -	50.9	45.0	23.3	14.3	15.1
5–14 years	- - -	- - -	- - -	23.4	20.7	12.9	9.9	10.3
15–24 years	- - -	- - -	- - -	80.8	76.0	55.2	44.7	48.6
25–34 years	- - -	- - -	- - -	83.5	79.6	55.0	54.1	55.7
35–44 years	- - -	- - -	- - -	128.3	130.8	104.9	83.0	84.5
45–54 years	- - -	- - -	- - -	342.3	287.1	249.7	212.3	205.3
55–64 years	- - -	- - -	- - -	881.1	789.1	642.4	519.9	507.9
65–74 years	- - -	- - -	- - -	2,236.1	2,041.4	1,661.0	1,107.1	1,130.7
75–84 years	- - -	- - -	- - -	5,389.5	5,008.6	4,328.2	3,047.8	3,091.6
85 years and over.	- - -	- - -	- - -	13,753.6	12,446.3	12,125.3	9,263.1	9,405.8
Hispanic or Latino male[3,6]								
All ages, age-adjusted[2]	- - -	- - -	- - -	- - -	886.4	818.1	626.8	628.9
All ages, crude	- - -	- - -	- - -	- - -	411.6	331.3	330.1	343.2
Under 1 year.	- - -	- - -	- - -	- - -	921.8	637.1	508.3	500.4
1–4 years.	- - -	- - -	- - -	- - -	53.8	31.5	20.1	22.0
5–14 years	- - -	- - -	- - -	- - -	26.0	17.9	12.5	12.2
15–24 years	- - -	- - -	- - -	- - -	159.3	107.7	75.4	82.2
25–34 years	- - -	- - -	- - -	- - -	234.0	120.2	103.6	111.8
35–44 years	- - -	- - -	- - -	- - -	341.8	211.0	149.4	152.8
45–54 years	- - -	- - -	- - -	- - -	533.9	439.0	341.0	340.2
55–64 years	- - -	- - -	- - -	- - -	1,123.7	965.7	787.7	788.2
65–74 years	- - -	- - -	- - -	- - -	2,368.2	2,287.9	1,655.1	1,674.3
75–84 years[5]	- - -	- - -	- - -	- - -	5,369.1	5,395.3	4,103.3	4,127.1
85 years and over.	- - -	- - -	- - -	- - -	12,272.1	13,086.2	10,318.0	10,145.7

See footnotes at end of table.

Table 21 (page 3 of 4). Death rates for all causes, by sex, race, Hispanic origin, and age: United States, selected years 1950–2015

Excel and PDF versions (with more data years and standard errors when available): *http://www.cdc.gov/nchs/hus/contents2016.htm#021.*

[Data are based on death certificates]

Sex, race, Hispanic origin, and age	1950[1]	1960[1]	1970	1980	1990	2000	2014	2015
White, not Hispanic or Latino male[6]				Deaths per 100,000 resident population				
All ages, age-adjusted[2]	- - -	- - -	- - -	- - -	1,170.9	1,035.4	872.3	881.3
All ages, crude	- - -	- - -	- - -	- - -	985.9	978.5	1,045.4	1,072.5
Under 1 year.	- - -	- - -	- - -	- - -	865.4	658.7	549.9	541.1
1–4 years.	- - -	- - -	- - -	- - -	43.8	32.4	24.9	25.5
5–14 years	- - -	- - -	- - -	- - -	25.7	20.0	14.2	14.5
15–24 years	- - -	- - -	- - -	- - -	123.4	103.5	90.6	93.4
25–34 years	- - -	- - -	- - -	- - -	165.3	123.0	155.8	168.1
35–44 years	- - -	- - -	- - -	- - -	257.1	233.9	227.4	238.1
45–54 years	- - -	- - -	- - -	- - -	544.5	497.7	511.2	510.0
55–64 years	- - -	- - -	- - -	- - -	1,479.7	1,170.9	1,085.3	1,093.3
65–74 years	- - -	- - -	- - -	- - -	3,434.5	2,930.5	2,170.0	2,184.0
75–84 years	- - -	- - -	- - -	- - -	7,920.4	6,977.8	5,499.0	5,500.5
85 years and over.	- - -	- - -	- - -	- - -	18,505.4	17,853.2	15,286.4	15,526.0
White female[3]								
All ages, age-adjusted[2]	1,198.0	1,074.4	944.0	796.1	728.8	715.3	617.6	627.0
All ages, crude	803.3	800.9	812.6	806.1	846.9	912.3	876.7	899.2
Under 1 year.	2,566.8	2,007.7	1,614.6	962.5	690.0	550.5	457.6	455.1
1–4 years.	112.2	85.2	66.1	49.3	36.1	25.5	19.6	19.7
5–14 years	45.1	34.7	29.9	22.9	17.9	14.1	10.0	10.6
15–24 years	71.5	54.9	61.6	55.5	45.9	41.1	35.5	37.8
25–34 years	112.8	85.0	84.1	65.4	61.5	55.1	66.9	72.0
35–44 years	235.8	191.1	193.3	138.2	117.4	125.7	130.7	131.7
45–54 years	546.4	458.8	462.9	372.7	309.3	281.4	305.8	306.6
55–64 years	1,293.8	1,078.9	1,014.9	876.2	822.7	730.9	635.1	640.4
65–74 years	3,242.8	2,779.3	2,470.7	2,066.6	1,923.5	1,868.3	1,433.1	1,443.8
75–84 years	8,481.5	7,696.6	6,698.7	5,401.7	4,839.1	4,785.3	4,001.3	4,028.0
85 years and over.	19,679.5	19,477.7	15,980.2	14,979.6	14,400.6	14,890.7	13,079.1	13,442.5
Black or African American female[3]								
All ages, age-adjusted[2]	1,545.5	1,369.7	1,228.7	1,033.3	975.1	927.6	713.3	710.8
All ages, crude	1,002.0	905.0	829.2	733.3	747.9	733.0	655.5	665.7
Under 1 year.	- - -	4,162.2	3,368.8	2,123.7	1,735.5	1,279.8	956.3	970.0
1–4 years[4]	1,139.3	173.3	129.4	84.4	67.6	45.3	31.9	32.0
5–14 years	72.8	53.8	43.8	30.5	27.5	20.0	14.3	15.0
15–24 years	213.1	107.5	111.9	70.5	68.7	58.3	42.5	45.8
25–34 years	393.3	273.2	231.0	150.0	159.5	121.8	88.6	92.9
35–44 years	758.1	568.5	533.0	323.9	298.6	271.9	193.9	191.8
45–54 years	1,576.4	1,177.0	1,043.9	768.2	639.4	588.3	455.8	447.0
55–64 years	3,089.4	2,510.9	1,986.2	1,561.0	1,452.6	1,227.2	974.8	969.6
65–74 years	4,000.2	4,064.2	3,860.9	3,057.4	2,865.7	2,689.6	1,880.2	1,864.4
75–84 years[5]	8,347.0	6,730.0	6,691.5	6,212.1	5,688.3	5,696.5	4,356.8	4,310.0
85 years and over.	- - -	13,052.6	10,706.6	12,367.2	13,309.5	13,941.3	11,656.8	11,741.3
American Indian or Alaska Native female[3]								
All ages, age-adjusted[2]	- - -	- - -	- - -	662.4	561.8	604.5	514.1	511.3
All ages, crude	- - -	- - -	- - -	380.1	330.4	346.1	363.5	375.8
Under 1 year.	- - -	- - -	- - -	1,352.6	688.7	492.2	412.5	431.0
1–4 years.	- - -	- - -	- - -	87.5	37.8	39.8	20.4	26.5
5–14 years	- - -	- - -	- - -	33.5	25.5	17.7	10.8	13.7
15–24 years	- - -	- - -	- - -	90.3	69.0	58.9	46.8	47.1
25–34 years	- - -	- - -	- - -	178.5	102.3	84.8	88.0	104.7
35–44 years	- - -	- - -	- - -	286.0	156.4	171.9	179.0	170.5
45–54 years	- - -	- - -	- - -	491.4	380.9	284.9	354.3	354.2
55–64 years	- - -	- - -	- - -	837.1	805.9	772.1	606.2	622.2
65–74 years	- - -	- - -	- - -	1,765.5	1,679.4	1,899.8	1,368.6	1,360.3
75–84 years	- - -	- - -	- - -	3,612.9	3,073.2	3,850.0	3,226.6	3,192.5
85 years and over.	- - -	- - -	- - -	8,567.4	8,201.1	9,118.2	7,893.5	7,636.6

See footnotes at end of table.

Excel and PDF versions (with more data years and standard errors when available): http://www.cdc.gov/nchs/hus/contents2016.htm#021.

[Data are based on death certificates]

Sex, race, Hispanic origin, and age	1950 [1]	1960 [1]	1970	1980	1990	2000	2014	2015
Asian or Pacific Islander female [3]				Deaths per 100,000 resident population				
All ages, age-adjusted [2]	- - -	- - -	- - -	425.9	469.3	416.8	331.1	338.0
All ages, crude	- - -	- - -	- - -	222.5	234.3	262.3	295.5	310.8
Under 1 year	- - -	- - -	- - -	755.8	518.2	434.3	338.6	358.1
1–4 years	- - -	- - -	- - -	35.4	32.0	20.0	12.5	15.0
5–14 years	- - -	- - -	- - -	21.5	13.0	11.7	6.5	7.3
15–24 years	- - -	- - -	- - -	32.3	28.8	22.4	17.8	19.1
25–34 years	- - -	- - -	- - -	45.4	37.5	27.6	24.8	26.2
35–44 years	- - -	- - -	- - -	89.7	69.9	65.6	49.1	51.1
45–54 years	- - -	- - -	- - -	214.1	182.7	155.5	122.3	127.6
55–64 years	- - -	- - -	- - -	440.8	483.4	390.9	283.2	288.0
65–74 years	- - -	- - -	- - -	1,027.7	1,089.2	996.4	700.5	704.8
75–84 years	- - -	- - -	- - -	2,833.6	3,127.9	2,882.4	2,237.5	2,263.5
85 years and over	- - -	- - -	- - -	7,923.3	10,254.0	9,052.2	7,945.3	8,142.0
Hispanic or Latina female [3,6]								
All ages, age-adjusted [2]	- - -	- - -	- - -	- - -	537.1	546.0	437.5	438.3
All ages, crude	- - -	- - -	- - -	- - -	285.4	274.6	281.0	290.4
Under 1 year	- - -	- - -	- - -	- - -	746.6	553.6	432.1	436.6
1–4 years	- - -	- - -	- - -	- - -	42.1	27.5	17.2	17.5
5–14 years	- - -	- - -	- - -	- - -	17.3	13.4	9.7	8.6
15–24 years	- - -	- - -	- - -	- - -	40.6	31.7	27.2	28.5
25–34 years	- - -	- - -	- - -	- - -	62.9	43.4	41.3	44.8
35–44 years	- - -	- - -	- - -	- - -	109.3	100.5	78.5	77.7
45–54 years	- - -	- - -	- - -	- - -	253.3	223.8	185.3	184.0
55–64 years	- - -	- - -	- - -	- - -	607.5	548.4	443.3	434.6
65–74 years	- - -	- - -	- - -	- - -	1,453.8	1,423.2	1,036.7	1,048.7
75–84 years	- - -	- - -	- - -	- - -	3,351.3	3,624.5	2,931.3	2,937.3
85 years and over	- - -	- - -	- - -	- - -	10,098.7	11,202.8	9,250.2	9,266.4
White, not Hispanic or Latina female [6]								
All ages, age-adjusted [2]	- - -	- - -	- - -	- - -	734.6	721.5	633.8	644.1
All ages, crude	- - -	- - -	- - -	- - -	903.6	1,007.3	1,011.3	1,038.5
Under 1 year	- - -	- - -	- - -	- - -	655.3	530.9	451.0	445.7
1–4 years	- - -	- - -	- - -	- - -	34.0	24.4	20.2	20.1
5–14 years	- - -	- - -	- - -	- - -	17.6	13.9	9.8	11.2
15–24 years	- - -	- - -	- - -	- - -	46.0	42.6	37.5	40.1
25–34 years	- - -	- - -	- - -	- - -	60.6	56.8	73.2	78.8
35–44 years	- - -	- - -	- - -	- - -	116.8	128.1	143.8	145.7
45–54 years	- - -	- - -	- - -	- - -	312.1	285.0	325.5	327.7
55–64 years	- - -	- - -	- - -	- - -	834.5	742.1	653.5	661.0
65–74 years	- - -	- - -	- - -	- - -	1,940.2	1,891.0	1,462.9	1,472.8
75–84 years	- - -	- - -	- - -	- - -	4,887.3	4,819.3	4,078.9	4,103.1
85 years and over	- - -	- - -	- - -	- - -	14,533.1	14,971.7	13,290.4	13,682.6

- - - Data not available.

[1] Includes deaths of persons who were not residents of the 50 states and the District of Columbia (D.C.).

[2] Age-adjusted rates are calculated using the year 2000 standard population. Prior to 2001, age-adjusted rates were calculated using standard million proportions based on rounded population numbers. Starting with 2001 data, unrounded population numbers are used to calculate age-adjusted rates. See Appendix II, Age adjustment.

[3] The race groups, white, black, Asian or Pacific Islander, and American Indian or Alaska Native, include persons of Hispanic and non-Hispanic origin. Persons of Hispanic origin may be of any race. Death rates for Hispanic, American Indian or Alaska Native, and Asian or Pacific Islander persons should be interpreted with caution because of inconsistencies in reporting Hispanic origin or race on the death certificate (death rate numerators) compared with population figures (death rate denominators). The net effect of misclassification is an underestimation of deaths and death rates for races other than white and black. See Appendix II, Race, for a detailed discussion of sources of bias in death rates by race and Hispanic origin.

[4] In 1950, rate is for the age group under 5 years.

[5] In 1950, rate is for the age group 75 years and over.

[6] Prior to 1997, data from states that did not report Hispanic origin on the death certificate were excluded. See Appendix II, Hispanic origin.

NOTES: Starting with *Health, United States, 2003*, rates for 1991–1999 were revised using intercensal population estimates based on the 1990 and 2000 censuses. For 2000, population estimates are bridged-race April 1 census counts. Starting with *Health, United States, 2012*, rates for 2001–2009 were revised using intercensal population estimates based on the 2000 and 2010 censuses. For 2010, population estimates are bridged-race April 1 census counts. Rates for 2011 and beyond were computed using 2010-based postcensal estimates. See Appendix I, Population Census and Population Estimates. Starting with 2003 data, some states began to collect information on more than one race on the death certificate, according to 1997 Office of Management and Budget (OMB) standards. The multiple-race data for these states were bridged to the single-race categories of the 1977 OMB standards, for comparability with other states. See Appendix II, Race. Data for additional years are available. See the Excel spreadsheet on the *Health, United States* website at: http://www.cdc.gov/nchs/hus.htm.

SOURCE: NCHS, National Vital Statistics System; Grove RD, Hetzel AM. Vital statistics rates in the United States, 1940–1960. Washington, DC: U.S. Government Printing Office, 1968; numerator data from National Vital Statistics System, annual public-use Mortality Files; denominator data from national population estimates for race groups from Table 1 and unpublished Hispanic population estimates for 1985–1996 prepared by the Housing and Household Economic Statistics Division, U.S. Census Bureau; Murphy SL, Kochanek KD, Xu JQ, Curtin SC. Deaths: Final data for 2015. National vital statistics reports. Hyattsville, MD: NCHS; 2017. Available from: http://www.cdc.gov/nchs/products/nvsr.htm. See Appendix I, National Vital Statistics System (NVSS).

Table 22 (page 1 of 3). Death rates for diseases of heart, by sex, race, Hispanic origin, and age: United States, selected years 1950–2015

Excel and PDF versions (with more data years and standard errors when available): http://www.cdc.gov/nchs/hus/contents2016.htm#022.

[Data are based on death certificates]

Sex, race, Hispanic origin, and age	1950 [1,2]	1960 [1,2]	1970 [2]	1980 [2]	1990 [2]	2000 [3]	2014 [3]	2015 [3]
All persons	Deaths per 100,000 resident population							
All ages, age-adjusted [4]	588.8	559.0	492.7	412.1	321.8	257.6	167.0	168.5
All ages, crude	356.8	369.0	362.0	336.0	289.5	252.6	192.7	197.2
Under 1 year.	4.1	6.6	13.1	22.8	20.1	13.0	8.0	7.3
1–4 years.	1.6	1.3	1.7	2.6	1.9	1.2	0.9	0.9
5–14 years	3.9	1.3	0.8	0.9	0.9	0.7	0.5	0.5
15–24 years	8.2	4.0	3.0	2.9	2.5	2.6	2.2	2.3
25–34 years	20.9	15.6	11.4	8.3	7.6	7.4	7.7	8.0
35–44 years	88.3	74.6	66.7	44.6	31.4	29.2	25.6	25.6
45–54 years	309.2	271.8	238.4	180.2	120.5	94.2	80.1	79.3
55–64 years	804.3	737.9	652.3	494.1	367.3	261.2	185.8	188.1
65–74 years	1,857.2	1,740.5	1,558.2	1,218.6	894.3	665.6	385.2	389.5
75–84 years	4,311.0	4,089.4	3,683.8	2,993.1	2,295.7	1,780.3	1,070.2	1,071.6
85 years and over.	9,152.5	9,317.8	7,891.3	7,777.1	6,739.9	5,926.1	3,920.9	3,986.5
Male								
All ages, age-adjusted [4]	699.0	687.6	634.0	538.9	412.4	320.0	210.9	211.8
All ages, crude	424.7	439.5	422.5	368.6	297.6	249.8	207.1	211.7
Under 1 year.	4.7	7.8	15.1	25.5	21.9	13.3	8.6	7.5
1–4 years.	1.7	1.4	1.9	2.8	1.9	1.4	0.9	1.0
5–14 years	3.5	1.4	0.9	1.0	0.9	0.8	0.5	0.5
15–24 years	8.3	4.2	3.7	3.7	3.1	3.2	2.7	3.0
25–34 years	24.4	20.1	15.2	11.4	10.3	9.6	10.3	10.3
35–44 years	120.4	112.7	103.2	68.7	48.1	41.4	34.8	35.1
45–54 years	441.2	420.4	376.4	282.6	183.0	140.2	113.5	112.1
55–64 years	1,100.5	1,066.9	987.2	746.8	537.3	371.7	268.1	269.4
65–74 years	2,310.2	2,291.3	2,170.3	1,728.0	1,250.0	898.3	525.7	529.7
75–84 years	4,825.8	4,742.4	4,534.8	3,834.3	2,968.2	2,248.1	1,354.8	1,354.4
85 years and over.	9,661.4	9,788.9	8,426.2	8,752.7	7,418.4	6,430.0	4,453.4	4,495.1
Female								
All ages, age-adjusted [4]	486.6	447.0	381.6	320.8	257.0	210.9	131.8	133.6
All ages, crude	289.7	300.6	304.5	305.1	281.8	255.3	178.6	183.1
Under 1 year.	3.4	5.4	10.9	20.0	18.3	12.5	7.4	7.2
1–4 years.	1.6	1.1	1.6	2.5	1.9	1.0	0.9	0.9
5–14 years	4.3	1.2	0.8	0.9	0.8	0.5	0.4	0.5
15–24 years	8.2	3.7	2.3	2.1	1.8	2.1	1.6	1.5
25–34 years	17.6	11.3	7.7	5.3	5.0	5.2	5.0	5.6
35–44 years	57.0	38.2	32.2	21.4	15.1	17.2	16.4	16.2
45–54 years	177.8	127.5	109.9	84.5	61.0	49.8	47.5	47.4
55–64 years	507.0	429.4	351.6	272.1	215.7	159.3	109.3	112.3
65–74 years	1,434.9	1,261.3	1,082.7	828.6	616.8	474.0	261.7	266.2
75–84 years	3,873.0	3,582.7	3,120.8	2,497.0	1,893.8	1,475.1	854.8	855.9
85 years and over.	8,798.1	9,016.8	7,591.8	7,350.5	6,478.1	5,720.9	3,643.8	3,717.6
White male [5]								
All ages, age-adjusted [4]	701.4	694.5	640.2	539.6	409.2	316.7	210.0	211.2
All ages, crude	434.2	454.6	438.3	384.0	312.7	265.8	223.9	229.1
45–54 years	424.1	413.2	365.7	269.8	170.6	130.7	107.7	106.6
55–64 years	1,082.6	1,056.0	979.3	730.6	516.7	351.8	255.9	256.5
65–74 years	2,309.4	2,297.9	2,177.2	1,729.7	1,230.5	877.8	512.7	516.8
75–84 years	4,908.0	4,839.9	4,617.6	3,883.2	2,983.4	2,247.0	1,361.5	1,362.9
85 years and over.	9,952.3	10,135.8	8,818.0	8,958.0	7,558.7	6,560.8	4,603.9	4,663.2
Black or African American male [5]								
All ages, age-adjusted [4]	641.5	615.2	607.3	561.4	485.4	392.5	259.5	258.6
All ages, crude	348.4	330.6	330.3	301.0	256.8	211.1	178.7	182.8
45–54 years	624.1	514.0	512.8	433.4	328.9	247.2	179.5	177.3
55–64 years	1,434.0	1,236.8	1,135.4	987.2	824.0	631.2	425.5	430.9
65–74 years	2,140.1	2,281.4	2,237.8	1,847.2	1,632.9	1,268.8	794.6	801.5
75–84 years [6]	4,107.9	3,533.6	3,783.4	3,578.8	3,107.1	2,597.6	1,651.4	1,644.6
85 years and over.	- - -	6,037.9	5,367.6	6,819.5	6,479.6	5,633.5	3,693.0	3,583.2

See footnotes at end of table.

Excel and PDF versions (with more data years and standard errors when available): http://www.cdc.gov/nchs/hus/contents2016.htm#022.

[Data are based on death certificates]

Sex, race, Hispanic origin, and age	1950[1,2]	1960[1,2]	1970[2]	1980[2]	1990[2]	2000[3]	2014[3]	2015[3]
American Indian or Alaska Native male[5]			Deaths per 100,000 resident population					
All ages, age-adjusted[4]	- - -	- - -	- - -	320.5	264.1	222.2	149.7	148.0
All ages, crude	- - -	- - -	- - -	130.6	108.0	90.1	84.4	87.4
45–54 years	- - -	- - -	- - -	238.1	173.8	108.5	95.9	102.2
55–64 years	- - -	- - -	- - -	496.3	411.0	285.0	217.2	231.7
65–74 years	- - -	- - -	- - -	1,009.4	839.1	748.2	444.0	408.5
75–84 years	- - -	- - -	- - -	2,062.2	1,788.8	1,655.7	978.2	1,042.1
85 years and over.	- - -	- - -	- - -	4,413.7	3,860.3	3,318.3	2,415.9	2,184.3
Asian or Pacific Islander male[5]								
All ages, age-adjusted[4]	- - -	- - -	- - -	286.9	220.7	185.5	109.1	109.7
All ages, crude	- - -	- - -	- - -	119.8	88.7	90.6	78.4	80.9
45–54 years	- - -	- - -	- - -	112.0	70.4	61.1	53.4	49.0
55–64 years	- - -	- - -	- - -	306.7	226.1	182.6	121.4	121.2
65–74 years	- - -	- - -	- - -	852.4	623.5	482.5	250.5	254.1
75–84 years	- - -	- - -	- - -	2,010.9	1,642.2	1,354.7	726.6	718.6
85 years and over.	- - -	- - -	- - -	5,923.0	4,617.8	4,154.2	2,459.7	2,543.8
Hispanic or Latino male[5,7]								
All ages, age-adjusted[4]	- - -	- - -	- - -	- - -	270.0	238.2	145.7	146.4
All ages, crude	- - -	- - -	- - -	- - -	91.0	74.7	67.4	70.7
45–54 years	- - -	- - -	- - -	- - -	116.4	84.3	64.0	64.8
55–64 years	- - -	- - -	- - -	- - -	363.0	264.8	169.5	176.4
65–74 years	- - -	- - -	- - -	- - -	829.9	684.8	391.6	395.6
75–84 years	- - -	- - -	- - -	- - -	1,971.3	1,733.2	1,019.7	1,046.6
85 years and over.	- - -	- - -	- - -	- - -	4,711.9	4,897.5	2,987.5	2,883.7
White, not Hispanic or Latino male[7]								
All ages, age-adjusted[4]	- - -	- - -	- - -	- - -	413.6	319.9	215.2	216.3
All ages, crude	- - -	- - -	- - -	- - -	336.5	297.5	261.0	267.0
45–54 years	- - -	- - -	- - -	- - -	172.8	134.3	115.0	113.8
55–64 years	- - -	- - -	- - -	- - -	521.3	356.3	263.6	263.4
65–74 years	- - -	- - -	- - -	- - -	1,243.4	885.1	518.9	522.2
75–84 years	- - -	- - -	- - -	- - -	3,007.7	2,261.9	1,382.1	1,379.4
85 years and over.	- - -	- - -	- - -	- - -	7,663.4	6,606.6	4,703.8	4,781.2
White female[5]								
All ages, age-adjusted[4]	479.2	441.7	376.7	315.9	250.9	205.6	130.0	132.4
All ages, crude	290.5	306.5	313.8	319.2	298.4	274.5	195.1	200.6
45–54 years	142.4	103.4	91.4	71.2	50.2	40.9	42.2	42.4
55–64 years	460.7	383.0	317.7	248.1	192.4	141.3	98.8	101.6
65–74 years	1,401.6	1,229.8	1,044.0	796.7	583.6	445.2	247.6	253.8
75–84 years	3,926.2	3,629.7	3,143.5	2,493.6	1,874.3	1,452.4	849.0	855.3
85 years and over.	9,086.9	9,280.8	7,839.9	7,501.6	6,563.4	5,801.4	3,746.8	3,835.1
Black or African American female[5]								
All ages, age-adjusted[4]	538.9	488.9	435.6	378.6	327.5	277.6	167.7	165.7
All ages, crude	289.9	268.5	261.0	249.7	237.0	212.6	152.3	153.9
45–54 years	526.8	360.7	290.9	202.4	155.3	125.0	94.9	92.4
55–64 years	1,210.7	952.3	710.5	530.1	442.0	332.8	211.0	214.3
65–74 years	1,659.4	1,680.5	1,553.2	1,210.3	1,017.5	815.2	437.9	433.5
75–84 years[6]	3,499.3	2,926.9	2,964.1	2,707.2	2,250.9	1,913.1	1,085.7	1,050.5
85 years and over.	- - -	5,650.0	5,003.8	5,796.5	5,766.1	5,298.7	3,269.8	3,282.5

See footnotes at end of table.

Table 22 (page 3 of 3). Death rates for diseases of heart, by sex, race, Hispanic origin, and age: United States, selected years 1950–2015

Excel and PDF versions (with more data years and standard errors when available): http://www.cdc.gov/nchs/hus/contents2016.htm#022.

[Data are based on death certificates]

Sex, race, Hispanic origin, and age	1950 [1,2]	1960 [1,2]	1970 [2]	1980 [2]	1990 [2]	2000 [3]	2014 [3]	2015 [3]
American Indian or Alaska Native female [5]				Deaths per 100,000 resident population				
All ages, age-adjusted [4]	- - -	- - -	- - -	175.4	153.1	143.6	94.0	94.0
All ages, crude	- - -	- - -	- - -	80.3	77.5	71.9	61.0	63.8
45–54 years	- - -	- - -	- - -	65.2	62.0	40.2	40.8	44.0
55–64 years	- - -	- - -	- - -	193.5	197.0	149.4	90.4	93.9
65–74 years	- - -	- - -	- - -	577.2	492.8	391.8	269.0	247.5
75–84 years	- - -	- - -	- - -	1,364.3	1,050.3	1,044.1	657.3	690.7
85 years and over	- - -	- - -	- - -	2,893.3	2,868.7	3,146.3	1,931.7	1,813.0
Asian or Pacific Islander female [5]								
All ages, age-adjusted [4]	- - -	- - -	- - -	132.3	149.2	115.7	68.2	68.5
All ages, crude	- - -	- - -	- - -	57.0	62.0	65.0	59.2	61.9
45–54 years	- - -	- - -	- - -	28.6	17.5	15.9	11.9	12.3
55–64 years	- - -	- - -	- - -	92.9	99.0	68.8	34.9	40.6
65–74 years	- - -	- - -	- - -	313.3	323.9	229.6	124.8	122.1
75–84 years	- - -	- - -	- - -	1,053.2	1,130.9	866.2	485.4	469.3
85 years and over	- - -	- - -	- - -	3,211.0	4,161.2	3,367.2	2,097.2	2,131.6
Hispanic or Latina female [5,7]								
All ages, age-adjusted [4]	- - -	- - -	- - -	- - -	177.2	163.7	92.4	93.0
All ages, crude	- - -	- - -	- - -	- - -	79.4	71.5	55.3	57.8
45–54 years	- - -	- - -	- - -	- - -	43.5	28.2	21.3	21.8
55–64 years	- - -	- - -	- - -	- - -	153.2	111.2	70.2	64.7
65–74 years	- - -	- - -	- - -	- - -	460.4	366.3	190.0	196.6
75–84 years	- - -	- - -	- - -	- - -	1,259.7	1,169.4	657.5	654.8
85 years and over	- - -	- - -	- - -	- - -	4,440.3	4,605.8	2,558.9	2,599.1
White, not Hispanic or Latina female [7]								
All ages, age-adjusted [4]	- - -	- - -	- - -	- - -	252.6	206.8	133.0	135.6
All ages, crude	- - -	- - -	- - -	- - -	320.0	304.9	226.9	233.6
45–54 years	- - -	- - -	- - -	- - -	50.2	41.9	45.8	46.3
55–64 years	- - -	- - -	- - -	- - -	193.6	142.9	101.4	105.5
65–74 years	- - -	- - -	- - -	- - -	584.7	448.5	251.3	257.3
75–84 years	- - -	- - -	- - -	- - -	1,890.2	1,458.9	862.1	867.6
85 years and over	- - -	- - -	- - -	- - -	6,615.2	5,822.7	3,813.8	3,907.6

- - - Data not available.

[1] Includes deaths of persons who were not residents of the 50 states and the District of Columbia (D.C.).

[2] Underlying cause of death was coded according to the 6th Revision of the *International Classification of Diseases* (ICD) in 1950, 7th Revision in 1960, 8th Revision in 1970, and 9th Revision in 1980–1998. See Appendix II, Cause of death; Table III; Table IV.

[3] Starting with 1999 data, cause of death is coded according to ICD–10. See Appendix II, Cause of death; Comparability ratio; Table IV; Table V.

[4] Age-adjusted rates are calculated using the year 2000 standard population. Prior to 2001, age-adjusted rates were calculated using standard million proportions based on rounded population numbers. Starting with 2001 data, unrounded population numbers are used to calculate age-adjusted rates. See Appendix II, Age adjustment.

[5] The race groups, white, black, Asian or Pacific Islander, and American Indian or Alaska Native, include persons of Hispanic and non-Hispanic origin. Persons of Hispanic origin may be of any race. Death rates for Hispanic, American Indian or Alaska Native, and Asian or Pacific Islander persons should be interpreted with caution because of inconsistencies in reporting Hispanic origin or race on the death certificate (death rate numerators) compared with population figures (death rate denominators). The net effect of misclassification is an underestimation of deaths and death rates for races other than white and black. See Appendix II, Race, for a detailed discussion of sources of bias in death rates by race and Hispanic origin.

[6] In 1950, rate is for the age group 75 years and over.

[7] Prior to 1997, data from states that did not report Hispanic origin on the death certificate were excluded. See Appendix II, Hispanic origin.

NOTES: Starting with *Health, United States, 2003*, rates for 1991–1999 were revised using intercensal population estimates based on the 1990 and 2000 censuses. For 2000, population estimates are bridged-race April 1 census counts. Starting with *Health, United States, 2012*, rates for 2001–2009 were revised using intercensal population estimates based on the 2000 and 2010 censuses. For 2010, population estimates are bridged-race April 1 census counts. Rates for 2011 and beyond were computed using 2010-based postcensal estimates. See Appendix I, Population Census and Population Estimates. Age groups were selected to minimize the presentation of unstable age-specific death rates based on small numbers of deaths and for consistency among comparison groups. Starting with 2003 data, some states began to collect information on more than one race on the death certificate, according to 1997 Office of Management and Budget (OMB) standards. The multiple-race data for these states were bridged to the single-race categories of the 1977 OMB standards, for comparability with other states. See Appendix II, Race. Data for additional years are available. See the Excel spreadsheet on the *Health, United States* website at: http://www.cdc.gov/nchs/hus.htm.

SOURCE: NCHS, National Vital Statistics System; numerator data from National Vital Statistics System, annual public-use Mortality Files; denominator data from national population estimates for race groups from Table 1 and unpublished Hispanic population estimates for 1985–1996 prepared by the Housing and Household Economic Statistics Division, U.S. Census Bureau; Murphy SL, Kochanek KD, Xu JQ, Curtin SC. Deaths: Final data for 2015. National vital statistics reports. Hyattsville, MD: NCHS; 2017. Available from: http://www.cdc.gov/nchs/products/nvsr.htm. See Appendix I, National Vital Statistics System (NVSS).

Table 23 (page 1 of 3). Death rates for cerebrovascular diseases, by sex, race, Hispanic origin, and age: United States, selected years 1950–2015

Excel and PDF versions (with more data years and standard errors when available): http://www.cdc.gov/nchs/hus/contents2016.htm#023.

[Data are based on death certificates]

Sex, race, Hispanic origin, and age	1950 [1,2]	1960 [1,2]	1970 [2]	1980 [2]	1990 [2]	2000 [3]	2014 [3]	2015 [3]
All persons	Deaths per 100,000 resident population							
All ages, age-adjusted [4]	180.7	177.9	147.7	96.2	65.3	60.9	36.5	37.6
All ages, crude	104.0	108.0	101.9	75.0	57.8	59.6	41.7	43.7
Under 1 year	5.1	4.1	5.0	4.4	3.8	3.3	2.4	2.2
1–4 years	0.9	0.8	1.0	0.5	0.3	0.3	0.2	0.3
5–14 years	0.5	0.7	0.7	0.3	0.2	0.2	0.2	0.2
15–24 years	1.6	1.8	1.6	1.0	0.6	0.5	0.4	0.4
25–34 years	4.2	4.7	4.5	2.6	2.2	1.5	1.3	1.3
35–44 years	18.7	14.7	15.6	8.5	6.4	5.8	4.3	4.4
45–54 years	70.4	49.2	41.6	25.2	18.7	16.0	12.3	12.3
55–64 years	194.2	147.3	115.8	65.1	47.9	41.0	29.3	29.6
65–74 years	554.7	469.2	384.1	219.0	144.2	128.6	74.5	75.5
75–84 years	1,499.6	1,491.3	1,254.2	786.9	498.0	461.3	265.7	273.0
85 years and over	2,990.1	3,680.5	3,014.3	2,283.7	1,628.9	1,589.2	929.7	975.8
Male								
All ages, age-adjusted [4]	186.4	186.1	157.4	102.2	68.5	62.4	36.9	37.8
All ages, crude	102.5	104.5	94.5	63.4	46.7	46.9	35.3	36.8
Under 1 year	6.4	5.0	5.8	5.0	4.4	3.8	2.6	2.6
1–4 years	1.1	0.9	1.2	0.4	0.3	*	*	0.3
5–14 years	0.5	0.7	0.8	0.3	0.2	0.2	0.2	0.2
15–24 years	1.8	1.9	1.8	1.1	0.7	0.5	0.5	0.4
25–34 years	4.2	4.5	4.4	2.6	2.1	1.5	1.5	1.4
35–44 years	17.5	14.6	15.7	8.7	6.8	5.8	5.0	4.9
45–54 years	67.9	52.2	44.4	27.2	20.5	17.5	14.0	13.6
55–64 years	205.2	163.8	138.7	74.6	54.3	47.2	35.2	35.4
65–74 years	589.6	530.7	449.5	258.6	166.6	145.0	85.1	86.3
75–84 years	1,543.6	1,555.9	1,361.6	866.3	551.1	490.8	272.8	282.2
85 years and over	3,048.6	3,643.1	2,895.2	2,193.6	1,528.5	1,484.3	832.0	863.3
Female								
All ages, age-adjusted [4]	175.8	170.7	140.0	91.7	62.6	59.1	35.6	36.9
All ages, crude	105.6	111.4	109.0	85.9	68.4	71.8	47.9	50.3
Under 1 year	3.7	3.2	4.0	3.8	3.1	2.7	2.1	1.9
1–4 years	0.7	0.7	0.7	0.5	0.3	0.4	*	*
5–14 years	0.4	0.6	0.6	0.3	0.2	0.2	0.2	0.2
15–24 years	1.5	1.6	1.4	0.8	0.6	0.5	0.3	0.4
25–34 years	4.3	4.9	4.7	2.6	2.2	1.5	1.2	1.1
35–44 years	19.9	14.8	15.6	8.4	6.1	5.7	3.7	3.9
45–54 years	72.9	46.3	39.0	23.3	17.0	14.5	10.7	11.0
55–64 years	183.1	131.8	95.3	56.8	42.2	35.3	23.8	24.3
65–74 years	522.1	415.7	333.3	188.7	126.7	115.1	65.2	66.0
75–84 years	1,462.2	1,441.1	1,183.1	740.1	466.2	442.1	260.3	266.0
85 years and over	2,949.4	3,704.4	3,081.0	2,323.1	1,667.6	1,632.0	980.6	1,035.3
White male [5]								
All ages, age-adjusted [4]	182.1	181.6	153.7	98.7	65.5	59.8	35.2	36.1
All ages, crude	100.5	102.7	93.5	63.1	46.9	48.4	36.7	38.2
45–54 years	53.7	40.9	35.6	21.7	15.4	13.6	11.9	11.2
55–64 years	182.2	139.0	119.9	64.0	45.7	39.7	29.6	29.8
65–74 years	569.7	501.0	420.0	239.8	152.9	133.8	77.3	78.2
75–84 years	1,556.3	1,564.8	1,361.6	852.7	539.2	480.0	265.3	273.5
85 years and over	3,127.1	3,734.8	3,018.1	2,230.8	1,545.4	1,490.7	841.4	878.9
Black or African American male [5]								
All ages, age-adjusted [4]	228.8	238.5	206.4	142.0	102.2	89.6	55.1	55.5
All ages, crude	122.0	122.9	108.8	73.0	53.0	46.1	36.5	37.5
45–54 years	211.9	166.1	136.1	82.1	68.4	49.5	29.6	30.4
55–64 years	522.8	439.9	343.4	189.7	141.7	115.4	79.4	78.4
65–74 years	783.6	899.2	780.1	472.3	326.9	268.5	169.8	169.9
75–84 years [6]	1,504.9	1,475.2	1,445.7	1,066.3	721.5	659.2	393.2	410.8
85 years and over	- - -	2,700.0	1,963.1	1,873.2	1,421.5	1,458.8	827.6	804.3

See footnotes at end of table.

Table 23 (page 2 of 3). Death rates for cerebrovascular diseases, by sex, race, Hispanic origin, and age: United States, selected years 1950–2015

Excel and PDF versions (with more data years and standard errors when available): http://www.cdc.gov/nchs/hus/contents2016.htm#023.

[Data are based on death certificates]

Sex, race, Hispanic origin, and age	1950[1,2]	1960[1,2]	1970[2]	1980[2]	1990[2]	2000[3]	2014[3]	2015[3]
American Indian or Alaska Native male[5]				Deaths per 100,000 resident population				
All ages, age-adjusted[4]	- - -	- - -	- - -	66.4	44.3	46.1	25.3	24.5
All ages, crude	- - -	- - -	- - -	23.1	16.0	16.8	13.0	13.4
45–54 years	- - -	- - -	- - -	*	*	13.3	8.4	10.9
55–64 years	- - -	- - -	- - -	72.0	39.8	48.6	29.8	23.8
65–74 years	- - -	- - -	- - -	170.5	120.3	144.7	74.7	76.5
75–84 years	- - -	- - -	- - -	523.9	325.9	373.3	193.0	183.3
85 years and over	- - -	- - -	- - -	1,384.7	949.8	834.9	463.9	424.5
Asian or Pacific Islander male[5]								
All ages, age-adjusted[4]	- - -	- - -	- - -	71.4	59.1	58.0	29.4	31.3
All ages, crude	- - -	- - -	- - -	28.7	23.3	27.2	20.7	22.8
45–54 years	- - -	- - -	- - -	17.0	15.6	15.0	11.0	11.9
55–64 years	- - -	- - -	- - -	59.9	51.8	49.3	30.0	32.2
65–74 years	- - -	- - -	- - -	197.9	167.9	135.6	66.4	73.0
75–84 years	- - -	- - -	- - -	619.5	483.9	438.7	217.2	239.8
85 years and over	- - -	- - -	- - -	1,399.0	1,196.6	1,415.6	666.1	669.1
Hispanic or Latino male[5,7]								
All ages, age-adjusted[4]	- - -	- - -	- - -	- - -	46.5	50.5	32.1	34.2
All ages, crude	- - -	- - -	- - -	- - -	15.6	15.8	14.6	15.9
45–54 years	- - -	- - -	- - -	- - -	20.0	18.1	13.3	11.5
55–64 years	- - -	- - -	- - -	- - -	49.2	48.8	33.2	32.7
65–74 years	- - -	- - -	- - -	- - -	126.4	136.1	77.0	86.4
75–84 years	- - -	- - -	- - -	- - -	356.6	392.9	245.8	265.9
85 years and over	- - -	- - -	- - -	- - -	866.3	1,029.9	656.6	706.9
White, not Hispanic or Latino male[7]								
All ages, age-adjusted[4]	- - -	- - -	- - -	- - -	66.3	59.9	35.1	35.8
All ages, crude	- - -	- - -	- - -	- - -	50.6	53.9	41.8	43.5
45–54 years	- - -	- - -	- - -	- - -	14.9	13.0	11.3	10.9
55–64 years	- - -	- - -	- - -	- - -	45.1	38.7	28.7	28.9
65–74 years	- - -	- - -	- - -	- - -	154.5	133.1	76.7	76.5
75–84 years	- - -	- - -	- - -	- - -	547.3	482.3	265.8	272.0
85 years and over	- - -	- - -	- - -	- - -	1,578.7	1,505.9	851.2	887.3
White female[5]								
All ages, age-adjusted[4]	169.7	165.0	135.5	89.0	60.3	57.3	34.7	35.9
All ages, crude	103.3	110.1	109.8	88.6	71.6	76.9	51.8	54.4
45–54 years	55.0	33.8	30.5	18.6	13.5	11.2	8.8	9.5
55–64 years	156.9	103.0	78.1	48.6	35.8	30.2	20.4	21.1
65–74 years	498.1	383.3	303.2	172.5	116.1	107.3	60.2	61.4
75–84 years	1,471.3	1,444.7	1,176.8	728.8	456.5	434.2	257.1	260.1
85 years and over	3,017.9	3,795.7	3,167.6	2,362.7	1,685.9	1,646.7	995.7	1,055.0
Black or African American female[5]								
All ages, age-adjusted[4]	238.4	232.5	189.3	119.6	84.0	76.2	45.2	46.7
All ages, crude	128.3	127.7	112.2	77.8	60.7	58.3	40.5	42.5
45–54 years	248.9	166.2	119.4	61.8	44.1	38.1	22.4	21.3
55–64 years	567.7	452.0	272.4	138.4	96.9	76.4	48.4	48.1
65–74 years	754.4	830.5	673.5	361.7	236.7	190.9	112.6	110.1
75–84 years[6]	1,496.7	1,413.1	1,338.3	917.5	595.0	549.2	322.6	345.3
85 years and over	- - -	2,578.9	2,210.5	1,891.6	1,495.2	1,556.5	934.0	977.5

See footnotes at end of table.

Excel and PDF versions (with more data years and standard errors when available): http://www.cdc.gov/nchs/hus/contents2016.htm#023.

[Data are based on death certificates]

Sex, race, Hispanic origin, and age	1950 [1,2]	1960 [1,2]	1970 [2]	1980 [2]	1990 [2]	2000 [3]	2014 [3]	2015 [3]
American Indian or Alaska Native female [5]				Deaths per 100,000 resident population				
All ages, age-adjusted [4]	- - -	- - -	- - -	51.2	38.4	43.7	25.0	24.4
All ages, crude	- - -	- - -	- - -	22.0	19.3	21.5	15.7	16.1
45–54 years	- - -	- - -	- - -	*	*	14.4	11.2	11.2
55–64 years	- - -	- - -	- - -	*	40.7	37.9	21.6	19.8
65–74 years	- - -	- - -	- - -	128.3	100.5	79.5	52.4	58.2
75–84 years	- - -	- - -	- - -	404.2	282.0	391.1	183.2	176.0
85 years and over.	- - -	- - -	- - -	1,095.5	776.2	931.5	618.8	559.4
Asian or Pacific Islander female [5]								
All ages, age-adjusted [4]	- - -	- - -	- - -	60.8	54.9	49.1	27.2	28.3
All ages, crude	- - -	- - -	- - -	26.4	24.3	28.7	23.8	25.5
45–54 years	- - -	- - -	- - -	20.3	19.7	13.3	8.6	7.6
55–64 years	- - -	- - -	- - -	43.7	42.1	33.3	18.4	18.3
65–74 years	- - -	- - -	- - -	136.1	124.0	102.8	52.3	51.3
75–84 years	- - -	- - -	- - -	446.6	396.6	386.0	197.9	219.2
85 years and over.	- - -	- - -	- - -	1,545.2	1,395.0	1,246.6	747.4	757.6
Hispanic or Latina female [5,7]								
All ages, age-adjusted [4]	- - -	- - -	- - -	- - -	43.7	43.0	28.3	30.4
All ages, crude	- - -	- - -	- - -	- - -	20.1	19.4	16.9	18.8
45–54 years	- - -	- - -	- - -	- - -	15.2	12.4	7.7	8.8
55–64 years	- - -	- - -	- - -	- - -	38.5	31.9	17.2	19.3
65–74 years	- - -	- - -	- - -	- - -	102.6	95.2	54.7	54.0
75–84 years	- - -	- - -	- - -	- - -	308.5	311.3	219.7	230.0
85 years and over.	- - -	- - -	- - -	- - -	1,055.3	1,108.9	744.6	831.1
White, not Hispanic or Latina female [7]								
All ages, age-adjusted [4]	- - -	- - -	- - -	- - -	61.0	57.6	35.0	36.2
All ages, crude	- - -	- - -	- - -	- - -	77.2	85.5	59.7	62.4
45–54 years	- - -	- - -	- - -	- - -	13.2	10.9	8.9	9.4
55–64 years	- - -	- - -	- - -	- - -	35.7	29.9	20.6	21.0
65–74 years	- - -	- - -	- - -	- - -	116.9	107.6	60.3	61.5
75–84 years	- - -	- - -	- - -	- - -	461.9	438.3	259.0	260.9
85 years and over.	- - -	- - -	- - -	- - -	1,714.7	1,661.6	1,009.2	1,066.0

* Rates based on fewer than 20 deaths are considered unreliable and are not shown.

- - - Data not available.

[1] Includes deaths of persons who were not residents of the 50 states and the District of Columbia (D.C.).

[2] Underlying cause of death was coded according to the 6th Revision of the *International Classification of Diseases* (ICD) in 1950, 7th Revision in 1960, 8th Revision in 1970, and 9th Revision in 1980–1998. See Appendix II, Cause of death; Table III; Table IV.

[3] Starting with 1999 data, cause of death is coded according to ICD–10. See Appendix II, Cause of death; Comparability ratio; Table IV; Table V.

[4] Age-adjusted rates are calculated using the year 2000 standard population. Prior to 2001, age-adjusted rates were calculated using standard million proportions based on rounded population numbers. Starting with 2001 data, unrounded population numbers are used to calculate age-adjusted rates. See Appendix II, Age adjustment.

[5] The race groups, white, black, Asian or Pacific Islander, and American Indian or Alaska Native, include persons of Hispanic and non-Hispanic origin. Persons of Hispanic origin may be of any race. Death rates for Hispanic, American Indian or Alaska Native, and Asian or Pacific Islander persons should be interpreted with caution because of inconsistencies in reporting Hispanic origin or race on the death certificate (death rate numerators) compared with population figures (death rate denominators). The net effect of misclassification is an underestimation of deaths and death rates for races other than white and black. See Appendix II, Race, for a detailed discussion of sources of bias in death rates by race and Hispanic origin.

[6] In 1950, rate is for the age group 75 years and over.

[7] Prior to 1997, data from states that did not report Hispanic origin on the birth certificate were excluded. See Appendix II, Hispanic origin.

NOTES: Starting with *Health, United States, 2003*, rates for 1991–1999 were revised using intercensal population estimates based on the 1990 and 2000 censuses. For 2000, population estimates are bridged-race April 1 census counts. Starting with *Health, United States, 2012*, rates for 2001–2009 were revised using intercensal population estimates based on the 2000 and 2010 censuses. For 2010, population estimates are bridged-race April 1 census counts. Rates for 2011 and beyond were computed using 2010-based postcensal estimates. See Appendix I, Population Census and Population Estimates. Age groups were selected to minimize the presentation of unstable age-specific death rates based on small numbers of deaths and for consistency among comparison groups. Starting with 2003 data, some states began to collect information on more than one race on the death certificate, according to 1997 Office of Management and Budget (OMB) standards. The multiple-race data for these states were bridged to the single-race categories of the 1977 OMB standards, for comparability with other states. See Appendix II, Race. Data for additional years are available. See the Excel spreadsheet on the *Health, United States* website at: http://www.cdc.gov/nchs/hus.htm.

SOURCE: NCHS, National Vital Statistics System; Grove RD, Hetzel AM. Vital statistics rates in the United States, 1940–1960. Washington, DC: U.S. Government Printing Office. 1968; numerator data from National Vital Statistics System, annual public-use Mortality Files; denominator data from national population estimates for race groups from Table 1 and unpublished Hispanic population estimates for 1985–1996 prepared by the Housing and Household Economic Statistics Division, U.S. Census Bureau; Murphy SL, Kochanek KD, Xu JQ, Curtin SC. Deaths: Final data for 2015. National vital statistics reports. Hyattsville, MD: NCHS; 2017. Available from: http://www.cdc.gov/nchs/products/nvsr.htm. See Appendix I, National Vital Statistics System (NVSS).

Table 24 (page 1 of 4). Death rates for malignant neoplasms, by sex, race, Hispanic origin, and age: United States, selected years 1950–2015

Excel and PDF versions (with more data years and standard errors when available): http://www.cdc.gov/nchs/hus/contents2016.htm#024.

[Data are based on death certificates]

Sex, race, Hispanic origin, and age	1950[1,2]	1960[1,2]	1970[2]	1980[2]	1990[2]	2000[3]	2014[3]	2015[3]
All persons	Deaths per 100,000 resident population							
All ages, age-adjusted[4]	193.9	193.9	198.6	207.9	216.0	199.6	161.2	158.5
All ages, crude	139.8	149.2	162.8	183.9	203.2	196.5	185.6	185.4
Under 1 year	8.7	7.2	4.7	3.2	2.3	2.4	1.3	1.3
1–4 years	11.7	10.9	7.5	4.5	3.5	2.7	2.0	2.2
5–14 years	6.7	6.8	6.0	4.3	3.1	2.5	2.1	2.1
15–24 years	8.6	8.3	8.3	6.3	4.9	4.4	3.6	3.4
25–34 years	20.0	19.5	16.5	13.7	12.6	9.8	8.3	8.4
35–44 years	62.7	59.7	59.5	48.6	43.3	36.6	27.8	26.9
45–54 years	175.1	177.0	182.5	180.0	158.9	127.5	103.2	99.7
55–64 years	390.7	396.8	423.0	436.1	449.6	366.7	287.6	284.1
65–74 years	698.8	713.9	754.2	817.9	872.3	816.3	603.1	594.3
75–84 years	1,153.3	1,127.4	1,169.2	1,232.3	1,348.5	1,335.6	1,125.9	1,100.8
85 years and over	1,451.0	1,450.0	1,320.7	1,594.6	1,752.9	1,819.4	1,632.9	1,628.6
Male								
All ages, age-adjusted[4]	208.1	225.1	247.6	271.2	280.4	248.9	192.9	189.2
All ages, crude	142.9	162.5	182.1	205.3	221.3	207.2	198.4	198.3
Under 1 year	9.7	7.7	4.4	3.7	2.4	2.6	1.1	1.5
1–4 years	12.5	12.4	8.3	5.2	3.7	3.0	2.2	2.4
5–14 years	7.4	7.6	6.7	4.9	3.5	2.7	2.3	2.2
15–24 years	9.7	10.2	10.4	7.8	5.7	5.1	4.2	3.9
25–34 years	17.7	18.8	16.3	13.4	12.6	9.2	8.2	8.2
35–44 years	45.6	48.9	53.0	44.0	38.5	32.7	24.0	23.0
45–54 years	156.2	170.8	183.5	188.7	162.5	130.9	102.9	99.4
55–64 years	413.1	459.9	511.8	520.8	532.9	415.8	330.3	325.5
65–74 years	791.5	890.5	1,006.8	1,093.2	1,122.2	1,001.9	711.9	701.7
75–84 years	1,332.6	1,389.4	1,588.3	1,790.5	1,914.4	1,760.6	1,387.5	1,355.8
85 years and over	1,668.3	1,741.2	1,720.8	2,369.5	2,739.9	2,710.7	2,250.4	2,220.2
Female								
All ages, age-adjusted[4]	182.3	168.7	163.2	166.7	175.7	167.6	138.1	135.9
All ages, crude	136.8	136.4	144.4	163.6	186.0	186.2	173.2	172.9
Under 1 year	7.6	6.8	5.0	2.7	2.2	2.3	1.6	1.1
1–4 years	10.8	9.3	6.7	3.7	3.2	2.5	1.8	2.0
5–14 years	6.0	6.0	5.2	3.6	2.8	2.2	1.8	2.0
15–24 years	7.6	6.5	6.2	4.8	4.1	3.6	2.9	2.8
25–34 years	22.2	20.1	16.7	14.0	12.6	10.4	8.5	8.6
35–44 years	79.3	70.0	65.6	53.1	48.1	40.4	31.6	30.7
45–54 years	194.0	183.0	181.5	171.8	155.5	124.2	103.4	100.0
55–64 years	368.2	337.7	343.2	361.7	375.2	321.3	247.9	245.4
65–74 years	612.3	560.2	557.9	607.1	677.4	663.6	507.5	499.8
75–84 years	1,000.7	924.1	891.9	903.1	1,010.3	1,058.5	928.0	906.4
85 years and over	1,299.7	1,263.9	1,096.7	1,255.7	1,372.1	1,456.4	1,311.7	1,315.8
White male[5]								
All ages, age-adjusted[4]	210.0	224.7	244.8	265.1	272.2	243.9	193.0	189.7
All ages, crude	147.2	166.1	185.1	208.7	227.7	218.1	214.4	214.7
25–34 years	17.7	18.8	16.2	13.6	12.3	9.2	8.4	8.4
35–44 years	44.5	46.3	50.1	41.1	35.8	30.9	24.0	23.1
45–54 years	150.8	164.1	172.0	175.4	149.9	123.5	102.3	98.8
55–64 years	409.4	450.9	498.1	497.4	508.2	401.9	323.5	320.5
65–74 years	798.7	887.3	997.0	1,070.7	1,090.7	984.3	707.6	698.7
75–84 years	1,367.6	1,413.7	1,592.7	1,779.7	1,883.2	1,736.0	1,400.4	1,369.4
85 years and over	1,732.7	1,791.4	1,772.2	2,375.6	2,715.1	2,693.7	2,279.7	2,251.6
Black or African American male[5]								
All ages, age-adjusted[4]	178.9	227.6	291.9	353.4	397.9	340.3	231.9	224.8
All ages, crude	106.6	136.7	171.6	205.5	221.9	188.5	165.1	163.8
25–34 years	18.0	18.4	18.8	14.1	15.7	10.1	8.3	8.7
35–44 years	55.7	72.9	81.3	73.8	64.3	48.4	28.8	26.3
45–54 years	211.7	244.7	311.2	333.0	302.6	214.2	128.8	123.8
55–64 years	490.8	579.7	689.2	812.5	859.2	626.4	450.5	437.4
65–74 years	636.5	938.5	1,168.9	1,417.2	1,613.9	1,363.8	925.8	895.8
75–84 years[6]	853.5	1,053.3	1,624.8	2,029.6	2,478.3	2,351.8	1,569.4	1,526.9
85 years and over	- - -	1,155.2	1,387.0	2,393.9	3,238.3	3,264.8	2,378.6	2,316.0

See footnotes at end of table.

Table 24 (page 2 of 4). Death rates for malignant neoplasms, by sex, race, Hispanic origin, and age: United States, selected years 1950–2015

Excel and PDF versions (with more data years and standard errors when available): *http://www.cdc.gov/nchs/hus/contents2016.htm#024.*

[Data are based on death certificates]

Sex, race, Hispanic origin, and age	1950 [1,2]	1960 [1,2]	1970 [2]	1980 [2]	1990 [2]	2000 [3]	2014 [3]	2015 [3]
American Indian or Alaska Native male [5]				Deaths per 100,000 resident population				
All ages, age-adjusted [4]	- - -	- - -	- - -	140.5	145.8	155.8	130.4	127.1
All ages, crude	- - -	- - -	- - -	58.1	61.4	67.0	76.1	77.5
25–34 years	- - -	- - -	- - -	*	*	*	*	5.4
35–44 years	- - -	- - -	- - -	*	22.8	21.4	15.2	14.7
45–54 years	- - -	- - -	- - -	86.9	86.9	70.3	58.7	70.0
55–64 years	- - -	- - -	- - -	213.4	246.2	255.6	221.2	202.7
65–74 years	- - -	- - -	- - -	613.0	530.6	648.0	520.7	505.3
75–84 years	- - -	- - -	- - -	936.4	1,038.4	1,152.5	1,015.8	971.8
85 years and over	- - -	- - -	- - -	1,471.2	1,654.4	1,584.2	1,256.3	1,229.2
Asian or Pacific Islander male [5]								
All ages, age-adjusted [4]	- - -	- - -	- - -	165.2	172.5	150.8	116.4	116.7
All ages, crude	- - -	- - -	- - -	81.9	82.7	85.2	90.2	92.5
25–34 years	- - -	- - -	- - -	6.3	9.2	7.4	6.0	5.3
35–44 years	- - -	- - -	- - -	29.4	27.7	26.1	15.9	18.0
45–54 years	- - -	- - -	- - -	108.2	92.6	78.5	64.6	61.6
55–64 years	- - -	- - -	- - -	298.5	274.6	229.2	190.7	179.8
65–74 years	- - -	- - -	- - -	581.2	687.2	559.4	399.6	410.2
75–84 years	- - -	- - -	- - -	1,147.6	1,229.9	1,086.1	839.8	843.2
85 years and over	- - -	- - -	- - -	1,798.7	1,837.0	1,823.2	1,468.0	1,492.8
Hispanic or Latino male [5,7]								
All ages, age-adjusted [4]	- - -	- - -	- - -	- - -	174.7	171.7	135.9	133.8
All ages, crude	- - -	- - -	- - -	- - -	65.5	61.3	68.0	69.4
25–34 years	- - -	- - -	- - -	- - -	8.0	6.9	7.1	7.7
35–44 years	- - -	- - -	- - -	- - -	22.5	20.1	17.2	17.0
45–54 years	- - -	- - -	- - -	- - -	96.6	79.4	65.1	63.3
55–64 years	- - -	- - -	- - -	- - -	294.0	253.1	207.8	208.8
65–74 years	- - -	- - -	- - -	- - -	655.5	651.2	497.9	487.9
75–84 years	- - -	- - -	- - -	- - -	1,233.4	1,306.4	1,026.5	1,016.4
85 years and over	- - -	- - -	- - -	- - -	2,019.4	2,049.7	1,624.9	1,573.7
White, not Hispanic or Latino male [7]								
All ages, age-adjusted [4]	- - -	- - -	- - -	- - -	276.7	247.7	197.7	194.3
All ages, crude	- - -	- - -	- - -	- - -	246.2	244.4	249.3	249.7
25–34 years	- - -	- - -	- - -	- - -	12.8	9.7	8.6	8.4
35–44 years	- - -	- - -	- - -	- - -	36.8	32.3	25.6	24.5
45–54 years	- - -	- - -	- - -	- - -	153.9	127.2	108.5	105.0
55–64 years	- - -	- - -	- - -	- - -	520.6	412.0	335.0	331.7
65–74 years	- - -	- - -	- - -	- - -	1,109.0	1,002.1	722.1	713.1
75–84 years	- - -	- - -	- - -	- - -	1,906.6	1,750.2	1,424.1	1,391.1
85 years and over	- - -	- - -	- - -	- - -	2,744.4	2,714.1	2,319.1	2,294.1
White female [5]								
All ages, age-adjusted [4]	182.0	167.7	162.5	165.2	174.0	166.9	138.8	136.8
All ages, crude	139.9	139.8	149.4	170.3	196.1	199.4	187.2	187.1
25–34 years	20.9	18.8	16.3	13.5	11.9	10.1	8.3	8.6
35–44 years	74.5	66.6	62.4	50.9	46.2	38.2	31.2	29.9
45–54 years	185.8	175.7	177.3	166.4	150.9	120.1	101.8	98.7
55–64 years	362.5	329.0	338.6	355.5	368.5	319.7	244.9	242.1
65–74 years	616.5	562.1	554.7	605.2	675.1	665.6	512.4	505.9
75–84 years	1,026.6	939.3	903.5	905.4	1,011.8	1,063.4	943.2	922.7
85 years and over	1,348.3	1,304.9	1,126.6	1,266.8	1,372.3	1,459.1	1,329.0	1,338.3

See footnotes at end of table.

Excel and PDF versions (with more data years and standard errors when available): http://www.cdc.gov/nchs/hus/contents2016.htm#024.

[Data are based on death certificates]

Sex, race, Hispanic origin, and age	1950[1,2]	1960[1,2]	1970[2]	1980[2]	1990[2]	2000[3]	2014[3]	2015[3]
Black or African American female[5]				Deaths per 100,000 resident population				
All ages, age-adjusted[4]	174.1	174.3	173.4	189.5	205.9	193.8	156.8	152.2
All ages, crude	111.8	113.8	117.3	136.5	156.1	151.8	147.5	146.2
25–34 years	34.3	31.0	20.9	18.3	18.7	13.5	11.2	10.9
35–44 years	119.8	102.4	94.6	73.5	67.4	58.9	40.5	40.9
45–54 years	277.0	254.8	228.6	230.2	209.9	173.9	133.4	126.2
55–64 years	484.6	442.7	404.8	450.4	482.4	391.0	321.9	317.2
65–74 years	477.3	541.6	615.8	662.4	773.2	753.1	583.7	566.7
75–84 years[6]	605.3	696.3	763.3	923.9	1,059.9	1,124.0	960.8	925.2
85 years and over	- - -	728.9	791.5	1,159.9	1,431.3	1,527.7	1,297.5	1,267.9
American Indian or Alaska Native female[5]								
All ages, age-adjusted[4]	- - -	- - -	- - -	94.0	106.9	108.3	88.5	93.0
All ages, crude	- - -	- - -	- - -	50.4	62.1	61.3	63.4	69.2
25–34 years	- - -	- - -	- - -	*	*	*	*	6.5
35–44 years	- - -	- - -	- - -	36.9	31.0	23.7	17.5	18.0
45–54 years	- - -	- - -	- - -	96.9	104.5	59.7	67.1	62.7
55–64 years	- - -	- - -	- - -	198.4	213.3	200.9	139.5	161.3
65–74 years	- - -	- - -	- - -	350.8	438.9	458.3	359.8	350.7
75–84 years	- - -	- - -	- - -	446.4	554.3	714.0	611.5	654.8
85 years and over	- - -	- - -	- - -	786.5	843.7	983.2	817.9	884.0
Asian or Pacific Islander female[5]								
All ages, age-adjusted[4]	- - -	- - -	- - -	93.0	103.0	100.7	86.2	86.2
All ages, crude	- - -	- - -	- - -	54.1	60.5	72.1	80.6	82.7
25–34 years	- - -	- - -	- - -	9.5	7.3	8.1	6.2	5.3
35–44 years	- - -	- - -	- - -	38.7	29.8	28.9	21.7	21.7
45–54 years	- - -	- - -	- - -	99.8	93.9	78.2	64.1	67.1
55–64 years	- - -	- - -	- - -	174.7	196.2	176.5	143.8	146.6
65–74 years	- - -	- - -	- - -	301.9	346.2	357.4	278.8	279.5
75–84 years	- - -	- - -	- - -	522.1	641.4	650.1	597.1	589.1
85 years and over	- - -	- - -	- - -	800.0	971.7	988.5	963.7	941.5
Hispanic or Latina female[5,7]								
All ages, age-adjusted[4]	- - -	- - -	- - -	- - -	111.9	110.8	95.7	93.6
All ages, crude	- - -	- - -	- - -	- - -	60.7	58.5	63.6	64.2
25–34 years	- - -	- - -	- - -	- - -	9.7	7.8	7.2	8.3
35–44 years	- - -	- - -	- - -	- - -	34.8	30.7	25.4	25.2
45–54 years	- - -	- - -	- - -	- - -	100.5	84.7	68.6	67.9
55–64 years	- - -	- - -	- - -	- - -	205.4	192.5	163.2	161.4
65–74 years	- - -	- - -	- - -	- - -	404.8	410.0	335.9	330.6
75–84 years	- - -	- - -	- - -	- - -	663.0	716.5	636.6	621.7
85 years and over	- - -	- - -	- - -	- - -	1,022.7	1,056.5	1,004.3	946.7
White, not Hispanic or Latina female[7]								
All ages, age-adjusted[4]	- - -	- - -	- - -	- - -	177.5	170.0	142.7	140.6
All ages, crude	- - -	- - -	- - -	- - -	210.6	220.6	215.1	215.1
25–34 years	- - -	- - -	- - -	- - -	11.9	10.5	8.4	8.4
35–44 years	- - -	- - -	- - -	- - -	47.0	38.9	32.3	30.6
45–54 years	- - -	- - -	- - -	- - -	154.9	123.0	107.1	103.7
55–64 years	- - -	- - -	- - -	- - -	379.5	328.9	253.3	250.6
65–74 years	- - -	- - -	- - -	- - -	688.5	681.0	527.0	520.4
75–84 years	- - -	- - -	- - -	- - -	1,027.2	1,075.3	967.1	945.6
85 years and over	- - -	- - -	- - -	- - -	1,385.7	1,468.7	1,345.8	1,360.0

See footnotes at end of table.

Table 24 (page 4 of 4). Death rates for malignant neoplasms, by sex, race, Hispanic origin, and age: United States, selected years 1950–2015

Excel and PDF versions (with more data years and standard errors when available): *http://www.cdc.gov/nchs/hus/contents2016.htm#024.*

[Data are based on death certificates]

- - - Data not available.

* Rates based on fewer than 20 deaths are considered unreliable and are not shown.

[1] Includes deaths of persons who were not residents of the 50 states and the District of Columbia (D.C.).

[2] Underlying cause of death was coded according to the 6th Revision of the *International Classification of Diseases* (ICD) in 1950, 7th Revision in 1960, 8th Revision in 1970, and 9th Revision in 1980–1998. See Appendix II, Cause of death; Table III; Table IV.

[3] Starting with 1999 data, cause of death is coded according to ICD–10. See Appendix II, Cause of death; Comparability ratio; Table IV; Table V.

[4] Age-adjusted rates are calculated using the year 2000 standard population. Prior to 2001, age-adjusted rates were calculated using standard million proportions based on rounded population numbers. Starting with 2001 data, unrounded population numbers are used to calculate age-adjusted rates. See Appendix II, Age adjustment.

[5] The race groups, white, black, Asian or Pacific Islander, and American Indian or Alaska Native, include persons of Hispanic and non-Hispanic origin. Persons of Hispanic origin may be of any race. Death rates for Hispanic, American Indian or Alaska Native, and Asian or Pacific Islander persons should be interpreted with caution because of inconsistencies in reporting Hispanic origin or race on the death certificate (death rate numerators) compared with population figures (death rate denominators). The net effect of misclassification is an underestimation of deaths and death rates for races other than white and black. See Appendix II, Race, for a detailed discussion of sources of bias in death rates by race and Hispanic origin.

[6] In 1950, rate is for the age group 75 years and over.

[7] Prior to 1997, data from states that did not report Hispanic origin on the death certificate were excluded. See Appendix II, Hispanic origin.

NOTES: Starting with *Health, United States, 2003*, rates for 1991–1999 were revised using intercensal population estimates based on the 1990 and 2000 censuses. For 2000, population estimates are bridged-race April 1 census counts. Starting with *Health, United States, 2012*, rates for 2001–2009 were revised using intercensal population estimates based on the 2000 and 2010 censuses. For 2010, population estimates are bridged-race April 1 census counts. Rates for 2011 and beyond were computed using 2010-based postcensal estimates. See Appendix I, Population Census and Population Estimates. Age groups were selected to minimize the presentation of unstable age-specific death rates based on small numbers of deaths and for consistency among comparison groups. Starting with 2003 data, some states began to collect information on more than one race on the death certificate, according to 1997 Office of Management and Budget (OMB) standards. The multiple-race data for these states were bridged to the single-race categories of the 1977 OMB standards, for comparability with other states. See Appendix II, Race. Data for additional years are available. See the Excel spreadsheet on the *Health, United States* website at: http://www.cdc.gov/nchs/hus.htm.

SOURCE: NCHS, National Vital Statistics System; Grove RD, Hetzel AM. Vital statistics rates in the United States, 1940–1960. Washington, DC: U.S. Government Printing Office. 1968; numerator data from National Vital Statistics System, annual public-use Mortality Files; denominator data from national population estimates for race groups from Table 1 and unpublished Hispanic population estimates for 1985–1996 prepared by the Housing and Household Economic Statistics Division, U.S. Census Bureau; Murphy SL, Kochanek KD, Xu JQ, Curtin SC. Deaths: Final data for 2015. National vital statistics reports. Hyattsville, MD: NCHS; 2017. Available from: http://www.cdc.gov/nchs/products/nvsr.htm. See Appendix I, National Vital Statistics System (NVSS).

Table 25 (page 1 of 3). Death rates for malignant neoplasms of trachea, bronchus, and lung, by sex, race, Hispanic origin, and age: United States, selected years 1950–2015

Excel and PDF versions (with more data years and standard errors when available): http://www.cdc.gov/nchs/hus/contents2016.htm#025.

[Data are based on death certificates]

Sex, race, Hispanic origin, and age	1950 [1,2]	1960 [1,2]	1970 [2]	1980 [2]	1990 [2]	2000 [3]	2014 [3]	2015 [3]
All persons	Deaths per 100,000 resident population							
All ages, age-adjusted [4]	15.0	24.1	37.1	49.9	59.3	56.1	42.1	40.5
All ages, crude	12.2	20.3	32.1	45.8	56.8	55.3	48.8	47.9
Under 25 years	0.1	0.0	0.1	0.0	0.0	0.0	0.0	0.0
25–34 years	0.8	1.0	0.9	0.6	0.7	0.5	0.3	0.3
35–44 years	4.5	6.8	11.0	9.2	6.8	6.1	2.7	2.5
45–54 years	20.4	29.6	43.4	54.1	46.8	31.6	22.4	20.5
55–64 years	48.7	75.3	109.1	138.2	160.6	122.4	78.5	76.8
65–74 years	59.7	108.1	164.5	233.3	288.4	284.2	189.4	181.0
75–84 years	55.8	91.5	163.2	240.5	333.3	370.8	321.2	306.4
85 years and over	42.3	65.6	101.7	176.0	242.5	302.1	311.7	316.1
Male								
All ages, age-adjusted [4]	24.6	43.6	67.5	85.2	91.1	76.7	51.7	49.5
All ages, crude	19.9	35.4	53.4	68.6	75.1	65.5	54.1	52.9
Under 25 years	0.0	0.0	0.1	0.1	0.0	*	*	*
25–34 years	1.1	1.4	1.3	0.8	0.9	0.5	0.3	0.3
35–44 years	7.1	10.5	16.1	11.9	8.5	6.9	2.9	2.6
45–54 years	35.0	50.6	67.5	76.0	59.7	38.5	23.8	22.1
55–64 years	83.8	139.3	189.7	213.6	222.9	154.0	93.8	92.1
65–74 years	98.7	204.3	320.8	403.9	430.4	377.9	229.5	217.1
75–84 years	82.6	167.1	330.8	488.8	572.9	532.2	395.7	378.3
85 years and over	62.5	107.7	194.0	368.1	513.2	521.2	442.8	434.4
Female								
All ages, age-adjusted [4]	5.8	7.5	13.1	24.4	37.1	41.3	34.7	33.5
All ages, crude	4.5	6.4	11.9	24.3	39.4	45.4	43.7	43.0
Under 25 years	0.1	0.0	0.0	*	*	*	*	0.0
25–34 years	0.5	0.5	0.5	0.5	0.5	0.5	0.3	0.3
35–44 years	1.9	3.2	6.1	6.5	5.2	5.3	2.6	2.4
45–54 years	5.8	9.2	21.0	33.7	34.5	25.0	21.0	18.8
55–64 years	13.6	15.4	36.8	72.0	105.0	93.3	64.2	62.7
65–74 years	23.3	24.4	43.1	102.7	177.6	206.9	154.2	149.1
75–84 years	32.9	32.8	52.4	94.1	190.1	265.6	264.8	251.5
85 years and over	28.2	38.8	50.0	91.9	138.1	212.8	243.5	253.6
White male [5]								
All ages, age-adjusted [4]	25.1	43.6	67.1	83.8	89.0	75.7	51.8	49.7
All ages, crude	20.8	36.4	54.6	70.2	77.8	69.4	58.7	57.4
45–54 years	35.1	49.2	63.3	70.9	55.2	35.7	23.7	22.0
55–64 years	85.4	139.2	186.8	205.6	213.7	150.8	92.1	91.1
65–74 years	101.5	207.5	325.0	401.0	422.1	374.9	230.2	216.9
75–84 years	85.5	170.4	336.7	493.5	572.2	529.9	400.4	383.5
85 years and over	67.4	109.4	199.6	374.1	516.3	522.4	446.6	439.6
Black or African American male [5]								
All ages, age-adjusted [4]	17.8	42.6	75.4	107.6	125.4	101.1	61.9	58.6
All ages, crude	12.1	28.1	47.7	66.6	73.7	58.3	45.0	43.7
45–54 years	34.4	68.4	115.4	133.8	114.9	70.7	31.0	28.8
55–64 years	68.3	146.8	234.3	321.1	358.6	223.5	131.4	124.4
65–74 years	53.8	168.3	300.5	472.3	585.4	488.8	287.7	275.3
75–84 years [6]	36.2	107.3	271.6	472.9	645.4	642.5	435.1	407.5
85 years and over	- - -	82.8	137.0	311.3	499.5	562.8	456.0	433.4
American Indian or Alaska Native male [5]								
All ages, age-adjusted [4]	- - -	- - -	- - -	31.7	47.5	42.9	34.1	32.1
All ages, crude	- - -	- - -	- - -	14.2	20.0	18.1	19.8	19.0
45–54 years	- - -	- - -	- - -	*	26.6	14.5	8.8	13.1
55–64 years	- - -	- - -	- - -	72.0	97.8	86.0	53.2	42.0
65–74 years	- - -	- - -	- - -	202.8	194.3	184.8	177.8	160.5
75–84 years	- - -	- - -	- - -	*	356.2	367.9	292.1	276.2
85 years and over	- - -	- - -	- - -	*	*	*	193.3	229.9

See footnotes at end of table.

Table 25 (page 2 of 3). **Death rates for malignant neoplasms of trachea, bronchus, and lung, by sex, race, Hispanic origin, and age: United States, selected years 1950–2015**

Excel and PDF versions (with more data years and standard errors when available): http://www.cdc.gov/nchs/hus/contents2016.htm#025.

[Data are based on death certificates]

Sex, race, Hispanic origin, and age	1950 [1,2]	1960 [1,2]	1970 [2]	1980 [2]	1990 [2]	2000 [3]	2014 [3]	2015 [3]
Asian or Pacific Islander male [5]				Deaths per 100,000 resident population				
All ages, age-adjusted [4]	- - -	- - -	- - -	43.3	44.2	40.9	29.6	29.5
All ages, crude	- - -	- - -	- - -	22.1	20.7	22.7	22.4	23.0
45–54 years	- - -	- - -	- - -	33.3	18.8	17.2	13.1	11.2
55–64 years	- - -	- - -	- - -	94.4	74.4	61.4	44.7	44.5
65–74 years	- - -	- - -	- - -	174.3	215.8	183.2	108.9	116.5
75–84 years	- - -	- - -	- - -	301.3	307.5	323.2	239.8	239.4
85 years and over	- - -	- - -	- - -	*	421.3	378.0	363.2	347.3
Hispanic or Latino male [5,7]								
All ages, age-adjusted [4]	- - -	- - -	- - -	- - -	44.1	39.0	25.0	24.3
All ages, crude	- - -	- - -	- - -	- - -	16.2	13.3	11.6	11.7
45–54 years	- - -	- - -	- - -	- - -	21.5	14.8	7.2	6.0
55–64 years	- - -	- - -	- - -	- - -	80.7	58.6	31.4	32.8
65–74 years	- - -	- - -	- - -	- - -	195.5	167.3	107.0	103.4
75–84 years	- - -	- - -	- - -	- - -	313.4	327.5	216.1	211.0
85 years and over	- - -	- - -	- - -	- - -	420.7	368.8	276.0	267.7
White, not Hispanic or Latino male [7]								
All ages, age-adjusted [4]	- - -	- - -	- - -	- - -	91.1	77.9	54.4	52.2
All ages, crude	- - -	- - -	- - -	- - -	84.7	78.9	70.2	68.6
45–54 years	- - -	- - -	- - -	- - -	57.8	37.7	26.9	25.2
55–64 years	- - -	- - -	- - -	- - -	221.0	157.7	99.0	98.0
65–74 years	- - -	- - -	- - -	- - -	431.4	387.3	240.3	226.1
75–84 years	- - -	- - -	- - -	- - -	580.4	537.7	414.3	396.2
85 years and over	- - -	- - -	- - -	- - -	520.9	527.3	457.5	451.0
White female [5]								
All ages, age-adjusted [4]	5.9	6.8	13.1	24.5	37.6	42.3	36.0	34.9
All ages, crude	4.7	5.9	12.3	25.6	42.4	49.9	48.7	48.1
45–54 years	5.7	9.0	20.9	33.0	34.6	24.8	21.7	19.7
55–64 years	13.7	15.1	37.2	71.9	105.7	96.1	66.3	64.8
65–74 years	23.7	24.8	42.9	104.6	181.3	213.2	161.4	156.2
75–84 years	34.0	32.7	52.6	95.2	194.6	272.7	275.3	263.0
85 years and over	29.3	39.1	50.6	92.4	138.3	215.9	247.7	260.2
Black or African American female [5]								
All ages, age-adjusted [4]	4.5	6.8	13.7	24.8	36.8	39.8	32.7	30.7
All ages, crude	2.8	4.3	9.4	18.3	28.1	30.8	30.7	29.5
45–54 years	7.5	11.3	23.9	43.4	41.3	32.9	23.2	18.8
55–64 years	12.9	17.9	33.5	79.9	117.9	95.3	69.8	67.4
65–74 years	14.0	18.1	46.1	88.0	164.3	194.1	142.3	136.2
75–84 years [6]	*	31.3	49.1	79.4	148.1	224.3	227.5	209.6
85 years and over	- - -	34.2	44.8	85.8	134.9	185.9	220.8	218.6
American Indian or Alaska Native female [5]								
All ages, age-adjusted [4]	- - -	- - -	- - -	11.7	19.3	24.8	22.7	22.5
All ages, crude	- - -	- - -	- - -	6.0	11.2	14.0	15.8	16.9
45–54 years	- - -	- - -	- - -	*	22.9	12.1	14.4	12.3
55–64 years	- - -	- - -	- - -	*	53.7	52.6	28.0	44.5
65–74 years	- - -	- - -	- - -	*	78.5	151.5	114.4	103.2
75–84 years	- - -	- - -	- - -	*	111.8	136.3	179.3	159.0
85 years and over	- - -	- - -	- - -	*	*	*	161.4	179.8

See footnotes at end of table.

Table 25 (page 3 of 3). Death rates for malignant neoplasms of trachea, bronchus, and lung, by sex, race, Hispanic origin, and age: United States, selected years 1950–2015

Excel and PDF versions (with more data years and standard errors when available): http://www.cdc.gov/nchs/hus/contents2016.htm#025.

[Data are based on death certificates]

Sex, race, Hispanic origin, and age	1950 [1,2]	1960 [1,2]	1970 [2]	1980 [2]	1990 [2]	2000 [3]	2014 [3]	2015 [3]
Asian or Pacific Islander female [5]				Deaths per 100,000 resident population				
All ages, age-adjusted [4]	- - -	- - -	- - -	15.4	18.9	18.4	17.6	16.8
All ages, crude	- - -	- - -	- - -	8.4	10.5	12.6	16.0	15.8
45–54 years	- - -	- - -	- - -	13.5	11.3	9.9	9.0	9.7
55–64 years	- - -	- - -	- - -	24.6	38.3	30.4	25.2	24.2
65–74 years	- - -	- - -	- - -	62.4	71.6	77.0	59.3	64.4
75–84 years	- - -	- - -	- - -	117.7	137.9	135.0	149.3	134.7
85 years and over.	- - -	- - -	- - -	*	172.9	175.3	199.6	183.2
Hispanic or Latina female [5,7]								
All ages, age-adjusted [4]	- - -	- - -	- - -	- - -	14.1	14.7	13.3	12.9
All ages, crude	- - -	- - -	- - -	- - -	7.2	7.2	8.3	8.4
45–54 years	- - -	- - -	- - -	- - -	8.7	7.1	5.1	5.3
55–64 years	- - -	- - -	- - -	- - -	25.1	22.2	19.3	19.5
65–74 years	- - -	- - -	- - -	- - -	66.8	66.0	53.0	51.1
75–84 years	- - -	- - -	- - -	- - -	94.3	112.3	109.7	104.7
85 years and over.	- - -	- - -	- - -	- - -	118.2	137.5	151.9	139.5
White, not Hispanic or Latina female [7]								
All ages, age-adjusted [4]	- - -	- - -	- - -	- - -	39.0	44.1	38.4	37.3
All ages, crude	- - -	- - -	- - -	- - -	46.2	56.4	58.1	57.6
45–54 years	- - -	- - -	- - -	- - -	36.6	26.4	24.8	22.5
55–64 years	- - -	- - -	- - -	- - -	111.3	102.2	72.1	70.4
65–74 years	- - -	- - -	- - -	- - -	186.4	222.9	171.6	166.2
75–84 years	- - -	- - -	- - -	- - -	199.1	279.2	289.7	277.0
85 years and over.	- - -	- - -	- - -	- - -	139.0	218.0	253.1	267.8

0.0 Quantity more than zero but less than 0.05.

* Rates based on fewer than 20 deaths are considered unreliable and are not shown.

- - - Data not available.

[1] Includes deaths of persons who were not residents of the 50 states and the District of Columbia (D.C.).

[2] Underlying cause of death was coded according to the 6th Revision of the *International Classification of Diseases* (ICD) in 1950, 7th Revision in 1960, 8th Revision in 1970, and 9th Revision in 1980–1998. See Appendix II, Cause of death; Table III; Table IV.

[3] Starting with 1999 data, cause of death is coded according to ICD–10. See Appendix II, Cause of death; Comparability ratio; Table IV; Table V.

[4] Age-adjusted rates are calculated using the year 2000 standard population. Prior to 2001, age-adjusted rates were calculated using standard million proportions based on rounded population numbers. Starting with 2001 data, unrounded population numbers are used to calculate age-adjusted rates. See Appendix II, Age adjustment.

[5] The race groups, white, black, Asian or Pacific Islander, and American Indian or Alaska Native, include persons of Hispanic and non-Hispanic origin. Persons of Hispanic origin may be of any race. Death rates for Hispanic, American Indian or Alaska Native, and Asian or Pacific Islander persons should be interpreted with caution because of inconsistencies in reporting Hispanic origin or race on the death certificate (death rate numerators) compared with population figures (death rate denominators). The net effect of misclassification is an underestimation of deaths and death rates for races other than white and black. See Appendix II, Race, for a detailed discussion of sources of bias in death rates by race and Hispanic origin.

[6] In 1950, rate is for the age group 75 years and over.

[7] Prior to 1997, data from states that did not report Hispanic origin on the death certificate were excluded. See Appendix II, Hispanic origin.

NOTES: Starting with *Health, United States, 2003*, rates for 1991–1999 were revised using intercensal population estimates based on the 1990 and 2000 censuses. For 2000, population estimates are bridged-race April 1 census counts. Starting with *Health, United States, 2012*, rates for 2001–2009 were revised using intercensal population estimates based on the 2000 and 2010 censuses. For 2010, population estimates are bridged-race April 1 census counts. Rates for 2011 and beyond were computed using 2010-based postcensal estimates. See Appendix I, Population Census and Population Estimates. Age groups were selected to minimize the presentation of unstable age-specific death rates based on small numbers of deaths and for consistency among comparison groups. Starting with 2003 data, some states began to collect information on more than one race on the death certificate, according to 1997 Office of Management and Budget (OMB) standards. The multiple-race data for these states were bridged to the single-race categories of the 1977 OMB standards, for comparability with other states. See Appendix II, Race. Data for additional years are available. See the Excel spreadsheet on the *Health, United States* website at: http://www.cdc.gov/nchs/hus.htm.

SOURCE: NCHS, National Vital Statistics System; Grove RD, Hetzel AM. Vital statistics rates in the United States, 1940–1960. Washington, DC: U.S. Government Printing Office. 1968; numerator data from National Vital Statistics System, annual public-use Mortality Files; denominator data from national population estimates for race groups from Table 1 and unpublished Hispanic population estimates for 1985–1996 prepared by the Housing and Household Economic Statistics Division, U.S. Census Bureau; Murphy SL, Kochanek KD, Xu JQ, Curtin SC. Deaths: Final data for 2015. National vital statistics reports. Hyattsville, MD: NCHS; 2017. Available from: http://www.cdc.gov/nchs/products/nvsr.htm. See Appendix I, National Vital Statistics System (NVSS).

Table 26 (page 1 of 2). Death rates for malignant neoplasm of breast among females, by race, Hispanic origin, and age: United States, selected years 1950–2015

Excel and PDF versions (with more data years and standard errors when available): http://www.cdc.gov/nchs/hus/contents2016.htm#026.

[Data are based on death certificates]

Race, Hispanic origin, and age	1950[1,2]	1960[1,2]	1970[2]	1980[2]	1990[2]	2000[3]	2010[3]	2014[3]	2015[3]
All females	Deaths per 100,000 resident population								
All ages, age-adjusted[4]	31.9	31.7	32.1	31.9	33.3	26.8	22.1	20.6	20.3
All ages, crude	24.7	26.1	28.4	30.6	34.0	29.2	26.1	25.5	25.4
Under 25 years	*	*	*	*	*	*	*	*	*
25–34 years	3.8	3.8	3.9	3.3	2.9	2.3	1.6	1.6	1.8
35–44 years	20.8	20.2	20.4	17.9	17.8	12.4	9.8	9.7	9.0
45–54 years	46.9	51.4	52.6	48.1	45.4	33.0	25.7	23.8	23.7
55–64 years	69.9	70.8	77.6	80.5	78.6	59.3	47.7	43.3	43.3
65–74 years	95.0	90.0	93.8	101.1	111.7	88.3	73.9	67.5	66.7
75–84 years	139.8	129.9	127.4	126.4	146.3	128.9	109.1	104.2	101.7
85 years and over	195.5	191.9	157.1	169.3	196.8	205.7	185.8	174.0	173.3
White[5]									
All ages, age-adjusted[4]	32.4	32.0	32.5	32.1	33.2	26.3	21.5	20.1	19.8
All ages, crude	25.7	27.2	29.9	32.3	35.9	30.7	27.3	26.6	26.6
35–44 years	20.8	19.7	20.2	17.3	17.1	11.3	8.8	8.9	8.2
45–54 years	47.1	51.2	53.0	48.1	44.3	31.2	23.9	22.0	22.0
55–64 years	70.9	71.8	79.3	81.3	78.5	57.9	45.9	41.4	41.4
65–74 years	96.3	91.6	95.9	103.7	113.3	89.3	73.3	67.4	66.4
75–84 years	143.6	132.8	129.6	128.4	148.2	130.2	110.2	105.2	102.5
85 years and over	204.2	199.7	161.9	171.7	198.0	205.5	186.8	175.9	175.4
Black or African American[5]									
All ages, age-adjusted[4]	25.3	27.9	28.9	31.7	38.1	34.5	30.3	28.1	27.7
All ages, crude	16.4	18.7	19.7	22.9	29.0	27.9	27.5	27.0	27.0
35–44 years	21.0	24.8	24.4	24.1	25.8	20.9	18.3	16.0	15.1
45–54 years	46.5	54.4	52.0	52.7	60.5	51.5	40.9	39.1	38.2
55–64 years	64.3	63.2	64.7	79.9	93.1	80.9	70.5	64.4	63.8
65–74 years	67.0	72.3	77.3	84.3	112.2	98.6	97.4	85.9	86.6
75–84 years[6]	81.0	87.5	101.8	114.1	140.5	139.8	123.2	122.6	117.8
85 years and over	- - -	92.1	112.1	149.9	201.5	238.7	214.6	196.4	196.4
American Indian or Alaska Native[5]									
All ages, age-adjusted[4]	- - -	- - -	- - -	10.8	13.7	13.6	11.5	10.8	12.8
All ages, crude	- - -	- - -	- - -	6.1	8.6	8.7	8.0	8.0	9.7
35–44 years	- - -	- - -	- - -	*	*	*	*	*	*
45–54 years	- - -	- - -	- - -	*	23.9	14.4	13.2	9.4	11.5
55–64 years	- - -	- - -	- - -	*	*	40.0	25.2	19.3	22.5
65–74 years	- - -	- - -	- - -	*	*	42.5	34.3	40.2	42.6
75–84 years	- - -	- - -	- - -	*	*	71.8	61.1	61.7	71.9
85 years and over	- - -	- - -	- - -	*	*	*	*	*	144.8
Asian or Pacific Islander[5]									
All ages, age-adjusted[4]	- - -	- - -	- - -	11.9	13.7	12.3	11.9	11.6	11.7
All ages, crude	- - -	- - -	- - -	8.2	9.3	10.2	10.8	11.5	11.7
35–44 years	- - -	- - -	- - -	10.4	8.4	8.1	5.4	6.4	5.9
45–54 years	- - -	- - -	- - -	23.4	26.4	22.3	17.0	16.8	15.7
55–64 years	- - -	- - -	- - -	35.7	33.8	31.3	28.4	27.6	29.1
65–74 years	- - -	- - -	- - -	*	38.5	34.7	37.9	35.1	34.3
75–84 years	- - -	- - -	- - -	*	48.0	37.5	53.2	47.7	55.9
85 years and over	- - -	- - -	- - -	*	*	68.2	77.5	81.3	74.0
Hispanic or Latina[5,7]									
All ages, age-adjusted[4]	- - -	- - -	- - -	- - -	19.5	16.9	14.4	14.5	13.5
All ages, crude	- - -	- - -	- - -	- - -	11.5	9.7	9.2	10.3	9.8
35–44 years	- - -	- - -	- - -	- - -	11.7	8.7	6.2	7.7	7.1
45–54 years	- - -	- - -	- - -	- - -	32.8	23.9	18.6	17.4	15.7
55–64 years	- - -	- - -	- - -	- - -	45.8	39.1	32.7	31.5	30.9
65–74 years	- - -	- - -	- - -	- - -	64.8	54.9	49.0	47.0	40.0
75–84 years	- - -	- - -	- - -	- - -	67.2	74.9	61.8	69.3	67.1
85 years and over	- - -	- - -	- - -	- - -	102.8	105.8	117.8	116.3	108.5

See footnotes at end of table.

Table 26 (page 2 of 2). Death rates for malignant neoplasm of breast among females, by race, Hispanic origin, and age: United States, selected years 1950–2015

Excel and PDF versions (with more data years and standard errors when available): http://www.cdc.gov/nchs/hus/contents2016.htm#026.

[Data are based on death certificates]

Race, Hispanic origin, and age	1950 [1,2]	1960 [1,2]	1970 [2]	1980 [2]	1990 [2]	2000 [3]	2010 [3]	2014 [3]	2015 [3]
White, not Hispanic or Latina [7]				Deaths per 100,000 resident population					
All ages, age-adjusted [4]	- - -	- - -	- - -	- - -	33.9	26.8	22.1	20.6	20.4
All ages, crude	- - -	- - -	- - -	- - -	38.5	33.8	31.0	30.2	30.4
35–44 years	- - -	- - -	- - -	- - -	17.5	11.6	9.3	9.1	8.3
45–54 years	- - -	- - -	- - -	- - -	45.2	31.7	24.5	22.6	23.0
55–64 years	- - -	- - -	- - -	- - -	80.6	59.2	47.1	42.2	42.3
65–74 years	- - -	- - -	- - -	- - -	115.7	91.4	75.1	69.1	68.7
75–84 years	- - -	- - -	- - -	- - -	151.4	132.2	113.6	108.1	105.2
85 years and over.	- - -	- - -	- - -	- - -	201.5	208.3	189.9	179.4	179.5

* Rates based on fewer than 20 deaths are considered unreliable and are not shown.

- - - Data not available.

[1] Includes deaths of persons who were not residents of the 50 states and the District of Columbia (D.C.).

[2] Underlying cause of death was coded according to the 6th Revision of the *International Classification of Diseases* (ICD) in 1950, 7th Revision in 1960, 8th Revision in 1970, and 9th Revision in 1980–1998. See Appendix II, Cause of death; Table III; Table IV.

[3] Starting with 1999 data, cause of death is coded according to ICD–10. See Appendix II, Cause of death; Comparability ratio; Table IV; Table V.

[4] Age-adjusted rates are calculated using the year 2000 standard population. Prior to 2001, age-adjusted rates were calculated using standard million proportions based on rounded population numbers. Starting with 2001 data, unrounded population numbers are used to calculate age-adjusted rates. See Appendix II, Age adjustment.

[5] The race groups, white, black, Asian or Pacific Islander, and American Indian or Alaska Native, include persons of Hispanic and non-Hispanic origin. Persons of Hispanic origin may be of any race. Death rates for Hispanic, American Indian or Alaska Native, and Asian or Pacific Islander persons should be interpreted with caution because of inconsistencies in reporting Hispanic origin or race on the death certificate (death rate numerators) compared with population figures (death rate denominators). The net effect of misclassification is an underestimation of deaths and death rates for races other than white and black. See Appendix II, Race, for a detailed discussion of sources of bias in death rates by race and Hispanic origin.

[6] In 1950, rate is for the age group 75 years and over.

[7] Prior to 1997, data from states that did not report Hispanic origin on the death certificate were excluded. See Appendix II, Hispanic origin.

NOTES: Starting with *Health, United States, 2003*, rates for 1991–1999 were revised using intercensal population estimates based on the 1990 and 2000 censuses. For 2000, population estimates are bridged-race April 1 census counts. Starting with *Health, United States, 2012*, rates for 2001–2009 were revised using intercensal population estimates based on the 2000 and 2010 censuses. For 2010, population estimates are bridged-race April 1 census counts. Rates for 2011 and beyond were computed using 2010-based postcensal estimates. See Appendix I, Population Census and Population Estimates. Age groups were selected to minimize the presentation of unstable age-specific death rates based on small numbers of deaths and for consistency among comparison groups. Starting with 2003 data, some states began to collect information on more than one race on the death certificate, according to 1997 Office of Management and Budget (OMB) standards. The multiple-race data for these states were bridged to the single-race categories of the 1977 OMB standards, for comparability with other states. See Appendix II, Race. Data for additional years are available. See the Excel spreadsheet on the *Health, United States* website at: http://www.cdc.gov/nchs/hus.htm.

SOURCE: NCHS, National Vital Statistics System; numerator data from National Vital Statistics System, annual public-use Mortality Files; denominator data from national population estimates for race groups from Table 1 and unpublished Hispanic population estimates for 1985–1996 prepared by the Housing and Household Economic Statistics Division, U.S. Census Bureau; Murphy SL, Kochanek KD, Xu JQ, Curtin SC. Deaths: Final data for 2015. National vital statistics reports. Hyattsville, MD: NCHS; 2017. Available from: http://www.cdc.gov/nchs/products/nvsr.htm. See Appendix I, National Vital Statistics System (NVSS).

Table 27 (page 1 of 4). Death rates for drug poisoning and drug poisoning involving opioid analgesics and heroin, by sex, age, race, and Hispanic origin: United States, selected years 1999–2015

Excel and PDF versions (with more data years and standard errors when available): http://www.cdc.gov/nchs/hus/contents2016.htm#027.

[Data are based on death certificates]

Sex, age, race, and Hispanic origin	1999	2000	2005	2010	2011	2012	2013	2014	2015
All persons	Drug poisoning deaths per 100,000 resident population [1]								
All ages, age-adjusted [2]	6.1	6.2	10.1	12.3	13.2	13.1	13.8	14.7	16.3
All ages, crude	6.0	6.2	10.1	12.4	13.3	13.2	13.9	14.8	16.3
Under 15 years	0.1	0.1	0.2	0.2	0.2	0.2	0.2	0.2	0.2
15–24 years	3.2	3.7	6.9	8.2	8.6	8.0	8.3	8.6	9.7
25–34 years	8.1	7.9	13.6	18.4	20.2	20.1	20.9	23.1	26.9
35–44 years	14.0	14.3	19.6	20.8	22.5	22.1	23.0	25.0	28.3
45–54 years	11.1	11.6	21.1	25.1	26.7	26.9	27.5	28.2	30.0
55–64 years	4.2	4.2	9.0	15.0	15.9	16.6	19.2	20.3	21.8
65–74 years	2.4	2.0	3.2	4.7	5.4	5.8	6.4	6.9	7.2
75–84 years	2.8	2.4	3.1	3.4	3.4	3.4	3.6	3.6	3.6
85 years and over	3.8	4.4	4.1	4.7	4.2	4.3	4.3	4.1	4.4
Male									
All ages, age-adjusted [2]	8.2	8.3	12.8	15.0	16.1	16.1	17.0	18.3	20.8
All ages, crude	8.2	8.4	12.9	15.2	16.3	16.3	17.2	18.4	20.8
Under 15 years	0.1	0.2	0.2	0.3	0.2	0.2	0.2	0.2	0.2
15–24 years	4.5	5.3	10.0	11.6	12.4	11.4	11.7	12.1	13.3
25–34 years	11.5	11.3	18.7	25.0	27.5	27.0	28.6	31.9	37.9
35–44 years	19.2	19.5	24.4	24.9	26.8	27.1	28.1	30.8	36.3
45–54 years	15.2	15.7	25.8	28.5	30.4	30.4	31.5	32.9	35.3
55–64 years	4.9	4.4	10.6	17.3	18.5	19.4	22.7	23.5	26.2
65–74 years	2.7	2.1	3.3	4.5	5.4	6.2	6.9	7.3	8.5
75–84 years	2.5	2.5	3.4	3.6	3.4	3.2	3.7	3.8	3.9
85 years and over	4.4	5.9	5.2	5.1	4.3	5.3	5.9	4.3	5.0
Female									
All ages, age-adjusted [2]	3.9	4.1	7.3	9.6	10.2	10.2	10.6	11.1	11.8
All ages, crude	3.9	4.1	7.4	9.8	10.3	10.3	10.7	11.3	11.9
Under 15 years	0.1	0.1	0.2	0.2	0.2	0.2	0.2	0.2	0.3
15–24 years	1.8	1.9	3.5	4.6	4.6	4.4	4.8	5.0	5.9
25–34 years	4.6	4.6	8.5	11.9	12.8	13.1	13.0	14.1	15.7
35–44 years	8.7	9.2	14.8	16.8	18.2	17.1	18.0	19.2	20.5
45–54 years	7.2	7.7	16.5	21.8	23.1	23.4	23.6	23.7	24.9
55–64 years	3.5	3.9	7.5	12.9	13.5	14.0	15.9	17.2	17.6
65–74 years	2.1	2.0	3.1	4.8	5.3	5.5	5.9	6.5	6.1
75–84 years	3.0	2.3	2.9	3.3	3.4	3.5	3.4	3.5	3.3
85 years and over	3.5	3.9	3.7	4.5	4.2	3.8	3.5	4.0	4.1
All ages, age-adjusted [2,3]									
Male:									
White	8.1	8.4	13.6	16.8	18.1	18.1	19.0	20.4	23.2
Black or African American	11.5	10.8	12.8	10.1	11.0	11.3	12.9	13.8	16.8
American Indian or Alaska Native	5.7	6.1	10.8	11.8	12.9	12.8	12.9	15.9	16.0
Asian or Pacific Islander	1.5	1.4	2.2	2.5	3.2	3.1	3.2	3.3	4.1
Hispanic or Latino	8.6	7.1	8.4	7.6	8.1	8.5	9.2	9.3	10.9
White, not Hispanic or Latino	8.0	8.6	14.7	19.0	20.5	20.4	21.4	23.2	26.2
Female:									
White	4.0	4.3	8.0	10.9	11.7	11.6	12.1	12.7	13.6
Black or African American	3.9	4.1	6.0	5.7	5.9	6.0	6.3	7.0	7.5
American Indian or Alaska Native	4.6	3.7	8.6	9.7	10.7	12.2	11.6	11.2	11.3
Asian or Pacific Islander	1.0	0.8	1.3	1.5	1.6	1.4	1.5	1.7	1.5
Hispanic or Latina	2.2	2.0	3.0	3.6	4.0	4.0	4.1	4.1	4.4
White, not Hispanic or Latina	4.3	4.5	8.8	12.5	13.3	13.2	13.8	14.6	15.8

See footnotes at end of table.

Table 27 (page 2 of 4). Death rates for drug poisoning and drug poisoning involving opioid analgesics and heroin, by sex, age, race, and Hispanic origin: United States, selected years 1999–2015

Excel and PDF versions (with more data years and standard errors when available): http://www.cdc.gov/nchs/hus/contents2016.htm#027.

[Data are based on death certificates]

Sex, age, race, and Hispanic origin	1999	2000	2005	2010	2011	2012	2013	2014	2015
All persons	Drug poisoning deaths involving opioid analgesics (other than heroin) per 100,000 resident population [4]								
All ages, age-adjusted [2]	1.4	1.5	3.7	5.4	5.4	5.1	5.1	5.9	7.0
All ages, crude	1.4	1.6	3.7	5.4	5.4	5.1	5.1	5.9	7.0
Under 15 years	*	0.0	0.1	0.1	0.1	0.1	0.1	0.1	0.1
15–24 years	0.7	0.8	2.7	3.9	3.6	2.8	2.6	3.1	3.9
25–34 years	1.9	1.9	5.3	8.5	8.5	7.7	7.5	9.0	11.8
35–44 years	3.5	3.7	6.9	9.1	9.3	8.8	8.6	10.3	12.6
45–54 years	2.9	3.2	7.9	10.9	11.2	10.6	10.6	11.7	12.9
55–64 years	1.0	1.1	3.1	6.2	6.3	6.6	7.5	8.5	9.5
65–74 years	0.4	0.4	1.0	1.5	1.8	2.0	2.3	2.7	2.9
75–84 years	0.3	0.2	0.6	0.7	0.7	0.9	0.8	0.9	1.0
85 years and over.	*	*	0.9	1.1	0.8	0.8	0.9	0.9	0.9
Male									
All ages, age-adjusted [2]	2.0	2.0	4.6	6.5	6.5	6.0	5.9	6.9	8.7
All ages, crude	2.0	2.1	4.6	6.6	6.5	6.0	5.9	7.0	8.7
Under 15 years	*	*	0.1	0.2	0.1	0.1	0.1	0.1	0.1
15–24 years	1.0	1.2	4.2	5.6	5.3	4.2	3.9	4.4	5.4
25–34 years	2.7	2.7	7.2	11.7	11.4	10.0	10.0	12.2	16.7
35–44 years	5.0	4.9	8.3	10.9	10.9	10.3	9.6	11.9	15.7
45–54 years	3.9	4.3	9.4	12.0	12.1	11.1	11.1	12.5	14.2
55–64 years	1.1	1.0	3.5	7.0	6.9	7.3	8.0	9.2	10.7
65–74 years	0.5	0.3	0.7	1.2	1.7	2.0	2.2	2.5	3.4
75–84 years	*	*	0.6	0.7	0.7	0.7	0.9	0.8	1.0
85 years and over.	*	*	*	1.3	*	1.0	1.3	*	*
Female									
All ages, age-adjusted [2]	0.9	1.1	2.8	4.2	4.3	4.2	4.3	4.9	5.4
All ages, crude	0.9	1.1	2.8	4.2	4.4	4.2	4.4	4.9	5.4
Under 15 years	*	*	*	0.1	0.1	0.1	0.1	0.1	0.1
15–24 years	0.3	0.4	1.2	2.1	1.9	1.5	1.4	1.7	2.3
25–34 years	1.1	1.2	3.4	5.3	5.5	5.3	5.0	5.7	6.9
35–44 years	2.1	2.5	5.6	7.3	7.8	7.3	7.6	8.7	9.6
45–54 years	1.9	2.2	6.5	9.8	10.2	10.1	10.1	10.9	11.6
55–64 years	0.8	1.1	2.8	5.5	5.7	6.0	6.9	7.8	8.4
65–74 years	0.3	0.4	1.2	1.7	1.8	2.0	2.4	2.9	2.4
75–84 years	0.4	*	0.6	0.7	0.7	0.9	0.7	1.0	1.0
85 years and over.	*	*	0.8	1.1	0.8	0.7	0.8	1.0	0.9
All ages, age-adjusted [2,3]									
Male:									
White	2.2	2.3	5.3	7.7	7.6	7.0	6.8	8.0	10.1
Black or African American	1.2	1.2	2.1	2.2	2.4	2.3	2.7	3.9	5.3
American Indian or Alaska Native. . . .	*	1.9	4.4	5.3	5.5	5.8	4.8	6.4	6.1
Asian or Pacific Islander	*	*	0.5	0.8	1.0	0.7	0.9	0.9	1.0
Hispanic or Latino	2.9	1.7	2.2	2.4	2.6	2.5	2.7	2.7	3.4
White, not Hispanic or Latino	2.1	2.3	5.9	9.0	8.8	8.1	7.9	9.3	11.8
Female:									
White	1.0	1.2	3.2	4.8	5.1	4.9	5.0	5.6	6.3
Black or African American	0.6	0.6	1.4	2.0	2.0	2.0	2.2	2.6	2.9
American Indian or Alaska Native. . . .	*	*	3.8	4.9	4.6	5.4	5.4	4.6	4.7
Asian or Pacific Islander	*	*	0.4	0.5	0.4	0.4	0.3	0.5	0.4
Hispanic or Latina	0.5	0.5	1.0	1.3	1.4	1.5	1.5	1.6	1.6
White, not Hispanic or Latina	1.1	1.3	3.5	5.6	5.8	5.6	5.8	6.5	7.4

See footnotes at end of table.

Table 27 (page 3 of 4). Death rates for drug poisoning and drug poisoning involving opioid analgesics and heroin, by sex, age, race, and Hispanic origin: United States, selected years 1999–2015

Excel and PDF versions (with more data years and standard errors when available): http://www.cdc.gov/nchs/hus/contents2016.htm#027.

[Data are based on death certificates]

Sex, age, race, and Hispanic origin	1999	2000	2005	2010	2011	2012	2013	2014	2015
All persons	Drug poisoning deaths involving heroin per 100,000 resident population [4]								
All ages, age-adjusted [2]	0.7	0.7	0.7	1.0	1.4	1.9	2.7	3.4	4.1
All ages, crude	0.7	0.7	0.7	1.0	1.4	1.9	2.6	3.3	4.0
Under 15 years	*	*	*	*	*	*	*	*	*
15–24 years	0.5	0.6	0.7	1.2	1.8	2.2	2.9	3.3	3.8
25–34 years	1.0	1.0	1.2	2.2	3.4	4.6	6.3	8.0	9.7
35–44 years	1.8	1.5	1.2	1.6	2.2	3.1	4.4	5.9	7.4
45–54 years	1.3	1.2	1.4	1.4	2.0	2.8	3.7	4.7	5.6
55–64 years	0.3	0.3	0.4	0.7	1.0	1.3	2.1	2.7	3.4
65–74 years	*	*	*	*	0.2	0.1	0.3	0.5	0.6
75–84 years	*	*	*	*	*	*	*	*	*
85 years and over	*	*	*	*	*	*	*	*	*
Male									
All ages, age-adjusted [2]	1.2	1.1	1.1	1.6	2.3	3.1	4.2	5.2	6.3
All ages, crude	1.2	1.1	1.1	1.6	2.3	3.0	4.2	5.2	6.2
Under 15 years	*	*	*	*	*	*	*	*	*
15–24 years	0.8	0.9	1.0	1.9	2.8	3.2	4.2	4.8	5.2
25–34 years	1.6	1.7	2.0	3.5	5.4	7.1	9.9	12.3	14.8
35–44 years	3.0	2.6	1.9	2.8	3.6	5.1	6.9	9.2	11.4
45–54 years	2.3	2.2	2.3	2.4	3.2	4.5	6.0	7.2	8.7
55–64 years	0.5	0.4	0.7	1.1	1.7	2.3	3.6	4.4	5.6
65–74 years	*	*	*	*	0.3	0.3	0.5	0.9	1.1
75–84 years	*	*	*	*	*	*	*	*	*
85 years and over	*	*	*	*	*	*	*	*	*
Female									
All ages, age-adjusted [2]	0.2	0.2	0.3	0.4	0.6	0.8	1.2	1.6	2.0
All ages, crude	0.2	0.2	0.3	0.4	0.6	0.8	1.1	1.5	1.9
Under 15 years	*	*	*	*	*	*	*	*	*
15–24 years	0.2	0.2	0.3	0.6	0.9	1.1	1.5	1.7	2.2
25–34 years	0.3	0.4	0.5	0.9	1.4	2.0	2.6	3.7	4.6
35–44 years	0.6	0.5	0.5	0.6	0.8	1.1	1.9	2.6	3.5
45–54 years	0.3	0.3	0.5	0.5	0.8	1.1	1.6	2.2	2.7
55–64 years	*	*	*	0.3	0.3	0.4	0.7	1.0	1.5
65–74 years	*	*	*	*	*	*	*	*	0.2
75–84 years	*	*	*	*	*	*	*	*	*
85 years and over	*	*	*	*	*	*	*	*	*
All ages, age-adjusted [2,3]									
Male:									
White	1.2	1.1	1.1	1.8	2.6	3.5	4.7	6.0	7.2
Black or African American	1.4	1.6	1.3	1.2	1.6	2.1	3.4	4.1	5.0
American Indian or Alaska Native	*	*	*	*	1.3	1.7	2.6	3.5	4.0
Asian or Pacific Islander	*	*	*	*	0.3	0.3	0.5	0.6	0.8
Hispanic or Latino	2.0	1.6	1.4	1.5	1.7	2.2	2.6	3.2	3.8
White, not Hispanic or Latino	1.1	1.0	1.1	1.9	2.9	3.9	5.3	6.7	8.1
Female:									
White	0.2	0.2	0.3	0.4	0.6	0.9	1.3	1.8	2.3
Black or African American	0.3	0.3	0.3	0.3	0.4	0.5	0.7	1.1	1.3
American Indian or Alaska Native	*	*	*	*	1.0	*	1.0	1.2	1.8
Asian or Pacific Islander	*	*	*	*	*	*	*	*	0.2
Hispanic or Latina	0.2	0.1	0.2	0.2	0.3	0.4	0.5	0.7	0.8
White, not Hispanic or Latina	0.2	0.2	0.3	0.5	0.7	1.1	1.5	2.1	2.7

See footnotes at end of table.

Excel and PDF versions (with more data years and standard errors when available): http://www.cdc.gov/nchs/hus/contents2016.htm#027.

[Data are based on death certificates]

* Rates based on fewer than 20 deaths are considered unreliable and are not shown.

0.0 Rate more than zero but less than 0.05.

[1] Drug poisoning was coded using underlying cause of death according to the 10th Revision of the *International Classification of Diseases* (ICD–10). See Appendix II, Cause of death; Table IV. Drug poisoning deaths include those resulting from accidental or intentional overdoses of a drug, being given the wrong drug, taking the wrong drug in error, taking a drug inadvertently, or other misuses of drugs. These deaths are from all manners and intents, including unintentional, suicide, homicide, undetermined intent, legal intervention, and operations of war.

[2] Age-adjusted rates are calculated using the year 2000 standard population with unrounded population numbers. See Appendix II, Age adjustment.

[3] The race groups, white, black, Asian or Pacific Islander, and American Indian or Alaska Native, include persons of Hispanic and non-Hispanic origin. Persons of Hispanic origin may be of any race. Death rates for Hispanic, American Indian or Alaska Native, and Asian or Pacific Islander persons should be interpreted with caution because of inconsistencies in reporting Hispanic origin or race on the death certificate (death rate numerators) compared with population figures (death rate denominators). The net effect of misclassification is an underestimation of deaths and death rates for races other than white and black. See Appendix II, Race, for a detailed discussion of sources of bias in death rates by race and Hispanic origin.

[4] Opioid analgesics include opioids such as hydrocodone, codeine, and methadone, and synthetic narcotics such as fentanyl, tramadol, and propoxyphene (removed from the market in 2010). Drug poisoning deaths involving opioid analgesics include those with an underlying cause of drug poisoning and with an opioid analgesic mentioned in the ICD–10 multiple causes of death. Drug poisoning deaths involving heroin include those with an underlying cause of drug poisoning and with heroin mentioned in the ICD–10 multiple causes of death. See Appendix I, National Vital Statistics System (NVSS), Mortality Multiple Cause-of-Death File, See Appendix II, Cause of death; Table IV. Drug-poisoning deaths may involve multiple drugs. Deaths involving both opioid analgesics and heroin are included in the death rate for opioid analgesics and the death rate for heroin. Opioid analgesic death rates include deaths involving fentanyl, a synthetic opioid. A sharp increase in deaths involving synthetic opioids, other than methadone, in 2014 coincided with law enforcement reports of increased availability of illicitly manufactured, or non-pharmaceutical, fentanyl. Illicitly manufactured fentanyl cannot be distinguished from pharmaceutical fentanyl in death certificate data. For more information, see CDC health advisory: Increases in fentanyl drug confiscations and fentanyl-related overdose fatalities. Available from: http://emergency.cdc.gov/han/han00384.asp, and Rudd RA, Aleshire N, Zibbell JE, Gladden M. Increases in drug and opioid overdose deaths—United States, 2000–2014. MMWR 2016;64(50):1378–82. Available from: http://www.cdc.gov/mmwr/preview/mmwrhtml/mm6450a3.htm?s_cid=mm6450a3_w. For more information on the type of drugs commonly involved in drug overdose deaths, see: Warner M, Trinidad JP, Bastian BA, et al. Drugs most frequently involved in drug overdose deaths: United States, 2010–2014. National vital statistics reports; vol 65 no 10. Hyattsville, MD: NCHS. 2016. Available from: https://www.cdc.gov/nchs/data/nvsr/nvsr65_10.pdf. Metabolic breakdown of heroin into morphine in the body can make it difficult to distinguish between deaths from heroin and deaths from morphine based on the information on the death certificate. Some deaths reported to involve morphine could be deaths from heroin. This may result in an undercount of heroin-related deaths. For more information, see Hedegaard H, Chen LH, Warner M. Drug-poisoning deaths involving heroin: United States, 2000–2013. NCHS data brief, no 190. Hyattsville, MD: NCHS. 2015. Available from: http://www.cdc.gov/nchs/data/databriefs/db190.htm. In 1999–2015, 17%–25% of drug poisoning deaths did not include specific information on the death certificate on the type of drug that was involved. Some of these deaths could have potentially involved heroin or opioid analgesics. For more information, see NCHS Health E-Stat available from: http://www.cdc.gov/nchs/data/hestat/drug_poisoning/drug_poisoning.htm. For more information on the enhancement of mortality statistics using information from the death certificate, see: Trinidad JP, Warner M, Bastian BA, et al. Using literal text from the death certificate to enhance mortality statistics: Characterizing drug involvement in deaths. National vital statistics reports; vol 65 no 9. Hyattsville, MD: NCHS. 2016. Available from: https://www.cdc.gov/nchs/data/nvsr/nvsr65_09.pdf.

NOTES: Rates for 1999 were computed using intercensal population estimates based on the 1990 and 2000 censuses. Rates for 2000 were computed based on 2000 bridged-race April 1 census counts. Starting with *Health, United States, 2012*, rates for 2001–2009 were revised using intercensal population estimates based on the 2000 and 2010 censuses. Rates for 2010 were based on 2010 bridged-race April 1 census counts. Rates for 2011 and beyond were computed using 2010-based postcensal estimates. See Appendix I, Population Census and Population Estimates. Age groups were selected to minimize the presentation of unstable age-specific death rates based on small numbers of deaths and for consistency among comparison groups. For additional injury-related statistics, see the Web-based Injury Statistics Query and Reporting System (WISQARS), available from: http://www.cdc.gov/injury/wisqars/index.html. Starting with 2003 data, some states allowed the reporting of more than one race on the death certificate. The multiple-race data for these states were bridged to the single-race categories of the 1977 Office of Management and Budget standards, for comparability with other states. See Appendix II, Race. Data for additional years are available. See the Excel spreadsheet on the *Health, United States* website at: http://www.cdc.gov/nchs/hus.htm.

SOURCE: NCHS, National Vital Statistics System; numerator data from National Vital Statistics System, annual public-use Mortality Files; denominator data from national population estimates for race groups from Table 1; Deaths: Final data for 2015. National vital statistics reports Hyattsville, MD: NCHS; 2017. Available from: http://www.cdc.gov/nchs/products/nvsr.htm. See Appendix I, National Vital Statistics System (NVSS).

Table 28 (page 1 of 4). Death rates for motor vehicle-related injuries, by sex, race, Hispanic origin, and age: United States, selected years 1950–2015

Excel and PDF versions (with more data years and standard errors when available): http://www.cdc.gov/nchs/hus/contents2016.htm#028.

[Data are based on death certificates]

Sex, race, Hispanic origin, and age	1950[1,2]	1960[1,2]	1970[2]	1980[2]	1990[2]	2000[3]	2010[3]	2014[3]	2015[3]
All persons			Deaths per 100,000 resident population						
All ages, age-adjusted[4]	24.6	23.1	27.6	22.3	18.5	15.4	11.3	10.8	11.4
All ages, crude	23.1	21.3	26.9	23.5	18.8	15.4	11.4	11.1	11.7
Under 1 year	8.4	8.1	9.8	7.0	4.9	4.4	2.0	1.7	1.8
1–14 years	9.8	8.6	10.5	8.2	6.0	4.3	2.3	2.2	2.2
1–4 years	11.5	10.0	11.5	9.2	6.3	4.2	2.8	2.5	2.6
5–14 years	8.8	7.9	10.2	7.9	5.9	4.3	2.2	2.0	2.1
15–24 years	34.4	38.0	47.2	44.8	34.1	26.9	16.6	15.3	15.9
15–19 years	29.6	33.9	43.6	43.0	33.1	26.0	13.6	11.9	12.4
20–24 years	38.8	42.9	51.3	46.6	35.0	28.0	19.7	18.3	19.2
25–34 years	24.6	24.3	30.9	29.1	23.6	17.3	14.0	13.9	14.7
35–44 years	20.3	19.3	24.9	20.9	16.9	15.3	11.6	11.1	11.9
45–64 years	25.2	23.0	26.5	18.0	15.7	14.3	11.9	12.0	12.8
45–54 years	22.2	21.4	25.5	18.6	15.6	14.2	12.0	12.1	12.8
55–64 years	29.0	25.1	27.9	17.4	15.9	14.4	11.9	11.9	12.7
65 years and over	43.1	34.7	36.2	22.5	23.1	21.4	16.0	14.8	15.3
65–74 years	39.1	31.4	32.8	19.2	18.6	16.5	12.3	11.9	12.8
75–84 years	52.7	41.8	43.5	28.1	29.1	25.7	18.8	17.5	17.5
85 years and over	45.1	37.9	34.2	27.6	31.2	30.4	23.8	20.9	21.7
Male									
All ages, age-adjusted[4]	38.5	35.4	41.5	33.6	26.5	21.7	16.2	15.8	16.7
All ages, crude	35.4	31.8	39.7	35.3	26.7	21.3	16.3	16.0	17.0
Under 1 year	9.1	8.6	9.3	7.3	5.0	4.6	2.2	1.9	2.2
1–14 years	12.3	10.7	13.0	10.0	7.0	4.9	2.7	2.5	2.5
1–4 years	13.0	11.5	12.9	10.2	6.9	4.7	3.0	2.8	2.9
5–14 years	11.9	10.4	13.1	9.9	7.0	5.0	2.5	2.4	2.4
15–24 years	56.7	61.2	73.2	68.4	49.5	37.4	23.1	21.5	22.2
15–19 years	46.3	51.7	64.1	62.6	45.5	33.9	17.8	16.1	16.3
20–24 years	66.7	73.2	84.4	74.3	53.3	41.2	28.5	26.5	27.7
25–34 years	40.8	40.1	49.4	46.3	35.7	25.5	21.0	20.8	21.8
35–44 years	32.5	29.9	37.7	31.7	24.7	22.0	16.9	16.4	17.9
45–64 years	37.7	33.3	38.9	26.5	21.9	20.2	17.9	18.1	19.4
45–54 years	33.6	31.6	37.2	27.6	22.0	20.4	17.9	18.2	19.1
55–64 years	43.1	35.6	40.9	25.4	21.7	19.8	17.8	18.1	19.8
65 years and over	66.6	52.1	54.4	33.9	32.1	29.5	22.2	21.0	22.1
65–74 years	59.1	45.8	47.3	27.3	24.2	21.7	17.1	17.0	18.5
75–84 years	85.0	66.0	68.2	44.3	41.2	35.6	25.9	24.8	24.9
85 years and over	78.1	62.7	63.1	56.1	64.5	57.5	40.2	34.0	35.6
Female									
All ages, age-adjusted[4]	11.5	11.7	14.9	11.8	11.0	9.5	6.5	6.1	6.4
All ages, crude	10.9	11.0	14.7	12.3	11.3	9.7	6.8	6.3	6.7
Under 1 year	7.6	7.5	10.4	6.7	4.9	4.2	1.8	1.5	1.3
1–14 years	7.2	6.3	7.9	6.3	4.9	3.7	2.0	1.8	1.9
1–4 years	10.0	8.4	10.0	8.1	5.6	3.8	2.5	2.3	2.3
5–14 years	5.7	5.4	7.2	5.7	4.7	3.6	1.8	1.6	1.8
15–24 years	12.6	15.1	21.6	20.8	17.9	15.9	9.9	8.7	9.3
15–19 years	12.9	16.0	22.7	22.8	20.0	17.5	9.2	7.6	8.4
20–24 years	12.2	14.0	20.4	18.9	16.0	14.2	10.5	9.7	10.2
25–34 years	9.3	9.2	13.0	12.2	11.5	8.8	6.9	6.8	7.5
35–44 years	8.5	9.1	12.9	10.4	9.2	8.8	6.2	5.8	6.1
45–64 years	12.6	13.1	15.3	10.3	10.1	8.7	6.3	6.2	6.4
45–54 years	10.9	11.6	14.5	10.2	9.6	8.2	6.3	6.2	6.7
55–64 years	14.9	15.2	16.2	10.5	10.8	9.5	6.3	6.1	6.1
65 years and over	21.9	20.3	23.1	15.0	17.2	15.8	11.3	9.9	10.0
65–74 years	20.6	19.0	21.6	13.0	14.1	12.3	8.2	7.5	7.8
75–84 years	25.2	23.0	27.2	18.5	21.9	19.2	13.7	12.0	11.9
85 years and over	22.1	22.0	18.0	15.2	18.3	19.3	15.9	14.1	14.4
White male[5]									
All ages, age-adjusted[4]	37.9	34.8	40.4	33.8	26.3	21.8	16.7	16.1	17.0
All ages, crude	35.1	31.5	39.1	35.9	26.7	21.6	17.0	16.5	17.4
Under 1 year	9.1	8.8	9.1	7.0	4.8	4.2	2.0	1.8	1.9
1–14 years	12.4	10.6	12.5	9.8	6.6	4.8	2.7	2.4	2.5
15–24 years	58.3	62.7	75.2	73.8	52.5	39.6	24.6	23.0	23.3
25–34 years	39.1	38.6	47.0	46.6	35.4	25.1	21.4	20.8	22.1
35–44 years	30.9	28.4	35.2	30.7	23.7	21.8	17.4	16.6	18.0
45–64 years	36.2	31.7	36.5	25.2	20.6	19.7	18.3	18.3	19.5
65 years and over	67.1	52.1	54.2	32.7	31.4	29.4	22.7	21.5	22.7

See footnotes at end of table.

Table 28 (page 2 of 4). Death rates for motor vehicle-related injuries, by sex, race, Hispanic origin, and age: United States, selected years 1950–2015

Excel and PDF versions (with more data years and standard errors when available): http://www.cdc.gov/nchs/hus/contents2016.htm#028.

[Data are based on death certificates]

Sex, race, Hispanic origin, and age	1950 [1,2]	1960 [1,2]	1970 [2]	1980 [2]	1990 [2]	2000 [3]	2010 [3]	2014 [3]	2015 [3]
Black or African American male [5]				Deaths per 100,000 resident population					
All ages, age-adjusted [4]	34.8	39.6	51.0	34.2	29.9	24.4	16.7	17.4	19.1
All ages, crude	37.2	33.1	44.3	31.1	28.1	22.5	15.9	16.8	18.7
Under 1 year.	- - -	*	10.6	7.8	*	6.7	*	*	*
1–14 years [6]	10.4	11.2	16.3	11.4	8.9	5.5	3.0	2.9	3.2
15–24 years	42.5	46.4	58.1	34.9	36.1	30.2	19.4	18.7	21.8
25–34 years	54.4	51.0	70.4	44.9	39.5	32.6	24.9	25.7	26.7
35–44 years	46.7	43.6	59.5	41.2	33.5	27.2	19.4	21.2	23.7
45–64 years	54.6	47.8	61.7	39.5	33.3	27.1	19.1	21.1	24.5
65 years and over.	52.6	48.2	53.4	42.4	36.3	32.1	20.0	19.8	19.6
American Indian or Alaska Native male [5]									
All ages, age-adjusted [4]	- - -	- - -	- - -	78.9	48.3	35.8	21.1	23.4	22.8
All ages, crude	- - -	- - -	- - -	74.6	47.6	33.6	19.8	22.2	22.1
1–14 years	- - -	- - -	- - -	15.1	11.6	7.8	*	4.2	4.4
15–24 years	- - -	- - -	- - -	126.1	75.2	56.8	31.9	27.3	24.9
25–34 years	- - -	- - -	- - -	107.0	78.2	49.8	23.8	31.8	32.4
35–44 years	- - -	- - -	- - -	82.8	57.0	36.3	24.5	24.2	30.3
45–64 years	- - -	- - -	- - -	77.4	45.9	32.0	23.2	30.5	26.6
65 years and over.	- - -	- - -	- - -	97.0	43.0	48.5	26.6	26.8	26.3
Asian or Pacific Islander male [5]									
All ages, age-adjusted [4]	- - -	- - -	- - -	19.0	17.9	10.6	6.5	6.2	6.3
All ages, crude	- - -	- - -	- - -	17.1	15.8	9.8	6.2	6.0	6.1
1–14 years	- - -	- - -	- - -	8.2	6.3	2.5	*	1.2	*
15–24 years	- - -	- - -	- - -	27.2	25.7	17.0	9.6	8.6	9.7
25–34 years	- - -	- - -	- - -	18.8	17.0	10.4	7.8	8.0	6.7
35–44 years	- - -	- - -	- - -	13.1	12.2	6.9	4.1	4.1	3.8
45–64 years	- - -	- - -	- - -	13.7	15.1	10.1	6.0	5.7	6.4
65 years and over.	- - -	- - -	- - -	37.3	33.6	21.1	14.6	13.1	13.5
Hispanic or Latino male [5,7]									
All ages, age-adjusted [4]	- - -	- - -	- - -	- - -	29.5	21.3	14.0	14.3	15.2
All ages, crude	- - -	- - -	- - -	- - -	29.2	20.1	12.8	13.5	14.4
1–14 years	- - -	- - -	- - -	- - -	7.2	4.4	2.5	2.5	2.6
15–24 years	- - -	- - -	- - -	- - -	48.2	34.7	20.2	22.0	22.8
25–34 years	- - -	- - -	- - -	- - -	41.0	24.9	18.0	19.6	21.2
35–44 years	- - -	- - -	- - -	- - -	28.0	21.6	13.9	13.4	14.8
45–64 years	- - -	- - -	- - -	- - -	28.9	21.7	14.3	14.9	15.9
65 years and over.	- - -	- - -	- - -	- - -	35.3	28.9	20.7	19.5	20.1
White, not Hispanic or Latino male [7]									
All ages, age-adjusted [4]	- - -	- - -	- - -	- - -	25.7	21.7	17.1	16.2	17.0
All ages, crude	- - -	- - -	- - -	- - -	26.0	21.5	17.6	16.9	17.9
1–14 years	- - -	- - -	- - -	- - -	6.4	4.9	2.7	2.3	2.4
15–24 years	- - -	- - -	- - -	- - -	52.3	40.3	25.4	22.6	22.8
25–34 years	- - -	- - -	- - -	- - -	34.0	24.7	21.9	20.7	21.7
35–44 years	- - -	- - -	- - -	- - -	23.1	21.6	18.0	17.2	18.6
45–64 years	- - -	- - -	- - -	- - -	19.8	19.3	18.6	18.6	19.8
65 years and over.	- - -	- - -	- - -	- - -	31.1	29.3	22.7	21.5	22.8
White female [5]									
All ages, age-adjusted [4]	11.4	11.7	14.9	12.2	11.2	9.8	6.8	6.3	6.6
All ages, crude	10.9	11.2	14.8	12.8	11.6	10.0	7.1	6.6	6.9
Under 1 year.	7.8	7.5	10.2	7.1	4.7	3.5	1.9	1.5	*
1–14 years	7.2	6.2	7.5	6.2	4.8	3.7	2.1	1.8	1.8
15–24 years	12.6	15.6	22.7	23.0	19.5	17.1	10.8	9.2	9.8
25–34 years	9.0	9.0	12.7	12.2	11.6	8.9	7.1	7.1	7.7
35–44 years	8.1	8.9	12.3	10.6	9.2	8.9	6.5	6.1	6.4
45–64 years	12.7	13.1	15.1	10.4	9.9	8.7	6.4	6.3	6.6
65 years and over.	22.2	20.8	23.7	15.3	17.4	16.2	11.5	10.3	10.3

See footnotes at end of table.

Table 28 (page 3 of 4). **Death rates for motor vehicle-related injuries, by sex, race, Hispanic origin, and age: United States, selected years 1950–2015**

Excel and PDF versions (with more data years and standard errors when available): http://www.cdc.gov/nchs/hus/contents2016.htm#028.

[Data are based on death certificates]

Sex, race, Hispanic origin, and age	1950 [1,2]	1960 [1,2]	1970 [2]	1980 [2]	1990 [2]	2000 [3]	2010 [3]	2014 [3]	2015 [3]
Black or African American female [5]				Deaths per 100,000 resident population					
All ages, age-adjusted [4]	9.3	10.4	14.1	8.5	9.6	8.4	5.9	5.6	6.1
All ages, crude	10.2	9.7	13.4	8.3	9.4	8.2	5.8	5.6	6.1
Under 1 year.	- - -	8.1	11.9	*	7.0	*	*	*	*
1–14 years [6]	7.2	6.9	10.2	6.3	5.3	3.9	2.0	2.3	2.6
15–24 years	11.6	9.9	13.4	8.0	9.9	11.7	7.8	7.7	8.9
25–34 years	10.8	9.8	13.3	10.6	11.1	9.4	6.8	6.9	7.8
35–44 years	11.1	11.0	16.1	8.3	9.4	8.2	5.8	5.7	6.1
45–64 years	11.8	12.7	16.7	9.2	10.7	9.0	6.3	6.2	6.3
65 years and over.	14.3	13.2	15.7	9.5	13.5	10.4	8.6	6.4	6.8
American Indian or Alaska Native female [5]									
All ages, age-adjusted [4]	- - -	- - -	- - -	32.0	17.5	19.5	10.6	10.1	11.2
All ages, crude	- - -	- - -	- - -	32.0	17.3	18.6	10.0	10.0	11.2
1–14 years	- - -	- - -	- - -	15.0	8.1	6.5	*	*	*
15–24 years	- - -	- - -	- - -	42.3	31.4	30.3	13.4	16.5	13.8
25–34 years	- - -	- - -	- - -	52.5	18.8	22.3	17.7	13.4	21.2
35–44 years	- - -	- - -	- - -	38.1	18.2	22.0	13.1	12.0	12.6
45–64 years	- - -	- - -	- - -	32.6	17.6	17.8	8.4	9.7	11.9
65 years and over.	- - -	- - -	- - -	*	*	24.0	14.8	*	*
Asian or Pacific Islander female [5]									
All ages, age-adjusted [4]	- - -	- - -	- - -	9.3	10.4	6.7	3.9	3.2	3.6
All ages, crude	- - -	- - -	- - -	8.2	9.0	5.9	3.6	3.2	3.6
1–14 years	- - -	- - -	- - -	7.4	3.6	2.3	*	*	*
15–24 years	- - -	- - -	- - -	7.4	11.4	6.0	3.3	3.0	3.4
25–34 years	- - -	- - -	- - -	7.3	7.3	4.5	3.1	2.5	2.6
35–44 years	- - -	- - -	- - -	8.6	7.5	4.9	2.0	2.0	1.7
45–64 years	- - -	- - -	- - -	8.5	11.8	6.4	4.3	3.3	4.0
65 years and over.	- - -	- - -	- - -	18.6	24.3	18.5	12.2	9.4	11.2
Hispanic or Latina female [5,7]									
All ages, age-adjusted [4]	- - -	- - -	- - -	- - -	9.6	7.9	5.3	5.0	5.2
All ages, crude	- - -	- - -	- - -	- - -	8.9	7.2	4.9	4.7	5.0
1–14 years	- - -	- - -	- - -	- - -	4.8	3.9	2.0	1.9	1.8
15–24 years	- - -	- - -	- - -	- - -	11.6	10.6	7.7	7.5	7.7
25–34 years	- - -	- - -	- - -	- - -	9.4	6.5	5.0	5.3	6.1
35–44 years	- - -	- - -	- - -	- - -	8.0	7.3	4.5	4.1	4.6
45–64 years	- - -	- - -	- - -	- - -	11.4	8.3	5.6	5.3	5.2
65 years and over.	- - -	- - -	- - -	- - -	14.9	13.4	9.4	8.1	8.3
White, not Hispanic or Latina female [7]									
All ages, age-adjusted [4]	- - -	- - -	- - -	- - -	11.3	10.0	7.0	6.5	6.8
All ages, crude	- - -	- - -	- - -	- - -	11.7	10.3	7.5	7.0	7.3
1–14 years	- - -	- - -	- - -	- - -	4.7	3.5	2.0	1.7	1.8
15–24 years	- - -	- - -	- - -	- - -	20.4	18.4	11.4	9.6	10.3
25–34 years	- - -	- - -	- - -	- - -	11.7	9.3	7.6	7.5	8.0
35–44 years	- - -	- - -	- - -	- - -	9.3	9.0	6.9	6.6	6.8
45–64 years	- - -	- - -	- - -	- - -	9.7	8.7	6.4	6.4	6.7
65 years and over.	- - -	- - -	- - -	- - -	17.5	16.3	11.6	10.4	10.5

See footnotes at end of table.

Excel and PDF versions (with more data years and standard errors when available): *http://www.cdc.gov/nchs/hus/contents2016.htm#028.*

[Data are based on death certificates]

- - - Data not available.

* Rates based on fewer than 20 deaths are considered unreliable and are not shown.

[1] Includes deaths of persons who were not residents of the 50 states and the District of Columbia (D.C.).

[2] Underlying cause of death was coded according to the 6th Revision of the *International Classification of Diseases* (ICD) in 1950, 7th Revision in 1960, 8th Revision in 1970, and 9th Revision in 1980–1998. See Appendix II, Cause of death; Table III; Table IV.

[3] Starting with 1999 data, cause of death is coded according to ICD–10. See Appendix II, Cause of death; Comparability ratio; Table IV; Table V.

[4] Age-adjusted rates are calculated using the year 2000 standard population. Prior to 2001, age-adjusted rates were calculated using standard million proportions based on rounded population numbers. Starting with 2001 data, unrounded population numbers are used to calculate age-adjusted rates. See Appendix II, Age adjustment.

[5] The race groups, white, black, Asian or Pacific Islander, and American Indian or Alaska Native, include persons of Hispanic and non-Hispanic origin. Persons of Hispanic origin may be of any race. Death rates for Hispanic, American Indian or Alaska Native, and Asian or Pacific Islander persons should be interpreted with caution because of inconsistencies in reporting Hispanic origin or race on the death certificate (death rate numerators) compared with population figures (death rate denominators). The net effect of misclassification is an underestimation of deaths and death rates for races other than white and black. See Appendix II, Race, for a detailed discussion of sources of bias in death rates by race and Hispanic origin.

[6] In 1950, rate is for the age group under 15 years.

[7] Prior to 1997, data from states that did not report Hispanic origin on the death certificate were excluded. See Appendix II, Hispanic origin.

NOTES: Starting with *Health, United States, 2003*, rates for 1991–1999 were revised using intercensal population estimates based on the 1990 and 2000 censuses. For 2000, population estimates are bridged-race April 1 census counts. Starting with *Health, United States, 2012*, rates for 2001–2009 were revised using intercensal population estimates based on the 2000 and 2010 censuses. For 2010, population estimates are bridged-race April 1 census counts. Rates for 2011 and beyond were computed using 2010-based postcensal estimates. See Appendix I, Population Census and Population Estimates. Age groups were selected to minimize the presentation of unstable age-specific death rates based on small numbers of deaths and for consistency among comparison groups. For additional injury-related statistics, see Web-based Injury Statistics Query and Reporting System (WISQARS), available from: http://www.cdc.gov/injury/wisqars/index.html. Starting with 2003 data, some states began to collect information on more than one race on the death certificate, according to 1997 Office of Management and Budget (OMB) standards. The multiple-race data for these states were bridged to the single-race categories of the 1977 OMB standards, for comparability with other states. See Appendix II, Race. Data for additional years are available. See the Excel spreadsheet on the *Health, United States* website at: http://www.cdc.gov/nchs/hus.htm.

SOURCE: NCHS, National Vital Statistics System; Grove RD, Hetzel AM. Vital statistics rates in the United States, 1940–1960. Washington, DC: U.S. Government Printing Office, 1968; numerator data from National Vital Statistics System, annual public-use Mortality Files; denominator data from national population estimates for race groups from Table 1 and unpublished Hispanic population estimates for 1985–1996 prepared by the Housing and Household Economic Statistics Division, U.S. Census Bureau; Murphy SL, Kochanek KD, Xu JQ, Curtin SC. Deaths: Final data for 2015. National vital statistics reports. Hyattsville, MD: NCHS; 2017. Available from: http://www.cdc.gov/nchs/products/nvsr.htm. See Appendix I, National Vital Statistics System (NVSS).

Table 29 (page 1 of 4). Death rates for homicide, by sex, race, Hispanic origin, and age: United States, selected years 1950–2015

Excel and PDF versions (with more data years and standard errors when available): *http://www.cdc.gov/nchs/hus/contents2016.htm#029.*

[Data are based on death certificates]

Sex, race, Hispanic origin, and age	1950 [1,2]	1960 [1,2]	1970 [2]	1980 [2]	1990 [2]	2000 [3]	2010 [3]	2014 [3]	2015 [3]
All persons	Deaths per 100,000 resident population								
All ages, age-adjusted [4]	5.1	5.0	8.8	10.4	9.4	5.9	5.3	5.1	5.7
All ages, crude	5.0	4.6	8.1	10.6	9.9	6.0	5.3	5.0	5.5
Under 1 year	4.4	4.8	4.3	5.9	8.4	9.2	7.9	6.3	6.6
1–14 years	0.6	0.6	1.1	1.5	1.8	1.3	1.1	1.1	1.2
1–4 years	0.6	0.7	1.9	2.5	2.5	2.3	2.4	2.3	2.3
5–14 years	0.5	0.5	0.9	1.2	1.5	0.9	0.6	0.7	0.7
15–24 years	5.8	5.6	11.3	15.4	19.7	12.6	10.7	9.5	10.8
15–19 years	3.9	3.9	7.7	10.5	16.9	9.5	8.3	6.7	7.5
20–24 years	8.5	7.7	15.6	20.2	22.2	16.0	13.2	12.1	13.8
25–44 years	8.9	8.5	14.9	17.5	14.7	8.7	8.2	8.1	9.2
25–34 years	9.3	9.2	16.2	19.3	17.4	10.4	10.4	9.6	11.0
35–44 years	8.4	7.8	13.5	14.9	11.6	7.1	6.0	6.4	7.1
45–64 years	5.0	5.3	8.7	9.0	6.3	4.0	3.8	3.7	4.1
45–54 years	5.9	6.1	10.0	11.0	7.5	4.7	4.4	4.5	4.9
55–64 years	3.9	4.1	7.1	7.0	5.0	3.0	2.9	2.9	3.2
65 years and over	3.0	2.7	4.6	5.5	4.0	2.4	2.0	2.0	2.0
65–74 years	3.2	2.8	4.9	5.7	3.8	2.4	2.1	2.1	2.0
75–84 years	2.5	2.3	4.0	5.2	4.3	2.4	1.9	2.0	2.1
85 years and over	2.3	2.4	4.2	5.3	4.6	2.4	2.0	1.9	1.7
Male									
All ages, age-adjusted [4]	7.9	7.5	14.3	16.6	14.8	9.0	8.4	8.0	9.1
All ages, crude	7.7	6.8	13.1	17.1	15.9	9.3	8.4	8.0	9.0
Under 1 year	4.5	4.7	4.5	6.3	8.8	10.4	8.8	7.1	7.1
1–14 years	0.6	0.6	1.2	1.6	2.0	1.5	1.4	1.2	1.5
1–4 years	0.5	0.7	1.9	2.7	2.7	2.5	2.8	2.4	2.8
5–14 years	0.6	0.5	1.0	1.2	1.7	1.1	0.8	0.8	0.9
15–24 years	8.6	8.4	18.2	24.0	32.5	20.9	18.2	16.1	18.4
15–19 years	5.5	5.7	12.1	15.9	27.8	15.5	14.0	11.2	12.7
20–24 years	13.5	11.8	25.6	32.2	36.9	26.7	22.6	20.6	23.7
25–44 years	13.8	12.8	24.4	28.9	23.5	13.3	13.3	13.2	15.1
25–34 years	14.4	13.9	26.8	31.9	27.7	16.7	17.3	15.9	18.4
35–44 years	13.2	11.7	21.7	24.5	18.6	10.3	9.2	10.3	11.5
45–64 years	8.1	8.1	14.8	15.2	10.2	6.0	5.6	5.7	6.3
45–54 years	9.5	9.4	16.8	18.4	11.9	6.9	6.7	6.9	7.6
55–64 years	6.3	6.4	12.1	11.8	8.0	4.6	4.3	4.3	4.8
65 years and over	4.8	4.3	7.7	8.8	5.8	3.3	2.6	2.7	2.7
65–74 years	5.2	4.6	8.5	9.2	5.8	3.4	2.9	2.9	2.9
75–84 years	3.9	3.7	5.9	8.1	5.7	3.2	2.1	2.2	2.3
85 years and over	2.5	3.6	7.4	7.5	6.7	3.3	2.2	2.2	1.9
Female									
All ages, age-adjusted [4]	2.4	2.6	3.7	4.4	4.0	2.8	2.3	2.1	2.2
All ages, crude	2.4	2.4	3.4	4.5	4.2	2.8	2.2	2.1	2.2
Under 1 year	4.2	4.9	4.1	5.6	8.0	7.9	6.9	5.4	6.1
1–14 years	0.6	0.5	1.0	1.4	1.6	1.1	0.9	1.0	0.9
1–4 years	0.7	0.7	1.9	2.2	2.3	2.1	1.9	2.2	1.8
5–14 years	0.5	0.4	0.7	1.1	1.2	0.7	0.5	0.6	0.5
15–24 years	3.0	2.8	4.6	6.6	6.2	3.9	2.9	2.5	2.8
15–19 years	2.4	1.9	3.2	4.9	5.4	3.1	2.3	1.9	2.1
20–24 years	3.7	3.8	6.2	8.2	7.0	4.7	3.4	3.1	3.5
25–44 years	4.2	4.3	5.8	6.4	6.0	4.0	3.1	2.9	3.1
25–34 years	4.5	4.6	6.0	6.9	7.1	4.1	3.3	3.2	3.5
35–44 years	3.8	4.0	5.7	5.7	4.8	4.0	2.9	2.6	2.8
45–64 years	1.9	2.5	3.1	3.4	2.8	2.1	2.0	1.8	1.9
45–54 years	2.3	2.9	3.7	4.1	3.2	2.5	2.3	2.2	2.2
55–64 years	1.4	2.0	2.5	2.8	2.3	1.6	1.7	1.5	1.7
65 years and over	1.4	1.3	2.3	3.3	2.8	1.8	1.6	1.5	1.5
65–74 years	1.3	1.3	2.2	3.0	2.2	1.6	1.4	1.3	1.2
75–84 years	1.4	1.3	2.7	3.5	3.4	2.0	1.8	1.8	1.9
85 years and over	2.1	1.6	2.5	4.3	3.8	2.0	2.0	1.8	1.7

See footnotes at end of table.

Table 29 (page 2 of 4). Death rates for homicide, by sex, race, Hispanic origin, and age: United States, selected years 1950–2015

Excel and PDF versions (with more data years and standard errors when available): http://www.cdc.gov/nchs/hus/contents2016.htm#029.

[Data are based on death certificates]

Sex, race, Hispanic origin, and age	1950 [1,2]	1960 [1,2]	1970 [2]	1980 [2]	1990 [2]	2000 [3]	2010 [3]	2014 [3]	2015 [3]
White male [5]				Deaths per 100,000 resident population					
All ages, age-adjusted [4]	3.8	3.9	7.2	10.4	8.3	5.2	4.7	4.3	4.7
All ages, crude	3.6	3.6	6.6	10.7	8.8	5.2	4.7	4.3	4.6
Under 1 year	4.3	3.8	2.9	4.3	6.4	8.2	8.5	5.8	5.9
1–14 years [6]	0.4	0.5	0.7	1.2	1.3	1.2	1.0	0.9	1.0
15–24 years	3.2	5.0	7.6	15.1	15.2	9.9	8.2	6.5	7.3
25–44 years	5.4	5.5	11.6	17.2	13.0	7.4	6.9	6.8	7.2
25–34 years	4.9	5.7	12.5	18.5	14.7	8.4	8.3	7.5	8.0
35–44 years	6.1	5.2	10.8	15.2	11.1	6.5	5.5	6.0	6.3
45–64 years	4.8	4.6	8.3	9.8	6.9	4.1	4.1	4.0	4.4
65 years and over	3.8	3.1	5.4	6.7	4.1	2.5	2.1	2.2	2.3
Black or African American male [5]									
All ages, age-adjusted [4]	47.0	42.3	78.2	69.4	63.1	35.4	31.5	30.6	35.4
All ages, crude	44.7	35.0	66.0	65.7	68.5	37.2	33.4	32.1	37.3
Under 1 year	- - -	10.3	14.3	18.6	21.4	23.3	12.3	13.9	13.4
1–14 years [6]	1.8	1.5	4.4	4.1	5.8	3.1	3.4	3.1	3.7
15–24 years	53.8	43.2	98.3	82.6	137.1	85.3	71.0	65.0	74.9
25–44 years	92.8	80.5	140.2	130.0	105.4	55.8	55.9	54.8	65.5
25–34 years	104.3	86.4	154.5	142.9	123.7	73.9	76.1	67.7	81.4
35–44 years	80.0	74.4	124.0	109.3	81.2	38.5	34.5	39.7	46.4
45–64 years	46.0	44.6	82.3	70.6	41.4	21.9	17.6	18.2	20.4
65 years and over	16.5	17.3	33.3	30.9	25.7	12.8	8.0	8.4	7.2
American Indian or Alaska Native male [5]									
All ages, age-adjusted [4]	- - -	- - -	- - -	23.3	16.7	10.7	8.8	9.1	9.8
All ages, crude	- - -	- - -	- - -	23.1	16.6	10.7	9.5	9.2	9.9
15–24 years	- - -	- - -	- - -	35.4	25.1	17.0	17.6	12.1	15.2
25–44 years	- - -	- - -	- - -	39.2	25.7	17.0	14.8	13.6	15.1
45–64 years	- - -	- - -	- - -	22.1	14.8	*	6.5	9.7	10.1
Asian or Pacific Islander male [5]									
All ages, age-adjusted [4]	- - -	- - -	- - -	9.1	7.3	4.3	2.6	2.2	2.3
All ages, crude	- - -	- - -	- - -	8.3	7.9	4.4	2.7	2.3	2.4
15–24 years	- - -	- - -	- - -	9.3	14.9	7.8	4.0	3.4	2.9
25–44 years	- - -	- - -	- - -	11.3	9.6	4.6	3.3	3.0	3.1
45–64 years	- - -	- - -	- - -	10.4	7.0	6.1	3.1	2.5	2.8
Hispanic or Latino male [5,7]									
All ages, age-adjusted [4]	- - -	- - -	- - -	- - -	27.4	11.8	8.7	7.2	7.9
All ages, crude	- - -	- - -	- - -	- - -	31.0	13.4	9.5	7.6	8.4
Under 1 year	- - -	- - -	- - -	- - -	8.7	6.6	7.0	4.5	*
1–14 years	- - -	- - -	- - -	- - -	3.1	1.7	1.1	0.7	1.2
15–24 years	- - -	- - -	- - -	- - -	55.4	28.5	19.7	14.2	16.5
25–44 years	- - -	- - -	- - -	- - -	46.4	17.2	13.2	11.6	12.2
25–34 years	- - -	- - -	- - -	- - -	50.9	19.9	16.8	13.1	14.3
35–44 years	- - -	- - -	- - -	- - -	39.3	13.5	8.9	9.9	9.9
45–64 years	- - -	- - -	- - -	- - -	20.5	9.1	6.9	5.6	6.3
65 years and over	- - -	- - -	- - -	- - -	9.4	4.4	3.2	3.3	2.9
White, not Hispanic or Latino male [7]									
All ages, age-adjusted [4]	- - -	- - -	- - -	- - -	5.6	3.6	3.3	3.3	3.6
All ages, crude	- - -	- - -	- - -	- - -	5.8	3.6	3.3	3.3	3.5
Under 1 year	- - -	- - -	- - -	- - -	5.4	8.3	8.7	6.5	7.0
1–14 years	- - -	- - -	- - -	- - -	0.9	1.0	0.9	0.9	1.0
15–24 years	- - -	- - -	- - -	- - -	7.5	4.7	4.1	3.5	3.8
25–44 years	- - -	- - -	- - -	- - -	8.7	5.2	4.7	4.9	5.3
25–34 years	- - -	- - -	- - -	- - -	9.3	5.2	5.0	5.3	5.5
35–44 years	- - -	- - -	- - -	- - -	8.0	5.2	4.4	4.6	5.0
45–64 years	- - -	- - -	- - -	- - -	5.7	3.6	3.6	3.6	3.9
65 years and over	- - -	- - -	- - -	- - -	3.7	2.3	2.0	2.0	2.2

See footnotes at end of table.

Table 29 (page 3 of 4). Death rates for homicide, by sex, race, Hispanic origin, and age: United States, selected years 1950–2015

Excel and PDF versions (with more data years and standard errors when available): *http://www.cdc.gov/nchs/hus/contents2016.htm#029.*

[Data are based on death certificates]

Sex, race, Hispanic origin, and age	1950 [1,2]	1960 [1,2]	1970 [2]	1980 [2]	1990 [2]	2000 [3]	2010 [3]	2014 [3]	2015 [3]
White female [5]				Deaths per 100,000 resident population					
All ages, age-adjusted [4]	1.4	1.5	2.3	3.2	2.7	2.1	1.8	1.7	1.8
All ages, crude	1.4	1.4	2.1	3.2	2.8	2.1	1.8	1.7	1.7
Under 1 year.	3.9	3.5	2.9	4.3	5.1	5.0	5.8	4.5	4.2
1–14 years [6]	0.4	0.4	0.7	1.1	1.0	0.8	0.7	0.8	0.7
15–24 years	1.3	1.5	2.7	4.7	4.0	2.7	2.0	1.7	1.9
25–44 years	2.0	2.1	3.3	4.2	3.8	2.9	2.4	2.3	2.5
45–64 years	1.5	1.7	2.1	2.6	2.3	1.8	1.7	1.5	1.7
65 years and over.	1.2	1.2	1.9	2.9	2.2	1.6	1.6	1.5	1.4
Black or African American female [5]									
All ages, age-adjusted [4]	11.1	11.4	14.7	13.2	12.5	7.1	5.0	4.7	4.9
All ages, crude	11.5	10.4	13.2	13.5	13.4	7.2	5.1	4.7	4.9
Under 1 year.	- - -	13.8	10.7	12.8	22.8	22.2	13.9	10.8	15.8
1–14 years [6]	1.8	1.2	3.1	3.3	4.7	2.7	2.0	2.2	1.9
15–24 years	16.5	11.9	17.7	18.4	18.9	10.7	7.5	7.0	7.5
25–44 years	22.5	22.7	25.3	22.6	21.0	11.0	7.4	6.7	7.4
45–64 years	6.8	10.3	13.4	10.8	6.5	4.5	4.2	3.7	3.7
65 years and over.	3.6	3.0	7.4	8.0	9.4	3.5	1.8	2.4	2.0
American Indian or Alaska Native female [5]									
All ages, age-adjusted [4]	- - -	- - -	- - -	8.1	4.6	3.0	2.5	2.5	2.5
All ages, crude	- - -	- - -	- - -	7.7	4.8	2.9	2.5	2.4	2.5
15–24 years	- - -	- - -	- - -	*	*	*	*	*	*
25–44 years	- - -	- - -	- - -	13.7	6.9	5.9	4.7	4.2	4.1
45–64 years	- - -	- - -	- - -	*	*	*	*	*	*
Asian or Pacific Islander female [5]									
All ages, age-adjusted [4]	- - -	- - -	- - -	3.1	2.8	1.7	1.2	1.0	1.0
All ages, crude	- - -	- - -	- - -	3.1	2.8	1.7	1.2	1.0	1.0
15–24 years	- - -	- - -	- - -	*	*	*	*	*	*
25–44 years	- - -	- - -	- - -	4.6	3.8	2.2	1.3	0.8	1.0
45–64 years	- - -	- - -	- - -	*	*	2.0	1.4	1.5	1.0
Hispanic or Latina female [5,7]									
All ages, age-adjusted [4]	- - -	- - -	- - -	- - -	4.3	2.8	1.8	1.7	1.8
All ages, crude	- - -	- - -	- - -	- - -	4.7	2.8	1.8	1.8	1.8
Under 1 year.	- - -	- - -	- - -	- - -	*	7.4	6.6	4.6	4.2
1–14 years	- - -	- - -	- - -	- - -	1.9	1.0	0.5	1.0	0.5
15–24 years	- - -	- - -	- - -	- - -	8.1	3.7	2.6	2.7	2.4
25–44 years	- - -	- - -	- - -	- - -	6.1	3.7	2.5	2.3	2.5
45–64 years	- - -	- - -	- - -	- - -	3.3	2.9	1.6	1.4	1.7
65 years and over.	- - -	- - -	- - -	- - -	*	2.4	1.3	*	1.2
White, not Hispanic or Latina female [7]									
All ages, age-adjusted [4]	- - -	- - -	- - -	- - -	2.5	1.9	1.8	1.6	1.7
All ages, crude	- - -	- - -	- - -	- - -	2.5	1.9	1.7	1.6	1.7
Under 1 year.	- - -	- - -	- - -	- - -	4.4	4.1	5.3	4.4	4.4
1–14 years	- - -	- - -	- - -	- - -	0.8	0.8	0.7	0.7	0.7
15–24 years	- - -	- - -	- - -	- - -	3.3	2.3	1.8	1.3	1.7
25–44 years	- - -	- - -	- - -	- - -	3.5	2.7	2.4	2.3	2.4
45–64 years	- - -	- - -	- - -	- - -	2.2	1.6	1.7	1.5	1.7
65 years and over.	- - -	- - -	- - -	- - -	2.2	1.6	1.6	1.5	1.4

See footnotes at end of table.

Table 29 (page 4 of 4). Death rates for homicide, by sex, race, Hispanic origin, and age: United States, selected years 1950–2015

Excel and PDF versions (with more data years and standard errors when available): http://www.cdc.gov/nchs/hus/contents2016.htm#029.

[Data are based on death certificates]

- - - Data not available.

* Rates based on fewer than 20 deaths are considered unreliable and are not shown.

[1] Includes deaths of persons who were not residents of the 50 states and the District of Columbia (D.C.).

[2] Underlying cause of death was coded according to the 6th Revision of the *International Classification of Diseases* (ICD) in 1950, 7th Revision in 1960, 8th Revision in 1970, and 9th Revision in 1980–1998. See Appendix II, Cause of death; Table III; Table IV.

[3] Starting with 1999 data, cause of death is coded according to ICD–10. See Appendix II, Cause of death; Comparability ratio; Table IV; Table V.

[4] Age-adjusted rates are calculated using the year 2000 standard population. Prior to 2001, age-adjusted rates were calculated using standard million proportions based on rounded population numbers. Starting with 2001 data, unrounded population numbers are used to calculate age-adjusted rates. See Appendix II, Age adjustment.

[5] The race groups, white, black, Asian or Pacific Islander, and American Indian or Alaska Native, include persons of Hispanic and non-Hispanic origin. Persons of Hispanic origin may be of any race. Death rates for Hispanic, American Indian or Alaska Native, and Asian or Pacific Islander persons should be interpreted with caution because of inconsistencies in reporting Hispanic origin or race on the death certificate (death rate numerators) compared with population figures (death rate denominators). The net effect of misclassification is an underestimation of deaths and death rates for races other than white and black. See Appendix II, Race, for a detailed discussion of sources of bias in death rates by race and Hispanic origin.

[6] In 1950, rate is for the age group under 15 years.

[7] Prior to 1997, data from states that did not report Hispanic origin on the death certificate were excluded. See Appendix II, Hispanic origin.

NOTES: Starting with *Health, United States, 2003*, rates for 1991–1999 were revised using intercensal population estimates based on the 1990 and 2000 censuses. For 2000, population estimates are bridged-race April 1 census counts. Starting with *Health, United States, 2012*, rates for 2001–2009 were revised using intercensal population estimates based on the 2000 and 2010 censuses. For 2010, population estimates are bridged-race April 1 census counts. Rates for 2011 and beyond were computed using 2010-based postcensal estimates. See Appendix I, Population Census and Population Estimates. Figures for 2001 include September 11-related deaths for which death certificates were filed as of October 24, 2002. See Appendix II, Cause of death; Table IV for terrorism-related ICD–10 codes. Age groups were selected to minimize the presentation of unstable age-specific death rates based on small numbers of deaths and for consistency among comparison groups. For additional injury-related statistics, see Web-based Injury Statistics Query and Reporting System (WISQARS), available from: http://www.cdc.gov/injury/wisqars/index.html. Starting with 2003 data, some states began to collect information on more than one race on the death certificate, according to 1997 Office of Management and Budget (OMB) standards. The multiple-race data for these states were bridged to the single-race categories of the 1977 OMB standards, for comparability with other states. See Appendix II, Race. Data for additional years are available. See the Excel spreadsheet on the *Health, United States* website at: http://www.cdc.gov/nchs/hus.htm. Some data have been revised and differ from previous editions of *Health, United States*.

SOURCE: NCHS, National Vital Statistics System; Grove RD, Hetzel AM. Vital statistics rates in the United States, 1940–1960. Washington, DC: U.S. Government Printing Office, 1968; numerator data from National Vital Statistics System, annual public-use Mortality Files; denominator data from national population estimates for race groups from Table 1 and unpublished Hispanic population estimates for 1985–1996 prepared by the Housing and Household Economic Statistics Division, U.S. Census Bureau; Murphy SL, Kochanek KD, Xu JQ, Curtin SC. Deaths: Final data for 2015. National vital statistics reports. Hyattsville, MD: NCHS; 2017. Available from: http://www.cdc.gov/nchs/products/nvsr.htm. See Appendix I, National Vital Statistics System (NVSS).

Table 30 (page 1 of 3). Death rates for suicide, by sex, race, Hispanic origin, and age: United States, selected years 1950–2015

Excel and PDF versions (with more data years and standard errors when available): http://www.cdc.gov/nchs/hus/contents2016.htm#030.

[Data are based on death certificates]

Sex, race, Hispanic origin, and age	1950[1,2]	1960[1,2]	1970[2]	1980[2]	1990[2]	2000[3]	2010[3]	2014[3]	2015[3]
All persons	Deaths per 100,000 resident population								
All ages, age-adjusted[4]	13.2	12.5	13.1	12.2	12.5	10.4	12.1	13.0	13.3
All ages, crude	11.4	10.6	11.6	11.9	12.4	10.4	12.4	13.4	13.7
Under 1 year.	. . .	. . .	. . .	. . .	. . .	. . .	. . .	. . .	. . .
1–4 years.	. . .	. . .	. . .	. . .	. . .	. . .	. . .	. . .	. . .
5–14 years.	0.2	0.3	0.3	0.4	0.8	0.7	0.7	1.0	1.0
15–24 years	4.5	5.2	8.8	12.3	13.2	10.2	10.5	11.6	12.5
15–19 years.	2.7	3.6	5.9	8.5	11.1	8.0	7.5	8.7	9.8
20–24 years.	6.2	7.1	12.2	16.1	15.1	12.5	13.6	14.2	15.1
25–44 years	11.6	12.2	15.4	15.6	15.2	13.4	15.0	15.8	16.4
25–34 years.	9.1	10.0	14.1	16.0	15.2	12.0	14.0	15.1	15.7
35–44 years.	14.3	14.2	16.9	15.4	15.3	14.5	16.0	16.6	17.1
45–64 years	23.5	22.0	20.6	15.9	15.3	13.5	18.6	19.5	19.6
45–54 years.	20.9	20.7	20.0	15.9	14.8	14.4	19.6	20.2	20.3
55–64 years.	26.8	23.7	21.4	15.9	16.0	12.1	17.5	18.8	18.9
65 years and over.	30.0	24.5	20.8	17.6	20.5	15.2	14.9	16.7	16.6
65–74 years.	29.6	23.0	20.8	16.9	17.9	12.5	13.7	15.6	15.2
75–84 years.	31.1	27.9	21.2	19.1	24.9	17.6	15.7	17.5	17.9
85 years and over	28.8	26.0	19.0	19.2	22.2	19.6	17.6	19.3	19.4
Male									
All ages, age-adjusted[4]	21.2	20.0	19.8	19.9	21.5	17.7	19.8	20.7	21.1
All ages, crude	17.8	16.5	16.8	18.6	20.4	17.1	19.9	21.1	21.5
Under 1 year.	. . .	. . .	. . .	. . .	. . .	. . .	. . .	. . .	. . .
1–4 years.	. . .	. . .	. . .	. . .	. . .	. . .	. . .	. . .	. . .
5–14 years	0.3	0.4	0.5	0.6	1.1	1.2	0.9	1.3	1.2
15–24 years	6.5	8.2	13.5	20.2	22.0	17.1	16.9	18.2	19.4
15–19 years.	3.5	5.6	8.8	13.8	18.1	13.0	11.7	13.0	14.2
20–24 years.	9.3	11.5	19.3	26.8	25.7	21.4	22.2	22.9	24.2
25–44 years	17.2	17.9	20.9	24.0	24.4	21.3	23.6	24.4	25.2
25–34 years.	13.4	14.7	19.8	25.0	24.8	19.6	22.5	23.8	24.7
35–44 years.	21.3	21.0	22.1	22.5	23.9	22.8	24.6	25.0	25.9
45–64 years	37.1	34.4	30.0	23.7	24.3	21.3	29.2	29.7	29.5
45–54 years.	32.0	31.6	27.9	22.9	23.2	22.4	30.4	30.0	30.1
55–64 years.	43.6	38.1	32.7	24.5	25.7	19.4	27.7	29.4	28.9
65 years and over.	52.8	44.0	38.4	35.0	41.6	31.1	29.0	31.4	31.0
65–74 years.	50.5	39.6	36.0	30.4	32.2	22.7	23.9	26.6	26.2
75–84 years.	58.3	52.5	42.8	42.3	56.1	38.6	32.3	34.9	35.2
85 years and over	58.3	57.4	42.4	50.6	65.9	57.5	47.3	49.9	48.2
Female									
All ages, age-adjusted[4]	5.6	5.6	7.4	5.7	4.8	4.0	5.0	5.8	6.0
All ages, crude	5.1	4.9	6.6	5.5	4.8	4.0	5.2	6.0	6.2
Under 1 year.	. . .	. . .	. . .	. . .	. . .	. . .	. . .	. . .	. . .
1–4 years.	. . .	. . .	. . .	. . .	. . .	. . .	. . .	. . .	. . .
5–14 years	0.1	0.1	0.2	0.2	0.4	0.3	0.4	0.7	0.8
15–24 years	2.6	2.2	4.2	4.3	3.9	3.0	3.9	4.6	5.3
15–19 years.	1.8	1.6	2.9	3.0	3.7	2.7	3.1	4.2	5.1
20–24 years.	3.3	2.9	5.7	5.5	4.1	3.2	4.7	5.0	5.5
25–44 years	6.2	6.6	10.2	7.7	6.2	5.4	6.4	7.2	7.5
25–34 years.	4.9	5.5	8.6	7.1	5.6	4.3	5.3	6.3	6.6
35–44 years.	7.5	7.7	11.9	8.5	6.8	6.4	7.5	8.2	8.4
45–64 years	9.9	10.2	12.0	8.9	7.1	6.2	8.6	9.8	10.2
45–54 years.	9.9	10.2	12.6	9.4	6.9	6.7	9.0	10.7	10.7
55–64 years.	9.9	10.2	11.4	8.4	7.3	5.4	8.0	8.9	9.7
65 years and over.	9.4	8.4	8.1	6.1	6.4	4.0	4.2	5.0	5.1
65–74 years.	10.1	8.4	9.0	6.5	6.7	4.0	4.8	5.9	5.7
75–84 years.	8.1	8.9	7.0	5.5	6.3	4.0	3.7	4.3	4.6
85 years and over	8.2	6.0	5.9	5.5	5.4	4.2	3.3	3.4	4.2
White male[5]									
All ages, age-adjusted[4]	22.3	21.1	20.8	20.9	22.8	19.1	22.0	23.3	23.6
All ages, crude	19.0	17.6	18.0	19.9	22.0	18.8	22.6	24.2	24.6
15–24 years	6.6	8.6	13.9	21.4	23.2	17.9	18.3	19.9	20.9
25–44 years	17.9	18.5	21.5	24.6	25.4	22.9	26.2	27.5	28.6
45–64 years	39.3	36.5	31.9	25.0	26.0	23.2	33.0	34.0	33.8
65 years and over.	55.8	46.7	41.1	37.2	44.2	33.3	31.7	34.7	34.3
65–74 years.	53.2	42.0	38.7	32.5	34.2	24.3	26.3	29.5	29.1
75–84 years.	61.9	55.7	45.5	45.5	60.2	41.1	34.9	38.3	38.6
85 years and over	61.9	61.3	45.8	52.8	70.3	61.6	50.8	54.4	52.5

See footnotes at end of table.

Table 30 (page 2 of 3). Death rates for suicide, by sex, race, Hispanic origin, and age: United States, selected years 1950–2015

Excel and PDF versions (with more data years and standard errors when available): http://www.cdc.gov/nchs/hus/contents2016.htm#030.

[Data are based on death certificates]

Sex, race, Hispanic origin, and age	1950[1,2]	1960[1,2]	1970[2]	1980[2]	1990[2]	2000[3]	2010[3]	2014[3]	2015[3]
Black or African American male[5]				Deaths per 100,000 resident population					
All ages, age-adjusted[4]	7.5	8.4	10.0	11.4	12.8	10.0	9.1	9.5	9.6
All ages, crude	6.3	6.4	8.0	10.3	12.0	9.4	8.7	9.2	9.4
15–24 years	4.9	4.1	10.5	12.3	15.1	14.2	11.1	12.0	12.9
25–44 years	9.8	12.6	16.1	19.2	19.6	14.3	14.5	14.4	14.8
45–64 years	12.7	13.0	12.4	11.8	13.1	9.9	9.5	9.9	9.7
65 years and over	9.0	9.9	8.7	11.4	14.9	11.5	8.3	8.9	8.6
65–74 years	10.0	11.3	8.7	11.1	14.7	11.1	7.6	7.7	7.3
75–84 years[6]	*	*	*	10.5	14.4	12.1	9.9	11.0	11.2
85 years and over	- - -	*	*	*	*	*	*	*	*
American Indian or Alaska Native male[5]									
All ages, age-adjusted[4]	- - -	- - -	- - -	19.3	20.1	16.0	15.5	16.4	18.8
All ages, crude	- - -	- - -	- - -	20.9	20.9	15.9	16.1	16.0	18.5
15–24 years	- - -	- - -	- - -	45.3	49.1	26.2	30.6	23.5	29.5
25–44 years	- - -	- - -	- - -	31.2	27.8	24.5	20.9	26.2	27.3
45–64 years	- - -	- - -	- - -	*	*	15.4	17.8	15.1	20.8
65 years and over	- - -	- - -	- - -	*	*	*	*	13.4	13.2
Asian or Pacific Islander male[5]									
All ages, age-adjusted[4]	- - -	- - -	- - -	10.7	9.6	8.6	9.5	8.9	9.1
All ages, crude	- - -	- - -	- - -	8.8	8.7	7.9	9.3	9.0	9.2
15–24 years	- - -	- - -	- - -	10.8	13.5	9.1	10.9	12.9	15.6
25–44 years	- - -	- - -	- - -	11.0	10.6	9.9	10.6	9.7	9.6
45–64 years	- - -	- - -	- - -	13.0	9.7	9.7	12.8	12.1	10.9
65 years and over	- - -	- - -	- - -	18.6	16.8	15.4	14.9	11.6	12.6
Hispanic or Latino male[5,7]									
All ages, age-adjusted[4]	- - -	- - -	- - -	- - -	13.7	10.3	9.9	10.3	9.9
All ages, crude	- - -	- - -	- - -	- - -	11.4	8.4	8.5	9.2	9.0
15–24 years	- - -	- - -	- - -	- - -	14.7	10.9	10.7	11.6	12.8
25–44 years	- - -	- - -	- - -	- - -	16.2	11.2	11.2	12.6	12.2
45–64 years	- - -	- - -	- - -	- - -	16.1	12.0	12.9	12.4	11.4
65 years and over	- - -	- - -	- - -	- - -	23.4	19.5	15.7	15.9	14.5
White, not Hispanic or Latino male[7]									
All ages, age-adjusted[4]	- - -	- - -	- - -	- - -	23.5	20.2	24.2	25.9	26.6
All ages, crude	- - -	- - -	- - -	- - -	23.1	20.4	25.7	27.7	28.3
15–24 years	- - -	- - -	- - -	- - -	24.4	19.5	20.4	22.4	23.4
25–44 years	- - -	- - -	- - -	- - -	26.4	25.1	30.3	31.8	33.5
45–64 years	- - -	- - -	- - -	- - -	26.8	24.0	35.4	37.2	37.2
65 years and over	- - -	- - -	- - -	- - -	45.4	33.9	32.7	36.1	35.9
White female[5]									
All ages, age-adjusted[4]	6.0	5.9	7.9	6.1	5.2	4.3	5.6	6.6	6.9
All ages, crude	5.5	5.3	7.1	5.9	5.3	4.4	5.9	6.9	7.2
15–24 years	2.7	2.3	4.2	4.6	4.2	3.1	4.2	5.0	5.6
25–44 years	6.6	7.0	11.0	8.1	6.6	6.0	7.3	8.4	8.7
45–64 years	10.6	10.9	13.0	9.6	7.7	6.9	9.9	11.5	11.9
65 years and over	9.9	8.8	8.5	6.4	6.8	4.3	4.5	5.5	5.6
Black or African American female[5]									
All ages, age-adjusted[4]	1.8	2.0	2.9	2.4	2.4	1.8	1.8	2.1	2.0
All ages, crude	1.5	1.6	2.6	2.2	2.3	1.7	1.8	2.1	2.1
15–24 years	1.8	*	3.8	2.3	2.3	2.2	2.0	2.6	3.6
25–44 years	2.3	3.0	4.8	4.3	3.8	2.6	2.8	2.9	2.7
45–64 years	2.7	3.1	2.9	2.5	2.9	2.1	2.1	2.7	2.6
65 years and over	*	*	2.6	*	1.9	1.3	*	1.3	0.9

See footnotes at end of table.

Excel and PDF versions (with more data years and standard errors when available): http://www.cdc.gov/nchs/hus/contents2016.htm#030.

[Data are based on death certificates]

Sex, race, Hispanic origin, and age	1950[1,2]	1960[1,2]	1970[2]	1980[2]	1990[2]	2000[3]	2010[3]	2014[3]	2015[3]
American Indian or Alaska Native female[5]				Deaths per 100,000 resident population					
All ages, age-adjusted[4]	- - -	- - -	- - -	4.7	3.6	3.8	6.1	5.5	6.5
All ages, crude	- - -	- - -	- - -	4.7	3.7	4.0	5.9	5.6	6.6
15–24 years	- - -	- - -	- - -	*	*	*	10.4	9.6	11.7
25–44 years	- - -	- - -	- - -	10.7	*	7.2	7.4	9.7	8.8
45–64 years	- - -	- - -	- - -	*	*	*	6.2	*	6.9
65 years and over	- - -	- - -	- - -	*	*	*	*	*	*
Asian or Pacific Islander female[5]									
All ages, age-adjusted[4]	- - -	- - -	- - -	5.5	4.1	2.8	3.4	3.4	4.0
All ages, crude	- - -	- - -	- - -	4.7	3.4	2.7	3.4	3.5	4.1
15–24 years	- - -	- - -	- - -	*	3.9	2.7	3.5	4.1	4.9
25–44 years	- - -	- - -	- - -	5.4	3.8	3.3	4.1	4.0	4.5
45–64 years	- - -	- - -	- - -	7.9	5.0	3.2	4.7	4.2	5.2
65 years and over	- - -	- - -	- - -	*	8.5	5.2	4.3	5.2	5.2
Hispanic or Latina female[5,7]									
All ages, age-adjusted[4]	- - -	- - -	- - -	- - -	2.3	1.7	2.1	2.5	2.6
All ages, crude	- - -	- - -	- - -	- - -	2.2	1.5	2.0	2.4	2.6
15–24 years	- - -	- - -	- - -	- - -	3.1	2.0	3.1	3.4	3.9
25–44 years	- - -	- - -	- - -	- - -	3.1	2.1	2.4	3.0	3.2
45–64 years	- - -	- - -	- - -	- - -	2.5	2.5	2.8	3.5	3.8
65 years and over	- - -	- - -	- - -	- - -	*	*	2.2	2.1	1.9
White, not Hispanic or Latina female[7]									
All ages, age-adjusted[4]	- - -	- - -	- - -	- - -	5.4	4.7	6.2	7.5	7.8
All ages, crude	- - -	- - -	- - -	- - -	5.6	4.9	6.7	7.9	8.3
15–24 years	- - -	- - -	- - -	- - -	4.3	3.3	4.4	5.4	6.1
25–44 years	- - -	- - -	- - -	- - -	7.0	6.7	8.6	9.8	10.3
45–64 years	- - -	- - -	- - -	- - -	8.0	7.3	10.7	12.6	13.1
65 years and over	- - -	- - -	- - -	- - -	7.0	4.4	4.7	5.8	6.0

. . . Category not applicable.

* Rates based on fewer than 20 deaths are considered unreliable and are not shown.

- - - Data not available.

[1] Includes deaths of persons who were not residents of the 50 states and the District of Columbia (D.C.).

[2] Underlying cause of death was coded according to the 6th Revision of the *International Classification of Diseases* (ICD) in 1950, 7th Revision in 1960, 8th Revision in 1970, and 9th Revision in 1980–1998. See Appendix II, Cause of death; Table III; Table IV.

[3] Starting with 1999 data, cause of death is coded according to ICD–10. See Appendix II, Cause of death; Comparability ratio; Table IV; Table V.

[4] Age-adjusted rates are calculated using the year 2000 standard population. Prior to 2001, age-adjusted rates were calculated using standard million proportions based on rounded population numbers. Starting with 2001 data, unrounded population numbers are used to calculate age-adjusted rates. See Appendix II, Age adjustment.

[5] The race groups, white, black, Asian or Pacific Islander, and American Indian or Alaska Native, include persons of Hispanic and non-Hispanic origin. Persons of Hispanic origin may be of any race. Death rates for Hispanic, American Indian or Alaska Native, and Asian or Pacific Islander persons should be interpreted with caution because of inconsistencies in reporting Hispanic origin or race on the death certificate (death rate numerators) compared with population figures (death rate denominators). The net effect of misclassification is an underestimation of deaths and death rates for races other than white and black. See Appendix II, Race, for a detailed discussion of sources of bias in death rates by race and Hispanic origin.

[6] In 1950, rate is for the age group 75 years and over.

[7] Prior to 1997, data from states that did not report Hispanic origin on the death certificate were excluded. See Appendix II, Hispanic origin.

NOTES: Starting with *Health, United States, 2003*, rates for 1991–1999 were revised using intercensal population estimates based on the 1990 and 2000 censuses. For 2000, population estimates are bridged-race April 1 census counts. Starting with *Health, United States, 2012*, rates for 2001–2009 were revised using intercensal population estimates based on the 2000 and 2010 censuses. For 2010, population estimates are bridged-race April 1 census counts. Rates for 2011 and beyond were computed using 2010-based postcensal estimates. See Appendix I, Population Census and Population Estimates. Figures for 2001 include September 11-related deaths for which death certificates were filed as of October 24, 2002. See Appendix II, Cause of death; Table IV for terrorism-related ICD–10 codes. Age groups were selected to minimize the presentation of unstable age-specific death rates based on small numbers of deaths and for consistency among comparison groups. For additional injury-related statistics, see Web-based Injury Statistics Query and Reporting System (WISQARS), available from: http://www.cdc.gov/injury/wisqars/index.html. Starting with 2003 data, some states began to collect information on more than one race on the death certificate, according to 1997 Office of Management and Budget (OMB) standards. The multiple-race data for these states were bridged to the single-race categories of the 1977 OMB standards, for comparability with other states. See Appendix II, Race. Data for additional years are available. See the Excel spreadsheet on the *Health, United States* website at: http://www.cdc.gov/nchs/hus.htm. Some data have been revised and differ from previous editions of *Health, United States*.

SOURCE: NCHS, National Vital Statistics System; Grove RD, Hetzel AM. Vital statistics rates in the United States, 1940–1960. Washington, DC: U.S. Government Printing Office, 1968; numerator data from National Vital Statistics System, annual public-use Mortality Files; denominator data from national population estimates for race groups from Table 1 and unpublished Hispanic population estimates for 1985–1996 prepared by the Housing and Household Economic Statistics Division, U.S. Census Bureau; Murphy SL, Kochanek KD, Xu JQ, Curtin SC. Deaths: Final data for 2015. National vital statistics reports. Hyattsville, MD: NCHS; 2017. Available from: http://www.cdc.gov/nchs/products/nvsr.htm. See Appendix I, National Vital Statistics System (NVSS).

Table 31 (page 1 of 3). Death rates for firearm-related injuries, by sex, race, Hispanic origin, and age: United States, selected years 1970–2015

Excel and PDF versions (with more data years and standard errors when available): http://www.cdc.gov/nchs/hus/contents2016.htm#031.

[Data are based on death certificates]

Sex, race, Hispanic origin, and age	1970[1]	1980[1]	1990[1]	1995[1]	2000[2]	2010[2]	2014[2]	2015[2]
All persons								
	Deaths per 100,000 resident population							
All ages, age-adjusted[3]	14.3	14.8	14.6	13.4	10.2	10.1	10.3	11.1
All ages, crude	13.1	14.9	14.9	13.5	10.2	10.3	10.5	11.3
Under 1 year	*	*	*	*	*	*	*	*
1–14 years	1.6	1.4	1.5	1.6	0.7	0.6	0.8	0.8
1–4 years	1.0	0.7	0.6	0.6	0.3	0.4	0.4	0.5
5–14 years	1.7	1.6	1.9	1.9	0.9	0.7	0.9	0.9
15–24 years	15.5	20.6	25.8	26.7	16.8	14.2	14.0	15.7
15–19 years	11.4	14.7	23.3	24.1	12.9	10.6	9.9	11.3
20–24 years	20.3	26.4	28.1	29.2	20.9	17.9	17.7	19.8
25–44 years	20.9	22.5	19.3	16.9	13.1	13.3	13.4	15.0
25–34 years	22.2	24.3	21.8	19.6	14.5	15.0	14.7	16.8
35–44 years	19.6	20.0	16.3	14.3	11.9	11.7	12.1	13.1
45–64 years	17.6	15.2	13.6	11.7	10.0	11.6	11.8	12.0
45–54 years	18.1	16.4	13.9	12.0	10.5	12.0	12.2	12.4
55–64 years	17.0	13.9	13.3	11.3	9.4	11.1	11.4	11.7
65 years and over	13.8	13.5	16.0	14.1	12.2	11.7	12.7	12.7
65–74 years	14.5	13.8	14.4	12.8	10.6	10.7	11.5	11.3
75–84 years	13.4	13.4	19.4	16.3	13.9	12.7	13.9	14.5
85 years and over	10.2	11.6	14.7	14.4	14.2	13.2	15.0	14.5
Male								
All ages, age-adjusted[3]	24.8	25.9	26.1	23.8	18.1	17.9	18.0	19.4
All ages, crude	22.2	25.7	26.2	23.6	17.8	18.0	18.3	19.6
Under 1 year	*	*	*	*	*	*	*	*
1–14 years	2.3	2.0	2.2	2.3	1.1	1.0	1.1	1.1
1–4 years	1.2	0.9	0.7	0.8	0.4	0.6	0.5	0.6
5–14 years	2.7	2.5	2.9	2.9	1.4	1.1	1.3	1.2
15–24 years	26.4	34.8	44.7	46.5	29.4	25.0	24.3	27.4
15–19 years	19.2	24.5	40.1	41.6	22.4	18.4	17.2	19.5
20–24 years	35.1	45.2	49.1	51.5	37.0	31.8	30.8	34.7
25–44 years	34.1	38.1	32.6	28.4	22.0	22.9	22.8	25.6
25–34 years	36.5	41.4	37.0	33.2	24.9	26.4	25.2	28.8
35–44 years	31.6	33.2	27.4	23.6	19.4	19.3	20.1	22.1
45–64 years	31.0	25.9	23.4	20.0	17.1	19.9	19.8	20.2
45–54 years	30.7	27.3	23.2	20.1	17.6	20.3	19.9	20.5
55–64 years	31.3	24.5	23.7	19.8	16.3	19.3	19.8	19.9
65 years and over	29.7	29.7	35.3	30.7	26.4	24.1	25.7	25.5
65–74 years	29.5	27.8	28.2	25.1	20.3	20.0	21.5	21.1
75–84 years	31.0	33.0	46.9	37.8	32.2	27.5	29.2	30.2
85 years and over	26.2	34.9	49.3	47.1	44.7	37.4	40.7	38.9
Female								
All ages, age-adjusted[3]	4.8	4.7	4.2	3.8	2.8	2.7	3.0	3.2
All ages, crude	4.4	4.7	4.3	3.8	2.8	2.7	3.0	3.2
Under 1 year	*	*	*	*	*	*	*	*
1–14 years	0.8	0.7	0.8	0.8	0.3	0.3	0.5	0.5
1–4 years	0.9	0.5	0.5	0.5	*	0.3	0.4	0.4
5–14 years	0.8	0.7	1.0	0.9	0.4	0.3	0.5	0.5
15–24 years	4.8	6.1	6.0	5.9	3.5	2.9	3.1	3.4
15–19 years	3.5	4.6	5.7	5.6	2.9	2.3	2.3	2.7
20–24 years	6.4	7.7	6.3	6.1	4.2	3.5	3.9	4.1
25–44 years	8.3	7.4	6.1	5.5	4.2	3.8	4.0	4.4
25–34 years	8.4	7.5	6.7	5.8	4.0	3.5	3.9	4.5
35–44 years	8.2	7.2	5.4	5.2	4.4	4.1	4.1	4.3
45–64 years	5.4	5.4	4.5	3.9	3.4	3.7	4.1	4.3
45–54 years	6.4	6.2	4.9	4.2	3.6	3.8	4.7	4.5
55–64 years	4.2	4.6	4.0	3.5	3.0	3.4	3.6	4.0
65 years and over	2.4	2.5	3.1	2.8	2.2	2.2	2.5	2.5
65–74 years	2.8	3.1	3.6	3.0	2.5	2.6	2.7	2.7
75–84 years	1.7	1.7	2.9	2.8	2.0	2.1	2.4	2.6
85 years and over	*	1.3	1.3	1.8	1.7	1.5	1.6	1.7
White male[4]								
All ages, age-adjusted[3]	19.7	22.1	22.0	20.1	15.9	16.1	16.3	17.0
All ages, crude	17.6	21.8	21.8	19.9	15.6	16.5	17.0	17.7
1–14 years	1.8	1.9	1.9	1.9	1.0	0.8	1.0	0.9
15–24 years	16.9	28.4	29.5	30.8	19.6	16.2	16.1	17.5
25–44 years	24.2	29.5	25.7	23.2	18.0	18.6	18.4	20.0
25–34 years	24.3	31.1	27.8	25.2	18.1	19.1	18.7	20.5
35–44 years	24.1	27.1	23.3	21.2	17.9	18.0	18.2	19.4
45–64 years	27.4	23.3	22.8	19.5	17.4	21.3	21.4	21.6
65 years and over	29.9	30.1	36.8	32.2	28.2	26.5	28.3	28.3

See footnotes at end of table.

Table 31 (page 2 of 3). **Death rates for firearm-related injuries, by sex, race, Hispanic origin, and age: United States, selected years 1970–2015**

Excel and PDF versions (with more data years and standard errors when available): http://www.cdc.gov/nchs/hus/contents2016.htm#031.

[Data are based on death certificates]

Sex, race, Hispanic origin, and age	1970[1]	1980[1]	1990[1]	1995[1]	2000[2]	2010[2]	2014[2]	2015[2]
Black or African American male[4]				Deaths per 100,000 resident population				
All ages, age-adjusted[3]	70.8	60.1	56.3	49.2	34.2	31.8	31.5	36.4
All ages, crude	60.8	57.7	61.9	52.9	36.1	33.4	32.9	38.1
1–14 years	5.3	3.0	4.4	4.4	1.8	1.9	1.9	2.1
15–24 years	97.3	77.9	138.0	138.7	89.3	73.2	68.9	79.7
25–44 years	126.2	114.1	90.3	70.2	54.1	57.3	57.4	68.1
25–34 years.	145.6	128.4	108.6	92.3	74.8	78.2	71.3	84.9
35–44 years.	104.2	92.3	66.1	46.3	34.3	35.2	41.0	47.9
45–64 years	71.1	55.6	34.5	28.3	18.4	16.5	16.9	18.7
65 years and over.	30.6	29.7	23.9	21.8	13.8	9.4	10.9	10.0
American Indian or Alaska Native male[4]								
All ages, age-adjusted[3]	- - -	24.0	19.4	19.4	13.1	11.7	12.9	14.4
All ages, crude	- - -	27.5	20.5	20.9	13.2	12.5	12.4	14.2
15–24 years	- - -	55.3	49.1	40.9	26.9	26.0	17.7	26.4
25–44 years	- - -	43.9	25.4	31.2	16.6	16.9	19.3	18.7
45–64 years	- - -	*	*	14.2	12.2	11.1	12.6	14.0
65 years and over.	- - -	*	*	*	*	*	*	*
Asian or Pacific Islander male[4]								
All ages, age-adjusted[3]	- - -	7.8	8.8	9.2	6.0	4.2	3.7	4.4
All ages, crude	- - -	8.2	9.4	10.0	6.2	4.4	3.8	4.7
15–24 years	- - -	10.8	21.0	24.3	9.3	6.8	6.3	8.0
25–44 years	- - -	12.8	10.9	10.6	8.1	6.0	4.8	6.0
45–64 years	- - -	10.4	8.1	8.2	7.4	4.4	4.1	5.0
65 years and over.	- - -	*	*	*	*	3.9	3.4	3.7
Hispanic or Latino male[4,5]								
All ages, age-adjusted[3]	- - -	- - -	27.6	23.8	13.6	10.5	9.4	10.1
All ages, crude	- - -	- - -	29.9	26.2	14.2	10.5	9.4	10.2
1–14 years	- - -	- - -	2.6	2.8	1.0	0.6	0.5	0.5
15–24 years	- - -	- - -	55.5	61.7	30.8	20.9	17.2	19.6
25–44 years	- - -	- - -	42.7	31.4	17.3	14.4	14.1	15.0
25–34 years.	- - -	- - -	47.3	36.4	20.3	18.0	15.7	17.7
35–44 years.	- - -	- - -	35.4	24.2	13.2	10.2	12.3	11.9
45–64 years	- - -	- - -	21.4	17.2	12.0	9.1	7.9	8.0
65 years and over.	- - -	- - -	19.1	16.5	12.2	9.9	7.8	9.1
White, not Hispanic or Latino male[5]								
All ages, age-adjusted[3]	- - -	- - -	20.6	18.6	15.5	16.6	17.3	18.0
All ages, crude	- - -	- - -	20.4	18.5	15.7	17.6	18.7	19.4
1–14 years	- - -	- - -	1.6	1.6	1.0	0.9	1.2	1.0
15–24 years	- - -	- - -	24.1	23.5	16.2	14.2	15.4	16.4
25–44 years	- - -	- - -	23.3	21.4	17.9	19.4	19.4	21.2
25–34 years.	- - -	- - -	24.7	22.5	17.2	18.9	19.2	20.9
35–44 years.	- - -	- - -	21.6	20.4	18.4	19.9	19.7	21.5
45–64 years	- - -	- - -	22.7	19.5	17.8	22.8	23.4	23.7
65 years and over.	- - -	- - -	37.4	32.5	29.0	27.6	29.9	29.8
White female[4]								
All ages, age-adjusted[3]	4.0	4.2	3.8	3.5	2.7	2.7	3.1	3.2
All ages, crude	3.7	4.1	3.8	3.5	2.7	2.8	3.2	3.3
15–24 years	3.4	5.1	4.8	4.5	2.8	2.3	2.6	2.8
25–44 years	6.9	6.2	5.3	4.9	3.9	3.7	4.0	4.4
45–64 years	5.0	5.1	4.5	4.0	3.5	4.1	4.7	4.9
65 years and over.	2.2	2.5	3.1	2.8	2.4	2.5	2.7	2.8

See footnotes at end of table.

Excel and PDF versions (with more data years and standard errors when available): http://www.cdc.gov/nchs/hus/contents2016.htm#031.

[Data are based on death certificates]

Sex, race, Hispanic origin, and age	1970[1]	1980[1]	1990[1]	1995[1]	2000[2]	2010[2]	2014[2]	2015[2]
Black or African American female [4]			Deaths per 100,000 resident population					
All ages, age-adjusted [3]	11.1	8.7	7.3	6.2	3.9	3.3	3.2	3.6
All ages, crude	10.0	8.8	7.8	6.5	4.0	3.3	3.2	3.7
15–24 years	15.2	12.3	13.3	13.2	7.6	6.4	6.2	6.8
25–44 years	19.4	16.1	12.4	9.8	6.5	5.6	5.3	6.2
45–64 years	10.2	8.2	4.8	4.1	3.1	2.2	2.1	2.3
65 years and over	4.3	3.1	3.1	2.6	1.3	*	1.4	1.1
American Indian or Alaska Native female [4]								
All ages, age-adjusted [3]	- - -	5.8	3.3	3.8	2.9	2.6	2.4	2.6
All ages, crude	- - -	5.8	3.4	4.1	2.9	2.4	2.4	2.5
15–24 years	- - -	*	*	*	*	*	*	*
25–44 years	- - -	10.2	*	7.0	5.5	3.7	5.6	4.3
45–64 years	- - -	*	*	*	*	*	*	*
65 years and over	- - -	*	*	*	*	*	*	*
Asian or Pacific Islander female [4]								
All ages, age-adjusted [3]	- - -	2.0	1.9	2.0	1.1	0.6	0.7	0.8
All ages, crude	- - -	2.1	2.1	2.1	1.2	0.6	0.8	0.8
15–24 years	- - -	*	*	3.9	*	*	*	*
25–44 years	- - -	3.2	2.7	2.7	1.5	1.1	0.8	1.0
45–64 years	- - -	*	*	*	*	*	1.3	0.8
65 years and over	- - -	*	*	*	*	*	*	*
Hispanic or Latina female [4,5]								
All ages, age-adjusted [3]	- - -	- - -	3.3	3.1	1.8	1.3	1.4	1.5
All ages, crude	- - -	- - -	3.6	3.3	1.8	1.3	1.4	1.5
15–24 years	- - -	- - -	6.9	6.1	2.9	2.1	2.6	2.5
25–44 years	- - -	- - -	5.1	4.7	2.5	1.8	1.9	2.2
45–64 years	- - -	- - -	2.4	2.4	2.2	1.5	1.2	1.6
65 years and over	- - -	- - -	*	*	*	*	*	*
White, not Hispanic or Latina female [5]								
All ages, age-adjusted [3]	- - -	- - -	3.7	3.4	2.8	3.0	3.4	3.6
All ages, crude	- - -	- - -	3.7	3.5	2.9	3.1	3.6	3.7
15–24 years	- - -	- - -	4.3	4.1	2.7	2.3	2.6	2.9
25–44 years	- - -	- - -	5.1	4.8	4.2	4.2	4.6	5.0
45–64 years	- - -	- - -	4.6	4.1	3.6	4.4	5.2	5.4
65 years and over	- - -	- - -	3.2	2.8	2.4	2.6	2.9	3.0

* Rates based on fewer than 20 deaths are considered unreliable and are not shown.

- - - Data not available.

[1] Underlying cause of death was coded according to the 8th Revision of the *International Classification of Diseases* (ICD) in 1970 and 9th Revision in 1980–1998. See Appendix II, Cause of death; Table III; Table IV.

[2] Starting with 1999 data, cause of death is coded according to ICD–10. See Appendix II, Cause of death; Comparability ratio; Table IV; Table V.

[3] Age-adjusted rates are calculated using the year 2000 standard population. Prior to 2001, age-adjusted rates were calculated using standard million proportions based on rounded population numbers. Starting with 2001 data, unrounded population numbers are used to calculate age-adjusted rates. See Appendix II, Age adjustment.

[4] The race groups, white, black, Asian or Pacific Islander, and American Indian or Alaska Native, include persons of Hispanic and non-Hispanic origin. Persons of Hispanic origin may be of any race. Death rates for Hispanic, American Indian or Alaska Native, and Asian or Pacific Islander persons should be interpreted with caution because of inconsistencies in reporting Hispanic origin or race on the death certificate (death rate numerators) compared with population figures (death rate denominators). The net effect of misclassification is an underestimation of deaths and death rates for races other than white and black. See Appendix II, Race, for a detailed discussion of sources of bias in death rates by race and Hispanic origin.

[5] Prior to 1997, data from states that did not report Hispanic origin on the death certificate were excluded. See Appendix II, Hispanic origin.

NOTES: Starting with *Health, United States, 2003*, rates for 1991–1999 were revised using intercensal population estimates based on the 1990 and 2000 censuses. For 2000, population estimates are bridged-race April 1 census counts. Starting with *Health, United States, 2012*, rates for 2001–2009 were revised using intercensal population estimates based on the 2000 and 2010 censuses. For 2010, population estimates are bridged-race April 1 census counts. Rates for 2011 and beyond were computed using 2010-based postcensal estimates. See Appendix I, Population Census and Population Estimates. Age groups were selected to minimize the presentation of unstable age-specific death rates based on small numbers of deaths and for consistency among comparison groups. For additional injury-related statistics, see Web-based Injury Statistics Query and Reporting System (WISQARS), available from: http://www.cdc.gov/injury/wisqars/index.html. Starting with 2003 data, some states began to collect information on more than one race on the death certificate, according to 1997 Office of Management and Budget (OMB) standards. The multiple-race data for these states were bridged to the single-race categories of the 1977 OMB standards, for comparability with other states. See Appendix II, Race. Data for additional years are available. See the Excel spreadsheet on the *Health, United States* website at: http://www.cdc.gov/nchs/hus.htm. Some data have been revised and differ from previous editions of *Health, United States*.

SOURCE: NCHS, National Vital Statistics System; numerator data from National Vital Statistics System, annual public-use Mortality Files; denominator data from national population estimates for race groups from Table 1 and unpublished Hispanic population estimates for 1985–1996 prepared by the Housing and Household Economic Statistics Division, U.S. Census Bureau; Murphy SL, Kochanek KD, Xu JQ, Curtin SC. Deaths: Final data for 2015. National vital statistics reports. Hyattsville, MD: NCHS; 2017. Available from: http://www.cdc.gov/nchs/products/nvsr.htm. See Appendix I, National Vital Statistics System (NVSS).

Table 32 (page 1 of 2). Occupational fatal injuries, by industry, sex, age, race, and Hispanic origin: United States, selected years 2003–2015

Excel and PDF versions (with more data years and standard errors when available): http://www.cdc.gov/nchs/hus/contents2016.htm#032.

[Data are compiled from various federal, state, and local administrative sources]

Characteristic	2003	2005	2010	2012	2013	2014	2015
				Number of deaths			
Total workforce	5,575	5,734	4,690	4,628	4,585	4,821	4,836
Sex							
Male	5,129	5,328	4,322	4,277	4,265	4,454	4,492
Female	446	406	368	351	319	367	344
Unspecified	0	0	0	0	1	0	0
Age							
Under 16 years	25	23	16	19	5	8	12
16–17 years	28	31	18	10	9	14	12
18–19 years	84	111	56	59	57	42	50
20–24 years	462	403	245	287	279	292	329
25–34 years	1,018	1,017	785	736	777	753	758
35–44 years	1,329	1,243	868	829	853	860	864
45–54 years	1,301	1,389	1,169	1,161	1,115	1,161	1,130
55–64 years	802	933	948	936	933	1,007	1,031
65 years and over.	523	578	582	588	557	684	650
Unspecified	3	6	3	3	0	0	0
Race and Hispanic origin							
Hispanic or Latino	794	923	707	748	817	804	903
Not Hispanic or Latino	4,781	4,811	3,983	3,880	3,768	4,017	3,933
White	3,988	3,977	3,363	3,177	3,125	3,332	3,241
Black or African American	543	584	412	486	439	475	495
American Indian or Alaska Native.	42	50	32	37	35	34	36
Asian.	147	154	143	147	125	137	114
Native Hawaiian or Other Pacific Islander .	11	9	6	7	7	5	9
Multiple races	3	*	8	5	12	20	12
Other races or not reported	47	35	19	21	25	14	26
Industry [1]							
Private sector	5,043	5,214	4,206	4,175	4,101	4,386	4,379
Agriculture, forestry, fishing, and hunting .	709	715	621	509	500	584	570
Mining [2]	141	159	172	181	155	183	120
Utilities	32	30	26	23	24	17	22
Construction	1,131	1,192	774	806	828	899	937
Manufacturing	420	393	329	327	312	349	353
Wholesale trade	191	209	191	204	201	191	175
Retail trade	344	400	311	273	263	272	269
Transportation and warehousing	808	885	661	741	733	766	765
Information	64	65	43	42	40	35	42
Finance and insurance	45	42	24	21	21	29	19
Real estate and rental and leasing	84	57	89	64	66	88	64
Professional and technical services	97	83	76	57	87	80	76
Management, administrative, and waste services [3].	- - -	- - -	- - -	352	343	345	401
Educational services	41	46	30	34	32	40	30
Health care and social assistance	102	104	141	107	103	106	109
Arts, entertainment, and recreation.	88	77	84	80	69	81	82
Accommodation and food services.	187	136	154	152	138	135	143
Other services (except public administration)	194	210	192	199	186	186	202
Government [4]	532	520	484	453	484	435	457

See footnotes at end of table.

Excel and PDF versions (with more data years and standard errors when available): *http://www.cdc.gov/nchs/hus/contents2016.htm#032.*

[Data are compiled from various federal, state, and local administrative sources]

- - - Data not available.

* Estimates are unreliable or data do not meet publication criteria.

[1] Industry data from 2003 to 2008 (shown in spreadsheet version) are based on the North American Industry Classification System (NAICS) 2002. Industry data from 2009 to 2013 are based on NAICS 2007. Industry data from 2014 to the present are based on NAICS 2012. NAICS replaces the Standard Industrial Classification (SIC) system. Because of substantial differences between NAICS and SIC, industry data classified by these two systems are not comparable. See Appendix II, Table VIII.

[2] Includes fatal injuries at all establishments categorized as Mining (Sector 21) in the NAICS, including establishments not governed by the Mine Safety and Health Administration (MSHA) rules and reporting, such as those in Oil and Gas Extraction.

[3] Starting with 2011 data, CFOI combined the categories "Management of companies and enterprises" and "Administrative and support and waste management and remediation services" into one category entitled "Management, administrative, and waste services."

[4] Includes fatal work injuries to workers employed by governmental organizations, regardless of industry.

NOTES: Fatal work injuries are based on revised data and may differ from originally published data from CFOI. See Appendix I, Census of Fatal Occupational Injuries (CFOI). Private sector totals include injuries with unknown industry. Data for additional years are available. See the Excel spreadsheet on the *Health, United States* website at: http://www.cdc.gov/nchs/hus.htm.

SOURCE: Department of Labor, Bureau of Labor Statistics, Census of Fatal Occupational Injuries. Revised annual data. See Appendix I, Census of Fatal Occupational Injuries (CFOI).

Excel and PDF versions (with more data years and standard errors when available): http://www.cdc.gov/nchs/hus/contents2016.htm#033.

[Data are based on reporting by state health departments]

Disease	1950	1960	1970	1980	1990	2000	2010	2014	2015
	New cases per 100,000 population								
Acute hepatitis A viral infection.	- - -	- - -	27.87	12.84	12.64	4.91	0.54	0.39	–
Acute hepatitis B viral infection.	- - -	- - -	4.08	8.39	8.48	2.95	1.10	0.88	–
Acute hepatitis C viral infection [1]	- - -	- - -	- - -	- - -	1.03	1.17	0.29	0.73	–
Diphtheria	3.83	0.51	0.21	0.00	0.00	0.00	–	0.00	–
Haemophilus influenzae, invasive	- - -	- - -	- - -	- - -	- - -	0.51	1.03	1.11	–
Lyme disease [2]	- - -	- - -	- - -	- - -	- - -	- - -	9.86	10.54	–
Measles (Rubeola)	211.01	245.42	23.23	5.96	11.17	0.03	0.02	0.21	–
Meningococcal disease	- - -	- - -	1.23	1.25	0.99	0.83	0.27	0.14	–
Mumps	- - -	- - -	55.55	3.86	2.17	0.13	0.85	0.38	–
Pertussis (whooping cough).	79.82	8.23	2.08	0.76	1.84	2.88	8.97	10.34	–
Poliomyelitis, paralytic [3]	- - -	1.40	0.02	0.00	0.00	–	–	–	–
Rubella (German measles).	- - -	- - -	27.75	1.72	0.45	0.06	0.00	0.00	–
Salmonellosis, excluding typhoid fever.	- - -	3.85	10.84	14.88	19.54	14.51	17.73	16.14	–
Shigellosis	15.45	6.94	6.79	8.41	10.89	8.41	4.82	6.51	–
Spotted fever rickettsiosis [4]	- - -	- - -	0.19	0.52	0.26	0.18	0.65	1.18	–
Tuberculosis [5]	- - -	30.83	18.28	12.25	10.33	6.01	3.64	2.95	–
Sexually transmitted diseases: [6]									
Syphilis [7].	146.02	68.78	44.80	30.30	54.32	11.20	14.93	19.90	23.43
Primary and secondary	16.73	9.06	10.80	12.00	20.26	2.12	4.49	6.27	7.49
Early latent.	39.71	10.11	8.00	8.90	22.19	3.35	4.43	6.10	7.58
Late and late latent [8]	70.22	45.91	24.70	9.20	10.32	5.53	5.89	7.38	8.21
Congenital [9]	368.30	103.70	52.30	7.70	92.95	14.29	8.73	11.72	12.38
Chlamydia [10]	- - -	- - -	- - -	- - -	160.19	251.38	426.01	452.17	478.79
Gonorrhea [11]	192.50	145.40	294.20	442.10	276.43	128.67	100.76	109.79	123.95
Chancroid.	3.34	0.94	0.70	0.30	1.69	0.03	0.01	0.00	0.00
	Number of new cases								
Acute hepatitis A viral infection.	- - -	- - -	56,797	29,087	31,441	13,397	1,670	1,239	–
Acute hepatitis B viral infection.	- - -	- - -	8,310	19,015	21,102	8,036	3,374	2,791	–
Acute hepatitis C viral infection [1]	- - -	- - -	- - -	- - -	2,553	3,197	849	2,204	–
Diphtheria	5,796	918	435	3	4	1	–	1	–
Haemophilus influenzae, invasive	- - -	- - -	- - -	- - -	- - -	1,398	3,151	3,541	–
Lyme disease [2]	- - -	- - -	- - -	- - -	- - -	- - -	30,158	33,461	–
Measles (Rubeola)	319,124	441,703	47,351	13,506	27,786	86	63	667	–
Meningococcal disease	- - -	- - -	2,505	2,840	2,451	2,256	833	433	–
Mumps	- - -	- - -	104,953	8,576	5,292	338	2,612	1,223	–
Pertussis (whooping cough).	120,718	14,809	4,249	1,730	4,570	7,867	27,550	32,971	–
Poliomyelitis, paralytic [3]	- - -	2,525	31	4	6	–	–	–	–
Rubella (German measles).	- - -	- - -	56,552	3,904	1,125	176	5	6	–
Salmonellosis, excluding typhoid fever.	- - -	6,929	22,096	33,715	48,603	39,574	54,424	51,455	–
Shigellosis	23,367	12,487	13,845	19,041	27,077	22,922	14,786	20,745	–
Spotted fever rickettsiosis [4]	464	- - -	380	1,163	651	495	1,985	3,757	–
Tuberculosis [5]	- - -	55,494	37,137	27,749	25,701	16,377	11,182	9,421	–
Sexually transmitted diseases: [6]									
Syphilis [7].	217,558	122,538	91,382	68,832	135,590	31,618	45,844	63,450	74,702
Primary and secondary	23,939	16,145	21,982	27,204	50,578	5,979	13,774	19,999	23,872
Early latent.	59,256	18,017	16,311	20,297	55,397	9,465	13,604	19,452	24,173
Late and late latent [8]	113,569	81,798	50,348	20,979	25,750	15,594	18,079	23,541	26,170
Congenital [9]	13,377	4,416	1,953	277	3,865	580	387	458	487
Chlamydia [10]	- - -	- - -	- - -	- - -	323,663	709,452	1,307,893	1,441,789	1,526,658
Gonorrhea [11]	286,746	258,933	600,072	1,004,029	690,042	363,136	309,341	350,062	395,216
Chancroid.	4,977	1,680	1,416	788	4,212	78	24	6	11

See footnotes at end of table.

Table 33 (page 2 of 2). Selected nationally notifiable disease rates and number of new cases: United States, selected years 1950–2015

Excel and PDF versions (with more data years and standard errors when available): *http://www.cdc.gov/nchs/hus/contents2016.htm#033.*

[Data are based on reporting by state health departments]

0.00 Rate more than zero but less than 0.005.

– Quantity zero.

- - - Data not available.

[1] Anti-HCV antibody test became available May 1990.

[2] Not nationally notifiable. National surveillance case definition revised in 2008; probable cases not previously reported.

[3] Cases of vaccine-associated paralytic poliomyelitis caused by polio vaccine virus.

[4] Prior to 2010 data, cases of spotted fever rickettsiosis were reported as Rocky Mountain spotted fever (RMSF). Because serologic tests commonly used to diagnose RMSF exhibit cross-reactivity between spotted fever rickettsial pathogens, some cases reported as RMSF might actually be disease caused by other spotted fever rickettsial infections, and therefore are more correctly referred to as spotted fever rickettsiosis starting with 2010 data.

[5] Case reporting for tuberculosis began in 1953. Data prior to 1975 are not comparable with subsequent years because of changes in reporting criteria effective in 1975.

[6] For 1950, data for Alaska and Hawaii were not included. Starting with 1991, data include both civilian and military cases. Cases and rates shown do not include U.S. outlying areas of Guam, Puerto Rico, and the Virgin Islands.

[7] Includes stage of syphilis not stated.

[8] Includes cases of unknown duration.

[9] Rates include all cases of congenitally acquired syphilis per 100,000 live births. Cases of congenitally acquired syphilis were reported through 1994. Starting with 1995 data, only congenital syphilis for cases under 1 year of age were reported. See STD Surveillance Report for congenital syphilis rates.

[10] Prior to 1994, chlamydia was not notifiable. In 1994–1999, cases for New York were exclusively reported by New York City. Starting with 2000 data, cases for New York include the entire state.

[11] Data for 1994 do not include cases from Georgia.

NOTES: The total resident population was used to calculate all rates except for sexually transmitted disease rates prior to 1991; STD rates prior to 1991 used the civilian resident population. See Appendix I, Sexually Transmitted Disease (STD) Surveillance; Population Census and Population Estimates. Population data from states where diseases were not notifiable or not available were excluded from the rate calculation; see Appendix II, Notifiable disease. See Appendix I, National Notifiable Disease Surveillance System (NNDSS), for information on underreporting of notifiable diseases. Data for additional years are available. See the Excel spreadsheet on the *Health, United States* website at: http://www.cdc.gov/nchs/hus.htm.

SOURCE: CDC, Office of Public Health Scientific Services (OPHSS); Center for Surveillance, Epidemiology and Laboratory Services (CSELS); Division of Health Informatics and Surveillance (DHIS). MMWR 2016;63(54):1–152 and CDC. Available from: http://www.cdc.gov/mmwr/mmwr_nd/index.html. Sexually transmitted disease surveillance, 2015. Atlanta, GA: U.S. Department of Health and Human Services, 2016. Available from: http://www.cdc.gov/std/stats/. See Appendix I, National Notifiable Diseases Surveillance System (NNDSS); Sexually Transmitted Disease (STD) Surveillance.

Excel and PDF versions (with more data years and standard errors when available): http://www.cdc.gov/nchs/hus/contents2016.htm#034.

[Data are based on reporting by 50 states and the District of Columbia]

Sex, age at diagnosis, Hispanic origin and race, and region of residence	Year of diagnosis [1]					
	2010	2011	2012	2013	2014	2015 [2]
	Number of HIV diagnoses [3]					
All persons [4]	43,978	42,120	41,265	39,632	40,234	39,513
Male, 13 years and over	34,100	33,051	32,720	31,720	32,390	31,991
Female, 13 years and over.	9,642	8,868	8,303	7,723	7,668	7,402
Age at diagnosis						
Under 13 years	236	201	242	189	176	120
13–14 years	42	43	48	42	35	25
15–19 years	2,087	2,005	1,881	1,693	1,726	1,698
20–24 years	7,082	7,078	7,181	7,040	7,312	7,084
25–29 years	6,353	6,381	6,476	6,676	7,156	7,510
30–34 years	5,527	5,282	5,481	5,185	5,458	5,437
35–39 years	5,080	4,476	4,161	3,989	4,283	4,194
40–44 years	5,239	4,814	4,456	3,946	3,787	3,418
45–49 years	4,887	4,583	4,319	3,938	3,633	3,302
50–54 years	3,507	3,371	3,215	2,987	2,916	3,010
55–59 years	2,082	1,990	1,929	2,017	1,952	1,860
60–64 years	1,062	1,074	1,059	1,072	977	996
65 years and over.	794	822	817	858	823	859
Hispanic origin and race [5]						
Not Hispanic or Latino:						
White	11,802	11,311	11,198	10,758	10,769	10,509
Black or African American	20,447	19,323	18,583	17,698	17,842	17,670
American Indian or Alaska Native.	168	151	182	168	200	209
Asian.	697	764	803	816	949	955
Native Hawaiian or Other Pacific Islander	55	56	56	52	43	79
Multiple race	1,643	1,518	1,437	1,318	1,080	801
Hispanic or Latino [6]	9,166	8,997	9,006	8,822	9,351	9,290
Region of residence						
Northeast.	8,362	7,798	7,608	7,052	7,039	6,516
Midwest	5,551	5,411	5,477	5,302	5,090	5,157
South	22,008	21,333	20,477	20,015	20,343	20,408
West	8,057	7,578	7,703	7,263	7,762	7,432

See footnotes at end of table.

Excel and PDF versions (with more data years and standard errors when available): http://www.cdc.gov/nchs/hus/contents2016.htm#034.

[Data are based on reporting by 50 states and the District of Columbia]

Sex, age at diagnosis, Hispanic origin and race, and region of residence	Year of diagnosis [1]					
	2010	2011	2012	2013	2014	2015 [2]
	Number of HIV diagnoses per 100,000 resident population [3]					
All persons [4]	14.2	13.5	13.1	12.5	12.6	12.3
Male, 13 years and over	27.3	26.2	25.7	24.6	24.9	24.4
Female, 13 years and over	7.3	6.7	6.2	5.7	5.6	5.4
Age at diagnosis						
Under 13 years	0.4	0.4	0.5	0.4	0.3	0.2
13–14 years	0.5	0.5	0.6	0.5	0.4	0.3
15–19 years	9.5	9.3	8.8	8.0	8.2	8.0
20–24 years	32.6	31.9	31.8	30.8	31.9	31.2
25–29 years	30.0	30.0	30.3	30.9	32.5	33.4
30–34 years	27.5	25.7	26.2	24.3	25.3	25.1
35–39 years	25.3	22.8	21.3	20.3	21.5	20.6
40–44 years	25.1	22.9	21.2	18.9	18.4	16.9
45–49 years	21.6	20.7	19.9	18.5	17.4	15.8
50–54 years	15.7	14.9	14.2	13.2	12.9	13.5
55–59 years	10.5	9.8	9.3	9.5	9.1	8.5
60–64 years	6.3	6.0	5.9	5.9	5.3	5.2
65 years and over	2.0	2.0	1.9	1.9	1.8	1.8
Hispanic origin and race [5]						
Not Hispanic or Latino:						
White	6.0	5.7	5.7	5.4	5.4	5.3
Black or African American	53.8	50.3	47.9	45.2	45.1	44.3
American Indian or Alaska Native	7.4	6.6	7.9	7.2	8.5	8.8
Asian	4.7	5.0	5.1	5.0	5.6	5.5
Native Hawaiian or Other Pacific Islander	11.0	11.0	10.7	9.7	7.9	14.1
Multiple race	29.1	26.0	23.9	21.3	16.9	12.2
Hispanic or Latino [6]	18.1	17.3	17.0	16.3	16.9	16.4
Region of residence						
Northeast	15.1	14.0	13.6	12.6	12.5	11.6
Midwest	8.3	8.1	8.1	7.8	7.5	7.6
South	19.2	18.4	17.5	16.9	17.0	16.8
West	11.2	10.4	10.5	9.8	10.3	9.8

[1] Based on diagnoses during 2010–2015 that were reported to CDC through June 30, 2016. Includes persons with a diagnosis of HIV infection regardless of the stage of disease (stage 0, 1, 2, 3 [AIDS], or unknown). In 2014, the criteria used to define HIV diagnoses changed. Cases diagnosed before 2014 were classified according to the 2008 HIV case definition. Starting with 2014 data, cases were classified according to the new definition. Because of the change in case definition, HIV diagnoses prior to 2014 are not strictly comparable to HIV diagnoses for 2014. The vertical line in the table represents the discontinuity in the HIV diagnosis trend. See Appendix II, Human immunodeficiency virus (HIV) disease and Acquired immunodeficiency syndrome (AIDS) for discussion of HIV diagnoses reporting definitions and other issues affecting interpretation of trends.

[2] Data for 2015 are preliminary; CDC cautions against using the 2015 data in this report for assessments of trends.

[3] Numbers and rates are point estimates that result from statistical adjustments for missing risk factor information. See Appendix I, National HIV Surveillance System.

[4] All persons totals were calculated independent of values for subpopulations. Consequently, sums of subpopulations may not equal totals for all persons.

[5] Hispanic origin and race categories are mutually exclusive.

[6] Persons of Hispanic origin may be of any race. See Appendix II, Hispanic origin.

NOTES: Data shown are for the 50 states and the District of Columbia, and include newly diagnosed and reported cases. This table does not present HIV incidence or prevalence data. Rates were calculated using vintage 2015 population estimates from the U.S. Census Bureau. Variations in trends among subpopulations may be due to differences in testing behaviors, targeted HIV testing initiatives, or the numbers of new HIV infections in some subpopulations. Caution should be used when interpreting data on diagnoses of HIV infection. HIV surveillance reports may not be representative of all persons with HIV for several reasons: not all infected persons have been tested and diagnosed; results of anonymous tests are not reported to the name-based HIV registries of state and local health departments; testing patterns are influenced by the extent to which testing is routinely offered to specific groups; and surveillance and reporting practices among jurisdictions differ. The data presented here are estimates of the minimum number of persons for whom HIV infection has been diagnosed and reported to the surveillance system. Data have been revised and differ from previous editions of *Health, United States*.

SOURCE: CDC, National Center for HIV/AIDS, Viral Hepatitis, STD, and TB Prevention. Division of HIV/AIDS Prevention. HIV Surveillance Report. Diagnoses of HIV infection in the United States and Dependent Areas, 2015 (vol. 27). Atlanta, GA: U.S. Department of Health and Human Services, CDC. Published November 2016. Available from: https://www.cdc.gov/hiv/pdf/library/reports/surveillance/cdc-hiv-surveillance-report-2015-vol-27.pdf. See Appendix I, National HIV Surveillance System.

Table 35 (page 1 of 5). Health conditions among children under age 18, by selected characteristics: United States, average annual, selected years 1997–1999 through 2013–2015

Excel and PDF versions (with more data years and standard errors when available): http://www.cdc.gov/nchs/hus/contents2016.htm#035.

[Data are based on household interviews of a sample of the civilian noninstitutionalized population]

Characteristic	Current asthma [1]				Asthma attack in the past 12 months [2]			
	1997–1999	*2000–2002*	*2003–2005*	*2013–2015*	*1997–1999*	*2000–2002*	*2003–2005*	*2013–2015*
	Percent of children							
Under 18 years [3]	- - -	- - -	8.7	8.5	5.4	5.7	5.4	4.5
Age								
0–4 years	- - -	- - -	6.1	4.4	4.3	4.7	4.2	2.9
5–17 years	- - -	- - -	9.6	10.0	5.7	6.1	5.8	5.1
5–9 years	- - -	- - -	9.1	9.4	5.6	6.3	6.1	5.5
10–17 years	- - -	- - -	9.9	10.3	5.8	5.9	5.7	4.8
Sex								
Male	- - -	- - -	9.9	9.8	6.2	6.6	6.3	5.2
Female	- - -	- - -	7.3	7.1	4.5	4.7	4.4	3.8
Race [4]								
White only	- - -	- - -	7.7	7.5	5.0	5.2	4.9	4.1
Black or African American only	- - -	- - -	13.0	13.4	7.0	8.0	7.6	6.8
American Indian or Alaska Native only . .	- - -	- - -	12.2	8.9	6.4	*8.7	*6.1	*4.6
Asian only	- - -	- - -	4.8	5.2	4.3	4.7	3.3	2.9
Native Hawaiian or Other Pacific Islander only	- - -	- - -	*	*	- - -	*	*	*
2 or more races	- - -	- - -	13.5	10.9	- - -	7.3	8.8	6.1
Hispanic origin and race [4]								
Hispanic or Latino	- - -	- - -	7.6	7.9	4.8	4.2	4.6	4.2
Not Hispanic or Latino	- - -	- - -	8.9	8.6	5.5	6.0	5.6	4.6
White only	- - -	- - -	7.9	7.5	5.1	5.5	5.0	4.0
Black or African American only	- - -	- - -	13.0	13.4	7.0	7.9	7.5	6.8
Percent of poverty level [5]								
Below 100%	- - -	- - -	10.4	10.9	6.1	7.1	6.5	6.2
100%–199%	- - -	- - -	8.6	8.5	5.3	5.4	5.2	4.4
200%–399%	- - -	- - -	8.3	7.9	5.0	5.3	5.2	4.0
400% or more	- - -	- - -	7.9	6.9	5.2	5.5	4.9	3.7
Health insurance status at the time of interview [6]								
Insured	- - -	- - -	9.0	8.5	5.6	5.9	5.6	4.5
Private	- - -	- - -	8.0	7.4	5.0	5.3	5.0	3.9
Medicaid	- - -	- - -	11.4	10.2	7.7	7.7	7.1	5.5
Uninsured	- - -	- - -	5.6	6.9	3.9	4.3	3.3	3.7

See footnotes at end of table.

Table 35 (page 2 of 5). Health conditions among children under age 18, by selected characteristics: United States, average annual, selected years 1997–1999 through 2013–2015

Excel and PDF versions (with more data years and standard errors when available): http://www.cdc.gov/nchs/hus/contents2016.htm#035.

[Data are based on household interviews of a sample of the civilian noninstitutionalized population]

Characteristic	Attention-deficit/hyperactivity disorder [7]				Serious emotional or behavioral difficulties [8]			
	1997–1999	2000–2002	2003–2005	2013–2015	1997–1999	2000–2002	2003–2005	2013–2015
Age	Percent of children							
5–17 years [3]	6.5	7.5	7.6	10.4	- - -	- - -	5.1	5.7
5–9 years	4.8	5.2	5.6	7.6	- - -	- - -	4.3	5.4
10–17 years	7.6	9.0	8.9	12.1	- - -	- - -	5.6	5.9
Sex								
Male	9.6	10.8	10.7	14.2	- - -	- - -	6.1	7.1
Female	3.2	4.2	4.4	6.4	- - -	- - -	4.1	4.2
Race [4]								
White only	7.1	8.1	7.8	10.8	- - -	- - -	5.1	5.7
Black or African American only	5.0	7.0	7.7	10.2	- - -	- - -	5.3	5.5
American Indian or Alaska Native only	*8.5	*	*9.4	*6.5	- - -	- - -	*	*5.9
Asian only	*1.7	*	*1.6	2.0	- - -	- - -	*1.7	*2.2
Native Hawaiian or Other Pacific Islander only	- - -	*	*	*	- - -	- - -	*	*
2 or more races	- - -	7.4	9.7	15.4	- - -	- - -	8.2	8.9
Hispanic origin and race [4]								
Hispanic or Latino	3.6	4.2	4.6	6.6	- - -	- - -	3.8	4.4
Not Hispanic or Latino	7.0	8.2	8.3	11.6	- - -	- - -	5.4	6.1
White only	7.7	9.0	8.8	12.6	- - -	- - -	5.6	6.4
Black or African American only	5.0	6.8	7.5	10.3	- - -	- - -	5.2	5.5
Percent of poverty level [5]								
Below 100%	7.2	8.2	8.4	12.7	- - -	- - -	7.4	8.1
100%–199%	6.7	7.5	7.8	10.9	- - -	- - -	5.4	6.1
200%–399%	6.2	7.7	7.8	9.4	- - -	- - -	4.9	4.9
400% or more	6.1	7.1	6.9	9.2	- - -	- - -	3.7	4.3
Health insurance status at the time of interview [6]								
Insured	6.7	7.8	7.8	10.7	- - -	- - -	5.2	5.8
Private	5.9	7.0	7.0	9.1	- - -	- - -	4.1	4.3
Medicaid	10.5	10.7	10.3	13.2	- - -	- - -	8.5	8.2
Uninsured	4.8	5.4	6.1	4.9	- - -	- - -	4.6	3.8

See footnotes at end of table.

Table 35 (page 3 of 5). Health conditions among children under age 18, by selected characteristics: United States, average annual, selected years 1997–1999 through 2013–2015

Excel and PDF versions (with more data years and standard errors when available): http://www.cdc.gov/nchs/hus/contents2016.htm#035.

[Data are based on household interviews of a sample of the civilian noninstitutionalized population]

Characteristic	Food allergy[9]				Skin allergy[10]			
	1997–1999	2000–2002	2003–2005	2013–2015	1997–1999	2000–2002	2003–2005	2013–2015
	Percent of children							
Under 18 years[3]	3.4	3.6	3.8	5.6	7.4	8.1	9.6	11.8
Age								
0–4 years	3.8	4.0	4.3	5.7	8.1	8.7	11.0	13.2
5–17 years	3.3	3.4	3.6	5.6	7.2	7.9	9.1	11.3
5–9 years	3.1	3.6	3.5	6.0	7.5	8.6	10.0	12.7
10–17 years	3.4	3.3	3.6	5.3	7.1	7.5	8.6	10.4
Sex								
Male	3.4	3.7	3.8	5.6	7.3	7.9	9.5	11.8
Female	3.5	3.4	3.8	5.6	7.6	8.4	9.8	11.8
Race[4]								
White only	3.5	3.6	3.8	5.4	7.1	7.6	9.0	10.7
Black or African American only	3.1	3.0	3.7	5.8	9.0	10.4	12.4	16.4
American Indian or Alaska Native only	*	*4.8	*	*4.0	*4.1	*9.1	11.3	9.0
Asian only	3.9	4.4	4.3	6.0	8.0	8.4	7.5	11.4
Native Hawaiian or Other Pacific Islander only	- - -	*	*	*	- - -	*	*	*
2 or more races	- - -	5.2	4.6	7.8	- - -	10.9	14.0	15.6
Hispanic origin and race[4]								
Hispanic or Latino	2.1	2.5	2.8	4.6	5.5	5.6	7.2	9.8
Not Hispanic or Latino	3.7	3.8	4.0	5.9	7.8	8.7	10.2	12.5
White only	3.8	3.9	4.1	5.8	7.5	8.2	9.7	11.3
Black or African American only	3.1	3.1	3.7	5.6	9.0	10.4	12.4	16.5
Percent of poverty level[5]								
Below 100%	3.3	3.2	3.3	5.1	7.3	7.1	9.0	11.8
100%–199%	3.0	3.4	3.8	5.4	7.2	7.6	8.7	11.2
200%–399%	3.2	3.4	3.8	5.5	7.3	8.5	10.0	12.0
400% or more	4.2	4.0	4.1	6.3	7.9	8.8	10.5	12.2
Health insurance status at the time of interview[6]								
Insured	3.5	3.7	3.9	5.7	7.7	8.5	10.0	12.0
Private	3.5	3.7	4.0	5.9	7.4	8.5	10.1	12.0
Medicaid	3.6	3.7	3.6	5.2	8.4	8.4	9.5	11.9
Uninsured	2.6	2.4	3.0	4.4	5.9	5.3	6.8	9.1

See footnotes at end of table.

Table 35 (page 4 of 5). Health conditions among children under age 18, by selected characteristics: United States, average annual, selected years 1997–1999 through 2013–2015

Excel and PDF versions (with more data years and standard errors when available): http://www.cdc.gov/nchs/hus/contents2016.htm#035.

[Data are based on household interviews of a sample of the civilian noninstitutionalized population]

Characteristic	Hay fever or respiratory allergy [11]				Three or more ear infections [12]			
	1997–1999	2000–2002	2003–2005	2013–2015	1997–1999	2000–2002	2003–2005	2013–2015
	Percent of children							
Under 18 years [3]	17.5	17.7	17.3	15.6	7.1	6.7	5.8	5.0
Age								
0–4 years.	10.7	10.4	10.1	9.1	13.7	12.8	11.0	9.2
5–17 years	19.9	20.3	20.0	18.0	4.8	4.5	3.8	3.4
5–9 years	17.3	18.1	17.9	16.7	7.1	6.9	5.7	5.2
10–17 years.	21.6	21.7	21.2	18.9	3.2	2.9	2.7	2.3
Sex								
Male.	18.6	18.8	18.9	17.3	7.3	6.9	5.9	5.1
Female	16.3	16.5	15.6	13.9	6.9	6.5	5.6	4.8
Race [4]								
White only	17.9	18.5	17.8	15.7	7.4	7.2	6.3	5.4
Black or African American only.	16.2	15.6	15.2	15.1	5.9	5.0	4.1	3.5
American Indian or Alaska Native only	15.2	16.4	16.5	12.9	*10.8	*6.3	*5.1	7.2
Asian only	15.3	12.6	11.3	12.2	3.7	2.6	3.3	2.1
Native Hawaiian or Other Pacific								
Islander only	- - -	*	*	*	- - -	*	*	*
2 or more races	- - -	20.9	20.8	20.3	- - -	7.4	5.0	5.0
Hispanic origin and race [4]								
Hispanic or Latino	12.4	12.4	12.8	12.8	6.1	6.7	6.2	5.5
Not Hispanic or Latino	18.4	18.8	18.3	16.5	7.3	6.7	5.7	4.8
White only	19.1	19.9	19.4	17.0	7.7	7.3	6.3	5.4
Black or African American only	16.3	15.5	15.1	15.2	5.9	4.9	4.0	3.4
Percent of poverty level [5]								
Below 100%.	14.3	14.0	14.2	13.3	8.3	7.9	6.7	6.2
100%–199%.	15.4	15.6	16.0	14.2	7.1	6.8	5.7	4.9
200%–399%.	18.5	18.1	17.7	16.2	6.8	6.5	5.6	4.7
400% or more.	20.3	21.1	19.7	18.1	6.6	6.1	5.5	4.3
Health insurance status at the time of interview [6]								
Insured	18.0	18.3	17.7	15.7	7.3	6.9	5.8	5.0
Private.	18.8	19.2	18.5	16.9	6.6	6.4	5.2	4.5
Medicaid	15.0	16.0	16.1	14.1	10.2	8.7	7.4	5.7
Uninsured	14.3	12.6	13.5	14.1	5.9	4.9	5.4	4.4

See footnotes at end of table.

Table 35 (page 5 of 5). Health conditions among children under age 18, by selected characteristics: United States, average annual, selected years 1997–1999 through 2013–2015

Excel and PDF versions (with more data years and standard errors when available): http://www.cdc.gov/nchs/hus/contents2016.htm#035.

[Data are based on household interviews of a sample of the civilian noninstitutionalized population]

- - - Data not available.

* Estimates are considered unreliable. Data preceded by an asterisk have a relative standard error (RSE) of 20%–30%. Data not shown have an RSE greater than 30%.

[1] Based on parent or knowledgeable adult responding to both questions, "Has a doctor or other health professional ever told you that your child had asthma?" and "Does your child still have asthma?"

[2] Based on parent or knowledgeable adult responding to both questions, "Has a doctor or other health professional ever told you that your child had asthma?" and "During the past 12 months, did your child have an episode of asthma or an asthma attack?"

[3] Includes all other races not shown separately and unknown health insurance status.

[4] The race groups, white, black, American Indian or Alaska Native, Asian, Native Hawaiian or Other Pacific Islander, and 2 or more races, include persons of Hispanic and non-Hispanic origin. Persons of Hispanic origin may be of any race. Starting with 1999 data, race-specific estimates are tabulated according to the 1997 *Revisions to the Standards for the Classification of Federal Data on Race and Ethnicity* and are not strictly comparable with estimates for earlier years. The five single-race categories plus multiple-race categories shown in the table conform to the 1997 Standards. Starting with 1999 data, race-specific estimates are for persons who reported only one racial group; the category 2 or more races includes persons who reported more than one racial group. Prior to 1999, data were tabulated according to the 1977 Standards with four racial groups, and the Asian only category included Native Hawaiian or Other Pacific Islander. Estimates for single-race categories prior to 1999 included persons who reported one race or, if they reported more than one race, identified one race as best representing their race. Starting with 2003 data, race responses of other race and unspecified multiple race were treated as missing, and then race was imputed if these were the only race responses. Almost all persons with a race response of other race were of Hispanic origin. See Appendix II, Hispanic origin; Race.

[5] Percent of poverty level is based on family income and family size and composition using U.S. Census Bureau poverty thresholds. Missing family income data were imputed for 1997 and beyond. See Appendix II, Family income; Poverty; Table VI.

[6] Health insurance categories are mutually exclusive. Persons who reported both Medicaid and private coverage are classified as having private coverage. Starting with 1997 data, state-sponsored health plan coverage is included as Medicaid coverage. Starting with 1999 data, coverage by the Children's Health Insurance Program (CHIP) is included as Medicaid coverage. In addition to private and Medicaid, the insured category also includes military, other government, and Medicare coverage. Persons not covered by private insurance, Medicaid, CHIP, state-sponsored or other government-sponsored health plans, Medicare, or military plans are considered to have no health insurance coverage. Persons with only Indian Health Service coverage are considered to have no health insurance coverage. See Appendix II, Health insurance coverage.

[7] Based on parent or knowledgeable adult responding to the question, "Has a doctor or health professional ever told you that your child had attention-deficit/hyperactivity disorder (ADHD) or attention deficit disorder (ADD)?"

[8] Based on parent or knowledgeable adult responding to the question, "Overall, do you think that [child] has difficulties in any of the following areas: emotions, concentration, behavior, or being able to get along with other people?"

[9] Based on parent or knowledgeable adult responding to the question, "During the past 12 months, has your child had any kind of food or digestive allergy?"

[10] Based on parent or knowledgeable adult responding to the question, "During the past 12 months, has your child had any eczema or any kind of skin allergy?"

[11] Based on parent or knowledgeable adult responding to the questions, "During the past 12 months, has your child had hay fever?" or to the question, "During the past 12 months, has your child had any kind of respiratory allergy?"

[12] Based on parent or knowledgeable adult responding to the question, "During the past 12 months, has your child had three or more ear infections?"

NOTES: Standard errors are available in the spreadsheet version of this table. Available from: http://www.cdc.gov/nchs/hus.htm. Data for additional years are available. See the Excel spreadsheet on the *Health, United States* website at: http://www.cdc.gov/nchs/hus.htm.

SOURCE: NCHS, National Health Interview Survey, family core and sample child questionnaires. See Appendix I, National Health Interview Survey (NHIS).

Table 36 (page 1 of 4). Age-adjusted cancer incidence rates for selected cancer sites, by sex, race, and Hispanic origin: United States, selected geographic areas, selected years 1990–2013

Excel and PDF versions (with more data years and standard errors when available): http://www.cdc.gov/nchs/hus/contents2016.htm#036.

[Data are based on the Surveillance, Epidemiology, and End Results (SEER) Program's 13 population-based cancer registries]

Site, sex, race, and Hispanic origin	1990	1995	2000	2003	2005	2010	2011	2012	2013	1990–2013 APC[1]
All sites	Number of new cases per 100,000 population[2]									
All persons.	475.8	471.4	475.2	463.4	460.8	450.7	443.0	429.3	419.5	†–0.5
White	483.3	477.4	485.8	474.1	473.1	462.0	454.8	439.5	429.9	†–0.4
Black or African American	515.2	539.4	525.9	514.3	505.3	483.9	476.8	464.4	444.2	†–0.7
American Indian or Alaska Native[3]	348.1	371.7	365.9	380.6	404.1	406.8	377.7	357.0	367.6	0.1
Asian or Pacific Islander	335.4	340.6	341.5	334.4	331.9	324.1	321.8	310.5	305.3	†–0.5
Hispanic or Latino[4]	356.1	359.9	362.0	358.3	365.0	348.9	351.3	336.7	327.4	†–0.3
White, not Hispanic or Latino[4].	495.2	491.2	503.6	492.4	491.3	482.7	474.6	459.5	451.1	†–0.3
Male	584.1	564.7	565.6	545.9	534.9	512.8	498.3	468.5	454.4	†–1.0
White	591.1	563.5	569.8	550.9	543.6	519.9	506.6	475.1	460.4	†–1.0
Black or African American	688.5	742.9	707.2	669.6	637.6	596.0	571.6	548.4	523.1	†–1.5
American Indian or Alaska Native[3]	395.1	424.0	374.7	448.0	426.4	456.7	403.9	350.0	377.3	–0.3
Asian or Pacific Islander	386.0	398.9	400.4	387.5	371.8	347.2	343.9	317.3	309.9	†–1.1
Hispanic or Latino[4]	417.5	440.7	436.6	423.9	426.9	398.8	392.1	365.6	343.9	†–0.9
White, not Hispanic or Latino[4].	606.7	577.3	588.9	569.3	561.8	540.8	526.9	495.4	483.2	†–0.9
Female	411.5	410.6	414.0	407.1	409.8	406.6	404.6	403.7	397.6	†–0.1
White	421.3	423.2	430.0	422.3	424.8	421.2	419.1	417.2	412.0	0.0
Black or African American	406.5	403.2	404.0	410.1	416.2	406.0	411.6	406.8	389.9	0.0
American Indian or Alaska Native[3]	316.5	338.6	366.2	336.1	389.0	378.3	364.1	370.2	365.7	†0.6
Asian or Pacific Islander	295.7	297.8	300.9	299.7	306.9	312.0	310.0	310.3	307.3	†0.2
Hispanic or Latina[4]	322.7	310.5	317.9	318.0	326.3	318.4	327.6	321.9	322.7	0.1
White, not Hispanic or Latina[4].	430.7	436.7	446.0	439.9	442.4	440.8	437.8	436.3	431.5	0.1
Lung and bronchus										
Male	95.0	86.9	77.8	75.5	71.5	63.1	60.8	58.8	55.9	†–2.1
White	94.1	85.0	76.3	74.3	70.8	62.8	60.3	58.0	55.1	†–2.1
Black or African American	134.2	137.0	111.7	112.1	98.0	82.2	82.7	81.6	74.1	†–2.6
American Indian or Alaska Native[3]	77.3	82.8	62.6	74.2	67.4	67.1	55.6	45.2	53.2	†–1.2
Asian or Pacific Islander	64.4	60.1	63.9	58.7	58.2	51.0	50.0	48.8	48.5	†–1.3
Hispanic or Latino[4]	59.4	52.4	45.2	46.5	43.9	34.5	35.6	33.9	33.8	†–2.1
White, not Hispanic or Latino[4].	97.4	88.4	80.2	77.9	74.6	67.2	64.2	62.0	58.8	†–1.9
Female	47.2	49.3	48.6	49.8	50.0	46.1	44.9	44.4	43.2	†–0.4
White	48.5	51.7	50.7	52.4	51.9	48.1	46.6	46.1	45.1	†–0.3
Black or African American	52.9	50.0	55.1	55.5	58.4	52.9	50.0	52.0	48.1	–0.1
American Indian or Alaska Native[3]	30.4	46.1	38.5	41.4	45.5	37.2	42.1	34.6	27.5	0.5
Asian or Pacific Islander	28.4	27.6	27.3	29.1	30.8	29.2	31.3	29.0	29.2	†0.3
Hispanic or Latina[4]	26.2	25.2	24.3	24.4	22.9	24.8	23.8	22.8	24.5	†–0.4
White, not Hispanic or Latina[4].	50.8	54.8	54.4	56.6	56.4	52.0	50.8	50.3	49.1	–0.1
Colon and rectum										
Male	72.3	63.2	62.6	58.4	54.7	46.9	45.4	43.6	42.3	†–2.1
White	73.0	62.5	62.0	57.1	54.1	45.4	43.6	42.1	40.3	†–2.3
Black or African American	73.1	75.2	73.6	76.3	67.0	57.7	57.0	55.7	55.8	†–1.4
American Indian or Alaska Native[3]	61.9	66.2	48.7	70.4	65.6	64.7	65.0	57.7	53.6	–0.2
Asian or Pacific Islander	60.9	58.8	58.0	53.3	47.7	45.5	45.6	42.3	42.5	†–1.6
Hispanic or Latino[4]	47.7	46.0	50.5	47.4	47.4	42.0	43.5	40.2	38.2	†–0.9
White, not Hispanic or Latino[4].	75.0	63.9	63.4	58.1	54.8	46.0	43.6	42.4	40.8	†–2.4
Female	50.2	45.9	46.1	43.6	41.4	36.0	34.7	33.6	32.1	†–1.6
White	49.7	45.4	45.6	42.9	40.3	34.5	33.8	32.8	31.5	†–1.7
Black or African American	61.3	54.9	58.1	55.4	54.2	46.5	42.5	41.5	38.6	†–1.4
American Indian or Alaska Native[3]	45.8	47.9	39.1	45.1	48.3	42.9	46.0	45.4	48.9	–0.2
Asian or Pacific Islander	37.8	38.9	37.5	36.4	36.9	34.6	31.6	28.8	27.5	†–1.4
Hispanic or Latina[4]	34.5	31.9	34.1	33.6	33.7	30.7	29.3	28.1	26.8	†–0.7
White, not Hispanic or Latina[4].	50.9	46.7	46.7	44.0	41.3	35.0	34.6	33.7	32.5	†–1.7
Prostate										
Male	166.9	166.6	179.0	165.5	154.1	143.8	137.2	111.5	104.6	†–2.0
White	168.5	161.3	174.9	161.7	150.1	139.3	132.9	105.6	99.6	†–2.1
Black or African American	219.5	279.7	291.6	253.7	243.8	219.9	208.2	181.4	170.0	†–2.0
American Indian or Alaska Native[3]	98.3	93.5	71.5	113.1	94.4	83.8	66.6	62.0	58.9	†–2.2
Asian or Pacific Islander	88.6	104.7	108.1	105.2	95.8	79.2	79.6	63.9	56.7	†–2.1
Hispanic or Latino[4]	119.2	141.2	150.6	139.3	132.8	118.9	110.2	94.5	83.1	†–1.8
White, not Hispanic or Latino[4].	172.2	163.6	178.7	165.3	152.7	143.2	137.3	108.3	103.4	†–2.0

See footnotes at end of table.

Table 36 (page 2 of 4). Age-adjusted cancer incidence rates for selected cancer sites, by sex, race, and Hispanic origin: United States, selected geographic areas, selected years 1990–2013

Excel and PDF versions (with more data years and standard errors when available): http://www.cdc.gov/nchs/hus/contents2016.htm#036.

[Data are based on the Surveillance, Epidemiology, and End Results (SEER) Program's 13 population-based cancer registries]

Site, sex, race, and Hispanic origin	1990	1995	2000	2003	2005	2010	2011	2012	2013	1990–2013 APC[1]
Breast	Number of new cases per 100,000 population[2]									
Female	129.4	130.9	134.2	124.2	124.5	123.5	126.7	126.3	126.2	†–0.3
White	134.2	136.3	140.6	129.1	129.6	127.3	130.5	129.3	129.1	†–0.3
Black or African American	117.4	123.0	122.8	123.3	119.3	123.5	129.2	130.8	126.4	†0.3
American Indian or Alaska Native[3]	69.6	96.7	100.2	94.1	105.6	91.7	105.3	97.2	89.7	0.3
Asian or Pacific Islander	88.1	88.4	94.9	92.2	95.7	100.7	102.7	104.3	107.4	†0.7
Hispanic or Latina[4]	91.0	89.4	97.0	88.0	93.0	87.3	96.0	91.7	93.4	0.1
White, not Hispanic or Latina[4].	138.6	141.9	147.0	135.8	136.2	135.5	137.4	137.1	137.0	–0.2
Cervix uteri										
Female	11.9	9.9	8.9	8.2	7.9	7.2	7.0	6.9	6.6	†–2.4
White	11.2	9.2	8.9	7.9	7.8	7.2	7.2	6.8	6.5	†–2.1
Black or African American	16.7	14.9	10.7	10.8	9.3	8.5	7.8	7.7	8.1	†–3.5
American Indian or Alaska Native[3]	14.7	*	*	*	10.7	8.3	9.5	*	9.4	†–1.9
Asian or Pacific Islander	12.2	11.2	8.0	8.1	7.8	6.5	5.4	6.7	5.7	†–3.8
Hispanic or Latina[4]	21.3	17.4	17.1	14.0	13.7	10.5	9.3	9.4	8.2	†–3.9
White, not Hispanic or Latina[4].	9.7	7.8	7.1	6.5	6.4	6.2	6.5	6.0	5.9	†–1.9
Corpus and uterus, not otherwise specified										
Female	24.7	24.9	23.9	23.6	24.1	26.7	26.6	27.0	26.4	†0.4
White	26.4	26.4	25.6	25.0	25.4	27.6	27.2	28.0	26.9	†0.2
Black or African American	17.0	17.9	17.4	20.3	21.5	24.6	27.7	25.1	27.0	†2.2
American Indian or Alaska Native[3]	19.3	*	18.5	19.5	14.4	27.6	20.5	19.3	27.1	*
Asian or Pacific Islander	13.5	17.8	16.6	16.6	18.9	22.5	21.7	22.3	22.4	†1.8
Hispanic or Latina[4]	17.7	16.5	15.8	17.8	19.3	20.4	22.1	23.9	23.3	†1.6
White, not Hispanic or Latina[4].	27.1	27.5	26.9	26.0	26.2	28.6	27.7	28.4	27.2	0.1
Ovary										
Female	15.6	14.6	14.2	13.6	13.2	12.5	12.2	12.3	11.4	†–1.1
White	16.4	15.4	15.0	14.3	13.9	13.4	12.9	13.0	11.9	†–1.1
Black or African American	11.3	10.8	10.9	11.6	10.8	9.6	10.0	10.6	8.8	†–0.5
American Indian or Alaska Native[3]	21.9	*	18.9	13.4	12.2	11.9	11.6	15.7	10.9	*
Asian or Pacific Islander	11.1	10.4	10.4	10.2	11.0	9.8	9.6	9.6	9.7	†–0.5
Hispanic or Latina[4]	12.2	11.7	10.6	11.6	11.8	11.8	11.2	12.2	10.0	–0.4
White, not Hispanic or Latina[4].	16.8	15.9	15.6	14.7	14.1	13.4	13.1	13.0	12.1	†–1.1
Oral cavity and pharynx										
Male	18.5	16.5	15.8	15.2	15.1	15.5	15.9	15.6	16.3	†–0.6
White	18.0	16.4	15.6	15.3	15.5	16.1	16.9	16.4	16.9	–0.3
Black or African American	25.4	22.3	19.4	17.6	15.9	13.8	13.9	14.0	14.2	†–2.7
American Indian or Alaska Native[3]	*	*	*	16.3	10.4	21.3	16.0	15.4	12.8	*
Asian or Pacific Islander	14.9	11.8	13.7	11.9	11.5	11.7	10.9	10.7	12.5	†–0.9
Hispanic or Latino[4]	10.7	12.3	9.1	8.8	9.8	8.9	10.8	10.0	8.9	†–0.6
White, not Hispanic or Latino[4].	18.8	16.9	16.6	16.3	16.4	17.5	18.1	17.6	18.5	0.0
Female	7.3	7.0	6.2	6.0	6.1	6.1	6.1	6.3	6.1	†–0.8
White	7.4	7.1	6.2	5.9	6.0	6.3	6.3	6.5	6.3	†–0.7
Black or African American	6.4	6.7	5.4	6.7	6.9	5.4	5.2	4.5	5.2	†–1.5
American Indian or Alaska Native[3]	*	*	*	*	*	*	*	7.4	8.8	*
Asian or Pacific Islander	6.1	5.2	6.3	5.1	5.9	5.2	4.8	5.9	5.2	†–0.8
Hispanic or Latina[4]	4.0	3.7	3.7	3.9	3.5	4.2	3.7	3.9	4.1	–0.3
White, not Hispanic or Latina[4].	7.8	7.5	6.6	6.2	6.4	6.7	6.9	7.0	6.8	†–0.6
Stomach										
Male	14.6	13.5	12.6	11.8	11.4	10.5	10.6	10.1	10.0	†–1.7
White	12.8	11.9	10.6	10.1	9.6	9.3	9.5	8.8	8.7	†–1.6
Black or African American	21.5	18.6	18.6	18.7	17.4	13.3	14.1	14.8	14.2	†–2.1
American Indian or Alaska Native[3]	*	24.1	20.2	*	20.8	20.7	21.2	16.1	22.8	–0.3
Asian or Pacific Islander	26.8	24.5	23.0	19.2	20.2	15.3	14.2	14.9	14.3	†–2.9
Hispanic or Latino[4]	20.2	19.3	16.1	16.2	15.5	14.9	14.2	13.0	12.1	†–1.9
White, not Hispanic or Latino[4].	12.1	11.1	10.0	9.2	8.7	8.3	8.5	7.9	7.8	†–1.9

See footnotes at end of table.

Table 36 (page 3 of 4).

Table 36 (page 3 of 4). Age-adjusted cancer incidence rates for selected cancer sites, by sex, race, and Hispanic origin: United States, selected geographic areas, selected years 1990–2013

Excel and PDF versions (with more data years and standard errors when available): http://www.cdc.gov/nchs/hus/contents2016.htm#036.

[Data are based on the Surveillance, Epidemiology, and End Results (SEER) Program's 13 population-based cancer registries]

Site, sex, race, and Hispanic origin	1990	1995	2000	2003	2005	2010	2011	2012	2013	1990–2013 APC[1]
Stomach	Number of new cases per 100,000 population[2]									
Female	6.7	6.2	6.1	6.0	5.7	5.7	5.6	5.9	5.4	†–0.8
White	5.7	5.1	5.0	5.0	4.7	4.7	4.8	5.0	4.5	†–0.8
Black or African American	10.0	9.8	8.7	9.5	8.1	8.5	9.4	8.1	6.9	†–1.2
American Indian or Alaska Native[3]	*	*	*	*	*	13.0	*	12.1	12.3	*
Asian or Pacific Islander	15.4	13.0	12.9	11.1	10.3	8.9	7.8	8.8	8.8	†–2.7
Hispanic or Latina[4]	10.8	11.2	10.6	10.3	10.2	9.4	8.8	9.6	8.8	†–1.0
White, not Hispanic or Latina[4]	5.1	4.5	4.2	4.1	3.8	3.6	3.9	3.9	3.5	†–1.5
Pancreas										
Male	13.0	12.8	12.8	12.5	13.7	13.7	14.2	14.0	14.1	†0.6
White	12.7	12.4	12.6	12.3	13.4	13.5	14.2	14.5	14.0	†0.7
Black or African American	19.3	19.1	18.2	17.4	18.3	18.6	17.0	16.1	17.8	–0.3
American Indian or Alaska Native[3]	*	*	*	*	21.2	17.4	17.7	*	13.0	*
Asian or Pacific Islander	11.0	10.3	10.7	10.2	11.8	11.4	12.2	10.3	12.1	0.2
Hispanic or Latino[4]	10.7	12.0	12.2	10.1	12.3	11.5	13.4	10.7	11.8	†0.7
White, not Hispanic or Latino[4]	12.8	12.4	12.7	12.7	13.6	13.8	14.3	15.0	14.3	†0.7
Female	10.0	9.9	9.9	10.4	10.8	11.2	10.6	11.3	11.0	†0.6
White	9.7	9.6	9.6	10.2	10.6	10.9	10.4	11.0	11.0	†0.7
Black or African American	12.9	15.5	12.8	14.4	16.4	15.1	15.1	15.1	13.3	–0.1
American Indian or Alaska Native[3]	*	*	20.4	*	12.4	12.9	*	12.1	*	*
Asian or Pacific Islander	9.9	8.1	9.2	8.1	8.0	10.5	9.1	10.3	9.4	†1.0
Hispanic or Latina[4]	9.9	9.0	9.1	8.6	11.1	9.9	10.2	10.4	11.2	0.3
White, not Hispanic or Latina[4]	9.7	9.7	9.6	10.5	10.6	11.1	10.4	11.1	10.9	†0.7
Urinary bladder										
Male	37.2	35.4	36.8	37.0	37.0	35.9	33.9	34.2	32.7	†–0.3
White	40.7	38.8	40.8	40.8	40.9	40.0	38.1	38.0	36.2	†–0.2
Black or African American	19.7	19.7	20.2	23.2	23.2	22.2	20.7	23.3	22.6	†0.5
American Indian or Alaska Native[3]	*	*	*	*	16.8	17.4	17.7	*	13.7	*
Asian or Pacific Islander	15.4	17.2	16.9	18.1	17.5	17.3	14.9	16.4	15.5	0.2
Hispanic or Latino[4]	22.4	17.8	20.4	20.2	20.2	18.5	19.9	18.8	18.1	–0.4
White, not Hispanic or Latino[4]	42.4	40.9	43.2	43.4	43.6	43.2	41.0	41.0	39.3	–0.1
Female	9.5	9.3	9.1	9.2	9.0	8.6	8.3	8.3	7.8	†–0.6
White	10.0	10.1	10.0	10.0	9.7	9.4	9.1	9.3	8.5	†–0.5
Black or African American	8.7	7.3	7.8	7.8	7.9	7.0	7.1	6.0	7.7	–0.5
American Indian or Alaska Native[3]	*	*	*	*	*	*	*	*	*	
Asian or Pacific Islander	5.2	4.5	4.3	5.0	5.2	4.7	4.4	4.1	3.8	–0.3
Hispanic or Latina[4]	5.8	5.3	5.8	4.7	5.9	4.7	5.6	4.8	4.4	†–0.6
White, not Hispanic or Latina[4]	10.3	10.6	10.5	10.8	10.3	10.2	9.8	10.1	9.3	†–0.3
Non-Hodgkin lymphoma										
Male	22.6	25.1	23.6	24.3	24.7	25.4	23.7	23.6	23.6	0.1
White	23.6	26.2	25.0	25.7	25.9	26.6	25.0	24.9	24.7	†0.2
Black or African American	17.7	21.7	17.6	19.4	19.6	21.4	17.4	17.4	17.6	–0.1
American Indian or Alaska Native[3]	*	*	15.3	*	23.2	19.6	10.8	13.8	10.4	*
Asian or Pacific Islander	16.7	16.5	16.4	16.4	17.9	17.5	18.1	17.6	17.9	0.3
Hispanic or Latino[4]	17.3	21.0	20.5	19.5	19.9	22.8	19.9	19.4	19.6	0.3
White, not Hispanic or Latino[4]	24.3	26.7	25.5	26.5	27.0	27.2	25.7	25.9	25.7	†0.3
Female	14.5	15.2	16.0	17.2	16.5	17.0	15.8	16.1	15.6	†0.5
White	15.4	15.9	16.9	18.0	17.7	18.1	16.6	17.1	16.5	†0.6
Black or African American	10.4	10.3	11.9	13.5	13.3	12.7	12.9	13.6	12.8	†1.2
American Indian or Alaska Native[3]	*	*	13.5	*	12.2	13.0	16.5	11.1	12.8	*
Asian or Pacific Islander	9.5	12.2	11.5	12.7	9.7	11.9	12.0	11.4	10.8	0.4
Hispanic or Latina[4]	13.6	13.1	13.8	15.3	15.0	15.5	14.6	15.2	14.5	†0.7
White, not Hispanic or Latina[4]	15.6	16.2	17.3	18.4	18.1	18.4	17.0	17.2	16.9	†0.6

See footnotes at end of table.

Table 36 (page 4 of 4). Age-adjusted cancer incidence rates for selected cancer sites, by sex, race, and Hispanic origin: United States, selected geographic areas, selected years 1990–2013

Excel and PDF versions (with more data years and standard errors when available): http://www.cdc.gov/nchs/hus/contents2016.htm#036.

[Data are based on the Surveillance, Epidemiology, and End Results (SEER) Program's 13 population-based cancer registries]

Site, sex, race, and Hispanic origin	1990	1995	2000	2003	2005	2010	2011	2012	2013	1990–2013 APC [1]
Leukemia	Number of new cases per 100,000 population [2]									
Male	17.2	17.7	17.2	17.4	17.5	18.1	17.7	17.3	16.8	0.1
White	18.0	19.0	18.2	18.5	19.1	19.6	19.0	18.2	18.1	[†]0.2
Black or African American	16.2	13.4	14.3	15.1	12.9	13.7	14.3	14.9	14.0	0.1
American Indian or Alaska Native [3]	*	*	*	*	12.3	*	9.8	14.6	11.4	*
Asian or Pacific Islander	8.4	10.2	10.6	10.5	9.4	10.1	10.4	10.5	8.7	−0.1
Hispanic or Latino [4]	12.2	14.6	13.3	12.3	13.2	13.2	13.8	11.5	12.7	0.3
White, not Hispanic or Latino [4]	18.3	19.3	18.7	19.1	19.5	20.1	19.6	19.0	18.6	[†]0.2
Female	9.9	10.3	10.4	10.1	10.1	10.7	10.5	10.6	10.3	[†]0.3
White	10.3	10.9	11.0	10.7	10.7	11.5	11.4	11.3	11.2	[†]0.4
Black or African American	8.5	8.4	9.8	9.1	9.6	9.1	9.4	9.2	8.4	0.1
American Indian or Alaska Native [3]	*	*	*	*	*	8.7	*	7.0	8.1	*
Asian or Pacific Islander	5.7	6.4	6.4	6.5	6.4	6.1	6.4	6.6	6.2	0.0
Hispanic or Latina [4]	8.5	8.2	7.8	7.2	8.3	8.7	8.7	8.8	9.6	[†]0.6
White, not Hispanic or Latina [4]	10.3	11.1	11.1	11.2	10.7	11.8	11.6	11.4	11.2	[†]0.5

[†] Annual percent change (APC) is significantly different from zero (p < 0.05).

0.0 APC is greater than –0.05 but less than 0.05.

* Estimates are considered unreliable. Data not shown if the rate is based on fewer than 16 cases for the time interval. The trend is not shown if it is based on fewer than 10 cases for at least 1 year within the time interval.

[1] APC was calculated by fitting a linear regression model to the natural logarithm of the yearly rates from 1990–2013.

[2] Age-adjusted by 5-year age groups to the year 2000 U.S. standard population. Age-adjusted rates are based on at least 16 cases. See Appendix II, Age adjustment.

[3] Estimates for the American Indian or Alaska Native populations are based on the Contract Health Service Delivery Area (CHSDA) counties within SEER areas.

[4] Hispanic data exclude cases from Alaska. The race groups, white, black, Asian or Pacific Islander, and American Indian or Alaska Native, include persons of Hispanic and non-Hispanic origin. Persons of Hispanic origin may be of any race. The North American Association of Central Cancer Registries (NAACCR) Hispanic Identification Algorithm was used on a combination of variables to classify cases as Hispanic for analytic purposes. See the report, NAACCR guideline for enhancing Hispanic-Latino identification, for more information. Available from: http://seer.cancer.gov/seerstat/variables/seer/yr1973_2006/race_ethnicity/. See Appendix II, Hispanic origin.

NOTES: See Appendix II, Incidence. Estimates are based on 13 SEER areas (November 2015 submission) and differ from published estimates based on 9 SEER areas or other submission dates. See Appendix I, Surveillance, Epidemiology, and End Results Program (SEER). The site variable distinguishes Kaposi Sarcoma and Mesothelioma as individual cancer sites. As a result, Kaposi Sarcoma and Mesothelioma cases do not contribute to other cancer sites. Estimates for 2001–2009 were computed using intercensal population estimates based on the 2000 and 2010 censuses. Data have been revised and differ from previous editions of *Health, United States*. Data for additional years are available. See the Excel spreadsheet on the *Health, United States* website at: http://www.cdc.gov/nchs/hus.htm.

SOURCE: National Institutes of Health, National Cancer Institute, Surveillance, Epidemiology, and End Results Program. Available from: http://www.seer.cancer.gov. See Appendix I, Surveillance, Epidemiology, and End Results Program (SEER).

Table 37. Five-year relative cancer survival rates for selected cancer sites, by race and sex: United States, selected geographic areas, selected years 1975–1977 through 2006–2012

Excel and PDF versions (with more data years and standard errors when available): http://www.cdc.gov/nchs/hus/contents2016.htm#037.

[Data are based on the Surveillance, Epidemiology, and End Results (SEER) Program's nine population-based cancer registries]

Sex and site	White					Black or African American				
	1975–1977	1981–1983	1987–1989	1999–2001	2006–2012	1975–1977	1981–1983	1987–1989	1999–2001	2006–2012
Both sexes					Percent of patients					
All sites	49.8	51.3	56.7	67.2	70.0	39.0	38.8	43.0	57.9	62.7
Oral cavity and pharynx	54.1	54.0	55.9	62.2	68.7	36.0	30.8	34.0	44.6	47.2
Esophagus.	5.5	7.3	10.5	18.8	21.7	3.5	4.3	6.6	12.5	12.5
Stomach.	14.1	16.2	18.3	22.3	30.2	16.1	16.4	18.8	23.0	30.3
Colon	50.9	55.4	60.6	66.6	66.7	44.7	48.5	52.3	52.5	56.9
Rectum	48.3	52.0	58.7	66.5	68.0	44.4	40.3	52.3	59.2	64.7
Pancreas	2.5	2.5	3.2	5.0	8.5	2.3	3.6	5.5	5.6	8.0
Lung and bronchus	12.2	13.3	13.3	15.5	19.0	11.2	11.3	10.9	12.6	15.9
Urinary bladder	73.3	77.4	79.8	81.0	78.9	50.3	59.5	62.6	67.4	66.1
Non-Hodgkin lymphoma	46.8	50.8	51.3	64.9	73.6	48.6	49.5	46.0	55.7	65.2
Leukemia	34.6	38.0	43.9	51.8	63.5	33.4	33.9	35.0	43.2	57.5
Male										
All sites	42.7	46.6	52.8	67.5	70.3	32.7	34.2	38.9	61.0	65.6
Oral cavity and pharynx	53.8	52.8	54.1	62.0	68.3	29.7	25.3	30.0	39.4	44.5
Esophagus.	4.8	6.5	11.0	18.6	21.8	2.0	3.7	5.3	10.6	10.5
Stomach.	13.1	15.4	15.5	21.0	28.8	16.1	16.2	16.6	25.0	24.1
Colon	50.5	56.1	61.4	67.8	67.0	44.0	44.6	50.7	53.6	56.8
Rectum	47.3	51.0	58.9	66.5	67.6	41.4	38.1	47.7	60.0	59.4
Pancreas	2.7	2.1	3.1	5.5	8.9	2.5	3.7	5.1	3.7	8.6
Lung and bronchus	11.1	11.7	12.0	13.3	16.4	10.5	10.1	10.8	10.8	13.3
Prostate gland.	68.5	73.1	84.4	99.7	99.7	60.7	62.8	71.1	97.3	97.3
Urinary bladder	74.3	78.5	82.0	81.5	80.2	56.5	64.9	67.5	71.6	70.9
Non-Hodgkin lymphoma	46.3	50.5	48.1	62.8	72.9	42.6	49.2	41.7	48.9	61.3
Leukemia	33.6	37.8	45.5	52.7	64.7	30.4	33.4	32.7	44.2	60.1
Female										
All sites	56.5	56.0	60.6	66.8	69.7	46.2	44.4	47.7	54.3	59.5
Colon	51.3	54.8	59.9	65.5	66.3	45.3	51.5	53.7	51.6	57.0
Rectum	49.4	53.2	58.4	66.4	68.7	46.8	42.5	56.9	58.2	70.1
Pancreas	2.3	3.0	3.3	4.4	8.0	1.9	3.2	5.8	7.4	7.4
Lung and bronchus	15.4	16.6	15.3	18.0	21.8	13.8	14.9	11.1	15.2	19.0
Melanoma of skin	86.2	87.2	91.3	94.6	95.1	*	*	89.5	76.1	76.2
Breast	75.6	77.1	85.1	90.8	92.0	62.2	63.4	71.1	78.8	81.5
Cervix uteri	69.7	67.8	72.5	73.4	70.6	64.6	59.2	57.0	66.0	58.4
Corpus and uterus, not otherwise specified	88.0	82.2	83.9	85.9	85.6	60.0	50.7	56.7	61.4	65.7
Ovary	35.3	38.4	38.1	43.5	46.0	41.9	37.5	33.7	35.6	38.1
Non-Hodgkin lymphoma	47.3	51.1	55.2	67.5	74.5	55.3	49.8	51.0	63.8	69.2

* Data for population groups with fewer than 25 cases are not shown because estimates are considered unreliable.

NOTES: Rates are based on follow-up of patients through 2013. The rate is the ratio of the observed survival rate for the patient group to the expected survival rate for persons in the general population similar to the patient group with respect to age, sex, race, and calendar year of observation. It estimates the chance of surviving the effects of cancer. See Appendix II, Relative survival rate. The site variable distinguishes Kaposi Sarcoma and Mesothelioma as individual cancer sites. As a result, Kaposi Sarcoma and Mesothelioma cases are excluded from each of the sites shown except all sites combined. The race groups, white and black, include persons of Hispanic and non-Hispanic origin. Due to death certificate race-ethnicity classification and other methodological issues related to developing life tables, relative survival rates for race-ethnicity groups other than white and black are not calculated. Data have been revised and differ from previous editions of *Health, United States*. Data for additional years are available. See the Excel spreadsheet on the *Health, United States* website at: http://www.cdc.gov/nchs/hus.htm.

SOURCE: National Institutes of Health, National Cancer Institute, Surveillance, Epidemiology, and End Results Program. Available from: http://www.seer.cancer.gov. See Appendix I, Surveillance, Epidemiology, and End Results Program (SEER).

Table 38 (page 1 of 2). **Respondent-reported prevalence of heart disease, cancer, and stroke among adults aged 18 and over, by selected characteristics: United States, average annual, selected years 1997–1998 through 2014–2015**

Excel and PDF versions (with more data years and standard errors when available): http://www.cdc.gov/nchs/hus/contents2016.htm#038.

[Data are based on household interviews of a sample of the civilian noninstitutionalized population]

Characteristic	Heart disease[1]				Cancer[2]				Stroke[3]			
	1997–1998	1999–2000	2010–2011	2014–2015	1997–1998	1999–2000	2010–2011	2014–2015	1997–1998	1999–2000	2010–2011	2014–2015
	Percent of adults											
18 years and over, age-adjusted[4,5]	12.0	11.1	11.1	10.7	4.9	5.1	6.0	5.9	2.3	2.2	2.6	2.4
18 years and over, crude[5].	11.6	10.9	11.6	11.6	4.8	4.9	6.3	6.5	2.2	2.1	2.7	2.7
Age												
18–44 years	4.6	4.3	4.0	4.3	1.7	1.7	1.7	1.6	0.4	0.4	0.6	0.5
18–24 years.	3.2	3.3	3.0	3.3	0.8	1.0	0.7	*0.5	*	*	*	*
25–44 years.	5.0	4.6	4.4	4.7	2.0	1.9	2.0	2.0	0.4	0.5	0.7	0.7
45–64 years	13.5	12.6	13.0	11.9	5.4	5.2	6.9	6.6	2.3	2.0	2.9	2.8
45–54 years.	10.9	10.0	9.6	8.5	4.0	4.0	4.9	4.2	1.4	1.3	2.1	1.8
55–64 years.	17.4	16.6	17.1	15.5	7.4	7.2	9.3	9.1	3.8	3.1	3.9	3.9
65 years and over	31.8	29.6	30.5	29.2	14.1	15.2	18.5	18.4	8.1	8.1	8.2	7.5
65–74 years.	27.8	25.8	25.6	25.3	12.4	13.1	15.9	15.0	6.7	6.2	6.3	5.5
75 years and over.	37.0	34.3	36.5	34.8	16.2	17.7	21.7	23.2	9.8	10.3	10.6	10.5
Sex[4]												
Male	12.3	11.9	12.4	11.9	4.1	4.4	5.5	5.3	2.6	2.4	2.6	2.5
Female.	11.8	10.5	10.2	9.8	5.8	5.8	6.6	6.5	2.1	2.1	2.6	2.3
Sex and age												
Male:												
18–44 years.	3.7	3.6	3.7	4.2	0.8	0.8	0.9	0.9	0.3	0.3	0.5	0.5
45–54 years.	11.0	10.0	9.5	8.4	2.0	2.0	3.1	2.7	1.2	1.3	1.9	1.7
55–64 years.	18.7	19.7	19.1	17.4	5.8	5.9	7.5	7.4	4.6	3.7	4.0	4.1
65–74 years.	32.0	30.4	31.3	31.2	12.8	13.9	16.9	14.6	8.1	6.7	6.6	6.6
75 years and over.	40.8	39.2	44.7	41.5	18.3	20.3	26.1	26.1	11.2	11.3	10.6	10.6
Female:												
18–44 years.	5.5	4.9	4.3	4.4	2.6	2.5	2.5	2.2	0.4	0.4	0.6	0.6
45–54 years.	10.8	9.9	9.6	8.6	6.0	5.9	6.6	5.6	1.5	1.4	2.2	1.9
55–64 years.	16.2	13.8	15.3	13.9	8.8	8.4	10.9	10.6	3.2	2.6	3.9	3.8
65–74 years.	24.5	22.0	20.6	20.2	12.1	12.5	15.0	15.3	5.5	5.8	6.1	4.6
75 years and over.	34.6	31.2	30.9	30.1	14.9	16.1	18.7	21.2	9.0	9.6	10.6	10.3
Race[4,6]												
White only	12.2	11.3	11.2	11.0	5.2	5.4	6.3	6.3	2.2	2.1	2.3	2.3
Black or African American only	11.4	10.6	10.7	9.7	3.5	3.5	5.1	4.5	3.3	3.5	4.1	3.8
American Indian or Alaska Native only . .	18.6	14.7	12.5	13.4	*6.5	*5.7	6.5	5.3	*5.0	*5.4	*4.7	*2.6
Asian only	6.9	6.3	7.2	6.5	2.4	*2.3	3.0	2.9	*1.2	*1.2	2.4	1.4
Native Hawaiian or Other Pacific Islander only	- - -	*	*	*	- - -	*	*	*	- - -	*	*	*
2 or more races	- - -	17.0	16.7	16.5	- - -	*4.7	7.9	6.0	- - -	*4.0	*3.9	3.7
Hispanic origin and race[4,6]												
Hispanic or Latino	8.7	8.0	8.4	8.0	2.9	3.0	3.4	3.9	2.1	1.9	2.7	2.4
Mexican.	7.5	7.4	8.4	7.7	3.0	2.8	3.2	3.7	2.5	2.0	2.6	2.7
Not Hispanic or Latino.	12.2	11.4	11.4	11.1	5.1	5.2	6.3	6.1	2.3	2.2	2.6	2.4
White only.	12.5	11.6	11.7	11.5	5.4	5.5	6.7	6.6	2.2	2.1	2.3	2.3
Black or African American only.	11.4	10.5	10.8	9.8	3.6	3.6	5.1	4.4	3.3	3.5	4.2	3.9
Education[7,8]												
No high school diploma or GED.	15.1	13.8	14.6	13.8	5.3	5.5	5.8	5.8	3.9	3.8	4.4	4.1
High school diploma or GED	12.8	11.9	12.4	12.0	5.5	5.8	6.8	6.8	2.5	2.5	3.4	3.1
Some college or more.	12.7	12.0	11.9	11.5	6.0	5.9	7.4	7.1	2.1	1.9	2.3	2.2

See footnotes at end of table.

Table 38 (page 2 of 2). Respondent-reported prevalence of heart disease, cancer, and stroke among adults aged 18 and over, by selected characteristics: United States, average annual, selected years 1997–1998 through 2014–2015

Excel and PDF versions (with more data years and standard errors when available): http://www.cdc.gov/nchs/hus/contents2016.htm#038.

[Data are based on household interviews of a sample of the civilian noninstitutionalized population]

Characteristic	Heart disease [1]				Cancer [2]				Stroke [3]			
	1997–1998	1999–2000	2010–2011	2014–2015	1997–1998	1999–2000	2010–2011	2014–2015	1997–1998	1999–2000	2010–2011	2014–2015
Percent of poverty level [4,9]					Percent of adults							
Below 100%.	15.3	13.6	13.9	13.7	4.9	4.9	5.3	5.8	4.3	3.7	4.6	4.3
100%–199%.	13.2	12.0	12.3	12.0	4.8	5.3	5.9	5.5	3.1	3.2	3.7	3.6
200%–399%.	11.5	11.0	11.3	10.7	4.9	5.1	6.2	5.9	2.1	2.1	2.5	2.4
400% or more	11.0	10.2	9.8	9.5	5.2	5.1	6.2	6.2	1.6	1.5	1.5	1.4
Hispanic origin and race and percent of poverty level [4,6,9]												
Hispanic or Latino:												
Below 100%	9.7	9.7	9.4	10.2	2.2	2.3	2.9	4.3	3.0	2.0	3.4	3.5
100%–199%	8.7	8.4	8.3	8.0	2.8	3.2	2.6	3.4	2.2	2.2	3.2	2.7
200%–399%	8.4	8.2	8.5	6.8	2.7	2.7	4.7	4.6	*1.8	*2.3	2.2	*2.0
400% or more	8.4	5.6	7.5	7.8	*5.5	*4.5	3.3	3.8	*	*	*2.1	*1.1
Not Hispanic or Latino:												
White only:												
Below 100%	17.8	15.2	15.8	16.2	6.3	6.2	6.8	7.4	4.4	3.8	4.4	4.2
100%–199%.	14.1	12.8	13.8	13.7	5.6	6.2	7.3	6.7	3.2	3.0	3.6	3.6
200%–399%.	12.2	11.6	11.8	11.8	5.2	5.5	6.8	6.5	2.1	2.1	2.3	2.4
400% or more	11.3	10.6	10.2	9.9	5.4	5.3	6.6	6.7	1.6	1.5	1.4	1.4
Black or African American only:												
Below 100%.	14.6	13.0	14.7	12.8	4.4	4.0	4.5	4.5	5.0	4.5	6.2	5.8
100%–199%.	12.9	11.2	11.2	11.4	3.3	3.2	5.2	4.4	4.2	5.1	4.6	5.0
200%–399%.	9.2	10.2	10.5	8.5	3.2	3.7	5.3	4.4	2.5	2.7	3.9	2.9
400% or more	9.5	8.9	7.3	7.4	4.0	4.3	5.6	4.3	*	*	*2.1	2.4
Geographic region [4]												
Northeast	11.6	10.6	10.1	10.1	4.5	5.0	5.6	5.6	1.8	1.8	2.0	1.9
Midwest	12.1	11.4	11.5	12.3	5.1	5.2	6.7	5.9	2.3	2.2	2.6	2.7
South	12.5	11.5	12.1	10.9	5.0	5.0	6.2	6.1	2.6	2.5	2.9	2.6
West	11.1	10.4	9.9	9.3	5.1	5.0	5.5	5.8	2.1	2.0	2.4	2.2
Location of residence [4,10]												
Within MSA	11.7	10.7	10.8	10.3	4.9	5.0	5.9	5.8	2.2	2.1	2.4	2.3
Outside MSA	12.8	12.5	13.0	13.1	5.1	5.5	6.7	6.3	2.7	2.5	3.4	2.9

* Estimates are considered unreliable. Data preceded by an asterisk have a relative standard error (RSE) of 20%–30%. Data not shown have an RSE greater than 30%.
- - - Data not available.

[1] Heart disease is based on self-reported responses to questions about whether respondents had ever been told by a doctor or other health professional that they had coronary heart disease, angina (angina pectoris), a heart attack (myocardial infarction), or any other kind of heart disease or heart condition.

[2] Cancer is based on self-reported responses to a question about whether respondents had ever been told by a doctor or other health professional that they had cancer or a malignancy of any kind. Excludes squamous cell and basal cell carcinomas.

[3] Stroke is based on self-reported responses to a question about whether respondents had ever been told by a doctor or other health professional that they had a stroke.

[4] Estimates are age-adjusted to the year 2000 standard population using five age groups: 18–44 years, 45–54 years, 55–64 years, 65–74 years, and 75 years and over. Age-adjusted estimates in this table may differ from other age-adjusted estimates based on the same data and presented elsewhere if different age groups are used in the adjustment procedure. See Appendix II, Age adjustment.

[5] Includes all other races not shown separately and unknown education level.

[6] The race groups, white, black, American Indian or Alaska Native, Asian, Native Hawaiian or Other Pacific Islander, and 2 or more races, include persons of Hispanic and non-Hispanic origin. Persons of Hispanic origin may be of any race. Starting with 1999 data, race-specific estimates are tabulated according to the 1997 *Revisions to the Standards for the Classification of Federal Data on Race and Ethnicity* and are not strictly comparable with estimates for earlier years. The five single-race categories plus multiple-race categories shown in the table conform to the 1997 Standards. Starting with 1999 data, race-specific estimates are for persons who reported only one racial group; the category 2 or more races includes persons who reported more than one racial group. Prior to 1999, data were tabulated according to the 1977 Standards with four racial groups, and the Asian only category included Native Hawaiian or Other Pacific Islander. Estimates for single-race categories prior to 1999 included persons who reported one race or, if they reported more than one race, identified one race as best representing their race. Starting with 2003 data, race responses of other race and unspecified multiple race were treated as missing, and then race was imputed if these were the only race responses. Almost all persons with a race response of other race were of Hispanic origin. See Appendix II, Hispanic origin; Race.

[7] Estimates are for persons aged 25 and over and are age-adjusted to the year 2000 standard population using five age groups: 25–44 years, 45–54 years, 55–64 years, 65–74 years, and 75 years and over. See Appendix II, Age adjustment.

[8] GED is General Educational Development high school equivalency diploma. See Appendix II, Education.

[9] Percent of poverty level is based on family income and family size and composition using U.S. Census Bureau poverty thresholds. Missing family income data were imputed for 1997–1998 and beyond. See Appendix II, Family income; Poverty; Table VI.

[10] MSA is metropolitan statistical area. Starting with 2006 data, MSA status is determined using 2000 census data and the 2000 standards for defining MSAs. For data prior to 2006, see Appendix II, Metropolitan statistical area (MSA) for the applicable standards.

NOTES: Standard errors are available in the spreadsheet version of this table. Available from: http://www.cdc.gov/nchs/hus.htm. Data for additional years are available. See the Excel spreadsheet on the *Health, United States* website at: http://www.cdc.gov/nchs/hus.htm.

SOURCE: NCHS, National Health Interview Survey, family core and sample adult questionnaires. See Appendix I, National Health Interview Survey (NHIS).

Table 39 (page 1 of 2). Number of respondent-reported chronic conditions from 10 selected conditions among adults aged 18 and over, by selected characteristics: United States, selected years 2002–2015

Excel and PDF versions (with more data years and standard errors when available): http://www.cdc.gov/nchs/hus/contents2016.htm#039.

[Data are based on household interviews of a sample of the civilian noninstitutionalized population]

| Characteristic | Number of respondent-reported chronic conditions from 10 selected conditions [1] | | | | | | | | | | | |
| | 0–1 chronic conditions | | | | 2–3 chronic conditions | | | | 4 or more chronic conditions | | | |
	2002	2010	2013	2015	2002	2010	2013	2015	2002	2010	2013	2015
	Percent distribution											
Total, age-adjusted [2,3]	78.5	75.4	76.7	76.7	17.9	19.9	19.0	18.8	3.6	4.6	4.3	4.5
Total, crude [2]	78.5	74.0	74.5	74.1	17.9	21.1	20.8	20.7	3.6	4.9	4.7	5.1
Age												
18–64 years	85.1	81.3	82.4	82.6	12.9	16.0	14.9	14.7	2.0	2.8	2.6	2.7
18–44 years	93.3	92.2	93.2	92.8	6.2	7.2	6.3	6.7	0.5	0.6	0.4	0.5
18–24 years.	96.4	96.6	97.1	97.2	3.5	3.3	2.8	2.8	*	*	*	*
25–44 years.	92.3	90.7	91.8	91.3	7.1	8.6	7.6	8.1	0.7	0.8	0.6	0.7
45–64 years	71.4	66.2	67.7	68.8	24.2	28.1	26.6	25.5	4.4	5.7	5.6	5.7
45–54 years.	78.4	74.1	76.2	77.3	18.6	22.3	20.1	19.3	3.1	3.6	3.7	3.3
55–64 years.	60.9	56.4	58.4	59.8	32.7	35.3	33.8	32.0	6.4	8.3	7.8	8.2
65 years and over	44.6	37.9	39.1	38.4	43.4	46.5	46.8	46.3	12.0	15.6	14.1	15.3
65–74 years.	47.6	41.2	42.6	42.5	41.4	45.5	45.2	44.4	11.0	13.2	12.2	13.1
75 years and over.	41.1	33.8	34.4	32.4	45.8	47.7	48.9	49.0	13.2	18.6	16.7	18.5
Sex [3]												
Male	79.7	76.2	77.6	77.4	16.5	19.3	18.2	18.1	3.8	4.5	4.3	4.6
Female.	77.3	74.7	75.9	76.1	19.1	20.5	19.8	19.4	3.6	4.8	4.3	4.5
Race [3,4]												
White only	78.8	76.0	76.9	77.1	17.7	19.5	19.0	18.5	3.5	4.5	4.1	4.4
Black or African American only	74.3	70.4	72.9	71.9	21.3	23.8	21.4	22.5	4.4	5.8	5.7	5.6
American Indian or Alaska Native only . .	69.5	64.7	71.4	71.5	25.5	28.8	21.4	20.1	*	*	*7.2	*8.4
Asian only	86.5	82.9	84.6	83.5	11.3	14.4	12.8	14.7	*	2.8	2.7	*1.8
Native Hawaiian or Other Pacific Islander only	*	*	*	*	*	*	*	*	*	*	*	*
2 or more races	72.3	66.6	70.3	72.5	20.2	23.2	21.4	17.1	*7.6	*10.2	8.3	10.4
Hispanic origin and race [3,4]												
Hispanic or Latino	82.2	78.0	80.0	79.7	14.8	17.9	16.1	16.2	3.0	4.1	3.9	4.1
Mexican.	81.8	77.7	80.0	79.2	15.0	18.0	15.9	16.3	3.2	4.3	4.1	4.5
Not Hispanic or Latino.	78.0	75.1	76.2	76.3	18.3	20.2	19.5	19.2	3.7	4.7	4.3	4.6
White only.	78.3	75.6	76.2	76.4	18.1	19.8	19.6	19.1	3.6	4.5	4.2	4.5
Black or African American only.	74.3	70.1	72.6	71.9	21.3	24.0	21.7	22.6	4.4	5.8	5.7	5.5
Percent of poverty level [3,5]												
Below 100%.	71.9	69.2	69.7	68.1	21.3	22.7	21.9	23.3	6.8	8.1	8.4	8.6
100%–199%.	76.4	72.6	73.6	73.3	18.6	21.0	20.7	20.6	5.0	6.4	5.7	6.1
200%–399%.	77.8	75.6	76.9	76.6	18.9	19.9	18.9	18.9	3.3	4.5	4.2	4.5
400% or more	81.2	78.3	80.0	80.5	15.9	18.7	17.5	16.6	2.8	3.0	2.5	2.9
Health insurance status at the time of interview [6,7]												
18–64 years:												
Insured	85.1	82.5	84.1	84.4	13.0	15.0	13.5	13.4	1.9	2.5	2.4	2.3
Private	86.9	84.9	87.0	87.3	11.8	13.6	11.7	11.4	1.2	1.5	1.3	1.3
Medicaid	69.2	69.6	71.4	71.9	22.3	22.3	20.8	21.1	8.5	8.1	7.8	6.9
Uninsured.	87.5	85.9	86.6	88.0	10.7	12.4	12.0	10.4	1.8	1.7	1.4	1.5

See footnotes at end of table.

Table 39 (page 2 of 2). Number of respondent-reported chronic conditions from 10 selected conditions among adults aged 18 and over, by selected characteristics: United States, selected years 2002–2015

Excel and PDF versions (with more data years and standard errors when available): http://www.cdc.gov/nchs/hus/contents2016.htm#039.

[Data are based on household interviews of a sample of the civilian noninstitutionalized population]

| | Number of respondent-reported chronic conditions from 10 selected conditions [1] | | | | | | | | | | | |
| | 0–1 chronic conditions | | | | 2–3 chronic conditions | | | | 4 or more chronic conditions | | | |
Characteristic	2002	2010	2013	2015	2002	2010	2013	2015	2002	2010	2013	2015
Geographic region [3]				Percent distribution								
Northeast	79.4	77.7	78.3	78.4	17.4	18.1	17.4	18.0	3.1	4.1	4.3	3.5
Midwest	78.4	73.7	75.5	75.0	17.9	21.2	20.2	19.8	3.7	5.1	4.3	5.3
South	77.3	73.9	75.4	75.9	18.6	21.0	20.0	19.2	4.0	5.2	4.6	4.9
West	79.7	77.6	78.9	78.7	17.0	18.5	17.4	17.5	3.3	3.9	3.6	3.8
Location of residence [3,8]												
Within MSA	79.1	76.1	77.5	77.6	17.5	19.5	18.5	18.2	3.4	4.4	4.0	4.3
Outside MSA	76.0	71.7	72.3	72.0	19.6	22.6	22.2	22.2	4.4	5.7	5.6	5.8

* Estimates are considered unreliable. Data preceded by an asterisk have a relative standard error (RSE) of 20%–30%. Data not shown have an RSE greater than 30%.

[1] Adults were categorized as having 0–1, 2–3, or 4 or more of the following chronic conditions: hypertension, coronary heart disease, stroke, diabetes, cancer, arthritis, hepatitis, weak or failing kidneys, chronic obstructive pulmonary disease, or current asthma. Data from the National Health Interview Survey capture 10 of 20 chronic conditions used in a standardized approach for defining chronic conditions in the United States. Thus, these estimates are conservative in nature. For more information, see: Goodman RA, Posner SF, Huang ES, Parekh AK, Koh HK. Defining and measuring chronic conditions: imperatives for research, policy, program, and practice. Prev Chronic Dis 2013;10:120239. Available from: http://www.cdc.gov/pcd/issues/2013/12_0239.htm, and Ward BW, Schiller JS. Prevalence of multiple chronic conditions among US adults: estimates from the National Health Interview Survey, 2010. Prev Chronic Dis 2013;10:120203. Available from: http://www.cdc.gov/pcd/issues/2013/12_0203.htm.

[2] Includes all other races not shown separately and unknown health insurance status.

[3] Estimates are age-adjusted to the year 2000 standard population using five age groups: 18–44 years, 45–54 years, 55–64 years, 65–74 years, and 75 years and over. See Appendix II, Age adjustment.

[4] The race groups, white, black, American Indian or Alaska Native, Asian, Native Hawaiian or Other Pacific Islander, and 2 or more races, include persons of Hispanic and non-Hispanic origin. Persons of Hispanic origin may be of any race. Race-specific estimates are tabulated according to the 1997 *Revisions to the Standards for the Classification of Federal Data on Race and Ethnicity*. The five single-race categories plus multiple-race categories shown in the table conform to the 1997 Standards. Race-specific estimates are for persons who reported only one racial group; the category 2 or more races includes persons who reported more than one racial group. Starting with 2003 data, race responses of other race and unspecified multiple race were treated as missing, and then race was imputed if these were the only race responses. Almost all persons with a race response of other race were of Hispanic origin. See Appendix II, Hispanic origin; Race.

[5] Percent of poverty level is based on family income and family size and composition using U.S. Census Bureau poverty thresholds. Missing family income data were imputed. See Appendix II, Family income; Poverty; Table VI.

[6] Estimates are age-adjusted to the year 2000 standard population using three age groups: 18–44 years, 45–54 years, and 55–64 years. See Appendix II, Age adjustment.

[7] Health insurance categories are mutually exclusive. Persons who reported both Medicaid and private coverage are classified as having private coverage. State-sponsored health plan coverage is included as Medicaid coverage. Coverage by the Children's Health Insurance Program (CHIP) is included with Medicaid coverage. In addition to private and Medicaid, the insured category also includes military plans, other government-sponsored health plans, and Medicare, not shown separately. Persons not covered by private insurance, Medicaid, CHIP, state-sponsored or other government-sponsored health plans (starting in 1997), Medicare, or military plans are considered to have no health insurance coverage. Persons with only Indian Health Service coverage are considered to have no health insurance coverage. See Appendix II, Health insurance coverage.

[8] MSA is metropolitan statistical area. Starting with 2006 data, MSA status is determined using 2000 census data and the 2000 standards for defining MSAs. For data prior to 2006, see Appendix II, Metropolitan statistical area (MSA) for the applicable standards.

NOTES: Standard errors are available in the spreadsheet version of this table. See http://www.cdc.gov/nchs/hus.htm. Data for additional years are available. See the Excel spreadsheet on the *Health, United States* website at: http://www.cdc.gov/nchs/hus.htm.

SOURCE: NCHS, National Health Interview Survey, family core and sample adult questionnaires. See Appendix I, National Health Interview Survey (NHIS).

Table 40 (page 1 of 3). Diabetes prevalence and glycemic control among adults aged 20 and over, by sex, age, and race and Hispanic origin: United States, selected years 1988–1994 through 2011–2014

Excel and PDF versions (with more data years and standard errors when available): http://www.cdc.gov/nchs/hus/contents2016.htm#040.

[Data are based on interviews and physical examinations of a sample of the civilian noninstitutionalized population]

Sex, age, and race and Hispanic origin [3]	Physician-diagnosed and undiagnosed diabetes [1,2]				Physician-diagnosed diabetes [1]				Undiagnosed diabetes [2]			
	1988– 1994	1999– 2002	2007– 2010	2011– 2014	1988– 1994	1999– 2002	2007– 2010	2011– 2014	1988– 1994	1999– 2002	2007– 2010	2011– 2014
20 years and over, age-adjusted [4]	Percent of population											
All persons [5]	8.8	9.9	11.4	11.9	5.2	6.6	8.1	9.0	3.6	3.2	3.3	2.9
Male.	9.6	11.2	13.2	12.8	5.5	7.3	8.8	9.4	4.1	3.9	4.4	3.3
Female	8.2	8.6	9.8	11.2	5.1	5.9	7.4	8.7	3.2	2.7	2.4	2.4
Not Hispanic or Latino:												
White only.	7.7	8.5	9.6	9.6	4.8	5.5	6.7	7.6	2.9	3.0	2.8	2.0
Black or African American only . .	16.3	14.0	18.4	18.0	9.1	9.2	13.2	13.4	7.2	4.8	5.1	4.6
Asian only.	- - -	- - -	- - -	16.3	- - -	- - -	- - -	10.4	- - -	- - -	- - -	5.9
Hispanic or Latino	- - -	- - -	17.1	16.8	- - -	- - -	12.3	12.1	- - -	- - -	4.8	4.7
Mexican origin	15.6	13.9	18.9	18.0	10.7	10.8	13.4	13.0	5.0	3.1	5.5	5.1
Percent of poverty level: [6]												
Below 100%	14.2	14.6	13.8	17.4	8.8	9.0	10.1	13.4	*5.4	5.6	3.7	3.9
100% or more	8.1	9.3	10.9	11.2	4.8	6.4	7.6	8.5	3.3	2.9	3.3	2.7
100%–199%	9.7	13.1	14.8	15.0	5.2	9.4	11.0	10.5	4.4	*3.6	3.8	4.5
200% or more.	7.8	8.2	10.0	9.7	4.7	5.5	6.8	7.7	3.1	2.7	3.2	2.1
200%–399%	7.8	10.5	12.3	11.4	4.3	7.3	8.9	8.6	3.6	3.2	3.3	2.8
400% or more	7.8	6.7	7.9	8.6	5.3	4.3	4.9	7.2	2.5	2.3	3.0	*1.4
20 years and over, crude												
All persons [5]	8.3	9.8	12.0	12.6	4.9	6.6	8.5	9.6	3.4	3.2	3.5	3.0
Male.	8.6	10.8	13.4	13.2	4.9	7.1	8.9	9.7	3.7	3.7	4.5	3.5
Female	8.0	8.9	10.7	12.1	5.0	6.1	8.2	9.5	3.1	2.8	2.5	2.5
Not Hispanic or Latino:												
White only.	7.6	8.9	10.9	11.0	4.7	5.6	7.6	8.7	2.9	3.2	3.2	2.3
Black or African American only . .	13.3	12.5	17.0	17.5	7.2	8.3	12.3	13.0	6.1	4.2	4.6	4.6
Asian only.	- - -	- - -	- - -	15.1	- - -	- - -	- - -	9.3	- - -	- - -	- - -	5.8
Hispanic or Latino	- - -	- - -	13.6	13.8	- - -	- - -	9.5	9.8	- - -	- - -	4.1	4.0
Mexican origin	10.4	9.3	13.7	14.3	6.3	7.2	9.4	10.1	4.1	2.0	4.3	4.2
Percent of poverty level: [6]												
Below 100%	11.6	13.4	11.4	15.0	7.2	8.4	8.3	11.2	4.4	5.1	3.1	3.7
100% or more	7.6	9.2	11.8	12.3	4.5	6.3	8.3	9.4	3.1	2.9	3.6	2.9
100%–199%	9.1	12.9	15.8	16.8	5.2	9.3	11.7	12.1	3.9	*3.6	4.1	4.7
200% or more.	7.1	8.0	10.6	10.8	4.3	5.4	7.2	8.4	2.8	2.6	3.4	2.3
200%–399%	6.8	10.2	13.0	12.3	3.7	7.0	9.4	9.3	3.1	*3.1	3.5	3.0
400% or more	7.6	6.4	8.7	9.5	5.2	4.1	5.4	7.7	*2.5	2.3	3.2	*1.8
Age												
20–44 years	*2.1	4.4	3.3	4.0	*	3.2	2.1	2.6	1.1	*	1.1	1.4
45–64 years	14.0	12.8	15.3	16.6	7.9	8.3	11.4	12.3	6.0	4.5	3.9	4.3
65 years and over.	19.4	20.4	28.1	26.3	12.7	13.7	19.3	21.9	6.7	6.7	8.8	4.3

See footnotes at end of table.

Table 40 (page 2 of 3). Diabetes prevalence and glycemic control among adults aged 20 and over, by sex, age, and race and Hispanic origin: United States, selected years 1988–1994 through 2011–2014

Excel and PDF versions (with more data years and standard errors when available): http://www.cdc.gov/nchs/hus/contents2016.htm#040.

[Data are based on interviews and physical examinations of a sample of the civilian noninstitutionalized population]

Sex, age, and race and Hispanic origin [3]	Poor glycemic control (A1c greater than 9%) among persons with physician-diagnosed diabetes			
	1988–1994	1999–2002	2007–2010	2011–2014
20 years and over, age-adjusted [4]	Percent of population with physician-diagnosed diabetes			
All persons [5]	26.3	24.7	18.3	20.6
Male.	22.4	27.7	20.8	24.1
Female	29.4	*20.3	15.8	18.0
Not Hispanic or Latino:				
White only.	23.7	*22.9	*11.2	*16.6
Black or African American only . .	38.9	25.4	30.4	23.9
Asian only.	- - -	- - -	- - -	*17.3
Hispanic or Latino	- - -	- - -	26.9	29.8
Mexican origin	29.8	28.0	*24.3	27.6
Percent of poverty level: [6]				
Below 100%	37.2	30.6	22.9	27.3
100% or more	22.8	*22.6	17.2	18.3
100%–199%	*	*	*	21.7
200% or more.	21.2	*25.6	18.0	*16.6
200%–399%	*24.2	*27.0	*20.2	*13.5
400% or more	*	*	*	*
20 years and over, crude				
All persons [5]	23.3	18.4	12.5	15.6
Male.	20.2	20.2	14.0	15.4
Female	25.8	16.7	11.0	15.7
Not Hispanic or Latino:				
White only.	20.6	13.6	9.5	12.0
Black or African American only . .	34.2	25.4	19.0	19.0
Asian only.	- - -	- - -	- - -	*12.8
Hispanic or Latino	- - -	- - -	19.8	25.5
Mexican origin	29.2	26.8	19.6	22.9
Percent of poverty level: [6]				
Below 100%	30.2	25.6	18.5	23.2
100% or more	21.4	15.9	11.1	13.6
100%–199%	24.2	*14.9	9.8	13.9
200% or more.	20.0	16.4	11.8	13.4
200%–399%	*21.2	*17.5	12.4	13.1
400% or more	*18.3	*	*11.2	*13.8
Age				
20–44 years	29.5	*32.7	24.9	26.2
45–64 years	26.0	19.9	14.1	17.8
65 years and over.	18.0	*10.2	6.8	9.2

See footnotes at end of table.

Excel and PDF versions (with more data years and standard errors when available): http://www.cdc.gov/nchs/hus/contents2016.htm#040.

[Data are based on interviews and physical examinations of a sample of the civilian noninstitutionalized population]

- - - Data not available.

* Estimates are considered unreliable. Data preceded by an asterisk have a relative standard error (RSE) of 20%–30%. Data not shown have an RSE greater than 30%.

[1] Physician-diagnosed diabetes was obtained by self-report and excludes women who were pregnant.

[2] Undiagnosed diabetes is defined as a fasting plasma glucose (FPG) of at least 126 mg/dL or a hemoglobin A1c of at least 6.5% and no reported physician diagnosis. Respondents had fasted for at least 8 hours and less than 24 hours. Pregnant females are excluded. Estimates in some prior editions of *Health, United States* included data from respondents who had fasted for at least 9 hours and less than 24 hours. Starting in 2005–2006, testing was performed at a different laboratory and using different instruments than testing in earlier years. The National Health and Nutrition Examination Survey (NHANES) conducted crossover studies to evaluate the impact of these changes on FPG and A1c measurements and recommended adjustments to the FPG data. The adjustments recommended by NHANES were incorporated into the data presented here. For more information, see http://wwwn.cdc.gov/nchs/nhanes/2005-2006/GLU_D.htm. Prior to *Health, United States, 2010*, the definition of undiagnosed diabetes did not consider hemoglobin A1c. The revised definition of undiagnosed diabetes was based on recommendations from the American Diabetes Association. For more information, see Standards of medical care in diabetes—2010. Diabetes Care 2010;33(suppl 1):S11-S61. To ensure data comparability, the revised definition of undiagnosed diabetes was applied to all data in this table. Also see Appendix II, Diabetes.

[3] Persons of Hispanic and Mexican origin may be of any race. Starting with 1999 data, race-specific estimates are tabulated according to the 1997 *Revisions to the Standards for the Classification of Federal Data on Race and Ethnicity* and are not strictly comparable with estimates for earlier years. The non-Hispanic race categories shown in the table conform to the 1997 Standards. Starting with 1999 data, race-specific estimates are for persons who reported only one racial group. Prior to data year 1999, estimates were tabulated according to the 1977 Standards. Estimates for single-race categories prior to 1999 included persons who reported one race or, if they reported more than one race, identified one race as best representing their race. See Appendix II, Hispanic origin; Race.

[4] Estimates are age-adjusted to the year 2000 standard population using three age groups: 20–44 years, 45–64 years, and 65 years and over. Age-adjusted estimates in this table may differ from other age-adjusted estimates based on the same data and presented elsewhere if different age groups are used in the adjustment procedure. See Appendix II, Age adjustment.

[5] Includes persons of all other races and Hispanic origins not shown separately.

[6] Percent of poverty level was calculated by dividing family income by the U.S. Department of Health and Human Services' poverty guideline specific to family size, as well as the appropriate year, and state. Persons with unknown percent of poverty level are excluded (6% in 2011–2014). See Appendix II, Family income; Poverty.

NOTES: Excludes pregnant women. Fasting weights were used to obtain estimates of total, physician-diagnosed, and undiagnosed diabetes prevalence. Examination weights were used to obtain the poor glycemic control estimates. Estimates in this table may differ from other estimates based on the same data and presented elsewhere if different weights, age adjustment groups, definitions, or trend adjustments are used. Standard errors are available in the spreadsheet version of this table. Available from: http://www.cdc.gov/nchs/hus.htm. Data for additional years are available. See the Excel spreadsheet on the *Health, United States* website at: http://www.cdc.gov/nchs/hus.htm.

SOURCE: NCHS, National Health and Nutrition Examination Survey. See Appendix I, National Health and Nutrition Examination Survey (NHANES).

Table 41 (page 1 of 3). Severe headache or migraine, low back pain, and neck pain among adults aged 18 and over, by selected characteristics: United States, selected years 1997–2015

Excel and PDF versions (with more data years and standard errors when available): http://www.cdc.gov/nchs/hus/contents2016.htm#041.

[Data are based on household interviews of a sample of the civilian noninstitutionalized population]

Characteristic	Severe headache or migraine[1]			Low back pain[1]			Neck pain[1]		
	1997	2010	2015	1997	2010	2015	1997	2010	2015
	Percent of adults with pain during the past 3 months								
18 years and over, age-adjusted[2,3]	15.8	16.6	15.4	28.2	28.4	29.1	14.7	15.4	15.7
18 years and over, crude[3]	16.0	16.4	15.0	28.1	28.8	29.8	14.6	15.8	16.1
Age									
18–44 years	18.7	20.4	17.9	26.1	25.2	23.9	13.3	13.1	12.9
18–24 years	18.7	19.6	15.4	21.9	19.4	16.2	9.8	8.3	7.8
25–44 years	18.7	20.7	18.8	27.3	27.2	26.7	14.3	14.8	14.8
45–64 years	15.8	15.6	15.9	31.3	32.4	35.4	17.0	20.0	20.1
45–54 years	17.8	16.7	17.6	31.3	31.3	34.6	17.3	19.1	19.8
55–64 years	12.7	14.1	14.2	31.2	33.8	36.1	16.6	21.0	20.5
65 years and over	7.0	6.4	6.4	29.5	31.8	34.4	15.0	14.8	16.6
65–74 years	8.2	7.4	7.3	30.2	32.5	34.0	15.0	15.5	16.9
75 years and over	5.4	5.1	5.1	28.6	30.9	34.9	15.0	14.0	16.2
Sex[2]									
Male	9.9	11.0	9.7	26.5	26.3	27.6	12.6	13.1	13.9
Female	21.4	22.1	20.9	29.6	30.3	30.4	16.6	17.6	17.4
Sex and age									
Male:									
18–44 years	11.9	13.5	11.0	24.8	23.2	22.3	11.6	11.0	11.2
45–54 years	10.3	10.4	10.7	29.4	29.6	34.1	13.9	16.3	17.4
55–64 years	8.8	9.6	10.5	30.7	32.8	35.5	14.6	17.6	19.1
65–74 years	5.0	5.5	5.0	29.0	28.4	31.7	13.6	12.8	14.4
75 years and over	*2.4	4.0	3.4	22.5	27.4	32.1	12.6	13.0	14.9
Female:									
18–44 years	25.4	27.3	24.7	27.3	27.1	25.5	14.9	15.2	14.6
45–54 years	24.9	22.9	24.2	33.1	33.0	35.2	20.6	21.8	22.0
55–64 years	16.3	18.2	17.6	31.7	34.7	36.7	18.4	24.1	21.8
65–74 years	10.7	9.1	9.3	31.1	36.1	35.9	16.1	17.8	19.0
75 years and over	7.4	5.8	6.3	32.4	33.2	36.9	16.5	14.6	17.0
Race[2,4]									
White only	15.9	16.7	15.5	28.7	29.1	29.9	15.1	16.0	16.3
Black or African American only	16.7	18.2	16.3	26.9	27.2	28.1	13.3	13.3	13.8
American Indian or Alaska Native only	18.9	18.8	18.7	33.3	33.6	34.1	16.2	16.9	20.4
Asian only	11.7	10.1	11.3	21.0	19.1	19.3	9.2	9.6	11.5
Native Hawaiian or Other Pacific Islander only	- - -	*	*	- - -	*	*	- - -	*	*
2 or more races	- - -	21.5	20.7	- - -	35.6	33.7	- - -	22.0	19.0
Hispanic origin and race[2,4]									
Hispanic or Latino	15.5	16.2	14.9	26.4	27.4	27.4	13.9	15.1	14.2
Mexican	14.6	15.7	14.1	25.2	26.5	26.4	12.9	14.7	12.9
Not Hispanic or Latino	15.9	16.8	15.6	28.4	28.7	29.4	14.9	15.5	16.1
White only	16.1	17.0	16.0	29.1	29.7	30.5	15.4	16.3	17.1
Black or African American only	16.8	18.4	16.1	26.9	27.1	27.9	13.3	13.3	13.6
Education[5,6]									
25 years and over:									
No high school diploma or GED	19.2	18.2	19.4	33.6	34.5	34.6	16.5	18.9	18.1
High school diploma or GED	16.0	17.4	14.9	30.2	31.9	34.8	15.5	16.8	17.3
Some college or more	13.8	15.1	14.9	26.9	28.0	29.3	14.6	15.8	16.5

See footnotes at end of table.

Table 41 (page 2 of 3). Severe headache or migraine, low back pain, and neck pain among adults aged 18 and over, by selected characteristics: United States, selected years 1997–2015

Excel and PDF versions (with more data years and standard errors when available): http://www.cdc.gov/nchs/hus/contents2016.htm#041.

[Data are based on household interviews of a sample of the civilian noninstitutionalized population]

Characteristic	Severe headache or migraine [1]			Low back pain [1]			Neck pain [1]		
	1997	2010	2015	1997	2010	2015	1997	2010	2015
Percent of poverty level [2,7]			Percent of adults with pain during past 3 months						
Below 100%.	23.3	22.7	21.8	35.4	34.9	36.8	18.6	20.2	19.9
100%–199%.	18.9	19.5	19.0	30.8	32.5	33.8	16.1	17.7	18.3
200%–399%.	15.5	16.6	15.5	27.9	28.5	28.7	14.8	15.2	14.9
400% or more	12.4	13.3	11.9	24.8	24.7	25.1	12.8	13.1	14.3
Hispanic origin and race and percent of poverty level [2,4,7]									
Hispanic or Latino:									
Below 100%	18.9	19.6	19.9	29.5	29.0	33.4	16.4	17.4	17.8
100%–199%	15.7	15.1	14.2	26.8	27.2	25.9	12.9	15.7	15.9
200%–399%	14.0	16.5	13.6	25.0	27.5	25.0	13.8	12.9	11.4
400% or more	13.0	14.0	12.9	21.6	25.6	27.5	12.1	15.3	12.0
Not Hispanic or Latino:									
White only:									
Below 100%	26.1	24.8	25.5	38.9	40.5	42.0	20.5	23.7	23.6
100%–199%	20.4	22.0	22.8	33.3	35.9	38.6	18.0	19.9	21.5
200%–399%	16.3	16.9	16.4	29.1	30.5	30.9	15.9	16.8	16.8
400% or more	12.5	13.8	11.8	25.4	25.2	25.9	13.1	13.6	15.1
Black or African American only:									
Below 100%	22.7	24.0	19.8	34.5	32.5	33.1	17.9	18.6	17.3
100%–199%	17.6	19.6	16.4	27.7	31.2	33.7	14.0	14.4	15.1
200%–399%	14.0	17.6	15.7	24.3	23.7	24.9	10.2	11.7	12.0
400% or more	12.9	12.2	13.6	21.5	21.0	22.2	11.9	8.5	11.8
Disability measure [2,8]									
Any basic actions difficulty or complex activity limitation	29.3	30.1	29.5	48.0	49.5	51.7	27.2	28.1	30.1
Any basic actions difficulty	30.0	30.9	30.4	49.3	51.1	53.0	27.9	29.0	30.7
Any complex activity limitation	34.6	36.0	34.6	55.1	54.5	57.5	33.1	34.3	37.1
No disability	11.0	11.7	10.6	19.4	19.0	19.4	9.1	9.7	9.7
Geographic region [2]									
Northeast	14.5	15.4	14.6	27.1	28.0	28.8	14.0	14.9	15.8
Midwest	15.6	16.8	15.9	28.7	28.1	29.0	15.3	16.0	14.9
South	17.1	18.2	15.8	27.5	28.3	28.6	13.9	14.6	14.9
West	15.3	15.1	15.2	30.0	29.3	29.9	16.1	16.5	17.5
Location of residence [2,9]									
Within MSA	15.2	16.3	15.1	27.0	27.5	28.2	14.2	14.9	15.3
Outside MSA	18.1	18.6	17.9	32.5	33.8	34.5	16.4	18.1	18.2

See footnotes at end of table.

Table 41 (page 3 of 3). Severe headache or migraine, low back pain, and neck pain among adults aged 18 and over, by selected characteristics: United States, selected years 1997–2015

Excel and PDF versions (with more data years and standard errors when available): http://www.cdc.gov/nchs/hus/contents2016.htm#041.

[Data are based on household interviews of a sample of the civilian noninstitutionalized population]

- - - Data not available.

* Estimates are considered unreliable. Data preceded by an asterisk have a relative standard error (RSE) of 20%–30%. Data not shown have an RSE greater than 30%.

[1] In three separate questions, respondents were asked, "During the past 3 months, did you have a severe headache or migraine? . . .low back pain? . . .neck pain?" Respondents were instructed to report pain that had lasted a whole day or more, and not to report fleeting or minor aches or pains. Persons may be represented in more than one column.

[2] Estimates are age-adjusted to the year 2000 standard population using five age groups: 18–44 years, 45–54 years, 55–64 years, 65–74 years, and 75 years and over. Age-adjusted estimates in this table may differ from other age-adjusted estimates based on the same data and presented elsewhere if different age groups are used in the adjustment procedure. See Appendix II, Age adjustment.

[3] Includes all other races not shown separately, unknown education level, and unknown disability status.

[4] The race groups, white, black, American Indian or Alaska Native, Asian, Native Hawaiian or Other Pacific Islander, and 2 or more races, include persons of Hispanic and non-Hispanic origin. Persons of Hispanic origin may be of any race. Starting with 1999 data, race-specific estimates are tabulated according to the 1997 *Revisions to the Standards for the Classification of Federal Data on Race and Ethnicity* and are not strictly comparable with estimates for earlier years. The five single-race categories plus multiple-race categories shown in the table conform to the 1997 Standards. Starting with 1999 data, race-specific estimates are for persons who reported only one racial group; the category 2 or more races includes persons who reported more than one racial group. Prior to 1999, data were tabulated according to the 1977 Standards with four racial groups, and the Asian only category included Native Hawaiian or Other Pacific Islander. Estimates for single-race categories prior to 1999 included persons who reported one race or, if they reported more than one race, identified one race as best representing their race. Starting with 2003 data, race responses of other race and unspecified multiple race were treated as missing, and then race was imputed if these were the only race responses. Almost all persons with a race response of other race were of Hispanic origin. See Appendix II, Hispanic origin; Race.

[5] Estimates are for persons aged 25 and over and are age-adjusted to the year 2000 standard population using five age groups: 25–44 years, 45–54 years, 55–64 years, 65–74 years, and 75 years and over. See Appendix II, Age adjustment.

[6] GED is General Educational Development high school equivalency diploma. See Appendix II, Education.

[7] Percent of poverty level is based on family income and family size and composition using U.S. Census Bureau poverty thresholds. Missing family income data were imputed for 1997 and beyond. See Appendix II, Family income; Poverty; Table VI.

[8] Any basic actions difficulty or complex activity limitation is defined as having one or more of the following limitations or difficulties: movement difficulty, emotional difficulty, sensory (seeing or hearing) difficulty, cognitive difficulty, self-care (activities of daily living or instrumental activities of daily living) limitation, social limitation, or work limitation. For more information, see Appendix II, Basic actions difficulty; Complex activity limitation. Starting with 2007 data, the hearing question, a component of the basic actions difficulty measure, was revised. Consequently, data prior to 2007 are not comparable with data for 2007 and beyond. For more information on the impact of the revised hearing question, see Appendix II, Hearing trouble.

[9] MSA is metropolitan statistical area. Starting with 2006 data, MSA status is determined using 2000 census data and the 2000 standards for defining MSAs. For data prior to 2006, see Appendix II, Metropolitan statistical area (MSA) for the applicable standards

NOTES: Standard errors are available in the spreadsheet version of this table. Available from: http://www.cdc.gov/nchs/hus.htm. Data for additional years are available. See the Excel spreadsheet on the *Health, United States* website at: http://www.cdc.gov/nchs/hus.htm.

SOURCE: NCHS, National Health Interview Survey, sample adult questionnaire. See Appendix I, National Health Interview Survey (NHIS).

Excel and PDF versions (with more data years and standard errors when available): http://www.cdc.gov/nchs/hus/contents2016.htm#042.

[Data are based on household interviews of a sample of the civilian noninstitutionalized population]

Characteristic	18 years and over				18–64 years				65 years and over			
	1997	2000	2010[1]	2015[1]	1997	2000	2010[1]	2015[1]	1997	2000	2010[1]	2015[1]
	Number, in millions											
At least one basic actions difficulty or complex activity limitation [2,3]	60.9	59.0	73.7	77.0	41.3	39.3	50.7	50.5	19.6	19.7	23.0	26.5
At least one basic actions difficulty [2]	56.7	55.2	69.2	72.6	38.1	36.4	47.2	47.1	18.6	18.7	22.0	25.4
At least one complex activity limitation [3]	29.0	27.2	35.0	38.6	18.1	16.7	22.9	24.2	11.0	10.5	12.1	14.4
	At least one basic actions difficulty or complex activity limitation [2,3]											
	Percent											
Total, age-adjusted [4,5]	32.5	29.9	31.9	31.5	. . .	. . .	. . .	. . .	. . .	. . .	. . .	. . .
Total, crude [4]	31.8	29.5	32.8	33.2	25.8	23.5	27.1	26.9	62.2	60.8	61.7	59.8
	At least one basic actions difficulty [2]											
	Percent											
Total, age-adjusted [4,5]	30.1	27.9	29.9	29.6	. . .	. . .	. . .	. . .	. . .	. . .	. . .	. . .
Total, crude [4]	29.4	27.5	30.8	31.2	23.6	21.7	25.1	25.1	58.8	58.1	59.3	57.5
Sex												
Male	25.6	23.8	26.3	26.6	20.7	18.9	21.4	21.1	54.5	53.4	53.8	52.0
Female	32.9	31.0	35.1	35.6	26.4	24.3	28.8	28.8	61.9	61.5	63.6	61.9
Race [6]												
White only	29.6	28.1	31.2	31.6	23.5	21.8	25.1	25.1	58.5	58.0	59.2	57.2
Black or African American only	31.4	27.2	32.3	33.5	26.9	22.7	28.4	28.8	64.4	60.6	62.9	62.4
American Indian or Alaska Native only	43.8	36.8	41.6	41.2	41.9	34.1	38.5	37.6	66.0	70.2	74.0	65.4
Asian only	15.5	15.5	17.5	19.3	13.0	12.6	12.8	14.8	46.4	44.7	50.1	47.0
Native Hawaiian or Other Pacific Islander only	- - -	*	*	*	- - -	*	*	*	- - -	*	*	*
2 or more races	- - -	38.0	36.3	33.5	- - -	34.4	33.9	27.6	- - -	70.7	65.4	74.4
Hispanic origin and race [6]												
Hispanic or Latino	23.8	19.6	24.7	24.1	21.0	16.6	21.2	20.5	54.6	57.5	61.5	57.1
Not Hispanic or Latino.	30.0	28.5	31.8	32.6	23.9	22.4	25.9	26.0	59.0	58.2	59.1	57.5
White only.	30.3	29.1	32.4	33.4	23.8	22.5	26.0	26.4	58.7	58.2	59.0	57.2
Black or African American only	31.5	27.3	32.6	33.8	27.0	22.9	28.6	29.0	64.4	60.4	63.2	62.6
Percent of poverty level [7]												
Below 100%.	41.9	38.4	40.6	42.8	36.2	31.9	36.3	37.8	74.1	71.6	72.7	76.8
100%–199%.	38.2	37.1	38.7	41.0	29.2	26.5	30.5	33.3	66.6	69.4	69.5	69.0
200%–399%.	28.4	28.2	31.1	32.4	22.0	22.1	24.1	24.6	56.1	53.9	58.9	60.5
400% or more	21.0	19.4	23.0	22.1	18.2	16.8	19.3	17.5	45.5	44.7	47.0	43.7
Location of residence [8]												
Within MSA	27.7	25.9	29.2	29.9	22.3	20.3	23.6	23.9	56.6	56.7	59.2	56.9
Outside MSA	35.6	33.6	39.3	39.3	28.6	26.8	33.8	32.7	65.8	62.6	59.9	60.1

See footnotes at end of table.

Table 42 (page 2 of 2). Disability measures among adults aged 18 and over, by selected characteristics: United States, selected years 1997–2015

Excel and PDF versions (with more data years and standard errors when available): http://www.cdc.gov/nchs/hus/contents2016.htm#042.

[Data are based on household interviews of a sample of the civilian noninstitutionalized population]

Characteristic	18 years and over				18–64 years				65 years and over			
	1997	2000	2010[1]	2015[1]	1997	2000	2010[1]	2015[1]	1997	2000	2010[1]	2015[1]
	At least one complex activity limitation[3]											
	Percent											
Total, age-adjusted[4,5]	15.6	13.7	14.9	15.1	. . .	. . .	. . .	. . .	. . .	. . .	. . .	. . .
Total, crude[4].	15.1	13.4	15.5	16.1	11.2	9.8	12.1	12.5	35.1	32.0	32.3	31.7
Sex												
Male	13.7	12.0	14.0	15.1	10.6	9.4	11.3	12.0	31.9	28.1	30.1	29.6
Female.	16.5	14.7	16.8	17.1	11.9	10.3	12.9	12.9	37.4	34.9	34.0	33.4
Race[6]												
White only	15.0	13.6	15.2	16.2	10.9	9.8	11.7	12.5	34.3	31.5	31.7	30.8
Black or African American only	19.0	15.0	19.7	19.1	15.2	11.7	17.0	15.8	47.1	40.4	39.9	40.0
American Indian or Alaska Native only	23.7	20.6	15.4	15.5	22.1	17.8	14.5	10.4	*42.6	*54.9	*	*48.9
Asian only	5.7	4.7	7.7	7.8	4.9	3.6	5.0	4.7	*14.8	*15.5	26.7	26.6
Native Hawaiian or Other Pacific Islander only	- - -	*	*	*	- - -	*	*	*	- - -	*	*	*
2 or more races	- - -	22.5	19.6	20.3	- - -	20.3	17.0	16.5	- - -	*42.2	53.6	46.2
Hispanic origin and race[6]												
Hispanic or Latino	11.9	9.1	10.4	10.4	9.8	7.3	7.9	8.1	33.9	32.4	37.6	32.1
Not Hispanic or Latino.	15.5	14.0	16.3	17.2	11.4	10.2	12.9	13.4	35.1	32.0	31.9	31.7
White only.	15.4	14.1	16.1	17.5	11.1	10.1	12.5	13.7	34.4	31.5	31.1	30.7
Black or African American only	18.8	15.1	20.0	19.3	15.0	11.7	17.3	15.9	46.8	40.3	40.0	40.2
Percent of poverty level[7]												
Below 100%.	30.0	26.0	27.5	29.3	25.2	22.0	24.0	25.5	56.9	46.7	54.5	55.6
100%–199%.	23.3	22.0	23.7	24.2	16.7	15.1	18.4	19.7	43.9	42.8	43.7	40.6
200%–399%.	13.3	12.8	14.5	16.1	9.3	9.2	10.8	11.2	30.6	27.5	29.3	33.5
400% or more	7.3	6.4	7.7	8.3	5.8	5.0	5.8	5.8	20.2	19.6	19.8	19.8
Location of residence[8]												
Within MSA	14.1	12.1	14.2	15.1	10.6	8.9	10.9	11.5	32.7	29.8	31.6	30.9
Outside MSA	19.0	18.2	22.2	22.7	13.6	13.4	18.8	18.6	42.8	38.8	35.2	35.6

. . . Category not applicable.

* Estimates are considered unreliable. Data preceded by an asterisk have a relative standard error (RSE) of 20%–30%. Data not shown have an RSE greater than 30%.

- - - Data not available.

[1] Starting with 2007 data (shown in spreadsheet version), the hearing question, a component of the basic actions difficulty measure, was revised. Consequently, data for basic actions difficulty prior to 2007 are not comparable with 2007 data and beyond. For more information on the impact of the revised hearing question, see Appendix II, Hearing trouble.

[2] A basic actions difficulty is defined as having difficulties in one or more of the following areas of functioning: movement, emotional, sensory (seeing or hearing), or cognitive. For more information, see Appendix II, Basic actions difficulty. Starting with 2007 data, the hearing question, a component of basic actions difficulty, was revised. Consequently, data prior to 2007 are not comparable with data for 2007 and beyond. For more information on the impact of the revised hearing question, see Appendix II, Hearing trouble.

[3] A complex activity limitation is defined as having one or more of the following limitations: maintaining independence (performing activities of daily living or instrumental activities of daily living), socializing, or working. For more information, see Appendix II, Complex activity limitation.

[4] Includes all other races not shown separately.

[5] Estimates are age-adjusted to the year 2000 standard population using five age groups: 18–44 years, 45–54 years, 55–64 years, 65–74 years, and 75 years and over. See Appendix II, Age adjustment.

[6] The race groups, white, black, American Indian or Alaska Native, Asian, Native Hawaiian or Other Pacific Islander, and 2 or more races, include persons of Hispanic and non-Hispanic origin. Persons of Hispanic origin may be of any race. Starting with 1999 data, race-specific estimates are tabulated according to the 1997 *Revisions to the Standards for the Classification of Federal Data on Race and Ethnicity* and are not strictly comparable with estimates for earlier years. The five single-race categories plus multiple-race categories shown in the table conform to the 1997 Standards. Starting with 1999 data, race-specific estimates are for persons who reported only one racial group; the category 2 or more races includes persons who reported more than one racial group. Prior to 1999, data were tabulated according to the 1977 Standards with four racial groups, and the Asian only category included Native Hawaiian or Other Pacific Islander. Estimates for single-race categories prior to 1999 included persons who reported one race or, if they reported more than one race, identified one race as best representing their race. Starting with 2003 data, race responses of other race and unspecified multiple race were treated as missing, and then race was imputed if these were the only race responses. Almost all persons with a race response of other race were of Hispanic origin. See Appendix II, Hispanic origin; Race.

[7] Percent of poverty level is based on family income and family size and composition using U.S. Census Bureau poverty thresholds. Missing family income data were imputed for 1997 and beyond. See Appendix II, Family income; Poverty; Table VI.

[8] MSA is metropolitan statistical area. Starting with 2006 data, MSA status is determined using 2000 census data and the 2000 standards for defining MSAs. For data prior to 2006, see Appendix II, Metropolitan statistical area (MSA) for the applicable standards.

NOTES: Standard errors are available in the spreadsheet version of this table. Available from: http://www.cdc.gov/nchs/hus.htm. Data for additional years are available. See the Excel spreadsheet on the *Health, United States* website at: http://www.cdc.gov/nchs/hus.htm.

SOURCE: NCHS, National Health Interview Survey, sample adult questionnaire. See Appendix I, National Health Interview Survey (NHIS).

Table 43 (page 1 of 2). Vision limitations among adults aged 18 and over, by selected characteristics: United States, selected years 1997–2015

Excel and PDF versions (with more data years and standard errors when available): http://www.cdc.gov/nchs/hus/contents2016.htm#043.

[Data are based on household interviews of a sample of the civilian noninstitutionalized population]

Characteristic	Any trouble seeing, even with glasses or contacts [1]									
	1997	2000	2005	2007	2010	2011	2012	2013	2014	2015
	Percent of adults									
18 years and over, age-adjusted [2,3]	10.0	9.0	9.2	9.9	9.1	8.8	8.4	8.7	8.7	9.0
18 years and over, crude [3]	9.8	8.9	9.3	10.0	9.4	9.2	8.8	9.1	9.1	9.4
Age										
18–44 years	6.2	5.3	5.5	6.9	6.2	5.5	5.4	5.5	5.6	5.6
18–24 years.	5.4	4.2	5.0	6.9	5.8	5.2	5.1	5.5	4.9	4.9
25–44 years.	6.5	5.7	5.7	6.8	6.3	5.6	5.5	5.5	5.9	5.8
45–64 years	12.0	10.7	11.2	12.2	11.6	12.0	11.3	11.1	11.3	11.6
45–54 years	12.2	10.9	11.0	12.3	10.7	11.7	11.2	10.6	11.5	11.2
55–64 years	11.6	10.5	11.5	12.1	12.7	12.4	11.5	11.7	11.0	12.1
65 years and over	18.1	17.4	17.4	15.3	13.9	13.6	12.7	14.3	13.5	14.9
65–74 years.	14.2	13.6	13.2	12.9	12.2	12.2	11.0	11.5	11.5	11.9
75 years and over.	23.1	21.9	22.0	17.9	16.1	15.2	14.9	18.0	16.5	19.1
Sex [2]										
Male	8.8	7.9	7.9	8.5	7.9	7.6	7.1	7.5	7.6	7.4
Female.	11.1	10.1	10.5	11.2	10.3	10.1	9.7	9.8	9.8	10.6
Sex and age										
Male:										
18–44 years.	5.3	4.4	4.5	5.6	5.2	4.2	4.4	4.5	4.3	4.0
45–54 years.	10.1	8.8	8.8	10.6	9.1	10.4	9.3	9.4	10.7	8.9
55–64 years.	10.5	9.5	10.5	10.0	10.7	11.8	9.8	10.4	9.6	10.2
65–74 years.	13.2	12.8	11.4	11.4	10.5	9.7	9.9	10.9	10.3	10.0
75 years and over.	21.4	20.7	20.4	17.2	15.7	14.9	12.8	14.7	17.0	18.8
Female:										
18–44 years.	7.1	6.2	6.5	8.1	7.1	6.9	6.4	6.5	7.0	7.1
45–54 years.	14.2	12.8	13.2	13.9	12.3	13.0	12.9	11.8	12.2	13.4
55–64 years.	12.6	11.5	12.4	14.2	14.6	13.0	13.1	12.9	12.3	13.8
65–74 years.	15.0	14.4	14.8	14.2	13.6	14.5	11.9	12.1	12.5	13.5
75 years and over.	24.2	22.7	23.0	18.4	16.4	15.4	16.4	20.3	16.1	19.4
Race [2,4]										
White only	9.7	8.8	9.1	9.9	8.8	8.6	8.4	8.7	8.5	9.0
Black or African American only	12.8	10.6	10.9	10.5	12.1	10.8	9.2	10.0	11.1	10.3
American Indian or Alaska Native only	19.2	16.6	*14.9	18.0	15.0	15.0	13.0	13.7	16.9	*10.9
Asian only	6.2	6.3	5.5	5.7	5.3	6.3	5.7	4.9	5.7	6.3
Native Hawaiian or Other Pacific Islander only	- - -	*	*	*	*	*	*	*	*	*
2 or more races	- - -	16.2	16.4	16.9	13.1	12.4	15.6	11.8	11.4	12.4
Hispanic origin and race [2,4]										
Hispanic or Latino.	10.0	9.7	9.6	9.9	9.2	9.4	9.4	9.7	8.8	9.3
Mexican.	10.2	8.3	9.9	10.1	9.0	10.4	9.3	10.9	9.3	9.3
Not Hispanic or Latino.	10.0	9.1	9.2	10.0	9.2	8.8	8.4	8.6	8.8	9.0
White only.	9.8	8.9	9.1	10.1	8.9	8.6	8.4	8.6	8.5	9.1
Black or African American only	12.8	10.6	10.9	10.6	12.2	10.7	9.3	10.1	11.3	10.2
Education [5,6]										
25 years of age and over:										
No high school diploma or GED	15.0	12.2	13.5	13.4	14.1	13.9	12.9	12.8	13.1	13.4
High school diploma or GED	10.6	9.5	10.3	10.9	10.5	10.4	9.3	10.0	9.3	9.5
Some college or more	8.9	8.9	8.6	9.2	8.0	7.9	7.9	8.0	8.4	8.9

See footnotes at end of table.

Table 43 (page 2 of 2). Vision limitations among adults aged 18 and over, by selected characteristics: United States, selected years 1997–2015

Excel and PDF versions (with more data years and standard errors when available): http://www.cdc.gov/nchs/hus/contents2016.htm#043.

[Data are based on household interviews of a sample of the civilian noninstitutionalized population]

Characteristic	Any trouble seeing, even with glasses or contacts [1]									
	1997	2000	2005	2007	2010	2011	2012	2013	2014	2015
Percent of poverty level [2,7]	Percent of adults									
Below 100%.	17.0	12.9	15.3	15.0	14.8	14.2	13.7	15.6	13.2	14.2
100%–199%.	12.9	11.6	11.5	13.0	12.2	11.5	10.9	11.2	10.9	11.8
200%–399%.	9.1	8.8	8.9	9.4	9.0	8.7	7.9	7.6	8.8	9.4
400% or more	7.3	7.1	6.9	7.8	6.4	6.0	6.1	6.4	6.4	6.3
Hispanic origin and race and percent of poverty level [2,4,7]										
Hispanic or Latino:										
Below 100%	12.8	11.0	13.6	13.4	10.8	13.9	13.1	13.1	10.2	15.1
100%–199%	11.2	9.4	8.8	11.1	10.8	9.6	10.0	10.6	9.3	10.1
200%–399%	8.1	9.2	8.2	7.2	8.9	8.3	6.8	7.4	9.2	7.2
400% or more	*8.1	10.5	8.0	10.6	5.3	5.1	7.8	9.0	6.6	5.2
Not Hispanic or Latino:										
White only:										
Below 100%	17.9	13.1	16.2	16.3	16.8	14.4	14.5	17.7	14.6	14.8
100%–199%	13.1	12.0	12.7	14.2	12.6	12.3	11.7	11.8	11.3	12.9
200%–399%	9.2	9.2	9.0	10.3	8.8	9.0	8.5	7.8	8.7	10.3
400% or more	7.3	7.0	6.9	7.7	6.7	5.9	6.0	6.4	6.3	6.4
Black or African American only:										
Below 100%	17.9	13.6	16.0	15.1	15.8	15.5	13.7	15.3	14.2	13.6
100%–199%	16.0	12.9	11.3	14.0	14.9	12.3	11.3	11.4	12.1	12.4
200%–399%	9.3	7.7	9.7	7.3	12.0	8.5	6.8	8.0	10.8	9.5
400% or more	7.7	8.3	6.4	6.9	6.6	8.6	6.4	6.7	8.6	6.1
Geographic region [2]										
Northeast	8.6	7.4	8.1	8.1	7.8	7.6	6.4	7.4	7.0	7.9
Midwest	9.5	9.6	9.7	10.3	9.1	8.7	8.7	9.0	9.0	9.3
South	11.4	9.2	9.8	10.1	10.6	9.4	9.1	8.9	9.1	9.4
West	9.7	9.9	8.6	10.5	8.0	9.1	8.9	9.1	9.3	8.9
Location of residence [2,8]										
Within MSA	9.5	8.5	8.6	9.6	8.6	8.6	8.2	8.4	8.4	8.7
Outside MSA	12.0	11.1	11.7	11.4	11.6	10.3	9.8	10.6	10.3	11.0

* Estimates are considered unreliable. Data preceded by an asterisk have a relative standard error (RSE) of 20%–30%. Data not shown have an RSE greater than 30%.
- - - Data not available.
[1] Respondents were asked, "Do you have any trouble seeing, even when wearing glasses or contact lenses?" Respondents were also asked, "Are you blind or unable to see at all?" In this analysis, any trouble seeing and blind are combined into one category.
[2] Estimates are age-adjusted to the year 2000 standard population using five age groups: 18–44 years, 45–54 years, 55–64 years, 65–74 years, and 75 years and over. Age-adjusted estimates in this table may differ from other age-adjusted estimates based on the same data and presented elsewhere if different age groups are used in the adjustment procedure. See Appendix II, Age adjustment.
[3] Includes all other races not shown separately and unknown education level.
[4] The race groups, white, black, American Indian or Alaska Native, Asian, Native Hawaiian or Other Pacific Islander, and 2 or more races, include persons of Hispanic and non-Hispanic origin. Persons of Hispanic origin may be of any race. Starting with 1999 data, race-specific estimates are tabulated according to the 1997 *Revisions to the Standards for the Classification of Federal Data on Race and Ethnicity* and are not strictly comparable with estimates for earlier years. The five single-race categories plus multiple-race categories shown in the table conform to the 1997 Standards. Starting with 1999 data, race-specific estimates are for persons who reported only one racial group; the category 2 or more races includes persons who reported more than one racial group. Prior to 1999, data were tabulated according to the 1977 Standards with four racial groups, and the Asian only category included Native Hawaiian or Other Pacific Islander. Estimates for single-race categories prior to 1999 included persons who reported one race or, if they reported more than one race, identified one race as best representing their race. Starting with 2003 data, race responses of other race and unspecified multiple race were treated as missing, and then race was imputed if these were the only race responses. Almost all persons with a race response of other race were of Hispanic origin. See Appendix II, Hispanic origin; Race.
[5] Estimates are for persons aged 25 and over and are age-adjusted to the year 2000 standard population using five age groups: 25–44 years, 45–54 years, 55–64 years, 65–74 years, and 75 years and over. See Appendix II, Age adjustment.
[6] GED is General Educational Development high school equivalency diploma. See Appendix II, Education.
[7] Percent of poverty level is based on family income and family size and composition using U.S. Census Bureau poverty thresholds. Missing family income data were imputed for 1997 and beyond. See Appendix II, Family income; Poverty; Table VI.
[8] MSA is metropolitan statistical area. Starting with 2006 data, MSA status is determined using 2000 census data and the 2000 standards for defining MSAs. For data prior to 2006, see Appendix II, Metropolitan statistical area (MSA) for the applicable standards.

NOTES: Standard errors are available in the spreadsheet version of this table. Available from: http://www.cdc.gov/nchs/hus.htm. Data for additional years are available. See the Excel spreadsheet on the *Health, United States* website at: http://www.cdc.gov/nchs/hus.htm.

SOURCE: NCHS, National Health Interview Survey, sample adult questionnaire. See Appendix I, National Health Interview Survey (NHIS). See footnotes at end of table.

Table 44 (page 1 of 2). Hearing limitations among adults aged 18 and over, by selected characteristics: United States, selected years 2007–2015

Excel and PDF versions (with more data years and standard errors when available): http://www.cdc.gov/nchs/hus/contents2016.htm#044.

[Data are based on household interviews of a sample of the civilian noninstitutionalized population]

| | Level of hearing trouble | | | | | | | | | | | |
| | Any hearing trouble (a little, moderate, a lot of trouble, or deaf)[1] | | | | Moderate, a lot of trouble, or deaf[1] | | | | A lot of trouble or deaf[1] | | | |
Characteristic	2007	2010	2014	2015	2007	2010	2014	2015	2007	2010	2014	2015
	Percent of adults											
18 years and over, age-adjusted[2,3]	14.7	15.6	15.6	14.2	5.6	5.7	5.8	5.2	2.3	2.1	2.3	2.0
18 years and over, crude[3].	14.9	16.2	16.8	15.3	5.7	5.9	6.3	5.6	2.3	2.2	2.4	2.1
Age												
18–44 years	6.0	6.7	6.3	5.8	1.3	1.7	1.7	1.1	0.4	0.5	0.6	0.4
18–24 years.	4.1	5.4	4.1	4.5	*	*1.2	*	*0.8	*	*	*	*
25–44 years.	6.6	7.2	7.2	6.2	1.6	1.8	1.9	1.2	0.5	0.5	0.6	0.4
45–64 years	17.6	18.9	19.2	16.2	6.0	6.1	5.9	4.9	2.0	1.9	2.0	1.5
45–54 years.	14.7	15.6	15.4	12.8	4.1	4.8	3.9	3.3	1.2	1.2	1.3	1.1
55–64 years.	21.5	23.2	23.3	19.9	8.5	7.8	8.2	6.5	3.0	2.7	2.7	1.9
65 years and over.	36.9	37.5	38.7	36.9	18.6	17.7	18.5	18.1	8.7	7.6	7.8	7.4
65–74 years.	29.8	31.2	33.1	30.2	11.9	12.9	13.5	12.5	4.7	4.6	5.0	4.2
75 years and over	45.0	45.2	46.7	46.5	26.3	23.7	25.7	26.0	13.3	11.1	11.8	11.9
Sex[2]												
Male	18.3	18.9	19.1	17.4	7.7	7.4	7.7	6.8	3.1	2.8	2.9	2.6
Female	11.5	12.7	12.6	11.4	3.9	4.3	4.3	3.8	1.6	1.6	1.7	1.5
Sex and age												
Male:												
18–44 years.	6.8	7.7	7.4	6.4	1.6	1.9	2.0	1.1	*0.5	*0.7	*0.6	*0.3
45–54 years.	18.7	18.2	18.1	16.1	5.3	5.7	4.9	4.6	1.5	*1.1	1.4	*1.6
55–64 years.	28.4	30.1	30.2	25.7	12.9	11.5	10.9	9.6	4.7	3.9	3.8	2.9
65–74 years.	39.4	41.0	41.9	40.8	17.7	17.9	19.3	17.6	7.0	6.7	6.9	5.8
75 years and over	54.6	53.1	57.0	54.5	34.8	29.7	33.2	33.1	16.9	14.5	15.5	15.8
Female:												
18–44 years.	5.1	5.8	5.3	5.2	1.0	1.4	1.3	1.1	*0.3	*0.3	*0.5	*0.5
45–54 years.	11.0	13.0	12.8	9.7	2.9	3.9	2.9	2.1	*1.0	*1.3	*1.2	*0.7
55–64 years.	15.0	16.7	16.9	14.5	4.3	4.4	5.7	3.7	*1.3	1.6	1.7	*1.0
65–74 years.	21.8	22.8	25.5	21.0	6.9	8.6	8.4	8.0	2.8	2.9	3.3	2.9
75 years and over	38.8	39.9	39.5	40.8	20.9	19.7	20.4	21.0	11.1	8.9	9.2	9.1
Race[2,4]												
White only	15.6	16.5	16.7	15.2	6.0	6.1	6.3	5.5	2.4	2.3	2.4	2.1
Black or African American only.	8.5	10.3	10.3	8.8	2.7	3.3	3.5	2.6	1.2	1.1	1.2	0.9
American Indian or Alaska Native only	17.9	21.1	13.5	22.8	*8.8	*7.1	*8.2	10.0	*3.8	*	*	*6.3
Asian only	8.0	8.0	9.5	9.1	2.8	2.6	2.7	3.5	*	*1.0	*1.3	*1.4
Native Hawaiian or Other Pacific Islander only	*	*	*	*	*	*	*	*	*	*	*	*
2 or more races	24.4	23.3	20.1	17.6	11.5	8.7	7.1	7.9	*4.9	*	*	*
Hispanic origin and race[2,4]												
Hispanic or Latino	10.9	10.9	12.2	9.3	4.3	3.5	4.7	2.8	2.5	1.4	1.9	1.3
Mexican.	11.8	11.5	13.8	10.5	4.4	3.5	6.2	3.2	2.5	*1.5	2.6	1.5
Not Hispanic or Latino	15.2	16.2	16.2	14.9	5.8	6.0	6.0	5.5	2.3	2.2	2.3	2.0
White only.	16.5	17.5	17.6	16.3	6.3	6.5	6.5	5.9	2.5	2.4	2.5	2.2
Black or African American only	8.4	10.3	10.4	8.7	2.7	3.3	3.4	2.6	1.2	1.1	1.2	*0.9
Education[5,6]												
25 years and over:												
No high school diploma or GED.	17.9	19.7	17.2	17.1	7.6	8.1	6.7	6.3	4.1	3.2	3.3	2.9
High school diploma or GED.	17.2	18.1	18.9	16.3	6.4	6.5	7.4	6.4	2.8	2.5	2.8	2.8
Some college or more	15.4	16.2	16.8	15.2	6.1	6.0	6.1	5.5	1.9	2.0	2.1	1.8

See footnotes at end of table.

Table 44 (page 2 of 2). Hearing limitations among adults aged 18 and over, by selectedcharacteristics: United States, selected years 2007–2015

Excel and PDF versions (with more data years and standard errors when available): http://www.cdc.gov/nchs/hus/contents2016.htm#044.

[Data are based on household interviews of a sample of the civilian noninstitutionalized population]

	Level of hearing trouble											
	Any hearing trouble (a little, moderate, a lot of trouble, or deaf)[1]				Moderate, a lot of trouble, or deaf[1]				A lot of trouble or deaf[1]			
Characteristic	2007	2010	2014	2015	2007	2010	2014	2015	2007	2010	2014	2015
Percent of poverty level[2,7]					Percent of adults							
Below 100%.	16.2	16.7	16.5	15.4	6.8	6.8	6.3	5.6	3.4	2.7	2.8	2.3
100%–199%.	15.5	17.2	16.6	15.8	5.8	6.6	6.3	6.0	2.8	2.5	2.4	2.6
200%–399%.	15.1	15.7	16.0	14.9	5.8	5.6	6.2	5.8	2.4	2.1	2.3	2.2
400% or more	13.6	14.5	14.7	12.6	5.3	5.0	5.2	4.2	1.6	1.8	2.0	1.4
Hispanic origin and race and percent of poverty level[2,4,7]												
Hispanic or Latino:												
Below 100%	12.7	9.1	13.0	9.7	*6.1	*3.5	4.4	3.0	*	*	*	*1.7
100%–199%	9.7	11.8	12.0	10.8	*3.1	4.3	4.6	3.8	*2.1	*2.3	*2.1	*1.8
200%–399%	9.8	10.3	12.2	8.2	*3.9	*2.6	5.0	*1.8	*	*	*	*
400% or more	13.3	12.4	12.3	8.0	*5.6	*3.2	*5.6	*2.2	*	*	*	*
Not Hispanic or Latino:												
White only:												
Below 100%	20.9	21.7	19.9	20.3	8.8	9.2	8.2	8.0	4.3	3.7	3.9	3.2
100%–199%.	18.8	20.8	21.0	19.7	7.2	8.3	7.8	7.6	3.3	3.0	2.9	3.2
200%–399%.	17.2	17.9	18.0	17.8	6.4	6.5	7.0	6.9	2.6	2.3	2.5	2.6
400% or more	14.3	15.4	16.0	13.8	5.6	5.4	5.7	4.5	1.7	2.0	2.1	1.4
Black or African American only:												
Below 100%	9.3	11.6	13.9	10.9	*2.8	4.0	4.5	2.3	*	*1.5	*1.9	*
100%–199%.	9.8	11.1	11.3	9.8	*3.1	3.0	3.9	3.3	*	*0.7	*1.1	*
200%–399%.	7.8	10.4	9.4	7.7	*2.2	3.6	*2.9	2.7	*	*	*	*
400% or more	7.1	7.7	6.6	7.0	*	*2.8	*	*2.0	*	*	*	*
Geographic region[2]												
Northeast	13.3	13.9	12.3	12.4	5.2	4.4	4.5	3.9	1.7	1.4	1.6	1.4
Midwest	16.0	17.5	17.4	16.0	6.1	6.3	6.1	5.8	2.3	2.3	2.3	2.2
South	14.0	16.0	16.1	13.9	5.4	6.3	6.1	5.3	2.5	2.6	2.3	2.1
West	15.5	14.4	15.8	14.4	5.9	5.3	6.2	5.4	2.4	1.9	2.6	1.9
Location of residence[2,8]												
Within MSA	14.0	14.7	14.9	13.5	5.3	5.4	5.5	4.9	2.1	1.9	2.1	1.9
Outside MSA	18.0	20.1	19.8	18.6	7.2	7.5	7.3	6.6	3.3	3.0	2.9	2.6

* Estimates are considered unreliable. Data preceded by an asterisk have a relative standard error (RSE) of 20%–30%. Data not shown have an RSE greater than 30%.

[1] Starting in 2007, respondents were asked questions about their hearing WITHOUT the use of hearing aids or other listening devices. "Is your hearing excellent, good, a little trouble hearing, moderate trouble, a lot of trouble, or are you deaf?" Hearing limitation questions differed slightly on the National Health Interview Survey across the years for which data are shown. See Appendix II, Hearing trouble.

[2] Estimates are age-adjusted to the year 2000 standard population using five age groups: 18–44 years, 45–54 years, 55–64 years, 65–74 years, and 75 years and over. Age-adjusted estimates in this table may differ from other age-adjusted estimates based on the same data and presented elsewhere if different age groups are used in the adjustment procedure. See Appendix II, Age adjustment.

[3] Includes all other races not shown separately and unknown education level.

[4] The race groups, white, black, American Indian or Alaska Native, Asian, Native Hawaiian or Other Pacific Islander, and 2 or more races, include persons of Hispanic and non-Hispanic origin. Persons of Hispanic origin may be of any race. Starting with 1999 data, race-specific estimates are tabulated according to the 1997 *Revisions to the Standards for the Classification of Federal Data on Race and Ethnicity* and are not strictly comparable with estimates for earlier years. The five single-race categories plus multiple-race categories shown in the table conform to the 1997 Standards. Starting with 1999 data, race-specific estimates are for persons who reported only one racial group; the category 2 or more races includes persons who reported more than one racial group. Prior to 1999, data were tabulated according to the 1977 Standards with four racial groups, and the Asian only category included Native Hawaiian or Other Pacific Islander. Estimates for single-race categories prior to 1999 included persons who reported one race or, if they reported more than one race, identified one race as best representing their race. Starting with 2003 data, race responses of other race and unspecified multiple race were treated as missing, and then race was imputed if these were the only race responses. Almost all persons with a race response of other race were of Hispanic origin. See Appendix II, Hispanic origin; Race.

[5] Estimates are for persons aged 25 and over and are age-adjusted to the year 2000 standard population using five age groups: 25–44 years, 45–54 years, 55–64 years, 65–74 years, and 75 years and over. See Appendix II, Age adjustment.

[6] GED is General Educational Development high school equivalency diploma. See Appendix II, Education.

[7] Percent of poverty level is based on family income and family size and composition using U.S. Census Bureau poverty thresholds. Missing family income data were imputed for 1997 and beyond. See Appendix II, Family income; Poverty; Table VI.

[8] MSA is metropolitan statistical area. Starting with 2006 data, MSA status is determined using 2000 census data and the 2000 standards for defining MSAs. For data prior to 2006, see Appendix II, Metropolitan statistical area (MSA) for the applicable standards.

NOTES: Starting with *Health, United States, 2013*, the hearing measures shown in this table were revised to provide a consistent definition over time. For a longer trend, see *Health, United States, 2012*. Available from: http://www.cdc.gov/nchs/hus.htm. Standard errors are available in the spreadsheet version of this table. Available from: http://www.cdc.gov/nchs/hus.htm. Data for additional years are available. See the Excel spreadsheet on the *Health, United States* website at: http://www.cdc.gov/nchs/hus.htm.

SOURCE: NCHS, National Health Interview Survey, sample adult questionnaire. See Appendix I, National Health Interview Survey (NHIS).

Table 45 (page 1 of 2). Respondent-assessed fair-poor health status, by selected characteristics: United States, selected years 1991–2015

Excel and PDF versions (with more data years and standard errors when available): http://www.cdc.gov/nchs/hus/contents2016.htm#045.

[Data are based on household interviews of a sample of the civilian noninstitutionalized population]

Characteristic	1991[1]	1995[1]	1997	2000	2005	2010	2014	2015
	Percent of persons with fair or poor health[2]							
All ages, age-adjusted [3,4]	10.4	10.6	9.2	9.0	9.2	9.6	8.9	9.2
All ages, crude [4]	10.0	10.1	8.9	8.9	9.3	10.1	9.8	10.1
Age								
Under 18 years	2.6	2.6	2.1	1.7	1.8	2.0	1.6	1.8
Under 6 years	2.7	2.7	1.9	1.5	1.6	1.8	1.3	1.2
6–17 years	2.6	2.5	2.1	1.8	1.9	2.2	1.8	2.1
18–44 years	6.1	6.6	5.3	5.1	5.5	6.3	6.1	6.3
18–24 years	4.8	4.5	3.4	3.3	3.3	3.9	3.7	3.8
25–44 years	6.4	7.2	5.9	5.7	6.3	7.2	7.0	7.2
45–54 years	13.4	13.4	11.7	11.9	11.6	13.3	12.8	13.5
55–64 years	20.7	21.4	18.2	17.9	18.3	19.4	18.4	18.7
65 years and over	29.0	28.3	26.7	26.9	26.6	24.4	21.7	21.8
65–74 years	26.0	25.6	23.1	22.5	23.4	21.2	19.5	19.0
75 years and over	33.6	32.2	31.5	32.1	30.2	28.3	24.9	25.8
Sex [3]								
Male	10.0	10.1	8.8	8.8	8.8	9.2	8.7	8.9
Female	10.8	11.1	9.7	9.3	9.5	10.0	9.2	9.5
Race [3,5]								
White only	9.6	9.7	8.3	8.2	8.6	8.8	8.3	8.5
Black or African American only	16.8	17.2	15.8	14.6	14.3	14.9	13.6	13.6
American Indian or Alaska Native only	18.3	18.7	17.3	17.2	13.2	17.8	14.1	16.6
Asian only	7.8	9.3	7.8	7.4	6.8	8.1	7.3	7.8
Native Hawaiian or Other Pacific Islander only	- - -	- - -	- - -	*	*	*	*	*
2 or more races	- - -	- - -	- - -	16.2	14.5	15.6	12.8	14.4
Black or African American; White	- - -	- - -	- - -	*14.5	8.3	*16.7	11.9	*13.7
American Indian or Alaska Native; White	- - -	- - -	- - -	18.7	17.2	19.0	17.6	18.2
Hispanic origin and race [3,5]								
Hispanic or Latino	15.6	15.1	13.0	12.8	13.3	13.1	12.2	12.7
Mexican	17.0	16.7	13.1	12.8	14.3	13.7	13.0	12.7
Not Hispanic or Latino	10.0	10.1	8.9	8.7	8.7	9.2	8.5	8.7
White only	9.1	9.1	8.0	7.9	8.0	8.2	7.7	7.9
Black or African American only	16.8	17.3	15.8	14.6	14.4	14.9	13.6	13.4
Percent of poverty level [3,6]								
Below 100%	22.8	23.7	20.8	19.6	20.4	20.9	19.8	21.2
100%–199%	14.7	15.5	13.9	14.1	14.4	15.2	14.2	14.9
200%–399%	7.9	7.9	8.2	8.4	8.3	8.3	7.9	8.4
400% or more	4.9	4.7	4.1	4.5	4.7	4.3	3.9	4.0
Hispanic origin and race and percent of poverty level [3,5,6]								
Hispanic or Latino:								
Below 100%	23.6	22.7	19.9	18.7	20.2	19.2	18.7	21.3
100%–199%	18.0	16.9	13.5	15.3	15.3	15.6	14.1	14.4
200%–399%	10.3	10.1	10.0	10.3	10.3	10.3	9.4	9.7
400% or more	6.6	4.0	5.7	5.5	7.6	6.4	5.5	5.7
Not Hispanic or Latino:								
White only:								
Below 100%	21.9	22.8	19.7	18.8	20.1	20.9	20.3	20.7
100%–199%	14.0	14.8	13.3	13.4	13.8	14.8	14.1	15.0
200%–399%	7.5	7.3	7.7	7.9	7.9	7.7	7.4	8.0
400% or more	4.7	4.6	3.9	4.2	4.3	4.0	3.5	3.7
Black or African American only:								
Below 100%	25.8	27.7	25.3	23.8	23.3	23.9	21.8	23.3
100%–199%	17.0	19.3	19.2	18.2	17.6	18.3	16.8	17.0
200%–399%	12.0	11.4	12.2	11.7	11.2	11.2	9.8	9.8
400% or more	5.9	6.5	6.1	7.3	7.1	6.8	5.7	6.3

See footnotes at end of table.

Table 45 (page 2 of 2). Respondent-assessed fair-poor health status, by selected characteristics: United States, selected years 1991–2015

Excel and PDF versions (with more data years and standard errors when available): http://www.cdc.gov/nchs/hus/contents2016.htm#045.

[Data are based on household interviews of a sample of the civilian noninstitutionalized population]

Characteristic	1991[1]	1995[1]	1997	2000	2005	2010	2014	2015
Disability measure among adults 18 years and over[3,7]	Percent of persons with fair or poor health[2]							
Any basic actions difficulty or complex activity limitation	- - -	- - -	27.0	27.6	28.5	28.7	28.8	29.1
Any basic actions difficulty	- - -	- - -	27.3	27.7	29.1	28.9	29.1	29.9
Any complex activity limitation	- - -	- - -	42.9	45.6	46.3	46.0	47.6	46.3
No disability	- - -	- - -	3.4	3.8	3.6	3.5	3.8	3.5
Geographic region[3]								
Northeast	8.3	9.1	8.0	7.6	7.5	7.9	7.2	8.2
Midwest	9.1	9.7	8.1	8.0	8.3	9.0	8.5	8.8
South	13.1	12.3	10.8	10.7	11.0	11.1	10.2	10.0
West	9.7	10.1	8.8	8.8	8.6	9.2	8.6	9.1
Location of residence[3,8]								
Within MSA	9.9	10.1	8.7	8.5	8.7	9.2	8.5	8.8
Outside MSA	11.9	12.6	11.1	11.1	11.2	11.9	11.4	11.8

- - - Data not available.

* Estimates are considered unreliable. Data preceded by an asterisk have a relative standard error (RSE) of 20%–30%. Data not shown have an RSE greater than 30%.

[1] Data prior to 1997 are not strictly comparable with data for later years due to the 1997 questionnaire redesign. See Appendix I, National Health Interview Survey (NHIS).

[2] See Appendix II, Health status, respondent-assessed.

[3] Estimates are age-adjusted to the year 2000 standard population using six age groups: under 18 years, 18–44 years, 45–54 years, 55–64 years, 65–74 years, and 75 years and over. The disability measure is age-adjusted using the five adult age groups. See Appendix II, Age adjustment.

[4] Includes all other races not shown separately and unknown disability status.

[5] The race groups, white, black, American Indian or Alaska Native, Asian, Native Hawaiian or Other Pacific Islander, and 2 or more races, include persons of Hispanic and non-Hispanic origin. Persons of Hispanic origin may be of any race. Starting with 1999 data, race-specific estimates are tabulated according to the 1997 *Revisions to the Standards for the Classification of Federal Data on Race and Ethnicity* and are not strictly comparable with estimates for earlier years. The five single-race categories plus multiple-race categories shown in the table conform to the 1997 Standards. Starting with 1999 data, race-specific estimates are for persons who reported only one racial group; the category 2 or more races includes persons who reported more than one racial group. Prior to 1999, data were tabulated according to the 1977 Standards with four racial groups, and the Asian only category included Native Hawaiian or Other Pacific Islander. Estimates for single-race categories prior to 1999 included persons who reported one race or, if they reported more than one race, identified one race as best representing their race. Starting with 2003 data, race responses of other race and unspecified multiple race were treated as missing, and then race was imputed if these were the only race responses. Almost all persons with a race response of other race were of Hispanic origin. See Appendix II, Hispanic origin; Race.

[6] Percent of poverty level is based on family income and family size and composition using U.S. Census Bureau poverty thresholds. Missing family income data were imputed for 1991 and beyond. See Appendix II, Family income; Poverty; Table VI.

[7] Any basic actions difficulty or complex activity limitation is defined as having one or more of the following limitations or difficulties: movement difficulty, emotional difficulty, sensory (seeing or hearing) difficulty, cognitive difficulty, self-care (activities of daily living or instrumental activities of daily living) limitation, social limitation, or work limitation. For more information, see Appendix II, Basic actions difficulty; Complex activity limitation. Starting with 2007 data, the hearing question, a component of the basic actions difficulty measure, was revised. Consequently, data prior to 2007 are not comparable with data for 2007 and beyond. For more information on the impact of the revised hearing question, see Appendix II, Hearing trouble.

[8] MSA is metropolitan statistical area. Starting with 2006 data, MSA status is determined using 2000 census data and the 2000 standards for defining MSAs. For data prior to 2006, see Appendix II, Metropolitan statistical area (MSA) for the applicable standards.

NOTES: Standard errors for selected years are available in the spreadsheet version of this table. Available from: http://www.cdc.gov/nchs/hus.htm. Data for additional years are available. See the Excel spreadsheet on the *Health, United States* website at: http://www.cdc.gov/nchs/hus.htm.

SOURCE: NCHS, National Health Interview Survey, family core and sample adult questionnaires. See Appendix I, National Health Interview Survey (NHIS).

Table 46 (page 1 of 2). Serious psychological distress in the past 30 days among adults aged 18 and over, by selected characteristics: United States, average annual, selected years 1997–1998 through 2014–2015

Excel and PDF versions (with more data years and standard errors when available): http://www.cdc.gov/nchs/hus/contents2016.htm#046.

[Data are based on household interviews of a sample of the civilian noninstitutionalized population]

Characteristic	1997–1998	1999–2000	2001–2002	2004–2005	2010–2011	2014–2015[1]
	Percent of adults with serious psychological distress[2]					
18 years and over, age-adjusted[3,4]	3.2	2.6	3.1	3.0	3.3	3.3
18 years and over, crude[4].	3.2	2.6	3.1	3.0	3.4	3.4
Age						
18–44 years	2.9	2.3	2.9	2.8	2.9	3.3
18–24 years.	2.7	2.2	2.8	2.5	2.4	3.2
25–44 years.	3.0	2.4	3.0	2.9	3.1	3.3
45–64 years	3.7	3.2	3.9	3.7	4.5	4.1
45–54 years.	3.9	3.5	4.2	3.9	4.2	3.9
55–64 years.	3.4	2.6	3.4	3.4	4.7	4.3
65 years and over	3.1	2.4	2.4	2.5	2.4	2.2
65–74 years.	2.5	2.3	2.4	2.2	2.6	2.4
75 years and over.	3.8	2.5	2.4	2.9	2.1	1.9
Sex[3]						
Male	2.5	2.0	2.4	2.3	2.8	2.7
Female.	3.8	3.1	3.8	3.7	3.7	3.9
Race[3,5]						
White only	3.1	2.5	3.0	2.9	3.2	3.3
Black or African American only	4.0	2.9	3.5	3.6	3.7	3.4
American Indian or Alaska Native only	7.8	*7.2	8.1	*3.5	5.6	*11.8
Asian only	2.0	*1.4	*1.8	1.7	1.7	1.9
Native Hawaiian or Other Pacific Islander only	- - -	*	*	*	*	*
2 or more races	- - -	4.8	5.0	7.9	5.6	8.4
Hispanic origin and race[3,5]						
Hispanic or Latino.	5.0	3.5	4.0	3.7	4.0	4.4
Mexican.	5.2	2.9	3.8	3.6	3.6	4.3
Not Hispanic or Latino.	3.0	2.5	3.1	3.0	3.2	3.2
White only.	2.9	2.4	3.0	2.9	3.2	3.1
Black or African American only.	3.9	2.9	3.5	3.6	3.7	3.4
Percent of poverty level[3,6]						
Below 100%.	9.1	6.8	8.4	8.6	8.2	8.3
100%–199%.	5.0	4.4	5.2	5.0	5.0	5.3
200%–399%.	2.5	2.3	2.8	2.5	2.9	2.8
400% or more	1.3	1.2	1.3	1.1	1.2	1.3
Hispanic origin and race and percent of poverty level[3,5,6]						
Hispanic or Latino:						
Below 100%	8.6	6.1	7.5	6.6	7.5	7.4
100%–199%	5.4	3.8	4.1	3.9	4.3	5.1
200%–399%	3.4	2.1	3.5	2.6	3.1	3.0
400% or more	*	2.3	*	*1.9	*1.4	2.7
Not Hispanic or Latino:						
White only:						
Below 100%	9.6	7.8	9.2	10.2	9.6	9.8
100%–199%	5.2	4.9	5.9	5.6	5.6	6.0
200%–399%	2.5	2.3	2.9	2.6	3.2	2.9
400% or more	1.3	1.1	1.3	1.1	1.1	1.2
Black or African American only:						
Below 100%	8.7	6.0	7.2	7.6	7.7	6.9
100%–199%	4.3	3.6	4.9	4.8	4.4	3.2
200%–399%	2.2	*1.7	2.3	2.1	1.9	2.6
400% or more	*	*1.0	*	*	*1.5	*1.0

See footnotes at end of table.

Table 46 (page 2 of 2). Serious psychological distress in the past 30 days among adults aged 18 and over, by selected characteristics: United States, average annual, selected years 1997–1998 through 2014–2015

Excel and PDF versions (with more data years and standard errors when available): http://www.cdc.gov/nchs/hus/contents2016.htm#046.

[Data are based on household interviews of a sample of the civilian noninstitutionalized population]

Characteristic	1997–1998	1999–2000	2001–2002	2004–2005	2010–2011	2014–2015[1]
Geographic region[3]	Percent of adults with serious psychological distress[2]					
Northeast	2.7	1.9	2.8	2.5	3.0	2.7
Midwest	2.6	2.5	2.9	2.7	3.1	3.3
South	3.8	2.9	3.5	3.7	3.6	3.4
West	3.3	2.8	3.0	2.8	3.3	3.7
Location of residence[3,7]						
Within MSA	3.0	2.3	3.0	2.8	3.1	3.2
Outside MSA	3.9	3.5	3.8	4.0	4.0	4.3

* Estimates are considered unreliable. Data preceded by an asterisk have a relative standard error (RSE) of 20%–30%. Data not shown have an RSE greater than 30%.

- - - Data not available.

[1] Starting in 2013 (shown in spreadsheet version), the six psychological distress questions were moved to the adult selected items section of the sample adult questionnaire. Observed differences between the 2012 and earlier estimates and the 2013 and later estimates may be partially or fully attributable to this change in question placement within the sample adult questionnaire.

[2] Serious psychological distress is measured by a six-question scale that asks respondents how often they experienced each of the six symptoms of psychological distress in the past 30 days. Respondents must have answered all six questions to have a computed K6 score. Only those with K6 scores were included in this analysis. See Appendix II, Serious psychological distress.

[3] Estimates are age-adjusted to the year 2000 standard population using five age groups: 18–44 years, 45–54 years, 55–64 years, 65–74 years, and 75 years and over. See Appendix II, Age adjustment.

[4] Includes all other races not shown separately.

[5] The race groups, white, black, American Indian or Alaska Native, Asian, Native Hawaiian or Other Pacific Islander, and 2 or more races, include persons of Hispanic and non-Hispanic origin. Persons of Hispanic origin may be of any race. Starting with 1999 data, race-specific estimates are tabulated according to the 1997 Standards and are not strictly comparable with estimates for earlier years. The five single-race categories plus multiple-race categories shown in the table conform to the 1997 *Revisions to the Standards for the Classification of Federal Data on Race and Ethnicity*. Starting with 1999 data, race-specific estimates are for persons who reported only one racial group; the category 2 or more races includes persons who reported more than one racial group. Prior to 1999, data were tabulated according to the 1977 Standards with four racial groups, and the Asian only category included Native Hawaiian or Other Pacific Islander. Estimates for single-race categories prior to 1999 included persons who reported one race or, if they reported more than one race, identified one race as best representing their race. Starting with 2003 data, race responses of other race and unspecified multiple race were treated as missing, and then race was imputed if these were the only race responses. Almost all persons with a race response of other race were of Hispanic origin. See Appendix II, Hispanic origin; Race.

[6] Percent of poverty level is based on family income and family size and composition using U.S. Census Bureau poverty thresholds. Missing family income data were imputed for 1997 and beyond. See Appendix II, Family income; Poverty; Table VI.

[7] MSA is metropolitan statistical area. Starting with 2006–2007 data (shown in spreadsheet), MSA status is determined using 2000 census data and the 2000 standards for defining MSAs. For data prior to 2006, see Appendix II, Metropolitan statistical area (MSA) for the applicable standards.

NOTES: Standard errors for selected years are available in the spreadsheet version of this table. Available from: http://www.cdc.gov/nchs/hus.htm. Data for additional years are available. See the Excel spreadsheet on the *Health, United States* website at: http://www.cdc.gov/nchs/hus.htm.

SOURCE: NCHS, National Health Interview Survey, sample adult questionnaire. See Appendix I, National Health Interview Survey (NHIS).

Table 47 (page 1 of 2). Current cigarette smoking among adults aged 18 and over, by sex, race, and age: United States, selected years 1965–2015

Excel and PDF versions (with more data years and standard errors when available): http://www.cdc.gov/nchs/hus/contents2016.htm#047.

[Data are based on household interviews of a sample of the civilian noninstitutionalized population]

Sex, race, and age	1965[1]	1979[1]	1985[1]	1990[1]	2000	2005	2010	2012	2013	2014	2015
18 years and over, age-adjusted[2]	Percent of adults who were current cigarette smokers[3]										
All persons.	41.9	33.3	29.9	25.3	23.1	20.8	19.3	18.2	17.9	17.0	15.3
Male	51.2	37.0	32.2	28.0	25.2	23.4	21.2	20.6	20.5	19.0	16.8
Female.	33.7	30.1	27.9	22.9	21.1	18.3	17.5	15.9	15.5	15.1	13.8
White male[4]	50.4	36.4	31.3	27.6	25.4	23.3	21.4	20.7	20.5	18.8	16.8
Black or African American male[4]	58.8	43.9	40.2	32.8	25.7	25.9	23.3	22.0	21.8	21.7	20.3
White female[4]	33.9	30.3	27.9	23.5	22.0	19.1	18.3	16.9	16.3	16.0	14.8
Black or African American female[4]	31.8	30.5	30.9	20.8	20.7	17.1	16.6	14.2	14.9	13.4	13.2
18 years and over, crude											
All persons.	42.4	33.5	30.1	25.5	23.2	20.9	19.3	18.1	17.8	16.8	15.1
Male	51.9	37.5	32.6	28.4	25.6	23.9	21.5	20.5	20.5	18.8	16.7
Female.	33.9	29.9	27.9	22.8	20.9	18.1	17.3	15.8	15.3	14.8	13.6
White male[4]	51.1	36.8	31.7	28.0	25.7	23.6	21.4	20.3	20.3	18.5	16.5
Black or African American male[4]	60.4	44.1	39.9	32.5	26.2	26.5	24.3	22.0	21.9	21.8	20.6
White female[4]	34.0	30.1	27.7	23.4	21.4	18.7	17.9	16.6	15.9	15.5	14.3
Black or African American female[4]	33.7	31.1	31.0	21.2	20.8	17.3	17.0	14.7	15.1	13.5	13.1
All males											
18–44 years	57.9	40.4	35.2	31.4	29.2	27.1	23.9	24.0	22.9	21.7	18.5
18–24 years.	54.1	35.0	28.0	26.6	28.1	28.0	22.8	20.1	21.9	18.5	15.0
25–34 years.	60.7	43.9	38.2	31.6	28.9	27.7	26.1	28.0	24.4	23.7	21.3
35–44 years.	58.2	41.8	37.6	34.5	30.2	26.0	22.5	22.8	22.1	22.0	18.3
45–64 years	51.9	39.3	33.4	29.3	26.4	25.2	23.2	20.2	21.9	19.4	17.9
45–54 years.	55.9	42.0	34.9	32.1	28.8	28.1	25.2	21.4	21.4	19.9	18.3
55–64 years.	46.6	36.4	31.9	25.9	22.6	21.1	20.7	18.8	22.6	18.8	17.5
65 years and over	28.5	20.9	19.6	14.6	10.2	8.9	9.7	10.6	10.6	9.8	9.7
White male[4]											
18–44 years	57.1	40.0	34.6	31.3	30.2	27.7	24.6	24.8	23.4	21.7	18.9
18–24 years.	53.0	34.3	28.4	27.4	30.4	29.7	23.8	21.9	23.5	20.0	15.6
25–34 years.	60.1	43.6	37.3	31.6	29.7	27.7	26.6	28.4	24.6	23.4	20.9
35–44 years.	57.3	41.3	36.6	33.5	30.6	26.3	23.1	23.3	21.9	21.2	19.1
45–64 years	51.3	38.3	32.1	28.7	25.8	24.5	22.5	19.4	21.7	19.0	17.3
45–54 years.	55.3	40.9	33.7	31.3	28.0	27.4	24.5	20.7	21.2	19.7	17.8
55–64 years.	46.1	35.3	30.5	25.6	22.5	20.4	20.1	17.9	22.2	18.2	16.9
65 years and over	27.7	20.5	18.9	13.7	9.8	7.9	9.6	10.3	10.0	9.4	9.3
Black or African American male[4]											
18–44 years	66.3	45.2	39.6	32.9	25.5	25.1	22.6	21.3	20.9	22.2	20.2
18–24 years.	62.8	40.2	27.2	21.3	20.9	21.6	18.8	13.2	*13.2	*13.9	*15.9
25–34 years.	68.4	47.5	45.6	33.8	23.2	29.8	25.7	24.9	24.8	28.0	26.0
35–44 years.	67.3	48.6	45.0	42.0	30.7	23.3	22.6	24.7	24.0	24.0	17.9
45–64 years	57.9	50.0	46.1	36.7	32.2	32.4	31.8	24.6	25.7	24.0	22.8
45–54 years.	62.4	51.5	47.7	42.0	35.6	33.9	33.2	23.3	25.7	22.5	20.5
55–64 years.	51.8	47.9	44.4	30.2	26.3	29.8	29.6	26.4	25.6	25.9	25.5
65 years and over	36.4	26.2	27.7	21.5	14.2	16.8	10.0	17.4	15.5	13.9	16.0
All females											
18–44 years	42.1	34.7	31.4	25.6	24.5	21.2	19.1	16.9	16.6	16.6	14.5
18–24 years.	38.1	33.8	30.4	22.5	24.9	20.7	17.4	14.5	15.4	14.8	11.0
25–34 year	43.7	33.7	32.0	28.2	22.3	21.5	20.6	19.4	17.9	17.5	15.0
35–44 years.	43.7	37.0	31.5	24.8	26.2	21.3	19.0	16.1	16.3	17.0	16.5
45–64 years	32.0	30.7	29.9	24.8	21.7	18.8	19.1	18.9	18.1	16.8	16.1
45–54 years.	37.5	32.6	32.4	28.5	22.2	20.9	21.3	21.3	20.6	18.7	18.4
55–64 years.	25.0	28.6	27.4	20.5	20.9	16.1	16.5	16.2	15.2	14.8	13.7
65 years and over	9.6	13.2	13.5	11.5	9.3	8.3	9.3	7.5	7.5	7.5	7.3

See footnotes at end of table.

Table 47 (page 2 of 2). Current cigarette smoking among adults aged 18 and over, by sex, race, and age: United States, selected years 1965–2015

Excel and PDF versions (with more data years and standard errors when available): http://www.cdc.gov/nchs/hus/contents2016.htm#047.

[Data are based on household interviews of a sample of the civilian noninstitutionalized population]

Sex, race, and age	1965[1]	1979[1]	1985[1]	1990[1]	2000	2005	2010	2012	2013	2014	2015
White female[4]				Percent of adults who were current cigarette smokers[3]							
18–44 years	42.2	35.1	31.6	26.5	26.5	22.6	20.5	18.6	17.8	17.8	15.7
18–24 years	38.4	34.5	31.8	25.4	28.5	22.6	18.4	16.9	17.0	16.5	11.2
25–34 years	43.4	34.1	32.0	28.5	24.9	23.1	22.0	20.7	19.2	18.6	16.3
35–44 years	43.9	37.2	31.0	25.0	26.6	22.2	20.5	17.6	17.0	18.0	18.3
45–64 years	32.7	30.6	29.7	25.4	21.4	18.9	19.5	19.4	18.4	17.6	17.1
45–54 years	38.2	32.5	32.4	29.1	21.9	21.0	22.4	22.7	21.2	19.9	20.2
55–64 years	25.7	28.5	27.2	21.2	20.6	16.2	15.9	15.8	15.5	15.3	14.0
65 years and over	9.8	13.8	13.3	11.5	9.1	8.4	9.4	7.5	7.9	7.6	7.5
Black or African American female[4]											
18–44 years	42.9	34.7	33.5	22.8	20.8	16.9	17.1	12.3	15.1	13.9	13.3
18–24 years	37.1	31.8	23.7	10.0	14.2	14.2	14.2	*7.4	11.8	*9.3	*8.6
25–34 years	47.8	35.2	36.2	29.1	15.5	16.9	19.3	17.3	16.4	15.1	14.9
35–44 years	42.8	37.7	40.2	25.5	30.2	19.0	17.2	11.2	16.4	16.4	15.4
45–64 years	25.7	34.2	33.4	22.6	25.6	21.0	19.8	20.4	18.8	15.0	14.5
45–54 years	32.3	36.2	36.4	26.5	26.5	22.2	20.4	20.1	22.2	15.7	14.7
55–64 years	16.5	31.9	29.8	17.6	24.2	19.1	18.9	20.8	14.8	14.2	14.3
65 years and over	7.1	*8.5	14.5	11.1	10.2	10.0	9.4	9.1	6.5	8.1	9.7

* Estimates are considered unreliable. Data preceded by an asterisk have a relative standard error of 20%–30%.

[1] Data prior to 1997 are not strictly comparable with data for later years due to the 1997 questionnaire redesign. See Appendix I, National Health Interview Survey (NHIS).

[2] Estimates are age-adjusted to the year 2000 standard population using five age groups: 18–24 years, 25–34 years, 35–44 years, 45–64 years, and 65 years and over. Age-adjusted estimates in this table may differ from other age-adjusted estimates based on the same data and presented elsewhere if different age groups are used in the adjustment procedure. See Appendix II, Age adjustment.

[3] Starting with 1993 data (shown in spreadsheet version), current cigarette smokers were defined as ever smoking 100 cigarettes in their lifetime and smoking now every day or some days. For previous definition, see Appendix II, Cigarette smoking.

[4] The race groups, white and black, include persons of Hispanic and non-Hispanic origin. Starting with 1999 data, race-specific estimates are tabulated according to the 1997 *Revisions to the Standards for the Classification of Federal Data on Race and Ethnicity* and are not strictly comparable with estimates for earlier years. The single-race categories shown in the table conform to the 1997 Standards. Starting with 1999 data, race-specific estimates are for persons who reported only one racial group. Prior to 1999, data were tabulated according to the 1977 Standards. Estimates for single-race categories prior to 1999 included persons who reported one race or, if they reported more than one race, identified one race as best representing their race. Starting with 2003 data, race responses of other race and unspecified multiple race were treated as missing, and then race was imputed if these were the only race responses. Almost all persons with a race response of other race were of Hispanic origin. See Appendix II, Hispanic origin; Race.

NOTES: Standard errors for selected years are available in the spreadsheet version of this table. Available from: http://www.cdc.gov/nchs/hus.htm. Data for additional years are available. See the Excel spreadsheet on the *Health, United States* website at: http://www.cdc.gov/nchs/hus.htm.

SOURCE: NCHS, National Health Interview Survey. Data are from the core questionnaire (1965) and the following questionnaire supplements: hypertension (1974), smoking (1979), alcohol and health practices (1983), health promotion and disease prevention (1985, 1990–1991), cancer control and cancer epidemiology (1992), and year 2000 objectives (1993–1995). Starting with 1997, data are from the family core and sample adult questionnaires. See Appendix I, National Health Interview Survey (NHIS).

Table 48. Age-adjusted prevalence of current cigarette smoking among adults aged 25 and over, by sex, race, and education level: United States, selected years 1974–2015

Excel and PDF versions (with more data years and standard errors when available): http://www.cdc.gov/nchs/hus/contents2016.htm#048.

[Data are based on household interviews of a sample of the civilian noninstitutionalized population]

Sex, race, and education level	1974[1]	1979[1]	1985[1]	1990[1]	1995[1]	2000	2005	2010	2014	2015
25 years and over, age-adjusted[2]										
All persons[4]	36.9	33.1	30.0	25.4	24.5	22.6	20.3	19.2	17.1	15.6
No high school diploma or GED.	43.7	40.7	40.8	36.7	35.6	31.6	28.2	26.9	24.4	25.6
High school diploma or GED	36.2	33.6	32.0	29.1	29.1	29.2	27.0	27.0	25.9	22.9
Some college, no bachelor's degree	35.9	33.2	29.5	23.4	22.6	21.7	21.8	21.3	18.6	17.9
Bachelor's degree or higher.	27.2	22.6	18.5	13.9	13.6	10.9	9.1	8.3	7.0	5.9
All males[4]	42.9	37.3	32.8	28.2	26.4	24.7	22.7	21.0	19.1	17.1
No high school diploma or GED.	52.3	47.6	45.7	42.0	39.7	36.0	31.7	29.7	27.7	28.6
High school diploma or GED	42.4	38.9	35.5	33.1	32.7	32.1	29.9	29.3	28.2	24.3
Some college, no bachelor's degree	41.8	36.5	32.9	25.9	23.7	23.3	24.9	23.2	20.2	18.7
Bachelor's degree or higher.	28.3	22.7	19.6	14.5	13.8	11.6	9.7	8.7	7.9	6.6
White males[4,5]	41.9	36.7	31.7	27.6	25.9	24.7	22.4	21.0	18.6	16.9
No high school diploma or GED.	51.5	47.6	45.0	41.8	38.7	38.2	31.6	29.4	26.0	27.1
High school diploma or GED	42.0	38.5	34.8	32.9	32.9	32.4	30.0	29.6	27.9	25.3
Some college, no bachelor's degree	41.6	36.4	32.2	25.4	23.3	23.5	24.5	23.4	20.3	18.0
Bachelor's degree or higher.	27.8	22.5	19.1	14.4	13.4	11.3	9.3	8.8	7.4	6.6
Black or African American males[4,5]	53.4	44.4	42.1	34.5	31.6	26.4	26.5	23.9	22.9	20.9
No high school diploma or GED.	58.1	49.7	50.5	41.6	41.9	38.2	35.9	34.4	38.7	38.1
High school diploma or GED	*50.7	48.6	41.8	37.4	36.6	29.0	30.1	28.8	28.7	22.1
Some college, no bachelor's degree	*45.3	39.2	41.8	28.1	26.4	19.9	27.4	24.2	18.8	23.0
Bachelor's degree or higher.	*41.4	*36.8	*32.0	*20.8	*17.3	14.6	10.0	8.1	9.8	*6.9
All females[4]	32.0	29.5	27.5	22.9	22.9	20.5	18.0	17.5	15.2	14.3
No high school diploma or GED.	36.6	34.8	36.5	31.8	31.7	27.1	24.6	23.7	21.2	21.2
High school diploma or GED	32.2	29.8	29.5	26.1	26.4	26.6	24.1	24.9	23.5	21.2
Some college, no bachelor's degree	30.1	30.0	26.3	21.0	21.6	20.4	19.1	19.6	17.3	17.2
Bachelor's degree or higher.	25.9	22.5	17.1	13.3	13.3	10.1	8.5	7.9	6.2	5.3
White females[4,5]	31.7	29.7	27.3	23.3	23.1	21.0	18.6	18.3	16.0	15.3
No high school diploma or GED.	36.8	35.8	36.7	33.4	32.4	28.4	24.6	24.0	21.0	23.8
High school diploma or GED	31.9	29.9	29.4	26.5	26.8	27.8	25.9	25.8	25.4	22.7
Some college, no bachelor's degree	30.4	30.7	26.7	21.2	22.2	21.1	19.5	21.0	18.3	18.6
Bachelor's degree or higher.	25.5	21.9	16.5	13.4	13.5	10.2	9.1	8.7	6.6	5.9
Black or African American females[4,5]	35.6	30.3	32.0	22.4	25.7	21.6	17.5	17.0	14.0	13.9
No high school diploma or GED.	36.1	31.6	39.4	26.3	32.3	31.1	27.8	25.8	22.5	24.0
High school diploma or GED	40.9	32.6	32.1	24.1	27.8	25.4	18.2	22.9	15.9	18.0
Some college, no bachelor's degree	32.3	*28.9	23.9	22.7	20.8	20.4	17.5	15.0	14.4	14.5
Bachelor's degree or higher.	*36.3	*43.3	26.6	17.0	17.3	10.8	*6.6	*6.6	6.9	*4.5

---

* Estimates are considered unreliable. Data preceded by an asterisk have a relative standard error (RSE) of 20%–30%.

[1] Data prior to 1997 are not strictly comparable with data for later years due to the 1997 questionnaire redesign. See Appendix I, National Health Interview Survey (NHIS).

[2] Estimates are age-adjusted to the year 2000 standard population using four age groups: 25–34 years, 35–44 years, 45–64 years, and 65 years and over. See Appendix II, Age adjustment. For age groups where smoking was 0% or 100%, the age-adjustment procedure was modified to substitute the percentage smoking from the next lower education group.

[3] Starting with 1993 data (shown in spreadsheet version), current cigarette smokers were defined as ever smoking 100 cigarettes in their lifetime and smoking now every day or some days. For previous definition, see Appendix II, Cigarette smoking.

[4] Includes unknown education level. Education categories shown are for 1997 and subsequent years. GED is General Educational Development high school equivalency diploma. In 1974–1995 the following categories based on number of years of school completed were used: less than 12 years, 12 years, 13–15 years, 16 years or more. See Appendix II, Education.

[5] The race groups, white and black, include persons of Hispanic and non-Hispanic origin. Starting with 1999 data, race-specific estimates are tabulated according to the 1997 *Revisions to the Standards for the Classification of Federal Data on Race and Ethnicity* and are not strictly comparable with estimates for earlier years. The single-race categories shown in the table conform to the 1997 Standards. Starting with 1999 data, race-specific estimates are for persons who reported only one racial group. Prior to 1999, data were tabulated according to the 1977 Standards. Estimates for single-race categories prior to 1999 included persons who reported one race or, if they reported more than one race, identified one race as best representing their race. Starting with 2003 data, race responses of other race and unspecified multiple race were treated as missing, and then race was imputed if these were the only race responses. Almost all persons with a race response of other race were of Hispanic origin. See Appendix II, Hispanic origin; Race.

NOTES: Standard errors for selected years are available in the spreadsheet version of this table. Available from: http://www.cdc.gov/nchs/hus.htm. Data for additional years are available. See the Excel spreadsheet on the *Health, United States* website at: http://www.cdc.gov/nchs/hus.htm.

SOURCE: NCHS, National Health Interview Survey. Data are from the following questionnaire supplements: hypertension (1974), smoking (1979), alcohol and health practices (1983), health promotion and disease prevention (1985, 1990–1991), cancer control and cancer epidemiology (1992), and year 2000 objectives (1993–1995). Starting with 1997, data are from the family core and sample adult questionnaires. See Appendix I, National Health Interview Survey (NHIS).

Table 49 (page 1 of 3). Current cigarette smoking among adults aged 18 and over, by sex, race, Hispanic origin, age, and education level: United States, average annual, selected years 1990–1992 through 2013–2015

Excel and PDF versions (with more data years and standard errors when available): http://www.cdc.gov/nchs/hus/contents2016.htm#049.

[Data are based on household interviews of a sample of the civilian noninstitutionalized population]

Characteristic	Male			Female		
	1990–1992 [1]	1999–2001	2013–2015	1990–1992 [1]	1999–2001	2013–2015
18 years and over, age-adjusted [2]	Percent of adults who were current cigarette smokers [3]					
All persons [4]	27.9	25.0	18.8	23.7	21.1	14.8
Race [5]						
White only	27.4	25.1	18.7	24.3	22.2	15.7
Black or African American only	33.9	27.2	21.2	23.1	19.7	13.8
American Indian or Alaska Native only	34.2	30.3	20.6	36.7	34.7	19.8
Asian only	24.8	20.3	13.4	6.3	6.7	4.4
Native Hawaiian or Other Pacific Islander only	- - -	*	*	- - -	*	*
2 or more races	- - -	34.4	27.2	- - -	30.7	21.2
American Indian or Alaska Native; White	- - -	38.7	30.5	- - -	38.9	27.6
Hispanic origin and race [5]						
Hispanic or Latino	25.7	22.2	14.4	15.8	12.1	7.2
Mexican	26.2	21.9	14.6	14.8	10.6	6.7
Not Hispanic or Latino	28.1	25.5	19.8	24.4	22.3	16.4
White only	27.7	25.5	19.9	25.2	23.5	17.9
Black or African American only	33.9	27.2	21.4	23.2	19.7	14.0
18 years and over, crude						
All persons [4]	28.4	25.5	18.7	23.6	21.0	14.6
Race [5]						
White only	27.8	25.4	18.4	24.1	21.7	15.3
Black or African American only	33.2	27.5	21.4	23.3	19.8	13.9
American Indian or Alaska Native only	35.5	31.8	20.5	37.3	36.9	20.3
Asian only	24.9	21.4	13.8	6.3	6.9	4.4
Native Hawaiian or Other Pacific Islander only	- - -	*	*	- - -	*	*
2 or more races	- - -	35.9	27.1	- - -	31.5	20.6
American Indian or Alaska Native; White	- - -	41.1	28.0	- - -	40.1	27.6
Hispanic origin and race [5]						
Hispanic or Latino	26.5	23.2	15.0	16.6	12.6	7.2
Mexican	27.1	22.8	15.0	15.0	11.0	6.6
Not Hispanic or Latino	28.5	25.8	19.4	24.2	21.9	15.9
White only	28.0	25.5	19.2	24.8	22.7	17.0
Black or African American only	33.3	27.5	21.6	23.3	19.8	14.1
Age and Hispanic origin and race [5]						
18–24 years:						
Hispanic or Latino	19.3	22.6	13.6	12.8	12.9	5.0
Not Hispanic or Latino:						
White only	28.9	32.7	21.9	28.7	30.8	18.4
Black or African American only	17.7	21.9	14.2	10.8	13.0	10.1
25–34 years:						
Hispanic or Latino	29.9	23.2	18.7	19.2	12.5	7.0
Not Hispanic or Latino:						
White only	32.7	30.8	24.4	30.9	27.4	21.4
Black or African American only	34.6	23.3	27.2	29.2	16.9	15.7
35–44 years:						
Hispanic or Latino	32.1	25.3	13.9	19.9	14.1	7.7
Not Hispanic or Latino:						
White only	32.3	29.6	22.9	27.3	28.3	20.9
Black or African American only	44.1	32.0	22.2	31.3	27.5	16.4
45–64 years:						
Hispanic or Latino	26.6	24.7	15.0	17.1	13.5	9.5
Not Hispanic or Latino:						
White only	28.4	25.1	20.1	26.1	22.1	19.1
Black or African American only	38.0	34.0	24.0	26.1	23.6	16.3
65 years and over:						
Hispanic or Latino	16.1	12.6	9.9	6.6	5.9	4.1
Not Hispanic or Latino:						
White only	14.2	10.0	9.6	12.3	9.8	8.0
Black or African American only	25.2	17.6	15.0	10.7	11.0	8.1

See footnotes at end of table.

Table 49 (page 2 of 3). Current cigarette smoking among adults aged 18 and over, by sex, race, Hispanic origin, age, and education level: United States, average annual, selected years 1990–1992 through 2013–2015

Excel and PDF versions (with more data years and standard errors when available): http://www.cdc.gov/nchs/hus/contents2016.htm#049.

[Data are based on household interviews of a sample of the civilian noninstitutionalized population]

Characteristic	Male			Female		
	1990–1992[1]	1999–2001	2013–2015	1990–1992[1]	1999–2001	2013–2015
Percent of poverty level[2,6]	Percent of adults who were current cigarette smokers[3]					
Below 100%.	40.5	36.5	31.8	30.7	29.1	24.6
100%–199%.	35.0	32.8	26.0	26.9	25.6	19.8
200%–399%.	26.5	27.3	19.6	22.6	22.3	14.7
400% or more	22.5	18.8	11.9	19.0	15.9	8.5
Hispanic origin and race and percent of poverty level[2,5,6]						
Hispanic or Latino:						
Below 100%	29.2	25.3	18.0	16.3	14.4	10.3
100%–199%	29.5	22.0	14.7	16.0	11.8	7.3
200%–399%	23.7	23.6	14.2	15.9	12.0	5.8
400% or more	19.7	18.1	11.0	13.6	9.4	5.5
Not Hispanic or Latino:						
White only:						
Below 100%	44.2	40.7	41.2	37.8	38.3	36.8
100%–199%	36.3	37.5	33.3	31.1	32.0	28.6
200%–399%	26.4	28.5	21.0	23.7	24.8	18.5
400% or more	22.5	19.1	12.5	19.5	17.1	9.7
Black or African American only:						
Below 100%	43.5	40.6	35.8	28.9	27.7	23.8
100%–199%	36.0	33.9	25.5	20.3	21.3	15.0
200%–399%	31.4	24.9	20.3	21.4	17.3	9.6
400% or more	24.3	17.9	10.3	19.2	12.6	6.3
Disability measure[2,7]						
Any basic actions difficulty or complex activity limitation	- - -	33.1	27.9	- - -	28.1	22.9
Any basic actions difficulty	- - -	33.2	28.0	- - -	28.2	23.1
Any complex activity limitation	- - -	37.6	32.0	- - -	30.6	27.4
No disability	- - -	22.8	15.9	- - -	18.8	11.6
Education, Hispanic origin, and race[5,8]						
25 years and over, age-adjusted[9]						
No high school diploma or GED:						
Hispanic or Latino	30.2	24.3	17.2	15.8	12.1	7.2
Not Hispanic or Latino:						
White only	46.1	43.5	42.2	40.4	39.3	41.5
Black or African American only	45.4	40.0	40.5	31.3	29.4	26.0
High school diploma or GED:						
Hispanic or Latino	29.6	24.1	15.2	18.4	12.5	8.0
Not Hispanic or Latino:						
White only	32.9	31.8	30.5	28.4	29.2	29.2
Black or African American only	38.2	31.4	28.3	25.4	23.0	16.9
Some college or more:						
Hispanic or Latino	20.4	17.1	10.8	14.3	11.1	7.5
Not Hispanic or Latino:						
White only	19.3	17.6	13.4	18.1	16.7	13.0
Black or African American only	25.6	19.2	15.3	22.8	16.9	11.5

See footnotes at end of table.

Table 49 (page 3 of 3). Current cigarette smoking among adults aged 18 and over, by sex, race, Hispanic origin, age, and education level: United States, average annual, selected years 1990–1992 through 2013–2015

Excel and PDF versions (with more data years and standard errors when available): http://www.cdc.gov/nchs/hus/contents2016.htm#049.

[Data are based on household interviews of a sample of the civilian noninstitutionalized population]

- - - Data not available.

* Estimates are considered unreliable. Data preceded by an asterisk have a relative standard error (RSE) of 20%–30%. Data not shown have an RSE greater than 30%.

[1] Data prior to 1997 are not strictly comparable with data for later years due to the 1997 questionnaire redesign. See Appendix I, National Health Interview Survey (NHIS).

[2] Estimates are age-adjusted to the year 2000 standard population using five age groups: 18–24 years, 25–34 years, 35–44 years, 45–64 years, and 65 years and over. See Appendix II, Age adjustment. For age groups where smoking is 0% or 100%, the age-adjustment procedure was modified to substitute the percentage smoking from the previous 3-year period.

[3] Starting with 1993 data, current cigarette smokers were defined as ever smoking 100 cigarettes in their lifetime and smoking now every day or some days. For previous definition, see Appendix II, Cigarette smoking.

[4] Includes all other races not shown separately, unknown education level, and unknown disability measure.

[5] The race groups, white, black, American Indian or Alaska Native, Asian, Native Hawaiian or Other Pacific Islander, and 2 or more races, include persons of Hispanic and non-Hispanic origin. Persons of Hispanic origin may be of any race. Starting with 1999 data, race-specific estimates are tabulated according to the 1997 *Revisions to the Standards for the Classification of Federal Data on Race and Ethnicity* and are not strictly comparable with estimates for earlier years. The five single-race categories plus multiple-race categories shown in the table conform to the 1997 Standards. Starting with 1999–2001 data, race-specific estimates are for persons who reported only one racial group; the category 2 or more races includes persons who reported more than one racial group. Prior to 1999, data were tabulated according to the 1977 Standards with four racial groups, and the Asian only category included Native Hawaiian or Other Pacific Islander. Estimates for single-race categories prior to 1999 included persons who reported one race or, if they reported more than one race, identified one race as best representing their race. Starting with 2003 data, race responses of other race and unspecified multiple race were treated as missing, and then race was imputed if these were the only race responses. Almost all persons with a race response of other race were of Hispanic origin. See Appendix II, Hispanic origin; Race.

[6] Percent of poverty level is based on family income and family size and composition using U.S. Census Bureau poverty thresholds. Missing family income data were imputed for 1990 and beyond. See Appendix II, Family income; Poverty; Table VI.

[7] Any basic actions difficulty or complex activity limitation is defined as having one or more of the following limitations or difficulties: movement difficulty, emotional difficulty, sensory (seeing or hearing) difficulty, cognitive difficulty, self-care (activities of daily living or instrumental activities of daily living) limitation, social limitation, or work limitation. For more information, see Appendix II, Basic actions difficulty; Complex activity limitation. Starting with 2007 data, the hearing question, a component of the basic actions difficulty measure, was revised. Consequently, data prior to 2007 are not comparable with data for 2007 and beyond. For more information on the impact of the revised hearing question, see Appendix II, Hearing trouble.

[8] Education categories shown are for 1997 and subsequent years. GED is General Educational Development high school equivalency diploma. In years prior to 1997, the following categories based on number of years of school completed were used: less than 12 years, 12 years, 13 years or more. See Appendix II, Education.

[9] Estimates are age-adjusted to the year 2000 standard using four age groups: 25–34 years, 35–44 years, 45–64 years, and 65 years and over. See Appendix II, Age adjustment.

NOTES: Standard errors for selected years are available in the spreadsheet version of this table. Available from: http://www.cdc.gov/nchs/hus.htm. Data for additional years are available. See the Excel spreadsheet on the *Health, United States* website at: http://www.cdc.gov/nchs/hus.htm.

SOURCE: NCHS, National Health Interview Survey. Data are from the following questionnaire supplements: health promotion and disease prevention (1990–1991), cancer control and cancer epidemiology (1992), and year 2000 objectives (1993–1995). Starting with 1997, data are from the family core and sample adult questionnaires. See Appendix I, National Health Interview Survey (NHIS).

Table 50 (page 1 of 2). Use of selected substances in the past month among persons aged 12 and over, by age, sex, race, and Hispanic origin: United States, selected years 2002–2015

Excel and PDF versions (with more data years and standard errors when available): http://www.cdc.gov/nchs/hus/contents2016.htm#050.

[Data are based on household interviews of a sample of the civilian noninstitutionalized population aged 12 and over]

Age, sex, race, and Hispanic origin	Any illicit drug [1]			Marijuana			Misuse of prescription psychotherapeutic drugs [2]		
	2002	2014	2015	2002	2014	2015	2002	2014	2015
				Percent of population					
12 years and over	- - -	- - -	10.1	6.2	8.4	8.3	- - -	- - -	2.4
Age									
12–13 years	- - -	- - -	2.6	1.4	1.1	0.8	- - -	- - -	0.9
14–15 years	- - -	- - -	7.2	7.6	5.5	5.7	- - -	- - -	1.7
16–17 years	- - -	- - -	16.3	15.7	15.0	14.2	- - -	- - -	3.3
18–25 years	- - -	- - -	22.3	17.3	19.6	19.8	- - -	- - -	5.1
26–34 years	- - -	- - -	15.4	7.7	12.7	12.9	- - -	- - -	3.7
35 years and over	- - -	- - -	6.6	3.1	5.2	5.1	- - -	- - -	1.6
Sex									
Male	- - -	- - -	12.5	8.1	10.9	10.6	- - -	- - -	2.6
Female	- - -	- - -	7.9	4.4	6.0	6.2	- - -	- - -	2.2
Age and sex									
12–17 years	- - -	- - -	8.8	8.2	7.4	7.0	- - -	- - -	2.0
Male	- - -	- - -	8.8	9.1	7.9	7.5	- - -	- - -	1.7
Female	- - -	- - -	8.8	7.2	6.8	6.5	- - -	- - -	2.3
Hispanic origin and race [3]									
Not Hispanic or Latino:									
White only.	- - -	- - -	10.2	6.5	8.7	8.4	- - -	- - -	2.6
Black or African American only	- - -	- - -	12.5	7.4	10.3	10.7	- - -	- - -	1.8
American Indian or Alaska Native only . . .	- - -	- - -	14.2	6.7	11.8	11.2	- - -	- - -	2.6
Native Hawaiian or Other Pacific Islander only.	- - -	- - -	9.8	4.4	12.1	9.2	- - -	- - -	1.7
Asian only.	- - -	- - -	4.0	1.8	2.8	3.0	- - -	- - -	0.7
2 or more races	- - -	- - -	17.2	9.0	12.4	13.4	- - -	- - -	4.8
Hispanic or Latino	- - -	- - -	9.2	4.3	6.7	7.2	- - -	- - -	2.3

Age, sex, race, and Hispanic origin	Alcohol use			Binge alcohol use [4]			Heavy alcohol use [5]		
	2002	2014	2015	2002	2014	2015	2002	2014	2015
				Percent of population					
12 years and over	51.0	52.7	51.7	- - -	- - -	24.9	- - -	- - -	6.5
Age									
12–13 years	4.3	2.1	1.3	- - -	- - -	0.7	- - -	- - -	0.0
14–15 years	16.6	8.5	7.4	- - -	- - -	3.8	- - -	- - -	0.3
16–17 years	32.6	23.3	19.7	- - -	- - -	12.6	- - -	- - -	2.3
18–25 years	60.5	59.6	58.3	- - -	- - -	39.0	- - -	- - -	10.9
26–34 years	61.4	66.0	65.0	- - -	- - -	38.3	- - -	- - -	9.7
35 years and over	52.1	54.4	53.5	- - -	- - -	21.8	- - -	- - -	5.6
Sex									
Male	57.4	57.3	56.2	31.2	30.0	29.6	10.8	9.3	8.9
Female	44.9	48.4	47.4	- - -	- - -	20.5	- - -	- - -	4.2
Age and sex									
12–17 years	17.6	11.5	9.6	- - -	- - -	5.8	- - -	- - -	0.9
Male	17.4	10.8	9.3	11.4	6.4	5.8	3.1	1.2	1.1
Female	17.9	12.3	9.9	- - -	- - -	5.8	- - -	- - -	0.7
Hispanic origin and race [3]									
Not Hispanic or Latino:									
White only.	55.0	57.7	57.0	- - -	- - -	26.0	- - -	- - -	7.6
Black or African American only	39.9	44.2	43.8	- - -	- - -	23.4	- - -	- - -	4.8
American Indian or Alaska Native only . . .	44.7	42.3	37.9	- - -	- - -	24.1	- - -	- - -	4.7
Native Hawaiian or Other Pacific Islander only.	*	37.9	33.8	- - -	- - -	17.8	- - -	- - -	3.0
Asian only.	37.1	38.7	39.7	- - -	- - -	14.0	- - -	- - -	2.2
2 or more races	49.9	49.5	42.8	- - -	- - -	22.9	- - -	- - -	6.8
Hispanic or Latino	42.8	44.4	42.4	- - -	- - -	25.7	- - -	- - -	4.8

See footnotes at end of table.

Table 50 (page 2 of 2). Use of selected substances in the past month among persons aged 12 and over, by age, sex, race, and Hispanic origin: United States, selected years 2002–2015

Excel and PDF versions (with more data years and standard errors when available): http://www.cdc.gov/nchs/hus/contents2016.htm#050.

[Data are based on household interviews of a sample of the civilian noninstitutionalized population aged 12 and over]

Age, sex, race, and Hispanic origin	Any tobacco[6]			Cigarettes			Cigars		
	2002	2014	2015	2002	2014	2015	2002	2014	2015
	Percent of population								
12 years and over	30.4	25.2	23.9	26.0	20.8	19.4	5.4	4.5	4.7
Age									
12–13 years	3.8	1.1	0.6	3.2	0.7	0.5	0.7	0.3	0.2
14–15 years	13.4	5.1	4.6	11.2	3.4	3.1	3.8	1.5	1.2
16–17 years	29.0	14.4	12.4	24.9	10.2	8.7	9.3	4.4	4.8
18–25 years	45.3	35.0	33.0	40.8	28.4	26.7	11.0	9.7	8.9
26–34 years	38.2	34.8	35.1	32.7	29.4	29.3	6.6	6.8	7.8
35 years and over	27.9	23.7	22.1	23.4	19.7	17.9	4.1	3.3	3.5
Sex									
Male	37.0	31.1	29.6	28.7	23.2	21.8	9.4	7.5	7.6
Female.	24.3	19.7	18.5	23.4	18.6	17.1	1.7	1.7	2.0
Age and sex									
12–17 years	15.2	7.0	6.0	13.0	4.9	4.2	4.5	2.1	2.1
Male.	16.0	8.2	7.0	12.3	5.1	4.6	6.2	2.7	2.6
Female	14.4	5.8	4.9	13.6	4.6	3.8	2.7	1.5	1.5
Hispanic origin and race[3]									
Not Hispanic or Latino:									
White only.	32.0	27.6	25.9	26.9	22.3	20.7	5.5	4.6	4.5
Black or African American only	28.8	26.6	26.0	25.3	22.5	21.3	6.8	6.5	8.0
American Indian or Alaska Native only . . .	44.3	37.8	37.0	37.1	32.5	29.5	5.2	4.2	6.4
Native Hawaiian or Other Pacific Islander only.	*	30.6	19.2	*	25.4	16.3	4.1	3.2	4.2
Asian only.	18.6	10.2	11.4	17.7	9.2	10.0	1.1	1.2	2.2
2 or more races.	38.1	29.5	31.9	35.0	24.4	26.8	5.5	6.5	5.9
Hispanic or Latino	25.2	18.8	17.7	23.0	16.7	15.3	5.0	3.7	3.7

* Estimates are considered unreliable. Data not shown if the relative standard error is greater than 17.5% of the log transformation of the proportion, the minimum effective sample size is less than 68, the minimum nominal sample size is less than 100, or the prevalence is close to 0% or 100%.

- - - Data not available.

[1] Any illicit drug includes marijuana, cocaine (including crack), heroin, hallucinogens (including LSD, PCP, peyote, mescaline, psilocybin mushrooms, "Ecstasy," ketamine, DMT/AMT/"Foxy," and Salvia divinorum), inhalants, methamphetamine, or the misuse of prescription pain relievers, tranquilizers, stimulants, and sedatives. See Appendix II, Illicit drug use.

[2] Misuse of prescription psychotherapeutic drugs is defined as use in any way not directed by a doctor, including use without a prescription of one's own; use in greater amounts, more often, or longer than told to take a drug; or use in any other way not directed by a doctor.

[3] Persons of Hispanic origin may be of any race. Data on race and Hispanic origin were collected using the 1997 *Revisions to the Standards for the Classification of Federal Data on Race and Ethnicity*. Single-race categories shown include persons who reported only one racial group. The category 2 or more races includes persons who reported more than one racial group. See Appendix II, Hispanic origin; Race.

[4] Binge alcohol use for men is defined as drinking five or more drinks on the same occasion on at least 1 day in the past 30 days. Starting in 2015, binge alcohol use for women is defined as drinking four or more drinks on the same occasion on at least 1 day in the past 30 days. Occasion is defined as at the same time or within a couple of hours of each other. See Appendix II, Alcohol consumption; Binge drinking.

[5] Heavy alcohol use is defined as drinking five or more drinks on the same occasion on each of 5 or more days in the past 30 days. By definition, all heavy alcohol users are also binge alcohol users.

[6] Any tobacco product includes cigarettes, smokeless tobacco (such as snuff, dip, chewing tobacco, or "snus"), cigars, or pipe tobacco. See Appendix II, Cigarette smoking.

NOTES: The National Survey on Drug Use & Health (NSDUH), formerly called the National Household Survey on Drug Abuse (NHSDA), began a new baseline in 2002 and cannot be compared with previous years. The NSDUH questionnaire underwent a partial redesign in 2015, including changes to some questions. Consequently, for some categories, data for prior years are not comparable to 2015 estimates and are not shown in this table. Starting with 2011 data, 2010-census based control totals were used in the weighting process. Because of methodological differences among the National Survey on Drug Use & Health, the Monitoring the Future (MTF) Study, and the Youth Risk Behavior Survey (YRBS), rates of substance use measured by these surveys are not directly comparable. See Appendix I, Monitoring the Future (MTF) Study; National Survey on Drug Use & Health (NSDUH); Youth Risk Behavior Survey (YRBS). See Appendix II, Substance use. Data for additional years are available. See the Excel spreadsheet on the *Health, United States* website at: http://www.cdc.gov/nchs/hus.htm. Data have been revised and differ from previous editions of *Health, United States*.

SOURCE: Substance Abuse and Mental Health Services Administration, Center for Behavioral Health Statistics and Quality, National Survey on Drug Use & Health. Available from: http://www.samhsa.gov/data/population-data-nsduh. See Appendix I, National Survey on Drug Use & Health (NSDUH).

Table 51 (page 1 of 3). Use of selected substances in the past 30 days among 12th graders, 10th graders, and 8th graders, by sex and race: United States, selected years 1980–2015

Excel and PDF versions (with more data years and standard errors when available): http://www.cdc.gov/nchs/hus/contents2016.htm#051.

[Data are based on a survey of 12th graders, 10th graders, and 8th graders in the coterminous United States]

Substance, grade in school, sex, and race	1980	1990	2000	2005	2010	2011	2012	2013	2014	2015
Cigarettes				Percent using substance in the past 30 days						
All 12th graders	30.5	29.4	31.4	23.2	19.2	18.7	17.1	16.3	13.6	11.4
Male	26.8	29.1	32.8	24.8	21.9	21.5	19.3	18.4	15.2	13.0
Female.	33.4	29.2	29.7	20.7	15.7	15.1	14.5	13.2	11.6	9.1
White	31.0	32.5	36.6	27.0	22.2	22.2	20.1	18.5	16.5	13.4
Black or African American	25.2	12.0	13.6	10.0	10.7	8.7	8.4	10.8	7.5	6.4
All 10th graders	- - -	- - -	23.9	14.9	13.6	11.8	10.8	9.1	7.2	6.3
Male	- - -	- - -	23.8	14.5	15.0	13.4	12.0	10.5	7.7	6.1
Female.	- - -	- - -	23.6	15.1	12.1	10.0	9.6	7.5	6.6	6.3
White	- - -	- - -	27.3	17.0	14.8	13.7	12.2	10.4	8.5	7.3
Black or African American	- - -	- - -	11.3	7.7	7.0	7.2	6.2	4.2	4.2	3.5
All 8th graders.	- - -	- - -	14.6	9.3	7.1	6.1	4.9	4.5	4.0	3.6
Male	- - -	- - -	14.3	8.7	7.4	6.2	4.6	4.0	3.5	3.3
Female.	- - -	- - -	14.7	9.7	6.8	5.7	4.9	4.7	4.2	3.7
White	- - -	- - -	16.4	9.5	7.9	6.5	5.0	4.3	4.6	3.8
Black or African American	- - -	- - -	8.4	6.7	4.0	4.2	3.8	3.3	2.0	2.4
E-cigarettes										
All 12th graders	- - -	- - -	- - -	- - -	- - -	- - -	- - -	- - -	17.1	16.2
Male	- - -	- - -	- - -	- - -	- - -	- - -	- - -	- - -	20.1	21.5
Female.	- - -	- - -	- - -	- - -	- - -	- - -	- - -	- - -	13.7	10.9
White	- - -	- - -	- - -	- - -	- - -	- - -	- - -	- - -	19.5	19.0
Black or African American	- - -	- - -	- - -	- - -	- - -	- - -	- - -	- - -	7.1	7.4
All 10th graders	- - -	- - -	- - -	- - -	- - -	- - -	- - -	- - -	16.2	14.0
Male	- - -	- - -	- - -	- - -	- - -	- - -	- - -	- - -	19.2	15.9
Female.	- - -	- - -	- - -	- - -	- - -	- - -	- - -	- - -	13.1	12.0
White	- - -	- - -	- - -	- - -	- - -	- - -	- - -	- - -	16.8	15.7
Black or African American	- - -	- - -	- - -	- - -	- - -	- - -	- - -	- - -	9.8	8.3
All 8th graders.	- - -	- - -	- - -	- - -	- - -	- - -	- - -	- - -	8.7	9.5
Male	- - -	- - -	- - -	- - -	- - -	- - -	- - -	- - -	9.8	10.2
Female.	- - -	- - -	- - -	- - -	- - -	- - -	- - -	- - -	7.1	8.6
White	- - -	- - -	- - -	- - -	- - -	- - -	- - -	- - -	7.3	8.8
Black or African American	- - -	- - -	- - -	- - -	- - -	- - -	- - -	- - -	5.1	6.9
Marijuana										
All 12th graders	33.7	14.0	21.6	19.8	21.4	22.6	22.9	22.7	21.2	21.3
Male	37.8	16.1	24.7	23.6	25.2	26.4	26.5	26.4	24.3	23.1
Female.	29.1	11.5	18.3	15.8	16.9	18.4	18.8	18.7	17.9	19.2
White	34.2	15.6	22.0	21.7	21.6	22.9	22.3	21.3	21.4	20.6
Black or African American	26.5	5.2	17.5	15.1	19.7	22.2	22.4	25.7	20.7	20.9
All 10th graders	- - -	- - -	19.7	15.2	16.7	17.6	17.0	18.0	16.6	14.8
Male	- - -	- - -	23.3	16.7	20.1	20.8	19.8	20.6	17.4	15.6
Female.	- - -	- - -	16.2	13.4	13.3	14.5	14.4	15.3	15.7	13.7
White	- - -	- - -	20.1	15.7	15.9	16.9	16.6	16.5	15.8	13.7
Black or African American	- - -	- - -	17.0	13.5	15.9	20.0	17.6	20.7	17.4	17.5
All 8th graders.	- - -	- - -	9.1	6.6	8.0	7.2	6.5	7.0	6.5	6.5
Male	- - -	- - -	10.2	7.6	9.2	8.5	7.0	6.7	6.9	6.6
Female.	- - -	- - -	7.8	5.7	6.8	5.7	6.0	7.2	5.9	6.2
White	- - -	- - -	8.3	6.0	7.1	5.9	4.7	4.8	4.7	4.5
Black or African American	- - -	- - -	8.5	8.2	8.2	8.0	7.1	9.3	6.5	7.9

See footnotes at end of table.

Table 51 (page 2 of 3). Use of selected substances in the past 30 days among 12th graders, 10th graders, and 8th graders, by sex and race: United States, selected years 1980–2015

Excel and PDF versions (with more data years and standard errors when available): http://www.cdc.gov/nchs/hus/contents2016.htm#051.

[Data are based on a survey of 12th graders, 10th graders, and 8th graders in the coterminous United States]

Substance, grade in school, sex, and race	1980	1990	2000	2005	2010	2011	2012	2013	2014	2015
Cocaine			Percent using substance in the past 30 days							
All 12th graders	5.2	1.9	2.1	2.3	1.3	1.1	1.1	1.1	1.0	1.1
Male	6.0	2.3	2.7	2.6	1.9	1.5	1.5	1.4	1.5	1.4
Female.	4.3	1.3	1.6	1.8	0.7	0.7	0.6	0.5	0.5	0.8
White	5.4	1.8	2.2	2.3	1.2	1.2	1.0	0.7	0.8	1.0
Black or African American	2.0	0.5	1.0	0.5	0.9	0.8	0.5	0.6	1.4	0.4
All 10th graders	- - -	- - -	1.8	1.5	0.9	0.7	0.8	0.8	0.6	0.8
Male	- - -	- - -	2.1	1.9	1.1	0.8	0.8	1.2	0.8	0.9
Female.	- - -	- - -	1.4	1.2	0.5	0.5	0.7	0.5	0.4	0.6
White	- - -	- - -	1.7	1.5	0.7	0.5	0.5	0.6	0.5	0.7
Black or African American	- - -	- - -	0.4	0.8	0.6	0.6	1.2	0.9	0.5	0.7
All 8th graders.	- - -	- - -	1.2	1.0	0.6	0.8	0.5	0.5	0.5	0.5
Male	- - -	- - -	1.3	0.9	0.6	0.7	0.5	0.4	0.5	0.5
Female.	- - -	- - -	1.1	1.0	0.6	0.7	0.4	0.5	0.4	0.4
White	- - -	- - -	1.1	0.9	0.5	0.5	0.3	0.4	0.2	0.3
Black or African American	- - -	- - -	0.5	0.3	0.3	0.5	0.5	0.5	0.4	0.5
Inhalants										
All 12th graders	1.4	2.7	2.2	2.0	1.4	1.0	0.9	1.0	0.7	0.7
Male	1.8	3.5	2.9	2.4	2.1	1.1	0.9	1.2	1.0	0.8
Female.	1.0	2.0	1.7	1.6	0.7	0.9	0.8	0.7	0.5	0.6
White	1.4	3.0	2.1	2.1	1.1	0.9	0.6	0.6	0.6	0.5
Black or African American	1.0	1.5	2.1	1.4	1.5	1.3	0.9	1.3	1.4	0.8
All 10th graders	- - -	- - -	2.6	2.2	2.0	1.7	1.4	1.3	1.1	1.2
Male	- - -	- - -	3.0	1.9	1.6	1.5	1.2	1.4	0.9	1.1
Female.	- - -	- - -	2.2	2.5	2.4	2.0	1.6	1.3	1.2	1.2
White	- - -	- - -	2.8	2.2	1.7	1.4	1.1	1.0	0.9	0.8
Black or African American	- - -	- - -	1.5	1.4	1.8	1.6	1.2	1.9	1.4	1.4
All 8th graders.	- - -	- - -	4.5	4.2	3.6	3.2	2.7	2.3	2.2	2.0
Male	- - -	- - -	4.1	3.1	2.8	2.5	1.9	1.6	1.6	1.8
Female.	- - -	- - -	4.8	5.3	4.4	3.9	3.4	2.9	2.6	2.1
White	- - -	- - -	4.8	4.0	3.2	2.7	2.1	1.7	1.7	1.6
Black or African American	- - -	- - -	2.3	2.9	2.2	2.8	3.0	2.4	2.4	2.1
MDMA (Ecstasy) [1]										
All 12th graders	- - -	- - -	3.6	1.0	1.4	2.3	0.9	1.5	1.5	1.1
Male	- - -	- - -	4.1	1.0	1.5	2.8	1.2	2.1	2.2	1.2
Female.	- - -	- - -	3.1	1.0	1.2	1.8	0.6	0.9	0.9	1.0
White	- - -	- - -	3.9	1.0	0.9	2.1	0.9	1.5	0.7	1.0
Black or African American	- - -	- - -	1.9	0.9	1.1	1.1	0.4	0.7	2.6	1.2
All 10th graders	- - -	- - -	2.6	1.0	1.9	1.6	1.0	1.2	1.1	0.9
Male	- - -	- - -	2.5	1.0	2.3	1.7	1.1	1.5	1.4	1.0
Female.	- - -	- - -	2.5	0.9	1.5	1.3	1.0	1.0	0.9	0.6
White	- - -	- - -	2.5	1.0	1.5	1.1	1.0	0.9	1.3	0.8
Black or African American	- - -	- - -	1.8	0.3	1.1	1.1	1.1	0.4	1.3	0.7
All 8th graders.	- - -	- - -	1.4	0.6	1.1	0.6	0.5	0.5	0.7	0.5
Male	- - -	- - -	1.6	0.8	1.2	0.7	0.4	0.4	1.0	0.4
Female.	- - -	- - -	1.2	0.4	1.1	0.5	0.6	0.5	0.5	0.5
White	- - -	- - -	1.4	0.6	1.0	0.4	0.4	0.3	0.6	0.4
Black or African American	- - -	- - -	0.8	0.9	0.5	0.2	0.5	0.6	0.7	0.3

See footnotes at end of table.

Table 51 (page 3 of 3). Use of selected substances in the past 30 days among 12th graders, 10th graders, and 8th graders, by sex and race: United States, selected years 1980–2015

Excel and PDF versions (with more data years and standard errors when available): http://www.cdc.gov/nchs/hus/contents2016.htm#051.

[Data are based on a survey of 12th graders, 10th graders, and 8th graders in the coterminous United States]

Substance, grade in school, sex, and race	1980	1990	2000	2005	2010	2011	2012	2013	2014	2015
Alcohol[2]			Percent using substance in the past 30 days							
All 12th graders	72.0	57.1	50.0	47.0	41.2	40.0	41.5	39.2	37.4	35.3
Male	77.4	61.3	54.0	50.7	44.2	42.1	43.8	41.8	37.4	36.0
Female.	66.8	52.3	46.1	43.3	37.9	37.5	38.8	36.3	37.1	35.0
White	75.8	62.2	55.3	52.2	44.1	43.4	44.3	42.8	42.1	39.7
Black or African American	47.7	32.9	29.3	28.8	30.8	29.4	29.8	27.0	24.9	23.2
All 10th graders	- - -	- - -	41.0	33.2	28.9	27.2	27.6	25.7	23.5	21.5
Male	- - -	- - -	43.3	32.8	30.1	28.2	28.0	26.0	23.0	20.6
Female.	- - -	- - -	38.6	33.6	27.7	26.0	27.1	25.3	23.9	22.5
White	- - -	- - -	44.3	36.7	29.2	28.9	29.2	26.9	25.9	23.6
Black or African American	- - -	- - -	24.7	20.8	21.3	20.3	20.1	17.7	15.5	14.8
All 8th graders.	- - -	- - -	22.4	17.1	13.8	12.7	11.0	10.2	9.0	9.7
Male	- - -	- - -	22.5	16.2	13.2	12.1	10.3	9.3	8.2	9.1
Female.	- - -	- - -	22.0	17.9	14.3	12.8	11.5	11.2	9.5	9.9
White	- - -	- - -	23.9	17.3	12.8	11.8	9.6	9.4	8.7	9.2
Black or African American	- - -	- - -	15.1	13.9	12.7	10.5	9.4	9.9	7.9	8.5
Binge drinking[3]			Percent having 5 or more drinks in a row in the last 2 weeks							
All 12th graders	41.2	32.2	30.0	27.1	23.2	21.6	23.7	22.1	19.4	17.2
Male	52.1	39.1	36.7	32.6	28.0	25.5	27.2	26.1	22.3	19.3
Female.	30.5	24.4	23.5	21.6	18.4	17.6	19.7	18.1	16.6	14.9
White	44.6	36.2	34.4	31.8	26.5	25.3	26.2	25.0	22.5	19.8
Black or African American	17.0	11.6	11.0	10.9	12.6	10.0	13.0	12.0	10.6	9.1
All 10th graders	- - -	- - -	24.1	19.0	16.3	14.7	15.6	13.7	12.6	10.9
Male	- - -	- - -	27.6	19.9	17.9	16.5	16.4	14.7	13.1	11.3
Female.	- - -	- - -	20.6	17.9	14.6	12.7	14.8	12.5	12.2	10.6
White	- - -	- - -	26.6	21.5	16.0	16.1	16.5	14.7	14.1	12.1
Black or African American	- - -	- - -	10.6	8.4	11.5	7.3	9.3	7.9	7.2	6.6
All 8th graders.	- - -	- - -	11.7	8.4	7.2	6.4	5.1	5.1	4.1	4.6
Male	- - -	- - -	11.7	8.2	6.5	6.1	4.6	4.5	3.5	4.6
Female.	- - -	- - -	11.3	8.6	7.8	6.5	5.5	5.7	4.6	4.6
White	- - -	- - -	12.5	8.4	6.7	5.8	3.9	4.6	3.7	4.2
Black or African American	- - -	- - -	6.2	5.8	5.9	4.4	4.2	4.8	4.1	4.1

- - - Data not available.

[1] Starting in 2014, a revised question on the use of MDMA (ecstasy) including "Molly," a nickname for MDMA, was added to the questionnaire for each grade. The 2014 and 2015 data reported here are only for the revised question which includes "Molly."

[2] In 1993, the alcohol question was changed to indicate that a drink meant more than a few sips. Data for 1993, available in the spreadsheet version of this table, are based on a half sample. See Appendix II, Alcohol consumption.

[3] Five or more alcoholic drinks in a row at least once in the prior 2-week period. See Appendix II, Binge drinking.

NOTES: Estimates for Hispanic students are not shown due to small sample size. For 2-year estimates for Hispanic students, see Johnston LD, O'Malley PM, Miech RA, Bachman JG, Schulenberg JE. (2015). Demographic subgroup trends among adolescents in the use of various licit and illicit drugs 1975–2014 (Monitoring the Future Occasional Paper No. 83). Ann Arbor, MI: Institute for Social Research, University of Michigan, 530 pp. Available at: http://monitoringthefuture.org/pubs.html#papers. Because of methodological differences among the National Survey on Drug Use & Health (NSDUH), the Monitoring the Future (MTF) Study, and the Youth Risk Behavior Survey (YRBS), rates of substance use measured by these surveys are not directly comparable. See Appendix I, National Survey on Drug Use & Health (NSDUH); Monitoring the Future (MTF) Study; Youth Risk Behavior Survey (YRBS). See Appendix II, Cigarette smoking; Illicit drug use; Substance use. Data for additional years are available. See the Excel spreadsheet on the *Health, United States* website at: http://www.cdc.gov/nchs/hus.htm.

SOURCE: Monitoring the Future Study. Institute for Social Research, the University of Michigan. Supported by National Institutes of Health, National Institute on Drug Abuse. See Appendix I, Monitoring the Future (MTF) Study.

Table 52 (page 1 of 3). Health risk behaviors among students in grades 9–12, by sex, grade level, race, and Hispanic origin: United States, selected years 1991–2015

Excel and PDF versions (with more data years and standard errors when available): http://www.cdc.gov/nchs/hus/contents2016.htm#052.

[Data are based on a national sample of high school students, grades 9–12]

Sex, grade level, race, and Hispanic origin	Seriously considered suicide [1]				In a physical fight [1]				Carried a weapon [2,3]			
	1991	2001	2013	2015	1991	2001	2013	2015	1991	2001	2013	2015
	Percent of students											
Total	29.0	19.0	17.0	17.7	42.5	33.2	24.7	22.6	26.1	17.4	17.9	16.2
Male												
Total	20.8	14.2	11.6	12.2	50.2	43.1	30.2	28.4	40.6	29.3	28.1	24.3
9th grade.	17.6	14.7	9.9	10.7	57.8	50.0	33.2	32.5	44.4	33.7	26.4	24.6
10th grade	19.5	13.8	11.3	10.8	50.2	45.0	30.9	29.4	41.5	28.4	26.4	25.5
11th grade	25.3	14.1	14.0	13.3	51.0	38.0	31.6	27.1	44.0	28.1	30.5	23.0
12th grade	20.7	13.7	11.0	14.0	42.3	36.5	23.8	22.9	33.1	25.6	29.5	23.4
Not Hispanic or Latino:												
White	21.7	14.9	11.4	11.5	49.1	43.1	27.1	26.6	41.2	31.3	33.4	28.0
Black or African American . . .	13.3	9.2	10.2	11.0	58.4	43.9	37.5	38.6	43.4	22.4	18.2	17.6
Hispanic or Latino	18.0	12.2	11.5	12.4	48.5	42.4	34.2	27.3	40.0	26.0	23.8	20.2
Female												
Total	37.2	23.6	22.4	23.4	34.4	23.9	19.2	16.5	10.9	6.2	7.9	7.5
9th grade.	40.3	26.2	24.6	26.5	42.9	30.3	23.3	22.6	10.4	7.4	8.6	6.6
10th grade	39.7	24.1	23.4	25.7	35.4	24.9	21.9	17.6	11.1	5.4	9.2	7.2
11th grade	38.4	23.6	22.3	22.1	34.5	20.3	16.7	12.8	12.9	5.9	5.9	8.0
12th grade	30.7	18.9	18.7	18.6	25.4	16.9	13.9	12.0	9.5	5.3	7.5	8.0
Not Hispanic or Latina:												
White	38.6	24.2	21.1	22.8	32.2	21.7	14.6	13.5	7.5	5.1	8.3	8.1
Black or African American	29.4	17.2	18.6	18.7	43.8	29.6	32.1	25.4	23.6	8.6	7.2	6.2
Hispanic or Latina	34.6	26.5	26.0	25.6	34.8	29.3	22.8	18.6	12.9	7.4	7.7	7.1

Sex, grade level, race, and Hispanic origin	Rarely or never wore a seatbelt [4]				Rode with a driver who had been drinking alcohol [2,4]				Texted or e-mailed while driving a car or other vehicle [5]			
	1991	2001	2013	2015	1991	2001	2013	2015	1991	2001	2013	2015
	Percent of students											
Total	25.9	14.1	7.6	6.1	39.9	30.7	21.9	20.0	- - -	- - -	41.4	41.5
Male												
Total	30.0	18.1	9.1	7.2	40.0	31.8	21.4	19.6	- - -	- - -	41.8	42.4
9th grade.	30.0	19.4	9.8	7.0	33.9	29.2	18.1	19.1	- - -	- - -	18.3	17.4
10th grade	25.5	16.6	8.4	7.6	36.6	31.5	19.9	19.0	- - -	- - -	27.8	25.2
11th grade	29.5	17.5	9.7	7.1	45.0	32.8	23.4	20.4	- - -	- - -	49.6	50.1
12th grade	34.7	18.6	8.3	6.1	44.7	34.5	25.3	19.9	- - -	- - -	61.0	61.9
Not Hispanic or Latino:												
White	28.6	17.7	8.5	5.3	40.2	31.2	19.6	17.7	- - -	- - -	45.1	45.0
Black or African American	37.5	20.3	11.8	12.4	37.5	31.2	18.9	20.6	- - -	- - -	31.5	33.0
Hispanic or Latino	37.1	17.7	8.9	6.8	47.2	37.1	28.9	25.3	- - -	- - -	39.5	42.2
Female												
Total	21.6	10.2	6.1	4.9	39.8	29.6	22.4	20.2	- - -	- - -	40.9	40.4
9th grade.	25.0	10.8	7.1	5.5	36.0	31.3	20.8	21.3	- - -	- - -	15.1	14.4
10th grade	20.4	10.3	5.7	4.5	38.8	29.9	23.8	18.4	- - -	- - -	25.0	24.7
11th grade	20.8	9.7	6.3	4.1	39.7	25.4	21.8	20.1	- - -	- - -	48.7	45.1
12th grade	20.2	9.4	5.1	5.1	44.8	31.3	23.2	21.0	- - -	- - -	59.5	60.8
Not Hispanic or Latina:												
White	18.7	9.7	4.7	3.5	40.9	29.4	19.9	17.5	- - -	- - -	46.7	45.3
Black or African American	31.9	12.2	7.1	7.6	33.8	24.2	24.8	21.2	- - -	- - -	26.5	33.1
Hispanic or Latina	25.9	11.3	8.7	6.3	46.7	39.3	29.2	27.3	- - -	- - -	32.1	28.2

See footnotes at end of table.

Table 52 (page 2 of 3). Health risk behaviors among students in grades 9–12, by sex, grade level, race, and Hispanic origin: United States, selected years 1991–2015

Excel and PDF versions (with more data years and standard errors when available): http://www.cdc.gov/nchs/hus/contents2016.htm#052.

[Data are based on a national sample of high school students, grades 9–12]

Sex, grade level, race, and Hispanic origin	Ever had sexual intercourse				Did not use a condom at last sex [6,7]				Ever physically forced to have sex			
	1991	2001	2013	2015	1991	2001	2013	2015	1991	2001	2013	2015
	Percent of students											
Total	54.1	45.6	46.8	41.2	53.8	42.1	40.9	43.1	- - -	7.7	7.3	6.7
Male												
Total	57.4	48.5	47.5	43.2	45.5	34.9	34.2	38.5	- - -	5.1	4.2	3.1
9th grade.	45.6	40.5	32.0	27.3	44.1	31.1	30.5	36.7	- - -	5.9	3.8	2.1
10th grade	50.9	42.2	41.1	37.9	43.1	30.7	30.7	34.4	- - -	4.1	2.8	3.9
11th grade	64.5	54.0	54.3	51.2	43.2	34.7	29.4	37.5	- - -	4.3	4.7	2.8
12th grade	68.3	61.0	65.4	59.0	49.3	40.8	42.0	42.6	- - -	5.8	5.5	3.5
Not Hispanic or Latino:												
White	52.7	45.1	42.2	39.5	44.8	36.2	38.2	41.9	- - -	3.8	3.1	2.0
Black or African American	88.1	68.8	68.4	58.8	43.0	27.3	27.0	26.4	- - -	8.5	5.2	4.4
Hispanic or Latino	64.1	53.0	51.7	45.1	53.0	40.9	33.5	37.5	- - -	6.2	5.2	4.0
Female												
Total	50.8	42.9	46.0	39.2	62.0	48.7	46.9	48.0	- - -	10.3	10.5	10.3
9th grade.	32.2	29.1	28.1	20.7	49.7	33.4	43.5	43.3	- - -	8.6	8.3	9.4
10th grade	45.3	39.3	41.7	33.5	63.6	47.8	44.5	46.0	- - -	10.7	11.8	7.9
11th grade	60.2	49.7	53.9	48.2	59.3	47.3	45.2	47.1	- - -	9.9	10.5	12.0
12th grade	65.1	60.1	62.8	57.2	67.4	58.8	51.6	51.2	- - -	12.2	11.2	11.9
Not Hispanic or Latina:												
White	47.1	41.3	45.3	40.3	62.0	49.0	46.8	44.1	- - -	9.8	9.1	9.9
Black or African American	75.9	53.4	53.4	37.4	60.6	39.3	44.7	53.3	- - -	10.6	11.5	10.3
Hispanic or Latina	43.3	44.0	46.9	39.8	73.1	52.4	49.3	51.7	- - -	11.6	12.2	10.1

Sex, grade level, race, and Hispanic origin	Watched television 3 or more hours [8]				Played video or computer games or used a computer 3 or more hours [8,9]				Not physically active at least 60 minutes every day [7,10]			
	1991	2001	2013	2015	1991	2001	2013	2015	1991	2001	2013	2015
	Percent of students											
Total	- - -	38.3	32.5	24.7	- - -	- - -	41.3	41.7	- - -	- - -	72.9	72.9
Male												
Total	- - -	41.8	32.8	25.0	- - -	- - -	42.3	40.6	- - -	- - -	63.4	64.0
9th grade.	- - -	51.4	34.6	26.3	- - -	- - -	43.0	42.5	- - -	- - -	59.5	59.9
10th grade	- - -	42.3	32.4	24.6	- - -	- - -	44.9	43.4	- - -	- - -	65.4	63.3
11th grade	- - -	36.8	32.3	24.6	- - -	- - -	42.4	36.1	- - -	- - -	63.0	65.7
12th grade	- - -	33.5	31.9	24.4	- - -	- - -	38.4	40.8	- - -	- - -	66.5	67.4
Not Hispanic or Latino:												
White	- - -	35.7	25.7	21.4	- - -	- - -	39.1	38.9	- - -	- - -	62.5	61.5
Black or African American	- - -	69.1	55.3	37.0	- - -	- - -	51.9	41.2	- - -	- - -	62.8	69.2
Hispanic or Latino	- - -	49.7	36.5	27.4	- - -	- - -	42.0	45.1	- - -	- - -	66.1	65.8
Female												
Total	- - -	35.0	32.2	24.4	- - -	- - -	40.4	42.8	- - -	- - -	82.3	82.3
9th grade.	- - -	39.6	35.3	25.3	- - -	- - -	46.5	48.7	- - -	- - -	79.9	79.1
10th grade	- - -	36.2	32.2	24.1	- - -	- - -	41.0	43.3	- - -	- - -	79.5	81.0
11th grade	- - -	32.5	30.4	22.4	- - -	- - -	37.6	38.1	- - -	- - -	85.6	84.0
12th grade	- - -	29.2	30.6	25.9	- - -	- - -	35.4	40.4	- - -	- - -	84.7	85.7
Not Hispanic or Latina:												
White	- - -	26.5	24.3	18.8	- - -	- - -	35.6	38.3	- - -	- - -	81.3	80.5
Black or African American	- - -	68.6	52.2	41.5	- - -	- - -	46.6	48.4	- - -	- - -	84.0	83.4
Hispanic or Latina	- - -	46.0	39.0	29.2	- - -	- - -	44.8	47.4	- - -	- - -	82.6	85.3

See footnotes at end of table.

Table 52 (page 3 of 3). Health risk behaviors among students in grades 9–12, by sex, grade level, race, and Hispanic origin: United States, selected years 1991–2015

Excel and PDF versions (with more data years and standard errors when available): http://www.cdc.gov/nchs/hus/contents2016.htm#052.

[Data are based on a national sample of high school students, grades 9–12]

Sex, grade level, race, and Hispanic origin	Did not eat breakfast on all 7 days [7,10]				Got fewer than 8 hours of sleep [7,11]			
	1991	2001	2013	2015	1991	2001	2013	2015
	Percent of students							
Total	- - -	- - -	61.9	63.7	- - -	- - -	68.3	72.7
Male								
Total	- - -	- - -	57.6	59.5	- - -	- - -	65.5	69.9
9th grade.	- - -	- - -	51.1	53.4	- - -	- - -	55.0	60.7
10th grade	- - -	- - -	58.2	57.7	- - -	- - -	62.9	66.2
11th grade	- - -	- - -	60.4	62.9	- - -	- - -	70.6	77.1
12th grade	- - -	- - -	62.3	65.3	- - -	- - -	75.7	77.4
Not Hispanic or Latino:								
White	- - -	- - -	55.1	56.7	- - -	- - -	64.6	68.9
Black or African American	- - -	- - -	64.3	69.2	- - -	- - -	71.2	74.4
Hispanic or Latino	- - -	- - -	60.4	60.5	- - -	- - -	64.6	67.1
Female								
Total	- - -	- - -	66.2	67.9	- - -	- - -	71.1	75.6
9th grade.	- - -	- - -	67.5	68.1	- - -	- - -	65.2	70.9
10th grade	- - -	- - -	65.6	68.9	- - -	- - -	70.1	76.9
11th grade	- - -	- - -	65.2	67.6	- - -	- - -	72.4	77.0
12th grade	- - -	- - -	66.3	67.1	- - -	- - -	77.6	77.8
Not Hispanic or Latina:								
White	- - -	- - -	63.0	65.2	- - -	- - -	70.6	75.1
Black or African American	- - -	- - -	75.1	75.3	- - -	- - -	72.4	79.4
Hispanic or Latina	- - -	- - -	67.9	69.9	- - -	- - -	69.8	73.2

- - - Data not available.
[1] During the past 12 months.
[2] During the past 30 days.
[3] Such as a gun, knife, or club.
[4] When riding in a car driven by someone else.
[5] Among students who drove a vehicle on at least 1 day during the past 30 days.
[6] Among students who were currently sexually active.
[7] Percent is 100 minus percent presented in MMWR Youth Risk Behavior Surveillance Summaries. See Surveillance Summaries at https://www.cdc.gov/healthyyouth/data/yrbs/index.htm.
[8] On an average school day.
[9] For something that was not school work.
[10] During the past 7 days.
[11] On an average school night.

NOTES: Only youths attending school participated in the survey. YRBS is conducted biennially. Persons of Hispanic origin may be of any race. Not all questions were asked for all years. All available and comparable data are presented as shown. See Appendix II, Hispanic origin; Race; Suicidal ideation. Standard errors for selected years are available in the spreadsheet version of this table. Data for additional years are available. See the Excel spreadsheet on the *Health, United States* website at: http://www.cdc.gov/nchs/hus.htm.

SOURCE: CDC/National Center for HIV, Hepatitis, STD, and TB Prevention, Youth Risk Behavior Survey. See Youth Online website at http://nccd.cdc.gov/youthonline. See Appendix I, Youth Risk Behavior Survey (YRBS).

Table 53 (page 1 of 2). Selected health conditions and risk factors, by age: United States, selected years 1988–1994 through 2013–2014

Excel and PDF versions (with more data years and standard errors when available): http://www.cdc.gov/nchs/hus/contents2016.htm#053.

[Data are based on interviews and physical examinations of a sample of the civilian noninstitutionalized population]

Health condition	1988–1994	1999–2000	2001–2002	2003–2004	2005–2006	2007–2008	2009–2010	2011–2012	2013–2014
Diabetes [1]	Percent of adults aged 20 and over								
Total, age-adjusted [2]	8.8	9.0	10.6	10.9	10.4	11.4	11.5	11.9	11.9
Total, crude	8.3	8.6	10.3	10.9	10.9	11.9	12.1	12.5	12.7
Hypercholesterolemia [3]									
Total, age-adjusted [4]	22.8	25.5	24.6	27.9	27.4	27.6	27.2	28.2	27.4
Total, crude	21.5	24.5	24.2	27.9	28.1	28.8	28.6	30.4	29.3
High cholesterol [5]									
Total, age-adjusted [4]	20.8	18.3	16.5	16.9	15.6	14.2	13.2	12.7	11.1
Total, crude	19.6	17.7	16.4	17.0	15.9	14.6	13.6	13.1	11.1
Hypertension [6]									
Total, age-adjusted [4]	25.5	30.0	29.7	32.1	30.5	31.2	30.0	30.0	30.8
Total, crude	24.1	28.9	28.9	32.5	31.7	32.6	31.9	32.5	33.5
Uncontrolled high blood pressure among persons with hypertension [7]									
Total, age-adjusted [4]	77.2	71.9	68.3	63.8	63.0	56.2	55.7	54.6	51.3
Total, crude	73.9	69.1	65.4	60.8	56.6	51.8	46.7	48.0	46.1
Overweight (includes obesity) [8]									
Total, age-adjusted [4]	56.0	64.5	65.6	66.4	66.9	68.1	68.8	68.6	70.4
Total, crude	54.9	64.1	65.6	66.5	67.3	68.3	69.2	69.0	70.7
Obesity [9]									
Total, age-adjusted [4]	22.9	30.5	30.5	32.3	34.4	33.7	35.7	34.9	37.8
Total, crude	22.3	30.3	30.6	32.3	34.7	33.9	35.9	35.1	37.9
Untreated dental caries [10]									
Total, age-adjusted [4]	27.7	24.4	21.3	29.8	24.4	21.7	- - -	25.5	31.5
Total, crude	28.2	25.0	21.7	30.2	24.5	21.8	- - -	25.5	31.3
Obesity [11]	Percent of persons under age 20								
2–5 years.	7.2	10.3	10.6	14.0	11.0	10.1	12.1	8.4	9.4
6–11 years	11.3	15.1	16.3	18.8	15.1	19.6	18.0	17.7	17.4
12–19 years	10.5	14.8	16.7	17.4	17.8	18.1	18.4	20.5	20.6
Untreated dental caries [10]									
5–19 years	24.3	23.6	21.2	25.6	16.2	16.9	14.6	17.5	19.6

See footnotes at end of table.

Table 53 (page 2 of 2). Selected health conditions and risk factors, by age: United States, selected years 1988–1994 through 2013–2014

Excel and PDF versions (with more data years and standard errors when available): http://www.cdc.gov/nchs/hus/contents2016.htm#053.

[Data are based on interviews and physical examinations of a sample of the civilian noninstitutionalized population]

- - - Data not available.

[1] Includes physician-diagnosed and undiagnosed diabetes. Estimates were obtained using fasting weights. Physician-diagnosed diabetes was obtained by self-report and excludes women who reported having diabetes only during pregnancy. Undiagnosed diabetes is defined as a fasting plasma glucose (FPG) of at least 126 mg/dL or a hemoglobin A1c of at least 6.5% and no reported physician diagnosis. Pregnant women were excluded. Adjustments to FPG recommended by NHANES for trend analysis were incorporated into the data presented here. For more information, see https://wwwn.cdc.gov/nchs/nhanes/2005-2006/GLU_D.htm. See Appendix II, Diabetes. See related Table 40.

[2] Estimates are age-adjusted to the year 2000 standard population using three age groups: 20–44 years, 45–64 years, and 65 years and over. Age-adjusted estimates in this table may differ from other age-adjusted estimates based on the same data presented elsewhere if different age groups are used in the adjustment procedure. See Appendix II, Age adjustment.

[3] Hypercholesterolemia is defined as measured serum total cholesterol greater than or equal to 240 mg/dL or reporting taking cholesterol-lowering medication. Respondents were asked, "Are you now following this advice [from a doctor or health professional] to take prescribed medicine [to lower your cholesterol]?" See Appendix II, Cholesterol. See related Table 55.

[4] Estimates are age-adjusted to the year 2000 standard population using five age groups: 20–34 years, 35–44 years, 45–54 years, 55–64 years, and 65 years and over. Age-adjusted estimates in this table may differ from other age-adjusted estimates based on the same data and presented elsewhere if different age groups are used in the adjustment procedure. See Appendix II, Age adjustment.

[5] High cholesterol is defined as greater than or equal to 240 mg/dL (6.20 mmol/L). This second measure of cholesterol presented in *Health, United States* is based solely on measured high serum total cholesterol. See Appendix II, Cholesterol. See related Table 55.

[6] Hypertension is defined as having measured high blood pressure and/or taking antihypertensive medication. High blood pressure is defined as having measured systolic pressure of at least 140 mm Hg or diastolic pressure of at least 90 mm Hg. Those with high blood pressure also may be taking prescribed medicine for high blood pressure. For antihypertensive medication use, respondents were asked, "Are you now taking prescribed medicine for your high blood pressure?" Pregnant women were excluded. See Appendix II, Blood pressure, high. See related Table 54.

[7] Uncontrolled high blood pressure among persons with hypertension is defined as measured systolic pressure of at least 140 mm Hg or diastolic pressure of at least 90 mm Hg, among those with measured high blood pressure or reporting taking antihypertensive medication. Pregnant women were excluded. See Appendix II, Blood pressure, high. See related Table 54.

[8] Overweight is defined as body mass index (BMI) greater than or equal to 25, based on the NHANES variable, Body Mass Index. Excludes pregnant women. See Appendix II, Body mass index (BMI). See related Table 58.

[9] Obesity is defined as body mass index (BMI) greater than or equal to 30, based on the NHANES variable, Body Mass Index. Excludes pregnant women. See Appendix II, Body mass index (BMI). See related Table 58.

[10] Untreated dental caries refers to decay on the crown or enamel surface of a tooth (i.e., coronal caries) that has not been treated or filled. The presence of caries was evaluated in primary and permanent teeth for persons aged 5 and older. The third molars were not included. Persons without at least one natural tooth (primary or permanent) were excluded. Over time, there have been changes in the NHANES oral health examination process, ages examined, and methodology. For more information, see Appendix II, Dental caries. See related Table 60.

[11] Obesity is defined as body mass index (BMI) at or above the sex- and age-specific 95th percentile BMI (based on the variable BMXBMI) using cutoff points from the 2000 CDC growth charts for the United States: Methods and development. NCHS. Vital Health Stat 11(246). 2002. Available at: http://www.cdc.gov/nchs/data/series/sr_11/sr11_246.pdf. Excludes pregnant girls. See related Table 59.

NOTES: Standard errors are available in the spreadsheet version of this table. Available from: http://www.cdc.gov/nchs/hus.htm.

SOURCE: NCHS, National Health and Nutrition Examination Survey. See Appendix I, National Health and Nutrition Examination Survey (NHANES).

Table 54 (page 1 of 2). Hypertension among adults aged 20 and over, by selected characteristics: United States, selected years 1988–1994 through 2011–2014

Excel and PDF versions (with more data years and standard errors when available): http://www.cdc.gov/nchs/hus/contents2016.htm#054.

[Data are based on interviews and physical examinations of a sample of the civilian noninstitutionalized population]

Sex, age, race and Hispanic origin[1], and percent of poverty level	Hypertension[2,3] (measured high blood pressure and/or taking antihypertensive medication)				Uncontrolled high blood pressure among persons with hypertension[4]			
	1988–1994	1999–2002	2007–2010	2011–2014	1988–1994	1999–2002	2007–2010	2011–2014
20 years and over, age-adjusted[5]	*Percent of population*							
Both sexes[6]	25.5	30.0	30.6	30.4	77.2	70.6	55.8	52.8
Male	26.4	28.8	31.3	31.0	83.2	73.3	61.4	58.1
Female	24.4	30.6	29.6	29.7	68.5	61.8	46.3	45.5
Not Hispanic or Latino:								
White only	24.4	28.3	29.7	29.1	76.6	69.1	52.7	48.4
White only, male	25.6	27.6	31.1	30.2	82.6	70.3	57.3	53.5
White only, female	23.0	28.5	28.1	28.0	67.0	63.6	44.2	40.2
Black or African American only	38.1	42.3	42.7	43.3	77.5	71.5	59.7	58.7
Black or African American only, male	37.5	40.6	40.5	42.4	84.0	74.3	71.5	66.2
Black or African American only, female	38.3	43.5	44.3	44.0	71.1	67.2	51.0	52.8
Asian only	- - -	- - -	- - -	26.5	- - -	- - -	- - -	64.7
Asian only, male	- - -	- - -	- - -	28.0	- - -	- - -	- - -	68.6
Asian only, female	- - -	- - -	- - -	25.0	- - -	- - -	- - -	58.7
Hispanic or Latino	- - -	- - -	28.5	28.2	- - -	- - -	64.4	57.5
Hispanic or Latino, male	- - -	- - -	29.0	27.7	- - -	- - -	70.3	69.6
Hispanic or Latina, female	- - -	- - -	27.6	28.6	- - -	- - -	48.1	43.4
Mexican origin	26.1	27.6	28.5	28.4	85.7	84.1	69.5	59.3
Mexican origin, male	26.9	26.8	28.6	27.5	87.9	89.5	71.6	71.4
Mexican origin, female	25.0	27.9	27.8	29.4	77.6	71.5	56.4	40.7
Percent of poverty level:[7]								
Below 100%	31.7	33.9	33.8	34.1	75.0	71.2	54.5	54.8
100%–199%	26.6	33.5	33.4	33.4	76.0	73.4	60.4	56.4
200%–399%	24.7	30.2	31.7	30.0	76.2	67.8	51.9	51.5
400% or more	22.6	26.4	28.5	27.7	81.5	70.3	56.2	53.5
20 years and over, crude								
Both sexes[6]	24.1	30.2	32.2	33.0	73.9	67.3	49.3	47.0
Male	23.8	27.6	31.7	32.6	79.3	67.1	52.3	49.9
Female	24.4	32.7	32.8	33.4	68.8	67.4	46.4	44.3
Not Hispanic or Latino:								
White only	24.4	30.6	33.5	34.5	72.7	65.5	46.6	44.3
White only, male	24.3	28.3	33.7	34.6	78.0	64.0	48.7	46.0
White only, female	24.6	32.8	33.4	34.5	67.8	66.9	44.6	42.5
Black or African American only	31.8	39.1	41.3	43.0	75.9	69.1	54.6	52.6
Black or African American only, male	31.1	35.9	37.6	40.9	83.3	71.3	62.3	58.3
Black or African American only, female	32.5	41.9	44.4	44.8	70.0	67.5	49.2	48.1
Asian only	- - -	- - -	- - -	25.0	- - -	- - -	- - -	56.7
Asian only, male	- - -	- - -	- - -	25.7	- - -	- - -	- - -	61.2
Asian only, female	- - -	- - -	- - -	24.3	- - -	- - -	- - -	52.4
Hispanic or Latino	- - -	- - -	21.2	22.0	- - -	- - -	59.3	53.2
Hispanic or Latino, male	- - -	- - -	20.9	20.4	- - -	- - -	64.7	59.6
Hispanic or Latina, female	- - -	- - -	21.6	23.6	- - -	- - -	53.4	47.3
Mexican origin	16.2	17.5	20.6	21.3	83.8	80.9	62.6	55.4
Mexican origin, male	16.4	16.5	19.9	20.2	86.5	86.9	66.2	62.6
Mexican origin, female	15.9	18.8	21.4	22.5	80.6	74.5	58.6	47.8
Percent of poverty level:[7]								
Below 100%	25.7	30.3	27.5	29.1	74.0	71.3	54.4	52.4
100%–199%	26.7	34.8	36.2	36.5	75.1	70.7	54.5	48.3
200%–399%	22.4	29.9	34.2	33.2	73.4	64.4	46.3	46.7
400% or more	22.0	26.8	30.6	32.2	74.3	63.8	45.1	44.2

See footnotes at end of table.

Table 54 (page 2 of 2). Hypertension among adults aged 20 and over, by selected characteristics: United States, selected years 1988–1994 through 2011–2014

Excel and PDF versions (with more data years and standard errors when available): http://www.cdc.gov/nchs/hus/contents2016.htm#054.

[Data are based on interviews and physical examinations of a sample of the civilian noninstitutionalized population]

Sex, age, race and Hispanic origin[1], and percent of poverty level	Hypertension[2,3] (measured high blood pressure and/or taking antihypertensive medication)				Uncontrolled high blood pressure among persons with hypertension[4]			
	1988–1994	*1999–2002*	*2007–2010*	*2011–2014*	*1988–1994*	*1999–2002*	*2007–2010*	*2011–2014*
Male	Percent of population							
20–44 years	10.9	12.1	12.5	11.5	90.5	79.7	67.9	67.8
20–34 years.	7.1	*8.1	6.8	6.9	92.6	89.9	82.5	74.1
35–44 years.	17.1	17.1	20.7	18.8	89.0	73.3	60.8	64.2
45–64 years	34.2	36.4	41.2	43.8	73.1	61.4	50.6	49.7
45–54 years.	29.2	31.0	35.5	33.0	76.2	66.4	54.4	46.3
55–64 years.	40.6	45.0	49.5	54.9	70.3	55.9	46.7	51.7
65–74 years	54.4	59.6	64.1	63.4	74.3	59.1	42.2	38.2
75 years and over.	60.4	69.0	71.7	72.3	82.5	74.3	50.7	46.5
Female								
20–44 years	6.5	8.3	8.3	10.2	63.4	58.3	44.4	41.9
20–34 years.	2.9	*2.7	3.8	4.3	82.2	56.9	52.6	55.5
35–44 years.	11.2	15.1	14.2	18.6	56.8	58.6	41.6	37.7
45–64 years	32.8	40.0	39.7	39.5	62.1	60.5	42.9	36.8
45–54 years.	23.9	31.8	31.2	28.1	58.5	61.1	38.9	40.3
55–64 years.	42.6	53.9	50.4	52.1	64.3	60.0	46.1	34.8
65–74 years	56.2	72.7	69.3	64.3	68.7	73.5	44.9	44.5
75 years and over.	73.6	83.1	81.3	79.9	81.9	78.1	56.0	61.5

* Estimates are considered unreliable. Data preceded by an asterisk have a relative standard error of 20%–30%.

- - - Data not available.

[1] Persons of Hispanic and Mexican origin may be of any race. Starting with 1999 data, race-specific estimates are tabulated according to the 1997 *Revisions to the Standards for the Classification of Federal Data on Race and Ethnicity* and are not strictly comparable with estimates for earlier years. The non-Hispanic race categories shown in the table conform to the 1997 Standards. Starting with 1999 data, race-specific estimates are for persons who reported only one racial group. Prior to data year 1999, estimates were tabulated according to the 1977 Standards. Estimates for single-race categories prior to 1999 included persons who reported one race or, if they reported more than one race, identified one race as best representing their race. See Appendix II, Hispanic origin; Race.

[2] Hypertension is defined as having measured high blood pressure and/or taking antihypertensive medication. High blood pressure is defined as having measured systolic pressure of at least 140 mm Hg or diastolic pressure of at least 90 mm Hg. Those with high blood pressure also may be taking prescribed medicine for high blood pressure. Those taking antihypertensive medication may not have measured high blood pressure but are still classified as having hypertension. See Appendix II, Blood pressure, high.

[3] Respondents were asked, "Are you now taking prescribed medicine for your high blood pressure?"

[4] Uncontrolled high blood pressure among persons with hypertension is defined as measured systolic pressure of at least 140 mm Hg or diastolic pressure of at least 90 mm Hg, among those with measured high blood pressure or reporting taking antihypertensive medication. See Appendix II, Blood pressure, high.

[5] Estimates are age-adjusted to the year 2000 standard population using five age groups: 20–34 years, 35–44 years, 45–54 years, 55–64 years, and 65 years and over. Age-adjusted estimates in this table may differ from other age-adjusted estimates based on the same data and presented elsewhere if different age groups are used in the adjustment procedure. See Appendix II, Age adjustment.

[6] Includes persons of all races and Hispanic origins, not just those shown separately.

[7] Percent of poverty level was calculated by dividing family income by the U.S. Department of Health and Human Services' poverty guideline specific to family size, as well as the appropriate year, and state. Persons with unknown percent of poverty level are excluded (6% in 2011–2014). See Appendix II, Family income; Poverty.

NOTES: Percentages are based on the average of blood pressure measurements taken. In 2011–2014, 85% of participants had three systolic or diastolic blood pressure readings. Excludes pregnant women. Standard errors are available in the spreadsheet version of this table. Available from: http://www.cdc.gov/nchs/hus.htm. Data for additional years are available. See the Excel spreadsheet on the *Health, United States* website at: http://www.cdc.gov/nchs/hus.htm.

SOURCE: NCHS, National Health and Nutrition Examination Survey. See Appendix I, National Health and Nutrition Examination Survey (NHANES).

Table 55 (page 1 of 4). Cholesterol among adults aged 20 and over, by selected characteristics: United States, selected years 1988–1994 through 2011–2014

Excel and PDF versions (with more data years and standard errors when available): http://www.cdc.gov/nchs/hus/contents2016.htm#055.

[Data are based on interviews and laboratory data of a sample of the civilian noninstitutionalized population]

Sex, age, race and Hispanic origin [1], and percent of poverty level	1988–1994	1999–2002	2003–2006	2007–2010	2011–2014
20 years and over, age-adjusted [2]	Percent of population with hypercholesterolemia (serum total cholesterol greater than or equal to 240 mg/dL or taking cholesterol-lowering medications) [3]				
Both sexes [4]	22.8	25.0	27.7	27.4	27.8
Male	21.1	25.3	27.7	28.0	28.4
Female	24.0	24.3	27.4	26.7	27.3
Not Hispanic or Latino:					
White only	22.9	25.8	28.5	27.8	28.7
White only, male	21.1	26.0	28.7	28.1	29.4
White only, female	24.2	25.1	28.2	27.4	28.0
Black or African American only	21.3	21.3	23.2	25.6	25.2
Black or African American only, male	18.6	20.1	22.8	25.4	24.5
Black or African American only, female	23.1	22.0	23.3	25.6	25.7
Asian only	- - -	- - -	- - -	- - -	26.0
Asian only, male	- - -	- - -	- - -	- - -	27.4
Asian only, female	- - -	- - -	- - -	- - -	24.6
Hispanic or Latino	- - -	- - -	- - -	27.3	26.3
Hispanic or Latino, male	- - -	- - -	- - -	29.1	26.6
Hispanic or Latina, female	- - -	- - -	- - -	25.2	25.8
Mexican origin	20.0	20.6	24.2	27.4	24.8
Mexican origin, male	19.9	21.6	24.2	28.6	26.6
Mexican origin, female	19.8	19.3	24.1	25.5	22.7
Percent of poverty level: [5]					
Below 100%	23.0	25.0	27.9	26.5	29.2
100%–199%	22.1	25.9	27.6	27.6	25.4
200%–399%	23.1	26.5	27.5	28.9	29.0
400% or more	21.7	23.1	27.9	26.6	28.1
20 years and over, crude					
Both sexes [4]	21.5	25.0	28.0	28.7	29.8
Male	19.6	25.1	27.5	28.7	29.5
Female	23.2	24.8	28.5	28.7	30.1
Not Hispanic or Latino:					
White only	22.3	26.9	30.3	30.9	33.1
White only, male	20.0	26.8	29.7	30.4	32.6
White only, female	24.5	27.0	30.8	31.4	33.5
Black or African American only	18.1	19.3	21.7	24.4	24.8
Black or African American only, male	16.0	18.5	21.3	24.1	24.0
Black or African American only, female	19.7	19.9	21.9	24.7	25.4
Asian only	- - -	- - -	- - -	- - -	24.7
Asian only, male	- - -	- - -	- - -	- - -	25.9
Asian only, female	- - -	- - -	- - -	- - -	23.7
Hispanic or Latino	- - -	- - -	- - -	22.3	21.2
Hispanic or Latino, male	- - -	- - -	- - -	23.7	21.3
Hispanic or Latina, female	- - -	- - -	- - -	20.7	21.1
Mexican origin	15.6	15.5	19.0	22.4	19.1
Mexican origin, male	16.2	17.0	19.3	23.7	21.2
Mexican origin, female	14.9	13.8	18.7	21.0	16.8
Percent of poverty level: [5]					
Below 100%	19.4	21.6	24.1	22.3	25.3
100%–199%	21.3	25.4	28.3	28.7	27.4
200%–399%	21.3	26.2	28.1	30.6	31.6
400% or more	21.9	24.2	28.7	29.6	32.2
Male					
20–44 years	13.1	16.1	16.5	14.3	12.3
20–34 years	8.2	10.4	10.2	8.5	6.7
35–44 years	21.0	23.1	25.2	22.5	21.1
45–64 years	30.1	36.0	35.7	39.0	39.3
45–54 years	29.6	34.1	32.4	34.0	32.9
55–64 years	30.8	39.1	41.6	46.2	46.0
65–74 years	27.4	36.3	49.4	48.9	55.8
75 years and over	24.4	29.0	37.1	45.2	54.4

See footnotes at end of table.

Excel and PDF versions (with more data years and standard errors when available): http://www.cdc.gov/nchs/hus/contents2016.htm#055.

[Data are based on interviews and laboratory data of a sample of the civilian noninstitutionalized population]

Sex, age, race and Hispanic origin [1], and percent of poverty level	1988–1994	1999–2002	2003–2006	2007–2010	2011–2014
Female	Percent of population with hypercholesterolemia (serum total cholesterol greater than or equal to 240 mg/dL or taking cholesterol-lowering medications) [3]				
20–44 years	9.9	11.4	12.9	10.6	9.0
20–34 years.	7.3	9.1	10.8	6.8	6.1
35–44 years.	13.5	14.4	15.8	15.7	13.2
45–64 years	36.4	31.7	37.3	39.1	40.6
45–54 years.	28.2	27.2	29.6	29.1	31.2
55–64 years.	45.8	39.2	49.2	51.4	51.2
65–74 years	46.9	51.9	55.3	53.3	58.1
75 years and over.	41.2	44.0	47.3	52.5	59.1
20 years and over, age-adjusted [2]	Percent of population with high cholesterol (serum total cholesterol greater than or equal to 240 mg/dL) [6]				
Both sexes [4]	20.8	17.3	16.3	13.7	11.9
Male	19.0	16.4	15.1	12.6	10.8
Female	22.0	17.8	17.1	14.4	12.7
Not Hispanic or Latino:					
White only.	20.8	17.5	16.9	13.9	12.4
White only, male	18.8	16.5	15.5	12.2	11.2
White only, female	22.2	18.1	18.0	15.3	13.3
Black or African American only	19.5	15.5	12.2	11.3	8.6
Black or African American only, male . .	16.9	12.4	10.9	10.8	7.7
Black or African American only, female .	21.4	17.7	13.3	11.5	9.4
Asian only.	- - -	- - -	- - -	- - -	10.9
Asian only, male	- - -	- - -	- - -	- - -	10.6
Asian only, female	- - -	- - -	- - -	- - -	11.0
Hispanic or Latino	- - -	- - -	- - -	14.7	13.0
Hispanic or Latino, male.	- - -	- - -	- - -	15.5	13.1
Hispanic or Latina, female.	- - -	- - -	- - -	13.7	12.7
Mexican origin	18.7	15.8	16.1	14.6	11.2
Mexican origin, male.	18.5	17.4	17.6	15.1	12.8
Mexican origin, female.	18.7	13.8	14.4	13.6	9.3
Percent of poverty level: [5]					
Below 100%	20.6	18.3	18.1	14.4	12.3
100%–199%	20.6	19.1	16.7	15.0	11.3
200%–399%	20.8	18.9	15.8	14.4	13.0
400% or more	19.5	14.4	15.9	12.3	11.5
20 years and over, crude					
Both sexes [4]	19.6	17.3	16.4	14.1	12.1
Male	17.7	16.5	15.2	12.9	10.7
Female	21.3	18.0	17.5	15.2	13.5
Not Hispanic or Latino:					
White only.	20.3	18.0	17.4	14.7	12.9
White only, male	18.0	16.9	15.7	12.6	10.8
White only, female	22.5	19.1	18.9	16.7	14.9
Black or African American only	16.7	14.4	11.7	11.1	8.6
Black or African American only, male . .	14.7	12.2	10.8	10.9	7.4
Black or African American only, female .	18.2	16.1	12.5	11.3	9.5
Asian only.	- - -	- - -	- - -	- - -	10.9
Asian only, male	- - -	- - -	- - -	- - -	10.9
Asian only, female	- - -	- - -	- - -	- - -	10.9
Hispanic or Latino	- - -	- - -	- - -	13.5	12.1
Hispanic or Latino, male.	- - -	- - -	- - -	14.7	12.7
Hispanic or Latina, female.	- - -	- - -	- - -	12.2	11.6
Mexican origin	14.9	12.9	14.2	13.6	10.6
Mexican origin, male.	15.4	15.0	15.7	14.7	12.3
Mexican origin, female.	14.3	10.7	12.6	12.3	8.8
Percent of poverty level: [5]					
Below 100%	17.6	16.4	16.8	12.8	11.3
100%–199%	19.8	18.2	16.0	14.6	11.1
200%–399%	19.3	18.7	15.8	14.6	13.4
400% or more	19.9	15.5	17.1	13.7	12.5

See footnotes at end of table.

Excel and PDF versions (with more data years and standard errors when available): http://www.cdc.gov/nchs/hus/contents2016.htm#055.

[Data are based on interviews and laboratory data of a sample of the civilian noninstitutionalized population]

Sex, age, race and Hispanic origin [1], and percent of poverty level	1988–1994	1999–2002	2003–2006	2007–2010	2011–2014
Male	Percent of population with high cholesterol (serum total cholesterol greater than or equal to 240 mg/dL) [6]				
20–44 years	12.5	14.2	14.1	11.1	10.0
20–34 years	8.2	9.8	9.5	7.6	6.0
35–44 years	19.4	19.7	20.5	16.2	16.2
45–64 years	27.2	22.2	19.1	17.7	13.6
45–54 years	26.6	23.6	20.8	18.7	15.7
55–64 years	28.0	19.9	16.0	16.3	11.5
65–74 years	21.9	13.7	10.9	7.5	7.6
75 years and over	20.4	10.2	9.6	6.8	*3.6
Female					
20–44 years	9.4	10.4	11.3	8.4	7.2
20–34 years	7.3	8.9	10.3	5.8	5.4
35–44 years	12.3	12.4	12.7	11.9	9.8
45–64 years	33.4	23.0	23.9	21.3	19.9
45–54 years	26.7	21.4	19.7	17.7	18.0
55–64 years	40.9	25.6	30.5	25.6	22.1
65–74 years	41.3	32.3	24.2	20.6	15.8
75 years and over	38.2	26.5	18.6	20.2	16.1
20 years and over, age-adjusted [2]	Mean serum total cholesterol level, mg/dL				
Both sexes [4]	206	203	200	196	192
Male	204	202	198	194	189
Female	207	204	202	198	195
Not Hispanic or Latino:					
White only	206	204	201	196	193
White only, male	205	202	198	193	189
White only, female	208	205	203	199	196
Black or African American only	205	199	194	192	186
Black or African American only, male . .	202	195	193	191	183
Black or African American only, female .	207	202	195	192	189
Asian only	- - -	- - -	- - -	- - -	191
Asian only, male	- - -	- - -	- - -	- - -	189
Asian only, female	- - -	- - -	- - -	- - -	192
Hispanic or Latino	- - -	- - -	- - -	198	194
Hispanic or Latino, male	- - -	- - -	- - -	199	193
Hispanic or Latina, female	- - -	- - -	- - -	197	195
Mexican origin	206	202	202	198	192
Mexican origin, male	206	204	203	200	194
Mexican origin, female	206	199	200	196	191
Percent of poverty level: [5]					
Below 100%	205	201	203	196	191
100%–199%	205	204	201	198	191
200%–399%	207	205	199	196	193
400% or more	205	202	201	195	194

See footnotes at end of table.

Table 55 (page 4 of 4). Cholesterol among adults aged 20 and over, by selected characteristics: United States, selected years 1988–1994 through 2011–2014

Excel and PDF versions (with more data years and standard errors when available): http://www.cdc.gov/nchs/hus/contents2016.htm#055.

[Data are based on interviews and laboratory data of a sample of the civilian noninstitutionalized population]

Sex, age, race and Hispanic origin[1], and percent of poverty level	1988–1994	1999–2002	2003–2006	2007–2010	2011–2014
20 years and over, crude	Mean serum total cholesterol level, mg/dL				
Both sexes[4]	204	203	200	197	192
Male	202	202	198	194	188
Female	206	204	202	199	196
Not Hispanic or Latino:					
White only.	206	205	202	198	194
White only, male	203	203	198	193	188
White only, female	208	206	205	201	199
Black or African American only	200	197	193	191	186
Black or African American only, male . .	198	194	192	191	183
Black or African American only, female .	201	199	194	191	189
Asian only.	- - -	- - -	- - -	- - -	191
Asian only, male	- - -	- - -	- - -	- - -	190
Asian only, female	- - -	- - -	- - -	- - -	192
Hispanic or Latino	- - -	- - -	- - -	197	193
Hispanic or Latino, male.	- - -	- - -	- - -	199	193
Hispanic or Latina, female.	- - -	- - -	- - -	194	193
Mexican origin	199	197	198	198	192
Mexican origin, male.	199	200	200	200	194
Mexican origin, female.	198	194	196	195	189
Percent of poverty level:[5]					
Below 100%	200	198	200	194	189
100%–199%	202	202	199	197	190
200%–399%	205	204	199	197	193
400% or more	206	204	203	198	196
Male					
20–44 years	194	196	196	194	188
20–34 years.	186	188	186	186	179
35–44 years.	206	207	209	205	202
45–64 years	216	213	206	202	196
45–54 years.	216	215	208	204	200
55–64 years.	216	212	202	199	192
65–74 years	212	202	191	182	180
75 years and over.	205	195	187	176	168
Female					
20–44 years	189	191	192	187	184
20–34 years.	184	185	188	181	179
35–44 years.	195	198	197	195	193
45–64 years	225	215	213	211	209
45–54 years.	217	211	208	208	207
55–64 years.	235	221	219	214	210
65–74 years	233	224	214	207	200
75 years and over.	229	217	206	203	199

- - - Data not available.

[1] Persons of Hispanic and Mexican origin may be of any race. Starting with 1999 data, race-specific estimates are tabulated according to the 1997 *Revisions to the Standards for the Classification of Federal Data on Race and Ethnicity* and are not strictly comparable with estimates for earlier years. The non-Hispanic race categories shown in the table conform to the 1997 Standards. Starting with 1999 data, race-specific estimates are for persons who reported only one racial group. Prior to data year 1999, estimates were tabulated according to the 1977 Standards. Estimates for single-race categories prior to 1999 included persons who reported one race or, if they reported more than one race, identified one race as best representing their race. See Appendix II, Hispanic origin; Race.

[2] Estimates are age-adjusted to the year 2000 standard population using five age groups: 20–34 years, 35–44 years, 45–54 years, 55–64 years, and 65 years and over. Age-adjusted estimates may differ from other age-adjusted estimates based on the same data and presented elsewhere if different age groups are used in the adjustment procedure. See Appendix II, Age adjustment.

[3] Hypercholesterolemia is defined as measured serum total cholesterol greater than or equal to 240 mg/dL or reporting taking cholesterol-lowering medications. Respondents were asked, "Are you now following this advice [from a doctor or health professional] to take prescribed medicine [to lower your cholesterol]?"

[4] Includes persons of all races and Hispanic origins, not just those shown separately.

[5] Percent of poverty level was calculated by dividing family income by the U.S. Department of Health and Human Services' poverty guideline specific to family size, as well as the appropriate year, and state. Persons with unknown percent of poverty level are excluded (6% in 2011–2014). See Appendix II, Family income; Poverty.

[6] High cholesterol is defined as serum total cholesterol greater than or equal to 240 mg/dL (6.20 mmol/L), regardless of whether the respondent reported taking cholesterol-lowering medications.

NOTES: See Appendix II, Cholesterol. Standard errors for selected years are available in the spreadsheet version of this table. Available from: http://www.cdc.gov/nchs/hus.htm. Data for additional years are available. See the Excel spreadsheet on the *Health, United States* website at: http://www.cdc.gov/nchs/hus.htm.

SOURCE: NCHS, National Health and Nutrition Examination Survey. See Appendix I, National Health and Nutrition Examination Survey (NHANES).

Table 56 (page 1 of 2). Mean macronutrient intake among adults aged 20 and over, by sex and age: United States, selected years 1988–1994 through 2011–2014

Excel and PDF versions (with more data years and standard errors when available): http://www.cdc.gov/nchs/hus/contents2016.htm#056.

[Data are based on dietary recall interviews of a sample of the civilian noninstitutionalized population]

Sex and age	1988–1994	1999–2002	2003–2006	2007–2010	2011–2014
	Percent kcal from carbohydrates				
Both sexes, age-adjusted[1]	49.8	50.7	48.9	49.5	48.6
Both sexes, crude	49.8	50.7	48.9	49.4	48.5
20–44 years.	49.2	51.3	49.3	50.1	48.8
45–64 years.	49.7	49.3	47.5	48.2	47.9
65–74 years.	51.1	50.5	49.2	49.0	48.2
75 years and over	53.0	52.6	51.5	51.1	50.5
Male, age-adjusted[1]	48.5	49.5	47.8	48.0	47.5
Male, crude	48.4	49.4	47.7	47.9	47.4
20–44 years.	48.1	50.2	48.4	48.7	47.5
45–64 years.	48.3	48.0	46.3	46.4	47.2
65–74 years.	49.4	49.4	47.6	47.5	46.6
75 years and over	50.9	51.0	50.3	50.4	49.0
Female, age-adjusted[1].	51.0	51.9	49.9	50.8	49.7
Female, crude.	51.0	51.9	49.9	50.7	49.6
20–44 years.	50.3	52.5	50.2	51.4	50.0
45–64 years.	51.0	50.6	48.7	49.8	48.6
65–74 years.	52.5	51.4	50.6	50.4	49.6
75 years and over	54.2	53.7	52.4	51.6	51.6
	Percent kcal from protein				
Both sexes, age-adjusted[1]	15.5	15.3	15.6	15.8	15.8
Both sexes, crude	15.4	15.3	15.6	15.8	15.8
20–44 years.	15.0	14.9	15.3	15.6	15.7
45–64 years.	15.9	15.6	16.0	16.0	15.8
65–74 years.	16.2	16.3	15.9	16.2	16.3
75 years and over	16.0	15.4	15.6	15.8	15.7
Male, age-adjusted[1]	15.5	15.4	15.6	16.0	16.1
Male, crude	15.4	15.4	15.6	16.0	16.1
20–44 years.	15.0	15.0	15.4	15.8	16.1
45–64 years.	15.9	15.7	15.8	16.3	16.0
65–74 years.	15.9	16.3	16.0	16.3	16.6
75 years and over	16.3	15.7	15.8	15.9	16.1
Female, age-adjusted[1].	15.5	15.2	15.6	15.6	15.5
Female, crude.	15.4	15.2	15.6	15.6	15.6
20–44 years.	14.9	14.8	15.2	15.4	15.3
45–64 years.	15.9	15.5	16.1	15.8	15.7
65–74 years.	16.5	16.3	15.9	16.1	16.1
75 years and over	15.9	15.3	15.5	15.7	15.3
	Percent kcal from total fat				
Both sexes, age-adjusted[1]	33.5	33.0	33.7	33.1	33.6
Both sexes, crude	33.5	33.0	33.7	33.2	33.7
20–44 years.	34.0	32.4	33.1	32.3	33.2
45–64 years.	33.4	33.9	34.6	34.1	34.0
65–74 years.	32.3	33.4	34.3	34.1	34.4
75 years and over	32.0	32.8	33.1	33.3	33.7
Male, age-adjusted[1]	33.8	33.0	33.5	33.1	33.6
Male, crude	33.9	33.0	33.6	33.2	33.6
20–44 years.	34.1	32.2	32.6	32.2	33.0
45–64 years.	33.9	34.0	34.8	34.3	34.1
65–74 years.	33.0	33.4	34.5	34.4	34.5
75 years and over	33.0	33.2	33.3	33.2	34.1
Female, age-adjusted[1].	33.2	33.1	33.8	33.1	33.7
Female, crude.	33.2	33.1	33.9	33.2	33.7
20–44 years.	33.9	32.6	33.6	32.4	33.5
45–64 years.	32.9	33.9	34.4	33.9	33.9
65–74 years.	31.6	33.3	34.1	33.9	34.2
75 years and over	31.5	32.6	32.9	33.4	33.4

See footnotes at end of table.

Table 56 (page 2 of 2). Mean macronutrient intake among adults aged 20 and over, by sex and age: United States, selected years 1988–1994 through 2011–2014

Excel and PDF versions (with more data years and standard errors when available): *http://www.cdc.gov/nchs/hus/contents2016.htm#056.*

[Data are based on dietary recall interviews of a sample of the civilian noninstitutionalized population]

Sex and age	1988–1994	1999–2002	2003–2006	2007–2010	2011–2014
	Percent kcal from saturated fat				
Both sexes, age-adjusted[1]	11.2	10.7	11.2	10.8	10.8
Both sexes, crude	11.2	10.7	11.2	10.9	10.8
20–44 years.	11.5	10.8	11.1	10.6	10.7
45–64 years.	11.1	10.8	11.4	11.1	10.8
65–74 years.	10.7	10.5	11.2	11.1	10.8
75 years and over	10.7	10.3	11.0	10.9	11.1
Male, age-adjusted[1]	11.3	10.7	11.1	10.8	10.8
Male, crude	11.4	10.7	11.1	10.9	10.8
20–44 years.	11.5	10.8	11.0	10.6	10.6
45–64 years.	11.2	10.7	11.3	11.2	10.9
65–74 years.	10.9	10.6	11.2	11.0	11.0
75 years and over	11.2	10.7	11.2	10.9	11.1
Female, age-adjusted[1].	11.1	10.7	11.2	10.9	10.8
Female, crude.	11.1	10.7	11.3	10.9	10.8
20–44 years.	11.4	10.8	11.2	10.7	10.8
45–64 years.	10.9	10.9	11.5	11.0	10.7
65–74 years.	10.4	10.4	11.3	11.2	10.6
75 years and over	10.5	10.1	10.8	11.0	11.0

[1] Estimates are age-adjusted to the year 2000 standard population using four age groups: 20–44 years, 45–64 years, 65–74 years, and 75 years and over. Age-adjusted estimates in this table may differ from other age-adjusted estimates based on the same data and presented elsewhere if different age groups are used in the adjustment procedure. See Appendix II, Age adjustment.

NOTES: Starting in 2001, 24-hour dietary recall data were collected in the mobile examination center (day 1 file) and on a second day by telephone interview (day 2 file). For comparability across survey years, this table is based on day 1 data only. It is recognized that usual intake of macronutrients based on 2 or more days of dietary data would be more precise (Freedman LS, Guenther PM, Dodd KW, Krebs-Smith SM, Midthune D. The population distribution of ratios of usual intakes of dietary components that are consumed every day can be estimated from repeated 24-hour recalls. J Nutr 2010 Jan;140(1):111–6). Two days of data are available only in later years of the continuous NHANES survey. Thus, in order to present trends, macronutrient intake estimates on a given day are presented in this table. This table excludes individuals who reported no energy intake. Energy intake included kilocalories from all foods and beverages, including alcoholic beverages, consumed during the previous 24-hour period. Macronutrients (carbohydrates, protein, and fat) do not sum to 100% because information for alcohol is not shown in the table. See *Health, United States, 2013*, Table 67, for earlier data years. Standard errors are available in the spreadsheet version of this table. Available from: http://www.cdc.gov/nchs/hus.htm. Data for additional years are available. See the Excel spreadsheet on the *Health, United States* website at: http://www.cdc.gov/nchs/hus.htm.

SOURCE: NCHS, National Health and Nutrition Examination Survey. U.S. Department of Agriculture, Agriculture Research Service. Beltsville Human Nutrition Research Center, Food Surveys Research Group, What We Eat in America. See Appendix I, National Health and Nutrition Examination Survey (NHANES).

Table 57 (page 1 of 5). Participation in leisure-time aerobic and muscle-strengthening activities that meet the federal *2008 Physical Activity Guidelines for Americans* among adults aged 18 and over, by selected characteristics: United States, selected years 1998–2015

Excel and PDF versions (with more data years and standard errors when available): http://www.cdc.gov/nchs/hus/contents2016.htm#057.

[Data are based on household interviews of a sample of the civilian noninstitutionalized population]

| | 2008 Physical Activity Guidelines for Americans [1] | | | | | | | | | |
| | Met both aerobic activity and muscle-strengthening guidelines | | | | | Met neither aerobic activity nor muscle-strengthening guideline | | | | |
Characteristic	1998	2000	2010	2014	2015	1998	2000	2010	2014	2015
	Percent									
18 years and over, age-adjusted [2,3]	14.3	15.0	20.7	21.5	21.6	56.6	54.7	49.1	46.8	46.8
18 years and over, crude [3]	14.5	15.1	20.4	20.9	20.9	56.3	54.6	49.5	47.5	47.5
Age										
18–44 years	18.9	18.9	25.7	26.7	26.4	50.7	49.1	43.1	40.8	40.7
18–24 years.	23.8	23.8	29.6	31.1	29.8	46.5	44.5	39.4	38.0	37.8
25–44 years.	17.4	17.3	24.3	25.1	25.2	51.9	50.6	44.4	41.8	41.7
45–64 years	11.4	12.8	17.7	17.8	18.1	58.8	57.6	51.0	50.6	50.5
45–54 years.	13.2	14.5	19.2	19.3	19.3	56.9	55.4	48.9	49.2	49.0
55–64 years.	8.6	10.1	15.9	16.1	16.9	61.8	61.0	53.7	52.1	52.2
65 years and over	5.5	6.8	10.4	11.7	12.7	71.0	67.0	64.6	58.7	58.8
65–74 years.	7.0	8.4	13.6	14.4	15.5	65.6	60.3	59.9	53.1	52.4
75 years and over.	3.5	4.9	6.4	7.9	8.7	77.8	75.0	70.3	66.7	67.8
Sex [2]										
Male.	17.5	17.9	25.1	25.5	25.3	50.8	49.6	43.8	43.4	43.5
Female.	11.4	12.3	16.5	17.7	18.0	61.9	59.4	54.0	50.0	49.9
Sex and age										
Male:										
18–44 years.	23.0	23.0	31.8	32.3	32.1	44.3	43.0	37.1	36.2	36.8
45–54 years.	16.1	16.0	20.9	21.5	21.6	52.9	52.7	45.2	48.0	47.5
55–64 years.	9.4	11.3	19.1	17.6	18.9	58.2	58.7	50.1	52.1	50.3
65–74 years.	9.5	9.4	16.6	17.5	15.7	58.9	55.3	55.6	50.5	48.4
75 years and over.	4.9	7.1	9.1	10.7	9.4	69.5	66.7	62.8	60.3	63.2
Female:										
18–44 years.	14.9	15.0	19.6	21.3	20.9	56.9	55.0	49.0	45.2	44.5
45–54 years.	10.5	13.1	17.5	17.3	17.1	60.8	57.9	52.4	50.3	50.4
55–64 years.	7.8	9.0	13.1	14.8	15.0	65.0	63.1	57.0	52.2	53.9
65–74 years.	5.1	7.7	11.0	11.8	15.3	70.9	64.3	63.6	55.4	55.9
75 years and over.	2.6	3.6	4.6	5.9	8.2	83.0	80.0	75.3	71.3	71.1
Race [2,4]										
White only	14.8	15.7	21.4	22.1	22.0	55.2	53.1	47.6	45.6	45.7
Black or African American only	11.7	12.2	17.2	19.9	19.8	65.7	64.6	58.5	53.4	54.5
American Indian or Alaska Native only	16.0	*10.6	*12.7	24.1	18.8	57.6	67.1	54.0	51.5	47.0
Asian only	13.5	14.1	17.8	17.0	19.1	59.1	55.0	51.7	49.9	45.1
Native Hawaiian or Other Pacific Islander only	- - -	*	*	*	*	- - -	*	*	*	*
2 or more races	- - -	19.0	25.9	21.0	22.7	- - -	52.8	45.0	46.1	47.8
Hispanic origin and race [2,4]										
Hispanic or Latino	9.4	9.2	14.4	15.3	16.8	67.7	66.5	60.2	55.2	53.5
Mexican.	8.7	8.1	13.2	14.3	16.4	69.5	67.0	60.7	55.8	55.0
Not Hispanic or Latino.	14.9	15.8	21.9	22.7	22.6	55.3	53.2	47.2	45.2	45.4
White only.	15.5	16.5	22.9	23.7	23.5	53.6	51.4	45.0	43.3	43.6
Black or African American only	11.7	12.2	17.4	20.1	19.9	65.8	64.6	58.4	53.3	54.3
Education [5,6]										
No high school diploma or GED.	4.6	4.3	7.7	7.1	8.1	76.3	74.0	69.8	66.7	67.0
High school diploma or GED	8.6	9.5	12.7	13.1	13.2	64.6	61.7	59.0	57.2	58.1
Some college or more.	18.2	18.9	25.0	25.4	25.2	48.0	47.1	42.1	40.4	40.7

See footnotes at end of table.

Excel and PDF versions (with more data years and standard errors when available): http://www.cdc.gov/nchs/hus/contents2016.htm#057.

[Data are based on household interviews of a sample of the civilian noninstitutionalized population]

| | 2008 Physical Activity Guidelines for Americans [1] | | | | | | | | | |
| | Met both aerobic activity and muscle-strengthening guidelines | | | | | Met neither aerobic activity nor muscle-strengthening guideline | | | | |
Characteristic	1998	2000	2010	2014	2015	1998	2000	2010	2014	2015
Percent of poverty level [2,7]					Percent					
Below 100%.	8.0	9.3	12.0	13.1	13.1	71.3	68.0	63.9	60.2	60.1
100%–199%.	9.0	9.0	12.7	14.1	12.7	67.1	65.5	60.6	56.6	58.3
200%–399%.	12.6	13.2	19.2	19.7	20.1	58.0	56.8	50.6	49.0	49.2
400% or more	20.2	20.5	29.1	29.9	29.7	46.2	45.0	36.9	35.6	35.8
Hispanic origin and race and percent of poverty level [2,4,7]										
Hispanic or Latino:										
Below 100%	4.6	4.4	8.9	9.0	10.3	78.0	75.2	68.6	65.0	64.2
100%–199%	7.0	5.0	9.3	12.8	11.8	71.2	72.2	66.7	57.5	58.9
200%–399%	11.1	10.2	15.7	17.2	18.9	63.8	63.1	57.6	52.2	50.6
400% or more	17.4	19.6	28.1	26.1	28.4	55.6	52.8	42.5	41.3	38.7
Not Hispanic or Latino:										
White only:										
Below 100%	9.9	11.7	13.7	16.1	15.0	66.9	63.5	60.5	57.4	55.1
100%–199%.	9.6	10.3	14.1	14.7	12.5	65.1	62.6	56.4	54.8	58.4
200%–399%.	13.1	13.9	20.0	19.8	20.2	56.1	54.7	48.6	47.8	48.6
400% or more	20.2	21.0	29.9	31.0	30.6	45.2	43.7	35.2	33.6	34.1
Black or African American only:										
Below 100%	7.1	9.5	11.3	12.9	13.0	74.6	72.1	66.9	60.5	64.8
100%–199%	8.8	9.5	11.7	15.0	14.6	69.8	69.2	67.0	59.6	59.6
200%–399%	10.6	11.8	20.8	23.2	20.7	64.5	64.3	53.3	50.8	50.8
400% or more	21.2	17.6	26.1	30.4	30.1	54.2	54.9	47.7	41.7	44.9
Disability measure [2,8]										
Any basic actions difficulty or complex activity limitation	10.2	10.3	13.6	14.3	14.0	64.4	62.2	59.1	58.3	59.0
Any basic actions difficulty	9.8	10.3	13.8	14.2	13.7	64.8	62.1	59.2	58.6	59.6
Any complex activity limitation	7.7	7.2	8.9	10.7	9.6	71.9	71.2	67.2	66.3	68.5
No disability	16.0	17.0	24.2	24.5	25.3	52.5	50.6	43.3	41.2	39.9
Geographic region [2]										
Northeast	14.2	17.0	20.2	22.3	22.1	57.0	51.8	49.1	48.8	46.8
Midwest	15.0	16.4	20.7	20.8	21.0	54.9	53.4	49.7	47.7	48.2
South	11.8	12.1	18.8	20.1	20.7	61.4	59.7	51.8	48.2	48.4
West	18.5	16.7	24.0	24.0	23.2	49.5	50.1	44.5	42.3	42.8
Location of residence [2,9]										
Within MSA	14.9	15.7	21.8	22.4	22.4	55.8	54.1	47.8	45.9	45.5
Outside MSA	12.2	12.3	14.5	16.0	16.1	59.7	56.9	56.9	52.4	55.1

See footnotes at end of table.

Table 57 (page 3 of 5). Participation in leisure-time aerobic and muscle-strengthening activities that meet the federal *2008 Physical Activity Guidelines for Americans* among adults aged 18 and over, by selected characteristics: United States, selected years 1998–2015

Excel and PDF versions (with more data years and standard errors when available): http://www.cdc.gov/nchs/hus/contents2016.htm#057.

[Data are based on household interviews of a sample of the civilian noninstitutionalized population]

	2008 Physical Activity Guidelines for Americans [1]									
	Met aerobic activity guideline					Met muscle-strengthening guideline				
Characteristic	1998	2000	2010	2014	2015	1998	2000	2010	2014	2015
	Percent									
18 years and over, age-adjusted [2,3]	40.0	42.2	47.3	50.0	49.8	17.7	18.0	24.4	24.6	25.0
18 years and over, crude [3].	40.3	42.4	46.9	49.3	49.0	17.9	18.1	24.0	24.0	24.4
Age										
18–44 years	45.7	47.7	53.8	56.7	56.4	22.5	22.1	28.8	29.3	29.3
18–24 years.	49.3	52.2	57.2	59.5	59.0	28.0	27.2	32.8	33.8	32.9
25–44 years.	44.6	46.3	52.5	55.7	55.5	20.8	20.5	27.4	27.7	27.9
45–64 years	38.2	39.7	45.2	46.2	45.9	14.4	15.5	21.5	21.0	21.8
45–54 years.	40.1	42.1	47.6	47.8	47.9	16.2	17.0	22.6	22.4	22.5
55–64 years.	35.3	36.1	42.1	44.4	43.8	11.5	13.1	20.1	19.4	21.0
65 years and over	26.0	30.1	30.5	36.5	36.6	8.6	9.8	15.4	16.5	17.3
65–74 years.	31.7	36.8	35.9	42.4	43.3	9.7	11.3	17.9	19.0	19.8
75 years and over.	18.7	22.1	23.9	28.2	27.2	7.2	8.0	12.3	13.0	13.8
Sex [2]										
Male	45.4	47.4	52.1	53.3	53.0	21.2	20.8	29.1	28.8	28.8
Female.	35.1	37.6	42.7	47.0	46.9	14.4	15.4	19.8	20.7	21.2
Sex and age										
Male:										
18–44 years.	51.5	53.6	59.0	60.8	60.0	27.2	26.3	35.6	35.4	35.2
45–54 years.	44.3	45.2	50.7	48.9	49.3	18.8	18.0	24.8	24.5	25.0
55–64 years.	38.3	38.9	46.0	44.7	46.5	12.9	13.8	22.9	20.7	22.1
65–74 years.	38.5	41.8	40.7	45.6	47.2	12.0	12.2	20.6	21.5	20.1
75 years and over.	26.1	30.7	32.3	35.2	31.1	9.5	10.1	14.5	15.3	15.0
Female:										
18–44 years.	40.0	42.0	48.5	52.7	52.9	17.9	17.9	22.1	23.4	23.5
45–54 years.	36.1	39.1	44.7	46.7	46.6	13.7	16.1	20.4	20.4	20.1
55–64 years.	32.5	33.5	38.6	44.2	41.2	10.3	12.4	17.5	18.3	19.9
65–74 years.	26.2	32.6	31.8	39.7	39.9	7.8	10.5	15.6	16.8	19.5
75 years and over.	14.0	16.8	18.3	23.2	24.4	5.7	6.7	10.8	11.4	12.9
Race [2,4]										
White only	41.5	44.1	48.9	51.3	51.0	18.0	18.5	24.8	25.2	25.3
Black or African American only	30.4	31.7	37.3	43.6	42.0	15.6	16.0	21.4	23.1	23.5
American Indian or Alaska Native only	39.7	29.7	42.0	44.1	46.9	18.2	13.9	16.7	27.9	24.4
Asian only	37.1	41.7	44.2	47.5	51.4	17.2	17.2	21.9	19.5	22.6
Native Hawaiian or Other Pacific Islander only	- - -	*	*	*	*	- - -	*	*	*	*
2 or more races	- - -	43.9	50.2	50.5	49.0	- - -	22.2	30.4	24.8	26.3
Hispanic origin and race [2,4]										
Hispanic or Latino	29.1	30.8	36.2	41.3	43.3	12.7	11.9	18.1	19.0	20.0
Mexican.	27.4	30.0	35.9	40.6	42.3	11.9	11.3	16.7	18.1	19.2
Not Hispanic or Latino.	41.3	43.7	49.1	51.7	51.2	18.3	18.8	25.5	25.8	26.0
White only.	43.1	45.7	51.5	53.7	53.1	18.7	19.3	26.3	26.7	26.7
Black or African American only	30.4	31.7	37.3	43.6	42.1	15.6	16.0	21.6	23.3	23.7
Education [5,6]										
No high school diploma or GED.	21.4	23.9	27.1	31.2	30.1	7.0	6.6	10.9	9.3	11.0
High school diploma or GED	32.6	35.7	37.3	39.7	39.0	11.4	12.1	16.2	16.2	16.2
Some college or more.	48.1	49.4	53.9	56.1	55.5	22.1	22.4	28.9	28.9	29.0

See footnotes at end of table.

Table 57 (page 4 of 5). Participation in leisure-time aerobic and muscle-strengthening activities that meet the federal *2008 Physical Activity Guidelines for Americans* among adults aged 18 and over, by selected characteristics: United States, selected years 1998–2015

Excel and PDF versions (with more data years and standard errors when available): http://www.cdc.gov/nchs/hus/contents2016.htm#057.

[Data are based on household interviews of a sample of the civilian noninstitutionalized population]

| | 2008 Physical Activity Guidelines for Americans [1] | | | | | | | | | |
| | Met aerobic activity guideline | | | | | Met muscle-strengthening guideline | | | | |
Characteristic	1998	2000	2010	2014	2015	1998	2000	2010	2014	2015
Percent of poverty level [2,7]					Percent					
Below 100%.	25.9	29.3	32.2	36.7	37.1	10.8	12.3	15.8	16.2	16.0
100%–199%.	29.9	32.0	36.0	40.4	38.5	12.0	11.5	16.1	17.3	15.9
200%–399%.	38.8	39.9	45.5	47.8	47.4	15.9	16.5	23.1	23.0	23.6
400% or more.	50.0	52.0	59.3	61.4	60.7	24.0	23.4	32.8	32.9	33.2
Hispanic origin and race and percent of poverty level [2,4,7]										
Hispanic or Latino:										
Below 100%	19.5	22.1	27.8	31.2	33.1	7.1	7.2	12.4	13.0	13.4
100%–199%	25.6	25.8	30.1	39.0	38.9	10.2	7.1	12.6	16.3	14.2
200%–399%	33.1	33.0	38.8	43.5	45.3	14.6	14.0	19.5	21.8	22.8
400% or more	40.6	45.1	53.4	56.2	57.4	21.1	21.7	32.1	28.7	32.2
Not Hispanic or Latino:										
White only:										
Below 100%	30.2	34.0	35.5	39.7	41.8	12.8	14.7	17.5	18.9	18.1
100%–199%	32.2	34.8	40.6	42.5	38.0	12.5	12.9	17.0	17.6	15.9
200%–399%	40.8	42.3	47.8	49.0	48.3	16.2	16.9	23.6	22.9	23.3
400% or more	51.0	53.4	61.0	63.3	62.5	24.0	23.8	33.5	34.0	33.9
Black or African American only:										
Below 100%	22.7	25.4	29.3	37.0	32.9	10.0	12.1	15.3	15.7	15.3
100%–199%	26.9	28.0	28.5	37.4	37.3	12.1	12.3	16.0	18.1	18.0
200%–399%	30.6	31.4	41.9	45.6	45.2	15.5	16.2	25.7	26.9	25.3
400% or more	41.7	40.3	48.5	54.8	50.7	25.4	22.4	29.8	34.0	34.5
Disability measure [2,8]										
Any basic actions difficulty or complex activity limitation	31.8	34.2	36.4	38.1	37.4	13.9	14.0	18.0	18.0	17.4
Any basic actions difficulty	31.3	34.0	36.6	37.7	36.9	13.6	14.2	18.1	17.9	17.1
Any complex activity limitation	24.4	24.9	27.9	29.2	27.6	11.5	11.3	13.9	15.1	13.4
No disability	44.3	46.6	53.4	56.0	56.9	19.3	19.8	27.4	27.3	28.5
Geographic region [2]										
Northeast	39.6	45.3	46.9	48.6	49.8	17.5	20.0	24.3	24.9	25.5
Midwest	42.0	43.5	46.1	48.9	48.3	18.2	19.3	24.7	24.3	24.5
South	35.3	37.3	45.0	48.7	48.1	15.0	15.1	22.0	23.2	24.1
West	46.7	46.9	52.0	54.5	54.2	22.3	19.7	27.5	27.1	26.3
Location of residence [2,9]										
Within MSA	40.8	42.9	48.7	51.0	51.2	18.3	18.6	25.4	25.5	25.8
Outside MSA	37.1	39.9	39.1	44.6	41.1	15.4	15.5	18.5	19.0	19.7

See footnotes at end of table.

Table 57 (page 5 of 5). Participation in leisure-time aerobic and muscle-strengthening activities that meet the federal *2008 Physical Activity Guidelines for Americans* among adults aged 18 and over, by selected characteristics: United States, selected years 1998–2015

Excel and PDF versions (with more data years and standard errors when available): http://www.cdc.gov/nchs/hus/contents2016.htm#057.

[Data are based on household interviews of a sample of the civilian noninstitutionalized population]

---

* Estimates are considered unreliable. Data preceded by an asterisk have a relative standard error (RSE) of 20%–30%. Data not shown have an RSE greater than 30%.

- - - Data not available.

[1] Starting with *Health, United States, 2010*, measures of physical activity shown in this table changed to reflect the federal *2008 Physical Activity Guidelines for Americans* (available from: http://www.health.gov/PAGuidelines/). This table presents four measures of physical activity that are of interest to the public health community: the percentage of adults who met the federal 2008 guidelines for both aerobic activity and muscle strengthening; the percentage who met neither the aerobic activity guideline nor the muscle-strengthening guideline; the percentage who met the aerobic activity guideline; and the percentage who met the muscle-strengthening guideline. Persons who met neither the aerobic activity nor the muscle-strengthening guideline were unable to be active, were completely inactive, or had some aerobic or muscle-strengthening activities but amounts were insufficient to meet the guidelines. The percentage of persons who met the aerobic activity guideline includes those who may or may not have also met the muscle-strengthening guideline. Similarly, the percentage of persons who met the muscle-strengthening guideline includes those who may or may not have also met the aerobic activity guideline. The federal 2008 guidelines recommend that for substantial health benefits adults perform at least 150 minutes (2 hours and 30 minutes) a week of moderate-intensity, or 75 minutes (1 hour and 15 minutes) a week of vigorous-intensity aerobic physical activity, or an equivalent combination of moderate- and vigorous-intensity aerobic activity. Aerobic activity should be performed in episodes of at least 10 minutes, and preferably should be spread throughout the week. The 2008 guidelines also recommend that adults perform muscle-strengthening activities that are moderate or high intensity and involve all major muscle groups on 2 or more days a week, because these activities provide additional health benefits. See Appendix II, Physical activity, leisure-time.

[2] Estimates are age-adjusted to the year 2000 standard population using five age groups: 18–44 years, 45–54 years, 55–64 years, 65–74 years, and 75 years and over. Age-adjusted estimates in this table may differ from other age-adjusted estimates based on the same data and presented elsewhere if different age groups are used in the adjustment procedure. See Appendix II, Age adjustment.

[3] Includes all other races not shown separately, unknown education level, and unknown disability status.

[4] The race groups, white, black, American Indian or Alaska Native, Asian, Native Hawaiian or Other Pacific Islander, and 2 or more races, include persons of Hispanic and non-Hispanic origin. Persons of Hispanic origin may be of any race. Starting with 1999 data, race-specific estimates are tabulated according to the 1997 *Revisions to the Standards for the Classification of Federal Data on Race and Ethnicity* and are not strictly comparable with estimates for earlier years. The five single-race categories plus multiple-race categories shown in the table conform to the 1997 Standards. Starting with 1999 data, race-specific estimates are for persons who reported only one racial group; the category 2 or more races includes persons who reported more than one racial group. Prior to 1999, data were tabulated according to the 1977 Standards with four racial groups, and the Asian only category included Native Hawaiian or Other Pacific Islander. Estimates for single-race categories prior to 1999 included persons who reported one race or, if they reported more than one race, identified one race as best representing their race. Starting with 2003 data (shown in spreadsheet version), race responses of other race and unspecified multiple race were treated as missing, and then race was imputed if these were the only race responses. Almost all persons with a race response of other race were of Hispanic origin. See Appendix II, Hispanic origin; Race.

[5] Estimates are for persons aged 25 and over and are age-adjusted to the year 2000 standard population using five age groups: 25–44 years, 45–54 years, 55–64 years, 65–74 years, and 75 years and over. See Appendix II, Age adjustment.

[6] GED is General Educational Development high school equivalency diploma. See Appendix II, Education.

[7] Percent of poverty level is based on family income and family size and composition using U.S. Census Bureau poverty thresholds. Missing family income data were imputed for 1997 and beyond. See Appendix II, Family income; Poverty; Table VI.

[8] Any basic actions difficulty or complex activity limitation is defined as having one or more of the following limitations or difficulties: movement difficulty, emotional difficulty, sensory (seeing or hearing) difficulty, cognitive difficulty, self-care (activities of daily living or instrumental activities of daily living) limitation, social limitation, or work limitation. For more information, see Appendix II, Basic actions difficulty; Complex activity limitation. Starting with 2007 data, the hearing question, a component of the basic actions difficulty measure, was revised. Consequently, data prior to 2007 are not comparable with data for 2007 and beyond. For more information on the impact of the revised hearing question, see Appendix II, Hearing trouble.

[9] MSA is metropolitan statistical area. Starting with 2006 data, MSA status is determined using 2000 census data and the 2000 standards for defining MSAs. For data prior to 2006, see Appendix II, Metropolitan statistical area (MSA) for the applicable standards.

NOTES: Standard errors are available in the spreadsheet version of this table. Available from: http://www.cdc.gov/nchs/hus.htm. Data for additional years are available. See the Excel spreadsheet on the *Health, United States* website at: http://www.cdc.gov/nchs/hus.htm.

SOURCE: NCHS, National Health Interview Survey, family core and sample adult questionnaires. See Appendix I, National Health Interview Survey (NHIS).

Table 58 (page 1 of 7). Normal weight, overweight, and obesity among adults aged 20 and over, by selected characteristics: United States, selected years 1988–1994 through 2011–2014

Excel and PDF versions (with more data years and standard errors when available): http://www.cdc.gov/nchs/hus/contents2016.htm#058.

[Data are based on measured height and weight of a sample of the civilian noninstitutionalized population]

Sex, age, race and Hispanic origin [1], and percent of poverty level	Normal weight (BMI from 18.5 to 24.9) [2]				
	1988–1994	1999–2002	2003–2006	2007–2010	2011–2014
20 years and over, age-adjusted [3]	Percent of population				
Both sexes [4]	41.6	33.0	31.6	29.8	28.9
Male	37.9	30.2	26.6	25.7	26.0
Female	45.0	35.7	36.5	33.7	31.7
Not Hispanic or Latino:					
White only.	43.1	34.6	33.2	31.4	30.0
White only, male	37.3	29.6	26.8	25.5	25.6
White only, female	48.7	39.5	39.6	36.9	34.3
Black or African American only	33.9	27.6	22.7	22.7	22.0
Black or African American only, male . .	40.1	34.7	27.0	28.5	29.0
Black or African American only, female .	29.2	21.6	19.2	17.9	16.0
Asian only.	- - -	- - -	- - -	- - -	55.7
Asian only, male	- - -	- - -	- - -	- - -	50.2
Asian only, female	- - -	- - -	- - -	- - -	60.5
Hispanic or Latino	- - -	- - -	- - -	21.1	20.9
Hispanic or Latino, male.	- - -	- - -	- - -	19.0	19.5
Hispanic or Latina, female.	- - -	- - -	- - -	23.5	22.3
Mexican origin	30.1	26.9	24.4	19.6	17.7
Mexican origin, male.	30.2	26.5	23.8	18.5	16.5
Mexican origin, female.	29.8	27.5	25.1	21.3	19.1
Percent of poverty level: [5]					
Below 100%	37.5	32.7	32.1	27.3	28.1
100%–199%	39.3	30.5	31.3	27.6	24.6
200%–399%	41.8	29.6	29.7	29.7	27.5
400% or more	45.5	36.5	33.7	32.1	33.4
20 years and over, crude					
Both sexes [4]	42.6	32.9	31.4	29.6	28.6
Male	39.4	30.4	26.6	25.8	26.2
Female	45.7	35.4	35.9	33.2	31.0
Not Hispanic or Latino:					
White only.	43.6	34.0	32.3	30.4	29.0
White only, male	38.2	29.2	26.2	24.8	25.1
White only, female	48.8	38.7	38.2	35.7	32.8
Black or African American only	35.9	28.2	22.7	23.0	21.9
Black or African American only, male . .	41.5	35.9	27.1	29.4	29.3
Black or African American only, female .	31.2	21.8	19.2	17.6	15.8
Asian only.	- - -	- - -	- - -	- - -	55.8
Asian only, male	- - -	- - -	- - -	- - -	50.7
Asian only, female	- - -	- - -	- - -	- - -	60.3
Hispanic or Latino	- - -	- - -	- - -	22.3	21.7
Hispanic or Latino, male.	- - -	- - -	- - -	20.3	20.2
Hispanic or Latina, female.	- - -	- - -	- - -	24.6	23.1
Mexican origin	34.0	29.4	25.5	20.8	18.4
Mexican origin, male.	35.2	29.4	25.2	19.5	17.0
Mexican origin, female.	32.5	29.5	25.8	22.3	19.9
Percent of poverty level: [5]					
Below 100%	39.8	34.5	33.2	29.2	29.8
100%–199%	41.5	31.5	31.7	28.0	25.2
200%–399%	42.9	29.7	29.6	29.5	27.4
400% or more	44.6	35.3	32.1	30.5	31.3
Male					
20–34 years	51.1	40.3	35.9	37.5	37.6
35–44 years	33.4	29.0	24.1	19.8	20.5
45–54 years	33.6	24.0	20.8	21.8	18.7
55–64 years	28.6	23.8	19.3	19.4	22.7
65–74 years	30.1	22.8	21.2	21.6	22.2
75 years and over.	40.9	32.0	33.1	25.4	28.1
Female					
20–34 years	57.9	42.5	45.1	41.1	38.1
35–44 years	47.1	37.1	37.6	34.4	32.5
45–54 years	37.2	33.1	31.1	30.7	27.8
55–64 years	31.5	27.6	29.5	26.7	24.2
65–74 years	37.0	26.4	28.5	23.9	26.9
75 years and over.	43.0	36.9	35.4	35.4	32.9

See footnotes at end of table.

Table 58 (page 2 of 7). Normal weight, overweight, and obesity among adults aged 20 and over, by selected characteristics: United States, selected years 1988–1994 through 2011–2014

Excel and PDF versions (with more data years and standard errors when available): http://www.cdc.gov/nchs/hus/contents2016.htm#058.

[Data are based on measured height and weight of a sample of the civilian noninstitutionalized population]

Sex, age, race and Hispanic origin[1], and percent of poverty level	Overweight or obese (BMI greater than or equal to 25.0)[2]				
	1988–1994	1999–2002	2003–2006	2007–2010	2011–2014
20 years and over, age-adjusted[3]	Percent of population				
Both sexes[4]	56.0	65.1	66.7	68.5	69.5
Male	60.9	68.8	72.1	73.3	73.0
Female	51.4	61.6	61.3	63.9	66.2
Not Hispanic or Latino:					
White only.	54.4	63.3	64.8	66.8	68.5
White only, male	61.6	69.4	71.8	73.6	73.7
White only, female	47.5	57.2	57.9	60.3	63.5
Black or African American only	63.7	70.5	76.1	75.5	76.3
Black or African American only, male . .	57.8	62.6	71.6	70.0	69.6
Black or African American only, female .	68.2	77.2	79.8	80.0	82.0
Asian only.	- - -	- - -	- - -	- - -	40.3
Asian only, male	- - -	- - -	- - -	- - -	46.9
Asian only, female	- - -	- - -	- - -	- - -	34.4
Hispanic or Latino	- - -	- - -	- - -	78.4	78.4
Hispanic or Latino, male.	- - -	- - -	- - -	80.6	79.6
Hispanic or Latina, female.	- - -	- - -	- - -	75.7	77.1
Mexican origin	68.9	72.3	75.0	79.9	81.6
Mexican origin, male	68.9	73.2	75.8	81.3	82.7
Mexican origin, female.	68.9	71.2	73.9	78.0	80.3
Percent of poverty level:[5]					
Below 100%	59.6	64.7	65.7	69.7	69.1
100%–199%	58.0	67.3	66.5	70.5	73.9
200%–399%	56.0	68.6	69.0	68.6	71.6
400% or more	52.4	62.2	64.7	66.9	65.6
20 years and over, crude					
Both sexes[4]	54.9	65.2	66.9	68.7	69.8
Male	59.4	68.6	72.1	73.2	72.8
Female	50.7	62.0	61.9	64.5	67.0
Not Hispanic or Latino:					
White only.	53.8	63.9	65.8	67.8	69.6
White only, male	60.6	69.9	72.5	74.2	74.2
White only, female	47.4	58.2	59.4	61.7	65.2
Black or African American only	61.8	70.0	76.0	75.2	76.3
Black or African American only, male . .	56.7	61.7	71.6	69.1	69.1
Black or African American only, female .	66.0	76.9	79.7	80.2	82.3
Asian only.	- - -	- - -	- - -	- - -	40.0
Asian only, male	- - -	- - -	- - -	- - -	46.3
Asian only, female	- - -	- - -	- - -	- - -	34.5
Hispanic or Latino	- - -	- - -	- - -	77.1	77.5
Hispanic or Latino, male.	- - -	- - -	- - -	79.3	78.8
Hispanic or Latina, female.	- - -	- - -	- - -	74.6	76.3
Mexican origin	64.8	69.8	73.9	78.8	81.0
Mexican origin, male.	63.9	70.1	74.6	80.2	82.3
Mexican origin, female.	65.9	69.3	73.0	77.1	79.5
Percent of poverty level:[5]					
Below 100%	56.8	62.5	64.4	67.8	67.1
100%–199%	55.7	66.2	66.0	70.1	73.1
200%–399%	54.9	68.5	69.0	68.8	71.8
400% or more	53.3	63.7	66.5	68.5	67.7
Male					
20–34 years	47.5	57.4	61.6	61.1	60.4
35–44 years	65.5	70.5	75.2	80.2	79.3
45–54 years	66.1	75.7	78.5	76.8	80.8
55–64 years	70.5	75.4	79.7	79.8	76.7
65–74 years	68.5	76.2	78.0	77.5	76.1
75 years and over.	56.5	67.4	65.8	73.2	71.0
Female					
20–34 years	37.0	52.9	50.9	55.4	58.5
35–44 years	49.6	60.6	60.7	63.9	65.6
45–54 years	60.3	65.1	67.3	66.2	71.4
55–64 years	66.3	72.2	69.6	72.2	74.3
65–74 years	60.3	70.9	70.5	74.2	71.2
75 years and over.	52.3	59.9	62.6	63.2	64.6

See footnotes at end of table.

Table 58 (page 3 of 7). Normal weight, overweight, and obesity among adults aged 20 and over, by selected characteristics: United States, selected years 1988–1994 through 2011–2014

Excel and PDF versions (with more data years and standard errors when available): http://www.cdc.gov/nchs/hus/contents2016.htm#058.

[Data are based on measured height and weight of a sample of the civilian noninstitutionalized population]

Sex, age, race and Hispanic origin[1], and percent of poverty level	Obesity (BMI greater than or equal to 30.0)[2]				
	1988–1994	1999–2002	2003–2006	2007–2010	2011–2014
20 years and over, age-adjusted[3]	Percent of population				
Both sexes[4]	22.9	30.4	33.4	34.7	36.4
Male	20.2	27.5	32.4	33.9	34.5
Female	25.5	33.2	34.3	35.5	38.1
Not Hispanic or Latino:					
White only.	21.6	29.4	32.0	33.3	34.6
White only, male	20.2	28.0	32.4	34.1	34.0
White only, female	22.9	30.7	31.6	32.5	35.3
Black or African American only	30.7	39.2	45.5	47.0	48.0
Black or African American only, male . .	20.9	27.8	35.7	38.3	37.9
Black or African American only, female .	38.3	48.6	53.4	54.0	56.5
Asian only.	- - -	- - -	- - -	- - -	11.8
Asian only, male	- - -	- - -	- - -	- - -	11.3
Asian only, female	- - -	- - -	- - -	- - -	11.9
Hispanic or Latino	- - -	- - -	- - -	38.9	42.6
Hispanic or Latino, male.	- - -	- - -	- - -	35.7	39.1
Hispanic or Latina, female.	- - -	- - -	- - -	42.1	45.6
Mexican origin	29.3	32.7	35.3	40.3	46.4
Mexican origin, male.	23.8	27.8	29.5	36.3	43.3
Mexican origin, female.	35.2	38.0	41.8	44.6	49.6
Percent of poverty level:[5]					
Below 100%	28.1	34.7	35.0	37.2	39.2
100%–199%	26.1	34.1	35.9	37.3	42.6
200%–399%	22.7	32.1	35.7	36.8	38.8
400% or more	18.7	25.5	28.9	31.3	29.7
20 years and over, crude					
Both sexes[4]	22.3	30.5	33.5	34.9	36.5
Male	19.5	27.5	32.4	33.9	34.5
Female	25.0	33.4	34.6	35.9	38.5
Not Hispanic or Latino:					
White only.	21.3	29.8	32.4	33.8	35.3
White only, male	19.8	28.4	32.6	34.4	34.3
White only, female	22.7	31.3	32.2	33.2	36.2
Black or African American only	29.5	39.1	45.3	46.9	48.2
Black or African American only, male . .	20.7	27.5	35.8	38.1	37.6
Black or African American only, female .	36.7	48.7	53.2	54.2	56.9
Asian only.	- - -	- - -	- - -	- - -	11.8
Asian only, male	- - -	- - -	- - -	- - -	11.7
Asian only, female	- - -	- - -	- - -	- - -	11.9
Hispanic or Latino	- - -	- - -	- - -	38.0	42.3
Hispanic or Latino, male.	- - -	- - -	- - -	34.8	39.7
Hispanic or Latina, female.	- - -	- - -	- - -	41.5	45.0
Mexican origin	26.4	31.0	34.5	39.5	45.9
Mexican origin, male.	20.6	26.0	29.0	35.6	43.5
Mexican origin, female.	33.3	37.0	41.2	44.2	48.6
Percent of poverty level:[5]					
Below 100%	25.9	33.0	34.6	36.5	38.1
100%–199%	24.3	32.8	35.0	36.8	41.9
200%–399%	22.0	31.8	35.5	36.8	38.8
400% or more	19.3	27.2	30.7	32.4	31.1
Male					
20–34 years	14.1	21.7	26.2	27.1	28.5
35–44 years	21.3	28.5	37.0	37.2	39.8
45–54 years	23.2	30.6	34.6	36.6	36.6
55–64 years	27.2	35.5	39.3	37.3	38.1
65–74 years	24.1	31.9	33.0	41.5	36.2
75 years and over.	13.2	18.0	24.0	26.6	26.8
Female					
20–34 years	18.5	28.3	28.4	30.4	33.4
35–44 years	25.5	32.1	36.1	37.1	39.1
45–54 years	32.4	36.9	40.0	36.9	41.7
55–64 years	33.7	42.1	41.0	43.4	44.4
65–74 years	26.9	39.3	36.4	40.3	40.7
75 years and over.	19.2	23.6	24.2	28.7	30.5

See footnotes at end of table.

Excel and PDF versions (with more data years and standard errors when available): *http://www.cdc.gov/nchs/hus/contents2016.htm#058*.

[Data are based on measured height and weight of a sample of the civilian noninstitutionalized population]

Sex, age, race and Hispanic origin[1], and percent of poverty level	Grade 1 Obesity (BMI from 30.0 to 34.9)[2]				
	1988–1994	1999–2002	2003–2006	2007–2010	2011–2014
20 years and over, age-adjusted[3]	Percent of population				
Both sexes[4]	14.8	17.9	19.8	19.9	20.6
Male	14.9	18.2	21.8	22.3	22.0
Female	14.7	17.6	17.9	17.6	19.3
Not Hispanic or Latino:					
White only.	14.0	17.6	19.3	19.2	19.6
White only, male	14.9	18.9	21.6	22.7	21.4
White only, female	13.2	16.2	17.0	15.9	17.9
Black or African American only	17.3	19.0	23.1	23.0	23.5
Black or African American only, male . .	14.2	16.1	22.4	20.8	22.0
Black or African American only, female .	19.6	21.6	23.8	24.8	24.9
Asian only.	- - -	- - -	- - -	- - -	9.3
Asian only, male	- - -	- - -	- - -	- - -	9.4
Asian only, female	- - -	- - -	- - -	- - -	8.9
Hispanic or Latino	- - -	- - -	- - -	23.7	25.6
Hispanic or Latino, male.	- - -	- - -	- - -	23.9	27.2
Hispanic or Latina, female.	- - -	- - -	- - -	23.5	24.1
Mexican origin	20.3	21.1	22.8	24.8	26.9
Mexican origin, male.	18.9	19.5	22.0	24.7	29.7
Mexican origin, female.	22.0	22.9	23.6	24.9	23.8
Percent of poverty level:[5]					
Below 100%	16.6	17.3	19.3	19.8	20.7
100%–199%	16.1	17.7	20.6	19.8	21.7
200%–399%	14.5	19.8	21.6	20.2	22.7
400% or more	13.3	16.6	18.0	19.4	18.2
20 years and over, crude					
Both sexes[4]	14.4	17.9	19.8	20.0	20.7
Male	14.3	18.1	21.8	22.3	22.0
Female	14.5	17.7	18.0	17.9	19.4
Not Hispanic or Latino:					
White only.	13.8	17.8	19.5	19.6	20.2
White only, male	14.6	19.1	21.8	22.8	22.0
White only, female	13.2	16.6	17.3	16.6	18.5
Black or African American only	16.6	19.0	22.9	22.8	23.3
Black or African American only, male . .	14.0	15.8	22.2	20.6	21.4
Black or African American only, female .	18.7	21.7	23.5	24.6	24.9
Asian only.	- - -	- - -	- - -	- - -	9.4
Asian only, male	- - -	- - -	- - -	- - -	9.8
Asian only, female	- - -	- - -	- - -	- - -	9.0
Hispanic or Latino	- - -	- - -	- - -	22.9	25.4
Hispanic or Latino, male.	- - -	- - -	- - -	22.9	27.2
Hispanic or Latina, female.	- - -	- - -	- - -	22.9	23.7
Mexican origin	18.1	20.2	22.2	24.1	26.9
Mexican origin, male.	15.8	18.2	21.6	23.8	29.4
Mexican origin, female.	20.7	22.4	22.9	24.5	24.1
Percent of poverty level:[5]					
Below 100%	15.2	16.4	19.1	19.2	19.5
100%–199%	15.2	17.5	20.4	19.8	21.5
200%–399%	14.0	19.6	21.5	20.3	22.6
400% or more	13.5	17.4	18.6	19.9	19.0
Male					
20–34 years	9.8	13.7	18.1	19.0	16.7
35–44 years	14.7	19.3	24.9	23.2	23.9
45–54 years	17.3	17.8	22.4	22.6	25.8
55–64 years	20.6	25.3	27.0	25.2	25.1
65–74 years	19.4	22.1	20.5	26.1	22.5
75 years and over.	10.9	15.7	18.5	20.6	20.3
Female					
20–34 years	10.8	15.9	14.2	14.0	14.7
35–44 years	13.9	14.8	19.7	17.0	21.9
45–54 years	17.5	19.4	18.4	18.6	19.7
55–64 years	20.0	21.6	19.8	22.5	21.7
65–74 years	16.0	23.4	20.3	19.4	21.9
75 years and over.	14.4	14.1	18.2	19.8	19.9

See footnotes at end of table.

Table 58 (page 5 of 7). Normal weight, overweight, and obesity among adults aged 20 and over, by selected characteristics: United States, selected years 1988–1994 through 2011–2014

Excel and PDF versions (with more data years and standard errors when available): http://www.cdc.gov/nchs/hus/contents2016.htm#058.

[Data are based on measured height and weight of a sample of the civilian noninstitutionalized population]

Sex, age, race and Hispanic origin [1], and percent of poverty level	Grade 2 Obesity (BMI from 35.0 to 39.9) [2]				
	1988–1994	1999–2002	2003–2006	2007–2010	2011–2014
20 years and over, age-adjusted [3]	Percent of population				
Both sexes [4]	5.2	7.6	8.2	8.9	8.8
Male	3.5	5.9	7.1	7.4	7.6
Female	6.8	9.2	9.3	10.3	9.9
Not Hispanic or Latino:					
White only	4.9	7.4	7.8	8.6	8.5
White only, male	3.5	5.8	7.2	7.3	7.8
White only, female	6.3	9.0	8.4	9.9	9.1
Black or African American only	7.8	11.2	12.0	12.0	12.3
Black or African American only, male	4.1	8.3	7.6	10.2	8.9
Black or African American only, female	10.7	13.6	15.4	13.4	15.1
Asian only	- - -	- - -	- - -	- - -	1.9
Asian only, male	- - -	- - -	- - -	- - -	*
Asian only, female	- - -	- - -	- - -	- - -	*2.1
Hispanic or Latino	- - -	- - -	- - -	9.8	10.6
Hispanic or Latino, male	- - -	- - -	- - -	7.8	7.3
Hispanic or Latina, female	- - -	- - -	- - -	12.0	13.5
Mexican origin	6.1	7.4	8.0	9.8	12.4
Mexican origin, male	3.8	5.4	5.1	7.2	8.3
Mexican origin, female	8.4	9.4	11.2	12.9	16.6
Percent of poverty level: [5]					
Below 100%	6.8	9.6	8.6	10.0	10.1
100%–199%	6.5	9.7	9.0	9.4	11.0
200%–399%	5.2	7.5	8.8	10.3	9.4
400% or more	3.6	5.7	6.7	7.6	6.5
20 years and over, crude					
Both sexes [4]	5.1	7.7	8.2	8.8	8.8
Male	3.5	6.0	7.0	7.3	7.5
Female	6.6	9.3	9.4	10.3	10.1
Not Hispanic or Latino:					
White only	4.8	7.5	8.0	8.7	8.5
White only, male	3.4	5.9	7.4	7.4	7.6
White only, female	6.2	9.1	8.5	9.9	9.4
Black or African American only	7.6	11.1	11.7	11.9	12.5
Black or African American only, male	4.2	8.2	7.5	10.2	9.1
Black or African American only, female	10.4	13.5	15.3	13.3	15.4
Asian only	- - -	- - -	- - -	- - -	1.9
Asian only, male	- - -	- - -	- - -	- - -	*
Asian only, female	- - -	- - -	- - -	- - -	*2.1
Hispanic or Latino	- - -	- - -	- - -	9.7	10.3
Hispanic or Latino, male	- - -	- - -	- - -	7.6	7.6
Hispanic or Latina, female	- - -	- - -	- - -	12.0	13.1
Mexican origin	5.6	6.8	7.6	9.7	11.7
Mexican origin, male	3.7	5.1	4.7	7.0	8.6
Mexican origin, female	7.9	8.8	11.2	13.0	15.2
Percent of poverty level: [5]					
Below 100%	6.3	9.5	8.4	9.7	10.1
100%–199%	6.2	8.9	8.7	9.2	10.8
200%–399%	5.1	7.5	8.8	10.1	9.4
400% or more	3.8	6.4	7.4	7.9	6.5
Male					
20–34 years	2.9	4.1	4.5	4.7	7.0
35–44 years	*3.5	5.9	7.9	8.8	10.3
45–54 years	*3.5	8.5	8.3	8.9	6.1
55–64 years	5.5	*7.4	8.4	6.7	6.8
65–74 years	*3.8	6.9	10.3	11.8	8.9
75 years and over	*	*	*3.9	4.6	*4.9
Female					
20–34 years	5.1	8.0	7.9	8.6	9.6
35–44 years	7.1	9.4	9.2	12.6	8.1
45–54 years	8.4	10.4	12.4	10.6	11.5
55–64 years	9.4	10.9	11.4	11.5	11.2
65–74 years	6.7	9.8	9.6	11.7	12.4
75 years and over	3.7	7.2	*3.9	5.5	7.4

See footnotes at end of table.

Table 58 (page 6 of 7). **Normal weight, overweight, and obesity among adults aged 20 and over, by selected characteristics: United States, selected years 1988–1994 through 2011–2014**

Excel and PDF versions (with more data years and standard errors when available): http://www.cdc.gov/nchs/hus/contents2016.htm#058.

[Data are based on measured height and weight of a sample of the civilian noninstitutionalized population]

Sex, age, race and Hispanic origin[1], and percent of poverty level	Grade 3 Obesity (BMI greater than or equal to 40.0)[2]				
	1988–1994	1999–2002	2003–2006	2007–2010	2011–2014
20 years and over, age-adjusted[3]	Percent of population				
Both sexes[4]	2.9	4.9	5.4	6.0	6.9
Male	1.7	3.3	3.5	4.2	4.9
Female	4.0	6.4	7.2	7.6	8.9
Not Hispanic or Latino:					
White only	2.7	4.4	4.9	5.4	6.5
White only, male	*1.8	3.3	3.5	4.0	4.7
White only, female	3.5	5.5	6.3	6.7	8.2
Black or African American only	5.6	8.9	10.4	11.9	12.1
Black or African American only, male . .	2.5	3.4	5.6	7.3	7.0
Black or African American only, female .	8.0	13.4	14.2	15.8	16.5
Asian only	- - -	- - -	- - -	- - -	*
Asian only, male	- - -	- - -	- - -	- - -	*
Asian only, female	- - -	- - -	- - -	- - -	*
Hispanic or Latino	- - -	- - -	- - -	5.3	6.4
Hispanic or Latino, male	- - -	- - -	- - -	4.0	4.7
Hispanic or Latina, female	- - -	- - -	- - -	6.6	8.1
Mexican origin	2.9	4.2	4.6	5.6	7.1
Mexican origin, male	*	*2.9	*2.4	4.4	5.3
Mexican origin, female	4.9	5.7	6.9	6.8	9.2
Percent of poverty level:[5]					
Below 100%	4.7	7.8	7.0	7.5	8.5
100%–199%	3.6	6.7	6.3	8.1	9.8
200%–399%	3.0	4.8	5.2	6.3	6.7
400% or more	1.9	3.2	4.2	4.4	5.0
20 years and over, crude					
Both sexes[4]	2.8	4.9	5.4	6.0	7.0
Male	1.7	3.4	3.5	4.3	4.9
Female	3.8	6.4	7.2	7.7	9.0
Not Hispanic or Latino:					
White only	2.6	4.5	4.9	5.5	6.6
White only, male	*1.8	3.4	3.5	4.1	4.7
White only, female	3.3	5.6	6.3	6.8	8.3
Black or African American only	5.3	8.9	10.6	12.2	12.3
Black or African American only, male . .	2.6	3.5	6.1	7.2	7.1
Black or African American only, female .	7.6	13.4	14.4	16.3	16.7
Asian only	- - -	- - -	- - -	- - -	*
Asian only, male	- - -	- - -	- - -	- - -	*
Asian only, female	- - -	- - -	- - -	- - -	*
Hispanic or Latino	- - -	- - -	- - -	5.4	6.6
Hispanic or Latino, male	- - -	- - -	- - -	4.3	5.0
Hispanic or Latina, female	- - -	- - -	- - -	6.5	8.1
Mexican origin	2.7	4.1	4.7	5.7	7.3
Mexican origin, male	*1.1	*2.7	*2.7	4.9	*5.6
Mexican origin, female	4.7	5.7	7.0	6.6	9.3
Percent of poverty level:[5]					
Below 100%	4.3	7.1	7.1	7.5	8.5
100%–199%	3.0	6.4	5.9	7.9	9.6
200%–399%	2.9	4.7	5.2	6.3	6.7
400% or more	2.0	3.5	4.7	4.6	5.5
Male					
20–34 years	*1.3	3.9	3.6	3.4	4.7
35–44 years	*	*3.2	4.2	5.2	5.6
45–54 years	*	*4.2	*3.9	5.1	*4.6
55–64 years	*	*2.8	3.9	5.4	*6.2
65–74 years	*	*	*2.1	*3.6	*4.7
75 years and over	*	*	*	*	*
Female					
20–34 years	2.6	4.5	6.3	7.7	9.1
35–44 years	4.5	7.9	7.2	7.5	9.0
45–54 years	6.4	7.2	9.2	7.7	10.5
55–64 years	4.2	9.5	9.8	9.4	11.5
65–74 years	4.2	6.2	*6.4	9.2	6.5
75 years and over	*	*	*2.1	*3.4	*3.3

See footnotes at end of table.

Table 58 (page 7 of 7). Normal weight, overweight, and obesity among adults aged 20 and over, by selected characteristics: United States, selected years 1988–1994 through 2011–2014

Excel and PDF versions (with more data years and standard errors when available): http://www.cdc.gov/nchs/hus/contents2016.htm#058.

[Data are based on measured height and weight of a sample of the civilian noninstitutionalized population]

- - - Data not available.

* Estimates are considered unreliable. Data preceded by an asterisk have a relative standard error (RSE) of 20%–30%. Data not shown have an RSE greater than 30%.

[1] Persons of Hispanic and Mexican origin may be of any race. Starting with 1999 data, race-specific estimates are tabulated according to the 1997 *Revisions to the Standards for the Classification of Federal Data on Race and Ethnicity* and are not strictly comparable with estimates for earlier years. The non-Hispanic race categories shown in the table conform to the 1997 Standards. Starting with 1999 data, race-specific estimates are for persons who reported only one racial group. Prior to data year 1999, estimates were tabulated according to the 1977 Standards. Estimates for single-race categories prior to 1999 included persons who reported one race or, if they reported more than one race, identified one race as best representing their race. See Appendix II, Hispanic origin; Race.

[2] Body mass index (BMI) equals weight in kilograms divided by height in meters squared. In *Health, United States* the NHANES variable, Body Mass Index, is used to assign persons to BMI categories. See Appendix II, Body mass index (BMI).

[3] Estimates are age-adjusted to the year 2000 standard population using five age groups: 20–34 years, 35–44 years, 45–54 years, 55–64 years, and 65 years and over. Age-adjusted estimates in this table may differ from other age-adjusted estimates based on the same data and presented elsewhere if different age groups are used in the adjustment procedure. See Appendix II, Age adjustment.

[4] Includes persons of all races and Hispanic origins, not just those shown separately.

[5] Percent of poverty level was calculated by dividing family income by the U.S. Department of Health and Human Services' poverty guideline specific to family size, as well as the appropriate year, and state. Persons with unknown percent of poverty level are excluded (6% in 2011–2014). See Appendix II, Family income; Poverty.

NOTES: Percents do not sum to 100 because the percentage of persons with BMI less than normal weight (18.5 kilograms per meters squared) is not shown and the percentage of persons with obesity is a subset of the percentage with overweight. Height was measured without shoes. Excludes pregnant women.
See *Health, United States, 2013*, Table 69, for earlier data years. Standard errors for selected years are available in the spreadsheet version of this table. Available from: http://www.cdc.gov/nchs/hus.htm. Data for additional years are available. See the Excel spreadsheet on the *Health, United States* website at: http://www.cdc.gov/nchs/hus.htm.

SOURCE: NCHS, National Health and Nutrition Examination Survey. See Appendix I, National Health and Nutrition Examination Survey (NHANES).

Table 59 (page 1 of 2). Obesity among children and adolescents aged 2–19 years, by selected characteristics: United States, selected years 1988–1994 through 2011–2014

Excel and PDF versions (with more data years and standard errors when available): http://www.cdc.gov/nchs/hus/contents2016.htm#059.

[Data are based on measured height and weight of a sample of the civilian noninstitutionalized population]

Sex, age, race and Hispanic origin [1], and percent of poverty level	1988–1994	1999–2002	2003–2006	2007–2010	2011–2014
2–5 years			Percent of population		
Both sexes [2]	7.2	10.3	12.5	11.1	8.9
Not Hispanic or Latino:					
White only	5.2	8.7	10.8	9.0	*5.2
Black or African American only	7.8	8.8	14.9	15.0	10.4
Asian only	- - -	- - -	- - -	- - -	*
Hispanic or Latino	- - -	- - -	- - -	15.3	15.6
Mexican origin	12.3	13.1	16.7	14.6	15.3
Boys	6.2	10.0	12.8	11.9	9.2
Not Hispanic or Latino:					
White only	*4.5	*8.2	11.1	8.8	*
Black or African American only	7.9	*8.0	13.3	15.7	*9.0
Asian only	- - -	- - -	- - -	- - -	*
Hispanic or Latino	- - -	- - -	- - -	17.7	16.7
Mexican origin	12.4	14.1	18.8	19.1	*14.5
Girls	8.2	10.6	12.2	10.2	8.6
Not Hispanic or Latina:					
White only	5.9	*9.0	10.4	*9.2	*4.4
Black or African American only	7.6	9.6	16.6	*14.2	11.9
Asian only	- - -	- - -	- - -	- - -	*
Hispanic or Latina	- - -	- - -	- - -	12.7	14.6
Mexican origin	12.3	*12.2	14.5	*9.9	*16.1
Percent of poverty level: [3]					
Below 100%	9.7	10.9	14.3	13.2	11.6
100%–199%	7.3	*13.8	12.7	11.8	10.2
200%–399%	5.6	*7.6	11.9	13.9	*7.7
400% or more	*	*	*10.0	*5.8	*
6–11 years					
Both sexes [2]	11.3	15.9	17.0	18.8	17.5
Not Hispanic or Latino:					
White only	10.2	13.6	15.0	16.4	13.6
Black or African American only	14.6	19.8	21.3	23.9	21.4
Asian only	- - -	- - -	- - -	- - -	*9.8
Hispanic or Latino	- - -	- - -	- - -	23.8	25.0
Mexican origin	16.4	21.8	23.7	23.3	25.3
Boys	11.6	16.9	18.0	20.7	17.6
Not Hispanic or Latino:					
White only	10.7	14.0	15.5	18.6	13.0
Black or African American only	12.3	17.0	18.6	23.3	21.2
Asian only	- - -	- - -	- - -	- - -	*14.7
Hispanic or Latino	- - -	- - -	- - -	26.0	25.8
Mexican origin	17.5	26.5	27.5	24.3	25.3
Girls	11.0	14.7	15.8	16.9	17.5
Not Hispanic or Latina:					
White only	*9.8	13.1	14.4	14.0	14.4
Black or African American only	17.0	22.8	24.0	24.5	21.6
Asian only	- - -	- - -	- - -	- - -	*
Hispanic or Latina	- - -	- - -	- - -	21.5	24.1
Mexican origin	15.3	17.1	19.7	22.4	25.3
Percent of poverty level: [3]					
Below 100%	11.4	19.1	22.0	22.2	21.5
100%–199%	11.1	16.4	19.2	20.7	20.4
200%–399%	11.7	15.3	16.7	18.9	15.7
400% or more	*	*12.9	*9.2	*12.5	*12.2

See footnotes at end of table.

Table 59 (page 2 of 2). Obesity among children and adolescents aged 2–19 years, by selected characteristics: United States, selected years 1988–1994 through 2011–2014

Excel and PDF versions (with more data years and standard errors when available): http://www.cdc.gov/nchs/hus/contents2016.htm#059.

[Data are based on measured height and weight of a sample of the civilian noninstitutionalized population]

Sex, age, race and Hispanic origin[1], and percent of poverty level	1988–1994	1999–2002	2003–2006	2007–2010	2011–2014
12–19 years			Percent of population		
Both sexes[2]	10.5	16.0	17.6	18.2	20.5
Not Hispanic or Latino:					
White only	10.3	13.7	16.0	15.9	19.6
Black or African American only.	13.4	21.1	22.9	24.1	22.6
Asian only	- - -	- - -	- - -	- - -	9.4
Hispanic or Latino.	- - -	- - -	- - -	22.5	22.8
Mexican origin	13.8	22.3	21.1	23.1	23.5
Boys	11.3	16.7	18.2	19.4	20.1
Not Hispanic or Latino:					
White only	11.6	14.6	17.3	17.1	18.7
Black or African American only.	10.7	18.8	18.4	21.2	20.9
Asian only	- - -	- - -	- - -	- - -	12.9
Hispanic or Latino.	- - -	- - -	- - -	26.0	22.7
Mexican origin	14.1	24.7	22.1	27.9	22.8
Girls	9.7	15.3	16.8	16.9	21.0
Not Hispanic or Latina:					
White only	8.9	12.6	14.5	14.6	20.4
Black or African American only.	16.3	23.5	27.7	27.1	24.4
Asian only	- - -	- - -	- - -	- - -	*5.7
Hispanic or Latina.	- - -	- - -	- - -	18.7	22.8
Mexican origin	*13.4	19.6	19.9	18.0	24.2
Percent of poverty level:[3]					
Below 100%	15.8	19.8	19.3	24.3	22.4
100%–199%	11.2	15.1	18.4	20.1	25.7
200%–399%	9.4	15.7	19.3	16.3	19.7
400% or more	*	13.9	12.6	14.0	*13.7

- - - Data not available.

* Estimates are considered unreliable. Data preceded by an asterisk have a relative standard error (RSE) of 20%–30%. Data not shown have an RSE greater than 30%.

[1] Persons of Hispanic and Mexican origin may be of any race. Starting with 1999 data, race-specific estimates are tabulated according to the 1997 *Revisions to the Standards for the Classification of Federal Data on Race and Ethnicity* and are not strictly comparable with estimates for earlier years. The non-Hispanic race categories shown in the table conform to the 1997 Standards. Starting with 1999 data, race-specific estimates are for persons who reported only one racial group. Prior to data year 1999, estimates were tabulated according to the 1977 Standards. Estimates for single-race categories prior to 1999 included persons who reported one race or, if they reported more than one race, identified one race as best representing their race. See Appendix II, Hispanic origin; Race.

[2] Includes persons of all races and Hispanic origins, not just those shown separately.

[3] Percent of poverty level was calculated by dividing family income by the U.S. Department of Health and Human Services' poverty guideline specific to family size, as well as the appropriate year, and state. Persons with unknown percent of poverty level are excluded (6% in 2011–2014). See Appendix II, Family income; Poverty.

NOTES: Obesity is defined as body mass index (BMI) at or above the sex- and age-specific 95th percentile from the 2000 CDC Growth Charts: United States. Kuczmarski RJ, Ogden CL, Guo SS, Grummer-Strawn LM, Flegal KM, Mei Z, Wei R, Curtin LR, Roche AF, Johnson CL. 2000 CDC Growth Charts for the United States: methods and development. Vital Health Stat 11. 2002 May;(246):1–190. Available at: http://www.cdc.gov/nchs/data/series/sr_11/sr11_246.pdf. In *Health, United States* the NHANES variable, Body Mass Index, is used to assign persons to BMI categories. Age is at time of examination at the mobile examination center. Crude rates, not age-adjusted rates, are shown. Height was measured without shoes. Excludes pregnant females. See *Health, United States, 2013*, Table 70, for earlier data years. Standard errors for selected years are available in the spreadsheet version of this table. Available from: http://www.cdc.gov/nchs/hus.htm. Data for additional years are available. See the Excel spreadsheet on the *Health, United States* website at: http://www.cdc.gov/nchs/hus.htm. Data for 1988–1994 have been revised and differ from previous editions.

SOURCE: NCHS, National Health and Nutrition Examination Survey. See Appendix I, National Health and Nutrition Examination Survey (NHANES).

Table 60 (page 1 of 2). Untreated dental caries, by selected characteristics: United States, selected years 1988–1994 through 2011–2014

Excel and PDF versions (with more data years and standard errors when available): *http://www.cdc.gov/nchs/hus/contents2016.htm#060.*

[Data are based on dental examinations of a sample of the civilian noninstitutionalized population]

Sex, race and Hispanic origin [1], and percent of poverty level	Age 5–19 years				Age 20–44 years			
	1988–1994	1999–2002	2005–2008	2011–2014	1988–1994	1999–2002	2005–2008	2011–2014
	Percent of persons with untreated dental caries							
Total [2]	24.3	22.5	16.6	18.6	29.5	26.0	25.1	31.6
Sex								
Male	23.6	23.7	17.6	19.7	32.8	27.0	28.4	32.8
Female	25.0	21.3	15.5	17.4	26.4	24.9	21.8	30.3
Race and Hispanic origin								
Not Hispanic or Latino:								
White only.	19.4	18.5	13.3	16.7	24.8	20.7	21.1	27.1
Black or African American only	33.9	29.2	22.6	23.4	49.2	43.4	36.7	46.1
Asian only.	- - -	- - -	- - -	15.4	- - -	- - -	- - -	20.5
Hispanic or Latino	- - -	- - -	- - -	21.7	- - -	- - -	- - -	37.8
Mexican origin	37.9	33.9	22.4	23.8	40.0	35.6	35.1	40.0
Percent of poverty level: [3]								
Below 100%	39.0	31.9	25.4	24.7	47.8	42.4	39.8	47.0
100%–199%	29.6	29.7	19.3	22.3	43.7	36.7	37.7	40.8
200%–399%	16.6	18.0	14.7	16.0	24.5	24.9	22.3	28.1
400% or more	*10.4	8.9	9.3	9.1	12.5	9.8	12.4	14.8
Race and Hispanic origin, and percent of poverty level [3]								
Not Hispanic or Latino:								
White only:								
Below 100% of poverty level	33.8	28.0	25.0	24.5	42.9	36.9	37.7	47.4
100% or more of poverty level	17.3	16.5	11.6	14.8	22.7	18.5	18.6	23.0
Black or African American only:								
Below 100% of poverty level	37.4	36.7	27.3	27.5	60.0	55.3	48.7	56.0
100% or more of poverty level	31.2	25.0	19.5	19.3	44.8	37.6	33.8	41.3
Asian only:								
Below 100% of poverty level	- - -	- - -	- - -	*24.2	- - -	- - -	- - -	24.6
100% or more of poverty level	- - -	- - -	- - -	13.6	- - -	- - -	- - -	19.9
Hispanic or Latino:								
Below 100% of poverty level	- - -	- - -	- - -	23.6	- - -	- - -	- - -	43.4
100% or more of poverty level	- - -	- - -	- - -	19.7	- - -	- - -	- - -	33.3
Mexican origin:								
Below 100% of poverty level	47.5	40.2	25.9	23.1	52.7	42.2	42.1	44.4
100% or more of poverty level	28.0	27.0	20.5	23.7	31.2	32.5	31.0	35.8

See footnotes at end of table.

Table 60 (page 2 of 2). Untreated dental caries, by selected characteristics: United States, selected years 1988–1994 through 2011–2014

Excel and PDF versions (with more data years and standard errors when available): http://www.cdc.gov/nchs/hus/contents2016.htm#060.

[Data are based on dental examinations of a sample of the civilian noninstitutionalized population]

Sex, race and Hispanic origin [1], and percent of poverty level	Age 45–64 years				Age 65 years and over			
	1988–1994	1999–2002	2005–2008	2011–2014	1988–1994	1999–2002	2005–2008	2011–2014
	Percent of persons with untreated dental caries							
Total [2]	25.4	20.1	21.6	27.2	27.1	18.4	19.9	21.8
Sex								
Male	28.5	24.0	25.4	31.8	31.2	21.8	25.1	24.7
Female	22.6	16.5	18.0	22.9	24.1	15.7	15.6	19.4
Race and Hispanic origin								
Not Hispanic or Latino:								
White only.	21.7	15.6	17.1	23.4	24.6	16.0	17.8	18.6
Black or African American only	46.2	39.8	44.4	45.4	51.2	38.6	35.8	40.7
Asian only.	- - -	- - -	- - -	17.4	- - -	- - -	- - -	27.6
Hispanic or Latino	- - -	- - -	- - -	35.9	- - -	- - -	- - -	34.4
Mexican origin	41.4	34.3	35.4	40.8	46.3	37.9	36.4	46.3
Percent of poverty level: [3]								
Below 100%	49.5	39.3	47.6	54.2	46.8	30.5	41.3	44.0
100%–199%	42.5	35.9	37.7	45.0	37.6	25.3	22.5	36.8
200%–399%	25.0	24.8	27.6	29.2	24.1	15.6	16.6	18.3
400% or more	13.0	9.6	10.0	12.6	15.6	11.1	13.1	*9.5
Race and Hispanic origin, and percent of poverty level [3]								
Not Hispanic or Latino:								
White only:								
Below 100% of poverty level	47.6	31.2	45.4	52.2	38.5	*27.1	*35.6	46.7
100% or more of poverty level	19.7	14.2	15.4	20.9	23.9	15.4	16.1	17.2
Black or African American only:								
Below 100% of poverty level	62.9	52.5	61.0	71.7	56.3	40.1	55.7	52.9
100% or more of poverty level	41.2	37.7	41.4	37.9	47.8	40.3	30.6	38.6
Asian only:								
Below 100% of poverty level	- - -	- - -	- - -	*26.2	- - -	- - -	- - -	*
100% or more of poverty level	- - -	- - -	- - -	15.4	- - -	- - -	- - -	26.7
Hispanic or Latino:								
Below 100% of poverty level	- - -	- - -	- - -	45.6	- - -	- - -	- - -	39.0
100% or more of poverty level	- - -	- - -	- - -	33.6	- - -	- - -	- - -	33.1
Mexican origin:								
Below 100% of poverty level	52.7	49.0	51.6	49.9	62.8	46.8	56.3	58.7
100% or more of poverty level	34.5	31.1	30.9	38.5	35.4	36.2	26.2	42.3

- - - Data not available.

* Estimates are considered unreliable. Data preceded by an asterisk have a relative standard error (RSE) of 20%–30%. Data not shown have an RSE of greater than 30%.

[1] Persons of Hispanic and Mexican origin may be of any race. Starting with 1999 data, race-specific estimates are tabulated according to the 1997 *Revisions to the Standards for the Classification of Federal Data on Race and Ethnicity* and are not strictly comparable with estimates for earlier years. The non-Hispanic race categories shown in the table conform to the 1997 Standards. Starting with 1999 data, race-specific estimates are for persons who reported only one racial group. Prior to data year 1999, estimates were tabulated according to the 1977 Standards. Estimates for single-race categories prior to 1999 included persons who reported one race or, if they reported more than one race, identified one race as best representing their race. See Appendix II, Hispanic origin; Race.

[2] Includes persons of all races and Hispanic origins, not just those shown separately, and those with unknown percent of poverty level.

[3] Percent of poverty level was calculated by dividing family income by the U.S. Department of Health and Human Services' poverty guideline specific to family size, as well as the appropriate year, and state. Persons with unknown percent of poverty level are excluded (6% in 2011–2014). See Appendix II, Family income; Poverty.

NOTES: Untreated dental caries refers to decay on the crown or enamel surface of a tooth (i.e., coronal caries) that has not been treated or filled. Decay in the root (i.e., root caries) was not included. The presence of caries was evaluated in primary and permanent teeth for persons aged 5 and older. The third molars were not included. Persons without at least one natural tooth (primary or permanent) were classified as edentulous (without any teeth) and were excluded. The majority of edentulous persons are aged 65 and over. Estimates of edentulism among persons aged 65 and over are 33% in 1988–1994, 23% in 2005–2008, and 17% in 2011–2014. Over time, there have been changes in the NHANES oral health examination process, ages examined, and methodology. Therefore, data trends need to be interpreted with caution. For more information on the methodology changes, see Appendix II, Dental caries. Standard errors are available in the spreadsheet version of this table. Available from: http://www.cdc.gov/nchs/hus.htm. Data for additional years are available. See the Excel spreadsheet on the *Health, United States* website at: http://www.cdc.gov/nchs/hus.htm.

SOURCE: NCHS, National Health and Nutrition Examination Survey. See Appendix I, National Health and Nutrition Examination Survey (NHANES).

Table 61 (page 1 of 2). No usual source of health care among children under age 18, by selected characteristics: United States, average annual, selected years 1993–1994 through 2014–2015

Excel and PDF versions (with more data years and standard errors when available): http://www.cdc.gov/nchs/hus/contents2016.htm#061.

[Data are based on household interviews of a sample of the civilian noninstitutionalized population]

Characteristic	Under 18 years			Under 6 years			6–17 years		
	1993–1994[1]	1999–2000	2014–2015	1993–1994[1]	1999–2000	2014–2015	1993–1994[1]	1999–2000	2014–2015
	Percent of children without a usual source of health care[2]								
All children[3]	7.7	6.9	4.0	5.2	4.6	2.7	9.0	8.0	4.6
Sex									
Male	8.1	6.7	3.9	5.3	4.5	2.4	9.6	7.8	4.6
Female	7.3	7.1	4.1	5.0	4.7	3.0	8.5	8.2	4.6
Race[4]									
White only	7.0	6.3	3.7	4.7	4.4	2.4	8.3	7.2	4.3
Black or African American only	10.3	7.7	4.8	7.6	4.4	4.0	11.9	9.1	5.1
American Indian or Alaska Native only	*9.3	*9.4	*	*	*	*	*8.7	*9.4	*
Asian only	9.7	10.0	5.0	*3.4	*5.8	*4.2	13.5	12.2	5.4
Native Hawaiian or Other Pacific Islander only	- - -	*	*	- - -	*	*	- - -	*	*
2 or more races	- - -	*4.9	4.8	- - -	*	*3.3	- - -	*7.2	5.8
Hispanic origin and race[4]									
Hispanic or Latino	14.3	14.2	6.2	9.3	9.0	3.9	17.7	17.2	7.5
Not Hispanic or Latino	6.7	5.5	3.3	4.4	3.6	2.3	7.8	6.3	3.7
White only	5.7	4.7	2.6	3.7	3.3	1.7	6.7	5.4	3.0
Black or African American only	10.2	7.6	4.5	7.7	4.5	3.8	11.6	9.0	4.8
Percent of poverty level[5]									
Below 100%	13.9	13.1	6.5	9.4	7.6	4.4	16.8	16.2	7.6
100%–199%	9.8	10.6	5.4	6.7	7.5	3.7	11.6	12.2	6.2
200%–399%	3.7	4.8	3.4	1.9	3.2	2.3	4.5	5.6	3.9
400% or more	3.7	2.6	1.4	*1.6	1.5	*0.8	5.0	3.0	1.7
Hispanic origin and race and percent of poverty level[4,5]									
Hispanic or Latino:									
Below 100%	19.6	19.4	7.6	12.7	11.6	*4.8	24.8	24.5	9.3
100%–199%	15.3	17.1	6.9	9.9	11.3	*4.0	18.9	20.4	8.3
200%–399%	5.2	8.3	5.0	*	*5.0	*3.5	6.7	10.1	5.8
400% or more	*	*3.8	*2.4	*	*	*	*	*5.0	*3.0
Not Hispanic or Latino:									
White only:									
Below 100%	10.2	10.7	4.9	6.5	*6.3	*	12.7	13.1	*5.4
100%–199%	8.7	7.8	4.0	6.3	5.7	*3.2	10.1	8.8	4.5
200%–399%	3.3	4.0	2.6	1.6	2.7	*1.3	4.0	4.6	3.3
400% or more	4.0	2.3	1.1	*1.7	*1.5	*	5.4	2.6	1.4
Black or African American only:									
Below 100%	13.7	9.4	5.0	10.9	*4.7	*4.8	15.5	11.8	5.1
100%–199%	9.1	9.7	5.3	*6.0	*6.4	*	10.8	11.2	6.1
200%–399%	5.0	5.0	*4.1	*	*	*	6.2	5.7	*4.2
400% or more	*	*3.5	*	*	*	*	*	*4.0	*
Health insurance status at the time of interview[6]									
Insured	5.0	3.9	2.8	3.3	2.6	2.1	5.9	4.5	3.1
Private	3.8	3.4	2.1	1.9	2.2	1.5	4.6	3.9	2.3
Medicaid	8.9	5.3	3.7	6.4	3.5	2.8	11.3	6.7	4.3
Uninsured	23.5	29.3	27.9	18.0	20.8	20.3	26.0	32.9	30.3
Health insurance status prior to interview[6]									
Insured continuously all 12 months	4.6	3.6	2.5	3.1	2.3	1.9	5.5	4.2	2.8
Uninsured for any period up to 12 months	15.3	15.0	13.5	10.9	12.5	10.8	18.1	16.4	14.8
Uninsured more than 12 months	27.6	35.8	34.9	21.4	26.8	*23.5	30.0	39.1	37.5

See footnotes at end of table.

Table 61 (page 2 of 2). No usual source of health care among children under age 18, by selected characteristics: United States, average annual, selected years 1993–1994 through 2014–2015

Excel and PDF versions (with more data years and standard errors when available): http://www.cdc.gov/nchs/hus/contents2016.htm#061.

[Data are based on household interviews of a sample of the civilian noninstitutionalized population]

Characteristic	Under 18 years			Under 6 years			6–17 years		
	1993– 1994[1]	1999– 2000	2014– 2015	1993– 1994[1]	1999– 2000	2014– 2015	1993– 1994[1]	1999– 2000	2014– 2015
Percent of poverty level and health insurance status prior to interview[5,6]	Percent of children without a usual source of health care[2]								
Below 100%:									
Insured continuously all 12 months.	8.6	5.7	4.0	5.8	*2.7	2.9	10.7	7.5	4.5
Uninsured for any period up to 12 months . . .	21.7	19.8	20.8	18.0	*16.0	*	23.7	21.9	21.5
Uninsured more than 12 months	31.2	42.7	47.9	25.5	31.0	*	33.4	47.1	49.8
100%–199%:									
Insured continuously all 12 months.	5.6	5.2	3.0	3.7	3.7	2.4	6.7	6.0	3.3
Uninsured for any period up to 12 months . . .	14.5	15.4	14.8	*9.7	*14.4	*11.3	18.0	15.9	16.6
Uninsured more than 12 months	27.6	34.4	34.6	21.4	26.4	*	30.2	37.4	36.0
200%–399%:									
Insured continuously all 12 months.	2.8	3.2	2.3	1.5	2.1	1.9	3.4	3.7	2.5
Uninsured for any period up to 12 months . . .	9.1	11.1	9.4	*	*8.4	*	11.6	12.7	*11.4
Uninsured more than 12 months	18.2	27.1	26.5	*9.7	*20.3	*	21.0	29.4	30.1
400% or more:									
Insured continuously all 12 months.	3.1	2.0	1.2	*	*1.2	*	4.3	2.4	1.5
Uninsured for any period up to 12 months . . .	*	*10.3	*	*	*	*	*	*	*
Uninsured more than 12 months	*	*30.0	*	*	*	*	*	*33.3	*
Geographic region									
Northeast	4.1	2.8	1.7	2.9	2.3	*1.4	4.8	3.0	1.8
Midwest	5.2	5.3	3.5	4.1	3.7	2.7	5.9	6.0	3.8
South	10.9	8.5	4.5	7.3	5.8	3.0	12.7	9.8	5.3
West	8.6	9.7	5.1	5.3	5.7	3.1	10.6	11.7	6.1
Location of residence[7]									
Within MSA	7.7	6.8	4.0	5.0	4.7	2.7	9.2	7.8	4.7
Outside MSA	7.8	7.4	3.8	6.0	4.2	3.1	8.7	8.7	4.1

* Estimates are considered unreliable. Data preceded by an asterisk have a relative standard error (RSE) of 20%–30%. Data not shown have an RSE greater than 30%.

- - - Data not available.

[1] Data prior to 1997 are not strictly comparable with data for later years due to the 1997 questionnaire redesign. See Appendix I, National Health Interview Survey (NHIS).

[2] Persons who report the emergency department as their usual source of care are defined as having no usual source of care. See Appendix II, Usual source of care.

[3] Includes all other races not shown separately and unknown health insurance status.

[4] The race groups, white, black, American Indian or Alaska Native, Asian, Native Hawaiian or Other Pacific Islander, and 2 or more races, include persons of Hispanic and non-Hispanic origin. Persons of Hispanic origin may be of any race. Starting with 1999 data, race-specific estimates are tabulated according to the 1997 *Revisions to the Standards for the Classification of Federal Data on Race and Ethnicity* and are not strictly comparable with estimates for earlier years. The five single-race categories plus multiple-race categories shown in the table conform to the 1997 Standards. Starting with 1999 data, race-specific estimates are for persons who reported only one racial group; the category 2 or more races includes persons who reported more than one racial group. Prior to 1999, data were tabulated according to the 1977 Standards with four racial groups, and the Asian only category included Native Hawaiian or Other Pacific Islander. Estimates for single-race categories prior to 1999 included persons who reported one race or, if they reported more than one race, identified one race as best representing their race. Starting with 2003 data, race responses of other race and unspecified multiple race were treated as missing, and then race was imputed if these were the only race responses. Almost all persons with a race response of other race were of Hispanic origin. See Appendix II, Hispanic origin; Race.

[5] Percent of poverty level is based on family income and family size and composition using U.S. Census Bureau poverty thresholds. Missing family income data were imputed starting in 1993. See Appendix II, Family income; Poverty; Table VI.

[6] Health insurance categories are mutually exclusive. Persons who reported both Medicaid and private coverage are classified as having private coverage. Medicaid includes other public assistance through 1996. Starting with 1997 data, state-sponsored health plan coverage is included as Medicaid coverage. Starting with 1999 data, coverage by the Children's Health Insurance Program (CHIP) is included with Medicaid coverage. In addition to private and Medicaid, the insured category also includes military, other government, and Medicare coverage. Persons not covered by private insurance, Medicaid, CHIP, public assistance (through 1996), state-sponsored or other government-sponsored health plans (starting in 1997), Medicare, or military plans are considered to have no health insurance coverage. Persons with only Indian Health Service coverage are considered to have no health insurance coverage. Health insurance status was unknown for 8%–9% of children in 1993–1996 and about 1% in 1997–2015. See Appendix II, Health insurance coverage.

[7] MSA is metropolitan statistical area. Starting with 2005–2006 data, MSA status is determined using 2000 census data and the 2000 standards for defining MSAs. For data prior to 2005, see Appendix II, Metropolitan statistical area (MSA) for the applicable standards.

NOTES: Standard errors are available in the spreadsheet version of this table. Available from: http://www.cdc.gov/nchs/hus.htm. Data for additional years are available. See the Excel spreadsheet on the *Health, United States* website at: http://www.cdc.gov/nchs/hus.htm.

SOURCE: NCHS, National Health Interview Survey, access to care and health insurance supplements (1993–1996). Starting in 1997, data are from the family core and sample child questionnaires. See Appendix I, National Health Interview Survey (NHIS).

Table 62 (page 1 of 2). No usual source of health care among adults aged 18–64, by selected characteristics: United States, average annual, selected years 1993–1994 through 2014–2015

Excel and PDF versions (with more data years and standard errors when available): http://www.cdc.gov/nchs/hus/contents2016.htm#062.

[Data are based on household interviews of a sample of the civilian noninstitutionalized population]

Characteristic	1993–1994[1]	1999–2000	2004–2005	2007–2008	2009–2010	2011–2012	2014–2015
	Percent of adults without a usual source of health care[2]						
18–64 years[3]	18.9	17.8	18.0	18.5	20.3	19.5	17.3
Age							
18–44 years	21.7	21.6	22.8	23.6	26.0	25.0	22.5
18–24 years.	26.6	27.2	29.9	28.6	29.8	27.8	24.2
19–25 years.	28.0	29.0	31.3	30.0	33.1	30.3	26.9
25–44 years.	20.3	19.9	20.3	21.8	24.7	23.9	21.9
45–64 years	12.8	10.9	10.6	11.0	12.3	12.0	10.2
45–54 years.	14.1	12.0	11.9	13.1	14.7	14.2	12.1
55–64 years.	11.1	9.2	8.8	8.3	9.3	9.6	8.1
Sex							
Male	23.9	24.1	23.3	23.9	25.9	24.4	22.3
Female.	14.1	11.8	12.9	13.1	14.8	14.8	12.4
Race[4]							
White only	18.4	16.7	17.7	18.0	19.7	18.9	17.0
Black or African American only	20.0	19.2	19.3	20.5	22.4	21.9	18.0
American Indian or Alaska Native only . . .	19.7	19.2	22.8	24.4	26.7	23.6	20.1
Asian only	24.8	22.1	18.8	17.8	20.8	20.8	17.5
Native Hawaiian or Other Pacific Islander only	- - -	*	*	*	*	*	*
2 or more races	- - -	21.0	18.1	21.4	27.5	22.3	23.1
American Indian or Alaska Native; White	- - -	25.8	19.1	20.9	27.1	19.0	23.9
Hispanic origin and race[4]							
Hispanic or Latino	30.3	32.6	34.0	32.5	33.3	33.6	26.2
Mexican.	32.4	36.5	37.8	36.6	35.7	35.6	27.5
Not Hispanic or Latino.	17.7	15.8	15.4	16.0	17.9	16.8	15.4
White only.	17.1	14.9	14.6	15.1	16.8	15.5	14.6
Black or African American only.	19.7	19.2	19.0	20.2	22.2	21.6	18.0
Percent of poverty level[5]							
Below 100%.	29.5	29.6	31.8	30.4	33.8	32.1	27.3
100%–199%.	25.4	27.1	27.1	29.1	30.5	30.2	24.2
200%–399%.	15.6	17.2	17.9	18.9	20.5	19.3	18.1
400% or more	13.4	11.6	10.3	10.2	10.8	9.6	9.9
Hispanic origin and race and percent of poverty level[4,5]							
Hispanic or Latino:							
Below 100%	40.0	44.4	44.5	43.7	45.5	42.9	35.4
100%–199%	36.9	40.6	40.7	40.6	39.7	40.0	30.1
200%–399%	20.7	26.9	30.1	28.0	29.1	29.4	23.3
400% or more	13.8	16.1	16.2	16.9	14.0	15.4	13.1
Not Hispanic or Latino:							
White only:							
Below 100%.	28.2	24.2	26.8	25.2	28.8	27.0	24.2
100%–199%.	23.3	23.0	22.8	24.9	26.6	25.7	22.2
200%–399%.	14.8	15.3	15.6	16.7	18.6	16.9	16.4
400% or more	13.4	11.2	9.6	9.5	10.3	8.8	9.4
Black or African American only:							
Below 100%.	24.7	23.7	28.3	27.1	30.1	29.9	24.8
100%–199%.	22.3	24.4	22.1	25.7	28.5	28.2	20.3
200%–399%.	16.5	18.2	16.6	19.7	20.1	18.5	17.8
400% or more	11.7	12.0	11.3	10.2	10.5	10.1	9.0
Health insurance status at the time of interview[6]							
Insured.	13.3	10.9	9.7	10.1	10.6	10.5	11.2
Private	13.1	11.1	9.5	10.0	10.6	10.1	11.1
Medicaid	16.3	9.9	12.1	11.7	12.5	13.1	13.1
Uninsured	43.1	49.2	52.5	52.1	55.6	54.1	52.6
Health insurance status prior to interview[6]							
Insured continuously all 12 months	12.7	10.3	8.9	9.1	9.8	9.6	10.0
Uninsured for any period up to 12 months .	30.9	31.2	34.0	35.1	36.5	33.2	32.4
Uninsured more than 12 months	46.9	54.8	57.4	56.1	59.5	57.8	56.9

See footnotes at end of table.

Table 62 (page 2 of 2). No usual source of health care among adults aged 18–64, by selected characteristics: United States, average annual, selected years 1993–1994 through 2014–2015

Excel and PDF versions (with more data years and standard errors when available): *http://www.cdc.gov/nchs/hus/contents2016.htm#062*.

[Data are based on household interviews of a sample of the civilian noninstitutionalized population]

Characteristic	1993–1994[1]	1999–2000	2004–2005	2007–2008	2009–2010	2011–2012	2014–2015
Percent of poverty level and health insurance status prior to interview[5,6]	Percent of adults without a usual source of health care[2]						
Below 100%:							
Insured continuously all 12 months.	16.7	11.6	12.7	12.7	13.0	14.0	14.3
Uninsured for any period up to 12 months . .	33.6	31.9	39.4	37.4	37.8	35.6	34.6
Uninsured more than 12 months	50.1	57.1	61.6	61.1	65.3	61.3	56.1
100%–199%:							
Insured continuously all 12 months.	14.7	12.3	10.7	11.9	12.5	12.8	12.0
Uninsured for any period up to 12 months . .	30.9	34.6	37.1	35.9	38.1	35.9	31.9
Uninsured more than 12 months	47.6	54.9	56.0	56.8	58.5	57.9	58.6
200%–399%:							
Insured continuously all 12 months.	11.7	10.6	9.5	9.4	10.6	10.0	10.8
Uninsured for any period up to 12 months . .	29.2	29.0	31.9	36.3	37.6	33.2	32.9
Uninsured more than 12 months	44.5	53.6	55.6	54.2	56.6	55.3	57.2
400% or more:							
Insured continuously all 12 months.	11.8	9.3	7.4	7.5	7.9	7.4	7.9
Uninsured for any period up to 12 months . .	31.5	30.2	28.8	30.3	31.2	25.6	29.8
Uninsured more than 12 months	36.5	51.8	56.5	47.9	53.8	52.9	51.7
Disability measure[7]							
Any basic actions difficulty or complex activity limitation	- - -	14.1	15.0	16.6	16.8	16.5	14.1
Any basic actions difficulty	- - -	14.1	15.2	16.5	16.7	16.5	14.1
Any complex activity limitation	- - -	11.6	11.5	13.6	13.5	13.5	10.9
No disability	- - -	18.8	18.8	19.1	21.5	20.5	18.4
Geographic region							
Northeast	14.7	12.8	11.7	12.5	14.0	13.1	11.5
Midwest	16.2	17.0	15.4	16.6	17.5	17.1	16.3
South	21.8	19.7	21.0	21.4	23.5	22.2	19.6
West	21.1	20.1	21.2	20.0	22.9	22.8	18.7
Location of residence[8]							
Within MSA	19.3	18.1	18.3	18.7	20.3	19.8	17.5
Outside MSA	17.5	16.8	16.6	16.9	20.4	17.8	16.0

- - - Data not available.

* Estimates are considered unreliable. Data not shown have a relative standard error greater than 30%.

[1] Data prior to 1997 are not strictly comparable with data for later years due to the 1997 questionnaire redesign. See Appendix I, National Health Interview Survey (NHIS).

[2] Persons who report the emergency department as their usual source of care are defined as having no usual source of care. See Appendix II, Usual source of care.

[3] Includes all other races not shown separately, unknown health insurance status, and unknown disability status.

[4] The race groups, white, black, American Indian or Alaska Native, Asian, Native Hawaiian or Other Pacific Islander, and 2 or more races, include persons of Hispanic and non-Hispanic origin. Persons of Hispanic origin may be of any race. Starting with 1999 data, race-specific estimates are tabulated according to the 1997 *Revisions to the Standards for the Classification of Federal Data on Race and Ethnicity* and are not strictly comparable with estimates for earlier years. The five single-race categories plus multiple-race categories shown in the table conform to the 1997 Standards. Starting with 1999 data, race-specific estimates are for persons who reported only one racial group; the category 2 or more races includes persons who reported more than one racial group. Prior to 1999, data were tabulated according to the 1977 Standards with four racial groups, and the Asian only category included Native Hawaiian or Other Pacific Islander. Estimates for single-race categories prior to 1999 included persons who reported one race or, if they reported more than one race, identified one race as best representing their race. Starting with 2003 data (shown in spreadsheet version), race responses of other race and unspecified multiple race were treated as missing, and then race was imputed if these were the only race responses. Almost all persons with a race response of other race were of Hispanic origin. See Appendix II, Hispanic origin; Race.

[5] Percent of poverty level is based on family income and family size and composition using U.S. Census Bureau poverty thresholds. Missing family income data were imputed starting in 1993. See Appendix II, Family income; Poverty; Table VI.

[6] Health insurance categories are mutually exclusive. Persons who reported both Medicaid and private coverage are classified as having private coverage. Medicaid includes other public assistance through 1996. Starting with 1997 data, state-sponsored health plan coverage is included as Medicaid coverage. Starting with 1999 data, coverage by the Children's Health Insurance Program (CHIP) is included with Medicaid coverage. In addition to private and Medicaid, the insured category also includes military, other government, and Medicare coverage. Persons not covered by private insurance, Medicaid, CHIP, public assistance (through 1996), state-sponsored or other government-sponsored health plans (starting in 1997), Medicare, or military plans are considered to have no health insurance coverage. Persons with only Indian Health Service coverage are considered to have no health insurance coverage. In 1993–1996, health insurance status was unknown for 8%–9% of adults in the sample. In 1997–2015, health insurance status was unknown for about 1% of adults aged 18–64. See Appendix II, Health insurance coverage.

[7] Any basic actions difficulty or complex activity limitation is defined as having one or more of the following limitations or difficulties: movement difficulty, emotional difficulty, sensory (seeing or hearing) difficulty, cognitive difficulty, self-care (activities of daily living or instrumental activities of daily living) limitation, social limitation, or work limitation. For more information, see Appendix II, Basic actions difficulty; Complex activity limitation. Starting with 2007 data, the hearing question, a component of the basic actions difficulty measure, was revised. Consequently, data prior to 2007 are not comparable with data for 2007 and beyond. For more information on the impact of the revised hearing question, see Appendix II, Hearing trouble.

[8] MSA is metropolitan statistical area. Starting with 2005–2006 data, MSA status is determined using 2000 census data and the 2000 standards for defining MSAs. For data prior to 2005, see Appendix II, Metropolitan statistical area (MSA) for the applicable standards.

NOTES: Standard errors are available in the spreadsheet version of this table. Available from: http://www.cdc.gov/nchs/hus.htm. Data for additional years are available. See the Excel spreadsheet on the *Health, United States* website at: http://www.cdc.gov/nchs/hus.htm.

SOURCE: NCHS, National Health Interview Survey, access to care and health insurance supplements (1993–1996). Starting in 1997, data are from the family core and sample adult questionnaires. See Appendix I, National Health Interview Survey (NHIS).

Table 63 (page 1 of 3). Delay or nonreceipt of needed medical care, nonreceipt of needed prescription drugs, or nonreceipt of needed dental care during the past 12 months due to cost, by selected characteristics: United States, selected years 1997–2015

Excel and PDF versions (with more data years and standard errors when available): http://www.cdc.gov/nchs/hus/contents2016.htm#063.

[Data are based on household interviews of a sample of the civilian noninstitutionalized population]

Characteristic	Delay or nonreceipt of needed medical care due to cost[1]				Nonreceipt of needed prescription drugs due to cost[2]				Nonreceipt of needed dental care due to cost[3]			
	1997	2005	2010	2015	1997	2005	2010	2015	1997	2005	2010	2015
	Percent											
Total[4]	8.3	8.5	10.9	7.3	4.8	7.2	8.3	5.2	8.6	10.7	13.5	9.4
Age												
Under 19 years	4.5	4.3	4.5	2.8	2.1	3.0	2.8	1.6	6.0	7.3	6.6	4.1
Under 18 years	4.4	4.2	4.4	2.7	2.2	2.9	2.7	1.6	6.0	7.3	6.6	4.1
Under 6 years.	3.3	3.3	3.7	2.2	1.6	2.5	2.5	1.4	3.9	3.7	3.9	1.9
6–17 years	4.9	4.7	4.8	2.9	2.4	3.1	2.8	1.7	6.8	8.4	7.5	4.9
18–64 years	10.7	11.0	14.7	9.8	6.3	9.4	11.2	6.9	10.6	13.0	17.3	11.8
18–44 years.	11.0	11.3	14.5	9.5	6.9	9.8	11.2	6.2	11.7	14.1	17.9	11.6
18–24 years	10.2	11.3	13.5	7.5	6.7	9.6	9.7	4.5	11.6	13.7	17.4	9.4
25–34 years	11.4	11.8	15.3	10.3	6.9	10.2	12.0	6.6	12.3	15.1	18.3	12.4
35–44 years	11.0	10.8	14.4	10.1	7.1	9.6	11.3	6.9	11.2	13.3	17.8	12.4
19–25 years.	11.1	12.5	14.8	8.4	7.7	10.3	10.9	5.5	13.1	14.8	18.9	10.9
45–64 years.	10.1	10.6	14.9	10.3	5.1	8.7	11.3	8.0	8.4	11.5	16.5	12.1
45–54 years	10.6	10.8	15.0	10.3	5.6	9.2	11.5	8.0	9.4	12.1	17.8	12.1
55–64 years	9.3	10.4	14.6	10.2	4.2	8.0	11.0	8.0	7.0	10.7	14.9	12.2
65 years and over	4.6	4.6	5.0	4.1	2.8	5.1	4.7	3.9	3.5	5.2	6.9	7.0
65–74 years.	5.0	5.4	6.3	4.9	3.4	6.4	6.3	4.8	4.2	6.2	9.0	7.8
75 years and over.	4.1	3.7	3.4	3.0	2.0	3.6	2.8	2.8	2.6	4.0	4.3	5.8
18–64 years												
Sex												
Male	9.3	10.0	13.5	8.9	5.1	7.2	8.8	5.4	8.8	10.8	15.2	10.0
Female.	12.0	12.1	15.7	10.7	7.4	11.4	13.5	8.4	12.4	15.2	19.4	13.6
Race[5]												
White only	10.8	11.1	14.5	9.9	5.9	9.1	10.8	6.5	10.6	12.8	17.1	11.7
Black or African American only	10.8	12.0	17.4	11.0	9.5	11.6	15.6	10.1	10.8	15.2	20.7	13.6
American Indian or Alaska Native only .	14.5	13.2	*15.7	9.8	*10.1	*14.1	18.6	*13.4	18.8	19.2	23.1	17.7
Asian only	6.3	5.0	8.0	4.8	*2.8	*3.5	4.2	3.4	7.8	6.8	8.7	7.4
Native Hawaiian or Other Pacific Islander only	- - -	*	*	*	- - -	*	*	*	- - -	*	*	*
2 or more races	- - -	19.9	24.0	15.2	- - -	22.9	16.6	10.9	- - -	23.0	25.6	14.3
Hispanic origin and race[5]												
Hispanic or Latino	10.5	11.5	15.4	10.8	6.7	11.2	13.0	8.3	11.5	15.5	21.6	14.5
Mexican.	9.7	11.4	15.6	11.0	6.5	12.0	13.5	8.6	11.3	16.3	22.0	16.0
Not Hispanic or Latino.	10.7	11.0	14.5	9.6	6.3	9.0	10.9	6.6	10.5	12.6	16.6	11.3
White only.	10.9	11.1	14.3	9.7	5.9	8.7	10.3	6.1	10.5	12.3	16.2	11.1
Black or African American only	10.8	12.0	17.5	11.1	9.5	11.4	15.6	10.2	10.8	15.3	20.8	13.7
Education[6]												
No high school diploma or GED.	16.2	16.2	20.6	14.0	11.5	16.4	18.1	13.9	14.5	20.3	26.3	20.3
High school diploma or GED	11.1	11.7	16.1	11.4	7.0	10.5	13.8	9.2	11.4	14.6	20.1	14.2
Some college or more.	9.2	9.8	13.4	9.2	4.3	7.1	9.2	5.6	8.8	10.4	14.4	10.2
Percent of poverty level[7]												
Below 100%.	19.6	20.0	23.4	16.6	14.8	19.5	21.5	12.9	19.4	24.4	30.4	21.2
100%–199%.	17.9	18.9	24.0	15.9	11.6	16.3	18.4	12.7	18.3	21.0	29.2	20.9
200%–399%.	10.5	11.8	15.2	10.8	5.5	9.5	11.4	7.0	10.2	13.7	17.3	12.9
400% or more	4.6	5.0	6.8	4.2	1.7	3.3	3.9	2.3	4.5	5.9	7.0	4.0

See footnotes at end of table.

Table 63 (page 2 of 3). Delay or nonreceipt of needed medical care, nonreceipt of needed prescription drugs, or nonreceipt of needed dental care during the past 12 months due to cost, by selected characteristics: United States, selected years 1997–2015

Excel and PDF versions (with more data years and standard errors when available): http://www.cdc.gov/nchs/hus/contents2016.htm#063.

[Data are based on household interviews of a sample of the civilian noninstitutionalized population]

Characteristic	Delay or nonreceipt of needed medical care due to cost[1]				Nonreceipt of needed prescription drugs due to cost[2]				Nonreceipt of needed dental care due to cost[3]			
	1997	2005	2010	2015	1997	2005	2010	2015	1997	2005	2010	2015
Hispanic origin and race and percent of poverty level[5,7]					Percent							
Hispanic or Latino:												
Below 100%	14.6	14.8	19.0	16.0	10.6	17.3	18.9	13.1	16.1	23.5	30.5	20.9
100%–199%	12.2	14.5	18.6	12.5	8.1	13.0	14.7	10.8	13.5	18.2	25.2	18.8
200%–399%	8.0	9.6	13.9	8.9	4.4	9.1	11.5	6.3	9.2	12.5	18.1	12.1
400% or more	5.1	6.2	7.7	5.6	*	*4.2	4.6	*2.1	4.5	5.8	9.1	4.8
Not Hispanic or Latino:												
White only:												
Below 100%	24.3	23.6	26.1	19.0	17.3	20.5	24.6	12.9	23.4	25.1	31.8	22.9
100%–199%	20.9	21.8	27.6	18.7	12.4	18.2	19.9	13.5	20.6	22.9	31.7	23.3
200%–399%	11.4	13.1	16.0	11.7	5.4	10.0	11.3	6.7	10.6	14.4	18.0	13.5
400% or more	4.6	5.0	6.9	4.3	1.7	3.2	3.8	2.4	4.5	5.9	6.9	4.1
Black or African American only:												
Below 100%	16.1	20.1	24.4	15.2	14.9	21.7	21.1	13.8	14.8	25.5	29.7	19.6
100%–199%	14.3	16.2	22.9	14.0	13.9	14.3	21.3	14.3	16.4	19.0	28.2	18.7
200%–399%	8.8	9.2	14.6	11.2	7.0	7.9	13.7	9.9	8.6	12.0	16.1	13.8
400% or more	4.6	5.5	8.1	4.7	*2.9	*4.1	5.6	*	4.3	*7.0	9.1	*3.7
Health insurance status at the time of interview[8]												
Insured	6.8	6.8	9.1	7.2	3.7	6.0	7.3	5.4	7.2	8.7	11.8	9.4
Private	6.0	5.9	8.2	6.2	2.9	4.7	6.0	4.0	6.2	6.7	9.2	6.9
Medicaid	11.9	12.0	12.5	10.5	11.1	14.0	13.5	10.7	14.8	21.8	24.2	18.9
Uninsured	27.6	29.5	34.5	28.1	18.0	23.1	25.7	17.3	26.1	30.7	37.7	28.2
Health insurance status prior to interview[8]												
Insured continuously all 12 months	5.5	5.5	7.6	5.7	2.8	5.0	6.2	4.4	6.0	7.5	10.5	8.2
Uninsured for any period up to 12 months	28.7	31.7	35.1	30.7	17.7	23.5	25.1	19.6	25.2	30.3	33.6	27.6
Uninsured more than 12 months	30.6	31.1	35.9	28.9	18.9	24.5	26.2	17.4	28.0	32.1	39.4	29.6
Percent of poverty level and health insurance status prior to interview[7,8]												
Below 100%:												
Insured continuously all 12 months	9.4	9.4	10.1	9.1	8.1	10.8	11.4	8.2	10.7	15.0	20.7	15.6
Uninsured for any period up to 12 months	31.9	37.3	36.7	34.6	25.5	31.8	35.7	28.1	31.6	38.1	39.0	34.2
Uninsured more than 12 months	32.4	32.4	38.5	32.6	21.6	29.3	31.5	20.0	29.4	34.4	42.3	32.4
100%–199%:												
Insured continuously all 12 months	9.5	9.6	12.5	9.4	6.0	9.7	11.9	8.8	11.0	12.9	19.7	16.0
Uninsured for any period up to 12 months	33.6	35.1	38.5	34.0	20.5	28.4	26.5	22.3	28.2	35.0	38.9	33.6
Uninsured more than 12 months	30.0	32.7	37.4	28.1	19.5	24.2	26.1	20.0	29.3	31.4	40.7	30.8
200%–399%:												
Insured continuously all 12 months	6.1	6.6	9.5	7.0	2.9	6.0	7.4	4.9	6.8	8.8	11.6	9.5
Uninsured for any period up to 12 months	27.1	31.4	33.7	30.1	14.0	21.5	23.2	16.6	21.6	27.0	32.5	25.6
Uninsured more than 12 months	31.3	29.7	32.4	26.4	17.3	21.6	23.7	13.8	26.5	31.5	36.1	27.7
400% or more:												
Insured continuously all 12 months	3.1	3.1	4.6	3.0	0.8	2.1	2.9	1.7	3.1	4.0	5.2	3.1
Uninsured for any period up to 12 months	20.8	23.9	30.7	22.8	10.7	13.9	14.0	12.9	19.3	23.4	21.6	15.9
Uninsured more than 12 months	25.5	27.6	31.8	27.2	13.5	20.7	16.3	*	23.6	29.6	34.6	*20.0
Disability measure[9]												
Any basic actions difficulty or complex activity limitation	23.3	24.8	28.9	21.3	14.8	20.0	22.6	16.0	19.8	23.8	28.8	22.8
Any basic actions difficulty	24.2	26.1	28.9	22.3	15.3	20.5	23.3	16.4	20.1	24.4	29.2	23.2
Any complex activity limitation	25.7	26.9	30.8	22.4	19.4	25.3	27.3	19.8	23.2	27.3	33.7	27.6
No disability	9.0	9.8	13.2	8.5	3.4	5.7	7.0	3.7	7.5	9.4	13.1	7.9

See footnotes at end of table.

Table 63 (page 3 of 3). Delay or nonreceipt of needed medical care, nonreceipt of needed prescription drugs, or nonreceipt of needed dental care during the past 12 months due to cost, by selected characteristics: United States, selected years 1997–2015

Excel and PDF versions (with more data years and standard errors when available): http://www.cdc.gov/nchs/hus/contents2016.htm#063.

[Data are based on household interviews of a sample of the civilian noninstitutionalized population]

Characteristic	Delay or nonreceipt of needed medical care due to cost[1]				Nonreceipt of needed prescription drugs due to cost[2]				Nonreceipt of needed dental care due to cost[3]			
	1997	2005	2010	2015	1997	2005	2010	2015	1997	2005	2010	2015
Geographic region							Percent					
Northeast	8.8	8.7	10.2	7.7	4.9	7.2	7.7	5.2	8.9	10.6	12.9	9.1
Midwest	10.5	10.6	14.8	9.9	5.9	9.0	11.6	6.5	9.7	11.9	16.0	10.9
South	11.8	12.6	16.5	11.0	7.3	11.3	13.5	8.4	10.9	14.7	19.6	13.0
West	10.8	11.1	15.1	9.5	6.3	8.2	10.0	6.2	13.1	13.6	18.4	12.9
Location of residence[10]												
Within MSA	10.2	10.6	14.2	9.6	5.9	8.8	10.8	6.7	10.0	12.7	17.0	11.4
Outside MSA	12.5	12.8	17.4	11.0	7.9	11.8	13.6	8.3	12.9	14.6	19.1	14.5

* Estimates are considered unreliable. Data preceded by an asterisk have a relative standard error (RSE) of 20%–30%. Data not shown have an RSE greater than 30%.

- - - Data not available.

[1] Based on persons responding to the questions, "During the past 12 months was there any time when person needed medical care but did not get it because person couldn't afford it?" and "During the past 12 months has medical care been delayed because of worry about the cost?"

[2] Based on persons responding to the question, "During the past 12 months was there any time when person needed prescription medicine but didn't get it because person couldn't afford it?"

[3] Based on persons responding to the question, "During the past 12 months was there any time when person needed dental care (including checkups) but didn't get it because person couldn't afford it?"

[4] Includes all other races not shown separately, unknown health insurance status, unknown education level, and unknown disability status.

[5] The race groups, white, black, American Indian or Alaska Native, Asian, Native Hawaiian or Other Pacific Islander, and 2 or more races, include persons of Hispanic and non-Hispanic origin. Persons of Hispanic origin may be of any race. Starting with 1999 data, race-specific estimates are tabulated according to the 1997 *Revisions to the Standards for the Classification of Federal Data on Race and Ethnicity* and are not strictly comparable with estimates for earlier years. The five single-race categories plus multiple-race categories shown in the table conform to the 1997 Standards. Starting with 1999 data, race-specific estimates are for persons who reported only one racial group; the category 2 or more races includes persons who reported more than one racial group. Prior to 1999, data were tabulated according to the 1977 Standards with four racial groups, and the Asian only category included Native Hawaiian or Other Pacific Islander. Estimates for single-race categories prior to 1999 included persons who reported one race or, if they reported more than one race, identified one race as best representing their race. Starting with 2003 data, race responses of other race and unspecified multiple race were treated as missing, and then race was imputed if these were the only race responses. Almost all persons with a race response of other race were of Hispanic origin. See Appendix II, Hispanic origin; Race.

[6] Estimates are for persons aged 25–64. GED is General Educational Development high school equivalency diploma. See Appendix II, Education.

[7] Percent of poverty level is based on family income and family size and composition using U.S. Census Bureau poverty thresholds. Missing family income data were imputed for 1997 and beyond. See Appendix II, Family income; Poverty; Table VI.

[8] For information on the health insurance categories, see Appendix II, Health insurance coverage.

[9] Any basic actions difficulty or complex activity limitation is defined as having one or more of the following limitations or difficulties: movement difficulty, emotional difficulty, sensory (seeing or hearing) difficulty, cognitive difficulty, self-care (activities of daily living or instrumental activities of daily living) limitation, social limitation, or work limitation. For more information, see Appendix II, Basic actions difficulty; Complex activity limitation. Starting with 2007 data, the hearing question, a component of the basic actions difficulty measure, was revised. Consequently, data prior to 2007 are not comparable with data for 2007 and beyond. For more information on the impact of the revised hearing question, see Appendix II, Hearing trouble.

[10] MSA is metropolitan statistical area. Starting with 2006 data, MSA status is determined using 2000 census data and the 2000 standards for defining MSAs. For data prior to 2006, see Appendix II, Metropolitan statistical area (MSA) for the applicable standards.

NOTES: Standard errors and additional data years are available in the spreadsheet version of this table. Available from: http://www.cdc.gov/nchs/hus.htm. Data for additional years are available. See the Excel spreadsheet on the *Health, United States* website at: http://www.cdc.gov/nchs/hus.htm.

SOURCE: NCHS, National Health Interview Survey, family core, sample child, and sample adult questionnaires. See Appendix I, National Health Interview Survey (NHIS).

Table 64 (page 1 of 2). No health care visits to an office or clinic within the past 12 months among children under age 18, by selected characteristics: United States, average annual, selected years 1997–1998 through 2014–2015

Excel and PDF versions (with more data years and standard errors when available): http://www.cdc.gov/nchs/hus/contents2016.htm#064.

[Data are based on household interviews of a sample of the civilian noninstitutionalized population]

Characteristic	Under 18 years			Under 6 years			6–17 years		
	1997–1998	2001–2002	2014–2015	1997–1998	2001–2002	2014–2015	1997–1998	2001–2002	2014–2015
	Percent of children without a health care visit [1]								
All children [2]	12.8	12.1	8.5	5.7	6.3	5.1	16.3	14.9	10.2
Sex									
Male	12.9	12.3	8.5	4.9	6.4	5.0	16.8	15.1	10.2
Female	12.7	11.9	8.5	6.5	6.1	5.2	15.8	14.6	10.2
Race [3]									
White only	12.2	11.5	8.2	5.5	6.4	5.0	15.5	13.9	9.7
Black or African American only	14.3	13.3	9.8	6.5	5.9	6.1	18.1	16.8	11.6
American Indian or Alaska Native only	13.8	*18.6	15.6	*	*	*	*17.6	*23.0	20.0
Asian only	16.3	15.6	9.6	*5.6	*6.8	*6.0	22.1	20.5	11.5
Native Hawaiian or Other Pacific Islander only	- - -	*	*	- - -	*	*	- - -	*	*
2 or more races	- - -	8.3	6.5	- - -	*3.3	*	- - -	12.4	9.2
Hispanic origin and race [3]									
Hispanic or Latino	19.3	18.8	11.3	9.7	9.6	5.9	25.3	24.0	14.2
Not Hispanic or Latino	11.6	10.6	7.6	4.8	5.4	4.8	14.9	13.0	8.9
White only	10.7	9.7	6.8	4.3	5.3	4.6	13.7	11.7	7.9
Black or African American only	14.5	13.4	9.7	6.5	6.0	6.2	18.3	16.8	11.3
Percent of poverty level [4]									
Below 100%	17.6	17.3	10.3	8.1	9.1	6.7	23.6	21.8	12.3
100%–199%	16.2	14.8	10.4	7.2	7.4	5.9	20.8	18.7	12.6
200%–399%	11.7	11.2	8.8	4.9	5.4	5.3	14.8	13.8	10.5
400% or more	7.4	7.7	5.2	3.0	4.1	2.6	9.5	9.3	6.3
Hispanic origin and race and percent of poverty level [3,4]									
Hispanic or Latino:									
Below 100%	23.2	22.1	11.1	11.7	10.4	6.8	31.1	29.4	13.7
100%–199%	20.9	21.3	13.3	9.7	12.3	6.5	28.1	26.2	16.5
200%–399%	15.7	15.5	11.3	8.0	*7.3	5.9	19.7	20.0	14.1
400% or more	7.8	9.7	6.2	*	*	*	9.3	12.5	8.9
Not Hispanic or Latino:									
White only:									
Below 100%	14.0	13.2	8.3	*5.6	*8.6	*6.6	19.7	15.6	9.2
100%–199%	14.1	11.8	8.7	6.0	*6.0	6.5	18.0	14.8	9.8
200%–399%	10.9	10.2	7.5	4.3	4.8	4.8	13.9	12.5	8.9
400% or more	7.2	7.4	4.8	*2.8	4.2	*2.5	9.1	8.6	5.8
Black or African American only:									
Below 100%	15.8	16.1	10.5	7.6	*7.8	*7.1	20.5	20.3	12.4
100%–199%	16.4	13.3	9.1	*7.7	*4.4	*	20.4	17.5	11.4
200%–399%	13.3	12.2	10.6	*4.9	*6.5	*	16.7	14.6	11.6
400% or more	8.3	8.9	*6.5	*	*	*	10.7	11.5	*6.7
Health insurance status at the time of interview [5]									
Insured	10.4	9.8	7.5	4.5	4.7	4.8	13.4	12.3	8.9
Private	10.4	9.5	7.2	4.3	4.3	4.0	13.1	11.8	8.6
Medicaid	10.1	10.3	7.9	5.0	5.5	5.4	14.4	13.3	9.3
Uninsured	28.8	31.9	27.1	14.6	21.0	13.1	34.9	36.3	31.6
Health insurance status prior to interview [5]									
Insured continuously all 12 months	10.3	9.5	7.3	4.4	4.6	4.7	13.2	12.0	8.7
Uninsured for any period up to 12 months	15.9	17.7	14.6	7.7	10.3	*8.1	20.9	21.9	17.8
Uninsured more than 12 months	34.9	41.4	35.1	19.9	30.2	*18.2	40.2	45.3	39.0

See footnotes at end of table.

Table 64 (page 2 of 2). No health care visits to an office or clinic within the past 12 months among children under age 18, by selected characteristics: United States, average annual, selected years 1997–1998 through 2014–2015

Excel and PDF versions (with more data years and standard errors when available): http://www.cdc.gov/nchs/hus/contents2016.htm#064.

[Data are based on household interviews of a sample of the civilian noninstitutionalized population]

Characteristic	Under 18 years			Under 6 years			6–17 years		
	1997–1998	2001–2002	2014–2015	1997–1998	2001–2002	2014–2015	1997–1998	2001–2002	2014–2015
Percent of poverty level and health insurance status prior to interview [4,5]	Percent of children without a health care visit [1]								
Below 100%:									
Insured continuously all 12 months.	12.6	11.7	8.8	5.7	6.1	6.1	17.6	14.9	10.3
Uninsured for any period up to 12 months . . .	19.9	21.8	18.4	*9.9	*14.4	*	26.1	26.6	20.4
Uninsured more than 12 months	39.9	48.2	36.2	24.9	*28.0	*	45.2	55.7	40.1
100%–199%:									
Insured continuously all 12 months.	12.6	10.9	8.3	4.8	4.2	4.9	16.7	14.5	10.0
Uninsured for any period up to 12 months . . .	15.6	18.9	15.8	*8.7	*10.7	*8.0	20.2	23.2	19.7
Uninsured more than 12 months	33.7	41.3	39.0	21.3	35.4	*31.0	37.9	43.6	40.3
200%–399%:									
Insured continuously all 12 months.	10.5	10.0	7.9	4.5	4.6	5.2	13.2	12.4	9.3
Uninsured for any period up to 12 months . . .	12.8	14.5	11.5	*	*7.1	*	17.2	18.7	14.7
Uninsured more than 12 months	29.9	30.8	31.1	*11.8	*24.2	*	36.5	32.9	36.0
400% or more:									
Insured continuously all 12 months.	7.0	7.2	4.9	2.9	3.9	2.6	8.8	8.7	5.9
Uninsured for any period up to 12 months . . .	*10.8	*11.4	*10.7	*	*	*	*15.1	*14.1	*
Uninsured more than 12 months	*28.8	*38.4	*	*	*	*	*37.7	*40.3	*
Geographic region									
Northeast	7.0	6.0	5.1	3.1	3.9	*3.2	8.9	6.9	6.0
Midwest	12.2	10.3	7.5	5.9	5.1	4.9	15.3	12.8	8.8
South	14.3	14.0	9.2	5.6	7.0	6.0	18.5	17.4	10.7
West	16.3	16.0	10.5	7.9	8.1	5.0	20.7	20.0	13.3
Location of residence [6]									
Within MSA	12.3	11.7	8.2	5.4	6.1	5.1	15.9	14.5	9.8
Outside MSA	14.6	13.5	10.2	6.9	6.9	5.3	17.9	16.3	12.6

* Estimates are considered unreliable. Data preceded by an asterisk have a relative standard error (RSE) of 20%–30%. Data not shown have an RSE greater than 30%.

- - - Data not available.

[1] Respondents were asked how many times a doctor or other health care professional was seen in the past 12 months at a doctor's office, clinic, or some other place. Excluded are visits to emergency rooms, hospitalizations, home visits, and telephone calls. Starting with 2000 data, dental visits were also excluded. See Appendix II, Health care contact.

[2] Includes all other races not shown separately and unknown health insurance status.

[3] The race groups, white, black, American Indian or Alaska Native, Asian, Native Hawaiian or Other Pacific Islander, and 2 or more races, include persons of Hispanic and non-Hispanic origin. Persons of Hispanic origin may be of any race. Starting with 1999 data, race-specific estimates are tabulated according to the 1997 *Revisions to the Standards for the Classification of Federal Data on Race and Ethnicity* and are not strictly comparable with estimates for earlier years. The five single-race categories plus multiple-race categories shown in the table conform to the 1997 Standards. Starting with 1999 data, race-specific estimates are for persons who reported only one racial group; the category 2 or more races includes persons who reported more than one racial group. Prior to 1999, data were tabulated according to the 1977 Standards with four racial groups, and the Asian only category included Native Hawaiian or Other Pacific Islander. Estimates for single-race categories prior to 1999 included persons who reported one race or, if they reported more than one race, identified one race as best representing their race. Starting with 2003 data, race responses of other race and unspecified multiple race were treated as missing, and then race was imputed if these were the only race responses. Almost all persons with a race response of other race were of Hispanic origin. See Appendix II, Hispanic origin; Race.

[4] Percent of poverty level is based on family income and family size and composition using U.S. Census Bureau poverty thresholds. Missing family income data were imputed starting in 1997. See Appendix II, Family income; Poverty; Table VI.

[5] Health insurance categories are mutually exclusive. Persons who reported both Medicaid and private coverage are classified as having private coverage. Starting with 1997 data, state-sponsored health plan coverage is included as Medicaid coverage. Starting with 1999 data, coverage by the Children's Health Insurance Program (CHIP) is included with Medicaid coverage. In addition to private and Medicaid, the insured category also includes military, other government, and Medicare coverage. Persons not covered by private insurance, Medicaid, CHIP, state-sponsored or other government-sponsored health plans (starting in 1997), Medicare, or military plans are considered to have no health insurance coverage. Persons with only Indian Health Service coverage are considered to have no health insurance coverage. See Appendix II, Health insurance coverage.

[6] MSA is metropolitan statistical area. Starting with 2005–2006 data, MSA status is determined using 2000 census data and the 2000 standards for defining MSAs. For data prior to 2005, see Appendix II, Metropolitan statistical area (MSA) for the applicable standards.

NOTES: Standard errors for selected years are available in the spreadsheet version of this table. Available from: http://www.cdc.gov/nchs/hus.htm. Data for additional years are available. See the Excel spreadsheet on the *Health, United States* website at: http://www.cdc.gov/nchs/hus.htm.

SOURCE: NCHS, National Health Interview Survey, family core and sample child questionnaires. See Appendix I, National Health Interview Survey (NHIS).

Table 65 (page 1 of 3). Health care visits to doctor offices, emergency departments, and home visits within the past 12 months, by selected characteristics: United States, selected years 1997–2015

Excel and PDF versions (with more data years and standard errors when available): http://www.cdc.gov/nchs/hus/contents2016.htm#065.

[Data are based on household interviews of a sample of the civilian noninstitutionalized population]

| Characteristic | Number of health care visits[1] | | | | | | | | | | | |
| | None | | | 1–3 visits | | | 4–9 visits | | | 10 or more visits | | |
	1997	2010	2015	1997	2010	2015	1997	2010	2015	1997	2010	2015
	Percent distribution											
Total, age-adjusted[2,3]	16.5	15.6	15.0	46.2	45.4	48.4	23.6	25.8	23.7	13.7	13.2	12.8
Total, crude[2].	16.5	15.4	14.6	46.5	45.2	47.8	23.5	26.0	24.1	13.5	13.5	13.5
Age												
Under 18 years	11.8	8.1	7.9	54.1	55.6	59.7	25.2	28.2	25.7	8.9	8.2	6.7
Under 6 years.	5.0	3.7	4.7	44.9	48.9	52.2	37.0	36.8	35.7	13.0	10.6	7.5
6–17 years	15.3	10.4	9.5	58.7	59.1	63.3	19.3	23.6	20.9	6.8	6.9	6.4
18–44 years	21.7	24.2	23.3	46.7	43.9	46.9	19.0	20.6	18.7	12.6	11.3	11.1
18–24 years.	22.0	25.9	24.5	46.8	43.4	47.2	20.0	21.1	19.6	11.2	9.6	8.8
25–44 years.	21.6	23.6	22.9	46.7	44.1	46.8	18.7	20.5	18.3	13.0	11.9	11.9
45–64 years	16.9	14.8	13.7	42.9	42.8	45.5	24.7	26.1	24.5	15.5	16.4	16.3
45–54 years.	17.9	17.6	16.1	43.9	43.5	47.0	23.4	23.9	23.3	14.8	15.0	13.6
55–64 years.	15.3	11.1	11.2	41.3	41.9	43.8	26.7	28.8	25.9	16.7	18.2	19.1
65 years and over	8.9	5.3	5.5	34.7	33.8	35.5	32.5	36.7	33.9	23.8	24.2	25.1
65–74 years.	9.8	6.3	6.4	36.9	36.1	37.9	31.6	35.7	33.7	21.6	21.9	22.0
75 years and over.	7.7	4.1	4.2	31.8	31.0	32.0	33.8	38.0	34.2	26.6	27.0	29.6
Sex[3]												
Male	21.3	20.4	19.5	47.1	46.4	49.8	20.6	22.7	20.3	11.0	10.5	10.5
Female.	11.8	10.9	10.8	45.4	44.4	47.1	26.5	28.8	26.9	16.3	15.9	15.2
Race[3,4]												
White only	16.0	15.3	14.8	46.1	44.9	47.8	23.9	26.1	24.0	14.0	13.7	13.4
Black or African American only	16.8	15.7	14.5	46.1	47.2	50.2	23.2	24.7	24.1	13.9	12.4	11.2
American Indian or Alaska Native only . .	17.1	19.4	20.6	38.0	40.3	39.0	24.2	28.1	23.3	20.7	12.2	17.1
Asian only	22.8	20.4	18.2	49.1	49.9	54.7	19.7	22.1	18.7	8.3	7.6	8.5
Native Hawaiian or Other Pacific Islander only	- - -	*	*	- - -	*	*	- - -	*	*	- - -	*	*
2 or more races	- - -	13.9	17.3	- - -	42.3	41.5	- - -	25.2	25.0	- - -	18.6	16.2
Hispanic origin and race[3,4]												
Hispanic or Latino	24.9	23.5	22.3	42.3	43.2	45.9	20.3	22.6	21.9	12.5	10.7	9.9
Mexican.	28.9	25.2	24.8	40.8	43.3	44.8	18.5	21.4	20.7	11.8	10.1	9.7
Not Hispanic or Latino.	15.4	14.0	13.4	46.7	45.8	49.0	24.0	26.5	24.1	13.9	13.7	13.5
White only.	14.7	13.2	12.7	46.6	45.3	48.1	24.4	27.1	24.7	14.3	14.4	14.5
Black or African American only.	16.9	15.6	14.7	46.1	47.3	50.5	23.1	24.9	23.8	13.8	12.2	11.0
Percent of poverty level[3,5]												
Below 100%.	20.6	20.4	19.0	37.8	37.5	39.9	22.7	25.1	23.9	18.9	17.0	17.1
100%–199%.	20.1	20.8	18.4	43.3	42.1	45.1	21.7	23.1	22.9	14.9	13.9	13.6
200%–399%.	16.4	16.2	15.9	47.2	46.3	49.5	23.6	25.4	22.8	12.8	12.1	11.8
400% or more	12.8	10.2	11.2	49.8	49.4	51.8	24.9	27.6	24.7	12.5	12.7	12.3

See footnotes at end of table.

Excel and PDF versions (with more data years and standard errors when available): http://www.cdc.gov/nchs/hus/contents2016.htm#065.

[Data are based on household interviews of a sample of the civilian noninstitutionalized population]

Characteristic	Number of health care visits[1]											
	None			1–3 visits			4–9 visits			10 or more visits		
	1997	2010	2015	1997	2010	2015	1997	2010	2015	1997	2010	2015
Hispanic origin and race and percent of poverty level[3,4,5]	Percent distribution											
Hispanic or Latino:												
Below 100%	30.2	28.7	26.3	34.8	36.5	38.3	19.9	22.5	22.7	15.0	12.3	12.7
100%–199%	28.7	27.7	25.1	39.7	42.7	45.1	20.4	19.9	21.0	11.2	9.8	8.8
200%–399%	20.7	21.6	22.2	47.4	45.0	49.5	19.8	23.1	20.2	12.1	10.3	8.2
400% or more	15.2	11.3	13.3	50.4	51.1	50.2	22.6	26.1	25.1	11.8	11.5	11.4
Not Hispanic or Latino:												
White only:												
Below 100%	17.0	15.0	15.2	38.3	37.0	38.3	23.9	27.4	25.6	20.9	20.6	20.9
100%–199%	17.3	18.4	15.7	44.1	40.4	43.6	22.2	24.7	23.7	16.3	16.5	17.0
200%–399%	15.4	14.7	13.7	46.9	46.0	48.6	24.3	26.3	24.0	13.4	13.0	13.7
400% or more	12.5	9.9	10.6	49.1	48.2	51.1	25.5	28.4	25.2	13.0	13.5	13.2
Black or African American only:												
Below 100%	17.4	18.4	16.2	38.5	39.8	42.9	23.4	25.0	25.1	20.7	16.8	15.7
100%–199%	18.8	17.6	14.6	43.7	45.7	47.6	22.9	24.3	25.2	14.5	12.5	12.6
200%–399%	16.6	15.1	15.6	49.7	49.0	54.0	22.9	25.7	22.3	10.8	10.2	8.0
400% or more	14.0	10.0	11.7	54.3	58.2	55.9	22.7	22.5	23.2	9.0	9.3	9.2
Health insurance status at the time of interview[6,7]												
Under 65 years:												
Insured	14.3	12.3	13.3	49.0	48.5	51.7	23.6	26.1	23.3	13.1	13.1	11.7
Private	14.7	12.4	13.7	50.6	51.0	53.8	23.1	25.5	22.7	11.6	11.1	9.9
Medicaid	9.8	10.9	12.4	35.5	38.2	43.4	26.5	28.0	25.4	28.2	23.0	18.8
Uninsured	33.7	37.2	39.8	42.8	42.2	41.4	15.3	15.2	13.7	8.2	5.4	5.1
Health insurance status prior to interview[6,7]												
Under 65 years:												
Insured continuously all 12 months	14.1	12.1	12.9	49.2	48.6	52.0	23.6	26.2	23.4	13.0	13.0	11.7
Uninsured for any period up to 12 months	18.9	18.5	21.5	46.0	47.8	46.9	20.8	22.0	20.0	14.4	11.6	11.6
Uninsured more than 12 months	39.0	43.8	48.7	41.4	39.7	37.8	13.2	12.6	10.4	6.4	3.9	3.1
Percent of poverty level and health insurance status prior to interview[5,6,7]												
Under 65 years:												
Below 100%:												
Insured continuously all 12 months	13.8	12.7	14.3	39.7	39.5	42.3	25.2	27.5	25.9	21.4	20.3	17.5
Uninsured for any period up to 12 months	19.7	16.9	21.8	37.6	43.0	45.6	21.9	25.0	19.0	20.9	15.1	13.7
Uninsured more than 12 months	41.2	45.0	48.8	39.9	38.1	36.9	12.2	13.6	10.6	6.6	3.3	*3.8
100%–199%:												
Insured continuously all 12 months	16.0	14.8	13.3	46.4	44.4	49.1	21.9	24.8	23.8	15.8	16.0	13.8
Uninsured for any period up to 12 months	18.8	21.0	25.6	45.1	46.0	41.9	21.0	20.6	19.4	15.0	12.4	13.0
Uninsured more than 12 months	38.7	43.2	48.8	41.0	39.4	37.6	14.0	12.4	11.1	6.3	5.0	*
200%–399%:												
Insured continuously all 12 months	15.1	13.6	14.0	49.4	49.4	53.5	23.4	25.3	22.0	12.1	11.7	10.5
Uninsured for any period up to 12 months	17.9	18.8	19.8	49.3	49.7	49.0	20.0	19.7	21.1	12.8	11.8	10.0
Uninsured more than 12 months	37.0	43.8	50.7	43.8	40.7	38.5	12.6	13.3	8.7	6.6	*2.2	*2.2
400% or more:												
Insured continuously all 12 months	12.4	9.7	11.4	52.2	51.8	54.3	23.9	26.8	23.5	11.5	11.6	10.8
Uninsured for any period up to 12 months	17.2	16.6	16.6	50.0	53.5	54.1	24.2	23.9	20.2	*8.5	*6.0	9.0
Uninsured more than 12 months	35.1	39.2	39.3	44.1	46.0	41.1	15.1	*8.8	*	*5.7	*	*
Respondent-assessed health status[3]												
Fair or poor	7.8	8.4	8.0	23.3	24.0	25.3	29.0	30.2	28.7	39.9	37.3	38.0
Good to excellent	17.2	16.3	15.7	48.4	47.5	50.6	23.3	25.5	23.3	11.1	10.7	10.3

See footnotes at end of table.

Table 65 (page 3 of 3). Health care visits to doctor offices, emergency departments, and home visits within the past 12 months, by selected characteristics: United States, selected years 1997–2015

Excel and PDF versions (with more data years and standard errors when available): http://www.cdc.gov/nchs/hus/contents2016.htm#065.

[Data are based on household interviews of a sample of the civilian noninstitutionalized population]

| Characteristic | Number of health care visits [1] | | | | | | | | | | | |
| | None | | | 1–3 visits | | | 4–9 visits | | | 10 or more visits | | |
	1997	2010	2015	1997	2010	2015	1997	2010	2015	1997	2010	2015
Disability measure among adults 18 years of age and over [3,8]	Percent distribution											
Any basic actions difficulty or complex activity limitation	11.1	11.5	10.6	32.0	30.9	31.2	27.9	29.3	29.0	29.1	28.3	29.2
Any basic actions difficulty	11.1	11.5	10.5	31.9	30.3	31.1	27.5	29.2	28.9	29.4	29.0	29.5
Any complex activity limitation	7.1	6.9	6.8	23.7	23.0	22.4	27.5	29.1	28.8	41.7	41.0	41.9
No disability	20.9	20.5	20.1	49.6	47.5	50.9	20.8	23.4	20.8	8.7	8.5	8.2
Geographic region [3]												
Northeast	13.2	12.6	10.9	45.9	46.3	50.9	26.0	26.4	24.2	14.9	14.7	14.0
Midwest	15.9	13.4	14.5	47.7	46.8	48.9	22.8	26.4	23.3	13.6	13.3	13.3
South	17.2	16.1	15.9	46.1	44.2	47.2	23.3	26.6	24.4	13.5	13.2	12.5
West	19.1	19.1	17.1	44.8	45.2	48.3	22.8	23.5	22.5	13.3	12.2	12.1
Location of residence [3,9]												
Within MSA	16.2	15.6	14.9	46.4	45.8	49.0	23.7	25.6	23.4	13.7	13.0	12.6
Outside MSA	17.3	15.9	15.7	45.4	42.7	44.5	23.3	27.0	25.1	13.9	14.4	14.7

- - - Data not available.

* Estimates are considered unreliable. Data preceded by an asterisk have a relative standard error (RSE) of 20%–30%. Data not shown have an RSE greater than 30%.

[1] This table presents a summary measure of the number of visits to hospital emergency departments, home visits by a nurse or other health care professional, and visits to doctor offices, clinics, or some other place during a 12-month period. See Appendix II, Emergency department or emergency room visit; Health care contact; Home visit.

[2] Includes all other races not shown separately, unknown health insurance status, and unknown disability status.

[3] Estimates are age-adjusted to the year 2000 standard population using six age groups: Under 18 years, 18–44 years, 45–54 years, 55–64 years, 65–74 years, and 75 years and over. The disability measure is age-adjusted using the five adult age groups. See Appendix II, Age adjustment.

[4] The race groups, white, black, American Indian or Alaska Native, Asian, Native Hawaiian or Other Pacific Islander, and 2 or more races, include persons of Hispanic and non-Hispanic origin. Persons of Hispanic origin may be of any race. Starting with 1999 data, race-specific estimates are tabulated according to the 1997 *Revisions to the Standards for the Classification of Federal Data on Race and Ethnicity* and are not strictly comparable with estimates for earlier years. The five single-race categories plus multiple-race categories shown in the table conform to the 1997 Standards. Starting with 1999 data, race-specific estimates are for persons who reported only one racial group; the category 2 or more races includes persons who reported more than one racial group. Prior to 1999, data were tabulated according to the 1977 Standards with four racial groups, and the Asian only category included Native Hawaiian or Other Pacific Islander. Estimates for single-race categories prior to 1999 included persons who reported one race or, if they reported more than one race, identified one race as best representing their race. Starting with 2003 data, race responses of other race and unspecified multiple race were treated as missing, and then race was imputed if these were the only race responses. Almost all persons with a race response of other race were of Hispanic origin. See Appendix II, Hispanic origin; Race.

[5] Percent of poverty level is based on family income and family size and composition using U.S. Census Bureau poverty thresholds. Missing family income data were imputed for 1997 and beyond. See Appendix II, Family income; Poverty; Table VI.

[6] Estimates for persons under age 65 are age-adjusted to the year 2000 standard population using four age groups: Under 18 years, 18–44 years, 45–54 years, and 55–64 years. See Appendix II, Age adjustment.

[7] Health insurance categories are mutually exclusive. Persons who reported both Medicaid and private coverage are classified as having private coverage. Starting with 1997 data, state-sponsored health plan coverage is included as Medicaid coverage. Starting with 1999 data, coverage by the Children's Health Insurance Program (CHIP) is included with Medicaid coverage. In addition to private and Medicaid, the insured category also includes military plans, other government-sponsored health plans, and Medicare, not shown separately. Persons not covered by private insurance, Medicaid, CHIP, state-sponsored or other government-sponsored health plans (starting in 1997), Medicare, or military plans are considered to have no health insurance coverage. Persons with only Indian Health Service coverage are considered to have no health insurance coverage. See Appendix II, Health insurance coverage.

[8] Any basic actions difficulty or complex activity limitation is defined as having one or more of the following limitations or difficulties: movement difficulty, emotional difficulty, sensory (seeing or hearing) difficulty, cognitive difficulty, self-care (activities of daily living or instrumental activities of daily living) limitation, social limitation, or work limitation. For more information, see Appendix II, Basic actions difficulty; Complex activity limitation. Starting with 2007 data, the hearing question, a component of the basic actions difficulty measure, was revised. Consequently, data prior to 2007 are not comparable with data for 2007 and beyond. For more information on the impact of the revised hearing question, see Appendix II, Hearing trouble.

[9] MSA is metropolitan statistical area. Starting with 2006 data, MSA status is determined using 2000 census data and the 2000 standards for defining MSAs. For data prior to 2006, see Appendix II, Metropolitan statistical area (MSA) for the applicable standards.

NOTES: Standard errors are available in the spreadsheet version of this table. Available from http://www.cdc.gov/nchs/hus.htm. Data for additional years are available. See the Excel spreadsheet on the *Health, United States* website at: http://www.cdc.gov/nchs/hus.htm.

SOURCE: NCHS, National Health Interview Survey, family core and sample adult questionnaires. See Appendix I, National Health Interview Survey (NHIS).

Table 66 (page 1 of 3). Vaccination coverage for selected diseases among children aged 19–35 months, by race, Hispanic origin, poverty level, and location of residence in metropolitan statistical area: United States, selected years 1998–2015

Excel and PDF versions (with more data years and standard errors when available): http://www.cdc.gov/nchs/hus/contents2016.htm#066.

[Data are based on telephone interviews of a sample of the civilian noninstitutionalized population, supplemented by a survey of interview participants' immunization providers]

Vaccination and year	All	Race and Hispanic origin[1]							Poverty level[2]		Location of residence		
		Not Hispanic or Latino									Inside MSA[3]		
		White only	Black or African American only	American Indian or Alaska Native only	Asian only[4]	Native Hawaiian or Other Pacific Islander only[4]	2 or more races	Hispanic or Latino	Below poverty level	At or above poverty level	Central city	Remaining area	Outside MSA[3]
						Percent of children aged 19–35 months							
Combined 7-vaccine series:[5]													
2009	44.3	45.2	39.6	*	38.6	*	40.7	45.9	41.3	45.7	44.8	44.6	42.4
2010	56.6	56.9	54.5	64.1	59.3	*	61.3	55.5	52.8	58.7	56.5	57.2	55.2
2011	68.5	68.8	63.7	65.9	70.8	*	70.9	69.5	63.6	71.6	69.5	67.9	67.4
2012	68.4	69.3	64.8	*	71.6	*	71.5	67.8	63.4	71.6	67.6	69.4	68.0
2013	70.4	72.1	65.0	70.1	72.7	*	71.8	69.3	64.4	73.8	68.8	72.5	69.1
2014	71.6	72.6	65.4	*	69.5	*	68.5	74.3	65.7	75.4	70.8	72.7	71.2
2015	72.2	72.7	69.1	68.2	77.9	*	73.7	71.7	68.7	74.7	72.5	72.5	70.2
DTP/DT/DTaP (4 doses or more):[6]													
2000	81.7	84.4	76.1	77.8	84.5	*	81.5	78.6	76.2	83.5	79.9	82.8	82.9
2005	85.7	87.1	84.0	*	88.8	*	86.3	83.6	81.8	87.4	84.8	87.0	84.7
2009	83.9	85.8	78.6	82.1	86.6	93.1	81.8	82.9	80.1	85.7	83.8	84.2	84.2
2010	84.4	84.5	83.7	81.8	88.3	*	82.8	84.4	80.8	86.1	84.0	85.0	83.7
2011	84.6	85.0	81.3	72.7	92.0	93.0	87.1	84.1	81.0	86.8	86.1	83.8	82.2
2012	82.5	83.6	79.6	88.2	88.1	*	85.6	80.8	78.5	85.0	82.4	83.4	80.5
2013	83.1	85.3	74.7	78.1	89.0	*	83.1	82.3	77.8	86.0	81.8	84.7	82.4
2014	84.2	85.5	79.1	*	87.4	*	79.6	85.4	79.1	87.4	83.6	85.3	83.1
2015	84.6	85.2	82.0	79.6	90.0	*	82.5	84.5	80.2	87.1	85.4	84.3	82.7
Polio (3 doses or more):													
2000	89.5	90.6	86.6	90.8	92.7	91.2	91.2	87.9	86.9	89.9	88.1	90.1	91.1
2005	91.7	91.4	91.0	*	92.9	*	93.8	92.3	89.7	92.4	90.6	92.6	92.2
2009	92.8	93.3	90.9	92.2	94.0	97.3	92.8	92.5	92.0	93.3	93.5	92.1	92.1
2010	93.3	93.2	94.0	94.6	92.8	95.1	90.2	93.8	92.4	93.6	92.7	94.1	93.1
2011	93.9	93.9	93.9	88.1	96.5	96.6	93.5	93.8	93.6	94.2	94.3	93.4	94.2
2012	92.8	93.0	92.9	95.2	92.3	*	93.3	92.5	91.8	93.4	92.6	92.9	92.8
2013	92.7	93.7	91.2	92.2	95.5	*	90.8	91.6	89.2	94.4	91.9	93.2	93.4
2014	93.3	93.3	92.0	93.8	93.2	93.8	94.0	93.8	92.0	94.5	92.7	94.2	92.7
2015	93.7	93.1	93.3	91.8	96.9	92.8	92.4	94.5	91.8	94.6	93.9	94.0	91.7
Measles, Mumps, Rubella:													
2000	90.5	91.6	87.7	89.4	89.3	94.5	88.1	90.0	88.9	90.9	89.7	91.0	90.8
2005	91.5	91.4	91.9	89.7	91.9	90.3	93.7	91.1	89.3	92.1	91.6	91.8	90.4
2009	90.0	90.8	88.2	94.9	90.7	96.9	88.5	89.3	88.8	90.6	91.1	88.6	88.6
2010	91.5	90.6	92.1	93.4	91.7	96.9	89.7	92.9	91.3	91.4	92.4	90.5	91.4
2011	91.6	91.1	90.8	94.8	93.9	98.7	91.1	92.4	91.3	91.7	92.0	91.2	91.5
2012	90.8	90.9	90.9	92.0	89.8	*	92.3	90.7	89.9	91.4	90.1	91.0	92.4
2013	91.9	91.5	90.9	96.3	96.7	90.4	91.5	92.1	90.5	92.5	91.5	92.4	91.3
2014	91.5	91.2	90.3	96.5	95.7	95.7	90.5	91.9	89.5	92.8	91.9	91.2	91.2
2015	91.9	91.8	90.7	88.5	92.5	92.0	93.0	92.3	90.3	92.9	92.4	91.7	90.7
Hib (full series):[7]													
2009	54.8	55.3	51.2	*	54.6	*	53.7	55.4	51.4	56.5	55.5	54.9	53.0
2010	66.8	67.5	65.4	77.1	69.5	*	70.1	64.8	61.3	69.7	66.5	68.4	63.4
2011	80.4	81.0	74.6	73.7	83.5	*	82.0	81.6	75.5	83.4	81.4	80.3	77.8
2012	80.9	82.2	77.5	84.7	86.1	*	82.5	79.5	76.4	84.0	80.5	81.8	79.9
2013	82.0	84.2	74.9	82.9	82.0	*	84.9	80.9	75.8	85.3	80.6	84.3	79.7
2014	82.0	83.8	75.2	83.8	83.1	*	78.7	82.8	76.3	85.5	81.4	82.7	81.6
2015	82.7	83.0	78.9	81.4	87.0	*	82.4	83.0	78.1	85.5	82.3	83.6	80.9

See footnotes at end of table.

Excel and PDF versions (with more data years and standard errors when available): http://www.cdc.gov/nchs/hus/contents2016.htm#066.

[Data are based on telephone interviews of a sample of the civilian noninstitutionalized population, supplemented by a survey of interview participants' immunization providers]

| Vaccination and year | All | Race and Hispanic origin [1] | | | | | | | Poverty level [2] | | Location of residence | | |
| | | Not Hispanic or Latino | | | | | | | | | Inside MSA [3] | | |
		White only	Black or African American only	American Indian or Alaska Native only	Asian only [4]	Native Hawaiian or Other Pacific Islander only [4]	2 or more races	Hispanic or Latino	Below poverty level	At or above poverty level	Central city	Remaining area	Outside MSA [3]
					Percent of children aged 19–35 months								
Hepatitis A (2 doses or more):													
2009	46.6	46.2	41.3	33.2	50.9	*	47.8	49.3	47.3	46.2	48.2	46.9	42.0
2010	49.7	45.8	48.6	*	50.8	*	49.8	57.0	51.0	49.1	52.4	48.8	45.1
2011	52.2	50.0	50.9	*	56.9	*	50.2	56.3	50.7	53.4	55.0	50.9	47.6
2012	53.0	52.6	52.0	*	57.5	*	49.4	54.4	49.4	55.4	54.7	53.0	48.2
2013	54.7	53.4	49.1	*	67.3	*	57.8	56.6	53.5	56.1	55.5	55.2	50.1
2014	57.5	55.4	56.7	*	67.7	*	53.7	61.6	54.0	59.2	58.9	58.1	51.2
2015	59.6	58.7	59.3	61.3	67.8	*	54.1	60.9	56.0	61.7	60.5	59.6	55.7
Hepatitis B (3 doses or more):													
2000	90.3	91.4	88.8	91.9	89.5	93.1	92.6	88.2	87.3	91.4	89.4	90.3	92.3
2005	92.9	93.1	92.7	90.1	92.7	*	94.4	92.7	91.4	93.5	91.8	93.9	93.4
2009	92.4	92.3	91.6	92.5	93.1	96.2	93.3	92.6	92.3	92.7	92.8	91.8	91.8
2010	91.8	91.4	92.1	97.2	91.7	96.7	89.9	92.5	91.5	92.0	91.2	92.0	92.7
2011	91.1	90.3	92.1	92.6	95.5	91.1	90.7	91.5	91.8	91.2	91.0	90.7	92.5
2012	89.7	89.3	89.7	94.0	93.2	*	92.2	89.4	89.4	89.8	89.5	89.6	90.7
2013	90.8	91.0	91.1	96.1	92.0	94.9	90.7	89.7	88.3	92.0	89.6	91.8	91.4
2014	91.6	90.7	92.3	98.5	92.9	95.2	92.9	91.9	91.3	92.0	90.5	92.5	91.9
2015	92.6	92.0	93.3	92.4	95.5	94.1	91.4	93.2	92.5	92.7	92.9	92.5	92.1
Varicella: [8]													
1998	43.2	41.9	42.4	28.0	52.6	- - -	- - -	46.9	40.5	44.1	45.1	45.2	34.3
2000	67.8	66.3	67.6	65.8	76.3	*	69.7	70.2	63.5	69.2	69.0	69.8	60.2
2005	87.9	86.1	90.6	82.2	91.9	*	90.1	89.2	87.3	87.7	88.4	88.2	85.7
2009	89.6	89.2	88.2	89.2	89.5	97.5	90.6	90.7	89.0	90.2	90.6	88.5	88.5
2010	90.4	88.9	91.5	95.7	92.5	92.7	88.9	92.3	89.6	90.6	90.8	90.1	90.0
2011	90.8	89.6	91.2	90.1	93.5	99.0	91.9	92.0	90.2	90.9	90.9	91.0	89.8
2012	90.2	89.8	90.4	92.5	91.9	*	90.9	90.9	89.7	90.6	90.1	90.0	91.3
2013	91.2	90.0	92.1	95.4	96.0	88.7	91.0	92.0	90.3	91.6	91.1	91.6	90.3
2014	91.0	90.3	90.1	95.7	95.3	94.9	90.0	92.1	89.9	91.9	91.4	91.1	89.8
2015	91.8	91.2	91.8	87.8	93.4	91.8	92.1	92.7	90.6	92.5	92.5	91.5	89.9
PCV (4 doses or more): [9]													
2005	53.7	57.3	46.2	*	56.2	*	54.2	50.5	44.6	57.1	51.7	57.7	48.4
2009	80.4	83.4	73.2	76.2	72.5	*	73.1	80.6	74.8	83.2	79.7	81.8	81.8
2010	83.3	84.2	79.7	85.3	78.9	*	83.0	83.9	78.7	85.6	82.6	84.3	82.6
2011	84.4	85.3	81.3	75.3	84.9	93.1	84.0	84.6	80.6	86.9	85.0	84.6	82.3
2012	81.9	83.5	77.1	*	80.7	*	84.1	82.1	76.7	85.3	80.4	84.0	80.8
2013	82.0	84.1	76.1	79.0	85.6	*	83.0	80.4	74.5	86.1	80.7	84.1	79.9
2014	82.9	84.5	78.0	*	80.9	93.1	82.1	83.2	76.9	86.9	81.4	84.5	82.9
2015	84.1	85.0	81.4	77.1	85.0	*	83.7	84.0	78.9	87.2	83.9	85.5	80.4
Rotavirus vaccine: [10]													
2009	43.9	46.4	38.0	*	41.7	*	38.4	43.7	37.7	47.1	44.6	46.6	35.6
2010	59.2	60.2	52.7	*	62.6	*	57.7	60.5	51.5	62.9	59.2	62.2	51.6
2011	67.3	68.3	62.5	57.7	66.9	*	67.8	68.3	61.1	71.1	68.9	67.4	62.7
2012	68.6	70.5	60.4	*	69.9	*	69.3	70.0	63.0	72.5	68.8	70.5	62.5
2013	72.6	74.8	62.1	*	74.9	*	72.8	73.7	64.3	76.9	72.4	74.7	66.7
2014	71.7	74.8	61.6	*	72.4	*	73.9	71.3	62.8	76.9	71.2	73.2	68.4
2015	73.2	74.6	69.7	*	75.6	*	70.6	72.9	66.8	76.8	72.7	75.1	68.6

See footnotes at end of table.

Table 66 (page 3 of 3). Vaccination coverage for selected diseases among children aged 19–35 months, by race, Hispanic origin, poverty level, and location of residence in metropolitan statistical area: United States, selected years 1998–2015

Excel and PDF versions (with more data years and standard errors when available): http://www.cdc.gov/nchs/hus/contents2016.htm#066.

[Data are based on telephone interviews of a sample of the civilian noninstitutionalized population, supplemented by a survey of interview participants' immunization providers]

| | Not Hispanic or Latino | | | | Hispanic or Latino | |
| | White only | | Black or African American Only | | | |
Vaccination and year	Below poverty level[2]	At or above poverty level[2]	Below poverty level[2]	At or above poverty level[2]	Below poverty level[2]	At or above poverty level[2]
	Percent of children aged 19–35 months					
Combined 7-vaccine series: [5]						
2009	43.2	45.6	37.8	43.5	43.5	48.5
2010	48.7	59.0	53.4	56.3	55.0	55.2
2011	59.8	71.8	61.0	68.0	67.9	71.1
2012	58.2	72.1	62.7	68.5	68.1	68.3
2013	61.3	74.9	60.4	69.1	68.6	70.2
2014	61.2	75.4	61.5	71.0	71.8	79.4
2015	64.1	75.4	65.8	73.2	72.9	70.1

- - - Data not available.

* Estimates are considered unreliable. For data prior to 2007 (shown in spreadsheet version), percents not shown if the unweighted sample size for the numerator was less than 30, or the confidence interval half-width divided by the estimate was greater than 50%, or the confidence interval half-width was greater than 10. Starting with 2007 data, percents not shown if the unweighted sample size for the denominator was less than 30, or the confidence interval half-width divided by the estimate was greater than 58.8%, or the confidence interval half-width was greater than 10.

[1] Persons of Hispanic origin may be of any race. Starting with 2000 data, estimates were tabulated using the 1997 *Revisions to the Standards for the Classification of Federal Data on Race and Ethnicity*. Estimates for earlier years were tabulated using the 1977 Standards on Race and Ethnicity. See Appendix II, Hispanic origin; Race.

[2] Poverty level is based on family income and family size using U.S. Census Bureau poverty thresholds. In 2015, 3.5% of the 15,167 children with provider-reported vaccination history data, 5.8% of Hispanic, 2.3% of non-Hispanic white, and 5.9% of non-Hispanic black children, were missing information about poverty level and were omitted from the estimates of vaccination coverage by poverty level (unweighted percentages). See Appendix II, Family income; Poverty. See Appendix I, National Immunization Survey (NIS).

[3] MSA is metropolitan statistical area. See Appendix II, Metropolitan statistical area (MSA).

[4] Prior to data year 2000, the category Asian included Native Hawaiian or Other Pacific Islander.

[5] The combined 7-vaccine series consists of 4 or more doses of either the diphtheria, tetanus toxoids, and pertussis vaccine (DTP), the diphtheria and tetanus toxoids vaccine (DT), or the diphtheria, tetanus toxoids, and acellular pertussis vaccine (DTaP); 3 or more doses of any poliovirus vaccine; 1 or more doses of a measles-containing vaccine (MCV); 3 or more doses or 4 or more doses of *Haemophilus influenzae* type b vaccine (Hib) depending on Hib vaccine product type (full series Hib); 3 or more doses of hepatitis B vaccine; 1 or more doses of varicella vaccine; and 4 or more doses of pneumococcal conjugate vaccine (PCV). The vaccine shortage that ended in September 2004 might have reduced coverage with the fourth dose of PCV among children in the 2007 National Immunization Survey (NIS) cohort. Also see footnote 7 for additional information on (Hib) vaccination.

[6] Includes the diphtheria, tetanus toxoids, and pertussis vaccine (DTP), the diphtheria and tetanus toxoids vaccine (DT), and the diphtheria, tetanus toxoids, and acellular pertussis vaccine (DTaP).

[7] *Haemophilus influenzae* type b vaccine (Hib) full series includes primary series plus the booster dose. Before January 2009, NIS did not distinguish between Hib vaccine product types; therefore, children who received 3 doses of a vaccine product that requires 4 doses were misclassified as fully vaccinated. In addition, there was a Hib vaccine shortage during December 2007–September 2009. For more information, see Changes in measurement of *Haemophilus influenzae* serotype b (Hib) vaccination coverage—National Immunization Survey, United States, 2009. MMWR 59(33);1069-72. Available from: http://www.cdc.gov/mmwr/preview/mmwrhtml/mm5933a3.htm?s_cid=mm5933a3_e%0d%0a.

[8] Recommended in 1996. Data collection for varicella began in July 1996.

[9] PCV is pneumococcal conjugate vaccine. Recommended in 2000. Data collection for PCV began in July 2001. Data for 4 doses of PCV are not available prior to 2005.

[10] Rotavirus vaccine includes 2 or more or 3 or more doses, depending on the product type received. Recommended in 2006. Data collection for rotavirus began in 2009.

NOTES: Final estimates from the National Immunization Survey include an adjustment for children with missing immunization provider data. Additional information on childhood immunizations is available from: http://www.cdc.gov/vaccines/schedules/index.html. Data for additional years are available. See the Excel spreadsheet on the *Health, United States* website at: http://www.cdc.gov/nchs/hus.htm.

SOURCE: NCHS and National Center for Immunization and Respiratory Diseases (NCIRD) (data for 1998–2014); NCIRD (data for 2015 onwards), National Immunization Survey. Available from: https://www.cdc.gov/vaccines/imz-managers/nis/index.html. See Appendix I, National Immunization Survey (NIS).

Table 67. Vaccination coverage for selected diseases among adolescents aged 13–17, by selected characteristics: United States, selected years 2008–2015

Excel and PDF versions (with more data years and standard errors when available): http://www.cdc.gov/nchs/hus/contents2016.htm#067.

[Data are based on telephone interviews of a sample of the civilian noninstitutionalized population, supplemented by a survey of interview participants' immunization providers]

Vaccination coverage	2008	2010	2011	2012	2013[1]	2014[1]	2015[1]
	Percent of adolescents aged 13–17						
Measles, mumps, rubella (2 doses or more)	89.3	90.5	91.1	91.4	89.6	90.7	90.7
Hepatitis B (3 doses or more).	87.9	91.6	92.3	92.8	91.3	91.4	91.1
Varicella vaccine (2 doses or more) among those with no history of varicella[2]	34.1	58.1	68.3	74.9	78.5	81.0	83.1
Tdap (1 dose or more)[3]	40.8	68.7	78.2	84.6	84.7	87.6	86.4
Meningococcal conjugate vaccine (MenACWY) (1 dose or more)[4]	41.8	62.7	70.5	74.0	76.6	79.3	81.3
Human papillomavirus (HPV) (3 doses or more among females)[5].	17.9	32.0	34.8	33.4	36.8	39.7	41.9
Human papillomavirus (HPV) (3 doses or more among males)[5].	. . .	. . .	1.3	6.8	13.4	21.6	28.1

	Race and Hispanic origin[6]					Poverty level[7]		Location of residence		
	Not Hispanic or Latino							Inside MSA[8]		
Vaccination coverage, 2015	White only	Black or African American only	American Indian or Alaska Native only	Asian only	Hispanic or Latino	Below poverty level	At or above poverty level	Central city	Remaining area	Outside MSA[8]
	Percent of adolescents aged 13–17									
Measles, mumps, rubella (2 doses or more)	91.7	91.9	91.1	87.5	88.1	89.5	90.9	91.2	90.1	91.4
Hepatitis B (3 doses or more).	92.5	92.5	93.1	89.2	87.4	90.3	91.1	91.5	90.7	91.3
Varicella vaccine (2 doses or more) among those with no history of varicella[2]	82.8	84.9	86.9	84.5	82.3	85.4	82.2	84.6	83.1	78.3
Tdap (1 dose or more)[3]	86.6	86.0	87.6	86.0	85.3	85.0	87.0	88.1	86.0	82.7
Meningococcal conjugate vaccine (MenACWY) (1 dose or more)[4]	79.5	81.7	83.9	83.3	85.0	82.6	80.5	82.9	82.5	71.6
Human papillomavirus (HPV) (3 doses or more among females)[5].	39.6	40.8	38.7	53.5	46.2	44.4	41.3	44.6	41.3	35.8
Human papillomavirus (HPV) (3 doses or more among males)[5].	25.2	26.0	34.6	30.7	35.0	31.0	27.4	32.5	26.0	22.5

. . . Category not applicable.

[1] Starting in 2014, NIS-Teen implemented a new definition of adequate provider data. Data for 2013 shown in this table were revised based on the 2014 definition. In general, 2013 NIS-Teen vaccination coverage estimates using the revised adequate provider data definition were different, and generally lower, than original 2013 NIS-Teen estimates. Thus, data for 2013 and beyond are not directly comparable with data for 2008–2012. For more information on the new criteria and their effect on coverage levels, see Appendix I, National Immunization Survey (NIS).

[2] Denominator is comprised of adolescents aged 13–17 with no history of varicella disease. History of varicella disease was obtained by parent/guardian report or by provider records. Historically, report of varicella disease has been considered valid evidence of immunity under the Advisory Committee on Immunization Practices guidelines.

[3] Tdap refers to tetanus toxoid-diphtheria vaccine (Td) or tetanus toxoid, reduced diphtheria toxoid, and acellular pertussis vaccine (Tdap) or tetanus-unknown type vaccine received at or after the age of 10 years.

[4] Includes persons receiving MenACWY or meningococcal-unknown type vaccine.

[5] For 2008, refers to HPV vaccine quadrivalent; for 2009–2014, refers to HPV vaccine quadrivalent or bivalent; for 2015 and beyond, refers to HPV vaccine 9-valent, quadrivalent, or bivalent.

[6] Persons of Hispanic origin may be of any race. Estimates were tabulated using the 1997 *Revisions to the Standards for the Classification of Federal Data on Race and Ethnicity*. Data for Native Hawaiian or Other Pacific Islander persons and persons of multiple races were not included because of small sample sizes. See Appendix II, Hispanic origin; Race.

[7] Poverty level is based on family income and family size using U.S. Census Bureau poverty thresholds. In 2015, 3.5% (unweighted) of adolescents with provider-reported vaccination data were missing information about poverty level and were not included in the estimates of vaccination coverage by poverty level. See Appendix II, Family income; Poverty.

[8] MSA is metropolitan statistical area. See Appendix II, Metropolitan statistical area (MSA).

NOTES: Vaccination coverage estimates are based on provider-verified responses from parents who live in households with telephones. Complex statistical methods are used to adjust vaccination estimates to account for adolescents whose parents refuse to participate in the survey, for adolescents who live in households without telephones, or for adolescents whose vaccination histories cannot be verified through their providers. Starting in 2011, the NIS sampling frame was expanded from a single-landline frame to dual-landline and cellular telephone sampling frames. See Appendix I, National Immunization Survey (NIS). Detailed vaccination data among adolescents, by race and Hispanic origin, percent of poverty level, and MSA were not available prior to 2008. Interpretation of vaccination data needs to take into account when specific vaccines were licensed and recommended for use among adolescents. Quadrivalent HPV vaccine was licensed by the U.S. Food and Drug Administration (FDA) in June 2006. For the initial recommendations on HPV vaccination, see: CDC. Quadrivalent human papillomavirus vaccine: Recommendations of the Advisory Committee on Immunization Practices. MMWR 2007;56(RR-02):1–24. Available from: http://www.cdc.gov/mmwr/preview/mmwrhtml/rr5602a1.htm?s_cid=rr5602a1_e; HPV vaccine was recommended for males in October 2011. CDC. Recommendations on the use of quadrivalent human papillomavirus vaccine in males - Advisory Committee on Immunization Practices (ACIP), 2011. MMWR 2011;60(50):1705–8. Available from: http://www.cdc.gov/mmwr/preview/mmwrhtml/mm6050a3.htm. Meningococcal vaccine was licensed for use by the FDA in January 2005. For the initial recommendations on meningococcal vaccination, see: CDC. Prevention and control of meningococcal disease: Recommendations of the Advisory Committee on Immunization Practices. MMWR 2005;54(RR-07):1–21. Available from: http://www.cdc.gov/mmwr/preview/mmwrhtml/rr5407a1.htm. Tdap vaccines were licensed by the FDA in May and June of 2005. For the initial recommendations on Tdap vaccination, see: CDC. Preventing tetanus, diphtheria, and pertussis among adolescents: Use of tetanus toxoid, reduced diphtheria toxoid and acellular pertussis vaccines. Recommendations of the Advisory Committee on Immunization Practices. MMWR 2006;55(RR-03):1–34. Available from: http://www.cdc.gov/mmwr/preview/mmwrhtml/rr5503a1.htm. See Appendix I, National Immunization Survey (NIS). Additional information on the recommended schedule for adolescent vaccination is available from: http://www.cdc.gov/vaccines/schedules/index.html.

SOURCE: NCHS and National Center for Immunization and Respiratory Diseases (NCIRD) (data for 2008–2014); NCIRD (data for 2015 onwards), National Immunization Survey–Teen. Available from: https://www.cdc.gov/vaccines/vaxview/index.html. See Appendix I, National Immunization Survey (NIS).

Table 68 (page 1 of 2). Influenza vaccination among adults aged 18 and over, by selected characteristics: United States, selected years 1989–2015

Excel and PDF versions (with more data years and standard errors when available): http://www.cdc.gov/nchs/hus/contents2016.htm#068.

[Data are based on household interviews of a sample of the civilian noninstitutionalized population]

Characteristic	1989	1995	2000	2005	2010	2012	2013	2014	2015
	Percent receiving influenza vaccination during past 12 months[1]								
18 years and over, age-adjusted[2,3]	9.6	23.7	28.7	21.6	35.3	36.8	39.9	41.0	41.7
18 years and over, crude[3]	9.1	23.0	28.4	21.4	35.8	37.7	41.0	42.2	43.2
Age									
18–44 years	3.3	12.0	15.6	10.1	24.6	25.6	28.5	30.2	30.9
45–64 years	8.8	24.5	31.6	20.2	37.8	39.4	43.7	43.3	45.1
65 years and over	30.4	58.2	64.4	59.7	63.9	66.5	67.9	70.1	69.1
65–74 years	28.0	54.9	61.1	53.7	60.5	62.6	64.4	67.1	67.0
75 years and over	34.2	63.0	68.4	66.3	68.2	71.7	72.8	74.3	72.1
18 years and over									
Sex									
Male	8.5	21.5	26.7	18.4	31.3	33.4	37.0	37.9	39.2
Female	9.7	24.4	30.0	24.2	40.0	41.7	44.7	46.1	46.8
Race[4]									
White only	9.6	23.7	30.1	22.5	36.9	38.7	42.2	43.4	44.2
Black or African American only	6.4	19.0	19.8	15.5	28.1	30.6	33.0	34.1	35.7
American Indian or Alaska Native only	10.9	*16.5	31.1	16.2	36.3	37.2	37.9	42.6	39.3
Asian only	4.3	20.0	27.0	16.9	38.6	40.9	43.9	45.0	47.0
Native Hawaiian or Other Pacific Islander only	- - -	- - -	*	*	*	*	*	*	*
2 or more races	- - -	- - -	25.3	15.9	28.9	30.1	34.7	34.3	40.8
Hispanic origin and race[4]									
Hispanic or Latino	5.9	16.1	17.7	12.0	26.5	28.1	28.9	31.0	31.2
Mexican	5.2	16.0	16.6	10.9	25.1	26.8	29.2	31.2	30.4
Not Hispanic or Latino	9.4	23.7	29.8	22.8	37.3	39.4	43.1	44.2	45.4
White only	9.9	24.6	31.4	24.3	38.8	40.9	44.9	46.0	46.9
Black or African American only	6.4	19.2	19.9	15.6	28.0	30.9	33.2	34.4	36.0
Percent of poverty level[5]									
Below 100%	8.9	20.6	23.1	16.9	25.0	29.2	30.1	32.0	33.6
100%–199%	11.5	23.4	28.1	22.0	31.3	32.3	35.5	36.7	37.0
200%–399%	8.0	22.8	29.6	22.9	34.8	36.8	40.1	40.8	41.2
400% or more	9.0	24.3	29.2	21.3	42.7	44.5	48.6	49.7	50.4
Hispanic origin and race and percent of poverty level[4,5]									
Hispanic or Latino:									
Below 100%	5.1	13.3	14.5	9.5	21.9	25.4	25.8	26.8	29.9
100%–199%	7.5	17.8	15.8	11.9	23.3	25.7	25.4	29.6	27.7
200%–399%	6.3	15.7	19.3	11.8	27.5	28.6	29.4	30.8	30.0
400% or more	6.0	19.8	22.2	15.5	36.4	35.5	37.6	39.8	40.0
Not Hispanic or Latino:									
White only:									
Below 100%	10.6	23.9	27.8	20.6	26.5	31.3	32.4	35.1	34.9
100%–199%	13.2	25.6	33.1	27.4	35.0	35.8	40.7	41.2	41.7
200%–399%	8.3	23.8	32.5	26.3	37.5	38.9	42.9	44.0	44.4
400% or more	9.4	25.5	30.5	22.4	43.8	46.2	50.4	51.3	52.2
Black or African American only:									
Below 100%	7.5	19.8	20.0	17.0	24.0	27.7	28.3	29.4	30.2
100%–199%	6.4	18.8	21.3	15.4	28.6	29.9	30.9	33.0	33.9
200%–399%	6.9	20.4	19.5	15.1	27.4	31.8	35.2	34.6	36.1
400% or more	5.6	15.6	19.2	15.3	32.9	34.2	38.2	41.6	43.3

See footnotes at end of table.

Table 68 (page 2 of 2). Influenza vaccination among adults aged 18 and over, by selected characteristics: United States, selected years 1989–2015

Excel and PDF versions (with more data years and standard errors when available): http://www.cdc.gov/nchs/hus/contents2016.htm#068.

[Data are based on household interviews of a sample of the civilian noninstitutionalized population]

Characteristic	1989	1995	2000	2005	2010	2012	2013	2014	2015
Disability measure [6]	Percent receiving influenza vaccination during past 12 months [1]								
Any basic actions difficulty or complex activity limitation	- - -	- - -	40.8	34.1	44.6	47.3	50.6	51.4	52.2
Any basic actions difficulty	- - -	- - -	41.0	34.4	45.1	47.8	51.3	51.8	52.5
Any complex activity limitation	- - -	- - -	44.7	40.3	47.7	50.9	52.3	54.7	53.9
No disability	- - -	- - -	23.2	15.6	31.6	33.2	36.7	37.9	38.8
Geographic region									
Northeast	8.6	21.2	28.0	23.2	39.1	40.1	44.5	45.0	46.6
Midwest	8.8	22.7	28.5	22.6	37.6	38.4	41.4	43.6	43.1
South	9.5	24.7	28.7	20.3	35.1	37.2	40.1	41.5	42.4
West	9.4	22.3	28.1	20.2	32.6	36.0	39.4	39.7	41.8
Location of residence [7]									
Within MSA	8.5	22.3	27.5	20.4	35.7	37.7	40.8	41.9	43.4
Outside MSA	11.4	25.7	31.8	25.1	36.1	37.9	42.2	44.1	41.9

* Estimates are considered unreliable. Data preceded by an asterisk have a relative standard error (RSE) of 20%–30%. Data not shown have an RSE greater than 30%.

- - - Data not available.

[1] Questions concerning use of influenza vaccination differed slightly on the National Health Interview Survey across the years. See Appendix II, Vaccination. Data prior to 1997 are not strictly comparable with data for later years due to the 1997 questionnaire redesign. See Appendix I, National Health Interview Survey (NHIS).

[2] Estimates are age-adjusted to the year 2000 standard population using four age groups: 18–44 years, 45–64 years, 65–74 years, and 75 years and over. See Appendix II, Age adjustment.

[3] Includes all other races not shown separately and unknown disability status for all data years, and unknown poverty level in 1989.

[4] The race groups, white, black, American Indian or Alaska Native, Asian, Native Hawaiian or Other Pacific Islander, and 2 or more races, include persons of Hispanic and non-Hispanic origin. Persons of Hispanic origin may be of any race. Starting with 1999 data, race-specific estimates are tabulated according to the 1997 *Revisions to the Standards for the Classification of Federal Data on Race and Ethnicity* and are not strictly comparable with estimates for earlier years. The five single-race categories plus multiple-race categories shown in the table conform to the 1997 Standards. Starting with 1999 data, race-specific estimates are for persons who reported only one racial group; the category 2 or more races includes persons who reported more than one racial group. Prior to 1999, data were tabulated according to the 1977 Standards with four racial groups, and the Asian only category included Native Hawaiian or Other Pacific Islander. Estimates for single-race categories prior to 1999 included persons who reported one race or, if they reported more than one race, identified one race as best representing their race. Starting with 2003 data, race responses of other race and unspecified multiple race were treated as missing, and then race was imputed if these were the only race responses. Almost all persons with a race response of other race were of Hispanic origin. See Appendix II, Hispanic origin; Race.

[5] Percent of poverty level is based on family income and family size and composition using U.S. Census Bureau poverty thresholds. Poverty level was unknown for 11% of persons aged 18 and over in 1989. Missing family income data were imputed for 1991 and beyond. See Appendix II, Family income; Poverty; Table VI.

[6] Any basic actions difficulty or complex activity limitation is defined as having one or more of the following limitations or difficulties: movement difficulty, emotional difficulty, sensory (seeing or hearing) difficulty, cognitive difficulty, self-care (activities of daily living or instrumental activities of daily living) limitation, social limitation, or work limitation. For more information, see Appendix II, Basic actions difficulty; Complex activity limitation. Starting with 2007 data, the hearing question, a component of the basic actions difficulty measure, was revised. Consequently, data prior to 2007 are not comparable with data for 2007 and beyond. For more information on the impact of the revised hearing question, see Appendix II, Hearing trouble.

[7] MSA is metropolitan statistical area. Starting with 2006 data, MSA status is determined using 2000 census data and the 2000 standards for defining MSAs. For data prior to 2006, see Appendix II, Metropolitan statistical area (MSA) for the applicable standards.

NOTES: Interpretation of vaccination data needs to take into account when universal recommendations were issued. Medicare payment for the costs of the vaccine and its administration began in 1993. In 2000, CDC's Advisory Committee on Immunization Practices (ACIP) recommended universal influenza vaccination, with rare exceptions, for persons aged 50 and over. See, *Health, United States, 2014*, Table 74 for historical data for adults age 50 and over. In 2010, ACIP recommended universal influenza vaccination, with rare exceptions, for persons aged 6 months and over. For current ACIP vaccination recommendations, see: http://www.cdc.gov/flu/professionals/acip/index.htm. Standard errors for selected years are available in the spreadsheet version of this table. Available from http://www.cdc.gov/nchs/hus.htm. Data for additional years are available. See the Excel spreadsheet on the *Health, United States* website at: http://www.cdc.gov/nchs/hus.htm.

SOURCE: NCHS, National Health Interview Survey. Data are from the following questionnaire supplements: immunization (1989) and the year 2000 objectives (1995). Starting in 1997, data are from the sample adult questionnaire. See Appendix I, National Health Interview Survey (NHIS).

Table 69 (page 1 of 2). Pneumococcal vaccination among adults aged 18 and over, by selected characteristics: United States, selected years 1989–2015

Excel and PDF versions (with more data years and standard errors when available): http://www.cdc.gov/nchs/hus/contents2016.htm#069.

[Data are based on household interviews of a sample of the civilian noninstitutionalized population]

Characteristic	1989	1995	2000	2005	2010	2012	2013	2014	2015
	Percent of adults ever receiving pneumococcal vaccination [1]								
18 years and over, age-adjusted [2,3]	4.6	12.0	15.4	16.7	19.2	19.9	19.9	20.5	21.2
18 years and over, crude [3].	4.4	11.7	15.1	16.5	19.6	20.7	21.0	21.8	22.9
Age									
18–44 years	2.1	6.6	5.1	5.3	6.9	7.9	7.5	8.3	8.8
45–64 years	3.7	8.8	12.2	14.3	17.7	18.0	18.8	18.4	18.8
65 years and over	14.1	34.0	53.1	56.2	59.7	59.9	59.7	61.3	63.6
65–74 years.	13.1	31.4	48.2	49.4	54.6	55.0	54.4	55.8	60.2
75 years and over.	15.7	37.8	59.1	63.9	66.0	66.4	67.1	69.3	68.5
High-risk group [4]									
Total, 18–64 years	- - -	- - -	18.3	22.6	18.3	19.9	21.0	20.2	23.0
18–44 years.	- - -	- - -	11.3	13.8	9.8	11.3	11.7	11.3	12.8
45–64 years.	- - -	- - -	23.3	27.9	26.7	28.0	29.4	28.3	31.6
65 years and over									
Sex									
Male	13.9	34.6	52.1	53.4	57.6	55.8	57.1	58.4	62.9
Female.	14.3	33.6	53.9	58.4	61.3	63.1	61.8	63.7	64.2
Race [5]									
White only	14.8	35.3	55.6	58.4	61.6	62.3	61.7	63.1	65.8
Black or African American only	6.4	21.9	30.6	40.2	45.5	46.0	48.4	49.2	49.9
American Indian or Alaska Native only	31.2	*	70.1	*	*48.5	*36.3	52.9	57.1	60.3
Asian only	*	*23.4	40.9	35.0	47.9	41.1	45.0	47.7	49.3
Native Hawaiian or Other Pacific Islander only	- - -	- - -	*	*	*	*	*	*	*
2 or more races	- - -	- - -	55.6	64.8	65.5	45.4	50.8	71.2	60.4
Hispanic origin and race [5]									
Hispanic or Latino	9.8	23.2	30.4	27.5	39.0	43.4	39.2	45.2	41.7
Mexican.	12.9	*18.8	32.0	31.3	41.4	45.5	47.4	47.8	49.1
Not Hispanic or Latino.	14.3	34.5	54.4	58.1	61.3	61.2	61.4	62.7	65.5
White only.	15.0	35.9	56.8	60.6	63.5	64.0	63.6	64.7	68.1
Black or African American only.	6.2	21.8	30.6	40.4	46.2	46.1	48.7	49.8	50.2
Percent of poverty level [6]									
Below 100%.	11.2	28.7	40.6	46.7	42.6	39.5	50.5	47.3	48.7
100%–199%.	15.1	30.7	51.4	54.5	57.2	59.8	58.0	59.5	61.7
200%–399%.	15.1	36.1	55.8	60.8	62.2	63.6	61.7	64.5	64.8
400% or more	15.5	39.5	56.9	55.3	64.0	61.4	61.6	63.2	67.1
Hispanic origin and race and percent of poverty level [5,6]									
Hispanic or Latino:									
Below 100%	*	*14.1	23.8	20.9	30.2	30.9	35.3	34.1	31.0
100%–199%	*11.0	*15.6	32.3	26.9	36.9	42.0	39.1	44.4	45.2
200%–399%	*11.1	*34.4	37.6	35.2	45.8	54.5	36.1	52.1	43.9
400% or more	*	*55.1	*26.4	*25.2	43.0	46.4	49.1	54.0	44.3
Not Hispanic or Latino:									
White only:									
Below 100%	13.3	32.5	47.9	55.6	51.1	46.5	59.1	55.4	54.1
100%–199%	16.0	33.5	56.1	60.5	61.3	66.1	63.3	64.1	67.4
200%–399%	15.7	37.1	57.6	64.1	64.9	65.9	65.2	66.9	68.4
400% or more	15.9	39.3	59.5	57.4	66.0	63.5	63.2	64.5	70.2
Black or African American only:									
Below 100%	*5.0	*22.6	28.8	42.3	34.9	36.1	48.9	46.0	53.3
100%–199%	7.8	*20.9	28.1	36.6	46.4	44.5	46.9	49.1	46.9
200%–399%	*5.9	*21.7	35.5	41.6	51.8	54.1	49.4	47.9	44.1
400% or more	*	*	*32.6	44.6	50.1	45.4	50.3	56.0	61.8

See footnotes at end of table.

Table 69 (page 2 of 2). Pneumococcal vaccination among adults aged 18 and over, by selected characteristics: United States, selected years 1989–2015

Excel and PDF versions (with more data years and standard errors when available): http://www.cdc.gov/nchs/hus/contents2016.htm#069.

[Data are based on household interviews of a sample of the civilian noninstitutionalized population]

Characteristic	1989	1995	2000	2005	2010	2012	2013	2014	2015
Disability measure[7]	\multicolumn{9}{c}{Percent of adults ever receiving pneumococcal vaccination[1]}
Any basic actions difficulty or complex activity limitation	- - -	- - -	56.6	61.6	63.9	65.4	64.4	66.7	66.4
Any basic actions difficulty	- - -	- - -	56.8	61.6	64.2	66.0	64.9	66.7	66.6
Any complex activity limitation	- - -	- - -	58.0	63.3	65.2	65.7	66.1	67.6	67.1
No disability	- - -	- - -	47.9	47.8	53.3	53.2	53.1	53.7	59.4
Geographic region									
Northeast	10.4	28.2	51.2	55.8	56.7	58.0	59.1	59.6	60.8
Midwest	13.7	31.0	52.6	58.5	61.2	63.8	62.3	65.4	68.3
South	14.9	35.9	51.3	57.4	60.9	59.5	59.3	60.9	62.3
West	17.9	41.1	59.7	51.4	58.9	58.2	58.3	59.3	63.7
Location of residence[8]									
Within MSA	13.1	33.8	52.4	55.1	58.8	59.3	59.0	60.7	63.4
Outside MSA	16.9	34.7	55.4	59.8	63.3	62.4	62.8	64.0	64.7

- - - Data not available.

* Estimates are considered unreliable. Data preceded by an asterisk have a relative standard error (RSE) of 20%–30%. Data not shown have an RSE greater than 30%.

[1] Questions concerning receipt of pneumococcal vaccination differed slightly on the National Health Interview Survey across the years. See Appendix II, Vaccination. Data prior to 1997 are not strictly comparable with data for later years due to the 1997 questionnaire redesign. See Appendix I, National Health Interview Survey (NHIS).

[2] Estimates are age-adjusted to the year 2000 standard population using four age groups: 18–44 years, 45–64 years, 65–74 years, and 75 years and over. See Appendix II, Age adjustment.

[3] Includes all other races not shown separately and unknown disability status for all data years, and unknown poverty level in 1989.

[4] High-risk group membership is based on recommendations of CDC's Advisory Committee on Immunization Practices (ACIP). The high-risk group includes persons who reported diabetes, cancer, heart, lung, liver, or kidney disease. Starting with data year 2009, this definition was expanded to also include persons who reported asthma or cigarette smoking, to be consistent with the revised ACIP recommendation. Starting with data year 2012, the survey questionnaire changed and now asks respondents if a health professional had ever told them they had chronic obstructive pulmonary disease (COPD), and this information was added to the list of lung diseases used to construct the high-risk category. For more information on high-risk groups, see the 2009 ACIP recommendation. Available from: http://www.cdc.gov/mmwr/pdf/wk/mm5934.pdf.

[5] The race groups, white, black, American Indian or Alaska Native, Asian, Native Hawaiian or Other Pacific Islander, and 2 or more races, include persons of Hispanic and non-Hispanic origin. Persons of Hispanic origin may be of any race. Starting with 1999 data, race-specific estimates are tabulated according to the 1997 *Revisions to the Standards for the Classification of Federal Data on Race and Ethnicity* and are not strictly comparable with estimates for earlier years. The five single-race categories plus multiple-race categories shown in the table conform to the 1997 Standards. Starting with 1999 data, race-specific estimates are for persons who reported only one racial group; the category 2 or more races includes persons who reported more than one racial group. Prior to 1999, data were tabulated according to the 1977 Standards with four racial groups, and the Asian only category included Native Hawaiian or Other Pacific Islander. Estimates for single-race categories prior to 1999 included persons who reported one race or, if they reported more than one race, identified one race as best representing their race. Starting with 2003 data, race responses of other race and unspecified multiple race were treated as missing, and then race was imputed if these were the only race responses. Almost all persons with a race response of other race were of Hispanic origin. See Appendix II, Hispanic origin; Race.

[6] Percent of poverty level is based on family income and family size and composition using U.S. Census Bureau poverty thresholds. Poverty level was unknown for 11% of persons aged 18 and over in 1989. Missing family income data were imputed for 1991 and beyond. See Appendix II, Family income; Poverty; Table VI.

[7] Any basic actions difficulty or complex activity limitation is defined as having one or more of the following limitations or difficulties: movement difficulty, emotional difficulty, sensory (seeing or hearing) difficulty, cognitive difficulty, self-care (activities of daily living or instrumental activities of daily living) limitation, social limitation, or work limitation. For more information, see Appendix II, Basic actions difficulty; Complex activity limitation. Starting with 2007 data, the hearing question, a component of the basic actions difficulty measure, was revised. Consequently, data prior to 2007 are not comparable with data for 2007 and beyond. For more information on the impact of the revised hearing question, see Appendix II, Hearing trouble.

[8] MSA is metropolitan statistical area. Starting with 2006 data, MSA status is determined using 2000 census data and the 2000 standards for defining MSAs. For data prior to 2006, see Appendix II, Metropolitan statistical area (MSA) for the applicable standards.

NOTES: A pneumococcal polysaccharide vaccine was first licensed in 1977. Medicare payment for the costs of the vaccine and its administration began in 1981. In 1997, CDC's Advisory Committee on Immunization Practices (ACIP) recommended universal pneumonia vaccination for adults aged 65 and over. CDC. Prevention of pneumococcal disease: Recommendations of the Advisory Committee on Immunization Practices (ACIP). MMWR 1997;46(RR-08);1-24. Available from: http://www.cdc.gov/mmwr/preview/mmwrhtml/00047135.htm. For more information on the adult vaccination schedule, see: http://www.cdc.gov/vaccines/schedules/index.html. Standard errors for selected years are available in the spreadsheet version of this table. Available from: http://www.cdc.gov/nchs/hus.htm. Data for additional years are available. See the Excel spreadsheet on the *Health, United States* website at: http://www.cdc.gov/nchs/hus.htm. Some estimates have been revised and differ from previous editions of *Health, United States*.

SOURCE: NCHS, National Health Interview Survey. Data are from the following questionnaire supplements: immunization (1989) and the year 2000 objectives (1995). Starting in 1997, data are from the sample adult questionnaire. See Appendix I, National Health Interview Survey (NHIS).

Table 70 (page 1 of 3). Use of mammography among women aged 40 and over, by selected characteristics: United States, selected years 1987–2015

Excel and PDF versions (with more data years and standard errors when available): http://www.cdc.gov/nchs/hus/contents2016.htm#070.

[Data are based on household interviews of a sample of the civilian noninstitutionalized population]

Characteristic	1987	1993	1994	2000	2005	2008	2010	2013	2015
	Percent of women having a mammogram within the past 2 years[1]								
40 years and over, age-adjusted[2,3]	29.0	59.7	61.0	70.4	66.6	67.1	66.5	65.7	64.0
40 years and over, crude[2]	28.7	59.7	60.9	70.4	66.8	67.6	67.1	66.8	65.3
50 years and over, age-adjusted[2,3]	27.3	59.7	60.9	73.7	68.2	70.3	68.8	69.1	67.2
50 years and over, crude[2]	27.4	59.7	60.6	73.6	68.4	70.5	69.2	69.5	67.8
Age									
40–49 years	31.9	59.9	61.3	64.3	63.5	61.5	62.3	59.6	58.3
50–64 years	31.7	65.1	66.5	78.7	71.8	74.2	72.6	71.4	71.3
65 years and over	22.8	54.2	55.0	67.9	63.8	65.5	64.4	66.9	63.3
65–74 years	26.6	64.2	63.0	74.0	72.5	72.6	71.9	75.3	72.2
75 years and over	17.3	41.0	44.6	61.3	54.7	57.9	55.7	56.5	51.5
Race[4]									
40 years and over, crude:									
White only	29.6	60.0	60.6	71.4	67.4	67.9	67.4	66.8	65.3
Black or African American only	24.0	59.1	64.3	67.8	64.9	68.0	67.9	67.1	69.8
American Indian or Alaska Native only	*	49.8	65.8	47.4	72.8	62.7	71.2	62.6	51.5
Asian only	*	55.1	55.8	53.5	54.6	66.1	62.4	66.6	59.7
Native Hawaiian or Other Pacific Islander only	- - -	- - -	- - -	*	*	*	*	*	*
2 or more races	- - -	- - -	- - -	69.2	63.7	55.2	51.4	65.4	62.7
Hispanic origin and race[4]									
40 years and over, crude:									
Hispanic or Latina	18.3	50.9	51.9	61.2	58.8	61.2	64.2	61.4	60.9
Not Hispanic or Latina	29.4	60.3	61.5	71.1	67.5	68.3	67.4	67.5	65.9
White only	30.3	60.6	61.3	72.2	68.3	68.7	67.8	67.6	65.8
Black or African American only	23.8	59.2	64.4	67.9	65.2	68.3	67.4	67.2	69.7
Age and Hispanic origin and race[4]									
40–49 years:									
Hispanic or Latina	*15.3	52.6	47.5	54.1	54.2	54.1	59.8	56.4	50.3
Not Hispanic or Latina:									
White only	34.3	61.6	62.0	67.2	65.5	64.1	62.6	60.3	58.8
Black or African American only	27.8	55.6	67.2	60.9	62.1	59.5	63.5	59.4	67.8
50–64 years:									
Hispanic or Latina	23.0	59.2	60.1	66.5	61.5	71.3	68.6	65.6	71.6
Not Hispanic or Latina:									
White only	33.6	66.2	67.5	80.6	73.5	74.1	73.5	72.1	71.4
Black or African American only	26.4	65.5	63.6	77.7	71.6	76.7	74.0	71.7	73.5
65 years and over:									
Hispanic or Latina	*	*35.7	48.0	68.3	63.8	59.0	65.2	63.2	60.9
Not Hispanic or Latina:									
White only	24.0	54.7	54.9	68.3	64.7	66.1	65.0	67.3	63.9
Black or African American only	14.1	56.3	61.0	65.5	60.5	66.4	60.9	68.8	65.2
Age and percent of poverty level[5]									
40 years and over, crude:									
Below 100%	14.6	41.1	44.2	54.8	48.5	51.4	51.4	49.9	52.2
100%–199%	20.9	47.5	48.6	58.1	55.3	55.8	53.8	56.7	54.9
200%–399%	29.7	63.2	65.0	68.8	67.2	64.4	66.2	66.0	63.4
400% or more	42.9	74.1	74.1	81.5	76.6	79.0	78.1	77.2	74.7
40–49 years:									
Below 100%	18.6	36.1	43.0	47.4	42.5	46.6	48.1	43.3	45.8
100%–199%	18.4	47.8	47.6	43.6	49.8	46.5	46.2	52.0	47.5
200%–399%	31.2	63.0	64.5	60.2	61.8	56.8	59.2	58.5	55.6
400% or more	44.1	69.6	69.9	75.8	73.6	72.5	73.6	69.0	68.2
50–64 years:									
Below 100%	14.6	47.3	46.2	61.7	50.4	57.5	54.7	55.0	56.9
100%–199%	24.2	47.0	49.0	68.3	58.8	58.9	57.3	57.2	60.5
200%–399%	29.7	66.1	69.6	75.1	70.7	69.8	70.7	69.5	69.0
400% or more	44.7	78.7	78.0	86.9	80.6	84.3	82.8	80.9	79.2
65 years and over:									
Below 100%	13.1	40.4	43.9	54.8	52.3	49.1	50.6	49.8	52.7
100%–199%	19.9	47.6	48.8	60.3	56.1	59.4	55.5	59.3	54.4
200%–399%	27.7	60.3	61.0	71.1	68.6	65.0	67.2	68.1	63.3
400% or more	34.7	71.3	73.0	81.9	72.6	78.3	74.5	79.0	73.1

See footnotes at end of table.

Table 70 (page 2 of 3). Use of mammography among women aged 40 and over, by selected characteristics: United States, selected years 1987–2015

Excel and PDF versions (with more data years and standard errors when available): http://www.cdc.gov/nchs/hus/contents2016.htm#070.

[Data are based on household interviews of a sample of the civilian noninstitutionalized population]

Characteristic	1987	1993	1994	2000	2005	2008	2010	2013	2015
Health insurance status at the time of interview [6]				Percent of women having a mammogram within the past 2 years [1]					
40–64 years:									
Insured	- - -	66.2	68.3	76.0	72.5	73.4	74.1	72.1	69.7
Private	- - -	67.1	69.4	77.1	74.5	74.2	75.6	73.4	72.2
Medicaid	- - -	51.9	54.5	61.7	55.6	64.2	64.4	63.5	57.7
Uninsured	- - -	36.0	34.0	40.7	38.1	39.7	36.0	37.3	30.0
Health insurance status prior to interview [6]									
40–64 years:									
Insured continuously all 12 months	- - -	66.6	68.6	76.8	73.1	74.1	74.7	72.7	70.6
Uninsured for any period up to 12 months	- - -	49.4	49.9	53.0	51.3	55.3	57.3	54.5	50.0
Uninsured more than 12 months	- - -	28.4	26.6	34.0	32.9	34.6	30.0	32.8	23.9
Age and education [7]									
40 years and over, crude:									
No high school diploma or GED	17.8	46.4	48.2	57.7	52.8	53.8	53.0	53.6	51.7
High school diploma or GED	31.3	59.0	61.0	69.7	64.9	65.2	64.4	63.4	60.1
Some college or more	37.7	69.5	69.7	76.2	72.7	73.4	72.1	71.6	70.5
40–49 years:									
No high school diploma or GED	15.1	43.6	50.4	46.8	51.2	46.9	44.9	46.9	43.8
High school diploma or GED	32.6	56.6	55.8	59.0	58.8	57.2	58.4	51.8	47.5
Some college or more	39.2	66.1	68.7	70.6	68.3	66.3	66.5	64.3	64.0
50–64 years:									
No high school diploma or GED	21.2	51.4	51.6	66.5	56.9	64.9	56.7	58.2	58.1
High school diploma or GED	33.8	62.4	67.8	76.6	70.1	70.4	69.9	66.9	67.0
Some college or more	40.5	78.5	74.7	84.2	77.0	78.5	77.0	75.7	75.3
65 years and over:									
No high school diploma or GED	16.5	44.2	45.6	57.4	50.7	49.2	54.1	53.4	50.8
High school diploma or GED	25.9	57.4	59.1	71.8	64.3	65.7	62.5	66.5	60.0
Some college or more	32.3	64.8	64.3	74.1	73.0	75.6	70.9	73.6	69.8
Disability measure [8]									
40 years and over, crude:									
Any basic actions difficulty or complex activity limitation	- - -	- - -	- - -	67.8	63.5	63.9	63.3	63.5	62.2
Any basic actions difficulty	- - -	- - -	- - -	67.9	63.5	63.9	63.3	63.8	62.4
Any complex activity limitation	- - -	- - -	- - -	64.1	59.9	60.2	58.2	58.4	56.1
No disability	- - -	- - -	- - -	72.6	69.8	71.1	70.8	69.8	68.0

See footnotes at end of table.

Table 70 (page 3 of 3). Use of mammography among women aged 40 and over, by selected characteristics: United States, selected years 1987–2015

Excel and PDF versions (with more data years and standard errors when available): http://www.cdc.gov/nchs/hus/contents2016.htm#070.

[Data are based on household interviews of a sample of the civilian noninstitutionalized population]

---

* Estimates are considered unreliable. Data preceded by an asterisk have a relative standard error (RSE) of 20%–30%. Data not shown have an RSE greater than 30%.

- - - Data not available.

[1] Questions concerning use of mammography differed slightly on the National Health Interview Survey across survey years. See Appendix II, Mammography. Data prior to 1997 are not strictly comparable with data for later years due to the 1997 questionnaire redesign. See Appendix I, National Health Interview Survey (NHIS).

[2] Includes all other races not shown separately, unknown poverty level in 1987, unknown health insurance status, unknown education level, and unknown disability status.

[3] Estimates for women aged 40 and over are age-adjusted to the year 2000 standard population using four age groups: 40–49 years, 50–64 years, 65–74 years, and 75 years and over. Estimates for women 50 years of age and over are age-adjusted using three age groups. See Appendix II, Age adjustment.

[4] The race groups, white, black, American Indian or Alaska Native, Asian, Native Hawaiian or Other Pacific Islander, and 2 or more races, include persons of Hispanic and non-Hispanic origin. Persons of Hispanic origin may be of any race. Starting with 1999 data, race-specific estimates are tabulated according to the 1997 *Revisions to the Standards for the Classification of Federal Data on Race and Ethnicity* and are not strictly comparable with estimates for earlier years. The five single-race categories plus multiple-race categories shown in the table conform to the 1997 Standards. Starting with 1999 data, race-specific estimates are for persons who reported only one racial group; the category 2 or more races includes persons who reported more than one racial group. Prior to 1999, data were tabulated according to the 1977 Standards with four racial groups, and the Asian only category included Native Hawaiian or Other Pacific Islander. Estimates for single-race categories prior to 1999 included persons who reported one race or, if they reported more than one race, identified one race as best representing their race. Starting with 2003 data, race responses of other race and unspecified multiple race were treated as missing, and then race was imputed if these were the only race responses. Almost all persons with a race response of other race were of Hispanic origin. See Appendix II, Hispanic origin; Race.

[5] Percent of poverty level is based on family income and family size and composition using U.S. Census Bureau poverty thresholds. Poverty level was unknown for 11% of women aged 40 and over in 1987. Missing family income data were imputed for 1997 and beyond. See Appendix II, Family income; Poverty; Table VI.

[6] Health insurance categories are mutually exclusive. Persons who reported both Medicaid and private coverage are classified as having private coverage. Starting with 1997 data, state-sponsored health plan coverage is included as Medicaid coverage. Starting with 1999 data, coverage by the Children's Health Insurance Program (CHIP) is included with Medicaid coverage. In addition to private and Medicaid, the insured category also includes military plans, other government-sponsored health plans, and Medicare, not shown separately. Persons not covered by private insurance, Medicaid, CHIP, public assistance (through 1996), state-sponsored or other government-sponsored health plans (starting in 1997), Medicare, or military plans are considered to have no health insurance coverage. Persons with only Indian Health Service coverage are considered to have no health insurance coverage. See Appendix II, Health insurance coverage.

[7] Education categories shown are for 1998 and subsequent years. GED is General Educational Development high school equivalency diploma. In years prior to 1998, the following categories based on number of years of school completed were used: less than 12 years, 12 years, 13 years or more. See Appendix II, Education.

[8] Any basic actions difficulty or complex activity limitation is defined as having one or more of the following limitations or difficulties: movement difficulty, emotional difficulty, sensory (seeing or hearing) difficulty, cognitive difficulty, self-care (activities of daily living or instrumental activities of daily living) limitation, social limitation, or work limitation. For more information, see Appendix II, Basic actions difficulty; Complex activity limitation. Starting with 2007 data, the hearing question, a component of the basic actions difficulty measure, was revised. Consequently, data prior to 2007 are not comparable with 2007 data and beyond. For more information on the impact of the revised hearing question, see Appendix II, Hearing trouble.

NOTES: See Appendix II, Mammography, for a discussion of the U.S. Preventive Services Task Force recommendations for mammography screening. Standard errors are available in the spreadsheet version of this table. Available from: http://www.cdc.gov/nchs/hus.htm. Data starting in 1997 are not strictly comparable with data for earlier years due to the 1997 questionnaire redesign. See Appendix I, National Health Interview Survey (NHIS). Data for additional years are available. See the Excel spreadsheet on the *Health, United States* website at: http://www.cdc.gov/nchs/hus.htm.

SOURCE: NCHS, National Health Interview Survey. Data are from the following supplements: cancer control (1987), health promotion and disease prevention (1990–1991), year 2000 objectives (1993–1994), and prevention (1998). Starting from 1999, data are from either the cancer control module or the cancer screening supplement of the sample adult questionnaire, in addition to the family core questionnaire. See Appendix I, National Health Interview Survey (NHIS).

Table 71 (page 1 of 5). Use of Pap smears among women aged 18 and over, by selected characteristics: United States, selected years 1987–2015

Excel and PDF versions (with more data years and standard errors when available): http://www.cdc.gov/nchs/hus/contents2016.htm#071.

[Data are based on household interviews of a sample of the civilian noninstitutionalized population]

Characteristic	1987	1993	1999	2000	2005	2008	2010	2013	2015
	Percent of women having a Pap smear within the past 3 years [1]								
18 years and over, age-adjusted [2,3]	74.1	77.7	80.8	81.3	77.9	75.6	73.7	70.4	70.2
18 years and over, crude [2].	74.4	77.7	80.8	81.2	77.7	75.1	73.2	69.4	69.0
Age									
18–44 years	83.3	84.6	86.8	84.9	83.6	81.8	80.4	77.2	76.1
18–20 years.	59.4	66.8	65.3	59.8	61.1	57.5	52.0	38.6	34.0
21–44 years.	86.1	86.2	89.2	87.8	86.3	84.8	84.0	81.6	81.1
21–24 years	85.3	86.1	85.3	84.1	84.0	80.2	81.1	74.6	69.7
25–44 years	86.3	86.3	89.9	88.5	86.8	85.7	84.6	83.2	83.5
45–64 years	70.5	77.2	81.7	84.6	80.6	78.8	76.9	73.9	75.5
45–54 years.	75.7	82.1	83.8	86.3	83.4	81.0	79.9	78.6	79.7
55–64 years.	65.2	70.6	78.4	82.0	76.8	76.0	73.2	68.6	71.1
65 years and over	50.8	57.6	61.0	64.5	54.9	50.0	47.1	42.7	42.3
65–74 years.	57.9	64.7	70.0	71.6	66.3	61.6	58.0	54.5	52.9
75 years and over.	40.4	48.0	50.8	56.7	42.7	37.5	34.6	27.9	28.1
Race [4]									
18 years and over, crude:									
White only.	74.1	77.3	80.6	81.3	77.7	74.9	72.8	68.7	68.4
Black or African American only	80.7	82.7	85.7	85.1	81.1	80.1	77.9	75.3	74.6
American Indian or Alaska Native only . .	85.4	78.1	92.2	76.8	75.2	69.4	73.4	70.1	60.9
Asian only.	51.9	68.8	64.4	66.4	64.1	65.1	68.0	65.3	64.9
Native Hawaiian or Other Pacific									
Islander only.	- - -	- - -	*	*	*	*	*	*	*
2 or more races.	- - -	- - -	86.9	80.0	86.2	77.1	70.8	70.8	72.5
Hispanic origin and race [4]									
18 years and over, crude:									
Hispanic or Latina	67.6	77.2	76.3	77.0	75.5	75.4	73.6	70.5	68.6
Not Hispanic or Latina	74.9	77.8	81.3	81.7	78.0	75.1	73.1	69.2	69.0
White only	74.7	77.3	81.0	81.8	78.1	74.9	72.8	68.4	68.4
Black or African American only	80.9	82.7	86.0	85.1	81.2	80.0	77.4	75.1	74.6
Age, Hispanic origin, and race [4]									
18–44 years:									
Hispanic or Latina	73.9	80.9	77.0	78.1	76.5	77.9	75.9	72.3	70.2
Not Hispanic or Latina:									
White only	84.5	85.3	88.7	86.6	85.8	83.8	82.1	79.0	78.2
Black or African American only	89.1	88.0	90.8	88.5	86.4	83.5	84.2	82.8	82.1
45–64 years:									
Hispanic or Latina	57.7	75.8	79.5	77.8	78.4	78.2	75.4	74.4	74.0
Not Hispanic or Latina:									
White only	71.2	77.2	81.9	85.9	81.4	79.0	77.2	73.6	75.5
Black or African American only	76.2	80.3	84.6	85.7	80.5	82.1	78.2	76.0	77.4
65 years and over:									
Hispanic or Latina	41.7	57.1	63.7	66.8	60.0	52.6	54.2	49.4	46.2
Not Hispanic or Latina:									
White only	51.8	57.1	60.5	64.2	54.1	49.0	46.5	41.4	41.9
Black or African American only	44.8	61.2	64.5	67.2	60.1	58.7	48.0	45.8	43.5
Age and percent of poverty level [5]									
18 years and over, crude:									
Below 100%	64.3	70.3	73.6	72.0	68.7	68.9	65.1	60.6	63.2
100%–199%	68.2	71.2	72.5	73.4	69.0	65.0	64.3	59.8	60.3
200%–399%	77.6	80.6	80.6	80.2	77.9	72.5	71.3	68.5	66.6
400% or more	83.6	85.1	87.6	89.1	85.7	84.4	83.1	79.4	77.6
18–44 years:									
Below 100%	77.1	77.0	79.7	77.1	76.2	76.5	73.0	69.2	69.1
100%–199%	80.4	81.9	84.0	79.4	78.1	75.5	75.7	72.6	73.5
200%–399%	84.8	86.6	86.7	86.1	85.5	82.6	79.8	78.6	74.7
400% or more	88.9	91.3	91.1	89.8	88.7	87.0	88.9	84.5	83.2
45–64 years:									
Below 100%	53.6	66.5	73.1	73.6	65.9	66.2	61.7	54.9	63.7
100%–199%	60.4	64.8	70.4	76.1	69.6	65.6	63.2	61.2	64.2
200%–399%	71.0	79.5	79.9	80.0	79.3	75.3	75.2	73.7	73.5
400% or more	79.1	83.9	87.4	91.5	87.4	87.1	85.7	82.8	82.9
65 years and over:									
Below 100%	33.2	47.4	51.9	53.7	44.4	41.6	35.1	34.1	37.1
100%–199%	50.4	55.7	54.7	61.0	49.5	43.5	40.7	33.0	31.9
200%–399%	58.0	59.7	64.0	65.1	56.8	45.8	47.1	39.6	41.5
400% or more	65.2	67.5	70.4	75.4	64.6	65.7	57.7	58.1	52.3

See footnotes at end of table.

Table 71 (page 2 of 5). Use of Pap smears among women aged 18 and over, by selected characteristics: United States, selected years 1987–2015

Excel and PDF versions (with more data years and standard errors when available): http://www.cdc.gov/nchs/hus/contents2016.htm#071.

[Data are based on household interviews of a sample of the civilian noninstitutionalized population]

Characteristic	1987	1993	1999	2000	2005	2008	2010	2013	2015
Health insurance status at the time of interview [6]		Percent of women having a Pap smear within the past 3 years [1]							
18–64 years, crude:									
Insured	- - -	84.7	87.2	87.8	85.6	83.4	82.8	80.0	78.2
Private	- - -	84.8	87.5	88.0	86.5	84.2	84.2	81.3	79.6
Medicaid	- - -	82.7	84.2	85.8	80.9	80.3	78.0	75.7	72.6
Uninsured	- - -	69.4	73.3	70.4	67.7	67.1	61.9	57.6	57.3
Health insurance status prior to interview [6]									
18–64 years, crude:									
Insured continuously all 12 months.	- - -	84.8	87.3	88.0	85.8	83.7	83.2	80.4	78.5
Uninsured for any period up to 12 months .	- - -	81.8	83.5	83.7	81.3	78.9	78.3	72.3	72.0
Uninsured more than 12 months	- - -	65.1	68.8	65.1	62.0	62.1	55.2	52.7	51.0
Age and education [7]									
25 years and over, crude:									
No high school diploma or GED	57.1	61.9	66.1	69.9	64.1	60.6	56.7	56.2	55.9
High school diploma or GED	76.4	78.2	79.3	79.8	73.8	69.5	66.8	62.0	62.0
Some college or more	84.0	84.4	87.8	88.0	84.6	82.6	80.7	77.1	76.9
25–44 years:									
No high school diploma or GED	75.1	73.6	79.0	79.6	75.5	76.2	69.1	71.7	73.3
High school diploma or GED.	85.6	85.4	87.6	86.2	83.1	80.0	79.0	79.5	75.1
Some college or more	90.1	89.8	93.0	91.4	90.5	89.3	89.0	86.1	87.2
45–64 years:									
No high school diploma or GED	58.0	65.6	71.6	75.7	69.7	70.4	63.4	63.0	60.3
High school diploma or GED.	72.3	77.6	79.8	81.8	79.0	73.9	72.4	67.0	70.7
Some college or more	80.1	83.0	85.7	89.1	84.1	83.0	81.5	78.7	79.9
65 years and over:									
No high school diploma or GED	44.0	50.7	51.8	56.6	46.0	36.7	37.7	33.8	32.9
High school diploma or GED.	55.4	61.6	63.7	66.9	52.5	49.3	42.6	38.8	39.0
Some college or more	59.4	62.3	68.8	69.8	63.8	59.0	54.9	49.7	47.5
Disability measure [8]									
18 years and over, crude:									
Any basic actions difficulty or complex activity limitation.	- - -	- - -	74.4	75.4	69.1	66.1	63.8	59.3	59.9
Any basic actions difficulty.	- - -	- - -	74.3	75.1	69.1	66.2	63.6	59.2	59.9
Any complex activity limitation.	- - -	- - -	69.3	71.0	62.2	60.1	58.5	52.8	54.6
No disability.	- - -	- - -	83.8	84.1	82.6	80.4	78.9	75.2	74.5

See footnotes at end of table.

Table 71 (page 3 of 5). Use of Pap smears among women aged 18 and over, by selected characteristics: United States, selected years 1987–2015

Excel and PDF versions (with more data years and standard errors when available): http://www.cdc.gov/nchs/hus/contents2016.htm#071.

[Data are based on household interviews of a sample of the civilian noninstitutionalized population]

Characteristic	1987	1993	1999	2000	2005	2008	2010	2013	2015
	Percent of women having a Pap smear within the past 3 years, among those who have not had a hysterectomy [9]								
18 years and over, age-adjusted [2,3]	77.3	78.7	81.6	82.7	79.5	78.1	76.2	72.7	72.9
18 years and over, crude [2].	77.8	80.0	82.6	83.3	80.7	79.3	77.3	73.9	73.9
Age									
18–44 years	85.1	84.7	86.3	84.9	83.8	81.8	80.3	77.2	76.2
18–20 years	62.1	67.3	63.3	59.8	61.3	57.6	52.0	38.6	34.0
21–44 years	87.7	86.4	89.0	88.0	86.6	85.0	84.0	81.7	81.4
21–24 years	85.9	86.0	84.8	84.3	84.0	80.2	81.1	74.5	69.5
25–44 years	88.1	86.5	89.7	88.7	87.2	86.0	84.7	83.5	84.1
45–64 years	75.8	79.2	83.8	86.9	83.3	83.7	81.6	79.2	81.0
45–54 years	80.9	82.9	85.5	87.6	85.5	83.8	83.1	81.7	83.3
55–64 years	70.5	73.6	80.6	85.5	79.6	83.6	79.4	75.9	78.4
65 years and over	55.4	59.7	63.7	68.6	59.1	56.1	54.1	48.8	49.9
65–74 years	62.8	67.9	71.9	75.9	72.1	69.9	66.9	63.0	62.3
75 years and over	44.4	49.9	54.7	60.9	46.2	41.9	39.3	29.9	31.4
Race [4]									
18 years and over, crude:									
White only	77.8	79.9	82.8	83.7	81.1	79.6	77.4	73.8	73.9
Black or African American only	82.3	83.3	87.2	86.8	82.1	82.5	80.8	77.4	77.9
American Indian or Alaska Native only . .	85.9	78.2	94.1	77.7	75.6	74.8	78.9	74.3	65.5
Asian only	52.5	69.6	63.4	66.9	64.6	65.3	69.7	66.9	67.0
Native Hawaiian or Other Pacific Islander only	- - -	- - -	*	*	*	*	*	*	*
2 or more races	- - -	- - -	87.5	82.2	88.8	81.6	72.5	74.6	78.1
Hispanic origin and race [4]									
18 years and over, crude:									
Hispanic or Latina	69.8	77.3	75.1	78.0	75.9	77.3	74.7	71.6	70.3
Not Hispanic or Latina	78.5	80.2	83.5	84.0	81.4	79.6	77.8	74.3	74.6
White only	78.6	80.2	83.6	84.4	82.1	80.2	78.1	74.4	74.8
Black or African American only	82.4	83.4	87.5	86.8	82.3	82.4	80.4	77.2	77.9
Age, Hispanic origin, and race [4]									
18–44 years:									
Hispanic or Latina	75.1	80.2	76.0	77.9	76.5	78.3	75.6	72.0	69.9
Not Hispanic or Latina:									
White only	86.5	85.7	88.3	86.6	86.2	83.9	82.1	79.3	78.6
Black or African American only	90.3	87.6	90.6	88.7	86.1	83.3	84.0	82.5	81.9
45–64 years:									
Hispanic or Latina	62.4	75.3	77.8	81.0	78.6	81.0	77.7	77.3	77.6
Not Hispanic or Latina:									
White only	77.0	79.3	84.7	88.5	85.0	84.7	82.7	80.0	81.9
Black or African American only	78.0	81.1	86.6	87.4	80.7	85.6	81.7	77.6	81.6
65 years and over:									
Hispanic or Latina	43.8	58.9	60.9	71.2	60.0	53.7	56.4	49.4	51.1
Not Hispanic or Latina:									
White only	56.8	60.0	63.8	68.0	59.2	56.2	54.4	48.7	50.3
Black or African American only	46.3	55.8	65.1	72.1	59.3	64.1	52.7	45.6	46.2
Age and percent of poverty level [5]									
18 years and over, crude:									
Below 100%	67.5	71.7	74.8	73.8	70.3	72.3	67.6	62.7	66.1
100%–199%	71.6	73.7	75.2	75.7	72.6	69.6	69.3	64.7	66.2
200%–399%	81.0	83.0	82.5	83.0	81.4	77.3	76.0	73.9	71.6
400% or more	87.0	87.8	88.9	90.5	88.2	87.8	87.1	84.0	82.5
18–44 years:									
Below 100%	79.3	77.2	79.0	76.8	76.1	76.6	73.0	69.3	69.3
100%–199%	81.8	82.1	83.7	79.2	78.1	75.4	75.6	72.3	73.6
200%–399%	86.6	86.5	86.2	86.0	86.1	82.4	79.7	78.4	74.8
400% or more	90.2	91.9	90.6	90.0	88.8	87.3	88.9	84.7	83.4
45–64 years:									
Below 100%	58.0	65.8	74.7	75.6	64.8	70.7	63.7	54.9	67.8
100%–199%	66.1	64.2	72.2	78.2	71.3	70.0	67.8	65.6	70.0
200%–399%	76.9	82.2	81.2	81.7	81.7	79.5	79.5	81.0	79.6
400% or more	84.4	86.6	89.7	93.7	90.9	92.4	90.8	88.0	88.0
65 years and over:									
Below 100%	36.4	47.5	53.5	55.9	43.7	44.7	36.5	36.8	41.5
100%–199%	54.6	56.6	56.3	63.3	54.4	48.7	48.1	37.7	37.1
200%–399%	62.8	63.5	68.3	71.8	61.4	53.3	56.1	43.8	48.1
400% or more	73.0	71.7	72.9	78.6	70.1	70.9	63.7	67.6	62.4

See footnotes at end of table.

Table 71 (page 4 of 5). Use of Pap smears among women aged 18 and over, by selected characteristics: United States, selected years 1987–2015

Excel and PDF versions (with more data years and standard errors when available): http://www.cdc.gov/nchs/hus/contents2016.htm#071.

[Data are based on household interviews of a sample of the civilian noninstitutionalized population]

Characteristic	1987	1993	1999	2000	2005	2008	2010	2013	2015
Health insurance status at the time of interview [6]	Percent of women having a Pap smear within the past 3 years, among those who have not had a hysterectomy [9]								
18–64 years, crude:									
Insured	- - -	85.9	87.8	88.7	87.1	85.8	85.1	82.3	80.5
Private	- - -	86.0	88.1	88.8	87.9	86.6	86.2	83.5	81.8
Medicaid	- - -	83.9	84.2	86.9	82.6	82.4	79.7	77.6	74.8
Uninsured	- - -	70.2	74.3	70.8	68.0	67.9	63.1	59.6	59.3
Health insurance status prior to interview [6]									
18–64 years, crude:									
Insured continuously all 12 months	- - -	86.1	88.0	88.9	87.2	86.1	85.4	82.9	80.9
Uninsured for any period up to 12 months	- - -	81.7	84.4	84.4	82.7	80.9	79.7	74.5	73.9
Uninsured more than 12 months	- - -	66.5	69.9	65.5	62.7	62.4	56.6	54.6	52.8
Age and education [7]									
25 years and over, crude:									
No high school diploma or GED	61.7	63.2	68.3	72.5	66.9	67.5	61.0	60.2	61.7
High school diploma or GED	80.0	80.2	81.2	82.7	77.1	73.6	71.5	68.3	67.9
Some college or more	86.7	86.7	89.9	90.1	88.2	86.8	85.3	82.3	82.9
25–44 years:									
No high school diploma or GED	77.3	73.1	78.4	78.6	74.7	76.5	69.0	71.6	73.8
High school diploma or GED	87.6	85.6	87.4	86.2	83.4	79.5	78.8	79.6	75.5
Some college or more	91.5	90.0	92.9	91.7	91.1	89.7	89.2	86.5	87.8
45–64 years:									
No high school diploma or GED	63.9	65.5	73.2	77.5	70.5	74.8	66.8	65.7	65.3
High school diploma or GED	77.0	78.8	81.6	84.1	80.1	77.9	75.8	71.4	76.1
Some college or more	85.5	86.2	87.7	91.0	87.9	87.9	86.4	84.5	85.4
65 years and over:									
No high school diploma or GED	48.4	51.3	52.7	59.7	49.2	43.0	40.6	34.5	36.9
High school diploma or GED	60.4	63.8	65.0	71.3	56.5	53.6	48.7	45.3	43.4
Some college or more	63.6	65.7	75.6	74.9	69.9	66.1	64.0	57.6	58.2
Disability measure [8]									
18 years and over, crude:									
Any basic actions difficulty or complex activity limitation	- - -	- - -	77.8	78.6	73.7	73.4	70.6	66.1	67.1
Any basic actions difficulty	- - -	- - -	77.8	78.5	73.9	73.8	70.6	66.2	67.4
Any complex activity limitation	- - -	- - -	73.9	73.9	67.4	68.1	65.9	59.1	61.4
No disability	- - -	- - -	84.5	85.1	84.0	82.1	80.8	77.4	77.2

See footnotes at end of table.

Table 71 (page 5 of 5). Use of Pap smears among women aged 18 and over, by selected characteristics: United States, selected years 1987–2015

Excel and PDF versions (with more data years and standard errors when available): http://www.cdc.gov/nchs/hus/contents2016.htm#071.

[Data are based on household interviews of a sample of the civilian noninstitutionalized population]

- - - Data not available.

* Estimates are considered unreliable. Data not shown have a relative standard error greater than 30%.

[1] Includes all women aged 18 and over who had a Pap smear (Pap test) within the past 3 years, including women who reported having had a hysterectomy. Questions concerning use of Pap smears differed slightly on the National Health Interview Survey across survey years. See Appendix II, Pap smear. Data prior to 1997 are not strictly comparable with data for later years due to the 1997 questionnaire redesign. See Appendix I, National Health Interview Survey (NHIS).

[2] Includes all other races not shown separately, unknown poverty level in 1987, unknown health insurance status, unknown education level, and unknown disability status.

[3] Estimates are age-adjusted to the year 2000 standard population using five age groups: 18–44 years, 45–54 years, 55–64 years, 65–74 years, and 75 years and over. Age-adjusted estimates in this table may differ from other age-adjusted estimates based on the same data and presented elsewhere if different age groups are used in the adjustment procedure. See Appendix II, Age adjustment.

[4] The race groups, white, black, American Indian or Alaska Native, Asian, Native Hawaiian or Other Pacific Islander, and 2 or more races, include persons of Hispanic and non-Hispanic origin. Persons of Hispanic origin may be of any race. Starting with 1999 data, race-specific estimates are tabulated according to the 1997 *Revisions to the Standards for the Classification of Federal Data on Race and Ethnicity* and are not strictly comparable with estimates for earlier years. The five single-race categories plus multiple-race categories shown in the table conform to the 1997 Standards. Starting with 1999 data, race-specific estimates are for persons who reported only one racial group; the category 2 or more races includes persons who reported more than one racial group. Prior to 1999, data were tabulated according to the 1977 Standards with four racial groups, and the Asian only category included Native Hawaiian or Other Pacific Islander. Estimates for single-race categories prior to 1999 included persons who reported one race or, if they reported more than one race, identified one race as best representing their race. Starting with 2003 data, race responses of other race and unspecified multiple race were treated as missing, and then race was imputed if these were the only race responses. Almost all persons with a race response of other race were of Hispanic origin. See Appendix II, Hispanic origin; Race.

[5] Percent of poverty level is based on family income and family size and composition using U.S. Census Bureau poverty thresholds. Poverty level was unknown for 9% of women aged 18 and over in 1987. Missing family income data were imputed for 1993 and beyond. See Appendix II, Family income; Poverty; Table VI.

[6] Health insurance categories are mutually exclusive. Persons who reported both Medicaid and private coverage are classified as having private coverage. Starting with 1997 data, state-sponsored health plan coverage is included as Medicaid coverage. Starting with 1999 data, coverage by the Children's Health Insurance Program (CHIP) is included with Medicaid coverage. In addition to private and Medicaid, the insured category also includes military plans, other government-sponsored health plans, and Medicare, not shown separately. Persons not covered by private insurance, Medicaid, CHIP, public assistance (through 1996), state-sponsored or other government-sponsored health plans (starting in 1997), Medicare, or military plans are considered to have no health insurance coverage. Persons with only Indian Health Service coverage are considered to have no health insurance coverage. See Appendix II, Health insurance coverage.

[7] Education categories shown are for 1998 and subsequent years. GED is General Educational Development high school equivalency diploma. In years prior to 1998, the following categories based on number of years of school completed were used: less than 12 years, 12 years, 13 years or more. See Appendix II, Education.

[8] Any basic actions difficulty or complex activity limitation is defined as having one or more of the following limitations or difficulties: movement difficulty, emotional difficulty, sensory (seeing or hearing) difficulty, cognitive difficulty, self-care (activities of daily living or instrumental activities of daily living) limitation, social limitation, or work limitation. For more information, see Appendix II, Basic actions difficulty; Complex activity limitation. Starting with 2007 data, the hearing question, a component of the basic actions difficulty measure, was revised. Consequently, data prior to 2007 are not comparable with data for 2007 and beyond. For more information on the impact of the revised hearing question, see Appendix II, Hearing trouble.

[9] The U.S. Preventive Services Task Force recommends against routine Pap smear screening for women who have had a total hysterectomy for benign disease. Therefore, Pap smear screening estimates are presented in two ways: among all women and among women who have not had a hysterectomy. Note that it is not possible to determine whether the hysterectomy was for a benign disease using the National Health Interview Survey (NHIS) data. Questions concerning hysterectomy differed slightly on NHIS across survey years. See Appendix II, Pap smear.

NOTES: Currently, the U.S. Preventive Services Task Force (USPSTF) recommends Pap smears every three years for women aged 21 to 65, although the USPSTF recommendations have changed over time. See Appendix II, Pap smear. Standard errors are available in the spreadsheet version of this table. Available from: http://www.cdc.gov/nchs/hus.htm. Data for additional years are available. See the Excel spreadsheet on the *Health, United States* website at: http://www.cdc.gov/nchs/hus.htm.

SOURCE: NCHS, National Health Interview Survey. Data are from the following supplements: cancer control (1987), year 2000 objectives (1993–1994), and prevention (1998). Starting in 1999, data are either from the cancer control module or the cancer screening supplement of the sample adult questionnaire, in addition to the family core questionnaire. See Appendix I, National Health Interview Survey (NHIS).

Table 72 (page 1 of 2). Use of colorectal tests or procedures among adults aged 50–75, by selected characteristics: United States, selected years 2000–2015

Excel and PDF versions (with more data years and standard errors when available): http://www.cdc.gov/nchs/hus/contents2016.htm#072.

[Data are based on household interviews of a sample of the civilian noninstitutionalized population]

Characteristic	Any colorectal test or procedure [1,2]					Colonoscopy [2,3]				
	2000	2005	2010	2013	2015	2000	2005	2010	2013	2015
	Percent of adults aged 50–75									
All adults 50–75 years [4]	33.9	44.3	58.7	57.8	62.4	19.1	37.6	54.9	54.5	59.2
Sex										
Male	33.1	44.4	58.5	56.7	61.6	19.5	37.9	54.7	53.4	58.4
Female.	34.5	44.2	58.8	58.9	63.1	18.8	37.4	55.1	55.5	60.0
Race [5]										
White only	34.9	45.6	59.8	58.4	63.7	19.7	38.9	56.0	55.3	60.7
Black or African American only	29.6	38.1	55.2	58.0	59.6	17.4	32.2	51.8	54.1	56.3
American Indian or Alaska Native only	*35.2	*33.9	48.9	49.3	48.9	*	*	46.7	45.8	45.3
Asian only	20.4	30.8	47.1	49.8	52.3	*8.6	24.4	43.6	43.7	45.8
Native Hawaiian or Other Pacific Islander only	*	*	*	*	*	*	*	*	*	*
2 or more races	37.5	33.8	51.9	50.5	52.7	*25.1	29.6	48.4	48.4	49.8
Hispanic origin and race [5]										
Hispanic or Latino	21.7	28.5	46.5	41.5	47.4	13.3	23.1	43.9	37.5	44.0
Mexican.	19.3	24.6	44.6	39.2	41.2	11.2	18.2	41.3	35.2	37.6
Not Hispanic or Latino.	34.7	45.6	59.9	59.6	64.1	19.5	38.9	56.0	56.3	61.0
White only.	35.7	47.4	61.3	60.4	65.6	20.0	40.5	57.3	57.4	62.8
Black or African American only	29.7	38.0	55.3	58.2	60.3	17.5	32.0	52.0	54.6	56.9
Percent of poverty level [6]										
Below 100%.	26.5	28.7	37.9	43.7	45.6	16.3	23.6	34.8	40.5	42.8
100%–199%.	29.4	38.4	47.9	48.4	51.8	17.7	31.5	43.3	44.8	48.0
200%–399%.	33.7	43.6	58.0	55.8	61.3	18.6	37.0	54.6	52.0	58.6
400% or more	37.1	49.6	67.3	65.6	70.0	20.5	42.8	63.6	62.7	66.8
Hispanic origin and race and percent of poverty level [5,6]										
Hispanic or Latino:										
Below 100%	15.3	19.3	33.7	35.7	40.4	*9.3	13.1	32.1	32.0	37.0
100%–199%	16.8	24.6	39.6	35.1	37.7	8.6	19.4	36.3	31.2	34.0
200%–399%	23.6	28.3	47.5	41.5	48.9	*13.7	21.6	46.0	37.3	45.0
400% or more	31.1	42.1	63.3	53.0	61.5	22.4	39.3	59.5	48.8	58.7
Not Hispanic or Latino:										
White only:										
Below 100%	29.6	30.6	40.4	46.8	46.1	19.3	26.8	36.4	44.0	43.7
100%–199%	32.1	42.4	50.0	51.9	55.1	19.7	35.0	44.5	48.3	51.6
200%–399%	35.2	47.3	59.7	57.6	64.3	19.3	40.2	56.3	54.0	62.1
400% or more	37.9	50.6	68.0	66.2	71.3	20.7	43.8	64.3	63.6	68.3
Black or African American only:										
Below 100%	27.5	29.0	39.2	45.5	49.1	14.5	23.5	36.4	41.2	44.8
100%–199%	28.7	36.2	49.0	51.4	56.2	17.2	30.3	46.5	47.3	51.8
200%–399%	27.7	35.8	60.5	61.3	60.2	16.5	31.8	56.2	57.9	58.2
400% or more	33.9	48.9	68.1	70.5	71.9	20.7	40.2	64.6	67.5	68.5
Education [7]										
No high school diploma or GED.	25.9	34.5	44.6	43.5	46.6	14.9	29.0	41.5	39.9	43.7
High school diploma or GED	33.1	42.1	53.7	53.4	58.2	19.0	35.7	50.8	50.4	55.2
Some college or more.	37.8	48.7	64.7	63.1	67.2	20.9	41.6	60.4	59.6	63.9

See footnotes at end of table.

Table 72 (page 2 of 2). Use of colorectal tests or procedures among adults aged 50–75, by selected characteristics: United States, selected years 2000–2015

Excel and PDF versions (with more data years and standard errors when available): http://www.cdc.gov/nchs/hus/contents2016.htm#072.

[Data are based on household interviews of a sample of the civilian noninstitutionalized population]

Characteristic	Any colorectal test or procedure [1,2]					Colonoscopy [2,3]				
	2000	2005	2010	2013	2015	2000	2005	2010	2013	2015
Disability measure [8]	Percent of adults aged 50–75									
Any basic actions difficulty or complex activity limitation	37.8	47.7	59.5	61.0	64.9	22.1	40.1	55.5	57.6	61.8
Any basic actions difficulty	38.1	47.9	59.7	61.5	65.1	22.5	40.6	55.8	58.0	62.0
Any complex activity limitation	37.4	48.1	59.4	59.9	62.9	22.6	39.7	55.1	55.7	59.5
No disability	30.9	41.6	58.5	55.5	60.7	16.6	35.6	54.9	52.2	57.5
Geographic region										
Northeast	34.4	50.9	64.3	61.0	66.4	19.1	44.8	61.7	59.4	64.5
Midwest	35.2	43.5	58.4	59.5	63.1	19.8	36.6	55.2	57.3	61.7
South	32.5	43.9	57.4	56.4	60.4	20.0	38.1	54.4	53.8	57.8
West	34.1	39.6	56.3	55.9	61.8	16.3	31.3	49.7	48.7	54.9
Location of residence [9]										
Within MSA	34.1	44.7	59.6	58.3	63.2	19.0	37.9	55.8	54.8	59.8
Outside MSA	33.2	42.7	54.4	55.6	58.5	19.6	36.7	50.9	52.8	56.5

* Estimates are considered unreliable. Data preceded by an asterisk have a relative standard error (RSE) of 20%–30%. Data not shown have an RSE greater than 30%.

[1] Includes reports of home fecal occult blood test (FOBT) in the past year, sigmoidoscopy procedure in the past 5 years with FOBT in the past 3 years, or colonoscopy in the past 10 years. Colorectal procedures are performed for diagnostic and screening purposes.

[2] Questions differed slightly on the National Health Interview Survey across survey years. See Appendix II, Colorectal tests or procedures.

[3] Includes any colonoscopy in the past 10 years, alone or in addition to another type of colorectal test or procedure.

[4] Includes all other races not shown separately, unknown disability status, and unknown education level.

[5] The race groups, white, black, American Indian or Alaska Native, Asian, Native Hawaiian or Other Pacific Islander, and 2 or more races include persons of Hispanic and non-Hispanic origin. Persons of Hispanic origin may be of any race. The five single-race and multiple-race categories shown in the table conform to the 1997 *Revisions to the Standards for the Classification of Federal Data on Race and Ethnicity.* Starting with 2003 data, race responses of other race and unspecified multiple race were treated as missing, and then race was imputed if these were the only race responses. Almost all persons with a race response of other race were of Hispanic origin. See Appendix II, Hispanic origin; Race.

[6] Based on family income and family size and composition using U.S. Census Bureau poverty thresholds. Missing family income data were imputed. See Appendix II, Family income; Poverty; Table VI.

[7] GED is General Educational Development high school equivalency diploma. See Appendix II, Education.

[8] Any basic actions difficulty or complex activity limitation is defined as having one or more of the following limitations or difficulties: movement difficulty, emotional difficulty, sensory (seeing or hearing) difficulty, cognitive difficulty, self-care (activities of daily living or instrumental activities of daily living) limitation, social limitation, or work limitation. For more information, see Appendix II, Basic actions difficulty; Complex activity limitation. Starting with 2007 data, the hearing question, a component of the basic actions difficulty measure, was revised. Consequently, data prior to 2007 are not comparable with data for 2007 and beyond. For more information on the impact of the revised hearing question, see Appendix II, Hearing trouble.

[9] MSA is metropolitan statistical area. Starting with 2006 data, MSA status is determined using 2000 census data and the 2000 standards for defining MSAs. For data prior to 2006, see Appendix II, Metropolitan statistical area (MSA) for the applicable standards.

NOTES: In 2008, the U.S. Preventive Services Task Force (USPSTF) recommended screening for colorectal cancer annually using FOBT, every 5 years using sigmoidoscopy with FOBT every 3 years, or every 10 years using colonoscopy in adults, beginning at age 50 and continuing until age 75. The USPSTF recommendations were updated in 2016 to include additional screening methods but did not emphasize one method over another, as the risk and benefits vary from method to method. For more information, see: http://www.uspreventiveservicestaskforce.org/Page/Document/RecommendationStatementFinal/colorectal-cancer-screening2. Colonoscopy estimates are shown separately in the table because of the recent large increase in its utilization. The 2009 Colorectal Cancer Screening Guidelines from the American College of Gastroenterology recommended that African American persons start routine testing for colorectal cancer at age 45. See: http://www.acg.gi.org/patients/ccrk/ for more information. Standard errors for selected years are available in the spreadsheet version of this table. Available from: http://www.cdc.gov/nchs/hus.htm. Data for additional years are available. See the Excel spreadsheet on the *Health, United States* website at: http://www.cdc.gov/nchs/hus.htm.

SOURCE: NCHS, National Health Interview Survey. Data are from either the cancer control module or the cancer screening supplement of the sample adult questionnaire, in addition to the family core questionnaire. See Appendix I, National Health Interview Survey (NHIS).

Table 73 (page 1 of 4). Emergency department visits within the past 12 months among children under age 18, by selected characteristics: United States, selected years 1997–2015

Excel and PDF versions (with more data years and standard errors when available): http://www.cdc.gov/nchs/hus/contents2016.htm#073.

[Data are based on household interviews of a sample of the civilian noninstitutionalized population]

Characteristic	Under 18 years			Under 6 years			6–17 years		
	1997	2010	2015	1997	2010	2015	1997	2010	2015
	Percent of children with one or more emergency department visits [1]								
All children [2]	19.9	22.1	16.9	24.3	27.8	21.7	17.7	19.1	14.5
Sex									
Male	21.5	23.3	17.3	25.2	29.3	23.0	19.6	20.1	14.6
Female.	18.3	20.9	16.3	23.3	26.3	20.4	15.7	18.2	14.4
Race [3]									
White only	19.4	21.2	16.3	22.6	26.6	20.9	17.8	18.4	14.1
Black or African American only	24.0	27.6	21.6	33.1	34.0	27.4	19.4	24.2	18.8
American Indian or Alaska Native only	*24.1	20.9	23.3	*24.3	*35.4	*37.2	*24.0	*	*17.5
Asian only	12.6	15.0	9.2	20.8	18.4	13.9	8.6	13.3	*7.0
Native Hawaiian or Other Pacific Islander only	- - -	*	*	- - -	*	*	- - -	*	*
2 or more races	- - -	27.2	18.6	- - -	34.9	23.1	- - -	21.6	*15.8
Hispanic origin and race [3]									
Hispanic or Latino	21.1	23.6	18.8	25.7	30.2	25.9	18.1	19.4	15.2
Not Hispanic or Latino.	19.7	21.7	16.2	24.0	27.0	20.3	17.6	19.0	14.3
White only.	19.2	20.4	15.4	22.2	25.1	18.8	17.7	18.2	13.8
Black or African American only	23.6	27.2	21.3	32.7	34.4	27.2	19.2	23.3	18.4
Percent of poverty level [4]									
Below 100%.	25.1	30.6	23.1	29.5	35.4	28.8	22.2	27.6	19.9
100%–199%.	22.0	25.7	18.7	28.0	31.6	24.0	19.0	22.3	16.2
200%–399%.	18.0	18.4	14.7	21.4	22.7	20.8	16.4	16.4	11.8
400% or more	16.3	15.9	12.9	19.1	21.7	14.7	15.1	13.3	12.0
Hispanic origin and race and percent of poverty level [3,4]									
Hispanic or Latino:									
Percent of poverty level:									
Below 100%	21.9	27.0	21.7	25.0	32.0	27.9	19.6	23.4	18.2
100%–199%	20.8	23.3	18.1	28.8	31.6	24.9	15.6	18.0	15.3
200%–399%	21.4	19.5	17.0	24.6	25.2	28.2	19.6	16.1	11.0
400% or more	17.7	21.4	16.0	*20.2	28.6	*18.0	16.4	18.0	14.9
Not Hispanic or Latino:									
White only:									
Percent of poverty level:									
Below 100%.	25.5	33.7	24.7	27.2	37.4	26.8	24.4	31.6	23.6
100%–199%	22.3	26.3	17.8	25.8	29.2	21.5	20.7	24.7	15.9
200%–399%	17.8	17.6	13.9	20.9	21.2	18.3	16.3	15.9	11.8
400% or more	16.5	15.5	12.7	19.0	21.0	15.0	15.4	13.2	11.7
Black or African American only:									
Percent of poverty level:									
Below 100%.	29.3	32.4	23.7	39.5	41.6	30.8	23.0	26.6	20.1
100%–199%	22.5	27.5	23.5	31.7	34.5	29.3	18.5	23.7	20.6
200%–399%	18.5	22.3	17.4	23.9	24.6	*27.1	16.3	21.4	13.8
400% or more	16.1	18.9	16.3	*18.8	*24.1	*	15.2	16.1	*18.0
Health insurance status at the time of interview [5]									
Insured.	19.8	22.3	16.9	24.4	28.1	21.7	17.5	19.2	14.6
Private	17.5	17.1	12.5	20.9	21.8	16.7	15.9	14.9	10.6
Medicaid	28.2	30.0	22.8	33.0	35.5	27.3	24.1	26.4	20.4
Uninsured	20.2	19.4	14.3	23.0	24.0	*19.4	18.9	17.6	12.7
Health insurance status prior to interview [5]									
Insured continuously all 12 months	19.6	22.2	16.8	24.1	28.1	21.4	17.3	19.1	14.6
Uninsured for any period up to 12 months . . .	24.0	23.7	20.7	27.1	28.0	29.2	21.9	21.3	16.6
Uninsured more than 12 months	18.4	17.6	*10.4	19.3	*21.3	*	18.1	16.7	*9.8

See footnotes at end of table.

Table 73 (page 2 of 4). Emergency department visits within the past 12 months among children under age 18, by selected characteristics: United States, selected years 1997–2015

Excel and PDF versions (with more data years and standard errors when available): http://www.cdc.gov/nchs/hus/contents2016.htm#073.

[Data are based on household interviews of a sample of the civilian noninstitutionalized population]

Characteristic	Under 18 years			Under 6 years			6–17 years		
	1997	2010	2015	1997	2010	2015	1997	2010	2015
Percent of poverty level and health insurance status prior to interview [4,5]	Percent of children with one or more emergency department visits [1]								
Below 100%:									
Insured continuously all 12 months.	26.3	31.7	23.6	30.9	36.3	29.6	22.8	28.7	20.1
Uninsured for any period up to 12 months . .	26.5	30.3	23.8	29.7	34.7	*	24.4	27.5	*24.7
Uninsured more than 12 months	17.5	*19.6	*	*16.0	*	*	18.0	*16.0	*
100%–199%:									
Insured continuously all 12 months.	21.8	26.2	18.5	28.0	32.4	23.4	18.6	22.4	16.1
Uninsured for any period up to 12 months . .	24.5	28.4	23.2	29.7	30.9	*34.5	21.0	27.0	*17.8
Uninsured more than 12 months	19.5	17.6	*	*22.5	*	*	18.6	*17.2	*
200%–399%:									
Insured continuously all 12 months.	17.7	18.4	14.7	21.2	22.8	20.1	16.1	16.3	12.1
Uninsured for any period up to 12 months . .	21.1	16.2	15.5	*19.5	*22.7	*25.9	22.1	*12.6	*10.6
Uninsured more than 12 months	19.2	*17.4	*	*22.7	*	*	17.6	*18.7	*
400% or more:									
Insured continuously all 12 months.	16.2	16.1	12.8	18.9	22.0	14.3	15.1	13.5	12.0
Uninsured for any period up to 12 months . .	*19.2	*	*	*	*	*	*	*	*
Uninsured more than 12 months	*	*	*	*	*	*	*	*	*
Geographic region									
Northeast	18.5	22.3	16.5	20.7	27.8	22.4	17.4	19.6	13.7
Midwest	19.5	23.3	19.1	26.0	28.8	23.5	16.4	20.7	17.1
South	21.8	23.4	17.6	25.6	30.4	23.5	19.9	19.5	14.9
West	18.5	19.1	13.7	23.5	23.3	17.2	15.9	16.8	11.9
Location of residence [6]									
Within MSA	19.7	21.8	16.4	23.9	27.7	21.1	17.4	18.6	14.0
Outside MSA	20.8	24.2	20.0	26.2	28.6	25.6	18.6	22.1	17.3
	Percent of children with two or more emergency department visits [1]								
All children [2]	7.1	8.4	5.3	9.6	10.8	7.0	5.8	7.2	4.5
Sex									
Male	7.3	8.5	5.4	9.9	11.3	7.4	6.0	7.0	4.4
Female.	6.9	8.3	5.3	9.4	10.3	6.5	5.7	7.3	4.7
Race [3]									
White only	6.6	7.6	4.9	8.4	10.1	6.0	5.7	6.3	4.3
Black or African American only	9.6	12.6	7.6	14.9	15.7	10.0	6.9	11.0	6.3
American Indian or Alaska Native only	*	*	*13.5	*	*	*	*	*	*
Asian only	*5.7	7.3	*2.6	*12.9	*	*	*	*7.1	*
Native Hawaiian or Other Pacific Islander only	- - -	*	*	- - -	*	*	- - -	*	*
2 or more races	- - -	10.3	6.7	- - -	*11.7	*10.2	- - -	*9.2	*
Hispanic origin and race [3]									
Hispanic or Latino	8.9	8.6	6.2	11.8	11.7	8.6	7.0	6.6	5.0
Not Hispanic or Latino.	6.8	8.4	5.0	9.2	10.5	6.4	5.7	7.3	4.3
White only.	6.2	7.4	4.4	7.8	9.3	5.1	5.5	6.4	4.1
Black or African American only.	9.3	12.3	7.4	14.6	15.8	9.8	6.8	10.4	6.2
Percent of poverty level [4]									
Below 100%.	11.1	13.4	8.9	14.5	15.3	11.8	8.9	12.1	7.4
100%–199%.	8.3	10.3	7.2	12.2	13.4	9.7	6.3	8.4	6.0
200%–399%.	6.2	6.3	3.4	7.4	7.3	4.1	5.6	5.9	3.0
400% or more	4.0	5.0	3.0	5.0	7.3	*3.5	3.6	3.9	2.7

See footnotes at end of table.

Table 73 (page 3 of 4). Emergency department visits within the past 12 months among children under age 18, by selected characteristics: United States, selected years 1997–2015

Excel and PDF versions (with more data years and standard errors when available): http://www.cdc.gov/nchs/hus/contents2016.htm#073.

[Data are based on household interviews of a sample of the civilian noninstitutionalized population]

Characteristic	Under 18 years			Under 6 years			6–17 years		
	1997	2010	2015	1997	2010	2015	1997	2010	2015
Hispanic origin and race and percent of poverty level [3,4]	Percent of children with two or more emergency department visits [1]								
Hispanic or Latino:									
Percent of poverty level:									
Below 100%	10.4	9.9	7.0	13.9	10.9	*9.1	8.0	9.2	5.9
100%–199%	8.2	9.4	7.3	12.0	15.4	11.7	5.7	5.5	5.5
200%–399%	8.5	5.9	*4.0	10.0	*8.0	*5.7	*7.6	*4.6	*3.1
400% or more	*5.0	*6.5	*5.6	*	*	*	*	*5.2	*
Not Hispanic or Latino:									
White only:									
Percent of poverty level:									
Below 100%	10.7	14.0	9.6	12.2	15.5	*10.1	9.8	13.1	*9.4
100%–199%	8.0	10.4	7.7	11.2	12.3	*8.6	6.4	9.4	7.3
200%–399%	6.0	5.7	2.9	6.7	*6.5	*2.8	5.6	5.4	*3.0
400% or more	3.7	5.0	2.6	4.6	7.6	*3.5	3.3	3.9	*2.2
Black or African American only:									
Percent of poverty level:									
Below 100%	12.7	16.1	9.9	19.1	22.1	14.5	8.8	12.4	*7.5
100%–199%	9.2	12.4	6.9	*13.5	*14.6	*	*7.2	11.1	*6.5
200%–399%	5.8	9.9	*5.6	*8.9	*10.2	*	*4.5	*9.8	*
400% or more	*	*3.7	*	*	*	*	*	*	*
Health insurance status at the time of interview [5]									
Insured	7.0	8.5	5.4	9.6	11.0	7.1	5.7	7.1	4.6
Private	5.2	5.5	3.0	6.8	7.4	3.5	4.5	4.6	2.8
Medicaid	13.1	12.8	8.8	16.2	15.3	11.5	10.4	11.2	7.4
Uninsured	7.7	8.0	*3.5	9.8	*8.5	*	6.8	7.8	*3.5
Health insurance status prior to interview [5]									
Insured continuously all 12 months	6.9	8.4	5.3	9.4	10.8	6.9	5.7	7.1	4.5
Uninsured for any period up to 12 months	8.5	10.1	7.8	11.5	13.3	*10.1	6.6	8.4	*6.7
Uninsured more than 12 months	6.8	7.8	*	*8.6	*	*	6.2	*7.9	*
Geographic region									
Northeast	6.2	7.8	4.6	7.6	10.3	7.5	5.4	6.6	3.2
Midwest	6.6	9.1	5.7	10.4	11.4	6.5	4.8	8.0	5.3
South	8.0	9.1	5.9	10.1	12.9	7.6	6.9	7.1	5.1
West	7.1	7.2	4.5	10.0	7.6	6.2	5.6	7.0	3.6
Location of residence [6]									
Within MSA	7.2	8.3	5.0	9.6	10.6	6.6	5.9	7.0	4.2
Outside MSA	6.8	9.3	7.2	9.7	12.2	9.5	5.6	7.9	6.2

See footnotes at end of table.

Table 73 (page 4 of 4). Emergency department visits within the past 12 months among children under age 18, by selected characteristics: United States, selected years 1997–2015

Excel and PDF versions (with more data years and standard errors when available): http://www.cdc.gov/nchs/hus/contents2016.htm#073.

[Data are based on household interviews of a sample of the civilian noninstitutionalized population]

---

* Estimates are considered unreliable. Data preceded by an asterisk have a relative standard error (RSE) of 20%–30%. Data not shown have an RSE greater than 30%.

- - - Data not available.

[1] See Appendix II, Emergency department or emergency room visit.

[2] Includes all other races not shown separately and unknown health insurance status.

[3] The race groups, white, black, American Indian or Alaska Native, Asian, Native Hawaiian or Other Pacific Islander, and 2 or more races, include persons of Hispanic and non-Hispanic origin. Persons of Hispanic origin may be of any race. Starting with 1999 data, race-specific estimates are tabulated according to the 1997 *Revisions to the Standards for the Classification of Federal Data on Race and Ethnicity* and are not strictly comparable with estimates for earlier years. The five single-race categories plus multiple-race categories shown in the table conform to the 1997 Standards. Starting with 1999 data, race-specific estimates are for persons who reported only one racial group; the category 2 or more races includes persons who reported more than one racial group. Prior to 1999, data were tabulated according to the 1977 Standards with four racial groups, and the Asian only category included Native Hawaiian or Other Pacific Islander. Estimates for single-race categories prior to 1999 included persons who reported one race or, if they reported more than one race, identified one race as best representing their race. Starting with 2003 data, race responses of other race and unspecified multiple race were treated as missing, and then race was imputed if these were the only race responses. Almost all persons with a race response of other race were of Hispanic origin. See Appendix II, Hispanic origin; Race.

[4] Percent of poverty level is based on family income and family size and composition using U.S. Census Bureau poverty thresholds. Missing family income data were imputed for 1997 and beyond. See Appendix II, Family income; Poverty; Table VI.

[5] Health insurance categories are mutually exclusive. Persons who reported both Medicaid and private coverage are classified as having private coverage. Starting with 1997 data, state-sponsored health plan coverage is included as Medicaid coverage. Starting with 1999 data, coverage by the Children's Health Insurance Program (CHIP) is included with Medicaid coverage. In addition to private and Medicaid, the insured category also includes military, other government, and Medicare coverage. Persons not covered by private insurance, Medicaid, CHIP, state-sponsored or other government-sponsored health plans (starting in 1997), Medicare, or military plans are considered to have no health insurance coverage. Persons with only Indian Health Service coverage are considered to have no health insurance coverage. See Appendix II, Health insurance coverage.

[6] MSA is metropolitan statistical area. Starting with 2006 data, MSA status is determined using 2000 census data and the 2000 standards for defining MSAs. For data prior to 2006, see Appendix II, Metropolitan statistical area (MSA) for the applicable standards.

NOTES: Standard errors are available in the spreadsheet version of this table. Available from: http://www.cdc.gov/nchs/hus.htm. Data for additional years are available. See the Excel spreadsheet on the *Health, United States* website at: http://www.cdc.gov/nchs/hus.htm.

SOURCE: NCHS, National Health Interview Survey, family core and sample child questionnaires. See Appendix I, National Health Interview Survey (NHIS).

Table 74 (page 1 of 3). Emergency department visits within the past 12 months among adults aged 18 and over, by selected characteristics: United States, selected years 1997–2015

Excel and PDF versions (with more data years and standard errors when available): http://www.cdc.gov/nchs/hus/contents2016.htm#074.

[Data are based on household interviews of a sample of the civilian noninstitutionalized population]

Characteristic	One or more emergency department visits				Two or more emergency department visits			
	1997	2000	2010	2015	1997	2000	2010	2015
	Percent of adults with emergency department visits [1]							
18 years and over, age-adjusted [2,3]	19.6	20.2	21.4	18.8	6.7	6.9	7.8	6.9
18 years and over, crude [2]	19.6	20.1	21.3	18.8	6.7	6.8	7.7	6.9
Age								
18–44 years	20.7	20.5	22.0	18.6	6.8	7.0	8.4	6.9
18–24 years.	26.3	25.7	25.4	20.5	9.1	8.8	9.6	7.5
25–44 years.	19.0	18.8	20.7	17.9	6.2	6.4	8.0	6.7
45–64 years	16.2	17.6	19.2	17.4	5.6	5.6	6.7	6.1
45–54 years.	15.7	17.9	18.6	16.4	5.5	5.8	6.6	6.0
55–64 years.	16.9	17.0	19.8	18.4	5.7	5.3	6.8	6.2
65 years and over	22.0	23.7	23.7	21.8	8.1	8.6	7.7	8.2
65–74 years.	20.3	21.6	20.7	18.3	7.1	7.4	6.4	6.9
75 years and over.	24.3	26.2	27.4	26.7	9.3	10.0	9.4	10.0
Sex [3]								
Male	19.1	18.7	18.5	16.9	5.9	5.7	6.0	5.7
Female.	20.2	21.6	24.3	20.6	7.5	7.9	9.6	8.1
Race [3,4]								
White only	19.0	19.4	20.7	18.0	6.2	6.4	7.2	6.4
Black or African American only	25.9	26.5	28.6	26.6	11.1	10.8	12.6	10.9
American Indian or Alaska Native only	24.8	30.3	22.6	28.3	13.1	*12.6	*11.8	16.1
Asian only	11.6	13.6	13.3	9.4	*2.9	*3.8	3.3	2.7
Native Hawaiian or Other Pacific Islander only	- - -	*	*	*	- - -	*	*	*
2 or more races	- - -	32.5	29.7	27.1	- - -	11.3	11.1	12.4
American Indian or Alaska Native; White	- - -	33.9	31.1	29.0	- - -	*9.4	*15.2	*14.1
Hispanic origin and race [3,4]								
Hispanic or Latino.	19.2	18.3	19.8	17.3	7.4	7.0	6.9	6.4
Mexican.	17.8	17.4	18.1	16.0	6.4	7.1	6.1	6.0
Not Hispanic or Latino.	19.7	20.6	21.9	19.2	6.7	6.9	8.1	7.0
White only.	19.1	19.8	21.1	18.3	6.2	6.4	7.4	6.4
Black or African American only	25.9	26.5	29.0	26.5	11.0	10.8	12.7	10.8
Percent of poverty level [3,5]								
Below 100%.	28.1	29.0	30.6	29.5	12.8	13.3	14.9	14.7
100%–199%.	23.8	23.9	25.6	24.1	9.3	9.6	10.5	9.9
200%–399%.	18.3	19.8	20.4	17.1	5.9	6.3	6.8	6.2
400% or more	15.9	16.8	17.0	14.3	3.9	4.5	4.7	3.6
Hispanic origin and race and percent of poverty level [3,4,5]								
Hispanic or Latino:								
Below 100%	22.1	22.4	23.6	22.6	9.8	9.7	11.5	11.5
100%–199%	19.2	18.1	19.9	17.7	8.1	6.7	6.3	6.7
200%–399%	18.5	17.3	18.1	13.3	6.0	7.4	5.2	4.1
400% or more	14.6	16.4	18.8	17.5	*3.8	*4.3	*5.5	*4.4
Not Hispanic or Latino:								
White only:								
Below 100%	29.5	30.1	33.3	32.0	13.0	13.9	15.5	16.0
100%–199%	24.3	25.5	26.8	26.0	9.1	10.4	11.2	10.5
200%–399%	18.1	20.1	20.3	17.4	5.8	6.3	6.5	6.4
400% or more	15.8	16.3	16.9	14.0	3.8	4.1	4.9	3.5
Black or African American only:								
Below 100%	34.6	35.4	36.9	35.8	17.5	17.4	20.2	17.1
100%–199%	29.2	28.5	33.5	32.6	12.8	12.2	15.9	14.0
200%–399%	20.8	23.2	25.7	22.2	8.1	8.0	10.2	8.3
400% or more	18.2	22.6	18.8	18.3	5.9	8.8	*4.0	5.4

See footnotes at end of table.

Table 74 (page 2 of 3). Emergency department visits within the past 12 months among adults aged 18 and over, by selected characteristics: United States, selected years 1997–2015

Excel and PDF versions (with more data years and standard errors when available): http://www.cdc.gov/nchs/hus/contents2016.htm#074.

[Data are based on household interviews of a sample of the civilian noninstitutionalized population]

Characteristic	One or more emergency department visits				Two or more emergency department visits			
	1997	2000	2010	2015	1997	2000	2010	2015
Health insurance status at the time of interview [6,7]	Percent of adults with emergency department visits [1]							
18–64 years:								
Insured	18.8	19.5	20.8	18.0	6.1	6.4	7.5	6.5
Private	16.9	17.6	17.4	14.1	4.7	5.1	5.2	3.9
Medicaid	37.6	42.2	40.2	34.9	19.7	21.0	21.1	18.0
Uninsured	20.0	19.3	21.3	18.0	7.5	6.9	8.9	6.9
Health insurance status prior to interview [6,7]								
18–64 years:								
Insured continuously all 12 months	18.3	19.0	20.2	17.6	5.8	6.1	7.1	6.2
Uninsured for any period up to 12 months	25.5	28.2	26.0	22.6	9.4	10.3	12.5	9.9
Uninsured more than 12 months	18.9	17.3	20.6	16.6	7.1	6.4	8.1	6.4
Percent of poverty level and health insurance status prior to interview [5,6,7]								
18–64 years:								
Below 100%:								
Insured continuously all 12 months	30.2	31.6	35.2	31.7	14.7	15.4	18.3	16.7
Uninsured for any period up to 12 months	34.1	43.7	34.2	32.7	16.1	18.1	16.5	15.3
Uninsured more than 12 months	20.8	20.5	23.4	21.6	8.1	9.1	11.7	8.8
100%–199%:								
Insured continuously all 12 months	24.5	25.5	26.1	25.1	8.9	10.2	10.8	10.2
Uninsured for any period up to 12 months	28.7	27.7	29.7	26.7	12.3	11.7	15.6	13.8
Uninsured more than 12 months	19.0	17.4	21.2	17.4	8.3	6.4	7.8	6.6
200%–399%:								
Insured continuously all 12 months	17.5	19.5	19.6	15.7	5.3	6.3	6.0	5.5
Uninsured for any period up to 12 months	21.6	24.6	25.4	18.9	6.6	7.3	12.2	7.3
Uninsured more than 12 months	16.8	15.6	17.6	12.4	5.9	4.5	5.7	*5.7
400% or more:								
Insured continuously all 12 months	14.9	15.5	15.9	13.2	3.7	3.7	4.5	3.0
Uninsured for any period up to 12 months	18.0	20.1	12.5	*14.5	*3.1	6.4	*	*
Uninsured more than 12 months	19.1	15.8	19.4	*8.7	*	*5.2	*	*
Disability measure [3,8]								
Any basic actions difficulty or complex activity limitation	30.8	32.0	34.9	32.5	13.5	14.6	16.8	15.9
Any basic actions difficulty	30.5	32.4	35.0	32.8	13.5	14.9	17.2	16.4
Any complex activity limitation	39.7	41.5	43.8	41.0	19.9	21.2	24.5	22.4
No disability	14.5	15.3	16.1	12.9	3.7	3.9	4.4	3.4
Geographic region [3]								
Northeast	19.5	20.0	22.6	18.1	6.9	6.2	8.4	5.8
Midwest	19.3	20.1	22.3	20.5	6.2	6.9	8.2	8.1
South	20.9	21.2	22.1	19.5	7.3	7.6	8.0	7.0
West	17.7	18.6	18.9	16.6	6.0	6.3	6.7	6.4
Location of residence [3,9]								
Within MSA	19.1	19.6	20.8	18.2	6.4	6.6	7.5	6.5
Outside MSA	21.5	22.5	25.5	22.8	7.8	7.8	9.8	9.6

See footnotes at end of table.

Table 74 (page 3 of 3). Emergency department visits within the past 12 months among adults aged 18 and over, by selected characteristics: United States, selected years 1997–2015

Excel and PDF versions (with more data years and standard errors when available): http://www.cdc.gov/nchs/hus/contents2016.htm#074.

[Data are based on household interviews of a sample of the civilian noninstitutionalized population]

* Estimates are considered unreliable. Data preceded by an asterisk have a relative standard error (RSE) of 20%–30%. Data not shown have an RSE greater than 30%.

- - - Data not available.

[1] See Appendix II, Emergency department or emergency room visit.

[2] Includes all other races not shown separately, unknown health insurance status, and unknown disability status.

[3] Estimates are for persons aged 18 and over and are age-adjusted to the year 2000 standard population using five age groups: 18–44 years, 45–54 years, 55–64 years, 65–74 years, and 75 years and over. See Appendix II, Age adjustment.

[4] The race groups, white, black, American Indian or Alaska Native, Asian, Native Hawaiian or Other Pacific Islander, and 2 or more races, include persons of Hispanic and non-Hispanic origin. Persons of Hispanic origin may be of any race. Starting with 1999 data, race-specific estimates are tabulated according to the 1997 *Revisions to the Standards for the Classification of Federal Data on Race and Ethnicity* and are not strictly comparable with estimates for earlier years. The five single-race categories plus multiple-race categories shown in the table conform to the 1997 Standards. Starting with 1999 data, race-specific estimates are for persons who reported only one racial group; the category 2 or more races includes persons who reported more than one racial group. Prior to 1999, data were tabulated according to the 1977 Standards with four racial groups, and the Asian only category included Native Hawaiian or Other Pacific Islander. Estimates for single-race categories prior to 1999 included persons who reported one race or, if they reported more than one race, identified one race as best representing their race. Starting with 2003 data, race responses of other race and unspecified multiple race were treated as missing, and then race was imputed if these were the only race responses. Almost all persons with a race response of other race were of Hispanic origin. See Appendix II, Hispanic origin; Race.

[5] Percent of poverty level is based on family income and family size and composition using U.S. Census Bureau poverty thresholds. Missing family income data were imputed for 1997 and beyond. See Appendix II, Family income; Poverty; Table VI.

[6] Estimates for persons aged 18–64 are age-adjusted to the year 2000 standard population using three age groups: 18–44 years, 45–54 years, and 55–64 years. See Appendix II, Age adjustment.

[7] Health insurance categories are mutually exclusive. Persons who reported both Medicaid and private coverage are classified as having private coverage. Starting with 1997 data, state-sponsored health plan coverage is included as Medicaid coverage. Starting with 1999 data, coverage by the Children's Health Insurance Program (CHIP) is included with Medicaid coverage. In addition to private and Medicaid, the insured category also includes military plans, other government-sponsored health plans, and Medicare, not shown separately. Persons not covered by private insurance, Medicaid, CHIP, state-sponsored or other government-sponsored health plans (starting in 1997), Medicare, or military plans are considered to have no health insurance coverage. Persons with only Indian Health Service coverage are considered to have no health insurance coverage. See Appendix II, Health insurance coverage.

[8] Any basic actions difficulty or complex activity limitation is defined as having one or more of the following limitations or difficulties: movement difficulty, emotional difficulty, sensory (seeing or hearing) difficulty, cognitive difficulty, self-care (activities of daily living or instrumental activities of daily living) limitation, social limitation, or work limitation. For more information, see Appendix II, Basic actions difficulty; Complex activity limitation. Starting with 2007 data, the hearing question, a component of the basic actions difficulty measure, was revised. Consequently, data prior to 2007 are not comparable with data for 2007 and beyond. For more information on the impact of the revised hearing question, see Appendix II, Hearing trouble.

[9] MSA is metropolitan statistical area. Starting with 2006 data, MSA status is determined using 2000 census data and the 2000 standards for defining MSAs. For data prior to 2006, see Appendix II, Metropolitan statistical area (MSA) for the applicable standards.

NOTES: Standard errors are available in the spreadsheet version of this table. Available from: http://www.cdc.gov/nchs/hus.htm. Data for additional years are available. See the Excel spreadsheet on the *Health, United States* website at: http://www.cdc.gov/nchs/hus.htm.

SOURCE: NCHS, National Health Interview Survey, family core and sample adult questionnaires. See Appendix I, National Health Interview Survey (NHIS).

Table 75 (page 1 of 2). Initial injury-related visits to hospital emergency departments, by sex, age, and intent and mechanism of injury: United States, average annual, selected years 2005–2006 through 2012–2013

Excel and PDF versions (with more data years and standard errors when available): http://www.cdc.gov/nchs/hus/contents2016.htm#075.

[Data are based on reporting by a sample of hospital emergency departments]

Sex, age, and intent and mechanism of injury[1]	2005–2006	2010–2011	2012–2013	2005–2006	2010–2011	2012–2013
Both sexes	Initial injury-related visits, in thousands			Initial injury-related visits per 10,000 persons		
All ages, age-adjusted[2,3]	31,706	33,007	30,402	1,076.4	1,084.0	983.4
All ages, crude[2]	31,706	33,007	30,402	1,068.6	1,067.9	968.9
Unintentional injuries[4]	25,658	27,275	25,078	864.7	882.4	799.2
Falls	8,100	9,932	8,760	273.0	321.3	279.2
Struck by or against objects or persons . .	2,935	3,166	3,149	98.9	102.4	100.4
Motor vehicle traffic	3,714	3,557	3,207	125.2	115.1	102.2
Cut or pierce	2,145	1,922	1,699	72.3	62.2	54.1
Intentional injuries	1,977	2,446	1,692	66.6	79.1	53.9
Male						
All ages, age-adjusted[2,3]	16,966	17,483	15,184	1,166.1	1,164.5	1,000.4
All ages, crude[2]	16,966	17,483	15,184	1,164.2	1,150.5	985.9
Unintentional injuries[4]	13,736	14,451	12,447	942.5	951.0	808.1
Falls	3,685	4,689	3,649	252.9	308.6	236.9
Struck by or against objects or persons . .	1,833	2,008	1,781	125.8	132.2	115.6
Motor vehicle traffic	1,733	1,710	1,519	118.9	112.5	98.6
Cut or pierce	1,392	1,236	1,042	95.5	81.4	67.7
Intentional injuries	1,135	1,396	907	77.8	91.8	58.9
Under 18 years[2]	5,072	5,309	4,117	1,346.6	1,397.8	1,093.6
Unintentional injuries[4]	4,391	4,724	3,641	1,165.8	1,243.9	967.0
Falls	1,362	1,737	1,092	361.5	457.4	290.1
Struck by or against objects or persons . .	816	997	735	216.6	262.6	195.2
Motor vehicle traffic	357	301	198	94.8	79.1	52.6
Cut or pierce	291	238	265	77.3	62.7	70.5
Intentional injuries	190	167	*122	50.4	44.1	*32.5
18–24 years[2]	2,552	2,511	2,122	1,729.5	1,612.1	1,348.5
Unintentional injuries[4]	1,985	1,890	1,634	1,345.4	1,213.7	1,038.4
Falls	318	390	268	215.2	250.4	170.3
Struck by or against objects or persons . .	290	259	227	196.9	166.6	144.0
Motor vehicle traffic	386	357	343	261.6	229.3	217.9
Cut or pierce	265	192	152	179.5	123.5	96.8
Intentional injuries	273	403	216	185.2	258.7	137.3
25–44 years[2]	5,199	4,850	4,429	1,243.6	1,184.3	1,079.9
Unintentional injuries[4]	4,001	3,690	3,426	957.1	901.1	835.4
Falls	763	815	791	182.4	199.1	192.8
Struck by or against objects or persons . .	472	452	495	112.9	110.4	120.7
Motor vehicle traffic	629	591	509	150.5	144.3	124.1
Cut or pierce	480	423	354	114.8	103.2	86.4
Intentional injuries	436	589	424	104.4	143.8	103.4
45–64 years[2]	2,842	3,270	3,101	790.0	822.7	767.3
Unintentional injuries[4]	2,275	2,741	2,505	632.5	689.6	620.0
Falls	599	909	716	166.6	228.6	177.2
Struck by or against objects or persons . .	208	204	256	57.9	51.4	63.4
Motor vehicle traffic	262	334	389	72.9	84.0	96.3
Cut or pierce	285	294	190	79.2	73.9	47.1
Intentional injuries	205	219	130	57.1	55.2	32.1
65 years and over[2]	1,301	1,544	1,415	837.5	871.6	736.6
Unintentional injuries[4]	1,082	1,406	1,240	696.8	793.5	645.5
Falls	644	838	782	414.5	473.0	407.3
Struck by or against objects or persons . .	46	95	*67	29.8	53.6	*35.1
Motor vehicle traffic	98	128	*79	63.4	72.1	*41.4
Cut or pierce	70	90	*80	45.3	50.6	*41.7
Intentional injuries	*	*	*	*	*	*

See footnotes at end of table.

Excel and PDF versions (with more data years and standard errors when available): http://www.cdc.gov/nchs/hus/contents2016.htm#075.

[Data are based on reporting by a sample of hospital emergency departments]

Sex, age, and intent and mechanism of injury [1]	2005–2006	2010–2011	2012–2013	2005–2006	2010–2011	2012–2013
Female	Initial injury-related visits, in thousands			Initial injury-related visits per 10,000 persons		
All ages, age-adjusted [2,3]	14,740	15,524	15,218	980.5	997.2	959.0
All ages, crude [2]	14,740	15,524	15,218	976.3	988.0	952.6
Unintentional injuries [4]	11,922	12,824	12,632	789.7	816.1	790.7
Falls	4,415	5,243	5,111	292.4	333.6	319.9
Struck by or against objects or persons	1,102	1,158	1,368	73.0	73.7	85.7
Motor vehicle traffic	1,981	1,847	1,688	131.2	117.6	105.7
Cut or pierce	753	685	657	49.9	43.6	41.1
Intentional injuries	843	1,050	785	55.8	66.8	49.1
Under 18 years [2]	3,625	3,673	3,602	1,008.7	1,013.2	1,000.4
Unintentional injuries [4]	3,058	3,120	3,105	851.1	860.7	862.2
Falls	1,039	1,138	1,047	289.1	314.0	290.9
Struck by or against objects or persons	419	425	522	116.7	117.2	145.0
Motor vehicle traffic	367	302	273	102.1	83.4	75.8
Cut or pierce	160	158	*148	44.4	43.7	*41.0
Intentional injuries	188	196	144	52.3	54.1	39.9
18–24 years [2]	1,882	1,936	1,769	1,329.3	1,297.1	1,160.3
Unintentional injuries [4]	1,431	1,530	1,367	1,010.5	1,025.0	896.7
Falls	290	305	326	205.0	204.5	214.2
Struck by or against objects or persons	146	171	129	103.4	114.7	84.4
Motor vehicle traffic	397	460	372	280.6	308.1	244.3
Cut or pierce	116	*94	81	82.2	*63.3	53.2
Intentional injuries	176	251	151	124.2	168.4	99.2
25–44 years [2]	4,173	4,233	3,914	1,004.2	1,034.6	947.8
Unintentional injuries [4]	3,266	3,308	3,105	785.8	808.5	751.8
Falls	873	941	921	210.1	229.9	223.0
Struck by or against objects or persons	309	284	326	74.3	69.4	79.0
Motor vehicle traffic	719	616	529	173.1	150.5	128.0
Cut or pierce	269	219	215	64.7	53.6	52.1
Intentional injuries	313	408	310	75.4	99.8	75.0
45–64 years [2]	2,904	3,101	3,173	767.8	741.9	746.6
Unintentional injuries [4]	2,278	2,519	2,538	602.2	602.7	597.4
Falls	865	1,075	993	228.7	257.1	233.7
Struck by or against objects or persons	160	197	246	42.2	47.2	58.0
Motor vehicle traffic	359	345	388	94.8	82.6	91.2
Cut or pierce	158	157	159	41.7	37.6	37.4
Intentional injuries	149	182	*171	39.4	43.5	*40.2
65 years and over [2]	2,155	2,582	2,760	1,002.9	1,110.7	1,116.8
Unintentional injuries [4]	1,889	2,348	2,517	879.1	1,009.8	1,018.2
Falls	1,347	1,784	1,823	626.9	767.2	737.7
Struck by or against objects or persons	69	81	*145	31.9	34.7	*58.6
Motor vehicle traffic	139	124	127	64.5	53.5	51.2
Cut or pierce	*50	*56	*54	*23.3	*24.2	*21.8
Intentional injuries	*	*	*	*	*	*

*Estimates are considered unreliable. Data preceded by an asterisk have a relative standard error (RSE) of 20%–30%. Data not shown have an RSE greater than 30%.

[1] Intent and mechanism of injury are based on the first-listed external cause of injury code (E code). Intentional injuries include suicide attempts and assaults. See Appendix II, External cause of injury; Injury; Injury-related visit; Table IX for a listing of E codes.

[2] Includes all injury-related visits not shown separately in table, including those with undetermined intent (1% in 2012–2013) and insufficient or no information to code cause of injury (11% in 2012–2013).

[3] Rates are age-adjusted to the year 2000 standard population using six age groups: under 18 years, 18–24 years, 25–44 years, 45–64 years, 65–74 years, and 75 years and over. See Appendix II, Age adjustment.

[4] Includes unintentional injury-related visits with mechanism of injury not shown in table.

NOTES: An emergency department visit was considered injury-related if the first-listed diagnosis was injury-related (ICD–9–CM 800–909.2, 909.4, 909.9–994.9, 995.50–995.59, and 995.80–995.85) or the first-listed external cause code (E code) was injury-related (ICD–9–CM E800–E869, E880–E929, and E950–E999). See: http://www.cdc.gov/nchs/injury/injury_tools.htm for code used to classify injury-related visits in this table. Visits with a first-listed diagnosis or first-listed E code describing a complication or adverse effect of medical care were not considered injury related. For more information on injury-related visits, see Bergen G, Chen LH, Warner M, Fingerhut LA. Injury in the United States: 2007 Chartbook. Hyattsville, MD: NCHS. 2008. Available from: http://www.cdc.gov/nchs/data/misc/injury2007.pdf. Estimates for first-listed injury-related visits were further limited to those visits that were initial visits for the injury. This was determined using an imputed variable in 2005–2006; for 2007 and beyond this was determined by using the initial visit episode of care information collected on the questionnaire. Limiting the estimates to initial visits decreases the total number of injury-related visits by 9% in 2005–2006, 14% in 2007–2008 (shown in spreadsheet version), 10%–12% in 2008–2009, 2009–2010, and 2010–2011 (shown in spreadsheet version), 13% in 2011–2012, and 11% in 2012–2013. Rates were calculated using estimates of the civilian population of the United States including institutionalized persons. Population data are from unpublished tabulations provided by the U.S. Census Bureau. Rates for 2005–2010 were calculated using postcensal population estimates based on the 2000 census. Rates for 2011 and beyond were calculated using postcensal population estimates based on the 2010 census. Data for additional years are available. See the Excel spreadsheet on the *Health, United States* website at: http://www.cdc.gov/nchs/hus.htm.

SOURCE: NCHS, National Hospital Ambulatory Medical Care Survey. See Appendix I, National Hospital Ambulatory Medical Care Survey (NHAMCS).

Table 76 (page 1 of 3). Visits to physician offices, hospital outpatient departments, and hospital emergency departments, by age, sex, and race: United States, selected years 2000–2013

Excel and PDF versions (with more data years and standard errors when available): http://www.cdc.gov/nchs/hus/contents2016.htm#076.

[Data are based on reporting by a sample of office-based physicians, hospital outpatient departments, and hospital emergency departments]

Age, sex, and race	All places [1]				Physician offices			
	2000	2010	2011	2013 [2]	2000	2010	2011	2013 [2]
Age	Number of visits, in thousands							
Total	1,014,848	1,239,387	1,249,047	- - -	823,542	1,008,802	987,029	922,596
Under 18 years	212,165	246,228	263,387	- - -	163,459	191,500	206,285	151,036
18–44 years	315,774	342,797	333,427	- - -	243,011	261,941	239,224	224,256
45–64 years	255,894	352,001	353,591	- - -	216,783	296,385	285,784	282,109
45–54 years	142,233	171,039	173,334	- - -	119,474	140,819	136,429	131,013
55–64 years	113,661	180,962	180,258	- - -	97,309	155,566	149,355	151,096
65 years and over	231,014	298,362	298,642	- - -	200,289	258,976	255,736	265,195
65–74 years	116,505	151,075	151,970	- - -	102,447	132,201	131,233	141,507
75 years and over	114,510	147,287	146,672	- - -	97,842	126,775	124,503	123,688
	Number of visits per 100 persons							
Total, age–adjusted [3]	374	401	400	- - -	304	325	314	285
Total, crude	370	408	408	- - -	300	332	322	297
Under 18 years	293	331	357	- - -	226	257	280	206
18–44 years	291	310	302	- - -	224	237	216	201
45–64 years	422	441	431	- - -	358	371	349	343
45–54 years	385	388	392	- - -	323	320	309	303
55–64 years	481	505	477	- - -	412	434	395	387
65 years and over	706	767	745	- - -	612	666	638	611
65–74 years	656	713	683	- - -	577	624	590	566
75 years and over	766	831	822	- - -	654	715	698	672
Sex and age								
Male, age–adjusted [3]	325	350	354	- - -	261	283	280	250
Male, crude	314	350	356	- - -	251	283	281	256
Under 18 years	302	340	372	- - -	231	262	294	206
18–44 years	203	205	208	- - -	148	151	145	137
45–54 years	316	324	322	- - -	260	265	250	263
55–64 years	428	460	430	- - -	367	396	351	359
65–74 years	614	680	655	- - -	539	597	566	530
75 years and over	771	871	869	- - -	670	760	758	679
Female, age–adjusted [3]	420	452	444	- - -	345	367	348	318
Female, crude	424	464	457	- - -	348	379	361	336
Under 18 years	285	322	341	- - -	221	252	265	206
18–44 years	377	415	393	- - -	298	323	286	263
45–54 years	451	450	459	- - -	384	372	364	341
55–64 years	529	546	520	- - -	453	469	436	413
65–74 years	692	741	707	- - -	609	647	611	598
75 years and over	763	804	790	- - -	645	685	657	667
Race and age [4]								
White, age–adjusted [3]	380	408	411	- - -	315	336	333	304
White, crude	381	421	424	- - -	316	349	345	323
Under 18 years	306	341	397	- - -	243	270	324	230
18–44 years	301	319	312	- - -	239	249	233	218
45–54 years	386	389	378	- - -	330	326	305	318
55–64 years	480	505	474	- - -	416	440	400	405
65–74 years	641	727	677	- - -	568	642	594	582
75 years and over	764	838	815	- - -	658	723	698	701
Black or African American, age–adjusted [3] . .	353	439	430	- - -	239	316	277	243
Black or African American, crude	324	425	416	- - -	214	303	266	235
Under 18 years	264	351	275	- - -	167	241	153	158
18–44 years	257	339	350	- - -	149	222	199	170
45–54 years	383	466	550	- - -	269	339	378	284
55–64 years	495	617	566	- - -	373	481	412	339
65–74 years	656	715	733	- - -	512	565	539	527
75 years and over	745	845	821	- - -	568	682	605	542

See footnotes at end of table.

Excel and PDF versions (with more data years and standard errors when available): http://www.cdc.gov/nchs/hus/contents2016.htm#076.

[Data are based on reporting by a sample of office-based physicians, hospital outpatient departments, and hospital emergency departments]

Age, sex, and race	Hospital outpatient departments				Hospital emergency departments			
	2000	2010	2011	2013	2000	2010	2011	2013
Age	Number of visits, in thousands							
Total	83,289	100,742	125,721	- - -	108,017	129,843	136,296	130,353
Under 18 years	21,076	24,913	27,651	- - -	27,630	29,815	29,451	27,992
18–44 years	26,947	28,159	37,557	- - -	45,816	52,697	56,646	51,251
45–64 years	20,772	27,739	37,980	- - -	18,339	27,877	29,828	30,358
45–54 years.	11,558	13,639	19,310	- - -	11,201	16,581	17,595	17,358
55–64 years.	9,214	14,100	18,670	- - -	7,138	11,296	12,232	13,000
65 years and over	14,494	19,932	22,534	- - -	16,232	19,454	20,372	20,752
65–74 years.	7,515	10,675	12,529	- - -	6,543	8,199	8,208	9,354
75 years and over.	6,979	9,257	10,005	- - -	9,690	11,255	12,163	11,398
	Number of visits per 100 persons							
Total, age–adjusted [3]	31	33	40	- - -	40	43	45	42
Total, crude	30	33	41	- - -	39	43	44	42
Under 18 years	29	33	37	- - -	38	40	40	38
18–44 years	25	25	34	- - -	42	48	51	46
45–64 years	34	35	46	- - -	30	35	36	37
45–54 years.	31	31	44	- - -	30	38	40	40
55–64 years.	39	39	49	- - -	30	32	32	33
65 years and over	44	51	56	- - -	50	50	51	48
65–74 years.	42	50	56	- - -	37	39	37	37
75 years and over.	47	52	56	- - -	65	64	68	62
Sex and age								
Male, age–adjusted [3]	26	27	32	- - -	38	40	42	38
Male, crude	25	27	33	- - -	38	39	41	38
Under 18 years	29	34	37	- - -	41	43	41	39
18–44 years.	17	16	20	- - -	38	38	43	37
45–54 years.	26	24	34	- - -	30	35	38	37
55–64 years.	32	32	45	- - -	30	32	34	34
65–74 years.	38	47	52	- - -	36	37	37	36
75 years and over.	42	50	49	- - -	59	60	62	55
Female, age–adjusted [3]	35	38	48	- - -	41	47	48	47
Female, crude	35	39	49	- - -	41	46	48	46
Under 18 years	29	33	38	- - -	35	37	39	38
18–44 years.	33	35	47	- - -	46	57	59	55
45–54 years.	36	37	53	- - -	31	40	41	43
55–64 years.	45	46	54	- - -	31	31	31	33
65–74 years.	46	54	60	- - -	37	40	37	39
75 years and over.	49	53	61	- - -	69	66	72	67
Race and age [4]								
White, age–adjusted [3]	28	31	37	- - -	37	41	42	40
White, crude.	28	32	38	- - -	37	40	41	40
Under 18 years	27	33	37	- - -	36	39	37	37
18–44 years.	23	25	31	- - -	39	45	47	43
45–54 years.	28	28	37	- - -	28	34	35	36
55–64 years.	36	36	44	- - -	28	29	30	31
65–74 years.	38	48	49	- - -	35	37	34	35
75 years and over.	44	52	52	- - -	63	62	65	63
Black or African American, age–adjusted [3] . .	51	51	69	- - -	62	73	85	73
Black or African American, crude	48	50	68	- - -	62	72	83	72
Under 18 years	40	48	*50	- - -	57	62	72	60
18–44 years.	40	37	55	- - -	68	81	96	83
45–54 years.	61	54	89	- - -	53	73	83	77
55–64 years.	70	73	94	- - -	52	62	60	64
65–74 years.	85	*85	*121	- - -	59	66	73	63
75 years and over.	85	*74	*98	- - -	92	89	118	69

See footnotes at end of table.

Table 76 (page 3 of 3). Visits to physician offices, hospital outpatient departments, and hospital emergency departments, by age, sex, and race: United States, selected years 2000–2013

Excel and PDF versions (with more data years and standard errors when available): http://www.cdc.gov/nchs/hus/contents2016.htm#076.

[Data are based on reporting by a sample of office-based physicians, hospital outpatient departments, and hospital emergency departments]

- - - Data not available.

* Estimates are considered unreliable. Data preceded by an asterisk have a relative standard error (RSE) of 20%–30%. Data not shown have an RSE greater than 30%.

[1] All places includes visits to physician offices and hospital outpatient and emergency departments. See Appendix II, Emergency department; Emergency department or emergency room visit; Office visit; Outpatient department; Outpatient visit.

[2] In 2012 and 2013, data for all places and physician offices exclude visits to community health centers; in 2006–2011, data for all places and physician offices include visits to community health centers (2%–3% of visits to physician offices in 2006–2011 were to community health centers). Prior to 2006, visits to community health centers were not included in the survey.

[3] Estimates are age-adjusted to the year 2000 standard population using six age groups: under 18 years, 18–44 years, 45–54 years, 55–64 years, 65–74 years, and 75 years and over. See Appendix II, Age adjustment.

[4] Estimates by racial group should be used with caution because information on race was collected from medical records and race is imputed for records missing that information. Information on the race imputation process used in each data year is available in the public-use file documentation. Available from: http://www.cdc.gov/nchs/ahcd.htm. Starting with 1999 data, the instruction for the race item on the Patient Record Form was changed so that more than one race could be recorded. In previous years only one race could be recorded. Estimates for race in this table are for visits where only one race was recorded. Because of the small number of responses with more than one racial group recorded, estimates for visits with multiple races recorded are unreliable and are not presented.

NOTES: Rates for 1995–2000 were computed using 1990-based postcensal estimates of the civilian noninstitutionalized population as of July 1, adjusted for net underenumeration using the 1990 National Population Adjustment Matrix from the U.S. Census Bureau. For 2001–2010 data, rates were computed using 2000-based postcensal estimates of the civilian noninstitutionalized population as of July 1. For 2011 data and beyond, rates were computed using 2010-based postcensal estimates of the civilian noninstitutionalized population as of July 1. Rates using the civilian noninstitutionalized population will be overestimated to the extent that visits by institutionalized persons are counted in the numerator (for example, hospital emergency department visits by nursing home residents) but institutionalized persons are omitted from the denominator (the civilian noninstitutionalized population). Starting with *Health, United States, 2005*, data for physician offices for 2001 and beyond use a revised weighting scheme. See Appendix I, National Ambulatory Medical Care Survey (NAMCS); National Hospital Ambulatory Medical Care Survey (NHAMCS). Data for additional years are available. See the Excel spreadsheet on the *Health, United States* website at: http://www.cdc.gov/nchs/hus.htm.

SOURCE: NCHS, National Ambulatory Medical Care Survey and National Hospital Ambulatory Medical Care Survey. See Appendix I, National Ambulatory Medical Care Survey (NAMCS); National Hospital Ambulatory Medical Care Survey (NHAMCS).

Table 77 (page 1 of 2). Visits to primary care generalist and specialty care physicians, by selected characteristics and type of physician: United States, selected years 1980–2013

Excel and PDF versions (with more data years and standard errors when available): http://www.cdc.gov/nchs/hus/contents2016.htm#077.

[Data are based on reporting by a sample of office-based physicians]

| Age, sex, and race | Type of primary care generalist physician[1] | | | | | | | | | | | |
| | All primary care generalists | | | | General and family practice | | | | Internal medicine | | | |
	1980	2000	2010	2013[2]	1980	2000	2010	2013[2]	1980	2000	2010	2013[2]
Age					Percent distribution							
Total	66.2	58.9	55.2	49.1	33.5	24.1	21.1	18.9	12.1	15.3	13.9	13.7
Under 18 years	77.8	79.7	80.9	74.1	26.1	19.9	15.3	12.4	2.0	*	*	*0.6
18–44 years	65.3	62.1	62.7	53.7	34.3	28.2	27.8	20.9	8.6	12.7	11.6	12.8
45–64 years	60.2	51.2	46.7	42.1	36.3	26.4	23.1	21.5	19.5	20.1	18.5	16.4
45–54 years.	60.2	52.3	48.7	42.9	37.4	27.8	26.2	22.5	17.1	18.7	15.7	15.1
55–64 years.	60.2	49.9	44.8	41.3	35.4	24.7	20.4	20.6	21.8	21.7	21.0	17.6
65 years and over	61.6	46.5	38.3	38.3	37.5	20.2	16.4	18.0	22.7	24.5	20.5	18.8
65–74 years	61.2	46.6	37.3	37.5	37.4	19.7	17.5	17.6	22.1	24.5	18.2	18.2
75 years and over.	62.3	46.4	39.2	39.1	37.6	20.8	15.4	18.4	23.5	24.5	22.8	19.6
Sex and age												
Male:												
Under 18 years	77.3	77.7	80.1	73.8	25.6	18.3	15.7	12.1	2.0	*	*	*
18–44 years.	50.8	51.5	51.7	41.5	38.0	34.2	33.7	24.9	11.5	14.4	16.4	14.9
45–64 years.	55.6	49.4	43.7	38.9	34.4	28.7	24.4	21.4	20.5	19.8	19.1	17.4
65 years and over.	58.2	43.1	36.6	34.1	35.6	19.3	16.2	16.3	22.3	23.8	20.3	17.7
Female:												
Under 18 years	78.5	82.0	81.7	74.5	26.6	21.7	14.9	12.7	2.0	*	*	*0.6
18–44 years.	72.1	67.2	67.9	59.9	32.5	25.3	25.0	18.9	7.3	11.9	9.4	11.8
45–64 years.	63.4	52.5	48.9	44.6	37.7	24.9	22.2	21.6	18.9	20.2	18.1	15.7
65 years and over.	63.9	48.9	39.6	41.3	38.7	20.9	16.7	19.2	22.9	25.0	20.5	19.7
Race and age[3]												
White:												
Under 18 years	77.6	78.5	79.6	74.5	26.4	21.2	15.6	13.0	2.0	*	*	*
18–44 years.	64.8	61.4	61.2	52.4	34.5	29.2	27.9	21.5	8.6	11.0	11.1	12.7
45–64 years.	59.6	49.3	45.2	41.5	36.0	27.3	22.8	22.1	19.2	17.1	17.5	15.4
65 years and over.	61.4	45.1	37.6	38.1	36.6	20.3	16.6	18.2	23.3	23.0	19.7	18.5
Black or African American:												
Under 18 years	79.9	87.3	88.0	73.2	23.7	*	*16.5	*10.3	*2.2	*	*	*
18–44 years.	68.5	65.0	72.6	60.8	31.7	22.0	29.4	20.0	9.0	20.9	*14.0	11.8
45–64 years.	66.1	61.7	57.0	45.7	38.6	23.3	26.7	19.4	22.6	35.9	24.5	22.3
65 years and over.	64.6	52.8	45.2	41.9	49.0	*18.5	*18.6	15.6	14.2	33.4	*25.4	24.8

See footnotes at end of table.

Table 77 (page 2 of 2). Visits to primary care generalist and specialty care physicians, by selected characteristics and type of physician: United States, selected years 1980–2013

Excel and PDF versions (with more data years and standard errors when available): http://www.cdc.gov/nchs/hus/contents2016.htm#077.

[Data are based on reporting by a sample of office-based physicians]

| Age, sex, and race | Type of primary care generalist physician[1] | | | | | | | | Specialty care physicians | | | |
| | Obstetrics and gynecology | | | | Pediatrics | | | | | | | |
	1980	2000	2010	2013[2]	1980	2000	2010	2013[2]	1980	2000	2010	2013[2]
Age						Percent distribution						
Total	9.6	7.8	7.8	6.3	10.9	11.7	12.4	10.2	33.8	41.1	44.8	50.9
Under 18 years	1.3	*1.1	*1.3	*0.6	48.5	57.3	63.4	60.5	22.2	20.3	19.1	25.9
18–44 years	21.7	20.4	22.3	18.8	0.7	*0.9	1.0	1.1	34.7	37.9	37.3	46.3
45–64 years	4.2	4.5	4.9	4.1	*	*	*	*	39.8	48.8	53.3	57.9
45–54 years.	5.6	5.6	6.7	5.3	*	*	*	*	39.8	47.7	51.3	57.1
55–64 years.	2.9	3.3	3.3	3.1	*	*	*	*	39.8	50.1	55.2	58.7
65 years and over	1.4	1.5	1.3	1.4	*	*	*	*	38.4	53.5	61.7	61.7
65–74 years.	1.7	2.0	1.7	1.7	*	*	*	*	38.8	53.4	62.7	62.5
75 years and over.	1.0	*1.0	*1.0	1.1	*	*	*	*	37.7	53.6	60.8	60.9
Sex and age												
Male:												
Under 18 years	. . .	. . .	. . .	. . .	49.4	58.0	63.7	61.0	22.7	22.3	19.9	26.2
18–44 years.	. . .	. . .	. . .	. . .	1.0	*1.7	*1.4	1.6	49.2	48.5	48.3	58.5
45–64 years.	. . .	. . .	. . .	. . .	*	*	*	*	44.4	50.6	56.3	61.1
65 years and over.	. . .	. . .	. . .	. . .	*	*	*	*	41.8	56.9	63.4	65.9
Female:												
Under 18 years	2.5	2.1	*2.8	*1.1	47.4	56.5	63.1	60.0	21.5	18.0	18.3	25.5
18–44 years.	31.7	29.6	32.5	28.4	0.6	*	*0.9	0.9	27.9	32.8	32.1	40.1
45–64 years.	6.7	7.3	8.5	7.2	*	*	*	*	36.6	47.5	51.1	55.4
65 years and over.	2.1	2.6	2.4	2.4	*	*	*	*	36.1	51.1	60.4	58.7
Race and age[3]												
White:												
Under 18 years	1.1	*1.2	*1.3	*0.5	48.2	54.7	61.7	60.3	22.4	21.5	20.4	25.5
18–44 years.	21.0	20.4	21.1	17.1	0.7	*0.8	*1.1	1.1	35.2	38.6	38.8	47.6
45–64 years.	4.1	4.7	4.7	4.0	*	*	*	*	40.4	50.7	54.8	58.5
65 years and over.	1.4	1.5	*1.3	1.4	*	*	*	*	38.6	54.9	62.4	61.9
Black or African American:												
Under 18 years	2.8	*	*	*	51.2	75.0	70.2	61.3	20.1	*12.7	*12.0	26.8
18–44 years.	27.1	20.7	28.4	27.8	*	*	*	*1.2	31.5	35.0	27.4	39.2
45–64 years.	4.8	*2.4	*5.6	*4.0	*	*	*	0.0	33.9	38.3	43.0	54.3
65 years and over.	*	*	*1.2	*	*	*	*	0.0	35.4	47.2	54.8	58.1

* Estimates are considered unreliable. Data preceded by an asterisk have a relative standard error (RSE) of 20%–30%. Data not shown have a RSE greater than 30%.
. . . Category not applicable.

[1] Type of physician is based on physician's self-designated primary area of practice. Primary care generalist physicians are defined as practitioners in the fields of general and family practice, general internal medicine, general obstetrics and gynecology, and general pediatrics and exclude primary care specialists. Primary care generalists in general and family practice exclude primary care specialties, such as sports medicine and geriatrics. Primary care internal medicine physicians exclude internal medicine specialists, such as allergists, cardiologists, and endocrinologists. Primary care obstetrics and gynecology physicians exclude obstetrics and gynecology specialties, such as gynecological oncology, maternal and fetal medicine, obstetrics and gynecology critical care medicine, and reproductive endocrinology. Primary care pediatricians exclude pediatric specialists, such as adolescent medicine specialists, neonatologists, pediatric allergists, and pediatric cardiologists. See Appendix II, Physician specialty.

[2] In 2012 and 2013, data exclude visits to community health centers; in 2006–2011, data include visits to community health centers (2%–3% of visits to physician offices in 2006–2011 were to community health centers). Prior to 2006, visits to community health centers were not included in the survey.

[3] Estimates by racial group should be used with caution because information on race was collected from medical records. In 2013, race data were missing and imputed for 30% of visits. Information on the race imputation process used in each data year is available in the public-use file documentation. Available from: http://www.cdc.gov/nchs/ahcd.htm. Starting with 1999 data, the instruction for the race item on the Patient Record Form was changed so that more than one race could be recorded. In previous years only one racial category could be checked. Estimates for racial groups presented in this table are for visits where only one race was recorded. Because of the small number of responses with more than one racial group checked, estimates for visits with multiple races checked are unreliable and are not presented.

NOTES: This table presents data on visits to physician offices and excludes visits to other sites, such as hospital outpatient and emergency departments. See Appendix II, Office visit. In 1980, the survey excluded Alaska and Hawaii. Data for all other years include all 50 states and the District of Columbia. Visits with specialty of physician unknown are excluded. Starting with *Health, United States, 2005*, data for 2001 and later years for physician offices use a revised weighting scheme. See Appendix I, National Ambulatory Medical Care Survey (NAMCS). Data for additional years are available. See the Excel spreadsheet on the *Health, United States* website at: http://www.cdc.gov/nchs/hus.htm.

SOURCE: NCHS, National Ambulatory Medical Care Survey. See Appendix I, National Ambulatory Medical Care Survey (NAMCS).

Table 78 (page 1 of 2). Dental visits in the past year, by selected characteristics: United States, selected years 1997–2015

Excel and PDF versions (with more data years and standard errors when available): http://www.cdc.gov/nchs/hus/contents2016.htm#078.

[Data are based on household interviews of a sample of the civilian noninstitutionalized population]

Characteristic	2 years and over			2–17 years			18–64 years			65 years and over[1]		
	1997	2010	2015	1997	2010	2015	1997	2010	2015	1997	2010	2015
	Percent of persons with a dental visit in the past year[2]											
Total[3]	65.1	64.7	68.2	72.7	78.9	84.7	64.1	61.1	64.0	54.8	57.7	62.7
Sex												
Male	62.9	61.7	66.0	72.3	78.3	84.2	60.4	56.8	60.5	55.4	56.2	62.1
Female	67.1	67.5	70.3	73.0	79.6	85.2	67.7	65.4	67.3	54.4	58.9	63.2
Race[4]												
White only	66.4	65.6	68.8	74.0	79.2	84.8	65.7	62.4	64.6	56.8	59.3	64.9
Black or African American only	58.9	58.8	64.3	68.8	79.0	85.1	57.0	53.1	59.4	35.4	40.6	46.3
American Indian or Alaska Native only .	55.1	57.4	61.7	66.8	73.2	82.1	49.9	49.8	57.9	*	72.2	*36.1
Asian only	62.5	66.5	71.1	69.9	74.8	82.2	60.3	64.6	69.2	53.9	61.9	62.8
Native Hawaiian or Other Pacific Islander only	- - -	*	*	- - -	*	*	- - -	*	*	- - -	*	*
2 or more races	- - -	65.2	68.1	- - -	77.9	84.7	- - -	54.7	58.3	- - -	48.1	41.7
Black or African American; White . . .	- - -	72.5	71.6	- - -	78.4	84.2	- - -	62.1	50.7	- - -	*	*
American Indian or Alaska Native; White	- - -	54.7	56.9	- - -	70.0	83.1	- - -	49.0	51.5	- - -	*54.5	*41.9
Hispanic origin and race[4]												
Hispanic or Latino	54.0	56.5	62.2	61.0	74.8	83.8	50.8	48.5	53.2	47.8	42.1	52.2
Not Hispanic or Latino	66.4	66.2	69.5	74.7	80.1	85.0	65.7	63.4	66.2	55.2	59.0	63.6
White only	68.0	67.6	70.4	76.4	80.9	85.4	67.5	65.4	67.4	57.2	60.9	66.1
Black or African American only	58.8	58.7	64.3	68.8	79.2	85.1	56.9	53.1	59.4	35.3	40.5	46.8
Percent of poverty level[5]												
Below 100%	50.5	50.6	55.8	62.0	73.2	82.2	46.9	41.0	45.0	31.5	32.8	35.9
100%–199%	50.8	51.6	55.4	62.5	73.4	81.2	48.3	44.1	47.1	40.8	43.8	44.0
200%–399%	66.2	63.5	66.4	76.1	79.0	84.1	63.4	59.6	61.8	60.7	57.9	61.3
400% or more	78.9	79.3	81.2	85.7	88.0	90.1	77.7	77.5	79.2	74.7	77.2	80.8
Hispanic origin and race and percent of poverty level[4,5]												
Hispanic or Latino:												
Below 100%	45.7	50.8	58.5	55.9	74.3	85.2	39.2	34.7	40.8	33.6	32.4	41.3
100%–199%	47.2	50.8	57.1	53.8	71.1	83.8	43.5	40.2	44.7	47.9	39.5	42.9
200%–399%	61.2	59.1	61.8	70.5	76.5	79.1	57.5	54.1	56.4	57.0	46.0	54.2
400% or more	73.0	73.3	77.7	82.4	84.2	89.3	70.8	71.6	74.8	64.9	54.3	74.4
Not Hispanic or Latino:												
White only:												
Below 100%	51.7	49.3	52.6	64.4	69.1	78.5	50.6	44.4	46.9	32.0	36.4	35.4
100%–199%	52.4	52.7	52.4	66.1	75.3	78.7	50.4	47.2	45.3	42.2	45.4	45.2
200%–399%	67.5	64.7	67.5	77.1	79.6	85.1	65.0	61.4	62.9	61.9	59.8	63.7
400% or more	79.7	79.8	82.0	86.8	88.6	90.9	78.5	77.9	80.1	75.5	78.8	81.9
Black or African American only:												
Below 100%	52.8	52.0	57.1	66.1	78.0	82.9	46.2	39.7	44.8	27.7	20.9	31.2
100%–199%	48.7	50.0	58.7	61.2	75.9	84.0	46.3	41.5	52.3	26.9	33.6	36.7
200%–399%	63.3	61.2	65.5	75.0	81.2	88.2	60.7	57.2	62.0	41.5	45.3	48.0
400% or more	74.6	77.2	77.3	81.8	87.2	88.2	73.4	75.9	75.8	66.1	69.8	72.4

See footnotes at end of table.

Excel and PDF versions (with more data years and standard errors when available): http://www.cdc.gov/nchs/hus/contents2016.htm#078.

[Data are based on household interviews of a sample of the civilian noninstitutionalized population]

Characteristic	2 years and over			2–17 years			18–64 years			65 years and over[1]		
	1997	2010	2015	1997	2010	2015	1997	2010	2015	1997	2010	2015
Disability measure[6]	Percent of persons with a dental visit in the past year[2]											
Any basic actions difficulty or complex activity limitation	. . .	. . .	. . .	. . .	. . .	. . .	55.1	53.5	55.1	49.0	50.7	56.0
Any basic actions difficulty	. . .	. . .	. . .	. . .	. . .	. . .	54.7	53.2	55.1	48.7	50.5	55.7
Any complex activity limitation	. . .	. . .	. . .	. . .	. . .	. . .	51.0	47.4	48.4	44.6	43.1	49.1
No disability	. . .	. . .	. . .	. . .	. . .	. . .	67.4	64.2	67.2	64.2	68.8	73.3
Geographic region												
Northeast	69.6	70.1	72.6	77.5	83.8	86.8	69.6	67.9	70.9	55.5	61.5	62.8
Midwest	68.4	67.3	69.3	76.4	80.8	83.8	67.4	64.3	65.3	57.6	58.2	64.8
South	60.2	60.9	64.9	68.0	77.4	84.7	59.4	56.5	59.2	49.0	54.1	60.1
West	65.0	63.9	69.3	71.5	76.1	84.2	62.9	60.2	65.1	61.9	59.8	65.4
Location of residence[7]												
Within MSA	66.7	65.9	69.4	73.6	79.3	84.9	65.7	62.4	65.3	57.6	59.4	64.6
Outside MSA	59.1	58.4	60.8	69.3	76.4	83.3	58.0	53.8	55.0	46.1	51.3	54.2

* Estimates are considered unreliable. Data preceded by an asterisk have a relative standard error (RSE) of 20%–30%. Data not shown have an RSE greater than 30%.
- - - Data not available.
. . . Category not applicable.
[1] Based on the 1997–2015 National Health Interview Surveys, about 19%–30% of persons aged 65 and over were edentulous (having lost all their natural teeth). In 1997–2015, about 69%–73% of older dentate persons, compared with 17%–24% of older edentate persons, had a dental visit in the past year.
[2] Respondents were asked, "About how long has it been since you last saw or talked to a dentist?" See Appendix II, Dental visit.
[3] Includes all other races not shown separately and unknown disability status.
[4] The race groups, white, black, American Indian or Alaska Native, Asian, Native Hawaiian or Other Pacific Islander, and 2 or more races, include persons of Hispanic and non-Hispanic origin. Persons of Hispanic origin may be of any race. Starting with 1999 data, race-specific estimates are tabulated according to the 1997 *Revisions to the Standards for the Classification of Federal Data on Race and Ethnicity* and are not strictly comparable with estimates for earlier years. The five single-race categories plus multiple-race categories shown in the table conform to the 1997 Standards. Starting with 1999 data, race-specific estimates are for persons who reported only one racial group; the category 2 or more races includes persons who reported more than one racial group. Prior to 1999, data were tabulated according to the 1977 Standards with four racial groups, and the Asian only category included Native Hawaiian or Other Pacific Islander. Estimates for single-race categories prior to 1999 included persons who reported one race or, if they reported more than one race, identified one race as best representing their race. Starting with 2003 data, race responses of other race and unspecified multiple race were treated as missing, and then race was imputed if these were the only race responses. Almost all persons with a race response of other race were of Hispanic origin. See Appendix II, Hispanic origin; Race.
[5] Percent of poverty level is based on family income and family size and composition using U.S. Census Bureau poverty thresholds. Missing family income data were imputed for 1997 and beyond. See Appendix II, Family income; Poverty; Table VI.
[6] Any basic actions difficulty or complex activity limitation is defined as having one or more of the following limitations or difficulties: movement difficulty, emotional difficulty, sensory (seeing or hearing) difficulty, cognitive difficulty, self-care (activities of daily living or instrumental activities of daily living) limitation, social limitation, or work limitation. For more information, see Appendix II, Basic actions difficulty; Complex activity limitation. Starting with 2007 data, the hearing question, a component of the basic actions difficulty measure, was revised. Consequently, data prior to 2007 are not comparable with data for 2007 and beyond. For more information on the impact of the revised hearing question, see Appendix II, Hearing trouble.
[7] MSA is metropolitan statistical area. Starting with 2006 data, MSA status is determined using 2000 census data and the 2000 standards for defining MSAs. For data prior to 2006, see Appendix II, Metropolitan statistical area (MSA) for the applicable standards.

NOTES: Standard errors for selected years are available in the spreadsheet version of this table. Available from: http://www.cdc.gov/nchs/hus.htm. Data for additional years are available. See the Excel spreadsheet on the *Health, United States* website at: http://www.cdc.gov/nchs/hus.htm.

SOURCE: NCHS, National Health Interview Survey, sample child and sample adult questionnaires. See Appendix I, National Health Interview Survey (NHIS).

Table 79 (page 1 of 2). Prescription drug use in the past 30 days, by sex, race and Hispanic origin, and age: United States, selected years 1988–1994 through 2011–2014

Excel and PDF versions (with more data years and standard errors when available): http://www.cdc.gov/nchs/hus/contents2016.htm#079.

[Data are based on a sample of the civilian noninstitutionalized population]

Sex, race and Hispanic origin,[1] and age	At least one prescription drug in past 30 days				Three or more prescription drugs in past 30 days				Five or more prescription drugs in past 30 days			
	1988–1994	1999–2002	2007–2010	2011–2014	1988–1994	1999–2002	2007–2010	2011–2014	1988–1994	1999–2002	2007–2010	2011–2014
All ages, age-adjusted[2]	Percent of population											
Both sexes[3]	39.1	45.2	47.5	46.9	11.8	17.8	20.8	21.5	4.0	7.5	10.1	10.9
Male	32.7	39.8	42.8	42.6	9.4	14.8	19.1	19.7	2.9	6.1	9.2	9.7
Female.	45.0	50.3	52.0	51.2	13.9	20.4	22.5	23.2	4.9	8.7	11.0	12.0
Not Hispanic or Latino:												
White only.	41.1	48.7	52.8	51.9	12.4	18.9	22.4	23.1	4.2	7.8	10.7	11.5
White only, male	34.2	43.0	47.5	46.8	9.9	15.9	20.6	21.0	3.1	6.3	9.8	10.2
White only, female	47.6	54.3	57.9	57.0	14.6	21.8	24.3	25.1	5.1	9.2	11.6	12.8
Black or African American only	36.9	40.1	42.3	44.2	12.6	16.5	20.7	22.5	3.8	7.7	10.8	12.1
Black or African American only, male . .	31.1	35.4	36.7	38.3	10.2	14.5	17.7	19.4	2.9	6.4	9.1	10.1
Black or African American only, female .	41.4	43.8	46.8	49.0	14.3	18.1	22.9	24.9	4.5	8.7	12.0	13.7
Asian only.	- - -	- - -	- - -	34.3	- - -	- - -	- - -	14.3	- - -	- - -	- - -	6.2
Asian only, male	- - -	- - -	- - -	31.9	- - -	- - -	- - -	14.1	- - -	- - -	- - -	6.2
Asian only, female	- - -	- - -	- - -	36.3	- - -	- - -	- - -	14.6	- - -	- - -	- - -	6.1
Hispanic or Latino	- - -	- - -	35.2	35.7	- - -	- - -	15.7	16.0	- - -	- - -	8.4	8.4
Hispanic or Latino, male	- - -	- - -	31.7	32.1	- - -	- - -	14.0	15.0	- - -	- - -	7.3	7.9
Hispanic or Latina, female	- - -	- - -	38.8	39.2	- - -	- - -	17.4	17.1	- - -	- - -	9.5	8.8
Mexican origin	31.7	31.7	33.9	34.2	9.0	11.2	15.0	15.9	2.9	4.4	7.9	8.7
Mexican origin, male	27.5	25.8	31.0	31.8	7.0	9.5	13.4	14.9	2.0	3.5	7.2	8.2
Mexican origin, female	36.0	37.8	37.0	36.9	11.0	12.8	16.6	17.0	3.7	5.2	8.7	9.2
All ages, crude												
Both sexes[3]	37.8	45.0	48.5	48.9	11.0	17.6	21.7	23.1	3.6	7.4	10.6	11.9
Male	30.6	38.6	43.0	43.7	8.3	13.9	19.0	20.4	2.5	5.6	9.1	10.0
Female.	44.6	51.1	53.8	53.9	13.6	21.1	24.2	25.8	4.7	9.1	12.1	13.6
Not Hispanic or Latino:												
White only.	41.4	50.7	56.2	57.0	12.5	20.6	25.8	27.7	4.2	8.7	12.6	14.3
White only, male	33.5	43.8	50.3	51.4	9.5	16.5	22.9	24.6	2.9	6.6	11.0	12.1
White only, female	48.9	57.5	61.8	62.4	15.4	24.5	28.6	30.7	5.4	10.8	14.2	16.4
Black or African American only	31.2	36.0	40.2	42.8	9.2	13.5	18.6	21.1	2.6	6.2	9.4	11.2
Black or African American only, male . .	25.5	30.7	33.9	36.3	7.0	10.9	15.0	17.5	1.8	4.8	7.5	8.9
Black or African American only, female .	36.2	40.6	45.7	48.5	11.1	15.7	21.7	24.2	3.3	7.4	11.1	13.1
Asian only.	- - -	- - -	- - -	34.0	- - -	- - -	- - -	13.6	- - -	- - -	- - -	5.7
Asian only, male	- - -	- - -	- - -	30.5	- - -	- - -	- - -	12.6	- - -	- - -	- - -	5.5
Asian only, female	- - -	- - -	- - -	37.1	- - -	- - -	- - -	14.5	- - -	- - -	- - -	6.0
Hispanic or Latino	- - -	- - -	28.6	29.5	- - -	- - -	10.3	10.9	- - -	- - -	5.0	5.3
Hispanic or Latino, male	- - -	- - -	24.9	25.4	- - -	- - -	8.4	9.3	- - -	- - -	3.8	4.6
Hispanic or Latina, female	- - -	- - -	32.5	33.5	- - -	- - -	12.3	12.6	- - -	- - -	6.2	6.0
Mexican origin	24.0	23.6	26.4	27.0	4.8	6.1	9.0	9.8	1.4	2.1	4.1	4.9
Mexican origin, male	20.1	18.8	23.7	24.9	3.4	4.8	7.6	9.0	0.9	1.6	3.4	4.6
Mexican origin, female	28.1	28.9	29.4	29.3	6.4	7.5	10.6	10.8	1.9	2.7	4.9	5.4
Both sexes												
Under 18 years	20.5	23.8	24.0	21.5	2.4	4.1	3.8	3.9	*	*0.8	0.8	0.8
18–44 years	31.3	35.9	38.7	37.1	5.7	8.4	9.7	10.1	1.2	2.3	3.1	3.9
45–64 years	54.8	64.1	66.2	69.0	20.0	30.8	34.4	36.4	7.4	13.3	16.8	18.3
65 years and over	73.6	84.7	89.7	90.6	35.3	51.8	66.6	66.8	13.8	27.1	39.7	40.7
Male												
Under 18 years	20.4	25.7	24.5	21.1	2.6	4.3	4.4	4.3	*	*	0.8	0.9
18–44 years.	21.5	27.1	29.5	28.8	3.6	6.7	7.1	7.5	*0.8	1.7	2.1	3.0
45–64 years.	47.2	55.6	61.3	65.6	15.1	23.6	30.4	33.0	4.8	9.5	14.4	15.7
65 years and over.	67.2	80.1	88.8	88.7	31.3	46.3	66.8	65.2	11.3	24.7	39.5	38.4
Female												
Under 18 years	20.6	21.7	23.5	22.0	2.3	3.9	3.1	3.5	*	*0.8	*0.7	*
18–44 years.	40.7	44.6	47.6	45.3	7.6	10.2	12.2	12.6	1.7	2.8	4.0	4.8
45–64 years.	62.0	72.0	70.8	72.1	24.7	37.5	38.1	39.4	9.7	16.8	19.1	20.7
65 years and over.	78.3	88.1	90.4	92.1	38.2	55.9	66.4	68.1	15.6	28.9	39.8	42.6

See footnotes at end of table.

Table 79 (page 2 of 2). Prescription drug use in the past 30 days, by sex, race and Hispanic origin, and age: United States, selected years 1988–1994 through 2011–2014

Excel and PDF versions (with more data years and standard errors when available): http://www.cdc.gov/nchs/hus/contents2016.htm#079.

[Data are based on a sample of the civilian noninstitutionalized population]

- - - Data not available.

* Estimates are considered unreliable. Data preceded by an asterisk have a relative standard error (RSE) of 20%–30%. Data not shown have an RSE greater than 30%.

[1] Persons of Hispanic and Mexican origin may be of any race. Starting with 1999 data, race-specific estimates are tabulated according to the 1997 *Revisions to the Standards for the Classification of Federal Data on Race and Ethnicity* and are not strictly comparable with estimates for earlier years. The non-Hispanic race categories shown in the table conform to the 1997 Standards. Starting with 1999 data, race-specific estimates are for persons who reported only one racial group. Prior to data year 1999, estimates were tabulated according to the 1977 Standards. Estimates for single-race categories prior to 1999 included persons who reported one race or, if they reported more than one race, identified one race as best representing their race. See Appendix II, Hispanic origin; Race.

[2] Estimates are age-adjusted to the year 2000 standard population using four age groups: under 18 years, 18–44 years, 45–64 years, and 65 years and over. Age-adjusted estimates in this table may differ from other age-adjusted estimates based on the same data and presented elsewhere if different age groups are used in the adjustment procedure. See Appendix II, Age adjustment.

[3] Includes persons of all races and Hispanic origins, not just those shown separately.

NOTES: See Appendix II, Drug. Standard errors are available in the spreadsheet version of this table. Available from: http://www.cdc.gov/nchs/hus.htm. Data for additional years are available. See the Excel spreadsheet on the *Health, United States* website at: http://www.cdc.gov/nchs/hus.htm.

SOURCE: NCHS, National Health and Nutrition Examination Survey. See Appendix I, National Health and Nutrition Examination Survey (NHANES).

Table 80 (page 1 of 3). Selected prescription drug classes used in the past 30 days, by sex and age: United States, selected years 1988–1994 through 2011–2014

Excel and PDF versions (with more data years and standard errors when available): http://www.cdc.gov/nchs/hus/contents2016.htm#080.

[Data are based on a sample of the civilian noninstitutionalized population]

Age group and Multum Lexicon Plus therapeutic class [1] (common indications for use)	Total			Male			Female		
	1988–1994	1999–2002	2011–2014	1988–1994	1999–2002	2011–2014	1988–1994	1999–2002	2011–2014
All ages	Percent of population with at least one prescription drug in drug class in past 30 days								
Antihyperlipidemic agents (high cholesterol)	1.7	6.5	14.3	1.5	7.1	15.0	1.8	5.8	13.7
Analgesics (pain relief)	7.2	9.4	9.1	5.4	7.3	7.6	9.0	11.3	10.5
Antidepressants (depression and related disorders) . . .	1.8	6.4	10.7	1.2	4.4	7.3	2.3	8.3	13.9
Proton pump inhibitors or H2 antagonists (gastric reflux, ulcers) [2]	2.8	5.3	8.5	2.4	4.7	7.5	3.0	5.9	9.4
Beta-adrenergic blocking agents (high blood pressure, heart disease)	3.1	4.4	7.7	2.7	4.1	7.1	3.5	4.6	8.4
ACE inhibitors (high blood pressure, heart disease). . . .	2.4	4.6	7.3	2.4	4.7	8.1	2.4	4.5	6.6
Antidiabetic agents (diabetes)	2.6	3.7	6.6	2.5	3.7	6.8	2.6	3.8	6.3
Diuretics (high blood pressure, heart disease, kidney disease) [3]	3.4	4.1	5.6	2.3	3.1	4.4	4.4	5.1	6.7
Thyroid hormones (hypothyroidism)	2.3	3.9	5.1	0.8	1.5	1.9	3.7	6.2	8.0
Bronchodilators (asthma, breathing).	2.6	3.5	4.6	2.5	3.1	4.5	2.7	3.8	4.6
Sex hormones (contraceptives, menopause, hot flashes) [4]	. . .	. . .	. . .	. . .	. . .	. . .	9.8	15.2	8.7
Anxiolytics, sedatives, and hypnotics (anxiety, insomnia, and related disorders)	2.8	3.3	5.3	1.9	2.6	4.4	3.6	4.0	6.2
Antihypertensive combinations (high blood pressure) . .	2.4	2.9	4.1	1.4	1.9	3.3	3.3	3.8	4.8
Anticonvulsants (epilepsy, seizure, and related disorders).	1.4	2.4	4.9	1.2	2.1	4.3	1.6	2.7	5.5
Calcium channel blocking agents (high blood pressure, heart disease)	3.6	4.2	4.7	3.4	3.5	4.6	3.8	4.8	4.7
Under 18 years									
Bronchodilators (asthma, breathing).	3.0	4.0	4.4	3.3	4.4	4.9	2.7	3.6	3.9
CNS stimulants (attention-deficit/hyperactivity disorder).	*0.8	2.9	3.4	*1.2	4.4	5.0	*	1.4	1.7
Penicillins (bacterial infections)	6.1	5.1	2.6	5.9	5.2	2.0	6.4	5.0	3.2
Leukotriene modifiers (asthma, allergies)	. . .	0.7	2.1	. . .	*0.9	2.5	. . .	*	1.7
Antihistamines (allergies)	2.0	4.4	2.0	2.1	4.9	2.3	1.9	3.9	1.8
Respiratory inhalant products (asthma, chronic obstructive pulmonary disease, and related disorders).	*0.7	1.5	1.9	*	1.7	2.4	*	1.3	*1.3
Adrenal cortical steroids (anti-inflammatory)	*0.5	0.8	1.0	*	*0.7	*1.0	*0.5	0.9	*1.1
Nasal preparations (nose symptoms)	*	1.1	1.7	*	*1.3	2.2	*	1.0	*
Antidepressants (depression and related disorders) . . .	*	1.8	*1.3	*	2.2	*0.7	*	*1.5	*
Upper respiratory combinations (cough and cold, congestion).	2.3	2.3	*	2.6	*2.4	*	2.0	*2.2	*
Analgesics (pain relief)	1.2	1.4	1.1	*1.2	1.3	*1.0	1.4	1.6	*1.3
Dermatological agents (skin symptoms)	0.7	1.1	1.1	*	1.1	*0.9	*1.0	*1.1	1.4
18–44 years									
Analgesics (pain relief)	7.2	8.0	7.0	5.1	6.0	5.3	9.1	9.9	8.8
Antidepressants (depression and related disorders) . . .	1.6	6.0	8.8	*1.0	3.6	6.4	2.3	8.5	11.2
Sex hormones (contraceptives, menopause, hot flashes) [4]	. . .	. . .	. . .	. . .	. . .	. . .	11.5	13.5	13.4
Proton pump inhibitors or H2 antagonists (gastric reflux, ulcers) [2]	2.0	3.0	3.8	1.6	3.0	4.2	2.4	3.0	3.4
Anxiolytics, sedatives, and hypnotics (anxiety, insomnia, and related disorders)	1.4	2.1	4.2	*1.0	*1.7	3.5	1.9	2.5	5.0
Anticonvulsants (epilepsy, seizure, and related disorders).	0.8	1.6	4.1	*0.6	1.6	4.0	1.0	*1.5	4.2
Bronchodilators (asthma, breathing).	1.4	2.2	2.9	*1.1	1.6	2.6	*1.8	2.8	3.2
Antihyperlipidemic agents (high cholesterol)	*0.4	1.3	2.3	*	2.0	2.9	*	*	1.8
Antihistamines (allergies)	2.5	3.9	1.8	1.8	3.6	*1.6	3.2	4.2	*2.0
Thyroid hormones (hypothyroidism)	1.3	1.6	2.2	*	*	*0.7	2.1	2.8	3.6
ACE inhibitors (high blood pressure, heart disease). . . .	0.7	1.4	2.1	*0.9	1.5	2.1	*0.6	*1.2	2.2
Antidiabetic agents (diabetes)	*1.0	1.5	2.5	*	*1.5	2.1	*1.0	*1.6	2.9
Muscle relaxants (muscle spasm and related disorders).	1.0	1.3	1.7	*1.3	*1.1	1.4	*0.7	*1.4	2.1
Beta-adrenergic blocking agents (high blood pressure, heart disease)	1.1	*1.2	1.6	*0.9	*1.3	1.2	1.3	*	2.0
Nasal preparations (nose symptoms)	*0.6	1.5	1.4	*	*1.2	*0.8	*0.7	1.7	2.1

See footnotes at end of table.

Table 80 (page 2 of 3). Selected prescription drug classes used in the past 30 days, by sex and age: United States, selected years 1988–1994 through 2011–2014

Excel and PDF versions (with more data years and standard errors when available): http://www.cdc.gov/nchs/hus/contents2016.htm#080.

[Data are based on a sample of the civilian noninstitutionalized population]

Age group and Multum Lexicon Plus therapeutic class [1] (common indications for use)	Total			Male			Female		
	1988–1994	1999–2002	2011–2014	1988–1994	1999–2002	2011–2014	1988–1994	1999–2002	2011–2014
45–64 years	Percent of population with at least one prescription drug in drug class in past 30 days								
Antihyperlipidemic agents (high cholesterol)	4.3	13.8	25.6	4.4	17.2	28.2	4.2	10.7	23.1
Proton pump inhibitors or H2 antagonists (gastric reflux, ulcers) [2]	5.2	9.9	14.1	5.3	8.4	12.7	5.2	11.3	15.4
Antidepressants (depression and related disorders)	3.5	10.5	17.5	*2.3	7.0	12.5	4.6	13.8	22.2
Sex hormones (contraceptives, menopause, hot flashes) [4]	. . .	. . .	. . .	. . .	. . .	. . .	19.9	30.3	10.1
Analgesics (pain relief)	11.9	16.0	15.5	9.2	13.5	14.3	14.3	18.3	16.7
Beta-adrenergic blocking agents (high blood pressure, heart disease)	6.6	8.7	11.5	7.0	7.8	10.8	6.2	9.5	12.1
ACE inhibitors (high blood pressure, heart disease)	5.2	8.8	12.5	5.7	9.8	14.9	4.6	7.9	10.2
Antidiabetic agents (diabetes)	5.5	7.0	11.3	5.9	7.8	12.5	5.1	6.3	10.2
Thyroid hormones (hypothyroidism)	4.7	6.6	8.1	*1.2	*2.7	*2.6	8.1	10.1	13.2
Antihypertensive combinations (high blood pressure)	5.3	5.6	7.9	3.3	*3.7	7.4	7.1	7.3	8.3
Anxiolytics, sedatives, and hypnotics (anxiety, insomnia, and related disorders)	6.0	6.2	8.6	4.3	4.9	7.7	7.5	7.4	9.4
Diuretics (high blood pressure, heart disease, kidney disease) [3]	6.1	6.6	8.6	4.8	4.8	7.2	7.3	8.3	9.9
Anticonvulsants (epilepsy, seizure, and related disorders)	2.7	4.3	7.5	*2.5	3.5	6.3	2.9	5.1	8.6
Bronchodilators (asthma, breathing)	3.4	3.8	5.2	2.9	3.1	*4.6	3.8	4.5	5.8
Calcium channel blocking agents (high blood pressure, heart disease)	7.0	6.7	6.6	8.2	5.9	7.9	5.9	7.5	5.4
65 years and over									
Antihyperlipidemic agents (high cholesterol)	5.9	23.4	50.3	5.3	24.3	54.4	6.4	22.7	47.1
Beta-adrenergic blocking agents (high blood pressure, heart disease)	11.8	15.9	30.5	10.4	17.5	31.4	12.8	14.8	29.8
Diuretics (high blood pressure, heart disease, kidney disease) [3]	16.2	19.2	21.1	12.2	17.1	19.0	19.1	20.7	22.7
ACE inhibitors (high blood pressure, heart disease)	9.5	16.9	24.1	9.8	18.0	28.1	9.3	16.1	21.0
Proton pump inhibitors or H2 antagonists (gastric reflux, ulcers) [2]	7.5	14.6	23.2	7.2	14.1	19.8	7.7	15.0	25.9
Antidiabetic agents (diabetes)	9.0	12.4	19.5	9.0	12.9	22.6	9.0	12.0	17.1
Anticoagulants or antiplatelet agents (blood clot prevention) [5]	6.1	9.1	14.6	6.8	11.5	17.8	5.6	7.4	12.1
Analgesics (pain relief)	13.8	18.4	16.4	11.4	15.0	14.2	15.6	20.9	18.2
Calcium channel blocking agents (high blood pressure, heart disease)	16.1	19.1	17.8	14.5	17.4	16.7	17.3	20.4	18.7
Thyroid hormones (hypothyroidism)	7.0	14.3	15.5	3.3	6.7	7.7	9.7	19.8	21.7
Antihypertensive combinations (high blood pressure)	9.6	9.8	11.7	6.0	7.4	8.0	12.2	11.6	14.6
Antidepressants (depression and related disorders)	3.0	9.3	18.9	*2.3	7.2	12.0	3.5	10.8	24.4
Angiotensin II inhibitors (high blood pressure, heart disease)	. . .	4.8	12.2	. . .	4.1	11.8	. . .	5.3	12.6
Antiarrhythmic agents (heart rhythm irregularities)	23.1	16.6	8.8	21.6	17.9	8.4	24.3	15.6	9.0
65–74 years									
Antihyperlipidemic agents (high cholesterol)	7.3	26.2	49.1	6.2	26.6	51.9	8.1	25.9	46.7
Beta-adrenergic blocking agents (high blood pressure, heart disease)	11.3	14.8	25.8	10.6	16.0	27.9	11.9	13.9	24.1
ACE inhibitors (high blood pressure, heart disease)	9.6	17.2	23.5	10.6	18.1	28.9	8.9	16.4	18.9
Proton pump inhibitors or H2 antagonists (gastric reflux, ulcers) [2]	7.0	14.7	20.7	6.3	13.4	18.3	7.5	15.8	22.8
Antidiabetic agents (diabetes)	8.8	12.9	19.9	8.0	13.8	22.5	9.4	12.0	17.7
Diuretics (high blood pressure, heart disease, kidney disease) [3]	14.2	15.9	17.2	10.8	14.6	14.6	17.0	16.9	19.4
Analgesics (pain relief)	13.0	18.5	16.8	10.5	14.9	15.3	15.0	21.4	18.0
Antihypertensive combinations (high blood pressure)	8.1	8.0	11.8	4.8	*6.7	8.5	10.8	9.0	14.5
Anticoagulants or antiplatelet agents (blood clot prevention) [5]	5.4	6.7	10.7	6.3	9.8	*13.8	4.6	*4.2	8.1
Antidepressants (depression and related disorders)	2.8	9.3	18.7	*2.3	5.8	12.6	3.1	12.1	23.9
Calcium channel blocking agents (high blood pressure, heart disease)	15.0	16.1	14.4	14.0	15.3	15.0	15.8	16.8	13.9
Thyroid hormones (hypothyroidism)	6.4	13.0	14.6	*3.4	*5.0	*7.3	8.9	19.7	20.8
Angiotensin II inhibitors (high blood pressure, heart disease)	. . .	4.2	11.1	. . .	*3.5	9.5	. . .	4.9	12.4
Antiarrhythmic agents (heart rhythm irregularities)	20.2	13.0	6.4	19.0	15.5	*5.8	21.1	10.8	6.9

See footnotes at end of table.

Table 80 (page 3 of 3). Selected prescription drug classes used in the past 30 days, by sex and age: United States, selected years 1988–1994 through 2011–2014

Excel and PDF versions (with more data years and standard errors when available): http://www.cdc.gov/nchs/hus/contents2016.htm#080.

[Data are based on a sample of the civilian noninstitutionalized population]

Age group and Multum Lexicon Plus therapeutic class [1] (common indications for use)	Total			Male			Female		
	1988–1994	1999–2002	2011–2014	1988–1994	1999–2002	2011–2014	1988–1994	1999–2002	2011–2014
75 years and over	Percent of population with at least one prescription drug in drug class in past 30 days								
Antihyperlipidemic agents (high cholesterol)	3.8	19.9	48.2	*3.5	21.1	55.7	4.0	19.2	43.1
Beta-adrenergic blocking agents (high blood pressure, heart disease)	12.5	17.3	37.9	9.8	19.6	37.6	14.1	15.8	38.1
Diuretics (high blood pressure, heart disease, kidney disease.	19.2	23.2	25.4	14.7	20.5	24.5	21.9	24.9	26.1
ACE inhibitors (high blood pressure, heart disease). . . .	9.3	16.4	25.0	8.5	17.7	27.0	9.8	15.6	23.7
Anticoagulants or antiplatelet agents (blood clot prevention) [5]	7.2	12.0	20.1	7.8	13.9	24.1	6.9	10.9	17.4
Proton pump inhibitors or H2 antagonists (gastric reflux, ulcers) [2]	8.3	14.6	26.8	9.0	15.3	22.3	7.9	14.2	30.0
Calcium channel blocking agents (high blood pressure, heart disease)	17.8	22.8	22.6	15.3	20.5	19.4	19.2	24.2	24.9
Thyroid hormones (hypothyroidism)	7.9	15.8	16.8	3.0	9.2	8.2	10.9	20.0	22.9
Analgesics (pain relief)	15.1	18.4	16.0	13.0	15.1	12.6	16.3	20.4	18.3
Antidiabetic agents (diabetes)	9.3	11.8	18.9	10.7	11.5	22.8	8.5	12.0	16.3
Antihypertensive combinations (high blood pressure) . .	11.9	12.0	11.5	8.3	*8.2	7.1	14.0	14.4	14.6
Antiarrhythmic agents (heart rhythm irregularities)	27.7	21.0	12.1	26.3	21.3	12.6	28.6	20.7	11.7
Angiotensin II inhibitors (high blood pressure, heart disease)	. . .	5.4	13.9	. . .	*4.9	15.2	. . .	5.8	12.9
Antidepressants (depression and related disorders) . . .	3.4	9.3	19.2	*2.3	9.2	11.0	4.0	9.4	25.0

* Estimates are considered unreliable. Data preceded by an asterisk have a relative standard error (RSE) of 20%–30%. Data not shown have an RSE greater than 30%.
. . . Category not applicable.
[1] The drug therapeutic class is based on the December 2014 Lexicon Plus, a proprietary database of Cerner Multum, Inc. Lexicon Plus is a comprehensive database of all prescription and some nonprescription drug products available in the U.S. drug market. Data on prescription drug use are collected by the National Health and Nutrition Examination Survey. Respondents were asked if they had taken a prescription drug in the past 30 days. Those who answered "yes" were asked to show the interviewer the medication containers for all prescriptions. If no container was available, the respondent was asked to verbally report the name of the medication. Each drug's complete name was recorded and classified. Data presented here are based on the second level classification of prescription drugs. Up to four classes are assigned to each drug. Drugs classified into more than one class were counted in each class. For more information, see https://wwwn.cdc.gov/nchs/nhanes/1999-2000/RXQ_DRUG.htm. See Appendix II, Multum Lexicon Plus therapeutic class.
[2] The drugs classes proton pump inhibitors (272) and H2 antagonists (94) have been combined because of their similar indications for use.
[3] This category includes carbonic anhydrase inhibitors which are primarily used to treat glaucoma.
[4] Although sex hormones may be used by males, most are used by females. Therefore, data for sex hormones are only presented for females.
[5] The drugs classes anticoagulants (82) and antiplatelet agents (83) have been combined because of their similar indications for use.

NOTES: Some drug classes were not available in 1988–1994 and are coded as not applicable. See Appendix II, Drug. Standard errors are available in the spreadsheet version of this table. Available from: http://www.cdc.gov/nchs/hus.htm. Data have been revised and differ from previous editions of *Health, United States*.

SOURCE: NCHS, National Health and Nutrition Examination Survey. See Appendix I, National Health and Nutrition Examination Survey (NHANES).

Table 81 (page 1 of 4). Persons with hospital stays in the past year, by selected characteristics: United States, selected years 1997–2015

Excel and PDF versions (with more data years and standard errors when available): http://www.cdc.gov/nchs/hus/contents2016.htm#081.

[Data are based on household interviews of a sample of the civilian noninstitutionalized population]

Characteristic	One or more hospital stays[1]					Two or more hospital stays[1]				
	1997	2000	2010	2014	2015	1997	2000	2010	2014	2015
	Percent									
1 year and over, age-adjusted[2,3]	7.8	7.6	7.0	6.4	6.5	1.8	1.8	1.8	1.6	1.7
1 year and over, crude[2]	7.7	7.5	7.2	6.8	6.9	1.7	1.8	1.9	1.7	1.8
Age										
1–17 years.	2.8	2.5	2.4	2.0	2.1	0.5	0.4	0.5	0.4	0.3
1–5 years	3.9	3.8	3.4	3.0	3.1	0.7	0.7	0.6	0.7	*0.4
6–17 years	2.3	1.9	1.9	1.6	1.7	0.4	0.3	0.5	0.3	0.3
18–44 years	7.4	7.0	6.3	5.8	5.8	1.2	1.1	1.3	1.1	1.2
18–24 years	7.9	7.0	5.7	4.6	4.5	1.3	1.1	1.1	0.9	0.8
25–44 years.	7.3	7.0	6.6	6.2	6.3	1.2	1.2	1.3	1.1	1.3
45–64 years	8.2	8.4	8.3	7.4	7.7	2.2	2.2	2.5	2.3	2.3
45–54 years.	6.9	7.3	7.3	6.1	6.4	1.7	1.8	2.1	1.9	1.8
55–64 years.	10.2	10.0	9.5	8.7	9.2	2.9	2.8	2.9	2.6	2.7
65 years and over	18.0	18.2	16.1	15.3	15.2	5.4	5.8	4.9	4.3	4.9
65–74 years.	16.1	16.1	13.6	13.8	12.8	4.8	4.9	3.8	4.0	4.0
75 years and over.	20.4	20.7	19.0	17.5	18.8	6.2	6.8	6.2	4.8	6.2
75–84 years	19.8	20.1	18.3	16.1	17.3	6.1	6.2	6.1	4.2	5.7
85 years and over	22.8	23.4	20.8	20.9	22.5	6.2	9.0	6.6	6.3	7.3
1–64 years										
Total, 1–64 years[2,4]	6.3	6.1	5.7	5.1	5.2	1.3	1.2	1.3	1.2	1.2
Sex										
Male, crude	4.4	4.2	4.2	3.9	4.2	0.9	1.0	1.1	1.1	1.2
1–17 years	2.9	2.4	2.4	2.0	2.1	0.6	0.4	0.5	0.5	0.4
18–44 years	3.6	3.1	2.9	2.6	3.1	0.6	0.6	0.7	0.6	0.9
45–54 years	6.0	7.0	6.4	5.7	5.9	1.4	1.8	1.9	1.8	1.7
55–64 years	11.1	10.2	9.3	9.0	9.7	3.0	3.0	2.8	2.8	2.9
Female, crude	8.0	7.9	7.6	6.7	6.6	1.6	1.5	1.7	1.4	1.4
1–17 years	2.6	2.5	2.3	2.1	2.1	0.5	0.4	0.5	0.4	0.3
18–44 years	11.2	10.8	9.8	8.9	8.5	1.8	1.7	1.9	1.5	1.5
45–54 years	7.6	7.6	8.3	6.6	6.8	2.0	1.9	2.3	2.0	2.0
55–64 years	9.4	9.8	9.7	8.5	8.8	2.9	2.7	2.9	2.5	2.4
Race[4,5]										
White only	6.2	5.9	5.6	5.0	5.1	1.2	1.1	1.3	1.1	1.1
Black or African American only	7.6	7.4	6.7	6.2	6.4	1.9	1.9	1.9	2.1	2.0
American Indian or Alaska Native only	7.6	7.0	*7.6	6.6	5.7	*	*	*2.4	*	*
Asian only	3.9	3.9	3.6	3.1	3.3	*0.5	*0.6	*0.4	0.5	0.8
Native Hawaiian or Other Pacific Islander only	- - -	*	*	*	*	- - -	*	*	*	*
2 or more races	- - -	8.8	7.7	5.9	5.7	- - -	*1.6	*2.4	*1.4	*1.6
Hispanic origin and race[4,5]										
Hispanic or Latino	6.8	5.5	5.2	4.5	4.8	1.3	0.9	1.1	1.1	1.2
Not Hispanic or Latino.	6.2	6.1	5.8	5.2	5.3	1.3	1.3	1.4	1.2	1.2
White only.	6.1	6.0	5.7	5.2	5.3	1.2	1.2	1.3	1.1	1.1
Black or African American only	7.5	7.4	6.7	6.2	6.4	1.9	1.9	1.9	2.1	2.0
Percent of poverty level[4,6]										
Below 100%	10.3	9.1	8.3	8.1	8.3	2.8	2.6	2.7	2.7	2.9
100%–199%	7.3	7.3	7.0	6.1	6.1	1.7	1.9	1.9	1.7	1.7
200%–399%	6.0	6.0	5.2	4.7	4.9	1.2	1.1	1.1	1.0	1.1
400% or more	4.7	5.0	4.5	3.8	4.1	0.7	0.8	0.8	0.6	0.6

See footnotes at end of table.

Excel and PDF versions (with more data years and standard errors when available): http://www.cdc.gov/nchs/hus/contents2016.htm#081.

[Data are based on household interviews of a sample of the civilian noninstitutionalized population]

Characteristic	One or more hospital stays [1]					Two or more hospital stays [1]				
	1997	2000	2010	2014	2015	1997	2000	2010	2014	2015
Hispanic origin and race and percent of poverty level [4,5,6]	Percent									
Hispanic or Latino:										
Below 100%	9.1	7.4	7.3	6.6	6.7	2.0	1.6	2.0	2.0	2.1
100%–199%	5.9	5.4	4.8	4.4	4.8	1.0	0.8	1.1	1.1	1.1
200%–399%	5.9	4.6	4.3	3.8	3.7	1.1	0.7	0.7	0.8	0.9
400% or more	5.5	4.7	4.4	2.7	4.6	*1.1	*0.6	*0.8	*	*0.8
Not Hispanic or Latino:										
White only:										
Below 100%	10.7	9.6	8.8	8.8	9.1	3.2	2.7	2.9	2.9	3.3
100%–199%	7.7	7.8	7.8	6.8	7.0	1.8	2.2	2.2	1.7	1.8
200%–399%	6.1	6.1	5.5	5.1	5.2	1.2	1.1	1.2	1.0	1.0
400% or more	4.7	5.0	4.6	4.0	4.2	0.7	0.8	0.8	0.6	0.6
Black or African American only:										
Below 100%	11.4	10.8	9.4	8.8	9.4	3.3	3.4	3.1	3.6	3.1
100%–199%	8.0	8.5	7.7	7.2	6.8	2.1	2.3	2.3	2.6	2.6
200%–399%	6.2	6.1	5.3	4.2	5.7	1.5	1.3	1.4	1.3	1.7
400% or more	4.7	5.8	4.5	4.7	4.0	*0.9	*1.3	*1.0	*0.9	*1.0
Health insurance status at the time of interview [4,7]										
Insured	6.6	6.4	6.2	5.4	5.4	1.3	1.3	1.4	1.2	1.2
Private	5.6	5.5	5.0	4.2	4.3	1.0	1.0	0.9	0.7	0.7
Medicaid	16.1	15.9	12.7	10.4	10.3	4.9	4.7	4.5	3.6	3.4
Uninsured	4.8	4.5	4.0	3.5	3.7	1.0	0.9	0.9	0.8	1.0
Health insurance status prior to interview [4,7]										
Insured continuously all 12 months	6.5	6.3	6.0	5.3	5.4	1.3	1.2	1.4	1.2	1.2
Uninsured for any period up to 12 months	8.5	8.4	7.9	6.5	6.3	1.8	1.9	1.9	1.6	1.7
Uninsured more than 12 months	3.8	3.5	3.0	2.7	2.9	0.8	0.8	0.8	0.7	0.8
Percent of poverty level and health insurance status prior to interview [4,6,7]										
Below 100%:										
Insured continuously all 12 months	12.4	10.7	10.4	9.8	9.4	3.7	3.1	3.4	3.4	3.4
Uninsured for any period up to 12 months	13.7	13.4	10.4	10.2	10.2	3.4	*3.4	3.0	3.1	3.4
Uninsured more than 12 months	4.9	5.0	4.0	3.3	3.9	1.0	*1.6	1.3	*1.1	*1.1
100%–199%:										
Insured continuously all 12 months	8.5	8.6	8.5	7.1	7.0	2.0	2.3	2.5	2.0	1.9
Uninsured for any period up to 12 months	9.3	9.1	10.1	7.3	5.7	*1.9	*2.2	1.9	1.7	1.6
Uninsured more than 12 months	3.8	3.2	2.7	2.8	2.8	*0.7	*0.7	*0.5	*0.8	*0.7
200%–399%:										
Insured continuously all 12 months	6.3	6.4	5.6	5.0	5.0	1.3	1.2	1.2	1.0	1.0
Uninsured for any period up to 12 months	7.0	6.6	6.1	5.0	6.3	*1.5	*1.3	*1.6	*1.0	*1.6
Uninsured more than 12 months	3.3	2.8	2.6	2.0	2.1	*0.7	*0.4	*0.7	*	*
400% or more:										
Insured continuously all 12 months	4.9	5.1	4.7	3.9	4.2	0.7	0.8	0.8	0.6	0.6
Uninsured for any period up to 12 months	3.9	6.0	4.1	3.2	3.6	*	*	*	*	*
Uninsured more than 12 months	*	*2.1	*1.8	*2.5	*	*	*	*	*	*
Disability measure among adults 18–64 years [4,8]										
Any basic actions difficulty or complex activity limitation	14.1	15.1	14.3	13.4	12.9	4.1	4.4	5.2	4.6	4.4
Any basic actions difficulty	13.9	15.1	14.2	13.6	12.8	4.1	4.4	5.1	4.7	4.6
Any complex activity limitation	21.5	22.6	21.2	21.5	19.0	7.7	8.8	8.6	8.4	7.5
No disability	5.8	5.6	5.4	4.5	4.6	0.6	0.7	0.8	0.5	0.6

See footnotes at end of table.

Table 81 (page 3 of 4). Persons with hospital stays in the past year, by selected characteristics: United States, selected years 1997–2015

Excel and PDF versions (with more data years and standard errors when available): http://www.cdc.gov/nchs/hus/contents2016.htm#081.

[Data are based on household interviews of a sample of the civilian noninstitutionalized population]

Characteristic	One or more hospital stays [1]					Two or more hospital stays [1]				
	1997	2000	2010	2014	2015	1997	2000	2010	2014	2015
Geographic region [4]	Percent									
Northeast	6.0	5.5	5.2	5.1	5.3	1.2	1.0	1.2	1.1	1.2
Midwest.	6.5	6.3	6.3	5.3	5.8	1.5	1.3	1.5	1.3	1.3
South	6.8	6.6	6.0	5.2	5.3	1.4	1.5	1.5	1.3	1.3
West.	5.4	5.2	4.9	4.6	4.3	0.8	0.9	1.1	1.0	0.9
Location of residence [4,9]										
Within MSA	6.1	5.8	5.5	5.0	5.1	1.2	1.1	1.3	1.1	1.2
Outside MSA	7.0	6.9	6.9	5.8	5.7	1.6	1.5	1.6	1.4	1.4
65 years and over										
Total 65 years and over [2,10]	18.1	18.3	16.2	15.6	15.6	5.4	5.8	4.9	4.4	5.0
65–74 years.	16.1	16.1	13.6	13.8	12.8	4.8	4.9	3.8	4.0	4.0
75 years and over.	20.4	20.7	19.0	17.5	18.8	6.2	6.8	6.2	4.8	6.2
Sex [10]										
Male	19.0	19.5	16.2	16.6	17.0	5.8	5.8	5.4	4.7	5.6
Female.	17.5	17.4	16.2	14.8	14.6	5.1	5.7	4.6	4.1	4.6
Hispanic origin and race [5,10]										
Hispanic or Latino	17.3	16.6	13.9	14.7	14.7	6.2	6.4	5.0	4.2	5.2
Not Hispanic or Latino.	18.2	18.4	16.4	15.6	15.7	5.4	5.8	4.9	4.4	5.0
White only.	18.3	18.4	16.5	15.7	15.8	5.4	5.7	4.9	4.3	5.0
Black or African American only	18.9	19.8	16.9	16.7	16.2	5.5	7.5	5.5	5.5	5.5
Percent of poverty level [6,10]										
Below 100%.	20.9	20.9	18.8	17.5	18.0	6.4	7.5	5.1	6.1	8.1
100%–199%.	19.6	19.2	17.2	17.8	17.7	6.5	6.6	5.2	5.3	5.9
200%–399%.	17.3	18.1	16.0	15.5	15.9	4.9	5.8	5.5	4.5	5.0
400% or more	16.6	16.0	15.0	13.9	13.7	4.7	4.2	4.1	3.4	3.9
Disability measure [8,10]										
Any basic actions difficulty or complex activity limitation	22.6	24.7	20.2	19.9	21.9	7.2	8.6	6.4	6.2	7.9
Any basic actions difficulty	22.7	24.7	20.4	20.0	22.0	7.2	8.7	6.6	6.3	8.0
Any complex activity limitation	29.0	31.5	25.4	24.8	28.2	10.8	12.2	9.2	9.5	11.1
No disability	7.8	9.7	10.6	8.1	7.8	1.1	1.9	*1.6	*1.4	*1.8
Geographic region [10]										
Northeast	17.2	16.6	16.5	15.6	14.2	5.1	4.5	6.1	4.4	4.5
Midwest.	18.2	19.5	16.4	17.6	17.9	5.6	7.2	4.7	4.0	6.6
South	19.4	19.5	16.4	15.0	15.6	6.1	6.3	4.7	4.9	4.8
West.	16.5	16.4	15.3	14.3	14.6	4.4	4.4	4.5	3.9	4.3
Location of residence [9,10]										
Within MSA	17.8	17.8	15.9	15.4	15.5	5.2	5.4	4.8	4.5	5.1
Outside MSA	19.1	19.6	17.3	16.2	16.2	6.3	6.9	5.6	3.9	4.8

See footnotes at end of table.

Table 81 (page 4 of 4). Persons with hospital stays in the past year, by selected characteristics: United States, selected years 1997–2015

Excel and PDF versions (with more data years and standard errors when available): http://www.cdc.gov/nchs/hus/contents2016.htm#081.

[Data are based on household interviews of a sample of the civilian noninstitutionalized population]

---

* Estimates are considered unreliable. Data preceded by an asterisk have a relative standard error (RSE) of 20%–30%. Data not shown have an RSE greater than 30%.

- - - Data not available.

[1] These estimates exclude hospitalizations for institutionalized persons and those who died while hospitalized, because they are outside the scope of this survey. See Appendix II, Hospital utilization.

[2] Includes all other races not shown separately, unknown health insurance status, and unknown disability status.

[3] Estimates are for persons 1 year of age and over and are age-adjusted to the year 2000 standard population using six age groups: 1–17 years, 18–44 years, 45–54 years, 55–64 years, 65–74 years, and 75 years and over. See Appendix II, Age adjustment.

[4] Estimates are for persons aged 1–64 and are age-adjusted to the year 2000 standard population using four age groups: 1–17 years, 18–44 years, 45–54 years, and 55–64 years. The disability measure is age-adjusted using the three adult age groups. See Appendix II, Age adjustment.

[5] The race groups, white, black, American Indian or Alaska Native, Asian, Native Hawaiian or Other Pacific Islander, and 2 or more races, include persons of Hispanic and non-Hispanic origin. Persons of Hispanic origin may be of any race. Starting with 1999 data, race-specific estimates are tabulated according to the 1997 *Revisions to the Standards for the Classification of Federal Data on Race and Ethnicity* and are not strictly comparable with estimates for earlier years. The five single-race categories plus multiple-race categories shown in the table conform to the 1997 Standards. Starting with 1999 data, race-specific estimates are for persons who reported only one racial group; the category 2 or more races includes persons who reported more than one racial group. Prior to 1999, data were tabulated according to the 1977 Standards with four racial groups, and the Asian only category included Native Hawaiian or Other Pacific Islander. Estimates for single-race categories prior to 1999 included persons who reported one race or, if they reported more than one race, identified one race as best representing their race. Starting with 2003 data, race responses of other race and unspecified multiple race were treated as missing, and then race was imputed if these were the only race responses. Almost all persons with a race response of other race were of Hispanic origin. See Appendix II, Hispanic origin; Race.

[6] Percent of poverty level is based on family income and family size and composition using U.S. Census Bureau poverty thresholds. Missing family income data were imputed for 1997 and beyond. See Appendix II, Family income; Poverty; Table VI.

[7] Health insurance categories are mutually exclusive. Persons who reported both Medicaid and private coverage are classified as having private coverage. Starting with 1997 data, state-sponsored health plan coverage is included as Medicaid coverage. Starting with 1999 data, coverage by the Children's Health Insurance Program (CHIP) is included with Medicaid coverage. In addition to private and Medicaid, the insured category also includes military, other government, and Medicare coverage. Persons not covered by private insurance, Medicaid, CHIP, state-sponsored or other government-sponsored health plans (starting in 1997), Medicare, or military plans are considered to have no health insurance coverage. Persons with only Indian Health Service coverage are considered to have no health insurance coverage. See Appendix II, Health insurance coverage.

[8] Any basic actions difficulty or complex activity limitation is defined as having one or more of the following limitations or difficulties: movement difficulty, emotional difficulty, sensory (seeing or hearing) difficulty, cognitive difficulty, self-care (activities of daily living or instrumental activities of daily living) limitation, social limitation, or work limitation. For more information, see Appendix II, Basic actions difficulty; Complex activity limitation. Starting with 2007 data, the hearing question, a component of the basic actions difficulty measure, was revised. Consequently, data prior to 2007 are not comparable with data for 2007 and beyond. For more information on the impact of the revised hearing question, see Appendix II, Hearing trouble.

[9] MSA is metropolitan statistical area. Starting with 2006 data, MSA status is determined using 2000 census data and the 2000 standards for defining MSAs. For data prior to 2006, see Appendix II, Metropolitan statistical area (MSA) for the applicable standards.

[10] Estimates are for persons aged 65 and over and are age-adjusted to the year 2000 standard population using two age groups: 65–74 years and 75 years and over. See Appendix II, Age adjustment.

NOTES: Standard errors are available in the spreadsheet version of this table. Available from: http://www.cdc.gov/nchs/hus.htm. Data for additional years are available. See the Excel spreadsheet on the *Health, United States* website at: http://www.cdc.gov/nchs/hus.htm.

SOURCE: NCHS, National Health Interview Survey, family core and sample adult questionnaires. See Appendix I, National Health Interview Survey (NHIS).

Table 82. Hospital admissions, average length of stay, outpatient visits, and outpatient surgery, by type of ownership and size of hospital: United States, selected years 1975–2014

Excel and PDF versions (with more data years and standard errors when available): http://www.cdc.gov/nchs/hus/contents2016.htm#082.

[Data are based on reporting by a census of hospitals]

Type of ownership and size of hospital	1975	1980	1990	2000	2010	2012	2013	2014
Admissions	Number, in thousands							
All hospitals	36,157	38,892	33,774	34,891	36,915	36,156	35,416	34,879
Federal	1,913	2,044	1,759	1,034	911	901	949	936
Nonfederal [1]	34,243	36,848	32,015	33,946	36,004	35,256	34,467	33,943
Community [2]	33,435	36,143	31,181	33,089	35,149	34,422	33,609	33,067
Nonprofit	23,722	25,566	22,878	24,453	25,532	24,751	24,319	23,742
For profit	2,646	3,165	3,066	4,141	4,925	5,224	5,052	5,119
State-local government.	7,067	7,413	5,236	4,496	4,693	4,447	4,238	4,206
6–24 beds	174	159	95	141	199	197	189	185
25–49 beds	1,431	1,254	870	995	1,169	1,128	1,087	1,046
50–99 beds	3,675	3,700	2,474	2,355	2,173	2,017	2,021	1,925
100–199 beds	7,017	7,162	5,833	6,735	6,125	5,920	5,754	5,849
200–299 beds	6,174	6,596	6,333	6,702	6,569	6,298	6,156	5,759
300–399 beds	4,739	5,358	5,091	5,135	5,835	5,660	5,344	5,190
400–499 beds	3,689	4,401	3,644	3,617	3,869	3,966	3,750	3,899
500 beds or more	6,537	7,513	6,840	7,410	9,210	9,235	9,307	9,212
Average length of stay [3]	Number of days							
All hospitals	11.4	10.0	9.1	6.8	6.2	6.1	6.1	6.1
Federal	20.3	16.8	14.9	12.8	11.8	9.9	9.6	10.3
Nonfederal [1]	10.8	9.6	8.8	6.6	6.1	6.0	6.0	6.0
Community [2]	7.7	7.6	7.2	5.8	5.4	5.4	5.4	5.5
Nonprofit	7.8	7.7	7.3	5.7	5.3	5.2	5.3	5.3
For profit	6.6	6.5	6.4	5.4	5.3	5.3	5.5	5.5
State-local government.	7.6	7.3	7.7	6.7	6.2	6.3	6.3	6.4
6–24 beds	5.6	5.3	5.4	4.3	4.3	4.4	4.6	4.8
25–49 beds	6.0	5.8	6.1	5.1	5.2	5.3	5.5	5.5
50–99 beds	6.8	6.7	7.2	6.5	6.4	6.8	6.7	6.9
100–199 beds	7.1	7.0	7.1	5.7	5.3	5.2	5.2	5.3
200–299 beds	7.5	7.4	6.9	5.7	5.1	5.1	5.1	5.1
300–399 beds	7.8	7.6	7.0	5.5	5.1	5.1	5.1	5.1
400–499 beds	8.1	7.9	7.3	5.6	5.3	5.2	5.3	5.3
500 beds or more	9.1	8.7	8.1	6.3	5.7	5.7	5.7	5.7
Outpatient visits [4]	Number, in thousands							
All hospitals	254,844	262,951	368,184	592,673	750,408	777,961	787,422	802,680
Federal	51,957	50,566	58,527	63,402	90,134	92,891	98,676	100,263
Nonfederal [1]	202,887	212,385	309,657	531,972	660,274	685,070	688,746	702,417
Community [2]	190,672	202,310	301,329	521,405	651,424	674,971	677,951	693,107
Nonprofit	131,435	142,156	221,073	393,168	494,178	512,237	516,162	525,424
For profit	7,713	9,696	20,110	43,378	48,201	53,854	53,191	56,299
State-local government.	51,525	50,459	60,146	84,858	109,045	108,880	108,599	111,384
6–24 beds	915	1,155	1,471	4,555	9,934	10,628	10,888	11,314
25–49 beds	5,855	6,227	10,812	27,007	43,099	46,693	47,453	47,871
50–99 beds	16,303	17,976	27,582	49,385	57,701	56,800	58,123	59,361
100–199 beds	35,156	36,453	58,940	114,183	120,902	123,765	123,562	133,742
200–299 beds	32,772	36,073	60,561	99,248	110,661	111,664	112,921	105,764
300–399 beds	29,169	30,495	43,699	73,444	90,515	93,787	89,747	85,585
400–499 beds	22,127	25,501	33,394	52,205	65,543	72,413	71,359	77,947
500 beds or more	48,375	48,430	64,870	101,378	153,067	159,222	163,897	171,523
Outpatient surgery	Percent of total surgeries [5]							
Community hospitals [2]	- - -	16.3	50.5	62.7	63.6	64.5	65.6	65.9

- - - Data not available.

[1] The category of nonfederal hospitals comprises psychiatric hospitals, tuberculosis and other respiratory diseases hospitals, and long-term and short-term general and other special hospitals. See Appendix II, Hospital.
[2] Community hospitals are nonfederal short-term general and special hospitals whose facilities and services are available to the public. The types of facilities included in the community hospitals category have changed over time. See Appendix II, Hospital.
[3] Average length of stay is the number of inpatient days divided by the number of admissions. See Appendix II, Average length of stay.
[4] Outpatient visits include visits to the emergency department, outpatient department, referred visits (pharmacy, EKG, radiology), and outpatient surgery. See Appendix II, Outpatient visit.
[5] Total surgeries is a measure of patients with at least one surgical procedure. Persons with multiple surgical procedures during the same outpatient visit or inpatient stay are counted only once. See Appendix II, Outpatient surgery.

SOURCE: American Hospital Association (AHA). Annual Survey of Hospitals. Hospital Statistics, 1976, 1981, 1991–92, 2002, 2012, 2014, 2015, and 2016 editions. Chicago, IL. (Reprinted from AHA Hospital Statistics by permission, Copyright 1976, 1981, 1991–92, 2002, 2012, 2014, 2015, and 2016 editions by Health Forum, LLC, an American Hospital Association Company.) See Appendix I, American Hospital Association (AHA) Annual Survey of Hospitals.

Table 83. Active physicians and physicians in patient care, by state: United States, selected years 1975–2013

[Data are based on reporting by physicians]

State	Active physicians [1,2]						Physicians in patient care [1,2,3]					
	1975	1985	2000 [4]	2010	2012	2013	1975	1985	2000 [4]	2010	2012	2013
	Number per 10,000 civilian population											
United States	15.3	20.7	25.8	27.2	28.3	29.4	13.5	18.0	22.7	24.0	26.9	27.6
Alabama.	9.2	14.2	19.8	21.4	21.8	22.4	8.6	13.1	18.2	20.6	21.1	21.5
Alaska	8.4	13.0	18.5	24.3	24.2	25.0	7.8	12.1	16.3	23.3	23.2	23.7
Arizona	16.7	20.2	20.9	22.6	24.2	25.5	14.1	17.1	17.6	21.6	23.2	24.0
Arkansas	9.1	13.8	18.8	20.2	20.9	21.5	8.5	12.8	17.3	19.4	20.2	20.6
California	18.8	23.7	23.8	26.1	26.9	27.8	17.3	21.5	21.6	24.7	25.6	26.2
Colorado	17.3	20.7	24.0	26.9	27.6	29.1	15.0	17.7	20.9	25.5	26.3	27.4
Connecticut.	19.8	27.6	33.7	36.0	37.6	38.4	17.7	24.3	30.3	33.6	35.2	35.8
Delaware	14.3	19.7	24.7	26.3	26.4	27.4	12.7	17.1	21.0	25.2	25.3	25.8
District of Columbia	39.6	55.3	62.5	76.9	73.8	74.7	34.6	45.6	54.5	68.8	65.9	66.1
Florida.	15.2	20.2	24.1	26.0	26.5	27.2	13.4	17.8	21.2	25.0	25.5	25.7
Georgia	11.5	16.2	20.4	21.3	22.3	23.4	10.6	14.7	18.6	20.2	21.2	22.0
Hawaii	16.2	21.5	26.4	31.3	29.7	30.8	14.7	19.8	24.0	29.6	28.2	29.0
Idaho.	9.5	12.1	15.8	18.4	18.4	19.2	8.9	11.4	14.4	17.9	18.0	18.6
Illinois	14.5	20.5	26.1	27.9	28.7	30.1	13.1	18.2	23.1	26.6	27.5	28.5
Indiana.	10.6	14.7	20.0	22.2	22.6	23.3	9.6	13.2	18.0	21.3	21.7	22.2
Iowa	11.4	15.6	19.8	21.8	22.0	23.2	9.4	12.4	15.5	20.8	21.0	21.6
Kansas	12.8	17.3	21.8	24.0	24.5	25.4	11.2	15.1	18.8	23.1	23.6	24.1
Kentucky	10.9	15.1	20.6	23.1	23.3	24.6	10.1	13.9	19.1	22.2	22.5	23.6
Louisiana	11.4	17.3	23.8	25.4	26.8	27.2	10.5	16.1	22.4	24.5	25.9	26.3
Maine	12.8	18.7	26.8	31.8	32.0	33.7	10.7	15.6	21.7	30.2	30.5	31.7
Maryland	18.6	30.4	35.4	39.1	39.5	40.9	16.5	24.9	31.1	34.9	35.5	36.5
Massachusetts.	20.8	30.2	38.6	43.4	44.6	47.0	18.3	25.4	34.4	40.0	41.3	43.0
Michigan	15.4	20.8	26.3	28.9	30.1	31.5	12.0	16.0	20.2	27.6	28.8	29.4
Minnesota.	14.9	20.5	24.9	30.1	30.3	31.1	13.7	18.5	23.0	28.2	28.9	29.5
Mississippi	8.4	11.8	16.6	18.3	18.6	19.5	8.0	11.1	15.2	17.6	18.0	18.7
Missouri.	15.0	20.5	24.7	26.3	27.4	28.9	11.6	16.3	20.2	25.1	26.2	26.9
Montana.	10.6	14.0	20.4	22.5	22.4	23.1	10.1	13.2	18.8	21.8	21.7	22.3
Nebraska	12.1	15.7	21.7	24.5	24.8	26.0	10.9	14.4	20.1	23.4	23.8	24.8
Nevada	11.9	16.0	18.0	19.8	19.6	20.3	10.9	14.5	15.9	19.2	19.0	19.3
New Hampshire	14.3	18.1	23.8	29.5	30.6	32.0	13.1	16.7	21.7	28.2	29.3	30.4
New Jersey	16.2	23.4	31.1	31.8	32.5	33.5	14.0	19.8	26.2	30.1	30.9	31.5
New Mexico	12.2	17.0	20.9	23.8	24.1	25.2	10.1	14.7	18.5	22.5	22.9	23.6
New York	22.7	29.0	36.2	36.4	38.3	39.4	20.2	25.2	32.3	34.2	36.2	36.8
North Carolina	11.7	16.9	22.3	25.0	25.4	26.4	10.6	15.0	20.5	23.7	24.1	24.9
North Dakota.	9.7	15.8	19.2	25.0	25.0	25.3	9.2	14.9	19.8	24.1	24.2	24.4
Ohio	14.1	19.9	25.4	28.5	29.5	31.4	12.2	16.8	21.3	27.3	28.3	29.5
Oklahoma.	11.6	16.1	19.4	21.0	21.5	22.3	9.4	12.9	14.8	20.2	20.7	21.0
Oregon	15.6	19.7	22.9	28.3	29.1	30.7	13.8	17.6	20.5	26.9	27.8	29.0
Pennsylvania	16.6	23.6	31.6	32.6	33.1	35.1	13.9	19.2	25.4	30.7	31.2	32.5
Rhode Island	17.8	23.3	32.5	37.1	38.2	40.2	16.1	20.2	28.8	35.2	36.3	37.8
South Carolina	10.0	14.7	21.0	23.3	23.4	24.1	9.3	13.6	19.4	22.4	22.5	23.1
South Dakota.	8.2	13.4	19.2	23.0	23.8	24.6	7.7	12.3	17.7	22.2	22.8	23.6
Tennessee	12.4	17.7	23.6	26.0	26.8	27.7	11.3	16.2	21.8	24.8	25.6	26.3
Texas	12.5	16.8	20.3	21.5	22.3	23.2	11.0	14.7	17.9	20.6	21.5	22.1
Utah	14.1	17.2	19.6	21.0	21.9	22.6	13.0	15.5	17.8	20.0	21.0	21.5
Vermont.	18.2	23.8	32.0	35.7	36.2	38.2	15.5	20.3	28.8	33.4	34.0	35.6
Virginia	12.9	19.5	23.9	27.0	27.2	28.1	11.9	17.8	22.0	25.7	26.0	26.6
Washington.	15.3	20.2	23.7	27.1	27.4	28.4	13.6	17.9	21.2	25.5	25.8	26.5
West Virginia	11.0	16.3	23.5	25.5	26.0	27.1	10.0	14.6	19.5	24.5	24.9	25.4
Wisconsin.	12.5	17.7	23.1	26.8	27.3	27.9	11.4	15.9	20.9	25.6	26.2	26.6
Wyoming	9.5	12.9	17.3	19.7	19.2	19.5	8.9	12.0	15.7	19.1	18.8	18.9

[1] Includes active doctors of medicine (MDs) and active doctors of osteopathy (DOs). See Appendix II, Physician.
[2] Starting with 2003 data, federal and nonfederal physicians are included. Data prior to 2003 included nonfederal physicians only.
[3] Prior to 2006, excludes DOs. Excludes physicians in medical teaching, administration, research, and other nonpatient care activities. Includes residents.
[4] Data for DOs are as of January 2001.

NOTES: Data for MDs are as of December 31. Data for DOs are as of May 31, unless otherwise specified. Starting with Health, United States, 2012, data for DOs for 2009 and beyond are from the American Medical Association (AMA). Prior to 2009, data for DOs are from the American Osteopathic Association (AOA).

SOURCE: American Medical Association (AMA): Physician distribution and medical licensure in the U.S., 1975; Physician characteristics and distribution in the U.S., 1986, 2002–2003, 2012, 2014, and 2015 editions; Department of Physician Practice and Communications Information, Division of Survey and Data Resources, AMA. (Copyright 1976, 1986, 2003, 2012, 2014, and 2015: Used with permission of the AMA); American Osteopathic Association: 1975–1976 Yearbook and Directory of Osteopathic Physicians, 1985–1986 Yearbook and Directory of Osteopathic Physicians. See Appendix I, American Medical Association (AMA) Physician Masterfile; American Osteopathic Association (AOA).

Table 84. Doctors of medicine, by place of medical education and activity: United States and outlying U.S. areas, selected years 1975–2013

[Data are based on reporting by physicians]

Place of medical education and activity	1975	1985	1995	2000	2005	2010	2012	2013
	Number of doctors of medicine							
Total doctors of medicine	393,742	552,716	720,325	813,770	902,053	985,375	1,026,788	1,045,910
Active doctors of medicine [1]	340,280	497,140	625,443	692,368	762,438	794,862	826,001	854,698
Place of medical education:								
U.S. medical graduates.	- - -	392,007	481,137	527,931	571,798	595,908	615,100	636,707
International medical graduates [2]	- - -	105,133	144,306	164,437	190,640	198,954	210,901	217,991
Activity:								
Patient care [3,4]	287,837	431,527	564,074	631,431	718,473	752,572	784,633	809,845
Office-based practice	213,334	329,041	427,275	490,398	563,225	565,024	585,933	600,863
General and family practice	46,347	53,862	59,932	67,534	74,999	77,098	78,935	80,240
Cardiovascular diseases	5,046	9,054	13,739	16,300	17,519	17,454	17,512	17,657
Dermatology	3,442	5,325	6,959	7,969	8,795	9,272	9,669	9,910
Gastroenterology	1,696	4,135	7,300	8,515	9,742	10,466	10,985	11,322
Internal medicine	28,188	52,712	72,612	88,699	107,028	110,612	116,937	120,439
Pediatrics.	12,687	22,392	33,890	42,215	51,854	53,054	56,692	58,719
Pulmonary diseases.	1,166	3,035	4,964	6,095	7,321	7,846	8,365	8,870
General surgery	19,710	24,708	24,086	24,475	26,079	24,327	24,448	25,024
Obstetrics and gynecology	15,613	23,525	29,111	31,726	34,659	34,083	34,570	34,780
Ophthalmology.	8,795	12,212	14,596	15,598	16,580	15,723	16,002	16,331
Orthopedic surgery	8,148	13,033	17,136	17,367	19,115	19,325	19,581	20,013
Otolaryngology.	4,297	5,751	7,139	7,581	8,206	7,964	8,021	8,136
Plastic surgery	1,706	3,299	4,612	5,308	6,011	6,180	6,322	6,414
Urological surgery	5,025	7,081	7,991	8,460	8,955	8,606	8,558	8,563
Anesthesiology.	8,970	15,285	23,770	27,624	31,887	31,819	32,604	33,218
Diagnostic radiology	1,978	7,735	12,751	14,622	17,618	17,503	17,916	18,203
Emergency medicine	- - -	- - -	11,700	14,541	20,173	20,654	22,223	23,414
Neurology.	1,862	4,691	7,623	8,559	10,400	10,547	11,249	11,762
Pathology, anatomical/clinical.	4,195	6,877	9,031	10,267	11,747	10,688	10,648	10,481
Psychiatry.	12,173	18,521	23,334	24,955	27,638	25,690	26,171	26,696
Radiology	6,970	7,355	5,994	6,674	7,049	7,032	7,228	7,527
Other specialty	15,320	28,453	29,005	35,314	39,850	39,081	41,297	43,144
Hospital-based practice	74,503	102,486	136,799	141,033	155,248	187,548	198,700	208,982
Residents and interns [5]	53,527	72,159	93,650	95,125	95,391	108,142	116,460	117,203
Full-time hospital staff	20,976	30,327	43,149	45,908	59,857	79,406	82,240	91,779
Other professional activity [6]	24,252	44,046	40,290	41,556	43,965	42,290	41,368	44,853
Inactive.	21,449	38,646	72,326	75,168	99,823	125,928	142,716	147,676
Not classified	26,145	13,950	20,579	45,136	39,304	64,153	57,649	43,536
Unknown address	5,868	2,980	1,977	1,098	488	432	422	- - -

- - - Data not available.

[1] Doctors of medicine who are inactive, have unknown address, or primary specialty not classified are excluded. See Appendix II, Physician.

[2] International medical graduates received their medical education in schools outside of the United States and Canada.

[3] Specialty information is based on the physician's self-designated primary area of practice. Categories include generalists and specialists. See Appendix II, Physician specialty.

[4] Starting with 2003 data, federal and nonfederal doctors of medicine are included. Data prior to 2003 included nonfederal doctors of medicine only.

[5] Starting with 1990 data, clinical fellows are included in this category. In prior years, clinical fellows were included in the other professional activity category.

[6] Includes doctors of medicine in medical teaching, administration, research, and other nonpatient care activities. Prior to 1990, this category also included clinical fellows.

NOTES: Data for doctors of medicine are as of December 31. Outlying areas include Puerto Rico, the U.S. Virgin Islands, and the U.S. Pacific islands.

SOURCE: American Medical Association (AMA). Physician distribution and medical licensure in the U.S., 1975; Physician characteristics and distribution in the U.S., 1986, 1996–1997, 2002–2003, 2007, 2012, 2014, and 2015 editions, Department of Physician Practice and Communications Information, Division of Survey and Data Resources, AMA. (Copyright 1976, 1986, 1997, 2003, 2007, 2012, 2014, and 2015: Used with permission of the AMA.) See Appendix I, American Medical Association (AMA) Physician Masterfile.

Table 85. Doctors of medicine in primary care, by specialty: United States and outlying U.S. areas, selected years 1949–2013

[Data are based on reporting by physicians]

Specialty	1949[1]	1960[1]	1970	1980	1990	2000	2010	2012	2013
	Number								
Total doctors of medicine[2]	201,277	260,484	334,028	467,679	615,421	813,770	985,375	1,026,788	1,045,910
Active doctors of medicine[3]	191,577	247,257	310,845	414,916	547,310	692,368	794,862	826,001	854,698
General primary care specialists	113,222	125,359	134,354	170,705	213,514	274,653	304,687	313,793	319,881
General practice/family medicine	95,980	88,023	57,948	60,049	70,480	86,312	94,746	96,552	98,298
Internal medicine	12,453	26,209	39,924	58,462	76,295	101,353	113,591	118,504	121,127
Obstetrics/Gynecology	- - -	- - -	18,532	24,612	30,220	35,922	38,520	39,324	40,045
Pediatrics	4,789	11,127	17,950	27,582	36,519	51,066	57,830	59,413	60,411
Primary care subspecialists	- - -	- - -	3,161	16,642	30,911	52,294	76,122	83,532	90,147
Family medicine.	- - -	- - -	- - -	- - -	- - -	483	1,445	1,764	1,991
Internal medicine	- - -	- - -	1,948	13,069	22,054	34,831	50,730	55,357	59,256
Obstetrics/Gynecology	- - -	- - -	344	1,693	3,477	4,319	4,277	4,186	4,141
Pediatrics	- - -	- - -	869	1,880	5,380	12,661	19,670	22,225	24,759
	Percent of active doctors of medicine								
General primary care specialists	59.1	50.7	43.2	41.1	39.0	39.7	38.3	38.0	37.4
General practice/family medicine	50.1	35.6	18.6	14.5	12.9	12.5	11.9	11.7	11.5
Internal medicine	6.5	10.6	12.8	14.1	13.9	14.6	14.3	14.3	14.2
Obstetrics/Gynecology	- - -	- - -	6.0	5.9	5.5	5.2	4.8	4.8	4.7
Pediatrics	2.5	4.5	5.8	6.6	6.7	7.4	7.3	7.2	7.1
Primary care subspecialists	- - -	- - -	1.0	4.0	5.6	7.6	9.6	10.1	10.5
Family medicine.	- - -	- - -	- - -	- - -	- - -	0.1	0.2	0.2	0.2
Internal medicine	- - -	- - -	0.6	3.1	4.0	5.0	6.4	6.7	6.9
Obstetrics/Gynecology	- - -	- - -	0.1	0.4	0.6	0.6	0.5	0.5	0.5
Pediatrics	- - -	- - -	0.3	0.5	1.0	1.8	2.5	2.7	2.9

- - - Data not available.

0.0 Percentage greater than zero but less than 0.05.

[1] Estimated by the Bureau of Health Professions, Health Resources and Services Administration. Active doctors of medicine (MDs) include those with address unknown and primary specialty not classified.

[2] Data on federal and nonfederal doctors of medicine engaged in office- or hospital-based patient care and other professional activities.

[3] Starting with 1970 data, MDs who are inactive, have unknown address, or primary specialty not classified are excluded. See Appendix II, Physician.

NOTES: See Appendix II, Physician specialty. Data are as of December 31 except for 1990–1994 data, which are as of January 1, and 1949 data, which are as of midyear. Outlying areas include Puerto Rico, the U.S. Virgin Islands, and the U.S. Pacific islands.

SOURCE: Health Manpower Source Book: Medical Specialists, USDHEW, 1962; American Medical Association (AMA). Distribution of physicians in the United States, 1970; Physician characteristics and distribution in the U.S., 1981, 1992, 2002–2003, 2011, 2012, 2014, and 2015 editions, Department of Physician Practice and Communications Information, Division of Survey and Data Resources, AMA. (Copyright 1971, 1982, 1992, 2003, 2012, 2014, and 2015: Used with permission of the AMA.) See Appendix I, American Medical Association (AMA) Physician Masterfile.

Table 86. Active dentists, by state: United States, selected years 2001–2015

[Data are based on reporting by dentists]

State	2001	2006	2013	2014	2015	2001	2006	2013	2014	2015
	Number of dentists					Number of dentists per 100,000 civilian population				
United States	163,345	172,603	191,347	192,313	195,722	57.32	57.85	60.47	60.30	60.89
Alabama.	1,880	1,921	2,128	2,125	2,130	42.08	41.50	44.05	43.85	43.84
Alaska	457	489	577	588	597	72.11	72.41	78.24	79.78	80.85
Arizona	2,374	3,061	3,617	3,627	3,677	45.02	50.77	54.55	53.90	53.85
Arkansas	1,047	1,114	1,210	1,204	1,219	38.90	39.48	40.91	40.58	40.93
California	22,709	26,388	29,425	29,530	30,180	65.86	73.26	76.60	76.12	77.10
Colorado	2,844	3,098	3,623	3,692	3,801	64.26	65.63	68.73	68.94	69.66
Connecticut.	2,590	2,587	2,742	2,692	2,723	75.45	73.55	76.23	74.89	75.83
Delaware	352	383	420	426	431	44.24	44.57	45.39	45.51	45.56
District of Columbia	603	533	579	580	604	104.96	93.40	89.14	87.90	89.85
Florida	8,158	8,754	9,947	10,223	10,543	49.87	48.19	50.76	51.36	52.01
Georgia	3,614	4,115	4,701	4,731	4,805	43.14	44.94	47.05	46.85	47.04
Hawaii	1,022	1,009	1,060	1,069	1,083	83.36	77.04	75.24	75.27	75.65
Idaho.	690	864	932	907	939	52.27	58.83	57.79	55.48	56.74
Illinois	8,154	7,994	8,599	8,593	8,697	65.29	63.22	66.71	66.70	67.63
Indiana.	2,870	2,842	3,116	3,104	3,157	46.84	44.88	47.42	47.05	47.69
Iowa	1,516	1,526	1,604	1,611	1,652	51.71	51.16	51.87	51.81	52.88
Kansas	1,314	1,347	1,461	1,471	1,482	48.63	48.75	50.47	50.68	50.90
Kentucky	2,256	2,287	2,488	2,441	2,445	55.46	54.20	56.56	55.32	55.25
Louisiana	2,058	2,017	2,221	2,199	2,262	45.96	46.88	48.00	47.30	48.43
Maine	598	642	693	669	674	46.51	48.50	52.15	50.29	50.70
Maryland	3,955	3,989	4,268	4,260	4,322	73.59	70.89	71.90	71.29	71.96
Massachusetts.	4,898	4,797	5,232	5,303	5,319	76.56	74.84	77.99	78.50	78.28
Michigan	5,783	5,928	6,075	6,010	6,056	57.88	59.07	61.36	60.61	61.03
Minnesota.	2,880	3,105	3,284	3,288	3,312	57.80	60.13	60.58	60.25	60.33
Mississippi	1,117	1,140	1,275	1,264	1,284	39.15	39.24	42.63	42.23	42.91
Missouri.	2,634	2,666	2,900	2,952	2,943	46.69	45.63	47.98	48.68	48.38
Montana.	511	525	598	612	619	56.34	55.11	58.95	59.81	59.93
Nebraska	1,103	1,117	1,203	1,223	1,250	64.13	63.01	64.36	64.95	65.92
Nevada	846	1,177	1,448	1,446	1,525	40.32	46.66	51.89	50.95	52.75
New Hampshire	735	815	847	830	851	58.54	62.29	64.04	62.50	63.96
New Jersey.	6,054	6,922	7,238	7,256	7,303	71.28	79.92	81.26	81.17	81.52
New Mexico	814	861	1,062	1,065	1,060	44.44	43.88	50.89	51.07	50.84
New York	14,309	14,062	14,468	14,428	14,560	74.98	73.61	73.48	73.06	73.55
North Carolina	3,474	4,016	4,719	4,791	5,038	42.31	45.04	47.93	48.20	50.17
North Dakota.	305	311	394	405	419	47.73	47.89	54.45	54.73	55.36
Ohio.	5,929	5,797	6,003	5,978	6,078	52.07	50.49	51.87	51.55	52.34
Oklahoma.	1,664	1,749	1,943	1,937	1,966	47.99	48.66	50.42	49.93	50.26
Oregon	2,197	2,431	2,708	2,700	2,785	63.35	66.22	68.94	67.99	69.12
Pennsylvania	7,595	7,454	7,698	7,783	7,774	61.75	59.58	60.22	60.83	60.72
Rhode Island	588	576	566	553	572	55.62	54.18	53.76	52.42	54.15
South Carolina	1,839	1,958	2,288	2,229	2,350	45.24	44.93	47.98	46.16	48.00
South Dakota.	348	382	457	460	460	45.91	48.78	54.07	53.91	53.58
Tennessee	2,912	2,947	3,246	3,252	3,273	50.64	48.40	49.97	49.67	49.59
Texas	9,642	10,365	13,391	13,692	14,268	45.23	44.37	50.53	50.75	51.94
Utah	1,409	1,559	1,892	1,864	1,885	61.70	61.73	65.16	63.30	62.92
Vermont.	354	343	365	347	355	57.82	55.07	58.20	55.36	56.71
Virginia	4,189	4,367	5,194	5,277	5,329	58.19	56.91	62.82	63.36	63.57
Washington.	3,957	4,312	4,951	5,050	5,219	66.11	67.68	71.00	71.50	72.79
West Virginia	863	835	890	881	897	47.91	45.68	48.03	47.65	48.64
Wisconsin.	3,069	2,860	3,215	3,202	3,193	56.76	51.28	55.97	55.60	55.33
Wyoming	266	266	309	323	317	53.77	50.89	52.99	55.28	54.09

NOTES: Data include professionally active dentists only. Professionally active dentists include those whose primary occupation is one of the following: private practice (full- or part-time), dental school/faculty staff member, armed forces, other federal services (i.e., Veterans' Affairs, Public Health Service), state or local government employee, hospital staff dentist, graduate student/intern/resident, or other health/dental organization staff member. U.S. totals include dentists with unknown state of practice not shown separately and may include missing data. Starting with *Health, United States, 2016*, data on the number of dentists per 100,000 civilian population for 2011 and beyond are calculated using 2010-based postcensal estimates, data for 2010 are calculated using the April 1, 2010 census counts, and data for 2001–2009 are calculated using the the intercensal estimates based on the 2000 and 2010 censuses.

SOURCE: American Dental Association, Health Policy Institute, Dentist Supply in the US: 2001–2015, Tables 1 and 3 (Copyright 2016 American Dental Association. Reprinted with permission. All rights reserved.). Any form of reproduction is strictly prohibited without prior written permission of the American Dental Association. See Appendix I, American Dental Association (ADA).

Table 87. Healthcare employment and wages, by selected occupations: United States, selected years 2000–2015

Excel and PDF versions (with more data years and standard errors when available): http://www.cdc.gov/nchs/hus/contents2016.htm#087.

[Data are based on a semiannual mail survey of nonfarm establishments]

Occupation title	2000	2010	2014	2015	2000	2010	2014	2015
Healthcare practitioners and technical occupations	Employment[1]				Mean hourly wage[2]			
Audiologists	11,530	12,860	12,250	12,070	$22.92	$33.58	$36.92	$37.22
Cardiovascular technologists and technicians	40,080	48,720	51,080	51,400	16.81	24.38	26.54	26.97
Dental hygienists	148,460	177,520	196,520	200,550	24.99	33.02	34.60	34.96
Diagnostic medical sonographers	31,760	53,010	59,760	61,250	22.03	31.20	32.88	34.08
Dietetic technicians.	28,010	23,890	28,690	28,950	10.98	13.86	13.75	14.03
Dietitians and nutritionists	43,030	53,510	59,490	59,740	18.76	26.13	27.62	28.08
Emergency medical technicians and paramedics.	165,530	221,760	235,760	236,890	11.89	16.01	16.88	17.04
Licensed practical and licensed vocational nurses	679,470	730,290	695,610	697,250	14.65	19.88	20.87	21.17
Magnetic resonance imaging technologists	- - -	- - -	33,130	33,460	- - -	- - -	32.36	32.86
Medical and clinical laboratory technicians.	146,060	156,480	160,460	157,610	13.93	18.36	19.59	19.91
Medical and clinical laboratory technologists.	144,530	164,430	161,710	162,950	19.84	27.34	29.12	29.74
Medical records and health information technicians.	143,870	176,090	184,740	189,930	11.74	16.83	18.68	19.44
Nuclear medicine technologists	18,030	21,600	20,320	19,740	21.56	33.20	35.21	36.06
Nurse anesthetists	- - -	- - -	36,590	39,410	- - -	- - -	76.40	77.04
Nurse midwives	- - -	- - -	5,110	7,430	- - -	- - -	46.97	45.01
Nurse practitioners	- - -	- - -	122,050	136,060	- - -	- - -	47.11	48.68
Occupational therapists	75,150	100,300	110,520	114,660	24.10	35.28	38.46	39.27
Opticians, dispensing	66,580	62,200	73,110	73,520	12.67	16.73	17.43	17.70
Pharmacists	212,660	268,030	290,780	295,620	33.39	52.59	56.96	57.34
Pharmacy technicians	190,940	333,500	368,760	379,430	10.38	14.10	14.95	15.23
Physical therapists	120,410	180,280	200,670	209,690	27.62	37.50	40.35	41.25
Physician assistants	55,490	81,420	91,670	98,470	29.17	41.89	46.77	47.73
Psychiatric technicians	53,350	72,650	64,540	58,450	12.53	15.15	16.91	17.44
Radiation therapists	13,100	16,590	16,380	16,930	25.59	37.64	40.25	40.61
Radiologic technologists[3]	172,080	216,730	193,400	195,590	17.93	26.80	27.65	28.13
Recreational therapists	26,940	20,830	17,950	17,880	14.23	19.92	22.14	22.98
Registered nurses[4]	2,189,670	2,655,020	2,687,310	2,745,910	22.31	32.56	33.55	34.14
Respiratory therapists	82,670	109,270	119,410	120,330	18.37	26.54	28.12	28.67
Respiratory therapy technicians	28,230	13,570	10,610	10,000	16.46	22.28	23.46	23.90
Speech-language pathologists	82,850	112,530	126,500	131,450	23.31	33.60	36.01	36.97
Healthcare support occupations								
Dental assistants	250,870	294,030	314,330	323,110	12.86	16.41	17.43	17.75
Home health aides	561,120	982,840	799,080	820,630	8.71	10.46	10.77	11.00
Massage therapists.	24,620	60,040	87,670	92,090	15.51	19.12	20.09	20.76
Medical assistants	330,830	523,260	584,970	601,240	11.46	14.31	15.01	15.34
Medical equipment preparers.	32,760	47,310	50,550	50,330	10.68	14.59	16.28	16.80
Medical transcriptionists.	97,330	78,780	61,210	57,830	12.37	16.12	17.11	17.17
Nursing assistants[5].	1,273,460	1,451,090	1,427,740	1,420,570	9.18	12.09	12.62	12.89
Occupational therapy aides.	8,890	7,180	8,570	7,570	11.21	14.95	13.96	14.95
Occupational therapy assistants	15,910	27,720	32,230	35,460	16.76	24.66	27.53	28.05
Orderlies.	- - -	- - -	52,420	52,660	- - -	- - -	12.82	13.26
Pharmacy aides.	59,890	49,580	41,240	38,040	9.10	10.98	12.28	13.20
Physical therapist aides	34,620	45,900	48,730	50,540	10.06	12.02	12.82	13.19
Physical therapist assistants	44,120	65,960	76,910	81,230	16.52	23.95	26.12	26.56
Psychiatric aides	57,680	64,730	72,860	69,550	10.79	12.84	13.67	13.55

- - - Data not available.

[1] Employment is the number of filled positions. This table includes both full-time and part-time wage and salary positions. Estimates do not include the self-employed, owners and partners in unincorporated firms, household workers, or unpaid family workers. Estimates were rounded to the nearest 10.

[2] The mean hourly wage rate for an occupation is the total wages that all workers in the occupation earn in an hour, divided by the total number of employees in the occupation. More information is available from: http://www.bls.gov/oes/current/oes_tec.htm.

[3] Starting with 2012 data, the radiologic technologists and technicians occupation category was split into two occupations as part of the 2010 Standard Occupational Classification (SOC) revision: Radiologic technologists (29-2034) and Magnetic resonance imaging technologists (29-2035). Thus, data prior to 2012 include radiologic technologists as well as magnetic resonance imaging technologists and are not comparable with 2012–2015 data.

[4] Starting with 2012 data, the registered nurses occupation category was split into four occupations as part of the 2010 SOC revision: Registered nurses (29-1141), plus three advanced practice nursing occupations: Nurse anesthetists (29-1151), Nurse midwives (29-1161), and Nurse practitioners (29-1171). Thus, data prior to 2012 include registered nurses as well as nurse anesthetists, nurse midwives, and nurse practitioners and are not comparable with 2012–2015 data.

[5] Starting with 2012 data, the nursing aides, orderlies, and attendants occupation category was split into two occupations as part of the 2010 SOC revision: Nursing assistants (31-1014) and Orderlies (31-1015). Thus, data prior to 2012 include nursing assistants as well as orderlies and are not comparable with 2012–2015 data.

NOTES: This table excludes occupations such as dentists, physicians, and chiropractors, which have a large percentage of workers who are self-employed. Challenges in using Occupational Employment Statistics (OES) data as a time series include changes in the occupational, industrial, and geographical classification systems; changes in the way data are collected; changes in the survey reference period; and changes in mean wage estimation methodology, as well as permanent features of the methodology. See Appendix I, Occupational Employment Statistics (OES).

SOURCE: U.S. Department of Labor, Bureau of Labor Statistics. Occupational Employment Statistics. Available from: http://www.bls.gov/oes/current/oes_nat.htm#29-0000. See Appendix I, Occupational Employment Statistics (OES).

Table 88. First-year enrollment and graduates of health professions schools, and number of schools, by selected profession: United States, selected academic years 1980–1981 through 2014–2015

[Data are based on reporting by health professions associations]

Profession	Academic years						
	1980–1981	1990–1991	2000–2001	2010–2011	2012–2013	2013–2014	2014–2015
First-year enrollment	Number						
Dentistry	6,030	4,001	4,327	5,170	5,697	5,904	5,967
Medicine (Allopathic) [1,2]	17,186	16,876	16,699	19,082	20,279	20,803	21,036
Medicine (Osteopathic) [2]	1,496	1,950	2,927	5,428	5,986	6,636	7,012
Optometry [1]	1,174	1,245	1,384	1,661	1,760	1,818	1,789
Pharmacy [1,3]	7,377	8,267	8,382	13,077	14,011	14,008	14,276
Podiatry	695	561	475	671	687	671	647
Public Health: [1,4,5,6]							
Schools and programs	- - -	- - -	- - -	- - -	- - -	13,591	14,720
Schools	3,348	4,087	5,840	10,980	11,350	12,311	13,121
Graduates							
Dentistry [6]	5,256	5,550	4,367	5,106	5,390	5,530	5,811
Medicine (Allopathic) [1]	15,632	15,427	15,796	17,363	18,157	18,078	18,704
Medicine (Osteopathic)	1,151	1,534	2,510	4,159	4,806	4,997	5,323
Optometry [1,7]	1,092	1,224	1,310	1,308	1,545	1,541	1,531
Pharmacy [1]	7,323	7,122	7,000	11,931	13,207	13,838	13,994
Podiatry	597	591	531	543	572	564	557
Public Health: [1,5,6]							
Schools and programs	- - -	- - -	- - -	- - -	- - -	11,687	12,520
Schools	3,168	3,995	5,747	9,566	10,200	10,807	11,287
Schools							
Dentistry	60	56	55	58	62	65	65
Medicine (Allopathic) [1,8]	125	125	124	135	141	141	144
Medicine (Osteopathic)	14	15	19	34	37	40	42
Optometry [1]	13	17	17	20	21	21	21
Pharmacy [1,6]	72	74	82	120	129	130	133
Podiatry	5	7	7	9	9	9	9
Public Health: [1,9]							
Schools and programs	- - -	- - -	- - -	- - -	- - -	91	100
Schools	21	24	28	46	50	56	56

- - - Data not available.

[1] Includes data from schools in Puerto Rico. For Pharmacy, includes data from the University of Puerto Rico School of Pharmacy.

[2] Includes new entrants and those repeating the initial year.

[3] Starting with 2005–2006 data, first-year enrollment for pharmacy schools include Pharm.D.1 enrollments only. Pharm.D.1 refers to the Doctor of Pharmacy degree awarded as the first professional degree. Prior to 2005, first-year enrollment data included Pharm.D.1, B.S. Pharmacy, and B.Pharm. enrollments. It also included second from last year baccalaureate enrollees and third from last year Pharm.D.1 enrollees. It did not include first-year enrollees in accelerated programs.

[4] Prior to 2009–2010 data, enrollment is provided for the fall. For the 2009–2010 to 2013–2014 data, enrollment includes winter, spring, summer, and fall. For 2014–2015 data, enrollment is provided for the 2014–2015 academic year.

[5] ASPPH data is provided for U.S.-based ASPPH members. 2010–2011 data reported for 45 schools of public health. 2012–2013 data reported for 49 schools of public health. 2013–2014 data reported for 52 schools and 24 programs of public health. 2014–2015 data reported for 54 schools and 31 programs of public health.

[6] Data for the 2010–2011 academic year and beyond have been revised and differ from previous editions of *Health, United States*.

[7] Includes graduates receiving the O.D. degree but excludes those of "special" optometry degree programs which include, but are not limited to, accelerated programs for those entering optometry schools with a doctoral degree, foreign optometry programs, or modified extended programs for those returning to schools after an absence, changing professional fields, or taking a reduced course load for personal reasons.

[8] Includes schools with preliminary and provisional accreditation, in addition to fully accredited schools.

[9] Includes programs of public health as Association of Schools & Programs of Public Health members as of 2013 school year.

NOTE: Data on the number of schools and first-year enrollments are reported as of the beginning of the academic year, while data on the number of graduates are reported as of the end of the academic year.

SOURCE: American Dental Association: 2015–2016 Survey of Dental Education Series, Report 1: Academic Programs, Enrollment and Graduates. Available from: http://www.ada.org/en/science-research/health-policy-institute/data-center/dental-education (Copyright 2016 American Dental Association. Reprinted with permission. All rights reserved.) Any form of reproduction is strictly prohibited without prior written permission of the American Dental Association; Association of American Medical Colleges (AAMC): AAMC Data Book 2016 - Medical Schools and Teaching Hospitals by the Numbers, Washington, DC. 2016. Table A1 (number of schools) and Table B1 (number of first-year enrollment students and number of graduates). Used with permission of the AAMC; American Association of Colleges of Osteopathic Medicine: Trends in Osteopathic Medical School Applicants, Enrollment, and Graduates, 2016. Chevy Chase, MD. 2016. Available from: http://www.aacom.org/reports-programs-initiatives/aacom-reports. Reprinted with permission from AACOM, All rights reserved; Association of Schools and Colleges of Optometry: Annual Student Data Report Academic Years 2014–2015, Annual Student Data Report Academic Years 2015–2016. Available from: https://optometriceducation.org/data-surveys. Association of Schools and Colleges of Optometry: Annual Student Data Report Academic Years 2015–2016. Available from: https://optometriceducation.org/data-surveys. American Association of Colleges of Pharmacy: Fall 2014 Profile of Pharmacy Students, Fall 2015 Profile of Pharmacy Students. Available from: http://www.aacp.org/resources/research/institutionalresearch/Pages/StudentApplications,EnrollmentsandDegreesConferred.aspx; American Association of Colleges of Podiatric Medicine: Applicant, Matriculant, and Graduate Statistics, 2006 through 2014 and unpublished data. Available from: http://www.aacpm.org. Used with permission of the AACPM; Association of Schools & Programs of Public Health: unpublished data. Washington, DC. Used with permission of the ASPPH; Bureau of Health Professions: United States Health Personnel FACTBOOK. Health Resources and Services Administration. Rockville, MD. 2003. See Appendix I, American Dental Association (ADA); Association of American Medical Colleges (AAMC); American Association of Colleges of Osteopathic Medicine (AACOM); Association of Schools and Colleges of Optometry (ASCO); American Association of Colleges of Pharmacy (AACP); American Association of Colleges of Podiatric Medicine (AACPM); Association of Schools & Programs of Public Health (ASPPH).

Table 89. Hospitals, beds, and occupancy rates, by type of ownership and size of hospital: United States, selected years 1975–2014

[Data are based on reporting by a census of hospitals]

Type of ownership and size of hospital	1975	1980	1990	2000	2005	2010	2012	2013	2014
Hospitals					Number				
All hospitals	7,156	6,965	6,649	5,810	5,756	5,754	5,723	5,686	5,627
Federal	382	359	337	245	226	213	211	213	213
Nonfederal [1]	6,774	6,606	6,312	5,565	5,530	5,541	5,512	5,473	5,414
Community [2]	5,875	5,830	5,384	4,915	4,936	4,985	4,999	4,974	4,926
Nonprofit	3,339	3,322	3,191	3,003	2,958	2,904	2,894	2,904	2,870
For profit	775	730	749	749	868	1,013	1,068	1,060	1,053
State-local government. . .	1,761	1,778	1,444	1,163	1,110	1,068	1,037	1,010	1,003
6–24 beds	299	259	226	288	370	424	462	469	486
25–49 beds.	1,155	1,029	935	910	1,032	1,167	1,192	1,186	1,168
50–99 beds.	1,481	1,462	1,263	1,055	1,001	970	954	959	934
100–199 beds	1,363	1,370	1,306	1,236	1,129	1,029	1,012	995	1,013
200–299 beds	678	715	739	656	619	585	570	571	536
300–399 beds	378	412	408	341	368	352	348	334	328
400–499 beds	230	266	222	182	173	185	189	183	188
500 beds or more	291	317	285	247	244	273	272	277	273
Beds									
All hospitals	1,465,828	1,364,516	1,213,327	983,628	946,997	941,995	920,829	914,513	902,202
Federal	131,946	117,328	98,255	53,067	45,837	44,940	38,557	38,747	38,893
Nonfederal [1]	1,333,882	1,247,188	1,115,072	930,561	901,160	897,055	882,272	875,766	863,309
Community [2]	941,844	988,387	927,360	823,560	802,311	804,943	800,566	795,603	786,874
Nonprofit	658,195	692,459	656,755	582,988	561,106	555,768	545,287	543,929	534,554
For profit	73,495	87,033	101,377	109,883	113,510	124,652	135,008	134,643	135,909
State-local government. . .	210,154	208,895	169,228	130,689	127,695	124,523	120,271	117,031	116,411
6–24 beds	5,615	4,932	4,427	5,156	6,316	7,261	7,791	7,763	7,985
25–49 beds.	41,783	37,478	35,420	33,333	33,726	37,446	38,338	38,039	37,559
50–99 beds.	106,776	105,278	90,394	75,865	71,737	69,470	67,879	67,892	66,092
100–199 beds	192,438	192,892	183,867	175,778	161,593	148,090	145,556	143,760	147,188
200–299 beds	164,405	172,390	179,670	159,807	151,290	142,616	139,212	140,113	131,526
300–399 beds	127,728	139,434	138,938	117,220	126,899	121,749	120,554	115,511	112,909
400–499 beds	101,278	117,724	98,833	80,763	76,894	82,071	84,007	81,148	83,285
500 beds or more	201,821	218,259	195,811	175,638	173,856	196,240	197,229	201,377	200,330
Occupancy rate [3]					Percent				
All hospitals	76.7	77.7	69.5	66.1	69.3	66.6	65.2	64.7	64.8
Federal	80.7	80.1	72.9	68.2	66.0	65.3	63.5	64.5	68.0
Nonfederal [1]	76.3	77.4	69.2	65.9	69.5	66.6	65.3	64.7	64.6
Community [2]	75.0	75.2	66.8	63.9	67.3	64.5	63.4	62.9	62.8
Nonprofit	77.5	78.2	69.3	65.5	69.1	66.2	64.9	64.5	64.4
For profit	65.9	65.2	52.8	55.9	59.6	57.1	56.8	56.2	56.6
State-local government. . .	70.4	71.1	65.3	63.2	66.7	64.4	63.8	62.9	62.9
6–24 beds	48.0	46.8	32.3	31.7	33.5	32.3	30.8	30.5	30.3
25–49 beds.	56.7	52.8	41.3	41.3	47.1	44.8	43.1	42.7	42.1
50–99 beds.	64.7	64.2	53.8	54.8	59.0	55.1	55.2	55.1	54.7
100–199 beds	71.2	71.4	61.5	60.0	63.2	60.4	58.1	57.6	57.6
200–299 beds	77.1	77.4	67.1	65.0	67.7	64.0	63.2	61.6	61.6
300–399 beds	79.7	79.7	70.0	65.7	70.1	67.4	65.1	64.9	64.5
400–499 beds	81.1	81.2	73.5	69.1	71.2	68.5	67.5	67.6	67.9
500 beds or more	80.9	82.1	77.3	72.2	75.9	73.0	72.6	72.1	72.3

[1] The category of nonfederal hospitals comprises psychiatric hospitals, tuberculosis and other respiratory diseases hospitals, and long-term and short-term general and other special hospitals. See Appendix II, Hospital.
[2] Community hospitals are nonfederal short-term general and special hospitals whose facilities and services are available to the public. The types of facilities included in the community hospitals category have changed over time. See Appendix II, Hospital.
[3] Estimated percentage of staffed beds that are occupied. Occupancy rate is calculated as the average daily census (from the American Hospital Association) divided by the number of hospital beds. See Appendix II, Occupancy rate.

SOURCE: American Hospital Association (AHA). Annual Survey of Hospitals. Hospital Statistics, 1976, 1981, 1991–92, 2002, 2014, 2015, and 2016 editions. Chicago, IL. (Reprinted from AHA Hospital Statistics by permission, Copyright 1976, 1981, 1991–92, 2002, 2012, 2014, 2015, and 2016 editions by Health Forum, LLC, an American Hospital Association Company.) See Appendix I, American Hospital Association (AHA) Annual Survey of Hospitals.

Table 90. Community hospital beds and average annual percent change, by state: United States, selected years 1980–2014

[Data are based on reporting by a census of hospitals]

State	1980	1990	2000	2010	2013	2014	1980–1990	1990–2000	2000–2010	2010–2014
	Beds per 1,000 resident population						Average annual percent change[1]			
United States	4.5	3.7	2.9	2.6	2.5	2.5	−1.9	−2.4	−1.1	−1.0
Alabama.	5.1	4.6	3.7	3.2	3.1	3.1	−1.0	−2.2	−1.4	−0.8
Alaska	2.7	2.3	2.3	2.2	2.1	2.2	−1.6	–	−0.4	–
Arizona	3.6	2.7	2.1	2.0	2.0	2.0	−2.8	−2.5	−0.5	–
Arkansas	5.0	4.6	3.7	3.2	3.2	3.1	−0.8	−2.2	−1.4	−0.8
California	3.6	2.7	2.1	1.9	1.8	1.8	−2.8	−2.5	−1.0	−1.3
Colorado	4.2	3.2	2.2	2.0	2.0	2.0	−2.7	−3.7	−0.9	–
Connecticut.	3.5	2.9	2.3	2.3	2.2	2.2	−1.9	−2.3	–	−1.1
Delaware	3.6	3.0	2.3	2.4	2.2	2.2	−1.8	−2.6	0.4	−2.2
District of Columbia	7.3	7.6	5.8	5.7	5.6	5.4	0.4	−2.7	−0.2	−1.3
Florida.	5.1	3.9	3.2	2.9	2.7	2.7	−2.6	−2.0	−1.0	−1.8
Georgia	4.6	4.0	2.9	2.6	2.5	2.4	−1.4	−3.2	−1.1	−2.0
Hawaii	3.1	2.7	2.5	2.4	2.0	2.0	−1.4	−0.8	−0.4	−4.5
Idaho.	3.7	3.2	2.7	2.2	2.1	2.0	−1.4	−1.7	−2.0	−2.4
Illinois	5.1	4.0	3.0	2.6	2.5	2.5	−2.4	−2.8	−1.4	−1.0
Indiana.	4.5	3.9	3.2	2.8	2.6	2.6	−1.4	−2.0	−1.3	−1.8
Iowa	5.7	5.1	4.0	3.3	3.2	3.1	−1.1	−2.4	−1.9	−1.6
Kansas	5.8	4.8	4.0	3.5	3.5	3.5	−1.9	−1.8	−1.3	–
Kentucky	4.5	4.3	3.7	3.3	3.2	3.2	−0.5	−1.5	−1.1	−0.8
Louisiana	4.8	4.6	3.9	3.4	3.4	3.2	−0.4	−1.6	−1.4	−1.5
Maine	4.7	3.7	2.9	2.7	2.6	2.5	−2.4	−2.4	−0.7	−1.9
Maryland	3.6	2.8	2.1	2.0	2.1	2.0	−2.5	−2.8	−0.5	–
Massachusetts.	4.4	3.6	2.6	2.4	2.5	2.4	−2.0	−3.2	−0.8	–
Michigan	4.4	3.7	2.6	2.6	2.5	2.5	−1.7	−3.5	–	−1.0
Minnesota.	5.7	4.4	3.4	2.9	2.7	2.7	−2.6	−2.5	−1.6	−1.8
Mississippi	5.3	5.0	4.8	4.4	4.3	4.2	−0.6	−0.4	−0.9	−1.2
Missouri.	5.7	4.8	3.6	3.1	3.1	3.1	−1.7	−2.8	−1.5	–
Montana.	5.9	5.8	4.7	3.8	3.7	3.6	−0.2	−2.1	−2.1	−1.3
Nebraska	6.0	5.5	4.8	4.0	3.6	3.5	−0.9	−1.4	−1.8	−3.3
Nevada	4.2	2.8	1.9	2.0	2.0	2.0	−4.0	−3.8	0.5	–
New Hampshire	3.9	3.1	2.3	2.2	2.1	2.1	−2.3	−2.9	−0.4	−1.2
New Jersey	4.2	3.7	3.0	2.4	2.4	2.3	−1.3	−2.1	−2.2	−1.1
New Mexico	3.1	2.8	1.9	2.0	1.8	1.8	−1.0	−3.8	0.5	−2.6
New York	4.5	4.1	3.5	3.0	2.9	2.8	−0.9	−1.6	−1.5	−1.7
North Carolina	4.2	3.3	2.9	2.4	2.3	2.2	−2.4	−1.3	−1.9	−2.2
North Dakota	7.4	7.0	6.0	5.1	4.0	4.3	−0.6	−1.5	−1.6	−4.2
Ohio.	4.7	4.0	3.0	3.0	2.9	2.9	−1.6	−2.8	–	−0.8
Oklahoma.	4.6	4.0	3.2	3.0	3.0	2.9	−1.4	−2.2	−0.6	−0.8
Oregon	3.5	2.8	1.9	1.7	1.7	1.7	−2.2	−3.8	−1.1	–
Pennsylvania	4.8	4.4	3.4	3.2	3.1	3.0	−0.9	−2.5	−0.6	−1.6
Rhode Island	3.8	3.2	2.3	2.3	2.1	2.1	−1.7	−3.2	–	−2.2
South Carolina	3.9	3.3	2.9	2.7	2.7	2.5	−1.7	−1.3	−0.7	−1.9
South Dakota.	5.5	6.1	5.7	5.0	4.9	4.8	1.0	−0.7	−1.3	−1.0
Tennessee	5.5	4.8	3.6	3.3	3.1	3.1	−1.4	−2.8	−0.9	−1.6
Texas	4.7	3.5	2.7	2.4	2.3	2.3	−2.9	−2.6	−1.2	−1.1
Utah	3.1	2.6	1.9	1.8	1.8	1.8	−1.7	−3.1	−0.5	–
Vermont	4.4	3.0	2.7	2.1	1.9	1.9	−3.8	−1.0	−2.5	−2.5
Virginia	4.1	3.3	2.4	2.2	2.2	2.2	−2.1	−3.1	−0.9	–
Washington.	3.1	2.5	1.9	1.7	1.7	1.7	−2.1	−2.7	−1.1	–
West Virginia	5.5	4.7	4.4	4.0	3.8	3.7	−1.6	−0.7	−0.9	−1.9
Wisconsin.	4.9	3.8	2.9	2.4	2.2	2.2	−2.5	−2.7	−1.9	−2.2
Wyoming	3.6	4.8	3.9	3.6	3.3	3.1	2.9	−2.1	−0.8	−3.7

– Quantity zero.
[1] See Appendix II, Average annual rate of change (percent change).

NOTES: Community hospitals are nonfederal short-term general and special hospitals whose facilities and services are available to the public. The types of facilities included in the community hospitals category have changed over time. See Appendix II, Hospital. See *Health, United States, 2013*, Table 108, for 1970 hospital data.

SOURCE: American Hospital Association (AHA). Annual Survey of Hospitals. Hospital Statistics, 1981, 1991–92, 2002, 2012, 2014, 2015, and 2016 editions. Chicago, IL. (Reprinted from AHA Hospital Statistics by permission, Copyright 1981, 1991–92, 2002, 2012, 2014, 2015, and 2016 by Health Forum, LLC, an American Hospital Association Company.) See Appendix I, American Hospital Association (AHA) Annual Survey of Hospitals.

Table 91. Occupancy rates in community hospitals and average annual percent change, by state: United States, selected years 1980–2014

[Data are based on reporting by a census of hospitals]

State	1980	1990	2000	2010	2014	1980–1990	1990–2000	2000–2010	2010–2014
	\multicolumn{5}{c}{Occupancy rate[1]}		Average annual percent change[2]		
United States	75	67	64	65	63	−1.1	−0.5	0.2	−0.8
Alabama.	73	63	60	61	61	−1.5	−0.5	0.2	–
Alaska	58	50	57	61	63	−1.5	1.3	0.7	0.8
Arizona	74	62	63	65	59	−1.8	0.2	0.3	−2.4
Arkansas	70	62	59	55	52	−1.2	−0.5	−0.7	−1.4
California	69	64	66	68	64	−0.7	0.3	0.3	−1.5
Colorado	72	64	58	60	56	−1.2	−1.0	0.3	−1.7
Connecticut.	80	77	75	78	73	−0.4	−0.3	0.4	−1.6
Delaware	82	77	75	74	74	−0.6	−0.3	−0.1	–
District of Columbia	83	75	74	73	72	−1.0	−0.1	−0.1	−0.3
Florida.	72	62	61	63	63	−1.5	−0.2	0.3	–
Georgia	70	66	63	66	69	−0.6	−0.5	0.5	1.1
Hawaii	75	85	76	72	72	1.3	−1.1	−0.5	–
Idaho.	65	56	53	51	49	−1.5	−0.5	−0.4	−1.0
Illinois	75	66	60	62	59	−1.3	−0.9	0.3	−1.2
Indiana.	78	61	56	58	57	−2.4	−0.9	0.4	−0.4
Iowa	69	62	58	56	55	−1.1	−0.7	−0.4	−0.4
Kansas	69	56	53	54	52	−2.1	−0.5	0.2	−0.9
Kentucky	77	62	62	60	58	−2.1	–	−0.3	−0.8
Louisiana	70	57	56	59	56	−2.0	−0.2	0.5	−1.3
Maine	75	72	64	62	63	−0.4	−1.2	−0.3	0.4
Maryland	84	79	73	74	70	−0.6	−0.8	0.1	−1.4
Massachusetts.	82	74	71	73	70	−1.0	−0.4	0.3	−1.0
Michigan	78	66	65	66	64	−1.7	−0.2	0.2	−0.8
Minnesota.	74	67	67	64	63	−1.0	–	−0.5	−0.4
Mississippi	71	59	59	54	55	−1.8	–	−0.9	0.5
Missouri.	75	62	58	61	60	−1.9	−0.7	0.5	−0.4
Montana.	66	61	67	63	60	−0.8	0.9	−0.6	−1.2
Nebraska	67	58	59	55	55	−1.4	0.2	−0.7	–
Nevada	69	60	71	68	69	−1.4	1.7	−0.4	0.4
New Hampshire	73	67	59	60	61	−0.9	−1.3	0.2	0.4
New Jersey.	83	80	69	71	67	−0.4	−1.5	0.3	−1.4
New Mexico	66	58	58	57	60	−1.3	–	−0.2	1.3
New York	86	86	79	79	78	–	−0.8	–	−0.3
North Carolina	78	73	70	70	68	−0.7	−0.4	–	−0.7
North Dakota	69	64	60	59	56	−0.7	−0.6	−0.2	−1.3
Ohio	79	65	61	61	59	−1.9	−0.6	–	−0.8
Oklahoma.	68	58	56	57	53	−1.6	−0.4	0.2	−1.8
Oregon	69	57	59	59	59	−1.9	0.3	–	–
Pennsylvania	80	73	68	67	63	−0.9	−0.7	−0.1	−1.5
Rhode Island	86	79	72	69	67	−0.8	−0.9	−0.4	−0.7
South Carolina	77	71	69	66	62	−0.8	−0.3	−0.4	−1.6
South Dakota.	61	62	65	62	62	0.2	0.5	−0.5	–
Tennessee	76	64	56	60	61	−1.7	−1.3	0.7	0.4
Texas	70	57	59	60	59	−2.0	0.3	0.2	−0.4
Utah	70	59	56	53	52	−1.7	−0.5	−0.5	−0.5
Vermont.	74	67	67	65	66	−1.0	–	−0.3	0.4
Virginia	78	67	68	67	67	−1.5	0.1	−0.1	–
Washington.	72	63	60	63	62	−1.3	−0.5	0.5	−0.4
West Virginia	76	63	61	61	61	−1.9	−0.3	–	–
Wisconsin.	74	65	60	60	60	−1.3	−0.8	–	–
Wyoming	57	54	56	56	54	−0.5	0.4	–	−0.9

– Quantity zero.

[1] Estimated percent of staffed beds that are occupied. Occupancy rate is calculated as the average daily census (inpatient days divided by 365) divided by the number of hospital beds. See Appendix II, Occupancy rate.

[2] See Appendix II, Average annual rate of change (percent change).

NOTES: Community hospitals are nonfederal short-term general and special hospitals whose facilities and services are available to the public. The types of facilities included in the community hospitals category have changed over time. See Appendix II, Hospital. See *Health, United States, 2013*, Table 109, for 1970 hospital data.

SOURCE: American Hospital Association (AHA). Annual Survey of Hospitals. Hospital Statistics, 1981, 1991–92, 2002, 2012, 2014, 2015, and 2016 editions. Chicago, IL. (Reprinted from AHA Hospital Statistics by permission, Copyright 1981, 1991–92, 2002, 2012, 2014, 2015, and 2016 by Health Forum, LLC, an American Hospital Association Company.) See Appendix I, American Hospital Association (AHA) Annual Survey of Hospitals.

Table 92 (page 1 of 2). Nursing homes, beds, residents, and occupancy rates, by state: United States, selected years 1995–2015

Excel and PDF versions (with more data years and standard errors when available): http://www.cdc.gov/nchs/hus/contents2016.htm#092.

[Data are based on a census of certified nursing facilities]

State	Nursing homes				Beds			
	1995	2000	2014	2015	1995	2000	2014	2015
				Number				
United States	16,389	16,886	15,643	15,656	1,751,302	1,795,388	1,693,943	1,694,777
Alabama.	221	225	226	227	23,353	25,248	26,388	26,506
Alaska	15	15	18	18	814	821	693	693
Arizona	152	150	147	145	16,162	17,458	16,605	16,523
Arkansas	256	255	229	228	29,952	25,715	24,558	24,463
California	1,382	1,369	1,217	1,213	140,203	131,762	119,866	119,046
Colorado	219	225	214	217	19,912	20,240	20,431	20,560
Connecticut.	267	259	229	229	32,827	32,433	27,673	27,608
Delaware	42	43	46	45	4,739	4,906	4,876	4,791
District of Columbia	19	20	19	19	3,206	3,078	2,766	2,766
Florida.	627	732	689	689	72,656	83,365	83,545	83,668
Georgia	352	363	357	358	38,097	39,817	39,975	39,857
Hawaii	34	45	46	46	2,513	4,006	4,213	4,313
Idaho.	76	84	78	79	5,747	6,181	5,951	5,977
Illinois	827	869	761	762	103,230	110,766	98,348	98,489
Indiana.	556	564	528	541	59,538	56,762	59,555	61,048
Iowa	419	467	443	442	39,959	37,034	31,950	31,843
Kansas	429	392	345	344	30,016	27,067	25,730	25,756
Kentucky	288	307	287	289	23,221	25,341	26,300	27,060
Louisiana	337	337	280	279	37,769	39,430	35,066	34,537
Maine	132	126	105	103	9,243	8,248	6,953	6,904
Maryland	218	255	228	228	28,394	31,495	28,115	28,013
Massachusetts.	550	526	416	413	54,532	56,030	48,320	47,990
Michigan	432	439	433	437	49,473	50,696	46,521	46,669
Minnesota.	432	433	377	377	43,865	42,149	30,319	29,934
Mississippi	183	190	205	204	16,059	17,068	18,434	18,426
Missouri	546	551	512	512	52,679	54,829	55,273	55,245
Montana.	100	104	83	80	7,210	7,667	6,732	6,693
Nebraska	231	236	219	217	18,169	17,877	16,005	15,961
Nevada	42	51	52	54	3,998	5,547	6,040	6,256
New Hampshire	74	83	76	76	7,412	7,837	7,501	7,525
New Jersey	300	361	361	365	43,967	52,195	52,051	52,538
New Mexico	83	80	71	73	6,969	7,289	6,869	7,070
New York	624	665	628	626	107,750	120,514	117,131	116,666
North Carolina	391	410	422	423	38,322	41,376	45,088	45,221
North Dakota	87	88	81	80	7,125	6,954	6,131	6,009
Ohio	943	1,009	954	959	106,884	105,038	90,653	90,667
Oklahoma.	405	392	309	305	33,918	33,903	28,962	28,580
Oregon	161	150	137	137	13,885	13,500	12,210	12,274
Pennsylvania	726	770	699	699	92,655	95,063	88,236	88,133
Rhode Island	94	99	84	84	9,612	10,271	8,720	8,720
South Carolina	166	178	188	187	16,682	18,102	19,631	19,758
South Dakota.	114	114	111	111	8,296	7,844	6,945	6,893
Tennessee	322	349	321	319	37,074	38,593	37,268	36,719
Texas	1,266	1,215	1,212	1,222	123,056	125,052	136,000	137,396
Utah	91	93	99	100	7,101	7,651	8,577	8,639
Vermont.	23	44	37	37	1,862	3,743	3,174	3,174
Virginia	271	278	288	286	30,070	30,595	32,497	32,447
Washington.	285	277	221	220	28,464	25,905	21,286	21,145
West Virginia	129	139	127	126	10,903	11,413	10,888	10,858
Wisconsin.	413	420	389	388	48,754	46,395	33,959	33,800
Wyoming	37	40	39	38	3,035	3,119	2,965	2,950

See footnotes at end of table.

Excel and PDF versions (with more data years and standard errors when available): http://www.cdc.gov/nchs/hus/contents2016.htm#092.

[Data are based on a census of certified nursing facilities]

State	Residents				Occupancy rate [1]			
	1995	2000	2014	2015	1995	2000	2014	2015
	Number							
United States	1,479,550	1,480,076	1,368,667	1,360,970	84.5	82.4	80.8	80.3
Alabama.	21,691	23,089	22,731	22,721	92.9	91.4	86.1	85.7
Alaska	634	595	612	626	77.9	72.5	88.3	90.3
Arizona	12,382	13,253	11,428	11,588	76.6	75.9	68.8	70.1
Arkansas	20,823	19,317	17,688	17,655	69.5	75.1	72.0	72.2
California	109,805	106,460	102,245	102,674	78.3	80.8	85.3	86.2
Colorado	17,055	17,045	16,309	16,290	85.7	84.2	79.8	79.2
Connecticut.	29,948	29,657	24,250	24,018	91.2	91.4	87.6	87.0
Delaware	3,819	3,900	4,314	4,253	80.6	79.5	88.5	88.8
District of Columbia	2,576	2,858	2,539	2,540	80.3	92.9	91.8	91.8
Florida.	61,845	69,050	73,487	73,492	85.1	82.8	88.0	87.8
Georgia	35,933	36,559	33,930	33,399	94.3	91.8	84.9	83.8
Hawaii	2,413	3,558	3,663	3,568	96.0	88.8	86.9	82.7
Idaho.	4,697	4,640	3,841	3,881	81.7	75.1	64.5	64.9
Illinois	83,696	83,604	72,563	71,952	81.1	75.5	73.8	73.1
Indiana.	44,328	42,328	38,893	39,267	74.5	74.6	65.3	64.3
Iowa	27,506	29,204	24,859	24,585	68.8	78.9	77.8	77.2
Kansas	25,140	22,230	18,337	18,204	83.8	82.1	71.3	70.7
Kentucky	20,696	22,730	23,008	23,453	89.1	89.7	87.5	86.7
Louisiana	32,493	30,735	25,854	25,722	86.0	77.9	73.7	74.5
Maine	8,587	7,298	6,239	6,199	92.9	88.5	89.7	89.8
Maryland	24,716	25,629	24,430	24,572	87.0	81.4	86.9	87.7
Massachusetts.	49,765	49,805	41,255	40,794	91.3	88.9	85.4	85.0
Michigan	43,271	42,615	39,374	39,275	87.5	84.1	84.6	84.2
Minnesota.	41,163	38,813	26,695	25,725	93.8	92.1	88.0	85.9
Mississippi	15,247	15,815	16,129	16,026	94.9	92.7	87.5	87.0
Missouri.	39,891	38,586	38,326	38,418	75.7	70.4	69.3	69.5
Montana.	6,415	5,973	4,619	4,466	89.0	77.9	68.6	66.7
Nebraska	16,166	14,989	12,043	11,938	89.0	83.8	75.2	74.8
Nevada	3,645	3,657	4,821	4,827	91.2	65.9	79.8	77.2
New Hampshire	6,877	7,158	6,767	6,706	92.8	91.3	90.2	89.1
New Jersey.	40,397	45,837	45,185	44,998	91.9	87.8	86.8	85.6
New Mexico	6,051	6,503	5,439	5,502	86.8	89.2	79.2	77.8
New York	103,409	112,957	105,390	104,684	96.0	93.7	90.0	89.7
North Carolina	35,511	36,658	37,058	36,612	92.7	88.6	82.2	81.0
North Dakota.	6,868	6,343	5,664	5,571	96.4	91.2	92.4	92.7
Ohio	79,026	81,946	76,325	75,523	73.9	78.0	84.2	83.3
Oklahoma.	26,377	23,833	19,108	18,854	77.8	70.3	66.0	66.0
Oregon	11,673	9,990	7,343	7,379	84.1	74.0	60.1	60.1
Pennsylvania	84,843	83,880	79,598	78,822	91.6	88.2	90.2	89.4
Rhode Island	8,823	9,041	8,011	7,966	91.8	88.0	91.9	91.4
South Carolina	14,568	15,739	16,773	16,830	87.3	86.9	85.4	85.2
South Dakota.	7,926	7,059	6,381	6,301	95.5	90.0	91.9	91.4
Tennessee	33,929	34,714	28,897	28,246	91.5	89.9	77.5	76.9
Texas	89,354	85,275	93,170	93,316	72.6	68.2	68.5	67.9
Utah	5,832	5,703	5,515	5,518	82.1	74.5	64.3	63.9
Vermont.	1,792	3,349	2,686	2,628	96.2	89.5	84.6	82.8
Virginia	28,119	27,091	28,486	27,874	93.5	88.5	87.7	85.9
Washington.	24,954	21,158	17,005	16,969	87.7	81.7	79.9	80.3
West Virginia	10,216	10,334	9,535	9,471	93.7	90.5	87.6	87.2
Wisconsin.	43,998	38,911	27,485	26,804	90.2	83.9	80.9	79.3
Wyoming	2,661	2,605	2,364	2,268	87.7	83.5	79.7	76.9

- - - Data not available.

[1] Percentage of beds occupied (number of nursing home residents per 100 nursing home beds). See Appendix II, Occupancy rate.

NOTES: Annual numbers of nursing homes, beds, and residents are based on the Centers for Medicare & Medicaid Services' reporting cycle. Starting with 2013 data, a new editing rule was used for number of beds. For the U.S., the number of beds decreased by less than 1%. For most states, this caused little or no change in the data. The change in the number of beds also caused a change in some occupancy rates. Because of the methodology change, trends should be interpreted with caution. Data for additional years are available. See the Excel spreadsheet on the *Health, United States* website at: http://www.cdc.gov/nchs/hus.htm.

SOURCE: Cowles CM ed., 2015 Nursing Home Statistical Yearbook. Anacortes, WA: Cowles Research Group, 2016 and previous editions; and Cowles Research Group, unpublished data. Based on data from the Centers for Medicare & Medicaid Services' Quality Improvement Evaluation System (QIES) and its predecessor, the Online Survey Certification and Reporting Database (OSCAR). See Appendix I, Quality Improvement Evaluation System (QIES).

Table 93 (page 1 of 2). Gross domestic product, national health expenditures, per capita amounts, percent distribution, and average annual percent change: United States, selected years 1960–2015

Excel and PDF versions (with more data years and standard errors when available): http://www.cdc.gov/nchs/hus/contents2016.htm#093.

[Data are compiled from various sources by the Centers for Medicare & Medicaid Services]

Gross domestic product and national health expenditures	1960	1970	1975	1980	1990	2000	2009	2014	2015
	Amount, in billions								
Gross domestic product (GDP)	$543	$1,076	$1,689	$2,863	$5,980	$10,285	$14,419	$17,393	$18,037
	Deflator (2009 = 100.0)								
Price deflator for GDP [1]	17.5	22.8	31.4	44.5	66.8	81.9	100.0	108.8	110.0
	Amount, in billions								
National health expenditures	$27.2	$74.6	$133.3	$255.3	$721.4	$1,369.7	$2,494.7	$3,029.3	$3,205.6
Health consumption expenditures	24.7	67.0	121.1	235.5	674.1	1,286.4	2,355.7	2,878.4	3,050.8
Personal health care	23.3	63.1	113.2	217.0	615.3	1,162.0	2,114.2	2,562.8	2,717.2
Administration and net cost of private health insurance	1.1	2.6	4.9	12.1	38.7	81.3	167.4	236.6	252.7
Public health	0.4	1.4	3.0	6.4	20.0	43.0	74.1	79.0	80.9
Investment [2]	2.5	7.5	12.2	19.9	47.3	83.3	139.0	150.9	154.7
	Deflator (2009 = 100.0)								
Chain-weighted national health expenditure deflator [1]	- - -	- - -	- - -	- - -	- - -	- - -	100.0	110.2	111.5
	Per capita amount, in dollars								
National health expenditures	$146	$355	$605	$1,108	$2,843	$4,857	$8,141	$9,515	$9,990
Health consumption expenditures	133	319	550	1,022	2,657	4,562	7,687	9,041	9,508
Personal health care	125	300	514	942	2,425	4,121	6,899	8,050	8,468
Administration and net cost of private health insurance	6	13	22	52	153	288	546	743	787
Public health	2	6	13	28	79	153	242	248	252
Investment [2]	13	36	55	86	187	295	453	474	482
	Percent								
National health expenditures as percent of GDP	5.0	6.9	7.9	8.9	12.1	13.3	17.3	17.4	17.8
	Percent distribution								
National health expenditures	100.0	100.0	100.0	100.0	100.0	100.0	100.0	100.0	100.0
Health consumption expenditures	90.8	89.9	90.9	92.2	93.4	93.9	94.4	95.0	95.2
Personal health care	85.5	84.6	84.9	85.0	85.3	84.8	84.7	84.6	84.8
Administration and net cost of private health insurance	3.9	3.5	3.7	4.7	5.4	5.9	6.7	7.8	7.9
Public health	1.4	1.8	2.2	2.5	2.8	3.1	3.0	2.6	2.5
Investment [2]	9.2	10.1	9.1	7.8	6.6	6.1	5.6	5.0	4.8
	Average annual percent change from previous year shown [3]								
GDP	. . .	7.1	9.4	11.1	7.6	5.6	3.8	3.8	3.7
National health expenditures	. . .	10.6	12.3	13.9	10.9	6.6	6.9	4.0	5.8
Health consumption expenditures	. . .	10.5	12.6	14.2	11.1	6.7	7.0	4.1	6.0
Personal health care	. . .	10.5	12.4	13.9	11.0	6.6	6.9	3.9	6.0
Administration and net cost of private health insurance	. . .	9.4	13.3	19.6	12.4	7.7	8.4	7.2	6.8
Public health	. . .	13.8	17.0	16.8	12.0	8.0	6.2	1.3	2.4
Investment [2]	. . .	11.6	10.1	10.3	9.1	5.8	5.8	1.7	2.6
National health expenditures, per capita . . .	. . .	9.3	11.3	12.9	9.9	5.5	5.9	3.2	5.0
Health consumption expenditures	. . .	9.1	11.5	13.2	10.0	5.6	6.0	3.3	5.2
Personal health care	. . .	9.1	11.4	12.9	9.9	5.4	5.9	3.1	5.2
Administration and net cost of private health insurance	. . .	8.0	11.1	18.8	11.4	6.5	7.4	6.4	5.9
Public health	. . .	11.6	16.7	16.6	10.9	6.8	5.2	0.5	1.6
Investment [2]	. . .	10.7	8.8	9.4	8.1	4.7	4.9	0.9	1.7

See footnotes at end of table.

Table 93 (page 2 of 2). Gross domestic product, national health expenditures, per capita amounts, percent distribution, and average annual percent change: United States, selected years 1960–2015

Excel and PDF versions (with more data years and standard errors when available): http://www.cdc.gov/nchs/hus/contents2016.htm#093.

[Data are compiled from various sources by the Centers for Medicare & Medicaid Services]

- - - Data not available.
. . . Category not applicable.
[1] Year 2009 = 100.0. For more information on the detailed price series recommended for deflating each category of spending, see the National Health Expenditure Accounts Methodology Paper, 2015 and NHE Deflator Methodology paper. Available from:
  https://www.cms.gov/Research-Statistics-Data-and-Systems/Statistics-Trends-and-Reports/NationalHealthExpendData/NationalHealthAccountsHistorical.html.
[2] Investment consists of research and structures and equipment.
[3] See Appendix II, Average annual rate of change (percent change).

NOTES: Dollar amounts shown are in current dollars. See Appendix II, Gross domestic product (GDP); Health expenditures, national. Percents are calculated using unrounded data. Estimates may not add to totals because of rounding. Census resident-based population less armed forces overseas and population of outlying areas used to calculate per capita. For more information on NHE categories, sources, and methods, see the National Health Expenditure Accounts Methodology Paper, 2015. See Appendix I, National Health Expenditure Accounts (NHEA). Data have been revised and differ from previous editions of *Health, United States*.

SOURCE: Centers for Medicare & Medicaid Services, Office of the Actuary, National Health Statistics Group, National Health Expenditure Accounts, National health expenditures aggregate. Available from:
https://www.cms.gov/Research-Statistics-Data-and-Systems/Statistics-Trends-and-Reports/NationalHealthExpendData/NationalHealthAccountsHistorical.html, accessed on January 5, 2017. U.S. Department of Commerce Bureau of Economic Analysis, National Economic Accounts, National Income and Product Accounts, Table 1.1.4, accessed on January 5, 2017. Available from: http://www.bea.gov/iTable/iTable.cfm?ReqID=9&step=1. See Appendix I, National Health Expenditure Accounts (NHEA); National Income and Product Accounts (NIPA).

Table 94 (page 1 of 2). National health expenditures, average annual percent change, and percent distribution, by type of expenditure: United States, selected years 1960–2015

Excel and PDF versions (with more data years and standard errors when available): http://www.cdc.gov/nchs/hus/contents2016.htm#094.

[Data are compiled from various sources by the Centers for Medicare & Medicaid Services]

Type of national health expenditure	1960	1970	1975	1980	1990	2000	2009	2014	2015
	Amount, in billions								
National health expenditures	$27.2	$74.6	$133.3	$255.3	$721.4	$1,369.7	$2,494.7	$3,029.3	$3,205.6
Health consumption expenditures	24.7	67.0	121.1	235.5	674.1	1,286.4	2,355.7	2,878.4	3,050.8
Personal health care	23.3	63.1	113.2	217.0	615.3	1,162.0	2,114.2	2,562.8	2,717.2
Hospital care	9.0	27.2	51.2	100.5	250.4	415.5	779.7	981.0	1036.1
Professional services	7.9	19.8	34.7	64.5	207.3	387.5	668.2	792.8	840.2
Physician and clinical services	5.6	14.3	25.3	47.7	158.4	288.7	498.7	597.1	634.9
Other professional services	0.4	0.7	1.3	3.5	17.3	36.6	67.2	82.8	87.7
Dental services	2.0	4.7	8.0	13.3	31.6	62.1	102.3	112.8	117.5
Other health, residential, and personal care	0.4	1.3	2.9	8.4	23.8	63.9	123.4	151.5	163.3
Home health care [1]	0.1	0.2	0.6	2.4	12.5	32.3	67.3	83.6	88.8
Nursing care facilities and continuing care retirement communities [1]	0.8	4.0	8.0	15.3	44.7	85.0	134.9	152.6	156.8
Retail outlet sales of medical products	5.0	10.6	15.8	25.9	76.5	177.8	340.8	401.4	432.0
Prescription drugs	2.7	5.5	8.1	12.0	40.3	121.0	252.7	297.9	324.6
Durable medical equipment	0.7	1.7	2.8	4.1	13.8	25.2	37.8	46.6	48.5
Other nondurable medical products	1.6	3.3	4.9	9.8	22.4	31.6	50.3	56.9	59.0
Government administration [2]	0.1	0.7	1.5	2.8	7.2	17.1	29.6	41.2	42.6
Net cost of health insurance [3]	1.0	1.9	3.4	9.3	31.6	64.2	137.9	195.3	210.1
Government public health activities [4]	0.4	1.4	3.0	6.4	20.0	43.1	74.1	79.0	80.9
Investment	2.5	7.5	12.2	19.9	47.3	83.3	139.0	150.9	154.7
Research [5]	0.7	2.0	3.4	5.4	12.7	25.5	45.4	45.9	46.7
Structures and equipment	1.8	5.6	8.8	14.4	34.6	57.8	93.6	105.0	108.0
	Average annual percent change from previous year shown [6]								
National health expenditures	...	10.6	12.3	13.9	10.9	6.6	6.9	4.0	5.8
Health consumption expenditures	...	10.5	12.6	14.2	11.1	6.7	7.0	4.1	6.0
Personal health care	...	10.5	12.4	13.9	11.0	6.6	6.9	3.9	6.0
Hospital care	...	11.7	13.5	14.4	9.6	5.2	7.2	4.7	5.6
Professional services	...	9.6	11.9	13.2	12.4	6.5	6.2	3.5	6.0
Physician and clinical services	...	9.9	12.0	13.5	12.7	6.2	6.3	3.7	6.3
Other professional services	...	6.3	13.0	21.1	17.4	7.8	7.0	4.3	5.9
Dental services	...	9.0	11.2	10.7	9.0	7.0	5.7	2.0	4.2
Other health, residential, and personal care	...	11.5	17.2	23.9	11.0	10.4	7.6	4.2	7.8
Home health care [1]	...	14.5	23.2	30.7	18.1	9.9	8.5	4.4	6.3
Nursing care facilities and continuing care retirement communities [1]	...	17.4	14.7	13.7	11.4	6.6	5.3	2.5	2.7
Retail outlet sales of medical products	...	7.7	8.4	10.4	11.4	8.8	7.5	3.3	7.6
Prescription drugs	...	7.5	7.9	8.4	12.8	11.6	8.5	3.3	9.0
Durable medical equipment	...	9.0	9.9	7.7	13.0	6.2	4.6	4.3	3.9
Other nondurable medical products	...	7.4	8.3	14.6	8.6	3.5	5.3	2.5	3.7
Government administration [2]	...	30.0	15.1	13.2	10.0	9.0	6.3	6.9	3.2
Net cost of health insurance [3]	...	6.4	12.6	22.0	13.0	7.4	8.9	7.2	7.6
Government public health activities [4]	...	13.8	17.0	16.8	12.0	8.0	6.2	1.3	2.4
Investment	...	11.6	10.1	10.3	9.1	5.8	5.8	1.7	2.6
Research [5]	...	10.9	11.5	10.0	8.9	7.2	6.6	0.2	1.8
Structures and equipment	...	11.9	9.6	10.4	9.2	5.3	5.5	2.3	2.9
	Percent distribution								
National health expenditures	100.0	100.0	100.0	100.0	100.0	100.0	100.0	100.0	100.0
Health consumption expenditures	90.8	89.9	90.9	92.2	93.4	93.9	94.4	95.0	95.2
Personal health care	85.5	84.6	84.9	85.0	85.3	84.8	84.7	84.6	84.8
Hospital care	33.0	36.4	38.4	39.4	34.7	30.3	31.3	32.4	32.3
Professional services	29.1	26.5	26.0	25.3	28.7	28.3	26.8	26.2	26.2
Physician and clinical services	20.4	19.2	19.0	18.7	22.0	21.1	20.0	19.7	19.8
Other professional services	1.4	1.0	1.0	1.4	2.4	2.7	2.7	2.7	2.7
Dental services	7.3	6.3	6.0	5.2	4.4	4.5	4.1	3.7	3.7
Other health, residential, and personal care	1.6	1.7	2.2	3.3	3.3	4.7	4.9	5.0	5.1
Home health care [1]	0.2	0.3	0.5	0.9	1.7	2.4	2.7	2.8	2.8
Nursing care facilities and continuing care retirement communities [1]	3.0	5.4	6.0	6.0	6.2	6.2	5.4	5.0	4.9
Retail outlet sales of medical products	18.5	14.2	11.9	10.1	10.6	13.0	13.7	13.3	13.5
Prescription drugs	9.8	7.4	6.0	4.7	5.6	8.8	10.1	9.8	10.1
Durable medical equipment	2.7	2.3	2.1	1.6	1.9	1.8	1.5	1.5	1.5
Other nondurable medical products	6.0	4.5	3.7	3.8	3.1	2.3	2.0	1.9	1.8
Government administration [2]	0.2	1.0	1.1	1.1	1.0	1.2	1.2	1.4	1.3
Net cost of health insurance [3]	3.7	2.5	2.6	3.6	4.4	4.7	5.5	6.4	6.6
Government public health activities [4]	1.4	1.8	2.2	2.5	2.8	3.1	3.0	2.6	2.5
Investment	9.2	10.1	9.1	7.8	6.6	6.1	5.6	5.0	4.8
Research [5]	2.6	2.6	2.5	2.1	1.8	1.9	1.8	1.5	1.5
Structures and equipment	6.7	7.5	6.6	5.7	4.8	4.2	3.8	3.5	3.4

See footnotes at end of table.

Table 94 (page 2 of 2). National health expenditures, average annual percent change, and percent distribution, by type of expenditure: United States, selected years 1960–2015

Excel and PDF versions (with more data years and standard errors when available): http://www.cdc.gov/nchs/hus/contents2016.htm#094.

[Data are compiled from various sources by the Centers for Medicare & Medicaid Services]

Type of national health expenditure	1960	1970	1975	1980	1990	2000	2009	2014	2015
	Percent distribution								
Personal health care	100.0	100.0	100.0	100.0	100.0	100.0	100.0	100.0	100.0
Hospital care	38.6	43.1	45.3	46.3	40.7	35.8	36.9	38.3	38.1
Professional services	34.1	31.3	30.6	29.7	33.7	33.3	31.6	30.9	30.9
Physician and clinical services	23.9	22.7	22.4	22.0	25.7	24.8	23.6	23.3	23.4
Other professional services.	1.7	1.2	1.2	1.6	2.8	3.2	3.2	3.2	3.2
Dental services	8.5	7.5	7.1	6.1	5.1	5.3	4.8	4.4	4.3
Other health, residential, and personal care .	1.9	2.1	2.5	3.9	3.9	5.5	5.8	5.9	6.0
Home health care [1]	0.2	0.3	0.5	1.1	2.0	2.8	3.2	3.3	3.3
Nursing care facilities and continuing care retirement communities [1]	3.5	6.4	7.1	7.0	7.3	7.3	6.4	6.0	5.8
Retail outlet sales of medical products	21.7	16.8	14.0	11.9	12.4	15.3	16.1	15.7	15.9
Prescription drugs	11.5	8.7	7.1	5.6	6.5	10.4	12.0	11.6	11.9
Durable medical equipment	3.2	2.8	2.5	1.9	2.2	2.2	1.8	1.8	1.8
Other nondurable medical products	7.0	5.3	4.4	4.5	3.6	2.7	2.4	2.2	2.2

. . . Category not applicable.

[1] Includes expenditures for care in freestanding facilities only. Additional services of this type are provided in hospital-based facilities and are considered hospital care.

[2] Includes all administrative costs (federal and state and local employees' salaries; contracted employees, including fiscal intermediaries; rent and building costs; computer systems and programs; other materials and supplies; and other miscellaneous expenses) associated with insuring individuals enrolled in the following health insurance programs: Medicare, Medicaid, Children's Health Insurance Program, Department of Defense, Department of Veterans Affairs, Indian Health Service, workers' compensation, maternal and child health, vocational rehabilitation, Substance Abuse and Mental Health Services Administration, and other federal programs.

[3] Net cost of health insurance is calculated as the difference between calendar year incurred premiums earned and benefits incurred for private health insurance. This includes administrative costs, and in some cases additions to reserves, rate credits and dividends, premium taxes, and net underwriting gains or losses. Also included in this category is the difference between premiums earned and benefits incurred for the private health insurance companie that insure the enrollees of the following programs: Medicare, Medicaid, Children's Health Insurance Program, and workers' compensation (health portion only).

[4] Includes health care services delivered by government public health agencies.

[5] Research and development expenditures of drug companies and other manufacturers and providers of medical equipment and supplies are excluded. These are included in the expenditure class in which the product falls because such expenditures are covered by the payment received for that product.

[6] See Appendix II, Average annual rate of change (percent change).

NOTES: Percents and average annual percent change are calculated using unrounded data. For more information on NHE categories, sources, and methods, see the National Health Expenditure Accounts Methodology Paper, 2015. See Appendix I, National Health Expenditure Accounts (NHEA). Data have been revised and differ from previous editions of *Health, United States*.

SOURCE: Centers for Medicare & Medicaid Services, Office of the Actuary, National Health Statistics Group, National Health Expenditure Accounts, National health expenditures. Available from: https://www.cms.gov/Research-Statistics-Data-and-Systems/Statistics-Trends-and-Reports/NationalHealthExpendData/NationalHealthAccountsHistorical.html, accessed on January 5, 2017. See Appendix I, National Health Expenditure Accounts (NHEA).

Table 95 (page 1 of 3). Personal health care expenditures, by source of funds and type of expenditure: United States, selected years 1960–2015

Excel and PDF versions (with more data years and standard errors when available): http://www.cdc.gov/nchs/hus/contents2016.htm#095.

[Data are compiled from various sources by the Centers for Medicare & Medicaid Services]

Type of personal health care expenditure and source of funds	1960	1970	1975	1980	1990	2000	2009	2014	2015
					Amount				
Per capita	$125	$300	$514	$942	$2,425	$4,121	$6,899	$8,050	$8,468
					Amount, in billions				
All personal health care expenditures [1]	$23.3	$63.1	$113.2	$217.0	$615.3	$1,162.0	$2,114.2	$2,562.8	$2,717.2
Out-of-pocket payments	12.9	25.0	37.3	58.1	137.9	199.0	293.1	329.7	338.1
Health insurance	6.6	29.7	62.1	132.1	402.9	844.2	1,636.7	2,009.4	2,151.2
Private health insurance	5.0	14.1	27.7	61.5	204.8	406.1	734.4	875.2	944.7
Medicare	. . .	7.3	15.6	36.3	107.3	216.3	470.3	580.6	605.0
Medicaid	. . .	5.0	12.8	24.7	69.7	186.9	346.2	446.7	486.5
Federal	. . .	2.7	7.0	13.7	40.3	109.3	230.6	274.4	306.2
State and local	. . .	2.3	5.8	11.0	29.4	77.6	115.6	172.3	180.3
CHIP [2]	. . .	. . .	. . .	. . .	. . .	2.5	9.5	10.8	12.0
Federal	. . .	. . .	. . .	. . .	. . .	1.8	6.7	7.6	9.0
State and local	. . .	. . .	. . .	. . .	. . .	0.8	2.8	3.3	3.0
Other health insurance programs [3]	1.7	3.3	5.9	9.6	21.2	32.3	76.2	96.2	103.0
Other third-party payers and programs [4]	3.7	8.5	13.9	26.7	74.5	118.9	184.4	223.7	227.8
					Deflator (2009 = 100.0)				
Chain-weighted personal health care deflator [5]	9.3	13.5	18.6	28.5	56.3	75.7	100.0	109.9	111.0
					Percent distribution				
All sources of funds	100.0	100.0	100.0	100.0	100.0	100.0	100.0	100.0	100.0
Out-of-pocket payments	55.7	39.6	32.9	26.8	22.4	17.1	13.9	12.9	12.4
Health insurance	28.5	47.0	54.8	60.9	65.5	72.6	77.4	78.4	79.2
Private health insurance	21.3	22.3	24.5	28.4	33.3	34.9	34.7	34.1	34.8
Medicare	. . .	11.5	13.8	16.7	17.4	18.6	22.2	22.7	22.3
Medicaid	. . .	8.0	11.3	11.4	11.3	16.1	16.4	17.4	17.9
Federal	. . .	4.3	6.2	6.3	6.6	9.4	10.9	10.7	11.3
State and local	. . .	3.7	5.1	5.1	4.8	6.7	5.5	6.7	6.6
CHIP [2]	. . .	. . .	. . .	. . .	. . .	0.2	0.5	0.4	0.4
Federal	. . .	. . .	. . .	. . .	. . .	0.2	0.3	0.3	0.3
State and local	. . .	. . .	. . .	. . .	. . .	0.1	0.1	0.1	0.1
Other health insurance programs [3]	7.2	5.2	5.2	4.4	3.4	2.8	3.6	3.8	3.8
Other third-party payers and programs [4]	15.8	13.4	12.2	12.3	12.1	10.2	8.7	8.7	8.4
					Amount, in billions				
Hospital expenditures [6]	$9.0	$27.2	$51.2	$100.5	$250.4	$415.5	$779.7	$981.0	$1,036.1
					Percent distribution				
All sources of funds	100.0	100.0	100.0	100.0	100.0	100.0	100.0	100.0	100.0
Out-of-pocket payments	20.6	9.0	8.4	5.4	4.5	3.2	3.3	3.4	3.1
Health insurance	50.7	71.5	74.7	79.7	82.6	86.2	87.4	86.8	87.7
Private health insurance	35.6	32.5	33.2	36.6	38.5	33.9	36.6	37.7	39.0
Medicare	. . .	19.7	22.4	26.1	26.9	29.7	27.5	25.8	24.8
Medicaid	. . .	9.7	9.8	9.2	10.6	17.1	17.1	17.2	17.9
Federal	. . .	5.2	5.4	5.0	6.3	10.3	11.3	10.7	11.5
State and local	. . .	4.5	4.4	4.2	4.3	6.8	5.8	6.5	6.3
CHIP [2]	. . .	. . .	. . .	. . .	. . .	0.2	0.4	0.3	0.4
Federal	. . .	. . .	. . .	. . .	. . .	0.2	0.3	0.2	0.3
State and local	. . .	. . .	. . .	. . .	. . .	0.1	0.1	0.1	0.1
Other health insurance programs [3]	15.2	9.6	9.3	7.8	6.5	5.3	5.8	5.8	5.8
Other third-party payers and programs [4]	28.6	19.5	16.9	15.0	12.9	10.6	9.3	9.8	9.2
					Amount, in billions				
Physician and clinical expenditures	$5.6	$14.3	$25.3	$47.7	$158.4	$288.7	$498.7	$597.1	$634.9
					Percent distribution				
All sources of funds	100.0	100.0	100.0	100.0	100.0	100.0	100.0	100.0	100.0
Out-of-pocket payments	59.5	45.1	35.9	29.8	18.9	11.1	9.1	9.0	8.9
Health insurance	33.1	48.8	55.2	59.8	67.8	76.4	80.5	80.9	81.1
Private health insurance	28.7	29.4	31.4	34.8	42.1	47.1	45.9	42.8	42.9
Medicare	. . .	11.5	13.7	17.4	19.2	20.3	22.5	23.1	22.7
Medicaid	. . .	4.5	7.0	5.1	4.4	6.7	8.1	10.7	11.0
Federal	. . .	2.4	3.9	2.9	2.6	3.9	5.6	7.4	7.7
State and local	. . .	2.1	3.2	2.2	1.8	2.7	2.5	3.3	3.3
CHIP [2]	. . .	. . .	. . .	. . .	. . .	0.3	0.6	0.5	0.5
Federal	. . .	. . .	. . .	. . .	. . .	0.2	0.4	0.4	0.4
State and local	. . .	. . .	. . .	. . .	. . .	0.1	0.2	0.2	0.1
Other health insurance programs [3]	4.4	3.4	3.1	2.4	2.1	2.1	3.5	3.9	3.9
Other third-party payers and programs [4]	7.4	6.1	8.9	10.4	13.3	12.5	10.4	10.0	10.0

See footnotes at end of table.

Excel and PDF versions (with more data years and standard errors when available): http://www.cdc.gov/nchs/hus/contents2016.htm#095.

[Data are compiled from various sources by the Centers for Medicare & Medicaid Services]

Type of personal health care expenditure and source of funds	1960	1970	1975	1980	1990	2000	2009	2014	2015
	Amount, in billions								
Dental services expenditures	$2.0	$4.7	$8.0	$13.3	$31.6	$62.1	$102.3	$112.8	$117.5
	Percent distribution								
All sources of funds	100.0	100.0	100.0	100.0	100.0	100.0	100.0	100.0	100.0
Out-of-pocket payments	96.0	90.0	81.4	65.8	48.3	44.2	41.6	40.8	39.9
Health insurance	3.2	9.5	17.9	33.4	51.2	55.3	57.9	58.8	59.7
Private health insurance	1.9	4.5	11.7	28.4	47.9	50.3	48.3	47.1	46.5
Medicare	. . .	. . .	0.0	. . .	. . .	0.1	0.3	0.4	0.4
Medicaid	. . .	3.4	4.5	3.8	2.4	3.9	7.5	8.8	9.8
Federal	. . .	1.8	2.5	2.1	1.3	2.2	5.1	5.5	6.5
State and local	. . .	1.6	2.0	1.7	1.0	1.7	2.4	3.3	3.3
CHIP [2]	. . .	. . .	. . .	. . .	. . .	0.4	0.7	1.3	1.4
Federal	. . .	. . .	. . .	. . .	. . .	0.3	0.5	0.9	1.0
State and local	. . .	. . .	. . .	. . .	. . .	0.1	0.2	0.4	0.3
Other health insurance programs [3]	1.3	1.6	1.6	1.2	0.9	0.6	1.1	1.3	1.6
Other third-party payers and programs [4]	0.8	0.4	0.7	0.8	0.6	0.6	0.5	0.4	0.4
	Amount, in billions								
Home health care expenditures [7]	$0.1	$0.2	$0.6	$2.4	$12.5	$32.3	$67.3	$83.6	$88.8
	Percent distribution								
All sources of funds	100.0	100.0	100.0	100.0	100.0	100.0	100.0	100.0	100.0
Out-of-pocket payments	12.3	9.5	12.7	15.3	17.8	19.2	8.3	9.4	9.9
Health insurance	5.3	37.7	53.0	53.7	66.2	71.8	88.4	87.4	87.0
Private health insurance	1.8	3.2	7.7	14.7	22.8	24.0	7.3	9.8	10.6
Medicare	. . .	26.8	30.3	26.8	26.0	26.5	45.0	41.0	39.6
Medicaid	. . .	6.8	13.8	11.6	17.1	20.9	35.6	36.1	36.1
Federal	. . .	3.2	7.7	6.2	9.2	11.3	23.2	20.4	20.6
State and local	. . .	3.2	6.1	5.4	8.0	9.6	12.4	15.7	15.4
CHIP [2]	. . .	. . .	. . .	. . .	. . .	0.0	0.0	0.0	0.1
Federal	. . .	. . .	. . .	. . .	. . .	0.0	0.0	0.0	0.0
State and local	. . .	. . .	. . .	. . .	. . .	0.0	0.0	0.0	0.0
Other health insurance programs [3]	3.5	1.4	1.1	0.5	0.3	0.3	0.4	0.5	0.7
Other third-party payers and programs [4]	80.7	52.7	34.3	31.1	16.0	9.0	3.3	3.2	3.1
	Amount, in billions								
Nursing care facilities and continuing care retirement communities expenditures [8]	$0.8	$4.0	$8.0	$15.3	$44.7	$85.0	$134.9	$152.6	$156.8
	Percent distribution								
All sources of funds	100.0	100.0	100.0	100.0	100.0	100.0	100.0	100.0	100.0
Out-of-pocket payments	74.4	49.2	39.5	40.5	40.3	31.9	27.3	26.0	25.6
Health insurance	. . .	28.5	52.9	51.9	49.0	61.2	66.2	66.7	67.4
Private health insurance	. . .	0.2	0.5	1.3	6.2	8.8	7.3	8.0	8.6
Medicare	. . .	3.5	2.7	2.0	3.8	12.7	22.3	23.3	24.0
Medicaid	. . .	23.3	47.5	46.2	36.7	37.5	33.7	32.2	31.7
Federal	. . .	12.5	26.1	26.1	20.7	21.8	22.5	18.4	18.2
State and local	. . .	10.8	21.4	20.1	16.1	15.7	11.2	13.8	13.5
CHIP [2]	. . .	. . .	. . .	. . .	. . .	0.0	0.0	0.0	0.0
Federal	. . .	. . .	. . .	. . .	. . .	0.0	0.0	0.0	0.0
State and local	. . .	. . .	. . .	. . .	. . .	0.0	0.0	0.0	0.0
Other health insurance programs [3]	. . .	1.5	2.2	2.4	2.2	2.2	2.9	3.1	3.2
Other third-party payers and programs [4]	25.5	22.3	7.6	7.6	10.8	6.9	6.5	7.3	7.0
	Amount, in billions								
Prescription drug expenditures	$2.7	$5.5	$8.1	$12.0	$40.3	$121.0	$252.7	$297.9	$324.6
	Percent distribution								
All sources of funds	100.0	100.0	100.0	100.0	100.0	100.0	100.0	100.0	100.0
Out-of-pocket payments	96.0	82.4	75.7	71.3	56.8	27.8	19.4	15.0	14.0
Health insurance	1.5	16.5	23.1	26.9	40.3	70.3	79.2	84.3	85.4
Private health insurance	1.3	8.8	12.0	15.0	27.0	50.5	45.9	43.0	43.1
Medicare	. . .	. . .	0.0	. . .	0.5	1.7	21.6	28.5	29.0
Medicaid	. . .	7.6	10.8	11.7	12.6	16.3	8.1	9.4	9.8
Federal	. . .	4.1	5.9	6.8	7.2	9.3	5.4	6.0	6.5
State and local	. . .	3.5	4.9	4.9	5.4	7.0	2.7	3.3	3.3
CHIP [2]	. . .	. . .	. . .	. . .	. . .	0.2	0.5	0.5	0.5
Federal	. . .	. . .	. . .	. . .	. . .	0.2	0.4	0.3	0.3
State and local	. . .	. . .	. . .	. . .	. . .	0.1	0.2	0.1	0.1
Other health insurance programs [3]	0.1	0.1	0.2	0.2	0.2	1.5	3.1	2.9	3.0
Other third-party payers and programs [4]	2.5	1.1	1.3	1.8	3.0	1.9	1.4	0.7	0.6

See footnotes at end of table.

Table 95 (page 3 of 3). Personal health care expenditures, by source of funds and type of expenditure: United States, selected years 1960–2015

Excel and PDF versions (with more data years and standard errors when available): *http://www.cdc.gov/nchs/hus/contents2016.htm#095.*

[Data are compiled from various sources by the Centers for Medicare & Medicaid Services]

Type of personal health care expenditure and source of funds	1960	1970	1975	1980	1990	2000	2009	2014	2015
					Amount, in billions				
All other personal health care expenditures[9]	$3.2	$7.1	$12.0	$25.7	$77.3	$157.3	$278.7	$337.8	$358.5
					Percent distribution				
All sources of funds	100.0	100.0	100.0	100.0	100.0	100.0	100.0	100.0	100.0
Out-of-pocket payments	84.6	74.2	66.8	56.9	49.7	37.6	31.6	30.8	30.2
Health insurance	4.1	9.1	16.6	25.7	33.7	45.0	52.2	53.9	55.0
Private health insurance	3.1	4.6	6.6	7.8	13.0	13.7	14.3	14.2	14.4
Medicare	. . .	1.0	1.9	2.8	5.5	8.1	10.3	10.3	10.1
Medicaid	. . .	3.0	7.6	14.8	15.0	22.8	27.0	28.7	29.7
Federal	. . .	1.6	4.2	8.1	8.5	13.0	18.0	16.6	17.4
State and local	. . .	1.4	3.4	6.7	6.4	9.8	9.0	12.1	12.4
CHIP[2]	. . .	. . .	. . .	. . .	. . .	0.2	0.4	0.4	0.5
Federal	. . .	. . .	. . .	. . .	. . .	0.1	0.3	0.3	0.4
State and local	. . .	. . .	. . .	. . .	. . .	0.1	0.1	0.1	0.1
Other health insurance programs[3].	1.1	0.5	0.4	0.3	0.2	0.2	0.2	0.3	0.3
Other third-party payers and programs[4]	11.2	16.7	16.6	17.4	16.6	17.4	16.2	15.3	14.8

. . . Category not applicable.

0.0 Quantity more than zero but less than 0.05.

[1] Includes all expenditures other than expenses for government administration, net cost of health insurance, public health activities, research, and structures and equipment.

[2] The Children's Health Insurance Program (CHIP) including Medicaid CHIP expansions.

[3] Includes Department of Defense and Department of Veterans Affairs.

[4] Includes worksite health care, other private revenues, Indian Health Service, workers' compensation, general assistance, maternal and child health, vocational rehabilitation, other federal programs, Substance Abuse and Mental Health Services Administration, other state and local programs, and school health.

[5] The personal health care deflator is calculated as a chain weighted price index using the Producer Price Indexes for hospitals, offices of physicians, medical and diagnostic laboratories, home health care services, and nursing care facilities; and Consumer Price Indices specific to each of the remaining personal health care components. For more information on the detailed price series recommended for deflating each category of spending see the National Health Expenditure Accounts Methodology Paper, 2015 and NHE Deflator Methodology paper.

[6] Includes expenditures for hospital-based nursing home and home health agency care.

[7] Includes expenditures for care in freestanding facilities only. Additional services of this type are provided in hospital-based facilities and are considered hospital care.

[8] Includes expenditures for care in freestanding nursing homes. Expenditures for care in hospital-based nursing homes are included with hospital care.

[9] Includes expenditures for other professional services, other nondurable medical products, durable medical equipment, and other health, residential, and personal care, not shown separately. See Appendix II, Health expenditures, national.

NOTES: Percents may not add to totals because of rounding. Census resident-based population less armed forces overseas and population of outlying areas used to calculate per capita. The Medicare and Medicaid programs began coverage in 1965. The Children's Health Insurance Program began coverage in 1997. For more information on NHE sources and methods, see the National Health Expenditure Accounts Methodology Paper, 2015. Available from: https://www.cms.gov/Research-Statistics-Data-and-Systems/Statistics-Trends-and-Reports/NationalHealthExpendData/Downloads/DSM-15.pdf. See Appendix I, National Health Expenditure Accounts (NHEA). Data have been revised and differ from previous editions of *Health, United States*.

SOURCE: Centers for Medicare & Medicaid Services, Office of the Actuary, National Health Statistics Group, National Health Expenditure Accounts, National health expenditures. Available from: https://www.cms.gov/Research-Statistics-Data-and-Systems/Statistics-Trends-and-Reports/NationalHealthExpendData/NationalHealthAccountsHistorical.html, accessed on January 13, 2017. Martin AB, Hartman M, Washington B, Catlin A. National health spending: Faster growth in 2015 as coverage expands and utilization increases. Health Aff 2016;36(1):1–11. See Appendix I, National Health Expenditure Accounts (NHEA).

Excel and PDF versions (with more data years and standard errors when available): http://www.cdc.gov/nchs/hus/contents2016.htm#096.

[Data are compiled by the Agency for Healthcare Research and Quality using discharge data from participating states]

Age and principal operating room procedure [1]	Mean inflation-adjusted cost per hospitalization: 2014 dollars [2]			Number of discharges with operating room principal procedure			Total inflation-adjusted national costs: 2014 dollars (in millions) [2]		
	2000	2010	2014	2000	2010	2014	2000	2010	2014
All ages									
Hospital discharges with an operating room principal procedure [3].	$13,782	$19,186	$19,266	8,743,631	9,637,687	8,308,949	$119,757	$184,725	$159,951
Laminectomy (back surgery)	8,493	11,920	14,883	285,636	204,786	151,705	2,436	2,440	2,268
Heart valve procedures	44,609	56,426	51,896	79,719	98,101	110,915	3,550	5,541	5,756
Coronary artery bypass graft (CABG)	32,520	41,897	41,932	337,972	164,801	160,240	11,028	6,907	6,717
Percutaneous coronary angioplasty (PTCA) (balloon angioplasty of heart)	15,587	20,957	21,448	581,183	488,521	377,475	9,057	10,240	8,104
Insertion, revision, replacement, removal of cardiac pacemaker or cardioverter/defibrillator	28,757	38,023	34,974	66,286	122,847	78,970	1,921	4,667	2,762
Colorectal resection (removal of part of the bowel)	20,241	25,560	23,616	253,780	261,401	234,290	5,244	6,678	5,529
Appendectomy	7,616	9,934	10,657	269,089	273,753	177,550	2,027	2,719	1,897
Cholecystectomy (gall bladder removal)	10,811	13,767	13,327	389,079	379,753	300,245	4,170	5,232	4,006
Hysterectomy	6,790	9,617	10,394	580,019	354,313	184,950	3,910	3,411	1,923
Cesarean section	5,646	6,313	6,150	898,859	1,226,435	1,142,680	4,956	7,750	7,032
Treatment, fracture or dislocation of hip and femur.	13,072	18,814	17,286	237,615	248,777	246,135	3,159	4,678	4,255
Arthroplasty knee (knee replacement).	14,357	17,592	16,292	318,854	693,086	723,086	4,551	12,198	11,783
Hip replacement	15,568	18,820	17,079	295,940	437,380	487,625	4,664	8,229	8,328
Spinal fusion.	18,119	30,933	28,949	204,320	444,508	413,206	3,614	13,755	11,970
Under 18 years									
Hospital discharges with an operating room principal procedure [3].	13,831	21,126	28,582	382,455	413,852	297,290	5,112	8,759	8,457
Incision and excision of CNS (a type of brain surgery).	30,026	44,269	47,633	6,352	8,925	7,870	184	396	372
Tonsillectomy and/or adenoidectomy.	4,597	6,465	7,897	12,045	13,000	8,635	57	85	69
Small bowel resection (removal of part of the small bowel)	37,710	44,954	60,727	1,712	2,694	1,855	64	120	112
Appendectomy	6,833	9,206	10,336	75,481	79,575	46,745	502	733	483
Cesarean section	6,269	6,718	6,594	23,690	22,582	12,090	134	152	80
Spinal fusion.	30,463	56,100	60,000	7,463	10,628	10,995	224	596	658
18–44 years									
Hospital discharges with an operating room principal procedure [3].	9,107	12,588	12,289	2,806,078	2,842,807	2,339,211	25,005	35,784	28,735
Incision and excision of CNS (a type of brain surgery).	26,477	39,120	37,330	19,510	22,908	18,660	497	902	699
Laminectomy (back surgery)	7,643	11,222	14,038	95,687	44,303	27,800	736	498	392
Appendectomy	7,014	9,112	9,519	133,662	116,699	71,470	924	1,064	683
Cholecystectomy (gall bladder removal)	8,855	10,939	10,747	132,538	139,244	102,825	1,127	1,526	1,108
Oophorectomy (removal of one or both ovaries).	6,602	9,584	10,800	38,252	32,130	17,915	255	308	193
Ligation of fallopian tubes ("tying" of fallopian tubes)	4,882	5,546	7,516	75,221	44,524	31,045	346	247	230
Hysterectomy	6,296	8,729	9,481	291,704	149,442	72,870	1,811	1,306	691
Cesarean section	5,628	6,300	6,141	873,231	1,198,961	1,126,890	4,809	7,561	6,925
Treatment, fracture or dislocation of lower extremity (other than hip or femur)	9,702	15,136	17,248	68,015	59,800	45,040	648	904	776
Spinal fusion.	17,033	29,044	27,341	73,228	89,655	64,600	1,206	2,605	1,768

See footnotes at end of table.

Table 96 (page 2 of 3). **Cost of hospital discharges with common hospital operating room procedures in nonfederal community hospitals, by age and selected principal procedure: United States, selected years 2000–2014**

Excel and PDF versions (with more data years and standard errors when available): http://www.cdc.gov/nchs/hus/contents2016.htm#096.

[Data are compiled by the Agency for Healthcare Research and Quality using discharge data from participating states]

Age and principal operating room procedure [1]	Mean inflation-adjusted cost per hospitalization: 2014 dollars [2]			Number of discharges with operating room principal procedure			Total inflation-adjusted national costs: 2014 dollars (in millions) [2]		
	2000	2010	2014	2000	2010	2014	2000	2010	2014
45–64 years									
Hospital discharges with an operating room principal procedure [3]	$15,076	$21,513	$21,420	2,435,212	3,085,028	2,636,652	$36,552	$66,262	$56,404
Laminectomy (back surgery)	8,567	12,311	15,482	107,720	80,487	59,585	924	990	927
Heart valve procedures	41,898	54,544	50,655	22,849	28,546	28,045	951	1,558	1,421
Coronary artery bypass graft (CABG)	30,385	40,362	39,934	139,897	73,265	67,165	4,271	2,958	2,682
Percutaneous coronary angioplasty (PTCA) (balloon angioplasty of heart)	15,086	20,557	20,751	252,151	224,713	170,935	3,796	4,620	3,550
Insertion, revision, replacement, removal of cardiac pacemaker or cardioverter/defibrillator .	35,219	40,063	37,584	15,957	36,456	23,770	558	1,460	893
Colorectal resection (removal of part of the bowel)	18,207	23,500	22,622	76,604	99,837	90,725	1,422	2,349	2,050
Cholecystectomy (gall bladder removal)	10,197	13,874	13,322	117,432	120,321	97,220	1,198	1,670	1,297
Oophorectomy (removal of one or both ovaries). .	7,903	10,736	13,172	21,232	37,253	22,565	168	400	297
Hysterectomy	6,926	9,742	10,369	231,498	164,344	88,465	1,601	1,603	918
Arthroplasty knee (knee replacement).	14,687	17,632	16,404	95,902	291,502	303,150	1,402	5,141	4,973
Hip replacement	16,180	18,471	16,915	65,118	150,253	176,055	1,061	2,774	2,976
Spinal fusion.	17,391	29,546	27,210	87,388	218,349	193,710	1,480	6,454	5,272
65–74 years									
Hospital discharges with an operating room principal procedure [3]	16,890	22,719	22,079	1,511,467	1,648,763	1,623,736	25,661	37,391	35,822
Laminectomy (back surgery)	8,975	11,479	14,571	45,976	43,879	36,780	413	503	538
Heart valve procedures	45,656	56,733	50,565	23,236	26,078	29,145	1,052	1,481	1,473
Coronary artery bypass graft (CABG)	33,093	41,966	42,230	112,652	53,818	56,070	3,726	2,258	2,367
Percutaneous coronary angioplasty (PTCA) (balloon angioplasty of heart)	15,519	21,035	21,929	166,497	125,005	99,675	2,579	2,629	2,189
Insertion, revision, replacement, removal of cardiac pacemaker or cardioverter/defibrillator .	31,418	39,604	36,477	19,096	32,601	20,425	603	1,290	746
Endarterectomy (plaque removal from artery lining of brain, head, neck).	9,044	10,830	10,809	51,292	34,638	30,055	476	375	325
Colorectal resection (removal of part of the bowel)	20,355	26,106	23,350	63,693	59,112	58,000	1,336	1,539	1,354
Cholecystectomy (gall bladder removal)	11,945	15,967	15,122	65,953	52,412	48,435	801	836	733
Arthroplasty knee (knee replacement).	14,623	17,438	16,075	110,961	232,195	264,425	1,607	4,053	4,253
Hip replacement	15,508	18,526	16,729	71,986	106,955	135,840	1,133	1,981	2,273
Spinal fusion.	19,151	32,385	29,609	23,419	84,861	100,785	446	2,748	2,986
75–84 years									
Hospital discharges with an operating room principal procedure [3]	17,144	22,844	22,152	1,224,573	1,189,769	1,010,816	21,299	27,126	22,392
Laminectomy (back surgery)	9,684	11,627	14,173	31,059	28,311	21,510	304	329	307
Heart valve procedures	47,093	58,243	52,058	21,004	26,690	30,675	1,001	1,555	1,597
Coronary artery bypass graft (CABG)	35,880	44,789	45,596	68,750	29,874	29,395	2,486	1,339	1,340
Percutaneous coronary angioplasty (PTCA) (balloon angioplasty of heart)	16,431	21,714	22,467	111,169	87,441	63,865	1,838	1,899	1,437
Insertion, revision, replacement, removal of cardiac pacemaker or cardioverter/defibrillator .	25,771	36,946	33,177	19,975	33,287	19,725	524	1,228	654
Endarterectomy (plaque removal from artery lining of brain, head, neck).	9,395	11,012	11,049	45,337	28,078	23,495	439	309	260
Colorectal resection (removal of part of the bowel)	22,198	28,167	24,861	62,096	48,800	39,230	1,416	1,372	975
Cholecystectomy (gall bladder removal)	13,689	18,110	16,705	52,448	42,922	33,660	733	777	563
Treatment, fracture or dislocation of hip and femur.	12,310	17,392	16,203	73,332	66,038	63,765	930	1,150	1,034
Arthroplasty knee (knee replacement).	14,615	17,530	16,188	79,138	133,319	123,855	1,158	2,338	2,006
Hip replacement	15,321	19,155	17,336	92,715	102,563	100,695	1,443	1,964	1,746
Spinal fusion.	19,927	32,830	29,844	11,770	36,462	39,065	233	1,197	1,166

See footnotes at end of table.

Table 96 (page 3 of 3). Cost of hospital discharges with common hospital operating room procedures in nonfederal community hospitals, by age and selected principal procedure: United States, selected years 2000–2014

Excel and PDF versions (with more data years and standard errors when available): http://www.cdc.gov/nchs/hus/contents2016.htm#096.

[Data are compiled by the Agency for Healthcare Research and Quality using discharge data from participating states]

Age and principal operating room procedure [1]	Mean inflation-adjusted cost per hospitalization: 2014 dollars [2]			Number of discharges with operating room principal procedure			Total inflation-adjusted national costs: 2014 dollars (in millions) [2]		
	2000	2010	2014	2000	2010	2014	2000	2010	2014
85 years and over									
Hospital discharges with an operating room principal procedure [3].	$15,718	$20,752	$20,304	382,341	445,658	399,570	$6,104	$9,247	$8,120
Heart valve procedures	49,507	52,561	50,551	2,985	5,639	13,005	147	297	658
Coronary artery bypass graft (CABG)	40,365	52,110	48,287	5,280	2,955	3,170	211	154	153
Percutaneous coronary angioplasty (PTCA) (balloon angioplasty of heart)	18,647	22,360	22,746	16,682	23,538	20,930	308	527	476
Insertion, revision, replacement, removal of cardiac pacemaker or cardioverter/defibrillator	15,294	28,712	25,877	7,071	11,702	8,845	111	335	229
Colorectal resection (removal of part of the bowel)	23,987	30,829	25,933	20,729	18,420	15,005	508	568	389
Cholecystectomy (gall bladder removal)	16,660	19,751	18,071	15,698	16,524	13,485	265	326	243
Treatment, fracture or dislocation of hip and femur.	11,986	16,550	15,737	76,900	76,798	77,365	949	1,273	1,219
Arthroplasty knee (knee replacement).	14,819	18,543	17,068	10,122	18,713	17,250	151	347	294
Hip replacement	14,899	19,487	17,855	50,005	57,878	56,850	757	1,128	1,015
Amputation of lower extremity (amputation of leg, foot or toe)	13,752	18,157	18,145	12,855	8,243	8,315	179	150	151

[1] Data are based on valid operating room procedures. Analysis is limited to procedures identified as operating room procedures based on the Centers for Medicare & Medicaid Services' Diagnosis Related Groups (DRGs). For DRGs, physician panels identified *International Classification of Diseases* (ICD–9–CM) procedure codes that would be performed in operating rooms in most hospitals. Operating room procedures are classified by the Clinical Classifications Software (CCS) that group ICD–9– CM procedure codes into 1 of 231 clinically meaningful categories. Mean costs per hospitalization are based on the principal procedure as determined by the CCS. The number of discharges is based on the first-listed (principal) operating room procedure. See Appendix II, Procedure.

[2] Charges (the amount billed by the hospital) were converted to costs using cost-to-charge ratios from the Centers for Medicare & Medicaid Services. Costs are for the entire hospitalization including the principal procedure. Costs were adjusted for inflation to 2014 dollars using the gross domestic product deflator Table 1.1.4. Price Indexes downloaded from https://www.bea.gov/iTable/iTable.cfm?ReqID=9&step=1 on November 21, 2016. See Appendix II, Cost to charge ratio.

[3] Includes discharges for operating room principal procedures not shown separately.

NOTES: Excludes newborn infants. The number of states participating in the sample varied over time from 28 states in 2000 to 46 in 2011, 44 in 2012, 43 states and D.C. in 2013, and 44 states and D.C. in 2014. See Appendix I, Healthcare Cost and Utilization Project (HCUP), National (Nationwide) Inpatient Sample, for a list of states available in each year. In 2012, the HCUP-NIS was redesigned and changed from a sample of hospitals to a sample of discharges from all participating community hospitals. For this report, the statistics for years prior to 2012 were regenerated using new trend weights taking into account the 2012 redesign. For more information on the 2012 redesign, see: Houchens R, Ross D, Elixhauser A, Jiang J. Nationwide Inpatient Sample (NIS) redesign final report. 2014. HCUP methods series report # 2014-04 ONLINE. April 4, 2014. U.S. Agency for Healthcare Research and Quality. Available from: http://www.hcup-us.ahrq.gov/reports/methods/2014-04.pdf. The estimates are weighted to provide national estimates. Standard errors are available in the spreadsheet version of this table. Available from: http://www.cdc.gov/nchs/hus.htm. Data for additional years are available. See the Excel spreadsheet on the *Health, United States* website at: http://www.cdc.gov/nchs/hus.htm. Data have been revised and differ from previous editions of *Health, United States*.

SOURCE: Agency for Healthcare Research and Quality, Healthcare Cost and Utilization Project, National (Nationwide) Inpatient Sample. See Appendix I, Healthcare Cost and Utilization Project (HCUP), National (Nationwide) Inpatient Sample.

Table 97 (page 1 of 3). Expenses for health care and prescribed medicine, by selected population characteristics: United States, selected years 1987–2013

Excel and PDF versions (with more data years and standard errors when available): http://www.cdc.gov/nchs/hus/contents2016.htm#097.

[Data are based on household interviews of a sample of the civilian noninstitutionalized population and a sample of medical providers]

| | Population in millions [2] | | | Total expenses [1] | | | | | | | |
| | | | | Percent of persons with expense | | | | Mean annual expense per person with expense [3] | | | |
Characteristic	1997	2000	2013	1987	1997	2000	2013	1987	1997	2000	2013
All ages.	271.3	278.4	315.7	84.5	84.1	83.5	84.4	$3,193	$3,518	$3,653	$5,256
Under 65 years:											
Total.	237.1	243.6	269.3	83.2	82.5	81.8	82.5	2,482	2,668	2,877	4,282
Under 6 years.	23.8	24.1	23.9	88.9	88.0	86.7	90.3	2,118	1,245	1,520	2,850
6–17 years.	48.1	48.4	50.1	80.2	81.7	80.0	85.4	1,380	1,398	1,512	2,044
18–44 years.	108.9	109.0	112.1	81.5	78.3	77.7	75.4	2,180	2,417	2,577	3,655
45–64 years.	56.3	62.1	83.2	87.0	89.2	88.5	88.0	4,231	4,682	4,819	6,737
Sex											
Male.	118.0	120.9	133.7	78.8	77.6	76.6	77.6	2,345	2,411	2,754	3,835
Female.	119.1	122.7	135.6	87.5	87.4	87.0	87.3	2,601	2,894	2,984	4,673
Hispanic origin and race [4]											
Hispanic or Latino.	29.4	32.0	51.0	71.0	69.5	69.0	72.2	1,986	2,220	1,960	2,995
Not Hispanic or Latino:											
White.	166.2	169.2	160.4	86.9	87.2	86.6	87.7	2,488	2,862	3,011	4,712
Black or African American.	31.3	32.1	34.0	72.2	72.1	71.3	77.2	3,016	2,139	3,056	4,332
Asian.	. . .	. . .	14.8	. . .	. . .	. . .	73.5	. . .	. . .	. . .	2,912
American Indian, Alaska Native, Native Hawaiian, Other Pacific Islander, and Multiple Race.	. . .	. . .	9.1	. . .	. . .	. . .	83.0	. . .	. . .	. . .	4,347
Insurance status [5]											
Any private insurance.	174.0	181.6	174.3	86.5	86.5	85.9	88.0	2,379	2,719	2,741	4,401
Public insurance only.	29.8	29.7	54.6	82.4	83.3	83.6	85.2	4,006	3,243	4,368	4,777
Uninsured all year.	33.3	32.3	40.3	61.8	61.1	57.3	54.9	1,529	1,593	2,029	2,416
65 years and over:											
Total.	34.2	34.8	46.5	93.7	95.2	95.5	95.6	7,902	8,632	8,306	10,125
Sex											
Male.	14.6	15.0	20.4	92.0	94.5	93.4	94.6	8,085	9,700	8,907	10,471
Female.	19.6	19.8	26.0	94.9	95.7	97.1	96.4	7,776	7,846	7,870	9,859
Hispanic origin and race [4]											
Hispanic or Latino.	1.7	1.9	3.6	82.5	94.2	92.5	92.1	7,516	9,032	7,454	8,247
Not Hispanic or Latino:											
White.	28.8	28.9	36.1	94.9	95.9	95.9	96.1	7,777	8,676	8,432	10,354
Black or African American.	2.8	2.9	4.0	88.5	92.2	94.0	94.6	9,551	8,501	7,988	10,357
Asian.	. . .	. . .	1.9	. . .	. . .	. . .	93.5	. . .	. . .	. . .	6,585
American Indian, Alaska Native, Native Hawaiian, Other Pacific Islander, and Multiple Race.	. . .	. . .	*	. . .	. . .	. . .	*	. . .	. . .	. . .	*
Insurance status [6]											
Medicare only.	8.8	12.0	16.9	85.9	92.1	94.8	93.3	6,221	7,952	7,131	9,271
Medicare and private insurance.	21.7	19.2	21.9	95.4	97.0	96.0	97.3	7,818	8,418	8,517	9,980
Medicare and other public coverage.	3.2	3.2	6.8	94.4	93.2	96.3	96.8	12,154	12,166	11,398	13,176

See footnotes at end of table.

Table 97 (page 2 of 3). Expenses for health care and prescribed medicine, by selected population characteristics: United States, selected years 1987–2013

Excel and PDF versions (with more data years and standard errors when available): http://www.cdc.gov/nchs/hus/contents2016.htm#097.

[Data are based on household interviews of a sample of the civilian noninstitutionalized population and a sample of medical providers]

| | Prescribed medicine expenses [7] | | | | | | | |
| | Percent of persons with expense | | | | Mean annual out-of-pocket expenses for prescribed medicine per person with prescribed medicine expenses [3] | | | |
Characteristic	1987	1997	2000	2013	1987	1997	2000	2013
All ages.	57.3	62.1	62.3	60.7	$189	$294	$371	$265
Under 65 years:								
Total	54.0	58.7	58.5	55.6	139	208	269	217
Under 6 years	61.8	61.3	56.9	48.6	49	51	50	28
6–17 years.	44.3	48.2	46.2	43.2	93	78	95	84
18–44 years	51.3	55.9	56.0	50.6	109	176	205	155
45–64 years	65.3	71.8	73.3	71.8	265	386	508	361
Sex								
Male.	46.5	51.5	51.3	49.5	129	185	236	214
Female.	61.4	65.8	65.6	61.6	147	225	295	220
Hispanic origin and race [4]								
Hispanic or Latino	41.6	47.7	45.0	42.9	101	138	198	142
Not Hispanic or Latino:								
White.	57.7	63.1	63.8	61.9	146	224	289	248
Black or African American.	44.1	50.0	47.6	52.0	124	167	222	160
Asian	. . .	. . .	. . .	40.6	. . .	. . .	. . .	193
American Indian, Alaska Native, Native Hawaiian, Other Pacific Islander, and Multiple Race.	. . .	. . .	. . .	52.2	. . .	. . .	. . .	160
Insurance status [5]								
Any private insurance.	56.5	61.6	61.6	59.6	144	197	231	224
Public insurance only	56.5	62.0	62.4	56.9	96	204	385	114
Uninsured all year	35.1	40.2	37.6	36.1	153	300	446	388
65 years and over:								
Total	81.6	86.0	88.3	90.3	434	701	843	434
Sex								
Male.	78.0	82.8	83.9	89.8	404	631	632	438
Female.	84.0	88.3	91.5	90.7	453	749	989	432
Hispanic origin and race [4]								
Hispanic or Latino	74.7	87.5	83.9	84.4	*575	571	710	246
Not Hispanic or Latino:								
White.	82.3	86.7	89.0	91.3	443	724	874	468
Black or African American.	79.5	85.3	85.3	89.5	340	582	720	355
Asian	. . .	. . .	. . .	84.4	. . .	. . .	. . .	247
American Indian, Alaska Native, Native Hawaiian, Other Pacific Islander, and Multiple Race.	. . .	. . .	. . .	*	. . .	. . .	. . .	*
Insurance status [6]								
Medicare only	70.6	82.1	87.7	88.6	480	810	1,007	423
Medicare and private insurance.	83.4	88.1	89.0	91.9	452	711	780	518
Medicare and other public coverage	88.2	85.0	88.5	91.9	163	392	668	211

See footnotes at end of table.

Table 97 (page 3 of 3). Expenses for health care and prescribed medicine, by selected population characteristics: United States, selected years 1987–2013

Excel and PDF versions (with more data years and standard errors when available): http://www.cdc.gov/nchs/hus/contents2016.htm#097.

[Data are based on household interviews of a sample of the civilian noninstitutionalized population and a sample of medical providers]

. . . Category not applicable.

* Estimates are considered unreliable. Data preceded by an asterisk have a relative standard error equal to or greater than 30%. Data not shown if based on fewer than 100 sample cases.

[1] Includes expenses for inpatient hospital and physician services, ambulatory physician and nonphysician services, prescribed medicines, home health services, dental services, and other medical equipment, supplies, and services that were purchased or rented during the year. Excludes expenses for over-the-counter medications, phone contacts with health providers, and premiums for health insurance.

[2] Includes persons in the civilian noninstitutionalized population for all or part of the year. Expenditures for persons in this population for only part of the year are restricted to those incurred during periods of eligibility (e.g., expenses incurred during periods of institutionalization and military service are not included in estimates).

[3] Estimates of expenses were converted to 2013 dollars using the Consumer Price Index (all items). See Appendix II, Consumer Price Index (CPI).

[4] Persons of Hispanic origin may be of any race. Estimates for Asian persons as well as for American Indian, Alaska Native, Native Hawaiian, Other Pacific Islander, and Multiple Race persons are not available for years prior to 2002 because Asian persons could not be distinguished separately and multiple race information was not collected.

[5] Any private insurance includes individuals with insurance that provided coverage for hospital and physician care at any time during the year, other than Medicare, Medicaid, or other public coverage for hospital or physician services. Public insurance only includes individuals who were not covered by private insurance at any time during the year but were covered by Medicare, Medicaid, other public coverage for hospital or physician services, and/or CHAMPUS/CHAMPVA (TRICARE) at any point during the year. Uninsured includes persons not covered by either private or public insurance throughout the entire year or period of eligibility for the survey. Individuals with Indian Health Service coverage only are considered uninsured.

[6] Populations do not add to total because uninsured persons and persons with unknown insurance status were excluded.

[7] Includes expenses for all prescribed medications that were purchased or refilled during the survey year.

NOTES: Estimates for 1987 are based on the National Medical Expenditure Survey (NMES); estimates for other years are based on the Medical Expenditure Panel Survey (MEPS). Because expenditures in NMES were based primarily on charges and those for MEPS were based on payments, NMES data were adjusted to be more comparable with MEPS by using estimated charge-to-payment ratios for 1987. Overall, this resulted in an approximate 11% reduction from the unadjusted 1987 NMES expenditure estimates. For a detailed explanation of this adjustment, see Zuvekas S, Cohen J. A guide to comparing health care expenditures in the 1996 MEPS to the 1987 NMES. Inquiry 2002;39(1):76-86. See Appendix I, Medical Expenditure Panel Survey (MEPS). Data for additional years are available. See the Excel spreadsheet on the *Health, United States* website at: http://www.cdc.gov/nchs/hus.htm. Data have been revised and differ from previous editions of *Health, United States*.

SOURCE: Agency for Healthcare Research and Quality, Center for Financing, Access, and Cost Trends. 1987 National Medical Expenditure Survey and 1996–2013 Medical Expenditure Panel Surveys. See Appendix I, Medical Expenditure Panel Survey (MEPS).

Table 98 (page 1 of 3). Sources of payment for health care, by selected population characteristics: United States, selected years 1987–2013

Excel and PDF versions (with more data years and standard errors when available): http://www.cdc.gov/nchs/hus/contents2016.htm#098.

[Data are based on household interviews of a sample of the civilian noninstitutionalized population and a sample of medical providers]

Characteristic	All sources	Source of payment for health care							
		Out of pocket				Private insurance [1]			
		1987	1997	2000	2013	1987	1997	2000	2013
		Percent distribution							
All ages.	100.0	24.8	19.4	19.4	13.8	36.6	40.3	40.3	39.6
Under 65 years:									
Total	100.0	26.2	21.1	20.3	14.5	46.6	53.1	52.5	52.6
Under 6 years	100.0	18.5	14.2	10.3	6.0	39.5	49.3	51.2	52.9
6–17 years	100.0	35.7	29.0	27.7	17.7	47.3	53.2	48.8	50.9
18–44 years	100.0	27.4	21.1	19.9	15.2	46.8	52.9	51.2	54.6
45–64 years	100.0	24.0	20.1	20.2	14.6	47.8	53.6	54.5	51.6
Sex									
Male	100.0	24.5	21.3	18.1	13.8	44.6	50.3	52.2	50.1
Female.	100.0	27.5	21.0	22.1	15.0	48.1	55.1	52.7	54.4
Hispanic origin and race [2]									
Hispanic or Latino	100.0	22.0	18.8	20.5	12.3	36.1	42.3	45.8	34.4
Not Hispanic or Latino:									
White	100.0	28.2	21.8	21.7	15.8	50.1	55.8	55.1	58.3
Black or African American.	100.0	15.5	17.1	11.8	8.2	30.0	42.3	40.5	38.7
Asian	100.0	. . .	. . .	. . .	18.4	. . .	. . .	. . .	59.4
American Indian, Alaska Native, Native Hawaiian, Other Pacific Islander, and Multiple Race.	100.0	. . .	. . .	. . .	13.6	. . .	. . .	. . .	40.8
Insurance status [3]									
Any private insurance	100.0	29.0	21.6	21.2	16.3	60.0	67.6	70.2	73.7
Public insurance only	100.0	8.9	10.6	9.8	4.5	. . .	. . .	. . .	. . .
Uninsured all year	100.0	40.6	41.3	40.4	33.8	. . .	. . .	. . .	. . .
65 years and over.	100.0	22.0	16.3	17.5	12.2	15.8	16.5	14.9	12.0
Sex									
Male	100.0	21.7	14.2	14.2	11.6	17.6	20.1	16.8	11.2
Female.	100.0	22.2	18.1	20.2	12.7	14.4	13.2	13.3	12.6
Hispanic origin and race [2]									
Hispanic or Latino	100.0	*13.5	13.6	13.9	6.4	*4.7	5.9	8.4	5.4
Not Hispanic or Latino:									
White	100.0	23.7	17.0	18.3	13.2	16.7	17.9	15.2	12.7
Black or African American.	100.0	11.2	11.4	13.6	8.3	*11.9	8.8	9.3	8.9
Asian	100.0	. . .	. . .	. . .	10.0	. . .	. . .	. . .	*20.1
American Indian, Alaska Native, Native Hawaiian, Other Pacific Islander, and Multiple Race.	100.0	. . .	. . .	. . .	*	. . .	. . .	. . .	*
Insurance status									
Medicare only	100.0	29.8	19.8	22.2	12.6	. . .	. . .	. . .	. . .
Medicare and private insurance.	100.0	23.4	17.3	17.0	14.8	18.9	25.7	25.3	24.3
Medicare and other public coverage	100.0	*6.2	5.2	9.1	5.1	. . .	. . .	. . .	. . .

See footnotes at end of table.

Table 98 (page 2 of 3). Sources of payment for health care, by selected population characteristics: United States, selected years 1987–2013

Excel and PDF versions (with more data years and standard errors when available): http://www.cdc.gov/nchs/hus/contents2016.htm#098.

[Data are based on household interviews of a sample of the civilian noninstitutionalized population and a sample of medical providers]

| | Source of payment for health care | | | | | | | |
| | Public sources [4] | | | | Other [5] | | | |
Characteristic	1987	1997	2000	2013	1987	1997	2000	2013
	Percent distribution							
All ages.	34.1	34.4	35.4	42.1	4.5	5.9	5.0	4.6
Under 65 years:								
Total	21.3	18.1	21.3	27.3	6.0	7.7	6.0	5.5
Under 6 years	35.8	25.4	33.6	37.6	6.2	11.2	4.9	*3.4
6–17 years	11.8	14.1	20.1	29.6	5.2	3.7	3.4	1.8
18–44 years	19.4	15.7	21.1	24.0	6.4	10.3	7.8	6.2
45–64 years	22.4	20.3	20.2	27.8	5.8	6.0	5.2	6.0
Sex								
Male	23.9	19.5	23.5	29.7	7.1	8.9	6.3	6.4
Female.	19.2	17.0	19.5	25.7	5.2	6.8	5.7	4.9
Hispanic origin and race [2]								
Hispanic or Latino	35.8	28.9	27.5	42.4	6.0	10.0	6.2	10.8
Not Hispanic or Latino:								
White	15.9	15.3	18.0	21.3	5.8	7.1	5.2	4.6
Black or African American.	47.2	30.7	38.8	46.4	7.3	9.9	8.8	6.8
Asian	. . .	. . .	. . .	17.9	. . .	. . .	. . .	4.4
American Indian, Alaska Native, Native Hawaiian, Other Pacific Islander, and Multiple Race.	. . .	. . .	. . .	42.8	. . .	. . .	. . .	*2.8
Insurance status [3]								
Any private insurance	6.2	6.6	5.3	8.1	4.8	4.2	3.3	1.9
Public insurance only	87.2	80.7	84.4	90.6	3.9	8.7	5.8	*4.8
Uninsured all year	28.6	7.5	*21.2	7.7	30.9	51.1	38.4	58.5
65 years and over.	60.8	64.8	64.7	73.3	1.5	2.5	2.9	2.5
Sex								
Male	58.8	63.4	66.9	74.7	*1.9	2.3	2.2	2.5
Female.	62.3	65.9	63.0	72.2	1.1	2.7	3.5	2.6
Hispanic origin and race [2]								
Hispanic or Latino	80.2	77.8	75.6	86.2	*1.6	*2.7	*2.2	2.0
Not Hispanic or Latino:								
White	58.0	62.6	64.1	71.4	1.6	2.5	2.4	2.7
Black or African American.	76.3	77.6	68.3	80.7	0.6	2.2	*8.9	*2.0
Asian	. . .	. . .	. . .	68.3	. . .	. . .	. . .	1.6
American Indian, Alaska Native, Native Hawaiian, Other Pacific Islander, and Multiple Race.	. . .	. . .	. . .	*	. . .	. . .	. . .	*
Insurance status								
Medicare only	68.8	72.4	72.2	81.1	1.4	7.7	5.7	6.4
Medicare and private insurance.	56.1	56.3	57.1	60.6	1.6	0.6	*0.6	*0.2
Medicare and other public coverage	92.9	92.7	87.3	93.5	1.0	*2.3	*4.0	1.3

See footnotes at end of table.

Table 98 (page 3 of 3). Sources of payment for health care, by selected population characteristics: United States, selected years 1987–2013

Excel and PDF versions (with more data years and standard errors when available): http://www.cdc.gov/nchs/hus/contents2016.htm#098.

[Data are based on household interviews of a sample of the civilian noninstitutionalized population and a sample of medical providers]

. . . Category not applicable.

* Estimates are considered unreliable. Data preceded by an asterisk have a relative standard error equal to or greater than 30%. Data not shown if based on fewer than 100 sample cases.

[1] Private insurance includes any type of private insurance payments reported for people with private health insurance coverage during the year.

[2] Persons of Hispanic origin may be of any race. Estimates for Asian persons as well as for American Indian, Alaska Native, Native Hawaiian, Other Pacific Islander, and Multiple Race persons are not available for years prior to 2002 because Asian persons could not be distinguished separately and multiple race information was not collected.

[3] Any private insurance includes individuals with insurance that provided coverage for hospital and physician care at any time during the year, other than Medicare, Medicaid, or other public coverage for hospital or physician services. Public insurance only includes individuals who were not covered by private insurance at any time during the year but were covered by Medicare, Medicaid, other public coverage for hospital or physician services, and/or CHAMPUS/CHAMPVA (TRICARE) at any point during the year. Uninsured includes persons not covered by either private or public insurance throughout the entire year or period of eligibility for the survey. However, some expenses for the uninsured were paid by sources that were not defined as health insurance coverage, such as the Department of Veterans Affairs, community and neighborhood clinics, the Indian Health Service, state and local health departments, state programs other than Medicaid, workers' compensation, and other unclassified sources (e.g., automobile, home, or liability insurance). Individuals with Indian Health Service coverage only are considered uninsured.

[4] Public sources include payments made by Medicare, Medicaid, the Department of Veterans Affairs, other federal sources (e.g., Indian Health Service, military treatment facilities, and other care provided by the federal government), CHAMPUS/CHAMPVA (TRICARE), and various state and local sources (e.g., community and neighborhood clinics, state and local health departments, and state programs not already included under the Medicaid program).

[5] Other sources includes workers' compensation, unclassified sources (automobile, home, or liability insurance, and other miscellaneous or unknown sources), Medicaid payments reported for people who were not enrolled in the program at any time during the year, and any type of private insurance payments reported for people without private health insurance coverage during the year.

NOTES: Includes persons in the civilian noninstitutionalized population for all or part of the year. Expenses for persons in this population for only part of the year are restricted to those incurred during periods of eligibility (e.g., expenses incurred during periods of institutionalization and military service are not included in estimates). Estimates for 1987 are based on the National Medical Expenditure Survey (NMES); estimates for other years are based on the Medical Expenditure Panel Survey (MEPS). Because expenditures in NMES were based primarily on charges and those for MEPS were based on payments, NMES data were adjusted to be more comparable with MEPS using estimated charge-to-payment ratios for 1987. Overall, this resulted in an approximate 11% reduction from the unadjusted 1987 NMES expenditure estimates. For a detailed explanation of this adjustment, see Zuvekas S, Cohen J. A guide to comparing health care expenditures in the 1996 MEPS to the 1987 NMES. Inquiry 2002;39(1):76-86. Percents sum to 100 across sources within years. See Appendix I, Medical Expenditure Panel Survey (MEPS). Data for additional years are available. See the Excel spreadsheet on the *Health, United States* website at: http://www.cdc.gov/nchs/hus.htm.

SOURCE: Agency for Healthcare Research and Quality, Center for Financing, Access, and Cost Trends. 1987 National Medical Expenditure Survey and 1996–2013 Medical Expenditure Panel Surveys. See Appendix I, Medical Expenditure Panel Survey (MEPS).

Table 99. Out-of-pocket health care expenses among persons with medical expenses, by age: United States, selected years 1987–2013

Excel and PDF versions (with more data years and standard errors when available): http://www.cdc.gov/nchs/hus/contents2016.htm#099.

[Data are based on household interviews of a sample of the civilian noninstitutionalized population and a sample of medical providers]

Age and year	Percent of persons with expenses	Amount paid out of pocket among persons with expenses [1]						
		Total	$0	$1–$99	$100–$499	$500–$999	$1,000–$1,999	$2,000 or more
All ages		*Percent distribution*						
1987	84.5	100.0	10.4	18.6	36.1	15.6	10.8	8.6
1997	84.1	100.0	8.5	24.8	34.5	14.7	10.1	7.4
2000	83.5	100.0	6.9	25.2	33.6	15.3	10.3	8.7
2005	84.7	100.0	8.7	20.2	30.7	16.0	12.5	11.9
2012	84.7	100.0	12.2	23.3	31.4	13.9	10.6	8.6
2013	84.4	100.0	13.4	22.0	31.7	14.0	10.3	8.7
Under 6 years								
1987	88.9	100.0	19.2	26.6	39.2	9.9	3.0	2.1
1997	88.0	100.0	20.0	42.9	29.7	4.2	2.3	0.8
2000	86.7	100.0	16.7	48.9	27.7	4.7	1.4	*0.6
2005	88.9	100.0	27.2	35.3	27.8	6.7	2.1	0.9
2012	88.8	100.0	38.4	35.1	19.8	3.9	2.4	*0.4
2013	90.3	100.0	41.4	29.6	21.1	3.4	2.6	2.0
6–17 years								
1987	80.2	100.0	15.5	25.8	37.8	9.4	6.1	5.5
1997	81.7	100.0	16.5	34.6	32.6	7.8	4.2	4.2
2000	80.0	100.0	14.7	35.3	33.4	7.6	4.1	4.9
2005	83.0	100.0	18.6	31.0	31.2	9.9	5.1	4.3
2012	85.7	100.0	29.0	28.2	26.8	6.4	3.7	6.0
2013	85.4	100.0	30.8	26.9	26.2	7.8	3.9	4.4
18–44 years								
1987	81.5	100.0	10.1	20.4	38.9	15.5	9.1	6.1
1997	78.3	100.0	7.3	27.0	39.0	14.6	7.7	4.4
2000	77.7	100.0	5.8	27.7	38.8	15.1	7.7	4.9
2005	77.1	100.0	7.0	23.7	36.8	15.7	9.6	7.2
2012	75.5	100.0	9.6	28.5	35.1	12.5	8.3	6.0
2013	75.4	100.0	10.6	27.3	36.7	11.8	8.1	5.5
45–64 years								
1987	87.0	100.0	5.6	11.6	34.6	20.5	15.9	11.9
1997	89.2	100.0	3.4	15.7	34.5	20.1	15.9	10.3
2000	88.5	100.0	2.6	14.8	33.4	21.1	15.9	12.1
2005	89.7	100.0	2.4	12.1	28.5	21.0	19.4	16.6
2012	88.9	100.0	3.8	17.7	33.3	17.8	15.4	11.9
2013	88.0	100.0	4.4	17.5	32.4	18.0	14.9	12.8
65–74 years								
1987	92.8	100.0	5.3	8.8	26.1	21.6	20.1	18.0
1997	94.6	100.0	3.2	10.3	29.8	22.6	17.7	16.4
2000	94.7	100.0	1.5	9.5	25.4	21.8	21.0	20.9
2005	95.9	100.0	1.7	6.1	23.1	20.2	22.6	26.3
2012	95.5	100.0	1.9	12.0	32.0	21.6	17.8	14.6
2013	94.9	100.0	2.8	11.3	31.1	22.6	18.0	14.2
75 years and over								
1987	95.1	100.0	5.6	7.2	23.3	19.3	19.6	24.9
1997	95.8	100.0	2.4	9.0	25.9	20.1	21.4	21.2
2000	96.5	100.0	2.6	9.0	24.0	21.4	19.3	23.7
2005	97.4	100.0	1.6	6.0	19.7	19.4	19.8	33.4
2012	97.4	100.0	2.3	11.6	30.0	22.8	18.1	15.2
2013	96.5	100.0	3.4	10.2	31.5	22.6	15.3	17.0

* Estimates are considered unreliable. Data preceded by an asterisk have a relative standard error equal to or greater than 30%.

[1] Estimates of expenses were converted to 2013 dollars using the Consumer Price Index (all items). See Appendix II, Consumer Price Index (CPI).

NOTES: Includes persons in the civilian noninstitutionalized population for all or part of the year. Expenses for persons in this population for only part of the year are restricted to those incurred during periods of eligibility (e.g., expenses incurred during periods of institutionalization and military service are not included in estimates). Out-of-pocket expenses include expenditures for inpatient hospital and physician services, ambulatory physician and nonphysician services, prescribed medicines, home health services, dental services, and various other medical equipment, supplies, and services that were purchased or rented during the year. Out-of-pocket expenses for over-the-counter medications, phone contacts with health providers, and premiums for health insurance policies are not included in these estimates. Estimates for 1987 are based on the National Medical Expenditure Survey (NMES); estimates for other years are based on the Medical Expenditure Panel Survey (MEPS). Because expenditures in NMES were based primarily on charges and those for MEPS were based on payments, NMES data were adjusted to be more comparable with MEPS using estimated charge-to-payment ratios for 1987. Overall, this resulted in an approximate 11% reduction from the unadjusted 1987 NMES expenditure estimates. For a detailed explanation of this adjustment, see Zuvekas S, Cohen J. A guide to comparing health care expenditures in the 1996 MEPS to the 1987 NMES. Inquiry 2002;39(1):76-86. See Appendix I, Medical Expenditure Panel Survey (MEPS). Data for additional years are available. See the Excel spreadsheet on the *Health, United States* website at: http://www.cdc.gov/nchs/hus.htm. Data have been revised and differ from previous editions of *Health, United States*.

SOURCE: Agency for Healthcare Research and Quality, Center for Financing, Access, and Cost Trends. 1987 National Medical Expenditure Survey and 1997–2013 Medical Expenditure Panel Surveys. See Appendix I, Medical Expenditure Panel Survey (MEPS).

Table 100 (page 1 of 2). National health expenditures and percent distribution, by sponsor: United States, selected years 1987–2015

Excel and PDF versions (with more data years and standard errors when available): http://www.cdc.gov/nchs/hus/contents2016.htm#100.

[Data are compiled from various sources by the Centers for Medicare & Medicaid Services]

Type of sponsor	1987	1990	2000	2009	2012	2013	2014	2015
				Amount, in billions				
National health expenditures	$516.5	$721.4	$1,369.7	$2,494.7	$2,795.4	$2,877.6	$3,029.3	$3,205.6
Businesses, households, and other private revenues	353.6	488.2	883.0	1,409.4	1,576.2	1,611.1	1,662.8	1,739.4
Private business	115.9	170.6	335.2	513.7	567.0	578.5	605.6	637.5
Private business contribution to employer-sponsored private health insurance premiums[1]	78.1	121.8	244.1	397.0	433.5	440.5	460.5	484.8
Employer Medicare hospital insurance trust fund payroll taxes[2]	24.4	29.4	61.8	77.1	87.3	89.7	94.3	98.8
Workers' compensation and temporary disability insurance	11.7	17.1	25.9	35.0	41.1	42.9	45.1	47.9
Worksite health care	1.7	2.2	3.5	4.6	5.2	5.4	5.7	6.1
Household	196.6	261.1	443.5	728.1	807.2	824.9	846.6	886.8
Household contribution to employer-sponsored private health insurance premiums[3]	29.4	48.9	102.3	213.0	233.7	236.3	235.2	251.3
Household contribution to direct purchase insurance	11.5	15.7	25.8	38.7	48.1	50.0	54.3	59.5
Medical portion of property and casualty insurance[4]	10.5	12.8	17.6	27.8	29.0	30.4	32.4	34.5
Employee and self-employment payroll taxes and voluntary premiums paid to Medicare hospital insurance trust fund[5]	29.4	35.7	82.5	108.2	125.5	123.7	132.2	139.3
Premiums paid by individuals to Medicare supplementary medical insurance trust fund and the pre-existing condition insurance plan[6]	6.2	10.2	16.3	47.3	53.4	59.3	62.9	64.1
Out-of-pocket health spending	109.7	137.9	199.0	293.1	317.6	325.1	329.7	338.1
Other private revenues[7]	41.1	56.5	104.2	167.6	201.9	207.7	210.5	215.1
Governments	162.9	233.2	486.7	1,085.3	1,219.2	1,266.5	1,366.5	1,466.2
Federal government	85.2	124.1	260.7	680.2	731.2	759.4	843.1	918.5
Federal government contribution to employer-sponsored private health insurance premiums	4.9	9.9	14.3	26.8	31.0	32.4	33.2	33.9
Employer Medicare hospital insurance trust fund payroll taxes	1.7	2.0	2.7	3.9	4.1	4.1	4.1	4.2
Marketplace tax credits and subsidies[8]	. . .	. . .	. . .	. . .	. . .	. . .	17.3	29.2
Federal general revenue and Medicare net trust fund expenditures[9]	17.7	27.7	49.4	231.7	265.9	278.9	289.6	303.6
Federal portion of Medicaid payments	27.9	42.6	116.8	247.3	243.3	256.9	305.5	344.0
Medicare buy-in premiums[10]	0.3	0.7	2.5	7.7	7.8	8.3	8.4	8.6
Retiree drug subsidy payments to employer-sponsored health insurance plans	. . .	. . .	. . .	3.9	3.0	1.7	1.6	1.4
Other federal health insurance and programs[11]	32.7	41.3	75.1	158.9	176.0	177.1	183.5	193.6
State and local government	77.7	109.1	226.0	405.1	488.1	507.1	523.4	547.7
State and local government contribution to employer-sponsored private health insurance premiums[12]	14.8	24.8	54.4	123.2	146.6	153.4	165.1	177.0
Employer Medicare hospital insurance trust fund payroll taxes	3.1	4.1	7.9	12.0	12.0	12.2	12.5	12.9
State portion of Medicaid payments	22.5	31.1	83.5	127.1	179.5	188.5	191.7	201.1
Medicare buy-in premiums[10]	0.2	0.5	1.8	3.5	5.4	5.7	5.8	5.9
Other programs[13]	37.0	48.6	78.4	139.2	144.5	147.4	148.3	150.8
				Percent distribution				
National health expenditures	100.0	100.0	100.0	100.0	100.0	100.0	100.0	100.0
Businesses, households, and other private revenues	68.5	67.7	64.5	56.5	56.4	56.0	54.9	54.3
Private business	22.4	23.6	24.5	20.6	20.3	20.1	20.0	19.9
Private business contribution to employer-sponsored private health insurance premiums[1]	15.1	16.9	17.8	15.9	15.5	15.3	15.2	15.1
Employer Medicare hospital insurance trust fund payroll taxes[2]	4.7	4.1	4.5	3.1	3.1	3.1	3.1	3.1
Workers' compensation and temporary disability insurance	2.3	2.4	1.9	1.4	1.5	1.5	1.5	1.5
Worksite health care	0.3	0.3	0.3	0.2	0.2	0.2	0.2	0.2
Household	38.1	36.2	32.4	29.2	28.9	28.7	27.9	27.7
Household contribution to employer-sponsored private health insurance premiums[3]	5.7	6.8	7.5	8.5	8.4	8.2	7.8	7.8
Household contribution to direct purchase insurance	2.2	2.2	1.9	1.6	1.7	1.7	1.8	1.9
Medical portion of property and casualty insurance[4]	2.0	1.8	1.3	1.1	1.0	1.1	1.1	1.1
Employee and self-employment payroll taxes and voluntary premiums paid to Medicare hospital insurance trust fund[5]	5.7	4.9	6.0	4.3	4.5	4.3	4.4	4.3
Premiums paid by individuals to Medicare supplementary medical insurance trust fund and the pre-existing condition insurance plan[6]	1.2	1.4	1.2	1.9	1.9	2.1	2.1	2.0
Out-of-pocket health spending	21.2	19.1	14.5	11.7	11.4	11.3	10.9	10.5
Other private revenues[7]	8.0	7.8	7.6	6.7	7.2	7.2	6.9	6.7

See footnotes at end of table.

Table 100 (page 2 of 2). National health expenditures and percent distribution, by sponsor: United States, selected years 1987–2015

Excel and PDF versions (with more data years and standard errors when available): http://www.cdc.gov/nchs/hus/contents2016.htm#100.

[Data are compiled from various sources by the Centers for Medicare & Medicaid Services]

Type of sponsor	1987	1990	2000	2009	2012	2013	2014	2015
	\multicolumn{8}{c}{Percent distribution}							
Governments	31.5	32.3	35.5	43.5	43.6	44.0	45.1	45.7
Federal government	16.5	17.2	19.0	27.3	26.2	26.4	27.8	28.7
Federal government contribution to employer-sponsored private health insurance premiums	0.9	1.4	1.0	1.1	1.1	1.1	1.1	1.1
Employer Medicare hospital insurance trust fund payroll taxes	0.3	0.3	0.2	0.2	0.1	0.1	0.1	0.1
Marketplace tax credits and subsidies[8].	. . .	. . .	. . .	. . .	. . .	. . .	0.6	0.9
Federal general revenue and Medicare net trust fund expenditures[9]	3.4	3.8	3.6	9.3	9.5	9.7	9.6	9.5
Federal portion of Medicaid payments	5.4	5.9	8.5	9.9	8.7	8.9	10.1	10.7
Medicare buy-in premiums[10]	0.1	0.1	0.2	0.3	0.3	0.3	0.3	0.3
Retiree drug subsidy payments to employer-sponsored health insurance plans	. . .	. . .	. . .	0.2	0.1	0.1	0.1	0.0
Other federal health insurance and programs[11].	6.3	5.7	5.5	6.4	6.3	6.2	6.1	6.0
State and local government	15.0	15.1	16.5	16.2	17.5	17.6	17.3	17.1
State and local government contribution to employer-sponsored private health insurance premiums[12]	2.9	3.4	4.0	4.9	5.2	5.3	5.5	5.5
Employer Medicare hospital insurance trust fund payroll taxes	0.6	0.6	0.6	0.5	0.4	0.4	0.4	0.4
State portion of Medicaid payments	4.4	4.3	6.1	5.1	6.4	6.6	6.3	6.3
Medicare buy-in premiums[10]	0.0	0.1	0.1	0.1	0.2	0.2	0.2	0.2
Other programs[13]	7.2	6.7	5.7	5.6	5.2	5.1	4.9	4.7

. . . Category not applicable.

[1] Excludes Medicare Retiree Drug Subsidy (RDS) payments to private plans beginning in 2006, small-business tax credits beginning in 2010, and Early Retirement Reinsurance Program (ERRP) payments for 2010–2011.

[2] Includes one-half of self-employment contribution to the Medicare hospital insurance (HI) trust fund.

[3] Excludes government-subsidized Consolidated Omnibus Budget Reconciliation Act (COBRA) payments in 2009–2011.

[4] Includes property and casualty insurance premium portions that are used to pay medical claims for automobile, homeowners, or other liability insurance.

[5] Includes one-half of self-employment contributions to the Medicare hospital insurance trust fund and income taxation of Social Security benefits.

[6] Includes premiums paid for the Pre-Existing Condition Insurance Plan (PCIP) in 2010–2015.

[7] Includes health-related philanthropic support, nonoperating revenue, investment income, and privately funded structures and equipment.

[8] Includes Affordable Care Act (ACA) health insurance premium tax credits and cost-sharing subsidies beginning in 2014.

[9] Excludes Medicare hospital trust fund payroll taxes and premiums, Medicare supplementary medical insurance premiums, Part D state phase-down payments to Medicare beginning in 2006, Medicare premium buy-in programs by Medicaid for people eligible for both Medicaid and Medicare (dual eligibles), and trust fund revenues from the income taxation of Social Security benefits.

[10] Medicare premium buy-in programs are for people eligible for both Medicaid and Medicare (dual eligibles).

[11] Includes maternal and child health, vocational rehabilitation, Substance Abuse and Mental Health Services Administration, Indian Health Service, federal workers' compensation, and other programs, public health activities, Department of Defense, Department of Veterans Affairs, Children's Health Insurance Program (CHIP), and investment (research, structures and equipment). Also includes government-subsidized COBRA payments in 2009–2011, small business tax credits beginning in 2010, and ERRP payments in 2010–2011. Excludes premiums paid for the Pre-Existing Condition Insurance Plan (PCIP) premiums in 2010–2015.

[12] Excludes Medicare RDS payments to state and local government employer plans beginning in 2006 and ERRP payments in 2010–2011.

[13] Includes maternal and child health, vocational rehabilitation, general assistance, school health, CHIP, public health activities, other state and local programs, investment (research, structures and equipment). Also includes Part D state phase-down payments to Medicare beginning in 2006. See Appendix II, Health expenditures, national.

NOTES: This table disaggregates health expenditures according to five classes of sponsors: businesses, households (individuals), federal government, state and local governments, and nonpatient revenue sources such as philanthropy. Where businesses or households pay dedicated funds into government health programs (for example, Medicare) or employers and employees share in the cost of health premiums, these costs are assigned to businesses or households accordingly. This results in a lower share of expenditures being assigned to the federal government than for tabulations of expenditures by source of funds. Estimates of national health expenditure by source of funds aim to track government-sponsored health programs over time and do not delineate the role of business employers in paying for health care. Some of the sponsor categories were revised or added in 2014 to account for changes in the health care system. See Appendix I, National Health Expenditure Accounts (NHEA). Estimates may not sum to totals because of rounding. For more information on NHE categories, sources, and methods, see the National Health Expenditure Accounts Methodology Paper, 2015. Data have been revised and differ from previous editions of Health, United States.

SOURCE: Centers for Medicare & Medicaid Services, Office of the Actuary, National Health Statistics Group. Businesses, Households, and Governments. National Health Expenditure Accounts, National health expenditures. Available from: https://www.cms.gov/Research-Statistics-Data-and-Systems/Statistics-Trends-and-Reports/NationalHealthExpendData/NationalHealthAccountsHistorical.html, accessed on January 14, 2017. See Appendix I, National Health Expenditure Accounts (NHEA).

Table 101. Employers' costs per employee-hour worked for total compensation, wages and salaries, and health insurance, by selected characteristics: United States, selected years 1999–2016

Excel and PDF versions (with more data years and standard errors when available): http://www.cdc.gov/nchs/hus/contents2016.htm#101.

[Data are based on surveys of a sample of employers]

Characteristic	1999	2000	2005	2008	2010	2013	2014	2015	2016
	Total compensation per employee-hour worked								
State and local government.	$28.00	$29.05	$35.50	$37.84	$39.81	$42.12	$43.10	$44.25	$45.23
Total private industry.	19.00	19.85	24.17	26.76	27.73	29.13	29.99	31.65	32.06
Census region:									
Northeast	20.94	22.67	27.09	30.56	32.13	33.43	34.79	38.93	39.06
Midwest	18.36	19.22	24.23	25.98	26.75	27.93	28.71	29.08	29.40
South.	16.97	17.81	21.36	23.90	24.72	26.60	27.14	29.04	29.48
West	20.74	20.88	25.98	28.70	29.52	30.54	31.59	32.23	33.13
Union status:									
Union	24.75	25.88	33.17	36.28	37.16	40.43	43.84	46.62	45.72
Nonunion.	18.20	19.07	23.09	25.64	26.67	28.02	28.63	30.18	30.72
Establishment employment size:									
1–99 employees	16.27	17.16	20.22	22.23	22.84	23.92	25.03	26.45	27.04
100 or more	21.88	22.81	28.94	31.68	33.33	35.25	35.76	37.78	38.14
100–499.	18.14	19.30	24.44	26.80	28.55	29.71	29.92	32.07	32.62
500 or more	26.37	26.93	34.59	37.60	39.76	43.05	44.04	46.19	46.85
	Wages and salaries as a percent of total compensation								
State and local government.	70.6	70.8	68.3	65.9	65.9	64.8	64.4	64.0	63.6
Total private industry.	73.0	73.0	71.0	70.6	70.6	70.3	69.9	69.3	69.7
Census region:									
Northeast	72.0	72.2	70.4	69.8	69.0	68.8	68.4	66.9	67.0
Midwest	71.9	72.4	70.1	69.8	70.0	69.5	69.5	69.2	69.4
South.	74.0	73.5	72.1	71.8	71.8	71.6	71.2	70.8	70.9
West	74.1	74.0	70.9	70.8	71.1	70.6	70.0	69.9	70.7
Union status:									
Union	65.5	65.2	62.6	61.9	61.6	59.8	60.0	59.8	60.2
Nonunion.	74.4	74.4	72.4	72.1	72.0	71.8	71.4	70.8	71.0
Establishment employment size:									
1–99 employees	75.5	75.5	73.9	73.8	73.6	74.0	73.5	72.5	72.6
100 or more	71.0	71.0	68.5	68.2	68.2	67.3	66.9	66.7	67.1
100–499.	72.6	72.8	70.2	69.8	70.0	69.1	68.8	68.5	69.1
500 or more	69.7	69.4	67.0	66.9	66.5	65.6	65.1	64.9	64.9
	Health insurance as a percent of total compensation								
State and local government.	7.6	7.8	10.2	11.0	11.4	11.7	11.7	11.6	11.7
Total private industry.	5.4	5.5	6.8	7.2	7.5	7.8	7.9	7.7	7.6
Census region:									
Northeast	5.7	5.6	6.8	6.9	7.5	8.1	8.2	7.7	7.7
Midwest	5.8	5.8	7.3	7.9	8.3	8.6	8.6	8.5	8.5
South.	5.2	5.4	6.6	6.9	7.2	7.2	7.3	7.1	7.2
West	4.8	5.0	6.3	6.9	7.1	7.4	7.5	7.7	7.3
Union status:									
Union	8.2	8.4	10.3	10.9	11.8	12.9	12.6	12.1	12.6
Nonunion.	4.9	5.0	6.2	6.5	6.8	7.0	7.1	7.0	6.9
Establishment employment size:									
1–99 employees	4.7	4.8	5.9	6.1	6.4	6.5	6.6	6.4	6.4
100 or more	5.9	6.0	7.5	8.0	8.4	8.8	8.9	8.7	8.7
100–499.	5.6	5.6	7.5	7.9	8.3	8.7	8.7	8.5	8.3
500 or more	6.2	6.4	7.6	8.0	8.5	8.9	9.1	8.9	9.1

NOTES: Costs are calculated annually from March survey data. Total compensation includes wages, salaries and benefits. See Appendix II, Employer costs for employee compensation. See *Health, United States, 2013*, Table 121 for prior years of data. Data for additional years are available. See the Excel spreadsheet on the *Health, United States* website at: http://www.cdc.gov/nchs/hus.htm.

SOURCE: U.S. Department of Labor, Bureau of Labor Statistics, National Compensation Survey: Employer Costs for Employee Compensation Annual, 1999–2001; Quarterly, 2002–2003; March release, 2004–2016. Available from: http://www.bls.gov/ncs/ect/. See Appendix I, National Compensation Survey (NCS).

Table 102 (page 1 of 3). Private health insurance coverage among persons under age 65, by selected characteristics: United States, selected years 1984–2015

Excel and PDF versions (with more data years and standard errors when available): http://www.cdc.gov/nchs/hus/contents2016.htm#102.

[Data are based on household interviews of a sample of the civilian noninstitutionalized population]

Characteristic	Private health insurance [1]								
	1984 [2]	1997	2000 [3]	2005	2010	2012	2013	2014	2015
	Number, in millions								
Total [4]	157.5	165.8	174.0	174.7	163.9	164.9	165.3	170.7	176.6
	Percent of population								
Total [4]	76.8	70.7	71.5	68.2	61.7	61.8	61.8	63.7	65.5
Age									
Under 19 years	72.6	66.1	66.7	62.3	54.3	53.6	53.5	54.1	55.0
Under 6 years	68.1	61.3	62.7	56.6	48.3	48.4	47.3	50.2	51.0
6–18 years	74.8	68.4	68.5	64.9	57.2	56.0	56.3	55.9	56.7
Under 18 years	72.6	66.1	66.6	62.1	54.1	53.4	53.2	53.7	54.6
6–17 years	74.9	68.5	68.5	64.7	57.2	55.8	56.0	55.4	56.2
18–64 years	78.6	72.7	73.5	70.7	64.7	65.1	65.1	67.4	69.7
18–44 years	76.5	69.4	70.5	66.6	60.0	61.4	61.8	64.3	66.8
18–24 years	67.4	59.3	60.3	58.0	52.3	58.1	59.0	62.0	64.8
19–25 years	67.4	58.3	59.1	56.3	51.8	58.1	58.9	62.2	65.5
25–34 years	77.4	68.1	70.1	65.1	58.7	58.7	59.0	62.0	65.1
35–44 years	83.9	76.4	77.0	73.7	66.9	66.7	67.0	68.6	70.0
45–64 years	83.3	79.0	78.7	76.9	71.3	70.0	69.5	71.7	73.6
45–54 years	83.3	80.4	80.0	77.4	70.9	69.6	69.8	71.6	74.1
55–64 years	83.3	76.9	76.7	76.2	71.8	70.4	69.1	71.7	73.1
Sex									
Male	77.3	70.9	71.6	68.0	61.1	61.8	61.9	63.8	65.4
Female	76.2	70.5	71.3	68.4	62.4	61.9	61.7	63.5	65.6
Sex and marital status [5]									
Male:									
Married	85.0	81.6	81.5	79.6	75.1	74.9	74.8	77.1	78.3
Divorced, separated, widowed	65.5	59.9	62.2	56.7	50.6	51.0	50.9	54.0	56.6
Never married	71.3	63.3	63.8	60.2	52.5	54.7	55.8	58.2	60.6
Female:									
Married	83.8	81.0	81.0	79.3	75.6	75.0	74.3	75.9	78.0
Divorced, separated, widowed	63.1	59.1	63.2	59.9	53.9	51.8	52.1	55.1	58.1
Never married	72.2	63.8	64.2	61.5	54.1	56.2	56.2	58.4	60.4
Race [6]									
White only	79.9	74.2	75.7	70.9	64.9	64.8	64.7	66.6	68.2
Black or African American only	58.1	54.7	55.9	52.9	44.8	45.8	45.4	47.1	50.6
American Indian or Alaska Native only	49.1	39.4	43.7	43.0	31.7	34.9	36.0	34.7	41.1
Asian only	69.9	68.0	72.1	72.2	68.1	67.6	69.4	72.5	73.8
Native Hawaiian or Other Pacific Islander only	- - -	- - -	*	*	*	*	*	*	*
2 or more races	- - -	- - -	61.4	57.6	52.4	52.9	50.0	55.4	55.3
Hispanic origin and race [6]									
Hispanic or Latino	55.7	46.4	47.8	42.4	36.8	36.7	37.3	41.2	43.8
Mexican	53.3	42.3	45.4	39.7	33.4	34.1	34.9	39.0	40.9
Puerto Rican	48.4	47.0	51.1	48.5	46.0	43.7	42.1	46.8	48.0
Cuban	72.5	71.0	63.9	58.1	53.8	49.1	45.3	56.6	61.7
Other Hispanic or Latino	61.6	49.9	50.7	45.6	40.9	39.5	41.2	43.1	47.8
Not Hispanic or Latino	78.7	74.0	75.2	73.0	67.0	67.5	67.4	68.9	70.7
White only	82.4	78.1	79.5	77.3	72.0	72.6	72.4	73.7	75.2
Black or African American only	58.2	54.9	56.0	53.1	45.1	46.4	45.7	48.0	51.2
Age and percent of poverty level [7]									
Under 65 years:									
Below 100%	32.2	23.3	25.2	21.4	16.0	16.5	15.5	17.4	18.6
100%–199%	70.3	53.5	50.1	44.7	34.8	36.7	35.1	38.2	39.8
100%–133%	59.4	39.7	39.3	36.0	24.4	26.9	25.3	26.5	30.6
134%–199%	75.2	60.1	55.3	49.4	40.3	42.4	40.8	45.1	45.1
200%–399%	89.3	80.8	78.1	74.8	70.7	71.3	71.3	73.6	73.4
400% or more	95.4	91.8	91.9	90.6	89.9	90.6	90.4	91.5	91.9

See footnotes at end of table.

Table 102 (page 2 of 3). Private health insurance coverage among persons under age 65, by selected characteristics: United States, selected years 1984–2015

Excel and PDF versions (with more data years and standard errors when available): http://www.cdc.gov/nchs/hus/contents2016.htm#102.

[Data are based on household interviews of a sample of the civilian noninstitutionalized population]

Characteristic	Private health insurance [1]								
	1984 [2]	1997	2000 [3]	2005	2010	2012	2013	2014	2015
	Percent of population								
Under 19 years:									
Below 100%	29.6	19.3	20.3	15.0	9.8	10.0	9.3	9.5	10.6
100%–199%	73.6	54.7	49.5	41.6	31.5	32.4	29.2	30.4	30.3
100%–133%	63.8	39.3	37.1	32.6	20.1	22.3	18.3	18.2	22.3
134%–199%	78.4	62.4	56.1	47.0	38.1	38.4	36.2	38.6	35.5
200%–399%	91.1	83.5	80.8	76.6	72.6	72.5	71.8	73.5	71.1
400% or more	96.2	93.3	93.0	92.5	91.2	91.2	92.3	92.5	92.7
Under 18 years:									
Below 100%	28.5	18.3	19.5	14.2	9.2	9.1	8.4	8.6	9.3
100%–199%	73.9	54.7	49.4	41.4	31.5	32.1	28.5	30.2	30.1
100%–133%	63.9	38.7	36.8	32.0	19.9	21.6	17.8	18.2	21.9
134%–199%	78.6	62.8	56.2	47.0	38.3	38.4	35.3	38.3	35.3
200%–399%	91.3	83.7	81.1	76.6	72.6	72.5	71.9	73.2	71.1
400% or more	96.1	93.5	93.1	92.5	91.4	91.4	92.2	92.6	92.7
18–64 years:									
Below 100%	35.0	26.8	29.1	25.9	20.4	20.9	19.9	22.7	24.3
100%–199%	68.3	52.8	50.5	46.5	36.4	38.9	38.2	42.1	44.6
100%–133%	56.6	40.3	40.9	38.3	26.9	29.6	29.2	31.1	35.4
134%–199%	73.3	58.6	54.9	50.7	41.3	44.2	43.2	48.2	49.8
200%–399%	88.3	79.4	76.7	74.0	70.0	70.8	71.1	73.7	74.3
400% or more	95.2	91.3	91.6	90.1	89.5	90.4	89.9	91.2	91.8
Disability measure among adults 18–64 years [8]									
Any basic actions difficulty or complex activity limitation	- - -	61.6	63.1	58.1	53.0	50.8	48.6	51.1	53.6
Any basic actions difficulty	- - -	62.3	63.9	58.8	53.8	51.7	49.2	51.8	54.0
Any complex activity limitation	- - -	47.9	48.4	44.0	38.6	36.0	34.8	34.7	38.3
No disability	- - -	77.4	77.2	73.7	69.3	70.2	70.7	72.5	75.3
Geographic region									
Northeast	80.5	74.2	76.3	74.0	68.2	67.2	66.1	67.7	70.2
Midwest	80.6	77.1	78.8	74.6	66.7	68.4	68.0	68.7	70.1
South	74.3	67.3	66.8	62.5	57.5	57.3	57.4	59.4	62.5
West	71.9	65.4	66.5	65.6	58.9	58.5	59.6	62.9	62.6
Location of residence [9]									
Within MSA	77.5	71.2	72.3	69.0	62.9	63.0	63.0	64.8	66.7
Outside MSA	75.2	68.4	67.8	64.6	55.1	55.3	54.7	56.2	57.8

See footnotes at end of table.

Table 102 (page 3 of 3). Private health insurance coverage among persons under age 65, by selected characteristics: United States, selected years 1984–2015

Excel and PDF versions (with more data years and standard errors when available): http://www.cdc.gov/nchs/hus/contents2016.htm#102.

[Data are based on household interviews of a sample of the civilian noninstitutionalized population]

- - - Data not available.

* Estimates are considered unreliable. Data not shown have a relative standard error greater than 30%.

[1] Any private health insurance coverage (both individual and insurance obtained through the workplace) at the time of interview; includes those who also had another type of coverage.

[2] Data prior to 1997 are not strictly comparable with data for later years due to the 1997 questionnaire redesign. See Appendix I, National Health Interview Survey (NHIS) and Appendix II, Health insurance coverage.

[3] Estimates for 2000–2002 were calculated using 2000-based sample weights and may differ from estimates in other reports that used 1990-based sample weights for 2000–2002 estimates.

[4] Includes all other races not shown separately, those with unknown marital status, unknown disability status, and, in 1984 and 1989, persons with unknown poverty level.

[5] Includes persons aged 14–64.

[6] The race groups, white, black, American Indian or Alaska Native, Asian, Native Hawaiian or Other Pacific Islander, and 2 or more races, include persons of Hispanic and non-Hispanic origin. Persons of Hispanic origin may be of any race. Starting with 1999 data, race-specific estimates are tabulated according to the 1997 *Revisions to the Standards for the Classification of Federal Data on Race and Ethnicity* and are not strictly comparable with estimates for earlier years. The five single-race categories plus multiple-race categories shown in the table conform to the 1997 Standards. Starting with 1999 data, race-specific estimates are for persons who reported only one racial group; the category 2 or more races includes persons who reported more than one racial group. Prior to 1999, data were tabulated according to the 1977 Standards with four racial groups, and the Asian only category included Native Hawaiian or Other Pacific Islander. Estimates for single-race categories prior to 1999 included persons who reported one race or, if they reported more than one race, identified one race as best representing their race. Starting with 2003 data, race responses of other race and unspecified multiple race were treated as missing, and then race was imputed if these were the only race responses. Almost all persons with a race response of other race were of Hispanic origin. See Appendix II, Hispanic origin; Race.

[7] Percent of poverty level is based on family income and family size and composition using U.S. Census Bureau poverty thresholds. Poverty level was unknown for 10%–11% of persons under age 65 in 1984 and 1989. Missing family income data were imputed for 1995 and beyond. See Appendix II, Family income; Poverty; Table VI.

[8] Any basic actions difficulty or complex activity limitation is defined as having one or more of the following limitations or difficulties: movement difficulty, emotional difficulty, sensory (seeing or hearing) difficulty, cognitive difficulty, self-care (activities of daily living or instrumental activities of daily living) limitation, social limitation, or work limitation. For more information, see Appendix II, Basic actions difficulty; Complex activity limitation. Starting with 2007 data, the hearing question, a component of the basic actions difficulty measure, was revised. Consequently, data prior to 2007 are not comparable with data for 2007 and beyond. For more information on the impact of the revised hearing question, see Appendix II, Hearing trouble.

[9] MSA is metropolitan statistical area. Starting with 2006 data, MSA status is determined using 2000 census data and the 2000 standards for defining MSAs. For data prior to 2006, see Appendix II, Metropolitan statistical area (MSA) for the applicable standards.

NOTES: This table includes persons who had private coverage through the workplace in addition to other types of health insurance coverage. Private health insurance coverage is at the time of interview. The number of persons with private coverage was calculated by multiplying the percentage with private coverage by the number of persons under age 65 in the civilian noninstitutionalized U.S. population, which was determined from the post-stratification Census control total for each survey year. Percentages of persons with private coverage were calculated with unknown values excluded from denominators. See Appendix II, Health insurance coverage. Standard errors are available in the spreadsheet version of this table. Available from: http://www.cdc.gov/nchs/hus.htm. Data for additional years are available. See the Excel spreadsheet on the *Health, United States* website at: http://www.cdc.gov/nchs/hus.htm.

SOURCE: NCHS, National Health Interview Survey, health insurance supplements (1984, 1989, 1994–1996). Starting with 1997, data are from the family core and the sample adult questionnaires. See Appendix I, National Health Interview Survey (NHIS).

Table 103 (page 1 of 3). Private health insurance coverage obtained through the workplace among persons under age 65, by selected characteristics: United States, selected years 1984–2015

Excel and PDF versions (with more data years and standard errors when available): http://www.cdc.gov/nchs/hus/contents2016.htm#103.

[Data are based on household interviews of a sample of the civilian noninstitutionalized population]

Characteristic	Private insurance obtained through workplace [1]								
	1984 [2]	1997	2000 [3]	2005	2010	2012	2013	2014	2015
	Number, in millions								
Total [4]	141.8	153.6	160.8	160.1	147.6	148.6	148.3	146.4	151.2
	Percent of population								
Total [4]	69.1	66.4	67.1	63.6	56.6	56.9	56.6	56.4	57.4
Age									
Under 19 years	66.4	62.8	63.1	58.7	50.9	50.1	49.6	49.6	49.8
Under 6 years.	62.1	58.3	58.9	53.4	44.9	45.0	44.2	45.7	46.6
6–18 years	68.4	64.9	64.9	61.1	53.8	52.4	52.0	51.3	51.2
Under 18 years	66.5	62.8	63.0	58.6	50.7	49.9	49.3	49.3	49.6
6–17 years	68.7	65.1	65.0	61.1	53.8	52.3	51.8	51.1	51.0
18–64 years	70.3	68.0	68.8	65.7	58.9	59.6	59.5	59.2	60.4
18–44 years.	69.6	65.7	66.5	62.2	54.6	56.7	56.9	57.0	58.6
18–24 years	58.7	54.9	55.5	52.1	45.3	52.7	53.1	53.9	55.8
19–25 years	59.0	53.7	54.2	50.6	44.1	52.7	53.0	54.0	56.7
25–34 years	71.2	64.6	66.4	61.1	53.3	53.8	53.8	54.2	56.9
35–44 years	77.4	72.7	73.2	69.9	62.8	62.7	63.1	62.2	62.4
45–64 years.	71.8	72.8	72.9	70.9	64.8	63.6	62.9	62.2	62.8
45–54 years	74.6	75.6	75.6	72.6	65.9	64.4	64.3	63.8	65.0
55–64 years	69.0	68.4	68.6	68.6	63.4	62.6	61.3	60.4	60.5
Sex									
Male	69.8	66.7	67.3	63.6	56.1	57.1	56.9	56.9	57.6
Female.	68.4	66.2	66.9	63.6	57.1	56.8	56.4	56.0	57.3
Sex and marital status [5]									
Male:									
Married	77.9	77.4	77.5	75.3	70.1	69.9	69.8	69.6	70.3
Divorced, separated, widowed	58.0	55.2	57.4	51.9	45.3	46.2	45.3	45.7	45.3
Never married.	61.5	58.4	58.8	54.9	46.2	49.6	50.0	50.1	51.6
Female:									
Married	76.1	76.4	76.3	74.2	69.8	69.3	68.5	67.7	69.2
Divorced, separated, widowed	51.9	53.8	57.8	54.3	48.1	46.3	46.3	45.8	46.2
Never married.	63.5	59.6	60.1	56.3	48.2	50.9	50.6	50.7	51.7
Race [6]									
White only	72.0	69.7	71.0	66.1	59.3	59.6	59.2	59.2	59.9
Black or African American only	52.4	52.6	53.4	50.6	42.3	43.2	42.9	42.0	44.8
American Indian or Alaska Native only	45.8	37.2	41.7	39.9	*29.4	34.0	34.2	30.9	35.9
Asian only	59.0	61.7	65.8	64.4	60.6	60.1	61.4	61.4	62.2
Native Hawaiian or Other Pacific Islander only	- - -	- - -	*	*	*	*	*	*	*
2 or more races	- - -	- - -	59.8	54.8	49.5	48.8	46.9	50.9	47.8
Hispanic origin and race [6]									
Hispanic or Latino	52.0	43.9	45.3	40.0	34.6	34.6	34.9	36.5	37.4
Mexican.	50.5	40.8	43.6	37.6	31.6	32.5	32.5	35.1	36.2
Puerto Rican	45.9	45.1	49.4	46.2	43.6	41.6	40.8	42.6	41.6
Cuban.	57.4	58.4	53.6	53.5	47.4	42.8	41.2	42.7	40.6
Other Hispanic or Latino	57.4	47.0	47.3	42.6	37.8	36.7	38.6	37.3	38.8
Not Hispanic or Latino.	70.7	69.5	70.6	68.0	61.3	62.0	61.7	61.2	62.2
White only	74.0	73.3	74.5	71.9	65.7	66.6	66.1	65.5	66.3
Black or African American only	52.5	52.9	53.6	50.9	42.6	43.6	43.2	42.9	45.4
Age and percent of poverty level [7]									
Under 65 years:									
Below 100%	24.1	20.0	21.0	17.8	12.4	13.6	12.2	12.2	12.7
100%–199%	61.7	48.9	45.4	40.1	30.2	32.2	31.0	31.0	30.2
100%–133%	50.0	35.4	35.0	31.3	20.6	23.0	21.7	20.5	22.7
134%–199%	66.9	55.4	50.5	44.8	35.3	37.5	36.3	37.3	34.5
200%–399%	82.8	76.5	73.4	69.8	65.3	65.9	65.6	65.4	64.0
400% or more	88.8	87.4	87.9	86.1	84.2	85.1	84.6	84.5	84.8

See footnotes at end of table.

Table 103 (page 2 of 3). Private health insurance coverage obtained through the workplace among persons under age 65, by selected characteristics: United States, selected years 1984–2015

Excel and PDF versions (with more data years and standard errors when available): http://www.cdc.gov/nchs/hus/contents2016.htm#103.

[Data are based on household interviews of a sample of the civilian noninstitutionalized population]

Characteristic	Private insurance obtained through workplace [1]								
	1984 [2]	1997	2000 [3]	2005	2010	2012	2013	2014	2015
	Percent of population								
Under 19 years:									
Below 100%	23.6	17.0	17.1	13.3	8.2	8.7	7.8	7.2	7.8
100%–199%	67.0	51.2	45.8	38.3	28.8	29.7	26.6	26.8	26.1
100%–133%	56.1	35.8	33.6	29.1	17.9	20.5	16.4	15.6	19.7
134%–199%	72.3	59.0	52.2	43.7	35.1	35.2	33.1	34.4	30.3
200%–399%	85.7	80.0	76.9	72.4	68.7	68.0	66.7	67.6	64.4
400% or more	90.8	89.7	89.5	88.3	86.5	86.3	86.9	87.1	86.9
Under 18 years:									
Below 100%	23.0	16.2	16.6	12.5	7.8	8.1	7.2	6.7	6.9
100%–199%	67.5	51.2	45.8	38.2	28.8	29.4	26.0	26.7	26.0
100%–133%	56.3	35.2	33.5	28.6	17.8	19.8	16.0	15.6	19.7
134%–199%	72.8	59.4	52.4	43.9	35.2	35.2	32.4	34.3	30.1
200%–399%	85.9	80.2	77.1	72.4	68.7	68.1	66.8	67.5	64.4
400% or more	90.7	89.8	89.7	88.5	86.6	86.4	86.8	87.2	87.0
18–64 years:									
Below 100%	24.8	22.7	24.0	21.2	15.4	16.9	15.2	15.6	16.3
100%–199%	58.3	47.6	45.2	41.1	30.9	33.6	33.3	33.1	32.2
100%–133%	46.0	35.5	35.9	32.9	22.1	24.6	24.7	23.2	24.4
134%–199%	63.6	53.2	49.5	45.3	35.3	38.7	38.0	38.6	36.6
200%–399%	81.4	74.7	71.7	68.7	63.9	65.0	65.2	64.7	63.8
400% or more	88.5	86.8	87.5	85.4	83.6	84.7	84.0	83.8	84.3
Disability measure among adults 18–64 years [8]									
Any basic actions difficulty or complex activity limitation	- - -	57.3	58.5	53.3	48.0	45.8	44.0	43.0	44.6
Any basic actions difficulty	- - -	58.0	59.1	54.0	48.9	46.7	44.6	43.8	45.0
Any complex activity limitation	- - -	43.3	43.5	38.9	32.8	30.5	29.6	26.1	29.3
No disability	- - -	72.5	72.5	68.5	63.5	64.7	64.7	64.2	65.8
Geographic region									
Northeast	74.0	71.0	72.5	70.6	64.4	63.4	62.3	61.5	62.9
Midwest	72.0	72.6	74.9	70.1	61.8	63.8	62.6	61.5	62.7
South	66.2	62.9	62.5	58.0	52.2	52.2	52.4	52.3	54.3
West	64.7	60.7	61.1	59.7	52.7	52.8	53.6	54.7	53.5
Location of residence [9]									
Within MSA	70.9	67.3	68.2	64.5	57.9	58.1	57.8	57.8	58.6
Outside MSA	65.3	62.8	62.6	59.6	49.4	50.3	49.4	48.0	50.0

See footnotes at end of table.

Excel and PDF versions (with more data years and standard errors when available): http://www.cdc.gov/nchs/hus/contents2016.htm#103.

[Data are based on household interviews of a sample of the civilian noninstitutionalized population]

- - - Data not available.

* Estimates are considered unreliable. Data preceded by an asterisk have a relative standard error (RSE) of 20%–30%. Data not shown have an RSE greater than 30%.

[1] Any private insurance at the time of interview that was originally obtained through a present or former employer or union, or, starting with 1997 data, through the workplace, self-employment, or a professional association; includes those who also had another type of coverage. Starting in 2014, an additional question on the health insurance marketplace was added to the questionnaire for those respondents who did not indicate that their health plan was obtained through a present/former employer, union, self-employment, or professional association. Starting in 2015, an additional answer category was added to the question on how a health plan was originally obtained to allow a respondent to indicate that their plan was obtained through the Health Insurance Marketplace or state-based exchange.

[2] Data prior to 1997 are not strictly comparable with data for later years due to the 1997 questionnaire redesign. See Appendix I, National Health Interview Survey (NHIS) and Appendix II, Health insurance coverage.

[3] Estimates for 2000–2002 were calculated using 2000-based sample weights and may differ from estimates in other reports that used 1990-based sample weights for 2000–2002 estimates.

[4] Includes all other races not shown separately, those with unknown marital status, unknown disability status, and, in 1984 and 1989, persons with unknown poverty level.

[5] Includes persons aged 14–64.

[6] The race groups, white, black, American Indian or Alaska Native, Asian, Native Hawaiian or Other Pacific Islander, and 2 or more races, include persons of Hispanic and non-Hispanic origin. Persons of Hispanic origin may be of any race. Starting with 1999 data, race-specific estimates are tabulated according to the 1997 *Revisions to the Standards for the Classification of Federal Data on Race and Ethnicity* and are not strictly comparable with estimates for earlier years. The five single-race categories plus multiple-race categories shown in the table conform to the 1997 Standards. Starting with 1999 data, race-specific estimates are for persons who reported only one racial group; the category 2 or more races includes persons who reported more than one racial group. Prior to 1999, data were tabulated according to the 1977 Standards with four racial groups, and the Asian only category included Native Hawaiian or Other Pacific Islander. Estimates for single-race categories prior to 1999 included persons who reported one race or, if they reported more than one race, identified one race as best representing their race. Starting with 2003 data, race responses of other race and unspecified multiple race were treated as missing, and then race was imputed if these were the only race responses. Almost all persons with a race response of other race were of Hispanic origin. See Appendix II, Hispanic origin; Race.

[7] Percent of poverty level is based on family income and family size and composition using U.S. Census Bureau poverty thresholds. Poverty level was unknown for 10%–11% of persons under age 65 in 1984 and 1989. Missing family income data were imputed for 1995 and beyond. See Appendix II, Family income; Poverty; Table VI.

[8] Any basic actions difficulty or complex activity limitation is defined as having one or more of the following limitations or difficulties: movement difficulty, emotional difficulty, sensory (seeing or hearing) difficulty, cognitive difficulty, self-care (activities of daily living or instrumental activities of daily living) limitation, social limitation, or work limitation. For more information, see Appendix II, Basic actions difficulty; Complex activity limitation. Starting with 2007 data, the hearing question, a component of the basic actions difficulty measure, was revised. Consequently, data prior to 2007 are not comparable with data for 2007 and beyond. For more information on the impact of the revised hearing question, see Appendix II, Hearing trouble.

[9] MSA is metropolitan statistical area. Starting with 2006 data, MSA status is determined using 2000 census data and the 2000 standards for defining MSAs. For data prior to 2006, see Appendix II, Metropolitan statistical area (MSA) for the applicable standards.

NOTES: This table includes persons who had private coverage through the workplace in addition to other types of health insurance coverage. Private coverage through the workplace is at the time of interview. The number of persons with private coverage through the workplace was calculated by multiplying the percentage with private coverage through the workplace by the number of persons under age 65 in the civilian noninstitutionalized U.S. population, which was determined from the post-stratification Census control total for each survey year. Percentages of persons with private coverage obtained through the workplace were calculated with unknown values excluded from denominators. See Appendix II, Health insurance coverage. Standard errors are available in the spreadsheet version of this table. Available from: http://www.cdc.gov/nchs/hus.htm. Data for additional years are available. See the Excel spreadsheet on the *Health, United States* website at: http://www.cdc.gov/nchs/hus.htm.

SOURCE: NCHS, National Health Interview Survey, health insurance supplements (1984, 1989, 1994–1996). Starting with 1997, data are from the family core and the sample adult questionnaires. See Appendix I, National Health Interview Survey (NHIS).

Table 104 (page 1 of 3). Medicaid coverage among persons under age 65, by selected characteristics: United States, selected years 1984–2015

Excel and PDF versions (with more data years and standard errors when available): *http://www.cdc.gov/nchs/hus/contents2016.htm#104.*

[Data are based on household interviews of a sample of the civilian noninstitutionalized population]

Characteristic	1984[1]	1997	2000[2]	2005[3]	2010[3]	2012[3]	2013[3]	2014[3]	2015[3]
	Number, in millions								
Total[4]	14.0	22.9	23.2	33.2	44.8	48.1	48.5	52.6	55.4
	Percent of population								
Total[4]	6.8	9.7	9.5	12.9	16.9	18.0	18.1	19.6	20.6
Age									
Under 19 years	11.7	18.0	19.2	26.6	35.7	38.1	38.1	38.6	39.2
Under 6 years	15.5	24.7	24.7	34.0	43.7	45.7	45.9	43.8	44.2
6–18 years	9.8	14.9	16.8	23.3	31.8	34.7	34.6	36.3	36.9
Under 18 years	11.9	18.4	19.6	27.2	36.4	38.9	38.9	39.4	39.9
6–17 years	10.1	15.2	17.2	23.9	32.5	35.5	35.5	37.3	37.9
18–64 years	4.5	5.9	5.2	7.2	9.2	10.0	10.2	12.1	13.2
18–44 years	5.1	6.6	5.6	8.3	10.9	11.6	11.6	13.8	15.0
18–24 years	6.4	8.8	8.1	11.3	14.5	15.4	14.2	17.9	18.5
19–25 years	6.3	8.5	7.3	10.3	12.6	13.4	12.1	16.1	16.3
25–34 years	5.3	6.8	5.5	8.0	11.1	11.4	11.7	13.3	14.7
35–44 years	3.5	5.2	4.3	6.6	8.1	8.8	9.6	11.3	12.8
45–64 years	3.4	4.6	4.5	5.5	6.8	8.0	8.4	9.9	10.8
45–54 years	3.2	4.0	4.2	5.2	7.0	8.2	8.6	9.8	11.2
55–64 years	3.6	5.6	4.9	5.8	6.6	7.7	8.2	9.9	10.4
Sex									
Male	5.4	8.4	8.2	11.6	15.2	16.3	16.5	17.8	19.1
Female	8.1	11.1	10.8	14.3	18.5	19.7	19.8	21.4	22.0
Sex and marital status[5]									
Male:									
Married	1.9	2.5	2.2	3.5	4.0	4.8	5.3	6.2	7.0
Divorced, separated, widowed	4.9	5.7	6.1	7.0	9.3	9.7	10.3	12.0	12.6
Never married	4.8	7.0	7.2	10.4	13.5	15.1	14.8	17.6	19.6
Female:									
Married	2.6	3.5	3.1	4.7	5.7	6.2	6.9	8.1	8.8
Divorced, separated, widowed	16.0	14.7	12.7	14.6	17.6	18.8	18.8	21.6	23.3
Never married	10.7	14.2	13.2	17.3	22.2	22.6	22.2	24.9	25.7
Race[6]									
White only	4.6	7.4	7.1	11.0	14.5	15.5	15.6	16.9	17.9
Black or African American only	20.5	22.4	21.2	24.9	30.4	31.6	31.6	34.1	34.3
American Indian or Alaska Native only	*28.2	19.6	15.1	24.2	21.6	36.5	32.0	35.5	34.3
Asian only	*8.7	9.6	7.5	8.2	12.0	13.0	13.2	14.7	16.5
Native Hawaiian or Other Pacific Islander only	- - -	- - -	*	*	*	*	*	*	*
2 or more races	- - -	- - -	19.1	22.0	27.4	29.1	30.4	30.2	31.5
Hispanic origin and race[6]									
Hispanic or Latino	13.3	17.6	15.5	22.9	28.6	30.5	29.5	31.3	33.5
Mexican	12.2	17.2	14.0	23.0	29.5	31.0	29.8	32.1	34.2
Puerto Rican	31.5	31.0	29.4	31.9	35.7	35.3	36.9	35.7	38.9
Cuban	*4.8	7.3	9.2	17.7	17.3	22.9	23.3	22.4	22.8
Other Hispanic or Latino	7.9	15.3	14.5	19.7	24.5	28.3	27.0	28.6	30.7
Not Hispanic or Latino	6.2	8.7	8.5	11.1	14.4	15.2	15.5	16.9	17.5
White only	3.7	6.1	6.1	8.5	11.0	11.5	11.9	13.0	13.6
Black or African American only	20.7	22.1	21.0	24.8	30.0	31.3	31.3	33.4	33.6
Age and percent of poverty level[7]									
Under 65 years:									
Below 100%	33.0	40.5	38.4	45.7	50.8	52.5	53.7	56.5	60.6
100%–199%	5.3	13.0	16.2	23.4	28.5	30.1	30.8	34.0	38.1
100%–133%	8.7	20.1	22.4	30.6	36.3	38.0	38.8	43.9	47.6
134%–199%	3.7	9.5	13.1	19.5	24.4	25.5	26.2	28.1	32.6
200%–399%	0.8	2.7	4.0	6.6	8.4	9.0	9.0	9.9	11.3
400% or more	0.2	0.8	0.9	1.5	2.0	1.7	1.9	2.2	2.2

See footnotes at end of table.

Table 104 (page 2 of 3). Medicaid coverage among persons under age 65, by selected characteristics: United States, selected years 1984–2015

Excel and PDF versions (with more data years and standard errors when available): http://www.cdc.gov/nchs/hus/contents2016.htm#104.

[Data are based on household interviews of a sample of the civilian noninstitutionalized population]

Characteristic	1984[1]	1997	2000[2]	2005[3]	2010[3]	2012[3]	2013[3]	2014[3]	2015[3]
					Percent of population				
Under 19 years:									
Below 100%	42.0	56.4	56.9	69.4	78.4	82.1	82.1	83.3	84.8
100%–199%	6.5	20.3	27.8	41.7	53.5	56.3	58.9	59.1	61.9
100%–133%	10.3	31.1	36.4	51.0	63.5	68.8	70.3	71.7	70.9
134%–199%	4.7	14.8	23.3	36.2	47.7	48.8	51.6	50.6	55.9
200%–399%	1.0	4.4	7.6	13.0	17.7	18.8	19.1	18.5	20.9
400% or more	*	1.3	2.1	2.9	4.3	3.6	3.2	3.8	4.3
Under 18 years:									
Below 100%	43.3	58.0	58.5	71.2	79.8	83.7	83.9	84.7	86.7
100%–199%	6.6	20.8	28.4	42.5	54.3	57.3	60.1	60.0	62.6
100%–133%	10.4	32.0	36.9	52.0	64.6	70.1	71.2	72.3	72.0
134%–199%	4.8	15.1	23.8	36.9	48.2	49.6	52.9	51.6	56.5
200%–399%	1.0	4.5	7.6	13.3	18.0	19.1	19.5	18.9	21.2
400% or more	*	1.3	2.2	2.9	4.3	3.6	3.3	4.0	4.3
18–64 years:									
Below 100%	25.3	28.0	24.9	29.6	32.4	34.0	35.4	39.7	44.8
100%–199%	4.5	8.6	9.1	13.1	15.7	16.8	17.1	21.4	25.9
100%–133%	7.6	13.0	13.2	17.9	21.0	21.8	22.0	28.3	34.2
134%–199%	3.1	6.5	7.2	10.7	13.0	13.9	14.4	17.6	21.3
200%–399%	0.7	1.9	2.4	3.8	4.8	5.1	5.1	6.7	7.6
400% or more	0.2	0.7	0.6	1.1	1.3	1.2	1.6	1.7	1.7
Disability measure among adults 18–64 years[8]									
Any basic actions difficulty or complex activity limitation	- - -	13.2	12.8	16.4	17.8	19.3	21.1	22.9	25.1
Any basic actions difficulty	- - -	12.7	12.2	15.5	16.7	18.4	20.6	22.0	24.6
Any complex activity limitation	- - -	22.9	23.2	28.5	30.0	30.8	32.3	35.6	36.9
No disability	- - -	3.5	3.0	4.9	6.8	7.0	6.8	8.7	9.2
Geographic region									
Northeast	8.6	11.3	10.6	13.3	17.9	19.3	20.8	21.4	21.6
Midwest	7.4	8.4	8.0	12.3	17.3	16.3	16.9	18.6	19.8
South	5.1	8.7	9.4	12.7	16.0	17.8	17.8	18.7	18.4
West	7.0	11.7	10.4	13.8	17.1	19.1	18.0	20.9	24.0
Location of residence[9]									
Within MSA	7.1	9.7	8.9	12.4	16.1	17.4	17.4	18.9	19.8
Outside MSA	6.1	10.1	11.9	15.5	21.4	21.4	22.5	24.4	25.4

See footnotes at end of table.

Table 104 (page 3 of 3). Medicaid coverage among persons under age 65, by selected characteristics: United States, selected years 1984–2015

Excel and PDF versions (with more data years and standard errors when available): http://www.cdc.gov/nchs/hus/contents2016.htm#104.

[Data are based on household interviews of a sample of the civilian noninstitutionalized population]

- - - Data not available.

* Estimates are considered unreliable. Data preceded by an asterisk have a relative standard error (RSE) of 20%–30%. Data not shown have an RSE greater than 30%.

[1] Data prior to 1997 are not strictly comparable with data for later years due to the 1997 questionnaire redesign. See Appendix I, National Health Interview Survey (NHIS) and Appendix II, Health insurance coverage.

[2] Estimates for 2000–2002 were calculated using 2000-based sample weights and may differ from estimates in other reports that used 1990-based sample weights for 2000–2002 estimates.

[3] Beginning in quarter 3 of the 2004 NHIS, persons under age 65 with no reported coverage were asked explicitly about Medicaid coverage. Estimates were calculated without and with the additional information from this question in the columns labeled 2004(1) and 2004(2) (in spreadsheet version), respectively, and estimates were calculated with the additional information starting with 2005 data.

[4] Includes all other races not shown separately, those with unknown marital status, unknown disability status, and, in 1984 and 1989, persons with unknown poverty level.

[5] Includes persons aged 14–64.

[6] The race groups, white, black, American Indian or Alaska Native, Asian, Native Hawaiian or Other Pacific Islander, and 2 or more races, include persons of Hispanic and non-Hispanic origin. Persons of Hispanic origin may be of any race. Starting with 1999 data, race-specific estimates are tabulated according to the 1997 *Revisions to the Standards for the Classification of Federal Data on Race and Ethnicity* and are not strictly comparable with estimates for earlier years. The five single-race categories plus multiple-race categories shown in the table conform to the 1997 Standards. Starting with 1999 data, race-specific estimates are for persons who reported only one racial group; the category 2 or more races includes persons who reported more than one racial group. Prior to 1999, data were tabulated according to the 1977 Standards with four racial groups, and the Asian only category included Native Hawaiian or Other Pacific Islander. Estimates for single-race categories prior to 1999 included persons who reported one race or, if they reported more than one race, identified one race as best representing their race. Starting with 2003 data, race responses of other race and unspecified multiple race were treated as missing, and then race was imputed if these were the only race responses. Almost all persons with a race response of other race were of Hispanic origin. See Appendix II, Hispanic origin; Race.

[7] Percent of poverty level is based on family income and family size and composition using U.S. Census Bureau poverty thresholds. Poverty level was unknown for 10%–11% of persons under age 65 in 1984 and 1989. Missing family income data were imputed for 1995 and beyond. See Appendix II, Family income; Poverty; Table VI.

[8] Any basic actions difficulty or complex activity limitation is defined as having one or more of the following limitations or difficulties: movement difficulty, emotional difficulty, sensory (seeing or hearing) difficulty, cognitive difficulty, self-care (activities of daily living or instrumental activities of daily living) limitation, social limitation, or work limitation. For more information, see Appendix II, Basic actions difficulty; Complex activity limitation. Starting with 2007 data, the hearing question, a component of the basic actions difficulty measure, was revised. Consequently, data prior to 2007 are not comparable with data for 2007 and beyond. For more information on the impact of the revised hearing question, see Appendix II, Hearing trouble.

[9] MSA is metropolitan statistical area. Starting with 2006 data, MSA status is determined using 2000 census data and the 2000 standards for defining MSAs. For data prior to 2006, see Appendix II, Metropolitan statistical area (MSA) for the applicable standards.

NOTES: The category Medicaid coverage includes persons who had any of the following at the time of interview: Medicaid, other public assistance through 1996, state-sponsored health plan starting in 1997, or Children's Health Insurance Program (CHIP) starting in 1999; it includes those who also had another type of coverage in addition to one of these. In 2015, 18.4% of persons under age 65 reported being covered by Medicaid, 1.1% by state-sponsored health plans, and 1.1% by CHIP. Estimates may not sum to total because of rounding. The number of persons with Medicaid coverage was calculated by multiplying the percentage with Medicaid coverage by the number of persons under age 65 in the civilian noninstitutionalized U.S. population, which was determined from the post-stratification Census control total for each survey year. Percentages of persons with Medicaid coverage were calculated with unknown values excluded from denominators. See Appendix II, Health insurance coverage; Medicaid. Standard errors are available in the spreadsheet version of this table. Available from: http://www.cdc.gov/nchs/hus.htm. Data for additional years are available. See the Excel spreadsheet on the *Health, United States* website at: http://www.cdc.gov/nchs/hus.htm.

SOURCE: NCHS, National Health Interview Survey, health insurance supplements (1984, 1989, 1994–1996). Starting with 1997, data are from the family core and the sample adult questionnaires. See Appendix I, National Health Interview Survey (NHIS).

Table 105 (page 1 of 3). No health insurance coverage among persons under age 65, by selected characteristics: United States, selected years 1984–2015

Excel and PDF versions (with more data years and standard errors when available): http://www.cdc.gov/nchs/hus/contents2016.htm#105.

[Data are based on household interviews of a sample of the civilian noninstitutionalized population]

Characteristic	1984[1]	1997	2000[2]	2005[3]	2010[3]	2012[3]	2013[3]	2014[3]	2015[3]
	Number, in millions								
Total[4]	29.8	41.0	41.4	42.1	48.3	45.2	44.6	35.7	28.7
	Percent of population								
Total[4]	14.5	17.5	17.0	16.4	18.2	16.9	16.7	13.3	10.6
Age									
Under 19 years	14.1	14.4	12.9	9.7	8.3	7.0	7.1	5.7	4.8
Under 6 years	14.9	12.5	11.8	7.7	6.3	4.6	5.0	4.1	3.3
6–18 years	13.8	15.2	13.4	10.6	9.2	8.1	8.0	6.5	5.5
Under 18 years	13.9	14.0	12.6	9.3	7.8	6.6	6.6	5.4	4.5
6–17 years	13.4	14.7	13.0	10.1	8.6	7.6	7.4	6.1	5.1
18–64 years	14.8	19.0	18.9	19.3	22.3	20.9	20.5	16.3	13.0
18–44 years	17.1	22.4	22.4	23.5	27.1	24.8	24.2	19.7	15.9
18–24 years	25.0	30.1	30.4	29.1	31.4	24.5	24.6	18.1	14.6
19–25 years	25.1	31.5	32.3	31.7	33.8	26.3	26.7	19.7	16.0
25–34 years	16.2	23.8	23.3	25.6	28.3	28.1	27.1	22.7	18.0
35–44 years	11.2	16.7	16.9	17.9	22.6	21.7	21.0	17.7	14.6
45–64 years	9.6	12.4	12.6	12.9	15.7	15.6	15.4	11.8	9.0
45–54 years	10.5	12.8	12.8	14.2	17.9	17.7	17.1	13.7	10.2
55–64 years	8.7	11.8	12.4	11.1	12.8	13.2	13.5	9.7	7.7
Sex									
Male	15.3	18.7	18.1	17.9	20.3	18.5	18.1	14.7	12.0
Female	13.8	16.3	15.9	15.0	16.1	15.4	15.2	11.9	9.3
Sex and marital status[5]									
Male:									
Married	11.1	13.9	14.1	14.4	17.2	16.2	15.9	12.6	10.6
Divorced, separated, widowed	24.9	28.8	25.8	28.6	31.4	29.3	28.1	23.2	20.0
Never married	22.4	27.9	27.2	27.6	31.1	27.5	26.9	21.9	17.4
Female:									
Married	11.2	13.0	13.3	13.0	14.7	14.6	14.6	11.6	8.8
Divorced, separated, widowed	19.2	23.2	21.3	22.1	23.6	24.2	22.8	17.7	13.4
Never married	16.3	20.5	21.1	20.0	21.9	19.6	19.6	15.1	12.1
Race[6]									
White only	13.6	16.4	15.4	15.9	17.6	16.7	16.3	13.3	10.7
Black or African American only	19.9	20.1	19.5	18.4	20.6	18.0	18.9	13.7	11.3
American Indian or Alaska Native only	22.5	38.1	38.4	32.2	44.0	27.0	29.4	28.3	21.4
Asian only	18.5	19.5	17.6	17.1	17.1	16.8	14.2	10.8	7.5
Native Hawaiian or Other Pacific Islander only	- - -	- - -	*	*	*	*	*	*	*
2 or more races	- - -	- - -	16.8	16.5	15.8	14.5	15.3	10.1	9.5
Hispanic origin and race[6]									
Hispanic or Latino	29.5	34.5	35.6	33.0	32.0	30.4	30.7	25.5	21.1
Mexican	33.8	39.4	39.9	36.0	34.8	33.2	33.4	27.2	23.5
Puerto Rican	18.3	19.0	16.4	16.3	13.7	14.4	15.6	13.0	9.6
Cuban	21.6	21.1	25.4	23.2	26.5	24.3	26.6	19.4	14.2
Other Hispanic or Latino	27.4	33.0	33.4	32.6	32.4	30.1	28.8	26.2	19.7
Not Hispanic or Latino	13.2	15.2	14.0	13.4	15.2	13.9	13.4	10.5	8.2
White only	11.9	13.8	12.5	12.0	13.7	12.7	12.2	9.7	7.5
Black or African American only	19.7	20.0	19.5	18.3	20.7	17.8	18.8	13.5	11.2
Age and percent of poverty level[7]									
Under 65 years:									
Below 100%	33.9	33.7	34.2	30.6	30.3	28.2	28.0	23.0	18.2
100%–199%	21.8	30.6	31.0	28.6	32.4	29.3	29.3	23.4	18.3
100%–133%	28.8	36.6	35.7	30.1	34.9	31.1	30.4	25.0	18.4
134%–199%	18.7	27.7	28.7	27.8	31.0	28.4	28.6	22.4	18.1
200%–399%	7.6	14.2	15.4	15.7	17.4	16.2	16.1	12.6	11.1
400% or more	3.2	6.1	5.9	6.3	5.6	4.9	4.8	3.8	3.3

See footnotes at end of table.

Table 105 (page 2 of 3). No health insurance coverage among persons under age 65, by selected characteristics: United States, selected years 1984–2015

Excel and PDF versions (with more data years and standard errors when available): http://www.cdc.gov/nchs/hus/contents2016.htm#105.

[Data are based on household interviews of a sample of the civilian noninstitutionalized population]

Characteristic	1984[1]	1997	2000[2]	2005[3]	2010[3]	2012[3]	2013[3]	2014[3]	2015[3]
				Percent of population					
Under 19 years:									
Below 100%	29.0	23.8	22.6	15.2	11.3	8.3	8.9	6.7	5.4
100%–199%	18.0	23.7	22.1	15.6	13.5	11.1	11.7	9.3	7.4
100%–133%	24.4	28.2	26.5	15.6	15.9	9.6	11.6	9.4	7.7
134%–199%	14.9	21.4	19.7	15.6	12.0	12.0	11.7	9.3	7.2
200%–399%	5.1	9.7	9.6	8.2	7.4	6.8	6.7	5.7	5.4
400% or more	1.8	4.0	3.5	3.3	2.3	2.2	1.9	1.7	1.6
Under 18 years:									
Below 100%	28.9	23.2	22.0	14.3	10.6	7.6	8.2	6.4	4.9
100%–199%	17.5	23.2	21.7	15.0	12.7	10.4	11.1	8.7	6.9
100%–133%	24.0	28.1	26.4	15.1	15.1	9.0	11.2	8.9	7.3
134%–199%	14.4	20.7	19.1	15.0	11.3	11.3	11.1	8.5	6.7
200%–399%	4.9	9.4	9.3	7.8	7.0	6.7	6.3	5.5	5.2
400% or more	1.8	3.9	3.3	3.2	2.1	2.1	1.8	*1.6	1.6
18–64 years:									
Below 100%	37.6	41.2	42.4	40.9	42.7	40.5	40.0	32.9	26.2
100%–199%	24.4	34.7	36.4	35.9	42.1	38.6	37.8	30.5	23.9
100%–133%	31.9	41.7	41.7	38.9	45.7	42.2	40.4	33.9	24.5
134%–199%	21.1	31.5	34.0	34.4	40.3	36.5	36.4	28.7	23.6
200%–399%	8.9	16.4	18.2	19.0	21.3	19.8	19.7	15.3	13.3
400% or more	3.4	6.7	6.6	7.1	6.5	5.6	5.6	4.3	3.8
Disability measure among adults 18–64 years[8]									
Any basic actions difficulty or complex activity limitation	- - -	20.1	17.6	19.6	20.8	20.4	20.4	16.2	11.6
Any basic actions difficulty	- - -	20.1	17.6	19.8	20.9	20.3	20.4	16.3	11.8
Any complex activity limitation	- - -	20.2	16.1	16.9	17.2	18.3	17.1	12.5	9.2
No disability	- - -	17.6	18.5	19.5	21.6	20.4	19.9	16.3	13.1
Geographic region									
Northeast	10.2	13.5	12.2	11.3	12.4	11.5	11.2	9.3	6.8
Midwest	11.3	13.2	12.3	11.9	14.1	13.6	13.1	10.3	8.2
South	17.7	20.9	20.5	21.0	21.9	20.3	19.9	16.9	14.2
West	18.2	20.6	20.7	18.4	20.6	19.0	18.9	13.3	10.1
Location of residence[9]									
Within MSA	13.6	16.9	16.6	16.1	17.8	16.4	16.2	13.0	10.3
Outside MSA	16.6	19.8	18.6	17.8	20.4	19.9	19.3	15.2	12.8

See footnotes at end of table.

Table 105 (page 3 of 3). No health insurance coverage among persons under age 65, by selected characteristics: United States, selected years 1984–2015

Excel and PDF versions (with more data years and standard errors when available): http://www.cdc.gov/nchs/hus/contents2016.htm#105.

[Data are based on household interviews of a sample of the civilian noninstitutionalized population]

- - - Data not available.

* Estimates are considered unreliable. Data preceded by an asterisk have a relative standard error (RSE) of 20%–30%. Data not shown have an RSE greater than 30%.

[1] Data prior to 1997 are not strictly comparable with data for later years due to the 1997 questionnaire redesign. See Appendix I, National Health Interview Survey (NHIS) and Appendix II, Health insurance coverage.

[2] Estimates for 2000–2002 were calculated using 2000-based sample weights and may differ from estimates in other reports that used 1990-based sample weights for 2000–2002 estimates.

[3] Beginning in quarter 3 of the 2004 NHIS, persons under age 65 with no reported coverage were asked explicitly about Medicaid coverage. Estimates were calculated without and with the additional information from this question in the columns labeled 2004(1) and 2004(2) (in spreadsheet version), respectively, and estimates were calculated with the additional information starting with 2005 data.

[4] Includes all other races not shown separately, those with unknown marital status, unknown disability status, and, in 1984 and 1989, persons with unknown poverty level.

[5] Includes persons aged 14–64.

[6] The race groups, white, black, American Indian or Alaska Native, Asian, Native Hawaiian or Other Pacific Islander, and 2 or more races, include persons of Hispanic and non-Hispanic origin. Persons of Hispanic origin may be of any race. Starting with 1999 data, race-specific estimates are tabulated according to the 1997 *Revisions to the Standards for the Classification of Federal Data on Race and Ethnicity* and are not strictly comparable with estimates for earlier years. The five single-race categories plus multiple-race categories shown in the table conform to the 1997 Standards. Starting with 1999 data, race-specific estimates are for persons who reported only one racial group; the category 2 or more races includes persons who reported more than one racial group. Prior to 1999, data were tabulated according to the 1977 Standards with four racial groups, and the Asian only category included Native Hawaiian or Other Pacific Islander. Estimates for single-race categories prior to 1999 included persons who reported one race or, if they reported more than one race, identified one race as best representing their race. Starting with 2003 data, race responses of other race and unspecified multiple race were treated as missing, and then race was imputed if these were the only race responses. Almost all persons with a race response of other race were of Hispanic origin. See Appendix II, Hispanic origin; Race.

[7] Percent of poverty level is based on family income and family size and composition using U.S. Census Bureau poverty thresholds. Poverty level was unknown for 10%–11% of persons under age 65 in 1984 and 1989. Missing family income data were imputed for 1995 and beyond. See Appendix II, Family income; Poverty; Table VI.

[8] Any basic actions difficulty or complex activity limitation is defined as having one or more of the following limitations or difficulties: movement difficulty, emotional difficulty, sensory (seeing or hearing) difficulty, cognitive difficulty, self-care (activities of daily living or instrumental activities of daily living) limitation, social limitation, or work limitation. For more information, see Appendix II, Basic actions difficulty; Complex activity limitation. Starting with 2007 data, the hearing question, a component of the basic actions difficulty measure, was revised. Consequently, data prior to 2007 are not comparable with data for 2007 and beyond. For more information on the impact of the revised hearing question, see Appendix II, Hearing trouble.

[9] MSA is metropolitan statistical area. Starting with 2006 data, MSA status is determined using 2000 census data and the 2000 standards for defining MSAs. For data prior to 2006, see Appendix II, Metropolitan statistical area (MSA) for the applicable standards.

NOTES: Persons not covered by private insurance, Medicaid, Children's Health Insurance Program (CHIP), public assistance (through 1996), state-sponsored or other government-sponsored health plans (starting in 1997), Medicare, or military plans are considered to have no health insurance coverage. Persons with only Indian Health Service coverage are considered to have no health insurance coverage. Health insurance coverage is at the time of interview. The number of persons with no health insurance coverage was calculated by multiplying the percentage with no coverage by the number of persons under age 65 in the civilian noninstitutionalized U.S. population, which was determined from the post-stratification Census control total for each survey year. Percentages of persons without coverage were calculated with unknown values excluded from denominators. See Appendix II, Children's Health Insurance Program (CHIP); Health insurance coverage; Medicaid. Standard errors are available in the spreadsheet version of this table. Available from: http://www.cdc.gov/nchs/hus.htm. Data for additional years are available. See the Excel spreadsheet on the *Health, United States* website at: http://www.cdc.gov/nchs/hus.htm.

SOURCE: NCHS, National Health Interview Survey, health insurance supplements (1984, 1989, 1994–1996). Starting with 1997, data are from the family core and the sample adult questionnaires. See Appendix I, National Health Interview Survey (NHIS).

Table 106 (page 1 of 2). Health insurance coverage of noninstitutionalized Medicare beneficiaries aged 65 and over, by type of coverage and selected characteristics: United States, selected years 1992–2013

Excel and PDF versions (with more data years and standard errors when available): http://www.cdc.gov/nchs/hus/contents2016.htm#106.

[Data are based on household interviews of a sample of noninstitutionalized Medicare beneficiaries]

Characteristic	Medicare Advantage plan [1]					Medicaid [2]				
	1992	1995	2000	2012	2013	1992	1995	2000	2012	2013
Age					Number, in millions					
65 years and over.	1.1	2.6	5.9	12.4	13.8	2.7	2.8	2.7	3.6	3.6
					Percent distribution					
65 years and over.	3.9	8.9	19.3	29.1	31.2	9.4	9.6	9.0	8.5	8.1
65–74 years.	4.2	9.5	20.6	29.1	30.3	7.9	8.8	8.5	7.6	7.2
75–84 years.	3.7	8.3	18.5	30.1	33.8	10.6	9.6	8.9	9.2	8.6
85 years and over	*	7.3	16.3	26.3	29.4	16.6	13.6	11.2	10.3	11.4
Sex										
Male	4.6	9.2	19.3	28.9	30.0	6.3	6.2	6.3	5.6	5.7
Female	3.4	8.6	19.3	29.2	32.3	11.6	12.0	10.9	10.7	10.1
Race and Hispanic origin										
White, not Hispanic or Latino	3.6	8.4	18.4	26.9	29.1	5.6	5.4	5.1	5.1	4.9
Black, not Hispanic or Latino	*	7.9	20.7	30.3	33.4	28.5	30.3	23.6	19.0	17.8
Hispanic	*	15.5	27.5	45.5	46.7	39.0	40.5	28.7	20.2	20.1
Percent of poverty level [3]										
Below 100%.	3.6	7.7	18.4	- - -	- - -	22.3	17.2	15.9	- - -	- - -
100%–less than 200%.	3.7	9.5	23.4	- - -	- - -	6.7	6.3	8.4	- - -	- - -
200% or more.	4.2	10.1	18.0	- - -	- - -	*	*	*	- - -	- - -
Marital status										
Married	4.6	9.5	18.7	28.6	30.2	4.0	4.3	4.3	3.9	3.5
Widowed.	2.3	7.7	19.4	28.6	31.2	14.9	15.0	13.6	13.8	12.5
Divorced	*	9.7	24.4	32.4	35.2	23.4	24.5	20.2	15.7	16.0
Never married	*	*	15.8	27.4	32.1	19.2	19.0	17.0	14.5	17.9

Characteristic	Employer-sponsored plan [4]					Medigap [5]				
	1992	1995	2000	2012	2013	1992	1995	2000	2012	2013
Age					Number, in millions					
65 years and over.	12.5	11.3	10.7	12.0	12.1	9.9	9.5	7.6	8.0	8.2
					Percent distribution					
65 years and over.	42.8	38.6	35.2	28.1	27.4	33.9	32.5	25.0	18.9	18.7
65–74 years.	46.9	41.1	36.6	29.8	29.5	31.4	29.9	21.7	17.5	17.5
75–84 years.	38.2	37.1	35.0	25.9	24.4	37.5	35.2	27.8	20.2	19.8
85 years and over	31.6	30.2	29.4	26.1	24.9	38.3	37.6	31.1	22.1	21.1
Sex										
Male	46.3	42.1	37.7	30.2	29.1	30.6	30.0	23.4	17.2	17.2
Female	40.4	36.0	33.4	26.4	25.9	36.2	34.4	26.2	20.3	19.9
Race and Hispanic origin										
White, not Hispanic or Latino	45.9	41.3	38.6	30.6	29.5	37.2	36.2	28.3	22.4	22.1
Black, not Hispanic or Latino	25.9	26.7	22.0	27.4	26.7	13.6	10.2	7.5	5.7	5.3
Hispanic	20.7	16.9	15.8	13.1	13.9	15.8	10.1	11.3	6.3	5.6
Percent of poverty level [3]										
Below 100%.	29.0	32.1	28.1	- - -	- - -	30.8	29.8	22.6	- - -	- - -
100%–less than 200%.	37.5	32.0	27.0	- - -	- - -	39.3	39.1	28.4	- - -	- - -
200% or more.	58.4	52.8	49.0	- - -	- - -	32.8	32.2	26.2	- - -	- - -
Marital status										
Married	49.9	44.6	41.0	32.9	33.0	33.0	32.6	25.6	20.1	19.6
Widowed.	34.1	30.3	28.7	22.6	21.3	37.5	35.2	26.7	19.9	19.9
Divorced	27.3	26.6	22.4	19.7	17.2	27.9	24.1	16.9	13.0	14.8
Never married	38.0	35.1	28.5	24.3	21.5	29.1	26.2	21.9	16.7	13.1

See footnotes at end of table.

Table 106 (page 2 of 2). Health insurance coverage of noninstitutionalized Medicare beneficiaries aged 65 and over, by type of coverage and selected characteristics: United States, selected years 1992–2013

Excel and PDF versions (with more data years and standard errors when available): http://www.cdc.gov/nchs/hus/contents2016.htm#106.

[Data are based on household interviews of a sample of noninstitutionalized Medicare beneficiaries]

Characteristic	Medicare fee-for-service only or Other[6]				
	1992	1995	2000	2012	2013
Age	Number, in millions				
65 years and over.	2.9	3.1	3.5	6.6	6.4
	Percent distribution				
65 years and over.	9.9	10.5	11.5	15.5	14.6
65–74 years.	9.7	10.7	12.6	16.0	15.5
75–84 years.	10.1	9.9	9.9	14.6	13.5
85 years and over	10.8	11.3	12.1	15.1	13.3
Sex					
Male	12.2	12.6	13.3	18.0	18.0
Female	8.3	8.9	10.2	13.4	11.9
Race and Hispanic origin					
White, not Hispanic or Latino. . . .	7.7	8.7	9.6	15.1	14.3
Black, not Hispanic or Latino. . . .	26.7	25.0	26.1	17.6	16.8
Hispanic	18.3	17.1	16.7	14.9	13.7
Percent of poverty level[3]					
Below 100%.	14.3	13.3	15.1	- - -	- - -
100%–less than 200%.	12.9	13.1	12.7	- - -	- - -
200% or more.	4.0	4.5	6.3	- - -	- - -
Marital status					
Married	8.5	9.0	10.5	14.6	13.8
Widowed.	11.2	11.9	11.6	15.1	15.2
Divorced	15.7	15.1	16.1	19.3	16.9
Never married	*	13.1	16.8	17.2	15.4

* Estimates are considered unreliable if the sample cell size is 50 or fewer.

- - - Data not available.

[1] Enrollee has a Medicare Advantage plan regardless of other insurance. Medicare Advantage plans include health maintenance organizations, preferred provider organizations, private fee-for-service plans, special needs plans, and Medicare medical savings account plans. Starting with 2013 data, the term Medicare Risk Health Maintenance Organization was replaced with Medicare Advantage plan. See Appendix II, Managed care.

[2] Enrolled in Medicaid and not enrolled in a Medicare Advantage plan. See Appendix II, Managed care.

[3] Percent of poverty level is based on family income and family size and composition using U.S. Census Bureau poverty thresholds. See Appendix II, Family income; Poverty.

[4] Private insurance plans purchased through employers (own, current, or former employer, family business, union, or former employer or union of spouse) and not enrolled in a Medicare Advantage plan or Medicaid.

[5] Supplemental insurance purchased privately or through organizations such as American Association of Retired Persons or professional organizations, and not enrolled in a Medicare Advantage plan, Medicaid, or employer-sponsored plan.

[6] Medicare fee-for-service only or other public plans (except Medicaid).

NOTES: Data for noninstitutionalized Medicare beneficiaries. Insurance categories are mutually exclusive. Persons with more than one type of coverage are categorized according to the order in which the health insurance categories appear in the table. See Appendix I, Medicare Current Beneficiary Survey (MCBS). Data for additional years are available. See the Excel spreadsheet on the *Health, United States* website at: http://www.cdc.gov/nchs/hus.htm.

SOURCE: Centers for Medicare & Medicaid Services, Medicare Current Beneficiary Survey, Access to Care file. See Appendix I, Medicare Current Beneficiary Survey (MCBS).

Table 107 (page 1 of 2). Medicare enrollees and expenditures and percent distribution, by Medicare program and type of service: United States and other areas, selected years 1970–2015

Excel and PDF versions (with more data years and standard errors when available): http://www.cdc.gov/nchs/hus/contents2016.htm#107.

[Data are compiled from various sources by the Centers for Medicare & Medicaid Services]

Medicare program and type of service	1970	1980	1990	1995	2000	2005	2010	2012	2013	2014	2015[1]
Enrollees					Number, in millions						
Total Medicare[2]	20.4	28.4	34.3	37.6	39.7	42.6	47.7	50.9	52.5	54.1	55.3
Hospital insurance	20.1	28.0	33.7	37.2	39.3	42.2	47.4	50.5	52.1	53.7	54.9
Supplementary medical insurance (SMI)[3]	19.5	27.3	32.6	35.6	37.3	- - -	- - -	- - -	- - -	- - -	- - -
Part B	19.5	27.3	32.6	35.6	37.3	39.8	43.9	46.5	48.0	49.4	50.7
Part D[4]	- - -	- - -	- - -	- - -	- - -	1.8	34.8	37.4	39.1	40.5	41.8
Expenditures					Amount, in billions						
Total Medicare	$7.5	$36.8	$111.0	$184.2	$221.8	$336.4	$522.9	$574.2	$582.9	$613.3	$647.6
Total hospital insurance (HI)	5.3	25.6	67.0	117.6	131.1	182.9	247.9	266.8	266.2	269.3	278.9
HI payments to managed care organizations[5]	- - -	0.0	2.7	6.7	21.4	24.9	60.7	70.2	73.1	74.0	78.5
HI payments for fee-for-service utilization	5.1	25.0	63.4	109.5	105.1	156.6	183.3	189.2	184.7	186.4	191.5
Inpatient hospital	4.8	24.1	56.9	82.3	87.1	123.3	136.1	138.9	134.2	136.2	139.2
Skilled nursing facility	0.2	0.4	2.5	9.1	11.1	19.3	27.0	28.4	28.4	28.5	29.7
Home health agency	0.1	0.5	3.7	16.2	4.0	6.0	7.1	6.8	6.8	6.5	6.6
Hospice	- - -	- - -	0.3	1.9	2.9	8.0	13.1	15.0	15.2	15.2	15.9
Other programs[6]	- - -	- - -	- - -	- - -	- - -	- - -	- - -	2.8	3.5	3.7	2.6
Home health agency transfer[7]	- - -	- - -	- - -	- - -	1.7	- - -	- - -	- - -	- - -	- - -	- - -
Medicare Advantage premiums[8]	- - -	- - -	- - -	- - -	- - -	- - -	0.2	0.2	0.3	0.3	0.3
Accounting error (CY 2005–2008)[9]	- - -	- - -	- - -	- - -	- - -	−1.9	- - -	- - -	- - -	- - -	- - -
Administrative expenses[10]	0.2	0.5	0.9	1.4	2.9	3.3	3.8	4.3	4.7	4.9	5.9
Total supplementary medical insurance (SMI)[3]	2.2	11.2	44.0	66.6	90.7	153.5	274.9	307.4	316.7	344.0	368.8
Total Part B	2.2	11.2	44.0	66.6	90.7	152.4	212.9	240.5	247.1	265.9	279.0
Part B payments to managed care organizations[5]	0.0	0.2	2.8	6.6	18.4	22.0	55.2	66.0	72.7	85.7	93.8
Part B payments for fee-for-service utilization[11]	1.9	10.4	39.6	58.4	72.2	125.0	154.3	170.3	170.8	175.8	181.5
Physician/supplier[12]	1.8	8.2	29.6	- - -	- - -	- - -	- - -	- - -	- - -	- - -	- - -
Outpatient hospital[13]	0.1	1.9	8.5	- - -	- - -	- - -	- - -	- - -	- - -	- - -	- - -
Independent laboratory[14]	0.0	0.1	1.5	- - -	- - -	- - -	- - -	- - -	- - -	- - -	- - -
Physician fee schedule	- - -	- - -	- - -	31.7	37.0	57.7	63.9	69.5	68.6	69.2	70.3
Durable medical equipment	- - -	- - -	- - -	3.7	4.7	8.0	8.3	8.2	7.2	6.3	6.8
Laboratory[15]	- - -	- - -	- - -	4.3	4.4	6.9	8.4	9.2	9.1	8.2	8.5
Other[16]	- - -	- - -	- - -	9.9	13.6	26.7	34.2	38.4	38.3	39.5	41.1
Hospital[17]	- - -	- - -	- - -	8.7	8.1	18.7	27.6	33.6	36.2	41.5	43.7
Home health agency	0.0	0.2	0.1	0.2	4.5	7.1	12.0	11.4	11.4	11.1	11.1
Home health agency transfer[7]	- - -	- - -	- - -	- - -	−1.7	- - -	- - -	- - -	- - -	- - -	- - -
Medicare Advantage premiums[8]	- - -	- - -	- - -	- - -	- - -	- - -	0.2	0.2	0.3	0.3	0.4
Accounting error (CY 2005–2008)[9]	- - -	- - -	- - -	- - -	- - -	1.9	- - -	- - -	- - -	- - -	- - -
Administrative expenses[10]	0.2	0.6	1.5	1.6	1.8	2.8	3.2	4.0	3.4	4.1	3.3
Part D start-up costs[18]	- - -	- - -	- - -	- - -	- - -	0.7	- - -	- - -	- - -	- - -	- - -
Total Part D[4]	- - -	- - -	- - -	- - -	- - -	1.1	62.1	66.9	69.7	78.1	89.8
					Percent distribution of expenditures						
Total hospital insurance (HI)	100.0	100.0	100.0	100.0	100.0	100.0	100.0	100.0	100.0	100.0	100.0
HI payments to managed care organizations[5]	- - -	0.0	4.0	5.7	16.3	13.6	24.5	26.3	27.5	27.5	28.2
HI payments for fee-for-service utilization	97.0	97.9	94.6	93.1	80.2	85.6	73.9	70.9	69.4	69.2	68.6
Inpatient hospital	91.4	94.3	85.0	70.0	66.4	67.4	54.9	52.1	50.4	50.6	49.9
Skilled nursing facility	4.7	1.5	3.7	7.8	8.5	10.6	10.9	10.7	10.7	10.6	10.7
Home health agency	1.0	2.1	5.5	13.8	3.1	3.3	2.9	2.6	2.6	2.4	2.4
Hospice	- - -	- - -	0.5	1.6	2.2	4.4	5.3	5.6	5.7	5.6	5.7
Other programs[6]	- - -	- - -	- - -	- - -	- - -	- - -	- - -	1.1	1.3	1.4	0.9
Home health agency transfer[7]	- - -	- - -	- - -	- - -	1.3	- - -	- - -	- - -	- - -	- - -	- - -
Medicare Advantage premiums[8]	- - -	- - -	- - -	- - -	- - -	- - -	0.1	0.1	0.1	0.1	0.1
Accounting error (CY 2005–2008)[9]	- - -	- - -	- - -	- - -	- - -	−1.0	- - -	- - -	- - -	- - -	- - -
Administrative expenses[10]	3.0	2.1	1.4	1.2	2.2	1.8	1.5	1.6	1.8	1.8	2.1

See footnotes at end of table.

Table 107 (page 2 of 2). Medicare enrollees and expenditures and percent distribution, by Medicare program and type of service: United States and other areas, selected years 1970–2015

Excel and PDF versions (with more data years and standard errors when available): *http://www.cdc.gov/nchs/hus/contents2016.htm#107*.

[Data are compiled from various sources by the Centers for Medicare & Medicaid Services]

Medicare program and type of service	1970	1980	1990	1995	2000	2005	2010	2012	2013	2014	2015 [1]
					Percent distribution of expenditures						
Total supplementary medical insurance (SMI) [3] .	100.0	100.0	100.0	100.0	100.0	100.0	100.0	100.0	100.0	100.0	100.0
Total Part B	100.0	100.0	100.0	100.0	100.0	99.3	77.4	78.2	78.0	77.3	75.6
Part B payments to managed care organizations [5]	1.2	1.8	6.4	9.9	20.2	14.3	20.1	21.5	22.9	24.9	25.4
Part B payments for fee-for-service utilization [11]	88.1	92.8	90.1	87.6	79.6	81.5	56.1	55.4	53.9	51.1	49.2
Physician/supplier [12]	80.9	72.8	67.3	- - -	- - -	- - -	- - -	- - -	- - -	- - -	- - -
Outpatient hospital [13]	5.2	16.9	19.3	- - -	- - -	- - -	- - -	- - -	- - -	- - -	- - -
Independent laboratory [14]	0.5	1.0	3.4	- - -	- - -	- - -	- - -	- - -	- - -	- - -	- - -
Physician fee schedule	- - -	- - -	- - -	47.5	40.8	37.6	23.2	22.6	21.7	20.1	19.1
Durable medical equipment	- - -	- - -	- - -	5.5	5.2	5.2	3.0	2.7	2.3	1.8	1.8
Laboratory [15]	- - -	- - -	- - -	6.4	4.8	4.5	3.1	3.0	2.9	2.4	2.3
Other [16]	- - -	- - -	- - -	14.8	15.0	17.4	12.4	12.5	12.1	11.5	11.1
Hospital [17]	- - -	- - -	- - -	13.0	8.9	12.2	10.0	10.9	11.4	12.1	11.9
Home health agency	1.5	2.1	0.2	0.3	4.9	4.6	4.4	3.7	3.6	3.2	3.0
Home health agency transfer [7]	- - -	- - -	- - -	- - -	-1.9	- - -	- - -	- - -	- - -	- - -	- - -
Medicare Advantage premiums [8]	- - -	- - -	- - -	- - -	- - -	- - -	0.1	0.1	0.1	0.1	0.1
Accounting error (CY 2005–2008) [9]	- - -	- - -	- - -	- - -	- - -	1.2	- - -	- - -	- - -	- - -	- - -
Administrative expenses [10]	10.7	5.4	3.5	2.4	2.0	1.8	1.2	1.3	1.1	1.2	0.9
Part D start-up costs [18]	- - -	- - -	- - -	- - -	- - -	0.4	- - -	- - -	- - -	- - -	- - -
Total Part D [4]	- - -	- - -	- - -	- - -	- - -	0.7	22.6	21.8	22.0	22.7	24.4

- - - Category not applicable or data not available.

0.0 Quantity more than zero but less than 0.05.

[1] Preliminary estimates.

[2] Average number enrolled in the hospital insurance (HI) and/or supplementary medical insurance (SMI) programs for the period. See Appendix II, Medicare.

[3] Starting with 2004 data, the SMI trust fund consists of two separate accounts: Part B (which pays for a portion of the costs of physicians' services, outpatient hospital services, and other related medical and health services for voluntarily enrolled individuals) and Part D (Medicare Prescription Drug Account, which pays private plans to provide prescription drug coverage).

[4] The Medicare Modernization Act, enacted December 8, 2003, established within SMI two Part D accounts related to prescription drug benefits: the Medicare Prescription Drug Account and the Transitional Assistance Account. The Medicare Prescription Drug Account is used in conjunction with the broad, voluntary prescription drug benefits that began in 2006. The Transitional Assistance Account was used to provide transitional assistance benefits, beginning in 2004 and extending through 2005, for certain low-income beneficiaries prior to the start of the new prescription drug benefit. The amounts shown for Total Part D expenditures— and thus for total SMI expenditures and total Medicare expenditures—for 2006 and later years include estimated amounts for premiums paid directly from Part D beneficiaries to Part D prescription drug plans.

[5] Medicare-approved managed care organizations. See Appendix II, Managed care.

[6] Includes Community-Based Care Transitions Program ($0.1 billion in each of 2011–2015) and Electronic Health Records Incentive Program ($0.7 billion in 2011, $2.7 billion in 2012, $3.4 billion in 2013, $3.6 billion in 2014, and $2.5 billion in 2015).

[7] For 1998 to 2003, data reflects annual home health HI to SMI transfer amounts.

[8] When a beneficiary chooses a Medicare Advantage plan whose monthly premium exceeds the benchmark amount, the additional premiums (that is, amounts beyond those paid by Medicare to the plan) are the responsibility of the beneficiary. Beneficiaries subject to such premiums may choose to either reimburse the plans directly or have the additional premiums deducted from their Social Security checks. The amounts shown here are only those additional premiums deducted from Social Security checks. These amounts are transferred to the HI trust and SMI trust funds and then transferred from the trust funds to the plans.

[9] Represents misallocation of benefit payments between the HI trust fund and the Part B account of the SMI trust fund from May 2005 to September 2007, and the transfer made in June 2008 to correct the misallocation.

[10] Includes expenditures for research, experiments and demonstration projects, peer review activity (performed by Peer Review Organizations from 1983 to 2001 and by Quality Review Organizations from 2002 to present), and to combat and prevent fraud and abuse.

[11] Type-of-service reporting categories for fee-for-service reimbursement differ before and after 1991.

[12] Includes payment for physicians, practitioners, durable medical equipment, and all suppliers other than independent laboratory through 1990. Starting with 1991 data, physician services subject to the physician fee schedule are shown. Payments for laboratory services paid under the laboratory fee schedule and performed in a physician office are included under Laboratory beginning in 1991. Payments for durable medical equipment are shown separately beginning in 1991. The remaining services from the Physician/supplier category are included in Other.

[13] Includes payments for hospital outpatient department services, skilled nursing facility outpatient services, Part B services received as an inpatient in a hospital or skilled nursing facility setting, and other types of outpatient facilities. Starting with 1991 data, payments for hospital outpatient department services, except for laboratory services, are listed under Hospital. Hospital outpatient laboratory services are included in the Laboratory line.

[14] Starting with 1991 data, those independent laboratory services that were paid under the laboratory fee schedule (most of the independent laboratory category) are included in the Laboratory line; the remaining services are included in the Physician fee schedule and Other lines.

[15] Payments for laboratory services paid under the laboratory fee schedule performed in a physician office, independent laboratory, or in a hospital outpatient department.

[16] Includes payments for physician-administered drugs; freestanding ambulatory surgical center facility services; ambulance services; supplies; freestanding end-stage renal disease (ESRD) dialysis facility services; rural health clinics; outpatient rehabilitation facilities; psychiatric hospitals; and federally qualified health centers.

[17] Includes the hospital facility costs for Medicare Part B services that are predominantly in the outpatient department, with the exception of hospital outpatient laboratory services, which are included on the Laboratory line. Physician reimbursement is included on the Physician fee schedule line.

[18] Part D start-up costs were funded through the SMI Part B account in 2004–2008.

NOTES: Estimates are subject to change as more recent data become available. Totals may not equal the sum of the components because of rounding. Estimates are for Medicare-covered services furnished to Medicare enrollees residing in the United States, Puerto Rico, Virgin Islands, Guam, other outlying areas, foreign countries, and unknown residence. Data for additional years are available. See the Excel spreadsheet on the *Health, United States* website at: http://www.cdc.gov/nchs/hus.htm. Estimates in this table have been revised and differ from previous editions of *Health, United States*.

SOURCE: Centers for Medicare & Medicaid Services (CMS), Office of the Actuary, Medicare and Medicaid Cost Estimates Group. Estimates are based on unpublished data from CMS, the Office of the Actuary, and Treasury Department financial statements.

Excel and PDF versions (with more data years and standard errors when available): http://www.cdc.gov/nchs/hus/contents2016.htm#108.

[Data are based on household interviews of a sample of Medicare beneficiaries and Medicare administrative records]

	All			Not Hispanic or Latino White			Black or African American			Hispanic or Latino		
Characteristic	1992	2012	2013	1992	2012	2013	1992	2012	2013	1992	2012	2013
	Number of beneficiaries, in millions											
All Medicare beneficiaries	36.8	52.0	53.9	30.9	39.4	40.2	3.3	4.9	5.1	1.9	5.0	5.5
	Percent distribution of beneficiaries											
All Medicare beneficiaries	100.0	100.0	100.0	84.2	75.6	74.6	8.9	9.4	9.5	5.2	9.7	10.1
Medical care use	Percent of beneficiaries with at least one service											
All Medicare beneficiaries:												
Long-term care facility stay . . .	7.7	8.4	8.6	8.0	9.2	9.1	6.2	6.8	7.8	4.2	5.2	6.6
Community-only residents:												
Inpatient hospital	17.9	15.4	15.7	18.1	15.4	15.3	18.4	16.2	18.2	16.6	14.4	17.0
Outpatient hospital	57.9	68.8	75.1	57.8	70.4	75.1	61.1	70.0	76.0	53.1	58.7	75.6
Physician/supplier[1]	92.4	96.4	97.0	93.0	96.9	97.1	89.1	94.5	96.4	87.9	94.9	97.5
Dental	40.4	48.4	49.0	43.1	52.9	52.9	23.5	30.2	32.5	29.1	39.3	39.8
Prescription medicine.	85.2	94.7	95.8	85.5	94.6	95.7	83.1	95.1	95.4	84.6	94.5	97.0
Expenditures	Expenditures per beneficiary											
All Medicare beneficiaries:												
Total health care[2]	$6,716	$17,197	$17,645	$6,816	$17,064	$17,367	$7,043	$19,975	$19,961	$5,784	$16,656	$18,651
Long-term care facility[3]	1,581	2,767	2,903	1,674	3,053	3,078	1,255	2,424	2,991	*758	1,823	2,159
Community-only residents:												
Total personal health care	5,054	12,880	13,108	4,988	12,556	12,651	5,530	15,887	15,039	4,938	13,218	15,070
Inpatient hospital	2,098	2,128	2,431	2,058	2,035	2,262	2,493	2,781	2,690	1,999	2,385	3,703
Outpatient hospital	504	1,568	1,659	478	1,545	1,597	668	2,297	2,246	511	1,024	1,756
Physician/supplier[1].	1,524	3,553	3,503	1,525	3,672	3,664	1,398	3,605	3,206	1,587	2,939	3,070
Dental	142	455	464	153	499	518	70	298	253	97	375	327
Prescription medicine	468	3,261	3,351	481	3,155	3,209	417	3,755	3,805	389	3,461	3,889
Long-term care facility residents only:												
Long-term care facility[4].	23,054	47,332	48,918	23,177	46,684	49,313	21,272	50,600	51,159	*25,026	*51,241	47,967
Sex	Percent distribution of beneficiaries											
Both sexes.	100.0	100.0	100.0	100.0	100.0	100.0	100.0	100.0	100.0	100.0	100.0	100.0
Male	42.9	45.5	45.6	42.7	45.1	45.8	42.0	45.5	42.2	46.7	48.6	46.6
Female.	57.1	54.5	54.4	57.3	54.9	54.2	58.0	54.5	57.8	53.3	51.4	53.4
Eligibility criteria and age												
All Medicare beneficiaries[5]	100.0	100.0	100.0	100.0	100.0	100.0	100.0	100.0	100.0	100.0	100.0	100.0
Disabled.	10.2	16.7	16.8	8.6	13.7	13.5	19.1	31.6	30.8	16.5	22.1	23.6
Under 45 years	3.5	3.6	3.6	2.9	2.8	2.9	7.6	7.7	7.1	6.9	4.4	4.1
45–64 years	6.5	13.1	13.2	5.8	10.9	10.6	11.5	23.9	23.7	9.6	17.7	19.5
Aged.	89.8	83.2	83.2	91.4	86.2	86.5	81.0	68.4	69.2	83.5	77.9	76.3
65–74 years	51.5	46.6	47.0	52.0	47.7	48.3	48.0	38.6	39.8	49.4	46.0	45.1
75–84 years	28.8	24.9	24.4	29.5	25.7	25.3	24.0	21.8	21.0	27.1	23.2	23.1
85 years and over	9.7	11.7	11.8	9.9	12.8	12.9	9.0	8.0	8.4	6.9	8.7	8.1
Living arrangement[6]												
All living arrangements.	100.0	100.0	100.0	100.0	100.0	100.0	100.0	100.0	100.0	100.0	100.0	100.0
Alone	27.0	28.1	26.5	27.5	28.8	27.2	27.7	30.9	28.5	20.2	23.6	22.5
With spouse	51.2	48.5	48.6	53.3	50.6	51.2	33.3	31.7	31.0	50.4	45.9	46.6
With children	9.1	10.4	10.8	7.7	8.2	8.5	16.8	19.1	20.3	16.6	17.0	16.0
With others	7.6	9.5	10.6	6.2	8.4	9.2	18.1	15.1	16.8	10.8	11.2	12.4
Long-term care facility	5.1	3.6	3.5	5.3	3.9	3.9	4.0	3.3	3.3	*2.0	*2.3	*2.5

See footnotes at end of table.

Table 108 (page 2 of 2). Medicare beneficiaries, by race, Hispanic origin, and selected characteristics: United States, selected years 1992–2013

Excel and PDF versions (with more data years and standard errors when available): http://www.cdc.gov/nchs/hus/contents2016.htm#108.

[Data are based on household interviews of a sample of Medicare beneficiaries and Medicare administrative records]

| | All | | | Not Hispanic or Latino | | | | | | Hispanic or Latino | | |
| | | | | White | | | Black or African American | | | | | |
Characteristic	1992	2012	2013	1992	2012	2013	1992	2012	2013	1992	2012	2013
Age and limitation of activity[7]					Percent distribution of beneficiaries							
Disabled, under age 65	100.0	100.0	100.0	100.0	100.0	100.0	100.0	100.0	100.0	100.0	100.0	100.0
None.	22.7	24.0	25.9	21.8	23.1	24.9	26.2	30.3	31.1	21.2	22.4	24.4
IADL only	39.0	32.7	33.9	38.9	33.7	33.6	35.8	32.4	36.5	46.1	29.3	32.6
1 or 2 ADLs.	21.2	25.4	24.9	21.5	26.2	26.1	21.2	20.5	20.8	*20.9	*25.9	24.7
3–5 ADLs	17.2	17.9	15.4	17.9	17.0	15.5	*16.8	16.8	*11.5	*11.9	22.4	*18.3
65–74 years	100.0	100.0	100.0	100.0	100.0	100.0	100.0	100.0	100.0	100.0	100.0	100.0
None.	67.0	68.5	70.5	68.7	70.1	73.0	55.1	62.9	61.1	59.2	65.0	62.3
IADL only	17.8	15.1	14.7	17.0	14.8	14.4	22.9	18.9	17.2	*20.9	14.5	16.0
1 or 2 ADLs.	10.4	11.3	9.8	9.6	10.4	8.3	14.4	*13.4	14.9	*15.7	*12.1	14.9
3–5 ADLs	4.8	5.1	5.0	4.6	4.7	4.3	*7.6	*4.8	*6.8	*4.2	*8.4	*6.7
75–84 years	100.0	100.0	100.0	100.0	100.0	100.0	100.0	100.0	100.0	100.0	100.0	100.0
None.	46.6	52.9	53.6	47.5	53.4	55.6	42.0	55.2	49.5	44.3	46.1	44.2
IADL only	23.9	21.6	21.8	23.6	22.1	21.4	26.7	*15.0	21.9	*27.8	22.5	21.7
1 or 2 ADLs.	16.5	16.0	15.8	16.8	15.5	15.1	15.3	19.0	18.9	*14.9	17.2	18.8
3–5 ADLs	13.0	9.5	8.8	12.2	8.9	7.9	*15.9	*10.9	*9.7	*13.0	*14.3	15.3
85 years and over.	100.0	100.0	100.0	100.0	100.0	100.0	100.0	100.0	100.0	100.0	100.0	100.0
None.	19.9	25.7	27.7	20.2	27.0	29.4	*19.6	*18.7	*22.4	*19.7	*16.1	*16.7
IADL only	20.9	25.6	26.5	20.2	26.2	27.0	*22.1	*25.5	*21.8	*24.7	*19.9	*17.0
1 or 2 ADLs.	23.5	22.5	21.1	23.5	23.0	20.8	*24.3	*18.4	*18.6	*23.7	*26.3	*30.1
3–5 ADLs	35.8	26.1	24.7	36.1	23.9	22.8	*34.0	*37.4	37.2	*31.8	*37.7	*36.2

---

* Estimates are based on 50 persons or fewer or have a relative standard error of 30% or higher and are considered unreliable.

[1] Physician/supplier services include medical and osteopathic doctor and health practitioner visits, diagnostic laboratory and radiology services, medical and surgical services, and durable medical equipment and nondurable medical supplies.

[2] Total health care expenditures by Medicare beneficiaries. Includes expenses paid by Medicare and all other sources of payment for the following services: inpatient hospital, outpatient hospital, physician/supplier, dental, prescription medicine, home health, and hospice and long-term care facility care. Excludes health insurance premiums.

[3] Expenditures for long-term care in facilities for all beneficiaries. Includes facility room and board expenses for beneficiaries who resided in a facility for the full year and for beneficiaries who resided in a facility for part of the year and in the community for part of the year. Also includes expenditures for short-term facility stays for full-year or part-year community residents. See Appendix II, Long-term care facility.

[4] Expenditures for facility-based long-term care for facility-based beneficiaries. Includes facility room and board expenses for beneficiaries who resided in a facility for the full year and for beneficiaries who resided in a facility for part of the year and in the community for part of the year. Excludes expenditures for short-term facility stays for full-year community residents. See Appendix II, Long-term care facility.

[5] Medicare beneficiaries with end-stage renal disease (ESRD) are included within the subgroups Aged and Disabled. In 2013, less than 1% of Medicare beneficiaries qualified because of ESRD. See Appendix II, Medicare.

[6] In 2013, less than 1% of Medicare beneficiaries had an unknown living arrangement.

[7] IADL is instrumental activities of daily living; ADL is activities of daily living. Includes data for both community and long-term care facility residents. See Appendix II, Activities of daily living (ADL); Instrumental activities of daily living (IADL).

NOTES: Percentages and percent distributions are calculated using unrounded numbers. Expenditures include expenses for Medicare beneficiaries paid by Medicare and all other sources of payment. Estimates include individuals enrolled in the hospital insurance (HI) and/or supplementary medical insurance (SMI) programs at any time during the calendar year. A new imputation methodology was used starting with 2012 estimates; therefore some utilization estimates may not be comparable to previous years.

SOURCE: Centers for Medicare & Medicaid Services, Medicare Current Beneficiary Survey, Cost and Use file, Health and Health Care of the Medicare Population. Available from: http://www.cms.hhs.gov/mcbs and unpublished data. See Appendix I, Medicare Current Beneficiary Survey (MCBS).

Table 109 (page 1 of 2). Medicaid and Children's Health Insurance Program beneficiaries and payments, by basis of eligibility, and race and Hispanic origin: United States, selected fiscal years 1999–2013

Excel and PDF versions (with more data years and standard errors when available): http://www.cdc.gov/nchs/hus/contents2016.htm#109.

[Data are compiled by the Centers for Medicare & Medicaid Services from the Medicaid Data System]

Basis of eligibility and race and Hispanic origin	1999	2000	2005	2008	2009	2010	2011[1]	2012[1]	2013[1]
Beneficiaries[2]				Number, in millions					
All beneficiaries	40.1	42.8	57.7	58.8	62.6	65.7	71.4	71.6	73.7
				Percent of beneficiaries					
Basis of eligibility:									
Aged (65 years and over)	9.4	8.7	7.6	7.1	6.7	6.5	5.7	5.7	5.6
Blind and disabled	16.7	16.1	14.2	14.8	14.4	14.3	13.1	13.2	13.0
Adults in families with dependent children[3]	18.7	20.5	21.8	22.0	23.1	23.7	18.9	19.5	19.0
Children under age 21[4]	46.9	46.1	47.2	47.8	47.7	48.3	40.5	40.6	40.4
Other Title XIX[5]	8.4	8.6	9.1	8.4	8.1	7.2	9.6	8.7	9.8
Separate CHIP[6]	- - -	- - -	- - -	- - -	- - -	- - -	12.2	12.3	12.1
Race and Hispanic origin:[7]									
White	- - -	- - -	39.3	38.1	38.2	38.9	37.2	37.2	36.1
Black or African American	- - -	- - -	21.5	21.1	20.7	20.6	19.8	20.1	19.5
American Indian or Alaska Native	- - -	- - -	1.2	1.3	1.2	1.2	1.1	1.1	1.1
Asian or Pacific Islander	- - -	- - -	3.5	3.5	3.6	3.6	3.6	3.8	3.8
Asian	- - -	- - -	2.5	2.6	2.7	2.7	2.8	2.9	3.0
Pacific Islander	- - -	- - -	0.9	0.9	0.9	0.9	0.9	0.8	0.8
Hispanic or Latino	- - -	- - -	20.6	21.7	22.3	22.3	17.4	17.4	17.4
Multiple race or unknown	- - -	- - -	13.9	14.3	14.0	13.3	20.9	20.4	22.0
Payments[8]				Amount, in billions					
All payments	$153.5	$168.3	$274.9	$296.8	$326.0	$339.0	$368.6	$363.9	$375.3
				Percent distribution					
Total	100.0	100.0	100.0	100.0	100.0	100.0	100.0	100.0	100.0
Basis of eligibility:									
Aged (65 years and over)	27.7	26.4	23.1	20.6	19.7	19.4	16.6	16.7	16.7
Blind and disabled	42.9	43.2	43.4	43.5	43.4	43.4	40.8	41.2	41.0
Adults in families with dependent children[3]	10.3	10.6	11.8	12.7	13.9	14.2	12.6	13.3	13.1
Children under age 21[4]	15.7	15.9	17.2	19.2	19.6	19.8	18.1	18.2	18.4
Other Title XIX[5]	3.4	3.9	4.6	4.0	3.3	3.1	4.5	3.5	3.5
Separate CHIP[6]	- - -	- - -	- - -	- - -	- - -	- - -	7.4	7.2	7.4
Race and Hispanic origin:[7]									
White	- - -	- - -	53.0	50.2	50.0	50.2	48.1	48.3	47.5
Black or African American	- - -	- - -	19.8	20.6	20.7	20.5	20.3	20.8	20.3
American Indian or Alaska Native	- - -	- - -	1.2	1.3	1.2	1.3	1.2	1.3	1.3
Asian or Pacific Islander	- - -	- - -	2.7	2.9	3.1	3.0	3.1	3.2	3.5
Asian	- - -	- - -	1.9	2.1	2.3	2.3	2.4	2.5	2.7
Pacific Islander	- - -	- - -	0.8	0.8	0.8	0.7	0.7	0.7	0.7
Hispanic or Latino	- - -	- - -	12.2	13.7	14.2	14.2	9.9	9.7	10.1
Multiple race or unknown	- - -	- - -	11.1	11.4	10.8	10.8	17.4	16.7	17.4
Payments per beneficiary[8]				Amount					
All beneficiaries	$3,819	$3,936	$4,768	$5,051	$5,209	$5,160	$5,159	$5,082	$5,094
Basis of eligibility:									
Aged (65 years and over)	11,268	11,929	14,427	14,742	15,337	15,286	15,073	14,862	15,194
Blind and disabled	9,832	10,559	14,531	14,843	15,670	15,695	16,104	15,825	16,115
Adults in families with dependent children[3]	2,104	2,030	2,583	2,912	3,144	3,095	3,443	3,460	3,503
Children under age 21[4]	1,282	1,358	1,732	2,035	2,145	2,122	2,300	2,281	2,315
Other Title XIX[5]	1,532	1,778	2,380	2,407	2,104	2,219	2,402	2,030	1,803
Separate CHIP[6]	- - -	- - -	- - -	- - -	- - -	- - -	3,125	2,979	3,083
Race and Hispanic origin:[7]									
White	- - -	- - -	6,422	6,657	6,809	6,663	6,677	6,598	6,691
Black or African American	- - -	- - -	4,397	4,928	5,216	5,142	5,308	5,266	5,314
American Indian or Alaska Native	- - -	- - -	4,626	5,218	5,382	5,421	5,461	5,649	5,824
Asian or Pacific Islander	- - -	- - -	3,710	4,133	4,402	4,300	4,483	4,365	4,585
Asian	- - -	- - -	3,624	4,123	4,386	4,307	4,482	4,383	4,575
Pacific Islander	- - -	- - -	3,947	4,161	4,448	4,275	4,484	4,302	4,624
Hispanic or Latino	- - -	- - -	2,822	3,175	3,322	3,276	2,944	2,821	2,958
Multiple race or unknown	- - -	- - -	3,816	4,014	4,025	4,173	4,298	4,161	4,025

See footnotes at end of table.

Table 109 (page 2 of 2). Medicaid and Children's Health Insurance Program beneficiaries and payments, by basis of eligibility, and race and Hispanic origin: United States, selected fiscal years 1999–2013

Excel and PDF versions (with more data years and standard errors when available): http://www.cdc.gov/nchs/hus/contents2016.htm#109.

[Data are compiled by the Centers for Medicare & Medicaid Services from the Medicaid Data System]

- - - Data not available.

[1] Starting with 2011, a new tabular methodology was used. Therefore, estimates may not be comparable to earlier data and caution should be used with trend analysis.

[2] Beneficiaries include those who were enrolled or received services through Medicaid or the Children's Health Insurance Program (CHIP). Beneficiary counts for 2011 and subsequent years were derived from MSIS claims files. Separate CHIP beneficiaries are included for 2011 and subsequent years.

[3] Includes adults who meet the requirements for the Aid to Families with Dependent Children (AFDC) program that were in effect in their state on July 16, 1996, or, at state option, meet more liberal criteria (with some exceptions). Includes adults in the Temporary Assistance for Needy Families (TANF) program. Starting with 2001 data, includes women in the Breast and Cervical Cancer Prevention and Treatment Program and unemployed adults. For more information on the eligibility requirements, see Appendix II, Medicaid.

[4] Includes children (including those in the foster care system) in the TANF program. For more information on the eligibility requirements, see Appendix II, Medicaid.

[5] Includes some participants in the Supplemental Security Income program and other people deemed medically needy in participating states. Excludes foster care children and includes unknown eligibility. Prior to 2001, includes unemployed adults.

[6] CHIP is Children's Health Insurance Program. CHIP provides federal funds for states to provide health care coverage to eligible low-income, uninsured children who do not qualify for Medicaid. Some states use CHIP funds to expand Medicaid. For 2012 data, all states except Colorado and Idaho had separate CHIP beneficiaries. See Appendix II, Children's Health Insurance Program (CHIP).

[7] Race and Hispanic origin are as determined based on the last best eligibility record of the beneficiary. Categories are mutually exclusive. Starting with 2001 data, the Hispanic category included Hispanic persons, regardless of race. Persons indicating more than one race or missing race information were included in the multiple race category.

[8] Payments for 2011 and subsequent years were derived from MSIS claims files. Medicaid payment data for 2010 and earlier excluded disproportionate share hospital (DSH) payments ($14.7 billion in FY2010) and DSH mental health facility payments ($2.9 billion in FY2010).

NOTES: Data are for fiscal year ending September 30. See Appendix II, Medicaid; Medicaid payments. For more information, see: http://www.medicaid.gov. Colorado and Idaho had not reported 2012 data as of the date 2012 data were accessed. Colorado, District of Columbia, Idaho, and Rhode Island had not reported 2013 data and Kansas had only reported partial 2013 data as of the date accessed. For more information on data quality and analytic issues, see: https://www.cms.gov/Research-Statistics-Data-and-Systems/Computer-Data-and-Systems/MedicaidDataSourcesGenInfo/MSIS-Tables.html.

SOURCE: Centers for Medicare & Medicaid Services, Center for Medicaid and CHIP Services, Medicaid Statistical Information System (MSIS), granular file. MSIS data for 2013 were accessed October 5, 2016. See Appendix I, Medicaid Statistical Information System (MSIS).

Table 110 (page 1 of 2). Medicaid and Children's Health Insurance Program beneficiaries and payments, by type of service: United States, selected fiscal years 1999–2013

Excel and PDF versions (with more data years and standard errors when available): http://www.cdc.gov/nchs/hus/contents2016.htm#110.

[Data are compiled by the Centers for Medicare & Medicaid Services from the Medicaid Data System]

Type of service	1999	2000	2005	2008	2009	2010	2011[1]	2012[1]	2013[1]
Beneficiaries[2]					**Number, in millions**				
All beneficiaries	40.2	42.8	57.7	58.8	62.6	65.7	71.4	71.6	73.7
					Percent of beneficiaries				
Inpatient hospital	11.2	11.5	9.5	8.9	8.7	6.9	11.4	11.8	12.5
Mental health facility	0.2	0.2	0.2	0.2	0.2	0.2	0.2	0.2	0.2
Intermediate care facility for individuals with intellectual disabilities[3]	0.3	0.3	0.2	0.2	0.2	0.2	0.1	0.1	0.1
Nursing facility	4.0	4.0	3.0	2.7	2.6	2.4	2.5	2.3	2.3
Physician.	45.7	44.7	42.0	36.9	36.9	36.9	62.6	64.4	65.5
Dental.	14.0	13.8	16.2	16.7	17.8	19.1	26.6	27.4	28.3
Other practitioner	9.9	11.1	10.2	8.8	8.8	9.2	13.6	14.2	14.3
Outpatient hospital	30.9	30.9	28.2	25.2	26.4	24.2	38.8	39.5	40.1
Clinic	16.8	17.9	20.7	20.2	20.6	20.7	24.4	23.6	23.9
Laboratory and radiological.	25.4	26.6	27.7	26.6	26.2	25.8	41.6	42.0	42.5
Home health.	2.0	2.3	2.1	1.9	1.7	1.7	2.4	2.5	2.4
Prescribed drugs	49.4	48.0	49.2	41.8	42.6	44.7	56.8	57.2	57.5
Capitated care	51.5	49.7	58.1	64.9	66.6	70.8	93.6	86.9	88.4
Primary care case management	9.7	13.0	15.1	14.9	13.1	13.3	13.3	13.6	11.4
Personal support	10.1	10.6	11.8	10.8	10.7	11.0	1.7	1.7	1.6
Other care[4]	21.6	21.4	21.9	21.3	20.6	19.9	47.6	47.9	49.3
Payments[5]					**Amount, in billions**				
All payments.	$153.5	$168.3	$274.9	$296.8	$326.0	$339.0	$368.6	$363.9	$375.3
					Percent distribution				
Total	100.0	100.0	100.0	100.0	100.0	100.0	100.0	100.0	100.0
Inpatient hospital	14.5	14.4	12.8	12.5	11.8	9.9	10.7	10.3	9.5
Mental health facility	1.1	1.1	0.8	0.8	0.8	0.7	0.7	0.6	0.6
Intermediate care facility for individuals with intellectual disabilities[3]	6.1	5.6	4.3	4.2	3.9	3.7	3.6	3.3	3.1
Nursing facility	21.7	20.5	16.3	16.1	14.9	14.4	13.1	13.0	12.5
Physician.	4.3	4.0	4.1	3.5	3.5	3.5	3.3	3.0	2.8
Dental.	0.8	0.8	1.1	1.3	1.4	1.6	1.6	1.3	1.0
Other practitioner	0.3	0.4	0.4	0.3	0.3	0.3	0.5	0.5	0.5
Outpatient hospital	4.0	4.2	3.6	3.7	3.7	3.8	3.5	3.5	3.3
Clinic	3.8	3.7	3.2	3.1	3.1	3.2	3.4	3.2	3.3
Laboratory and radiological.	0.8	0.8	1.1	1.0	1.0	1.0	1.0	0.8	0.8
Home health.	1.9	1.9	2.0	2.2	2.2	2.1	2.0	1.8	1.7
Prescribed drugs	10.8	11.9	15.6	7.9	7.8	8.0	7.9	6.1	4.9
Capitated care	14.0	14.5	16.9	23.0	25.5	27.2	29.5	33.6	37.8
Primary care case management	0.3	0.1	0.1	0.1	0.1	0.1	0.1	0.1	0.1
Personal support	6.9	6.9	7.5	8.3	8.0	7.7	3.3	3.3	3.0
Other care[4]	8.6	8.8	10.2	12.0	11.9	12.7	15.9	15.6	15.0

See footnotes at end of table.

Table 110 (page 2 of 2). Medicaid and Children's Health Insurance Program beneficiaries and payments, by type of service: United States, selected fiscal years 1999–2013

Excel and PDF versions (with more data years and standard errors when available): http://www.cdc.gov/nchs/hus/contents2016.htm#110.

[Data are compiled by the Centers for Medicare & Medicaid Services from the Medicaid Data System]

Type of service	1999	2000	2005	2008	2009	2010	2011[1]	2012[1]	2013[1]
Payments per beneficiary[5]					Amount				
Total payment per beneficiary	$3,819	$3,936	$4,768	$5,051	$5,209	$5,160	$5,159	$5,082	$5,094
Inpatient hospital	4,943	4,919	6,411	7,083	7,070	7,347	4,858	4,437	3,885
Mental health facility	18,094	17,800	19,252	21,975	21,404	20,782	14,557	13,221	12,691
Intermediate care facility for individuals with intellectual disabilities[3]	76,443	79,330	107,028	123,053	127,837	125,851	129,806	119,903	120,995
Nursing facility	20,568	20,220	26,185	29,533	29,551	31,617	26,995	28,060	27,808
Physician.	357	356	465	485	496	492	271	238	219
Dental.	214	238	326	389	423	432	301	245	181
Other practitioner	118	139	200	171	171	190	186	183	173
Outpatient hospital	491	533	617	736	735	803	470	454	424
Clinic	860	805	749	772	792	791	712	680	709
Laboratory and radiological.	114	113	183	188	198	205	119	102	91
Home health.	3,571	3,135	4,487	5,789	6,628	6,375	4,286	3,565	3,581
Prescribed drugs	837	975	1,509	957	951	926	719	540	432
Capitated care	1,040	1,148	1,386	1,786	1,991	1,983	1,627	1,964	2,178
Primary care case management	119	30	27	32	41	49	45	47	50
Personal support	2,583	2,543	3,035	3,852	3,903	3,593	9,959	9,619	9,588
Other care[4]	1,508	1,600	2,228	2,856	3,015	3,289	1,724	1,653	1,554

[1] Starting with 2011, a new tabular methodology was used. Therefore, estimates may not be comparable to earlier data and caution should be used with trend analysis.
[2] Beneficiaries include those who were enrolled or received services through Medicaid or the Children's Health Insurance Program (CHIP). Separate CHIP beneficiaries are included for 2011 and subsequent years.
[3] This category was previously known as Intermediate care facility for the mentally retarded. This is a change in terminology only and not measurement.
[4] Estimates for 2010 and earlier include unknown services and payments with Other care.
[5] Medicaid payment data for 2010 and earlier exclude disproportionate share hospital (DSH) payments ($14.7 billion in FY2010) and DSH mental health facility payments ($2.9 billion in FY2010).

NOTES: Data are for fiscal year ending September 30. See Appendix II, Medicaid; Medicaid payments. Beneficiaries receiving more than one type of service appear in multiple categories. Therefore, percents may not add up to 100%. For more information, see: http://www.medicaid.gov. Colorado and Idaho had not reported 2012 data as of the date 2012 data were accessed. Colorado, District of Columbia, Idaho, and Rhode Island had not reported 2013 data and Kansas had only reported partial 2013 data as of the date accessed. For more information on data quality and analytic issues, see: https://www.cms.gov/Research-Statistics-Data-and-Systems/Computer-Data-and-Systems/MedicaidDataSourcesGenInfo/MSIS-Tables.html.

SOURCE: Centers for Medicare & Medicaid Services, Center for Medicaid and CHIP Services, Medicaid Statistical Information System (MSIS), granular file. MSIS data for 2013 were accessed October 5, 2016. See Appendix I, Medicaid Statistical Information System (MSIS).

Table 111. Department of Veterans Affairs health care expenditures and use, and persons treated, by selected characteristics: United States, selected fiscal years 2005–2015

Excel and PDF versions (with more data years and standard errors when available): http://www.cdc.gov/nchs/hus/contents2016.htm#111.

[Data are compiled from patient records, enrollment information, and budgetary data by the Department of Veterans Affairs]

Type of expenditure and use	2005	2008	2009	2010	2011	2012	2013	2014	2015
Health care expenditures	Amount, in millions								
All expenditures[1]	$30,291	$38,282	$42,955	$47,280	$50,575	$51,880	$54,738	$58,010	$64,688
	Percent distribution								
All services	100.0	100.0	100.0	100.0	100.0	100.0	100.0	100.0	100.0
Inpatient hospital	24.3	23.5	22.7	21.4	20.6	20.1	19.8	19.8	18.4
Outpatient care	53.4	53.2	53.5	52.5	52.6	53.8	53.2	55.5	59.6
Nursing home care	8.4	8.1	7.8	7.4	7.2	7.3	7.0	7.0	6.4
All other[2]	13.9	15.2	16.0	18.8	19.6	18.8	20.0	17.7	15.6
Health care use	Number, in thousands								
Inpatient hospital discharges[3]	614	622	640	656	653	646	632	619	592
Outpatient visits[4]	57,169	66,484	73,969	79,457	83,146	87,370	90,226	93,852	101,791
Nursing home discharges[5]	61	64	65	67	63	67	69	68	68
Inpatients[6]									
Total	488	492	512	532	540	546	545	558	566
	Percent distribution								
Total	100.0	100.0	100.0	100.0	100.0	100.0	100.0	100.0	100.0
Veterans with service-connected disability	37.6	41.1	42.6	43.5	44.9	46.5	48.3	50.0	52.0
Veterans without service-connected disability	61.5	58.0	56.4	55.6	54.3	52.6	50.8	49.1	47.2
Low income	39.9	35.4	34.8	34.6	33.4	32.1	30.4	28.8	28.2
Veterans receiving aid and attendance or housebound benefits or who are catastrophically disabled	12.1	11.1	10.5	10.1	9.8	9.6	9.4	9.0	8.3
Veterans receiving medical care subject to copayments[7]	8.6	10.0	9.5	9.3	9.3	9.2	9.3	9.6	9.1
Other and unknown[8]	1.0	1.6	1.6	1.6	1.7	1.7	1.7	1.6	1.5
Nonveterans	0.9	0.9	1.0	0.9	0.9	0.9	0.9	0.9	0.9
Outpatients[6]	Number, in thousands								
Total	5,077	5,291	5,439	5,631	5,789	5,903	6,009	6,176	6,296
	Percent distribution								
Total	100.0	100.0	100.0	100.0	100.0	100.0	100.0	100.0	100.0
Veterans with service-connected disability	31.6	34.7	37.1	38.6	39.8	41.7	44.0	45.8	47.6
Veterans without service-connected disability	62.7	59.7	57.2	56.4	55.1	53.3	51.1	49.0	46.9
Low income	31.8	27.2	25.9	25.7	24.9	24.0	22.6	21.3	21.0
Veterans receiving aid and attendance or housebound benefits or who are catastrophically disabled	3.5	3.5	3.4	3.4	3.3	3.2	3.2	3.1	2.9
Veterans receiving medical care subject to copayments[7]	25.4	25.2	23.8	23.0	22.3	21.4	20.7	20.1	18.8
Other and unknown[8]	2.0	3.8	4.0	4.3	4.6	4.6	4.6	4.5	4.2
Nonveterans	5.7	5.7	5.7	5.1	5.1	5.1	4.9	5.3	5.5

[1] Health care expenditures exclude construction, medical administration, and miscellaneous operating expenses at Department of Veterans Affairs (VA) headquarters.
[2] Includes expenditures for miscellaneous benefits and services, contract hospitals, education and training, subsidies to state veterans hospitals, nursing homes and residential rehabilitation treatment programs (formerly domiciliaries), and the Civilian Health and Medical Program of the Department of Veterans Affairs.
[3] Discharges from medicine, surgery, psychiatry, rehabilitation medicine, spinal cord, and neurology units, and residential rehabilitation treatment programs (formerly, domiciliary care). Does not include long-term stays.
[4] Hospital outpatient care. Includes the following services: physicians, laboratory tests, home-based primary care, or outpatient fee-basis care.
[5] Includes VA-covered state nursing home veteran patients.
[6] Individuals receiving services. Individuals with multiple discharges or visits are only counted once in the inpatient or outpatient category. The inpatient and outpatient totals are not additive because most inpatients are also treated as outpatients.
[7] Includes veterans who receive medical care subject to copayments according to income level, based on financial means testing.
[8] Includes expenditures for services for veterans who were prisoners of war, exposed to Agent Orange, and other. Veterans reporting Agent Orange exposure but were not treated for it were means tested and placed in the low income or other group depending on income.

NOTES: Some veterans have multiple sources of health coverage, including Medicare or private insurance. Estimates in this table relate only to health care use paid for by the Veteran's Administration. At the end of FY2015, the veteran population was estimated at 21.7 million, with 46% aged 65 and over. Of all living veterans, 4% had served during World War II, 8% during the Korean conflict, 32% during the Vietnam era, 33% during the Persian Gulf War (service from August 2, 1990 to present), and 24% during peacetime. Percentages sum to more than 100% because some veterans serve during more than one war. See Appendix I, Department of Veterans Affairs National Enrollment and Patient Databases. Data for additional years are available. See the Excel spreadsheet on the *Health, United States* website at: http://www.cdc.gov/nchs/hus.htm.

SOURCE: Department of Veterans Affairs (VA), Office of the Assistant Deputy Under Secretary for Health, National Patient Care Database, National Enrollment Database, budgetary data, and unpublished data. Veteran population estimates were provided by the VA's Office of the Actuary. See Appendix I, Department of Veterans Affairs National Enrollment and Patient Databases.

Table 112 (page 1 of 2). Medicare enrollees, enrollees in managed care, payment per fee-for-service enrollee, and short-stay hospital utilization, by state: United States, 1994 and 2015

Excel and PDF versions (with more data years and standard errors when available): http://www.cdc.gov/nchs/hus/contents2016.htm#112.

[Data are compiled from administrative data by the Centers for Medicare & Medicaid Services]

State	Enrollment, in thousands[1]		Percent of enrollees in managed care[2]		Average payment per fee-for-service enrollee		Short-stay hospital utilization for Part A fee-for-service enrollees			
							Discharges per 1,000 enrollees[3]		Average length of stay, in days[3]	
	1994	2015	1994	2015	1994	2015	1994	2015	1994	2015
United States[4]	36,190	54,286	7.9	31.3	$4,375	$9,635	345	282	7.5	5.3
Alabama.	633	968	0.8	25.3	4,454	8,611	413	313	7.0	5.5
Alaska	33	84	0.6	1.0	3,687	8,301	269	181	6.3	6.0
Arizona	578	1,140	24.8	38.1	4,442	8,728	292	228	5.9	4.9
Arkansas	416	594	0.2	20.1	3,719	8,360	366	288	7.0	5.3
California	3,582	5,645	30.0	40.5	5,219	10,294	366	242	6.1	5.4
Colorado	413	786	17.2	36.9	3,935	7,914	302	218	6.0	4.7
Connecticut.	497	630	2.6	25.6	4,426	10,636	287	293	8.1	5.7
Delaware	99	181	0.2	8.3	4,712	9,803	326	278	8.1	5.5
District of Columbia	80	88	3.9	13.1	5,655	10,058	376	320	10.1	6.3
Florida.	2,584	4,040	13.8	39.8	5,027	10,715	326	324	7.1	5.3
Georgia	819	1,521	0.4	31.5	4,402	9,042	378	275	6.9	5.4
Hawaii.	146	244	29.8	45.8	3,069	6,459	301	162	9.1	6.4
Idaho.	146	283	2.5	32.6	3,045	7,706	274	181	5.2	4.6
Illinois	1,605	2,063	5.5	21.0	4,324	9,910	374	308	7.3	5.1
Indiana.	805	1,151	2.6	23.8	3,945	9,332	345	293	6.9	5.1
Iowa	470	572	3.1	14.9	3,080	8,286	322	235	6.6	5.1
Kansas	378	487	3.3	13.7	3,847	8,652	348	261	6.5	4.9
Kentucky	578	863	2.3	26.2	3,862	9,012	396	315	7.2	5.2
Louisiana	572	793	0.4	30.1	5,468	10,047	399	301	7.2	5.4
Maine	198	306	0.1	22.9	3,464	8,232	322	218	7.6	5.3
Maryland	596	930	1.4	8.7	4,997	11,010	362	293	7.5	5.5
Massachusetts.	924	1,217	6.1	20.9	5,147	10,394	350	295	7.6	5.2
Michigan	1,331	1,894	0.7	33.3	4,307	10,381	328	336	7.6	5.2
Minnesota.	625	912	19.6	53.8	3,394	12,904	334	405	5.7	4.9
Mississippi	391	560	0.1	14.7	4,189	9,659	423	319	7.4	5.6
Missouri.	821	1,136	3.4	28.3	4,191	9,042	349	306	7.3	5.1
Montana.	128	201	0.4	18.3	3,114	7,277	306	185	5.9	4.9
Nebraska	247	314	2.2	12.3	2,926	8,948	281	239	6.3	5.0
Nevada	187	455	19.0	33.1	4,306	9,216	291	248	7.0	5.7
New Hampshire	152	266	0.2	7.5	3,414	8,374	281	218	7.6	5.4
New Jersey.	1,158	1,489	2.6	15.4	4,531	10,898	354	294	10.2	5.8
New Mexico	205	373	13.6	31.7	3,110	7,680	301	208	6.0	5.0
New York	2,601	3,339	6.2	37.0	4,855	10,572	334	290	11.2	6.7
North Carolina	1,001	1,771	0.5	29.8	3,465	8,858	314	277	8.0	5.3
North Dakota	101	119	0.6	16.9	3,218	8,723	327	247	6.3	5.4
Ohio	1,649	2,153	2.4	41.0	3,982	9,613	350	309	7.1	5.0
Oklahoma.	481	679	2.5	16.9	4,098	9,348	355	295	7.0	5.3
Oregon	469	756	27.7	43.8	3,285	7,842	305	191	5.2	4.8
Pennsylvania.	2,053	2,531	3.3	39.9	5,212	9,687	379	304	8.0	5.3
Rhode Island	166	203	7.0	35.1	4,148	9,224	312	296	8.1	5.3
South Carolina	497	943	0.1	23.2	3,777	8,635	319	265	8.3	5.4
South Dakota.	114	156	0.1	19.0	2,952	8,969	356	258	6.1	4.9
Tennessee	754	1,236	0.3	34.3	4,441	8,963	375	300	7.1	5.3
Texas	2,029	3,636	4.1	31.8	4,703	10,603	333	289	7.2	5.3
Utah	182	346	9.4	33.8	3,443	8,187	238	207	5.4	4.3
Vermont.	82	131	0.1	7.5	3,182	7,917	283	179	7.6	5.5
Virginia	803	1,349	1.5	18.1	3,748	8,280	348	273	7.3	5.1
Washington.	676	1,192	12.5	30.0	3,401	7,920	269	207	5.3	4.9
West Virginia	326	416	8.3	26.8	3,798	8,641	420	312	7.1	5.4
Wisconsin.	752	1,050	2.0	37.9	3,246	8,746	310	253	6.8	4.9
Wyoming	58	95	3.3	3.9	3,537	8,235	315	205	5.6	4.8

See footnotes at end of table.

Excel and PDF versions (with more data years and standard errors when available): http://www.cdc.gov/nchs/hus/contents2016.htm#112.

[Data are compiled from administrative data by the Centers for Medicare & Medicaid Services]

[1] Total persons enrolled in the hospital insurance (Part A) program, supplementary medical insurance (Part B) program, or both, as of July 1. Includes fee-for-service and managed care enrollees.
[2] See Appendix II, Managed care.
[3] Data are for fee-for-service enrollees only.
[4] Includes residents of the 50 states and the District of Columbia.

NOTES: In 1994, 92% of Medicare enrollees were in fee-for-service; in 2015, 69% of enrollees were in fee-for-service. See Appendix II, Medicare; Fee-for-service health insurance. Prior to 2004, enrollment and percentage of enrollees in managed care were based on a 5% annual Denominator File derived from the Centers for Medicare & Medicaid Services' (CMS) Enrollment Database. Starting with 2004 data, the enrollee counts were pulled from the 100% Denominator File. Payments per fee-for-service enrollee are based on fee-for-service billing reimbursement for a 5% sample of Medicare beneficiaries as recorded in CMS' National Claims History File. Prior to 2011, short-stay hospital utilization is based on the Medicare Provider Analysis and Review (MedPAR) stay records for a 20% sample of Medicare beneficiaries. Beginning in 2011, short-stay hospital utilization is based on the MedPAR stay records for 100% of Medicare beneficiaries. Estimates may not sum to totals because of rounding. State based on residence of the beneficiary. Data for additional years are available. See the Excel spreadsheet on the *Health, United States* website at: http://www.cdc.gov/nchs/hus.htm.

SOURCE: Centers for Medicare & Medicaid Services; Office of Research, Development, and Information. Health Care Financing Review: Medicare and Medicaid Statistical Supplements for publication years 1996 to 2010; Center for Strategic Planning. Medicare & Medicaid Research Review: Medicare and Medicaid Statistical Supplement for publication year 2011; Office of Information Products and Data Analytics; Medicare and Medicaid Statistical Supplements for publication year 2012; Data for 2013 and 2014 (shown in spreadsheet version), and 2015 are unpublished. See Appendix I, Medicare Administrative Data.

Table 113 (page 1 of 2). **Medicaid and Children's Health Insurance Program beneficiaries, beneficiaries in managed care, and payments per beneficiary, by state: United States, selected fiscal years 2000–2013**

Excel and PDF versions (with more data years and standard errors when available): http://www.cdc.gov/nchs/hus/contents2016.htm#113.

[Data are compiled by the Centers for Medicare & Medicaid Services from the Medicaid Data System]

State	Beneficiaries, in thousands [1]			Percent of beneficiaries in managed care [2]		Payments per beneficiary [3]		
	2000	2012 [4]	2013 [4]	2000	2013	2000	2012 [4]	2013 [4]
United States	42,763	71,604	73,669	56	73	$3,936	$5,082	$5,094
Alabama.	619	964	972	60	59	3,860	4,261	4,297
Alaska	96	138	147	–	–	4,876	9,638	9,260
Arizona	681	1,698	1,629	92	84	3,100	4,843	5,050
Arkansas	489	810	821	57	78	3,086	4,425	4,406
California	7,915	10,987	12,329	50	67	2,155	3,232	3,418
Colorado	381	- - -	- - -	90	95	4,747	- - -	- - -
Connecticut.	420	774	770	72	–	6,762	7,603	8,104
Delaware	115	246	253	79	84	4,584	6,383	6,558
District of Columbia	139	250	- - -	66	68	5,715	6,509	- - -
Florida.	2,360	4,052	4,292	60	63	3,114	4,657	4,731
Georgia	1,290	2,296	2,266	96	65	2,774	3,963	4,109
Hawaii	204	335	338	74	99	2,626	4,466	4,459
Idaho.	131	- - -	- - -	30	95	4,530	- - -	- - -
Illinois	1,516	3,089	3,184	10	70	5,150	4,349	4,379
Indiana.	705	1,342	1,332	67	68	4,224	4,882	5,032
Iowa	314	562	577	90	82	4,707	6,093	6,209
Kansas	263	435	- - -	56	82	4,670	5,883	- - -
Kentucky	771	1,108	1,030	81	85	3,780	5,114	5,542
Louisiana	761	1,343	1,389	6	88	3,456	4,318	4,109
Maine	192	370	359	35	64	6,820	5,248	5,732
Maryland	665	1,127	1,206	81	79	5,396	6,611	6,162
Massachusetts.	1,047	1,542	1,586	64	64	5,153	7,009	7,178
Michigan	1,352	2,355	2,382	100	83	3,611	4,996	4,849
Minnesota.	559	1,106	1,195	63	70	5,857	7,825	7,166
Mississippi	605	897	779	39	23	2,987	4,160	4,932
Missouri.	890	1,206	1,204	40	97	3,673	5,466	6,045
Montana.	104	141	147	61	66	4,173	5,856	6,038
Nebraska	229	311	312	77	76	4,185	5,441	5,845
Nevada	138	390	408	39	55	3,733	3,526	3,621
New Hampshire	97	165	162	6	–	6,712	6,387	6,605
New Jersey.	822	1,596	1,633	59	88	5,724	5,896	6,020
New Mexico	376	633	648	64	74	3,325	4,009	4,062
New York	3,420	6,076	6,542	25	75	7,646	7,954	7,779
North Carolina	1,209	2,071	2,023	68	76	3,996	4,829	3,843
North Dakota	61	92	93	55	56	5,852	8,474	8,823
Ohio.	1,305	2,574	2,685	21	70	5,434	6,289	6,114
Oklahoma.	507	997	1,072	69	94	3,163	3,894	3,814
Oregon	542	787	798	83	90	3,135	4,776	5,006
Pennsylvania	1,492	2,578	2,590	73	88	4,266	6,901	7,239
Rhode Island	179	234	- - -	69	75	5,982	6,769	- - -
South Carolina	685	1,005	1,058	6	64	3,900	4,739	4,721
South Dakota.	102	136	136	93	75	3,935	5,626	5,732
Tennessee	1,568	1,683	1,545	100	100	2,226	7,305	8,833
Texas	2,603	6,021	6,294	34	77	3,487	3,673	3,509
Utah	224	443	434	90	98	4,277	5,344	6,079
Vermont.	139	189	191	47	56	3,451	5,690	5,945
Virginia	627	1,077	1,134	59	68	3,960	5,605	5,636
Washington.	895	1,487	1,474	100	67	2,717	4,208	4,534
West Virginia	335	411	417	35	53	4,154	7,426	7,712
Wisconsin.	577	1,398	1,390	44	63	5,039	4,070	4,128
Wyoming	46	78	78	–	–	4,609	7,425	7,770

See footnotes at end of table.

Table 113 (page 2 of 2). Medicaid and Children's Health Insurance Program beneficiaries, beneficiaries in managed care, and payments per beneficiary, by state: United States, selected fiscal years 2000–2013

Excel and PDF versions (with more data years and standard errors when available): *http://www.cdc.gov/nchs/hus/contents2016.htm#113.*

[Data are compiled by the Centers for Medicare & Medicaid Services from the Medicaid Data System]

- - - Data not available.
– Quantity zero.

[1] Beneficiaries include those who were enrolled or received services through Medicaid or the Children's Health Insurance Program (CHIP). Separate CHIP beneficiaries are included for 2011 and subsequent years.

[2] Medicaid managed care enrollment data include individuals in state health care reform programs that expand eligibility beyond traditional Medicaid eligibility standards. The managed care enrollment data include enrollees receiving comprehensive and limited benefits. Managed care enrollment for 2000 is as of June 30 and the U.S. total includes data for the territories. Data for 2010 and 2011 are as of June 30. Data for 2012 are not available. Data for 2013 are as of July 1. Michigan's 2013 enrollment data are derived from two data sources and may not be consistent with earlier years. Managed care enrollment data may change year to year due to a variety of factors, including changes in waiver programs, outreach efforts, and data reporting practices. For more information, see: http://www.medicaid.gov.

[3] Medicaid payment data for 2010 and earlier exclude disproportionate share hospital (DSH) payments ($14.7 billion in FY2010) and DSH mental health facility payments ($2.9 billion in FY2010).

[4] Starting with 2011, a new tabular methodology was used. Therefore, estimates may not be comparable to earlier data and caution should be used with trend analysis.

NOTES: See Appendix II, Children's Health Insurance Program (CHIP); Medicaid; Medicaid payments. Colorado and Idaho had not reported 2012 payment data as of the date 2012 data were accessed. Colorado, District of Columbia, Idaho, and Rhode Island had not reported and Kansas had only reported partial 2013 payment data as of the date accessed. For more information on data quality and analytic issues, see: https://www.cms.gov/Research-Statistics-Data-and-Systems/Computer-Data-and-Systems/MedicaidDataSourcesGenInfo/MSIS-Tables.html.

SOURCE: Centers for Medicare & Medicaid Services, Center for Medicaid and CHIP Services, Medicaid Statistical Information System (MSIS), granular file and Medicaid Managed Care Reports. MSIS data for 2013 were accessed October 5, 2016. See Appendix I, Medicaid Statistical Information System (MSIS).

Table 114 (page 1 of 3). Persons under age 65 without health insurance coverage, by age, state, and territory: United States and Puerto Rico, 2009–2015

Excel and PDF versions (with more data years and standard errors when available): http://www.cdc.gov/nchs/hus/contents2016.htm#114.

[Data are based on household interviews of a sample of the civilian noninstitutionalized population in the United States and Puerto Rico]

Age, state, and territory	2009	2010	2011	2012	2013	2014	2015
Under 65 years				Percent			
United States[1]	17.2	17.6	17.2	16.9	16.7	13.4	10.9
Alabama	16.0	16.9	16.3	15.4	15.9	14.0	11.9
Alaska	22.0	19.4	21.7	22.0	20.3	19.2	16.0
Arizona	19.8	19.5	19.9	20.3	20.3	16.0	13.1
Arkansas	19.3	20.2	19.7	19.0	18.8	13.8	11.0
California	20.1	20.7	20.3	20.0	19.3	14.0	9.6
Colorado	17.4	17.6	17.0	16.3	15.7	11.9	9.2
Connecticut	10.1	10.3	9.8	10.6	10.8	8.0	7.0
Delaware	11.9	11.5	10.2	9.9	11.7	8.7	6.5
District of Columbia	7.8	8.4	8.3	6.1	7.1	6.1	4.0
Florida	24.8	25.4	25.0	24.0	24.2	20.1	16.2
Georgia	21.0	21.9	21.8	20.8	21.1	17.8	15.7
Hawaii	7.9	8.7	8.4	7.7	8.3	5.7	4.5
Idaho	19.1	20.3	17.8	18.3	18.5	15.4	13.1
Illinois	14.9	15.7	14.5	14.6	14.4	11.2	8.1
Indiana	15.8	17.0	16.6	16.6	16.2	13.8	11.4
Iowa	10.1	10.8	10.4	9.7	10.2	6.7	5.7
Kansas	14.5	15.6	14.4	14.6	14.3	12.2	10.8
Kentucky	16.5	17.5	16.6	15.8	16.8	10.2	7.1
Louisiana	19.5	20.1	19.9	19.0	19.2	16.6	13.9
Maine	11.9	12.5	13.1	12.4	13.3	11.8	10.4
Maryland	12.5	12.7	11.5	11.5	11.4	9.0	7.6
Massachusetts	4.9	4.9	4.8	4.5	4.4	3.9	3.2
Michigan	14.1	14.3	13.6	13.4	12.8	9.8	7.1
Minnesota	10.2	10.1	9.9	9.4	9.5	6.8	5.2
Mississippi	20.0	20.7	20.2	19.7	19.6	16.8	14.7
Missouri	15.3	15.2	15.7	16.1	15.2	13.5	11.3
Montana	21.9	19.6	21.8	21.4	19.7	16.2	13.8
Nebraska	13.1	13.4	13.6	12.7	12.2	10.8	9.1
Nevada	24.6	25.4	24.7	25.0	23.4	17.5	14.1
New Hampshire	12.0	12.7	11.4	12.8	12.6	10.9	8.1
New Jersey	14.2	15.0	14.7	14.5	15.3	12.6	10.1
New Mexico	23.1	22.8	22.8	21.6	22.2	17.3	12.7
New York	13.0	13.5	13.0	12.5	12.4	9.9	8.1
North Carolina	18.2	19.2	18.7	18.9	18.0	15.2	13.1
North Dakota	11.4	11.5	11.5	12.4	11.9	9.2	9.4
Ohio	14.0	14.1	13.9	13.4	12.8	9.7	7.5
Oklahoma	21.3	22.0	21.3	21.1	20.4	17.7	16.5
Oregon	19.8	19.7	18.0	16.9	17.4	11.5	8.3
Pennsylvania	11.3	11.9	11.8	11.3	11.3	10.1	7.4
Rhode Island	12.8	13.7	12.6	13.3	13.9	8.3	6.1
South Carolina	19.2	20.2	19.4	19.3	18.4	16.0	12.8
South Dakota	15.6	13.6	13.4	12.3	14.3	11.6	13.1
Tennessee	16.3	16.4	17.0	16.1	16.2	13.9	12.0
Texas	26.3	26.3	25.5	24.8	24.5	21.2	19.0
Utah	15.7	17.0	16.5	15.3	14.7	13.6	11.7
Vermont	9.9	9.0	8.3	7.7	8.1	5.4	5.0
Virginia	13.3	14.5	14.1	14.2	14.1	12.4	10.7
Washington	15.3	16.1	16.0	15.7	16.1	10.5	7.5
West Virginia	16.7	17.2	18.2	16.9	16.1	10.7	6.6
Wisconsin	10.4	10.9	10.6	10.6	10.4	8.7	6.7
Wyoming	17.5	16.6	17.5	18.3	14.6	14.1	12.0
Puerto Rico[2]	9.4	9.4	8.9	8.5	7.7	7.2	6.7

See footnotes at end of table.

Table 114 (page 2 of 3). Persons under age 65 without health insurance coverage, by age, state, and territory: United States and Puerto Rico, 2009–2015

Excel and PDF versions (with more data years and standard errors when available): http://www.cdc.gov/nchs/hus/contents2016.htm#114.

[Data are based on household interviews of a sample of the civilian noninstitutionalized population in the United States and Puerto Rico]

Age, state, and territory	2009	2010	2011	2012	2013	2014	2015
Under 18 years				Percent			
United States[1]	8.5	8.0	7.5	7.1	7.1	6.0	4.8
Alabama	6.1	5.9	5.2	4.0	4.5	3.7	2.7
Alaska	12.8	9.3	13.9	13.3	11.7	12.3	9.2
Arizona	12.1	13.0	12.8	12.8	12.1	10.0	8.7
Arkansas	6.2	6.3	5.5	5.4	5.7	4.5	4.9
California	9.4	9.0	8.0	8.0	7.3	5.4	3.3
Colorado	9.8	9.8	9.3	8.1	8.4	6.0	4.1
Connecticut	3.9	2.9	2.5	3.7	4.1	3.9	3.5
Delaware	5.7	5.6	3.5	3.6	5.1	*5.0	*2.7
District of Columbia	*	*2.0	*4.1	*	*2.2	*2.6	*1.5
Florida	14.7	12.7	11.9	10.8	11.0	9.2	6.8
Georgia	10.7	9.8	9.5	8.9	9.5	7.5	7.0
Hawaii	2.4	3.7	3.9	2.9	3.2	2.0	*1.4
Idaho	10.7	10.6	8.5	7.6	8.3	7.2	6.0
Illinois	4.4	4.8	3.4	3.2	4.3	3.8	2.5
Indiana	8.5	8.9	8.4	8.0	8.4	7.2	7.1
Iowa	4.4	4.3	4.6	4.3	4.8	3.2	3.3
Kansas	8.1	7.7	6.1	6.9	6.6	6.1	5.2
Kentucky	5.8	5.8	5.9	5.9	5.9	4.3	4.4
Louisiana	6.4	5.6	5.7	5.3	5.6	5.0	3.5
Maine	5.7	3.8	5.5	4.2	5.1	6.1	6.2
Maryland	4.7	4.9	4.5	3.8	4.3	3.4	4.2
Massachusetts	1.7	1.4	1.6	1.3	1.5	1.6	1.2
Michigan	4.3	4.2	3.9	4.2	4.2	3.6	3.3
Minnesota	7.0	6.3	6.1	5.7	6.1	3.5	3.2
Mississippi	10.1	8.2	7.4	7.2	7.3	5.4	4.0
Missouri	7.2	6.3	6.7	7.2	7.3	6.8	5.8
Montana	13.4	12.7	12.8	10.9	10.4	8.6	7.4
Nebraska	6.3	5.2	7.3	5.4	5.9	5.0	4.7
Nevada	18.0	17.9	16.1	16.5	13.9	9.7	7.6
New Hampshire	4.6	4.9	3.2	4.2	3.5	5.2	3.2
New Jersey	6.2	6.0	5.2	5.1	5.7	4.5	3.8
New Mexico	12.0	9.9	9.1	8.1	9.0	7.6	4.4
New York	4.8	4.8	4.4	4.0	4.1	3.4	2.5
North Carolina	7.9	8.1	7.8	7.3	5.9	5.3	4.5
North Dakota	6.3	6.6	7.6	7.4	7.7	6.7	8.5
Ohio	6.4	5.9	6.1	5.4	5.1	4.9	4.3
Oklahoma	11.1	10.4	10.9	9.9	10.5	8.7	8.1
Oregon	10.8	8.8	7.0	5.6	6.3	4.3	3.4
Pennsylvania	5.0	5.2	5.4	5.1	5.0	5.4	4.0
Rhode Island	4.9	4.8	3.9	5.1	6.0	3.3	3.2
South Carolina	9.5	9.8	8.7	7.8	7.0	5.2	4.2
South Dakota	6.8	7.2	5.6	3.9	7.2	7.2	7.2
Tennessee	5.7	5.3	5.8	5.6	5.7	5.2	4.3
Texas	16.3	14.7	13.3	12.3	12.5	11.2	9.4
Utah	10.2	11.1	11.1	9.3	9.0	9.2	7.6
Vermont	*3.3	*2.7	*	*3.0	*	*	*
Virginia	6.7	6.4	5.8	5.6	5.7	5.9	4.9
Washington	7.0	6.4	6.1	5.5	6.3	4.4	2.8
West Virginia	5.4	4.7	5.0	3.9	4.0	3.0	2.6
Wisconsin	4.6	5.2	4.6	4.7	4.4	4.9	3.6
Wyoming	9.0	7.4	8.7	9.9	6.3	6.7	6.2
Puerto Rico[2]	4.2	4.5	4.0	4.3	3.5	3.1	2.7

See footnotes at end of table.

Table 114 (page 3 of 3). Persons under age 65 without health insurance coverage, by age, state, and territory: United States and Puerto Rico, 2009–2015

Excel and PDF versions (with more data years and standard errors when available): http://www.cdc.gov/nchs/hus/contents2016.htm#114.

[Data are based on household interviews of a sample of the civilian noninstitutionalized population in the United States and Puerto Rico]

Age, state, and territory	2009	2010	2011	2012	2013	2014	2015
18–64 years				Percent			
United States[1]	20.6	21.4	21.0	20.6	20.3	16.2	13.1
Alabama	19.8	21.2	20.5	19.7	20.2	17.9	15.4
Alaska.	25.8	23.6	24.8	25.5	23.9	22.0	18.8
Arizona	23.3	22.3	22.8	23.4	23.7	18.5	14.8
Arkansas	24.6	25.8	25.4	24.5	24.0	17.6	13.5
California	24.5	25.3	25.1	24.7	23.8	17.3	12.0
Colorado	20.3	20.5	19.9	19.4	18.5	14.0	11.0
Connecticut.	12.4	13.0	12.4	13.1	13.1	9.4	8.2
Delaware	14.3	13.7	12.7	12.2	14.1	10.1	7.9
District of Columbia.	9.2	9.9	9.3	7.1	8.3	7.0	4.6
Florida.	28.6	29.9	29.5	28.6	28.8	23.8	19.5
Georgia	25.4	26.9	26.8	25.6	25.8	21.9	19.2
Hawaii.	9.9	10.5	10.1	9.4	10.1	7.1	5.7
Idaho	22.8	24.7	22.0	23.1	23.1	19.2	16.3
Illinois	19.0	20.0	18.8	19.0	18.1	13.9	10.1
Indiana	18.8	20.3	19.8	20.0	19.2	16.4	13.1
Iowa.	12.2	13.3	12.6	11.8	12.3	8.0	6.6
Kansas	17.1	18.9	17.9	17.8	17.4	14.8	13.1
Kentucky	20.6	22.0	20.7	19.5	20.8	12.4	8.2
Louisiana	24.8	25.8	25.6	24.4	24.5	21.2	18.0
Maine	14.0	15.4	15.5	15.1	15.8	13.7	11.8
Maryland	15.4	15.5	14.0	14.3	14.0	11.0	8.8
Massachusetts	5.9	6.1	5.8	5.5	5.3	4.6	3.9
Michigan	17.8	18.1	17.3	16.8	16.0	12.1	8.5
Minnesota.	11.4	11.6	11.3	10.9	10.8	8.1	5.9
Mississippi	24.3	26.0	25.6	25.0	24.6	21.4	19.0
Missouri.	18.4	18.7	19.2	19.5	18.2	16.0	13.4
Montana	25.0	22.1	25.0	25.1	23.0	18.9	16.1
Nebraska	15.9	16.8	16.2	15.7	14.8	13.1	10.9
Nevada	27.3	28.4	28.1	28.4	27.1	20.4	16.5
New Hampshire.	14.4	15.3	14.1	15.6	15.6	12.6	9.6
New Jersey	17.2	18.3	18.2	17.9	18.7	15.5	12.3
New Mexico.	27.8	28.2	28.5	27.2	27.6	21.1	16.1
New York	16.0	16.6	16.0	15.4	15.2	12.1	10.0
North Carolina	22.2	23.5	22.9	23.3	22.6	19.0	16.3
North Dakota	13.2	13.3	12.9	14.1	13.4	10.1	9.7
Ohio.	16.9	17.2	16.8	16.4	15.6	11.5	8.7
Oklahoma.	25.6	26.8	25.6	25.6	24.5	21.4	19.9
Oregon	23.1	23.6	21.9	20.9	21.2	14.0	9.9
Pennsylvania	13.6	14.2	14.0	13.4	13.5	11.7	8.6
Rhode Island	15.5	16.7	15.5	16.0	16.4	9.8	7.0
South Carolina	23.0	24.2	23.5	23.6	22.5	19.9	15.9
South Dakota	19.1	16.3	16.6	15.7	17.2	13.4	15.5
Tennessee	20.4	20.7	21.2	20.0	20.1	17.1	14.9
Texas	30.9	31.5	30.9	30.4	29.7	25.6	23.1
Utah.	18.6	20.1	19.3	18.4	17.7	16.0	13.8
Vermont.	12.0	11.1	10.3	9.2	9.6	6.8	6.2
Virginia	15.8	17.4	17.1	17.3	17.1	14.7	12.8
Washington	18.4	19.7	19.6	19.4	19.8	12.7	9.2
West Virginia	20.5	21.5	22.7	21.2	20.2	13.3	8.0
Wisconsin.	12.5	13.1	12.8	12.8	12.7	10.1	7.8
Wyoming	20.7	20.2	20.7	21.5	17.8	16.9	14.2
Puerto Rico[2].	11.5	11.3	10.9	10.0	9.2	8.7	8.2

* Estimates are considered unreliable. Data preceded by an asterisk have a relative standard error of 20%–30%. Data not shown have an RSE greater than 30%.
[1] Excludes data for Puerto Rico.
[2] Data for Puerto Rico are collected in the Puerto Rico Community Survey. Data are not collected for the other territories.

NOTES: Health insurance estimates are shown for the civilian noninstitutionalized population. Data for 2009 use Census 2000 population controls, and data for 2010 and beyond use Census 2010 population controls. Questions on health insurance coverage ask about current coverage as of the day of American Community Survey (ACS) interview. Persons were considered uninsured if they were not covered by private health insurance, Medicare, Medicaid, Medical Assistance, TRICARE or other military health care, veteran's coverage through the Veteran's Administration, or other government coverage. People with Indian Health Service coverage only are considered uninsured by ACS. Standard errors for selected years are available in the spreadsheet version of this table. Available from: http://www.cdc.gov/nchs/hus. htm. Standard errors were computed with replicate weights using 80 balanced repeated replicate weights (BRR) with a Fay-modified BRR adjustment factor of 0.5.

SOURCE: U.S. Census Bureau, American Community Survey, public-use microdata sample. See Appendix I, American Community Survey (ACS).

Appendixes

Appendix Contents

Appendix II: Tables

Appendix II: Figure

Appendix I. Data Sources

Health, United States consolidates the most current data on the health of the population of the United States, the availability and use of health care resources, and health care expenditures. Information was obtained from the data files and published reports of many federal government, private, and global agencies and organizations. In each case, the sponsoring agency or organization collected data using its own methods and procedures. Therefore, data in this report may vary considerably with respect to source, method of collection, definitions, and reference period.

Although a detailed description and comprehensive evaluation of each data source are beyond the scope of this appendix, readers should be aware of the general strengths and weaknesses of the different data collection systems shown in *Health, United States*. For example, population-based surveys are able to collect socioeconomic data and information on the impact of an illness, such as limitation of activity. These data are limited by the amount of information a respondent remembers or is willing to report. For example, a respondent may not know detailed medical information, such as a precise diagnosis or the type of medical procedure performed, and therefore cannot report that information. In contrast, records-based surveys, which collect data from physician and hospital records, usually contain good diagnostic information but little or no information about the socioeconomic characteristics of individuals or the impact of illnesses on individuals.

Different data collection systems may cover different populations, and understanding these differences is critical to interpreting the resulting data. Data on vital statistics and national expenditures cover the entire population. However, most data on morbidity cover only the civilian noninstitutionalized population and thus may not include data for military personnel, who are usually young; for institutionalized people, including the prison population, who may be of any age; or for nursing home residents, who are usually older.

All data collection systems are subject to error, and records may be incomplete or contain inaccurate information. Respondents may not remember essential information, a question may not mean the same thing to different respondents, and some institutions or individuals may not respond at all. It is not always possible to measure the magnitude of these errors or their effect on the data. Where possible, table notes describe the universe and method of data collection, to assist users in evaluating data quality.

Some information is collected in more than one survey, and estimates of the same statistic may vary among surveys because of different survey methodologies, sampling frames, questionnaires, definitions, and tabulation categories. For example, cigarette use is measured by the National Health Interview Survey, the National Survey on Drug Use & Health, the Monitoring the Future Study, and the Youth Risk Behavior Survey. These surveys use slightly different questions, cover persons of differing ages, and interview in diverse settings (e.g., at school compared with at home), so estimates may differ.

Overall estimates generally have relatively small sampling errors, but estimates for certain population subgroups may be based on a small sample size and have relatively large sampling errors. Numbers of births and deaths from the National Vital Statistics System represent complete counts (except for births in those states where data are based on a 50% sample for certain years). Therefore, these data are not subject to sampling error. However, when the figures are used for analytical purposes, such as the comparison of rates over a period, the number of events that actually occurred may be considered as one of a large series of possible results that could have arisen under the same circumstances. When the number of events is small and the probability of such an event is rare, estimates may be unstable, and considerable caution must be used in interpreting the statistics. Estimates that are unreliable because of large sampling errors or small numbers of events are noted with asterisks in tables, and the criteria used to determine unreliable estimates are indicated in an accompanying footnote.

In this appendix, government data sources are listed alphabetically by data set name, and private and global sources are listed separately. To the extent possible, government data systems are described using a standard format. The *Overview* is a brief, general statement about the purpose or objectives of the data system. The *Coverage* section describes the population or events that the data system covers: for example, residents of the United States, the noninstitutionalized population, persons in specific population groups, or other entities that are included in the survey or data system. The *Methodology* section presents a short description of the methods used to collect the data. The *Sample Size and Response Rate* section provides these statistics for surveys. The *Issues Affecting Interpretation* section describes major changes in the data collection methodology or other factors that must be considered when analyzing trends shown in *Health, United States*: for example, a major survey redesign that may introduce a discontinuity in the trend. For additional information about the methodology, data files, and history of a data source, consult the *References* and *For More Information* sections that follow each summary.

Government Sources

Abortion Surveillance System

CDC/National Center for Chronic Disease Prevention and Health Promotion (NCCDPHP)

Overview. The Abortion Surveillance System documents the number and characteristics of women obtaining legal induced abortions in the United States.

Coverage. The system includes women of all ages, including adolescents, who obtain legal induced abortions.

Methodology. Each year, CDC requests tabulated data from the central health agencies of 52 reporting areas (the 50 states, the District of Columbia [D.C.], and New York City) to document the number and characteristics of women obtaining abortions in the United States. For the purpose of surveillance, a legal induced abortion is defined as an intervention performed by a licensed clinician (e.g., a physician, nurse-midwife, nurse practitioner, or physician assistant) that is intended to terminate a suspected or known ongoing intrauterine pregnancy and produce a nonviable fetus.

In most states, collection of abortion data is facilitated by the legal requirement for hospitals, facilities, and physicians to report abortions to a central health agency. These central health agencies voluntarily report abortion data to CDC and provide only the aggregate numbers for the abortion data they have collected through their independent surveillance systems. Although reporting to CDC is voluntary, most reporting areas provide aggregate abortion numbers; during 2003–2012, a total of 47 reporting areas provided CDC a continuous annual record of abortion numbers.

Issues Affecting Interpretation. Because reporting areas establish their own reporting requirements for abortion and send their data to CDC voluntarily, CDC is unable to obtain the total number of abortions performed in the United States. Although most states legally require medical providers to submit a report for all the abortions they perform, enforcement of this requirement varies. Additionally, although most reporting areas collect and send abortion data to CDC, during 2004–2013, 5 of the 52 reporting areas did not provide CDC with data on a consistent annual basis (the five states that did not report continuously for the period 2004–2013 were California, Louisiana, Maryland, New Hampshire, and West Virginia). Because of these limitations, during the period covered by this report the total annual number of abortions recorded by CDC was consistently approximately 70% of the number recorded by the Guttmacher Institute, which uses numerous active follow-up techniques to increase the completeness of the data obtained through its periodic national census of abortion providers. (See Appendix I, Guttmacher Institute Abortion Provider Census.)

Reference

Jatlaoui TC, Ewing A, Mandel MG, Simmons KB, Suchdev DB, Jamieson DJ, Pazol K. Abortion surveillance—United States, 2013. MMWR Surveill Summ 2016;65(SS–12):1–44. Available from: http://www.cdc.gov/mmwr/volumes/65/ss/ss6512a1.htm.

For More Information. See the NCCDPHP surveillance and research website at: http://www.cdc.gov/reproductivehealth/Data_Stats/index.htm.

American Community Survey (ACS)

U.S. Census Bureau

Overview. ACS provides annual estimates of income, education, employment, health insurance coverage, and housing costs and conditions for U.S. residents. Estimates from ACS complement population data collected by the U.S. Census Bureau during the decennial census. Topics currently included on an annual basis in ACS were previously collected once a decade through the decennial census long form.

Coverage. ACS covers U.S. residents residing in all 3,141 counties in the 50 states and D.C., and all 78 municipalities in Puerto Rico. ACS began data collection for U.S. residents residing in housing units in January 2005 and for residents residing in group quarters facilities in January 2006. Annual ACS estimates are available every year for states and for specific geographic areas with populations of 65,000 or more.

Methodology. Starting with 2013 data, the ACS data collection operation uses up to four modes to collect information: Internet, mail, telephone, and personal visit interviews. The first mode includes a mailed request to respond to the ACS questionnaire over the Internet, followed later by an option to complete a paper questionnaire and return it by mail. If neither an Internet nor mail questionnaire is received, a follow-up interview by phone or personal visit is attempted for a sample of nonrespondents. Prior to 2013, Internet collection was not used, and only three modes of collection were used. Each month, a sample of housing unit addresses and residents of group quarters facilities receive questionnaires. Housing units include a house, apartment, mobile home or trailer, a group of rooms, or a single room occupied as separate living quarters, or if vacant, intended for occupancy as separate living quarters. Group quarters are places where people live or stay that are normally owned or managed by an entity or organization providing housing and services for the residents. These services may include custodial or medical care as well as other types of assistance, and residency is commonly restricted to persons receiving these services. The group quarters population comprises both the institutional and noninstitutional group quarters populations. The institutional group quarters population includes residents under formally authorized supervised care, such as those in skilled nursing facilities, adult correctional facilities, and psychiatric hospitals. The noninstitutional group quarters population includes residents of colleges or university housing, military barracks, and group homes.

ACS creates two sets of weights: a weight to each sample person record (both household and group quarters persons) and a weight to each sample housing unit record. For information on the weighting procedure, see the ACS methodology website at: https://www.census.gov/programs-surveys/acs/methodology.html.

Sample Size and Response Rate. Each year from 2005 through 2010, approximately 2.9 million housing unit addresses in the U.S. and 36,000 in Puerto Rico were selected to participate in ACS. Starting in 2011, the housing unit sample was increased to 3.54 million addresses per year. For 2005–2012, the housing unit response rate was 97%–98%; in 2013, the housing unit response rate was 90%; in 2014 and 2015, it was 97% and 96%, respectively. Beginning in 2006, the ACS sample was expanded to include 2.5% of the population living in group quarters, which included approximately 20,000 group quarters facilities and 195,000 residents of group quarters in the United States and Puerto Rico. In 2013, the group quarters sample for college dormitories was restricted to the nonsummer months. The group quarters response rate ranged between 95% and 98% for 2005–2015. For year-specific response rates, see: http://www.census.gov/acs/www/methodology/sample-size-and-data-quality/response-rates/index.php.

Issues Affecting Interpretation. Several changes were made to the ACS questionnaire at the beginning of 2008, including the introduction of new questions on health insurance coverage. Health insurance coverage estimates are methodologically consistent for data year 2009 and subsequent years (O'Hara and Medalia). In addition, the methodology for weighting the group quarters survey changed starting in 2011.

References

Torrieri N, Program Staff. American Community Survey design and methodology (January 2014). Washington, D.C.: U.S. Census Bureau; 2014. Available from: http://www2.census.gov/programs-surveys/acs/methodology/design_and_methodology/acs_design_methodology_report_2014.pdf.

O'Hara B, Medalia C. CPS and ACS health insurance estimates: Consistent trends from 2009–2012. SEHSD working paper 2014–29. Washington, D.C.: U.S. Census Bureau, Social, Economic, and Housing Statistics Division; 2014. Available from: http://www.census.gov/content/dam/Census/library/working-papers/2014/demo/sehsd_wp_2014-29.pdf.

For More Information. See the ACS website at: http://www.census.gov/programs-surveys/acs/.

Behavioral Health Spending and Use Accounts (BHSUA)

Substance Abuse and Mental Health Services Administration (SAMHSA)

Overview. BHSUA measures aggregate spending for the treatment of mental health (MH) and/or substance use disorders (SUD) in the United States. Spending for MH and SUD services was based on the principal diagnosis using the *International Classification of Diseases, Ninth Revision, Clinical Modification* (ICD–9–CM) codes for mental disorders and excluded comorbid health costs resulting from MH and SUD. BHSUA provides expenditures across four dimensions: diagnosis (MH, SUD); providers and products (hospitals, physician services, other professional services including psychologists and clinical social workers, nursing home care, home health care, center-based providers, prescription drugs, insurance administration); setting (inpatient, outpatient, residential); and payment source (private insurance, out of pocket, other private including foundations and charities, Medicare, Medicaid/Children's Health Insurance Program [CHIP]). A consistent set of definitions is used in the BHSUA allowing for comparisons over time.

Methodology. BHSUA spending estimates were designed to closely mirror the National Health Expenditure Accounts (NHEA) constructed by CMS and to allow for comparisons between MH and SUD spending and overall health expenditures. (See Appendix I, National Health Expenditure Accounts [NHEA]). Estimates for MH and SUD spending for nonspecialty providers were carved out of estimates of total national health consumption expenditures developed by CMS. Estimates for specialty MH and SUD facilities were developed from SAMHSA data. Duplicate expenditures between specialty and nonspecialty providers were removed.

Issues Affecting Interpretation. In the 2009 comprehensive revisions to the NHEA, spending was broadened to encompass residential treatment facilities that included residential SUD and MH facilities. Some residential treatment centers that previously were not included in BHSUA were included starting in 2009, raising the overall level of MH/SUD spending.

Reference

Substance Abuse and Mental Health Services Administration. Behavioral Health Spending & Use Accounts 1986–2014. Rockville, MD: SAMHSA; 2016. Available from: http://store.samhsa.gov/shin/content/SMA16-4975/SMA16-4975.pdf.

For More Information. See the SAMHSA website at: https://www.samhsa.gov/.

Census of Fatal Occupational Injuries (CFOI)

Bureau of Labor Statistics (BLS)

Overview. CFOI compiles comprehensive and timely information on fatal work injuries, to monitor workplace safety and to inform private and public health efforts to improve workplace safety.

Coverage. The data cover all 50 states and D.C. In selected years, data are available for Puerto Rico, the Virgin Islands, and Guam but are not included in *Health, United States* because of data comparability issues.

Methodology. CFOI is administered by BLS, in conjunction with participating state agencies, to compile counts that are as complete as possible to identify, verify, and profile fatal work injuries. Key information about each workplace fatal injury (occupation and other worker characteristics, equipment or machinery involved, and circumstances of the event) is obtained by cross-referencing source documents. For a fatal occupational injury to be included in the census, the decedent must have been employed (i.e., self-employed, working for pay, or volunteering) at the time of the event, engaged in a legal work activity, or present at the site of the incident as a requirement of his or her job. These criteria are generally broader than those used by federal and state agencies administering specific laws and regulations. Fatal work injuries that occur during a person's commute to or from work are excluded from the census counts. Fatal work injuries to volunteer workers who are exposed to the same work hazards and perform the same duties or functions as paid employees and who meet the CFOI work relationship criteria are included. For more information on workplace fatalities included in CFOI, see: https://www.bls.gov/iif/cfoiscope.htm.

Data for CFOI are compiled from various federal, state, and local administrative sources, including death certificates, workers' compensation reports and claims, reports to various regulatory agencies, medical examiner reports, police reports, and news reports. Diverse sources are used because studies have shown that no single source captures all job-related fatal injuries. Source documents are matched so that each fatal work injury is counted only once. To ensure that a fatal work injury occurred while the decedent was at work, information is verified from two or more independent source documents or from a source document and a follow-up questionnaire.

Issues Affecting Interpretation. Prior to the release of 2015 data, the numbers of fatal occupational injuries were revised once after the initial preliminary release. States had up to

eight months to identify additional cases following their initial published counts before data collection closed for a reference year. Fatal work injuries initially excluded from the published count due to insufficient information may have been subsequently verified as work-related and included in the revised counts. Increases in the published counts from 2010–2014 based on additional information averaged 159 fatal occupational injuries per year, or less than 4% of the annual total. Beginning with 2015 data, preliminary releases were no longer produced, and only final CFOI data were produced.

CFOI classifies industries by the North American Industry Classification System (NAICS), which is revised periodically. Industry data for the reference years 2003 to 2008 were classified based on the 2002 NAICS, while industry data for reference years 2009 to 2013 were classified based on the 2007 NAICS. For reference year 2014 onwards, CFOI used the 2012 NAICS. In *Health, United States*, industry data are presented at the two-digit level. Most of the differences between the versions of NAICS were at a more detailed level; therefore, changes in NAICS over time are unlikely to affect the trend of CFOI data presented in *Health, United States*. (See Appendix II, Industry of employment.)

References

Bureau of Labor Statistics. Census of Fatal Occupational Injuries Summary, 2015. Washington, D.C.: U.S. Department of Labor; 2016. Available from: https://www.bls.gov/news.release/archives/cfoi_12162016.htm.

Bureau of Labor Statistics. Revisions to the 2014 Census of Fatal Occupational Injuries (CFOI) counts. Washington, D.C.: U.S. Department of Labor; 2016. Available from: https://www.bls.gov/iif/oshwc/cfoi/cfoi_revised14.htm.

For More Information. See the CFOI website at: https://www.bls.gov/iif/oshcfoi1.htm and the CFOI section of the BLS Handbook of Methods at: https://www.bls.gov/opub/hom/pdf/homch9.pdf.

Current Population Survey (CPS)

Bureau of Labor Statistics (BLS) and U.S. Census Bureau

Overview. CPS provides current estimates and trends in employment, unemployment, and other characteristics of the general labor force. The Annual Social and Economic (ASEC) Supplement—commonly called the March CPS supplement—of the CPS provides supplemental data on work experience, income, noncash benefits, and migration and is the source of the poverty estimates presented in *Health, United States*.

Coverage. The CPS sample, referred to as the basic CPS, is based on the results of the decennial census, with coverage in all 50 states and D.C. When files from the most recent decennial census become available, the Census Bureau gradually introduces a new sample design for the CPS. The CPS sample based on Census 2000 was introduced in April 2004 and implemented by July 2005. The CPS sample based on Census 2010 was introduced in April 2014 and implemented by July 2015.

For the basic CPS, persons aged 15 and over in the civilian noninstitutionalized population are eligible to participate; persons living in institutions such as prisons, long-term care hospitals, and nursing homes are not eligible for the survey. The CPS ASEC sample size is slightly larger than that of the basic CPS because it includes members of the Armed Forces living in civilian housing units on a military base or in households not on a military base. The CPS ASEC sample also includes additional Hispanic households that are not included in the monthly CPS estimates.

Methodology. The basic CPS sample is selected from multiple frames using multiple stages of selection. Each unit is selected with a known probability to represent similar units in the universe. The sample design is state-based, with the sample in each state being independent of the others. One person generally responds for all eligible members of a household.

The CPS interview is divided into three parts: (a) household and demographic information, (b) labor force information, and (c) supplement information for months that include supplements.

Estimates of poverty presented in *Health, United States* from CPS are derived from ASEC. ASEC collects the usual monthly labor force data in addition to data on migration, longest held job during the year, weeks worked, time spent looking for work or on layoff from a job, and income from all sources including noncash sources (e.g., food stamps, school lunch program, employer-provided group health insurance plan, personal health insurance, Medicaid, Medicare, TRICARE or military health care, and energy assistance).

The additional Hispanic sample in CPS ASEC is based on the previous November's basic CPS sample. If a person is identified as being of Hispanic origin from the November interview and is still residing at the same address in March, that housing unit is eligible for the March survey. This amounts to a near-doubling of the Hispanic sample because there is no overlap of housing units between the basic CPS samples in November and March.

The ASEC sample weight is an adjusted version of the final CPS sample weight. The final CPS sample weight is the product of the basic weight, the adjustments for special weighting, the noninterview adjustment, the first-stage ratio adjustment factor, and the second-stage ratio adjustment

factor. Due to differences in the questionnaire, sample, and data uses for the ASEC supplement, the ASEC sample weight should be used for poverty estimates.

Sample Size and Response Rate. The 2015 data from the 2016 CPS ASEC were based on a sample of about 95,000 addresses collected in the 50 states and D.C. In an average month, the nonresponse rate for the basic CPS is about 7%–8%; supplements tend to have higher nonresponse rates.

Beginning with 2001, the Children's Health Insurance Program (CHIP) sample expansion was introduced. This included an increase in the basic CPS sample to about 60,000 households per month in 2001. Prior to 2001, estimates were based on about 50,000 households per month. The expansion also included an additional 12,000 households that were allocated differentially across states based on prior information about the low-income, uninsured children in each state. This expansion was made to improve the reliability of state estimates on the number of children who lived in low-income families and lacked health insurance coverage.

Issues Affecting Interpretation. Over the years, the number of income questions has expanded, questions on work experience and other characteristics have been added, and the month of interview was moved to March. In 2002, an ASEC sample increase was implemented, requiring more time for data collection. Thus, additional ASEC interviews are now taking place in February and April. However, even with this sample increase, most of the data collection still occurs in March.

In 1994, major changes were introduced that included a complete redesign of the questionnaire and the introduction of computer-assisted interviewing for the entire survey. In addition, some of the labor force concepts and definitions were revised. Prior to this redesign, CPS data were primarily collected using a paper-and-pencil form. Beginning in 1994, population controls were based on the 1990 census and adjusted for the estimated population undercount. Starting with *Health, United States, 2003*, poverty estimates for data years 2000 and beyond were recalculated based on the expanded CHIP sample, and Census 2000-based population controls were implemented. Starting with 2002 data, race-specific estimates are tabulated according to the 1997 *Revisions to the Standards for the Classification of Federal Data on Race and Ethnicity* and are not strictly comparable with estimates for earlier years. Starting with *Health, United States, 2012*, Census 2010-based population controls were implemented for poverty estimates for 2010 and beyond. For a discussion of the impact of the implementation of the Census 2010-based controls on poverty estimate trends, see: DeNavas-Walt, Proctor, and Smith (2012).

For 2013 data, the CPS ASEC used a split panel to test a new set of income questions. Starting with *Health, United States, 2015*, estimates for 2013 are presented two ways:

using questions consistent with previous ASEC surveys and using the new set of income questions. Because data for 2013 (using the new income questions) and data for 2014 and beyond are based on the new set of income questions from the redesigned questionnaire, data trends need to be interpreted with caution.

References

U.S. Census Bureau. Current Population Survey: Design and methodology. Technical paper no 66. Washington, D.C.: U.S. Census Bureau; 2006. Available from: http://www.census.gov/prod/2006pubs/tp-66.pdf.

DeNavas-Walt C, Proctor BD, Smith JC. Income, poverty, and health insurance coverage in the United States: 2011. Current Population Reports, P60–243. Washington, D.C.: U.S. Government Printing Office; 2012. Available from: https://www.census.gov/prod/2012pubs/p60-243.pdf.

Proctor BD, Semega JL, Kollar MA. Income and poverty in the United States: 2015. Current Population Reports, P60–256. Washington, D.C.: U.S. Government Printing Office; 2016. Available from: http://www.census.gov/content/dam/Census/library/publications/2016/demo/p60-256.pdf.

For More Information. See the CPS website at: http://www.census.gov/cps.

Department of Veterans Affairs National Enrollment and Patient Databases

Department of Veterans Affairs (VA)

Overview. The VA compiles and analyzes multiple data sets on the health and health care of its clients and other veterans. Monitoring access and quality of care enables the VA to conduct program and policy evaluations. The VA maintains nationwide systems that contain a statistical record for each episode of care provided under VA auspices as well as in VA and non-VA hospitals, nursing homes, VA residential rehabilitation treatment programs (formerly called domiciliaries), and VA outpatient clinics. The VA also maintains enrollment information for each veteran enrolled in the VA health care system.

Coverage. U.S. veterans who receive services within the VA medical system are included. Data are available for some nonveterans who receive care at VA facilities.

Methodology. Encounter data from VA clinical information systems are collected locally at each VA medical center and transmitted electronically to the VA's Austin Automation Center for use in providing nationwide statistics, reports, and comparisons.

Issues Affecting Interpretation. The databases include users of the VA health care system. VA eligibility is a hierarchy based on service-connected disabilities, income, age, and availability of services. Therefore, different VA programs may serve populations with different sociodemographic characteristics in contrast with populations served by other health care systems.

For More Information. See the VA Information Resource Center website at: http://www.virec.research.va.gov/.

Employee Benefits Survey—See Appendix I, National Compensation Survey (NCS).

Healthcare Cost and Utilization Project (HCUP), National (Nationwide) Inpatient Sample

Agency for Healthcare Research and Quality (AHRQ)

Overview. HCUP is a family of health care databases and related software tools developed through a federal-state-industry partnership to build a multistate health data system for health care research and decision making. The National (Nationwide) Inpatient Sample (HCUP–NIS), a component of HCUP, is the largest all-payer inpatient care database that is publicly available in the United States.

HCUP–NIS contains a core set of clinical and nonclinical information found in a typical discharge abstract, including all-listed diagnoses and procedures, discharge status, patient demographics, and charges for all patients regardless of payer (e.g., persons covered by Medicare, Medicaid, and private insurance, as well as those without insurance coverage).

Coverage. In 2014, HCUP–NIS covered about 95% of all U.S. community hospital discharges (excluding discharges from rehabilitation or long-term acute care hospitals) from 44 states and D.C. Community hospitals are defined by the American Hospital Association as nonfederal, short-term, general, and other specialty hospitals, excluding hospital units of institutions.

The number of states participating in HCUP–NIS has generally increased each year. In the years of data presented in *Health, United States*, the number of states participating was 28 in 2000, 37 in 2005, 45 in 2010, 46 in 2011, 44 in 2012, 43 states and D.C. in 2013, and 44 states and D.C. in 2014. In 2014, all states except Alabama, Alaska, Delaware, Idaho, Mississippi, and New Hampshire were included.

Methodology. In 2012, HCUP–NIS was redesigned to improve national estimates. To highlight the design change, beginning with 2012 data, AHRQ renamed HCUP–NIS from the "Nationwide Inpatient Sample" to the "National Inpatient Sample." The redesigned HCUP–NIS is now a sample of discharge records from all HCUP-participating hospitals. It approximates a 20% stratified sample of discharges from U.S. community hospitals, excluding rehabilitation and long-term acute care hospitals. The information abstracted from hospital discharge records is translated into a uniform format to facilitate both multistate and national-state comparisons and analyses.

Prior to 2012, HCUP–NIS was designed to approximate a 20% stratified sample of U.S. community hospitals, rather than a sample of discharges. The pre-2012 HCUP–NIS was a stratified probability sample of hospitals in the frame, with sampling probabilities proportional to the number of U.S. community hospitals in each stratum (ownership and control, bed size, teaching status, urban or rural location, and U.S. region). Discharge records for all patients in the sampled hospitals were included in the pre-2012 HCUP–NIS. To permit longitudinal analysis, the statistics for years prior to 2012 presented in *Health, United States* were regenerated using new trend weights taking into account the redesign.

Hospital costs are derived from total hospital charges using hospital-specific cost-to-charge ratios based on hospital cost reports from the Centers for Medicare & Medicaid Services. Hospital charges reflect the amount the hospital billed for the entire hospital stay and do not include professional (physician) fees. Costs will tend to reflect the actual costs to produce hospital services, whereas charges represent what the hospital billed for the care. Costs are adjusted for economy-wide inflation using the Bureau of Economic Analysis Gross Domestic Product Price Index to remove economy-wide inflation that reflect the effect of changing average prices for the same goods and services. Additional inflation that is specific to the hospital sector is not removed in this calculation.

Sample Size and Response Rate. The 2014 HCUP–NIS contains data from 7.1 million hospital stays sampled from 4,411 hospitals.

Issues Affecting Interpretation. Weights are produced to create national estimates, but because the number of participating states has increased over time, estimates from earlier years may be biased if omitted states have substantially different hospitalization patterns than states that provided data. In 2012, the survey was redesigned. HCUP–NIS is now a sample of discharge records from all HCUP-participating hospitals, rather than a sample of hospitals from which all discharges were retained. The statistics for years prior to 2012 presented in *Health, United States* were regenerated using new trend weights taking into account the redesign.

References

Agency for Healthcare Research and Quality. Introduction to the HCUP National Inpatient Sample (NIS), 2014. In: Healthcare Cost and Utilization Project—HCUP: A federal-state-industry partnership in health data. Rockville, MD: AHRQ; 2016. Available from: https://www.hcup-us.ahrq.gov/db/nation/nis/NISIntroduction2014.pdf.

Houchens R, Ross D, Elixhauser A, Jiang J. Nationwide Inpatient Sample (NIS) redesign final report; 2014. HCUP Methods Series Report # 2014–04 ONLINE. April 4, 2014. U.S. Agency for Healthcare Research and Quality. Available from: https://www.hcup-us.ahrq.gov/reports/methods/2014-04.pdf.

For More Information. See the HCUP website at: http://www.hcup-us.ahrq.gov/.

Medicaid Statistical Information System (MSIS)

Centers for Medicare & Medicaid Services (CMS)

Overview. CMS works with its state partners to collect data on each person served by the Medicaid program in order to monitor and evaluate access to and quality of care, trends in program eligibility, characteristics of enrollees, changes in payment policy, and other program-related issues. MSIS is the primary data source for Medicaid statistical information. Data collected include claims for services and their associated payments for each Medicaid beneficiary, by type of service. MSIS also collects information on the characteristics of every Medicaid-eligible individual, including eligibility and demographic information.

Coverage. Medicaid data for all 50 states and D.C. are available starting from 1999. The data include information about all individuals enrolled in the Medicaid program, the services they receive, and the payments made for those services.

Methodology. Beginning in FY 1999, as a result of legislation enacted from the Balanced Budget Act of 1997, states were required to submit individual eligibility and claims data tapes to CMS quarterly, through MSIS. Prior to FY 1999, states were required to submit an annual HCFA–2082 report, designed to collect aggregated statistical data on eligibles, recipients, services, and expenditures during a federal fiscal year (October 1 through September 30) or, at state option, to submit eligibility data and claims through MSIS. The claims data reflect bills adjudicated or processed during the year, rather than services used during the year.

Issues Affecting Interpretation. Starting with 2011 data, estimates were derived from Medicaid claims files and a new methodology was used to obtain estimates. Therefore, caution should be used when comparing data for 2010 and earlier with more recent data. Not all states had reported data as of the date the statistics were obtained. States not reporting are listed in the table notes. For more information on data and analytic issues, see: https://www.cms.gov/Research-Statistics-Data-and-Systems/Computer-Data-and-Systems/MedicaidDataSourcesGenInfo/MSIS-Tables.html.

For More Information. See the CMS website at: https://www.medicaid.gov/index.html and http://www.medicaid.gov/Medicaid-CHIP-Program-Information/By-Topics/Data-and-Systems/Data-and-Systems.html and the Research Data Assistance Center (ResDAC) website at: http://cms.gov/Research-Statistics-Data-and-Systems/Research/ResearchGenInfo/ResearchDataAssistanceCenter.html. (Also see Appendix II, Medicaid.)

Medical Expenditure Panel Survey (MEPS)

Agency for Healthcare Research and Quality (AHRQ)

Overview. MEPS produces nationally representative estimates of health care use, expenditures, sources of payment, insurance coverage, and quality of care. MEPS consists of three components: the Household Component (HC), the Medical Provider Component (MPC), and the Insurance Component (IC). Data from MEPS–HC and MEPS–MPC are used in *Health, United States*.

Coverage. The U.S. civilian noninstitutionalized population is the primary population represented.

Methodology. MEPS–HC is a national probability survey conducted annually since 1996. The panel design of the survey features five rounds of interviewing covering two full calendar years. The HC is a nationally representative survey of the civilian noninstitutionalized population drawn from a subsample of households that participated in the prior year's National Health Interview Survey. Missing expenditure data in the HC are imputed largely from data collected in the MPC.

The MPC collects data from hospitals, physicians, home health care providers, and pharmacies that were reported in the HC as providing care to MEPS sample persons. Data are collected in the MPC to improve the accuracy of the expenditure estimates that would be obtained if derived solely from the HC. The MPC is particularly useful in obtaining expenditure information for persons enrolled in managed care plans and Medicaid recipients. Sample sizes for the MPC vary from year to year depending on the HC sample size and the MPC sampling rates for providers.

The MEPS predecessor, the 1987 National Medical Expenditure Survey (NMES), consisted of two components: the Household Survey (HS) and the Medical Provider Survey (MPS). The NMES–HS component was designed to provide nationally representative estimates for the U.S. civilian noninstitutionalized population for the calendar year 1987. Data from the NMES–MPS component were used in conjunction with HS data to produce estimates of health care expenditures. The NMES–HS consisted of four rounds of household interviews. Income information was collected in a special supplement administered early in 1988. Events under the scope of the NMES–MPS included medical services provided by or under the direction of a physician, all hospital events, and home health care.

Sample Size and Response Rate. In the 2013 MEPS, there were 13,936 families covered, and 35,068 respondents over the course of the year. For the same year, the overall annual response rate was 52.8%, reflecting nonresponse to the National Health Interview Survey from which the MEPS sample was selected, as well as nonresponse and attrition in MEPS.

Issues Affecting Interpretation. The 1987 estimates are based on NMES, and 1996 and later years' estimates are based on MEPS. Because expenditures in NMES were based primarily on charges, whereas those for MEPS were based on payments, data for NMES were adjusted to be more comparable with MEPS by using estimated charge-to-payment ratios for 1987. For a detailed explanation of this adjustment, see Zuvekas and Cohen (2002).

References

Ezzati-Rice TM, Rohde F, Greenblatt J. Sample design of the Medical Expenditure Panel Survey Household Component, 1998–2007. Methodology report no 22. Rockville, MD: Agency for Healthcare Research and Quality; 2008. Available from: https://meps.ahrq.gov/mepsweb/data_files/publications/mr22/mr22.shtml.

Zuvekas SH, Cohen JW. A guide to comparing health care expenditures in the 1996 MEPS to the 1987 NMES. Inquiry 2002;39(1):76–86.

For More Information. See the MEPS website at: https://meps.ahrq.gov/mepsweb/.

Medicare Administrative Data

Centers for Medicare & Medicaid Services (CMS)

Overview. CMS collects and synthesizes Medicare enrollment, spending, and claims data to monitor and evaluate access to and quality of care, trends in utilization, changes in payment policy, and other program-related issues. Data include claims information for services furnished to Medicare fee-for-service beneficiaries and Medicare enrollment data. Claims data include type of service, procedures, diagnoses, dates of service, charge amounts, and payment amounts. Enrollment data include date of birth, sex, race, and reason for entitlement.

Coverage. Enrollment data are for all persons enrolled in the Medicare program. Claims data include data for Medicare fee-for-service beneficiaries who received services and for whom claims were filed. Claims data are not included for beneficiaries enrolled in managed care plans.

Methodology. The claims and utilization data files contain extensive utilization information at various levels of summarization for a variety of providers and services. There are many types and levels of these files: National Claims History (NCH) files, Standard Analytic files (SAFs), Medicare Provider and Analysis Review (MedPAR) files, Medicare enrollment files, and various other files.

The NCH files contain all institutional and noninstitutional claims submitted during a calendar year, including adjustment claims. SAFs contain "final action" claims data in which all adjustments have been resolved. Both the NCH and SAF files contain information collected by Medicare to pay for health care services provided to a Medicare beneficiary. SAFs are available for each institutional (inpatient, outpatient, skilled nursing facility, hospice, or home health agency) and noninstitutional (physician and durable medical equipment providers) claim type. The record unit of SAFs is the claim (some episodes of care may have more than one claim).

MedPAR files contain inpatient hospital and skilled nursing facility (SNF) final action stay records. Each MedPAR record represents a stay in an inpatient hospital or SNF. An inpatient stay record summarizes all services rendered to a beneficiary from the time of admission to a facility, through discharge. Each MedPAR record may represent one claim or multiple claims, depending on the length of a beneficiary's stay and the amount of inpatient services used throughout the stay.

The Denominator file contains demographic and enrollment information about each beneficiary enrolled in Medicare during a calendar year. The information in the Denominator file is frozen in March of the following calendar year. Some of the information contained in this file includes the beneficiary unique identifier, state and county codes, ZIP code, date of birth, date of death, sex, race, age, monthly entitlement indicators (for Medicare Part A, Medicare Part B, or Part A and Part B), reasons for entitlement, state buy-in indicators, and monthly managed care indicators (yes or no). The Denominator file is used to determine beneficiary demographic characteristics, entitlement, and beneficiary participation in Medicare managed care organizations (MCOs).

Issues Affecting Interpretation. Because Medicare MCOs might not file claims, files based only on claims data will exclude care for persons enrolled in Medicare MCOs. In addition, to maintain a manageable file size, some files are based on a sample of enrollees rather than on all Medicare enrollees. Coding and the interpretation of Medicare coverage rules have also changed over the life of the Medicare program.

For More Information. See the CMS Research Data Assistance Center (ResDAC) website at: http://www.resdac.org and the CMS website at: http://www.cms.gov/Research-Statistics-Data-and-Systems/Research-Statistics-Data-and-Systems.html. (Also see Appendix II, Medicare.)

Medicare Current Beneficiary Survey (MCBS)

Centers for Medicare & Medicaid Services (CMS)

Overview. MCBS produces nationally representative estimates of health and functional status, health care use and expenditures, health insurance coverage, and socioeconomic and demographic characteristics of Medicare beneficiaries. It is used to estimate expenditures and sources of payment for all services used by Medicare beneficiaries, including copayments, deductibles, and noncovered services; to ascertain all types of health insurance coverage and relate coverage to sources of payment; and to trace processes over time, such as changes in health status and the effects of program changes.

Coverage. MCBS is a continuous survey of a nationally representative sample of aged, institutionalized, and disabled Medicare beneficiaries.

Methodology. The overlapping panel design of the survey allows each sample person (or his or her proxy) to be interviewed three times a year for four years, regardless of whether he or she resides in the community, resides in a facility, or moves between the two settings—the version of the questionnaire appropriate to the setting is used. Sampled people are interviewed using computer-assisted personal interviewing (CAPI) survey instruments. Because residents of long-term care facilities are often in poor health, information about institutionalized residents is collected from proxy respondents such as nurses and other primary caregivers affiliated with the facility. The sample is selected from the Medicare enrollment files, with oversampling among disabled persons under age 65 and among persons aged 85 and over.

MCBS has two components: the Cost and Use file and the Access to Care file. Medicare claims are linked to survey-reported events to produce the Cost and Use file, which provides complete expenditure and source-of-payment data on all health care services, including those not covered by Medicare. The Access to Care file contains information on beneficiaries' access to health care, satisfaction with care, and usual source of care. The sample for this file represents the always-enrolled population—those who participated in the Medicare program for the entire year. In contrast, the Cost and Use file represents the ever-enrolled population, including those who entered Medicare and those who died during the year.

Sample Size and Response Rate. Each fall, about one-third of the MCBS sample is retired and roughly 6,000 new sample persons are included in the survey; the exact number chosen is based on projections of target samples of 12,000 persons with 3 years of cost and use information distributed appropriately across the sample cells. In the community, response rates for initial interviews are approximately 80%; once respondents have completed the first interview, their participation in subsequent rounds is 95% or more. In recent rounds, data have been collected from approximately 16,000 beneficiaries. Roughly 90% of the sample is made up of persons who live in the community, with the remaining made up of persons living in long-term care facilities. Response rates for facility interviews approach 100%.

Issues Affecting Interpretation. Because only Medicare beneficiaries are included in MCBS, the survey excludes a small proportion of persons aged 65 and over who are not enrolled in Medicare. This should be noted when using MCBS to make estimates of the entire population aged 65 and over in the United States. Starting with 2012 data, the Cost and Use file estimates were created with a new imputation methodology; therefore some utilization estimates may not be comparable with previous years.

References

Adler GS. A profile of the Medicare Current Beneficiary Survey. Health Care Financ Rev 1994;15(4):153–63.

Lo A, Chu A, Apodaca R. Redesign of the Medicare Current Beneficiary Survey sample. Rockville, MD: Westat, Inc.; 2003. Available from: http://www.amstat.org/sections/srms/Proceedings/y2002/Files/JSM2002-000662.pdf.

For More Information. See the MCBS website at: http://www.cms.hhs.gov/MCBS.

Monitoring the Future (MTF) Study

University of Michigan, supported by the National Institute on Drug Abuse (NIDA)

Overview. MTF is an ongoing study that uses annual surveys to track the behaviors, attitudes, and values of U.S. secondary school students, college students, and adults through age 55. Data collected include lifetime, annual, and 30-day prevalence of use of many illegal drugs, inhalants, tobacco, and alcohol.

Coverage. MTF surveys a sample of 12th, 10th, and 8th graders in public and private high schools in the coterminous United States. Follow-up questionnaires are mailed to a sample of each graduating class for a number of years after their initial participation, to gather information on college students, young adults, and older adults.

Methodology. The survey design is a multistage random sample, with stage 1 being the selection of particular geographic areas, stage 2 the selection of one or more schools in each area, and stage 3 the selection of students within each school. Data are collected using self-administered questionnaires conducted in the classroom by representatives of the University of Michigan's Institute for Social Research. Dropouts and students who are absent on the day of the survey are excluded. Recognizing that the dropout population is at higher risk for drug use, MTF was expanded in 1991 to include similar nationally representative samples of 8th and 10th graders, who have lower dropout rates than seniors and include future high-risk 12th grade dropouts. For more information on MTF adjustments for absentees and dropouts, see Johnston et al. (2014 and preceding); and Miech et al. (2015 onwards).

Sample Size and Response Rate. In 2015, a total of 44,892 students in 382 public and private schools in the coterminous United States participated. The annual senior samples comprised 13,730 12th graders in 121 public and private high schools nationwide. The 10th-grade samples involved 16,147 students in 120 schools, and the 8th-grade samples had 15,015 students in 141 schools. Student response rates were 89% for grade 8, 87% for grade 10, and 83% for grade 12 and have been relatively constant across time. Absentees constitute virtually all of the nonresponding students.

Issues Affecting Interpretation. Estimates of substance use among youth based on the National Survey on Drug Use & Health (NSDUH) are not directly comparable with estimates based on MTF and the Youth Risk Behavior Survey (YRBS). In addition to the fact that MTF excludes dropouts and absentees, rates are not directly comparable across these surveys because of differences in populations covered, sample design, questionnaires, interview setting, and data cleaning procedures. NSDUH collects data in residences, whereas MTF and YRBS collect data in school classrooms. In addition, NSDUH estimates are tabulated by age, whereas MTF and YRBS estimates are tabulated by grade, representing different ages as well as different populations.

References

Miech RA, Johnston LD, O'Malley PM, Bachman JG, Schulenberg JE. Monitoring the Future National Survey results on drug use: 1975–2015. Vol I, Secondary school students. Ann Arbor, MI: Institute for Social Research, The University of Michigan; 2016. Available from: http://www.monitoringthefuture.org/pubs/monographs/mtf-vol1_2015.pdf.

Cowan CD. Coverage, sample design, and weighting in three federal surveys. J Drug Issues 2001;31(3):599–614.

Johnston LD, O'Malley PM, Bachman JG, Schulenberg JE, Miech, RA. Monitoring the Future National Survey results on drug use, 1975–2013: Vol I, Secondary school students. Ann Arbor, MI: Institute for Social Research, The University of Michigan; 2014. Available from: http://monitoringthefuture.org/pubs/monographs/mtf-vol1_2013.pdf.

For More Information. See the NIDA website at: http://www.nida.nih.gov/Infofax/HSYouthtrends.html and the MTF website at: http://www.monitoringthefuture.org.

National Ambulatory Medical Care Survey (NAMCS)

NCHS

Overview. NAMCS provides national data about the provision and use of medical care services in office-based physician practices in the United States, using information collected from medical records. Data are collected on type of providers seen; reason for visit; diagnoses; drugs ordered, provided, or continued; and selected procedures and tests ordered or performed during the visit. Patient data include age, sex, race, and expected source of payment. Data are also collected on selected characteristics of physician practices, including the adoption and use of electronic health record (EHR) systems.

Coverage. NAMCS covers patient encounters in the offices of nonfederally employed physicians classified by the American Medical Association (AMA) or American Osteopathic Association (AOA) as office-based patient care physicians in the United States. Patient encounters with physicians engaged in prepaid practices (health maintenance organizations [HMOs], independent practice organizations [IPAs], and other prepaid practices) are included in NAMCS. Excluded are visits to hospital-based physicians; visits to specialists in anesthesiology, pathology, or radiology; and visits to physicians who are principally engaged in teaching, research, or administration. Telephone contacts and nonoffice visits are also excluded. Starting in 2006, NAMCS includes visits to a separate sample of community health centers (CHCs). In 2012, the NAMCS survey sample size was increased to allow for state-level estimates in the 34 most populous states and the U.S. Census Bureau divisions.

Methodology. A multistage probability design is employed. Beginning in 1989–2011, the first-stage sample consisted of 112 primary sampling units (PSUs), which were selected from about 1,900 such units into which the United States had been divided. In each sample PSU, a sample of practicing nonfederal, office-based physicians was selected from master files maintained by AMA and AOA. The final stage involved systematic random samples of office visits during randomly assigned 7-day reporting periods. Starting with the 2012 survey, the sampling design was changed

to a list sample of physicians, instead of an area sample, to ensure adequate representation for state-level estimates. Starting in 1989, the survey included all 50 states and D.C.

Starting in 2006–2011, a dual-sampling procedure was used to select CHC physicians and nonphysician clinicians. First, the traditional NAMCS sample was selected using the methods described above. Second, information from the Health Resources and Services Administration and the Indian Health Service was used to select a sample of CHCs. Within CHCs, a maximum of three health care providers were selected, including physicians, physician assistants, nurse practitioners, or nurse midwives. After selection, CHC providers followed traditional NAMCS methods for selecting patient visits. Another major change starting in 2012 was the mode of data collection—from in-person interviews with a paper questionnaire to obtain physician practice information to laptop-assisted data collection using automated survey instruments. Over time, interviewer abstraction from visit records has been increasing. In 2012, medical abstraction by interviewers was the predominant method of data collection.

Since 2008, a supplemental mail survey on EHR systems has been conducted in addition to the core NAMCS. This supplement is known as the National Ambulatory Medical Care Survey–National Electronic Health Records Survey (NEHRS). Starting in 2010, the mail NEHRS sample size was increased five-fold to allow for state-level estimates without needing to combine NEHRS with the core NAMCS. Survey questions have been added since the introduction of NEHRS.

The U.S. Census Bureau acts as the data collection agent for NAMCS. Starting in 2012, Census field representatives have used laptops containing an automated version of each survey instrument to (a) conduct induction interviews with the physician or his or her representative to obtain information about the practice and ensure that it is within the scope of the survey; (b) determine which visits to sample; and (c) abstract and record data from medical charts. Prior to 2012, physicians were asked to perform their own visit sampling and record abstraction using a paper-and-pencil mode of data collection, but Census field representatives were available to perform these tasks if needed. Beginning in 2012, abstraction by field representatives became the preferred mode of data collection, accounting for 98% of 2012 and 99% of 2013 records collected.

Sample data are weighted to produce national estimates. The estimation procedure used in NAMCS has four basic components: inflation by the reciprocal of the probability of selection, adjustment for nonresponse, ratio adjustment to fixed totals, and weight smoothing.

Sample Size and Response Rate. In 2011, a sample of 3,819 physicians was selected: 2,555 were in-scope and 1,400 participated, for an unweighted response rate of 54%

(54% weighted). Data were provided for 30,872 visits. In 2012, a sample of 15,740 physicians was selected: 9,574 were in-scope and 3,010 participated, for an unweighted response rate of 39% (39% weighted). Data were provided for 76,330 visits. The response rates have been modified to accommodate the mixture of one- and two-stage samples of providers. The 2013 NAMCS–NEHRS had a sample of 10,302 physicians. The unweighted response rate was 70% (67% weighted).

Issues Affecting Interpretation. The NAMCS patient record form is modified approximately every 2–4 years to reflect changes in physician practice characteristics, patterns of care, and technological innovations. Examples of recent changes include increasing the number of drugs recorded on the patient record form and adding checkboxes for specific tests or procedures performed. Sample sizes vary by survey year. For some years it is suggested that analysts combine two or more years of data if they wish to examine relatively rare populations or events. Starting with *Health, United States, 2005*, data for survey years 2001–2002 were revised to be consistent with the weighting scheme introduced in the 2003 NAMCS data. For more information on the new weighting scheme, see Hing et al. (2005). The 2012 sampling design change may affect trending 2012 and subsequent data with earlier data. For more information on the new sampling design, see Hing et al. (2016).

References

Hing E, Cherry DK, Woodwell DA. National Ambulatory Medical Care Survey: 2003 summary. Advance data from vital and health statistics; no 365. Hyattsville, MD: NCHS; 2005. Available from: http://www.cdc.gov/nchs/data/ad/ad365.pdf.

Hing E, Shimizu IM, Talwalkar A. Nonresponse bias in estimates from the 2012 National Ambulatory Medical Care Survey. Vital Health Stat 2(171). Hyattsville, MD: NCHS; 2016. Available from: http://www.cdc.gov/nchs/data/series/sr_02/sr02_171.pdf.

For More Information. See the National Health Care Surveys website at: http://www.cdc.gov/nchs/dhcs.htm and the Ambulatory Health Care Data website at: http://www.cdc.gov/nchs/ahcd.htm.

National Compensation Survey (NCS)

Bureau of Labor Statistics (BLS)

Overview. NCS provides comprehensive measures of occupational earnings, compensation cost trends, benefit incidence, and detailed health and retirement plan provisions based on surveys of a sample of employers.

Coverage. NCS provides information for the nation, for the nine census divisions, and for 152 smaller geographic areas. NCS includes both full- and part-time workers who are paid a wage or salary and includes data for the civilian economy, including both private industry and state and local government. It excludes agriculture, private household workers, the self-employed, and the federal government.

Methodology. NCS is conducted quarterly by BLS' Office of Compensation and Working Conditions. The sample consists of 152 geographic areas, selected using a three-stage design. The first stage is the selection of geographic areas for the state and local government sample and the private industry sample. In the second stage, establishments are selected systematically, with the probability of selection proportionate to their relative employment size within sampled areas. Use of this technique means that the larger an establishment's employment, the greater its chance of selection. The third stage of sampling is a probability sample of occupations within a sampled establishment. This step is performed by the BLS field economist during an interview with the respondent establishment in which selection of an occupation is based on probability of selection proportionate to employment in the establishment, and each occupation is classified under its corresponding major occupational group.

Data collection is conducted by BLS field economists. Data are gathered from each establishment on the primary business activity of the establishment; types of occupations; number of employees; wages, salaries, and benefits; hours of work; and duties and responsibilities. Data are collected for the pay period including the 12th day of the survey months of March, June, September, and December.

Sample Size and Response Rate. The March 2016 sample consists of about 6,900 establishments in private industry and about 1,500 establishments in state and local government.

Issues Affecting Interpretation. Prior to 1999, estimates were based on multiple surveys that were replaced by NCS; therefore, trend analyses based on estimates prior to 1999 should be interpreted with care.

The state and local government sample is revised every 10 years and was replaced in its entirety in December 2007. As a result of this update, the number of state and local government occupations and establishments increased substantially. The private industry sample is fully replaced over an approximately 5-year period, which makes the sample more representative of the economy and reduces respondent burden. The sample is replaced on a cross-area, cross-establishment basis.

Compensation cost levels in state and local government should not be directly compared with levels in private industry. Differences between these sectors stem

---

from factors such as variation in work activities and occupational structures.

References

Bureau of Labor Statistics. Employer costs for employee compensation—March 2016 [press release USDL–16–1808]. Washington, D.C.: U.S. Department of Labor; 2016 June 09. Available from: http://www.bls.gov/news.release/pdf/ecec.pdf.

Wiatrowski WJ. The National Compensation Survey: Compensation statistics for the 21st century. Washington, D.C.: U.S. Department of Labor, Bureau of Labor Statistics. Compensation and Working Conditions (CWC) Online 2000;Winter:5–14. Available from: http://www.bls.gov/opub/mlr/cwc/the-national-compensation-survey-compensation-statistics-for-the-21st-century.pdf.

U.S. Bureau of Labor Statistics. BLS handbook of methods, Ch. 8: National compensation measures; 2007. Available from: http://www.bls.gov/opub/hom/pdf/homch8.pdf.

For More Information. See the NCS website at: http://www.bls.gov/ncs/.

National Health and Nutrition Examination Survey (NHANES)

NCHS

Overview. NHANES is designed to assess the health and nutritional status of adults and children in the United States. The survey is unique in that it combines interviews and physical examinations. NHANES collects data on the prevalence of chronic diseases and conditions (including undiagnosed conditions) and on risk factors such as obesity, elevated serum cholesterol levels, hypertension, diet and nutritional status, and numerous other measures.

Coverage. NHANES III, conducted during 1988–1994, and the continuous NHANES, begun in 1999, target the civilian noninstitutionalized U.S. population.

Methodology. NHANES includes clinical examinations, selected medical and laboratory tests, and self-reported data. NHANES interviews persons in their homes and conducts medical examinations in a mobile examination center (MEC), including laboratory analysis of blood, urine, and other tissue samples. Medical examinations and laboratory tests follow very specific protocols and are standardized as much as possible to ensure comparability across sites and providers. In 1988–1994, as a substitute for the MEC examinations, a small number of survey participants received an abbreviated health examination in their homes if they were unable to come to the MEC.

The survey for NHANES III was conducted from 1988 to 1994 using a stratified, multistage probability design to sample the civilian noninstitutionalized U.S. population. About 40,000 persons aged 2 months and over were selected and asked to complete an extensive interview and a physical examination. Participants were selected from households in 81 survey units across the United States. Children aged 2 months to 5 years, persons aged 60 and over, black persons, and persons of Mexican origin were oversampled to provide precise descriptive information on the health status of selected population groups in the United States.

Beginning in 1999, NHANES became a continuous annual survey, collecting data every year from a representative sample of the civilian noninstitutionalized U.S. population, newborns and older, through in-home personal interviews and physical examinations in the MEC. The sample design is a complex, multistage, clustered design using unequal probabilities of selection. The first-stage sample frame for continuous NHANES during 1999–2001 was the list of primary sampling units (PSUs) selected for the design of the National Health Interview Survey. Typically, an NHANES PSU is a county. For 2002, an independent sample of PSUs (based on current census data) was selected. This independent design was used for the period 2002–2006. In 2007–2010 and 2011–2014, the sample was redesigned. For 1999, because of a delay in the start of data collection, 12 distinct PSUs were in the annual sample. For each year in 2000–2014, 15 PSUs were selected. The within-PSU design involves forming secondary sampling units that are nested within census tracts, selecting dwelling units within secondary units, and then selecting sample persons within dwelling units. Selection of the final sample person involves differential probabilities of selection according to the demographic variables of sex (male or female), race and ethnicity, and age. Because of the differential probabilities of selection, dwelling units are screened for potential sample persons.

Beginning in 1999, NHANES oversampled low-income persons, adolescents aged 12–19, persons aged 60 and over, African American persons, and persons of Mexican origin. The sample for data years 1999–2006 was not designed to give a nationally representative sample for the total Hispanic population residing in the United States. Starting with 2007–2010 data collection, all Hispanic persons were oversampled, not just persons of Mexican origin, and adolescents were no longer oversampled. In 2011–2014, the sampling design was changed and the following groups were oversampled: Hispanic persons; non-Hispanic black persons; non-Hispanic Asian persons; non-Hispanic white and other persons at or below 130% of poverty; and non-Hispanic white and other persons aged 80 and over. For more information on the sample design for 1999–2006, see: http://www.cdc.gov/nchs/data/series/sr_02/sr02_155.pdf; for 2007–2010, see: http://www.cdc.gov/nchs/data/series/sr_02/sr02_160.pdf; and for 2011–2014, see: http://www.cdc.gov/nchs/data/series/sr_02/sr02_162.pdf.

The estimation procedure used to produce national statistics for all NHANES involved inflation by the reciprocal of the probability of selection, adjustment for nonresponse, and poststratified ratio adjustment to population totals. Sampling errors also were estimated, to measure the reliability of the statistics.

Sample Size and Response Rate. Over the 6-year survey period of NHANES III, 39,695 persons were selected; the household interview response rate was 86% (33,994); and the medical examination response rate was 78% (30,818). For NHANES 2011–2012, a total of 13,431 persons were eligible, of which 73% (9,756) were interviewed and 70% (9,338) completed the health examination component. For NHANES 2013–2014, a total of 14,332 persons were eligible, of which 71% (10,175) were interviewed and 68% (9,813) completed the health examination component. For more information on unweighted NHANES response rates and response weights using sample size weighted to Current Population Survey population totals, see: http://www.cdc.gov/nchs/nhanes/response_rates_CPS.htm.

Issues Affecting Interpretation. Data elements, laboratory tests performed, and the technological sophistication of medical examination and laboratory equipment have changed over time. Therefore, trend analyses should carefully examine how specific data elements were collected across the various survey years. Data files are revised periodically. If the file changes are minor and the impact on estimates small, then the data are not revised in *Health, United States.* Major data changes are incorporated.

Periodically, NHANES changes its sampling design to oversample different groups. Because the total sample size in any year is fixed due to operational constraints, sample sizes for the other oversampled groups (including Hispanic persons and non-low-income white and other persons) were decreased. Therefore, trend analyses on demographic subpopulations should be carefully evaluated to determine if the sample sizes meet the NHANES Analytic Guidelines. In general, any 2-year data cycle in NHANES can be combined with adjacent 2-year data cycles to create analytic data files based on 4 or more years of data, in order to improve precision. However, because of the sample design change in 2011–2012, the data user should be aware of the implications if these data are combined with data from earlier survey cycles. Users are advised to examine their estimates carefully to see if the 4-year estimates (and sampling errors) are consistent with each set of 2-year estimates.

References

Ezzati TM, Massey JT, Waksberg J, et al. Sample design: Third National Health and Nutrition Examination Survey. NCHS. Vital Health Stat 1992;2(113). Available from: http://www.cdc.gov/nchs/data/series/sr_02/sr02_113.pdf.

NCHS. Plan and operation of the Third National Health and Nutrition Examination Survey, 1988–94. Vital Health Stat 1994;1(32). Available from: http://www.cdc.gov/nchs/data/series/sr_01/sr01_032.pdf.

Johnson CL, Paulose-Ram R, Ogden CL, et al. National Health and Nutrition Examination Survey: Analytic guidelines, 1999–2010. NCHS. Vital Health Stat 2013;2(161). Available from: http://www.cdc.gov/nchs/data/series/sr_02/sr02_161.pdf.

Johnson CL, Dohrmann SM, Burt VL, Mohadjer LK. National Health and Nutrition Examination Survey: Sample design, 2011–2014. Vital Health Stat 2014;2(162). Available from: http://www.cdc.gov/nchs/data/series/sr_02/sr02_162.pdf.

For More Information. See the NHANES website at: http://www.cdc.gov/nchs/nhanes.htm.

National Health Expenditure Accounts (NHEA)

Centers for Medicare & Medicaid Services (CMS)

Overview. NHEA provide estimates of aggregate health care expenditures in the United States from 1960 onward. NHEA contain all of the main components of the health care system within a unified, mutually-exclusive, and exhaustive structure. The accounts measure spending for health care in the United States by type of good or service delivered (e.g., hospital care, physician and clinical services, or retail prescription drugs) and by the source of funds that pay for that care (e.g., private health insurance, Medicare, Medicaid, or out-of-pocket). A consistent set of definitions is used for health care goods and services and for sources of funds that finance health care expenditures, allowing for comparisons over time.

Methodology. The primary data sources used to estimate hospital care spending are the American Hospital Association's (AHA) Annual Survey and the U.S. Census Bureau's Services Annual Survey (SAS). These sources are supplemented by data on federal hospital spending. Expenditures for physician and clinical services are estimated using data from SAS and the U.S. Census Bureau's quinquennial Economic Census. Expenditures for nursing care facilities and continuing care retirement communities, home health care, dentists, and the services of other professionals (e.g., chiropractors, private duty nurses, therapists, and podiatrists) are estimated using data from SAS and the quinquennial Economic Census. The estimate of retail spending for prescription drugs is based on prescription drug data from the U.S. Census Bureau's Census of Retail Trade and data from IMS Health (Parsippany, NJ), an organization that collects data on retail sales of prescription drugs.

Expenditures for durable and other nondurable medical products purchased in retail outlets are based on input-output and personal consumption expenditure data (Bureau of Economic Analysis), the Economic Census and Annual Retail Trade Survey (ARTS) data (U.S. Census Bureau), Consumer Expenditure Survey data (Bureau of Labor Statistics [BLS]), Medical Expenditure Panel Surveys (MEPS) data (Agency for Healthcare Research and Quality [AHRQ]), and over-the-counter sales data from Kline and Company, Inc. Durable and nondurable products provided to inpatients in hospitals or nursing homes, and those provided by licensed health professionals or through home health care agencies, are excluded from NHEA estimates of durable and nondurable medical products but are included with the expenditure estimates for the provider service category.

The Structures and Equipment component of NHEA includes estimates of the value of new construction put in place and new capital equipment (including software) purchased by the medical sector during the year. These estimates are based on a variety of data from the U.S. Census Bureau and the Bureau of Economic Analysis, including the Annual Capital Expenditures Survey, the C–30 Survey, and data from the National Income and Product Accounts.

Expenditures for noncommercial research are included in the Investment category of NHEA and are developed primarily from information gathered by the National Institutes of Health and the National Science Foundation. The cost of commercial research (such as by drug companies) is assumed to be embedded in the price charged for the product and therefore is not included in the noncommercial research category.

Private health insurance spending for health care goods and services is derived using data from the U.S. Census Bureau, the American Medical Association (AMA), the American Hospital Association (AHA), and IMS Health, as well as household data from surveys such as the National Medical Care Expenditure Survey (National Center for Health Services Research, 1987) and later, MEPS (AHRQ, 1996–2015). The net cost of private health insurance (which includes administrative costs, additions to reserves, rate credits and dividends, premium taxes, and net underwriting gains or losses) is estimated using data from A.M. Best (Oldwick, NJ), the National Association of Insurance Commissioners, BLS surveys on the cost of employer-sponsored health insurance and consumer expenditures, MEPS data for self-insured plans, data from privately funded surveys, and numerous consulting firms and private health insurance trade organizations.

Estimates of federal health care program spending (e.g., Medicare, Medicaid, and Department of Defense) were developed using administrative records maintained by the servicing agencies. Out-of-pocket spending (direct spending by consumers for copayments, coinsurance, deductibles, and payments for goods and services not covered by insurance) was estimated using data from SAS (U.S. Census

Bureau), the Consumer Expenditure Survey (BLS), MEPS (AHRQ), the AHA Annual Survey, and IMS Health.

Issues Affecting Interpretation. Every 5 years, NHEA undergo a comprehensive revision that includes the incorporation of newly available source data, methodological and definitional changes, and benchmark estimates from the Economic Census. During these comprehensive revisions, the entire NHEA time series is opened for revision.

References

Martin AB, Hartman M, Benson J, Caitlin A, the National Health Expenditure Accounts Team. National health spending: Faster growth in 2015 as coverage expands and utilization increases. Health Aff (Millwood) 2017;36(1):166–76.

Centers for Medicare & Medicaid Services. National Health Expenditure Accounts: Methodology paper, 2015: Definitions, sources, and methods. Baltimore, MD: CMS; 2016. Available from: https://www.cms.gov/Research-Statistics-Data-and-Systems/Statistics-Trends-and-Reports/NationalHealthExpendData/downloads/dsm-15.pdf.

Centers for Medicare & Medicaid Services. Summary of 2014 comprehensive revision to National Health Expenditure Accounts. Baltimore, MD: CMS; 2015. Available from: https://www.cms.gov/Research-Statistics-Data-and-Systems/Statistics-Trends-and-Reports/NationalHealthExpendData/Downloads/benchmark2014.pdf.

For More Information. See the CMS National Health Expenditure Accounts website at: http://www.cms.gov/Research-Statistics-Data-and-Systems/Statistics-Trends-and-Reports/NationalHealthExpendData/NationalHealthAccountsHistorical.html.

National Health Interview Survey (NHIS)
NCHS

Overview. NHIS monitors the health of the U.S. population through the collection and analysis of data on a broad range of health topics. A major strength of this survey lies in the ability to analyze health measures by many demographic and socioeconomic characteristics. During household interviews, NHIS obtains information on activity limitation, illnesses, injuries, chronic conditions, health insurance coverage (or lack thereof), utilization of health care, and other health topics.

Coverage. The survey covers the civilian noninstitutionalized population of the United States. Among those excluded are patients in long-term care facilities, persons on active duty with the Armed Forces (although their dependents are included), incarcerated persons, and U.S. nationals living in foreign countries.

Methodology. NHIS is a cross-sectional household interview survey. Sampling and interviewing are continuous throughout each year. The sampling plan follows a multistage area probability design that permits the representative sampling of households. Traditionally, the sample for NHIS is redesigned and redrawn about every 10 years to better measure the changing U.S. population and to meet new survey objectives. A new sample design was implemented in the 2006 survey and will be used through the 2015 survey year. A new sample design will be used in 2016. The fundamental structure of the 2006 design is very similar to the previous design for the 1995–2005 surveys. Only the current sampling plan covering design years 2006–2015 is addressed here. The first stage of the current sampling plan consists of a sample of 428 primary sampling units (PSUs) drawn from approximately 1,900 geographically defined PSUs that cover the 50 states and D.C. A PSU consists of a county, a small group of contiguous counties, or a metropolitan statistical area.

Within a PSU, two types of second-stage units are used: area segments and permit segments. Area segments are defined geographically and contain an expected 8, 12, or 16 addresses. Permit segments cover housing units built after the 2000 census. The permit segments are defined using updated lists of building permits issued in the PSU since 2000 and contain an expected four addresses. Within each segment, all occupied households at the sample addresses are targeted for interview.

The total NHIS sample of PSUs is subdivided into four separate panels, or subdesigns, such that each panel is a representative sample of the U.S. population. This design feature has a number of advantages, including flexibility for the total sample size. The households selected for interview each week in NHIS are a probability sample representative of the target population.

Oversampling of the black and Hispanic populations was retained in the 2006–2015 design to allow for more precise estimation of health characteristics in these populations. The current sample design also oversamples the Asian population. In addition, the sample adult selection process was revised so that when black, Hispanic, or Asian persons aged 65 and over are present, they have an increased chance of being selected as the sample adult.

The current NHIS questionnaire, implemented in 1997, has two basic parts: a Basic Module or Core and one or more supplements that vary by year. The Core remains largely unchanged from year to year and allows for trend analysis and for data from more than one year to be pooled to increase the sample size for analytic purposes. The Core contains three components: the Family, the Sample Adult, and the Sample Child. The Family component collects information on everyone in the family. From each family in NHIS, one sample adult is randomly selected to participate in the Sample Adult questionnaire. For families with children under age 18, one sample child is randomly selected to participate in the Sample Child questionnaire. For children, information is provided by a knowledgeable family member aged 18 or over residing in the household. Because some health issues are different for children and adults, these two questionnaires differ in some items, but both collect basic information on health status, use of health care services, health conditions, and health behaviors.

Sample Size and Response Rate. The NHIS sample size varies from year to year. It may be reduced for budgetary reasons or may be augmented if supplementary funding is available. Between 1997 and 2005, the sample numbered about 100,000 persons annually, with about 30,000–36,000 persons participating in the Sample Adult and about 12,000–14,000 in the Sample Child questionnaires. In the 2006–2015 redesign, the NHIS sample was reduced by 13% compared with the 1995–2005 design. With four sample panels and no sample cuts or augmentations, the expected annual NHIS sample size (completed interviews) during survey years 2006–2010 was on average 37,000 households containing about 81,000 persons.

In 2011–2015, the NHIS sample size was augmented in 32 states and D.C. The main goal of the augmentation was to increase the number of states for which reliable state-level estimates can be made. In 2011, the sample size was augmented by approximately 13%; in 2012, by approximately 21%; in 2013, by approximately 18%; in 2014, by approximately 28%; and in 2015, by approximately 19%. In 2015, the sample numbered 103,789 persons, with 33,672 persons participating in the Sample Adult and 12,291 in the Sample Child questionnaires. In 2015 the total household response rate was 70%. The final response rate in 2015 was 55% for the Sample Adult file and 63% for the Sample Child file.

Issues Affecting Interpretation. In 1997, the questionnaire was redesigned: some basic concepts were changed, and other concepts were measured in different ways. For some questions there was a change in the reference period. Also in 1997, the collection methodology changed from paper-and-pencil questionnaires to computer-assisted personal interviewing (CAPI). Because of the major redesign of the questionnaire in 1997, most NHIS trend tables in *Health, United States* begin with 1997 data. Starting with *Health, United States, 2005*, estimates for 2000–2002 were revised to use 2000-based weights and differ from previous editions of *Health, United States* that used 1990-based weights for those data years. The weights available on the public-use NHIS files for 2000–2002 are 1990-based. Data for 2003–2011 use weights derived from the 2000 census. Data for 2012 and beyond use weights derived from the 2010 census. In 2006–2010, the sample size was reduced, and this is associated with slightly larger variance estimates than in other years when a larger sample was fielded. Starting in 2010, a geographic nonresponse adjustment was made to both the sample adult weight and the sample child weight. See Moriarity (2009).

References

Moriarity C. 2009 National Health Interview Survey sample adult and sample child nonresponse bias analysis. Hyattsville, MD: NCHS; 2010. Available from: http://www.cdc.gov/nchs/data/nhis/nr_bias_analysis_report_2009_NHIS.pdf.

Parsons VL, Moriarity C, Jonas K, et al. Design and estimation for the National Health Interview Survey, 2006–2015. NCHS. Vital Health Stat 2(165); 2014.

For More Information. See the NHIS website at: http://www.cdc.gov/nchs/nhis.htm.

National HIV Surveillance System

CDC/National Center for HIV/AIDS, Viral Hepatitis, STD, and TB Prevention (NCHHSTP)

Overview. Human immunodeficiency virus (HIV) surveillance data are used to detect and monitor cases of HIV infection in the United States, evaluate epidemiologic trends, identify unusual cases requiring follow-up, and inform public health efforts to prevent and control the disease. Data collected on persons diagnosed with HIV infection include age, sex, race, ethnicity, mode of exposure, and geographic region.

Coverage. All 50 states, D.C., and six U.S. dependent areas (American Samoa, Guam, Northern Mariana Islands, Puerto Rico, Republic of Palau, and the U.S. Virgin Islands) report confirmed diagnoses of HIV infection to CDC using a uniform surveillance case definition and case report form. As of April 2008, all reporting areas had implemented confidential, name-based HIV infection reporting and agreed to participate in CDC's National HIV Surveillance System. *Health, United States* only presents data for the 50 states and D.C.

Methodology. HIV surveillance includes case report data from 50 states, D.C., and six dependent areas. Using a standard confidential case report form, the health departments collect information that is then transmitted electronically, without personal identifiers, to CDC.

The 2015 HIV Surveillance Report marks the transition to presenting diagnosis, death, and prevalence data without statistical adjustments for delays in reporting of cases to CDC.

Because a substantial proportion of cases of HIV infection are reported to CDC without an identified risk factor, multiple imputation is used to assign a transmission category. Multiple imputation is a statistical approach in which each missing transmission category is replaced with a set of plausible values that represent the uncertainty about the true, but missing, value. The plausible values are analyzed by using standard procedures, and the results from these analyses are then combined to produce the final results. In tables displaying transmission categories, multiple imputation was used for adults and adolescents, but not for children (because the number of cases in children is small, missing transmission categories were not imputed). For more information, see Harrison KM, Kajese T, Hall HI, Song R. Risk factor redistribution of the national HIV/AIDS surveillance data: an alternative approach. Public Health Rep 2008;123(5):618–627; and see: Rubin DB. Multiple Imputation for Nonresponse in Surveys. New York: John Wiley & Sons Inc.; 1987.

Issues Affecting Interpretation. Although the completeness of reporting of cases of HIV infection to state and local health departments differs by geographic region and patient population, studies conducted by state and local health departments indicate that the reporting of cases of HIV infection in most areas of the United States is more than 80% complete.

Reference

CDC. HIV surveillance report. Atlanta, GA; [published annually]. Available from: http://www.cdc.gov/hiv/library/reports/hiv-surveillance.html.

For More Information. See the NCHHSTP website at: http://www.cdc.gov/nchhstp.

National Hospital Ambulatory Medical Care Survey (NHAMCS)

NCHS

Overview. NHAMCS provides national data on the provision and use of medical care services in hospital emergency and outpatient departments, using information collected from medical records. Data are collected on types of providers seen; reason for visit; diagnoses; drugs ordered, provided, or continued; and selected procedures and tests performed during the visit. Patient data include age, sex, race, and expected source of payment. Data are also collected on selected characteristics of the hospitals included in the survey.

Coverage. NHAMCS covers visits to emergency departments (EDs) and outpatient departments (OPDs) of nonfederal, short-stay, or general hospitals in the United States. Telephone contacts are excluded. Starting in 2009, the survey includes visits to hospital-based ambulatory surgery centers (ASCs). Starting in 2010, visits to freestanding ASCs are included in the survey.

Methodology. The four-stage probability sample design used in NHAMCS involves samples of (a) geographically defined primary sampling units (PSUs), (b) hospitals within PSUs, (c) clinics or emergency service areas within OPDs or EDs, and (d) patient visits within clinics or emergency service areas. EDs are treated as their own stratum, and all service areas within EDs are included. The first-stage sample of NHAMCS consists of 112 PSUs selected from 1,900 such units that make up the United States. Within PSUs, 600 general and short-stay hospitals were sampled and assigned to 1 of 16 panels. In any given year, 13 panels are included. Each panel is assigned to a 4-week reporting period during the survey year.

In the NHAMCS OPD, a clinic is defined as an administrative unit of the OPD in which ambulatory medical care is provided under the supervision of a physician. Clinics where only ancillary services (e.g., radiology, laboratory services, physical rehabilitation, renal dialysis, and pharmacy) are provided, or other settings in which physician services are not typically provided, are considered out of scope. If a hospital OPD has five or fewer in-scope clinics, all are included in the sample. If an OPD has more than five clinics, the clinics are assigned to one of six specialty groups: general medicine, surgery, pediatrics, obstetrics and gynecology, substance abuse, and other. Within these specialty groups, clinics are grouped into clinic sampling units (SUs). A clinic SU is generally one clinic, except when a clinic expects fewer than 30 visits. In that case, it is grouped with one or more other clinics to form a clinic SU. If the grouped SU is selected, all clinics included in that SU are included in the sample. Prior to 2001, generally a sample of five clinic SUs was selected per hospital, based on probability proportional to the total expected number of patient visits to the clinic during the assigned 4-week reporting period. Starting in 2001, clinic sampling within each hospital was stratified. If an OPD had more than five clinics, two clinic SUs were selected from each of the six specialty groups with a probability proportional to the total expected number of visits to the clinic. The change was made to ensure that at least two SUs were sampled from each of the specialty group strata.

The U.S. Census Bureau acts as the data collection agent for NHAMCS. Census field representatives contact sample hospitals to determine whether they have a 24-hour ED or an OPD that offers physician services. Visits to eligible EDs and OPDs are systematically sampled over the 4-week reporting period such that about 100 ED encounters and about 150–200 OPD encounters are selected. Hospital staff are asked to complete patient record forms (PRFs) for each sampled visit, but census field representatives typically abstract data for approximately two-thirds of these visits.

Sample data are weighted to produce national estimates. The estimation procedure used in NHAMCS has three basic components: inflation by the reciprocal of the probability of selection, adjustment for nonresponse, and population weighting ratio adjustment.

Sample Size and Response Rate. In any given year, the hospital sample consists of approximately 500 hospitals, of which 80% have EDs and about one-half have eligible OPDs. Typically, about 1,000 clinics are selected from participating hospital OPDs.

In 2011, the number of PRFs completed for EDs was 31,084 and for OPDs was 32,233, and the hospital response rate was 80% for EDs and 67% for OPDs. In 2012, the number of PRFs completed for EDs was 29,453 and the hospital response rate was 64% for EDs. In 2013, the number of PRFs completed for EDs was 24,777 and the hospital response rate was 66% for EDs. OPD data for years after 2011 are not currently available and at present there is no timeline for their release.

Issues Affecting Interpretation. The NHAMCS PRF is modified approximately every 2 to 4 years to reflect changes in physician practice characteristics, patterns of care, and technological innovations. Examples of recent changes include an increase in the number of drugs recorded on the PRF and adding checkboxes for specific tests or procedures performed.

Reference

McCaig LF, McLemore T. Plan and operation of the National Hospital Ambulatory Medical Care Survey. NCHS. Vital Health Stat 1994;1(34). Available from: http://www.cdc.gov/nchs/data/series/sr_01/sr01_034acc.pdf.

For More Information. See the National Health Care Surveys website at: http://www.cdc.gov/nchs/dhcs.htm and the Ambulatory Health Care Data website at: http://www.cdc.gov/nchs/ahcd.htm.

National Immunization Survey (NIS)

CDC/National Center for Immunization and Respiratory Diseases (NCIRD) and NCHS

Overview. NIS is a continuing nationwide telephone sample survey to monitor vaccination coverage rates among children aged 19–35 months and among teenagers (NIS–Teen) aged 13–17. Data collection for children aged 19–35 months started in 1994, and data collection for teenagers aged 13–17 started in 2006.

Coverage. Children aged 19–35 months and adolescents aged 13–17 in the civilian noninstitutionalized population are represented in this survey. Estimates of vaccine-specific coverage are available for the nation, the 50 states, and selected local areas and territories.

Methodology. NIS is a nationwide telephone sample survey of households with age-eligible children. The survey uses a two-phase sample design. First, a random-digit-dialing sample of telephone numbers is drawn. When households with at least one age-eligible child are contacted, the interviewer collects demographic and access-related information on all age-eligible children, the mother, and the household and obtains permission to contact the children's vaccination providers. Second, identified providers are sent vaccination history questionnaires by mail. Final weighted estimates are adjusted for households without telephones and for nonresponse. All vaccination coverage estimates are based on provider-reported vaccination histories. NIS–Teen followed the same sample design and data collection procedures as NIS except that only one age-eligible adolescent was selected from each screened household for data collection.

Starting in 2011, the NIS sampling frame was expanded from a single-landline frame to dual-landline and cellular telephone sampling frames. This change increased the representativeness of the sample characteristics but had little effect on the final 2011 NIS and NIS–Teen national estimates of vaccination coverage overall and when stratified by poverty status. See details of the dual-frame sample design in the annual NIS Data User's Guide on the NIS website. Available from: https://www.cdc.gov/vaccines/imz-managers/nis/datasets.html.

Sample Size and Response Rate. In 2015, the overall Council of American Survey Research Organizations (CASRO) response rate for NIS was 34.9%. Response rates for the landline and cellular telephone samples were 59.2% and 32.2%, respectively. Of the 4,522 age-eligible children with completed household interviews from the landline sample, 2,700 (59.7%) had adequate provider data. From the cellular telephone sample, 12,467 (55.5%) of the 22,453 eligible children with completed household interviews had adequate provider data.

The overall CASRO response rate for the 2015 NIS–Teen was 33.0%. Response rates for the landline and cellular telephone samples were 56.4% and 29.8%, respectively. Of the 8,961 age-eligible adolescents with completed household interviews from the landline sample, 4,784 (53.4%) had adequate provider data. From the cellular telephone sample, 17,091 (48.9%) of the 34,965 eligible adolescents with completed household interviews had adequate provider data.

Issues Affecting Interpretation. Starting with *Health, United States, 2015*, estimates are from the NIS website and may differ slightly from estimates published previously in *Morbidity and Mortality Weekly Report* (MMWR) articles.

The findings in recent years are subject to several limitations. Data year 2011 was the first year that NIS and NIS–Teen used a dual-frame sampling scheme that included landline and cellular telephone households. Estimates from 2011 and subsequent years might not be comparable with those from prior to 2011, when surveys were conducted via landline telephone only. NIS is a telephone survey, and statistical adjustments might not compensate fully for nonresponse and for households without landline telephones prior to 2011. Underestimates of vaccination coverage might have resulted in exclusive use of provider-reported vaccination histories because completeness of records is unknown. Finally, although national coverage estimates are precise, annual estimates and trends for state and local areas should be interpreted with caution because of smaller sample sizes and wider confidence intervals.

Before January 2009, NIS did not distinguish between Hib vaccine production types; therefore, children who received three doses of a vaccine product that requires four doses were misclassified as fully vaccinated. For more information, see "Changes in measurement of *Haemophilus influenzae* serotype b (Hib) vaccination coverage—National Immunization Survey, United States, 2009. MMWR 2010;59:1069–72."

Starting in 2014, NIS–Teen defined an adolescent's vaccination record as having adequate provider data if that adolescent had vaccination history data from one or more of the named vaccination providers, or if the parent reported that the adolescent was completely unvaccinated. Prior to 2014, the adequate provider data definition had more criteria, and it was based on a comparison of provider report of vaccination history with parental report of vaccination history, either by shot card report or recall.

To assess the effect of the change in the adequate provider definition criteria on vaccination coverage estimates, NIS recomputed estimates from the 2006–2013 survey. In general, 2013 NIS–Teen vaccination coverage estimates using the revised adequate provider data definition were different, and generally lower, than original 2013 NIS–Teen estimates. Differences between revised and original 2013 national vaccination estimates ranged from –0.1 percentage point to –2.2 percentage points. For more information on the revised adequate provider data criteria, see: http://www.cdc.gov/vaccines/imz-managers/coverage/nis/teen/apd-report.html, and for revised 2013 estimates based on the 2014 criteria, see: CDC. National, regional, state, and selected local area vaccination coverage among adolescents aged 13–17 years—United States, 2014. MMWR 2015;64(29):784-92. Available from: http://www.cdc.gov/mmwr/preview/mmwrhtml/mm6429a3.htm. Because of the revision in the adequate provider definition, NIS–Teen vaccination coverage estimates for 2013 and beyond cannot be directly compared with previously published 2006–2013 NIS–Teen survey vaccination coverage estimates based on the previous adequate provider definition.

References

CDC. Vaccination coverage among children aged 19–35 months—United States, 2015. MMWR 2016;65(39):1065–71. Available from: http://www.cdc.gov/mmwr/volumes/65/wr/pdfs/mm6539a4.pdf.

CDC. National, regional, state, and selected local area vaccination coverage among adolescents aged 13–17 years—United States, 2015. MMWR 2016;65(33):850–58. Available from: http://www.cdc.gov/mmwr/volumes/65/wr/pdfs/mm6533a4.pdf.

Smith PJ, Hoaglin DC, Battaglia MP, et al. Statistical methodology of the National Immunization Survey, 1994–2002. NCHS. Vital Health Stat 2005;2(138). Available from: http://www.cdc.gov/nchs/data/series/sr_02/sr02_138.pdf.

CDC. Announcement: Addition of households with only cellular telephone service to the National Immunization Survey, 2011. Available from: http://www.cdc.gov/mmwr/preview/mmwrhtml/mm6134a5.htm?s_cid=mm6134a5_e%0d%0a.

CDC. Changes in measurement of *Haemophilus influenzae* serotype b (Hib) vaccination coverage—National Immunization Survey, United States, 2009. MMWR 2010;59(33):1069–72. Available from: http://www.cdc.gov/mmwr/preview/mmwrhtml/mm5933a3.htm?s_cid=mm5933a3_e%0d%0a.

For More Information. See the NIS website at: http://www.cdc.gov/vaccines/nis.

National Income and Product Accounts (NIPA)

Bureau of Economic Analysis (BEA)

Overview. NIPA are a set of economic accounts that provide detailed measures of the value and composition of national output and the incomes generated in the production of that output. Essentially, NIPA provide a detailed snapshot of the myriad transactions that make up the economy—buying and selling goods and services, hiring of labor, investing, renting property, paying taxes, and the like. NIPA estimates show U.S. production, distribution, consumption, investment, and saving.

The best-known NIPA measure is the gross domestic product (GDP), which is defined as the market value of the goods and services produced by labor and property located in the United States. NIPA calculate GDP as the sum of familiar final expenditure components: personal consumption expenditures, private investment, government spending (consumption and investment), and net exports. However, GDP is just one of many economic measures presented in NIPA. Another key NIPA indicator presented in *Health, United States* is the implicit price deflator for GDP.

The conceptual framework of NIPA is illustrated by seven summary accounts: the domestic income and product account, the private enterprise income account, the personal income and outlay account, the government receipts and expenditures account, the foreign transactions current account, the domestic capital account, and the foreign transactions capital account. These summary accounts record a use (or expenditure) in one account for one sector and a corresponding source (or receipt) in an account of another sector or of the same sector. This integrated system provides a comprehensive measure of economic activity in a consistently defined framework without double counting.

Coverage. Source data for NIPA domestic estimates cover all 50 states and the D.C. The U.S. national income and product statistics were first presented as part of a complete and consistent double-entry accounting system in the summer of 1947.

Methodology. NIPA estimates are revised on a quarterly, annual, and quinquennial basis. For GDP and most other NIPA series, a set of three current quarterly estimates is released each year. Quarterly estimates provide the first look at the path of U.S. economic activity. Annual revisions of NIPA are usually carried out each summer. These revisions incorporate source data that are based on more extensive annual surveys, on annual data from other sources, and on later revisions to the monthly and quarterly source data, and they generally cover the three previous calendar years. Comprehensive revisions are carried out at about 5-year intervals and may result in revisions that extend back many years. These estimates incorporate all of the best available source data, such as data from the quinquennial U.S. Economic Census.

NIPA measures are built up from a wide range of source data using a variety of estimating methods. To ensure consistency and accuracy, NIPA use various adjustment and estimation techniques to estimate data. Three general types of adjustments are made to the source data that are incorporated into the NIPA estimates. The first consists of adjustments that are needed so that the data conform to appropriate NIPA concepts and definitions. The second type of adjustment involves filling gaps in coverage. The third type of adjustment involves time of recording and valuation. Source data must occasionally be adjusted to account for special circumstances that affect the accuracy of the data. For example, quarterly and monthly NIPA estimates are seasonally adjusted at the detailed-series level when the series demonstrate statistically significant seasonal patterns. Source data may also be used as indicators to extrapolate annual estimates. For more information, see "An introduction to the National Income and Product Accounts methodology papers: U.S. National Income and Product Accounts," available from: http://www.bea.gov/scb/pdf/national/nipa/methpap/mpi1_0907.pdf; and "Concepts and methods of the U.S. National Income and Product Accounts," available from: http://www.bea.gov/national/pdf/NIPAhandbookch1-4.pdf.

Issues Affecting Interpretation. NIPA source data and estimates are revised frequently. Data are released at different times, estimates are updated as they become available, new concepts and definitions are incorporated, and source data may change due to improvements in collection and new methodologies. As a result, major estimates such as GDP and its major components undergo frequent revision, and historical data are changed. For more information, see the BEA (NIPA) website at: http://www.bea.gov/scb/pdf/2013/03%20March/0313_nipa_comprehensive_revision_preview.pdf.

Reference

U.S. Bureau of Economic Analysis. A guide to the National Income and Product Accounts of the United States. Washington, D.C.: BEA; 2006. Available from: http://www.bea.gov/national/pdf/nipaguid.pdf.

For More Information. See the BEA (NIPA) website at: http://www.bea.gov/national/index.htm.

National Medical Expenditure Survey (NMES)—See Appendix I, Medical Expenditure Panel Survey (MEPS).

National Notifiable Diseases Surveillance System (NNDSS)

CDC

Overview. The CDC National Notifiable Diseases Surveillance System (NNDSS) is a nationwide collaboration that enables all levels of public health (local, state, territorial, federal, and international) to share health information to monitor, control, and prevent the occurrence and spread of state-reportable and nationally notifiable infectious and some noninfectious diseases and conditions. NNDSS is a multifaceted program that includes the surveillance system for collection, analysis, and sharing of health data, resources, and information about policies and standards, at the local, state, and national levels. NNDSS provides weekly provisional and annual finalized information on the occurrence of diseases defined as notifiable by the Council of State and Territorial Epidemiologists (CSTE). Data include incidence of reportable diseases, which are nationally notifiable using uniform surveillance case definitions.

Coverage. Notifiable disease reports are received from health departments in the 50 states, five territories, D.C., and New York City. Policies for reporting notifiable disease cases can vary by disease or reporting jurisdiction, depending on case status classification (i.e., confirmed, probable, or suspect).

Methodology. CDC, in partnership with CSTE, administers NNDSS. Reportable disease surveillance is conducted by public health practitioners at local, state, and national levels to support disease prevention and control. Data on a subset of reportable conditions that have been designated nationally notifiable are then submitted to CDC without personal identifiers. The system also provides annual summaries of the finalized data. CSTE and CDC annually review the status of national infectious disease surveillance and recommend additions or deletions to the list of nationally notifiable diseases, based on the need to respond to emerging priorities. For example, Q fever and tularemia became nationally notifiable in 2000. However, reporting nationally notifiable diseases to CDC is voluntary. Because reporting is currently mandated by law or regulation only at the local and state levels, the list of diseases that are considered reportable varies by state. For example, reporting of cyclosporiasis to CDC is not done by some states in which this disease is not reportable to local or state authorities.

State epidemiologists report cases of nationally notifiable diseases to CDC, which tabulates and publishes these data in Morbidity and Mortality Weekly Report (MMWR) and in Summary of Notifiable Diseases, United States (before 1985, titled Annual Summary).

Issues Affecting Interpretation. NNDSS data must be interpreted in light of reporting practices. Some diseases that cause severe clinical illness (for example, plague and rabies) are likely reported accurately if diagnosed by a clinician. However, persons who have diseases that are clinically mild and infrequently associated with serious consequences (e.g., salmonellosis) may not seek medical care from a health care provider. Even if these less severe diseases are diagnosed, they are less likely to be reported.

The degree of completeness of data reporting is also influenced by the diagnostic facilities available, the control measures in effect, public awareness of a specific disease, and the interests, resources, and priorities of state and local officials responsible for disease control and public health surveillance. Finally, factors such as changes in case definitions for public health surveillance, introduction of new diagnostic tests, or discovery of new disease entities can cause changes in disease reporting that are independent of the true incidence of disease.

Reference

CDC. Summary of notifiable diseases—United States, 2014. MMWR 2016;63(54):1–152. Available from: http://www.cdc.gov/mmwr/mmwr_nd/index.html.

For More Information. See the NNDSS website at: http://wwwn.cdc.gov/nndss/.

National Nursing Home Survey (NNHS)

NCHS

Overview. NNHS collected data from a nationally representative sample of nursing homes and provided national estimates on the characteristics of nursing homes and their residents and staff. Data about the facilities include characteristics such as bed size, ownership, Medicare/Medicaid certification, services offered, staff characteristics, expenses, and charges. Data about the current residents and discharges include demographic characteristics, health status, services received, and sources of payment.

Coverage. The initial NNHS, conducted in 1973–1974, included the universe of nursing homes that provided some level of nursing care and excluded homes providing only personal or domiciliary care. The 1977 NNHS encompassed all types of nursing homes, including personal care and domiciliary care homes. The 1985, 1995, 1997, 1999, and 2004 NNHS included only nursing homes that provided some level of nursing care and excluded homes providing only personal or domiciliary care, similar to the 1973–1974 survey.

Methodology. The survey used a stratified two-stage probability design. The first stage was the selection of facilities, and the second stage was the selection of residents and discharges. Prior to the 2004 NNHS, up to six current residents and/or six discharges were selected for each facility. The 2004 survey was designed to select only current residents, 12 from each facility, to participate in the survey. Information on the facility was collected through a personal interview with the administrator or with staff designated by the administrator. Resident data were provided by staff familiar with the care provided to the resident. Staff relied on the medical record and personal knowledge of the resident. Both live and deceased discharges were included. Residents were counted more than once if they were discharged more than once during the reference period. Resident rates are calculated using estimates of the civilian population of the United States, including institutionalized persons.

Sample Size and Response Rates. In 1973–1974, the sample of 2,118 homes was selected from nursing homes open for business in 1972. The 1977 NNHS sampled 1,698 homes. The sample for the 1985 survey consisted of 1,220 facilities. The 1995 sample was 1,500 nursing homes. For the 1997 survey, data were obtained from 1,488 nursing homes. The 1999 sample consisted of 1,496 nursing homes. In 1995, 1997, and 1999, facility-level response rates were over 93%. For the final NNHS in 2004, 1,500 nursing homes were selected and a facility response rate of 81% was achieved.

Issues Affecting Interpretation. Samples of discharges and residents contain different populations with different characteristics. The resident sample is more likely to contain long-term nursing home residents and, conversely, to underestimate short nursing home stays. Because short-term residents are less likely to be on the nursing home rolls on a given night, they are less likely to be sampled. Estimates of discharges underestimate long nursing home stays. The last NNHS was conducted in 2004; nursing home data is now available from the National Study of Long-Term Care Providers (NSLTCP).

References

Van Nostrand JF, Zappolo A, Hing E, Bloom B, Hirsch B, Foley DJ. The National Nursing Home Survey: 1977 summary for the United States. Vital Health Stat 13(43). Hyattsville, MD: NCHS; 1979. Available from: http://www.cdc.gov/nchs/data/series/sr_13/sr13_043.pdf.

Hing E, Sekscenski E, Strahan G. The National Nursing Home Survey: 1985 summary for the United States. Vital Health Stat 13(97). Hyattsville, MD: NCHS; 1989. Available from: http://www.cdc.gov/nchs/data/series/sr_13/sr13_097.pdf.

Strahan GW. An overview of nursing homes and their current residents: Data from the 1995 National Nursing Home Survey. Advance data from vital and health statistics; no 280. Hyattsville, MD: NCHS; 1997. Available from: http://www.cdc.gov/nchs/data/ad/ad280.pdf.

Jones AL, Dwyer LL, Bercovitz AR, Strahan GW. The National Nursing Home Survey: 2004 overview. Vital Health Stat 13(167). Hyattsville, MD: NCHS; 2009. Available from: http://www.cdc.gov/nchs/data/series/sr_13/sr13_167.pdf.

For More Information. See the NNHS website at: http://www.cdc.gov/nchs/nnhs.htm.

National Study of Long-Term Care Providers (NSLTCP)

NCHS

Overview. NSLTCP is a biennial study to monitor the major sectors of paid, regulated long-term care services. NSLTCP uses administrative data from the Centers for Medicare & Medicaid Services (CMS) about the home health, nursing home, and hospice sectors and collects survey data on the residential care community and adult day services sectors. Information includes the supply, organizational characteristics, staffing, and services offered by providers of long-term care services and the demographic, health, and functional status of users of these services. NSLTCP replaces NCHS' periodic National Nursing Home Survey and National Home and Hospice Care Survey, and the one-time National Survey of Residential Care Facilities.

Coverage. The initial NSLTCP, conducted in 2012, included providers that were licensed, registered, listed, certified, or otherwise regulated by the federal or state governments.

Methodology. Data on adult day services centers and residential care communities were obtained through surveys. Information on nursing homes, home health agencies, or hospices was obtained from CMS administrative records.

Survey data were collected through three modes: self-administered, hard copy mail questionnaires; self-administered web questionnaires; and computer-assisted telephone interview (CATI) interviews. To the extent possible, the questionnaires included topics comparable across all five LTC sectors, as well as topics specific to the particular sector.

The sampling frame from the National Adult Day Services Association (NADSA) contained 5,678 self-identified adult day services centers; duplicates were removed from the frame, leaving 5,443 centers. Centers were eligible if they: 1) were licensed or certified by the state or Medicaid; 2) had average daily attendance of at least one participant based on a typical week; and 3) had at least one participant enrolled at the center at the time of the survey.

Data from residential care communities included a mix of sampled communities from states that had enough residential care communities to produce reliable state estimates and a census of residential care communities in states that did not have enough communities to produce reliable state estimates. The sampling frame of 40,583 residential care communities was constructed from lists of licensed residential care communities obtained from the state licensing agencies in each of the 50 states and the District of Columbia. Sampling weights were used only for residential care communities where a sample was drawn. To be eligible for the survey, residential communities had to be state-licensed with four or more licensed beds; provide room and board of at least two meals a day, around-the-clock supervision, and offer assistance with personal care (like dressing) or health-related services (such as medication management); have at least one resident; and serve primarily an adult population.

Every nursing home, home health agency, or hospice in the United States that was certified to provide services under Medicare, Medicaid, or both, and had user data, was included in the data. Facility data was obtained from the CMS' administrative records in Certification and Survey Provider Enhanced Reporting ([CASPER], formerly known as Online Survey Certification and Reporting); the third quarter file of the data year was used. User data were obtained from the assessment and beneficiary files that CMS has for each of the three provider types and aggregated to the provider level.

Sample Size and Response Rates. Every certified nursing home, home health agency, and hospice with user information, and all users during the data time frame, was included. Of the 4,751 in-scope and presumed in-scope adult day services centers in 2014, 2,763 completed the questionnaire, for a response rate of 58.0%. Although a census of all adult day services centers was attempted, estimates were subject to variability due to the amount of nonresponse; this variability associated with the nonresponse was treated as if it were from a stratified (by state) sample without replacement. From 40,583 residential communities in the sampling frame, 11,618 residential care communities were sampled of which 10,415 were deemed eligible; 5,380 communities could not be contacted by the end of data collection. This yielded a weighted response rate of 49.6%.

Issues Affecting Interpretation. The estimates for adult day services center participants, nursing home residents, and residential care community residents are for current service users on any given day, rather than all users in a year. The estimate for home health patients includes only those who ended care in the prior year (discharges). The same person may be included in this sum more than once, if a person received care in more than one sector in a similar time period (e.g., a residential care resident receiving care from a home health agency). While every effort was made to match question wording in the NSLTCP surveys to the administrative data available through CMS, some differences remained and may affect comparisons between these two data sources. For example, because not all LTC providers are residential, information on capacity is not comparable across provider types. In addition, different data sources used different reference periods. For instance, user-level data used for home health agencies and hospices were from patients who received home health or hospice care services at any time in calendar year prior to the survey. In contrast, survey data on residential care community residents and adult day services center participants, and CMS data on nursing home residents, were from current users on any given day or active residents on the last day of the third quarter of the data year.

References

Harris-Kojetin L, Sengupta M, Park-Lee E, Valverde R, Caffrey C, Rome V, Lendon J. Long-term care providers and services users in the United States: Data from the National Study of Long-Term Care Providers, 2013–2014. National Center for Health Statistics. Vital Health Stat 3(38). 2016. Available from: http://www.cdc.gov/nchs/data/series/sr_03/sr03_038.pdf.

Harris-Kojetin L, Sengupta M, Park-Lee E, Valverde R. Long-term care services in the United States: 2013 overview. National Center for Health Statistics. Vital Health Stat 3(37). 2013. Available from: http://www.cdc.gov/nchs/data/series/sr_03/sr03_037.pdf.

Sengupta M, Valverde R, Lendon JP, Rome V, Caffrey C, Harris-Kojetin L. Long-term care providers and services users in the United States—State estimates supplement: National Study of Long-Term Care Providers, 2013– 2014. Hyattsville, MD: National Center for Health Statistics. 2016. Available from: http://www.cdc.gov/nchs/data/nsltcp/2014_nsltcp_state_tables.pdf.

For More Information. See the NSLTCP website at: http://www.cdc.gov/nchs/nsltcp/index.htm.

National Survey of Family Growth (NSFG)

NCHS

Overview. NSFG gathers information on family life, marriage and divorce, pregnancy, infertility, use of contraception, and men's and women's health. NSFG provides national data on factors affecting birth and pregnancy rates, adoption, and maternal and infant health. Data collected include sexual activity, marriage, divorce and remarriage, unmarried cohabitation, forced sexual intercourse, contraception and sterilization, infertility, breastfeeding, pregnancy loss, low birthweight, and use of medical care for family planning and infertility.

Coverage. Prior to the 2002 NSFG, the survey population of NSFG included women aged 15–44 in the household population of the United States (50 states and D.C.). Starting with the 2002 NSFG, the survey population additionally included men aged 15–44 in the household population. Excluded from the survey population were those living in institutions—such as prisons and long-term psychiatric hospitals—or on military bases.

Methodology. The NSFG moved from a periodically conducted survey—conducted six times from 1973 to 2002—to a continuous survey design in 2006. NSFG data are currently based on a multi-stage probability-based, nationally representative sample of the household population aged 15–44. Black and Hispanic adults, as well as all 15- to 19-year-olds are oversampled. Interviews are administered in person by trained female interviewers using a laptop or notebook computer with computer-assisted personal interviewing (CAPI) or audio computer-assisted self-interview (ACASI) programs.

To produce national estimates from the sample for the millions of women aged 15–44 in the United States, data for the interviewed sample women were (a) inflated by the reciprocal of the probability of selection at each stage of sampling (for example, if there was a 1 in 5,000 chance that a woman would be selected for the sample, her sampling weight was 5,000); (b) adjusted for nonresponse; and (c) poststratified, or aligned with benchmark population sizes based on data from the U.S. Census Bureau.

For more information on the methodology for prior NSFG surveys, see: https://www.cdc.gov/nchs/nsfg/nsfg_products.htm.

Sample Size and Response Rate. For the 2011–2013 and 2013–2015 NSFG surveys, the sample size for women respondents was 5,601 and 5,699, respectively. The response rate for women respondents was 73% for the 2011–2013 NSFG and 71% for the 2013–2015 NSFG. Sample sizes and response rates for respondents have varied across survey years. For more information on sample size and response rates for past surveys, see the 2013–2015 NSFG User's Guide at: https://www.cdc.gov/nchs/data/nsfg/nsfg_2013_2015_userguide_maintext.pdf.

References

Public Use Data File Documentation: 2011–2013 National Survey of Family Growth User's Guide. Hyattsville, MD: NCHS; 2014. Available from: https://www.cdc.gov/nchs/data/nsfg/nsfg_2011-2013_userguide_maintext.pdf.

Public Use Data File Documentation: 2013–2015 National Survey of Family Growth User's Guide. Hyattsville, MD: NCHS; 2016. Available from: https://www.cdc.gov/nchs/data/nsfg/nsfg_2013_2015_userguide_maintext.pdf.

For More Information. See the NSFG website at: http://www.cdc.gov/nchs/nsfg.htm.

National Survey on Drug Use & Health (NSDUH)

Substance Abuse and Mental Health Services Administration (SAMHSA)

Overview. NSDUH reports on the prevalence, incidence, and patterns of drug and alcohol use and abuse in the general U.S. civilian noninstitutionalized population aged 12 and over. NSDUH also reports on substance use disorders, substance use treatment, health care, mental disorders, and mental health service utilization.

Coverage. NSDUH is representative of persons aged 12 and over in the civilian noninstitutionalized population of the United States, and in each state and D.C.
The survey covers residents of households (including those living in houses, townhouses, apartments, and condominiums), persons in noninstitutional group quarters (including those in shelters, boarding houses, college dormitories, migratory work camps, and halfway houses), and civilians living on military bases. Persons excluded from the survey include people experiencing homelessness who do not use shelters, active military personnel, and residents of institutional group quarters such as jails and hospitals.

Methodology. The data collection method is in-person interviews conducted with a sample of individuals at their place of residence. Computer-assisted interviewing (CAI) methods, including audio computer-assisted self-interviewing (ACASI), are used to provide a private and confidential setting to complete the interview.

NSDUH uses a 50-state (and D.C.) sample design that is revised periodically. In 2014, NSDUH introduced an independent multistage area probability sample within each state and D.C. States are the first level of stratification. Each state was stratified into approximately equally populated state sampling regions (SSRs), and then census tracts within each SSR were selected, census block groups within census tracts, and area segments (i.e., a collection of census blocks) within census block groups. Finally, dwelling units (DUs) were selected within segments, and within each selected DU, up to two residents who were at least 12 years old were selected for the interview.

In addition, in 2014, changes were made in the sample sizes allocated to each state and to different age groups, in order to increase the precision of national and many state estimates as well as estimates for older adults. In particular, samples sizes were increased in the 12 most populous states. States with sample increases will have more precise estimates than in previous years, whereas states with smaller sample sizes will have some reductions in precision. However, all states will still have reasonable levels of precision. This allocation of sample to states is also thought to be more cost-efficient. Starting in 2014, the sample size was redistributed by age group so that 25% of the sample is allocated to those aged 12–17, 25% to those aged 18–25, and 50% to those aged 26 or older. Although the sample sizes for age groups 12–17 and 18–25 were reduced, these two groups are still considered to be oversampled since they represent approximately 10% and 13% of the total population, respectively.

Sample Size and Response Rate. Nationally, 132,210 household addresses were successfully screened for the 2015 survey, conducted from January to December 2015. In 2015, screening was completed at 132,210 addresses, and 68,073 completed interviews were obtained, including 16,955 interviews from adolescents aged 12–17 and 51,118 interviews from adults aged 18 or over. Weighted response rates were 79.7% for household screening and 69.3% for interviewing.

Issues Affecting Interpretation. Several improvements to the NSDUH were implemented in 2002. The data collected in 2002 represent a new baseline for tracking trends in substance use and other measures. Special questions on methamphetamine were added in 2005 and 2006. Data for years prior to 2007 were adjusted for comparability. Starting with 2011 data, 2010-census based control totals were used in the weighting process. Analysis weights in the 2002 through 2010 NSDUHs were derived from the 2000 census data. This reweighting to the 2010 census data could affect

comparisons between estimates for 2011 and subsequent years and those from prior years. However, an analysis of the impact of reweighting showed that the percentages of substance users were largely unaffected. For more information, see: http://www.samhsa.gov/data/NSDUH/NSDUHCensusEffects/Index.aspx.

The NSDUH questionnaire underwent a partial redesign in 2015 to improve the quality of NSDUH data and to address the changing needs of policymakers and researchers with regard to substance use and mental health issues. Due to the changes, only 2015 data are presented for certain estimates until comparability with prior years can be established. Trends continue to be presented for estimates that are assumed to have remained comparable with those in earlier years. For more information, see: https://www.samhsa.gov/data/sites/default/files/NSDUH-TrendBreak-2015.pdf.

Estimates of substance use for youth based on NSDUH are not directly comparable with estimates based on the Monitoring the Future (MTF) Study and the Youth Risk Behavior Survey (YRBS). In addition to the fact that MTF excludes dropouts and absentees, rates are not directly comparable across these surveys because of differences in the populations covered, sample design, questionnaires, and interview setting. NSDUH collects data in residences, whereas MTF and YRBS collect data in school classrooms. Further, NSDUH estimates are tabulated by age, whereas MTF and YRBS estimates are tabulated by grade, representing different ages as well as different populations.

References

Substance Abuse and Mental Health Services Administration. 2014 National Survey on Drug Use and Health: Methodological summary and definitions. Rockville, MD: SAMHSA; 2015. Available from: http://www.samhsa.gov/data/sites/default/files/NSDUH-MethodSummDefs2014/NSDUH-MethodSummDefs2014.pdf.

Substance Abuse and Mental Health Services Administration. Results from the 2014 National Survey on Drug Use and Health: Detailed tables. Rockville, MD: SAMHSA; 2015. Available from: http://www.samhsa.gov/data/sites/default/files/NSDUH-DetTabs2014/NSDUH-DetTabs2014.htm.

Substance Abuse and Mental Health Services Administration. Key substance use and mental health indicators in the United States: Results from the 2015 National Survey on Drug Use and Health. Rockville, MD: SAMHSA; 2016. Available from: https://www.samhsa.gov/data/sites/default/files/NSDUH-FFR1-2015/NSDUH-FFR1-2015/NSDUH-FFR1-2015.pdf.

Substance Abuse and Mental Health Services Administration. Results from the 2015 National Survey on Drug Use and Health: Detailed tables. Rockville, MD: SAMHSA; 2016. Available from: https://www.samhsa.gov/data/sites/default/files/NSDUH-DetTabs-2015/NSDUH-DetTabs-2015/NSDUH-DetTabs-2015.htm.

For More Information. See the NSDUH website at: http://www.samhsa.gov/data/population-data-nsduh and the Center for Behavioral Health Statistics and Quality (the data collection agency) website at: http://www.samhsa.gov/about-us/who-we-are/offices-centers/cbhsq.

National Vital Statistics System (NVSS)

NCHS

Overview. NVSS collects and publishes official national statistics on births, deaths, fetal deaths, and, prior to 1996, marriages and divorces occurring in the United States, based on U.S. Standard Certificates. Fetal deaths are classified and tabulated separately from other deaths. The vital statistics files—Birth, Fetal Death, Mortality Multiple Cause-of-Death, Linked Birth/Infant Death, and Compressed Mortality—are described in detail below.

Coverage. NVSS collects and presents U.S. resident data for the aggregate of 50 states, New York City, and D.C., as well as for each individual state, D.C., and the U.S. dependent areas of Puerto Rico, Virgin Islands, Guam, American Samoa, and Northern Marianas. Vital events occurring in the United States to non-U.S. residents and vital events occurring abroad to U.S. residents are excluded. Starting with *Health, United States, 2013*, information on vital events for Puerto Rico, Virgin Islands, Guam, American Samoa, and Northern Marianas is shown in selected state tables but is not included in U.S. totals.

Methodology. NCHS' Division of Vital Statistics obtains information on births and deaths from the registration offices of each of the 50 states, New York City, D.C., Puerto Rico, Virgin Islands, Guam, American Samoa, and Northern Marianas. Until 1972, microfilm copies of all death certificates and a 50% sample of birth certificates were received from all registration areas and processed by NCHS. In 1972, some states began sending their data to NCHS through the Cooperative Health Statistics System (CHSS). States that participated in the CHSS program processed 100% of their death and birth records and sent the entire data file to NCHS on computer tapes. Currently, data are sent to NCHS through the Vital Statistics Cooperative Program (VSCP) following procedures similar to those under CHSS. The number of participating states grew from 6 in 1972 to 46 in 1984. Starting in 1985, all 50 states and D.C. participated in VSCP.

U.S. Standard Certificates. U.S. Standard Certificates of Live Birth and Death and Fetal Death Reports are revised periodically, allowing evaluation and addition, modification, and deletion of items. Beginning with 1989,

revised Standard Certificates replaced the 1978 versions. The 1989 revision of the birth certificate included items to identify the Hispanic parentage of newborns and to expand information about maternal and infant health characteristics. The 1989 revision of the death certificate included items on educational attainment and Hispanic origin of decedents, as well as changes to improve the medical certification of cause of death. Standard Certificates recommended by NCHS are modified in each registration area to serve the area's needs. However, most certificates conform closely in content and arrangement to the Standard Certificate, and all certificates contain a minimum data set specified by NCHS. The 2003 revision of vital records went into effect in some states and territories beginning in 2003, but full implementation in all states and territories will be phased in over several years. The 2003 revision of the birth certificate included changes in ascertainment of education level, prenatal care, and tobacco use during pregnancy. The 2003 revision of the death certificate included changes in the ascertainment of multiple races, education level, tobacco use, and maternal mortality.

Birth File

Overview. Vital statistics natality data are a fundamental source of demographic, geographic, and medical and health information on all births occurring in the United States. This is one of the few sources of comparable health-related data for small geographic areas over an extended time period. The data are used to present the characteristics of babies and their mothers, track trends such as birth rates for teenagers, and compare natality trends with those in other countries.

The Birth file includes characteristics of the baby, such as sex, birthweight, and weeks of gestation; demographic information about the parents, such as age, race, Hispanic origin, parity, educational attainment, marital status, and state of residence; medical and health information, such as prenatal care, based on hospital records; and behavioral risk factors for the birth, such as mother's tobacco use during pregnancy.

Coverage. Birth data presented in *Health, United States* are based on reporting from all 50 states and D.C. Data for Puerto Rico, Virgin Islands, Guam, American Samoa, and Northern Marianas are shown in selected state tables but are not included in U.S. totals. Beginning with 1970, births to nonresidents of the United States are excluded.

Methodology. In the United States, state laws require birth certificates to be completed for all births. The registration of births is the responsibility of the professional attendant at birth, generally a physician or midwife. The birth certificate must be filed with the local registrar of the district in which the birth occurs. Each birth must be reported promptly; the reporting requirements vary from state to state, ranging from 24 hours to as much as 10 days after the birth.

Federal law mandates national collection and publication of birth and other vital statistics data. NVSS is the result of cooperation between NCHS and the states to provide access to statistical information from birth certificates. Standard forms for the collection of the data, and model procedures for the uniform registration of the events, are developed and recommended for state use through cooperative activities of the states and NCHS. NCHS shares the costs incurred by the states in providing vital statistics data for national use.

Issues Affecting Interpretation. Two-thirds (66%) of all births in 2009, 76% in 2010, 83% in 2011, 86% in 2012, 90% in 2013, 96% in 2014, and 97% in 2015 were reported using the 2003 revision of the U.S. Standard Certificate of Live Birth. Interpretation of trend data should take into consideration changes to reporting areas. For methodological and reporting area changes for the following birth certificate items, see Appendix II, Age; Hispanic origin; Marital status; Race.

Reference

> Martin JA, Hamilton BE, Osterman MJK, Driscoll AK, Mathews TJ. Births: Final data for 2015. National vital statistics report, vol 66, no 1. Hyattsville, MD: NCHS. 2017. Available from: https://www.cdc.gov/nchs/data/nvsr/nvsr66/nvsr66_01.pdf.

For More Information. See the Birth Data website at: http://www.cdc.gov/nchs/births.htm, and Vitalstats at: http://www.cdc.gov/nchs/data_access/Vitalstatsonline.htm.

Fetal Death Data Set

Overview. Fetal mortality refers to the intrauterine death of a fetus at any gestational age. In *Health, United States*, data are presented for fetal deaths at 20 weeks or more. The Fetal Death data set includes characteristics of the fetus, such as sex, birthweight, and weeks of gestation; demographic information about the mother, such as age, race, Hispanic origin, and live-birth order; and medical and health information, such as maternal diabetes and hypertension.

Coverage. Data presented in *Health, United States* are based on reporting from all 50 states and D.C. Data for Puerto Rico, Virgin Islands, Guam, American Samoa, and Northern Marianas are not included in U.S. totals but are included in the Fetal Death User Guide available from the NCHS website at: http://www.cdc.gov/nchs/data_access/VitalStatsOnline.htm, and in periodic reports.

Methodology. Fetal death means the death of a fetus prior to delivery from the mother, irrespective of the duration of pregnancy. Fetal deaths do not include induced

terminations of pregnancy. This definition of fetal death, adopted by NCHS as the nationally recommended standard, is based on the definition published by the World Health Organization in 1950 and revised in 1988. The term fetal death encompasses other commonly used terms, including stillbirth, spontaneous abortion, and miscarriage. All U.S. states and registration areas have definitions similar to the standard definition, except for Puerto Rico and Wisconsin, which have no formal definition.

State laws require the reporting of fetal deaths, and federal law mandates national collection and publication of fetal death data. States and reporting areas submit fetal mortality data to NCHS as part of a cooperative agreement. Standard forms and procedures for the collection of the data are developed and recommended for state use through cooperative activities of the states and NCHS. NCHS shares the costs incurred by the states in providing vital statistics data for national use.

In addition to fetal mortality rates, perinatal mortality rates are also presented in *Health, United States*. Perinatal mortality includes both late fetal deaths (of at least 28 weeks of gestation) and early infant (neonatal) deaths (within 7 days of birth). Data on early infant deaths come from the Linked Birth/Infant Death data set.

Issues Affecting Interpretation. Reporting requirements for fetal deaths vary by state, and these differences have important implications for comparisons of fetal mortality rates by state. The majority of states require reporting of fetal deaths at 20 weeks of gestation or more, or a minimum of 350 grams birthweight (roughly equivalent to 20 weeks), or some combination of the two. In 2014, seven states required reporting of fetal deaths at all periods of gestation, and one state required reporting beginning at 16 weeks of gestation. Further, one state required the reporting of fetal deaths with birthweights of 500 grams or more (roughly equivalent to 22 weeks of gestation).

Starting with 2014 data, the obstetric estimate of gestation at delivery (OE) is used to determine gestational age, instead of the last normal menses (LMP), which was used for earlier years. The adoption of OE for gestational age had no or negligible impact on total fetal mortality rates. However, late fetal mortality rates based on the OE were lower than those based on the LMP. For more information, see User guide to the 2014 Fetal Death public use file.

There is substantial evidence that not all fetal deaths for which reporting is required are, in fact, reported. Underreporting of fetal deaths is most likely to occur in the earlier part of the required reporting period for each state. For example, in 2013, for those states requiring reporting of fetal deaths at all periods of gestation, 56.4% of fetal deaths at 20 weeks of gestation or more were at 20–27 weeks, whereas for states requiring reporting of fetal deaths of 500 grams or more, only 33.8% were at 20–27 weeks, thus indicating substantial underreporting of early fetal deaths in some states.

References

NCHS. User guide to the 2014 Fetal Death public use file. Hyattsville, MD. Available from: ftp://ftp.cdc.gov/pub/Health_Statistics/NCHS/Dataset_Documentation/DVS/fetaldeath/2014FetalUserGuide.pdf.

MacDorman MF, Gregory ECW. Fetal and perinatal mortality: United States, 2013. National vital statistics reports; vol 64 no 8. Hyattsville, MD: NCHS; 2015. Available from: http://www.cdc.gov/nchs/data/nvsr/nvsr64/nvsr64_08.pdf.

Gregory ECW, MacDorman MF, Martin JA. Trends in fetal and perinatal mortality in the United States, 2006–2012. NCHS data brief, no 169. Hyattsville, MD: NCHS; 2014. Available from: http://www.cdc.gov/nchs/data/databriefs/db169.htm.

MacDorman MF, Kirmeyer SE, Wilson EC. Fetal and perinatal mortality, United States, 2006. National vital statistics report; vol 60 no 8. Hyattsville, MD: NCHS; 2012. Available from: http://www.cdc.gov/nchs/data/nvsr/nvsr60/nvsr60_08.pdf.

For More Information. See the NCHS Fetal Deaths data website at: http://www.cdc.gov/nchs/fetal_death.htm.

Mortality Multiple Cause-of-Death File

Overview. Vital statistics mortality data are a fundamental source of demographic, geographic, and underlying and multiple cause-of-death information. Multiple cause-of-death data reflect all medical information reported on death certificates and complement traditional underlying cause-of-death data. Multiple-cause data give information on diseases that are a factor in death, whether or not they are the underlying cause of death; on associations among diseases; and on injuries leading to death.

The Mortality multiple cause-of-death file includes demographic information on age, sex, race, Hispanic origin, state of residence, and educational attainment, as well as medical information on causes of death. This data set is one of the few sources of comparable health-related data for small geographic areas over an extended time period. The data are used to present the characteristics of those dying in the United States, to determine life expectancy, and to compare mortality trends with those in other countries.

Coverage. Mortality data presented in *Health, United States* are based on reporting from all 50 states and D.C. Data for Puerto Rico, Virgin Islands, Guam, American Samoa, and Northern Marianas are shown in selected state tables, but are not included in U.S. totals. Beginning with 1970, mortality statistics for the U.S. exclude deaths of nonresidents of the U.S. Mortality statistics for Puerto Rico, Virgin Islands, American Samoa, and Northern Marianas excluded deaths of nonresidents for each area. For Guam, mortality statistics exclude deaths that occurred to a resident of any place other than Guam or the U.S. (50 states and D.C.).

Methodology. By law, the registration of deaths is the responsibility of the funeral director. The funeral director obtains demographic data for the death certificate from an informant. The physician in attendance at the death is required to certify the cause of death. Where death is from other than natural causes, a coroner or medical examiner may be required to examine the body and certify the cause of death.

NCHS is responsible for compiling and publishing annual national statistics on causes of death. In carrying out this responsibility, NCHS adheres to the World Health Organization (WHO) Nomenclature Regulations. These regulations require (a) that cause of death be coded in accordance with the applicable revision of the *International Classification of Diseases* (ICD) (see Appendix II, *International Classification of Diseases* [ICD]; Table III); and (b) that underlying cause of death be selected in accordance with international rules. Traditionally, national mortality statistics have been based on a count of deaths, with one underlying cause assigned for each death.

Prior to 1968, mortality medical data were based on manual coding of an underlying cause of death for each certificate in accordance with WHO rules. Starting with 1968, NCHS converted to computerized coding of the underlying cause and manual coding of all causes (multiple causes) on the death certificate. In this system, called Automated Classification of Medical Entities (ACME), multiple-cause codes serve as inputs to the computer software, which employs WHO rules to select the underlying cause. ACME is used to select the underlying cause of death for all death certificates in the United States, and cause-of-death data in *Health, United States* are coded using ACME.

In addition, NCHS has developed two computer systems as inputs to ACME. Beginning with 1990 data, the Mortality Medical Indexing, Classification, and Retrieval system (MICAR) was introduced to automate coding of multiple causes of death. MICAR provides more detailed information on the conditions reported on death certificates than is available through the ICD code structure. Then, beginning with data year 1993, SuperMICAR, an enhancement of MICAR, was introduced. SuperMICAR allows for literal entry of the multiple cause-of-death text as reported by the certifier. This information is then processed automatically by the MICAR and ACME computer systems. Records that cannot be processed automatically by MICAR or SuperMICAR are multiple-cause-coded manually and then further processed through ACME. Starting in 2003, SuperMICAR was used to process all of the nation's death records.

Data for the entire United States refer to events occurring within the United States; data for geographic areas are by place of residence. For methodological and reporting area changes for the following death certificate items, see Appendix II, Hispanic origin; Race.

Issues Affecting Interpretation. The ICD, by which cause of death is coded and classified, is revised approximately every 10–20 years. Because revisions of the ICD may cause discontinuities in trend data by cause of death, comparison of death rates by cause of death across ICD revisions should be done with caution and with reference to the comparability ratio. (See Appendix II, Comparability ratio.) Prior to 1999, modifications to the ICD were made only when a new revision of the ICD was implemented. A process for updating the ICD was introduced with the 10th revision (ICD–10) that allows for mid-revision changes. These changes, however, may affect comparability of data between years for select causes of death. Minor changes may be implemented every year, whereas major changes may be implemented every 3 years (e.g., 2003 data year). In data year 2006, major changes were implemented, including the addition and deletion of several ICD codes. For more information, see Heron et al. (2009).

Multiple-cause data were obtained from all certificates for 1968–1971, 1973–1980, and 1983–present. Data were obtained from a 50% sample of certificates for 1972. Multiple-cause data for 1981 and 1982 were obtained from a 50% sample of certificates from 19 registration areas. For the other states, data were obtained from all certificates.

The death certificate has been revised periodically. A revised U.S. Standard Certificate of Death was recommended for state use beginning January 1, 1989. Among the changes were the addition of a new item on educational attainment and Hispanic origin of the decedent and changes to improve the medical certification of cause of death. The U.S. Standard Certificate of Death was revised again in 2003; states are adopting this new certificate on a rolling basis.

The 2003 revision permits reporting of more than one race (multiple races). This change was implemented to reflect the increasing diversity of the U.S. population and to be consistent with the decennial census. Some states, however, are still using the 1989 revision of the U.S. Standard Certificate of Death, which allows only a single race to be reported. Until all states adopt the new death certificate, the race data reported using the 2003 revision are "bridged" for those for whom more than one race was reported (multiple race) to one single race, to provide comparability with race data reported on the 1989 revision. For more information on the impact of the 2003 certificate revisions on mortality data presented in *Health, United States*, see Appendix II, Race.

References

Murphy SL, Kochanek KD, Xu JQ, Curtin SC. Deaths: Final data for 2015. Hyattsville, MD: NCHS; 2017. Available from: http://www.cdc.gov/nchs/products/nvsr.htm.

Kochanek KD, Murphy SL, Xu JQ, Tejada-Vera B. Deaths: Final data for 2014. National vital statistics reports; vol 65 no 4. Hyattsville, MD: NCHS; 2016. Available from: https://www.cdc.gov/nchs/data/nvsr/nvsr65/nvsr65_04.pdf.

Heron M, Hoyert DL, Murphy SL, et al. Deaths: Final data for 2006. National vital statistics reports; vol 57 no 14. Hyattsville, MD: NCHS; 2009. Available from: http://www.cdc.gov/nchs/data/nvsr/nvsr57/nvsr57_14.pdf.

NCHS. Multiple causes of death in the United States. Monthly vital statistics report; vol 32 no 10 suppl 2. Hyattsville, MD: NCHS; 1984. Available from: http://www.cdc.gov/nchs/data/mvsr/supp/mv32_10s2.pdf.

For More Information. See the Mortality Data website at: http://www.cdc.gov/nchs/deaths.htm.

Linked Birth/Infant Death Data Set

Overview. National linked files of live births and infant deaths are used for research on infant mortality. The Linked Birth/Infant Death data set links information from the birth certificate to information from the death certificate for each infant death in the United States. The purpose of the linkage is to use the many additional variables from the birth certificate, including the more accurate race and ethnicity data, for more detailed analyses of infant mortality patterns. The Linked Birth/Infant Death data set includes all variables on the natality (Birth) file, including racial and ethnic information, birthweight, and maternal smoking, as well as variables on the Mortality file, including cause of death and age at death.

Coverage. To be included in the U.S. linked file, both the birth and death must have occurred in the 50 states, D.C., Puerto Rico, Virgin Islands, or Guam. Data for Puerto Rico, Virgin Islands, and Guam are shown in selected state tables but are not included in U.S. totals. Linked birth/infant death data are not available for American Samoa and Northern Marianas.

Methodology. Infant deaths are defined as a death before the infant's first birthday. About 98%–99% of infant death records can be linked to their corresponding birth certificates. The linkage makes available extensive information from the birth certificate about the pregnancy, maternal risk factors, infant characteristics, and health items at birth that can be used for more detailed analyses of infant mortality. The linked file is used for calculating infant mortality rates by race and ethnicity, which are more accurately measured from the birth certificate.

Starting with 1995 data, linked birth/infant death data files are available in two different formats: period data and birth cohort data. The numerator for the period linked file consists of all infant deaths occurring in a given data year linked to their corresponding birth certificates, whether the birth occurred in that year or the previous year. The numerator for the birth cohort linked file consists of deaths to infants born in a given year. In both cases, the denominator is all births occurring in the year. For example, the 2013 period linked file contains a numerator file that consists of all infant deaths occurring in 2013 that have been linked to their corresponding birth certificates, whether the birth occurred in 2012 or 2013. In contrast, the 2013 birth cohort linked file will contain a numerator file that consists of all infant deaths to babies born in 2013, whether the death occurred in 2013 or 2014. Although the birth cohort format has methodological advantages, it creates substantial delays in data availability because it is necessary to wait until the close of the following data year to include all infant deaths in the birth cohort. Starting with 1995 data, period linked files are used for infant mortality rate tables in *Health, United States*.

Other changes to the data set starting with 1995 include the addition of record weights to compensate for the 1%–2% of infant death records that could not be linked to their corresponding birth records. In addition, not-stated birthweight was imputed if the period of gestation was known. This imputation was done to improve the accuracy of birthweight-specific infant mortality rates because the percentage of records with not-stated birthweight is generally higher for infant deaths (4.0% in 2014) than for live births (0.1% in 2014). In 2014, not-stated birthweight was imputed for 0.10% of births.

Issues Affecting Interpretation. Period linked file data starting with 1995 are not strictly comparable with birth cohort data for 1983–1991. A new revision of the birth certificate was introduced in 2003 and is being adopted by states on a voluntary, rolling basis.

Reference

Mathews TJ, Driscoll AK. Trends in infant mortality in the United States, 2005-2014. NCHS data brief, no 279. Hyattsville, MD: NCHS; 2017. Available from: https://www.cdc.gov/nchs/products/databriefs.htm.

Mathews TJ, MacDorman MF, Thoma ME. Infant mortality statistics from the 2013 period Linked Birth/Infant Death data set. National vital statistics report; vol 64 no 9. Hyattsville, MD: NCHS; 2015. Available from: http://www.cdc.gov/nchs/data/nvsr/nvsr64/nvsr64_09.pdf.

For More Information. See the NCHS Linked Birth and Infant Death Data website at: http://www.cdc.gov/nchs/linked.htm.

Occupational Employment Statistics (OES)

Bureau of Labor Statistics (BLS)

Overview. The OES program conducts a semiannual survey designed to produce estimates of employment and wages for specific occupations. The program collects data on wage and salary workers in nonfarm establishments, producing employment and wage estimates for over 800 occupations. The OES program produces these occupational estimates for all industries combined at different geographic levels— for the nation; the 50 states and D.C.; metropolitan and nonmetropolitan areas; and Guam, Puerto Rico, and the U.S. Virgin Islands. National occupational employment and wage estimates are also available by industry for more than 430 industry aggregations and by public/private ownership across all industries and for schools and hospitals.

Coverage. The OES survey covers all full-time and part-time wage and salary workers in nonfarm establishments. The survey does not cover the self-employed, owners and partners in unincorporated firms, household workers, or unpaid family workers.

Methodology. The OES program surveys approximately 200,000 establishments per panel (every 6 months), taking 3 years to fully collect the sample of 1.2 million establishments. The estimates for occupations in nonfarm establishments are based on OES data collected for the reference months of May and November. May 2015 employment and wage estimates are based on all data collected from establishments sampled in the May 2015, November 2014, May 2014, November 2013, May 2013, and November 2012 semiannual panels. The overall national response rate for the six panels is 73.5% based on establishments and 69.6% based on weighted sampled employment in the 50 states and D.C.

The OES survey is a federal-state cooperative program between BLS and state workforce agencies (SWAs). BLS provides the procedures and technical support, draws the sample, and produces the survey materials, while SWAs collect most of the data. SWAs from all 50 states plus D.C., Puerto Rico, Guam, and the U.S. Virgin Islands participate in the survey. Occupational employment and wage rate estimates at the national level are produced by BLS using data from the 50 states and D.C. Employers who respond to states' requests to participate in the OES survey make these estimates possible.

Issues Affecting Interpretation. Over time, OES data have had changes in the occupational, industrial, and geographical classification systems; data collection methods; survey reference period; and mean wage estimation methodology. Because of these changes as well as permanent features of the OES methodology, caution should be used in trend analysis.

OES occupational estimates are based on the Office of Management and Budget's Standard Occupational Classification (SOC) system. The OES survey classifies workers into more than 800 detailed occupations; these detailed occupations are aggregated into 23 SOC major groups. Only 22 SOC major groups are included in OES; Major group 55, Military Specific Occupations, is not included. Data on selected healthcare occupations are presented in *Health, United States*.

OES estimates for 1999 through 2009 classified occupations according to the 2000 SOC system. OES estimates for 2010 and 2011 were based on a hybrid structure using both the 2000 and 2010 SOC systems. For more information about the hybrid structure, see http://www.bls.gov/oes/oes_ques.htm. OES estimates for 2012 to 2015 classified occupations according to the 2010 SOC system.

Reference

Bureau of Labor Statistics. Occupational employment and wages, May 2015. Washington, D.C.: U.S. Department of Labor; 2016. Available from: http://www.bls.gov/OES/.

For More Information. See the OES website at: http://www.bls.gov/OES/.

Population Census and Population Estimates

U.S. Census Bureau

Decennial Census

The census of population (decennial census) has been held in the United States every 10 years since 1790. Since 1930, it has enumerated the resident population as of April 1 of the census year. Data on sex, race, Hispanic origin, age, and marital status are collected from 100% of the enumerated population.

Race Data on the 1990 Census

The question on race on the 1990 census was based on the Office of Management and Budget's (OMB) 1977 Race and Ethnic Standards for Federal Statistics and Administrative Reporting (Statistical Policy Directive 15). This document specified rules for the collection, tabulation, and reporting of racial and ethnic data within the federal statistical system. The 1977 Standards required federal agencies to report race-specific tabulations using four single-race categories: American Indian or Alaska Native, Asian or Pacific Islander, black, and white. Under the 1977 Standards, race and ethnicity were considered to be two separate and distinct concepts. Thus, persons of Hispanic origin may be of any race.

Race Data on the 2000 Census

The question on race on the 2000 census was based on OMB's 1997 Revisions to the Standards for the Classification of Federal Data on Race and Ethnicity (Fed Regist 1997 October 30;62:58781–90). (Also see Appendix II, Race.) The 1997 Standards incorporated two major changes in the collection, tabulation, and presentation of race data. First, the 1997 Standards increased the minimum set of categories to be used by federal agencies for identification of race from four to five: American Indian or Alaska Native, Asian, black or African American, Native Hawaiian or Other Pacific Islander, and white. Second, the 1997 Standards included the requirement that federal data collection programs allow respondents to select one or more race categories when responding to a query on their racial identity. This provision means that there are potentially 31 race groups, depending on whether an individual selects one, two, three, four, or all five of the race categories. The 1997 Standards continue to call for use, when possible, of a separate question on Hispanic or Latino ethnicity and specify that the ethnicity question should appear before the question on race. Thus, under the 1997 Standards, as under the 1977 Standards, persons of Hispanic origin may be of any race.

Race Data on the 2010 Census

Similar to race data on the 2000 census, the question on race on the 2010 census was based on OMB's 1997 Revisions to the Standards for the Classification of Federal Data on Race and Ethnicity (Fed Regist 1997 October 30;62:58781–90). (Also see Appendix II, Race.) The 1997 Standards required a minimum set of categories to be used by federal agencies for identification of race: American Indian or Alaska Native, Asian, black or African American, Native Hawaiian or Other Pacific Islander, and white and require that federal data collection programs allow respondents to select one or more race categories when responding to a query on their racial identity. The 1997 Standards continue to call for use, when possible, of a separate question on Hispanic or Latino ethnicity and specify that the ethnicity question should appear before the question on race. Thus, under the 1997 Standards, as under the 1977 Standards, persons of Hispanic origin may be of any race.

Modified Decennial Census Files

For several decades, the U.S. Census Bureau has produced Modified Decennial Census files. These modified files incorporate adjustments to the 100% April 1 count data for (a) errors in the census data discovered subsequent to publication, (b) misreported age data, and (c) nonspecified race.

For the 1990 census, the U.S. Census Bureau modified the age, race, and sex data on the census and produced the Modified Age-Race-Sex (MARS) file. The differences between the population counts in the original census file and the MARS file are primarily due to modification of the race data. Of the 248.7 million persons enumerated in 1990, 9.8 million did not specify their race (over 95% were of Hispanic origin). For the 1990 MARS file, these persons were assigned the race reported by a nearby person with an identical response to the Hispanic origin question.

For the 2000 and 2010 censuses, the U.S. Census Bureau modified the race data and produced the Modified Race Data Summary files. For these files, persons who did not report a race (reported only the category Some Other Race) as part of their race response were assigned by imputation to one of the 31 race groups, which are the single- and multiple-race combinations of the five race categories specified in the 1997 OMB race and ethnicity standards. For the 2000 census, 97% of the 15.4 million persons who did not report a race were of Hispanic origin. Because a large proportion of those identifying their race as Some Other Race are Hispanic, for the 2010 census, a new instruction was added that, for the census, Hispanic origins are not races. For the 2010 census, 97% of the 19.1 million persons who did not report a race (reported only the category Some Other Race) were of Hispanic origin.

Postcensal Population Estimates

Postcensal population estimates are estimates made for the years following a census, before the next census is taken. Postcensal population estimates are derived annually by updating the resident population enumerated in the decennial census using a components-of-population-change approach. Each annual series includes estimates for the current data year and revised estimates for the earlier years in the decade. The following formula is used to derive national estimates for a given year from those for the previous year, starting with the decennial census enumerated resident population as the base:

Resident population estimate

+ births to U.S. resident women

– deaths to U.S. residents

+ net international migration.

The postcensal estimates are consistent with official decennial census figures and do not reflect estimated decennial census underenumeration.

Estimates for the earlier years in a given series are revised to reflect changes in the components-of-change data sets (for example, births to U.S. resident women from a preliminary natality file are replaced with counts from a final natality file). To help users keep track of which postcensal estimate is being used, each annual series is referred to as a "vintage," and the last year in the series is used to name the series. For example, both the Vintage 2011 and the Vintage 2012 postcensal series have revised estimates for July 1, 2011, but

the estimates for July 1, 2011, from the Vintage 2011 and Vintage 2012 postcensal series differ.

The U.S. Census Bureau also produces postcensal estimates of the resident population of states and counties, using the components-of-population-change method. An additional component of population change—net internal migration—is involved.

Intercensal Population Estimates

Intercensal population estimates are estimates made for the years between two decennial censuses and are produced once the census at the end of the decade has been completed. They replace the postcensal estimates produced prior to the completion of the census at the end of the decade. Intercensal estimates are more accurate than postcensal estimates because they are based on both the census at the beginning and the census at the end of the decade. They are derived by adjusting the final postcensal estimates for the decade to correct for the error of closure (the difference between the estimated population at the end of the decade and the census count for that date). The patterns of population change observed over the decade are preserved. The intercensal estimates for the 1990s were produced using the same methodology used to generate the intercensal estimates for the 1980s. The revised intercensal population estimates for 2000–2009 were produced using a modified version of the methodology used previously. Vital rates calculated using postcensal population estimates are routinely revised when intercensal estimates become available.

Bridged-race Population Estimates

Race data on the 2000 and 2010 censuses are not comparable with race data on other data systems that are continuing to collect data using the 1977 OMB Standards on race and ethnicity during the transition to full implementation of the 1997 OMB Standards. For example, states are implementing the revised birth and death certificates—which have race and ethnicity items that are compliant with the 1997 OMB Standards—at different times, and to date some states are still using the 1989 certificates that collect race and ethnicity data in accordance with the 1977 OMB Standards. Thus, population estimates for 1990 and beyond with race categories comparable with the 1977 OMB categories are needed so that race-specific birth and death rates can be calculated. To meet this need, NCHS, in collaboration with the U.S. Census Bureau, developed methodology to bridge the 31 race groups in Census 2000 and Census 2010 to the four single-race categories specified under the 1977 OMB Standards.

The bridging methodology was developed using information from the 1997–2000 National Health Interview Survey (NHIS). NHIS provides a unique opportunity to investigate multiple-race groups because, since 1982, it has allowed respondents to choose more than one race but has also asked respondents reporting multiple races to choose a primary race. The bridging methodology developed by NCHS involved the application of regression models relating person-level and county-level covariates to the selection of a particular primary race by the multiple-race respondents. The bridging proportions derived from these models have been applied by the U.S. Census Bureau to various unbridged resident population files. These applications have resulted in bridged-race population estimates for each of the four single-race categories: American Indian or Alaska Native, Asian or Pacific Islander, black, and white.

In *Health, United States*, vital rates for 1991–1999 were calculated using the July 1, 1991–July 1, 1999 bridged-race intercensal estimates. Vital rates for 2000 were calculated using the bridged-race April 1, 2000, census counts, and those for 2010 were calculated using the bridged-race April 1, 2010, census counts. Starting with *Health, United States, 2012*, vital rates for 2001–2009 have been recalculated using the July 1, 2001–July 1, 2009, revised intercensal bridged-race population estimates. Vital rates for 2011 and beyond will be calculated using bridged-race estimates of the July 1 population from the corresponding postcensal vintage.

Reference

Ingram DD, Parker JD, Schenker N, et al. United States Census 2000 population with bridged race categories. NCHS. Vital Health Stat 2003;2(135). Available from: http://www.cdc.gov/nchs/data/series/sr_02/sr02_135.pdf.

For More Information. See the U.S. Census Bureau website at: http://www.census.gov and the NCHS website for U.S. Census populations with bridged race categories at: http://www.cdc.gov/nchs/nvss/bridged_race.htm.

Quality Improvement Evaluation System (QIES)

Centers for Medicare & Medicaid Services (CMS)

Overview. This administrative database, referred to in *Health, United States* as QIES, is created from the Certification and Survey Provider Enhanced Reporting (CASPER) and QIES systems. QIES is a CMS database that contains information from the standard annual facility survey data submitted by state survey agencies to CMS for certification to participate in the Medicare and Medicaid programs in the United States and territories. (Data for the territories are not shown in *Health, United States*.) The purpose of the facility survey certification process is to ensure that facilities meet current CMS care requirements and thus can be paid for services furnished to Medicare and Medicaid beneficiaries. In 2012, QIES replaced the Online Survey Certification and Reporting

Database (OSCAR). QIES (and its predecessor OSCAR) contain information on facility and patient characteristics and health deficiencies issued by the government during the survey process.

Coverage. Facilities in the United States that are certified to receive Medicare or Medicaid payments are included.

Methodology. QIES data are compiled by the state survey agency and a facility representative. The data are reviewed during the survey process and then submitted electronically to CMS. The information provided can be audited at any time.

All certified facilities are inspected periodically by representatives of the state survey agency (generally the department of health). Some facilities are inspected twice, or more often, during any given reporting cycle. To avoid overcounting, the data must be edited and duplicates removed. Data editing and compilation of nursing home data were performed by Cowles Research Group (CRG; Anacortes, WA) and published in the group's Nursing Home Statistical Yearbook series.

References

Cowles CM, ed. Nursing home statistical yearbooks for 2003–2015. Anacortes, WA: CRG; published 2004–2016, respectively. Available from: http://www.longtermcareinfo.com/publications/nursing-home-statistical-yearbook.php.

Centers for Medicare & Medicaid Services. Certification and compliance. Baltimore, MD: CMS; 2005. Available from: http://www.cms.gov/CertificationandComplianc/01_overview.asp.

For More Information. See the CMS website at: https://www.cms.gov/Research-Statistics-Data-and-Systems/Files-for-Order/NonIdentifiableDataFiles/index.html and the CRG website at: http://www.longtermcareinfo.com/index.html.

Sexually Transmitted Disease (STD) Surveillance

CDC/National Center for HIV/AIDS, Viral Hepatitis, STD, and TB Prevention (NCHHSTP)

Overview. Surveillance information on the incidence and prevalence of STDs is used to inform public and private health efforts to control these diseases. Case reporting data are available for nationally notifiable chancroid, chlamydia, gonorrhea, and syphilis. Enhanced surveillance of these conditions and surveillance of other STDs, such as genital herpes simplex virus, genital warts or other human papillomavirus infections, and trichomoniasis use data collected from other sources, including data from sentinel surveillance and national surveys.

Coverage. Case reports of STDs are reported to CDC by STD surveillance systems operated by state and local STD control programs and health departments in 50 states, D.C., selected cities, 3,142 U.S. counties, and outlying areas consisting of U.S. dependencies, possessions, and independent nations in free association with the United States. Data from outlying areas are not included in *Health, United States*.

Methodology. Information is obtained from the following data sources: (a) notifiable disease reporting from state and local STD programs; (b) projects that monitor STD positivity and prevalence in various settings, including the National Job Training Program, the National Notifiable Disease Surveillance System (NNDSS), and the Gonococcal Isolate Surveillance Project; and (c) national sample surveys implemented by federal and private organizations. STD data are submitted to CDC on a variety of hard-copy summary reporting forms (monthly, quarterly, and annually) and in electronic summary or individual case-specific (line-listed) formats through the National Electronic Telecommunications System for Surveillance.

Issues Affecting Interpretation. Because of incomplete diagnosis and reporting, the number of STD cases reported to CDC undercounts the actual number of infections occurring among the U.S. population.

Reference

> CDC. Sexually transmitted disease surveillance 2015. Atlanta, GA: CDC; 2016. Available from: http://www. cdc.gov/std/stats15/default.htm.

For More Information. See the STD Data and Statistics website at: http://www.cdc.gov/std/stats and the STD Diseases & Related Conditions website at: http://www.cdc. gov/std/default.htm.

Surveillance, Epidemiology, and End Results Program (SEER)

National Cancer Institute (NCI)

Overview. SEER tracks the incidence of new cancers each year and collects follow-up information on all previously diagnosed patients until their death. For each cancer, SEER registries routinely collect data on patient demographics, primary tumor site, morphology, stage at diagnosis, first course of treatment, and follow-up for vital status.

Coverage. The SEER 9 registries (Atlanta, Connecticut, Detroit, Hawaii, Iowa, New Mexico, San Francisco-Oakland, Seattle-Puget Sound, and Utah) have been part of the program continuously since 1975. The SEER 13 registries (the SEER 9 registries plus Los Angeles, San Jose-Monterey, rural Georgia, and the Alaska Native Tumor Registry) have been part of the program continuously since 1992. The SEER

18 registries (the SEER 13 plus Greater Georgia, Kentucky, Greater California, New Jersey, and Louisiana) have been part of the program continuously since 2000. SEER currently collects and publishes cancer incidence and survival data from 18 population-based cancer registries covering approximately 28% of the U.S. population.

Methodology. A cancer registry collects and stores data on cancers diagnosed in a specific hospital or medical facility (hospital-based registry) or in a defined geographic area (population-based registry). A population-based registry includes, but is not limited to, a number of hospital-based registries. In SEER registry areas, trained coders abstract medical records using the *International Classification of Diseases for Oncology, 3rd edition* (ICD–O–3) to classify site and tumor morphology. The ICD–O–3 coding also includes updates for hematopoietic codes based on WHO Classification of Tumours of Haematopoietic and Lymphoid Tissues (2008). All SEER data in this report were collected with or converted to ICD–O–3.

NCI obtains population counts from the U.S. Census Bureau and uses them to calculate incidence rates. It also uses estimation procedures as needed to obtain estimates for years and races not included in data provided by the Census Bureau. Life tables used to determine general population life expectancy when calculating relative survival rates were obtained from NCHS and in-house calculations. Separate life tables are used for each race-sex-specific group included in SEER.

Issues Affecting Interpretation. Because of the addition of registries over time, analysis of long-term incidence and survival trends is limited to those registries that have been in SEER for similar lengths of time. Analysis of Hispanic, and American Indian or Alaska Native data is limited to shorter trends. Starting with *Health, United States, 2006*, the North American Association of Central Cancer Registries (NAACCR) Hispanic Identification Algorithm was used on a combination of variables to classify cases as Hispanic for analytic purposes. Starting with *Health, United States, 2007*, Hispanic incidence data exclude data for Alaska. Earlier editions of *Health, United States* also excluded Hispanic data for Hawaii and Seattle. Starting with *Health, United States, 2007*, incidence estimates for the American Indian or Alaska Native population are limited to contract health service delivery area (CHSDA) counties within SEER reporting areas. This change is believed to produce estimates that more accurately reflect the incidence rates for this population group. More information on CHSDA is available from: http:// www.ihs.gov/chs/index.cfm?module=chs_requirements_ chsda. For more information on SEER estimates by race and ethnicity, see: http://seer.cancer.gov/seerstat/variables/seer/ race_ethnicity/index.html. Rates presented in this report may differ somewhat from those reported previously due to changes in population estimates and the addition and deletion of small numbers of incidence cases.

Reference

Howlader N, Noone AM, Krapcho M, Miller D, Bishop K, Altekruse SF, et al. (eds). SEER Cancer Statistics Review, 1975-2013, National Cancer Institute. Bethesda, MD, based on November 2015 SEER data submission, posted to the SEER website, April 2016. Available from: http://seer.cancer.gov/csr/1975_2013/.

For More Information. See the SEER website at: http://seer.cancer.gov.

Youth Risk Behavior Survey (YRBS)

CDC/National Center for HIV, Hepatitis, STD, and TB Prevention (NCHHSTP)

Overview. YRBS monitors health risk behaviors among students in grades 9–12 that contribute to morbidity and mortality in both adolescence and adulthood. The six areas monitored are behaviors that contribute to unintentional injuries and violence; tobacco use; alcohol and other drug use; sexual behaviors that contribute to unintended pregnancy and sexually transmitted diseases (STDs), including human immunodeficiency virus (HIV) infection; unhealthy dietary behaviors; and physical inactivity. In addition, YRBS monitors the prevalence of obesity, asthma, and sleep behaviors.

Coverage. National data are representative of high school students in public and private schools in the United States.

Methodology. The national YRBS school-based surveys have been conducted biennially since 1991. A three-stage cluster sample design is used to produce a nationally representative sample of students in grades 9–12 attending public and private schools. In 2013 and 2015, the first-stage sampling frame comprised primary sampling units (PSUs) consisting of counties, subareas of large counties, or groups of smaller, adjacent counties. PSUs were categorized into strata according to their metropolitan statistical area (MSA) status (e.g., urban city) and the percentages of non-Hispanic black and Hispanic students in the PSUs. PSUs were sampled with probability proportional to overall school enrollment size for the PSU. In the second stage of sampling, schools with any of grades 9–12 were sampled with probability proportional to school enrollment size. The third stage of sampling consisted of random sampling in each of grades 9–12, one or two classrooms from either a required subject (e.g., English or Social Studies) or a required period (e.g., Homeroom or second period).

All students in sampled classes were eligible to participate. Schools, classes, and students that refused to participate were not replaced. To enable a separate analysis of data for black and Hispanic students, two classes per grade, rather than one, were sampled in schools with a high enrollment of black and Hispanic students. Prior to 2013, three strategies were used to oversample black and Hispanic students: (a) larger sampling rates were used to select PSUs that were in high-black and high-Hispanic strata; (b) a modified measure of size was used to increase the probability of sampling schools with a disproportionately high minority enrollment; and (c) two classes per grade, rather than one, were sampled in schools with a high enrollment of black and Hispanic students. A weighting factor is applied to each student record to adjust for nonresponse and for the varying probabilities of selection, including those resulting from the oversampling of black and Hispanic students.

Sample Size and Response Rate. The sample size for the 2015 YRBS was 15,624 students in 180 schools. The school response rate was 69%, and the student response rate was 86%, for an overall response rate of 60%.

Issues Affecting Interpretation. National YRBS data are subject to at least two limitations. First, these data apply only to adolescents who attend regular high school, including some charter, public alternative, special education, and vocational schools. These students may not be representative of all persons in this age group because those who have dropped out of high school are not surveyed. Second, the extent of underreporting or overreporting cannot be determined, although the survey questions demonstrate good test-retest reliability.

Estimates of substance use for youth based on YRBS differ from the National Survey on Drug Use & Health (NSDUH) and the Monitoring the Future (MTF) Study. Rates are not directly comparable across these surveys because of differences in populations covered, sample designs, questionnaires, and interview settings. NSDUH collects data in residences, whereas MTF and YRBS collect data in school classrooms. In addition, NSDUH estimates are tabulated by age, whereas MTF and YRBS estimates are tabulated by grade, representing different ages as well as different populations. All YRBS data collection is anonymous.

References

Brener ND, Kann L, Shanklin SL, et al. Methodology of the Youth Risk Behavior Surveillance System—2013. MMWR 2013;62(RR01):1–23. Available from: http://www.cdc.gov/mmwr/preview/mmwrhtml/rr6201a1.htm.

Kann L, Kinchen S, Shanklin SL, et al. Youth Risk Behavior Surveillance—United States, 2013. MMWR Surveill Summ 2014;63(SS–4):1–172. Available from: http://www.cdc.gov/mmwr/pdf/ss/ss6304.pdf.

Kann L, McManus T, Harris WA, et al. Youth Risk Behavior Surveillance—United States, 2015. MMWR Surveill Summ 2016;65(SS–6):1–174. Available from: https://www.cdc.gov/healthyyouth/data/yrbs/pdf/2015/ss6506_updated.pdf.

Cowan CD. Coverage, sample design, and weighting in three federal surveys. J Drug Issues 2001;31(3):599–614.

For More Information. See the YRBS website at: http://www.cdc.gov/yrbs.

Private and Global Sources

American Association of Colleges of Osteopathic Medicine (AACOM)

AACOM compiles data on various aspects of osteopathic medical education for distribution to the profession, the government, and the public. Enrollment and graduate data are collected by the Annual Osteopathic Medical School Questionnaire, which is sent to schools of osteopathic medicine annually. The questionnaire requests information on the characteristics of applicants, students and graduates, faculty, curriculum, contract and grant activity, revenues and expenditures, and clinical facilities.

Reference

> American Association of Colleges of Osteopathic Medicine. Trends in osteopathic medical school applicants, enrollment, and graduates, 2016. Chevy Chase, MD: AACOM; 2016.

For More Information. See the AACOM website at: http://www.aacom.org.

American Association of Colleges of Pharmacy (AACP)

AACP compiles data on colleges and schools of pharmacy, including information on student enrollment and types of degrees conferred. Data are collected through five separate online survey instruments issued annually. Data on enrollments were collected using the Enrollment Survey–Fall 2014 Professional Pharmacy Degree Programs and the response rate was 99.2%. Data on graduates were collected using the Undergraduate and Professional Pharmacy Degrees Conferred Survey 2014–15 and the response rate was 97.8%.

Reference

> American Association of Colleges of Pharmacy. Fall 2014 profile of pharmacy students, Fall 2015 profile of pharmacy students. Available from: http://www.aacp.org/resources/research/institutionalresearch/Pages/StudentApplications,EnrollmentsandDegreesConferred.aspx.

For More Information. See the AACP website at: http://www.aacp.org.

American Association of Colleges of Podiatric Medicine (AACPM)

AACPM compiles data on colleges of podiatric medicine, including information on the schools and enrollment. Data are collected annually through written questionnaires. The response rate is 100%.

Reference

> American Association of Colleges of Podiatric Medicine. Applicant, matriculant, and graduate statistics. Available from: http://www.aacpm.org.

For More Information. See the AACPM website at: http://www.aacpm.org.

American Dental Association (ADA)

The ADA Masterfile contains the most up-to-date information on dentists in the United States. The Masterfile is a database of all dentists, both practicing and nonpracticing, in the United States. It is updated through a variety of methods including reconciliation with state licensure databases, death records, and various surveys and censuses of dentists carried out by ADA.

ADA's Health Policy Institute conducts annual surveys of predoctoral dental educational institutions. A questionnaire, mailed to all dental schools, collects information on academic programs, admissions, enrollment, attrition, graduates, educational expenses and financial assistance, patient care, advanced dental education, and faculty positions.

References

> American Dental Association, Health Policy Institute, Supply of dentists in the U.S.: 2001–2015, Tables 1 and 3. Available from: http://www.ada.org/en/science-research/health-policy-institute/data-center/supply-of-dentists.

> American Dental Association. 2015–2016 survey of dental education series. Report 1: Academic programs, enrollment and graduates. Chicago, IL: ADA; 2016. Available from: http://www.ada.org/en/science-research/health-policy-institute/data-center/dental-education.

For More Information. See the ADA website at: http://www.ada.org.

American Hospital Association (AHA) Annual Survey of Hospitals

Data from AHA's annual survey are based on questionnaires sent to all AHA-registered and nonregistered hospitals in the United States and its associated areas: American Samoa, Guam, the Marshall Islands, Puerto Rico, and the Virgin Islands. U.S. government hospitals located outside the United States are excluded. Overall, the average response rate over the past 5 years has been approximately 83%. For nonreporting hospitals and for the survey questionnaires of reporting hospitals on which some information was missing, estimates are made for all data except those on beds, bassinets, facilities, and services. Data for beds and bassinets of nonreporting hospitals are based on the most recent information available from those hospitals. Data for facilities and services are based only on reporting hospitals. Estimates of other types of missing data are based on data reported the previous year, if available. When unavailable, estimates are based on data furnished by reporting hospitals similar in size, control, major service provided, length of stay, and geographic and demographic characteristics.

Reference

American Hospital Association, Annual survey of hospitals. Hospital statistics, 2016. Chicago, IL: AHA; 2016.

For More Information. See the AHA website at: http://www. aha.org.

American Medical Association (AMA) Physician Masterfile

A master file of physicians has been maintained by AMA since 1906. The Physician Masterfile contains data on all physicians in the United States, both members and nonmembers of AMA, and on those graduates of American medical schools temporarily practicing overseas. The file also includes information on international medical graduates (IMGs) who are graduates of foreign medical schools, who reside in the United States, and who meet U.S. educational standards for primary recognition as physicians.

A file is initiated on each individual upon entry into medical school or, in the case of IMGs, upon entry into the United States. Between 1969 and 1985, a mail questionnaire survey was conducted every 4 years to update the file information on professional activities, self-designated area of specialization, and present employment status. Between 1985 and 2006, approximately one-third to one-fourth of all physicians were surveyed each year. Since then, AMA has employed a more diversified survey approach in which more than 500,000 active physicians are targeted each year through mail, telephone, and web-based surveys.

Reference

American Medical Association. Physician characteristics and distribution in the U.S., 2015. Chicago, IL: AMA Division of Survey and Data Resources; 2015.

For More Information. See the AMA website at: http://www. ama-assn.org.

American Osteopathic Association (AOA)

AOA was established to promote the public health, to encourage scientific research, and to maintain and improve high standards of medical education in osteopathic colleges. Among its activities, AOA compiles the number of osteopathic physicians (DOs); the number of active DOs by gender, age, and specialty and by 50 states and D.C.; and the number of osteopathic medical students, by selected characteristics.

Reference

American Osteopathic Association. 2015 osteopathic medical profession report. Chicago, IL: AOA; 2015. Available from: http://www.osteopathic.org/inside-aoa/about/aoa-annual-statistics/Pages/default.aspx.

For More Information. See the AOA website at: http://www. osteopathic.org.

Association of American Medical Colleges (AAMC)

As part of its mission to serve and lead the academic medicine community to improve the health of all, AAMC collects information on student enrollment in medical schools through a variety of sources. Among the data services and sources offered are the Medical College Admission Test (MCAT), the American Medical College Application Service (AMCAS), the Electronic Residency Application Service (ERAS), and the Student Records System (SRS). The AAMC Data Warehouse stores data relevant to both applicants and students, and from these two source files, the association derives summary statistics about accredited medical schools, applicants, accepted applicants, matriculants, enrollees, and graduates. AAMC has developed policies and procedures to ensure that the privacy of individual and institutional data are protected and meet federal, state, AAMC, and professional standards. Applicant, enrollment, and graduate statistical data are arranged by academic year, which begins July 1 and ends June 30.

Reference

Association of American Medical Colleges. AAMC data book: Medical schools and teaching hospitals by the numbers, 2016. Washington, D.C.: AAMC; 2016.

For More Information. See the AAMC website at: http://www.aamc.org.

Association of Schools and Colleges of Optometry (ASCO)

ASCO compiles data on various aspects of optometric education, including data on schools and enrollment. Schools and colleges complete an annual questionnaire. The response rate is 100%.

References

> Association of Schools and Colleges of Optometry. Annual student data report: Academic year 2014–2015 (updated August, 2016). Rockville, MD: ASCO; 2015. Available from: http://www.opted.org/student-data-reports/.

> Association of Schools and Colleges of Optometry. Annual student data report: Academic year 2015–2016. Rockville, MD: ASCO; 2016. Available from: http://www.opted.org/student-data-reports/.

For More Information. See the ASCO website at: http://www.opted.org.

Association of Schools & Programs of Public Health (ASPPH)

ASPPH compiles data on member schools and programs of public health accredited by the Council on Education for Public Health in the United States, Puerto Rico, Mexico, and Canada. Unlike health professional schools that emphasize specific clinical occupations, schools and programs of public health offer study in specialty areas such as biostatistics, epidemiology, environmental health, occupational health, health administration, health planning, nutrition, maternal and child health, social and behavioral sciences, and other population-based sciences. Data collection is conducted annually from all ASPPH member schools and programs and is reported in this report for U.S.-based institutions. The response rate in 2014–2015 was 85%.

Reference

> Association of Schools and Programs of Public Health [unpublished data]. Washington, D.C.: ASPPH; 2015.

For More Information. See the ASPPH website at: http://www.aspph.org.

Guttmacher Institute Abortion Provider Census

The Guttmacher Institute (previously called the Alan Guttmacher Institute, or AGI) is a not-for-profit organization for reproductive health research, policy analysis, and public education. Guttmacher has collected or estimated national abortion data since 1973 by conducting surveys every 3–4 years and extrapolating estimates for the intervening years. Guttmacher reports the number of legal induced abortions and the number, types, and locations of abortion providers by state and region.

The abortion data reported to Guttmacher contain data on women of all ages, including adolescents who obtain legal induced abortions, and includes both surgical and medication (e.g., using mifepristone, misoprostol, or methotrexate) abortion procedures. Data are collected from three major categories of providers that were identified as potential providers of abortion services: clinics, physicians, and hospitals.

Questionnaires are mailed to all potential providers, with two additional mailings and telephone follow-up for nonresponse. All questionnaires ask the number of induced abortions performed at the provider's location. State health statistics agencies are also contacted, requesting all available data reported by providers to each state health agency on the number of abortions performed in the survey year. For states that provide data to Guttmacher, the health agency figures are used for providers who do not respond to the survey. Estimates of the number of abortions performed by some providers are ascertained from knowledgeable sources, including other providers of reproductive health services.

In the 2012–2013 survey, respondents were asked to report the number of induced abortions performed in their facilities during 2010 and 2011. Of the 2,288 potential providers surveyed between April 2012 and May 2013, 1,222 responded directly or in follow-up; health department data were used for 470 providers; 71 facilities had closed or stopped offering abortion services during the survey period; knowledgeable sources were used for 51 providers; and Guttmacher made its own estimates for 474 facilities, usually relying on prior abortion census results. The level of internal estimation was higher than in the 2008 survey.

Between 2003 and 2011, the total number of abortions reported to CDC has been about one-third less than the total estimated by Guttmacher. (See Appendix I, Abortion Surveillance System.)

Reference

> Jones RK, Jerman J. Abortion incidence and service availability in the United States, 2011. Perspect Sex

Reprod Health 2014;46(1):3–14. Available from: http://
www.guttmacher.org/pubs/journals/psrh.46e0414.pdf.

For More Information. See The Guttmacher Institute website
at: http://www.guttmacher.org.

Organisation for Economic Co-operation and Development (OECD) Health Data

OECD provides annual data on statistical indicators for
health and health systems collected from 35 member
countries, with some time series going back to 1960.

OECD was established in 1961 with a mandate to promote
policies to achieve the highest sustainable economic
growth and a rising standard of living among member
countries. The organization now comprises 35 member
countries: Australia, Austria, Belgium, Canada, Chile, the
Czech Republic, Denmark, Estonia, Finland, France, Germany,
Greece, Hungary, Iceland, Ireland, Israel, Italy, Japan, Korea,
Latvia, Luxembourg, Mexico, the Netherlands, New Zealand,
Norway, Poland, Portugal, the Slovak Republic, Slovenia,
Spain, Sweden, Switzerland, Turkey, the United Kingdom,
and the United States.

Each year, OECD compiles cross-country data in the OECD
Health Data database, one of the most comprehensive
sources of comparable health-related statistics.

For More Information. See the OECD website at: http://www.
oecd.org/health.

Appendix II. Definitions and Methods

This appendix contains an alphabetical listing of terms used in *Health, United States*, and these definitions are specific to the data presented in this report. The methods used for calculating age-adjusted rates, average annual rates of change, relative standard errors, birth rates, death rates, and years of potential life lost are described. Included are standard populations used for age adjustment (Tables I and II), the years when the revisions for *International Classification of Diseases* (ICD) codes were in effect (Table III), codes for cause of death from the 6th through 10th revisions of ICD (Table IV), and comparability ratios between the 9th and 10th revisions (ICD–9 and ICD–10) for selected causes (Table V), imputed family income percentages from the National Health Interview Survey (NHIS) (Table VI), an analysis of the effect of added probe questions for Medicare and Medicaid coverage on health insurance rates in NHIS (Table VII), industry codes from the North American Industry Classification System (NAICS) (Table VIII), and ICD–9 Clinical Modification (ICD–9–CM) codes for external causes of injury and procedure categories (Tables IX and X). Standards for presenting federal data on race and ethnicity are described, and sample tabulations of NHIS data comparing the 1977 and 1997 Office of Management and Budget standards for the classification of federal data on race and ethnicity are presented in Tables XI and XII.

Acquired immunodeficiency syndrome (AIDS)—Human immunodeficiency virus (HIV) is the pathogen that causes AIDS, and HIV disease is the term that encompasses all of the condition's stages—from infection to the deterioration of the immune system and the onset of opportunistic diseases. However, AIDS is still the term most people use to refer to the immune deficiency caused by HIV. An AIDS diagnosis indicates that the person has reached the late stages of the disease and is given to people with HIV who have been diagnosed with at least one of a set of opportunistic diseases or whose laboratory values indicate advanced disease. All 50 states, the District of Columbia (D.C.), and six U.S. dependent areas (American Samoa, Guam, Northern Mariana Islands, Puerto Rico, Republic of Palau, and U.S. Virgin Islands) report confirmed diagnoses of HIV infection and AIDS cases to CDC using a uniform surveillance case definition and case report form. The case reporting definitions have changed over time to incorporate a broader range of AIDS-indicator diseases and conditions and use HIV diagnostic tests to improve the sensitivity and specificity of the definition. Because of these case definition changes, caution should be used when interpreting AIDS trends. (Also see Appendix II, Human immunodeficiency virus [HIV] disease.)

Active physician—See Appendix II, Physician.

Activities of daily living (ADL)—ADLs are activities related to personal care and include bathing or showering, dressing, getting into or out of bed or a chair, using the toilet, and eating. In the National Health Interview Survey, respondents were asked whether they or family members need the help of another person with personal care activities, such as eating, bathing, dressing, or getting around inside the home because of a physical, mental, or emotional problem.

In the Medicare Current Beneficiary Survey, the following personal care activities are defined as ADLs: bathing or showering, dressing, getting into or out of bed or a chair, using the toilet, and eating. If a sample person had any difficulty performing an activity by him- or herself and without special equipment, or did not perform the activity at all because of health problems, the person was categorized as having a limitation in that activity. The limitation may have been temporary or chronic at the time of interview. Sampled persons who were administered a community interview answered questions about health status and functioning themselves, if able to do so. If the sample person was not able to respond, a proxy answered the questions. For persons in a long-term care facility, a proxy, such as a nurse, answered questions about the sample person's health status and functioning. Starting in 1997, interview questions for people residing in long-term care facilities were changed slightly from those administered to people living in the community in order to differentiate residents who were independent from those who received supervision or assistance with transferring, locomotion on unit, dressing, eating, toilet use, and bathing. (Also see Appendix II, Basic actions difficulty; Complex activity limitation; Instrumental activities of daily living [IADL]; Limitation of activity.)

Admission—The American Hospital Association defines admissions as persons, excluding newborns, accepted for inpatient services during the survey reporting period. (Also see Appendix II, Days of care; Discharge; Inpatient.)

Age—Age is reported as age at last birthday (i.e., age in completed years), often calculated by subtracting the date of birth from the reference date, with the reference date being the date of the examination, interview, or other contact with an individual.

Mother's (maternal) age is reported on the birth certificate by all states. Birth statistics are presented for mothers aged 10–49 through 1996 and aged 10–54 starting in 1997, based on mother's date of birth or age as reported on the birth certificate. The age of the mother is edited for upper and lower limits. When the age of the mother is computed to be under 10 or 55 and over (50 and over in 1964–1996), it is considered not stated and is imputed according to the age of the mother from the previous birth record of the

Table I. United States projected year 2000 standard population and age groups used to age-adjust data

Data system and age	Population
DVS mortality data	
Total	274,633,642
Under 75 years	258,059,676
Under 1 year	3,794,901
1–4 years	15,191,619
5–14 years	39,976,619
15–24 years	38,076,743
25–34 years	37,233,437
35–44 years	44,659,185
45–54 years	37,030,152
55–64 years	23,961,506
65–74 years	18,135,514
75–84 years	12,314,793
85 years and over	4,259,173
DVS (Table 18)	
Under 75 years	258,059,676
Under 1 year	3,794,901
1–14 years	55,168,238
15–24 years	38,076,743
25–34 years	37,233,437
35–44 years	44,659,185
45–54 years	37,030,152
55–64 years	23,961,506
65–74 years	18,135,514
NHIS, NAMCS, and NHAMCS	
All ages.	274,633,642
18 years and over	203,852,188
25 years and over	177,593,760
40 years and over	118,180,367
65 years and over	34,709,480
Under 18 years	70,781,454
2–17 years	63,227,991
18–44 years	108,151,050
18–24 years	26,258,428
25–34 years	37,233,437
35–44 years	44,659,185
45–64 years	60,991,658
45–54 years	37,030,152
55–64 years	23,961,506
65–74 years	18,135,514
75 years and over	16,573,966
18–49 years	127,956,843
40–64 years:	
40–49 years	42,285,022
50–64 years	41,185,865

See footnotes at end of table.

Table I. United States projected year 2000 standard population and age groups used to age-adjust data —Con.

Data system and age	Population
NHANES	
20 years and over	195,850,985
20–34 years	55,490,662
35–44 years	44,659,185
45–54 years	37,030,152
55–64 years	23,961,506
65 years and over.	34,709,480
NHANES (Tables 40 and 53)	
20–44 years	100,149,847
45–64 years	60,991,658
65 years and over	34,709,480
NHANES (Table 56)	
20–44 years	100,149,847
45–64 years	60,991,658
65–74 years	18,135,514
75 years and over	16,573,966
NHANES (Table 79)	
Under 18 years	70,781,454
18–44 years	108,151,050
45–64 years	60,991,658
65 years and over	34,709,480

NOTES: DVS is Division of Vital Statistics.
NHIS is National Health Interview Survey.
NAMCS is National Ambulatory Medical Care Survey.
NHAMCS is National Hospital Ambulatory Medical Care Survey.
NHANES is National Health and Nutrition Examination Survey.

SOURCE: National Institutes of Health, National Cancer Institute, Surveillance, Epidemiology, and End Results (SEER). Standard populations—single ages. Available from: http://seer.cancer.gov/stdpopulations.

same race and total birth order (total of fetal deaths and live births). Before 1963, not-stated ages were distributed in proportion to the known ages for each racial group.

Beginning in 1997, the birth rate for the maternal age group 45–49 has included data for mothers aged 50–54 in the numerator and has been based on the population of women aged 45–49 in the denominator. Beginning with 2003 data, age of mother is imputed for stated ages 8 and under and 65 and over, for births occurring in states using the 2003 revision of the birth certificate. Starting with 2007 data, age of mother is imputed for all births for stated ages 8 and under and 65 and over, regardless of the birth certificate version used. As with data for earlier years, age is imputed according to the age of mother from the previous record with the same race and total birth order.

Age adjustment—Age adjustment is used to compare risks for two or more populations at one point in time or for one population at two or more points in time. Age-adjusted rates are computed by the direct method by applying age-specific rates in a population of interest to a standardized age distribution, to eliminate differences in observed rates that

Table II. United States projected year 2000 standard population and proportion distribution by age, for age-adjusting death rates prior to 2001

Age	Population	Proportion distribution (weight)	Standard million
Total	274,634,000	1.000000	1,000,000
Under 1 year	3,795,000	0.013818	13,818
1–4 years	15,192,000	0.055317	55,317
5–14 years.	39,977,000	0.145565	145,565
15–24 years.	38,077,000	0.138646	138,646
25–34 years.	37,233,000	0.135573	135,573
35–44 years.	44,659,000	0.162613	162,613
45–54 years.	37,030,000	0.134834	134,834
55–64 years.	23,961,000	0.087247	87,247
65–74 years.	18,136,000	0.066037	66,037
75–84 years.	12,315,000	*0.044842	44,842
85 years and over	4,259,000	0.015508	15,508

*Figure is rounded up instead of down to force total to 1.0.

SOURCE: NCHS. Anderson RN, Rosenberg HM. Age standardization of death rates: Implementation of the year 2000 standard. National vital statistics reports; vol 47 no 3. Hyattsville, MD: NCHS; 1998. Available from: http://www.cdc.gov/nchs/data/nvsr/nvsr47/nvs47_03.pdf.

result from age differences in population composition. Age-adjusted rates should be viewed as relative indexes rather than actual measures of risk.

Age-adjusted rates are calculated by the direct method, as follows:

$$\sum_{i=1}^{n} r_i \times (p_i / P)$$

where

r_i = rate in age group i in the population of interest

p_i = standard population in age group i

$$P = \sum_{i=1}^{n} p_i$$

n = total number of age groups over the age range of the age-adjusted rate.

Age adjustment by the direct method requires the use of a standard age distribution. The standard for age-adjusting death rates and estimates from surveys in *Health, United States* is the projected year 2000 U.S. resident population. Starting with *Health, United States, 2000*, the projected year 2000 U.S. standard population replaced the 1970 civilian noninstitutionalized population for age-adjusting estimates from most NCHS surveys; and starting with *Health, United States, 2001*, it was used uniformly and replaced the 1940 U.S. population for age-adjusting mortality statistics and the 1980 U.S. resident population, which previously had been used for age-adjusting estimates from the National Health and Nutrition Examination Survey.

Changing the standard population has implications for racial and ethnic differentials in mortality. For example, the mortality ratio for the black to white populations is reduced from 1.6 using the 1940 standard to 1.4 using the 2000

standard, reflecting the greater weight the 2000 standard gives to the older population, in which race differentials in mortality are smaller.

Age-adjusted estimates from any data source presented in *Health, United States* that use the projected year 2000 U.S. resident population may differ from age-adjusted estimates based on the same data presented in other reports if different age groups are used in the adjustment procedure.

For more information on implementing the 2000 population standard for age-adjusting death rates, see: Anderson RN, Rosenberg HM. Age standardization of death rates: Implementation of the year 2000 standard. National vital statistics reports; vol 47 no 3. Hyattsville, MD: NCHS; 1998. Available from: http://www.cdc.gov/nchs/data/nvsr/nvsr47/nvs47_03.pdf. For more information on the derivation of age-adjustment weights for use with NCHS survey data, see: Klein RJ, Schoenborn CA. Age adjustment using the 2000 projected U.S. population. Healthy People 2010 statistical notes, no 20. Hyattsville, MD: NCHS; 2001. Available from: http://www.cdc.gov/nchs/data/statnt/statnt20.pdf. The projected year 2000 U.S. standard population is available from the National Cancer Institute's Surveillance, Epidemiology, and End Results (SEER) Program: http://seer.cancer.gov/stdpopulations/stdpop.singleages.html.

Mortality data—Death rates are age-adjusted to the projected year 2000 U.S. standard population (Table I). Prior to 2001 data, age-adjusted rates were calculated using standard million proportions based on rounded population numbers (Table II). Starting with 2001 data, unrounded population numbers are used to age-adjust. Adjustment is based on 11 age groups, with two exceptions. First, age-adjusted death rates for black males and black females in 1950 are based on nine age groups, with under 1 and 1–4 combined as one group, and 75–84 and 85 and over combined as one group. Second, age-adjusted rates for years of potential life lost before age 75 also use the projected year 2000 standard population and are based on eight age groups: under 1, 1–14, 15–24, and 10-year age groups through 65–74.

National Health and Nutrition Examination Survey (NHANES)—Estimates based on the National Health Examination Survey and NHANES are generally age-adjusted to the projected year 2000 U.S. standard population by using five age groups: 20–34, 35–44, 45–54, 55–64, and 65–74 or 65 and over (Table I). Prior to *Health, United States, 2001*, these estimates were age-adjusted to the 1980 U.S. resident population.

National Health Care Surveys—Estimates based on the National Ambulatory Medical Care Survey, and the National Hospital Ambulatory Medical Care Survey are age-adjusted to the projected year 2000 U.S. standard population (Table I). Information on the age groups used in the age-adjustment procedure is contained in the footnotes to the specific tables.

National Health Interview Survey (NHIS)—Estimates based on NHIS are age-adjusted to the projected year 2000 U.S. standard population (Table I). Prior to *Health, United States, 2000*, NHIS estimates were age-adjusted to the 1970 civilian noninstitutionalized population. Information on the age groups used in the age-adjustment procedure is contained in the footnotes to the specific tables.

AIDS—See Appendix II, Acquired immunodeficiency syndrome (AIDS).

Alcohol consumption—Alcohol consumption is measured differently in the following data systems. (Also see Appendix II, Binge drinking.)

Monitoring the Future (MTF) Study—This school-based survey of secondary school students collects information on alcohol use by using self-completed questionnaires. To determine whether they have tried alcohol in their lifetime, students are asked a preliminary alcohol consumption (defined as beer, wine, liquor, and any other beverage that contains alcohol) screening question: "Have you ever had any alcoholic beverage to drink—more than just a few sips?" Students who reply in the affirmative are then asked additional questions about their alcohol consumption over different time frames: "On how many occasions (if any) have you had alcohol to drink—more than just a few sips… in your lifetime, …in the last 12 months, …in the last 30 days?" A subsequent question asks, "Think back over the last

two weeks. How many times have you had five or more drinks in a row?" A drink is defined as a bottle of beer, a glass of wine, a shot glass of liquor, a mixed drink, etc.

National Survey on Drug Use & Health (NSDUH)—Starting in 2002, NSDUH information about the frequency of the consumption of alcoholic beverages in the past 30 days has been obtained for all persons surveyed who are aged 12 and over. An extensive list of examples of the kinds of beverages covered is given to respondents prior to question administration. A drink is defined as a can or bottle of beer, a glass of wine or a wine cooler, a shot of liquor, or a mixed drink with liquor in it. Those times when the respondent had only a sip or two from a drink are not considered consumption. Alcohol use is based on the following questions: "During the past 30 days, on how many days did you drink one or more drinks of an alcoholic beverage?", "On the days that you drank during the past 30 days, how many drinks did you usually have?", and "During the past 30 days, on how many days did you have five or more drinks on the same occasion? By 'occasion,' we mean at the same time or within a couple of hours of each other."

Any-listed diagnosis—See Appendix II, Diagnosis.

Average annual rate of change (percent change)—In *Health, United States*, average annual rates of change, or growth rates, are calculated as follows:

$$[(P_n/P_o)^{1/N} - 1] \times 100$$

where

P_n = later time period
P_o = earlier time period
N = number of years in interval.

This geometric rate of change assumes that a variable increases or decreases at the same rate during each year between the two time periods.

Average length of stay—The American Hospital Association computes average length of stay by dividing the number of inpatient days by the number of admissions. (Also see Appendix II, Days of care; Discharge; Inpatient.)

Basic actions difficulty—Basic actions difficulty is a composite measure of disability designed to capture limitations or difficulties in movement, emotional, sensory, or cognitive functioning associated with a health problem. Persons with more than one of these difficulties are counted only once in the estimates. The full range of functional areas cannot be assessed on the basis of National Health Interview Survey (NHIS) questions; however, the available questions can identify difficulty in the following core areas of functioning:

- Movement (walking, standing, sitting, bending or kneeling, reaching overhead, grasping objects with fingers, and lifting).

- Selected elements of emotional functioning—in particular, feelings that interfere with accomplishing daily activities. Respondents were classified based on responses to a series of questions that measure psychological distress.

- Sensory functioning, based on difficulties seeing or hearing.

- Selected elements in cognitive functioning, specifically difficulties with remembering or experiencing confusion.

For many measures of disability, only disabilities resulting from an underlying condition that is chronic (based on nature and duration) are considered. However, whether the underlying conditions related to the core areas of basic actions difficulty were chronic was not a requirement in classifying persons. In *Health, United States*, respondents missing responses in a series of questions were classified as missing for that component. Respondents reporting that they "do not do this activity" were classified as missing for that activity. For hearing, respondents reporting that they were "deaf" or had "a lot of trouble" hearing without the use of hearing aids or other listening devices were coded as having a hearing limitation. For more information on how this measure was constructed using NHIS data, including the specific questions asked, see: Altman B, Bernstein A. Disability and health in the United States, 2001–2005. Hyattsville, MD: NCHS; 2008. Available from: http://www.cdc.gov/nchs/data/misc/disability2001-2005.pdf. (Also see Appendix II, Complex activity limitation; Hearing trouble.)

Bed, health facility—The American Hospital Association defines bed count as the number of beds, cribs, and pediatric bassinets that are set up and staffed for use by inpatients on the last day of the reporting period. In the Centers for Medicare & Medicaid Service's Quality Improvement Evaluation System (QIES) (formerly the Online Survey Certification and Reporting [OSCAR]) database, all beds in certified facilities are counted on the day of certification inspection. (Also see Appendix II, Hospital; Occupancy rate.)

Binge drinking—Binge drinking is measured in the following data systems. (Also see Appendix II, Alcohol consumption.)

Monitoring the Future (MTF) Study—This school-based survey of secondary school students collects information on alcohol use by using self-completed questionnaires. To determine whether they have tried alcohol, students are asked a preliminary screening question: "Have you ever had any alcoholic beverage to drink—more than just a few sips?" Students who reply in the affirmative are then asked additional questions about their alcohol consumption, including one on binge drinking: "Think back over the last two weeks. How many times have you had five or more drinks in a row?" A drink is defined as a bottle of beer, a glass of wine, a shot glass of liquor, a mixed drink, etc. Information on binge drinking is obtained for 12th graders (starting in 1975) and for 8th and 10th graders (starting in 1991).

National Survey on Drug Use & Health (NSDUH)—Starting in 2015, in NSDUH, binge alcohol use is defined as drinking five or more drinks on the same occasion on at least 1 day in the past 30 days for men. For women, binge drinking is defined as drinking four or more drinks on the same occasion on at least 1 day in the past 30 days. The threshold for determining binge alcohol use for women was lowered from five or more drinks on an occasion for the 2014 and earlier years to four or more drinks on an occasion for 2015. Heavy alcohol use is defined as binge drinking on five or more days in the past 30 days. Because heavy alcohol users are also binge alcohol users by definition, estimates of heavy alcohol use among women were also affected by the 2015 redesign. (Also see Appendix II, Alcohol consumption.)

Birth cohort—A birth cohort consists of all persons born within a given period of time, such as a calendar year.

Birth rate—See Appendix II, Rate: Birth and related rates.

Birthweight—Birthweight is the first weight of the newborn obtained after birth. Low birthweight is defined as weighing less than 2,500 grams (5 lb 8 oz). Very low birthweight is defined as weighing less than 1,500 grams (3 lb 4 oz). Prior to 1979, low birthweight was defined as weighing 2,500 grams or less, and very low birthweight as weighing 1,500 grams or less.

Blood pressure, high—In *Health, United States*, a person is considered to have hypertension if they have measured high blood pressure (i.e., average measured systolic blood pressure of at least 140 mm Hg or diastolic pressure of at least 90 mm Hg) and/or if they report that they are taking a prescription medicine for high blood pressure (respondents were asked, "Are you now taking prescribed medicine for your high blood pressure?"). Uncontrolled high blood pressure is defined as having an average measured systolic blood pressure of at least 140 mm Hg or diastolic pressure of at least 90 mm Hg, among those with hypertension. Those with uncontrolled high blood pressure also may be taking prescribed medicine for high blood pressure. These blood pressure definitions are consistent with the following: National Heart, Lung, and Blood Institute. Seventh report of the Joint National Committee on Prevention, Detection, Evaluation, and Treatment of High Blood Pressure. NIH pub no 04–5230. Bethesda, MD: National Institutes of Health;

2004. Available from: http://www.nhlbi.nih.gov/guidelines/hypertension/jnc7full.pdf; and Go AS, Bauman M, King SMC, Fonarow GC, Lawrence W, Williams KA, et al. AHA/ACC/CDC. An effective approach to high blood pressure control: A science advisory from the American Heart Association, the American College of Cardiology, and the Centers for Disease Control and Prevention. Hypertension 2014;63(4):878-85. Available from: https://www.ncbi.nlm.nih.gov/pubmed/24243703.

Blood pressure data presented in *Health, United States* are from the National Health and Nutrition Examination Survey (NHANES). Blood pressure is measured by averaging up to three blood pressure readings taken for an NHANES participant. Blood pressure readings of 0 mm Hg are not included in the estimates. The methods used to measure the blood pressure of participants have changed over the different NHANES survey years. Changes include the following:

- Number of blood pressure measurements taken (increased from one to four).

- Equipment maintenance procedures.

- Training of persons taking readings (physician, nurse, or interviewer).

- Proportion zero end-digits for systolic and diastolic readings.

- Published diastolic definition.

- Location where the measurements were taken (mobile examination center [MEC] or home).

In 1999 and subsequent years, blood pressure has been measured in the NHANES MEC by one of the MEC physicians. For people aged 8 and over, three consecutive blood pressure readings are obtained using the same arm. If a blood pressure measurement was interrupted or the measurer was unable to get one or more of the readings, a fourth attempt may be made. Both systolic and diastolic measurements are recorded to the nearest even number.

In NHANES III, three sets of blood pressure measurements were taken in the MEC for examinees aged 5 and over. Blood pressure measurements were also taken by trained interviewers during the household interview, on sample persons aged 17 and over. Systolic and diastolic average blood pressures were computed as the arithmetic mean of six or fewer measurements obtained at the household interview (maximum of three) and the MEC examination (maximum of three). If the examinee did not have blood pressure measurements taken in the MEC, this variable was calculated from measurements taken at the household interview. Both systolic and diastolic measurements were recorded to the nearest even number.

For more information on changes in blood pressure measurement in NHANES up to 1991, see: Burt VL, Cutler JA, Higgins M, Horan MJ, Labarthe D, Whelton P, et al. Trends in the prevalence, awareness, treatment, and control of hypertension in the adult U.S. population: Data from the health examination surveys, 1960 to 1991. Hypertension 1995;26(1):60–9.

Body mass index (BMI)—BMI is a measure that adjusts body weight for height. It is calculated as weight in kilograms divided by height in meters squared. Normal weight for adults is defined as a BMI of 18.5 to less than 25.0; overweight or obese is greater than or equal to 25.0; and obesity is greater than or equal to 30.0. Within the obesity category, Grade 1 obesity is defined as a BMI of 30.0 to less than 35.0; Grade 2 is 35.0 to less than 40.0; and Grade 3 is 40.0 or greater. Prior to assigning a person to a BMI category, BMI is rounded to one decimal place. In *Health, United States*, the NHANES variable Body Mass Index is used to assign persons to BMI categories. BMI cut points are defined in the following: National Heart, Lung, and Blood Institute. Managing overweight and obesity in adults: Systematic evidence review from the Obesity Expert Panel. Bethesda, MD: National Institutes of Health; 2013. Available from: https://www.nhlbi.nih.gov/health-pro/guidelines/in-develop/obesity-evidence-review; Jensen MD, Ryan DH, Apovian CM, Ard JD, Comuzzie AG, Donato KA, et al. 2013 AHA/ACC/TOS guideline for the management of overweight and obesity in adults: A report of the American College of Cardiology/American Heart Association Task Force on Practice Guidelines and the Obesity Society. Circulation; 2014;129(25 Suppl 2):S102-38. Available from: https://www.ncbi.nlm.nih.gov/pubmed/24222017; and HHS. Healthy People 2020: Nutrition, physical activity, and obesity; 2012. Available from: http://www.healthypeople.gov/2020/Leading-Health-Indicators. MEC weights were used to obtain estimates, and pregnant females were excluded. For 1988–1994 estimates for adults, almost 500 persons had an abbreviated exam in their home instead of going to the MEC. The MEC+home weight was used to include these persons in the estimates.

Obesity for children and adolescents is defined as a BMI at or above the sex- and age-specific 95th percentile from the 2000 CDC Growth Charts (http://www.cdc.gov/growthcharts/). The age used is age in months from the age at time of examination. Also see, Kuczmarski RJ, Ogden CL, Guo SS, et al. 2000 CDC Growth Charts for the United States: methods and development. Vital Health Stat 11. 2002 May; (246):1–190. Available at: http://www.cdc.gov/nchs/data/series/sr_11/sr11_246.pdf. MEC weights were used to obtain estimates, and pregnant girls were excluded. Starting with *Health, United States, 2010*, the terminology describing excess weight among children changed from previous editions. The term obesity now refers to children who were formerly labeled as overweight. This is a change in terminology only and not a change in measurement. For more information, see: Ogden CL, Flegal KM. Changes in terminology for childhood overweight and obesity. National health statistics report; no 25. Hyattsville, MD: NCHS; 2010. Available from: http://www.cdc.gov/nchs/data/nhsr/nhsr025.pdf.

Table III. Revision of the *International Classification of Diseases* (ICD), by year of conference in which adopted and years in use in the United States

ICD revision	Year of conference by which adopted	Years in use in United States
1st.	1900	1900–1909
2nd	1909	1910–1920
3rd	1920	1921–1929
4th.	1929	1930–1938
5th.	1938	1939–1948
6th.	1948	1949–1957
7th.	1955	1958–1967
8th.	1965	1968–1978
9th.	1975	1979–1998
10th.	1990	1999–present

SOURCE: NCHS. Available from: https://www.cdc.gov/nchs/icd/icd9.htm.

Cause of death—For the purpose of national mortality statistics, every death is attributed to one underlying condition, based on information reported on the death certificate and using the international rules for selecting the underlying cause of death from the conditions stated on the certificate. The underlying cause is defined by the World Health Organization (WHO) as "the disease or injury that initiated the train of events leading directly to death, or the circumstances of the accident or violence that produced the fatal injury." Generally, more medical information is reported on death certificates than is directly reflected in the underlying cause of death. Conditions that are not selected as the underlying cause of death constitute the nonunderlying causes of death, also known as multiple cause of death.

Cause of death is coded according to the appropriate revision of the *International Classification of Diseases* (ICD) (Table III). Effective with deaths occurring in 1999, the United States began using the 10th revision of the ICD (ICD–10); during the period 1979–1998, causes of death were coded and classified according to the 9th revision (ICD–9). Table IV lists ICD codes for the 6th through 10th revisions for causes of death shown in *Health, United States*. In *Health, United States*, common terms are sometimes used in the text in place of medical terminology. Examples include "cancer" for "malignant neoplasm" and "kidney disease" for "Nephritis, nephrotic syndrome, and nephrosis."

Each ICD revision has produced discontinuities in cause-of-death trends. These discontinuities are measured by using comparability ratios that are essential to the interpretation of mortality trends. For further discussion, see: http://www.cdc.gov/nchs/nvss/mortality/comparability_icd.htm. (Also see Appendix II, Comparability ratio; *International Classification of Diseases* [ICD]; and Appendix I, National Vital Statistics System [NVSS]; Multiple Cause-of-Death File.)

Cause-of-death ranking—Selected causes of death of public health and medical importance are compiled into tabulation lists and are ranked according to the number of deaths assigned to these causes. The top-ranking causes determine the leading causes of death. Certain causes on the tabulation lists are not ranked if, for example, the category title represents a group title (such as "Major cardiovascular diseases" and "Symptoms, signs, and abnormal clinical and laboratory findings, not elsewhere classified") or the category title begins with the words "Other" or "All other." In addition, when one of the titles that represents a subtotal (such as "Malignant neoplasms") is ranked, its component parts are not ranked. The tabulation lists used for ranking in the 10th revision of the *International Classification of Diseases* (ICD–10) include the List of 113 Selected Causes of Death, which replaces the ICD–9 List of 72 Selected Causes, HIV Infection and Alzheimer's Disease; and the ICD–10 List of 130 Selected Causes of Infant Death, which replaces the ICD–9 List of 60 Selected Causes of Infant Death and HIV Infection. Causes that are tied receive the same rank; the next cause is assigned the rank it would have received had the lower-ranked causes not been tied, that is, a rank is skipped. For more information, see the annual series of "Deaths: Final Data" and "Deaths: Leading Causes" reports, available from: http://www.cdc.gov/nchs/products/nvsr.htm. (Also see Appendix II, *International Classification of Diseases* [ICD].)

Children's Health Insurance Program (CHIP)—Title XXI of the Social Security Act, often referred to as the Children's Health Insurance Program (CHIP), is a program originally enacted by the Balanced Budget Act of 1997. The Children's Health Insurance Program Reauthorization Act of 2009 (CHIPRA, P.L. 111–3) reauthorized CHIP and appropriated funding for CHIP through FY 2013. The Affordable Care Act of 2010 (ACA, P.L. 111–148) extends CHIP funding through FY 2015, and the Medicare Access and CHIP Reauthorization Act of 2015 (P.L. 114–10) extended funding with no programmatic changes for CHIP through 2017. CHIP provides federal funds for states to provide health care coverage to eligible low-income, uninsured children whose income is too high to qualify for Medicaid. Generally, CHIP is only available through age 18. CHIP gives states broad flexibility in program design within a federal framework that includes important beneficiary protections. Funds from CHIP may be used for a separate child health program or to expand Medicaid. Although CHIP is not part of Medicaid, in some instances in *Health, United States*, data on CHIP and Medicaid are presented together, and those instances are discussed in the footnotes of the respective tables. For more information, see: https://www.medicaid.gov/chip/chip-program-information.html. (Also see Appendix II, Health insurance coverage; Medicaid.)

Cholesterol—Serum total cholesterol is a combination of high-density lipoprotein (HDL) cholesterol, low-density lipoprotein (LDL) cholesterol, and very low-density lipoprotein (VLDL) cholesterol and is highly correlated

Table IV. Cause-of-death codes, by applicable revision of the *International Classification of Diseases* (ICD)

Cause of death (10th Revision titles)	6th and 7th Revisions	8th Revision	9th Revision	10th Revision
Communicable diseases	. . .	. . .	001–139, 460–466, 480–487, 771.3	A00–B99, J00–J22
Chronic and noncommunicable diseases	. . .	. . .	140–459, 470–478, 490–799	C00–I99, J30–R99
Meningococcal Infection	. . .	. . .	036	A39
Septicemia	. . .	. . .	038	A40–A41
Human immunodeficiency virus (HIV) disease [1]	. . .	. . .	*042–*044	B20–B24
Malignant neoplasms	140–205	140–209	140–208	C00–C97
Colon, rectum, and anus	153–154	153–154	153, 154	C18–C21
Trachea, bronchus, and lung	162–163	162	162	C33–C34
Breast	170	174	174–175	C50
Prostate	177	185	185	C61
In situ neoplasms, benign neoplasms, and neoplasms of uncertain or unknown behavior	210–239	210–239	210–239	D00–D48
Diabetes mellitus	260	250	250	E10–E14
Anemias	. . .	. . .	280–285	D50–D64
Meningitis	. . .	. . .	320–322	G00, G03
Alzheimer's disease	. . .	. . .	331.0	G30
Diseases of heart	400–402, 410–443	390–398, 402, 404, 410–429	390–398, 402, 404, 410–429	I00–I09, I11, I13, I20–I51
Ischemic heart disease	. . .	. . .	410–414, 429.2	I20–I25
Essential hypertension and hypertensive renal disease	. . .	. . .	. . .	I10, I12, I15
Cerebrovascular diseases	330–334	430–438	430–434, 436–438	I60–I69
Atherosclerosis	. . .	. . .	440	I70
Influenza and pneumonia [2]	480–483, 490–493	470–474, 480–486	480–487	J09–J18
Chronic lower respiratory diseases	241, 501, 502, 527.1	490–493, 519.3	490–494, 496	J40–J47
Chronic liver disease and cirrhosis	581	571	571	K70, K73–K74
Nephritis, nephrotic syndrome, and nephrosis	. . .	. . .	580–589	N00–N07, N17–N19, N25–N27
Pregnancy, childbirth, and the puerperium	640–689	630–678	630–676	O00–O99
Congenital malformations, deformations and chromosomal abnormalities	. . .	. . .	740–759	Q00–Q99
Certain conditions originating in the perinatal period	. . .	. . .	760–779	P00–P96
Newborn affected by maternal complications of pregnancy	. . .	. . .	761	P01
Newborn affected by complications of placenta, cord and membranes	. . .	. . .	762	P02
Disorders related to short gestation and low birthweight, not elsewhere classified	. . .	. . .	765	P07
Birth trauma	. . .	. . .	767	P10–P15
Intrauterine hypoxia and birth asphyxia	. . .	. . .	768	P20–P21
Respiratory distress of newborn	. . .	. . .	769	P22
Bacterial sepsis of newborn	. . .	. . .	. . .	P36
Necrotizing enterocolitis of newborn	. . .	. . .	777.5	P77
Sudden infant death syndrome	. . .	. . .	798.0	R95

See footnotes at end of table.

Table IV. Cause-of-death codes, by applicable revision of the *International Classification of Diseases* (ICD)—Con.

Cause of death (10th Revision titles)	6th and 7th Revisions	8th Revision	9th Revision	10th Revision
Injuries[2]	. . .	. . .	E800–E869, E880–E929, E950–E999	*U01–*U03, V01–Y36, Y85–Y87, Y89
Unintentional injuries[3]	E800–E936, E960–E965	E800–E929, E940–E946	E800–E869, E880–E929	V01–X59, Y85–Y86
Motor vehicle-related injuries[3]	E810–E835	E810–E823	E810–E825	V02–V04, V09.0, V09.2, V12–V14, V19.0–V19.2, V19.4–V19.6, V20–V79, V80.3–V80.5, V81.0–V81.1, V82.0–V82.1, V83–V86, V87.0–V87.8, V88.0–V88.8, V89.0, V89.2
Poisoning	E870–E888, E890–E895	E850–E877	E850–E869	X40–X49
Suicide[2]	E963, E970–E979	E950–E959	E950–E959	*U03, X60–X84, Y87.0
Homicide[2]	E964, E980–E983	E960–E969	E960–E969	*U01–*U02, X85–Y09, Y87.1
Firearm-related injury	. . .	E922, E955, E965, E970, E985	E922, E955.0–E955.4, E965.0–E965.4, E970, E985.0–E985.4	*U01.4, W32–W34, X72–X74, X93–X95, Y22–Y24, Y35.0
Injury by drug poisoning	. . .	. . .	. . .	X40–X44, X60–64, X85, Y10–Y14
Heroin	. . .	. . .	. . .	X40–X44, X60–64, X85, Y10–Y14 (underlying cause) and T40.1 (multiple cause)
Opioid analgesics	. . .	. . .	. . .	X40–X44, X60–64, X85, Y10–Y14 (underlying cause) and T40.2–T40.4 (multiple cause)

. . . Cause-of-death codes are not provided for causes not shown in *Health, United States*.

[1] Categories for coding human immunodeficiency virus (HIV) infection were introduced in 1987. The asterisk (*) indicates codes that are not part of ICD–9.

[2] Starting with 2001 data, NCHS introduced categories *U01–*U03 for classifying and coding deaths due to acts of terrorism. The asterisk (*) indicates codes that are not part of ICD–10. Starting with 2007 data, NCHS introduced the category J09 for coding avian influenza virus. In 2009, the title for the ICD–10 code J09 was changed from Influenza due to identified avian influenza virus to Influenza due to certain identified influenza virus. This change was made to accommodate deaths from influenza A (H1N1) virus in the ICD–10 code J09 for data years 2009 and beyond.

[3] In the public health community, the term unintentional injuries is preferred to accidents, and the term motor vehicle-related injuries is preferred to motor vehicle accidents.

SOURCE: NCHS. Advance report: Final mortality statistics, 1974. Monthly vital statistics report; vol 24 no 11 suppl. Hyattsville, MD: NCHS; 1976. Available from: http://www.cdc.gov/nchs/data/mvsr/supp/mv24_11sacc.pdf. Hoyert DL, Kochanek KD, Murphy SL. Deaths: Final data for 1997. National vital statistics reports; vol 47 no 19. Hyattsville, MD: NCHS; 1999. Available from: http://www.cdc.gov/nchs/data/nvsr/nvsr47/nvs47_19.pdf. Hoyert DL, Heron MP, Murphy SL, Kung H-C. Deaths: Final data for 2003. National vital statistics reports; vol 54 no 13. Hyattsville, MD: NCHS; 2006. Available from: http://www.cdc.gov/nchs/data/nvsr/nvsr54/nvsr54_13.pdf. Murphy SL, Xu JQ, Kochanek KD. Deaths: Final data for 2010. National vital statistics reports; vol 61 no 4. Hyattsville, MD: NCHS; 2013. Available from: http://www.cdc.gov/nchs/data/nvsr/nvsr61/nvsr61_04.pdf. Murphy SL, Kochanek KD, Xu JQ, Curtin SC. Deaths: Final data for 2015. National vital statistics reports. Hyattsville, MD: NCHS; 2017. Available from: https://www.cdc.gov/nchs/products/nvsr.htm.

with LDL cholesterol. High serum total cholesterol is a risk factor for cardiovascular disease (see Wilson PW, D'Agostino RB, Levy D, Belanger AM, Silbershatz H, Kannel WB. Prediction of coronary heart disease using risk factor categories. Circulation 97(18):1837–47. 1998). In its 2002 report on high blood cholesterol, the National Cholesterol Education Program Expert Panel on Detection, Evaluation, and Treatment of High Blood Cholesterol in Adults (Adult Treatment Panel III, or ATP III) considered a serum total cholesterol value greater than or equal to 240 mg/dL (6.20 mmol/L) as high. A more recent set of guidelines—the result of a collaboration among the National Heart, Lung, and Blood Institute; the American College of Cardiology; and the American Heart Association—focused on which groups of people could benefit from statin use, based on their risk factors. Because *Health, United States* focuses on providing population-level prevalence data rather than individual-level estimates, three broad indicators of cholesterol are presented based on measured serum total cholesterol level and the reported use of cholesterol-lowering medications. Cholesterol levels are determined using the NHANES T_CHOL file. For more information on the current cholesterol guidelines, see: Management of blood cholesterol in adults: Systematic evidence review from the Cholesterol Expert Panel. Bethesda, MD: National Institutes of Health, National Heart, Lung, and Blood Institute; 2013. Available from: http://www.nhlbi.nih.gov/health-pro/guidelines/in-develop/cholesterol-in-adults; and Stone NJ, Robinson JG, Lichtenstein AH, Merz CNB, Blum CB, Eckel RH, et al. 2013 ACC/AHA guideline on the treatment of blood cholesterol to reduce atherosclerotic cardiovascular risk in adults: A report of the American College of Cardiology/American Heart Association Task Force on Practice Guidelines. Circulation. 2014;129:S1–45. Available from: http://circ.ahajournals.org/content/129/25_suppl_2/S1.full.

In *Health, United States*, three measures of total cholesterol are presented: hypercholesterolemia, high serum total cholesterol, and mean serum total cholesterol. Hypercholesterolemia is based on both laboratory testing and self-reported medication use. It is defined as measured serum total cholesterol greater than or equal to 240 mg/dL or reporting taking cholesterol-lowering medications. Respondents who were told by a doctor or health professional that their cholesterol was high, and were told by a doctor to take cholesterol-lowering medication and who answered "yes" to the question, "Are you now following this advice?" were classified as taking cholesterol-lowering medication. High serum total cholesterol is defined as measured serum total cholesterol greater than or equal to 240 mg/dL (6.20 mmol/L). Both high serum cholesterol and mean serum total cholesterol are based on serum samples collected during the National Health and Nutrition Examination Survey (NHANES) examination.

Venous blood serum samples collected from NHANES participants at mobile examination centers were frozen and shipped on dry ice to the laboratory conducting the lipid analyses. Serum total cholesterol was measured on all examined adults regardless of whether they had fasted, and data were analyzed regardless of fasting status. Cholesterol measurements are standardized according to the criteria of CDC—and later the CDC–National Heart, Lung, and Blood Institute Cholesterol Standardization Program—to ensure comparable and accurate measurements. For more information, see: Myers GL, Cooper GR, Winn CL, Smith SJ. The Centers for Disease Control–National Heart, Lung, and Blood Institute Lipid Standardization Program: An approach to accurate and precise lipid measurements. Clin Lab Med 1989;9(1):105–35. A detailed summary of the procedures used for measurement of total cholesterol in the earlier NHANES survey years has been published in: Carroll MD, Kit BK, Lacher DA, Shero ST, Mussolino ME. Trends in lipids and lipoproteins in US adults, 1988–2010. JAMA 2012;308(15):1545–54. A description of the laboratory procedures for the total cholesterol measurement for different NHANES survey years is published by NCHS and is available from: http://www.cdc.gov/nchs/nhanes.htm.

Cigarette smoking—Cigarette smoking and related tobacco use are measured in the following data systems.

Monitoring the Future (MTF) Study—Information on current cigarette smoking was obtained for 12th graders (starting in 1975) and for 8th and 10th graders (starting in 1991), based on the following question: "How frequently have you smoked cigarettes during the past 30 days?" Information on e-cigarette use was obtained for 8th, 10th, and 12th graders (starting in 2014), based on the following question: "During the last 30 days, on how many days (if any), have you used electronic cigarettes (e-cigarettes)?"

National Health Interview Survey (NHIS)—Information about cigarette smoking is obtained for adults aged 18 and over. Starting in 1993, current smokers are identified by asking the following two questions: "Have you smoked at least 100 cigarettes in your entire life?" and "Do you now smoke cigarettes every day, some days, or not at all?" Persons who smoked 100 cigarettes and who now smoke every day or some days were defined as current smokers. Before 1992, current smokers were identified based on positive responses to the following two questions: "Have you smoked 100 cigarettes in your entire life?" and "Do you smoke now?" (traditional definition). In 1992, the definition of current smoker in NHIS was modified to separately identify persons who smoked every day and those who smoked on some days (revised definition). In 1992, cigarette smoking data were collected for a half-sample, with one-half of respondents (one-quarter sample) answering the traditional smoking questions and the other one-half (one-quarter sample) answering the revised smoking question, "Do you smoke every day, some days, or not at all?" An unpublished analysis of the 1992 traditional smoking measure revealed that the crude percentage of current smokers aged 18 and over remained the same as for 1991. The estimates for 1992 shown in *Health, United States* combine data collected using both the traditional and revised questions. Estimates for 1993 and beyond use the revised questions.

In 1993–1995, estimates of cigarette smoking prevalence were based on a half-sample. Smoking data were not collected in 1996. Starting in 1997, smoking data were collected in the Sample Adult questionnaire. Starting in 2014, a question was added to the survey on the use of electronic cigarettes, often referred to as e-cigarettes. Electronic cigarette use was not considered in the definition of current cigarette smoking. For more information on e-cigarette use, see: Schoenborn CA, Gindi RM. Electronic cigarette use among adults: United States, 2014. NCHS data brief, no 217. Hyattsville, MD: NCHS. 2015. Available from: http://www.cdc.gov/nchs/data/databriefs/db217.htm. For more information on survey methodology and sample sizes pertaining to NHIS cigarette smoking data, see the NHIS Adult Tobacco Use Information website at: http://www.cdc.gov/nchs/nhis/tobacco.htm.

National Survey on Drug Use & Health (NSDUH)— Information on current cigarette smoking is obtained for all persons surveyed who are aged 12 and over, based on the following question: "Now think about the past 30 days, that is, from [DATE] up to and including today. During the past 30 days, have you smoked part or all of a cigarette?" Electronic cigarette use was not considered in the definition of current cigarette smoking.

Civilian noninstitutionalized population; Civilian population—See Appendix II, Population.

Colorectal tests or procedures—Colorectal tests or procedures are used to detect polyps, abnormal cell growth, lesions, and other gastrointestinal conditions, including colon cancer. These tests may include home fecal occult blood tests (FOBT), sigmoidoscopy, or colonoscopy. The time interval between screenings varies, depending on the type of test as well as individual risk factors and prior screening history.

In the National Health Interview Survey, questions about colorectal tests or procedures were asked of respondents aged 40 and over on an intermittent schedule, and the questions varied over time. Colorectal screening tests and procedures may be used for diagnostic or screening purposes, but the purpose cannot be determined from NHIS.

In 2000, 2003, 2005, and 2008, respondents were asked, "Have you ever had a sigmoidoscopy, colonoscopy, or proctoscopy?" In 2010, 2013, and 2015, respondents

were asked two separate questions: "Have you ever had a colonoscopy?" and "Have you ever had a sigmoidoscopy?" An additional question about colorectal testing, "Have you ever had a blood stool test using a home testing kit?" was asked in all of these survey years.

Respondents who replied that they had a colorectal test or procedure were asked subsequent questions about the month, year, and time since their most recent test or procedure. In 2000 and 2003, if respondents did not provide the year of, or the time since, their most recent colorectal exam, they were asked about the time frame of their most recent exam (i.e., whether they had the exam a year ago or less, more than 1 year ago but not more than 2 years ago, more than 2 years ago but not more than 3 years ago, more than 3 years ago but not more than 5 years ago, more than 5 years ago but not more than 10 years ago, or over 10 years ago). For adults who provided the year, but not the month, of their most recent exam, the exam date was coded as July 15 of the provided year.

In 2005, 2008, 2010, 2013, and 2015, the questionnaire skip pattern was modified so that respondents giving an incomplete or partial date (missing month or year) of their most recent colorectal exam were asked a follow-up question about the time since their most recent exam (i.e., whether they had the exam a year ago or less, more than 1 year ago but not more than 2 years ago, more than 2 years ago but not more than 3 years ago, more than 3 years ago but not more than 5 years ago, more than 5 years ago but not more than 10 years ago, or over 10 years ago). In 2015, the home FOBT questions were modified to include fecal immunochemical tests (FITs)—a type of FOBT ("Have you ever had a blood stool or FIT test, using a home test kit?"). In 2010 and 2015, additional questions on the use of virtual or CT colonoscopy were included in the questionnaire, but these questions were not used to determine whether respondents had a colorectal test or procedure in *Health, United States*.

In *Health, United States*, adults aged 50–75 were considered to have any colorectal test or procedure if they met the screening guidelines made by the U.S. Preventive Services Task Force (USPSTF) in 2008. These adults either reported (1) a home fecal occult blood test (FOBT) in the past year, (2) a sigmoidoscopy procedure in the past 5 years with FOBT in the past 3 years, or (3) a colonoscopy in the past 10 years.

The current USPSTF recommendations—made in 2016— have not been applied to *Health, United States* estimates. These guidelines recommend the use of screening in adults aged 50 to 75. Frequency of screening varies by test and procedure, and recommend strategies include: (1) annual or biennial screening with guaiac-based FOBT (gFOBT) in addition to flexible sigmoidoscopy every 3 to 5 years, (2) annual screening with FITs, (3) screening every 10 years with colonoscopy, or (4) screening every 5 years with CT colography. The recommendation does not emphasize a particular screening approach, as the risks and benefits may vary. For a summary of current colorectal screening recommendations and the status of the review, see: http://www.uspreventiveservicestaskforce.org/Page/Document/UpdateSummaryFinal/colorectal-cancer-screening2.

Community hospital—See Appendix II, Hospital.

Comparability ratio—About every 10 to 20 years, the *International Classification of Diseases* (ICD) is revised to stay abreast of advances in medical science and changes in medical terminology. Each of these revisions produces breaks in the continuity of cause-of-death statistics because of changes in classification and in the rules for selecting an underlying cause of death. Classification and rule changes affect cause-of-death trend data by shifting deaths away from some cause-of-death categories and into others. Comparability ratios measure the effect of changes in classification and coding rules. For the causes shown in Table V, comparability ratios range between 0.6974 and 1.5812. Influenza and pneumonia had the lowest comparability ratio (0.6974), indicating that this cause is about 30% less likely to be selected as the underlying cause of death under ICD–10 than under ICD–9. Alzheimer's disease had the highest comparability ratio (1.5812), indicating that Alzheimer's disease is 58% more likely to be selected as the underlying cause when ICD–10 coding is used.

For selected causes of death, the ICD–9 codes used to calculate death rates for 1980–1998 differ from the ICD–9 codes most nearly comparable with the corresponding ICD–10 cause-of-death category, which also affects the ability to compare death rates across ICD revisions. Examples of these causes are Ischemic heart disease; Cerebrovascular diseases; Trachea, bronchus, and lung cancer; Unintentional injuries; and Homicide. To address this source of discontinuity, mortality trends for 1980–1998 were recalculated using ICD–9 codes that are more comparable with codes for corresponding ICD–10 categories. Table IV shows the ICD–9 codes used for these causes. This modification may lessen the discontinuity between the 9th and 10th revisions, but the effect on the discontinuity between the 8th and 9th revisions is not measured.

Comparability ratios shown in Table V are based on a comparability study in which the same deaths were coded using both the 9th and 10th revisions. The comparability ratio was calculated by dividing the number of deaths classified by ICD–10 by the number of deaths classified by ICD–9. The resulting ratios represent the net effect of the 10th revision on cause-of-death statistics and can be used to adjust mortality statistics for causes of death classified by the 9th revision to be comparable with cause-specific mortality statistics classified by the 10th revision.

The application of comparability ratios to mortality statistics helps make the analysis of change between 1998 and 1999 more accurate and complete. The 1998 comparability-

Table V. Comparability of selected causes of death between the 9th and 10th revisions of the *International Classification of Diseases* (ICD)

Cause of death [1]	Final comparability ratio [2]
Human immunodeficiency virus (HIV) disease	1.0821
Malignant neoplasms	1.0093
Colon, rectum, and anus	0.9988
Trachea, bronchus, and lung	0.9844
Breast	1.0073
Prostate	1.0144
Diabetes mellitus	1.0193
Alzheimer's disease	1.5812
Diseases of heart	0.9852
Ischemic heart diseases	1.0006
Essential (primary) hypertension and hypertensive renal disease	1.1162
Cerebrovascular diseases	1.0502
Influenza and pneumonia	0.6974
Chronic lower respiratory diseases	1.0411
Chronic liver disease and cirrhosis	1.0321
Nephritis, nephrotic syndrome, and nephrosis	1.2555
Pregnancy, childbirth, and the puerperium	1.1404
Unintentional injuries	1.0251
Motor vehicle-related injuries	0.9527
Poisoning	1.0365
Suicide	1.0022
Homicide	1.0020
Firearm-related injury	1.0012
Chronic and noncommunicable diseases	1.0100
Injuries	1.0159

[1] See Table IV for ICD–9 and ICD–10 cause-of-death codes.
[2] Ratio of number of deaths classified by ICD–10 to number of deaths classified by ICD–9.

SOURCE: NCHS. Final comparability ratios for 113 selected causes of death. Available from: ftp://ftp.cdc.gov/pub/Health_Statistics/NCHS/Datasets/Comparability/icd9_icd10/Comparability_Ratio_tables.xls. Miniño AM, Anderson RN, Fingerhut LA, Boudreault MA, Warner M. Deaths: Injuries, 2002. National vital statistics reports; vol 54 no 10. Hyattsville, MD: NCHS; 2006. Available from: http://www.cdc.gov/nchs/data/nvsr/nvsr54/nvsr54_10.pdf.

modified death rate is calculated by multiplying the comparability ratio by the 1998 death rate. Comparability-modified rates should be used to estimate mortality change between 1998 and 1999.

Caution should be used when applying the comparability ratios presented in Table V to age-, race-, and sex-specific mortality data. Demographic subgroups may sometimes differ with regard to their cause-of-death distribution, and this would result in demographic variation in cause-specific comparability ratios.

For more information, see: Anderson RN, Miniño AM, Hoyert DL, Rosenberg HM. Comparability of cause of death between ICD–9 and ICD–10: Preliminary estimates. National vital statistics reports; vol 49 no 2. Hyattsville, MD: NCHS; 2001.

Available from: http://www.cdc.gov/nchs/data/nvsr/nvsr49/nvsr49_02.pdf; Kochanek KD, Smith BL, Anderson RN. Deaths: Preliminary data for 1999. National vital statistics reports; vol 49 no 3. Hyattsville, MD: NCHS; 2001. Available from: http://www.cdc.gov/nchs/data/nvsr/nvsr49/nvsr49_03.pdf; Final ratios for 113 selected causes of death, available from: ftp://ftp.cdc.gov/pub/Health_Statistics/NCHS/Datasets/Comparability/icd9_icd10/; and the ICD comparability ratio website at: http://www.cdc.gov/nchs/nvss/mortality/comparability_icd.htm. (Also see Appendix II, Cause of death; *International Classification of Diseases* [ICD].)

Compensation—See Appendix II, Employer costs for employee compensation.

Complex activity limitation—Complex activity limitation is a composite measure of disability constructed to measure disability as defined by the inability to function successfully in certain social roles. Complex activities consist of the tasks and organized activities that make up a number of social roles, such as working, maintaining a household, living independently, and participating in community activities. Complex activity performance requires the execution of a combination of core areas of functioning. Complex activities include the following:

- Maintaining independence, including self-care and the ability to carry out activities associated with maintaining a household, such as shopping, cooking, and taking care of bills. (Measures are based on questions commonly known as activities of daily living [ADLs] and instrumental activities of daily living [IADLs].) Limitations in these activities usually reflect severe restrictions and are associated with limitations in other complex activities.

- Difficulties experienced with social and leisure activities—represented in this measure by attending movies or sporting events, visiting friends, or pursuing hobbies or relaxation activities.

- Perceived limitation in the ability to work (a core aspect of social participation for the majority of the U.S. population)—represented by the respondent's self-defined limitation in the kind or amount of work they can do or their inability to work at a job or business.

For many measures of disability, only disabilities resulting from an underlying condition that is chronic (based on nature and duration) are considered. However, whether the underlying conditions related to the complex activities were chronic was not a requirement in classifying persons as having a complex activity limitation. In *Health, United States*, respondents missing responses in a series of questions were classified as missing for that component. Respondents reporting that they "do not do this activity" were classified as missing for that activity. For more information on how this measure was constructed using data from the National Health Interview Survey, including the specific questions asked, see: Altman B, Bernstein A. Disability and health

in the United States, 2001–2005. Hyattsville, MD: NCHS; 2008. Available from: http://www.cdc.gov/nchs/data/misc/disability2001-2005.pdf. (Also see Appendix II, Activities of daily living [ADL]; Basic actions difficulty; Instrumental activities of daily living [IADL].)

Consumer Price Index (CPI)—The CPI, prepared by the U.S. Bureau of Labor Statistics, is a monthly measure of the average change in prices of goods and services purchased by urban households. The medical care component of the CPI shows trends in medical care prices based on specific indicators of hospital, medical, and drug prices. A revised definition of the CPI has been in use since January 1988. (Also see Appendix II, Gross domestic product [GDP]; and Health expenditures, national.)

Contraception—The National Survey of Family Growth collects information on contraceptive use as reported by women aged 15–44. To determine current contraceptive use, women were asked to identify up to four, out of 21, contraceptive methods they had used during the month of interview. In the 2011–2015 NSFG, these methods included birth control pills, condoms, male sterilization, female sterilization, withdrawal, injectables, hormonal implants, calendar rhythm, natural family planning, diaphragm, female condoms, foams, jelly or creams, cervical caps, suppositories or inserts, sponge, intrauterine device, emergency contraception, contraceptive patches, vaginal contraceptive rings, or other methods.

Cost to charge ratio—The Agency for Healthcare Research and Quality's Healthcare Cost and Utilization Project (HCUP) contains data on total charges per discharge as reported on the hospital discharge record. This charge information represents the amount the hospital billed for services but does not reflect how much hospital services actually cost or the specific amounts that hospitals received in payment. Data on costs may be of more interest to some users. The HCUP Cost-to-Charge ratio files convert charges to costs. Each file contains hospital-specific cost-to-charge ratios based on all-payer inpatient cost for nearly every hospital in HCUP. Cost information was obtained from hospital cost reports collected by the Centers for Medicare & Medicaid Services. Some imputations for missing values were necessary. These files are unique by year.

Critical access hospital—See Appendix II, Hospital.

Crude birth rate; Crude death rate—See Appendix II, Rate: Birth and related rates; Rate: Death and related rates.

Days of care—Days of care is defined by the American Hospital Association as the number of adult and pediatric days of care rendered during the entire reporting period. Days of care for newborns are excluded. (Also see Appendix II, Admission; Average length of stay; Discharge; Hospital; Hospital utilization; Inpatient.)

Death rate—See Appendix II, Rate: Death and related rates.

Dental caries—Dental caries is evidence of decay on the crown or enamel surface of a tooth (i.e., coronal caries) and includes treated and untreated caries. Untreated dental caries refers to decay on the crown or enamel surface of a tooth (i.e., coronal caries) that has not been treated or filled. Decay in the root (i.e., root caries) was not included.

In *Health, United States*, estimates on the presence of caries are based on evaluation of primary and permanent teeth for persons aged 5 and over. The third molars were not included. Persons without at least one natural tooth (primary or permanent) were classified as edentulous (without any teeth) and were excluded. The majority of edentulous persons are aged 65 and over. Estimates of edentulism among persons aged 65 and over are 33% in 1988–1994, 23% in 2005–2008, and 17% in 2011–2014.

Dental caries was identified by an oral examination as part of the National Health and Nutrition Examination Survey (NHANES). Over time, there have been changes in the NHANES oral health examination process, ages examined, and methodology. During 1988–1994, a full-mouth complete oral health exam was conducted by a trained dentist on those aged 1 and over. During 1999–2004, a full-mouth complete oral health exam was conducted by a trained dentist on those aged 2 and over. During 2005–2008, data were collected for those aged 5 and over by a trained health technologist using the Basic Screening Examination (BSE), a simplified screening process to collect information on untreated caries, dental restorations, and dental sealants. During 2009–2010, the BSE was conducted by a trained dental hygienist on those aged 3–19. No data on adults were collected. During 2005–2008 and 2009–2010, the use of the BSE does not allow us to determine if untreated decay was found in permanent teeth or primary teeth. For 2011–2014 data, a full-mouth complete oral health exam was conducted by a trained dentist on those aged 1 and over.

For more information, see: Dye BA, Barker LK, Li X, Lewis BG, Beltrán-Aguilar ED. Overview and quality assurance for the oral health component of the National Health and Nutrition Examination Survey (NHANES), 2005–08. J Public Health Dent 2011;71(1):54–61; and the following NHANES resources: https://wwwn.cdc.gov/nchs/nhanes/2007-2008/OHX_E.htm, https://wwwn.cdc.gov/nchs/nhanes/2009-2010/OHXDEN_F.htm, and https://wwwn.cdc.gov/Nchs/Nhanes/2013-2014/OHXDEN_H.htm.

Dental visit—Starting in 1997, National Health Interview Survey respondents were asked, "About how long has it been since you last saw or talked to a dentist? Include all types of dentists, such as orthodontists, oral surgeons, and all other dental specialists as well as hygienists." Starting in 2001, the question was modified slightly to ask respondents how long it had been since they last saw a dentist. Questions about dental visits were not asked for children under age 2 for years 1997–1999 and under age 1 for years 2000 and beyond. Starting with 1997 data, estimates are presented for people with a dental visit in the past year.

Diabetes—Diabetes is a group of conditions in which insulin is not adequately secreted or utilized. Diabetes is a leading cause of disease and death in the United States. Using data from the National Health and Nutrition Examination Survey (NHANES), three measures of diabetes are presented in *Health, United States*: physician-diagnosed diabetes, undiagnosed diabetes, and total diabetes. Physician-diagnosed diabetes data were obtained by self-report. Respondents who answered "yes" to the question, "Other than during pregnancy, have you ever been told by a doctor or health professional that you have diabetes or sugar diabetes?" were classified as having physician-diagnosed diabetes.

Only respondents who were not classified as having physician-diagnosed diabetes were evaluated to determine if they had undiagnosed diabetes. Undiagnosed diabetes was based on the results of laboratory testing of whole blood and blood plasma samples collected from NHANES participants at mobile examination centers. Undiagnosed diabetes was defined as a fasting plasma glucose (FPG) of at least 126 mg/dL or a hemoglobin A1c of at least 6.5% and no reported physician diagnosis. Respondents had fasted for at least 8 hours and less than 24 hours at the time of the blood draw. Fasting is not necessary to measure hemoglobin A1c. However, to be consistent with the subsample of fasting respondents used for FPG, assessment of undiagnosed diabetes in *Health, United States* is limited to the fasting subsample. Total diabetes includes those who were classified as having either physician-diagnosed or undiagnosed diabetes. Fasting weights were used to obtain prevalence estimates, and pregnant women were excluded.

Starting with *Health, United States, 2010*, an elevated hemoglobin A1c (greater than or equal to 6.5%) was included as a component of the definition of undiagnosed diabetes, along with FPG. Previous editions of *Health, United States* did not evaluate hemoglobin A1c to classify respondents as having undiagnosed diabetes; undiagnosed diabetes was based solely on elevated FPG (greater than or equal to 126 mg/dL) among those without physician-diagnosed diabetes. The revised definition of undiagnosed diabetes was based on recommendations from the American Diabetes Association (ADA). Hemoglobin A1c was recommended as a component in diagnosing diabetes because recent improvements in assay standardization make A1c results more reliable. In addition, research has provided evidence linking elevated A1c levels with diabetic complications, thus allowing for a threshold to be set above which patients would be diagnosed as having diabetes. Although the ADA recommends using hemoglobin A1c greater than or equal to 6.5% as an indicator of undiagnosed diabetes, it cautions that A1c may be misleading in individuals with certain blood disorders (including sickle cell trait), which may have specific ethnic or geographic distributions. Therefore, clinicians may use other criteria and tests to diagnose a specific patient. For more information, see: Diagnosis and classification of diabetes mellitus. Diabetes Care 2015;38(suppl 1):S8–S16; Standards of medical care in diabetes—2010. Diabetes Care 2010;33(suppl 1):S11–S61; and International Expert Committee Report on the role of the A1c assay in the diagnosis of diabetes. Diabetes Care 2009;32(7):1327–34. To ensure data comparability over time, the revised definition of undiagnosed diabetes was applied to all estimates shown in *Health, United States*. As expected, this revised definition increased the percentage of respondents classified as having undiagnosed diabetes.

Periodically, NHANES laboratory testing is performed at different laboratories and using different instruments than testing in earlier years. In those instances, NHANES conducts crossover studies to evaluate the impact of these changes on laboratory measurements, and thus their impact on the evaluation of data over time. Crossover studies have been conducted to evaluate the impact of laboratory changes on both FPG and A1c. The recommended adjustments to FPG to account for laboratory changes from 2005–2006 to present have been incorporated in estimates presented in *Health, United States* so that these estimates are compatible with those from earlier years. NHANES does not recommend any adjustments to the A1c data.

Estimates presented in *Health, United States* may differ from other estimates based on the same data and presented elsewhere if different weights, age-adjustment groups, definitions, or trend adjustments are used.

For more information, see: https://wwwn.cdc.gov/Nchs/Nhanes/2013-2014/GHB_H.htm and https://wwwn.cdc.gov/Nchs/Nhanes/2013-2014/GLU_H.htm.

Diagnosis—Diagnosis is the act or process of identifying or determining the nature and cause of a disease or injury through evaluation of patient history, examination, and review of laboratory data. Diagnoses in the National Ambulatory Medical Care Survey and the National Hospital Ambulatory Medical Care Survey are abstracted from medical records and are currently coded to the *International Classification of Diseases, 9th Revision, Clinical Modification* (ICD–9–CM). Starting with 2016 data, diagnosis data will be classified using *International Classification of Diseases, 10th Revision, Clinical Modification/Procedure Coding System* (ICD–10–CM/PCS).

For a given medical care encounter, the first-listed diagnosis can be used to categorize the visit, or if more than one diagnosis is recorded on the medical record, the visit can be categorized based on all diagnoses recorded. Analyzing first-listed diagnoses avoids double-counting events such

as visits or hospitalizations; the first-listed diagnosis is often, but not always, considered the most important or dominant condition among all comorbid conditions. However, the choice of the first-listed diagnosis by the medical facility may be influenced by reimbursement or other factors. (Also see Appendix II, External cause of injury; Injury; Injury-related visit.)

Diagnostic and other nonsurgical procedure—See Appendix II, Procedure.

Discharge—The National Health Interview Survey defines a hospital discharge as the completion of any continuous period of stay of one night or more in a hospital as an inpatient. According to the Healthcare Cost and Utilization Project—National (Nationwide) Inpatient Sample, a discharge is a completed inpatient hospitalization. A hospitalization may be completed by death or by release of the patient to the customary place of residence, a nursing home, another hospital, or other locations. (Also see Appendix II, Admission; Average length of stay; Days of care; Hospital utilization; Inpatient.)

Domiciliary care home—See Appendix II, Long-term care facility; Nursing home.

Drug—Drugs are pharmaceutical agents, by any routes of administration, for the prevention, diagnosis, or treatment of medical conditions or diseases. Data on specific drug use are collected in several NCHS surveys. (Also see Appendix II, Multum Lexicon Plus therapeutic class.)

National Health and Nutrition Examination Survey (NHANES)—Drug information from NHANES III and from NHANES for 1999 and subsequent years was collected during in-person interviews conducted in participants' homes. Starting with 2001 data, participants were asked whether they had taken a medication in the past 30 days for which they needed a prescription. For 1988–1994 and 1999–2014 data, the question wording differed slightly; participants were asked whether they had taken a prescription medication in the past month. For all survey years, those who answered "yes" were asked to provide the prescription medication containers for the interviewer. For each medication reported, the interviewer entered the product's complete name from the container. If no container was available, the interviewer asked the participant to verbally report the name of the medication. In addition, participants were asked how long they had been taking the medication and the main reason for use.

All reported medication names were converted to their standard generic ingredient name. For multi-ingredient products, the ingredients were listed in alphabetical order and counted as one drug (e.g., Tylenol #3 was listed as acetaminophen; codeine). No trade or proprietary names were provided on the data file.

Drug data from NHANES provide a snapshot of all prescribed drugs reported by a sample of the civilian noninstitutionalized population for a 30-day period (or past month, for earlier survey years). Drugs taken on an irregular basis, such as every other day, once per week, or for a 10-day period, were captured in the 30-day recall period. Data shown in *Health, United States* for the percentage of the population reporting multiple prescription drugs during the past 30 days include a range of drug utilization patterns; for example, persons who took three or more drugs daily during the past 30 days or persons who took a different drug three separate times would be classified as taking three or more drugs in the past 30 days, as long as at least three drugs were taken at some time during the past 30 days.

For more information on prescription drug data collection and coding in NHANES, see: https://wwwn.cdc.gov/Nchs/Nhanes/2013-2014/RXQ_RX_H.htm and https://wwwn.cdc.gov/Nchs/Nhanes/1999-2000/RXQ_DRUG.htm.

For more information on NHANES III prescription drug data collection and coding, see: ftp://ftp.cdc.gov/pub/Health_Statistics/NCHS/nhanes/nhanes3/2A/pupremed.pdf. The small number of respondents (fewer than 10) who responded "unknown" to whether they were taking prescription medication were coded as not taking prescription drugs in the past month. (Also see Appendix I, National Health and Nutrition Examination Survey [NHANES].)

Drug abuse—See Appendix II, Illicit drug use.

Education—Several approaches to defining educational categories are used in *Health, United States*. Estimates are typically presented for adults aged 25 and over in order to give people time to complete their education.

National Health Interview Survey (NHIS)—Starting in 1997, the NHIS questionnaire was changed to ask, "What is the highest level of school [person] has completed or the highest degree received?" Responses were used to categorize adults according to educational credentials (i.e., no high school diploma or general educational development high school equivalency diploma [GED]; high school diploma or GED; some college, no bachelor's degree; bachelor's degree or higher).

Prior to 1997, the education variable in NHIS was measured by asking, "What is the highest grade or year of regular school [person] has ever attended?" and "Did [person] finish the grade/year?" Responses were used to categorize adults according to years of education completed (i.e., less than 12, 12, 13–15, or 16 years or more).

Data from the 1996 and 1997 NHIS were used to compare distributions of educational attainment for adults aged 25 and over, using categories based on educational credentials (1997) and categories based on years of education completed (1996). A larger percentage of persons reported some college than 13–15 years of education, and a correspondingly smaller percentage reported a high school diploma or GED than 12 years of education. In 1997, 19% of adults reported no high school diploma, 31% a high school diploma or GED, 26% some college, and 24% a bachelor's degree or higher. In 1996, 18% of adults reported less than 12 years of education, 37% reported 12 years, 20% reported 13–15 years, and 25% reported 16 or more years of education.

National Health and Nutrition Examination Survey (NHANES)—In 1988–1994 (NHANES III), the questionnaire asked, "What is the highest grade or year of regular school [person] has completed?" Responses were used to categorize adults according to educational credentials (i.e., no high school diploma or GED; high school diploma or GED; some college, no bachelor's degree; bachelor's degree or higher). Starting with 1999–2000 data, the questionnaire was changed to ask, "What is the highest grade or level of school [you have/(person) has] completed or the highest degree [you have/(person) has] received?" For data on children, education is based on the level of education completed by the head of the household. The question asked is, "What is the highest grade or level of school [you have/(person) has] completed or the highest degree [you have/(person) has] received?"

Emergency department—According to the National Hospital Ambulatory Medical Care Survey, an emergency department is a hospital facility that is staffed 24 hours a day and provides unscheduled outpatient services to patients whose condition requires immediate care. Emergency services provided under the "hospital as landlord" arrangement were also eligible. An emergency department was in scope if it was staffed 24 hours a day. If an in-scope emergency department had an emergency service area that was open less than 24 hours a day, then that area was included under the emergency department. If a hospital had an emergency department that was staffed less than 24 hours a day, that department was considered an outpatient clinic. (Also see Appendix II, Emergency department or emergency room visit; Outpatient department.)

Emergency department or emergency room visit—Starting with the 1997 National Health Interview Survey, respondents to the Sample Adult questionnaire and the Sample Child questionnaire (a knowledgeable adult, usually a parent) were asked about the number of visits to hospital emergency rooms during the past 12 months, including visits that resulted in hospitalization. In the National Hospital Ambulatory Medical Care Survey, an emergency department visit is a direct personal exchange between a patient and either a physician or a health care provider working under the physician's supervision, for the purpose of seeking care and receiving personal health services. (Also see Appendix II, Emergency department; Injury-related visit.)

Employer costs for employee compensation—Employer costs for employee compensation is a measure of the average cost per employee hour worked, to employers for wages, salaries, and benefits. Wages and salaries are defined as the hourly straight-time wage rate or, for workers not paid on an hourly basis, straight-time earnings divided by the corresponding hours. Straight-time wage and salary rates are total earnings before payroll deductions, excluding premium pay for work in addition to the regular work schedule (e.g., overtime, weekends, and holidays), shift differentials, and nonproduction bonuses such as discretionary holiday bonuses and lump-sum payments provided in lieu of wage increases. Production bonuses, incentive earnings, commission payments, and cost-of-living adjustments are included in straight-time wage and salary rates. Benefits included as compensation are paid leave (paid vacations, holidays, sick leave, and other leave), supplemental pay (premium pay for overtime, weekends, or holidays), shift differentials, nonproduction bonuses, insurance benefits (life, health, and short- and long-term disability), retirement and savings benefits (pension and other retirement plans and savings and thrift plans), and legally-required benefits (Social Security, Medicare, federal and state unemployment insurance, and workers' compensation). (Also see Appendix I, National Compensation Survey [NCS].)

Ethnicity—See Appendix II, Hispanic origin.

Exercise—See Appendix II, Physical activity, leisure-time.

Expenditures—See Appendix II, Health expenditures, national. (Also see Appendix I, National Health Expenditure Accounts [NHEA].)

External cause of injury—The external cause of injury is used for classifying the circumstances in which injuries occur. The *International Classification of Diseases, 9th Revision* (ICD–9), External Cause of Injury Matrix, is a two-dimensional array describing both the mechanism or external cause of the injury (e.g., fall, motor-vehicle traffic) and the manner or intent of the injury (e.g., unintentional, self-inflicted, or assault). Although this matrix was originally developed for mortality, it has been adapted for use with the ICD–9 Clinical Modification (ICD–9–CM) and will be used in *Health, United States* until 2016 data are available. Data for 2016 and beyond will be classified using the *International Classification of Diseases, 10th Revision, Clinical Modification/Procedure Coding System* (ICD–10–CM/PCS). For more information, see the NCHS website at: http://www.cdc.gov/nchs/injury/injury_tools.htm; and see: Bergen G, Chen LH, Warner M, Fingerhut LA. Injury in the United States: 2007 chartbook.

Hyattsville, MD: NCHS; 2008. Available from: http://www.cdc.gov/nchs/data/misc/injury2007.pdf.

Family income—For the National Health Interview Survey and the National Health and Nutrition Examination Survey, all people within a household who are related by blood, marriage or cohabitation, or adoption constitute a family. Each member of a family is classified according to the total income of the family. Unrelated individuals are classified according to their own income.

National Health Interview Survey (NHIS)—Prior to 1997, family income was the total income received by members of a family (or by an unrelated individual) in the 12 months before interview. Family income included wages, salaries, rents from property, interest, dividends, profits and fees from their own businesses, pensions, and help from relatives. Starting in 1997, NHIS collected family income data for the calendar year prior to interview (e.g., 2015 family income data were based on calendar year 2014 information). The 1997–2006 instrument allowed the respondent to supply a specific dollar amount (up to $999,995). Any family income responses greater than $999,995 were entered as $999,996. Respondents who did not know or refused to give a dollar amount in response to this question were asked if their total combined family income for the previous year was $20,000 or more, or less than $20,000. If the respondent answered this question, he or she was then given one of two flash cards and asked to indicate which income group listed on the card best represented the family's combined income during the previous calendar year. One flash card listed incomes that were $20,000 or more, and the other flash card listed incomes that were less than $20,000. Starting with the 2007 NHIS, the income amount follow-up questions that had been in place since 1997 were replaced with a series of unfolding bracket questions. The unfolding bracket method asked a series of closed-ended income range questions (e.g., "Is it less than $50,000?") if the respondent did not provide an answer to the exact income amount question. The closed-ended income range questions were constructed so that each successive question established a smaller range for the amount of the family's income. In 2011, 2012, and 2014, the unfolding-bracket income questions were further refined to improve the assignment of poverty status. For more information on this series of family income questions, see: 2015 NHIS public-use data release. NCHS. 2016. Available from: http://www.cdc.gov/nchs/nhis/nhis_2015_data_release.htm.

Also see: Pleis JR, Cohen RA. Impact of income bracketing on poverty measures used in the National Health Interview Survey's Early Release Program: Preliminary data from the 2007 NHIS. Hyattsville, MD: NCHS. 2007. Available from: http://www.cdc.gov/nchs/data/nhis/income.pdf.

For NHIS respondents, family income data are used in the computation of a poverty measure. Starting with *Health, United States, 2004*, a new methodology for imputing family income data for NHIS was implemented for data years 1997 and beyond. Multiple imputations were performed for survey years 1997 and beyond, with five sets of imputed values created to allow for the assessment of variability caused by imputation. A detailed description of the multiple imputation procedure, and data files for 1997 and beyond, are available from: http://www.cdc.gov/nchs/nhis/quest_data_related_1997_forward.htm through the Data Release or the Imputed Income Files link under that year. For data years 1990–1996, about 16%–18% of persons had missing data for family income. In those years, missing values were imputed for family income by using a sequential hot deck within matrix cells imputation approach. A detailed description of the imputation procedure and data files, with imputed annual family income for 1990–1996, is available from: ftp://ftp.cdc.gov/pub/Health_Statistics/NCHS/Datasets/NHIS/1990-96_Family_Income/. (Also see Appendix II, Poverty; Table VI.)

National Health and Nutrition Examination Survey (NHANES)—In NHANES 1999 and onward, family income is asked in a series of questions about possible sources of income, including wages, salaries, interest and dividends, federal programs, child support, rents, royalties, and other possible sources. After the information about sources of income was obtained in the family interview income section of the questionnaire, the respondent was asked to report total combined family income for him- or herself and the other members of their family, in dollars. If the respondent did not provide an answer or did not know the total combined family income, he or she was asked if the total family income was less than $20,000 or $20,000 or more. If the respondent answered, a follow-up question asked the respondent to select an income range from a list on a printed flash card. The midpoint of the income range was then used as the total family income value. Family income values are used to calculate a poverty measure. NHANES II (1976–1980) included questions on components of income; NHANES III (1988–1994) did not ask the detailed components-of-income questions but asked respondents to identify their income based on a set of ranges provided on a flash card. Family income was not imputed for individuals or families with no reported income information in any of the NHANES survey years. (Also see Appendix II, Poverty.)

National Immunization Survey (NIS)—Prior to 1998, family income was the total income received by all family members in the past 12 months at the time of interview. Following the changes in the NHIS income questions, NIS changed the reference period for 1998 onward and collected income received by all family members for the calendar year prior to the interview year for households with age-eligible children (e.g., 2015 NIS family income data are based on calendar year 2014 income). Family income is the combined total income received by all members of a family before taxes. For the family income questions, the household respondent is asked to include income received from jobs, Social Security, retirement income, unemployment payments, public assistance, interest, dividends, net income from business, farm, rent, or any other sources. Respondents who answered "don't know" or refused to give a dollar amount for the total family income were asked a cascading sequence of income questions—a total of 15 cascading questions—that attempt to place the family income into one of 15 income intervals ranging from less than or equal to $7,500 to greater than or equal to $75,000. The initial question asks if the family income for the prior year was more or less than $20,000. Subsequent sets of income range questions are asked so that each successive question establishes a narrower income range.

A family income variable is constructed from the total family income question and the cascading income questions. If an exact income is given, family income is set to this amount; otherwise it is set to the midpoint of the tightest bounds established by the cascading income questions. The values of total family income are used to calculate an income-to-poverty ratio. For NIS, this ratio is calculated only for households with age-eligible children, using either the actual family income value or the midpoint of the interval from the series of cascading questions in the numerator and the poverty threshold provided by the Census Bureau for the size of the family and the number of related children in the household in the denominator. Details of the income questions and computation of the income-to-poverty ratio for each data collection year can be found in the NIS data documentation (Data User's Guide and Household Interview Questionnaire) provided on the NIS website at: http://www.cdc.gov/vaccines/imz-managers/nis/data-tables.html.

For more information, see: Battaglia MP, Hoaglin DC, Izrael D, Khare M, Mokdad A. Improving income imputation by using partial income information and ecological variables. Presented at the American Statistical Association–Joint Statistical Meeting; 2002 Aug 11–15, New York, NY. Available from: http://www.cdc.gov/nchs/data/nis/estimation_weighting/Battaglia2002.pdf.

Federal hospital—See Appendix II, Hospital.

Fee-for-service health insurance—Fee-for-service health insurance is private (commercial) health insurance that reimburses health care providers on the basis of a fee for each health service provided to the insured person. In addition, "fee-for-service" is a term often applied to original Medicare, to distinguish it from Medicare managed-care plans and other new payment systems. (Also see Appendix II, Health insurance coverage; Managed care; Medicare.)

Fertility rate—See Appendix II, Rate: Birth and related rates.

General hospital—See Appendix II, Hospital.

Geographic region—The U.S. Census Bureau groups the 50 states and D.C., for statistical purposes, into four geographic regions (Northeast, Midwest, South, and West) and nine divisions based on geographic proximity. (See Figure I.)

Gestation—For the National Vital Statistics System and CDC's Abortion Surveillance System, the period of gestation is defined as beginning with the first day of the last normal menstrual period and ending with the day of birth or day of termination of pregnancy. Data on gestational age are subject to error for several reasons, including imperfect maternal recall or misidentification of the last menstrual period because of postconception bleeding, delayed ovulation, or intervening early miscarriage.

Gross domestic product (GDP)—The GDP is the market value of the goods and services produced by labor and property located in the United States. As long as the labor and property are located in the United States, the suppliers (i.e., the workers and, for property, the owners) may be U.S. residents or residents of other countries. (Also see Appendix II, Consumer Price Index [CPI]; Health expenditures, national.)

Health care contact—Starting in 1997, the National Health Interview Survey has collected information on health care contacts with doctors and other health care professionals by using the following series of questions: "During the past 12 months, how many times have you gone to a hospital emergency room about your own health?", "During the past 12 months, did you receive care at home from a nurse or other health care professional? What was the total number of home visits received?", and "During the past 12 months, how many times have you seen a doctor or other health care professional about your own health at a doctor's office, a clinic, or some other place? Do not include times you were hospitalized overnight, visits to hospital emergency rooms, home visits, or telephone calls." Starting with 2000 data, this question was amended to specifically exclude dental visits.

For 1997–1999, for each question, respondents were shown a flash card with response categories of 0, 1, 2–3, 4–9, 10–12, or 13 or more visits. For tabulation of the 1997–1999 data, responses of 2–3 were recoded to 2, responses of 4–9 were recoded to 6, responses of 10–12 were recoded to 11, and 13 or more visits were recoded to 13. The recoded values for the three types of visits were then added to yield an estimate of

total health care contacts. Starting with 2000 data, response categories were expanded to 0, 1, 2–3, 4–5, 6–7, 8–9, 10–12, 13–15, or 16 or more. For 2000 and more recent data, these response categories were recoded to the midpoint of the range. The category of 16 or more was recoded to 16. The recoded values for the three types of visits were then added to yield an estimate of the summary measure of health care contacts (including doctor's visits, hospital emergency room visits, and home visits). After summing the three component visit variables, respondents with values on the edge of the categories presented in *Health, United States* were rounded down to provide a more conservative estimate of the number of visits. For example, a respondent with 3.5 health care contacts was included in the 1–3 visits category, and a respondent with 9.5 health care contacts was included in the 4–9 visits category. Respondents were included in this analysis only if they were known on all three visit variables.

Analyses of the percentage of children without a health care visit are based on the following question: "During the past 12 months, how many times has [person] seen a doctor or other health care professional about [his/her] health at a doctor's office, a clinic, or some other place? Do not include times [person] was hospitalized overnight, visits to hospital emergency rooms, home visits, or telephone calls." Starting with 2000 data, this question was amended to specifically exclude dental visits. (Also see Appendix II, Emergency department or emergency room visit; Home visit.)

Health expenditures, national—National health expenditures are estimated by the Centers for Medicare & Medicaid Services (CMS) and measure calendar year spending for health care in the United States by type of service delivered (e.g., hospital care, physician services, nursing home care) and source of funding for those services (e.g., private health insurance, Medicare, Medicaid, out-of-pocket spending). CMS produces both historical and projected estimates of health expenditures by category. (Also see Appendix I, National Health Expenditure Accounts [NHEA]; Appendix II, Gross domestic product [GDP].) Types of national health expenditures include:

Health consumption expenditures are outlays for goods and services relating directly to patient care, plus expenses for administering health insurance programs, the net cost of health insurance, and public health activities. This category is equivalent to total national health expenditures minus expenditures for investment in noncommercial research and structures and equipment.

Personal health care expenditures are outlays for goods and services relating directly to patient care. These expenditures are total national health expenditures minus expenditures for investment, health insurance program administration and the net cost of insurance, and public health activities.

Table VI. Imputed family income percentages in the National Health Interview Survey, by selected characteristics: United States, 1990–2015

Year	All ages	Under 18 years	18 years and over	18-64 years	Under 65 years	1-64 years	65 years and over	Females 18 years and over	Females 40 years and over	2 years and over	45 years and over
					Percent						
1990	16	14	18	16	15	15	24	18	21	17	22
1991	18	15	19	17	17	17	26	19	23	18	23
1992	18	16	19	18	17	17	27	20	23	18	23
1993	16	14	17	16	15	15	23	17	19	16	20
1994	17	15	18	17	16	16	25	18	21	17	21
1995	16	14	16	15	15	15	22	17	19	16	19
1996	17	14	17	16	16	16	24	18	20	17	20
1997	24	21	26	24	23	23	34	26	30	25	30
1998	29	25	30	28	27	27	39	30	34	29	34
1999	31	27	32	30	29	29	43	33	37	31	37
2000	32	28	33	31	30	31	45	34	38	32	38
2001	32	27	33	31	30	30	44	34	37	32	38
2002	32	28	33	31	30	30	44	33	37	32	37
2003	33	30	35	33	32	32	44	35	38	34	38
2004	33	29	34	32	31	31	41	34	36	33	37
2005	33	29	34	32	31	31	44	35	37	33	38
2006	34	31	35	33	33	33	45	36	39	34	39
2007	33	29	34	32	31	31	43	35	38	33	37
2008	30	27	31	29	29	29	40	32	34	30	34
2009	25	21	26	24	23	23	34	26	29	25	29
2010	25	20	26	24	23	23	36	27	30	25	30
2011	22	19	23	22	21	21	31	24	26	23	26
2012	23	19	24	22	21	21	32	24	27	23	27
2013	23	19	24	23	22	22	31	25	27	23	27
2014	23	20	24	23	22	22	31	25	27	23	27
2015	23	20	24	22	22	22	31	24	26	23	26

NOTES: Weighted percentages. See Appendix II, Family income.

SOURCE: NCHS, National Health Interview Survey. See Appendix I, National Health Interview Survey (NHIS).

Business, household, and other private expenditures are outlays for services paid for by nongovernmental sources, such as consumers, private industry, and philanthropic and other non-patient-care sources.

Government expenditures are outlays for services paid for by federal, state, and local government agencies or expenditures required by governmental mandate (such as workers' compensation insurance payments).

Health insurance coverage—Health insurance is broadly defined to include both public and private payers who cover medical expenditures incurred by a defined population in a variety of settings. Estimates of health insurance are available from several different government surveys. Because of differences in methodology, question wording, and recall period, estimates from different sources may vary and are not directly comparable. For more information, see: Health insurance measurement and estimates. Available from: https://www.census.gov/content/dam/Census/library/working-papers/2015/demo/2015-Vornovitsy-Day-01.pdf

American Community Survey (ACS)—For point-in-time health insurance estimates, ACS respondents were asked about their coverage at the time of interview. Respondents were asked: "Is this person CURRENTLY covered by any of the following types of health insurance or health coverage plans? Mark yes or no for each type of coverage: Insurance through a current or former employer or union [of this person or another family member]; Insurance purchased directly from an insurance company [by this person or another family member]; Medicare, for people 65 and older, or people with certain disabilities; Medicaid, Medical Assistance, or any kind of government-assistance plan for those with low incomes or a disability; TRICARE or other military health care; VA (including those who have ever used or enrolled for VA health care); Indian Health Service; Any other type of health insurance or health coverage plan [specify plan]." In ACS, persons were considered uninsured if they were not covered by private health insurance, Medicare, Medicaid, Medical Assistance, TRICARE or other military health care, veteran's coverage through the Veteran's Administration, or other government coverage.

Figure I. U.S. Census Bureau: Four geographic regions and nine divisions of the United States

People with Indian Health Service coverage only were considered uninsured in ACS.

National Health Interview Survey (NHIS)—For point-in-time health insurance estimates, NHIS respondents were asked about their coverage at the time of interview. For 1993–1996, respondents were asked about their coverage in the previous month. Questions on health insurance coverage were expanded starting in 1993, compared with previous years. In 1997, the entire questionnaire was redesigned and data were collected using a computer-assisted personal interview (CAPI). In 2007, questions on health insurance coverage were expanded again to include three new questions on high-deductible health plans, health savings accounts, and flexible spending accounts.

Respondents were considered to be covered by private health insurance if they indicated private health insurance or, prior to 1997, if they were covered by a single-service hospital plan. Private health insurance includes managed care such as health maintenance organizations (HMOs).

Private insurance obtained through the workplace was defined as any private insurance that was originally obtained through a present or former employer or union or, starting in 1997, through the workplace, self-employment, or a professional association. Starting in 2011, respondents were also asked whether health insurance coverage was obtained through parents or another relative. Starting in 2014, an additional question on the health insurance marketplace was added to the questionnaire for those respondents who did not indicate that their health plan was obtained through a present or former employer, union, self-employment, or professional association. Starting in 2015, an additional answer category was added to the question on how a health plan was originally obtained to allow a respondent to indicate that their plan was obtained through the Health Insurance Marketplace or state-based exchange.

Until 1996, persons were defined as having Medicaid or other public assistance coverage if they indicated that they had either Medicaid or other public assistance or if they reported receiving Aid to Families with Dependent Children (AFDC) or Supplemental Security Income (SSI). After welfare reform in late 1996, Medicaid was delinked from AFDC and SSI. Starting in 1997, persons were considered to be covered by Medicaid if they reported Medicaid or a state-sponsored health program. Starting in 1999, persons also were considered covered by Medicaid if they reported coverage by the Children's Health Insurance Program (CHIP). Medicare or military health plan coverage was also determined in the interview and, starting in 1997, other government-sponsored program coverage was determined as well.

If respondents did not report coverage under one of the above types of plans and they had unknown coverage under either private health insurance or Medicaid, they were considered to have unknown coverage.

The remaining respondents without any indicated coverage were considered uninsured. The uninsured were persons who did not have coverage under private health insurance, Medicare, Medicaid, public assistance, a state-sponsored health plan, other government-sponsored programs, or a military health plan. Persons with only Indian Health Service (IHS) coverage were considered uninsured. Although NHIS respondents who report IHS coverage as their only source of coverage are currently recoded to being uninsured, IHS provides a comprehensive health service delivery system for approximately 2.2 million American Indian or Alaska Native persons. See: https://www.ihs.gov/newsroom/factsheets/ihsprofile/. Estimates of the percentage of persons who were uninsured based on NHIS may differ slightly from those based on other sources because of differences in survey questions, recall period, and other aspects of survey methodology.

In NHIS, on average less than 2% of people aged 65 and over reported no current health insurance coverage, but the small sample size precludes the presentation of separate estimates for this population. Therefore, the term "uninsured" refers only to the population under age 65.

Two additional questions were added to the health insurance section of NHIS beginning with the third quarter of 2004 (Table VII). One question was asked of persons aged 65 and over who had not indicated that they had Medicare: "People covered by Medicare have a card which looks like this. [Are/Is] [person] covered by Medicare?" The other question was asked of persons under age 65 who had not indicated any type of coverage: "There is a program called Medicaid that pays for health care for persons in need. In this state it is also called [state name]. [Are/Is] [person] covered by Medicaid?" Respondents who originally classified themselves as uninsured, but whose classification was changed to Medicare or Medicaid on the basis of a "yes" response to either question, subsequently received appropriate follow-up questions concerning periods of noncoverage for insured respondents. Of the 892 people (unweighted)

who were eligible to receive the Medicare probe question in the third and fourth quarters of 2004, 55% indicated that they were covered by Medicare. Of the 9,146 people (unweighted) who were eligible to receive the Medicaid probe question in the third and fourth quarters of 2004, 3% indicated that they were covered by Medicaid. From 2004 onwards, estimates in *Health, United States* were calculated using the responses to the two additional probe questions. For a complete discussion of the effect of the addition of these two probe questions on the estimates for insurance coverage, see: Cohen RA, Martinez ME. Impact of Medicare and Medicaid probe questions on health insurance estimates from the National Health Interview Survey, 2004. Health E-Stats. NCHS; 2005. Available from: http://www.cdc.gov/nchs/data/hestat/impact04/impact04.htm.

Survey respondents may be covered by health insurance at the time of interview but may have experienced one or more lapses in coverage during the 12 months prior to interview. Starting with *Health, United States, 2006*, NHIS estimates have been presented for the following three exhaustive categories: (a) people with health insurance continuously for the full 12 months prior to interview, (b) those who had a period of up to 12 months prior to interview without coverage, and (c) those who were uninsured for more than 12 months prior to interview. This stub variable has been added to selected tables. Two additional NHIS questions were used to determine the appropriate category for the survey respondents: (a) all persons without a known comprehensive health insurance plan were asked, "About how long has it been since [person] last had health care coverage?"; and (b) all persons with known health insurance coverage were asked, "In the past 12 months, was there any time when [person] did NOT have ANY health insurance coverage?"

(Also see Appendix II, Children's Health Insurance Program [CHIP]; Fee-for-service health insurance; Health maintenance organization [HMO]; Managed care; Medicaid; Medicare; Uninsured.)

Health maintenance organization (HMO)—An HMO is a health care system that assumes or shares both the financial risks and the delivery risks associated with providing comprehensive medical services to a voluntarily enrolled population in a particular geographic area, usually in return for a fixed, prepaid fee. Pure HMO enrollees use only the prepaid, capitated health services of the HMO panel of medical care providers. Open-ended HMO enrollees use the prepaid HMO health services but may also receive medical care from providers who are not part of the HMO panel. There is usually a substantial deductible, copayment, or coinsurance associated with use of nonpanel providers. HMO model types are as follows:

Group model HMO is an HMO that contracts with a single multispecialty medical group to provide care to the HMO's membership. The group practice may work exclusively with the HMO, or it may provide services to non-HMO patients as well. The HMO pays the medical group a negotiated per capita rate, which the group distributes among its physicians, usually on a salaried basis.

Staff model HMO is a closed-panel HMO (where patients can receive services only through a limited number of providers) in which physicians are HMO employees. The providers see members in the HMO's own facilities.

Network model HMO is an HMO that contracts with multiple physician groups to provide services to HMO members. It may include single or multispecialty groups.

Individual practice association (IPA) is a health care provider organization composed of a group of independent practicing physicians who maintain their own offices and band together for the purpose of contracting their services to HMOs, preferred provider organizations, and insurance companies. An IPA may contract with and provide services to both HMO and non-HMO plan participants.

Mixed model HMO is an HMO that combines features of more than one HMO model.

(Also see Appendix II, Managed care; Preferred provider organization [PPO].)

Health services and supplies expenditures—See Appendix II, Health expenditures, national.

Health status, respondent-assessed—Health status was measured in the National Health Interview Survey by asking the family respondent about his or her health or the health of a family member: "Would you say [person's] health in general is excellent, very good, good, fair, or poor?"

Hearing trouble—In the National Health Interview Survey, information about hearing trouble is obtained by asking respondents how well they hear without the use of hearing aids. Prior to 2007 data, respondents were asked, "Which statement best describes your hearing without a hearing aid: good, a little trouble, a lot of trouble, or deaf?" Starting with 2007 data, the question was revised to expand the response categories. Respondents were asked, "These next questions are about your hearing WITHOUT the use of hearing aids or other listening devices. Is your hearing excellent, good, [do you have] a little trouble hearing, moderate trouble, a lot of trouble, or are you deaf?" Starting with 2008 data, respondents were asked, "WITHOUT the use of hearing aids or other listening devices, is your hearing excellent, good,

[do you have] a little trouble hearing, moderate trouble, a lot of trouble, or are you deaf?" Because of the expanded response categories, 2007 and subsequent data are not strictly comparable with earlier years and caution is urged when interpreting trends. For example, in 2006, 3.5% of adults (aged 18 and over) were classified as having hearing difficulty (response categories: a lot of trouble or deaf). In 2007, 2.3% of adults (aged 18 and over) were classified as having hearing difficulty (response categories: a lot of trouble or deaf). This more than 30% decline from 2006 to 2007 in the estimate of those with hearing trouble is likely attributable to the addition of the moderate trouble response category, rather than changes in the prevalence of hearing trouble. Although all age groups saw a decline in the percentage reporting hearing trouble between 2006 and 2007, the amount of the decline varied. There was a 50% decline in reported hearing trouble among adults aged 18–44 (from 0.8% in 2006 to 0.4% in 2007). Among adults aged 45–64, the percentage that reported hearing trouble declined 43%, from 3.5% in 2006 to 2.0% in 2007. Among adults aged 65 and over, reported hearing trouble declined 24%, from 11.4% in 2006 to 8.7% in 2007.

For more information, see: Pleis JR, Lucas JW. Summary health statistics for U.S. adults: National Health Interview Survey, 2007. NCHS. Vital Health Stat 2009;10(240). Available from: http://www.cdc.gov/nchs/data/series/sr_10/sr10_240.pdf. (Also see Appendix II, Basic actions difficulty.)

Hispanic origin—Hispanic or Latino origin includes persons of Mexican, Puerto Rican, Cuban, Central and South American, and other or unknown Latin American or Spanish origin. Persons of Hispanic origin may be of any race.

Birth file—The reporting area for an Hispanic-origin item on the birth certificate expanded between 1980 and 1993 (when the Hispanic item was included on the birth certificate in all states and D.C.). Trend data on births of Hispanic and non-Hispanic parentage in *Health, United States* are affected by expansion of the reporting areas, which affects numbers of events, composition of the Hispanic population, and maternal and infant health characteristics.

In 1980 and 1981, information on births of Hispanic parentage was reported on the birth certificate by the following 22 states: Arizona, Arkansas, California, Colorado, Florida, Georgia, Hawaii, Illinois, Indiana, Kansas, Maine, Mississippi, Nebraska, Nevada, New Jersey, New Mexico, New York, North Dakota, Ohio, Texas, Utah, and Wyoming. In 1982 Tennessee, and in 1983 D.C., began reporting this information. Between 1983 and 1987, information on births of Hispanic parentage was available for 23 states and D.C. In 1988, this information became available for Alabama, Connecticut, Kentucky, Massachusetts, Montana, North Carolina, and Washington state, increasing the number of states reporting information on births of

Table VII. Percentage of persons under age 65 with Medicaid or who are uninsured, by selected demographic characteristics, using Method 1 and Method 2 estimation procedures: United States, 2004

Characteristic	Medicaid[1]		Uninsured[2]	
	Method 2[3]	Method 1[3]	Method 2[3]	Method 1[3]
Age	Percent (standard error)			
Under 65 years	12.0 (0.24)	11.8 (0.24)	16.4 (0.23)	16.6 (0.23)
Under 18 years	25.4 (0.49)	24.9 (0.49)	9.2 (0.30)	9.7 (0.29)
18–64 years	6.6 (0.17)	6.5 (0.17)	19.3 (0.26)	19.4 (0.26)
Percent of poverty level[4]				
Below 100%	47.5 (1.03)	46.6 (1.03)	29.6 (0.89)	30.5 (0.92)
100%–less than 200%	22.0 (0.59)	21.5 (0.60)	28.9 (0.66)	29.4 (0.66)
200% or more	2.9 (0.13)	2.8 (0.13)	9.4 (0.23)	9.5 (0.23)
Age and percent of poverty level[4]				
Under 18 years:				
Below 100%	71.9 (1.35)	70.2 (1.35)	14.5 (1.15)	16.2 (1.22)
100%–less than 200%	39.2 (1.13)	38.4 (1.14)	15.0 (0.81)	15.8 (0.82)
200% or more	6.2 (0.33)	6.1 (0.33)	4.9 (0.30)	4.9 (0.30)
18–64 years:				
Below 100%	31.2 (1.02)	30.8 (1.02)	39.7 (1.09)	40.1 (1.09)
100%–less than 200%	12.0 (0.48)	11.8 (0.48)	37.0 (0.72)	37.2 (0.72)
200% or more	1.7 (0.11)	1.7 (0.10)	11.0 (0.26)	11.1 (0.26)
Hispanic origin and race[5]				
Hispanic or Latino	22.2 (0.55)	21.5 (0.55)	34.4 (0.64)	35.1 (0.65)
Mexican	22.0 (0.63)	21.5 (0.63)	37.6 (0.82)	38.1 (0.83)
Not Hispanic or Latino	10.2 (0.25)	10.1 (0.25)	13.2 (0.23)	13.3 (0.23)
White only	7.4 (0.26)	7.4 (0.26)	12.0 (0.25)	12.1 (0.25)
Black or African American only	23.9 (0.80)	23.5 (0.79)	17.3 (0.58)	17.8 (0.58)

[1] Includes persons who do not have private coverage but who have Medicaid or other state-sponsored health plans, including the Children's Health Insurance Program (CHIP).

[2] Includes persons who have not indicated that they are covered at the time of interview under private health insurance, Medicare, Medicaid, CHIP, a state-sponsored health plan, other government programs, or military health plan (includes VA, TRICARE, and CHAMP-VA). This category includes persons who are only covered by Indian Health Service (IHS) or only have a plan that pays for one type of service, such as accidents or dental care.

[3] Starting with the third quarter of 2004, two additional questions were added to the National Health Interview Survey (NHIS) insurance section to reduce potential errors in reporting of Medicare and Medicaid status. Persons aged 65 and over not reporting Medicare coverage were asked explicitly about Medicare coverage, and persons under age 65 with no reported coverage were asked explicitly about Medicaid coverage. Estimates calculated without using the additional information from these questions are noted as Method 1. Estimates calculated using the additional information from these questions are noted as Method 2.

[4] Based on family income and family size and composition, using the U.S. Census Bureau's poverty thresholds. The percentage of respondents with unknown poverty level was 28.2% in 2004. See the *NHIS Survey Description* for 2004. Available from: http://www.cdc.gov/nchs/data/nhis/srvydesc.pdf.

[5] Persons of Hispanic origin may be of any race or combination of races. Similarly, the category Not Hispanic or Latino refers to all persons who are not of Hispanic or Latino origin, regardless of race.

SOURCE: NCHS, National Health Interview Survey, 2004. Family Core Component. Data are based on household interviews of a sample of the civilian noninstitutionalized population. Available from: http://www.cdc.gov/nchs/data/hestat/impact04/impact04.htm. See Appendix I, National Health Interview Survey (NHIS).

Hispanic parentage to 30 states and D.C. In 1989, this information became available from an additional 17 states, increasing the number of Hispanic-reporting states to 47 and D.C. In 1989, only Louisiana, New Hampshire, and Oklahoma did not report Hispanic parentage on the birth certificate. With the inclusion of Louisiana in 1989 and Oklahoma in 1990 as Hispanic-reporting states, 99% of birth records included information on mother's origin. Hispanic origin of the mother was reported on the birth certificates of 49 states and D.C. in 1991 and 1992; only New Hampshire did not provide this information. Starting in 1993, Hispanic origin of mother was reported by all 50 states and D.C.

Starting with 2003 data, some states began using the 2003 revision of the U.S. Standard Certificate of Live Birth. Hispanic origin and race are collected separately on the birth certificate. The Hispanic origin question on the 2003 revision of the birth certificate asks respondents to select only one response. Occasionally, more than one Hispanic origin response is given; that is, a specified Hispanic origin group (Mexican, Puerto Rican, Cuban, or Central and South American) in combination with one or more other specified Hispanic origin groups. From 2003 through 2012, respondents who selected more than one Hispanic origin on the birth certificate were classified as other Hispanic. In 2012, 0.4% of births in the revised-state reporting area, plus Massachusetts (unrevised state that also reported more than one Hispanic origin response), were to women reporting more than one Hispanic origin. Beginning with 2013 data, respondents who select more than one Hispanic origin are randomly assigned to a single Hispanic origin. The Hispanic origin question on the 1989 revision of the birth certificate also offers the opportunity to report more than one origin; however, NCHS processing guidelines for unrevised data allow for coding only the first Hispanic origin listed.

Linked birth/Infant death file—The linked birth/infant death file is particularly useful for computing accurate infant mortality rates by race and Hispanic origin because the race and Hispanic origin of the mother from the birth certificate are used in both the numerator and denominator of the linked birth/infant death infant mortality rate. In contrast, infant mortality rates based on the vital statistics mortality file use for the numerator race and Hispanic origin as reported on the death certificate and for the denominator the race and Hispanic origin of the mother as reported on the birth certificate. Race and Hispanic origin information from the birth certificate, which is reported by the mother, is considered more reliable than race and Hispanic origin information from the death certificate, which is reported by the funeral director based on information provided by an informant or by

observation. See Appendix II, Hispanic origin; sections for Birth file, Mortality file.

Mortality file—The reporting area for an Hispanic-origin item on the death certificate expanded between 1985 and 1997. In 1985, mortality data by Hispanic origin of decedent were based on deaths of residents of the following 17 states and D.C. whose data on the death certificate were at least 90% complete on a place-of-occurrence basis and of comparable format: Arizona, Arkansas, California, Colorado, Georgia, Hawaii, Illinois, Indiana, Kansas, Mississippi, Nebraska, New York, North Dakota, Ohio, Texas, Utah, and Wyoming. In 1986, New Jersey began reporting Hispanic origin of decedent, increasing the number of reporting states to 18 and D.C. in 1986 and 1987. In 1988, Alabama, Kentucky, Maine, Montana, North Carolina, Oregon, Rhode Island, and Washington state were added to the reporting area, increasing the number of states to 26 and D.C. In 1989, an additional 18 states were added, increasing the Hispanic reporting area to 44 states and D.C.; only Connecticut, Louisiana, Maryland, New Hampshire, Oklahoma, and Virginia were not included in the reporting area. Starting with 1990 data in Health, United States, the criterion was changed to include states whose data were at least 80% complete. In 1990, Maryland, Virginia, and Connecticut; in 1991 Louisiana; and in 1993 New Hampshire were added, increasing the reporting area for Hispanic origin of decedent to 47 states and D.C. in 1990; 48 states and D.C. in 1991 and 1992; and 49 states and D.C. in 1993–1996. Only Oklahoma did not provide this information in 1993–1996. Starting in 1997, Hispanic origin of decedent was reported by all 50 states and D.C. Based on data from the U.S. Census Bureau, the 1990 reporting area encompassed 99.6% of the U.S. Hispanic population. In 1990, more than 96% of death records included information on Hispanic origin of the decedent.

Starting with 2003 data, some states began using the 2003 revision of the U.S. Standard Certificate of Death, which allows the reporting of more than one race (multiple races) and includes some revisions in the item reporting Hispanic origin. The effect of the 2003 revision of the Hispanic origin item on the reporting of Hispanic origin on death certificates is presumed to be minor. For more information, see Appendix II, Race. Also see the Technical Notes section of the annual series of "Deaths: Final Data" reports, available from: http://www.cdc.gov/nchs/products/nvsr.htm; and NCHS procedures for multiple-race and Hispanic origin data: Collection, coding, editing, and transmitting. Hyattsville, MD: NCHS; 2004. Available from: http://www.cdc.gov/nchs/data/dvs/Multiple_race_docu_5-10-04.pdf.

National Health Interview Survey (NHIS) and *National Health and Nutrition Examination Survey (NHANES)*— Questions on Hispanic origin are self-reported in NHANES III and subsequent years, and since 1976 in NHIS, and precede questions on race. For 1999–2006 data, the NHANES sample was designed to provide estimates specifically for persons of Mexican origin and not for all Hispanic-origin persons in the United States. Persons of Hispanic origin other than Mexican were entered into the sample with different selection probabilities that are not nationally representative of the total U.S. Hispanic population. Starting with 2007–2008 data collection, all Hispanic persons were oversampled, not just persons of Mexican origin. In addition to allowing estimates for the total group of Hispanic persons, the sample size for Hispanic persons of Mexican origin is sufficient to continue to produce reliable estimates for this group. However, the methodology for the oversampling of Hispanic persons did not provide sufficient sample sizes for calculating estimates for other Hispanic subgroups besides Mexican origin. For more information on the NHANES sampling methodology changes, see https://wwwn.cdc.gov/nchs/data/series/sr02_160.pdf; and the series of NHANES analytic guidelines available from: http://www.cdc.gov/nchs/nhanes/survey_methods.htm. For more information on race and Hispanic origin in NHIS, see the NHIS Race and Hispanic Origin Information home page. Available from: http://www.cdc.gov/nchs/nhis/rhoi.htm.

Surveillance, Epidemiology, and End Results (SEER) Program—SEER data are available from the National Institutes of Health, National Cancer Institute. SEER Hispanic data used in *Health, United States* tables exclude data from Alaska. The North American Association of Central Cancer Registries, Inc. (NAACCR) Hispanic Identification Algorithm was used on a combination of variables to classify incidence cases as Hispanic for analytic purposes. See: NAACCR guideline for enhancing Hispanic–Latino identification. Bethesda, MD: National Cancer Institute; 2003. Available from: http://seer.cancer.gov/seerstat/variables/seer/yr1973_2004/race_ethnicity/.

Youth Risk Behavior Survey (YRBS)—Prior to 1999, a single question was asked about race and Hispanic origin, with the option of selecting one of the following categories: white not Hispanic, black not Hispanic, Hispanic or Latino, Asian or Other Pacific Islander, American Indian or Alaska Native, or other. Between 1999 and 2003, respondents were asked a single question about race and Hispanic origin with the option of choosing one or more of the following categories: white, black or African American, Hispanic or Latino, Asian, Native Hawaiian or Other Pacific Islander, or American Indian or Alaska Native. Beginning in 2005, respondents were asked a question

about Hispanic origin ("Are you Hispanic or Latino?") and a second separate question about race that included the option of selecting one or more of the following categories: American Indian or Alaska Native, Asian, black or African American, Native Hawaiian or Other Pacific Islander, or white. Because of the differences between questions, the data about race and Hispanic ethnicity for the years prior to 1999 are not strictly comparable with estimates for the subsequent years. However, analyses of data collected between 1991 and 2003 have indicated that the data are comparable across years and can be used to study trends. See Appendix II, Race; and see: Brener ND, Kann L, McManus T. A comparison of two survey questions on race and ethnicity among high school students. Public Opin Q 2003;67(2):227–36.

HIV—See Appendix II, Human immunodeficiency virus (HIV) disease.

Home visit—Starting in 1997, the National Health Interview Survey has been collecting information on home visits received during the 12 months prior to interview. Respondents are asked, "During the past 12 months, did you receive care at home from a nurse or other health care professional? What was the total number of home visits received?" These data are combined with data on visits to doctors' offices, clinics, and emergency departments to provide a summary measure of adult health care visits. (Also see Appendix II, Emergency department or emergency room visit; Health care contact.)

Hospital—According to the American Hospital Association (AHA), hospitals are licensed institutions with at least six beds whose primary function is to provide diagnostic and therapeutic patient services for medical conditions; they have an organized physician staff and provide continuous nursing services under the supervision of registered nurses. The World Health Organization (WHO) considers an establishment to be a hospital if it is permanently staffed by at least one physician, can offer inpatient accommodation, and can provide active medical and nursing care. Hospitals may be classified by type of service, ownership, size in terms of number of beds, and length of stay. In the National Hospital Ambulatory Medical Care Survey, hospitals include all those with an average length of stay for all patients of less than 30 days (short-stay) or hospitals whose specialty is general (medical or surgical) or children's general. Federal hospitals and hospital units of institutions and hospitals with fewer than six beds staffed for patient use are excluded. (Also see Appendix II, Average length of stay; Bed, health facility; Days of care; Emergency department; Inpatient; Outpatient department.)

Community hospital—Community hospitals, based on the AHA definition, include all nonfederal, short-term general and special hospitals whose facilities and services are available to the public. Special hospitals include obstetrics and gynecology; eye, ear, nose, and throat; rehabilitation; orthopedic; and other specialty services. Short-term general and special children's hospitals are also considered to be community hospitals. A hospital may include a nursing-home-type unit and still be classified as short-term, provided that the majority of its patients are admitted to units where the average length of stay is less than 30 days. Hospital units of institutions such as prisons and college infirmaries that are not open to the public and are contained within a nonhospital facility are not included in the category of community hospitals. Traditionally, the definition has included all nonfederal short-stay hospitals except facilities for persons with intellectual disabilities (formerly called mentally retarded). In a revised definition, the following additional sites were excluded: hospital units of institutions, and alcoholism and chemical dependency facilities.

Federal hospital—Federal hospitals are those operated by the federal government.

For-profit hospital—For-profit hospitals are operated for profit by individuals, partnerships, or corporations.

General hospital—General hospitals provide diagnostic, treatment, and surgical services for patients with a variety of medical conditions. According to WHO, these hospitals provide medical and nursing care for more than one category of medical discipline (e.g., general medicine, specialized medicine, general surgery, specialized surgery, and obstetrics). Excluded are hospitals, usually in rural areas, that provide a more limited range of care.

Nonprofit hospital—Nonprofit hospitals are those controlled by nonprofit organizations, such as religious organizations and fraternal societies.

Registered hospital—Registered hospitals are those registered with AHA. About 98% of U.S. hospitals are registered.

Short-stay hospital—In the National Health Interview Survey, short-stay hospitals are defined as any hospital or hospital department in which the type of service provided is general; maternity; eye, ear, nose, and throat; children's; or osteopathic.

Special hospital—Special hospitals are those, such as psychiatric, tuberculosis, chronic disease, rehabilitation, maternity, and alcoholic or narcotic dependency facilities, that provide a particular type of service to the majority of their patients.

Hospital-based physician—See Appendix II, Physician.

Hospital day—See Appendix II, Days of care.

Hospital utilization—Estimates of hospital utilization (such as hospital discharge rate, days of care rate, average length of stay, and percentage of the population with a hospitalization) presented in *Health, United States* are based on data from three sources: Healthcare Cost and Utilization Project, National (Nationwide) Inpatient Sample (HCUP–NIS); National Health Interview Survey (NHIS); and American Hospital Association (AHA). Beginning with the 2012 data year, HCUP–NIS is a 20% sample of discharges (alive or deceased) from all community hospitals participating in HCUP, excluding rehabilitation and long-term acute care hospitals. For prior years, HCUP–NIS estimates are based on hospital stays for persons discharged alive or deceased from about 1,000 hospitals sampled to approximate a 20% stratified sample of U.S. community hospitals, excluding rehabilitation hospitals and long-term acute care hospitals. NHIS hospital utilization data are based on household interviews with a sample of the civilian noninstitutionalized population. NHIS respondents were asked whether they had any hospital stays in the past year, excluding overnight stays in the emergency room. AHA data are from information reported by a census of hospitals. (Also see Appendix II, Average length of stay; Days of care; Discharge; and Appendix I, Healthcare Cost and Utilization Project [HCUP], National [Nationwide] Inpatient Sample; National Health Interview Survey [NHIS].)

Human immunodeficiency virus (HIV) disease—HIV disease is caused by infection with a cytopathic retrovirus, which in turn leads to destruction of parts of the immune system. A surveillance case for HIV requires laboratory-confirmed evidence of infection, including a positive result on a screening test for HIV antibody, followed by a positive result on a confirmatory test, or a positive result or detectable quantity on an HIV virologic test (see, CDC. HIV Surveillance Report, 2015; vol. 27. 2016. Available from: http://www.cdc.gov/hiv/library/reports/hiv-surveillance.html).

Since 1985, many states and U.S. dependent areas have implemented HIV case reporting as part of their comprehensive HIV and AIDS surveillance programs. As of April 2008, all reporting areas (50 states, D.C., and the six U.S. dependent areas of American Samoa, Guam, the Northern Mariana Islands, Puerto Rico, the Republic of Palau, and the U.S. Virgin Islands) had implemented HIV case surveillance using a confidential system for name-based case reporting for both HIV infection and AIDS. To better capture and characterize populations in which HIV infection has been newly diagnosed, including persons with evidence of recent HIV infection, many states report the prevalence of those living with a diagnosis of HIV infection, including those living with AIDS.

In 2008, changes were made to the case definition for HIV infection. The new case definition combined the two previous case definitions for HIV and AIDS and established a new disease staging classification. The term HIV/AIDS was replaced with the term "diagnosis of HIV infection," which is defined as diagnosis of HIV infection regardless of the stage of disease (stage 1, 2, 3 [AIDS], or unknown) and refers to all persons with a diagnosis of HIV infection (see MMWR 2008;57 [RR–10]:1–8).

In 2014, the HIV surveillance case definition was revised again to adapt to changes in diagnostic criteria used by laboratories and clinicians. The new case definition recognizes early HIV infection (stage 0); includes the distinction between HIV–1 and HIV–2 infections; consolidates staging systems for adults and children; simplifies surveillance criteria for opportunistic illnesses; and incorporates clinical criteria for reporting diagnoses without laboratory evidence. (See HIV Surveillance Report, 2014; vol. 26. 2015.)

The 2008 case definition was used to classify cases diagnosed from the beginning of the epidemic through 2013. In order to classify HIV infection among both adults and adolescents, the following HIV infection classification staging system was used:

- HIV infection, stage 1: No AIDS-defining condition and either a CD4 count of 500 cells/μL or more or a CD4 percentage of total lymphocytes of 29% or more.

- HIV infection, stage 2: No AIDS-defining condition and either a CD4 count of 200–499 cells/μL or a CD4 percentage of total lymphocytes of 14%–28%.

- HIV infection, stage 3 (AIDS): Documentation of an AIDS-defining condition, or either a CD4 count of less than 200 cells/μL or a CD4 percentage of total lymphocytes of less than 14%. Documentation of an AIDS-defining condition supersedes a CD4 count or percentage that would not by itself be the basis for a stage 3 (AIDS) classification.

- HIV infection, stage unknown: No reported information on AIDS-defining conditions and no information available on CD4 count or percentage (see MMWR 2008;57[RR–10]:1–8).

The 2014 case definition was used to classify cases diagnosed beginning in 2014 and is similar to the 2008 case definition except for the following: (a) inclusion of criteria for stage 0, (b) inclusion of CD4 testing criteria for stage 3 in children, and (c) changes in cutoffs for CD4 percentages of total lymphocytes used for classifications of stages 1 and 2 in persons aged 6 years and over. The 2014 case definition classifies HIV infection based on the following stages:

- HIV infection, stage 0: First positive HIV test result within 6 months after negative test result. After 6 months, the stage may be reclassified as 1, 2, 3, or unknown.

- HIV infection, stages 1, 2, and 3: Documentation of an AIDS-defining condition (excluding stage 0) is stage 3. Otherwise, the stage is determined by the lowest CD4 test result.

- HIV infection, stage unknown: No reported information on AIDS-defining conditions and no information available on CD4 count or percentage.

Mortality coding—Starting with 1999 data and the introduction of the 10th revision of the *International Classification of Diseases* (ICD–10), the title for this cause of death was changed from HIV infection to HIV disease, and the ICD codes were changed to B20–B24. Starting with 1987 data, NCHS introduced category numbers *042–*044 for classifying and coding HIV infection as a cause of death in ICD–9. The asterisks before the category numbers indicate that these codes were not part of the original ICD–9. HIV infection was formerly referred to as human T-cell lymphotropic virus-III/lymphadenopathy-associated virus (HTLV–III/LAV) infection. Before 1987, deaths involving HIV infection were classified to Deficiency of cell-mediated immunity (ICD–9, code 279.1) contained in the category All other diseases; to Pneumocystosis (ICD–9, code 136.3) contained in the category All other infectious and parasitic diseases; to Malignant neoplasms, including neoplasms of lymphatic and hematopoietic tissues; and to a number of other causes. Because of these coding changes, death statistics for HIV infection before 1987 are not strictly comparable with data for 1987 and subsequent years and therefore are not shown in *Health, United States*.

(Also see Appendix II, Acquired immunodeficiency syndrome [AIDS]; Cause of death; *International Classification of Diseases* [ICD]; *International Classification of Diseases, 9th Revision, Clinical Modification* [ICD–9–CM]; Table IV.)

Hypercholesterolemia—See Appendix II, Cholesterol.

Hypertension—See Appendix II, Blood pressure, high.

ICD; ICD codes—See Appendix II, Cause of death; *International Classification of Diseases* (ICD).

Illicit drug use—Illicit drug use refers to the use and misuse of illegal and controlled drugs.

Monitoring the Future (MTF) Study—In this school-based survey of secondary school students, information on illicit drug use is collected using self-completed questionnaires. The information is based on the following questions: "On how many occasions (if any) have you used marijuana in the last 30 days?" Similar questions are asked about lifetime and past year use of marijuana and a range of other drugs, including hallucinogens, inhalants, cocaine, heroin, and so on. Questions on cocaine use include the following: "On how many occasions (if any) have you taken crack (cocaine in chunk or rock form) during the last 30 days?" and "On how many occasions (if any) have you taken cocaine in any other form during the last 30 days?" Starting in 2014, the question on MDMA asks, "On how many occasions (if any) have you taken MDMA (ecstasy or Molly) during the past

30 days?" Previously, the question only asked about ecstasy use before Molly (a nickname for a supposedly stronger form of MDMA) became a popular form of the drug. Questions about prescription drugs—tranquilizers, sedatives, narcotic drugs other than heroin, and amphetamines—provide a description of the legitimate uses for those drugs and then ask respondents to include only use "…on your own, that is, without a doctor telling you to take them."

National Survey on Drug Use & Health (NSDUH)—Information on illicit drug use is collected for survey participants aged 12 and over. Information on any illicit drug use includes any use of marijuana or hashish, cocaine, crack, heroin, hallucinogens, inhalants, or methamphetamine, as well as misuse of prescription psychotherapeutic drugs. Current use (within the past month) is based on the question: "How long has it been since you last used [drug name]?" This answer is cross-checked with the following question: "Think specifically about the past 30 days, from [DATE] up to and including today. During the past 30 days, on how many days did you use [drug name]?" Starting in 2013, information about marijuana use that was recommended by a doctor or other health care professional has been collected; however, reported marijuana use is classified as illicit drug use. Starting in 2015, NSDUH questionnaire underwent a partial redesign, and changes in measurement for 7 of the 10 illicit drug categories—hallucinogens, inhalants, methamphetamine, and the misuse of prescription pain relievers, tranquilizers, stimulants, and sedatives—may have affected the comparability of the measurement of these illicit drugs and any illicit drug. (Also see Appendix II, Substance use.)

Immunization—See Appendix II, Vaccination.

Incidence—Incidence is the number of cases of disease having their onset during a prescribed period of time. It is often expressed as a rate (e.g., the incidence of measles per 1,000 children aged 5–15 during a specified year). Measuring incidence may be complicated because the population at risk for the disease may change during the period of interest due to births, deaths, or migration, for example. In addition, determining whether a case is new—that is, whether its onset occurred during the prescribed period of time—may be difficult. Because of these difficulties in measuring incidence, many health statistics are instead measured in terms of prevalence. (Also see Appendix II, Prevalence.)

Income—See Appendix II, Family income.

Individual practice association (IPA)—See Appendix II, Health maintenance organization (HMO).

Industry of employment—For the presentation of data in *Health, United States*, industries are classified according to the North American Industry Classification System (NAICS). NAICS groups establishments into industries based on their production or supply function. Establishments using similar raw material inputs, capital equipment, and labor are classified in the same industry. This approach creates homogeneous categories well suited for economic analysis. NAICS uses a six-digit hierarchical coding system to classify all economic activity. The first two digits of the six-digit code designate the highest level of aggregation, into the public administration (government) and 20 private industry sectors (Table VIII). Agriculture, forestry, fishing and hunting; mining, quarrying, and oil and gas extraction; construction; and manufacturing are primarily goods-producing sectors, and the remaining 16 sectors are entirely service providing. NAICS allows for the classification of more than 1,000 industries. For more information on NAICS, see: http://www.census.gov/eos/www/naics.

Starting in 1997, NAICS replaced the Standard Industrial Classification (SIC) system, which was last updated in 1987. The SIC system focused on the manufacturing sector of the economy and provided significantly less detail for the now-dominant service sector, including newly developed industries in information services, health care delivery, and high-technology manufacturing. Although some titles in SIC and NAICS are similar, there is little comparability between the two systems because industry groupings are defined differently. Estimates classified by NAICS should not be compared with estimates that used SIC.

Infant death—An infant death is the death of a live-born child before his or her first birthday. Age at death may be further classified as neonatal or postneonatal. Neonatal deaths are those that occur before the 28th day of life; postneonatal deaths are those that occur within 28 days to under 1 year of age. (Also see Appendix II, Rate: Death and related rates.)

Injury—The International Classification of External Causes of Injuries (ICECI) Coordination and Maintenance Group defines injury as a (suspected) bodily lesion resulting from acute overexposure to energy (this can be mechanical, thermal, electrical, chemical, or radiant) interacting with the body in amounts or rates that exceed the threshold of physiological tolerance. The time between exposure to the energy and the appearance of an injury is short. In some cases, an injury results from an insufficiency of any of the vital elements (i.e., air, water, or warmth), as in strangulation, drowning, or freezing. Acute poisonings and toxic effects, including overdoses of substances and wrong substances given or taken in error are included, as are adverse effects and complications of therapeutic, surgical, and medical care. Psychological harm is excluded. Injuries can be intentional or unintentional (i.e., accidental). In NCHS data systems, external causes of nonfatal injuries are currently coded to the *International Classification of Diseases, 9th Revision,*

Clinical Modification, Supplementary Classification of External Causes of Injury and Poisoning, and the codes are often referred to as E codes. See Table IX for a list of external causes of injury categories and E codes used in *Health, United States*. Also see the NCHS injury website at: http://www.cdc.gov/nchs/injury.htm; and see: ICECI Coordination and Maintenance Group. International Classification of External Causes of Injuries (ICECI), ver 1.2. Amsterdam, The Netherlands: Consumer Safety Institute; and Adelaide, Australia: Australian Institute of Health and Welfare National Injury Surveillance Unit, Flinders University; 2004. Available from: http://www.who.int/classifications/icd/adaptations/iceci/en/index.html. (Also see Appendix II, Diagnosis; Injury-related visit.)

Injury-related visit—In the National Hospital Ambulatory Medical Care Survey (NHAMCS), an emergency department visit was considered injury-related if the physician diagnosis was injury-related or an external cause-of-injury code (E code) was present (Table IX). Starting with *Health, United States, 2008*, an injury-related visit was redefined as an initial injury visit. In the 2001–2010 NHAMCS, an initial injury visit was the first visit to an emergency department for an injury that was characterized by either the first-listed diagnosis being a valid injury diagnosis or by a valid first-listed E code, regardless of the diagnosis code. Visits for which the first-listed diagnosis or the first-listed E code was for a complication of medical care or for an adverse event were not counted as injury visits. For 2001–2004 and 2007 and subsequent data years, the patient record form had a specific question on whether the episode of care was an initial visit for the problem. In the 2005 and 2006 surveys, this variable was not included, and in its place an imputed variable was constructed that indicated whether the visit was or was not the initial visit for the problem. For an explanation of the methodology used to create the imputed initial visit variable, see: http://www.cdc.gov/nchs/data/ahcd/initialvisit.pdf. For more information, see the NCHS Injury Data and Resources website at: http://www.cdc.gov/nchs/injury.htm; and Fingerhut LA. Recommended definition of initial injury visits to emergency departments for use with the NHAMCS–ED data. NCHS. Health E-Stats; 2006. Available from: http://www.cdc.gov/nchs/data/hestat/injury/injury.htm. (Also see Appendix II, Emergency department or emergency room visit; External cause of injury; Injury.)

Inpatient—An inpatient is a person who is formally admitted to the inpatient service of a hospital for observation, care, diagnosis, or treatment. (Also see Appendix II, Admission; Average length of stay; Days of care; Discharge; Hospital.)

Inpatient care—See Appendix II, Hospital utilization.

Inpatient day—See Appendix II, Days of care.

Table VIII. Codes for industries, based on the North American Industry Classification System (NAICS)

Industry	Code
Agriculture, forestry, fishing and hunting	11
Mining, quarrying, and oil and gas extraction	21
Utilities	22
Construction	23
Manufacturing	31–33
Wholesale trade	42
Retail trade	44–45
Transportation and warehousing	48–49
Information	51
Finance and insurance	52
Real estate and rental and leasing	53
Professional, scientific, and technical services	54
Management of companies and enterprises	55
Administrative and support and waste management and remediation services	56
Educational services	61
Health care and social assistance	62
Arts, entertainment, and recreation	71
Accommodation and food services	72
Other services, except public administration	81
Public administration	92

SOURCE: Bureau of Labor Statistics. Available from: http://www.census.gov/eos/www/naics/.

Instrumental activities of daily living (IADL)—IADLs are activities related to independent living and include preparing meals, managing money, shopping for groceries or personal items, performing light or heavy housework, and using a telephone. In the National Health Interview Survey, respondents are asked whether they or family members need the help of another person for handling routine IADL needs because of a physical, mental, or emotional problem.

In the Medicare Current Beneficiary Survey, if a sample person had any difficulty performing an activity by him- or herself and without special equipment or did not perform the activity at all because of health problems, the person was categorized as having a limitation in that activity. The limitation may have been temporary or chronic at the time of interview. Sampled persons in the community answered health status and functioning questions themselves, if able to do so. For sampled persons in a long-term care facility, a proxy, such as a nurse, answered questions about the sampled person's health status and functioning. (Also see Appendix II, Activities of daily living [ADL]; Complex activity limitation; Limitation of activity.)

Insurance—See Appendix II, Health insurance coverage.

Intermediate care facility—See Appendix II, Nursing home.

***International Classification of Diseases* (ICD)**—The ICD is used to code and classify cause-of-death data. The ICD is developed collaboratively by the World Health Organization and 10 international centers, one of which is housed at NCHS. The purpose of the ICD is to promote international

Table IX. Codes for external causes of injury, from the *International Classification of Diseases, 9th Revision, Clinical Modification*

External cause of injury category	E code
All injury	E800–E869, E880–E929, E950–E999
Unintentional	E800–E869, E880–E929
Motor vehicle traffic	E810–E819
Falls	E880–E886, E888
Struck by or against objects or persons	E916–E917
Caused by cutting and piercing instruments or objects	E920
Intentional (suicide and homicide)	E950–E969, E979, E999.1
Undetermined.	E980–E989
Other (includes legal intervention and operations of war)	E970–E978, E990–E999.0

SOURCE: Recommended framework of E code groupings for presenting injury morbidity data. Available from: http://www.cdc.gov/injury/wisqars/ecode_matrix.html, and the *International Classification of Diseases, 9th Revision, Clinical Modification*. Available from: http://www.cdc.gov/nchs/icd/icd9cm.htm.

comparability in the collection, classification, processing, and presentation of health statistics. Since 1900, the ICD has been modified about once every 10 years, except for the 20-year interval between the 9th and 10th revisions (ICD–9 and ICD–10) (Table III). The purpose of the revisions is to stay abreast of advances in medical science. New revisions usually introduce major disruptions in time series of mortality statistics (Tables IV and V). For more information, see the NCHS ICD–10 website at: http://www.cdc.gov/nchs/icd/icd10.htm. (Also see Appendix II, Cause of death; Comparability ratio; *International Classification of Diseases, 9th Revision, Clinical Modification* [ICD–9–CM].)

***International Classification of Diseases, 9th Revision, Clinical Modification* (ICD–9–CM)**—ICD–9–CM is based on, and is compatible with, the World Health Organization's ICD–9. The United States used ICD–9–CM to code morbidity diagnoses and inpatient procedures until October 1, 2015, when the *International Classification of Diseases, 10th Revision, Clinical Modification/Procedure Coding System* went into effect. ICD–9–CM consists of three volumes. Volumes 1 and 2 contain the diagnosis tabular list and index; Volume 3 contains the procedure classification (tabular list and index combined).

ICD–9–CM is divided into 17 chapters and two supplemental classifications. The chapters are arranged primarily by body system. In addition, there are chapters for Infectious and parasitic diseases; Neoplasms; Endocrine, nutritional, and metabolic diseases; Mental disorders; Complications of pregnancy, childbirth, and puerperium; Certain conditions originating in the perinatal period; Congenital anomalies; and Symptoms, signs, and ill-defined conditions. The two supplemental classifications are for factors influencing health status and contact with health services (V codes), and for external causes of injury and poisoning (E codes).

In *Health, United States*, morbidity data will be classified using ICD–9–CM until 2016 data are available and then morbidity data will be classified using *International Classification of Diseases, 10th Revision, Clinical Modification/ Procedure Coding System* (ICD–10–CM/PCS). ICD–9–CM procedure categories and codes are shown in Table X. For more information about ICD–9–CM, see the NCHS

Classification of Diseases, Functioning, and Disability website at: http://www.cdc.gov/nchs/icd.htm. (Also see Appendix II, *International Classification of Diseases* [ICD]; *International Classification of Diseases, 10th Revision, Clinical Modification/Procedure Coding System* [ICD–10–CM/PCS].)

***International Classification of Diseases, 10th Revision, Clinical Modification/Procedure Coding System* (ICD–10–CM/PCS)**—Use of ICD–10–CM/PCS to report medical diagnoses and inpatient procedures was implemented October 1, 2015. The transition to ICD–10 is required for everyone covered by the Health Insurance Portability and Accountability Act (HIPAA). This change to ICD–10 does not affect Current Procedural Terminology (CPT) coding for outpatient procedures and physician services. ICD–10–CM/PCS consists of two parts: ICD–10–CM for diagnosis coding, and ICD–10–PCS for inpatient procedure coding. For more information about ICD–10–CM/PCS, see the NCHS Classification of Diseases, Functioning, and Disability website at: http://www.cdc.gov/nchs/icd.htm and the Centers for Medicare & Medicaid Services ICD–10 transition website at: http://www.cms.gov/Medicare/Coding/ICD10/index.html.

Late fetal death rate—See Appendix II, Rate: Death and related rates.

Leading causes of death—See Appendix II, Cause-of-death ranking.

Length of stay—See Appendix II, Average length of stay.

Life expectancy—Life expectancy is the average number of years of life remaining to a person at a particular age and is based on a given set of age-specific death rates— generally the mortality conditions existing in the period mentioned. Life expectancy may be determined by sex, race and Hispanic origin, or other characteristics, by using age-specific death rates for the population with that characteristic. (Also see Appendix II, Rate: Death and related rates.)

U.S. life tables by Hispanic origin were available starting with 2006 data. Life expectancy data for the Hispanic population were not available before 2006 for three major reasons: (a) coverage of the Hispanic population in the U.S. mortality statistics system was incomplete, (b) misclassification of Hispanic persons on death certificate data underestimated deaths in the Hispanic population, and (c) misstatement of age at the oldest ages in the Hispanic population led to an underestimation of mortality at the oldest ages.

Hispanic origin was added to the U.S. standard death certificate in 1989, but it was not adopted by every state until 1997. By 1997, all states had reporting rates over 99%. Research on race and Hispanic origin reporting on U.S. death certificates found that misclassification of race and Hispanic origin accounts for a net underestimate of 5% for total Hispanic deaths and 1% for total non-Hispanic black deaths, and a net overestimate of 0.5% for non-Hispanic white deaths. To address the effects of age misstatement at the oldest ages, the probability of death for Hispanic persons over age 80 is estimated as a function of non-Hispanic white mortality with the use of the Brass relational logit model. For more information, see: Arias E. United States life tables by Hispanic origin. NCHS. Vital Health Stat 2010;2(152). Available from: http://www.cdc.gov/nchs/data/series/sr_02/sr02_152.pdf.

In 2000, the life table methodology was revised. The revised methodology is similar to that developed for the 1999–2001 decennial life tables. In 2008, the life table methodology was refined in two important ways. First, a logistic rather than a nonlinear least squares model was used to smooth and extrapolate the Vital and Medicare blended death rates at the older ages. Second, the age at which smoothing is begun was raised from 66 to 85 years or so, depending on the population. Values for 2001 and subsequent data years shown in *Health, United States* are based on the 2008 revision of the life table methodology. As a result, data post-2000 may differ from figures published previously. For a full description of the 2008 life table methodology, see: Arias E. United States life tables, 2008. National vital statistics reports; vol 61 no 3. Hyattsville, MD: NCHS; 2012. Available from: http://www.cdc.gov/nchs/data/nvsr/nvsr61/nvsr61_03.pdf. Starting with *Health, United States, 2016*, life expectancy estimates for 2010 and beyond were revised to reflect updated race and Hispanic origin classification ratios. See: Arias E, Heron M, Hakes JK. The validity of race and Hispanic-origin reporting on death certificates in the United States: An update. NCHS. Vital Health Stat 2(172). 2016. Available from: http://www.cdc.gov/nchs/data/series/sr_02/sr02_172.pdf. Additional life table estimates are available from the life table home page at: http://www.cdc.gov/nchs/products/life_tables.htm.

Limitation of activity—Limitation of activity may be defined in different ways, depending on the conceptual framework. In the National Health Interview Survey, limitation of activity refers to a long-term reduction in a person's capacity to perform the usual kind or amount of activities associated with his or her age group as a result of a chronic condition. Limitation of activity is assessed by asking persons a series of questions about limitations in their or a family member's ability to perform activities usual for their age group because of a physical, mental, or emotional problem. Persons are asked about limitations in activities of daily living, instrumental activities of daily living, play, school, work, difficulty walking or remembering, and any other activity limitations. For reported limitations, the causal health conditions are determined, and persons are considered limited if one or more of these conditions is chronic. Children under age 18 who receive special education or early intervention services are considered to have a limitation of activity. (Also see Appendix II, Activities of daily living [ADL]; Instrumental activities of daily living [IADL].)

Long-term care facility—A long-term care facility is a residence that provides a specific level of personal or medical care or supervision to residents. In the Medicare Current Beneficiary Survey, a residence is considered a long-term care facility if it has three or more long-term care beds and answers affirmatively to at least one of three questions: "Does this facility (a) provide personal care services to residents, (b) provide continuous supervision of residents, (c) provide any long-term care?" Types of long-term care facilities include licensed nursing homes, skilled nursing homes, intermediate care facilities, retirement homes (that provide services), domiciliary or personal care facilities, distinct long-term care units in a hospital complex, mental health facilities and centers, assisted and foster care homes, assisted living facilities, and institutions for persons with intellectual disabilities (formerly called mentally retarded) and the developmentally disabled. (Also see Appendix II, Nursing home.)

Low birthweight—See Appendix II, Birthweight.

Mammography—A mammogram is an x-ray image of the breast used to detect irregularities in breast tissue. In the National Health Interview Survey, questions concerning use of mammography are asked on an intermittent schedule, and question content has differed across years. Mammograms may be used for diagnostic or screening purposes, but the purpose cannot be determined from NHIS.

In *Health, United States*, use of mammography was defined as "percent of women having a mammogram within the past two years." Survey questions have changed over time as follows.

In 1987 and 1990, women were asked to report the number of days, weeks, months, or years that had passed since their most recent mammogram. In 1991, women were asked whether they had a mammogram in the past 2 years. In 1993 and 1994, women were asked whether they had a mammogram within the past year, between 1 and 2 years ago, or over 2 years ago. In 1998, women were asked whether they had a mammogram a year ago or less, more than 1 year but not more than 2 years, more than 2 years

Table X. Codes for procedure categories for Healthcare Cost and Utilization Project data, from the *International Classification of Diseases, 9th Revision, Clinical Modification*

Procedure category	Code
Amputation of lower extremity (amputation of lower limb)	84.10–84.19
Appendectomy	47.0, 47.01, 47.09, 47.1, 47.11, 47.19
Arthroplasty knee (knee replacement).	00.80–00.84, 81.41–81.44, 81.46, 81.47, 81.54, 81.55
Cesarean section	74.0, 74.1, 74.2, 74.4, 74.99
Cholecystectomy (gall bladder removal)	51.21–51.24, 51.41–51.43, 51.49, 51.51, 51.59
Colorectal resection (removal of part of the bowel)	17.31–17.36, 17.39, 45.71–45.76, 45.79, 45.8, 45.81–45.83, 48.40–48.43, 48.49, 48.5, 48.50–48.52, 48.59, 48.61–48.66, 48.69
Coronary artery bypass graft (CABG)	36.10–36.17, 36.19, 36.2, 36.3, 36.31–36.34, 36.39
Endarterectomy (plaque removal from artery lining of brain, head, neck)	38.11, 38.12
Heart valve procedures	35.00–35.14, 35.20–35.28, 35.96, 35.97, 35.99
Hip replacement.	00.70–00.77, 00.85–00.87, 81.51–81.53, 81.69
Hysterectomy	68.3, 68.31, 68.39, 68.4, 68.41, 68.49, 68.5, 68.51, 68.59, 68.6, 68.61, 68.69, 68.7, 68.71, 68.79, 68.9
Incision and excision of CNS (brain surgery)	01.01, 01.09, 01.21–01.28, 01.31, 01.32, 01.39, 01.41, 01.42, 01.51–01.53, 01.59
Insertion, revision, replacement, removal of cardiac pacemaker	00.50–00.54, 00.56, 00.57, 17.51, 17.52, 37.70–37.83, 37.85–37.87, 37.89, 37.94–37.98
Laminectomy (spine surgery)	03.02, 03.09, 80.5, 80.50, 80.51, 80.59, 84.59–84.69, 84.80–84.85
Ligation of fallopian tubes ("tying" of fallopian tubes).	66.21, 66.22, 66.29, 66.31, 66.32, 66.39
Oophorectomy (removal of one or both ovaries)	65.3, 65.31, 65.39, 65.4, 65.41, 65.49, 65.51–65.54, 65.61–65.64
Percutaneous coronary angioplasty (PTCA) (balloon angioplasty)	00.66, 17.55, 36.01, 36.02, 36.05
Small bowel resection (removal of part of the small bowel)	45.61–45.63
Spinal fusion.	81.00–81.09, 81.30–81.39, 81.61–81.64, 84.51
Tonsillectomy and/or adenoidectomy.	28.2, 28.3, 28.6, 28.7
Treatment, fracture or dislocation of hip and femur.	78.55, 78.65, 79.05, 79.15, 79.25, 79.35, 79.45, 79.55, 79.65, 79.75, 79.85, 79.95

NOTES: Procedures were classified by the Clinical Classifications Software (CCS). For more information, see: http://www.hcup-us.ahrq.gov/toolssoftware/ccs/AppendixBSinglePR.txt.

SOURCE: Agency for Healthcare Research and Quality.

ago but not more than 3 years, more than 3 years but not more than 5 years, or over 5 years ago.

In 1999, women were asked to report the number of days, weeks, months, or years that had passed since their most recent mammogram. Estimates for 1999 may be slightly overestimated in comparison with previous years: women who responded "2 years ago" (10% of women) may include those who received a mammogram more than 2 years but less than 3 years ago.

In 2000 and 2003, women were asked when they had their most recent mammogram (asked to give month and year). Women who did not respond were given a follow-up question that used the 1999 wording, and women who did not respond to the 1999 wording were asked a second follow-up question that used the 1998 wording. Estimates for 2000 and 2003 may be slightly overestimated in comparison with estimates prior to 1999: women who responded "2 years ago" (2% of women) may include those who received a mammogram more than 2 years but less than 3 years ago.

In 2005, women were asked the same series of mammography questions as in the 2000 and 2003 surveys, but the questionnaire skip pattern was modified so that more women were asked the follow-up question using the 1998 wording. Thus, estimates for 2005 and subsequent years are more precise than estimates for 1999, 2000, and 2003. SAS code to categorize mammography data for 2000 and beyond is available from: http://www.cdc.gov/nchs/nhis/nhis_2005_data_release.htm. In 2008, 2010, 2013, and 2015, the mammography questions were identical to those asked in 2005.

The recommended age to begin mammography screening and the interval between screenings has changed over time. The current recommendation, made by the U.S. Preventive Services Task Force in 2016, is the use of screening mammography for breast cancer every 2 years in women aged 50–74, with additional guidance provided for women aged 40–49. For additional information, see: U.S. Preventive Services Task Force. Breast cancer: Screening. Rockville, MD: Agency for Healthcare Research and Quality; 2016.

Available from: http://www.uspreventiveservicestaskforce.org/Page/Document/RecommendationStatementFinal/breast-cancer-screening1; and U.S. Preventive Services Task Force. Guide to clinical preventive services, 2014. Rockville, MD: Agency for Healthcare Research and Quality; 2014. Available from: http://www.ahrq.gov/professionals/clinicians-providers/guidelines-recommendations/guide/index.html.

Managed care—"Managed care" is a term originally used to refer to prepaid health plans (generally, health maintenance organizations, or HMOs) that furnish care through a network of providers under a fixed budget and "manage" costs. Increasingly, the term is also used to include preferred provider organizations (PPOs) and even forms of indemnity insurance coverage (i.e., "fee-for-service" insurance).

Medicare managed care includes a combination of risk- and cost-based plans. Risk-based plans receive a fixed prepayment per beneficiary per month to help pay for the cost of all covered services that a beneficiary may use. Each year, the Centers for Medicare & Medicaid Services (CMS) announces a "benchmark" amount for each county for coverage of Medicare Part A and Part B services. A managed care plan contracting with Medicare then submits a "bid," which represents the revenue it needs to cover these services. If the bid is above the benchmark, the difference must be charged in a premium to the enrollees of the plan. If the bid is below the benchmark, then a portion of the difference must be used to provide additional benefits to enrollees, with the Medicare trust funds receiving the remaining share. The term Medicare Advantage is used to refer to managed care plans, including HMOs, PPOs, private fee-for-service plans, special needs plans, Medicare medical savings account plans, and certain other types of plans.

Cost-based plans are offered by an HMO or a competitive medical plan and are paid for their "reasonable costs" in providing Medicare services to enrollees, based on annual cost reports filed with CMS. For current definitions of the various Medicare managed care plans, see the CMS Medicare Managed Care Manual. Ch 1, section 30, "Types of MA Plans," Baltimore, MD: CMS; 2011. Available from: https://www.cms.gov/Regulations-and-Guidance/Guidance/Manuals/Internet-Only-Manuals-IOMs-Items/CMS019326.html?DLPage=1&DLEntries=100&DLSort=0&DLS%20ortDir=ascending.

Medicare enrollees can choose to enroll in a managed care program (if available) or to receive services on a fee-for-service basis.

The two major Medicaid managed care categories are risk-based plans (managed care organizations, or MCOs) and primary care case management (PCCM) arrangements. Risk-based plans (MCOs) are paid a fixed monthly fee per enrollee. MCOs assume some or all of the financial risk for providing the services covered under the contract. PCCM providers are usually physicians, physician group practices, or entities employing or having other arrangements with such physicians, but they can also include nurse practitioners, nurse midwives, or physician assistants. These providers (also called gatekeepers) contract directly with the state to locate, coordinate, and monitor covered primary care (and sometimes additional services). PCCM providers are paid a per-patient case management fee and usually do not assume financial risk for the provision of services. Some states allow Medicaid enrollees to voluntarily enroll in managed care plans; most states require that at least certain categories of Medicaid beneficiaries join such plans. Both MCOs and PCCM arrangements include plans that provide specialized services to certain categories of Medicaid beneficiaries. For more information on state Medicaid managed care plans, see http://www.medicaid.gov/.

(Also see Appendix II, Health maintenance organization [HMO]; Medicare; Medicaid; Preferred provider organization [PPO].)

Marital status—Marital status is classified through self-reporting into the categories married and unmarried. The term "married" encompasses all married people, including those separated from their spouses. "Unmarried" includes those who are single (never married), divorced, or widowed.

Birth file—In 1970, 39 states and D.C., and in 1975, 38 states and D.C., included a direct question about mother's marital status on the birth certificate. Since 1980, national estimates of births to unmarried women have been based on two methods for determining marital status: a direct question in the birth registration process and inferential procedures. In 1980–1996, marital status was reported on the birth certificates of 41–45 states and D.C.; with the addition of California in 1997, 46 states and D.C.; and in 1998–2001, 48 states and D.C. In 1997, all but four states (Connecticut, Michigan, Nevada, and New York), and in 1998, all but two states (Michigan and New York) included a direct question about mother's marital status on their birth certificates. In 1998–2007, marital status was imputed as married on birth records with missing information in the 48 states and D.C. where this information was obtained by a direct question. In 2008–2013 for 49 states and D.C., marital status is reported in the birth registration process.

For states lacking a direct question, marital status was inferred. Before 1980, the incidence of births to unmarried women in states with no direct question on marital status was assumed to be the same as the incidence in reporting states in the same geographic division. Starting in 1980, for states without a direct question, marital status was inferred by comparing the parents' and child's surnames. For 1994–1996, birth certificates in 45 states and D.C. included a question about the mother's marital status. Beginning in 1997, the marital status of women giving birth in California and Nevada has been determined by a direct question in the birth registration process. Beginning in June 15, 1998, Connecticut discontinued inferring the mother's marital status and added a direct question regarding mother's marital status to the state's birth certificate.

In 2005, Michigan added a direct question to the birth registration process but uses inferential procedures to update information collected using the direct question. In both Michigan and New York, a birth is inferred as nonmarital if either of these factors, listed in priority-of-use order, is present: (a) a paternity acknowledgment was received or (b) the father's name is missing. For 2006–2008 data, inferential procedures were used to compile birth statistics by marital status, in full or in part, for New York and Michigan, respectively. For 2009–2014, mother's marital status is inferred for New York.

National Health Interview Survey (NHIS)—In NHIS, marital status is asked of, or about, all persons aged 14 and over. Respondents are asked, "Are you now married, widowed, divorced, separated, never married, or living with a partner?"

Maternal age—See Appendix II, Age.

Medicaid—Medicaid was authorized in 1965 and became Title XIX of the Social Security Act. Medicaid is a jointly funded cooperative venture between the federal and state governments to assist states in the provision of adequate medical care to eligible persons. Within broad federal guidelines, each state establishes its own eligibility standards; determines the type, amount, duration, and scope of services; sets the rate of payment for services; and administers its own program.

Medicaid is the largest program providing medical and health-related services to low income individuals. Medicaid was originally available only to individuals receiving cash assistance, but over time, Congress has expanded eligibility for children and selected adult groups. Most recently, the Affordable Care Act (ACA) and the Health Care and Education Reconciliation Act (HCERA) initiated significant changes to Medicaid. (Subsequent references to the ACA in this text will include changes enacted by either the ACA or HCERA.)

States are mandated by federal law to cover certain population groups (mandatory eligibility groups) but are granted flexibility in covering other groups (optional eligibility groups). In the standard benefit package, states must cover mandatory benefits (e.g., physician services) but may choose to cover optional benefits (e.g., tuberculosis-related services). Prior to the ACA, many states expanded Medicaid coverage above the federal minimums and many states have chosen to continue this additional coverage. The major coverage change introduced by the ACA was to create a new eligibility group—Medicaid Expansion to Low-Income Adults—for those with incomes up to 138% of the federal poverty level (FPL) (133% by statute with an additional 5% income disregard). This is discussed further below.

States set individual eligibility criteria within federal minimum standards. In addition to Medicaid's financial eligibility requirements, individuals must satisfy federal and state requirements regarding residency, immigration status, and documentation of U.S. citizenship. The ACA provided a standard application—available through the Medicaid program or through the Health Insurance Marketplace—and a standard method for calculating income eligibility for Medicaid, CHIP, and insurance affordability programs offered through the marketplace, based primarily on modified adjusted gross income (MAGI). Effective 2014, MAGI is used to determine Medicaid and CHIP eligibility for most nondisabled children and adults under age 65.

Broadly, there are four major eligibility groups covered by most states: Children, Adults with Disabilities, Aged Adults, and Nondisabled Adults. These are discussed in more detail below.

● *Major Eligibility Groups*

Children—Medicaid was originally available only to individuals receiving cash assistance, but Congress has since expanded eligibility for children and other populations, making individuals eligible based on income below a specified percentage of the FPL. The ACA raised the minimum Medicaid eligibility for nondisabled children to 138% FPL (133% by statute with an additional 5% income disregard). Other eligible child groups include: infants born to women covered by Medicaid (known as "deemed newborns"), certain children in foster care or adoption assistance programs, certain children with disabilities, and children who use long-term services and supports. Like disabled adults, most states automatically qualify disabled children in the Supplemental Security Income (SSI) program for Medicaid coverage; eligibility is not determined by the newly introduced MAGI. Some states use more restrictive criteria to determine Medicaid eligibility of children with SSI. These criteria are usually based on income relative to the FPL and assets. Regardless of how they qualify, all children enrolled in Medicaid are entitled to the comprehensive set of health care services known as Early, Periodic Screening, Diagnostic and Treatment (EPSDT). These services include screening for and treatment of any vision or hearing problems, coverage for eyeglasses and hearing aids, and regular preventive dental care and treatment.

Adults with Disabilities—Adults with disabilities from physical conditions, intellectual or development disabilities, serious behavioral disorders, or serious mental illness may be eligible for Medicaid. The

Supplemental Security Income (SSI) program pays benefits to disabled adults and children who have limited income and resources. Enrollment in SSI (or the Social Security Disability Insurance program, which provides Medicare to qualified individuals after a 24-month waiting period) automatically qualifies adults with disabilities for Medicaid in most states. However, some states use more restrictive criteria (known as 209(b) of the 1972 amendments to the Social Security Act) to determine Medicaid eligibility. These criteria are often based on income relative to the FPL and assets. As of December 2016, 10 states used more restrictive criteria than enrollment in SSI. Individuals with disabilities who are eligible for Medicaid are entitled to all services that are deemed medically necessary.

All states have the option of covering additional people with low incomes or high medical expenses through other eligibility pathways. These may include covering those at higher income levels; permitting persons with disabilities and high medical expenses to spend down until they are eligible for coverage; setting a special income level to cover institutionalized individuals with incomes up to 300% of the SSI benefit rate; extending coverage to individuals who receive home- and community-based waiver services as an alternative to institutionalization; permitting working individuals who are severely impaired but whose earnings would otherwise disqualify them from Medicaid to buy into Medicaid; covering adults with disabilities who use long-term services and supports based on their functional status (known as level-of-care) and use of services (e.g., residence in a nursing facility, intermediate care facility for persons with intellectual disabilities, or mental health facility; or requiring significant home-based services).

Aged Adults—The Supplemental Security Income (SSI) program covers those with disabilities and also people aged 65 and older without disabilities who meet the financial limits. In most states, SSI enrollment automatically qualified those aged 65 and older for Medicaid. However, some states use more restrictive criteria (known as 209(b)) to determine Medicaid eligibility. The more restrictive criteria may consider income and assets, disability, or both. Most Medicaid enrollees aged 65 or over are also Medicare beneficiaries. Members of this group are known as dual-eligible beneficiaries. Dual eligibles are eligible for the same Medicare benefits as other Medicare beneficiaries but have low incomes that make it difficult to afford the premiums and cost sharing required by Medicare, as well as the cost of services not covered by the Medicare program (e.g., long-term services and supports). Dual eligibles may qualify for partial Medicaid benefits (to cover Medicare premium and cost sharing) or full Medicaid benefits, in which case they get coverage for the full range of services offered by their state's Medicaid program.

Like coverage for adults with disabilities, states may extend Medicaid coverage to adults with low incomes or high medical expenses through other eligibility pathways, such as covering those with higher income levels or those with chronic conditions or low functional status requiring institutionalization or significant home-based services. There is considerable variation across states in the optional Medicaid services covered, which results in different benefits for dual-eligible beneficiaries depending on where they live.

Nondisabled Adults—Prior to the enactment of the ACA, most low-income nondisabled adults were not eligible for Medicaid unless they were in special groups (e.g., pregnant women, low-income parents, or other caretaker relatives with dependent children) or in states with demonstration programs that provided expanded coverage.

The major eligibility groups of nondisabled adults include the following: Medicaid Expansion Coverage to Low-income Adults (the new adult group), Pregnant Women, Parents and Caretaker Relatives, and Adults Without Dependent Children. These groups and some specialty eligible groups—Breast and Cervical Cancer Prevention and Treatment Program and Tuberculosis (TB)—are discussed below.

Medicaid Expansion to Low-income Adults—As of October 2016, 31 states and D.C. had chosen to expand their Medicaid programs. They are: Alaska, Arizona, Arkansas, California, Colorado, Connecticut, Delaware, Hawaii, Illinois, Indiana, Iowa, Kentucky, Louisiana, Maryland, Massachusetts, Michigan, Minnesota, Montana, Nevada, New Hampshire, New Jersey, New Mexico, New York, North Dakota, Ohio, Oregon, Pennsylvania, Rhode Island, Vermont, Washington, and West Virginia.

Pregnant Women—Since 1989, Congress has required Medicaid to cover pregnant women with low income. Currently, all but four states have extended Medicaid coverage to pregnant women above the currently required level of 138% FPL. Maternity-related services covered by the programs include prenatal care, labor and delivery, and 60 days of postpartum care. In Medicaid-expansion states, women at or below 138% FPL who are pregnant when they apply for Medicaid are not eligible for the new adult group. Medicaid coverage as a pregnant woman ends two months postpartum (after which the individual may be eligible in another Medicaid eligibility group).

Parents and Caretaker Relatives—Parents and caretaker relatives in low-income families with dependent children are eligible for coverage if their income meets the minimum eligibility levels established in 1996 for financial and medical assistance, which averages 41% of poverty. (1996 was the year of enactment for welfare reform, which held in place guaranteed Medicaid eligibility for those receiving cash benefits at that time.) States have the option to be more or less restrictive than the 1996 standards.

Adults without Dependent Children—Prior to the ACA, about one-half of states provided some coverage, through Medicaid demonstration projects or state-funded programs, for nondisabled adults who had limited incomes but did not otherwise qualify for Medicaid. Currently, 31 states and the District of Columbia have implemented the ACA Medicaid expansion for adults with incomes at or below 133% of the poverty line (with a 5% income disregard, so effectively 138%).

- *Other Eligibility Groups*

Breast and Cervical Cancer Prevention and Treatment Program—In 2000, Congress passed the Breast and Cervical Cancer Prevention and Treatment Act, which allowed states to offer eligible women, who were diagnosed with cancer through the CDC-funded screening program, access to treatment through Medicaid. All states and D.C. have chosen to provide this coverage. For a woman to be eligible under this option, she must be under age 65; been screened through CDC's National Breast and Cervical Cancer Early Detection Program; be diagnosed with either breast or cervical cancer, including precancerous conditions; need treatment for breast or cervical cancer; and be uninsured and otherwise not eligible for Medicaid.

Tuberculosis (TB)—States can choose to provide Medicaid coverage of TB-related services for low-income individuals who are infected with TB. This eligibility group serves individuals who are not otherwise eligible for Medicaid based on the traditional eligibility categories.

Medicaid operates as a vendor payment program. States may pay health care providers directly on a fee-for-service basis, or states may pay for Medicaid services through various prepayment arrangements, such as through Medicaid managed care organizations (MCOs) or other forms of managed care. Within federally imposed upper limits and restrictions, each state generally has broad discretion in determining both the payment method and rate for services. Thus, the Medicaid program varies considerably from state to state, as well as within each state over time. For more information, see: http://www.medicaid.gov/ and https://www.macpac.gov/.

(Also see Appendix II, Children's Health Insurance Program [CHIP]; Health expenditures, national; Health insurance coverage; Health maintenance organization [HMO]; Managed care; and Appendix I, Medicaid Statistical Information System [MSIS].)

Medicaid payments—Under the Medicaid program, medical vendor payments are payments (expenditures) to medical vendors from the state through a fiscal agent, or to a health insurance plan. Adjustments are made for cost settlements, third-party recoupments, refunds, voided checks, and financial settlements that cannot be related to specific provided claims. Medicaid medical vendor payments presented in *Health, United States* do not include payments made to providers from other federal programs or from third party payers for Medicaid-eligible individuals; payments made from state medical assistance funds that are not federally matchable; cost sharing or enrollment fees collected from recipients or a third party; and administration and training costs. Medicaid payment data presented in *Health, United States* are from the Medical Statistical Information System (MSIS), which obtains payment data from electronic Medicaid data submitted to the Centers for Medicare & Medicaid Services by each state. Payment data are based on adjudicated claims for medical services reimbursed with Title XIX funds.

Medical specialty—See Appendix II, Physician specialty.

Medicare—Medicare is a nationwide program providing health insurance coverage to selected groups, regardless of income. The covered groups are (a) most people aged 65 and over; (b) people entitled to Social Security or Railroad Retirement disability benefits for at least 24 months (with the waiting period waived or reduced in certain situations); (c) government employees or spouses with Medicare-only coverage who have been disabled for more than 29 months (with the waiting period waived or reduced in certain situations); (d) most people with end-stage renal disease; and (e) certain people in the Libby, Montana, vicinity who are diagnosed with asbestos-related conditions. The program was enacted on July 30, 1965, as Title XVIII of the Social Security Act, "Health Insurance for the Aged and Disabled," and became effective on July 1, 1966.

From its inception, Medicare has included two separate but coordinated programs: Hospital Insurance (Part A) and Supplementary Medical Insurance (Part B). Part C ("Medicare Advantage") was established by the Balanced Budget Act of 1997 (originally as "Medicare+Choice") as an expanded set of options for the delivery of health care under Medicare. Although all Medicare beneficiaries can receive their benefits through the original fee-for-service program, most beneficiaries enrolled in both Part A and Part B have the option to participate in a Medicare Advantage plan instead.

Organizations that seek to contract as Medicare Advantage plans must meet specific organizational, financial, and other requirements. Although most Medicare Advantage enrollees are in coordinated care plans, such as health maintenance organizations and preferred provider organizations, Medicare Advantage plans also include private fee-for-service plans, provider-sponsored organizations, special needs plans, medical savings account plans (MSA plans, which provide benefits after a single high deductible is met), and certain other types of plans. Medicare Advantage plans are generally paid on a capitation basis—that is, plans are paid a predetermined amount per member per month, which is adjusted according to the health status of the plans' members—and are required to provide at least those services covered by Parts A and B, except hospice services. Plans may (and in certain situations must) provide extra benefits (such as vision or hearing coverage) or reduce cost sharing or premiums.

The Medicare Prescription Drug, Improvement, and Modernization Act (also called the Medicare Modernization Act, or MMA) was passed on December 8, 2003. The MMA (Pub. L. 108–173) established a voluntary prescription drug benefit for Medicare beneficiaries and created a new Medicare Part D. People eligible for Medicare could begin to enroll in Part D beginning in January 2006. For more information on Medicare, see: https://www.medicare.gov/Pubs/pdf/10050.pdf and http://www.cms.gov/Research-Statistics-Data-and-Systems/Statistics-Trends-and-Reports/MedicareMedicaidStatSupp/2013.html. (Also see Appendix II, Fee-for-service health insurance; Health insurance coverage; Health maintenance organization [HMO]; Managed care; and Appendix I, Medicare Administrative Data.)

Metropolitan statistical area (MSA)—The Office of Management and Budget (OMB) defines MSAs according to published standards that are applied to U.S. Census Bureau data. The standards are revised periodically, generally prior to the decennial census, and are applied to the census data to delineate the statistical areas. Revisions to the areas are implemented between censuses by using updated population estimates. The most recent standards were released in June 2010 (available from: https://www.census.gov/programs-surveys/metro-micro.html). In July 2015, OMB released a new delineation of the nation's metropolitan and micropolitan statistical areas based on the 2010 standards (available from: https://www.census.gov/programs-surveys/metro-micro.html). New MSA delineations are incorporated into individual data systems at different times. In the 2000 and 2010 standards, an MSA is a county, or group of contiguous counties, that contains at least one urbanized area with a population of 50,000 or more. In addition to the county or counties that contain all or part of the urbanized area, an MSA may contain other counties if there are strong social and economic ties with the central county or counties, as measured by commuting. Counties that are not within an MSA are considered to be nonmetropolitan. For more information, see: https://www.census.gov/programs-surveys/metro-micro.html. Most data by MSA currently in *Health, United States* are based on the June 2003 OMB definitions (2000 OMB standards applied to 2000 census data). (Also see Appendix II, Urbanization.)

National Health Interview Survey (NHIS)—For respondents to NHIS, designation of place of residence as metropolitan or nonmetropolitan is based on the following MSA definitions: for 2006 and beyond, on the June 2003 OMB definitions (2000 OMB standards applied to 2000 census data); for 1995–2005, on the June 1993 OMB definitions (1990 OMB standards applied to 1990 census data); and for 1985–1994, on the June 1983 OMB definitions (1980 OMB standards applied to 1980 census data). For estimates based on 2006 NHIS data combined with earlier years of NHIS, metropolitan status of residence for all years involved is based on the June 2003 definitions. Introduction of each set of standards may create a discontinuity in trends.

National Immunization Survey (NIS)—Since 2013, designation of place of residence as metropolitan or nonmetropolitan for NIS respondents is based on 2010 Census data and the MSAs delineated in February 2013. For data prior to 2013, designation of place of residence as metropolitan or nonmetropolitan for NIS respondents was based on 2000 census data and the MSAs delineated in 2003, as well as the following versions and revisions of MSA definitions: for 2011 and 2012, on the December 2009 definitions; for 2010, on the November 2008 definitions, for New England, the county-based areas were used; for 2009, on the November 2007 definitions, for New England, the county-based areas were used; for 2008, on the December 2006 definitions, for New England, the county-based areas were used; for quarter 4 of 2007, on the December 2006 definitions; for quarters 1–3 of 2007, on the December 2005 definitions, for New England, the county-based areas were used in 2007; for 2006, on the November 2004 definitions, for New England, the county-based areas were used; for 2005, on the December 2003 definitions, for New England, the county-based areas were used; for quarters 3 and 4 of 2004, on the December 2003 definitions; and for quarters 1 and 2 of 2004 and quarter 4 of 2003, on the June 2003 definitions. For 2003–2004 for New England, the county-based areas were used. For more information, see: https://www.census.gov/programs-surveys/metro-micro.html.

Micropolitan statistical area—The Office of Management and Budget (OMB) defines a micropolitan statistical area as a nonmetropolitan county, or group of contiguous nonmetropolitan counties, that contains an urban cluster of 10,000–49,999 persons. A micropolitan statistical area may include surrounding counties that have strong social and economic ties with the central county or counties as measured by commuting. Nonmetropolitan counties that are not classified as part of a micropolitan statistical area are considered noncore.

OMB defines micropolitan statistical areas according to published standards that are applied to U.S. Census Bureau data. The standards are revised periodically, generally prior to the decennial census, and are applied to the census data to delineate the statistical areas. Revisions to the areas are implemented between censuses using updated population estimates. The most recent standards were released in June 2010 (available from: https://www.census.gov/programs-surveys/metro-micro.html). OMB released a new delineation of the nation's metropolitan and micropolitan statistical areas based on the 2010 standards in July 2015 (available from: https://www.census.gov/programs-surveys/metro-micro.html). Data for micropolitan statistical areas currently in *Health, United States* are based on the 2013-based delineation as part of the 2013 NCHS Urban–Rural Classification Scheme for Counties. The micropolitan statistical area data will be updated when the new delineation is incorporated into individual data systems.

For more information about micropolitan statistical areas, see https://www.census.gov/programs-surveys/metro-micro.html. (Also see Appendix II, Metropolitan statistical area [MSA]; Urbanization.)

Multum Lexicon Plus therapeutic class—Starting with 2003 data, NCHS used Lexicon Plus (Cerner Multum, Inc., Denver, CO.), a proprietary database, to assist with data editing and classification of human drugs. Starting with 2005 data, Lexicon Plus has also been used to assist with data collection. Data collected before 2003 were updated by adding a generic drug code from Lexicon Plus.

Lexicon Plus is a comprehensive database of all prescription and some nonprescription drug products available in the U.S. drug market. It uses a three-level nested category system to assign a therapeutic classification to each drug (e.g., for atenolol: cardiovascular agents [level 1]; beta-adrenergic blocking agents [level 2]; cardioselective beta blockers [level 3]). Not all drugs have three classification levels; some may only have two (e.g., for diltiazem: cardiovascular agents [level 1]; calcium channel blocking agents [level 2]). Other drugs may have only one classification level. All drugs in NCHS surveys were assigned into a Lexicon Plus drug category, even those drugs not found in the Lexicon Plus drug database. "Unspecified" drugs were assigned to their respective therapeutic category (e.g., hormones/hormone modifiers–unspecified: category ID = 97, category name = hormones/hormone modifiers).

Data presented in the *Health, United States* Trend Table on prescription drug use by drug class are based on the second level of the Lexicon Plus nested category system (e.g., calcium channel blocking agents). A drug may have up to four drug therapeutic categories; drugs classified into more than one class were counted in each class. For example, if a person reported taking lorazepam, that respondent was classified as taking an anticonvulsant; an antiemetic/antivertigo agent; and an anxiolytic, sedative, hypnotic drug.

The drug information file is updated along with each cycle of prescription medication data release. Some new therapeutic categories could be added, and a few assigned classification levels might be changed (e.g., alendronate now has three classification levels: metabolic agents [level 1], bone resorption inhibitors [level 2], and bisphosphonates [level 3]); under the prior drug information file, alendronate had two classification levels: hormones [level 1] and bisphosphonates [level 2]). Data presented in *Health, United States* used the most recent drug information file for all data years.

For more information, see: http://wwwn.cdc.gov/nchs/nhanes/1999-2000/RXQ_DRUG.htm.

Neonatal mortality rate—See Appendix II, Rate: Death and related rates.

Nonprofit hospital—See Appendix II, Hospital.

North American Industry Classification System (NAICS)—See Appendix II, Industry of employment.

Notifiable disease—A notifiable disease is one that, when diagnosed, health providers are required (usually by law) to report to state or local public health officials. Notifiable diseases are of public interest by reason of their contagiousness, severity, or frequency. For more information, see: http://www.cdc.gov/osels/ph_surveillance/nndss/nndsshis.htm.

Nursing home—In the Quality Improvement Evaluation System (QIES) (formerly the Online Survey Certification and Reporting [OSCAR]) database, a nursing home is a facility that is certified and meets the Centers for Medicare & Medicaid Services' long-term care requirements for Medicare and Medicaid eligibility.

After October 1, 1990, long-term care facilities that met the Omnibus Budget Reconciliation Act of 1987, Pub. L. No. 100–203, 101 Stat. 1330 nursing home reform requirements and were formerly certified under Medicaid as skilled nursing, nursing home, or intermediate care facilities were reclassified as nursing facilities. Medicare continues to certify skilled nursing facilities but not intermediate care facilities. State Medicaid programs can certify intermediate care facilities for individuals with intellectual disabilities (formerly called mentally retarded or developmentally disabled). To be certified for participation in Medicaid, nursing facilities must also be certified to participate in Medicare (except those facilities that have obtained waivers). Thus, most nursing home care is now provided in skilled care facilities.

(Also see Appendix II, Long-term care facility; Nursing home; Resident, health facility.)

Nursing home expenditures—See Appendix II, Health expenditures, national.

Obesity—See Appendix II, Body mass index (BMI).

Occupancy rate—In American Hospital Association statistics, hospital occupancy rate is calculated as the average daily census divided by the number of hospital beds, cribs, and pediatric bassinets set up and staffed on the last day of the reporting period, expressed as a percentage. Average daily census is calculated by dividing the total annual number of inpatients, excluding newborns, by 365 days to derive the number of inpatients receiving care on an average day during the annual reporting period. The occupancy rate for facilities other than hospitals is calculated as the number of residents at the facility reported on the day of interview, divided by the number of reported beds. In the Centers for Medicare & Medicaid Services' Quality Improvement Evaluation System (QIES) (formerly the Online Survey Certification and Reporting [OSCAR]) database, occupancy is determined as of the day of certification inspection as the total number of residents on that day divided by the total number of beds on that day.

Office-based physician—See Appendix II, Physician.

Office visit—In the National Ambulatory Medical Care Survey, a physician's ambulatory practice (office) can be in any location other than in a hospital, nursing home, other extended care facility, patient's home, industrial clinic, college clinic, or family planning clinic. Offices in health maintenance organizations and private offices in hospitals are included. An office visit is any direct personal exchange between an ambulatory patient and a physician or members of his or her staff for the purpose of seeking care and rendering health services. (Also see Appendix II, Outpatient visit.)

Operation—See Appendix II, Procedure.

Outpatient department—According to the National Hospital Ambulatory Medical Care Survey (NHAMCS), an outpatient department (OPD) is a hospital facility where nonurgent ambulatory medical care is provided. The following types of OPDs are excluded from NHAMCS: ambulatory surgical centers, chemotherapy, employee health services, renal dialysis, methadone maintenance, and radiology. (Also see Appendix II, Emergency department; Outpatient visit.)

Outpatient surgery—According to the American Hospital Association, outpatient surgery is a surgical operation, whether major or minor, performed on a patient who does not remain in the hospital overnight. Outpatient surgery may be performed in inpatient operating suites, outpatient surgery suites, or procedure rooms within an outpatient care facility. A surgical operation involving more than one surgical procedure is considered one surgical operation. (Also see Appendix II, Procedure.)

Outpatient visit—The American Hospital Association defines outpatient visits as visits for receipt of medical, dental, or other services at a hospital by patients who are not lodged in the hospital. Each appearance by an outpatient to each unit of the hospital is counted individually as an outpatient visit, including all clinic visits,

referred visits, observation services, outpatient surgeries, and emergency department visits. In the National Hospital Ambulatory Medical Care Survey, an outpatient department visit is a direct personal exchange between a patient and a physician or other health care provider working under the physician's supervision for the purpose of seeking care and receiving personal health services. (Also see Appendix II, Emergency department or emergency room visit; Outpatient department.)

Overweight—See Appendix II, Body mass index (BMI).

Pap smear—A Pap smear (also known as a Papanicolaou smear or Pap test) is a microscopic examination of cells scraped from the cervix that is used to detect cancerous or precancerous conditions of the cervix or other medical conditions.

In the National Health Interview Survey, questions concerning Pap smear use are asked on an intermittent schedule, and the question content has differed slightly across years. For 2015, women were asked when they had their most recent Pap smear, and use of Pap smears was defined as "percent of women having a Pap smear within the past three years." Survey questions have changed over time.

In 1987, women were asked to report either the month and year of their Pap smear or the amount of time (in days, weeks, months, or years) elapsed since their last Pap smear. Women who did not respond were asked, "Was it within the past year or a year or more ago?" Those who answered "within the past year" were asked to further clarify whether the Pap smear was less than 3 months or 3 more months ago, and those who answered "a year or more ago" were asked to further clarify whether the Pap smear was 3 years or less, between 3 and 5 years, or 5 or more years ago. In 1990 and 1991, Pap smear data in the past 3 years were not available. In 1993 and 1994, women were asked whether they had a Pap smear within the past year, between 1 and 3 years ago, or more than 3 years ago. In 1998, women were asked whether they had a Pap smear 1 year ago or less, more than 1 year but not more than 2 years ago, more than 2 years but not more than 3 years ago, more than 3 years but not more than 5 years ago, or more than 5 years ago.

In 1999, women were asked when they had their most recent Pap smear (time elapsed in days, weeks, months, or years). Women who did not respond were asked whether they had a Pap smear a year ago or less, more than 1 year but not more than 2 years ago, more than 2 years but not more than 3 years ago, more than 3 years but not more than 5 years ago, or over 5 years ago. Estimates for 1999 may be slightly overestimated in comparison with estimates for previous years due to the inclusion of women who responded "3 years ago" (4% of women), which could have included more than 3 years but less than 4 years.

In 2000 and 2003, women were asked when they had their most recent Pap smear (month and year). Women who did not respond were given a follow-up question that used the 1999 wording, and women who did not respond to the follow-up question were asked a second follow-up question that used the 1998 wording. Estimates for 2000 and 2003 may be slightly overestimated in comparison with years prior to 1999 due to the inclusion of women who responded "3 years ago" (less than 1% of women), which could have included more than 3 years but less than 4 years.

In 2005, women were asked the same series of questions about Pap smear use as in the 2000 and 2003 surveys, but the questionnaire skip pattern was modified so that more women were asked the follow-up question using the 1998 wording, and these women were not uniformly coded as having had a Pap smear within the past 3 years. Thus, estimates for 2005 are more precise than estimates for 1999, 2000, and 2003. SAS code to categorize Pap smear data for 2000 and beyond is available from: http://www.cdc.gov/ nchs/nhis/nhis_2005_data_release.htm.

In 2008, 2010, 2013, and 2015 Pap smear questions were similar to those asked in 2005.

All women aged 18 and over were asked the Pap smear question(s). Women who reported having had a hysterectomy (removal of the uterus, with or without removal of the ovaries and cervix) were still asked the Pap smear questions because a woman who has had a hysterectomy may still have had Pap smear testing.

The current general recommendation, made by the U.S. Preventive Services Task Force (USPSTF) in 2012, is the use of Pap smears for cervical cancer every 3 years in women aged 21–65, with additional recommendations available for women aged 30–65 who want to lengthen the recommended screening interval. In *Health, United States, 2014*, additional age groups (18–20, 21–24, and 21–44) were added to account for the new recommendation. However, these recommendations were undergoing review by the USPSTF at the time this report was prepared. For a summary of current Pap smear testing recommendations and the status of the review, see: https:// www.uspreventiveservicestaskforce.org/Page/Document/ UpdateSummaryFinal/cervical-cancer-screening.

The USPSTF recommends against routine Pap smear screening in women who have had a total hysterectomy for benign disease. Therefore, two measures of Pap smear screening are presented in *Health, United States*: one among all women and one among women who did not report having a hysterectomy, although it is not known from NHIS data whether, for women who did report a hysterectomy, it was for benign disease. Questions about whether the respondent had a hysterectomy were not asked in 2003. For other survey years, questions about hysterectomy in NHIS differed slightly, as follows.

In 1987, women who reported that they had not had a recent Pap smear were asked the most important reason

they had not had a Pap smear; one reason women could select was "had a hysterectomy". In 1993, 1994, 1998, 1999, 2013, and 2015, women were asked, "Have you had a hysterectomy?" In 2000, 2005, 2008, and 2010, two questions were used to determine whether women had had a hysterectomy. Women were asked, "Have you had a hysterectomy?" In addition, women who reported that they had not had a recent Pap smear were asked the most important reason they had not had a Pap smear; one reason women could select was "had hysterectomy". Women indicating in either of these questions that they had had a hysterectomy were excluded from the *Health, United States* estimates for the group "Percent of women having a Pap smear within the past 3 years, among those who have not had a hysterectomy".

Patient—See Appendix II, Inpatient; Office visit; Outpatient visit.

Percent change/percentage change—See Appendix II, Average annual rate of change (percent change).

Perinatal mortality rate; ratio—See Appendix II, Rate: Death and related rates.

Personal care home with or without nursing—See Appendix II, Nursing home.

Personal health care expenditures—See Appendix II, Health expenditures, national.

Physical activity, leisure-time—Starting with *Health, United States, 2010*, estimates on leisure-time physical activity changed to reflect the federal *2008 Physical Activity Guidelines for Americans* (available from: http://www.health. gov/PAGuidelines/guidelines/default.aspx). Adults who met the 2008 guidelines reported at least 150 minutes per week of moderate-intensity or 75 minutes per week of vigorous-intensity aerobic physical activity (or an equivalent combination of moderate- and vigorous-intensity aerobic activity) and muscle-strengthening activities at least twice a week. The estimates for the percentage of Americans who met the 2008 guidelines for aerobic physical activity and muscle strengthening are not comparable with estimates in previous editions of *Health, United States* that showed the percentage of Americans with regular leisure-time physical activity. For more information, see: Carlson SA, Fulton JE, Schoenborn CA, Loustalot F. Trend and prevalence estimates based on the 2008 Physical Activity Guidelines for Americans. Am J Prev Med 2010;39(4)305–13.

Starting with 1998 data, leisure-time physical activity has been assessed in the National Health Interview Survey (NHIS) by asking adults a series of questions about how often they do vigorous or light/moderate physical activity of at least 10 minutes duration and about how long these sessions generally last. All questions related to leisure-time physical activity were phrased in terms of current behavior and lack a specific reference period. Vigorous physical activity is described as causing heavy sweating or a large increase in breathing or heart rate and light/moderate as causing light sweating or a slight-to-moderate increase in breathing or heart rate. Adults were also asked about how often they did leisure-time physical activities specifically designed to strengthen their muscles, such as lifting weights or doing calisthenics. The 2008 guidelines recommend any kind of aerobic activity, not just leisure-time aerobic activity, so the leisure-time aerobic activity estimates presented in this report may underestimate the percentage of adults who met the 2008 guidelines for aerobic activity. For more information, see the NHIS Adult Physical Activity Information website at: http://www.cdc.gov/nchs/nhis/physical_activity.htm.

Physician—Data on physician characteristics are obtained through physician self-report from the American Medical Association's (AMA) Physician Masterfile. Although the AMA collects data for both doctors of medicine (MDs) and doctors of osteopathy (DOs), in *Health, United States* data for DOs come from the American Osteopathic Association.

Active (or professionally active) physician—These physicians are currently engaged in patient care or other professional activity for a minimum of 20 hours per week. Other professional activity includes administration, medical teaching, research, and other activities such as employment with insurance carriers, pharmaceutical companies, corporations, voluntary organizations, and medical societies. Physicians who are retired, semiretired, working part-time, or not practicing are classified as inactive and are excluded. Also excluded are physicians with unknown address and physicians who did not provide information on type of practice or present employment (not classified).

Hospital-based physician—These physicians are employed under contract with hospitals to provide direct patient care and include physicians in residency training (including clinical fellows) and full-time members of the hospital staff.

Office-based physician—These physicians are engaged in seeing patients in solo practice, group practice, two-physician practice, other patient care employment, or in providing inpatient services such as those offered by pathologists and radiologists.

Data for physicians are presented by type of education (doctor of medicine or doctor of osteopathy); place of education (U.S. medical graduates and international medical graduates); activity status (professionally active and inactive); area of specialty; and geographic area. (Also see Appendix II, Physician specialty.)

Physician specialty—A physician specialty is any specific branch of medicine in which a physician may concentrate. Data are based on physician self-reports of their primary area of specialty. Physician data are broadly categorized into two areas of practice: those who provide primary care and those who provide specialty care.

Primary care generalist—These physicians practice in the general fields of family medicine, general practice, internal medicine, obstetrics and gynecology, and pediatrics. Specifically excluded are primary care specialists associated with these generalist fields.

Primary care specialist—These specialists practice in the primary care subspecialties of family medicine, internal medicine, obstetrics and gynecology, and pediatrics. Family medicine subspecialties include geriatric medicine and sports medicine. Internal medicine subspecialties include adolescent medicine, critical care medicine, diabetes, endocrinology, diabetes and metabolism, hematology, hepatology, hematology/oncology, cardiac electrophysiology, infectious diseases, clinical and laboratory immunology, geriatric medicine, sports medicine, nephrology, nutrition, medical oncology, pulmonary critical care medicine, and rheumatology. Obstetrics and gynecology subspecialties include hospice and palliative medicine (obstetrics and gynecology), maternal and fetal medicine, critical care medicine (obstetrics and gynecology), and reproductive endocrinology. Pediatric subspecialties include adolescent medicine, pediatric critical care medicine, pediatrics/internal medicine, neonatal-perinatal medicine, pediatric allergy, pediatric cardiology, pediatric endocrinology, pediatric infectious disease, pediatric pulmonology, medical toxicology (pediatrics), pediatric emergency medicine, pediatric gastroenterology, pediatric hematology/oncology, clinical and laboratory immunology (pediatrics), pediatric nephrology, pediatric rheumatology, and sports medicine (pediatrics).

Specialty care physician—These physicians are sometimes called specialists and include primary care specialists listed above in addition to all other physicians not included in the generalist definition. Specialty fields include allergy and immunology, aerospace medicine, anesthesiology, cardiovascular diseases, child and adolescent psychiatry, colon and rectal surgery, dermatology, diagnostic radiology, forensic pathology, gastroenterology, general surgery, medical genetics, neurology, nuclear medicine, neurological surgery, occupational medicine, ophthalmology, orthopedic surgery, otolaryngology, psychiatry, public health and general preventive medicine, physical medicine and rehabilitation, plastic surgery, anatomic and clinical pathology, pulmonary diseases, radiation oncology, thoracic surgery, urology, addiction medicine, critical care medicine, legal medicine, and clinical pharmacology.

(Also see Appendix II, Physician.)

Population—The U.S. Census Bureau collects and publishes data on populations in the United States according to several different definitions. Various statistical systems then use the appropriate population for calculating rates. (Also see Appendix I, Population Census and Population Estimates.)

Resident population includes persons whose usual place of residence (i.e., the place where one usually lives and sleeps) is in one of the 50 states or D.C. It includes members of the Armed Forces stationed in the United States and their families. It excludes members of the Armed Forces stationed outside the United States and civilian U.S. citizens whose usual place of residence is outside the United States. The resident population is the denominator used to calculate birth and death rates and incidence of disease.

Civilian population is the resident population excluding members of the Armed Forces, although families of members of the Armed Forces are included. The civilian population is the denominator for emergency department visit rates using the National Hospital Ambulatory Medical Care Survey—Emergency Department Component.

Civilian noninstitutionalized population is the civilian population excluding persons residing in institutions (such as nursing homes, prisons, jails, mental hospitals, and juvenile correctional facilities). U.S. Census Bureau estimates of the civilian noninstitutionalized population are used to calculate sample weights for the National Health Interview Survey, the National Health and Nutrition Examination Survey, and the National Survey of Family Growth, and as denominators for rates calculated for the National Ambulatory Medical Care Survey and the National Hospital Ambulatory Medical Care Survey—Outpatient Department Component.

Postneonatal mortality rate—See Appendix II, Rate: Death and related rates.

Poverty—Two related versions of federal poverty measures are shown in *Health, United States*. The first measure—a ratio of family income to federal poverty threshold—is constructed using poverty thresholds from the U.S. Census Bureau. Poverty thresholds are updated annually for inflation by the Census Bureau using the Consumer Price Index for all urban consumers (CPI–U). Poverty thresholds include a set of money income thresholds that vary by family size and composition but do not vary geographically. Families or individuals with income below the appropriate threshold are classified as below poverty. For example, the weighted average poverty threshold for a family of four was $24,257 in 2015, $24,230 in 2014, $22,314 in 2010, $17,603 in 2000, and $13,359 in 1990. For more information, see the U.S.

Census Bureau's poverty threshold website at: http://www.census.gov/data/tables/time-series/demo/income-poverty/historical-poverty-thresholds.html.

The second poverty measure used in *Health, United States* is a ratio of family income to the HHS poverty guidelines. Poverty guidelines are derived from the U.S. Census Bureau's poverty thresholds and are issued annually by HHS. These guidelines are often used to determine eligibility in certain federal programs. The HHS poverty guidelines take into account family size and state (coterminous, Alaska, Hawaii), but not family composition. For more information, see HHS, Office of the Assistant Secretary for Planning and Evaluation. Poverty Guidelines, Research, and Measurement website at: http://aspe.hhs.gov/poverty/index.cfm.

National Health Interview Survey (NHIS)—For data years prior to 1997, a ratio of family income to U.S. Census Bureau poverty threshold was computed taking into account family income and family size. Starting with 1997 data, the poverty ratio was based on family income, family size, and family composition (number of children in the family, and for families with two or fewer adults the age of the adults in the family). (Also see Appendix II, Consumer Price Index [CPI]; Family income; and Appendix I, Current Population Survey [CPS]; National Health Interview Survey [NHIS].)

National Health and Nutrition Examination Survey (NHANES)—NHANES uses the U.S. Census Bureau's Current Population Survey (CPS) definition of family to group household members into a family unit. A poverty ratio is computed by dividing family income by the HHS poverty guidelines specific to family size, as well as the appropriate guideline year, and state. See: Johnson CL, Paulose-Ram R, Ogden CL, et al. National Health and Nutrition Examination Survey: Analytic guidelines, 1999–2010. NCHS. Vital Health Stat 2(161). 2013. Available from: http://www.cdc.gov/nchs/data/series/sr_02/sr02_161.pdf.

Preferred provider organization (PPO)—A PPO is a type of medical plan in which coverage is provided to participants through a network of selected health care providers, such as hospitals and physicians. Enrollees may seek care outside the network but pay a greater percentage of the cost of coverage than within the network. (Also see Appendix II, Health maintenance organization [HMO]; Managed care.)

Prevalence—Prevalence is the number of cases of a disease, number of infected persons, or number of persons with some other attribute present during a particular interval of time. It is often expressed as a rate (e.g., the prevalence of diabetes per 1,000 persons during a year). (Also see Appendix II, Incidence.)

Primary care specialty—See Appendix II, Physician specialty.

Private expenditures—See Appendix II, Health expenditures, national.

Procedure—Procedures can include surgical procedures (such as appendectomies), diagnostic procedures (such as spinal taps), and therapeutic treatments (such as infusion of a cancer chemotherapeutic substance) reported on a patient's medical record. In *Health, United States*, procedures are coded according to the *International Classification of Diseases, 9th Revision, Clinical Modification* (ICD–9–CM) until 2016 data are available, and then procedures will be classified using the *International Classification of Diseases, 10th Revision, Clinical Modification/Procedure Coding System* (ICD–10–CM/PCS).

Healthcare Cost and Utilization Project, National (Nationwide) Inpatient Sample (HCUP–NIS)—Currently, up to 15 procedures are coded using ICD–9–CM procedure codes per hospital stay in the HCUP–NIS database. Starting with 2016 data, procedures will be coded according to the *International Classification of Diseases, 10th Revision, Clinical Modification/Procedure Coding System*. For each record, a principal procedure is identified as the first procedure listed. HCUP–NIS procedure data presented in *Health, United States* are limited to operating room procedures that are principal procedures (first-listed). Valid operating room procedures were identified according to diagnosis-related groups (DRGs) software. For DRG development, physician panels classify all ICD–9–CM procedure codes based on whether the procedure would be performed in operating rooms in most hospitals. Clinical Classifications Software (CCS) was used to categorize ICD–9–CM principal operating room procedure codes into 1 of 231 clinically meaningful categories. CCS was developed at the Agency for Healthcare Research and Quality as a tool for clustering patient procedures into a manageable number of clinically meaningful categories. It is periodically updated. For more information on CCS, see: http://www.hcup-us.ahrq.gov/toolssoftware/ccs/AppendixBSinglePR.txt. The top-ranking operating room procedure categories by age group, based on the number of discharges and total national costs, are presented in *Health, United States* (Table X). CCS categories labeled "other" are not presented because these comprise miscellaneous procedures that do not form a homogeneous group.

(Also see Appendix II, Outpatient surgery.)

Proprietary hospital—See Appendix II, Hospital.

Public expenditures—See Appendix II, Health expenditures, national.

Purchasing power parities (PPPs)—PPPs are calculated rates of currency conversion that equalize the purchasing power of different currencies by eliminating the differences in price levels between countries. PPPs show the ratio of prices in national currencies for the same good or service in different countries. PPPs can be used to make intercountry comparisons of the gross domestic product (GDP) and its component expenditures. (Also see Appendix II, Gross domestic product [GDP].)

Race—In 1977, the Office of Management and Budget (OMB) issued "Race and Ethnic Standards for Federal Statistics and Administrative Reporting" (Statistical Policy Directive 15) to promote comparability of data among federal data systems. The 1977 Standards called for the federal government's data systems to classify individuals into the following four racial groups: American Indian or Alaskan Native, Asian or Pacific Islander, black, and white. Depending on the data source, the classification by race was based on self-classification or on observation by an interviewer or other person filling out the questionnaire.

In 1997, revisions were announced for classification of individuals by race within the federal government's data systems. (See: Revisions to the standards for the classification of federal data on race and ethnicity. Fed Regist 1997 October 30;62(210):58781–90.) The 1997 Standards specify five racial groups: American Indian or Alaska Native, Asian, black or African American, Native Hawaiian or Other Pacific Islander, and white. These five categories are the minimum set for data on race in federal statistics. The 1997 Standards also offer an opportunity for respondents to select more than one of the five groups, leading to many possible multiple-race categories. As with the single-race groups, data for the multiple-race groups are to be reported when estimates meet agency requirements for reliability and confidentiality. The 1997 Standards allow for observer or proxy identification of race but clearly state a preference for self-classification. The federal government considers race and Hispanic origin to be two separate and distinct concepts. Thus, Hispanic persons may be of any race. Federal data systems were required to comply with the 1997 Standards by 2003.

National Health Interview Survey (NHIS)—Starting with *Health, United States, 2002*, race-specific estimates based on NHIS were tabulated using the 1997 Standards for data year 1999 and beyond and are not strictly comparable with estimates for earlier years. The 1997 Standards specify five single-race categories plus multiple-race categories. Estimates for specific race groups are shown when they meet requirements for statistical reliability and confidentiality. The race categories white only, black or African American only, American Indian or Alaska Native only, Asian only, and Native Hawaiian or Other Pacific Islander only include persons who reported only one racial group; the category 2 or more races includes persons who reported more than one of the five racial groups in the 1997 Standards or one of the five racial groups and "some other race." In order to maintain consistency with the Census Bureau procedures for collecting and editing data on race and ethnicity, the NHIS made major changes to its editing procedures in the 2003 data year. Beginning in the 2003 NHIS, Other race was no longer available as a separate race response. This response category was treated as missing, and the race was imputed if this was the only race response. In cases where Other race was mentioned along with one or more race groups, the Other race response was dropped, and the race group information was retained.

Prior to data year 1999, data were tabulated according to the 1977 Standards, with four racial groups, and the Asian only category included Native Hawaiian or Other Pacific Islander. Estimates for single-race categories prior to 1999 included persons who reported one race or, if they reported more than one race, identified one race as best representing their race. Differences between estimates tabulated using the two standards for data year 1999 are discussed in the footnotes for each NHIS table in *Health, United States* 2002, 2003, and 2004 editions. Available from: https://www.cdc.gov/nchs/hus/previous.htm#editions.

Tables XI and XII illustrate NHIS data tabulated by race and Hispanic origin according to the 1997 and 1977 Standards for two health statistics (cigarette smoking and private health insurance coverage). In these examples, three separate tabulations using the 1997 Standards are shown: (a) Race: mutually exclusive race groups, including several multiple-race combinations; (b) Race, any mention: race groups that are not mutually exclusive because each race category includes all persons who mention that race; and (c) Hispanic origin and race: detailed race and Hispanic origin with a multiple-race total category.

Where applicable, comparison tabulations by race and Hispanic origin are shown based on the 1977 Standards. Because there are more race groups with the 1997 Standards, the sample size of each race group under the 1997 Standards is slightly smaller than the sample size under the 1977 Standards. Only those few multiple-race groups with sufficient numbers of observations to meet standards of statistical reliability are shown. These tables also illustrate changes in labels and group categories resulting from the 1997 Standards. The race designation black was changed to black or African American, and the ethnicity designation Hispanic was changed to Hispanic or Latino.

Survey data included in *Health, United States*, other than NHIS, the National Survey of Drug Use & Health (NSDUH), and the National Health and Nutrition Examination Survey (NHANES), generally do not permit tabulation of estimates for the detailed race and ethnicity categories shown in Tables XI and XII, either because race data based on the 1997 Standards categories are not yet available or because there are insufficient numbers of observations in certain subpopulation groups to meet statistical reliability or confidentiality requirements.

To improve the quality of data on ethnicity and race in NHIS, hot-deck imputation of selected race and ethnicity variables was done for the first time in the 2000 NHIS and continued to be used for subsequent data years. Starting with 2003 data, records for persons for whom "other race" was the only race response were treated as having missing data on race and were added to the pool of records for which selected race and ethnicity variables were imputed. Prior to the 2000 NHIS, a crude imputation method that assigned a race to persons with missing values for the variable MAINRACE (the respondent's classification of the race he or she most identified with) was used. Under these procedures, if an observed race was recorded by the interviewer, it was used to code a race value. If there was no observed race value, all persons who had a missing value for MAINRACE and were identified as Hispanic on the Hispanic origin question were coded as white. In all other cases, non-Hispanic persons were coded as "other race." Additional information on the NHIS methodology for imputing race and ethnicity is available from the survey documentation at: http://www.cdc.gov/nchs/nhis/quest_data_related_1997_forward.htm and from the NHIS race and Hispanic origin home page at: http://www.cdc.gov/nchs/nhis/rhoi.htm.

National Health and Nutrition Examination Survey (NHANES)—Starting with *Health, United States, 2003*, race-specific estimates based on NHANES were tabulated using the 1997 Standards for data years 1999 and beyond. Prior to data year 1999, the 1977 Standards were used. Because of the differences between the two standards, the race-specific estimates shown in Trend Tables based on NHANES for 1999 and beyond are not strictly comparable with estimates for earlier years. Race in NHANES I and II was determined primarily by interviewer observation; starting with NHANES III, race was self-reported by survey participants.

The NHANES sample for data years 1999–2006 was designed to provide estimates specifically for persons of Mexican origin and not for all Hispanic-origin persons in the United States. Persons of Hispanic origin other than Mexican origin were entered into the sample with different selection probabilities that are not nationally representative of the total U.S. Hispanic population. Starting with 2007–2008 data, all Hispanic persons were oversampled, not just persons of Mexican origin. Oversampling of the black population was continued. Starting in 2011, NHANES oversampled the non-Hispanic Asian population. In *Health, United States*, estimates are shown for non-Hispanic white, non-Hispanic black, and Mexican-origin persons, as well as Hispanic-origin and non-Hispanic Asian persons, where possible. Although data were collected according to the 1997 Standards, there are insufficient numbers of observations during this period to meet statistical reliability or confidentiality requirements for reporting estimates for additional race categories.

National Survey on Drug Use & Health (NSDUH)—Race-specific estimates based on NSDUH are tabulated using the 1997 Standards. Estimates in the NSDUH Trend Table begin with data year 2002. Estimates for specific race groups are shown when they meet requirements for statistical reliability and confidentiality. The race categories white only, black or African American only, American Indian or Alaska Native only, Asian only, and Native Hawaiian or Other Pacific Islander only include persons who reported only one racial group; the category 2 or more races includes persons who reported more than one of the five racial groups in the 1997 Standards or one of the five racial groups and "some other race."

National Vital Statistics System (NVSS)—Some of the states in the Vital Statistics Cooperative Program are still revising their birth and death records to conform to the 1997 Standards on race and ethnicity. During the transition to full implementation of the 1997 Standards, vital statistics data will continue to be presented for four major race groups (white, black or African American, American Indian or Alaska Native, and Asian or Pacific Islander) in accordance with the 1977 Standards.

Birth file—Information about the race and Hispanic origin of the mother and father is provided by the mother at the time of birth and is recorded on the birth certificate or fetal death record. Since 1980, birth rates, birth characteristics, and death rates for live-born infants and fetal deaths are presented in *Health, United States* according to race of the mother. Before 1980, data were tabulated by race of the newborn and fetus, taking into account the race of both parents. If the parents were of different races and one parent was white, the child was classified according to the race of the other parent. When neither parent was white, the child was classified according to the father's race, with one exception: if either parent was Hawaiian, the child was classified Hawaiian. Before 1964, if race was unknown, the birth was classified as white. Starting in 1964, unknown race was classified according to information on the birth record. Starting with the 2000 census, the race and ethnicity data used for denominators (population) to calculate birth and fertility rates have been collected in accordance with the 1997 revised OMB standards for race and ethnicity. However, the numerators (births) will not be compatible with the denominators until all the states revise their birth certificates to reflect the new standards. To compute rates, it is currently necessary to bridge population data for multiple-race persons to single-race categories. (Also see Appendix I, Population Census and Population Estimates, Bridged-race Population Estimates.)

Starting with 2003 data, some states began using the 2003 revision of the U.S. Standard Certificate of Live Birth, which allows the reporting of more than one race (multiple races). For 2014 data, 49 states, D.C., Guam, and Northern Marianas allowed the reporting of multiple-race data. The 49 states and D.C. represented 99% of all U.S. resident births. In 2014, multiple race was reported for slightly more than 2% of mothers in the states that permitted reporting of more than one race. In 2014, data from the vital records of the remaining state, and two territories, followed the 1977 OMB Standards and reported the minimum set of four race categories, compared with the minimum of five race categories for the 1997 Standards. To provide uniformity and comparability of data during the transition to the 2003 revision, before multiple-race data are available for all reporting areas, the responses of those who reported more than one race are bridged to a single race. For more information on the adoption of the 2003 revision of the U.S. Standard Certificate of Live Birth, see the Technical Notes section of the annual series of "Births: Final Data" reports, available from: http://www.cdc.gov/nchs/products/nvsr.htm.

Although the bridging procedure imputes multiple race of mothers to one of the four minimum races stipulated in the 1977 Standards, mothers of a specified Asian or Pacific Islander (API) subgroup (Chinese, Japanese, Hawaiian, or Filipino) in combination with another race (American Indian or Alaska Native, black, and/or white) or another API subgroup cannot be imputed to a single API subgroup. Data for the API subgroups are available in the 2014 Natality public-use data file at: http://www.cdc.gov/nchs/births.htm.

Mortality file—Information about the race and Hispanic origin of a decedent is reported by the funeral director as provided by an informant (often the surviving next of kin), or in the absence of an informant, on the basis of observation. Death rates by race and Hispanic origin are based on information from death certificates (numerators of the rates) and on population estimates from the Census Bureau (denominators). Race and ethnicity information from the census is by self-report. To the extent that race and Hispanic origin are inconsistent between these two data sources, death rates will be biased. Studies have shown that persons self-reported as American Indian, Asian, or Hispanic on census and survey records may sometimes be reported as white or non-Hispanic on the death certificate, resulting in an underestimation of deaths and death rates for the American Indian, Asian, and Hispanic groups. Bias also results from undercounts of some population groups in the census—particularly young black males, young white males, and elderly persons—resulting in an overestimation of death rates.

Table XI. Current cigarette smoking among adults aged 18 and over, by race and Hispanic origin under the 1997 and 1977 Standards for federal data on race and ethnicity: United States, average annual 1993–1995

1997 Standards	Sample size	Percent	Standard error	1977 Standards	Sample size	Percent	Standard error
White only	46,228	25.2	0.26	White	46,664	25.3	0.26
Black or African American only . .	7,208	26.6	0.64	Black	7,334	26.5	0.63
American Indian or Alaska Native only	416	32.9	2.53	American Indian or Alaskan Native	480	33.9	2.38
Asian only	1,370	15.0	1.19	Asian or Pacific Islander . . .	1,411	15.5	1.22
2 or more races total	786	34.5	2.00				
Black or African American; white.	83	*21.7	6.05				
American Indian or Alaska Native; white.	461	40.0	2.58				
Race, any mention							
White, any mention	46,882	25.3	0.26				
Black or African American, any mention.	7,382	26.6	0.63				
American Indian or Alaska Native, any mention	965	36.3	1.71				
Asian, any mention	1,458	15.7	1.20				
Native Hawaiian or Other Pacific Islander, any mention	53	*17.5	5.10				
Hispanic origin and race							
Not Hispanic or Latino:				Non-Hispanic:			
White only.	42,421	25.8	0.27	White	42,976	25.9	0.27
Black or African American only	7,053	26.7	0.65	Black.	7,203	26.7	0.64
American Indian or Alaska Native only.	358	33.5	2.69	American Indian or Alaskan Native	407	35.4	2.53
Asian only.	1,320	14.8	1.21	Asian or Pacific Islander. .	1,397	15.3	1.24
2 or more races total	687	35.6	2.15				
Hispanic or Latino	5,175	17.8	0.65	Hispanic	5,175	17.8	0.65

*Estimates are considered unreliable. Data preceded by an asterisk have a relative standard error of 20%–30%.

NOTES: The Office of Management and Budget's (OMB) 1997 *Revisions to the Standards for the Classification of Federal Data on Race and Ethnicity* specifies five race groups (white, black or African American, American Indian or Alaska Native, Asian, and Native Hawaiian or Other Pacific Islander) and allows respondents to report one or more race groups. Estimates for single-race and multiple-race groups not shown above do not meet standards for statistical reliability or confidentiality (relative standard error greater than 30%). Race groups under the 1997 Standards were based on the question, "What is the group or groups which represents [person's] race?" For persons who selected multiple groups, race groups under the OMB's 1977 *Race and Ethnic Standards for Federal Statistics and Administrative Reporting* were based on the additional question, "Which of those groups would you say best represents [person's] race?" Race-specific estimates in this table were calculated after excluding respondents of other and unknown race. Other published race-specific estimates are based on files in which such responses have been edited. Estimates are age-adjusted to the year 2000 standard population using five age groups: 18–24, 25–34, 35–44, 45–64, and 65 and over. See Appendix II, Age adjustment.

SOURCE: NCHS, National Health Interview Survey. See Appendix I, National Health Interview Survey (NHIS).

Race and ethnicity reporting on the death certificate continues to be excellent for the white and black populations. It remains poor for the American Indian or Alaska Native population but is reasonably good for the Hispanic and Asian or Pacific Islander populations. Decedent characteristics such as place of residence and nativity have an important effect on the quality of reporting on the death certificate. The effects of misclassification on mortality estimates were most pronounced for the American Indian or Alaska Native population, where correcting for misclassification reverses a large American Indian or Alaska Native-over-white mortality advantage to a relatively large disadvantage. Among the Hispanic and Asian or Pacific Islander populations, adjustment for death certificate misclassification did not significantly affect minority-majority mortality. For more information, see: Arias E, Heron M, Hakes JK. The validity of race and Hispanic-

origin reporting on death certificates in the United States: An update. NCHS. Vital Health Stat 2016:2 (172).

Available from: http://www.cdc.gov/nchs/data/series/sr_02/sr02_172.pdf; Arias E, Schauman WS, Eschbach K, et al. The validity of race and Hispanic origin reporting on death certificates in the United States. NCHS. Vital Health Stat 2008;2(148). Available from: http://www.cdc.gov/nchs/data/series/sr_02/sr02_148.pdf.

Denominators for infant mortality rates are based on the number of live births, rather than on population estimates. Race information for the denominator is supplied from the birth certificate. Before 1980, race of child for the denominator took into account the races of both parents. Starting in 1980, race information for the denominator has been based solely on the race of the mother. Race information for the numerator

Table XII. Private health care coverage among persons under age 65, by race and Hispanic origin under the 1997 and 1977 Standards for federal data on race and ethnicity: United States, average annual 1993–1995

1997 Standards	Sample size	Percent	Standard error	1977 Standards	Sample size	Percent	Standard error
White only	168,256	76.1	0.28	White	170,472	75.9	0.28
Black or African American only . .	30,048	53.5	0.63	Black	30,690	53.6	0.63
American Indian or Alaska Native only	2,003	44.2	1.97	American Indian or Alaskan Native	2,316	43.5	1.85
Asian only	6,896	68.0	1.39	Asian or Pacific Islander . . .	7,146	68.2	1.34
Native Hawaiian or Other Pacific Islander only	173	75.0	7.43				
2 or more races total	4,203	60.9	1.17				
Black or African American; white.	686	59.5	3.21				
American Indian or Alaska Native; white.	2,022	60.0	1.71				
Asian; white.	590	71.9	3.39				
Native Hawaiian or Other Pacific Islander; white	56	59.2	10.65				

	Race, any mention						
White, any mention	171,817	75.8	0.28				
Black or African American, any mention.	31,147	53.6	0.62				
American Indian or Alaska Native, any mention	4,365	52.4	1.40				
Asian, any mention	7,639	68.4	1.27				
Native Hawaiian or Other Pacific Islander, any mention	283	68.7	6.23				

	Hispanic origin and race						
Not Hispanic or Latino:				Non-Hispanic:			
White only.	146,109	78.9	0.27	White	149,057	78.6	0.27
Black or African American only	29,250	53.9	0.64	Black.	29,877	54.0	0.63
American Indian or Alaska Native only.	1,620	45.2	2.15	American Indian or Alaskan Native	1,859	44.6	2.05
Asian only	6,623	68.2	1.43	Asian or Pacific Islander. .	6,999	68.4	1.40
Native Hawaiian or Other Pacific Islander only	145	76.4	7.79				
2 or more races total	3,365	62.6	1.18				
Hispanic or Latino	31,040	48.8	0.74	Hispanic	31,040	48.8	0.74

NOTES: The Office of Management and Budget's (OMB) 1997 *Revisions to the Standards for the Classification of Federal Data on Race and Ethnicity* specifies five race groups (white, black or African American, American Indian or Alaska Native, Asian, and Native Hawaiian or Other Pacific Islander) and allows respondents to report one or more race groups. Estimates for single-race and multiple-race groups not shown above do not meet standards for statistical reliability or confidentiality (relative standard error greater than 30%). Race groups under the 1997 Standards were based on the question, "What is the group or groups which represents [person's] race?" For persons who selected multiple groups, race groups under the OMB's 1977 *Race and Ethnic Standards for Federal Statistics and Administrative Reporting* were based on the additional question, "Which of those groups would you say best represents [person's] race?" Race-specific estimates in this table were calculated after excluding respondents of other and unknown race. Other published race-specific estimates are based on files in which such responses have been edited. Estimates are age-adjusted to the year 2000 standard population using three age groups: under 18, 18–44, and 45–64. See Appendix II, Age adjustment.

SOURCE: NCHS, National Health Interview Survey. See Appendix I, National Health Interview Survey (NHIS).

is supplied from the death certificate. For the infant mortality rate, race information for the numerator is race of the deceased child.

Issues affecting the interpretation of vital event rates for the American Indian or Alaska Native population include (a) changes in the classification or self-identification of persons of American Indian or Alaska Native heritage over time, and (b) misclassification of American Indian or Alaska Native persons on death certificates by the funeral director or informant. Vital event rates for the American Indian or Alaska Native population shown in *Health, United States* are based on the total U.S. resident American Indian or Alaska Native

population, as enumerated by the U.S. Census Bureau. In contrast, the Indian Health Service calculates vital event rates for this population based on U.S. Census Bureau county data for American Indian or Alaska Native persons who reside on or near reservations. Because of misclassification of American Indian or Alaska Native persons on death certificates, American Indian or Alaska Native national and state-specific mortality estimates published in *Health, United States* should be interpreted with caution.

Interpretation of trends for the Asian population in the United States should take into account that this population more than doubled between 1980 and

1990, primarily because of immigration. Between 1990 and 2000, the increase in the Asian population was 48% for persons reporting that they were Asian alone and 72% for persons who reported they were either Asian alone or Asian in combination with another race.

For more information on coding race by using vital statistics, see: NCHS. Vital statistics of the United States, vol I, Natality, and vol II, Mortality, part A, Technical appendix. Hyattsville, MD; published annually. Available from: http://www.cdc.gov/nchs/nvss.htm.

Starting with 2003 data, some states began using the 2003 revision of the U.S. Standard Certificate of Death, which allows the reporting of more than one race (multiple races). This change was implemented to reflect the increasing diversity of the U.S. population and to be consistent with the decennial census. For more information on states' reporting of multiple-race data, see the annual series of "Deaths: Final Data" reports, available from: http://www.cdc.gov/nchs/products/nvsr.htm.

To provide uniformity and comparability of data until all states are reporting multiple-race data, it has been necessary to bridge the responses of those for whom more than one race is reported (multiple race) to one single race. For more information, see: NCHS procedures for multiple-race and Hispanic origin data: Collection, coding, editing, and transmitting. Hyattsville, MD: NCHS; 2004. Available from: http://www.cdc.gov/nchs/data/dvs/Multiple_race_docu_5-10-04.pdf; and NCHS. Vital statistics of the United States, vol I, Natality, and vol II, Mortality, part A, Technical appendix. Hyattsville, MD; published annually. Available from: http://www.cdc.gov/nchs/nvss.htm.

Youth Risk Behavior Survey (YRBS)—Prior to 1999, the 1977 OMB Standards were used. Respondents could select only one of the following categories: white (not Hispanic), black (not Hispanic), Hispanic or Latino, Asian or Pacific Islander, American Indian or Alaska Native, or other. Beginning in 1999, the 1997 OMB Standards were used for race-specific estimates, and respondents were given the option of selecting more than one category to describe their race and ethnicity. Between 1999 and 2003, students were asked a single question about race and Hispanic origin, with the option of choosing more than one of the following responses: white, black or African American, Hispanic or Latino, Asian, Native Hawaiian or Other Pacific Islander, or American Indian or Alaska Native. In 2005, students were asked a question about Hispanic origin ("Are you Hispanic or Latino?") and a second separate question about race that included the option of selecting more than one of the following categories: American Indian or Alaska Native, Asian, black or African American, Native Hawaiian or Other Pacific Islander, or white. Because of the differences between

questions, data about race and Hispanic ethnicity for the years prior to 1999 are not strictly comparable with estimates for the later years. However, analyses of data collected between 1991 and 2003 have indicated that the data are comparable across years and can be used to study trends. See: Brener ND, Kann L, McManus T. A comparison of two survey questions on race and ethnicity among high school students. Public Opin Q 2003;67(2):227–36.

(Also see Appendix II, Hispanic origin; and Appendix I, Population Census and Population Estimates.)

Rate—A rate is a measure of some event, disease, or condition in relation to a unit of population, along with some specification of time. (Also see Appendix II, Age adjustment; Population.)

- *Birth and related rates*

  Birth rate is calculated by dividing the number of live births in a population in a year by the resident population. For census years, rates are based on unrounded census counts of the resident population as of April 1. For the noncensus years 1981–1989, rates are based on national estimates of the resident population as of July 1, rounded to thousands. Rounded population estimates for 5-year age groups are calculated by summing unrounded population estimates before rounding to thousands. Starting in 1991, rates are based on unrounded national population estimates. Birth rates for 1991–1999 were revised based on the 1990 and 2000 censuses. The rates for 1990, 2000, and 2010 are based on populations from the censuses in those years as of April 1. Birth rates for 2001–2009 were revised based on the 2000 and 2010 censuses. Birth rates for 2011 and subsequent years were computed using 2010-based postcensal estimates. The population estimates have been provided by the U.S. Census Bureau and have been modified to be consistent with OMB racial categories as of 1977 and historical categories for birth data. Beginning in 1997, the birth rate for the maternal age group 45–49 includes data for mothers aged 50–54 in the numerator and is based on the population of women aged 45–49 in the denominator. Birth rates are expressed as the number of live births per 1,000 population. The rate may be restricted to births to women of specific age, race, marital status, or geographic location (specific rate), or it may be related to the entire population (crude rate).

  Fertility rate is the total number of live births, regardless of the age of the mother, per 1,000 women of reproductive age (aged 15–44). Beginning in 1997, the birth rate for the maternal age group 45–49 includes data for mothers aged 50–54 in the numerator and is based on the population of women aged 45–49 in the denominator.

- *Death and related rates*

  Death rate is calculated by dividing the number of deaths in a population in a year by the midyear resident population. For census years, rates are based on unrounded census counts of the resident population as of April 1. For the noncensus years 1981–1989, rates are based on national estimates of the resident population as of July 1, rounded to thousands. Rounded population estimates for 10-year age groups are calculated by summing unrounded population estimates before rounding to thousands. Starting in 1991, rates are based on unrounded national population estimates. Rates for the Hispanic and non-Hispanic white populations in each year are based on unrounded state population estimates for states in the Hispanic reporting area. Death rates are expressed as the number of deaths per 100,000 resident population. The rate may be restricted to deaths in specific age, race, sex, or geographic groups or from specific causes of death (specific rate), or it may be related to the entire population (crude rate). (Also see Appendix I, Population Census and Population Estimates.)

  Birth cohort infant mortality rates are based on the birth cohort linked birth and infant death files and are computed as the number of deaths under age 1 year to members of the birth cohort, divided by the number of live births, times 1,000. (Also see Appendix II, Birth cohort.)

  Fetal mortality rate is the number of fetal deaths with stated or presumed gestation of 20 weeks or more, divided by the sum of live births plus fetal deaths, times 1,000.

  Infant mortality rate is based on period files and is calculated by dividing the number of infant deaths during a calendar year by the number of live births reported in the same year. It is expressed as the number of infant deaths per 1,000 live births. Neonatal mortality rate is the number of deaths among infants under age 28 days per 1,000 live births. Postneonatal mortality rate is the number of infant deaths that occur between 28 days to under 1 year after birth, per 1,000 live births. (Also see Appendix II, Infant death.)

  Late fetal mortality rate is the number of fetal deaths with stated or presumed gestation of 28 weeks or more, divided by the sum of live births plus late fetal deaths, times 1,000. (Also see Appendix II, Gestation.)

  Perinatal mortality rates and ratios relate to the period surrounding the birth event. Rates and ratios are based on events reported in a calendar year. Although several different perinatal mortality definitions exist, the perinatal definition used in *Health, United States* (and used most commonly for international comparisons) is the sum of late fetal deaths at 28 weeks of gestation or more plus infant deaths within 7 days of birth, divided by the sum of live births plus late fetal deaths, times 1,000. Perinatal mortality ratio is the sum of late fetal deaths plus infant deaths within 7 days of birth, divided by the number of live births, times 1,000.

- *Visit rate*

  Visit rate is a basic measure of service utilization for event-based data. Examples of events include physician office visits with drugs provided, or hospital discharges. In the visit rate calculation, the numerator is the number of estimated events, and the denominator is the corresponding U.S. population estimate for those who possibly could have had events during a given period of time. The interpretation is that for every person in the population there were, on average, *x* events. It does not mean that *x* persons in the population had events, because some persons in the population had no events while others had multiple events. The only exception is when an event can occur just once for a person (e.g., if an appendectomy is performed during a hospital stay). The visit rate is best used to compare utilization across various subgroups of interest, such as age or race groups or geographic regions.

Region—See Appendix II, Geographic region.

Registered hospital—See Appendix II, Hospital.

Registration area—The United States has separate registration areas for birth, death, marriage, and divorce statistics. In general, registration areas correspond to states and include two separate registration areas for D.C. and New York City. The term "reporting area" may be used interchangeably with the term "registration area." All registration areas have adopted laws that require registration of births and deaths and the reporting of fetal deaths. It is believed that more than 99% of births and deaths occurring in this country are registered.

The death registration area was established in 1900 with 10 states and D.C., and the birth registration area was established in 1915, also with 10 states and D.C. Beginning in 1933, all states were included in the birth and death registration areas. The specific states added year by year are shown in: Hetzel AM. History and organization of the vital statistics system. Hyattsville, MD: NCHS; 1997. Available from: http://www.cdc.gov/nchs/data/misc/usvss.pdf. Currently, Puerto Rico, the U.S. Virgin Islands, and Guam each constitute a separate registration area, although their data are not included in statistical tabulations of U.S. resident data. (Also see Appendix II, Reporting area.)

Relative standard error (RSE)—RSE is a measure of an estimate's reliability. The RSE of an estimate is obtained by dividing the standard error of the estimate, SE(r), by the estimate itself, r. This quantity is expressed as a percentage of the estimate and is calculated as follows:

$$RSE = 100 \times [SE(r)/(r)]$$

Estimates with large RSEs are considered unreliable. In *Health, United States*, most statistics with large RSEs are preceded by an asterisk or are not presented. The criteria for evaluating RSEs is discussed in the footnotes accompanying each table.

Relative survival rate—The relative survival rate is the ratio of the observed survival rate for the patient group to the expected survival rate for persons in the general population similar to the patient group with respect to age, sex, race, and calendar year of observation. The 5-year relative survival rate estimates the proportion of cancer patients who have survived their cancer 5 years after diagnosis. Because more than one-half of all cancers occur in persons aged 65 and over, many of these individuals die of other causes with no evidence of recurrence of their cancer. However, by adjusting observed survival for the normal life expectancy of the general population of the same age, the relative survival rate gives a more specific estimate of the chance of surviving the effects of cancer alone.

Reporting area—In the National Vital Statistics System, the reporting area for such basic items on the birth and death certificates as age, race, and sex is based on data from residents of all 50 states in the United States, D.C., and New York City. The term "reporting area" may be used interchangeably with the term "registration area." (Also see Appendix II, Registration area; and Appendix I, National Vital Statistics System [NVSS].)

Resident, health facility—In the Centers for Medicare & Medicaid Services' Quality Improvement Evaluation System (QIES) (formerly the Online Survey Certification and Reporting [OSCAR]) database, all residents in certified facilities are counted on the day of certification inspection.

Resident population—See Appendix II, Population.

Rural—See Appendix II, Urbanization.

Self-assessment of health—See Appendix II, Health status, respondent-assessed.

Serious psychological distress—The K6 mental health screening instrument is a measure of psychological distress associated with unspecified but potentially diagnosable mental illness that may result in a higher risk for disability and higher utilization of health services. In the National Health Interview Survey, the K6 questions were asked of adults aged 18 and over. The K6 is designed to identify persons with serious psychological distress, using as few questions as possible. The six items included in the K6 are:

During the past 30 days, how often did you feel:

- So sad that nothing could cheer you up?
- Nervous?
- Restless or fidgety?
- Hopeless?
- That everything was an effort?
- Worthless?

Possible answers are "All of the time" (4 points), "Most of the time" (3 points), "Some of the time" (2 points), "A little of the time" (1 point), and "None of the time" (0 points).

To score the K6, the points are added together, yielding a possible total of 0–24 points. A threshold of 13 points or more is used to define serious psychological distress. Persons answering "Some of the time" to all six questions would not reach the threshold for serious psychological distress because they would need to answer "Most of the time" to at least one item to achieve a score of 13. Only respondents who answered all six psychological distress questions would have a computed K6 score for analysis. The version of the K6 used in NHIS provides 1-month prevalence rates because the reference period is the past 30 days. For more information, see: Kessler RC, Barker PR, Colpe LJ, Epstein JF, Gfroerer JC, Hiripi E, et al. Screening for serious mental illness in the general population. Arch Gen Psychiatry 2003;60(2):184–9. (Also see Appendix II, Basic actions difficulty.)

Starting in 2013, the K6 questions were moved to the adult selected items section of the Sample Adult questionnaire. Observed differences between the 2012 and earlier estimates and 2013 and later estimates may be partially or fully attributable to this change in question placement within the Sample Adult questionnaire.

Short-stay hospital—See Appendix II, Hospital.

Skilled nursing facility—See Appendix II, Nursing home.

Smoker—See Appendix II, Cigarette smoking.

Special hospital—See Appendix II, Hospital.

Substance use—Substance use refers to the use of selected substances, including alcohol, tobacco products, drugs, inhalants, and other substances that can be consumed, inhaled, injected, or otherwise absorbed into the body with possible dependence and other detrimental effects. (Also see Appendix II, Illicit drug use.)

Monitoring the Future (MTF) Study—MTF collects information on the use of selected substances by using self-completed questionnaires in a school-based survey of secondary school students. MTF has tracked 12th graders' illicit drug use and attitudes toward drugs since 1975. In 1991, 8th and 10th graders were added to the study. The survey includes questions on abuse of substances including (but not limited to) marijuana, inhalants, other illegal drugs, alcohol, cigarettes, and other tobacco products. (Also see Appendix I, Monitoring the Future [MTF] Study.)

National Survey on Drug Use & Health (NSDUH)—NSDUH conducts in-person, computer-assisted interviews of a sample of individuals aged 12 and over at their place of residence. For illicit drug use, alcohol use, and tobacco use, information is collected about use in the lifetime, past year, and past month. However, only estimates of use in the past month are presented in *Health, United States*. For illicit drug use, respondents in NSDUH are asked about use of marijuana/hashish, cocaine (including crack), inhalants, hallucinogens, heroin, and misuse of prescription-type psychotherapeutic drugs (pain relievers, tranquilizers, stimulants, and sedatives). A series of questions is asked about each substance: "Have you ever, even once, used [substance]?", and "How long has it been since you last used [substance]?" Numerous probes and checks are included in the computer-assisted interview system. Starting in 2013, information about marijuana use that was recommended by a doctor or other health care professional has been collected; however, any reported marijuana use is classified as illicit drug use. Summary measures, such as current illicit drug use, are produced. Starting in 2015, changes in measurement for 7 of the 10 illicit drug categories—hallucinogens, inhalants, methamphetamine, and the misuse of prescription pain relievers, tranquilizers, stimulants, and sedatives—may have affected the comparability of the measurement of these illicit drugs and any illicit drug between 2015 and prior years. (Also see Appendix II, Alcohol consumption; Cigarette smoking; Illicit drug use; and Appendix I, National Survey on Drug Use & Health [NSDUH].)

Suicidal ideation—Suicidal ideation means having thoughts of suicide or of taking action to end one's own life. Suicidal ideation includes all thoughts of suicide, both when the thoughts include a plan to commit suicide and when they do not include a plan. Suicidal ideation is measured in the Youth Risk Behavior Survey by the following three questions: "During the past 12 months, did you ever seriously consider attempting suicide?", "During the past 12 months, how many times did you actually attempt suicide?", and "If you attempted suicide during the past 12 months, did any attempt result in an injury, poisoning, or overdose that had to be treated by a doctor or nurse?" For more information, see: http://www.cdc.gov/HealthyYouth/yrbs/index.htm.

Surgery—See Appendix II, Outpatient surgery; Procedure.

Surgical specialty—See Appendix II, Physician specialty.

Tobacco use—See Appendix II, Cigarette smoking.

Uninsured—Broadly, persons are considered uninsured if they do not have coverage under private health insurance, Medicare, Medicaid, public assistance (through 1996), Children's Health Insurance Program (CHIP), a state-sponsored or other government-sponsored plan or program, or a military health plan. Because of differences in methodology, question wording, and recall period, estimates from different sources may vary and are not directly comparable. For more information, see: Health insurance measurement: Differences by data source. Available from: https://www2.census.gov/programs-surveys/demo/visualizations/p60/257/health_insurance_measurement.pdf.

American Community Survey (ACS)—In ACS, persons are considered uninsured if they do not have coverage through private health insurance, Medicare, Medicaid, CHIP, military/TRICARE or veterans coverage, another government program, or other insurance. Persons with only Indian Health Service coverage are considered uninsured. The questions on health insurance are administered throughout the year and ask about current health insurance coverage as of the day of the interview.

National Health Interview Survey (NHIS)—In NHIS, the uninsured are persons who do not have coverage under private health insurance, Medicare, Medicaid, public assistance (through 1996), CHIP, a state-sponsored health plan, other government-sponsored programs, or a military health plan. Persons with only Indian Health Service coverage are considered uninsured. Estimates for the uninsured are shown only for the population under age 65. Estimates of the percentage of persons who are uninsured based on NHIS may differ slightly from those based on the March Current Population Survey or the American Community Survey because of differences in survey questions, recall period, and other aspects of survey methodology.

Survey respondents may be covered by health insurance at the time of interview but may have experienced one or more lapses in coverage during the year prior to interview. Starting with *Health, United States, 2006*, NHIS estimates for people with health insurance coverage for all 12 months prior to interview, for those who were uninsured for any period up to 12 months, and for those who were uninsured for more than 12 months were added as stub variables to selected tables. (Also see Appendix II, Health insurance coverage.)

Urbanization—Urbanization is the degree of urban (city-like) character of a particular geographic area. Urbanization can be measured in a variety of ways. In *Health, United States*, the two measures currently used to categorize counties by urbanization level are the Office of Management and Budget's (OMB) metropolitan and micropolitan statistical area classification and the 2013 NCHS Urban–Rural Classification Scheme for Counties. For more information on the OMB classification of counties, see Appendix II, Metropolitan statistical area (MSA); Micropolitan statistical area.

The 2013 Urban–Rural Classification Scheme is based on the February 2013 OMB delineation of MSAs and micropolitan statistical areas, 2012 postcensal estimates of county and place population, and county-level data on selected settlement density, socioeconomic, and demographic variables from Census 2010. This is an updated version of NCHS' earlier scheme, the 2006 NCHS Urban–Rural Classification Scheme for Counties. The six categories of the NCHS scheme are large central metro (inner-city counties of MSAs of 1 million or more population), large fringe metro (suburban counties of MSAs of 1 million or more population), medium metro (counties of MSAs of 250,000–999,999 population), small metro (counties of MSAs with less than 250,000 population), nonmetropolitan micropolitan statistical areas, and nonmetropolitan noncore. For more information on the classification scheme, see: https://www.cdc.gov/nchs/data_access/urban_rural.htm.

Usual source of care—Usual source of care was measured in the National Health Interview Survey in 1993 and 1994 by asking the respondent, "Is there a particular person or place that [person] usually goes to when [person] is sick or needs advice about [person's] health?" In the 1995 and 1996 NHIS, the respondent was asked, "Is there one doctor, person, or place that [person] usually goes to when [person] is sick or needs advice about health?" Starting in 1997, the respondent was asked, "Is there a place that [person] usually goes when [he/she] is sick or you need advice about [his/her] health?" Persons who report the emergency department as their usual source of care are defined in *Health, United States* as having no usual source of care.

Vaccination—Vaccinations, or immunizations, work by stimulating the immune system—the natural disease-fighting system of the body. A healthy immune system is able to recognize invading bacteria and viruses and produce substances (antibodies) to destroy or disable these invaders. Vaccinations prepare the immune system to ward off a disease. In addition to the initial immunization process, the effectiveness of some immunizations can be improved by periodic repeat injections or "boosters." Vaccines are among the most successful and cost-effective public health tools available for reducing morbidity and mortality from vaccine-preventable diseases. For a comprehensive list of vaccine-preventable diseases, see: http://www.cdc.gov/vaccines/vpd-vac/vpd-list.htm and http://www.cdc.gov/vaccines/spec-grps/default.htm.

The currently recommended childhood vaccination schedule includes vaccines that prevent infectious diseases including hepatitis A and B, diphtheria, tetanus toxoids, acellular pertussis (whooping cough), measles, mumps, rubella (German measles), polio, varicella (chickenpox), and some forms of meningitis (HIB), influenza, and pneumococcal disease. In February 2006, a rotavirus vaccine (RotaTeq) was licensed for use in U.S. infants.

A vaccine that protects against the four types of human papillomavirus (HPV) that cause most cervical cancers and genital warts was marketed starting in 2006 and is now available for both females and males. Initially, the vaccine was recommended for girls aged 11 and 12 and for girls and women aged 13–26 who have not yet been vaccinated or completed the vaccine series. In October 2011, HPV vaccination also was recommended for males aged 11 and 12. Further information is available from: http://www.cdc.gov/mmwr/preview/mmwrhtml/mm6050a3.htm.

In addition to keeping current with the vaccines listed above, and annual influenza vaccination, some additional vaccinations are recommended for older adults, persons with specific health conditions, or health care workers who are likely to be exposed to infectious persons. For example, Herpes zoster vaccination is recommended for adults aged 60 and over, and pneumococcal vaccination is recommended for adults aged 65 and over and persons with specific health conditions.

For a full discussion of recommended vaccination schedules by age and population, see CDC's vaccination and immunization website at: http://www.cdc.gov/vaccines/schedules/index.html.

Influenza vaccination—In the National Health Interview Survey, questions concerning influenza vaccination differed slightly across the survey years. Prior to September 2003, respondents were asked, "During the past 12 months, have you had a flu shot? A flu shot is usually given in the fall and protects against influenza for the flu season." Starting in September 2003, respondents were asked about influenza vaccination by nasal spray (sometimes called by the brand name FluMist) during the past 12 months, in addition to the question regarding the flu shot. Starting with 2005 data, receipt of nasal spray or a flu shot was included in the calculation of influenza vaccination estimates presented in *Health, United States*. Starting with 2010 data, additional questions were asked about the receipt of the H1N1 flu shot and spray, including month and year received. These H1N1 questions and the original seasonal flu questions were asked only in quarters 1 and 2 and the first several weeks of quarter 3. Starting August 11, 2010, revised flu vaccination questions replaced all flu vaccination questions fielded earlier in 2010 and were used in 2011. The revised questions reflect the introduction of a new combined flu vaccination that protects against both the seasonal and H1N1 strains. For more information regarding the influenza questions that were introduced in 2010, see: ftp://ftp.cdc.gov/pub/Health_Statistics/NCHS/Dataset_Documentation/NHIS/2010/srvydesc.pdf.

The prevalence of influenza vaccination during the past 12 months may differ from season-specific coverage, and estimates from different data sources may differ (additional estimates are available from: http://www.cdc.gov/flu/fluvaxview/). See: CDC. Surveillance of influenza vaccination coverage—United States, 2007–08 through 2011–12 influenza seasons. MMWR 2013;62(ss04):1–29. Available from: http://www.cdc.gov/mmwr/preview/mmwrhtml/ss6204a1.htm?s_cid=ss6204a1_w.

The recommendations of the Advisory Committee on Immunization Practices regarding who should receive an influenza vaccination have changed over the years, and changes in coverage estimates may reflect changes in recommendations. An influenza vaccine shortage occurred during the 2004–2005 influenza season. Delays in the availability of influenza shots also occurred in fall 2000 and, to a lesser extent, in fall 2001. *Pneumococcal vaccination*—In the National Health Interview Survey, questions concerning pneumococcal vaccination differed slightly across the survey years. Prior to 1999, respondents were asked, "Have you EVER had a pneumonia vaccination? This shot is usually given only once in a person's lifetime and is different from the flu shot." Starting in 1999, respondents were asked, "Have you EVER had a pneumonia vaccination, sometimes called a pneumonia shot? This shot is usually given only once in a person's lifetime and is different from the flu shot." Starting in 2001, respondents were asked, "Have you EVER had a pneumonia shot? This shot is usually given only once or twice in a person's lifetime and is different from the flu shot. It is also called the pneumococcal vaccine."

Wages and salaries—See Appendix II, Employer costs for employee compensation.

Years of potential life lost (YPLL)—YPLL is a measure of premature mortality. Starting with *Health, United States, 1996*, YPLL has been presented for persons under age 75 because the average life expectancy in the United States is over 75 years. YPLL–75 is calculated using the following eight age groups: under 1, 1–14, 15–24, 25–34, 35–44, 45–54, 55–64, and 65–74. The number of deaths for each age group is multiplied by years of life lost, calculated as the difference between age 75 years and the midpoint of the age group. For the eight age groups, the midpoints are 0.5, 7.5, 19.5, 29.5, 39.5, 49.5, 59.5, and 69.5 years, respectively. For example, the death of a person aged 15–24 counts as 55.5 years of life lost. YPLL is derived by summing years of life lost over all age groups. In *Health, United States, 1995* and earlier editions, YPLL was presented for persons under

age 65. For more information, see: CDC. Premature mortality in the United States: Public health issues in the use of years of potential life lost. MMWR 1986;35(SS–02):1S–11S. Available from: http://www.cdc.gov/mmwr/preview/mmwrhtml/00001773.htm.

Index

(Numbers are table and figure numbers)